The Pathology of Fishes

Proceedings of a symposium sponsored by
The Registry of Comparative Pathology
The American Registry of Pathology
Armed Forces Institute of Pathology
and supported by
Universities Associated for Research
and Education in Pathology, Inc.
and the University of Wisconsin Sea Grant Program

THE

Pathology
of
Fishes

EDITED BY
William E. Ribelin
George Migaki

The University of Wisconsin Press

Published 1975

The University of Wisconsin Press
Box 1379, Madison, Wisconsin 53701

The University of Wisconsin Press, Ltd
70 Great Russell Street, London

Copyright © 1975
The Regents of the University of Wisconsin System
All rights reserved

First printing
Printed in the United States of America
For LC CIP information see the colophon

ISBN 0-299-06520-0

Preparation of this book was supported in part by Public Health Service Grant No. RR00301 from Division of Research Resources, United States Department of Health, Education, and Welfare, under the auspices of Universities Associated for Research and Education in Pathology, Inc.

Contents

v

PART V
NUTRITIONAL DISEASE

Foreword

Most scientists who are not engaged in the field of diseases of fishes still believe that fish pathology covers only a very insignificant area of comparative pathology. After Hofer published the first book on diseases of fishes in Munich in 1904, the growth of fish pathology was slow until the end of World War II. However, Marianne Plehn and W. Schäperclaus did make great contributions in this interim period.

During the last 20 years progress was as fast as that in other fields of biology and medicine. Conferences on diseases of fishes in America started in 1953 when the first symposium was sponsored by the American Fisheries Society. Since then, symposia have been held more often and on a larger scale. There were four symposia in the United States on various aspects of diseases of fishes, and one symposium on hepatoma of rainbow trout. Research on hepatoma is an excellent example of how a well-organized effort can solve a difficult problem in a very short time.

There have been three symposia in Europe, sponsored by the International Office of Epizootics and organized by Dr. P. Ghittino. Another symposium sponsored by the Fisheries Society of the British Isles and the London Zoological Society was organized by Lionel Mawdesley-Thomas and held in London in 1971. The last symposium was organized jointly by the United Nations Food and Agriculture Organization and the IOE and held in Amsterdam in 1972. There were also numerous fish disease conferences held in the Soviet Union, where there are many outstanding fish disease specialists, of whom Dogiel and Bauer are probably the most widely known. Fish disease symposia are also being held in Japan. Unfortunately, the language barrier and the lack of adequate translations stand in the way of full utilization of this information in the western world.

This present symposium was different because its organizers represent medical research. Utilization of fishes for research in comparative pathology was begun by Schlumberger and Lucké, whose monograph on tumors of cold-blooded vertebrates is a milestone in comparative pathology. Nigrelli, Scarpelli, Dawe, Ashley, Wood, Dunbar, Reichenbach-Klinke, and lately Mawdesley-Thomas, Roberts,

Mulcahy, Yasutake, Herman, and others have greatly contributed to comparative pathology by research on fishes. This symposium was the first international conference on contributions of fish pathology to comparative pathology and therefore is a milestone which will be long remembered.

S. F. Snieszko

August 9, 1972

Preface

The nine universities that make up Universities Associated for Research and Education in Pathology, Inc., take great pride in this timely and pioneering symposium on Fish Pathology.

In a very real sense the Registry of Comparative Pathology, which cosponsored this symposium, was developed because for many decades there has been a strong interest in comparative pathology at the Armed Forces Institute of Pathology and particularly in the Veterinary Pathology Division. At first this interest was fostered by the Committee on Pathology of the National Academy of Science–National Research Council, which I had the privilege of chairing. Now it is encouraged by the nine universities who joined together in the late 1960s to find ways and means of sustaining the American Registry of Pathology.

This has been a very rewarding effort in many ways and this symposium was a good example of the opportunities that present themselves for those who are interested in the broad interspecies approach to the study of disease.

On behalf of the nine universities I represent and on behalf of the Advisory Committee of the Registry of Comparative Pathology, which has representatives from three additional universities, I want to pay tribute to and to express our appreciation to the University of Wisconsin Sea Grant Program for joining hands with the Registry in sponsoring this symposium.

I want to pay special tribute to and to thank Drs. George Migaki and William E. Ribelin, who worked so hard in developing the program and making the arrangements. Also, thanks are due to Colonel R. W. Morrissey, Lt. Colonel F. R. Robinson, and Lt. Colonel P. K. Hildebrandt for the hospitality of the Armed Forces Institute of Pathology and the Walter Reed Army Institute of Research for the outstanding facilities that these Institutes made available for this conference.

I want to pay tribute to and to thank the Division of Research Resources, National Institutes of Health, United States Department of Health, Education, and Welfare, whose material support has made this Registry and this symposium possible. And last, but not least, I want to express our appreciation to the Armed

xi

Forces Institute of Pathology and its leadership on the Registry for their support and help not only here and now but over the years as the Registry of Comparative Pathology has had its birth and early development.

R. W. Wissler

August 7, 1972

The Pathology of Fishes

1

Comparative Fish Histology

LAURENCE M. ASHLEY

Comparative fish histology is of increasing importance today, as is comparative fish pathology. While the literature on this subject is still fragmentary and scattered, a considerable number of papers are available. An atlas of salmonid histology now in preparation by this author and two others (Joseph H. Wales and William T. Yasutake) promises useful supplementation of textbooks and courses in comparative vertebrate histology. In his excellent textbook of comparative histology (1), Warren Andrew remarked, "In the true sense each animal is a microcosm made up of marvels which lie beyond the field of vision of the naked eye." This is particularly true with fishes, among which specific variations worthy of histological comparison are legion. Common names of but a few fishes suggest interesting differences, e.g., seahorse, scorpionfish, boxfish, hatchetfish, porcupinefish, ribbonfish, climbing perch, fanged viperfish, four-eyed fish, anglerfish, lanternfish, and lungfish. All have differences in their morpho-histology.

THE INTEGUMENT

The skin may be naked or scaly. Dermal scales of several types may be present, depending on the species. Scales are enclosed in dermal scale pockets and are arranged in an imbricated pattern. The epidermis may be thin or thick, slightly keratinized and with an abundance of mucoid cells. An extensive lateral line system of canals, nerves, and neuromasts relays impulses induced by external stimuli via cranial nerves 9 and 10 to the brain. Taste buds occur on the lips, oral valves, and oral and pharyngeal mucosa of most fish, and in addition on the skin and barbels of catfishes and certain others. Several special cell types may occur in the

3

epidermis. Melanophores and other pigment cells may be seen below the epidermis and below the dermis, which typically contains both vascular and fibrous layers.

DIGESTIVE SYSTEM

Some species have membranous and bony devices which permit extraordinary protrusion of the lips for feeding. Others have fused jaws and must suck food into the mouth through slightly protruded lips (e.g., seahorses and pipefishes). Inside the mouth are upper and lower oral valves formed as U-shaped folds of oral mucosa to regulate ingress and egress of respiratory water. The slightly movable tongue may contain teeth on its upper surface. Heavy grasping and smaller teeth are set on bone in the jaws. The pharynx is perforated on each side by four pairs of gill slits, the first gills being modified as pseudobranch glands (described below). The caudal end of the pharynx often contains pharyngeal teeth which may aid in macerating food before it reaches the stomach. The very short esophagus typically has longitudinal folds of mucosa containing mucous cells but no discrete cardiac glands. The gastric mucosa contains tall columnar cells which are apically mucoid, but the mucus is different from that in the esophagus. A stomach is absent from Cyprinidae (e.g., carp, goldfish), Cyprinodontidae (e.g., mummichog), Poeciliidae (e.g., molly, guppy, mosquitofish), Scaridae (e.g., parrotfishes), and others, but is well developed in most fishes, wherein there are gastric pits and fundic glands but few pyloric glands, depending on species. An oblique muscle coat is variable in its development or absence. Brunner's duodenal glands are not found in fishes. The muscularis mucosae, usually very thin and difficult to demonstrate, varies with the species. In carp, skeletal muscle runs almost the entire length of the intestine, but in trout skeletal muscle is replaced by smooth muscle in the anterior stomach. A gizzard, devoid of gastric glands, occurs in the gizzard shad and related species. The intestine usually shows little differentiation into regions, and its mucosa exhibits short, rather wide villi. The hindgut is not enlarged into a colon as in mammals, but it does have many mucous cells in the mucosa. Spiral valves are common in some species and prominent folds of mucosa occur in others. The intestine is of various lengths in different species, while in one, the stoneroller sucker (*Campostoma anomalum*), the intestine is neatly wound around the air bladder in a series of coils. The submucosa differs from that of mammals in having a stratum compactum or dense fibroelastic layer next to the muscularis mucosae and a granular layer of mast cells or tissue eosinophils predominating. These are more obvious in certain species. There are no true glands in the intestine of carp and goldfish.

The number of caeca varies with the species from 0 to 100 or more. These are finger-like diverticula at or just beyond the pyloric sphincter. Their mucosa is longitudinally folded and goblet cells are common. Caeca are believed to aid in food digestion. The various coats or layers are similar to those in the intestine but the muscularis mucosae may be absent.

The pancreas is usually diffuse, scattered in the mesentery or fascia of the caeca, and fat is often interspersed among pancreatic acini. Pancreatic islets will be mentioned later. The acinar tissue of the pancreas is quite typical of that of higher vertebrates. In the channel catfish and certain other species, a hepato-pancreas occurs and is represented by a layer of pancreatic acini around each portal vein or hepatic triad. There are no islets in the hepatic pancreas. Some species have a splenopancreas with pancreatic acini similarly distributed in the spleen. The pancreas of lungfish lies within the intestinal wall between the serosa and muscularis.

The liver is generally less well organized into lobules than it is in higher verte-brates. Portal triads often have their hepatic arterioles removed some distance from the associated vein and bile duct. Central veins are rather irregularly dis-persed and the muralia (two-cell plates) of hepatocytes are often irregularly arrayed about the central veins. Thus, a zonal pattern is less distinct than in mam-mals. Sinusoids are often collapsed and hepatocytes are often filled with glyco-gen, giving a very vacuolated, pale appearance in hematoxylin and eosin (H&E) sections.

Kupffer cells are seldom seen clearly but bile canaliculi occur regularly and can be seen in well-fixed and stained H&E sections.

CIRCULATORY SYSTEM

Cardiac muscle in fishes resembles that of other vertebrates histologically, but the atrial and ventricular walls are relatively thinner and papillary muscles are poorly developed. The bulbus arteriosus is strongly elastic. Arteries and veins are thinner-walled, in keeping with a smaller blood volume per gram of tissue in fish as compared with terrestrial vertebrates. Arteries thus have poor smooth muscle coats as compared to their fibrous externas. The media and adventitia seem to blend. Lymphatic ducts and sinuses collect lymph from all parts of the body. Paired jugular and lateral lymph vessels return the lymph from head and trunk respectively, where the lymph and blood vessels unite at or near the common car-dinal vein. Dorsal and ventral longitudinal lymphatics may also occur. Cyclos-tomes differ from higher fishes in having several somewhat diffuse connections between lymph and blood vessels, and are therefore said to have a hemolymph system. Small flattened lymph hearts with valves and contractile muscle fibers occur in the tail of true eels (*Anguilla*) and trout (*Salmo*). Deep lymphatics col-lect the lymph from viscera (2).

SPLEEN

The spleen is much different morphologically from that in mammals but is similar cytologically in having a reticular stroma, white pulp and red pulp, and a network of blood vessels. It may be more active hematopoietically than spleens of higher vertebrates. Blood volume in the spleen is decreased as fish exercise. Trout in "dash" swimming (as to capture prey or to escape) use white skeletal muscle which has only one-third to one-fourth as many blood capillaries as the red muscle which is used continually in respiration, balance, and similar continuing activities.

The spleen is a hematopoietic organ which may also function in blood cell destruction. It lies next to the stomach in bony fishes and in ganoids. The red blood corpuscles are ovoid and nucleated in all vertebrates except mammals. Nucleated thrombocytes occur in fishes. There are no platelets. In fish, unlike mammals, lymphocytes are the most common type of white blood cell in the circulating blood, neutrophils come next, then eosinophils, monocytes, and basophils, the last three of which are uncommon in circulating blood. Plasma cells are seldom seen and rarely if ever in the circulation. Macrophages are common in the connective tissues, where they appear to originate. Red blood cells and white blood cells may mature in the circulating blood, where immature forms can often be seen. Lungfishes have two types of eosinophils and two types of basophils. The African lungfish has red blood cells up to 45 microns in length.

RESPIRATION

Because fishes breathe mainly by means of internal gills, these organs are of particular interest to comparative histologists. Bony fishes have five pairs of embryonic gill arches, the first of which becomes modified during development into a pseudobranch gland, thus leaving branchial arches 2 to 5 for the functional gills. Each gill filament contains an afferent and an efferent branch from the corresponding branchial artery. Each filament also contains a rod of hyaline cartilage between the afferent and efferent filamentar vessels. Gill lamellae are roughly semicircular, attached basally and partially overlapping one another in series along either side of the filament. In longitudinal section lamellae look like villi— a view that is deceiving to the uninitiated. Lamellae are covered with simple squamous epithelium on either side. Between these two thin layers are alternating pillar (pilaster) cells and blood capillaries in the form of a capillary plexus. Blood enters each plexus from the afferent and exits via the efferent filamentar artery. Respiratory gases, ammonia products, and various mineral nutrients enter or leave the respiratory blood stream by passing first through a doubled plasma membrane of a pillar cell, then through two roughly parallel plasma membranes of a squamous epithelial cell. Electron micrographs would probably reveal minute pores in these delicate membranes. A little work has been done along this line. At the bases of gill lamellae may be found special chloride cells and albuminous cells for secretion of these substances.

In lungfishes, the air bladder contains both alveolar "sacs" and capillary plexuses similar to amphibian lungs. Teleost gas bladders are generally only for hydrostatic functions and contain a "red" gland and sometimes a special "oval" structure, both of which are concerned with hydrostatic functions. In physostomatous fishes a patent (open) pneumatic duct connects the gas bladder to the anterior end of the esophagus or to the intestine, depending on the species.

EXCRETORY SYSTEM

While the degenerate parasitic hagfish has a functional pronephros, other fish have a functional mesonephros containing well-developed glomeruli with nephron tubules and a collecting duct system. There is no distinct cortex and medulla as there is in higher vertebrates. The nephron of teleosts consists of the glomerulus with Bowman's capsule, a short neck piece, a first and second portion of the proximal convoluted tubule, the distal convoluted tubule, which is followed by the collecting tubules which drain into the mesonephric duct. The mesonephric duct dilates into a sinus-like bladder and empties via a short duct through the urogenital sinus. The nephron of teleosts lacks a loop of Henle. Juxtaglomerular bodies have been described for many species. Some fish have aglomerular mesonephric kidneys and no functioning pronephric kidney. Lungfish *Ceratodus* sp. has short caudally-placed kidneys firmly attached to the ovary or testes.

REPRODUCTIVE SYSTEM

Ovaries and testes in young fishes are slender cords of delicate stroma and many gonia or developing sex cells. The ova develop from a delicate germinal epithelium and come to lie in "skeins" enveloped by a thin-walled capsule which ruptures when the eggs ripen. The eggs, now free in the peritoneal cavity, exit normally via genital pores beside or within a genital papilla. Pacific salmon spermatogonia develop in clusters of cysts which burst when the gonia have become spermatids or spermatozoa. After spawning, cells of testicular ducts and of ovarian tissues of Pacific salmon become necrotic. Vital signs deteriorate rapidly and the fish dies. Steelhead and sea-run cutthroat trout may survive two or three such spawning runs before showing signs of morbidity.

NERVOUS SYSTEM

The microscopic structure of the central nervous system of fishes is similar to that of mammals but morphologically much simpler. The retina of the eye contains more cones than rods in most teleost fishes but various species differ in this regard. The lens is spherical and fish are nearsighted. Ganglion cells are similar to those of higher vertebrates and most nerve endings are of the simple type. There are few specialized or encapsulated endings in teleosts. Unique giant neurons (Mauthner cells, Fig. 1.1) number from two dozen in cyclostomes to only

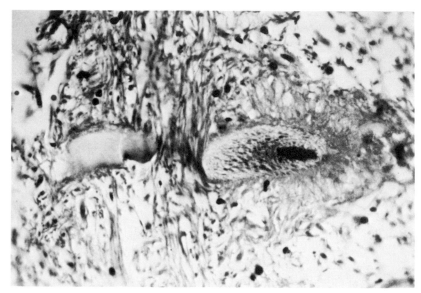

Fig. 1.1. Section through a Mauthner's giant neuron from the brain of a lake trout (*Salveli-nus namaycush*). (Courtesy of A. H. Walsh.) Hematoxylin and eosin (H&E); ×500.

two in teleosts; they occur near the cranial nerve roots in the medulla, and their giant axons (Fig. 1.2) course along the spinal cord. These carry high-velocity impulses similar to those carried by annelid giant nerve cells. An interesting crista with a delicately attached otolith occurs in each ampulla of the semicircular canals (Fig. 1.3) and a typical macula is present in the utriculus and sacculus. The laminations of otoliths are sometimes used to determine age. The meninges of teleosts are much simplified and exist as only one or two membranes instead of three. Elasmobranchs and cyclostomes have only one, the meninx primitiva. A mucoid parameningeal membrane may enclose the primitive meninx. The primitive paleothalamus lacks the higher coordination centers of most vertebrates.

SPECIAL SENSE ORGANS

The distribution of taste buds was noted above. Fish appear to utilize both taste and smell in relation to their homing instincts. In the eel, salmon, and steelhead, smell is well developed by a highly folded olfactory mucosa whose neuroepithelial cells sample the water passing through the nasal pits or capsules, most of which have anterior and posterior openings. Both chemical and vibratory sense may be mediated via the lateral line system of neuromasts, pits, and canals, and its cephalic branches (Figs. 1.4, 1.5). Further auditory sense is mediated via the eighth cranial nerve to the small legena, but the inner ear is mostly concerned with equilibratory sense originating with slight movements of otoliths over the

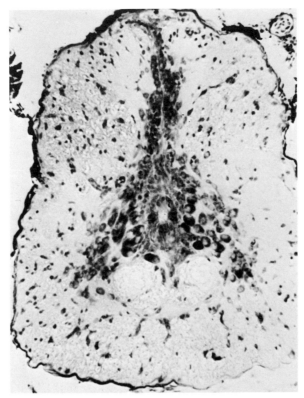

Fig. 1.2. Transverse section of spinal cord of coho salmon (*Oncorhynchus kisutch*), showing paired giant Mauthner's axons just below the central mass of neurons. The axons appear as pale circular areas. Giemsa; ×450.

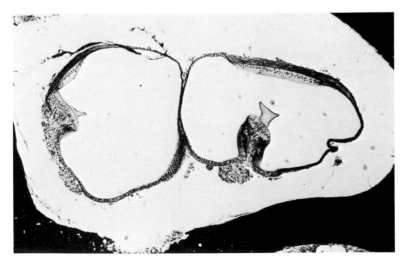

Fig. 1.3. Cristae with attached otoliths as seen in sections through two ampullae of a cutthroat trout (*Salmo clarki*). Giemsa; ×140.

9

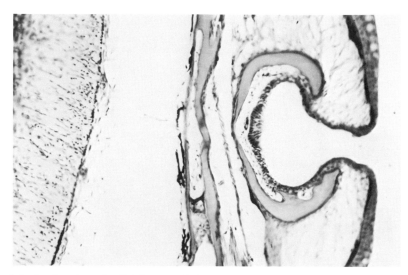

Fig. 1.4. Section through a "pit" organ of the lateral line system in cutthroat trout, showing small neuromast at bottom of the canal enclosed by bony trough. The cerebellum lies to the left of the broad space. H&E; ×280.

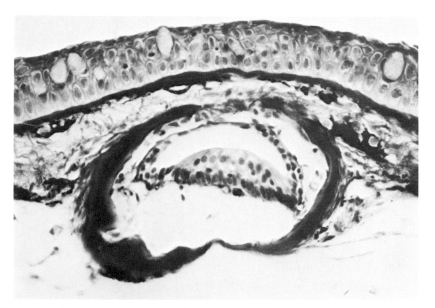

Fig. 1.5. Section of a mushroom-shaped neuromast in lateral line canal of head region in coho salmon. Detail of scaleless skin (above) includes several mucous cells within stratified squamous epidermis. Giemsa; ×700.

maculae and cristae of the utriculus, sacculus, and ampullae. A few species have special "hearing" apparatus involving a chain of Weberian ossicles connecting the internal ear with the gas bladder, which makes of the outer body wall a sort of eardrum.

The eye varies histologically with specific habits of life. Most teleosts have in common three types of visual cells: rods, single cones, and twin cones. The latter occur mostly in fishes that swim near the surface where they are exposed to bright light. The lens of most fish eyes is a near-perfect sphere, but exceptions occur, as in the four-eyed fish *Anableps,* which has its pupils divided, one part for aerial and the other for aquatic vision. The curvature of the upper part of the lens is much less than the lower, making it a truly amphibious eye. The "choroid" of some fishes is modified into an endocrine choroid gland with a "rete mirabile" circulation which lies dorsoposteriorly against the outside surface of the sclera. The sclera is cartilaginous in most teleosts.

BIOLUMINESCENT AND ELECTRIC ORGANS

Many kinds of fish have luminescent organs termed photophores, some of which contain silvery reflectors of guanine to focus or diffuse the luminescent effect. Battery-like bioelectric organs occur in several unrelated species of fish in various parts of the world. Electric tissues collectively known as the *electroplax* occur in such widely separated taxonomic groups and geographical locations as South America's electric eel (up to 6 feet in length), tropical Africa's electric catfish, and the electric ray (*Torpedo*) of tropical and subtropical Atlantic waters. In the eel the electroplax occupies most of the ventral region of the very long tail in the area usually occupied by hypaxial muscles in most fishes. In the torpedo, paired electric organs lie between gill chambers and the musculature of the pectoral fin of one side, filling the entire space between dorsal and ventral skin surfaces. In the electric catfish the potent tissue is between the skin and body muscles around the greater part of the body but thickest in the middle region.

The electric tissue in *Torpedo* is a syncytium of metamorphosed embryonic skeletal muscle cells derived from mesoderm. Layers of this syncytium alternate with gelatinous layers containing large nerve fibers and their branches. A pair of prominent electric lobes on the medulla form the motor centers for the electroplax.

ENDOCRINE SYSTEM

The endocrine system of fishes is histologically very interesting when one compares corresponding endocrine glands of fishes and higher vertebrates. The hypophysis of fishes resembles somewhat that of mammals but interesting differences occur with respect to most other fish endocrines. The number of histophysiological subdivisions of the adenohypophysis may vary from species to species. The neurohypophysis is quite similar in most species but in some there is a caudal extension. A saccus vasculosus (Fig. 1.6) lined by columnar or cuboidal ependyma-like cells lies caudal to the hypophysis.

The thyroid gland is usually very diffuse, the follicles being scattered mainly along the ventral aorta and its second and third branchial arteries. The thyroid follicles contain colloid and closely resemble those of higher vertebrates. In certain sharks the thyroid gland is a more compact, subspherical gland in the anterior midline just caudal to the lower jaw. There are no intrafollicular or "light" cells, as in mammals.

Parathyroids are not found in fishes but an ultimobranchial body is well de-

Fig. 1.6. Section through saccus vasculosus of coho salmon, which lies posteroventrally to the infundubulum and just posterior to the hypophysis. Note the venous sinuses alternating with parallel rows of columnar epithelium. Giemsa; ×350.

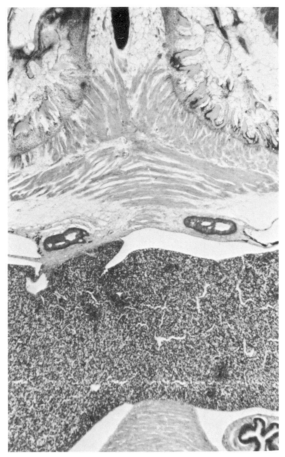

Fig. 1.7. Horizontal section of 27 gram fingerling rainbow trout (*Salmo gairdneri*), showing paired ultimobranchial bodies lying in the transverse septum. The pharyngeal floor of skeletal muscle lies anterior to these glands and the liver lies posteriorly. Giemsa; ×44.

veloped from paired primordia of the fifth pair of branchial pouches (Fig. 1.7). It lies in the transverse septum between the floor of the esophagus and the liver, just caudal to the heart. This gland has been shown to secrete calcitonin, an antagonist of parathormone. Histologically, the ultimobranchials consist of several small vesicles lined with tall columnar or pseudostratified columnar epithelium (Fig. 1.8). These glands are well vascularized with delicate vessels and capillary nets. They are considerably proliferated during prespawning runs of coho salmon.

Adrenal glands of most fishes are unlike those of higher vertebrates. The adrenal cortical tissue, often termed interrenal tissue (Fig. 1.9), lies in the anterior kidney, where adrenal cortical cells tend to surround the larger blood sinuses

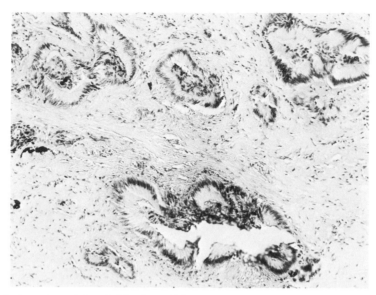

Fig. 1.8. Irregular vesicles of ultimobranchial gland with copious interstitial connective tissue from a spawned coho salmon. Note tall columnar epithelium lining vesicles which contain secretory residues. H&E; X450.

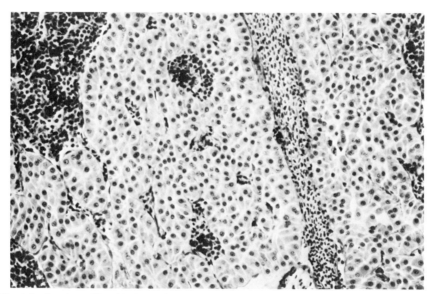

Fig. 1.9. Section of head kidney of 12-inch male rainbow trout, showing large mass of adrenal cortical ("interrenal") cells of pale color traversed by blood-filled vein. Small round (black) cells in corner are hematopoietic and are typical of head kidney. H&E; X450.

(branches of the postcardinal veins) and may be from one to many layers thick. They may also be scattered among the hematopoietic cells of the head kidney. Since these cells lie within the head kidney, the term *intrarenal* is more accurate for fishes. Adrenal medulla tissue, known as chromaffin tissue in fishes, occurs as pale-staining cells within the walls of the renal blood vessels (Fig. 1.10) and occasionally may be seen in slender cords similar to the neuron-containing sympathetic nerve trunks running just dorsal to the kidneys. Paraganglia or chromaffin tissue may also be found in these nerve chains, from which extensions of chromaffin tissue into the kidney are common. All groups of so-called ganglion cells in the fish heart have been held to be chromaffin rather than true ganglion cells.

The pineal gland (epiphysis) of teleosts is hollow, its walls consist of a much-folded columnar epithelium united by a tubular stalk with the diencephelon (Fig. 1.11), and it extends dorsally above the optic lobes, where it is thought to receive ultraviolet stimulation through the thin cranium of some fishes. Histologically, the pineal closely resembles a sensory structure. The structure of the vesicular epithelium resembles the retina except that the "pineal retina" is a reversed type with sensory cells in the "inner retinal" layer, but in cyclostomes there is a lens-like pellucida over the pineal body. The gland appears to have an endocrine function. There are three main types of cells: sensory, supporting, and ganglion cells. Much remains to be learned of the pineal gland of fishes.

The Islets of Langerhans in various classes of lower vertebrates differ from one

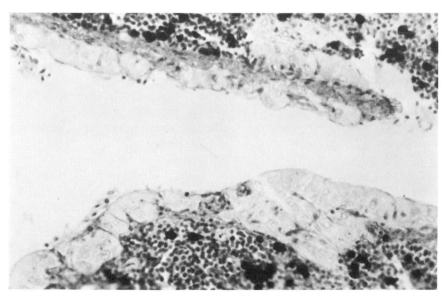

Fig. 1.10. Section of excretory kidney of 11-inch female rainbow trout, showing wide blood vessel lumen bordered by chromaffin cells (pale colored). Dark-staining tissue is hematopoietic and lies between renal tubules (not shown). H&E; ×280.

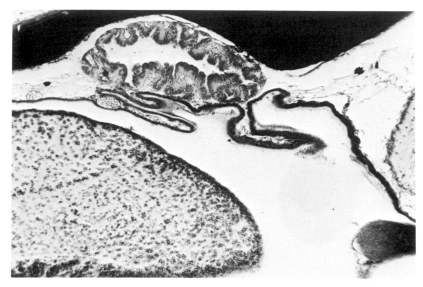

Fig. 1.11. Section of pineal body from cutthroat trout fingerling. The pineal lies below a curved depression in the cranial cartilage (black). A portion of the cerebrum appears below the pineal. Giemsa; ×180.

another, but all teleosts examined appear to have alpha, beta, and delta cells (as do higher vertebrates). The islet tissue is often diffuse, the islets being small and scattered, but bass and sunfishes (Centrarchidae) have rather large islets, sometimes encapsulated and surrounded by small amounts of pancreatic acinar tissue (Fig. 1.12).

Stannius corpuscles are from one to five in number on the dorsal or lateral aspect of the kidney (Fig. 1.13). There is no mammalian counterpart. These subspherical, encapsulated, well-vascularized glands contain septum-bound lobules alternating with wide interlobular spaces which contain blood. These are ductless glands whose parenchyma contains many secretory granules. The secretion has been described as proteinaceous. Removal of this gland in the eel causes a strong rise of blood calcium and a fall of the phosphate level. A decrease in osteoclastic resorption results in hypercalcemia and a stimulation of the ultimobranchial gland.

The urophysis is a caudal, neurosecretory organ. Its specific functions remain unknown although it occurs in most species of Chondrichthyes and Osteichthyes. It is believed to be endocrine in nature and is comparable to the cranial hypothalmo-neurohypophysial system. It consists of large Dahlgren cells to provide the neurosecretory nucleus. Their myelinated axons form a neurosecretory tract and the axon terminal in association with a capillary net has a storage release center for neurohumors.

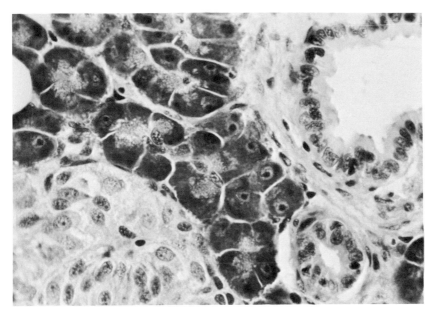

Fig. 1.12. Section of broodstock rainbow trout pancreas (dark cells), showing sector of pancreatic islet (Langerhans) in corner of picture. Opposite corner shows bile duct and smaller adjacent pancreatic duct. H&E; ×2600.

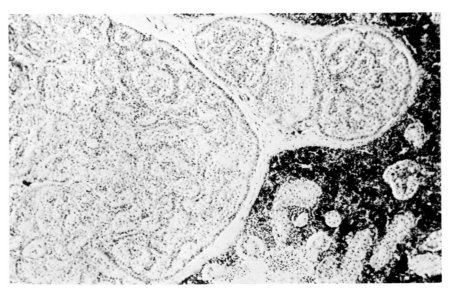

Fig. 1.13. Section of multilobed Stannius corpuscie and adjacent excretory kidney of channel catfish (*Ictalurus punctatus*). Note irregular cords of columnar cells interspersed with fine blood capillaries in the corpuscles of Stannius. Black tissue is hematopoietic. H&E; ×280.

17

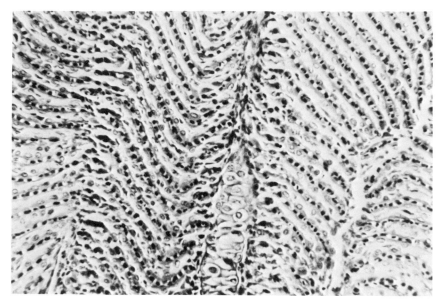

Fig. 1.14. Section of pseudobranch gland of rainbow trout fingerling. Note cartilage rod support in center and lamella-like pattern with contained blood capillaries suggestive of typical gill structure. H&E; ×450.

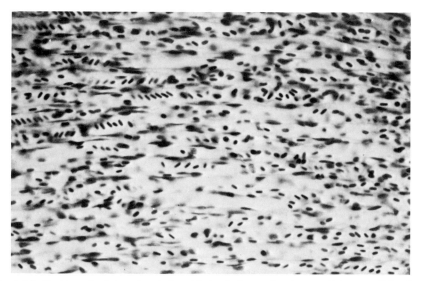

Fig. 1.15. Section of rainbow trout choroid gland of eye, showing parallel rows of blood capillaries alternating with slender cells resembling fibroblasts. H&E; ×600.

The pseudobranch gland, unique in fishes, is derived from the first gill and remains rudimentary (Fig. 1.14). Its structure resembles that of a compressed gill. An endocrine function is assumed for it. The pseudobranch is clearly concerned with active secretion of oxygen and is thus logically associated with the choroid gland. Those fishes that lack a pseudobranch invariably lack a choroid gland. The pseudobranch may produce or activate a hormonal principle, causing pigment aggregation in chromatophores. The entry of this hormone into the general circulation is thought to be regulated by the U-shaped choroid gland lying between the choroid and sclera around the exit of the optic nerve (Fig. 1.15). The specific functions of pseudobranch and choroid gland still require further investigation.

CONCLUSIONS

It is to be emphasized that fish histology and pathology are still infantile, compared with their mammalian and human counterparts. I do not know of a single fish species whose histology is fully known. An atlas of fish hematology is badly needed. The detailed histology of the fish nervous system is only partially recorded. The neurosecretory system and in particular the urophysis is but little known for fishes. Controversial reports in this and other areas need clarification. Recently considerable work has been done, and is being done, on fish endocrines. This is an area, as are several others, in which a harmonious blend of effort in histology, cytochemistry, physiology, and biochemistry are most desirable. The gill apparatus of fishes presents a case in point—its histomorphology is but scantily described, its histochemistry and biochemistry have only been touched upon. Numerous problems in enzymology and intermediary metabolism need to be resolved and the results correlated with gill microstructure. Much remains unknown concerning almost every major organ in fishes. The electron microscopist has only begun to discover the inmost secrets of fish fine structure. In pathology certain fish species are being identified as desirable animal models for the study of human and mammalian disease. Further research in fish histology is basic to future research in fish histopathology.

It should also be pointed out that in the future every available source of protein for human and animal nutrition must be fully developed, managed, and utilized if the earth's exploding populations are to survive. Fish protein is already supplementing that from other sources, as the burgeoning channel catfish industry now under way from Florida to California will testify. The survival of our sportfish and foodfish industries depends in large part upon the work of competent fish pathologists. It behooves us to battle against environmental pollution with increasing fervor so that earth's marine and aquatic environments will continue to yield their harvests of edible protein. Rehabilitation of several American streams has already shown promising results from efforts to restore important fish runs which were until recently threatened with extinction. In addition to environmentalists, deemed so essential today, we surely will need more well-trained fish histologists and fish pathologists tomorrow.

REFERENCES

References Cited

1. Andrew, W. *Textbook of Comparative Histology.* New York, Oxford Univ. Press, 1959.
2. Lagler, K. F., Bardach, J. E., and Miller, R. R. *Ichthyology,* pp. 219–221. New York, Wiley, 1962.

General

Colgrove, G. S. Histological and hematological changes in accompanying sexual maturation of sockeye salmon (*Oncorhynchus nerka*) in the Fraser River system. *Int. Pac. Salmon Fish. Comm. Bull. 20:* 1–28. 1966.

McKenzie, T. The blood-vascular system, ductless glands, and urogenital system of *Ameriurus catus. Proc. Can. Inst. 2:* 418–457. 1884.

Post. G. *Normal Histology of Fish.* Conservation Library Center, Denver Public Library, Denver. Colo. 1954.

Shellhamer, R. H. Histochemical studies of the lamprey. *Sport Fish. Abstr. 3(2):* #1629. 1958.

Shimomura, M. Histological changes of various organs in the fry of chum salmon and of rainbow trout during the seaward migration or following the experimental transference into sea water from fresh water. *Bull. Jap. Soc. Sci. Fish. 35(3):* 273–283. 1969.

Wood, E. M., Yasutake, W. T., Woodall, A. N., and Halver, J. E. The nutrition of salmonid fishes. I. Chemical and histological studies of wild and domestic fish. *J. Nutr. 61(4):* 465–478. 1957.

Wood, E. M., Yasutake, W. T., Halver, J. E., and Woodall, A. N. Chemical and histological studies of wild and hatchery salmon in fresh water. *Trans. Amer. Fish. Soc. 89(3):* 301–307. 1960.

Digestive

Barton, J. K. Contribution to the anatomy of the digestive tract in *Salmo salar. J. Anat. Physiol. (London) 34:* 294–304. 1899.

Baumgarten, H. G. On the muscles and nerves in the intestinal wall of tenches. *Z. Zellforsch. mikrosk. Anat. 68:* 116–137. 1965.

Bellisio, N. B. Anatomia e histologia del tracto digestive de algunos pimelodidos argentinos. *An. Congr. Lat.-Amer. Zool. 2:* 107–123. 1965.

Bernard, G. R., and Hartmann, J. F. Cytological and histochemical observations on the elasmobranch rectal gland. *Anat. Rec. 137(3):* 340. 1960.

Berry, P. Y., and Low, M. P. Comparative studies on some aspects of the morphology and histology of *Ctenopharyngodon idellus, Aristichthys nobilis,* and their hybrid (Cyprinidae). *Copeia 4:* 708–726. 1970.

Blake, I. H. Studies on the comparative histology of the digestive tube of certain teleost fishes. *J. Morphol. Physiol. 50:* 39–70. 1930.

Bucke, D.   The anatomy and histology of the alimentary tract of the carnivorous fish the pike *Esox lucius* L. *J. Fish Biol. 3:* 421–431. 1971.

Bulger, R. E.   Fine structure of the rectal (salt-secreting) gland of the spiny dogfish, *Squalus acanthias. Anat. Rec. 147*(1): 95–127. 1963.

Bulger, R. E.   Electron microscopy of the stratified epithelium lining the excretory canal of the dogfish rectal gland. *Anat. Rec. 151*(4): 589–608. 1965.

Bullock, W. L.   Intestinal histology of some salmonid fishes with particular reference to the histopathology of acanthocephalan infections. *J. Morphol. 112*(1): 23–44. 1963.

Bullock, W. L.   The intestinal histology of the mosquitofish, *Gambusia affinis* (Baird and Girard). *Acta zool. (Stockholm) 48*(1–2): 1–17. 1967.

Chaudry, H. S., and Khandelwal, O. P.   The anatomy and histology of the alimentary tract of *Oreinus plagiostoma* (Heckel). *Annot. zool. jap. 34*(3): 139–152. 1961.

Dawes, B.   The histology of the alimentary tract of the plaice (*Pleuronectes platessa*). *Quart. J. Microscop. Sci. 73*(2): 243–274. 1929.

de Oliveira e Silva, S. L.   Histologic aspects of the digestive tract (stomach intestine) of *Plecostomus* sp. (Pisces, Actinopterygii, Loricariidae). *Atas Soc. Biol. Rio de Janeiro 9*(4): 63–68. 1966.

Fahlen, G.   Histology of the posterior chamber of the fish swimbladder of *Argentina. Nature (London) 207*(4992): 94–95. 1965.

Fahlen, G.   The gas bladder as a hydrostatic organ in *Thymallus thymallus* L., *Osmerus eperlanus* L. and *Mallotus villosus* Mull. *Fiskeridir. skr. ser. havunders. 14*(4): 199–228. 1968.

Funge, R.   Anatomy and histology of the euphysoclist swimbladder. *Acta physiol. scand.* suppl. 108–113. 1954.

Greene, C. W.   Anatomy and histology of the alimentary tract of the king salmon. *Bull. Bur. Fish., Wash., 32:* 75–101. 1912.

Gulland, G. L.   The minute structure of the digestive tract of the Atlantic salmon and the changes which occur in it in fresh water. Anatomischer Anzeiger Centralblatt für die gesamte wissenschaftliche Anatomie. *Amtl. Organ anat. Ges. 14*(17–18): 441–455. 1898.

Gupta, O. P.   Studies on the morphology, histology and the swallowing mechanism of the digestive tract of a carnivorous fish, *Xenentodon cancila* (Ham.). *Okajimas folia anat. jap. 48*(1): 29–51. 1971.

Herold, R. C.   The fine structure of vasodentine in the teeth of the white hake, *Urophycis tenuis* (Pisces, Gadidae). *Arch. Oral Biol. 15*(4): 311–322. 1970.

Hussaini, A. H. al-.   On the functional morphology of the alimentary tract of some fish in relation to differences in their feeding habits: Anatomy and histology. *Quart. J. Microsc. Sci. 90*(2): 109–139. 1949.

Inui, Y., and Egusa, S.   Histological changes observed in glass eel liver during starvation. *Bull. Jap. Soc. Sci. Fish. 33*(3): 181–189. 1967.

Ishida, M., and Sato, M.   The anatomical and histological observations of the alimentary tract of a catfish, *Parasilurus asotus* (L.). *Sci. Rep. Hirosaki Univ. 7*(2): 57–63. 1960.

Isokawa, S., Van Huysen, G., and Kosakal, T.   Telemicroscopy of fish tooth tubular enamel. *J. Dent. Res. 44*(4): 449. 1965.

Iwai, T.   The pharyngeal pockets of the sardine, *Sardinops caerulea* (Girard). *Calif. Fish Game 41*(1): 113–116. 1955.

Iwai, T.   The comparative study of the digestive tract of teleost larvae. II. Ciliated cells of the gut epithelium in pond smelt larvae. *Bull. Jap. Soc. Sci. Fish. 33*(12): 1116–1119. 1967.

Iwai, T., and Tanaka, M.   The comparative study of the digestive tract of teleost larvae. III. Epithelial cells in the posterior gut of halfbeak larvae. *Bull. Jap. Soc. Sci. Fish. 34*(1): 44–48. 1968.

Jansson, B.-O., and Olsson, R.   The cytology of the caecal epithelial cells of *Perca*. *Acta zool. (Stockholm) 41*(3): 267–276, 1960.

Johansson, N.   Histological studies of the livers from 1½ year old salmon (*Salmo salar* L.) raised on different diets. *Swedish Salmon Res. Inst. Rep.,* 1965.

Kapoor, B. G.   The anatomy and histology of the pharyngeal organ in *Hilsa ilisha* (Ham.). *J. Zool. Soc. India 6*(2): 167–172. 1954.

Kappers, C. U. A.   FAS. 11, *Taste Buds,* 1: 378. New York, Macmillan, 1936.

Khalilov, F. K.   Some material on the histology and histochemistry of the pancreas and liver of teleost fishes. *Vop. Ikhtiol. 8*(2)49: 312–317. 1968.

Korovina, V. M., and Vasil'eva, N. E.   Comparative histologic studies on the mid-intestine of certain members of the salmon family (Salmonidae). *Vop. Ikhtiol. 11*(3): 502–508. 1971.

Macallum, A. B.   Alimentary canal, liver, pancreas, and air-bladder of *Ameiurus catus*. *Proc. Can. Inst. 2:* 387–417. 1884.

Maksimovich, A. A., and Korotaev, G. K.   Spawning-connected changes in the fine structure of the liver cells' nuclei and nucleoli in the Pacific salmon. *Tsitologiya 11*(11): 1393–1400. 1969.

Pascha, S. M. K.   The anatomy and histology of the alimentary canal of a herbivorous fish *Tilapia mossambica* (Peters). *Proc. Indian Acad. Sci.,* Sect. B *59*(6): 340–349. 1964.

Rahimullah (Quraishi), M.   A comparative study of the morphology, histology and probable functions of the pyloric caeca in Indian fishes, together with a discussion on their homology. D.Sc. thesis, 37 pp. University of Madras, 1944.

Saddler, J. B., and Ashley, L. M.   Comparative histology of the pyloric caeca of certain teleost fish. *Walla Walla Coll. Publ. (Washington), Dep. Biol. Sci. Biol. Sta. No. 27.* 1960.

Schmitz, E. H., and Baker, C. D.   Digestive anatomy of the gizzard shad, *Dorosoma cepedianum,* and the threadfin shad, *D. petenense*. *Trans. Amer. Microsc. Soc. 88*(4): 525–546. 1969.

Sivadas, P.   Absorption of fat in the alimentary canal of *Tilapia mossambica* (Peters) (Teleostei). *J. Cell. Comp. Physiol. 65:* 249–254. 1964.

Stolk, A.   Pharyngeal glands in the mouthbreeding anabantid *Betta anabatoides* Bleeker. *Acta morphol. Neer.-Scand. 5*(3): 252–260. 1963.

Vasil'eva, N. E., and Korovina, V. M.   A comparative histological study of the mid-intestine in a number of Salmonidae. *Vop. Ikhtiol. 9*(1): 191–196. 1969.

Verigina, I. A.   Structure of the alimentary tract in banded catfish (*Pseudobagrus fulvidraco*) and ussuri catfish (*Liocassis ussuriensis*) depending on the nature of nutrition. *Vop. Ikhtiol. 5*(1): 141–148. 1965.

Weinreb, E. L.   Studies on the histology and histopathology of the rainbow trout, *Salmo gairdneri irideus*. II. Effects. of induced inflammation and cortisone treatment on the digestive organs. *Zoologica (New York) 44*(2-5): 45-52. 1959.

Weinreb, E. L., and Bilstad, N. M.   Histology of the digestive tract and adjacent structures of the rainbow trout, *Salmo gairdneri irideus. Copeia 3:* 194-204. 1955.

Weisel, G. F.   Comparative study of the digestive tract of a sucker, *Catostomus catostomus*, and a predaceous minnow, *Phychocheilus oregonensis. Amer. Midl. Natur. 68*(2): 334-346. 1962.

Endocrine

Baker-Cohen, K. F.   Observations on the role of the thyroid in the development of platyfish. *Anat. Rec. 137*(3): 336. 1960.

Boddingius, J., and Fallaux, E. M.   Argyrophil adenohypophysial cells in the rainbow trout (*Salmo irideus*), demonstrated simultaneously with chromophil cells and with intracellular argyrophil fibrils by a new technique. *Neth. J. Zool. 20*(2): 291-297. 1970.

Cheze, G., Peyrand, C., Serfaty, A., and Seances, C. R.   A study of the effects of epiphysectomy on the retinal pigment dynamics of a teleost: The trout, *Salmo irideus* L. *Soc. Biol. Fil. 165*(9-10): 1985-1987. 1971.

Clement, J., Lecerf, J., and Fontaine, M.   Lipid constituents of the corpuscles of Stannius of *Anguilla anguilla* L. and *Salmo salar* L. *Ann. biol. anim. biochim. biophys. 10*(4): 631-642. 1971.

Cook, H., and Van Overbeeke, A. P.   Ultrastructure of the beta cells in the pituitary gland of adult migratory sockeye salmon (*Oncorhynchus nerka*). *Can. J. Zool. 47*(5): 937-941. 1969.

Cook, H., and Van Overbeeke, A. P.   Ultrastructure of the pituitary gland (pars distalis) in sockeye salmon (*Oncorhynchus nerka*) during gonad maturation. *Z. Zellforsch. mikrosk. Anat. 130*(3): 338-350. 1972.

Copeland, D. E., and Dalton, A. J.   An association between mitochondria and the endoplasmic reticulum in cells of the pseudobranch gland of a teleost. *J. Biophys. Biochem. Cytol. 5*(3): 393-396. 1959.

De Luise, M., Martin, T. J., and Melick, R. A.   Inactivation and degradation of porcine calcitonin by rat liver, and relative stability of salmon calcitonin. *J. Endocrinol. 48*(2): 181-188. 1970.

Fujita, H., Suemasa, H., and Honma, Y.   An electron microscopic study of the thyroid gland of the silver eel, *Anguilla japonica* (a part of phylogenetic studies of the fine structure of the thyroid). *Arch. histol. jap. 27*(1/5): 153-163. 1967.

Gardner, L. W., and Wachowski, H. E.   Histological study of the thyroid and pituitary in the minnow *Gambusia* after exposure to high temperature and treatment with thiourea. *Anat. Rec. 138*(3): 365, 1960.

Gupta, O. P., and Shrivastava, R. K.   Studies on the location, anatomy and histology of the endocrine glands of *Xenentodon cancila* (Ham.). *Okajimas folia anat. jap. 48*(4): 189-203. 1971.

Hafeez, M. A.   Light microscopic studies on the pineal organ in teleost fishes with special regard to its function. *J. Morphol. 134*(3): 281–314. 1971.

Hafeez, M. A., and Quay, W. B.   Histochemical and experimental studies of 5-hydroxytryptamine in pineal organs of teleosts (*Salmo gairdneri* and *Atherinopsis californiensis*). *Gen. Comp. Endocrinol. 13*(2): 211–217. 1969.

Keutmann, H. T., Parsons, J. A., Potts, J. T., Jr., and Schleuter, R. J.   Isolation and chemical properties of two calcitonins from salmon ultimobranchial glands. *J. Biol. Chem. 245*(6): 1491–1496. 1970.

Krishnamurthy, V. G.   Corpuscles of Stannius in *Colisa lalia* (Hamilton-Buchanan). *Naturwissenschaften 14:* 344–345. 1964.

Krishnamurthy, V. G., and Bern, H. A.   Innervation of corpuscles of Stannius. *Gen. Comp. Endocrinol. 16*(1): 162–165. 1971.

Lal, B.   Morphological, histological and histochemical studies of the pituitary gland of *Cirrhina mrigala* (Hamilton). *Proc. Indian Acad. Sci.,* Sect. B *59*(6): 297–317. 1964.

Lehri, G. K.   Correlative cyclical changes in the pituitary gland and the testis of a catfish, *Clarias batrachus* (Linn.). *Mikroskopie 26*(1/2): 50–56. 1970.

Lopez, E.   Histologic study of teleost cellular bone. II. Effect of ablation of the corpuscles of Stannius. *Z. Zellforsch. mikrosk. Anat. 109*(4): 566–572. 1971.

McBride, J. R., and Van Overbeeke, A. P.   Cytological changes in the pituitary gland of the adult sockeye salmon (*Oncorhynchus nerka*) after gonadectomy. *J. Fish. Res. Board Can. 26*(5): 1147–1156. 1969.

McBride, J. R., and Van Overbeeke, A. P.   Hypertrophy of the interrental tissue in sexually maturing sockeye salmon (*Oncorhynchus nerka*) and the effect of gonadectomy. *J. Fish. Res. Board Can. 26*(11): 2975–2985. 1969.

McBride, J. R., and Van Overbeeke, A. P.   Effects of androgens, estrogens, and cortisol on the skin, stomach, liver, pancreas, and kidney in gonadectomized adult sockeye salmon (*Oncorhynchus nerka*). *J. Fish. Res. Board Can. 28*(4): 485–490. 1971.

Moiseeva, E. B.   Identification and some morphological features of proadeno-hypophyseal cells of Gobiidae. *Dokl. Akad. Nauk. SSSR, Biol. Sci. Sect. 197*(2): 501–503, 1971.

Murphy, R. C.   The structure of the pineal organ of the bluefin tuna, *Thunnus thynnus. J. Morphol. 133*(1): 1–15. 1971.

Nagahama, Y., and Yamamoto, K.   Morphological studies on the pituitary of the chum salmon, *Oncorhynchus keta.* II. Changes of the prolactic cells during the life cycle. *Bull. Fac. Fish. Hokkaido Univ. 21*(3): 169–177. 1970.

Nandi, J.   The structure of the interrenal gland in teleost fishes. *Univ. Calif. Publ. Zool. 65:* 129–212. 1962.

Oguri, M.   Some histological observations on the interrenal bodies of elasmobranchs. *Bull. Jap. Soc. Sci. Fish. 26*(5): 481–485. 1960.

Oguri, M.   Histological study on the ACTH cells in the pituitary glands of freshwater teleosts. *Bull. Jap. Soc. Sci. Fish. 37*(7): 577–584. 1971.

Oguri, M., and Hibiya, T.   Studies on the adrenal gland of teleosts. II. On the adrenal tissues in 15 species of fishes. *Bull. Jap. Soc. Sci. Fish. 23*(3): 144–149. 1957.

Olivereau, M.   Anatomical and histological study of the thyroid gland of the tuna. *Bull. Soc. zool. Fr. 82*(5/6): 401–417. 1958.

Olivereau, M.   The histological structure of some endocrine glands of the eel following autotransplantation of the hypophysis. *Acta zool. (Stockholm) 52*(1): 69–83. 1971.

Olivereau. M.   Identification of the thyrotrophic cells in the hypophysis of the Pacific salmon (*Oncorhynchus tshawytscha* Walbaum) after radio thyroidectomy. *Z. Zellforsch. mikrosk. Anat. 128*(2): 175–187. 1972.

Olivereau, M., and Fromentin, H.   The effect of hypophysectomy on the histology of the anterior interrenal tissue in the eel, *Anguilla anguilla.   Ann. endocrinol. 15*(6): 805–826. 1954.

Olivereau, M., and Olivereau, J.   Effect of prolactin in intact and hypophysectomized eels.   VI.   Histological structure of interrenal and water and electrolyte metabolism. *Z. vgl. Physiol. 68*(4): 429–445. 1970.

Omura, Y., and Oguri, M.   The development and degeneration of the photoreceptor outer segment of the fish pineal organ. *Bull. Jap. Soc. Sci. Fish 37*(9): 851–856. 1971.

Rao, P. D. P.   Histology of the pituitary gland of six species of fishes belonging to the genus *Mystus scopoli* (Teleostomi). *Anat. Anz. 130*(3/4): 347–361. 1972.

Rasquin, P.   Undescribed glands in the kidney of the juvenile tarpon, *Megalops atlantica.   Copeia 1:* 83–91. 1969.

Robertson, D. R.   Some morphological observations of the ultimobranchial gland in the rainbow trout, *Salmo gairdneri. J. Anat. 105*(1): 115–127. 1969.

Robertson, D. R.   The ultimobranchial body of *Rana pipiens.* VIII.   Effects of extirpation upon calcium distribution and bone cell types. *Gen. Comp. Endocrinol. 12*(3): 479–490. 1969.

Robertson, O. H., and Wexler, B. C.   Histological changes in the pituitary gland of the Pacific salmon (genus *Oncorhynchus*) accompanying sexual maturation and spawning. *J. Morphol. 110*(2): 171–186. 1962.

Rucart, G., Payeur, C., and Germain, P.   Histochemical and experimental duality of the parathyroid epithelium. *Anat. Rec. 136*(2): 269. 1960.

Sathyanesan, A. G.   Histological changes in the pituitary and their correlation with the gonadal cycle in some teleosts. *Cellule 63*(2): 284–293. 1963.

Singh, T. P.   Seasonal variations in the cyanophils and the gonadotropic potency of the pituitary in relation to gonadal activity in the catfish, *Mystus vittatus* (Bloch). *Endokrinologie 56*(3): 292–303. 1971.

Swift, D. R.   Cyclical activity of the thyroid gland of fish in relation to environmental changes. *Symp. Zool. Soc. London 2:* 17–27, 1960.

Tan-Tue, V.   Histology of the ultimobranchial bodies of *Chimaera monstrosa. Arch. anat. microscop. morphol. exp. 59*(1): 21–36. 1970.

Van Overbeeke, A. P., and McBride, J. R.   The pituitary gland of the sockeye (*Oncorhynchus nerka*) during sexual maturation and spawning. *J. Fish. Res. Board Can. 24*(8): 1791–1810. 1967.

Van Overbeeke, A. P., and McBride, J. R.   Histological effects of 11-ketotestosterone, 17 α-methyltestosterone, estradiol, estradiol cypionate, and cortisol on the interrenal tissue, thyroid gland, and pituitary gland of the gonadectomized sockeye salmon (*Oncorhynchus nerka*). *J. Fish. Res. Board Can. 28*(4): 477–485. 1971.

Zaitsev, A. V.   Hypophyseal structures in bony fishes: Seasonal changes of hypophyseal and gonadal microstructures in relation to reproductive conditions. *Problemy Sovermennoi Embriologii* (*Problems in Presend-Day Embryology*): 304–310. 1964.

Genital

Flugel, H.   On the fine structure of the zona radiata of growing trout oocytes. *Naturwissenschaften 22:* 542. 1964.

Ivanova, S. A.   Histological study of gonads of the pink salmon and the summer chum. In *Pacific Salmon* (selected articles from Soviet periodicals–translated from Russian), 1956.

Robertson, O. H.   Accelerated development of testis after unilateral gonadectomy, with observations on normal testis of rainbow trout. *U. S. Fish Wildlife Serv. Fish. Bull. 127,* from Fish. Bull. 58: 9–30. 1958.

Sato, M.   The hatching and hatching glands of catfish, *Parasilurus asotus* (L.). *Sci. Rep. Hirosaki Univ. 7*(2): 48–56. 1960.

Excretory (Juxtaglomerular)

Beitch, I.   A histomorphological comparison of the urinary system in the serranid fishes, *Roccus saxatilis* and *R. americanus.   Chesapeake Sci. 4*(2): 75–83. 1963.

Bulger, R. E., and Trump, B. F.   Renal morphology of the English sole (*Parophrys vetulus*). *Amer. J. Anat. 123:* 195–226. 1963.

DeSmet, W.   The nephron of *Amia calva* (Protospondyli, Pisces). *Acta zool. (Stockholm) 44*(3): 269–298. 1963.

Ford, P., and Newstead, J. D.   Studies on the development of the kidney of the Pacific pink salmon (*Oncorhynchus gorbuscha* Walbaum). I. The development of the pronephros. *Can. J. Zool. 36*(1): 15–21. 1958.

Grafflin, A. L.   The problem of adaptation to fresh and salt water in the teleosts, viewed from the standpoint of the structure of the renal tubules. *J. Cell. Comp. Physiol. 9:* 469–476. 1937.

Gritzka, T. L.   The ultrastructure of the proximal convoluted tubule of a euryhaline teleost, *Fundulus heteroclitus. Anat. Rec. 145:* 235–236. 1968.

Maunsbach, A. B.   Comparison of renal tubule ultrastructure after perfusion fixation with different fixatives. *J. Cell Biol. 23*(2): 108A–109A. 1964.

Oguri, M., and Sokabe, H.   Juxtaglomerular cells in the teleost kidneys. *Bull. Jap. Soc. Sci. Fish. 34*(10): 882–888. 1968.

Oguri, M., Kamiya, K., and Sokabe, H.   A histological study of the juxtaglomerular cells in the kidney of Japanese mackerel. *Bull. Jap. Soc. Sci. Fish. 35*(8): 737–742. 1969.

Oguri, M., Ogawa, M., and Sokabe, H.   Absence of juxtaglomerular cells in the kidneys of Chondrichthyes and Cyclostomi. *Bull. Jap. Soc. Sci. Fish. 36*(9): 881–884. 1970.

Pak Poy, R. K. F.   Electron microscopy of the piscine (*Carassius auratus*) renal glomerulus. *Aust. J. Exp. Biol. Med. Sci. 36:* 191–210. 1958.

Tampi, P. R. S.   On the renal unit in some common teleosts. *Proc. Indian Acad. Sci.,* Sect. B *50*(2): 88–104, 1959.

Weatherley, A. H.   A note on the head kidney and kidney of the perch *Perca fluviatilis* (Linnaeus), with special reference to the blood vascular system. *J. Zool. (London) 140*(2): 161–167. 1963.

Hematopoietic, Blood, and Vascular

Downey, H.   The lymphatic tissue of the kidney of *Polyodon spathula. Folia haematol. (Leipzig) 8:* 415–466. 1909.

Drinker, C. K., and Yoffey, J. M.   Lymphatics, Lymph and Lymphoid Tissue. Cambridge, Harvard Univ. Press, 1941.

Drzewina, A.   Contribution. À l'étude du tissue lymphoide des ichthyopsides. *Arch. zool. exp. gen. 3:* 145–338. 1905.

Galer, B. B., and Billenstien, D. C.   Ultrastructural development of the saccus vasculosus in rainbow trout (*Salmo gairdneri*). *Z. Zellforsch. mikrosk. Anat. 128*(2): 162–174. 1972.

Jordan, H. E.   The reticulo-endothelial system with special reference to the lymphocyte. *Va. Med. 53:* 776–782. 1927.

Lansing, A. I., Lamy, F., and Malkoff, D.   Connective tissue fibers of the bulbus arteriosus. *Anat. Rec. 136*(2): 228. 1960.

Lanzing, W. J. R., and Van Lennep, E. W.   The ultrastructure of the saccus vasculosus of teleost fishes. I. The coronet cell. *Aust. J. Zool. 18*(4): 353–371. 1971.

Millot, J. M. M.   Suprabranchial blood regulating organ in *Latimeria chalumnae. C. r. séances Acad. Sci. 246.* 1958.

Ohara, T.   A study of the saccus vasculosus of fishes. *Acta med. (Fukuoka) 28*(3): 750–773. 1958.

Pestova, I. M.   The hemapoietic faculty of the vascular endothelium in the otogenesis of bony fish. *Arkh. anat. gistol. embriol. 31*(4): 17–24. 1956.

Remmele, W., and Rodrequez-Erdmann, F.   The kidneys and erythropoiesis. *Frankf. Z. Pathol. 70:* 152–173. 1959.

Robertson, O. H., Wexler, B. C., and Miller, B. F.   Degenerative changes in the cardiovascular system of the spawning Pacific salmon (*Oncorhynchus tshawytscha*). *Circ. Res. 9*(4): 826–834. 1961.

Rubashev, S. !.   Research on the physiology of fish blood, IV. White blood cells in some freshwater fishes. *Fish. Res. Board Can.,* Transl. Ser. No. 1312/1969. 1939.

Sundararaj, B. I., and Prasad, M. R. N.   The histochemistry of the saccus vasculosus of *Notopterus chitala* (Teleostei). *Quart. J. Microsc. Sci. 104*(4): 465–470, 1963.

Sundararaj, B. I. and Prasad, M. R. N.   The histophysiology of the saccus vasculosus of *Notopterus chitala* (Teleostei). *Quart. J. Microsc. Sci. 105*(1): 91–98. 1964.

Sundararaj, B. I., and Viswanathan, N.   Hypothalamo-hypophyseal neurosecretory and vascular systems in the catfish, *Heteropneustes fossilis* (Bloch). *J. Comp. Neurol. 141*(1): 95–106. 1971.

Weinreb, E. L.   Studies on the histology and histopathology of the rainbow trout, *Salmo gairdneri irideus*. I. Hematology under normal and experimental conditions of inflammation. *Zoologica (New York) 43*(4): 145–154. 1958.

Weinreb, E. L.   Electron microscope studies on teleost blood cells under normal and experimental conditions. *Anat. Rec. 145*(2): 369. 1963.

Yoffey, J. M.   A contribution to the study of the comparative histology and physiology of the spleen, with reference chiefly to its cellular constituents. I. In fishes. *J. Anat. 63:* 314–348. 1929.

Nervous and Special Sensory

Desgranges, J. C.   On the taste buds of the catfish *Ictalurus melas:* Ultrastructure of the basal cells. *C. r. hebd. séances Acad. Sci. (Paris),* Ser. D, Sci. Nat. *274*(12): 1814–1817. 1972.

Engstrom, K.   Cone types and cone arrangement in the retina of some cyprinids. *Acta zool. (Stockholm) 41*(3): 277–295. 1960.

Hall, A., Schulte, E., and Holl, W.   Crossing-over of olfactory fiber bundles within the olfactory bulb of catfishes. *Z. Naturforsch.,* Sect. B *26*(7): 739–740. 1971.

Moore, G. A., and Burris, W. E.   Description of the lateral-line system of the pirate perch, *Aphredoderus sayanus. Copeia 1:* 18–20. 1956.

Naka, K.   The horizontal cells. *Vision Res. 12*(4): 573–588. 1972.

Payrau, P., Offret, G., Faure, J. P., Pouliquen, Y., and Cuq, G.   On the lamellar structure of the corneas of certain fishes. *Arch. Ophthalmol. (Paris) 24*(8): 685–690. 1964.

Sato, M., and Katagiri, N.   Preliminary report on the fine structure of the receptor cells of the small pit organ of the catfish, *Parasilurus asotus. Jap. J. Ichthyol. 16*(3): 115–119. 1969.

Schuster, T.   Beitrag zur Architektonik der Riesensynapsen in Nucleus nervi oculomotorii bei *Salmo (trutta) irideus* (Gibbons, 1855). *Z. mikrosk.-anat. Forsch. 83*(4): 518–524. 1971.

Schuster, T., and Loetzke, H.   Cytoarchitektonik und Biomorphose des nc. n. oculomotorii bei *Salmo (trutta) irideus* (Gibbons, 1855). *Z. mikrosk.-anat. Forsch. 83*(2): 246–276. 1971.

Shibkova, S. A.   The innervation of the retina. *Probl. fiziol. optiki 12:* 422–428. 1958.

Stahl, A.   Neurosecretion and other neuronal elaborations in the brain of the teleostean fishes. *C. r. Ass. Anat. 44*(100): 699–708. 1958.

Wright, R. R.   On the skin and cutaneous sense organs of *Ameiurus. Proc. Canad. Inst. 2:* 251–269. 1884.

Respiratory

Brooks, R. E.   Ultrastructure of the physostomatous swimbladder of rainbow trout (*Salmo gairdneri*). *Z. Zellforsch. mikrosk. Anat. 106*(4): 473–483. 1970.

Fahlen, G. The functional morphology of the gas bladder of the genus *Salmo*. *Acta anat.* *78*(2): 161–184. 1971.

Fearnhead, E. A., and Fabian, B. C. The ultrastructure of the gill of *Monodactylus argenteus* (a euryhaline teleost fish) with particular reference to morphological changes associated with changes in salinity. *S. Afr. Ass. Mar. Biol. Res. Oceanogr. Res. Inst., Invest. Rep. No. 26*, pp. 1–40. 1971.

Kashiwagi, M., and Sato, R. Studies on the osmoregulation of the chum salmon, *Oncorhynchus keta* (Walbaum). II. Histological observations of the branchial epithelium according to the growth of the fish from hatching. *Tohoku J. Agr. Res. 20*(4): 212–221. 1970.

Monie, A. S. Goblet cells in the swimbladder of *Ophiocephalus striatus* (Bloch). *Nature (London) 192:* 1311. 1961.

Supportive Tissues

Hughes, G. M., and E. R. Weibel. Similarity of supporting tissue in fish gills and the mammalian reticuloendothelium. *J. Ultrastruct. Res. 39*(1–2): 106–114. 1972.

Lopez, E. Histological study on teleost cellular bone. I. *Z. Zellforsch. mikrosk. Anat. 109*(4): 552–565. 1971.

Moss, M. L. The biology of acellular teleost (fish) bone, pp. 337–350. In *Comparative Biology of Calcified Tissue, Ann. N. Y. Acad. Sci. 109*(1). 1963.

Moss, M. L. Studies of the acellular bone of teleost fish. V. Histology and mineral homeostasis of fresh-water species. *Acta anat. 60:* 262–276. 1965.

Integument

Bassot, J. Structure and ultrastructure of luminescent organs in some teleosts. *Proc. Int. Congr. Zool. 16*(2): 283. 1963.

Eastman, J. T., Moore, R. H., and Phillips, G. L. *Arius felis:* Pelvic fin modification in female. *Trans. Amer. Microsc. Soc. 89*(3): 427–430. 1970.

Thomson, D. A. A histological study and bioassay of the toxic stress secretion of the boxfish, *Ostracion lentiginosus*. *Diss. Abstr.* 3902. 1964.

(*Note:* Additional references can be seen in Hoar, W. S., and Randall, D. J., eds. *Fish Physiology*. 6 vols. New York and London, Academic Press, 1969–70.)

DISCUSSION OF COMPARATIVE FISH HISTOLOGY

Question: You mentioned that the carp has skeletal muscle the length of the intestine. This could have some very unique advantages in controlling the intestinal motility. Is it true that the carp can control the movement of food through the gut?

L. M. Ashley: Apparently so. I haven't worked with carp personally, but this is what is recorded.

R. C. Summerfelt: The question was asked about the occurrence of striated muscle in the carp gut. I don't know anything about the occurrence of this, but carp are capable of sorting and sifting through food very effectively. In fact, in efforts to control carp by scattering pills containing toxic substances, the carp would pick up these and sort through them and take the food out and reject the pill.

M. M. Sigel: I would like to make two points and ask questions pertaining to them. You state that the skin, while rich in goblet cells, does not contain any lymphocytes. Yet, we and others have found that the surface mucus of fish is very rich in IgM antibodies. We have also shown that these antibodies are produced locally and are not derived from the serum. We therefore assume that they are manufactured somewhere in the skin, yet I could not see any lymphoid cells in your section. This is one comment and question.

The other one has to do with the thymus. The thymus of fish is involved in both antibody synthesis and in antigen recognition, as shown by the blastogenic transformation of lymphocytes of the thymus. Our studies on the thymus show a very primitive thymus devoid of epithelium and Hassall's corpuscles. Have you seen Hassall's corpuscles or epithelium in fish thymuses?

L. M. Ashley: We see primitive Hassall's corpuscles occasionally in the thymus and some authors have identified them as Hassall's corpuscles. Their abundance may vary a great deal in different species. In salmonids I have recognized them occasionally and consider that they must be Hassall's corpuscles, but these are rather feeble attempts at reproducing the mammalian type. As far as lymphocytes in the skin are concerned, I think we do see them occasionally in the dermal area. In normal, healthy fish I don't find them there, and I have thought that they were there as a response to some irritant. It may be that in case of infection of the skin you would expect them to infiltrate the area. Otherwise I don't know where they would be except in the various depots where we have described them as commonly occurring.

R. L. Herman: In regard to the Hassall's bodies, my observations have been similar to Dr. Ashley's. I have the impression that in rainbow trout these Hassall's bodies appear as an indication of degeneration. At about two years of age the thymus in the trout begins to deteriorate and this is when I have seen these bodies, rather than in the younger fish.

L. M. Ashley: I think that's probably true but I haven't made any special study of this.

PART I
Specific Diseases

2

Pathology of Bacterial and Fungal
Diseases Affecting Fish

R . E . W O L K E

A classification of microbial diseases of fish useful to the pathologist and based upon organisms' ability to produce proliferative lesions can be constructed as follows:

The comparative pathologist seeks to diagnose disease on the basis of gross and histopathological lesions. He has other disciplines upon which he may call for assistance, such as clinical medicine, clinical pathology, and microbiology. But the findings of these disciplines are not always available and often he must depend solely on anatomic pathology to answer the question, "What disease process was responsible for the animal's death?"

He eagerly seeks to isolate and characterize the etiological agent involved in any disease outbreak, but should this be impossible it is his ability to interpret groups of gross and microscopic lesions which allows a diagnosis to be made. This approach is a well-recognized procedure in the diagnosis of disease in higher vertebrates, including man and domestic animals.

In the study of fish diseases the emphasis has been placed upon microbiology, while diagnosis by gross and histopathology has not been vigorously pursued. Changes do occur however within damaged fish tissue which are characteristic of specific disease processes.

Such tissue changes include three major categories of lesions: those associated with inflammation, those associated with cellular degeneration and necrosis, and abnormalities of cell growth, including neoplasia. These basic categories may be further subdivided to allow for the subtle differences elicited by various agents. Inflammatory responses, commonly associated with infectious agents, are categorized on the basis of cell type and vascular changes. Acute inflammation (of short duration) is characterized by sudden vascular insult resulting in congestion, edema, and hemorrhage and by an influx of polymorphonuclear cells (neutrophils, heterophils) at the point of damage. Chronic inflammation (of longer duration) is characterized by vascular proliferation and by an influx of mononuclear cells, such as lymphocytes and plasma cells. Granulomatous inflammation is a proliferative chronic inflammatory response characterized by reticulo-endothelial and phagocytic cells, especially the histiocyte (macrophage) and monocyte. In addition, epithelioid and giant cells are often present. A focus of granulomatous inflammation having a central area of necrosis surrounded by a zone of histiocytes and epithelioid cells in turn bound by fibroblastic proliferation and rimmed by lymphocytes and plasma cells is referred to as a granuloma. This structure may contain Langhans or foreign-body giant cells and/or infiltrating polymorphonuclear cells. Histopathological studies of the bacterial and mycotic diseases of fish yield examples of these major lesion categories and their subdivisions with the exception of autogenous neoplasia.

Data collected from studies of these diseases give credence to the hypothesis that fish tissue is capable of responding to pathological agents in much the same manner as the tissue of higher vertebrates except in the production of a true purulent response. The purulent inflammatory response is the product of enzyme systems present within the mammalian neutrophil and results in inflammatory exudate known as pus (39).

Pus is a product of necrotic tissue, body fluids, bacteria, and masses of neutrophils, many of which have phagocytized the invading bacteria. The whole suppurative process is therefore defined in terms of a mammalian response with specific cells (neutrophils) containing specific enzymes (lysosomal) and serving a specific function (enzyme production and phagocytosis). As we descend the phylogenetic scale we find that the bird is incapable of producing a true purulent response because its granulocytes (heterophils) are weakly phagocytic and lack the enzymes of higher vertebrates (31). On the basis of gross and histopathological examination of piscine inflammation, it appears that the fish granulocyte is similar to the avian heterophil. Although acute inflammations may occur, true pus is not a product of these inflammations. Fey (50) has reported the presence of acid and alkaline phosphatases in elasmobranch granulocytes, but Weinreb and Bilstad (176) found no evidence of these enzymes in trout digestive tract granulocytes. The presence of a true neutrophil in the fish is controversial. Recent evidence based upon the presence of chromatin bridges in certain carp granulocytes indicates that at least some species of fish may in fact have neutrophilic leukocytes (87). Whether or not these cells can function in a suppurative response is as yet unproven.

I have seen the production of a white to pink, creamy exudate resembling pus in *Pseudopleuronectes americanus* in natural infections, and 96 hours after intramuscular injection with a culture of *Vibrio anguillarum* suspended in Zobell's Marine Broth. Microscopic examination of exudate smears revealed necrotic tissue and masses of lymphocytes and macrophages. Granulocytes were present but no more than one or two per high-powered field. This exudate did not, therefore, fit the accepted definition of pus. Histologically the reaction was classified as a chronic inflammatory response and in no way resembled a suppurative process.

It would appear, therefore, that the fish responds more like the bird than the mammal in the production of pus or purulent exudate. For this reason, and with our present knowledge of piscine inflammation, classification of lesion types should not include purulent response but rather heterophilic or acute response.

These characteristic responses, then, once properly described and classified in association with their causative agents, allow the comparative pathologist to make positive diagnoses often without the aid of agent isolation. Further, such lesions allow the investigator to determine the mechanisms of disease development and the reasons for its manifestations.

A variable affecting tissue response which must be considered in any discussion of lesion development is that of the surrounding environmental temperature. Recent studies on inflammation in the rainbow trout indicate that the speed of inflammatory response and its severity depend to some extent on the temperature of the surrounding water (56). At a low temperature (5°C) lesions were identical to those elicited by the same agent at a higher temperature (15°C). However, quantitatively they differed, the reaction at the lower temperature being much less marked over a similar time period than the reaction at the higher temperature. After intraperitoneal injection of killed staphylococci, fibroblasts and fibroplasia which were present after 4 days at 15°C were not yet present after 16 days at 5°C. It appears, therefore, that the fish pathologist must consider the temperature of the surrounding water when he evaluates lesions in fish associated with infectious and noninfectious agents.

Some piscine bacterial and mycotic diseases lend themselves well to diagnosis by means of anatomic pathology. Others have not been sufficiently studied histopathologically to determine if they are responsible for the production of characteristic tissue lesions. However, present knowledge indicates that diagnosis of these diseases by means of classic pathological techniques warrants further investigation.

It is the purpose of this paper to describe these tissue changes and to add information regarding the pathogenesis of these diseases.

BACTERIAL DISEASES

The reported bacterial pathogens may be classified on the basis of their staining characteristics. This criterion separates the organisms into those which are gram-negative, those which are gram-positive, and those which are acid-fast. Further grouping may be made on the basis of the general tissue reaction which these organisms elicit. This general inflammatory response is either nonproliferative or proliferative in nature.

Nonproliferative may be defined as a tissue response which tends to be acute, vascular, characterized by necrosis, and nongranulomatous. In addition, the bacteria eliciting this type of response often produce dermal ulcers and tend to destroy elements of the hematopoietic system. *Proliferative* may be defined as a tissue response which tends to be more chronic, granulomatous, and characterized in some instances by hypertrophy and hyperplasia of epithelial and other tissue elements.

Combining these two criteria, staining reaction and general tissue response elicited, bacteria pathogenic to fish may be grouped as follows:

> NONPROLIFERATIVE
> > Gram-negative
> > > Brucellaceae
> > > > *Haemophilus piscium*
> > > > *Pasteurella piscicida*
> > > Cytophogaceae
> > > > *Cytophaga psychrophilia*
> > > Enterobacteriaceae
> > > > *Aerobacter cloacae*
> > > > *Paracolobactrum aerogenoides*
> > > > *"RM" bacterium*
> > > Myxococcaceae
> > > > *Chondrococcus columnaris*
> > > Pseudomonadaceae
> > > > *Aeromonas liquefaciens*
> > > > *A. salmonicida*
> > > > *Pseudomonas fluorescens*
> > > Spirillaceae
> > > > *Vibrio anguillarum*
> > Gram-positive
> > > Streptococcaceae
> > > > *Streptococcus faecalis*
> > > > *Streptococcus* sp.
> > > Streptomycetaceae
> > > > *Streptomyces salmonicida*

PROLIFERATIVE
    Gram-negative
        Achromobacteriaceae
            Flavobacterium sp.
        Cytophagaceae
            Cytophaga sp.
        Myxococcaceae
            Sporocytophaga sp.
    Gram-positive
        Corynebacteriaceae
            Corynebacterium sp.
        Micrococcaceae
            Staphylococcus sp.
    Acid-fast
        Actinomycetaceae
            Nocardia asteroides
            N. kampachi
        Mycobacteriaceae
            Mycobacterium fortuitum
            M. marinum
            M. platypoecilus

This grouping is based upon present knowledge of the histopathology associated with piscine bacterial diseases and is suggested as a convenient means of grouping these diseases for the histopathologist. For instance, it will be noted that the gram-negative organisms tend to be nonproliferative in their reaction whereas the gram-positive, acid-fast so-called higher bacteria are definitely granulomatous and proliferative in nature. A similar situation exists for the higher vertebrates as well. As we gather more histopathological information and as more experiments are conducted to study the pathogenesis of these diseases, the grouping of bacteria on the basis of generalized tissue reaction will undoubtedly need to be re-evaluated.

Pathogenic bacteria of fish were reviewed by Griffin (69) in 1954 and information concerning the advances in knowledge since that time was reviewed by Bullock and McLaughlin (24).

Gram-Negative Organisms Eliciting Nonproliferative Response

BRUCELLACEAE

Haemophilus piscium (ulcer disease)

Ulcer disease is a bacteremic disease of trout caused by the organism *Haemophilus piscium* and characterized by acute dermal ulceration, especially about the head and mouth.

The disease is confined to northeastern North America, and while it was relatively common two decades ago, its incidence has decreased significantly in recent years.

Early investigators encountered difficulty in isolating the causative agent but were able to differentiate the disease from furunculosis on the basis of gross lesions. Fish (56), describing an outbreak in a Cortland, New York, hatchery, noted proliferative epidermal changes preceding ulceration and a lack of secondary fungal invasion, two signs he felt absent from cases of furunculosis. Wolf (181) confirmed these findings and noted a propensity for ulcers to affect the skin of the head and mouth. He also reported differences in species susceptibility to infection. Rainbow trout (*Salmo gairdneri*) were found most resistant, brown trout (*S. trutta*) moderately resistant, and brook trout (*S. fontinalis*) most susceptible. The disease was not confined to hatcheries but was also present in wild trout (182).

The isolation of this fastidious organism was finally achieved, using a medium enriched with trout tissue extract (158, 160). The organism could be recovered from lesions, kidney, and blood. It was described as a small (1 to 2.0 X 0.6 to 0.8 microns), gram-negative, nonmotile, beta-hemolytic, aerobic rod for which the authors suggested the name *Haemophilus piscium.* A method of enriching commercial media to simplify isolation was described by Bullock (22).

Transmission occurs via contaminated food or water. The source of the organism may be ulcers or feces of affected fish. Experimental transmission by means of intraperitoneal or intramuscular inoculation followed by organism recovery has been successful. Both young and adult fish are susceptible, and older fish may recover from the disease. The condition often occurs in conjunction with *Aeromonas salmonicida.* Lowered water temperatures have been shown to retard disease development (182).

Gross lesions are confined to the external surface and are characterized by dermal ulceration especially along the edges of the jaw and the roof of the mouth. Fish (56) noted that ulcer development differed from that associated with furunculosis. In ulcer disease no "furuncle" is formed; rather, the ulcer is preceded by a thickening of epithelium referred to as an epithelial "tuft." This epithelial proliferation results in the presence of a white area which resembles a dermal fungal infection (saprolegniasis). The ulcer is sharply outlined, usually circular and up to 1 cm in diameter. Ulceration of the jaw may extend to the underlying bone, with its eventual destruction. The soft tissue between fin rays may also be destroyed. Here the proximal margin of the necrotic area is often bound by a distinct line of white tissue.

Microscopically the developed ulcer has sharp edges and extends through the dermis and hypodermis into the underlying skeletal muscle (Fig. 2.1). The epidermis bordering the ulcer is increased in thickness because of hyperplasia of epithelial cells just above the layer corresponding to the stratum germinativum of higher vertebrates. These cells are irregularly arranged, resulting in a loss of the normal strata organization. The inflammatory response at the center of the ulcer is within muscle and is subacute. It is characterized by hemorrhage, influx of lymphocytes, and muscle fiber necrosis (Fig. 2.2). In those areas closest to the

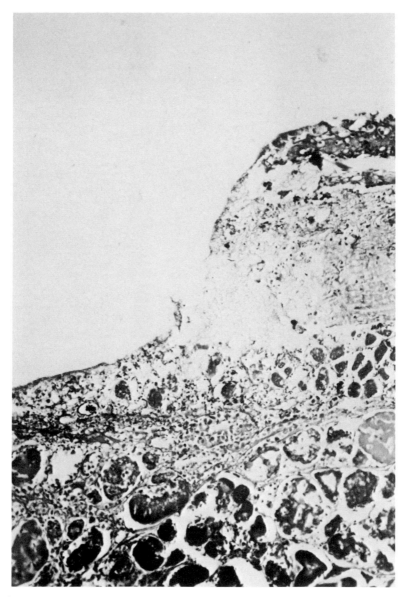

Fig. 2.1. Ulcer disease. Sharp-edged dermal ulcer extending into underlying skeletal muscle. (Tissue courtesy of Dr. G. Bullock.) Hematoxylin and eosin (H&E); ×65.

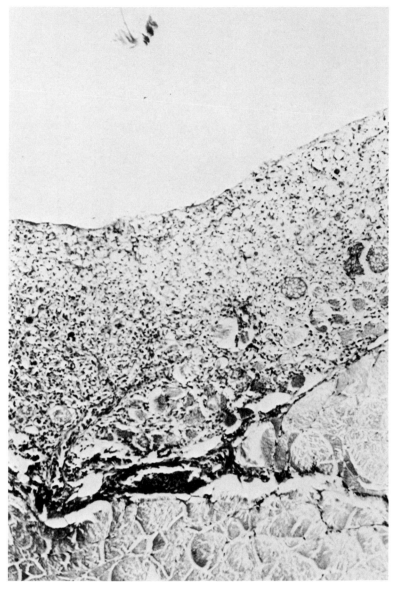

Fig. 2.2. Ulcer disease. Center of ulcer crater with muscle necrosis and lymphocytes in the base. (Tissue courtesy of Dr. G. Bullock.) H&E; ×65.

previously existing dermis there is a complete loss of muscle fibers, resulting in empty spaces surrounded by loosely arranged fibrous tissue and mononuclear cells. No regenerating muscle fibers are apparent. Lesions appear confined to skin, skeletal muscle, and bone.

A differential diagnosis of the ulcers associated with *Haemophilus* infection must consider ulcers produced by *A. salmonicida, A. liquefaciens,* and *V. anguillarum.* With present knowledge of the inflammatory response elicited by these agents, differential diagnosis based on histopathology does not appear possible. The ulcer of *A. salmonicida* differs from ulcers due to other agents in that inflammatory cell response is slight to absent after a 48-hour period. This lack of cell response can be attributed to the production of leukocytotoxin by the bacterium (90). However, since rate and severity of inflammatory reaction are so temperature-dependent, it is probable that a lesion due to *A. liquefaciens, Haemophilus,* or *Vibrio* could develop in the same time span but at a varying temperature and resemble the ulcer of furunculosis. I have produced ulcers and myositis by intramuscular injection of *V. anguillarum* at temperatures in excess of 18°C. These were essentially identical to those of *Haemophilus,* but those produced at lower temperatures resembled those of *A. salmonicida.* Differential diagnosis of these ulcerogenic diseases must, therefore, depend at present on anamnesis, clinical signs, other histopathological lesions, and agent isolation.

The economic importance, diagnosis, treatment, and prevention of ulcer disease is reviewed by Snieszko (155).

Pasteurella piscicida (pasteurellosis)

Pasteurellosis of fish was first reported by Snieszko et al. (162). These investigators recovered the organism from white perch (*Morone americana*) involved in a mass kill in Chesapeake Bay during the summer of 1963. Allen and Pelczar (6) studied the organism and found it unrelated to normal bacterial flora of the white perch and capable of disease production under experimental conditions. In 1968 the organism was named *Pasteurella piscicida* (86). It has also been recovered from striped bass (*M. saxatilis*) and is pathogenic to this species as well. Ajmal and Hobbs (4) isolated a small, nonhemolytic, gram-negative rod from the livers and kidneys of rudd and chub during a mass kill of these fish in Sussex lakes. The organism was identified as *Pasteurella* sp. Lesions included muscle hemorrhage and congestion of liver, spleen, and kidney. A greyish-brown fungus was present, usually at the base of the fins and caudal peduncle. Koch's postulates were not fulfilled. The histological lesions produced by *P. piscicida* or *Pasteurella* sp. have not been described.

I have examined formalin-fixed liver and spleen from a fish infected with *P. piscicida* obtained from the Eastern Fish Disease Laboratory, Leetown, West Virginia. Cut sections of the fixed spleen had white, circumscribed, 1 mm areas diffusely and irregularly distributed throughout the parenchyma. Histologically these areas were collections of necrotic lymphoid and peripheral blood cells (Fig. 2.3). The spleen was congested. Focal areas of hepatocytes undergoing co-

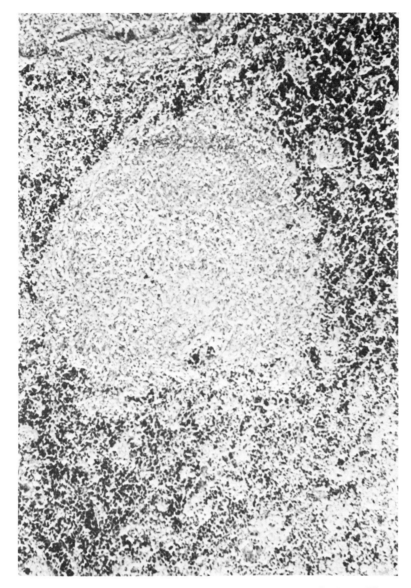

Fig. 2.3. Pasteurellosis of *Morone americana.*   Acute focal necrosis of spleen. (Tissue courtesy of Dr. G. Bullock.) H&E; ×65.

agulation necrosis were present throughout the liver. Increased Kupffer cell activity was present but an inflammatory cell response was conspicuously absent in both organs.

CYTOPHAGACEAE

Cytophaga psychrophilia (coldwater disease; peduncle disease)

In 1960 Borg (19) described a disease which had been observed among fingerling silver salmon 12 years previously in the state of Washington. Mortality among affected fish was as high as 31%. The outbreak occurred in water varying in temperature from 6° to 10°C and for this reason was referred to as a "low temperature" disease of salmonids. The primary gross lesion associated with the disease was dermal necrosis, occurring just anterior to the tail. The lesion progressed caudally, often resulting in destruction of the caudal fin and peduncle. A myxobacterium capable of reproducing the disease was isolated and named *Cytophaga psychrophilia.*

A similar disease described in 1946 had been observed as early as 1941 among fingerling rainbow trout at the Federal Hatchery in Leetown, West Virginia (44). The disease was named "peduncle disease." Bullock and Snieszko (25) have suggested that these two diseases may be identical, since, in both, lesions appear in similar locations, systemic myxobacteria are present, and the diseases occur at low water temperatures.

Coldwater disease is an acute septicemic process of fish caused by the bacterium *C. psychrophilia,* and characterized by dermal ulceration and necrosis of major organs.

C. psychrophilia is a bacterium of the order Myxobacteriales, family Cytophagaceae. These organisms are commonly known as myxobacteria or slime bacteria. They are elongate (0.3 to 0.5 × 2.0 to 10.0 microns), flexible, gram-negative rods which differ from other members of their order in that they do not produce fruiting bodies or resting cells. Isolation of the organism may be achieved using *Cytophaga* agar (9). Initial isolates of the organism would not grow above 25°C, and best growth was aerobically between 18° and 20°C (19). Colony, biochemical, and serological characteristics have been reviewed by Pacha and Ordal (116).

Coldwater disease affects young fish from yolk sac fry to fingerlings. The disease is reported in trout and three species of salmon (coho, chinook, and sockeye) (141). Outbreaks generally occur at low water temperatures from 4° to 12°C. Studies have shown a sharp decline in mortality in waters above 12.8°C (141).

While the disease is relatively common throughout the northwestern United States, its epidemiology is poorly understood. Borg (19) was able to pass on the disease by means of intramuscular injection and by exposing fish with abraded skin to dilute cultures for five minutes. The disease was not horizontally spread. The organism's natural reservoir is unknown, and it is suggested that resident fish might serve as carriers (115).

Anamnesis and clinical signs include an acute mortality (up to 50%) affecting fingerling or younger salmonids at low water temperatures (less than 55°F) and increased pigmentation of the caudal peduncle followed by ulceration, necrosis, and caudal fin destruction.

While gross lesions appear confined to the skin, muscle, and fins of affected fish, the causative organism may be recovered from internal organs, such as the spleen, liver, and kidney, as well as from external lesions.

Histologically, ulceration of the epidermis and underlying dermis is present. Early lesions have granulocytic infiltration of the dermis and outer muscle masses. As the lesion matures, more lymphocytes and then macrophages become apparent. Muscle fibers undergo necrosis, leaving empty spaces surrounded by perimysium. The lesion may be quite severe, with a good deal of connective tissue proliferation and attempts of muscle regeneration (Fig. 2.4). Long, slender gram-negative rods may be seen within the inflammatory tissue. Wood and Yasutake (185) state that the lesion of "red mouth" in trout is similar except that the inflammatory process is more extensive. Differentiation of the dermal ulcerations caused by *Cytophaga, A. liquefaciens, Haemophilus,* and *Vibrio* on the basis of present knowledge of histopathological changes in the fish would be extremely difficult if not impossible. The pathogenesis of these diseases must be studied at optimal, constant water temperatures over identical time spans in various species of fish before valid microscopic comparisons of lesions can be made.

Bacteria are also present within the heart, spleen, kidney glomeruli, and gill lamellar capillaries. This latter location of bacteria may be used to differentiate this disease from bacterial gill disease (185). In the latter case the bacteria are on the gill surface rather than within vessels. Necrosis of major organs is associated with the disease, especially in the kidney, where tubular elements are affected with greater frequency than the interstitial hematopoietic tissue.

ENTEROBACTERIACEAE

Aerobacter cloacae

In 1941 Reed and Toner (125) reported a disease of pike (*Esox lucius*) characterized by shallow grey dermal ulcers. *Proteus hydrophilus* (syn. *Aeromonas liquefaciens*) was recovered from the lesions, and the disease was referred to as "red sore" of pike. The entity was considered simply another manifestation of *Aeromonas* septicemia.

Clement and Gibbons (35) of the National Research Council, Ottawa, Ontario, Canada, reported in 1960 that cultures left from a large collection of *P. hydrophilus* isolated in studies of "red sore" disease and sent them by Reed were not, in fact, members of the genus *Pseudomonas* (*Proteus*), but were better classified as *Aerobacter* species *cloacae*. The authors further stated that either the original organisms were replaced by *Aerobacter* soon after receipt or that their presence was due to their greater hardiness.

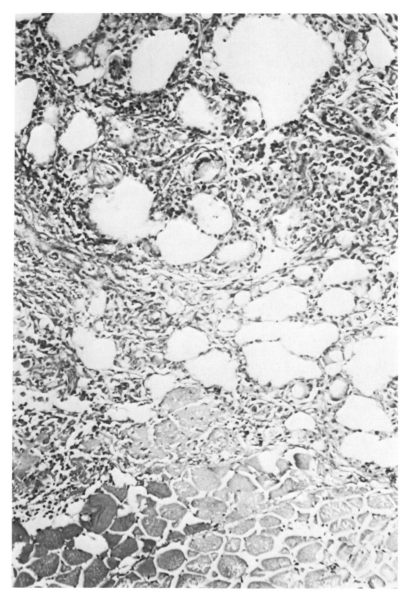

Fig. 2.4. Coldwater disease. Reaction at base of dermal ulcer. Note skeletal muscle necrosis resulting in empty spaces, connective tissue proliferation, and mixed inflammatory response. (Tissue courtesy of Dr. G. Bullock.) H&E; X65.

There is no experimental evidence that these cultures of *A. cloacae* are in fact infectious to fish, nor is there evidence that the original isolates were members of the genus *Aerobacter*. The possibility, however, that this organism is in fact a pathogen and may be a cause of "red sore" must not be overlooked. Its probable source and careful identification warrant its inclusion in a discussion of the bacterial pathogens of fish.

"RM" bacterium (redmouth)

A systemic, often epizootic, disease of trout resembling redmouth has existed for a number of years in hatcheries of the western United States (141). It is characterized by inflammatory lesions about the head and mouth and has therefore been referred to as redmouth, confusing it with another disease process known also as redmouth of trout due to bacteria of the genera *Aeromonas* and *Pseudomonas*. The causative agent has been isolated frequently in disease outbreaks and belongs to the Enterobacteriaceae rather than the Pseudomonadaceae. It is a peritrichous, gram-negative bacillus of uncertain classification, and the name *"RM" bacterium* has been suggested by Ross, Rucker, and Ewing (135) pending determination of taxonomic position. The organism is reported as the first enteric bacteria known pathogenic to fish, but Griffin and Snieszko (70) reported the isolation of an organism with the physical, biochemical, and antigenic properties of *Paracolobacterium aerogenoides* highly pathogenic to the aquarium fish *Corydoras aeneus, Xiphophorus helleri, Platypoecilus maculatus,* and *Poecilia reticulata* (*Lebistes reticulatus*). This organism was recovered from a fetid, purulent-like material in areas of greenish discoloration beneath the skin between the pectoral and ventral fins of affected fish. It grew at both 37° and 5°C and was pathogenic to both warm- and cold-blooded animals (mice and goldfish). The authors were uncertain of its classification because it possessed only a single flagellum and suggested that it might be a member of the Pseudomonadaceae. There are no reports of the histological lesions associated with this disease or with that caused by the *"RM" bacterium*.

MYXOCOCCACEAE

Chondrococcus columnaris (columnaris disease)

Chondrococcus columnaris is still another example of the Myxobacteriales or slime bacteria which include such pathogens as *C. psychrophilia, Cytophaga* sp., *Sporocytophaga* sp., and unidentified freshwater and saltwater myxobacteria found in association with disease processes. The disease syndrome was first described by Davis (41) and was apparently first observed in the Mississippi Valley in 1917. It was initially found in warmwater fishes and associated with higher water temperatures. The disease has been found to be pathogenic to many species, including members of the Salmonidae and to be widespread in its geographical distribution (3, 53, 60). It appears to be endemic in the major drainage systems of the temperate zone of North America (19).

Columnaris disease is an acute systemic disease of fish characterized by large areas of epidermal necrosis, dermal ulceration, and gill destruction and caused by the myxobacterium *C. columnaris.*

The causative agent of columnaris disease is a gram-negative, motile rod approximately 0.6 microns in diameter by 6 microns in length (116). It is unique in its tendency to form short, column-like masses on the edges of tissue when scrapings are examined under coverglass preparations. Bacteria in such preparations tend to glide back and forth with creeping motility (19). The organisms differ from members of the genus *Cytophaga* in their ability to produce fruiting bodies and microcysts, especially when cultured on sterile fish tissue (116).

The organism may be cultured aerobically using *Cytophaga* agar as described by Anacker and Ordal (9) between the temperatures of 4° and 30°C. Borg (19) describes growth in 48 hours on 0.9% agar and 0.5% tryptone of pH 7.3 either at room temperature or up to 30°C. Organisms are readily isolated from lesions and often may be recovered from the kidney of affected fish.

Studies of the disease among Pacific salmon have done much to elucidate the epizootiology of columnaris disease. Factors which appear to affect the frequency and distribution of the disease include water temperature, water hardness, water organic matter content, water pH, strain virulence, host condition, and crowding.

Water quality has always been recognized as a major factor in columnaris outbreaks. The disease is associated with high water temperature, usually in excess of 18°C (64.4°F). Evidence for this hypothesis is forthcoming from both field and laboratory studies. Incidence of disease in the Columbia River Basin was found related to increased water temperature (116). Similar findings among pond-cultured eels are reported by Wakabayashi, Kira, and Egusa (173), who observed increased incidence of disease signs, agent isolation, and agglutinins during summer months. Experimental evidence for this relationship is present in the work of Ordal and Rucker (111). These investigators showed a 70% increase in mortality among salmon when water temperatures were raised from 61° to 72°F.

The effects of water hardness, water organic matter content, and pH have been investigated (52). In hard water with increased organic matter the bacteria are able to persist for longer periods of time. If water pH was reduced to 6.0, bacterial survival time was also reduced. It appears, therefore, that a soft (< 10 ppm $CaCO_3$), acid-water low in organic matter does not provide a suitable environment for this pathogen.

Strain virulence also plays a role in the epizootiology of columnaris disease. Definite differences exist and the strains may be classified on the basis of acuteness of mortality after experimental infection (114). There is a further relationship between strain virulence and water temperature as well as route of infection. Strains of higher virulence appear able to produce disease at lower water temperatures (116).

Further, these highly virulent strains were found to produce disease readily by contact (fish placed in dilute solution of bacteria for 2 minutes) but were less virulent when administered intraperitoneally or intramuscularly. The reverse was true of strains considered low in virulence (113).

Host condition and crowding have also been recognized as factors affecting disease incidence. Wakabayashi, Kira, and Egusa (172) observed an increased resistance among thin, starved, cultured eel populations. Fujihara and Hungate (61) noted an increased incidence of organisms from fish ladder water samples on the Columbia River. They suggest that these sites, where crowding and confinement take place, may be important for transferring the disease from indigenous fish to migrating anadromous salmonids. Since it is known that scrap-fish may serve as carriers of the organism and remain with subclinical disease at lower temperatures, the epizootics among anadromous fish may be explained by sudden increases in water temperature resulting in disease among indigenous scrap-fish and rapid transmission to salmonids in areas of crowding, as in fish ladders (116).

The gross lesions of columnaris appear confined to the skin and gills of affected fish and may vary as to the species of fish involved. The most characteristic sign is the saddle lesion seen in scaleless fishes, such as the catfish. This lesion is characterized by a lighter-pigmented, smooth-edged patch usually occurring between the dorsal fin and the caudal fins and often extending down either side toward the lateral line. Its characteristic location and shape suggest the designation "saddle" lesion. These patches, however, may occur anywhere on the body and become confluent. Often they originate on the caudal fin and progress forward. Davis (41) in his original description of the disease states "centers of lesions are dark blue overlaid by a white veil or cloudiness." The patch is outlined by a thin zone of hyperemia and may resemble an early lesion of saprolegniasis. In scaled fish such as the black crappie (*Pomoxis nigromaculatus*), lesions tend to affect the fins and gills rather than the body proper. Hemorrhagic patches at the base of fins and about the mouth as well as ulcerations of the head are described in English roach and perch (3). In both scaled and scaleless fish, the dermal lesions may progress to ulcers extending into the underlying musculature.

Gill lesions include congestion, whitened discolored areas, and complete loss of gill filaments. In the latter case large areas of the gill arches are denuded. This lesion has been described in cultured eels (173). Rarely, gross lesions may be completely absent. The absence of lesions in young salmon may be associated with highly virulent strains of *C. columnaris.*

Microscopic changes present in the skin and associated with the lighter pigmented patches seen grossly include acute epidermal necrosis, swelling, acidophilia and necrosis of underlying muscle fibers, and little or no inflammatory response (Fig. 2.5). Long, slender bacteria may be present on the surface of the lesion, beneath scales, or within the intramuscular spaces. With Giemsa stain the bacteria are easily visualized. The lack of inflammatory response is striking and is well documented in the photomicrographs of skin lesions associated with the original

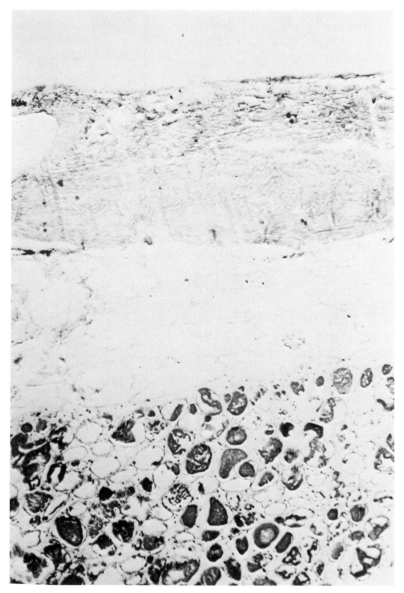

Fig. 2.5. Columnaris disease. Complete loss of epidermis, subdermal edema, and muscle necrosis. H&E; ×65.

outbreak of the disease (41). Studies of pathogenesis are needed to determine if early in lesion development an inflammatory response is present which disappears later with changes in tissue milieu.

Davis (41) described acute necrosis of the gill in warmwater fish with columnaris. A similar but more severe necrosis is reported by Wakabayashi, Kira, and Egusa (172) in the eel. In their experimental histopathological study using highly virulent strains of columnaris in young salmon, however, Pacha and Ordal (115) report only gill congestion and a lifting away of lamellar epithelium from the adjoining lamellar vessels. G. Gardner and P. Yevich (personal communication) report the presence of this lamellar epithelial change with great frequency in "normal" control *Fundulus heteroclitus* and suggest the change to be artifact. Blood-filled swollen lamellae, as reported by Wood and Yasutake (185), were also observed by Pacha and Ordal (115). This lesion has now also been reported in association with ammonia toxicity (23).

With the exception of the kidney lesions, lesions in other organ systems have not been reported. Ajmal and Hobbs (3) report "pathological changes" in liver and kidney of roach and perch but tissue was not examined by light microscopy. In young salmon, Bowman's space was distended and filled with an eosinophilic material (115).

PSEUDOMONADACEAE

Aeromonas liquefaciens (bauchwassersucht; hemorrhagic septicemia)

Hemorrhagic septicemia is a systemic disease of uncertain etiology associated with the organism *Aeromonas liquefaciens* and characterized by dermal ulceration, ascites, and necrosis of major organs.

The condition, as it affects European carp, was first thoroughly described by Schäperclaus (144). It was named *Bauchwassersucht* in reference to one of its clinical signs, ascites. Since that time, the disease has been found to be as ubiquitous as its suspected causative agent and has acquired a number of other names, such as infectious abdominal dropsy (carp), myoenterohepatic syndrome (carp), hydropigenous viral neurosis, rubella (all fish), redmouth (trout), and red pest or red sore (pike).

The bacterial organism consistently found in conjunction with outbreaks of hemorrhagic septicemia has also acquired a number of synonyms. Initially the agent was referred to as *Pseudomonas punctata*, which Schäperclaus (145) states is identical with the *Bacillus punctatus* described by Zimmermann in 1890. However, later isolates by other investigators were placed in other genera such as *Proteus, Aerobacter,* and *Aeromonas,* confusing the taxonomic position of the pathogen. Griffin (69) reported that Snieszko compared a number of isolates which had been variously known as *Pseudomonas punctata, P. hydrophilia, P. hirudinis, Proteus hydrophilia, P. melanovogenes,* and *Aerobacter liquefaciens* and concluded all these bacteria belonged to the same species. Other synonyms for the causative agent include *Bacterium punctatum, Bacillus ranicida, Aeromonas punctata,* and *A. hydrophilia* (157). Bullock and McLaughlin (24) have suggested the use of *Aeromonas liquefaciens,* since it is the type species.

Hemorrhagic septicemia is probably the most common and important disease of warmwater fish. It has also been reported affecting trout (105, 171). The disease is of worldwide distribution and affects a wide variety of fish, including both teleosts and elasmobranchs (66, 74, 97, 106, 129, 154). It is a disease of freshwater fish, but recoveries of the organism have been made in brackish water of less than 7 ppt salinity (109).

There is a good deal of controversy surrounding the etiology of the disease. As early as 1939 Schäperclaus recognized the possibility of a viral etiology because, while isolated epizootics occurred, the suspected pathogen was known to be of widespread distribution (145). Some experiments with bacteria-free filtrates from carp with dropsy injected into normal carp resulted in acute dropsy; however, it was impossible to exclude the presence of endo- and exotoxins as the cause of the observed disease. Schäperclaus (145) did not rule out the possibility that a virus might be an obligatory co-agent of *A. liquefaciens.* In order to accept the hypothesis that a bacterium is the primary cause of the disease, one must be prepared to recognize pathogenic variants which Schäperclaus has termed *forma ascitae.* Other investigators have presented evidence that the disease is of viral origin primarily and that the bacteria recovered are simply secondary invaders. The pathological manifestations of the disease which occurs under natural conditions differ from those of the disease when it is experimentally induced by injections of bacteria (66). Evidence for a viral etiology includes presence of intracellular inclusion bodies in epidermis and Purkinje cells (Epshtain-Pehkov inclusion), production of the disease by bacteria-free filtrates, and the presence of viral particles in abdominal exudate and ultrafiltrates from organs of diseased carp (66, 130). Tomašec and Fijan (167) were able to produce a cytopathogenic effect in carp kidney tissue cultures three days post-inoculation with 0.2 ml of skin filtrate from infected carp. The cultures were infectious in a period of one to two weeks to 67% of exposed carp. The signs of the disease were very slight and disappeared in a few days in the majority of cases.

A. liquefaciens is a motile, gram-negative bacillus, measuring approximately 0.5 × 1.0 microns, is cytochrome oxidase positive, and has the ability to produce 2,3-butanediol (20). The term includes both aerogenic and anaerogenic motile aeromonads (24). Organisms are readily isolated on either trypticase soy agar or sheep blood agar. Isolation and identification are reviewed by Bullock (20), Ojala (109), and Snieszko and Bullock (157).

The incidence of the disease appears related to environmental factors. Meyer (106), studying seasonal fluctuations in the incidence of disease on fish farms, noted that the infection incidence peaked in April and August and remained highest during the summer months. He attributed this to temperature stress in the spring when water temperatures rose sharply and to low oxygen levels later in the summer. Similar effects of oxygen depletion were reported by Haley, Davis, and Hyde (74) and Rock and Nelson (129) studying shad and channel catfish mortalities. It has further been observed that outbreaks often occur a few weeks after the stress of crowding or handling (157).

The source of infection appears to be water, pond mud, and latent carriers which have recovered from the disease. Infection may occur via ingestion (8). It has been suggested that the disease may also be transmitted by invertebrates such as leeches, *Argulus* sp. and *Gyrodactylus* sp. (69, 171).

Clinically the disease may manifest itself in epizootic proportions, resulting in high mortalities, or may affect a smaller portion of the fish exposed, with dermal ulcers followed by healing and recovery. Amlacher (8) recognizes three clinical syndromes in the carp. First, there exists a latent form with no external signs, although the fish may have altered behavior patterns, in that they separate themselves from the group and are feeble swimmers. Second, there is an acute ascitic form in which ascites is evident, as are exophthalmos and prolapsed anus. The third clinical manifestation is the chronic ulcerative form in which ulcers are present in the skin and often involve the musculature. Simultaneous manifestations of these forms are not unusual. Signs of ulceration and ascites, especially ulceration, occur in other species of fish as well (101, 125). Rock and Nelson (129) report ulceration about the head and mouth in a natural outbreak of the disease among channel catfish, and Wagner and Perkins (171) observed similar lesions in trout.

A number of clinical pathological parameters have been investigated in diseased carp and are reviewed by Amlacher (8). Erythrocyte counts and hemoglobin determinations reflected a severe anemia. There was an increase in total numbers of granulocytic cells and a relative decrease in the percentage of lymphocytes present. Decreases in blood glucose levels which correspond with a decrease in hepatic glycogen stores are also reported. Other blood components significantly decreased were total protein, albumin, globulin, and cholesterol values. Uric acid and bilirubin values were increased.

External gross lesions include petechiae, ecchymoses, ulcers, and abdominal distention. In carp recovering from the disease the ulcers undergo cicatrization with characteristic pigment changes including an outer black zone, an inner white zone, and a central red zone (8). Exophthalmos, anal prolapse, fin loss, and, rarely, skeletal deformities may be present. In experimental production of the disease by intramuscular injection, Gaines (63) reports deep, blood-free ulcers at the point of injection and occasional secondary infection by *Saprolegnia* sp.

Internal gross lesions reported are a yellow-to-serosanguineous ascitic fluid, peritoneal-visceral adhesions, splenomegaly, enteric hyperemia, yellowish-to-green liver coloration with occasional petechiae, and kidneys of an abnormally soft consistency (8). Similar findings are reported in acute experimental infections of channel catfish by *A. hydrophilia.* Livers are congested and darker in color than livers from control fish. Petechiae are present on the intestines and mesenteries, the spleen is dark in color, and the posterior kidney very friable (63).

Histopathological findings are compatible with the systemic nature of the disease. Lesions have been reported in skin, muscle, liver, intestine, heart, spleen, and pancreas. The petechiae and ecchymoses preceding dermal ulceration are characterized microscopically by subepidermal edema and hemorrhage. The epidermis and dermis then undergo necrosis, exposing the underlying musculature. Amlacher (8) describes the inflammatory response as mixed in natural outbreaks of the disease among carp. Discussing inflammation within the ulcer, he refers to a peripheral distribution of leukocytes and a more central influx of leukocytes and lymphocytes. In trout inoculated intramuscularly, I have observed a similar distribution of white cells, assuming that by *Leukocyten* Amlacher is referring to granulocytes and hence also mentions lymphocytes centrally. Inoculated trout have an infiltration of granulocytes within the epidermis. Epidermal cells undergo coagulation necrosis. Many are ballooned and contain pyknotic nuclei. Intermuscular congestion and hemorrhage are common. Underlying skeletal muscle fibers are swollen, acidophilic, and often surrounded by degenerating erythrocytes, thrombocytes, and some small lymphocytes (Fig. 2.6). Granulocytic cells are also present but are less numerous than in epidermal areas. Bacteria are plentiful within the muscle following inoculation and the reaction is more severe than that described by Gaines (63) following intraperitoneal inoculation. Following this route, necrosis appeared to occur from the peritoneal serous membrane outward with little inflammatory cell influx.

Microscopic lesions occur in other organs of the body as well. Fatty metamorphosis, coagulation and caseous necrosis, vasculitis and cirrhosis are described in livers of carp with the ascitic form of the disease (8). In channel catfish, Gaines (63) reports congestion and also necrosis of hepatocytes with loss of cell membranes. Experimentally infected brown trout (*S. trutta*) have a diffuse hepatitis characterized by hepatocyte necrosis, bacteria within sinusoids, and a lymphocytic infiltration (Fig. 2.7).

The most striking lesion in experimentally inoculated channel catfish is a massive hematopoietic and structural connective tissue (Fig. 2.8) necrosis of the spleen. Gaines (63) describes this aptly as a "honey-combed" appearance due to large areas of necrotic tissue surrounded by eosinophilic connective tissue fibers. Amlacher (8) does not report splenic lesions in the naturally occurring disease of carp, although Bullock, Conroy, and Snieszko (26) report necrosis of this organ in fish with hemorrhagic septicemia. No lesions of the spleen were present in brown trout inoculated intramuscularly. I have observed a similar hematopoietic necrosis in the spleens of *F. heteroclitus* inoculated intraperitoneally with *V. anguillarum.* Similar lesions did not develop when the fish were inoculated intramuscularly.

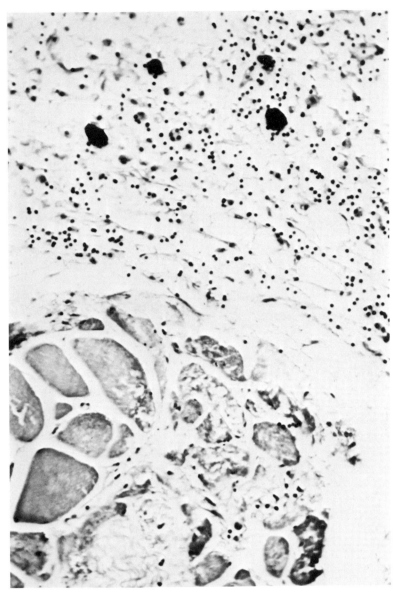

Fig. 2.6. Hemorrhagic septicemia. Reaction following intramuscular inoculation. Swollen, necrotic muscle fibers surrounded by degenerating erythrocytes, thrombocytes, and small lymphocytes. H&E; X160.

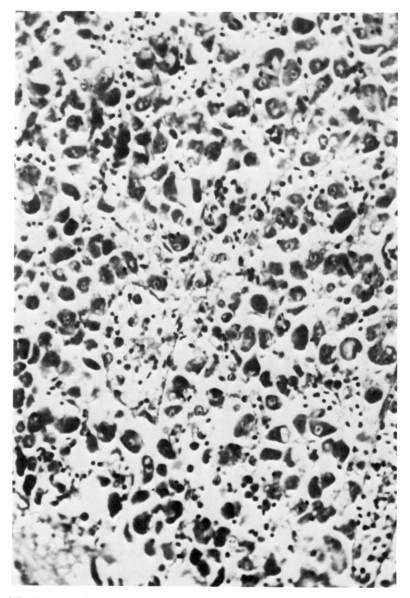

Fig. 2.7. Hemorrhagic septicemia. Brown trout (*Salmo trutta*), experimental inoculation. Diffuse hepatitis. H&E; ×160.

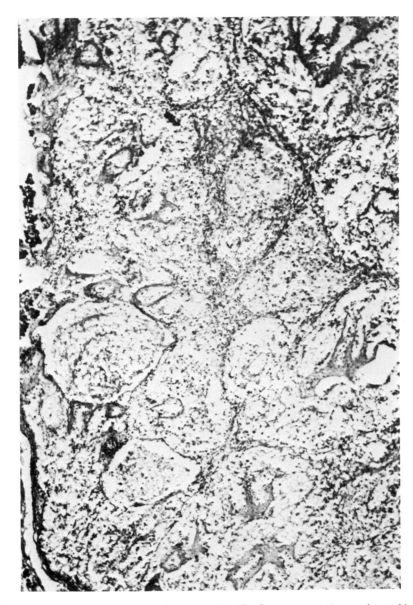

Fig. 2.8. Hemorrhagic septicemia. Channel catfish (*Ictalurus punctatus*), experimental inoculation. Massive structural and lymphoid necrosis of spleen. (Tissue courtesy of Dr. J. Gaines, Jr.) H&E; ✕65.

In the kidney, the major hematopoietic organ of fish, an increased production of lymphoid cells and occasional necrosis of both proximal and distal tubule segments have been reported (63).

Amlacher reported focal necrotic myocarditis in experimentally infected brown trout (*S. trutta*) with spaces of the cavernous internal musculature containing bacteria and an influx of small lymphocytes. He also noted bacteria in this latter area (8).

Intestinal lesions including mucosal necrosis, edema, and inflammatory cell infiltration of all gut layers are reported in the carp (8).

Aeromonas salmonicida (furunculosis; red plague)

Furunculosis is an acute systemic disease of fish characterized by a bacteremia due to *Aeromonas salmonicida*.

The disease was first described affecting trout in Germany in 1894 and is now recognized as worldwide in distribution. It has been reported in over 20 countries and was recently spread to Norway through the importation of infected fish (76, 81). The first description of the organism in the United States was that of Marsh (102), who observed the disease among hatchery trout in Michigan in the summer of 1901. Initially the disease was thought to occur only among hatchery-raised salmonids, but Fish (58) reported Plehn as describing the disease among wild fish in Bavarian rivers as early as 1909 and further reported the first instance of the disease in the United States in wild brown trout. It was long considered solely a disease of freshwater fish, but in 1971 Evelyn (48) reported isolation of aberrant strains of the pathogen from a marine host, *Anoplopoma fimbria* held in sea water (28 ppt salinity), which developed a ragged superficial hemorrhagic lesion on the caudal peduncle. Later, similar strains of bacteria were isolated from sockeye and chum salmon held in 9 ppt salinity.

Furunculosis is not confined in its pathogenicity to salmonids, but has been reported in at least 13 other genera of fish (76, 99, 103, 104). Its virulence varies among the species of fish affected. The eel appears quite resistant, while the eastern brook trout is most susceptible and the rainbow trout most resistant among salmonids (100, 156).

The disease has been and remains of great economic importance to those involved in trout and salmon culture (96, 100, 156). While its effect on other species in the natural environment is not as well documented, Mawdesley-Thomas (103) reported the recovery of *A. salmonicida* following mass mortalities of wild river fish in Great Britain.

A. salmonicida is a gram-negative, aerobic, nonmotile, nonspore-forming bacillus approximately 1 X 2 microns in size. Its classification in the genus *Aeromonas* was based on evidence presented by Griffin, Snieszko, and Friddle (71). The organism, however, lacks some of the characteristics of the genus, which led Smith (152) to suggest that it be placed in a new genus, that of *Necromonas*. The organism produces a brown, water-soluble pigment on solid media in the presence of tyrosine or phenylalanine. The pigment aids in identification and has led to the development of specific agars which enhance pigment production for use in presumptive diagnosis. Other tests for rapid diagnosis include a macroscopic slide agglutination test and the addition of 1% aqueous paraphenylene-diamine to agar colonies, with the production of a violet-black color indicating a positive reaction (68, 124). Klontz and Anderson (89) examined 24 geographically separate isolates of the organism by indirect immunofluorescence and found at least seven distinct serotypes.

Epizootiological studies indicate that the organism may be passed via water and feces from infected fish, through direct contact and through contaminated feed. There is no evidence that the disease is passed vertically in contaminated milt or ova (96). The role of latent carriers in the transmission of the disease is also of importance. The number of these fish increases when the temperature drops below 7°C, at which point infection may exist without symptoms or mortalities (156). According to McCraw (96) the organism is an obligate parasite persisting less than one week in water; however, Smith (152) was able to recover the organism three weeks after inoculating an artificial rock bottom stream. Cornick, Chudyk, and McDermott (40), examining hatcheries with endemic infections for possible sources other than fish, cultured 2954 vertebrates and invertebrates as well as 70 water and pond-bottom samples for the organism. The investigators found all samples negative for A. salmonicida. Viability studies indicated persistence in infected trout kept at −10°C for 49 days and in sterile moist soil for greater than 40 days. Disease transmission from stocked infected fish to wild populations was investigated by McDermott and Berst (98). In 1966 these investigators stocked 3000 marked yearling brook trout with a known infection incidence in an Ontario trout stream. The stream was electrofished for a two-year period and recovery rates of infected and noninfected trout were found to be similar. The authors concluded that there was no evidence that the disease was transmitted to stocked noninfected trout, resident trout, or other species.

The immunological aspects of the disease have been investigated and active and passive immunization attempted (10, 96, 163). Oral active immunization has not been successful as a practical means of protection; however, recent production of an oral toxoid appears promising (90, 163).

The clinical signs of A. salmonicida infection have been variously described by a number of authors (8, 96, 100). The classification suggested by Herman (76) incorporates his observations with those of others and concisely describes four clinical syndromes. These forms are a subclinical or latent form, an acute form lacking clinical signs, a subacute form characterized by dermal ecchymoses, vesicles, and ulcerations, and finally, a chronic form characterized by low mortality and hemorrhage at the base of fins. Of the three forms resulting in mortality the acute form appears most common. Mackie and Menzies (100) report the acute and subacute forms to be, under experimental conditions, dose-related, lower doses given parenterally resulting in typical vesicles and ulceration. These findings were confirmed by Klontz, Yasutake, and Johnross (90), who reproduced the subacute form by intramuscular injection of the least amount of organisms required for infection of all test animals.

Clinical pathological investigations have included determinations of sedimentation rate, hematocrit, hemoglobin, erythrocyte number, leukocyte number, total plasma protein, albumin, blood glucose, and nonprotein nitrogen. No changes were noted in hematocrit, hemoglobin, or erythrocyte counts (51, 90). Sedimentation rates were increased (146). Klontz, Yasutake, and Johnross (90) report an initial leukocytosis following experimental inoculation. Leukocytosis persisted for 48 hours and was followed by a severe leukopenia and shift in the differential count characterized by an increase in immature lymphocytes and the absence of heterophils. Total plasma protein and albumin remained within normal ranges, while blood glucose levels dropped sharply (100 mg% down to 9.0 mg%), and nonprotein nitrogen increased from 30 mg% to over 600 mg% (51).

In the acute and latent forms of furunculosis, gross lesions are absent. In the subacute form external lesions involving the skin and muscle are present. Focal zones of dermal hemorrhage are followed by raised fluctuating vesicles and eventual ulceration. The vesicles and ulcerations have been referred to as "boils," "abscesses," and "furuncles." None of these terms is readily applicable to the type of inflammatory reaction occurring within the skin and muscle of affected fish since they either refer to a specific disease entity in man (boil, furuncle) or describe a suppurative reaction with "pus" production (abscess). The vesicles contain an opaque serosanguineous material. Ulcers are variable in size, often irregular and ragged-edged, and may extend into the underlying musculature. Growths of fungi commonly cover ulcers and resemble areas of wet cotton when the fish is removed from water. On cut section muscles underlying skin lesions are often hemorrhagic or frankly necrotic.

Internal gross lesions are not striking. Mackie and Menzies (100) and Duff and Stewart (46) reported liquefactive necrosis of the kidney and spleen and petechial hemorrhage of the liver. In a study of the pathogenesis of this disease the only consistent lesion observed by Klontz and co-workers (90) was splenomegaly. Mawdesley-Thomas (104) reported congestion of viscera in goldfish with furunculosis. Amlacher (8) and Herman (76) both reported intestinal congestion and anal prolapse associated with the chronic form of the disease.

The most striking histopathological characteristic of tissue from diseased fish is the lack of inflammatory response. This lack of leukocytic response had long been recognized by investigators but its cause was not explained until Klontz, Yasutake, and Johnross (90) showed that a saline-soluble extract of the organism was capable of destroying leukocytes and depressing hematopoiesis. In their experiments an initial leukocytosis was observed followed by a depression of white cell production 56 hours post-inoculation. The inflammatory response in skin and muscle is therefore dependent upon the age of the lesion. Fish necropsied and examined in the later stages of disease have lesions characterized by acute necrosis with a minimum of lymphocytes and heterophils. It is for this reason that the pathologist commonly finds foci of bacteria in the parenchyma of major organs with no inflammatory response (Fig. 2.9).

Microscopic sections of ulcerated skin contain a complete loss of epidermis, little dermal inflammation, and a zone of edema between the dermis and underlying muscle which may contain a scattering of lymphocytes. In severe ulceration the dermis may also be absent. The underlying muscle is hemorrhagic and may undergo Zenker's necrosis. Secondary fungal infection is often present, with mycelia both overlying the lesion and within the zone of edema. Klontz, Yasutake, and Johnross (90) reported a marked inflammatory response in muscle and subcutis 32 to 48 hours post-inoculation with a decrease in white cells thereafter and a persistence of bacteria in zones of necrosis. Gram stains such as the Brown-Brenn reveal the presence of the causative agent.

Since furunculosis is bacteremic in nature, foci of the organisms are common in many of the major organs of the body. While renal elements are spared, the hematopoietic interstitial tissue of the kidney later in the disease may be seen to undergo necrosis. Marked changes in the hematopoietic elements of both the kidney and the spleen early in the course of infection are reported (90). Initially the hematopoietic elements were stimulated and an increase in macrophages was apparent. This was followed by necrosis and cessation of hematopoiesis. In conjunction with this early hematopoietic stimulation, these workers found an increased number of lymphocytes and macrophages in liver imprints. It is important that the diagnostic pathologist recognize that these lesions may or may not be present, depending upon the stage of disease at the time of examination.

With the exception of bacterial foci the hepatic parenchyma appears unaffected. The intestinal tract may be congested and edematous. Mawdesley-Thomas (104) reported a lymphocytic infiltration of the lamina propria and submucosa of the gut in a natural outbreak of the disease affecting *Carassius auratus.*

I have observed lesions in the gills of trout similar to those described by Mawdesley-Thomas (104) in goldfish. Bacteria were present within lamellar vessels, as was a slight-to-marked hypertophy and hyperplasia of lamellar epithelial cells. In addition there was an intralamellar infiltration of lymphocytes. No lesions have been reported in other organs, with the exception of bacterial foci.

In summation, furunculosis is a bacteremic disease characterized by an absence of inflammatory response (except in its initial stages), parenchymal bacterial foci, ulceration of the skin, necrosis of muscle, necrosis of the hematopoietic elements of the kidney and spleen, lymphocytic infiltration of gill lamellae, proliferation of lamellar epithelial cells and intestinal congestion. Since none of the pathological changes associated with this disease is specific, nor may they all be present in any one particular necropsy, diagnosis by means of gross and histopathological examination is difficult and a risky procedure. Presumptive diagnosis is possible but positive diagnosis must depend upon isolation of the causative agent.

Differential diagnosis must consider lesions caused by *H. piscium* in trout (ul-

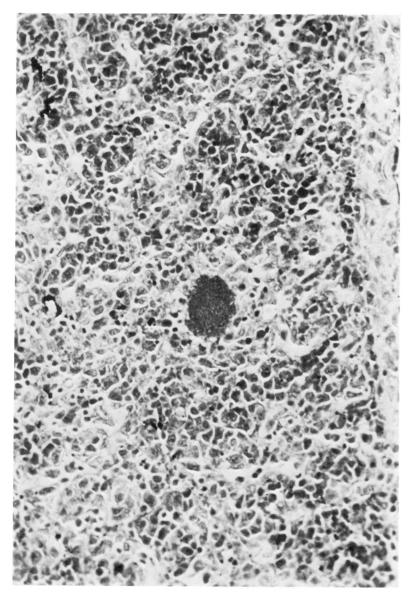

Fig. 2.9. Furunculosis. Foci of bacteria eliciting no inflammatory response in trout spleen.
H&E; ×160.

cer disease) and those resulting from infections by *A. liquefaciens* in salmonids and other species of fish.

Pseudomonas fluorescens

Pseudomonas fluorescens is the third member of the Pseudomonadaceae known pathogenic to fish (21, 27, 69, 136). It is responsible for a disease syndrome identical with that of *A. liquefaciens* and is an alternate cause of hemorrhagic septicemia (24, 161). Identification and separation of this bacterium from *A. liquefaciens* has been discussed by Bullock (20), while its pathogenicity has been attributed to its production of a proteolytic enzyme (95).

Recently André et al. (13) have reported an outbreak of hemorrhagic septicemia in European eels (*Anguilla vulgaris*) held in aerated freshwater tanks at 10° to 15°C. Gross lesions included erythema and ulceration of the skin, especially on the ventral surface. Petechiae were present on the peritoneal serosa, myocardium, and lower intestine. Microscopically, fragmentation of the hematopoietic melanin-macrophage centers and depletion of hematopoietic tissue were present. Of greatest interest, however, is the dermal lesion described in association with this epizootic. Epidermal changes occurring prior to ulceration closely resembled erythema exudativum multiforme of man (Fig. 2.10). Layers of the epidermis had extensive intra- and extracellular edema and capillaries were extremely congested. This condition in man may be secondary to toxemia of systemic infections (13).

Pseudomonas sp. was isolated from skin lesions and viscera. Koch's postulates were not fulfilled; however, the eels responded well to improved husbandry and antibiotic therapy.

SPIRILLACEAE

Vibrio anguillarum

Vibriosis is an acute, systemic disease of fish caused by the bacterium *Vibrio anguillarum* and characterized by dermal ulceration, hematopoietic necrosis, and anemia.

The causative agent of this disease is worldwide in its distribution and is known to be infectious to a large number of fish species (12, 49, 72). While it is primarily a disease of marine fish, there are reports in the literature of outbreaks in freshwater environments (73, 134, 138, 141). The outbreaks are often of epizootic proportions and are of economic importance when affecting species of sport fish or those used for human consumption (34, 81). Interest in the disease has been stimulated by an upsurge of maricultural endeavors during the past decade. The ubiquitous nature and virulence of the disease make it a factor which must be considered if any marine fish farming effort is to be a success. The literature is replete with reports of this disease as a limiting factor in the production of salmonids and other marine fish under cultural conditions. The extensive literature has been reviewed by Rucker (138) and by Anderson and Conroy (12).

The causative agent is a motile, gram-negative rod, anaerogenic, asporogenous, cytochrome oxidase-positive, and usually sensitive to the vibriostat 0/129. No

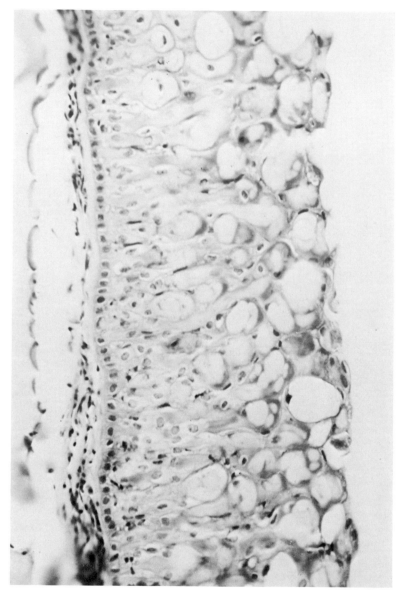

Fig. 2.10. *Pseudomonas fluorescens*. Intra- and extracellular edema of epidermis in eel (*Anguilla vulgaris*). (Tissue courtesy of Dr. R. Roberts.) H&E; ×160.

growth occurs at 37°C. Growth is completely absent or delayed in the presence of 8% NaCl. A scheme for the differentiation of marine vibrios pathogenic to fish and man is suggested by Levin, Wolke, and Cabelli (94).

The present classification of pathogenic fish vibrios is uncertain. The problem has recently been discussed by Hendrie, Hodgkiss, and Shewan (75), who suggest that the described pathogens *V. piscium, V. ichthyodermis,* and *V. anguillarum* be combined as a single species *V. anguillarum.* On the basis of biochemical reactions Nybelin (108) and Smith (151) were able to differentiate three biotypes, A, B, and C. Evelyn (49), however, points out that while such typing was of value in earlier investigations, with present methods of classification the advantages of the system are no longer as valid. A review of frequently reported biochemical properties of *V. anguillarum*-like bacteria collected from diseased marine animals from 1950 to 1970 is presented by Evelyn (49). Three distinct serotypes have been reported by Kiehn and Pacha (88), who were able to distinguish isolates from Pacific Northwest salmonids, Pacific Northwest herring, and European fish.

The means by which the disease is transmitted under natural conditions is unknown, although it has been suggested that the source may be water or feeding of uncooked frozen ocean fish (138). The disease is easily transmitted experimentally to winter flounder or *Fundulus* sp. by intramuscular injection of 0.1 ml of a 48-hour Zobell's broth culture. Lesions are apparent within a 24-hour period, as evidenced by swelling and hemorrhage at the point of inoculation. Similar observations are reported by Traxler and Li (168) in *F. heteroclitus* with isolates from a codfish nasal abscess. Experimental infection in juvenile chinook salmon by means of intraperitoneal inoculation has been reported (33).

Our work in Rhode Island with *P. americanus* shows a definite relationship between disease development and water temperature. This is in agreement with other investigators (5, 60). Flounder inoculated intramuscularly and kept in water at 20°C develop lesions within 24 hours, whereas those inoculated and kept at 10°C had no gross lesions after 120 hours.

Clinical pathological parameters which have been measured in various species of fish affected by vibriosis include hematocrit, total red blood cells (RBC), hemoglobin, mean corpuscular volume (MCV), mean corpuscular hemoglobin (MCH), mean corpuscular hemoglobin concentration (MCHC), total plasma dissolved solids (TDS), total serum protein, albumin, albumin/globulin ration (A/G), and total white blood cells (WBC).

There is a good deal of evidence that vibriosis is responsible for a severe anemia. Anderson and Conroy (12) observed a decrease in hematocrit, hemoglobin, and RBC members in cod, lemon sole, plaice, and turbot from the northeast of Scotland. Juvenile chinook salmon had similar changes (30). Normal, sexually intermixed fingerlings had a total RBC of 1.56×10^6 cells/cmm, while diseased fish had an RBC count of 1.13×10^6/cmm. Hemoglobin values were simultaneously decreased from a control of 8.05 grams % to 5.44 grams % in diseased fish. Hematocrits were depressed from 41.3% down to 26.9%. MCV and MCH were slightly decreased but MCHC was unchanged. These changes indicate a microcytic, normo-chromic anemia. These authors also report a reduction in TDS suggestive of de-creased plasma protein concentration, which they feel reflects a decreased albu-min level. Total WBC counts were also increased in diseased fish.

In our work with *P. americanus* from Rhode Island waters we have observed a similar change in blood parameters, indicating a severe anemia. In preliminary studies with sexually intermixed mature fish, hematocrit values are decreased from control levels of 35% down to 24.7%, total RBC from 2.44×10^6/cm and hemoglobin values from 6.2 grams % to 4.8 grams %. The correlation between hemoglobin and total red cells is statistically significant at the 1% level. Cardwell and Smith (30) in their work with salmon suggest that the observed anemia may be due to either erythropoietic destruction or accelerated destruction of red blood cells. It has also been suggested that the anemia may reflect a chronic blood loss from dermal ulcers. Under these latter circumstances higher vertebrates have a microcytic, hypochromic anemia indicative of chronic iron depletion. In our studies we have found a severe anemia within 72 hours of intramuscular injection of organisms and in the absence of any significant ulceration. Although focal necrosis of kidney hematopoietic tissue may be present, often the anemia exists in the absence of such necrosis. These findings, coupled with the acute onset of anemia, suggest that the bacteria are capable of producing a potent hemolytic toxin.

Winter flounders' total serum protein, albumin, and albumin/globulin ratios undergo seasonal fluctuations and vary further as to sex. The effect of vibriosis on these values, therefore, must be measured separately in both sexes and ideally on a monthly basis. Early data collections indicate that total serum proteins are drastically depressed in diseased fish. Albumin levels also appear slightly de-pressed. Statistical evaluation of these data must await further additional measurements.

Lesions associated with outbreaks of vibriosis may vary as to the species of fish affected and may vary within the same outbreaks (71, 80). In general, the characteristic gross lesions of the disease affect the skin. These include reddening at the base of fins, petechiae, ecchymoses, fluctuating vesicles, and frank ulcera-tion (12, 72). In the salmon the resemblance to furunculosis has been noted and the disease has, therefore, been referred to as "salt-water furunculosis" (139). Gross dermal lesions in *P. americanus* are most apparent on the ventral or non-pigmented side. These include randomly distributed petechiae and ecchymoses. Often there are raised fluctuating vesicles, also with a random distribution, which contain a clear-to-serosanguineous fluid. These vesicles rupture and are followed by ulcers which can extend into the underlying musculature. Frequently over the abdomen and caudal peduncle there are irregular zones of erythema which surround abnormally pale areas of epidermis lifted away from the subcutaneous tissue. Ulcers often develop in these areas as well. Sections of muscle underly-ing the ulcers are red in color and contrast sharply with the adjoining normal opalescent grey muscle. Necrosis of the dorsal and ventral fins is present in the majority of cases. Following intramuscular inoculation raised zones of intense erythema are present with hemorrhage throughout the musculature. After 48 to 72 hours vesicles develop, and when the area is sectioned a central zone of necrosis is present with a creamy grey exudate. Smears of the exudate contain necrotic muscle fibers, bacteria, and macrophages.

Other gross lesions include fin rot, ascites, congestion of spleen and liver, swelling of the kidney, intestinal hyperemia, and a clear viscous fluid within the gut (12, 72, 73). Rarely in acute outbreaks mortality may occur in the absence of gross lesions.

Few definitive histopathological studies of vibriosis have been conducted. In winter flounder I find the inflammatory response to be characterized by acute necrosis. Congestion and dilation of vessels characterize early skin lesions. This is followed by epidermal necrosis and Zenker's necrosis of underlying muscle. The inflammatory response is often minimal and primarily mononuclear. Bacteria may be present between muscle fibers. Lymphocytes and debris are present in empty scale pockets. The reaction following intramuscular inoculation at 20°C is far more severe and reveals the presence of a granulocytic influx early in lesion development. Lymphocytes and heterophils are seen in the subcutaneous tissue 24 hours post-inoculation. By 48 hours the lesion is primarily mononuclear with many macrophages in the area of muscle necrosis (Fig. 2.11).

The kidneys of affected flounder often have a proliferation of erythroblasts which may reflect the severe peripheral anemia. Discrete groups or islands of these large polygonal, basophilic cells are present in the kidney interstitial tissue. Within these groups individual cells are outlined by a clear zone (Fig. 2.12). Positive identification of these cells may be made by Wright's-stained impression smears. In addition to this compensatory hyperplasia, focal areas of hematopoietic necrosis and tubular necrosis may be present. Excessive Prussian blue-positive golden-brown to black pigment is often present in islands of macrophages diffusely distributed throughout the interstitial tissue.

Hacking and Budd (73) describe macrophage infiltration of the head kidney, cytoplasmic degeneration of hepatocytes, and focal areas of lymphocytes in the intestinal submucosa of goldfish inoculated intraperitoneally. In similarly inoculated *Lepomis gibbosus* a massive hemorrhage obliterated the normal leukocytic elements in the kidney and spleen. In addition, kidney tubules had degenerative changes.

Gram-Positive Organisms Eliciting Nonproliferative Response

STREPTOCOCCACEAE

Streptococcus faecalis

In the spring of 1957 in a Japanese hatchery a daily mortality of 0.3% was observed among rainbow trout 10 to 20 cm in length. A gram-positive coccoid or-

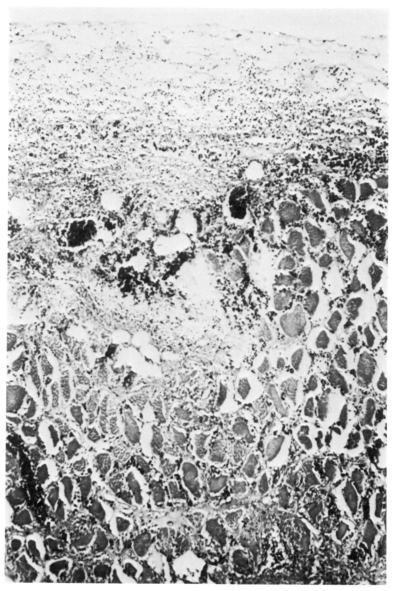

Fig. 2.11. Vibriosis. Base of ulcer with severe mononuclear reaction about necrotic muscle tissue. Hypodermis at top. H&E; ×65.

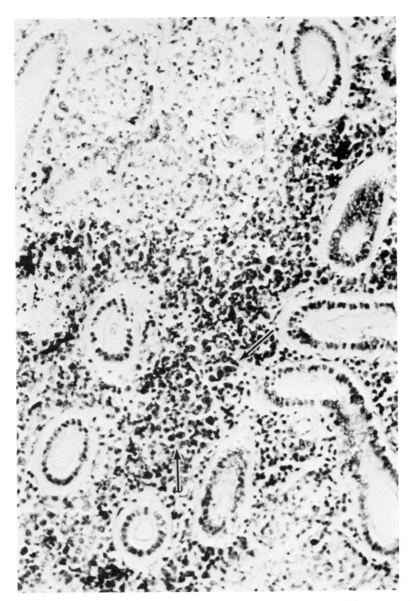

Fig. 2.12. Vibriosis. Kidney with foci of necrosis and proliferating erythroblasts (arrows). H&E; ×160.

ganism was present in smears of heart blood, spleen, liver, and kidney. The organism was isolated and identified as *Streptococcus faecalis* (83).

Robinson and Meyers (128) reported a group B, hemolytic *Streptococcus* sp. as the cause of death among *Notemigonus crysoleucas.* The organism was also pathogenic to members of the genus *Lepomis* and to *Bufo americanus,* but did not affect buffalo fish (*Ictiobus*), goldfish (*Carassius*), crappie (*Pomoxis*), and bass (*Micropterus*).

Two further outbreaks of mortality among trout due to *S. faecalis* were reported by Baker and Hagen (15). In both instances rainbow trout 3 to 5 cm in length were affected. At the height of the epizootic daily mortality was as high as 5%. The organism was isolated from body musculature.

The disease could be reproduced with the organisms isolated by Hoshina, Sano, and Morimoto (83) and Robinson and Meyers (128). Hoshina, Sano, and Morimoto (83), using intramuscular, intraperitoneal, intrarectal, and intragastric inoculations, produced death in 2 to 12 days. When the organism was introduced into new aquaria, death often occurred in as short a period as 48 hours (128).

Gross lesions include raised, inflamed areas behind the dorsal fin extending ventrally, congested intestines, hemorrhage about the anus, swollen kidneys, and congestion of the liver. It is interesting to note that the location of dermal lesions reported by Robinson and Meyers (128) in golden shiners is similar to that reported by S. R. Baker (personal communication) in trout.

Hoshina, Sano, and Morimoto (83) reported histological lesions, including necrosis of the endocardium, kidney, and liver. Microscopic lesions were most severe in the intestine and were characterized by mucosal necrosis and a cellular influx of the lamina propria and muscularis. Fish I have examined histologically (rainbow trout, golden shiners) had lesions in the skin and body musculature and were characterized by epidermal ulceration, an acute myolysis, and hemorrhage with a very slight mononuclear influx. Fungal hyphae were present within muscle tissue of trout with gross signs of mycoses. Tissue gram stains were negative.

Renal tubular epithelial cell degeneration and necrosis was present in kidneys of the golden shiners examined. A few foci of hematopoietic necrosis were also present in the mid-kidney area. Examination of the gill revealed areas of lamellar fusion with necrosis of cells at the base of filaments. This lesion is so nonspecific, however, that it is difficult to attribute it to the *Streptococcus* organism.

STREPTOMYCETACEAE

Streptomyces salmonicida
There is only one report in the literature of a streptomycete pathogenic to fish, that of Rucker (137). This organism, which was named *Streptomyces salmonicida,* was recovered from a group of hatchery blueback (sockeye) salmon (*Oncorhynchus nerka*) experiencing a low mortality. It was isolated on tryptone agar as was a pseudomonad. Both organisms were found to be infectious experimentally.

When fingerling salmon were inoculated with the streptomycete intramuscularly or intraperitoneally, mortality occurred after seven days. The organism in one instance was re-isolated from 9 of 20 kidney streaks. The disease could not be transmitted orally.

The streptomycete has branching, nonseptate hyphae 0.5 to 1 microns in diameter. It is gram-positive, non-acid-fast, and develops conidia when grown on agar.

Gross lesions associated with the initial outbreak included mycelial masses in the body cavity, congestion of the gastrointestinal tract, and in a few instances external ulceration of the body wall. The author states that lesions associated with the natural infection could not be determined because of the concurrent appearance of the pathogenic pseudomonad. Gross lesions following intramuscular injection included necrosis and bacteria at the site of inoculation. After intraperitoneal injection the presence of mycelial masses on the surface of the viscera was noted. These masses were raised, white, and circumscribed, and were reminiscent of miliary tubercles.

Histologically, there were zones of acute necrosis below masses of mycelia on the surface of affected organs. The inflammatory response was surprisingly slight and was characterized by the presence of a few mononuclear cells.

Gram-Negative Organisms Eliciting Proliferative Response

ACHROMOBACTERACEAE

Flavobacterium sp.

Flavobacterium disease is a systemic granulomatous disease with an apparent predilection for hepatic tissue, and is due to the bacterium *Flavobacterium* sp.

Kluge (91) reported an outbreak in the tropical aquarium fish, *Molliensia sphenops,* kept in indoor aquaria in Iowa. A total of 102 fish, including breeders and their progeny, contracted the disease and died approximately three months after developing clinical signs. The disease appeared confined to sexually mature animals.

The causative agent is a gram-negative, nonmotile pleomorphic rod, nitrate and cytochrome oxidase-positive, which grows at room temperature but not at 37°C and is a member of the genus *Flavobacterium* (91).

The disease was transmitted by inoculation of water with bacteria isolated from infected fish. The bacterium was not isolated from the experimentally infected fish.

Clinical signs included exophthalmos and emaciation. Gross lesions were confined to the liver, which was cystic and often contained mineralized nodules up to 3 mm in diameter. Microscopically, affected organs contained granulomas composed of histiocytes and macrophages rimmed by a thin layer of lymphocytes in turn bound by a fibrous capsule. Many of these granulomas had an eosinophilic central zone of coagulation necrosis (Fig. 2.13). Kluge (91) reported the frequency

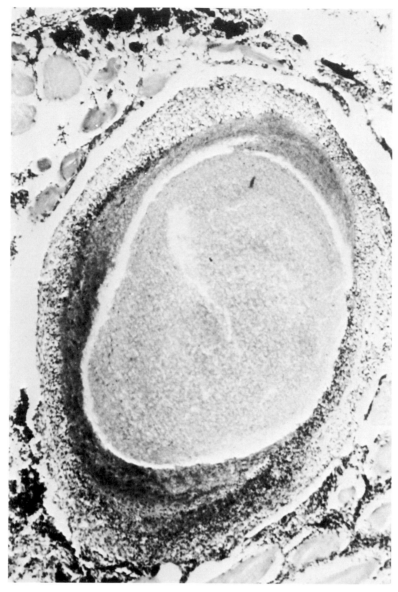

Fig. 2.13. *Flavobacterium* sp. Intermuscular granuloma with large acidophilic central zone of necrosis. H&E; ×65.

of organ involvement as liver 100%, brain and meninges 80%, kidney 70%, and pancreas 70%.

I have seen a lesion identical to those described by Kluge (91) in one of four *P. reticulata* (*L. reticulatus*) submitted in formalin by a breeder losing a small proportion of his fish monthly. Clinical signs included anorexia, fin necrosis, and a large swollen area on the dorsal caudal peduncle. Histologically, the swelling was a granuloma within skeletal muscle. No other organs were involved.

Another example of this disease was kindly provided by Dr. A. Jonas, Department of Pathology, Yale Medical School. Lesions were present within the mesentery, pancreas, and liver of a mature goldfish submitted for necropsy. This fish was not cultured, but histological lesions were characteristic of *Flavobacterium* infection. No organisms were apparent in the granulomas when sections were stained by Giemsa, Gram, or acid-fast methods.

Lesions resemble those caused by *Mycobacterium* sp., but are granulomas lacking acid-fast bacteria, having a larger central zone of acidophilic necrotic debris, and eliciting fewer epithelioid cells. Differential diagnosis included *Ichthyophonus hoferi,* Microsporidia, Myxosporidia, and migrating helminths.

The disease has been reviewed by Bullock, Conroy, and Snieszko (26).

CYTOPHAGACEAE

Cytophaga sp. (bacterial gill disease)

Bacterial gill disease (BGD) is a proliferative process affecting the gills of fish and is due to members of the order Myxobacteriales and characterized by hypertrophy and hyperplasia of lamellar epithelial cells.

A disease resulting in destruction of opercula with marked proliferation of gill epithelium was described by Osburn (112) in 1910, but the first description of the disease with reference to a bacterial etiology was that of Davis (42). He attributed the lesion to irritation by surface bacteria and further described the disease in 1927 (43). In 1935, Fish (57) described a Western form of BGD which he felt differed from Davis's Eastern form in the type of bacteria present and in its failure to respond to treatment. Ordal and Rucker (111) isolated myxobacteria from gill disease and were the first investigators to identify these bacteria in association with a disease outbreak. The disease is now a common and well-recognized entity affecting both warm- and coldwater fish and is responsible for tremendous losses annually (116).

While all the causative agents of the disease have not as yet been identified, two genera of myxobacteria have been found in frequent association with lesions. They are *Cytophaga* sp., family Cytophagaceae, and *Sporocytophaga* sp., family Myxococcaceae (23). Etiological studies indicate that the characteristic histopathological lesions associated with the disease are quite nonspecific. A number of essentially unrelated agents may elicit a similar tissue proliferation. Reported conditions capable of eliciting this reaction include excess organic matter, ammonia, parasites, *Branchiomyces* sp., *Dermocystidium* sp., pantothenic acid deficiency, and bacteria other than those of the order Myxobacteriales (8, 28, 57, 119, 174, 183, 187).

Bullock (23) states, "Bacterial gill disease is primarily an environmental disease and secondarily a bacterial disease of fingerling salmonids." His remark is based upon recognition of the role of other factors in production of the disease and of a failure to fulfill Koch's postulates with bacteria recovered from disease outbreaks. His studies of the production and transmission of the disease indicate a complex relationship between a virulent organism and environmental stress.

Experiments to stress fingerling trout, which included increases in ammonia, decreases in O_2, combinations of these factors, or addition of excess soil to the water, were not successful in producing gill disease (23). However, if trout were stressed by increased ammonia (0.5 to 1.5 ppm), decreased oxygen (4.0 to 5.0 ppm), and fecal material and food allowed to accumulate, typical lesions of bacterial gill disease appeared in 11 to 17 days. When live, diseased trout were placed in holding facilities with control trout, no disease developed. Yet stressed trout exposed to live, diseased trout developed the lesions in a much shorter period of time (3 to 5 days) than stressed trout without exposure (9 to 13 days). It is apparent, therefore, that conditions necessary to produce disease outbreaks are still not known in their entirety but that the presence of a virulent culture is a necessity (23).

It can be said with certainty that a variety of myxobacteria are involved in the disease process and since many may be recovered from completely normal fish gills it is apparent that they are "opportunistic" pathogens. Bullock (23) reported a serological relationship between his isolates and other known myxobacterial pathogens such as *C. columnaris* and *C. psychrophilia*. Slide-agglutination tests were also positive in the titer range of <1:10 to 1:40, which may indicate the ubiquitous nature and frequency of exposure to these organisms. There are no gross lesions associated with outbreaks of the disease with the exception of an occasional excess production of mucus. The presence of "short gill covers" or damaged opercula is probably not related to bacterial gill disease but certainly may be a predisposing factor to gill damage.

Histopathological changes are proliferative in nature. The epithelial cells lining lamellae undergo hyperplasia and hypertrophy. In severe cases the proliferation may be so extensive that adjoining lamellae become fused (Fig. 2.14). Early changes include a swelling and rounding of the cells. Rucker, Johnson, and Kaydas (142) report "plaque" cells as described by Burrows. These cells are basophilic with a granular cytoplasm and project above other lining cells. They appear only very early in the development of the disease. Wood and Yasutake (187) in an attempt to differentiate histopathologically between BGD and the identical lesions of nutritional gill disease (pantothenic acid deficiency) report differences in lesion development. In BGD, cell hyperplasia appears to begin at the tip of la-

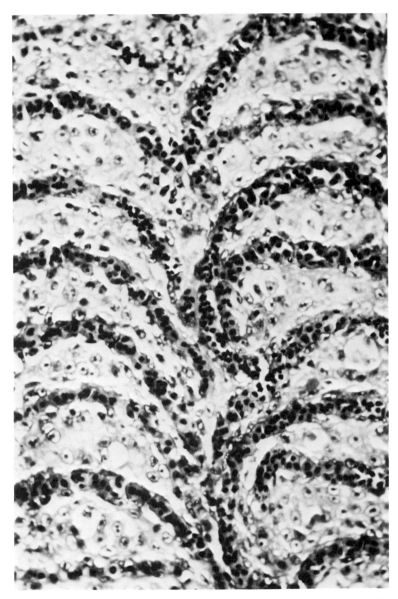

Fig. 2.14. Bacterial gill disease. Gill of brown trout (*S. trutta*) with lamellar epithelial cell hyperplasia and hypertrophy resulting in lamellar fusion. H&E; ×160.

mellae and is randomly scattered over the filament. In nutritional gill disease, however, the lesion begins at the base of lamellae and at the distal end of the filament. Once the lesion has become well developed, no differentiation is possible. Fish (57) in his description of Western BGD reports a progression of the lesion from the distal end of gill filaments.

The hyperplastic cells are round to ovoid with a weakly acidophilic cytoplasm, a large vesicular nucleus, and one to two nucleoli. Mitotic figures are not common. Focal areas of necrosis as evidenced by pyknosis may be present. Often the connective tissue of the filament is infiltrated by lymphocytes. Leukocytes containing large, strongly acidophilic intracytoplasmic granules and dense basophilic nuclei are found scattered between lamellae and below the layer of epithelial cells joining and lying at right angles to the lamellae. These cells are more acidophilic, have larger granules, and lack the apical crypt of the osmoregulatory chloride cells present at the base of teleosts' lamellae. Filamentous bacteria are present between lamellae and are often surrounded by proliferating cells.

There are reports that lesions may be present in other organs, specifically kidney hematopoietic tissue. Wood and Yasutake (187) report necrosis and inclusion-like particles in endothelial cells of this organ.

The lesion is reversible and with treatment the gill can be returned to normal.

Gram-Positive Organisms Eliciting Proliferative Response

CORYNEBACTERIACEAE

Corynebacterium sp. (kidney disease; Dee disease)

Kidney disease is a systemic, diffuse granulomatous inflammation of salmonids caused by a gram-positive, nonmotile diplobacillus of uncertain classification.

The first apparent outbreak of the disease was reported in salmon captured in the Aberdeenshire Dee, Scotland, in 1930 (62). The first probable record of the disease in North America occurred in 1935, affecting trout in a Massachusetts hatchery (17). It was not until the early 1950s, however, that a method was found for practical isolation of the organism and Koch's postulates were fulfilled (14, 141). The disease has been reported in three species of trout: *S. trutta, S. gairdneri,* and *Salvelinus fontinalis*, and five species of salmon: *S. salar, O. tshawytscha, O. nerka, O. kisutch,* and *O. gorbuscha* (18, 47, 153, 159). The disease is responsible for severe mortality rates among salmonids in the natural environment and under aquacultural conditions and has been reported to occur in both fresh and salt water (18, 153). During the past two decades there has been an increased incidence of the disease and it is now a well-recognized entity in hatcheries of the entire United States (179). The incidence of the disease appears related to water hardness. Warren (175) reported increased incidence in "soft" water with a mean total hardness below 13 ppm $CaCO_3$ (range 4.0 to 44.9). The effect of temperature on incidence is conflicting. Under experimental conditions Wolf and Dunbar (180) found the organism more virulent at 44.6° than at 54.5°F, while

Snieszko and Griffin (159) and Smith (153) reported the disease more prevalent in the natural environment when temperatures were rising during the spring and early summer, such that the incidence of lesions was greatest between 46° and 60°F.

The organism is a small bacillus measuring 0.5 to 0.9 microns in width and 0.8 to 2.8 microns in length, is gram-positive, aerobic, non-acid-fast, proteolytic, and catalase-positive (110, 153). On the basis of present data it best fits the classification of *Corynbacterium* sp., but Smith (153) points out its resemblance to *Brevibacteria* sp. It is fastidious in its growth requirements, growing in 7 to 10 days in an agar containing blood and 0.1% cysteine (110). Smith (153) reports a scanty growth at 5°C, best growth at 15°C, and no growth at 37°C.

The source of infection and means of transmission are at present unknown. There is no evidence of the Dee disease organism passing from fish to fish through water (153). Results of experimental transmission are conflicting. Both Earp, Ellis, and Ordal (47) and Wood and Wallis (189) report successful oral infection of salmon. Other investigators found it impossible to transmit the disease orally in brook trout but were successful by abrasion (161, 180).

Kidney disease is a chronic disease affecting both juvenile and adult fish. It may result in a slow progressive mortality or on occasion reach epizootic proportions. Clinical signs of the disease are variable and are reported to range from no external symptoms to signs including exophthalmos, abdominal distention, swollen raised areas in the musculature, and small dermal "blisters."

Clinical pathological examination of infected yearling brook trout revealed significant changes in hematocrit, total plasma protein values, and paper electrophoretic patterns. Packed cell volumes and total plasma protein values were decreased in diseased fish. Five electrophoretic fractions were present in normal male and female fish. In diseased fish fraction V (fastest migrating fraction; possible albumin fraction) was absent and fraction IV was significantly decreased (85).

Gross lesions are quite characteristic and allow for presumptive diagnosis. These lesions include focal cystic cavitations of body musculature, white foci of variable size (1 to 5 mm or more) extending into the parenchyma of the kidney, liver, and spleen, and often a fibrinous peritonitis resulting in a diphtheritic-like membrane covering the viscera. Skeletal muscle cavitations may be multiple and quite large (2 X 4 cm). The cystic spaces often contain an opaque grey serous fluid. The organisms appear to have a predilection for the kidney, so that this organ is commonly involved; however, Wood and Wallis (189) reported the liver to be the most affected organ in outbreaks among *O. tshawytscha*, while Bell (18) reported spleen and liver more commonly involved in pink salmon. Impression smears of infected organs may be made at the necropsy table, stained by the Gram method, and examined microscopically for the causative agent (159).

Histopathologically the disease is best described as a bacteremia characterized by a systemic diffuse granulomatous (histiocytic) inflammation. The first extensive microscopic description of the disease was that of Snieszko and Griffin (159), who described the tissue changes as granulomas similar to the reaction elicited by mycosis and tuberculosis in higher vertebrates. These workers reported typical well-defined tubercles with giant cells. Wood and Yasutake (186), comparing the Eastern and Western forms of the disease, reported granulomatous nodules, infrequent giant cells, and proliferation of reticulo-endothelial cells seen to be actively phagocytizing the bacillus. Microscopically the cellular reaction is histiocytic and should be classified as a diffuse granulomatous inflammation and differentiated from the classic focal granulomas of fungal or parasitic etiology. Marked reticulo-endothelial (RE) cell proliferation may be present in any organ of the body but is most commonly seen involving kidney, liver, spleen, skeletal musculature, and gill. Wood and Yasutake (186) report granulomatous nodules in the lamina propria of the gut, in myocardial tissue, and involving the brain. The inflammatory cells, which are large (20 microns) and polygonal, contain an eosinophilic granular cytoplasm and often an eccentric vesicular nucleus. They are distributed in sheets throughout the parenchyma of affected organs. Due to their eosinophilia the cells stand out as distinct islands among the interstitial hematopoietic cells of the kidney (Fig. 2.15). Similar infiltrations of cells are easily seen in liver, spleen, and intestinal lamina propria. RE cells are also present on occasion below the epithelial lining of the gill lamellae, resulting in a swelling of affected lamellae.

Examination of skeletal muscle cavitations reveals a central zone of debris surrounded by a zone of muscle undergoing Zenker's necrosis and finally an area of RE cell infiltration and fibroblast proliferation. The epidermis overlying these zones of necrosis remains intact.

The granular appearance of the inflammatory cell cytoplasm suggests that these cells are serving a phagocytic function. If tissue sections are stained by the Brown-Brenn or Gram method this assumption can be verified. Masses of the organisms are seen within the macrophages as well as extracellularly (Fig. 2.16). Organisms are also present within blood vessels, especially those of the terminal gill filaments, indicating the systemic nature of the disease (Fig. 2.17).

Smith (153) was the first to describe histologically the "false membrane" so apparent at necropsy. The membrane is composed, from within outward, of fibroblasts and histiocytes, degenerating leukocytes with macrophages, and finally a layer of fibrin. It lies superficially and does not penetrate the capsule of the organs it covers, differentiating it from the true diphtheritic membrane caused by *Corynebacterium diphtheriae*. Wood and Yasutake (186) also reported the presence of intracytoplasmic inclusions within pancreatic acinar cells, an eosinophilic infiltration of the muscular layers of the gut including the esophagus, and in some instances, a granulocytic peritonitis.

To the comparative pathologist, the inflammatory response of kidney disease brings to mind Johne's disease (paratuberculosis), histoplasmosis, and chronic granulomatous colitis of the Boxer dog.

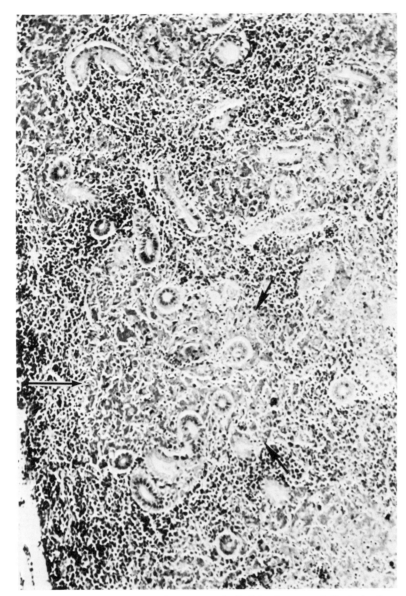

Fig. 2.15. Kidney disease. Islands of reticulo-endothelial cells (arrows) displacing hemato-poietic tissue of kidney. H&E; ×65.

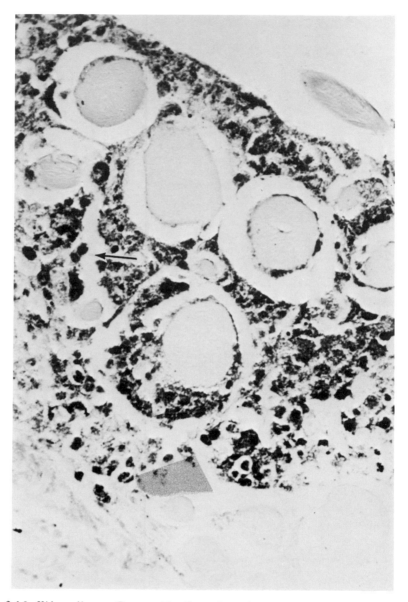

Fig. 2.16. Kidney disease. Gram-positive *Corynebacterium* organisms free and within macrophages (arrow) intermuscularly. Brown-Brenn; ×160.

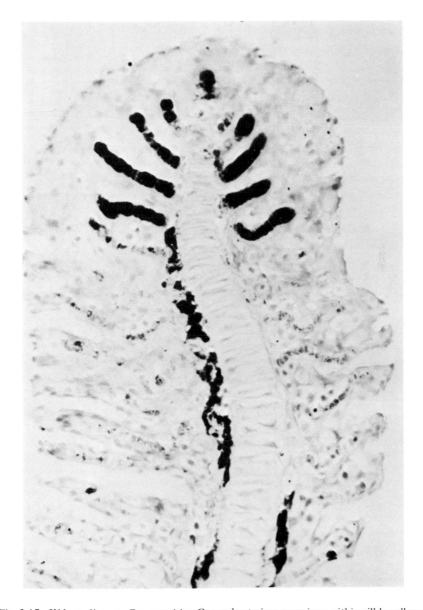

Fig. 2.17. Kidney disease. Gram-positive *Corynebacterium* organisms within gill lamellar vessels. Brown-Brenn; X65.

MICROCOCCACEAE

Staphylococcus sp.

R. J. Roberts (personal communication) reported an outbreak of mortality among caged saithe (*Pollachius virens*) in Scotland in which many of the affected fish had an ophthalmitis characterized by hypopion, keratitis, and retinal hemorrhage. *Staphylococcus* sp. was cultured from the eyes of moribund fish. Histological examination revealed the presence of both monogenetic trematodes (*Gyrodactylus* sp.) and metacercariae, possibly *Cryptocotyle* sp. A scleritis was present, unrelated to areas of parasite invasion. The lesion was composed of focal accumulations of epithelioid cells with a central zone of necrosis and scattered lymphocytes about the periphery of the nodule (Fig. 2.18). The response was reminiscent of a developing "coli-granuloma" seen in the chicken with Hjarre's disease. No giant cells were present.

Acid-Fast Organisms Eliciting Proliferative Response

ACTINOMYCETACEAE

Nocardia asteroides; N. kampachi

Nocardiosis is a systemic granulomatous disease of the fish caused by the higher bacterium *Nocardia asteroides.*

In 1963 Conroy (36) described an outbreak of disease among neon tetras (*Hyphessobrycon innesi*) kept in commercial aquaria in Argentina. The disease was characterized clinically by severe emaciation and pigmentation loss about the dorsal fin. An acid-fast, gram-positive organism was isolated and cultured on Lowenstein-Jensen media. Inoculations of this organism into gouramis (*Trichogaster trichopterus*) resulted in emaciation and death. Considering disease signs, pathogenicity, and organism characteristics, it was suggested that the causative agent might be a member of the genus *Mycobacterium.* Further characterization of the bacterium, however, revealed it to be the genus *Nocardia,* species *asteroides* (37, 169).

Snieszko et al. (161) reported nocardial infection in hatchery-reared fingerling rainbow trout observed from 1962 to 1963 at the National Fish Hatchery, Leetown, West Virginia. Both morbidity and mortality were slight and the disease did not spread. Attempts to transmit the disease by inoculation and feeding were seldom successful. Some fish developed lesions 30 to 90 days post-inoculation.

In 1965 and again in 1966 outbreaks of nocardiosis were described in seven species of fish, including rainbow trout (77, 78). The disease was described in brook trout approximately 22 cm in length by Campbell and MacKelvie (29). Intraperitoneal inoculations resulted in death in 40 to 60 days.

Gross lesions included cachexia, ascites, dermal ulceration, focal necrotic areas within skeletal muscle, and small white circumscribed masses in the kidney, spleen, heart, and liver. In cultured yellowtails the focal necrotic areas of skeletal muscle often contained a reddish-brown exudate (92).

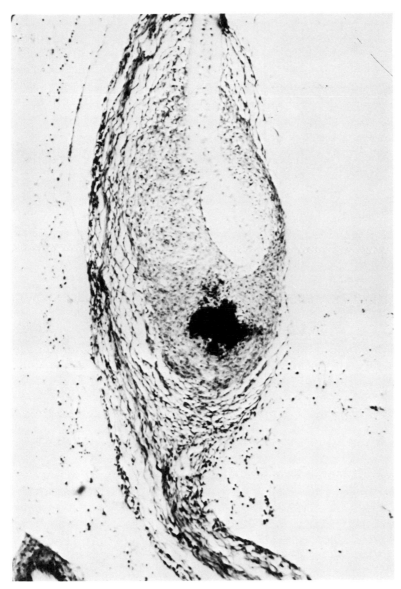

Fig. 2.18. *Staphylococcus* sp. Scleral granuloma of *Gadus pollachius.* (Tissue courtesy of Dr. R. Roberts.) H&E; ×65.

Focal granulomas are the predominant lesion present in cases of nocardiosis (*N. kampachi*) observed in *Seriola quinqueradiata* and *S. purpurascens*. More acute lesions, such as necrosis of muscle tissue, have also been reported and are characterized by hemorrhage, Zenker's necrosis, a mixed inflammatory response, and centrally located masses of the organism (92). Campbell and MacKelvie (29) reported nocardial organisms within the organs of trout inoculated intraperitoneally, while Snieszko et al. (161) reported large "colonies" of organisms and necrosis at the point of inoculation.

Examining a natural outbreak of the disease among rainbow trout 5 cm in length, I observed a diffuse granulomatous response within the mesentery and skeletal muscle. Large numbers of acid-fast bacteria were present, surrounded by loosely arranged histiocytes, macrophages, and scattered lymphocytes.

Conroy (36) has suggested that many cases of nocardiosis may have previously been misdiagnosed as tuberculosis. Considering the clinical signs and gross lesions associated with both these diseases this certainly is a possibility. Positive differentiation can only be made by isolation and identification of the causative agent; however, strongly presumptive diagnosis can be made by careful examination of lesion and organism morphology in fixed sections. *N. asteroides* is a gram-positive, acid-fast, filamentous, beaded, branching organism which is easily differentiated from the gram-positive, acid-fast, nonfilamentous, occasionally beaded, nonbranching bacillus of the mycobacteria. In addition, the granulomatous response elicited by *Nocardia,* in the cases which I have examined, was more diffuse and lacked encapsulation. Furthermore, unlike tuberculosis, nocardiosis may result in focal areas of necrosis in addition to its proliferative granulomatous reaction. The tremendous number of organisms associated with mycobacteriosis and nocardiosis in fish should allow for a relatively easy process of differentiation by histopathological examination.

MYCOBACTERIACEAE

Mycobacterium sp. (tuberculosis; fish mycobacteriosis)

Fish tuberculosis is a systemic, granulomatous disease characterized by the production of focal granulomas due to higher bacteria of the genus *Mycobacterium*.

Since its first report in carp (*Cyprinus carpio*) in 1897 by Bataillon, Dubart, and Terre (16) the disease has been recorded in 40 families and 151 species of fish and is worldwide in distribution (107). It is a disease of fresh- and saltwater fish and is present in both tropic and temperate zones. The exact effect of this disease on natural populations of fish is unknown; however, there is evidence that the disease may affect stocked, hatchery-reared salmonids and result in poor returns from the sea (188). Piscine tuberculosis is more often a problem faced by the aquarist and aquaculturist (107). The disease in salmonids was reviewed by Parisot (117) and again by Ross (132), while the problem affecting poikilotherms in general was considered by Conroy (38).

The causative agent is a gram-positive, acid-fast, nonmotile pleomorphic bacillus from 1 to 12 microns in length and belonging to the genus *Mycobacterium*. Classification of the species affecting fish is confused. The original isolate in 1897 was designated *Mycobacterium piscium*. The isolate, however, has been lost and is no longer included in Bergey's *Manual,* which at present lists three members of the genus as pathogenic to teleosts. *M. platypoecilus* was recovered from diseased *P. maculatus* (15). In 1955, Gordon and Smith (67) reported recovery from halibut of the third species listed in Bergey's *Manual, M. fortuitum.* This species has also been involved in infections of man and cattle. Ross (131) described a new species isolated from salmon and named it *M. salmoniphilum,* but it is still of uncertain classification. Isolation procedures for diagnosis have been described by Amlacher (8) and Nigrelli and Vogel (107). Both these investigators report little difficulty recovering the agent; however, Ross (132) states that organisms affecting salmon are extremely difficult to culture. Growth of the organism is slow, requiring 14 to 21 days for the colonies to become visible.

The epizootiology of piscine tuberculosis has been studied but the exact means of its transmission and spread are not known. The disease may be transmitted experimentally by injection and ingestion of contaminated feed (107). The latter method is responsible for disease problems in salmon hatcheries (188). Vertical transmission also seems possible. Nigrelli and Vogel (107) reported that transovarian passage in ovoviviparous fish is a strong possibility but passages via ova and milt in experiments with steelhead trout were negative (132).

Clinical signs of tuberculosis in fish are variable. An acute form exists, which may result in death without any external signs. Usually the disease is chronic and progressive, and affected animals are emaciated, ascitic, may have ulcerations, exophthalmos, lordosis or scoliosis, and frequently pigment changes (8). Pigment changes appear quite consistently in both tropical fish and salmonids. In the former, affected fish are reported to undergo loss of color, while among salmonids affected fish appeared brigher in color (8, 188).

Gross lesions include greyish-white raised areas of various size involving any organ. While a miliary form of the disease is not uncommon, no gross lesions may be present and immediate diagnosis may depend on Ziehl-Neelsen stains of impression smears. Microscopic examination reveals a classic focal granuloma composed of epithelioid cells (hypertrophied histiocytes with a ground glass cytoplasm resembling epithelial cells) and histiocytes occupying a central position surrounded by a wall of fibroblastic cells (Fig. 2.19). The histiocytes may serve a phagocytic function engulfing the bacillus, and are then referred to as macrophages. The piscine tubercle is similar to that in man, in that both the "soft" and "hard" tubercle are present. The "soft" tubercle has a center of caseous necrosis, while the "hard" tubercle lacks this central zone of necrosis. It differs from the human tubercle in that Langhans' giant cells are seldom present, calcification has not been reported, and the relative number of bacteria in the central zone far

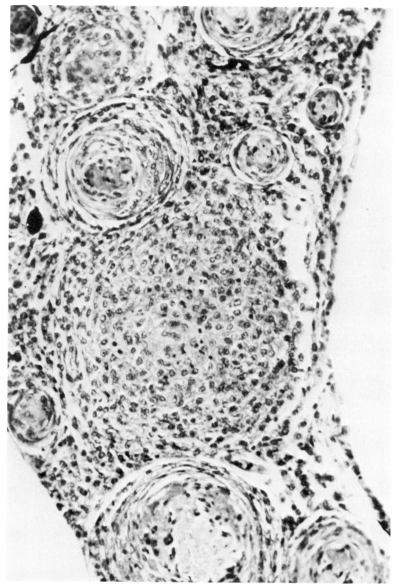

Fig. 2.19. Tuberculosis. Hard and soft tubercles in peri-orbital tissue of *Poecilia reticulata* (*Lebistes reticulatus*). H&E; ×160.

exceeds that found in higher vertebrates. Nigrelli and Vogel (107) state that the majority of lesions they observed in climbing perch, goldfish, and other species were of the "hard" tubercle form. Amlacher (8) reports the absence of giant cells in spontaneous cases but reports their presence occasionally in experimental cases and remarks on the rare appearance of eosinophilic granulocytes within tubercles. These focal granulomas may form conglomerate lesions, completely destroying the organ they occupy (8).

Positive diagnosis is possible by means of the Ziehl-Neelsen method for acid-fastness which reveals the presence of the bacillus in the central zone and within macrophages. This central zone of necrosis is also periodic acid-Schiff (PAS)-positive (8).

In salmonids, Parisot and Wood (118) reported the absence of inflammatory response among young fish and observed masses of bacteria in the peritoneum. In adult animals necrosis was present but the granulomatous response absent.

Differential diagnosis must consider other agents responsible for the formation of granulomas. These include the bacterium *Flavobacterium* sp., which produces a similar reaction but is negative for acid-fast organisms, *I. hoferi,* a fungus of marine fish which is more diffuse in its granulomatous reaction and whose mycelia and spore stages are PAS-positive, various migrating helminths which usually elicit an eosinophilic granulomatous response, and finally protozoans (microsporidians and myxosporidians), which may be identified by means of the Giemsa stain.

FUNGAL DISEASES

While mycotic diseases of fish are known to exist and have been reported in both fresh- and saltwater environments, far less is known about these diseases than is known about diseases of bacterial etiology. This lack of knowledge may well stem from the consensus that fungi infecting fish are secondary invaders and though they may eventually result in mortality, it is the underlying primary bacterial or viral disease which must be controlled and towards which major research efforts have been directed. There can be little question, however, that some piscine fungal disease outbreaks unassociated with other pathogenic agents have been epizootic in proportion and responsible for mass mortality. Such epizootics have been recorded under both aquacultural and natural conditions. Their usual manifestation is as a chronic dermal or branchial infection.

Any discussion of piscine mycoses is complicated by two factors. First is the problem of identification. Scott (147) reported that many of the organisms found in association with lesions have been incompletely or improperly identified. This has led to the lumping of the freshwater fungi affecting fish under the term *Saprolegnia.* Confusion exists not only as to species but also as to genera involved. The only information which can be gained from such reports is that a fungus was present in association with a pathogenic process or death. Questions of host and species specificity must remain unanswered. Further, this lack of proper identification gives rise to the second complicating factor in this discussion, the question of pathogenicity.

Not only are we faced with the problem of not knowing for certain what fungi have been reported, but we do not know whether the reported fungus was involved in the pathogenic process. We are at a loss to answer the question, "Is this organism sacrophytic, a primary pathogen, or simply an opportunist?"

This question can only be answered by proper gross and histopathological examination and description, isolation and identification of the organism, re-infection of fish of the same species, and re-isolation and identification. Such investigations have been conducted by Tiffney (166), Vishniac and Nigrelli (170), and Hoshina, Sano, and Sunayama (84).

The pathologist faced with the diagnosis of a mammalian mycotic disease is often able to identify the pathogenic agent in microscopic tissue sections. He is backed by a large body of knowledge regarding experimental reproduction of the disease and is able to reach a positive diagnosis with some certainty. The ichthyologist faced with the same problem is forced to ask himself what role these fungi may have played in the pathogenic processes he observes. He has no large body of experimental knowledge nor certain histopathological lesion descriptions on which to rely for presumptive diagnosis. It is imperative, therefore, that the comparative pathologist with the help of the mycologist isolate and identify fungi associated with lesions and carefully describe tissue changes present in relation to the organism. These isolates must then be classified as saprophytes, primary pathogens, or opportunists, by controlled experimentation.

Reported fungi of certain identification found in association with naturally occurring and experimentally induced disease in fish include the following isolates (7, 8, 45, 53, 55, 82, 84, 127, 133, 147, 148, 178):

PHYCOMYCETES
    Chytridiales
        Dermocystidium sp.
    Entomophthorales
        Ichthyophonus hoferi
        Basidiobolus intestinalis
        B. lotae
    Leptomitales
        Leptomitus lacteus
    Peronosporales
        Pythium sp.
        P. ultimum
        P. afertile
    Saprolegniales
        Achlya flagellata

A. nowickii
A. polyandra
A. prolifera
A. racemosa
A. ambisexualis
A. bisexualis
A. klebsiana
A. sparrowii
Aphanomyces laevis
A. stellatus
Calyptralegnia achlyoides
Dictyuchus monosporus
Isoachlya monolifera
I. parasitica
Leptolegnia caudata
Protoachlya paradoxa
Saprolegnia delica
S. ferax
S. invaderis
S. megasperma
S. mixta
S. monoica
S. parasitica
S. torolusa
Thraustotheca clavata
T. primoachlya

FUNGI IMPERFECTI
Sphaeropsidales
Phoma herbarum
Moniliales
Cladosporium sp.
Dematiaceae
Exophiala salmonis
Fusarium culmorum
Heterosporium tshawytscha
Scolecobasidium humicola
UNCERTAIN CLASS
Uncertain order
Branchiomyces sanguinus
B. demigrans
Cyclloptericola marina
Ichthyochytrium vulgare

Little-known fungi and those *non certae sedis* have been reviewed by Reichen-bach-Klinke (126).

CHYTRIDIALES

Dermocystidium sp.

This genus of organism is at present of uncertain classification and has been assigned by various investigators to either the lower fungi or to the Haplosporidia, an order of protozoans (64). Reichenbach-Klinke and Elkan (127), in their discussion of *Dermocystidium* pathogenic to fish, place them within the Haplosporidia on the basis of spore morphology, noting that the spores have a lid rather than a polar capsule. However, the *Dermocystidium* sp. which was infectious to Pacific salmon and was described by Pauley (119) and Allen et al. (7) was considered a fungus since it lacked a lid on the spore. Previous descriptions of *Dermocystidium* sp. isolated from coastal waters near Woods Hole, Massachusetts, also classified this organism as a member of the marine phycomycetes (64). Pauley (119) briefly reviewed the world literature regarding piscine *Dermocystidium* infections but made no reference to the fact that infections described before his 1967 report may have been due to organisms better classified as Haplosporidia. For the purposes of this discussion and because of the confusion regarding classification, only *Dermocystidium* sp. as described by Goldstein and Moriber (64), Pauley (119), and Allen et al. (7) will be considered as a member of the phycomycetes.

The first outbreak of mortality associated with the fungus *Dermocystidium* sp. occurred among prespawning adult salmon (*O. tshawytscha*) in the fall of 1965 at Priest Rapids Dam, Washington (119). Mortality was approximately 25% among 5000 adult fish. Another outbreak occurred in the same area in the fall of 1966 with a mortality of 21.8% among female fish (341 males and 655 females) and a morbidity of 77.3% among unspawned carcasses (7). In January 1967 Allen et al. (7) observed the disease in chinook salmon leaving the spawning areas and reported other outbreaks in hatcheries along the Columbia River. The disease was also found in spawning sockeye salmon.

Though little is known regarding the epidemiology of this disease, it is most frequent in water temperatures below 60°F. The life cycle of the parasite is unknown. Nutrition, respiration, and culturing of the organisms have been investigated by Goldstein, Belsky, and Chosak (65) and Allen et al. (7). The disease is apparently increasing in frequency throughout the Columbia River system (7).

The gross lesions associated with *Dermocystidium* sp. infections are confined to the gill, skin, and oral mucosa and are characterized by raised white shiny circumscribed masses 0.2 to 0.8 mm in diameter. Allen et al. (7) observed most of these masses on the anterior portion of affected fish. In severe cases the gill coverings are held open by the masses invading gill tissue. Histologically these masses are cysts containing the developmental stages of the organism. The cyst has a clear thin capsule and is often present within the gill lamellae, surrounded in turn by lamellar epithelium. The cysts, as they grow in size, push adjoining lamellae to one side and resemble balloon-like masses attached by the lamellae to the gill filament (Fig. 2.20). In this respect they are reminiscent, at low power, of swollen

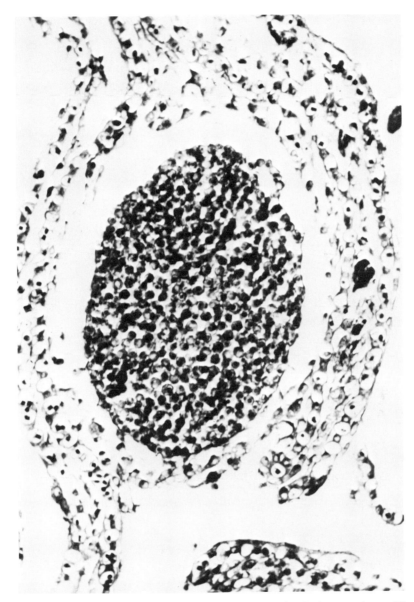

Fig. 2.20. *Dermocystidium* sp. Gill lamellar cyst containing developing organisms. (Tissue courtesy of Dr. G. Pauley.) H&E; ×160.

lamellae seen in hemorrhagic gill disease and in epitheliocystis infection (79, 184, 187). Pauley (119) reports congestion, hemorrhage, mixed inflammatory response, and lamellar epithelial hyperplasia and hypertrophy in association with the cysts. Diagnosis is possible by examination of the resting spores within the cysts. Developmental stages vary in size from 5 to 8 microns and the mature spores, when stained by the Giemsa method, are vacuolated, contain a pink, volutin body, and an eccentric vesicular nucleus (119). The disease is apparently systemic in nature, since both Pauley (119) and Allen et al. (7) report cysts suspected of containing developing stages of *Dermocystidium* sp. within the splenic parenchyma.

ENTOMOPHTHORALES

Ichthyophonus hoferi (ichthyosporidiosis; "staggers"; taumelkrankheit)

Ichthyophonus disease is a systemic granulomatous infection of both marine and freshwater fish due to the fungus *Ichthyophonus hoferi.*

The causative organism of this disease has been variously assigned to the genera *Ichthyosporidium* and *Ichthyophonus,* so that reports in the literature vary as to nomenclature. The disease was originally described in 1893 but the organism was assigned no name (127). Caullery and Mesnil (33) assigned a similar organism to the protozoan genus *Ichthyosporidium.* Later, both Pettit (120) and Plehn and Muslow (123) identified the organism as a fungus and the latter investigators assigned it the name *Ichthyophonus hoferi.* Pettit (121) challenged this nomenclature, changing the name to *Ichthyosporidium hoferi.* In a recent discussion of the *Ichthyosporidium,* Sprague (164) assigns this genus to the protozoans and Sindermann (148), discussing fungi pathogenic to fish, refers to the disease as *Ichthyophonus.*

I. hoferi is best known as the cause of periodic mass mortalities among North Atlantic herring (*Clupea harengus harengus*). The disease is of such importance that it may be a limiting factor to population growth of this fish (148). Within the Gulf of St. Lawrence four epizootics have been reported since 1898 and in the Gulf of Maine, two since 1931. Morbidity during epizootics was approximately 25% of sampled fish, and less than 1% in nonepizootic years (148). However, Fish (55) noted an incidence of 70% during the 1930–31 epizootic. He suggested a 16-year cycle between epizootics, but in recent years elapsed time between North Atlantic outbreaks has been 7 to 10 years. Outbreaks occur most frequently when water temperatures are lower, during the winter and spring (143). The disease is not confined to marine fish but has been reported in 48 species of freshwater fish as well as 35 species of marine fish (127). The literature up to 1954 is reviewed by Sindermann and Scattergood (150).

The life cycle of the organism is not completely understood and may vary as to the species of fish affected (127). In the herring, Sindermann and Scattergood (150) suggest the following cycle: spores are ingested by fish, germinate and penetrate gut, new hyphal bodies or spores enter blood stream for systemic distribution, germination and spore production in new organs, spores reach new host after release to external environment by ulceration or death and decay of original host. It is interesting to note that spores may remain viable and infectious in salt water under laboratory conditions for six months, which is evidence for the hypothesized means of passage among fish. The possibility exists that an intermediate host is involved in the cycle. The copepod *Calanus finmarchicus* has been found to harbor *Ichthyophonus* and can be experimentally infected. Herring fed samples of plankton exposed to the fungus were not infected in two series of experiments (150).

Transmission of the disease is easily accomplished by the feeding of infected material to fish. Transmission experiments involving exposure of wounded fish to the fungus or direct application to gill filaments were unsuccessful.

The fungus may be cultured after aseptic recovery from infected fish on Sabouraud dextrose agar slants to which 1% beef serum has been added. Growth is abundant in 7 to 10 days for up to 14 months at an optimum temperature of 10°C (150). Nonseptate hyphae grow down into the agar, where hyphal bodies and later spores are formed.

Gross lesions in the herring apparently occur as rapidly as 30 days after experimental feeding of the fungus and include raised round areas approximately 1 mm in diameter involving the skin, similar areas black in color, ulcers of varying size, and raised white sharply circumscribed nodules (1 to 3 mm) in internal organs, especially heart, mesentery, and liver. The blackened dermal areas result from a loss of the normal grossly silver epidermis as it covers proliferating fungal masses arising in the dermis. These pigmented areas impart a roughened texture to the skin, giving rise to the "sandpaper effect" described by Sindermann and Rosenfield (149). Other species of fish may lack external lesions but internal changes are common to all.

Microscopic appearance of the organism is dependent on its stage of development. Three basic stages can be recognized. Reichenbach-Klinke and Elkan (127) and Amlacher (8) discuss other possible stages and species variations. The stages include (1) spore or "resting" stage, (2) germinating spore, (3) hyphal stage.

The spores have been variously described as "resting" or quiescent stages but as suggested by Sindermann and Scattergood (150) are probably merely a developmental form in the life cycle. They range in size from 10 to 250 microns and possess a double wall. The outer wall thickness appears related to spore size, while the inner wall is consistently quite narrow. PAS and silver stains of both walls are positive and reveal the outer wall to be laminated and often rough on its outer contour. A thin clear area exists between the walls. The cytoplasm within the inner walls is often vacuolated, weakly basophilic, PAS-positive, argyophilic, and contains multiple nuclei (Fig. 2.21). Groups of these spores may be present in islands but frequently the larger spores are solitary.

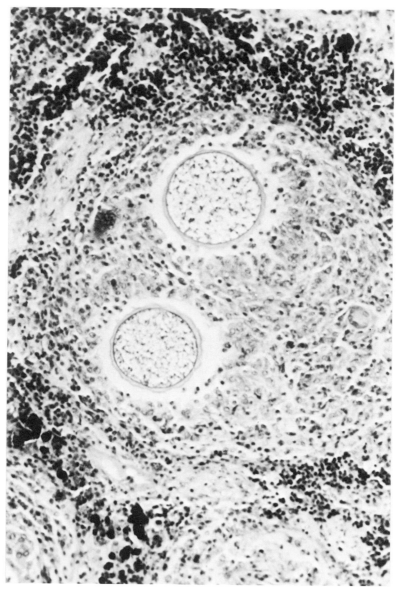

Fig. 2.21. *Ichthyophonus hoferi.* Spores or resting stage eliciting severe granulomatous re-action and giant cells in spleen. H&E; ×160.

The germinating spore is best defined as "flask" shaped, the "neck" of the structure constituting the forming hyphae. The "neck" breaks through the outer cell wall and the contained-cytoplasm is bounded solely by the inner spore wall (Fig. 2.22).

Less frequently elongate hyphal structures are present. These are nonseptate, vary in length to 2 mm, and often are of uneven width, varying from 5 to 40 microns. The cytoplasm within the hyphae resembles that within the spore. Hyphae give rise to new plasmodia after disintegration of the hyphal wall and the clumping together of the multinucleated cytoplasm. These plasmodia are termed *hyphal bodies* and in turn are capable of germination.

Rarely one may observe endogenous budding of the larger spores. Collections of plasmodia are present within the spore cytoplasm, often in close relation to the inner spore wall. This phenomenon has been described in tropical freshwater species (127).

Developmental stages may be found in any of the major organs of the body, including the blood. The most frequently involved organs in *C. harengus harengus* are the heart, skeletal muscle, liver, and kidney. Spores have been reported in branchial blood vessels and are occasionally seen in Giemsa-stained blood smears (150). The organisms elicit a severe focal granulomatous response which replaces much of the organ it occupies (Fig. 2.23). Masses of epithelioid cells surround developing and germinating spores. In acute infections the inflammatory cells closest to the spore are often radially arranged, their long axis at right angles to the cell wall. This layer may be three to four cells thick and is in turn bounded by concentric layers of epithelioid cells. The whole granuloma is bounded by a thin connective tissue capsule. Foreign body giant cells may rarely be present. A small percentage of the spores may be bound only by a thin layer of fibrous tissue, especially in areas such as the muscle layers of the intestine.

SAPROLEGNIALES

Saprolegnia sp.

The strict and proper definition of the term *Saprolegnia* is a genus of fungus, order Saprolegniales, class Phycomycetes. Used, however, in reference to mycotic disease it is an all-encompassing term which includes approximately 3 orders, 10 genera, and 22 species of fungi naturally or experimentally infectious to fish. The term is commonly used to refer to any cotton-like growth of fungi adherent to skin or gills. It is a problem of freshwater fish primarily, although some species may affect fish in waters of low salinity (165, 170).

Saprolegniasis is a localized, usually chronic disease of fish due to fungi of the orders Saprolegniales, Peronosporales, and Leptomitales, characterized by dermal ulceration and Zenker's necrosis of muscle in conjunction with a mononuclear inflammatory response.

The order Saprolegniales includes 29 genera and 90 species of fungi known as

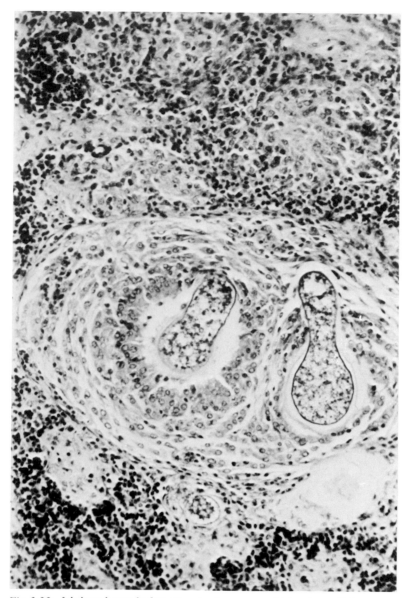

Fig. 2.22. *Ichthyophonus hoferi.* Germinating spores within spleen. H&E; ×160.

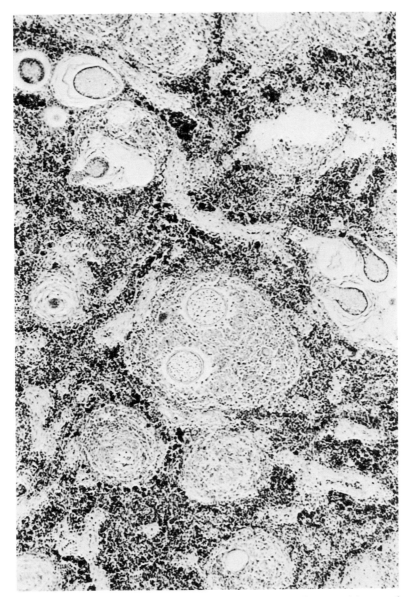

Fig. 2.23. *Ichthyophonus hoferi.* Low-power photomicrograph of spleen with severe focal granulomatous inflammation. H&E; ×65.

"water molds." Reproduction is both asexual by means of zoospores and sexual by oogonia and antheridia. Ainsworth (2) reports that the mycelial walls give a cellulose reaction which helps differentiate this order from other fungi. The nonsaprolegniaceous species of "water molds" responsible for saprolegniasis include three species of the genus *Pythium*, order Peronosporales and a single species, *Leptomitus lacteus*, of the order Leptomitales (147). The majority of the Saprolegniales and Leptomitales are ubiquitous aquatic forms, while members of the Peronosporales are soil inhabitants, with the exception of those species infectious to fish.

The fungal agents may be cultured in two general ways, an indirect method using "baits" and a direct method employing conventional nutrient agars. In the indirect method, pieces of infected tissue are placed in sterile fresh water with a "bait" such as sterile hempseed or insect parts. Fungal growths on the baits may then be transferred to diagnostic agar if necessary. Agars used for isolation which prevent bacterial contamination include GYS-tellurite or YpSs-tellurite (178).

Most of the fungi responsible for saprolegniasis are considered saprophytes, with the exception of *Saprolegnia parasitica.* The disease appears to be associated with some adverse environmental condition. For these reasons fish disease investigators have long felt that water molds affecting fish were simply secondary invaders; that they were, in short, opportunists. Outbreaks of disease are usually preceded by some environmental insult to the affected fish. Fungal lesions are commonly seen after handling, under conditions of crowding, trauma (spawning), and in conjunction with other viral and bacterial diseases (1, 93, 147, 166). Many of these conditions can disrupt the mucous covering on the surface of the fish. Willoughby (177) has suggested that this fish slime may serve as a barrier and possess some antifungal action. Further, there appears to be a relationship between disease incidence and water temperature. Disease incidence is greater at lower water temperatures (84, 165). Hoshina, Sano, and Sunayama (84) report a decrease in disease incidence among eels when temperatures exceed 18°C and further report that fungal isolations from eel ponds are most productive during the winter season.

Tiffney (166), Vishniac and Nigrelli (170), and Hoshina, Sano, and Sunayama (84) tested the hypothesis that some fungi isolated from infected fish were primary pathogens. *S. parasitica* was shown to be pathogenic to both uninjured and injured fish after exposure to zoospores, proving its primary pathogenicity. Differences in resistance were noted for different species of fish. The salmonidae were highly susceptible, while *C. auratus* and *Micropterus salmoides* were susceptible only after scale removal (166). Vishniac and Nigrelli (170) infected platyfish, following scale removal, with 16 species in 7 genera of Saprolegniales. Hoshina, Sano, and Sunayama (84) have reported primary saprolegniasis among cultured eels. The disease can be reproduced experimentally without prior injury to the fish. It would appear on the basis of present evidence that many of the fungi causing saprolegniasis are primary pathogens; that is to say, they are capable of infecting fish without the presence of a preceding bacterial or viral disease. However, they vary greatly in their virulence. *S. parasitica* and *S. ferax* are highly virulent and able to produce disease in the absence of any obvious insult to the host fish, whereas members of the genus *Pythium* may in fact be avirulent and simply saprophytes.

In addition to differences in virulence, Willoughby (178) suggests differences in host specificity. Studying a large outbreak of saprolegniasis among perch (50% morbidity) in Windemere, England, he found that *S. ferax*, the most common species in water samples, was unrecorded from the fish. However, there was a relationship between other fungi found in the water and those recovered from fish. In his etiological studies of ulcerative dermal necrosis of salmon, Willoughby (177) has isolated a single strain type of *Saprolegnia* which is sexually sterile and cannot be classified as to species. He notes that other forms of aquatic molds are rarely involved with this disease and states that such a high degree of selectivity is unexpected if the water molds are simply "secondary invaders."

The gross lesions of saprolegniasis are quite characteristic. These include focal, epidermal, white-to-brownish cotton-like masses randomly distributed on the surface of the fish. In specific disease outbreaks the distribution may not be random but may involve a particular region, for example, the head in "Sure" of the eel (84). This cotton-like appearance can only be seen when the fish is in water. When the animal is placed on the necropsy table the masses may be difficult to see but in severe cases resemble a ball of wet cotton adherent to the fish's side. The fungal growths are usually confined to the skin or gill but Agersborg (1) reported an outbreak of *S. ferax* in fingerling brook trout involving the gut lumen. There are no reports of systemic involvement. Beneath these accumulations of fungi the appearance of the skin may vary, depending upon the age of the lesions. Early lesions are often pale with peripheral areas of erythema and a central zone of scales lifted away from the body wall. Advanced lesions are frequently ulcerated with the underlying musculature exposed.

Histological examination of skin-sections stained with hematoxylin and eosin (H&E) reveals mycelial masses overlying zones of necrotic epithelium or overlying zones of frank ulceration. The mycelial masses are weakly eosinophilic, very irregular, and often contain unidentifiable debris (Fig. 2.24). Individual hyphae may be seen extending into the dermis and, if the lesion is far enough advanced, between muscle fibers. Inflammatory response to the invading hyphae is surprisingly slight. In addition to epithelial necrosis, Zenker's necrosis of muscle may be present. There is a lymphocytic and macrophagic infiltration of the affected area. When the infection is secondary to ulcers of furunculosis the reaction is less marked because of the production of leukocytotoxin by *A. salmonicida*. Invading hyphae are sparse, and, while they may be seen in routine H&E sections, special fungal stains are of value for certain identification. The hyphae are PAS-

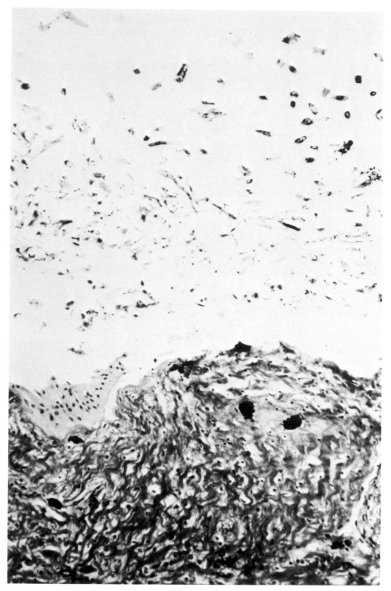

Fig. 2.24. Saprolegniasis. Mycelial mass above acute dermal ulcer. Some epidermis persists at left. Note lack of reaction. H&E; ×65.

positive but only weakly so, and I have found silver stains, especially the Grocott methenamine silver method, far superior for visualization. With this technique hyphae appear black against a light green background (Fig. 2.25). They are approximately 20 microns in diameter, irregularly branching and nonseptate. Their appearance is reminiscent of the hyphae of mucormycosis as seen in higher vertebrates.

SPHAEROPSIDALES

Phoma herbarum

H. Johnson and S. Leek of the Little White Salmon National Fish Hatchery, Cook, Washington, and L. M. Ashley of the Western Fish Nutrition Laboratory, Cook, have observed a fungal disease among coho and chinook fry which is responsible for mortality and has a morbidity varying from 1 to 5% (personal communication).

The causative agent has branching, septate hyphae and has been identified as a member of the order Sphaeropsidales genus *Phoma* and species *herbarum.* Little is known regarding epizootiology or pathogenesis.

Gross lesions include small (1 to 2 mm) white areas which are most commonly present at the anterior end of the gas bladder. Since the disease is systemic, similar areas may be found in the kidney, skeletal muscle, mesentery, and intestine. Ascites may be present. Smears of gas bladder fluid, ascitic fluid, and head kidney indicate the presence of structures varying in shape from round to elongate within degenerating red blood cells and erythroblasts. The organisms may also be found free of cells and vary in size as well as shape. The round forms are approximately 1 to 2 microns in diameter, while elongate forms may be up to 7 microns in length. Elongate forms often contain a purple central zone, while the round forms tend to be a uniform blue when stained by Leishman-Giemsa method. The relationship of these structures to *Phoma herbarum* is uncertain and there is a distinct possibility that they are not part of the fungal life cycle but are an unidentified protozoan. Hyphae are also present in smear preparations.

Microscopic lesions are characterized by a diffuse granulomatous reaction, necrosis, hemorrhage, and the presence of innumerable intertwining hyphae (Fig. 2.26).

The hyphae are PAS- and Giemsa-positive, from 50 to 100 microns in length by 2 to 3 microns in width, and have a beaded appearance because of a cytoplasmic variability in basophilia.

While the basic inflammatory response is that of macrophage infiltration, mats of hyphae may be associated with hemorrhage and necrosis within the kidney and other organs (Fig. 2.27).

The investigators suggest that the original site of infection is the gas bladder, from which the mold may extend ventrally into the mesentery, pancreas, or gastrointestinal tract, or dorsally into the kidney and eventually into the vertebral skele-

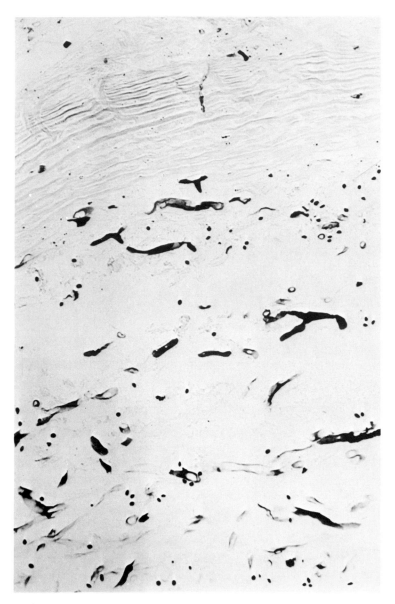

Fig. 2.25. Saprolegniasis. Subdermal nonseptate, irregular hyphae. Note lack of inflammatory response. Grocott methenamine silver; ×160.

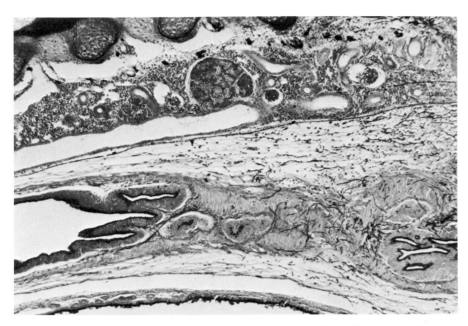

Fig. 2.26. *Phoma herbarum.* Diffuse granulomatous response within kidney and peritoneal cavity. Note mats of hyphae. (Photo courtesy of Dr. L. Ashley.) H&E; ×40.

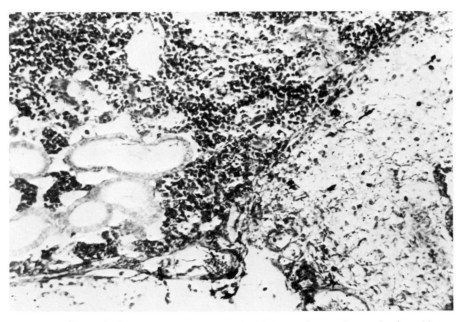

Fig. 2.27. *Phoma herbarum.* Hyphae associated with hemorrhage and necrosis of renal interstitial tissue. (Photo courtesy of Dr. L. Ashley.) H&E; ×100.

tal muscle. A distinct, diffuse granulomatous response may be elicited within the vertebral musculature.

MONILIALES

Exophiala salmonis
Three epizootics among hatchery-reared *S. clarki* fry and yearling lake trout have recently been described by Carmichael (32). The disease outbreaks occurred between 1948 and 1960 in an Alberta hatchery and the first one was associated with a 40% mortality. Clinical signs were similar in description to *Lentospora cerebralis* (Myxosoma) infections, including whirling, exophthalmos, and cranial ulcerations.

Brown, septate hyphae, recovered from skin ulcers, grew on Sabouraud's, Czapek's, cornmeal, and cereal agars. The fungus was described as a new genus and species, *Exophiala salmonis*, order Moniliales. Attempts to reproduce the disease were unsuccessful.

The author notes a similarity of this organism to *Phialophora verrucosa*, the cause of chromoblastoma in man, and refers to the lesions in affected fish as mycetomas. In the strict sense this is a clinical term referring to chronic mycoses characterized by swelling and by suppuration, with granules composed of fungal masses found within the resultant pus. The reaction described by Carmichael (32) does not indicate the presence of a true purulent response, and the term *mycetoma* may be ill-advised in reference to fungal diseases of the fish.

Histological examination revealed a chronic nonsuppurative granulomatous response with the presence of numerous giant cells. The lesions were confined to the brain and cranial area but were not present in the eyes, gills, or lower jaw.

Scolecobasidium humicola
Ross and Yasutake (133) described a systemic mycotic disease of juvenile coho salmon observed in fish held for experimental purposes. Isolates of the causative agent were made on Sabouraud-dextrose agar and identified as *Scolecobasidium humicola*.

The epizootiology of the disease is unclear and its transmission could not be accomplished unless ground glass was included in a dry meal diet. Fungus was recovered from 3 of 10 fish within a four-month period post-exposure.

Gross lesions include ascites, visceral adhesions, and grey areas in the organs, which the authors state resemble those of corynebacterial kidney disease.

Microscopic lesions are reported similar to those of *E. salmonis*, with the exception that no cerebral involvement was observed. The authors describe large areas of necrosis with lymphoid infiltration in association with many branching and fragmented fungal hyphae. No giant cells were present.

UNCERTAIN ORDER

Branchiomyces sp. (gill rot; branchiomycosis)

Gill rot is an acute, localized fungal infection of the gill of fish characterized by intravascular growth of the organisms *Branchiomyces sanguinis* and *B. demigrans*.

This interesting intravascular disease of European carp, tench, goldfish, and stickleback was apparently first described in 1912 by Plehn (122). She had observed a disease outbreak at the Munich Biologischen Versuchstation in the summer of 1911. Fungal hyphae were present within the branchial vessels, which resulted in respiratory embarrassment and death of affected carp. The agent was named *Branchiomyces sanguinis*.

Wundsch (190) reported a similar disease in pike occurring in a Prussian lake in the summer of 1929. He described the causative agent as a member of the same genus, *Branchiomyces,* but in reference to its characteristic extravascular growth assigned the species designation *demigrans*.

The organism produces nonseptate, branching hyphae and intrahyphal spores. The hyphae vary in width from 8 to 30 microns. *B. demigrans* has thicker hyphal walls (0.5 to 0.7 microns) and larger spores (8).

The means of natural transmission and the pathogenesis of the disease are not completely understood. Plehn (122) notes that spores are able to live in the water free of the host and suggests either direct gill invasion or ingestion, passage to circulation via intestinal lymph vessels, and eventual germination within gill vessels. She feels germination and growth can occur only in areas of high oxygen tension, hence localization of the fungus in the true sense, as evinced by the fact that the organism dies when it comes in contact with water.

This characteristic helps to differentiate *B. sanguinis* from *B. demigrans*. The latter organism commonly penetrates vessel walls and grows towards the gill exterior. Mortality may occur in two to four days, with an incidence as high as 50%.

Gross lesions include focal areas of hemorrhage as well as peripheral whitened necrotic patches due to thrombosis and ischemia. Microscopic lesions include lamellar epithelial cell proliferation and lamellar fusion, acute lamellar necrosis, and vascular necrosis. Hyphae are easily visualized within vessels, and spore formation within plasmodia is also readily apparent with routine staining methods. The reaction to *B. sanguinis* is surprisingly slight because of lack of tissue penetration (122). Reaction to *B. demigrans* is more severe, and hyphae may be seen to penetrate vessel walls and to grow into surrounding tissue.

In September and October 1972 two *L. gibbosus* and one *L. macrochirus* were captured in Worden's Pond, Kingston, Rhode Island. The fish were kept in a 30-gallon tank at 23°C at the Fish Pathology Laboratory, University of Rhode Island, for experimental purposes, by R. E. Richardson, a graduate student in the

Department of Animal Pathology, who kindly submitted tissue for examination. One *L. gibbosus* died seven days post-inoculation with 0.2 ml saline intramuscularly; the other, three weeks post-inoculation with 0.2 ml of a 48-hour *Staphylococcus* sp. culture. The bluegill became moribund while being held and was euthanized. All fish had raised white areas (1 mm) on major organs (parasitic granulomas); the bluegill had numerous gill copepods. Gross branchial lesions included focal red areas on filaments distal to which the tissue was pale.

Histological examination of the gills of all fish revealed an organism within lamellar and filament vessels. The distribution of the organism was random, involved all filaments examined, and 10 to 12 lamellae per filament. The organism was similar to that described by both Plehn (122) and Wundsch (190), having nonseptate branching hyphae containing intrahyphal round bodies called by the authors "spores." Both hyphal walls and spores were eosinophilic when stained with H&E and were strongly PAS-positive. In some instances the spores contained multiple basophilic granules, while in others they contained a few small round hyaline, highly eosinophilic areas. Since the width of the hyphae far exceeded that of the lamellar vessels, affected lamellae were swollen and distorted. Where massive proliferation occurred within filament vessels, the filament was markedly thickened. Lamellae overlying the area of thickened filament, and those lamellae penetrated by hyphae, often had hyperplastic and hypertrophied epithelial lining cells. At points of penetration of the vessels there were perivascular hemorrhage, fibroblastic proliferation, and collections of mononuclear cells with large vesicular nuclei and pale, poorly outlined cytoplasm which resemble primitive reticulo-endothelial cells. On the basis of histological findings the organism was identified as *Branchiomyces* sp.

It is of interest to note that Worden Pond has an introduced and thriving population of pike (*E. lucius*).

Acknowledgment. Contribution #1462 of the Rhode Island Agricultural Experiment Station. This study was supported in part by Sea Grant funds at the University of Rhode Island.

REFERENCES

1. Agersborg, H. P. K.   Salient problems in the artificial rearing of salmonoid fishes, with special reference to intestinal fungisitosis and the cause of white spot disease. *Trans. Amer. Fish. Soc. 63:* 240. 1933.

2. Ainsworth, G. C.   *Ainsworth and Bisby's Dictionary of the Fungi.* 6th ed. Kew, Surrey, Commonwealth Mycological Inst., 1971.

3. Ajmal, M., and Hobbs, B. C.   Columnaris disease in roach and perch from English waters. *Nature (London) 215:* 141. 1967.

4. Ajmal, M., and Hobbs, B. C.   Species of *Corynebacterium* and *Pasteurella* isolated from diseased salmon, trout and rudd. *Nature (London) 215:* 142. 1967.

5. Akazawa, H. Symposium of bacterial fish diseases. 2. Bacterial diseases of marine fishes. *Bull. Jap. Soc. Sci. Fish. 34:* 271. 1968.

6. Allen, N., and Pelczar, M. J. Bacteriological studies on the white perch *Roccus americanus. Chesapeake Sci. 8:* 135. 1967.

7. Allen, R. L., Meekin, T. K., Pauley, G. B., and Fujihara, M. P. Mortality among chinook salmon associated with the fungus *Dermocystidium. J. Fish. Res. Board Can. 25:* 2467. 1968.

8. Amlacher, E. *Taschenbuch der Fischkrankheiten.* Jena, Gustav Fischer Verlag, 1961.

9. Anacker, R. L., and Ordal, E. J. Studies on the myxobacterium *Chondrococcus columnaris.* I. Serological typing. *J. Bacteriol. 68:* 25. 1959.

10. Anderson, D. P., and Klontz, G. W. Precipitating antibody against *Aeromonas salmonicida* in serums of inbred albino rainbow trout (*Salmo gairdneri*). *J. Fish. Res. Board Can. 27:* 1389. 1970.

11. Anderson, J. I. W., and Conroy, D. A. The significance of disease in preliminary attempts to raise flatfish and salmonids in sea water. *Bull. Off. int. Épizoot. 69:* 1129. 1968.

12. Anderson, J. I. W., and Conroy, D. A. Vibrio disease in marine fishes. In *A Symposium on Diseases of Fishes and Shellfishes,* ed. S. F. Snieszko Amer. Fish. Soc., Spec. Publ. No. 5. Washington, D.C., 1970.

13. André, P. G., Conroy, D. A., McGregor, D., Roberts, R. J., and Young, H. Acute haemorrhagic septicaemia in captive European eels (*Anguilla vulgaris*): A clinical pathological study. *Vet. Rec.* in press. 1972.

14. Aronson, J. D. Spontaneous tuberculosis in saltwater fish. *J. Infec. Dis. 39:* 315. 1926.

15. Baker, J. A., and Hagen, W. A. Tuberculosis in Mexican platyfish (*Platypoecilus maculatus*). *J. Infec. Dis. 70:* 248. 1942.

16. Bataillon, E., Dubard, and Terre, L. Un Nouveau type de tuberculose. *C. r. séances Soc. Biol. 49:* 446. 1897.

17. Belding, D. L., and Merrill, B. A. A preliminary report upon a hatchery disease of the Salmonidae. *Trans. Amer. Fish. Soc. 65:* 76. 1935.

18. Bell, G. R. Two epidemics of apparent kidney disease in cultured pink salmon (*Oncorhynchus gorbuscha*). *J. Fish. Res. Board Can. 18:* 559. 1961.

19. Borg, A. F. Studies on myxobacteria associated with diseases in salmonid fishes. *Wildlife Dis. 8:* 1. 2 microcards. 1960.

20. Bullock, G. L. The identification and separation of *Aeromonas liquefaciens* from *Pseudomonas fluorescens* and related organisms occurring in diseased fish. *Appl. Microbiol. 9:* 587. 1961.

21. Bullock, G. L. Characteristics and pathogenicity of a capsulated *Pseudomonas* isolated from goldfish. *Appl. Microbiol. 13:* 89. 1965.

22. Bullock, G. L. Simple enrichment of commercial media for growth of *Hemophilus piscium. Progr. Fish-Cult. 27:* 163. 1965.

23. Bullock, G. L. Studies on selected myxobacteria pathogenic for fishes and on bacterial gill disease in hatchery-reared salmonids. *U. S. Bur. Sport Fish. Wildlife, Tech. Pap. 60.* 1972.

24. Bullock, G. L., and McLaughlin, J. J. A. Advances in knowledge concerning bacteria pathogenic to fishes (1954–1968). In *A Symposium on Diseases of*

Fishes and Shellfishes, ed. S. F. Snieszko. Amer. Fish. Soc., Spec. Publ. No. 5. Washington, D.C., 1970.

25. Bullock, G. L., and Snieszko, S. F.   Fin rot, coldwater disease, and peduncle disease of salmonid fishes. *U. S. Bur. Sport Fish. Wildlife, Fish Dis. Leafl. 25.* 1970.

26. Bullock, G. L., Conroy, D. A., and Snieszko, S. F.   Bacterial diseases of fishes. In *Diseases of Fishes,* ed. S. F. Snieszko and H. R. Axelrod. Jersey City, T.F.H. Publications, 1971.

27. Bullock, G. L., Snieszko, S. F., and Dunbar, C. E.   Characteristics and identification of exudative pseudomonads isolated from diseased fish. *J. Gen. Microbiol. 38:* 1. 1965.

28. Burrows, R. E.   Effects of accumulated excretory products on hatchery-reared salmonids. *U. S. Fish Wildlife Serv., Res. Rep. 66.* 1964.

29. Campbell, G., and MacKelvie, R. M.   Infection of brook trout (*Salvelinus fontinalis*) by Nocardiae. *J. Fish. Res. Board Can. 25:* 423. 1968.

30. Cardwell, R. D., and Smith, L. S.   Hematological manifestations of vibriosis on juvenile chinook salmon. *Progr. Fish-Cult. 33:* 232. 1971.

31. Carlson, H. C., and Allen, J. R.   The acute inflammatory reaction in chicken skin: Blood cellular response. *Avian Dis. 13:* 817. 1969.

32. Carmichael, J. W.   Cerebral mycetoma of trout due to a *Phialophora*-like fungus. *Sabouraudia 6:* 120. 1966.

33. Caullery, M., and Mesnil, F.   Recherches sur les Haplesporidies. *Arch. zool. exp. gen. 4:* 101. 1905.

34. Cisar, J. O., and Fryer, J. L.   An epizootic of vibriosis in chinook salmon. *Bull. Wildlife Dis. Ass. 5:* 73. 1969.

35. Clement, M. T., and Gibbons, N. E.   *Aeromonas hydrophilia* (*Pseudomonas hydrophilia*) NRC 491 and NRC 492 established as *Aerobacter cloacae.* *Can. J. Microbiol. 6:* 591. 1960.

36. Conroy, D. A.   The study of a tuberculosis-like condition in neon tetras (*Hyphessobrycon innesi*). Symptoms of the disease and preliminary description of the organism isolated. *Microbiol. Españ. 16:* 47. 1963.

37. Conroy, D. A.   Nocardiosis as a disease of tropical fish. *Vet. Rec. 76:* 676. 1964.

38. Conroy, D. A.   Tuberculosis of poikilotherms. *Fish Pathol. (Japan) 2.* 1967.

39. Copenhaver, W. M.   *Bailey's Textbook of Histology.* 15th ed. Baltimore, Williams and Wilkins, 1964.

40. Cornick, J. W., Chudyk, R. V., and McDermott, L. A.   Habitat and viability studies on *Aeromonas salmonicida,* causative agent of furunculosis. *Progr. Fish-Cult. 31:* 96. 1969.

41. Davis, H. S.   A new bacterial disease of freshwater fishes. *Bull. Bur. Fish., Wash. 38:* 261. 1924.

42. Davis, H. S.   A new gill disease of trout. *Trans. Amer. Fish. Soc. 56:* 156. 1926.

43. Davis. H. S.   Further observations on the gill disease of trout. *Trans. Amer. Fish. Soc. 57:* 210. 1927.

44. Davis, H. S.   Care and diseases of trout. *U. S. Fish Wildlife Serv., Res. Rep. 12.* 1946.
45. Doty, M. S., and Slater, D. W.   A new species of *Heterosporium* pathogenic on young chinook salmon. *Amer. Midland Natur. 36:* 663. 1946.
46. Duff, D. C. B., and Stewart, B. J.   Studies on furunculosis of fish in British Columbia. *Contrib. Can. Biol. Fish. 8:* 103. 1933.
47. Earp, B. J., Ellis, C. H., and Ordal, E. J.   Kidney disease in young salmon. *Wash. Dep. Fish., Spec. Rep. 1.* 1953.
48. Evelyn, T. P. T.   An aberrant strain of the bacterial fish pathogen *Aeromonas salmonicida* isolated from a marine host, the sablefish (*Anoplopoma fimbria*) and from two species of cultured Pacific salmon. *J. Fish. Res. Board Can. 28:* 1629. 1971.
49. Evelyn, T. P. T.   First records of vibriosis in Pacific salmon cultured in Canada, and taxonomic status of the responsible bacterium, *Vibrio anguillarum. J. Fish. Res. Board Can. 28:* 517. 1971.
50. Fey. F.   Cytochemische Untersuchungen an Selachierblutzellen. *Sonderdruck aus die Naturwissenschaften 204:* 604. Berlin, Gottingen, and Heidelberg, Springer Verlag, 1960.
51. Field, J. B., Gee, L. L., Elvehjem, C. A., and Juday. C.   The blood picture in furunculosis induced by *Bacterium salmonicida* in fish. *Arch. Biochem. Biophys. 3:* 277. 1944.
52. Fijan, N.   The survival of *Chondrococcus columnaris* in waters of different quality. *Bull. Off. int. Épizoot., 69:* 1159. 1968.
53. Fijan, N. N.   Systemic mycosis in channel catfish. *Bull. Wildlife Dis. Ass. 5:* 109. 1969.
54. Finn, J. P., and Nielsen, N. O.   The effect of temperature variation on the inflammatory response of rainbow trout. *J. Pathol. 105:* 257. 1971.
55. Fish, F. F.   A fungus disease in fishes of the Gulf of Maine. *Parasitology 26:* 1. 1934.
56. Fish. F. F.   Ulcer disease of trout. *Trans. Amer. Fish. Soc. 64:* 252. 1934.
57. Fish, F. F.   A western type of bacterial gill disease. *Trans. Amer. Fish. Soc. 65:* 85. 1935.
58. Fish, F. F.   Furunculosis in wild trout. *Copeia 1:* 37. 1937.
59. Fish, F. F., and Rucker, R. R.   Columnaris as a disease of cold water fishes. *Trans. Amer. Fish. Soc. 73:* 32. 1943.
60. Fryer, J. L., Nelson, J. S., and Garrison, R. L.   Vibriosis disease of fish. *Prog. Fish. Food Sci. 5:* 129. 1972.
61. Fujihara, M. P., and Hungate, F. P.   *Chondrococcus columnaris* disease of fishes: Influence of Columbia River fish ladders. *J. Fish. Res. Board Can. 28:* 533, 1971.
62. Furunculosis Committee. *Second Interim Report.* London, HMSO, 1933.
63. Gaines, J. L., Jr.   Pathology of experimental infection of *Aeromonas hydrophilia* (Chester) Stanier (Bacteria: Pseudomonadales), in the channel catfish *Ictalurus punctatus* (Rafinesque). Ph.D. thesis, Auburn Univ., Auburn, Ala., 1972.

64. Goldstein, S., and Moriber, L.   Biology of a problematic marine fungus, *Dermocystidium* sp. I. Development and cytology. *Arch. Mikrobiol. 53:* 1. 1966.

65. Goldstein, S., Belsky, N. N., and Chosak, R.   Biology of a problematic marine fungus, *Dermocystidium* sp. II. Nutrition and respiration. *Mycologia 61:* 468. 1969.

66. Goncharov, G. D.   Rubella, a viral fish disease. *Ann. N. Y. Acad. Sci. 126:* 598. 1965.

67. Gordon, R. E., and Smith, M. M.   Rapidly growing acid-fast bacteria. II. Species description of *Mycobacterium fortuitum* Cruz. *J. Bacteriol. 69:* 502. 1955.

68. Griffin, P. J.   A rapid presumptive test for furunculosis in fish. *Progr. Fish-Cult. 14:* 74. 1952.

69. Griffin, P. J.   The nature of bacteria pathogenic to fish. *Trans. Amer. Fish. Soc. 83:* 241. 1954.

70. Griffin, P. J., and Snieszko, S. F.   A unique bacterium pathogenic for warm-blooded and cold-blooded animals. *U. S. Fish Wildlife Serv., Fish. Bull. 68:* 187. 1951.

71. Griffin, P. J., Snieszko, S. F., and Friddle, S. B.   A more comprehensive description of *Bacterium salmonicida. Trans. Amer. Fish. Soc. 82:* 129. 1953.

72. Haastein, T., and Holt, G.   The occurrence of vibrio disease in wild Norwegian fish. *J. Fish Biol. 4:* 33. 1972.

73. Hacking, M. A., and Budd, J.   Vibrio infection in tropical fish in a freshwater aquarium. *J. Wildl. Dis., 7:* 273. 1971.

74. Haley, R., Davis, S. P., and Hyde, J. M.   Environmental stress and *Aeromonas liquefaciens* in American and threadfin shad mortalities. *Progr. Fish-Cult. 29:* 193. 1967.

75. Hendrie, M. S., Hodgkiss, W., and Shewan, J. M.   Proposal that the species *Vibrio anguillarum* Bergman 1909, *Vibrio piscium* David 1927 and *Vibrio ichthyodermis* (Wells and Zobell) Sherman, Hobbs and Hidgkiss 1960, be combined as a single series, *Vibrio anguillarium. Int. J. Syst. Bacteriol. 21:* 64. 1971.

76. Herman, R. L.   Fish furunculosis 1952–1966. *Trans. Amer. Fish. Soc. 97:* 221. 1968.

77. Heuschmann-Brunner, G.   Nocardiose bei Fischen des Susswassers und des Meeres. *Tierärztl. Wochenschr. 78 Jahrg. H. 5:* 94. 1965.

78. Heuschmann-Brunner, G.   Nocardia Infektion bei Regenbogenforellen (*Salmo gairdneri*). *Tierärztl. Wochenschr. 79 Jahrg. H. 5:* 96, 1966.

79. Hoffman, G. L., Dunbar, C. E., Wolf, K., and Zwillenberg, L. O.   Epitheliocystis, a new infectious disease of the bluegill (*Lepomis machrochirus*). *Antonie van Leeuwenhoek J. Microbiol. Serol. 35:* 146. 1969.

80. Holt, G.   Vibriosis (*Vibrio anguillarum*) as an epizootic disease in rainbow trout (*Salmo gairdneri*). *Acta. vet. scand. 11:* 600. 1970.

81. Holt, G., and Haastein, T.   Furunculosis in fish in Norway. *Nord. vet. med. 22:* 505. 1970.

82. Horter, R.   Fusarium als Erreger einer Hautmykose bei Karpfen. *Z. Parasitenk. 20:* 355. 1960.

83. Hoshina, T., Sano, T., and Morimoto, Y. A streptococcus pathogenic to fish. *J. Tokyo Univ. Fish. 44:* 57. 1958.

84. Hoshina, T., Sano, T., and Sunayama, M. Studies on the saprolegniasis of eel. *J. Tokyo Univ. Fish. 47:* 59. 1960.

85. Hunn, J. B. Some patho-physiologic effects of bacterial kidney disease in brook trout. *Proc. Soc. Exp. Biol. Med. 117:* 383. 1964.

86. Janssen, W. A., and Surgalla, M. J. Morphology, physiology and serology of a pasteurella species pathogenic for white perch. *J. Bacteriol. 96:* 1606. 1968.

87. Kelényu, G., and Németh, Á. Comparative histochemistry and electron microscopy of the eosinophil leucocytes of vertebrates. I. A study of avian, reptile, amphibian and fish leucocytes. *Acta. biol. Acad. Sci. Hung. 20:* 405. 1969.

88. Kiehn, E. D., and Pacha, R. E. Characterization and relatedness of marine vibrios pathogenic to fish: Deoxyribonucleic acid homology and base composition. *J. Bacteriol. 100:* 1248. 1969.

89. Klontz, G. W., and Anderson, D. P. Fluorescent antibody studies of isolates of *Aeromonas salmonicida. Bull. Off. int. Epizoot. 69:* 1149. 1968.

90. Klontz, G. W., Yasutake, W. T., and Johnross, A. Bacterial disease of the Salmonidae in the western United States: Pathogenesis of furunculosis in rainbow trout. *Amer. J. Vet. Res. 27:* 455. 1966.

91. Kluge, J.P. A granulomatous disease of fish produced by flavobacteria. *Pathol. vet. 2:* 545. 1965.

92. Kubota, S., Kariya, T., Nakamura, Y., and Kira, K. Nocardial infection in cultured yellowtails (*Seriola quinqueradiata* and *S. purpurescens*). II. Histological study. *Fish Pathol. Japan 3:* 24. 1968.

93. Lennon, R. E. Feeding mechanism of the sea lamprey and its effect on host fishes. *U. S. Fish Wildlife Serv., Fish. Bull. 56:* 245. 1954.

94. Levin, M. A., Wolke, R. E., and Cabelli, V. J. *Vibrio anguillarum* as a cause of disease in winter flounder (*Pseudopleuronectes americanus*). *Can. J. Microbiol. 18:* 1585. 1972.

95. Li, M. F., and Flemming, C. A proteolytic pseudomonad from skin lesions of rainbow trout (*Salmo gairdneri*). I. Characteristics of the pathogenic effects and the extracellular proteinase. *Can. J. Microbiol. 13:* 405. 1967.

96. McCraw, B. M. Furunculosis of fish. *U. S. Fish Wildlife Serv., Spec. Sci. Rep., Fish. 84.* 1952.

97. McDermott, L. A. *Aeromonas* sp. infection in Great Lakes lampreys. *J. Fish. Res. Board Can. 25:* 1521. 1968.

98. McDermott, L. A., and Berst, A. H. Experimental plantings of brook trout (*Salvelinus fontinalis*) from furunculosis-infected stock. *J. Fish. Res. Board Can. 25:* 2643. 1968.

99. McFadden, T. W. Furunculosis in non-salmonids. *J. Fish. Res. Board Can. 27:* 2365. 1970.

100. Mackie, T. H., and Menzies, W. J. M. Investigations in Great Britain of furunculosis of the Salmonidae. *J. Comp. Pathol. Therap. 51:* 225. 1938.

101. Margolis, L. "Red sore" disease of pike in Mont Trembaul Park District, Quebec, Canada. *Can. Fish Cult. 10:* 3. 1951.

102. Marsh, M. C. A more complete description of *Bacterium truttae*. *Bull. U. S. Fish. Comm. 22:* 411. 1902.
103. Mawdesley-Thomas, L. E. Salmon disease. *Lancet 2:* 616. 1967.
104. Mawdesley-Thomas, L. E. Furunculosis in the goldfish *Carassius auratus* (L.). *J. Fish Biol. 1:* 19. 1969.
105. Meyer, F. P. A review of the parasites and diseases of fishes in warm-water ponds in North America. *FAO (Food Agr. Organ. U. N.), Fish. Rep. 44* 5(IX/R-3): 290. 1968.
106. Meyer, F. P. Seasonal fluctuations in the incidence of disease on fish farms. In *A Symposium on Diseases of Fishes and Shellfishes,* ed. S. F. Snieszko. Amer. Fish. Soc., Spec. Publ. No. 5. Washington, D.C., 1970.
107. Nigrelli, R. F., and Vogel, H. Spontaneous tuberculosis in fishes and in other cold-blooded vertebrates with special reference to *Mycobacterium fortuitum* Cruz from fish and human lesions. *Zoologica (New York) 48:* 131. 1963.
108. Nybelin, O. Untersuchungen über den bei Fishkrankheiterregern Spaltpilz *Vibrio anguillarum.* *Medd. undersëkn aust. sötvatterfish (Stockholm) 8:* 62. 1935.
109. Ojala, O. Observations on the occurrence of *Aeromonas hydrophilia* and *A. punctata* in fish. *Bull. Off. int. Épizoot. 69:* 1107. 1968.
110. Ordal, E. J., and Earp, B. J. Cultivation and transmission of the etiological agent of kidney disease in salmonid fishes. *Proc. Soc. Exp. Biol. Med. 92:* 85. 1956.
111. Ordal, E. J., and Rucker, R. R. Pathogenic myxobacteria. *Proc. Soc. Exp. Biol. Med. 56:* 15. 1944.
112. Osburn, R. C. The effects of exposure on gill filaments of fishes. *Trans. Amer. Fish. Soc. 40:* 371–376. 1910.
113. Pacha, R. E., and Ordal, E. J. Columnaris disease in Columbia River salmon. *Bacteriol. Proc. 62:* 20. 1962.
114. Pacha, R. E., and Ordal, E. J. Epidemiology of columnaris disease in salmon. *Bacteriol. Proc. 63:* 3. 1963.
115. Pacha, R. E., and Ordal, E. J. Histopathology of experimental columnaris disease in young salmon. *J. Comp. Pathol. 77:* 419. 1967.
116. Pacha, R.E. and Ordal, E.J. Myxobacterial diseases of salmonids. In *A Symposium of Diseases of Fishes and Shellfishes,* ed. S. F. Snieszko. Amer. Fish. Soc., Spec. Publ. No. 5. Washington, D.C., 1970.
117. Parisot, T. J. Tuberculosis in fish: A review of the literature with a description of the disease in salmonid fish. *Bacteriol. Rev. 22:* 240. 1958.
118. Parisot, T. J., and Wood, E. M. A comparative study of the causative agent of the myxobacterial disease of salmonid fishes. II. A description of the histopathology of the disease in chinook salmon (*Oncorhynchus tshawytscha*) and a comparison of the staining characteristics of the fish disease with leprosy and human tuberculosis. *Amer. Rev. Resp. Dis. 82:* 212. 1960.
119. Pauley, G. B. Prespawning adult salmon mortality associated with a fungus of the genus *Dermocystidium.* *J. Fish. Res. Board Can. 24:* 843. 1967.
120. Pettit, A. À propos du microorganisme producteur de la Taumelkrankheit:

Ichthyosporidium ou Ichthyophonus. *C. r. séances Soc. Biol. 70:* 1045. 1911.

121. Pettit, A. Observations sur l'Ichthyosporidium et sur la maladie qu'il provoque chez la truite. *Ann. Inst. Pasteur (Paris) 27:* 986. 1913.

122. Plehn, M. Eine neue Karpfenkrankheit und ihr Erreger *Branchiomyces sanguinis. Zentralbl. Bakteriol. Pathologie, 62*(1–2): 129. 1912.

123. Plehn, M., and Muslow, K. Der Erreger der Taumelkrankheit der Salmoniden. *Zentralbl. Bakteriol. I. Abt. 59:* 63. 1911.

124. Rabb, L., Cornick, J. W., and McDermott, L. A. A macroscopic slide agglutination test for the presumptive diagnosis of furunculosis in fish. *Progr. Fish-Cult. 26:* 118. 1964.

125. Reed, G. B., and Toner, G. C. Red sore disease of pike. *Can. J. Res.,* Ser. D *19:* 139. 1941.

126. Reichenbach-Klinke, H.-H. Über einige bisher unbekannte Hyphomyceten bei verschieden Susswasser und Meeresfischen. *Mycopathol. mycol. appl. 7:* 333. 1956.

127. Reichenbach-Klinke, H.-H., and Elkan, E. *The Principal Diseases of Lower Vertebrates.* London and New York, Academic Press, 1965.

128. Robinson, J., and Meyers, F. Streptococcal fish pathogen. *J. Bacteriol. 92:* 512. 1966.

129. Rock, L. F., and Nelson, H. M. Channel catfish and gizzard shad mortality caused by *Aeromonas liquefaciens. Progr. Fish-Cult. 27:* 138. 1965.

130. Roegner-Aust, S., Brunner, G., and Jaxtheimer, R. Electromikroskopische Untersuchen über den Erreger der infektiösen Bauchwassersucht der Karpfen, Bakterium? Virus? *Allg. Fischerei-Ztg.* 1950.

131. Ross, A. J. *Mycobacterium salminophilum* sp. nov. from salmonid fishes. *Amer. Rev. Resp. Dis. 81:* 241. 1960.

132. Ross, A. J. Mycobacteriosis among Pacific salmonid fishes. In *A Symposium on Diseases of Fishes and Shellfishes,* ed. S. F. Snieszko. Amer. Fish. Soc., Spec. Publ. No. 5. Washington, D.C., 1970.

133. Ross, A. J., and Yasutake, W. T. *Scolecobasidium humicola,* a fungal pathogen of fish. In press, *J. Fish. Res. Board Can.* 1972.

134. Ross, A. J., Martin, J. E., and Bressler, V. *Vibrio anguillarum* from an epizootic in rainbow trout (*Salmo gairdneri*) in the U.S.A. *Bull. Off. int. Épizoot. 69:* 1139. 1968.

135. Ross, A. J., Rucker, R. R., and Ewing, W. H. Description of a bacterium associated with red mouth disease of rainbow trout (*Salmo gairdneri*). *Can. J. Microbiol. 12:* 763. 1966.

136. Ross, A. J., Nordstrom, P. R., Bailey, J. E., and Heaton, J. R. A bacterial disease of yellow perch (*Perca flavescens*). *Trans. Amer. Fish. Soc. 89:* 310. 1960.

137. Rucker, R. R. A streptomycete pathogenic to fish. *J. Bacteriol. 58:* 659. 1949.

138. Rucker, R. R. Vibrio infections among marine and freshwater fish. *Progr. Fish-Cult. 21:* 22. 1959.

139. Rucker, R. R. Status of fish diseases and relation to production. *Rep. Second Gov. Conf. Pac. Salmon,* Seattle, Jan. 1963.

140. Rucker, R. R.   Red mouth disease of rainbow trout (*Salmo gairdneri*). *Bull. Off. int. Épizoot. 65:* 825. 1966.

141. Rucker, R. R., Earp, B. J., and Ordal, E. J.   Infectious diseases of Pacific salmon. *Trans. Amer. Fish. Soc. 83:* 297. 1954.

142. Rucker, R. R., Johnson, H. E., and Kaydas, G. M.   An interim report on gill disease. *Progr. Fish-Cult. 14:* 10. 1952.

143. Scattergood, L. W.   A report on the appearance of the fungus *Ichthyosporidium hoferi* in the herring of the northwestern Atlantic. *U. S. Fish Wildlife Serv., Spec. Sci. Rep., Fish. 58.* 1948.

144. Schäperclaus, W.   *Pseudomonas punctata* als Krankheitserreger bei Fischen, Untersuchungen über Süsswasseraalrotseuche, Leibeshählenwassersucht der cypriniden, insbesondere des Karpfens und Flechenseuche der Weissfische. *Z. Fisch. Hilfswiss. 28:* 289. 1930.

145. Schäperclaus, W.   Etiology of infectious carp dropsy. *Ann. N. Y. Acad. Sci. 126:* 587. 1965.

146. Schumacher, R. E., Hamilton, C. H., and Longtien, E. J.   Blood sedimentation rates of brook trout as affected by furunculosis. *Progr. Fish-Cult. 18:* 147. 1956.

147. Scott, W. W.   Fungi associated with fish diseases. *Develop. Ind. Microbiol. 5:* 109. 1964.

148. Sindermann, C. J.   *Principal Diseases of Marine Fish and Shellfish.* 369 pp. New York and London, Academic Press, 1970.

149. Sindermann, C. J., and Rosenfield, A.   Diseases of fishes of the western North Atlantic. I. Diseases of the sea herring (*Clupea harengus*). *Maine Dep. Sea Shore Fish., Res. Bull. 18.* 1954.

150. Sindermann, C. J., and Scattergood, L. W.   Diseases of fishes of the western North Atlantic. II. Ichthyosporidium disease of the sea herring (*Clupea harengus*). *Maine Dep. Sea Shore Fish., Res. Bull. 19.* 1954.

151. Smith, I. W.   A disease of finnock due to *Vibrio anguillarum*. *J. Gen. Microbiol. 24:* 247. 1961.

152. Smith, I. W.   The classification of *Bacterium salmonida*. *J. Gen. Microbiol. 33:* 263. 1963.

153. Smith, I. W.   The occurrence and pathology of the Dee disease. *Scot. Dept. Agr. Fish., Freshwater Salmon Fish. Res. Rep. 34:* 3. 1964.

154. Snieszko, S. F.   A bacterial disease of carp in central Europe. *Progr. Fish-Cult. 52:* 12. 1940.

155. Snieszko, S. F.   Ulcer disease in brook trout (*Salvelinus fontinalis*): Its economic importance, diagnosis, treatment and prevention. *Progr. Fish-Cult. 14:* 43. 1952.

156. Snieszko, S. F.   Fish furunculosis. *U. S. Fish Wildlife Serv., Fish. Leafl. 467.* 1966.

157. Snieszko, S. F., and Bullock, G. L.   Freshwater fish diseases caused by bacteria belonging to the genera *Aeromonas* and *Pseudomonas*. *U. S. Bur. Sport Fish. Wildlife, Fish Dis. Leafl. 11.* 1968.

158. Snieszko, S. F., and Friddle, S. B.   A contribution to the etiology of ulcer disease of trout. *Trans. Amer. Fish. Soc. 78:* 56. 1948.

159. Snieszko, S. F., and Griffin, P. J.   Kidney disease in brook trout and its treatment. *Progr. Fish-Cult. 17:* 3. 1955.

160. Snieszko, S. F., Griffin, P. J., and Friddle, S. B.   A new bacterium (*Hemophilus piscium* n. sp.) from ulcer disease of trout. *J. Bacteriol. 59:* 699. 1950.

161. Snieszko, S. F., Bullock, G. L., Dunbar, C. E., and Pettijohn, J. L.   Nocardial infection in hatchery-reared fingerling rainbow trout (*Salmo gairdneri*). *J. Bacteriol. 88:* 1809. 1964.

162. Snieszko, S. F., Bullock, G. L., Hollis, E., and Boone, J. G.   *Pasteurella* sp. from an epizootic of white perch (*Roccus americanus*) in the Chesapeake Bay tidewater area. *J. Bacteriol. 88:* 1814. 1964.

163. Spence, K. D., Fryer, J. L., and Pilcher, K. S.   Active and passive immunization of certain salmonid fishes against *Aeromonas salmonicida*.   *Can. J. Microbiol. 11:* 397. 1965.

164. Sprague, V.   *Ichthyosporidium* Caullery and Mesnil, 1905, the name of a genus of fungi or a genus of sporozoans? *Syst. Zool. 14:* 110. 1965.

165. Stuart, M. R., and Fuller, H. T.   Mycological aspects of diseased Atlantic salmon. *Nature (London) 217:* 90. 1968.

166. Tiffney, W. N.   The host range of *Saprolegnia parasitica*.   *Mycologia 31:* 310. 1939.

167. Tomašec, I. I., and Fijan, N. N.   The etiology of infectious dropsy of carp. *Ann. N. Y. Acad. Sci. 126:* 606. 1965.

168. Traxler, G. S., and Li, M. F.   *Vibrio anguillarum* isolated from a nasal abscess of the cod fish (*Gadus morhua*). *J. Wildlife Dis. 8:* 207. 1972.

169. Valdez, I. E., and Conroy, D. A.   The study of a tuberculosis-like condition in neon tetras (*Hyphessobrycon innesi*). II. Characteristics of the bacterium isolated. *Microbiol. españ. 16:* 249. 1963.

170. Vishniac, J. F., and Nigrelli, R. F.   The ability of the Saprolegniaceae to parasitize platyfish. *Zoologica (New York) 43:* 131. 1957.

171. Wagner, E. D., and Perkins, C. L.   *Pseudomonas hydrophilia*, the cause of "red-mouth" disease in rainbow trout. *Progr. Fish-Cult. 14:* 127. 1952.

172. Wakabayashi, H., Kira, K., and Egusa, S.   Studies on columnaris disease of pond-cultured eels. I. Characteristics and pathogenicity of *Chondrococcus columnaris* isolated from pond-cultured eels. *Bull. Jap. Soc. Sci. Fish. 36:* 147. 1970.

173. Wakabayashi, H., Kira, K., and Egusa, S.   Studies on columnaris disease of pond-cultured eels. II. The relation between gill disease and *Chondrococcus columnaris*. *Bull. Jap. Soc. Sci. Fish. 36:* 678. 1970.

174. Wales, J. H., and Evins, D.   Sestonosis, a gill irritation in trout. *Calif. Fish Game 23:* 144. 1937.

175. Warren, J.   Kidney Disease of salmonid fishes and analysis of hatchery waters. *Progr. Fish-Cult. 25:* 121. 1963.

176. Weinreb, E. L., and Bilstad, N. M.   Histology of the digestive tract and adjacent structures of the rainbow trout, *Salmo gairdneri irideus*. *Copeia 3:* 194. 1955.

177. Willoughby, L. G.   Salmon disease in Windermere and the river Leven: The fungal aspect. *Salmon Trout Mag. 186:* 124. 1969.

178. Willoughby, L. G.   Mycological aspects of a disease of young perch in Windermere. *J. Fish Biol. 2:* 113. 1970.

179. Wolf, K.   Bacterial kidney disease of salmonid fishes. *U. S. Bur. Sport Fish. Wildlife, Fish Dis. Leafl. 8.* 1966.

180. Wolf, K., and Dunbar, C. E.   Methods of infecting trout with kidney disease and some effects of temperature on experimental infections. *U. S. Fish Wildlife Serv., Spec. Sci. Rep., Fish. 286.* 1959.

181. Wolf, L. E.   Observations on ulcer disease of trout. *Trans. Amer. Fish. Soc. 68:* 136. 1938.

182. Wolf, L. E.   Further observations on ulcer disease of trout. *Trans. Amer. Fish. Soc. 70:* 369. 1940.

183. Wolf, L. E.   Dietary gill disease of trout. *N. Y. Conserv. Dep., Fish. Res. Bull. 7.* 1945.

184. Wolke, R. E., Wyand, D. S., and Khairallah, L. H.   A light and electron microscopic study of epitheliocystis disease in the gills of Connecticut striped bass (*Morone saxatilis*) and white perch (*Morone americanus*). *J. Comp. Pathol. 80:* 559. 1970.

185. Wood, E. M., and Yasutake, W. T.   Histopathology of fish. III. Peduncle ("coldwater") disease. *Progr. Fish-Cult. 18:* 58. 1956.

186. Wood, E. M., and Yasutake, W. T.   Histopathology of kidney disease in fish. *Amer. J. Pathol. 32:* 845. 1956.

187. Wood, E. M., and Yasutake, W. T.   Histopathology of fish. V. Gill disease. *Progr. Fish-Cult. 19:* 7. 1957.

188. Wood, J. W., and Ordal, E. J.   Tuberculosis in Pacific salmon and steelhead trout. *Oreg. Fish Comm. Contrib. 25:* 1. 1958.

189. Wood, J. W., and Wallis, J.   Kidney disease in adult chinook salmon and its transmission by feeding to young chinook salmon. *Oreg. Fish Comm. Res. Briefs 6.* 1955.

190. Wundsch, H. H.   Weitere Beobachtungen an *Brancheomyces demigrans* als Erreger der Kiemenfaule beim Hecht. *Z. Fisch. Hilfswiss. 28:* 319. 1930.

3

Lesions of Protozoan Diseases in Fish

WILMER A. ROGERS
and JOHN L. GAINES, JR.

Protozoans are probably the most important group of animal parasites affecting fish. Fish culturists over the entire world report great losses caused by protozoans. Obligate parasites such as the ciliate *Ichthyophthirius* and certain of the cnidosporidians are responsible for many of these losses; however, many species that some protozoologists consider to be commensals become pathogenic under certain conditions.

Host-parasite relationships become very complex at times because such factors as environmental influences affect the hosts' susceptibility to certain protozoans. Well-being of the host is greatly correlated to its food supply and subsequent general condition.

Factors such as oxygen concentration and temperature affect both host and parasites. Fish population density is also an important factor, since many protozoans transfer from fish to fish through the water. The more fish that are present, the easier it is to find a new host, so that tremendous infestations of protozoans can occur in a relatively short time where fish populations are dense. Moreover, many of the protozoans that cause tremendous die-offs of fish in crowded conditions may never cause mortalities under less crowded conditions.

Host reaction to invasion by protozoans is highly variable. Many factors, such as host size, age, host specificity, immunity, the aforementioned influence

117

of host condition, and environmental factors, play an important part in this reaction.

Most literature concerning protozoans of fishes deals with taxonomy; however, several works cover pathological aspects. An excellent coverage of protozoans of marine fishes was given by Lom (21). A number of general and specific coverages of protozoans and the diseases they produce are available in books on fish diseases (2, 7, 10, 11, 13, 24, 31, 34, 39, 40, 43, 44, 51). For a comprehensive coverage of the biology and taxonomy of protozoans, one may consult Kudo (20) and Hyman (19).

The taxonomy of protozoans is by no means stable, but this situation is not unique to protozoans. Most protozoologists accept the classification of Protozoa by Honigberg et al. (18). For simplicity, and since taxonomy is not within the scope of this paper, we will discuss the pathological effects on fish-hosts of the six major classes of protozoans—flagellates, amebas, sporozoans, cnidosporidians, ciliates, and suctorians—as proposed by Shulman and Shtein (42) and Kudo (20), without considering taxonomy.

PARASITE-HOST RELATIONSHIPS

Lom (21), in his discussion of protozoans of marine fishes, proposed three groups of protozoans according to the relationship with these hosts. First were ecto- or endocommensals, in which there was no evidence of pathogenicity; second was the group that was somewhere between commensalism and parasitism and could be considered potential pathogens; third was the group of "true parasites" living exclusively at the expense of their hosts.

According to Bauer (3) every parasite living in or on a fish exerts some degree of harmful influence on its host. He warns that even though this influence is so slight that it does not cause the appearance of external signs, the parasite involved should not be considered nonpathogenic.

In determining the pathological effects of protozoans on or in the host, such factors as the morphological and physiological makeup of the host must be considered, as must environmental influences as well (21). Many irritating substances, such as chemical pollutants, may cause the same type of reaction in a host as protozoans or other parasites. Also, the degree of pathogenicity depends on numbers of parasites on or in the host. Most host reactions to invasion by protozoans are directed toward expelling or isolating the parasite. Mainly, harm done to the host is by mechanical damage, secretion of toxic substances, occlusion of the blood vessels, obtaining nutrition at the expense of the host, and rendering the host more susceptible to secondary infections by any, or by combinations, of the above factors. Most of the general references cited earlier describe clinical signs associated with disease conditions in fish. Some of the most common clinical signs are changes in swimming habits, such as loss of equilibrium, flashing, or scraping; loss of appetite; abnormal coloration; tissue erosion; excess mucus production; hemorrhaging; and swollen body or distended eyes. More specifically, according to Bauer (3) the host reacts by hypertrophy and proliferation of individual tissues to encapsulate the parasite; by metaplasia, where there is a change in structure and function of various cells; by inflammation, where there is an increased blood supply to the damaged part; and by immunity, or the ability of the host to resist infection by the pathogen of a definite disease. He did not stress hyperplasia, which is one of the common host reactions to protozoan invasions. Very often both hypertrophy and hyperplasia occur simultaneously.

FLAGELLATES

Hoffman (13) lists 10 genera of flagellates as parasites of fishes. Several of these genera have been reported only a few times and some have not been reported since their original description.

Species of the genus *Costia* are some of the most problematical flagellates parasitizing the gills and external surface of fish. A characteristic greyish-white to bluish film caused by excess mucus production appears on the skin of infected fish because of irritation caused by *Costia* spp.(Fig. 3.1). The attached form (Fig. 3.2) produces necrosis of epidermal cells and the dermis may be hyperemic (2). In some cases bacterial infection may occur secondarily. Schubert (41) conducted electron microscope studies on *Costia* sp. and showed that it attached to

Fig. 3.1. Catfish showing clinical signs of severe infestation of *Costia* sp.

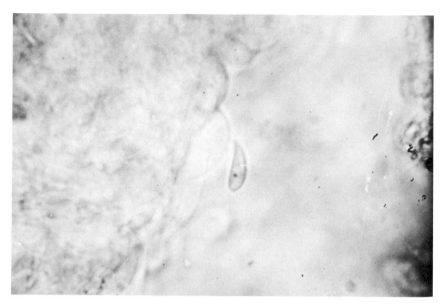

Fig. 3.2. Attached form of *Costia* sp.

the host by means of a flat disc. Small bundles of microtubules were extended into the host cell and portions of the cell were surrounded and brought back into the parasite as a food vacuole. The study also clarified the taxonomic status of *Costia.*

Two flagellates, *Trypanosoma* sp. and *Cryptobia* sp. (= *Trypanoplasma*), are quite commonly found in the blood of both freshwater and marine fishes. Life cycle of the parasites involves an alternation of hosts, with leeches being the alternate host and also the means of transfer from host to host. Wales and Wolf (52) found species of cryptobiids associated with serious mortality rates of salmonids in a hatchery. Amlacher (2) reports pale gills, sunken eyes, emaciation, and listlessness as clinical signs of *Cryptobia* sp. infection. One species, *Cryptobia branchialis,* is reported to attach to gill filaments, causing destruction of epithelium and formation of thrombi with resulting mortality of fish (42). *C. cyprini* is reported to cause acute anemia in young carp (24). A recent review of the literature on blood flagellates in fishes has been given by Becker (4).

Hexamita Dujardin, 1838 (= *Octomitis*) is a flagellate genus bearing four pairs of flagella; it lives in the intestine of salmonids and several other species of fish. There is much controversy over the pathogenicity of *Hexamita,* with some workers claiming that it causes extensive mortality and others claiming that it causes insignificant mortality. Uzmann, Paulik, and Hayduk (50), using experimental infections, suggest that at best it is a questionable pathogen and that its presence may not warrant routine countermeasures. Some earlier workers report what was

Fig. 3.3. Severe infestation of *Oodinium cyprinodontum* on gills.

believed to be intracellular reproductive stages of *Hexamita salmonis* in the cecal mucosa (8, 25). Uzmann, Paulik, and Hayduk (50) found no such cecal cell involvement. Sano (38) reported hexamitiasis of rainbow trout, with clinical signs being catarrhal enteritis with desquamation of the mucous membrane of the intestine. He also reported that histological examination showed the presence of the intracellular cysts of *H. salmonis* in the epithelium of the alimentary canal. Amlacher (2) reported a species of *Hexamita* that caused atrophy and necrosis of renal tubules.

Several species of dinoflagellates are capable of causing lesions in fishes. The names "velvet disease," "rust disease," "gold disease," and "coral fish disease" have been applied to disease caused by species of *Oodinium*. The first three are named because of the yellowish velvet appearance of the skin of fish infected with *Oodinium* spp. Brown (6) reported that in coral fish disease caused by *Oodinium ocellatum*, hemorrhaging and inflammation of gills with resulting necrosis of gill filaments may be observed, with bacterial or fungal infection often following. Lom (21) reported that he did not see penetration of *O.* (*Amyloocinium*) *ocellatum* cells beneath the epithelial layer, but Amlacher (2) reported that this species had been observed penetrating the subepithelial connective tissues of the gills. We have observed *O. cyprinodontum* Lawler infesting cyprinodontids of the Gulf of Mexico (55), with resultant hyperplasia and necrosis of gills (Figs. 3.3, 3.4). It appears that rather than *Oodinium* sp. penetrating the epithelium,

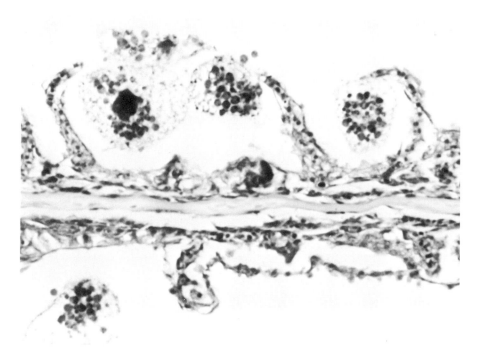

Fig. 3.4. Gill filament with necrosis caused by severe infestation of *Oodinium* sp.

there was a hyperplastic reaction which enclosed the parasite. The pseudopodia of attached *Oodinium* penetrate into the epidermal cells and seem to have histolytic power enabling them to liquefy and absorb the host's protoplasm (34).

The dinoflagellate *Glenodinium* sp. was reported by Rogers (35) as being associated with fish kills. Additional observations of *Glenodinium* sp. show it to produce clinical signs similar to those produced by *Oodinium* spp. Still other dinoflagellates will kill fish by secretion of toxins in both marine and fresh waters (2, 26).

AMEBAS

Noble and Noble (28) reviewed the literature on amebic parasites of marine fish and described a new species. Orias and Noble (29) described another new species from a fish but stated that there was no evidence of pathogenicity. Most authors report that the amebas they worked with apparently were not pathogenic. Sprague, Beckett, and Sawyer report a species of *Paramoeba* from the blue crab that apparently caused lysis of muscles and "grey crab" disease (46). Lopukhina (23) reported that carp infected with gill disease had ameboid cells abundantly present on the gills. Wild fish in the area also were infested with these ameboid

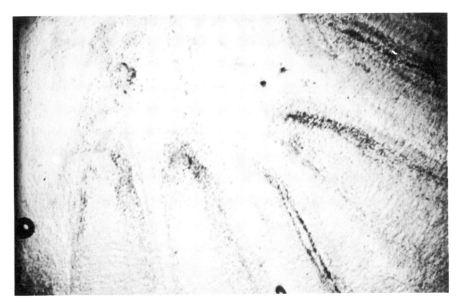

Fig. 3.5. Gills severely infested with amebas.

cells and it was concluded that these were protecting cells [*sic*] of the host. Rogers reported isolation of amebas from fish in 13 cases but in only one of these was there evidence that amebas were involved in *Tilapia* mortalities (35). The amebas were determined to be free-living forms in all except that one case. Amebas have subsequently been cultured at our laboratory from gills (Fig. 3.5) and body fluid of the abdominal cavity of *Tilapia aurea*, and attempts are being made to determine their pathogenicity to fish. Heavy infections of amebas in *T. aurea* were associated with ascites, and with hyperplasia and hypertrophy of gill tissues. These subsequent studies have also shown the presence of an unidentified *Eimeria* sp. and a *Henneguya* sp. in the visceral cavity, which may have contributed to the edematous condition of the host.

SPOROZOANS

Honigberg et al. (18) split the conventional taxon of "Sporozoa" into two groups, the Sporozoa and the Cnidospora. The genera *Haemogregarina*, *Dactylosoma*, and *Babesiosoma* are considered to be the only blood sporozoans of fishes established as valid taxa (4). Hemogregarines in marine fishes are evidently harmless, with no report existing on their pathogenicity (21).

Haemogregarina acipenseris has a severe pathogenic effect on fish in mass infections (24) and causes severe anemia and cachexia in fish (42).

Members of the genus *Eimeria* are coccidians that are intercellular parasites usually settling in intestinal epithelium, but they have been reported from virtually all visceral organs of fish. The disease they cause is accompanied by severe exhaustion, general edema, ascites, ruffling of scales, and exophthalmia (12, 24, 37). Many species are reported to cause a severe enteritis and anemia. Also, it is common to encounter secondary bacterial infections in fish infected with *Eimeria* (2). Serious deformities and lesions in the testes of clupeids infected with *Eimeria sardinae* indicate high pathogenicity and adverse effects on reproduction (21). Some cases of complete sterility by parasite castration were cited. *E. gadi* is reported to produce necrosis of cells of the swim bladder of the Baltic cod. *E. carpelli* causes coccidial enteritis in young carp, and serious mortality rates occur when infections are severe (42).

CNIDOSPORIDIANS

Members of this group form spores with polar filaments. Myxosporidians have spores of multicellular origin, while microsporidians have spores of unicellular origin (45). Host reaction to the histozoic forms is mainly by connective tissue encapsulation to form cysts, but some species elicit no host reactions. In the class Myxosporea, the coelozoic species are not considered to be particularly injurious to the host, but the histozoic forms are injurious and are of significant economic importance (43). Different species of myxosporidians have specific sites of infection, and they have been found in virtually all tissues and organs of fish. The gills and gall bladder are most frequently parasitized by myxosporidians in freshwater fishes, while the gall bladder and urinary bladder are the main sites of infection in marine fishes (20).

Twenty-three genera of myxosporidians have been listed from freshwater fishes of North America (13) and over 700 species parasitize fish (42). Some of the more important species parasitizing marine fishes are discussed by Lom (21) and Sindermann (43). Of great importance were members of the genera *Kudoa-Chloromyxum* complex, *Unicapsula* and *Hexacapsula*. These genera are associated with necrosis and liquefaction of flesh of living fish. Muscle degeneration, "wormy" or "mushy" appearance, jellied flesh, "milkiness," and ulcer disease are descriptive of conditions associated with the organisms. *Chloromyxum truttae* causes loss of appetite, chronic inflammation of the digestive tract, and diarrhea, and finally jaundice develops.

Members of the *Myxobolus-Myxosoma* group (we agree with Walliker (54) that *Myxosoma* should be synonymous with *Myxobolus*) are not as detrimental to the host in most cases as those genera mentioned earlier, but some species, such as *Myxosoma cerebralis*, causing whirling disease in salmonids (Fig. 3.6), are of great economic importance. Whirling disease is one of the most widespread diseases of rainbow trout (5). Hoffman, Dunbar, and Bradford (16) report on the pathology and other aspects of the disease in North America. The obvious clinical signs are

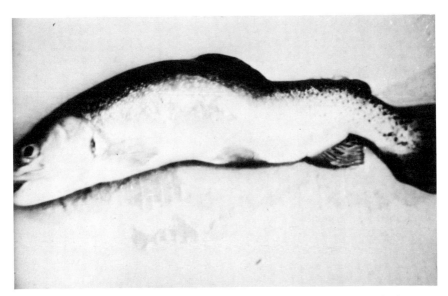

Fig. 3.6. Rainbow trout infected with whirling disease, *Myxosoma cerebralis.*

whirling, spinal curvature, and cranial deformities. Lesions of cartilage can be seen in histological preparations. Erosion of cartilage and weakening of the skeleton apparently cause pressure on the caudal nerves, and young fish may lose pigment control and thus a black tail is produced. An epithelioid granuloma type of tissue may proliferate and cause secondary damage. *M. cartilaginis* is reported from centrarchids (17). At first infection there was little host reaction, but after four to five months epithelioid granulomas appeared around some of the spore masses. Liquefaction of cartilage was present around the parasite for at least five weeks. *Myxobolus cyprini* parasitizes carp and several other species of cyprinids. It causes pernicious anemia and dropsy and eventually death when internal organs are infected; at other times kidney dysfunction, anemia, integmental hyperemia, scabrous scales, exophthalmia, ascites, and generalized hydrops of the body occur (42). Bubonic disease of barbel is caused by *M. pfeifferi.* Large cysts are formed to produce swellings, degeneration of muscle, sloughing of scales, and death of fish in heavy infestations. *M. dogieli* infects the heart of carp and is fatal (24). Clinical signs are inflammation, hyperplasia and hypertrophy, and formation of adhesions. Many species of myxosporidians infect gills (Fig. 3.7), and a number of species can cause death to the fish (24). An intralamellar form of *Henneguya* (Fig. 3.8) is believed to have caused extensive mortality among young channel catfish in the southeastern United States (F. P. Meyer, Bureau of Sport Fisheries and Wildlife, Fish Farming Experimental Station, Stuttgart, Ark., personal communication). A cutaneous form of *Henneguya* (Figs. 3.9, 3.10) causes lesions on

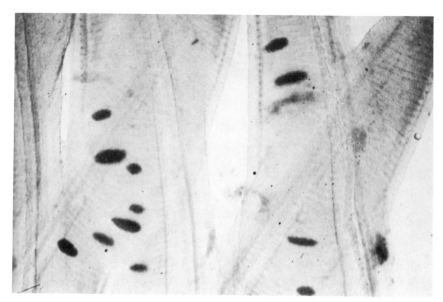

Fig. 3.7. Gills of channel catfish infected with intracapillary form of *Henneguya*.

Fig. 3.8. Gills of channel catfish infected with intralamellar form of *Henneguya*.

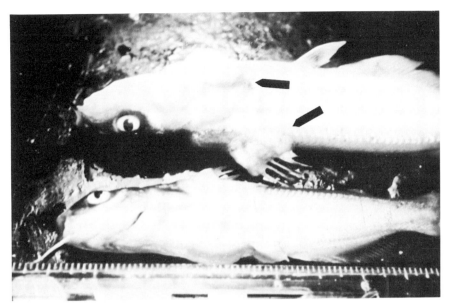

Fig. 3.9. Cutaneous form of *Henneguya* on channel catfish fins and body.

Fig. 3.10. Section through *Henneguya* cutaneous cyst. Note dense connective tissue cyst wall and parasites within.

the skin and body of channel catfish, but few mortalities seem to be associated with this form, and in those cases secondary invaders such as the bacterium *Aeromonas hydrophila* are probably always responsible. Certain members of the genus *Thelohanellus* produce subdermal cysts in connective tissue that become so changed that the cyst wall appears epithelioid in nature. *Thelohanellus pyriformis* causes "lumpy disease" or "boil disease" of cyprinids and whitefish in the Soviet Union (42).

The coelozoic myxosporidians generally do not produce significant pathological effects. Walliker (53) reported *Myxidium oviforme,* which normally infects the gall bladder, to produce abscesses in the liver, and it was suspected of being a contributory factor in extensive salmon mortalities. This species is also reported to cause intense inflammation in biliary ducts of the liver in severe infestations. *C. truttae,* found in the gall bladder of trout, is considered pathogenic, as mentioned earlier, but Davis (9) stated that it caused no appreciable injury. *Ceratomyxa shasta,* usually found in gall bladders of salmonids, is reported to cause extensive mortalities in fingerling rainbow trout (52) and may contribute to pre-spawning loss of adult chinook and coho salmon (37).

The microsporidians are intracellular parasites causing hypertrophy of affected cells, with some species causing severe epizootics (34). The genera *Glugea* and *Pleistophora* cause the greatest damage in fish (21). Most of the species parasitic in fishes belong to the genus *Nosema,* with the genus *Glugea* being a junior synonym of *Nosema.* Sindermann (43) and Lom (21) discuss several *Nosema* (= *Glugea*) species that occur commonly in marine fishes. *Nosema lophii* invades ganglion cells of the central nervous system, and the cysts which are produced are grouped into large grape-like tumors that are host cells without a cyst membrane. *N. stephani* invades connective tissue of the digestive tract, the surface of the liver, and the peritoneum of some flatfishes. In cases of heavy infection, the intestinal epithelium was reported to disappear, and ovaries, bile duct, liver, and mesenteries were affected. *N. anomala* produces hypertrophied host cells up to 4 mm in diameter and causes serious deformation of the body, dysfunctions of internal organs, and mass mortality. *N. hertwigi* (Fig. 3.11), along with several other species of *Nosema,* produces similar epizootics and can cause mass mortalities.

Species of *Pleistophora* occur in both marine and freshwater fishes. *Pleistophora macrozoarcidis* in the ocean pout produces large tumor-like cysts in muscle, with complete hyalinization and destruction of the muscle, and eventually only granular debris remains. *P. ehreubaumi* may produce a similar condition. Putz, Hoffman, and Dunbar (33) report that *P. cepedianum* was found killing gizzard shad in Ohio. This species produces large cysts that are located in the visceral cavity and often protrude from the body of the fish (Fig. 3.12). Wales and Wolf (52) report that *Pleistophora* sp. in steelhead fingerlings caused major losses. This species is reported to be synonymous with *P. salmonae* (33). Where cysts of this species were numerous, there was epithelial hyperplasia and fusion of gill lamellae. *P. ovariae* infects ovaries of golden shiners, and although no mortalities have been

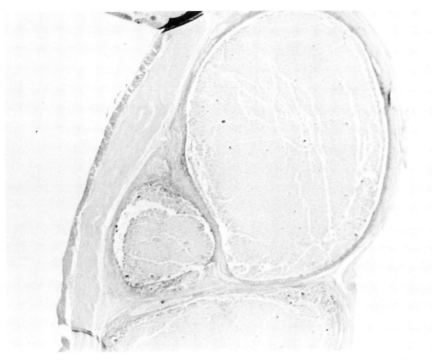

Fig. 3.11. Section through *Nosema* (= *Glugea*) *hertwigi* cyst in body wall of flounder.

Fig. 3.12. Gizzard shad with cyst of *Pleistophora cepedianum.*

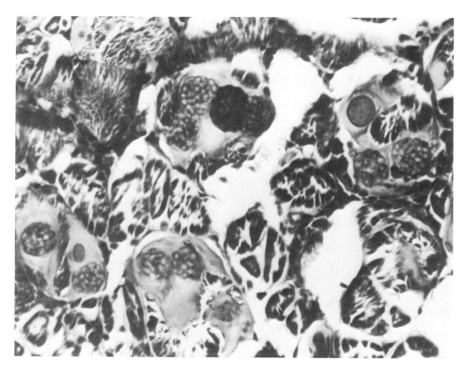

Fig. 3.13. Section through musculature of neon tetra with cysts of *Pleistophora hyphesso-bryconis.*

attributed to this species, it does reduce fecundity or may even sterilize the brood fish (47, 49). *P. tahoensis* infects muscles of the Piute sculpin and causes disintegration of the sarcoplasm and myofibrils (48). *P. hyphessobryconis* causes "neon fish disease" and often occurs among tropical species kept in aquaria. This species produces cysts in the musculature next to the skin and destroys parts of the muscle (Fig. 3.13), apparently by a chemical histolytic action on the muscle. The progressive disease causes congestion and muscular paralysis, with secondary loss of balance and fin degeneration (34). *Dermocystidium percae* produces cysts in the subcutis of *Perca fluviatilis* and is reported to cause deficiency of oxygen in blood and loss of tissue substance, but true epizootics have not been observed (34). Another haplosporidian, *Sporozoon tincae,* causes a lethal skin disease in tench. Tumor-like growths arise in the skin and break through the surface, causing severe ulceration (34).

CILIATES

The holotrichous ciliate, *Ichthyophthirius multifiliis* or "Ich," probably causes more damage to fish populations over the entire world than any other single parasite. "Ich" is an obligate parasite infesting the skin and gills of fishes.

The life cycle of "Ich" differs from most other ciliates in that numerous young individuals or "tomites" are produced from a single cell after the mature cell, the trophozoite, leaves the fish. The trophozoite encysts on the bottom on some substrate, and after a period of multiple fissions the tomites leave the cyst and seek a new host. They bore into the epidermis or gill epithelium, producing a severe irritation accompanied by an excess secretion of mucus and hyperplasia of the epithelium (Fig. 3.14). Small white pustules are produced where the parasite is located, giving ichthyophthiriasis the name "white spot." While most cases of "Ich" occur in aquaria or intensive fish culture situations, the disease has caused extensive fish kills in rivers and reservoirs (1).

Cryptocaryon irritans is a marine counterpart of *I. multifiliis*, having the same type of life cycle and producing the same type of lesion (21).

Chilodonella is a heart-shaped, flattened, holotrichous ciliate parasitizing the external surface of fish. Our observations and also reports in the literature indicate that this parasite causes problems mainly during winter months, especially in debilitated fish. It feeds on epithelial tissues of fish, causing severe irritation, excess mucus production, and desquamation. It may completely destroy gill epithelium, leaving nothing but the cartilaginous rays of the gill filaments (2, 3). The marine counterpart of *Chilodonella* is *Brooklynella,* which was found to produce severe lesions on gills of marine fish kept in aquaria (21).

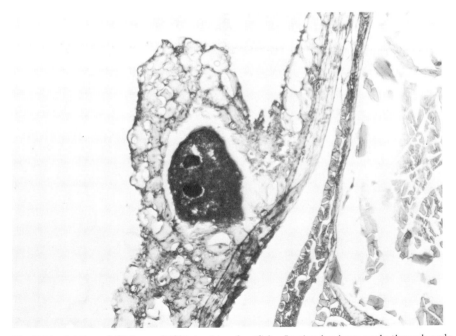

Fig. 3.14. *Ichthyophthirius multifiliis* in skin of catfish. Section has been made through ends of nucleus. Overlying epithelium is hypertrophic.

Hemiophrys is a ciliate that attaches to the host and may form round cysts under the skin or gill epithelium. It may also feed on epithelial cells (42).

Ophryoglena sp. has been reported as a pathogen from several species of fish (14) and we have observed several cases of this parasite infesting guppies (*Poecilia reticulata* = *Lebistes reticulatus*). The parasite invades the epithelium, causing necrosis and sloughing of tissues and excess mucus production. Death of the fish is probably caused by the loss and malfunction of invaded epithelium (14).

Tetrahymena sp. is a holotrichous parasite that has been reported from the gills, the surface of the body, and occasionally the internal organs of fish (13, 42). This parasite may enter through the yolk sacs of fish larvae and may sometimes devour the fry completely except for the denser tissues (42).

Members of the genus *Trichodina* and related peritrichous ciliates of the family Urceolariidae are some of the most common parasites of fishes over the entire world. Clinical signs of trichodinosis include excess mucus production ("blue slime"), flashing, debility (15), and hyperplasia and necrosis of the epidermis (9). The fins may become badly frayed in heavily infected fish and this may be accompanied by sluggishness and loss of appetite (9). Species parasitizing marine fishes attack mainly the gills (21) (Fig. 3.15), with complete destruction of gill epithelium reported in one case resulting in death of the host (21, 30). Trichodinids commonly are accompanied by other parasites, and it may be difficult to determine their relative importance as pathogens (9). Sarig (39) reports *Trichodina* sp., *Tripartiella* sp., and *Glossatella* sp. as being so abundant on gills and skin as to ob-

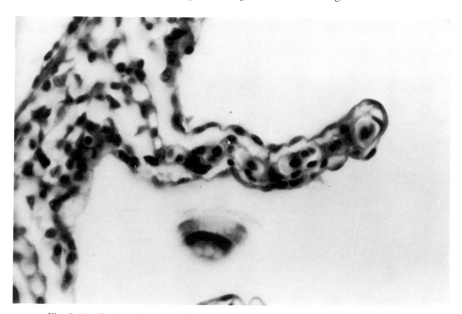

Fig. 3.15. Section through gill showing *Trichodina* sp. Note edematous cells.

scure the normal structure of the epithelium. Lom (21) reports no serious outbreaks of trichodinosis from marine aquaria although fishes brought freshly from
the sea were kept in aquaria for some time. Williams (56) reports that trichodinids greatly increased in numbers on marine fish cultured in cages on the United
States Gulf Coast.

Sessile peritrichs such as members of the genera *Scyphidia* and *Epistylis* and
their close relatives are considered to be harmless ectocommensals in marine fishes
(21); however, in freshwater fish populations they are capable of causing considerable injury and mortality (9, 22, 35, 36). Injury to the host is the result of large
numbers of the parasites on the gills interfering with respiration and causing suffo-
cation (Fig. 3.16). Most problems caused by these parasites are associated with
increased organic matter in the water as a result of feeding fish.

Members of the genus *Epistylis* may be extremely pathogenic under some circumstances. A species of *Epistylis* that we have observed frequently (Fig. 3.17)
from fishes in the southeastern United States causes large hemorrhagic lesions
with erosion of scales and hard-fin-rays and sometimes bone (36). The lesions begin as small hyperplastic protrusions of epithelium which later erode and become
hemorrhagic. Possibly most mortalities associated with *Epistylis* were caused by
secondary bacterial infections.

Other stalked ciliates such as *Vorticella, Carchesium,* and *Zoothamnium* have
been reported from fish and fish eggs (13).

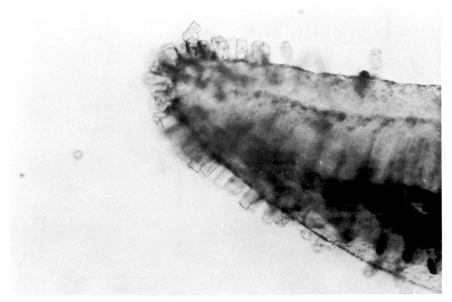

Fig. 3.16. Gill of channel catfish severely infested with *Scyphidia macropodia.*

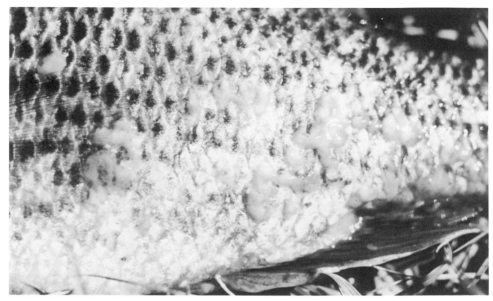

Fig. 3.17. *Epistylis* sp. colonies on warmouth.

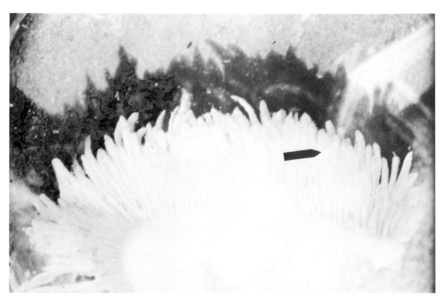

Fig. 3.18. Gills infested with *Trichophyra* sp. Note clubbing and swelling of gill filaments.

SUCTORIANS

Only one genus of this group, *Trichophyra,* is parasitic on fish, and it occurs on gills. The mature stage of this parasite possesses tentacles, while the juvenile stage is ciliated. Hoffman (13) states that there are apparently distinct physiological strains or species in spite of the morphological similarities and that the parasite has been observed on gills which were not heavily parasitized by other ectoparasites. It must have been feeding on fish mucus or other fish material.

We have on several occasions investigated epizootics caused by *Trichophyra ictaluri* on gills of channel catfish and we believe that this parasite was responsible for mortalities of both brood fish and fingerlings. In heavy infestations there is a severe hypertrophy of gill epithelium (Figs. 3.18-3.20). Shulman and Shtein (42) quote Chen as stating that *T. sinensis* may cause destruction of gill epithelium.

CONCLUSIONS

The protozoans are probably the most significant group of parasites of fishes. All organ systems are subject to being infested by protozoans and members of all major groups are capable of causing mortalities in fish. Most protozoans parasitizing the external surface of fish cause hyperplasia and hypertrophy of epithelium and excess mucus production. Gills and the body may be denuded of epithelium

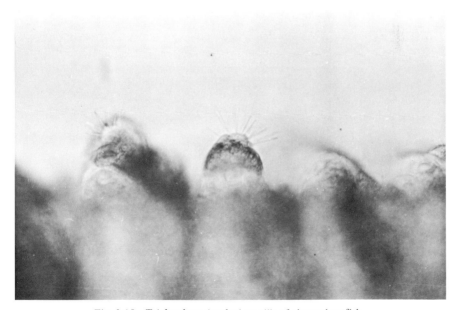

Fig. 3.19. *Trichophyra ictaluri* on gills of channel catfish.

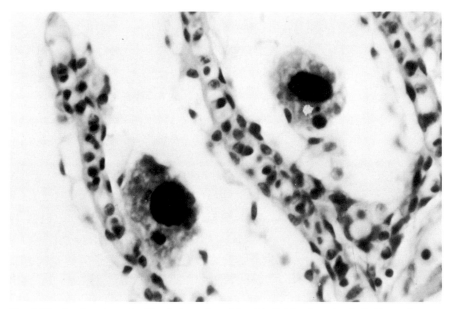

Fig. 3.20. Section through gills of channel catfish with *Trichophyra ictaluri.* Note edematous condition of cells.

by many of these parasites. Tissue-inhabiting forms may destroy cells, tissues, and organs.

General pathological changes associated with protozoan infestations are hypertrophy, hyperplasia, metaplasia, inflammation, edema, and hemorrhage.

Most works on protozoans of fishes deal with taxonomic problems. More attention should be given to host-parasite relationships and pathological effects of the parasites on the hosts.

Acknowledgment. Supported by the Southeastern Cooperative Fish Disease Project and in part by Sport Fish Restoration Funds.

REFERENCES

1. Allison, R., and Kelly, H. D.   An epizootic of *Ichthyophthirius multifiliis* in a river fish population. *Progr. Fish-Cult. 25*(3). 1963.
2. Amlacher, E.   *Textbook of Fish Diseases.* (Translated from German by D. A. Conroy and R. L. Herman.) 302 pp. Jersey City, T.F.H. Publications, 1970.
3. Bauer, O. N.   Parasites of freshwater fish and the biological basis for their control. *Bull. State Sci. Res. Inst. Lake River Fish. 49* (English transl., U. S. Dep. Commerce, Off. Tech. Serv., No. 61-31056, 236 pp., 1962). 1959.

4. Becker, C. D. Hematozoa of fishes, with emphasis on North American records. In *A Symposium on Diseases of Fishes and Shellfishes,* ed. S. F. Snieszko. Amer. Fish. Soc., Spec. Publ. No. 5. Washington, D.C., 1970.

5. Bogdanov, G. A. Modern data on the distribution and biology of *Myxosoma cerebralis* (Protozoa: Cnidosporidia) as agent of whirling disease of salmonids. *III Symp. Comm. Off. int. Épizoot. Étude Maladies Poissons.* Stockholm, 1968.

6. Brown, E. M. On *Oodinium ocellatum* Brown, a parasitic dinoflagellate causing epidemic disease in marine fish. *Proc. Zool. Soc. London 2:* 583–607. 1934.

7. Bykhovskaya-Pavlovskaya, I. E., et al. *Key to Parasites of Freshwater Fish of the U.S.S.R.* (Translated from Russian by the Israel program for scientific translations. Jerusalem, 1964.) 1962.

8. Davis, H. S. *Octomitis salmonis,* a parasitic flagellate of trout. *Bull. Bur. Fish., Wash. 42:* 9–26. 1926.

9. Davis, H. S. Studies of the protozoan parasites of freshwater fishes. *U. S. Fish Wildlife Serv., Fish. Bull. 41:* 1–29. 1947.

10. Davis, H. S. *Culture and Diseases of Game Fishes.* 332 pp. Berkeley, Univ. Calif. Press, 1953.

11. Dogiel, V. A., Petrushevskii, G. K., and Polyanski, Y. I. *Parasitology of Fishes.* (Translated from Russian by Z. Kabata.) 384 pp. Edinburgh, Oliver and Boyd, 1958.

12. Hoffman, G. L. *Eimeria aurati* n. sp. (Protozoa: Eimeriidae) from goldfish (*Carassius auratus*) in North America. *J. Protozool. 12:* 273–275. 1965.

13. Hoffman, G. L. *Parasites of North American Freshwater Fishes.* 486 pp. Berkeley and Los Angeles, Univ. Calif. Press, 1967.

14. Hoffman, G. L. An unusual case of fish disease caused by *Ophryoglena* sp. (Protozoa: Hymenostomatida). *Bull. Wildlife Dis. Ass. 3:* 111–112. 1967.

15. Hoffman, G. L., and Lom, J. Observations on *Tripartiella bursiformis, Trichodina nigra* and a pathogenic trichodinid, *Trichodina fultoni.* *Bull. Wildlife Dis. Ass. 3:* 156–159. 1967.

16. Hoffman, G. L., Dunbar, C. E., and Bradford, A. Whirling disease of trouts caused by *Myxosoma cerebralis* in the United States. *U. S. Fish Wildlife Serv., Spec. Sci. Rep., Fish. 427.* 1962.

17. Hoffman, G. L., Putz, R. E., and Dunbar, C. E. Studies on *Myxosoma cartilaginis* n. sp. (Protozoa: Myxosporidae) of centrarchid fish and a synopsis of the *Myxosoma* of North American freshwater fishes. *J. Protozool. 12:* 319–332. 1965.

18. Honigberg, B. M., Balamuth, W., Bovee, E. C., Corliss, J. O., Gojdics, M., Hall, R. P., Kudo, R. R., Levine, N. D., Loeblich, A. R., Jr., Weiser, J., and Wenrich, D. H. A revised classification of the phylum Protozoa. *J. Protozool. 11:* 7–20. 1964.

19. Hyman, L. H. *The Invertebrates.* Vol. 1, *Protozoa through Ctenophora.* 5 vols. New York, McGraw-Hill, 1940–59.

20. Kudo, R. R. *Protozoology.* 1184 pp. Springfield, Thomas, 1966.

21. Lom, J.   Protozoa causing diseases in marine fishes, pp. 101–123. In *Symposium on Fish Diseases*. Institute of Parasitology, Czech Academy of Sciences, Prague, 1970.

22. Lom, J., and Corliss, J. O.   Observations on the fine structure of two species of the peritrich ciliate genus *Scyphidia* and on their mode of attachment to their host. *Trans. Amer. Microsc. Soc. 87*(4): 493–509. 1968.

23. Lopukhina, A. M.   Data on the etiology and epizootiology of gill disease of the carp, pp. 124–137. In *Infectious Fish Diseases and Their Control*. (Translated from Russian by R. M. Howland, USFWS. Narragansett, R.I., 1971.) 1969.

24. Markevich, A. P.   *Parasitic Fauna of Freshwater Fish of the Ukrainian S.S.R.*, pp. 1–388. (Translated from Russian by the Israel Program for Scientific Translations. Jerusalem, 1963.) 1951.

25. Moore, E.   *Octomitis salmonis*, a new species of intestinal parasite in trout. *Trans. Amer. Fish. Soc. 52:* 74–93. 1922.

26. Muncy, R. J.   Observations on the factors involved with fish mortality as the result of dinoflagellate "bloom" in a freshwater lake. *Proc. Annu. Conf. Southeast. Ass. Game Fish Comm. 17:* 218–222. 1963.

27. Musselius, V. A., and Strelkov, J. A.   Diseases and control measures for fishes of Far-East complex in farms of the U.S.S.R. *III Symp. Comm. Off. int. Épizoot. Étude Maladies Poissons*. Stockholm, 1968.

28. Noble, E. R., and Noble, G. A.   Amebic parasites of fishes. *J. Protozool. 13:* 478–480. 1966.

29. Orias, J. D., and Noble, E. R.   *Entamoeba nezumia* sp. n. and other parasites from a North Atlantic fish. *J. Parasitol. 57:* 945–947. 1971.

30. Padnos, M., and Nigrelli, R.   *Trichodina spheroidesi* and *Trichodina halli* spp. nov. parasitic on the gills and skin of marine fishes with special reference to the life-history of *T. spheroidesi*. *Zoologica 27:* 65–72. 1942.

31. Petrushevskii, G. K.   *Parasites and Diseases of Fish*, pp. 1–338. (Translated from Russian by the Israel Program for Scientific Translations. Jerusalem, 1961.) 1957.

32. Polyanskii, Y. I.   *Parasites of the Fish of the Barents Sea*. (Translated from Russian by the Israel program for Scientific Translations. Jerusalem, 1966.) 1955.

33. Putz, R. E., Hoffman, G. L., and Dunbar, C. E.   Two new species of *Plistophora* (Microsporidea) from North American fish with a synopsis of Microsporidea of freshwater and euryhaline fishes. *J. Protozool. 12:* 228–236. 1965.

34. Reichenbach-Klinke, H.-H., and Elkan, E.   *The Principal Diseases of Lower Vertebrates*, pp. 1–205. New York and London, Academic Press, 1965.

35. Rogers, W. A.   A summary of fish disease cases received over a five year period at the Southeastern Cooperative Fish Disease Laboratory. *Proc. Annu. Conf. Southeast. Ass. Game Fish Comm. 23:* 353–358. 1969.

36. Rogers, W. A.   Disease in fish due to the protozoan *Epistylis* (Ciliata: Peritricha) in the southeastern U.S. *Proc. Annu. Conf. Southeast. Ass. Game Fish Comm. 25:* 493–496. 1971.

37. Sanders, J. E., Fryer, J. L., and Gould, R. W. Occurrence of the myxosporidian parasite *Ceratomyxa shasta* in salmonid fish from the Columbia River
basin and Oregon coastal streams. In *A Symposium on Diseases of Fishes and
Shellfishes*, ed. S. F. Snieszko. Amer. Fish. Soc., Spec. Publ. No. 5. Washington, D.C., 1970.

38. Sano, T. Etiology and histopathology of hexamitiasis and an IPN-like disease of rainbow trout. *J. Tokyo Univ. Fish. 56*(1-2): 23-30. 1970.

39. Sarig, S. Diseases of warmwater fishes with emphasis on intensive fish farming. In *Diseases of Fishes*, ed. S. F. Snieszko and H. R. Axelrod. Jersey City,
T.F.H. Publications, 1971.

40. Schäperclaus, W. *Fischkrankheiten.* 3d ed. 708 pp. Berlin, Akademie Verlag, 1954.

41. Schubert, G. The injurious effects of *Costia necatrix.* III *Symp. Comm.
Off. int. Épizoot. Étude Maladies Poissons.* Stockholm, 1968.

42. Shulman, S. S., and G. A. Shtein. Protozoa, pp. 5-236. In *Key to Parasites
of Freshwater Fish of the U.S.S.R.* (Translated from Russian by the Israel
Program for Scientific Translations. Jerusalem, 1964.) 1962.

43. Sindermann, C. J. *Principal Diseases of Marine Fish and Shellfish.* 369 pp.
New York and London, Academic Press, 1970.

44. Snieszko, S. F., ed. *A Symposium on Diseases of Fishes and Shellfishes.*
Amer. Fish. Soc., Spec. Publ. No. 5. Washington, D.C., 1970.

45. Sprague, V. Suggested changes in "A revised classification of the phylum
Protozoa," with particular reference to the position of the haplosporidians.
Syst. Zool. 15. 345-349. 1966.

46. Sprague, V., Beckett, R. L., and Sawyer, T. K. A new species of *Paramoeba*
(Amoebida, Paramoebidae) parasitic in the crab *Callinectes sapidus. J. In-
vertebr. Pathol. 14:* 167-174. 1969.

47. Summerfelt, R. C. A new microsporidian parasite from the golden shiner,
Notemigonus crysoleucas. Trans. Amer. Fish. Soc. 93: 6-10. 1964.

48. Summerfelt, R. C., and Ebert, V. W. *Plistophora tahoensis* sp. n. (Micro-
sporida, Nosematidae) in the body wall of the Piute sculpin (*Cottus beldingii*)
from Lake Tahoe, California-Nevada. *Bull. Wildlife Dis. Ass. 5:* 330-341.
1969.

49. Summerfelt, R. C., and Warner, M. C. Incidence and intensity of infection
of *Plistophora ovariae*, a microsporidian parasite of the golden shiner, *Notemigonus crysoleucas.* In *A Symposium on Diseases of Fishes and Shellfishes*,
ed. S. F. Snieszko, Amer. Fish. Soc., Spec. Publ. No. 5. Washington, D.C.,
1970.

50. Uzmann, J. R., Paulik, G. J., and Hayduk, S. H. Experimental hexamitiasis
in juvenile coho salmon (*Oncorhynchus kisutch*) and steelhead trout (*Salmo
gairdneri*). *Trans. Amer. Fish. Soc. 94:* 53-61. 1965.

51. Van Duijn, C., Jr. *Diseases of Fishes.* 309 pp. London, Iliffe Books, 1957.

52. Wales, J. H., and Wolf, H. Three protozoan diseases of trout in California.
Calif. Fish Game 41: 183-187. 1955.

53. Walliker, D. Studies on *Myxidium oviforme*, a myxosporidian parasite of
Irish salmon, *Salmo salar. Parasitology 58:* 839-844. 1965.

54. Walliker, D.   The nature of the iodinophilous vacuole of myxosporidian spores, and a proposal to synonymize the genus *Myxosoma* Thelohan, 1892 with the genus *Myxobolus* Butschli, 1882. *J. Parasitol. 15:* 571–575. 1968.
55. Williams, E. H., Jr.   *Oodinium cyprinodontum* Lawler (Dinoflagellida) on *Fundulus similis* (Baird and Girard) and *Cyprinodon variegatus* Lacépède from the Gulf of Mexico. *Ala. Mar. Resour. Bull. 8:* 32–33. 1972.
56. Williams, E. H., Jr.   Parasitic infestation of some marine fishes before and after confinement in feeding cages. *Ala. Mar. Resour. Bull. 8:* 25–31. 1972.

DISCUSSION OF LESIONS OF PROTOZOAN DISEASES IN FISH

W. E. Ribelin: The dark body discoloration that occurs in *Myxosoma* infections and other conditions has intrigued me for some time. As you know, blind fish get dark, and there are a number of diseases that produce darkening of fish. I suspect that rather than being due to the damage of nerves and loss of innervation it is probably due to stimulation of the nerves and thus the chromatophores, because if you anesthetize these fish or if they die the color rapidly disappears.

H.-H. Reichenbach-Klinke: The first parasite you have described resembles very much the new dinoflagellate parasite I described a year ago. It has dark brownish spots in the gills, and these spots were the dinospores. Propagation of this parasite is by means of two sorts of dinospores—macro- and micro-dinospores, and therefore this parasite belongs to the dinoflagellates. I ask if you have seen similar things in the propagation of the parasite you mentioned, and what is the systematic classification of this organism?

W. A. Rogers: I consider it to be an ameba. It is within the tissue, not on the outside, and the same form appears in the fluids of the body cavity, so we are pretty sure this is not a dinoflagellate. There are other organisms that we have seen numerous times that we consider to be algae and possibly a dinoflagellate. We have seen an organism which is granular and looks very similar to this. They are usually nonmotile, while this one is distinctly motile.

G. L. Hoffman: Did you see these amebas in any other tissues in addition to the gills? Did you make tissue sections of liver?

W. A. Rogers: Yes, we've sectioned tissues and the organism is pretty widespread in other tissues. We have found it in kidneys and submucosa of the intestine. We have isolated about half a dozen different genera of amebas but we really are not sure what we are dealing with yet.

R. F. Nigrelli: I would like to make one or two comments about protozoan diseases in general. There are many protozoan parasites that invade the various organs and get into every kind of tissue you can think of. There isn't a marine species which will not be infected with one or two of these protozoan parasites. Now the question that arises is, What do these parasites do to the fish? I am certain that under normal conditions the fish can get along very nicely with this parasitic load, but under stress I am certain the parasites are causing death of fishes. There are probably more species of myxosporidians that have not been described than have been described, so far. In my examination of fish from all over the world in the New York Aquarium, there isn't a species that doesn't have one or more species of either myxosporidian or microsporidian. I am sure that anyone who wants to get into this field will find it a most fruitful type of research, both as to the life cycles, the pathology, and the treatment one might apply. When you try to raise marine fish under captive conditions, you are going to encounter the same problems that you have for hatchery fish or pond fish, and I would certainly recommend that this particular area of pathology be investigated more thoroughly than has been done previously.

T. E. Murchison: I was interested in your comments on some of the amebas that invade the tissues of fish from the central Florida area. We have had several cases of *Acanthamoeba* that have invaded the human brain, of persons swimming in these lakes. Have you seen any of the amebas that invaded the brain of fish in the central Florida area?

W. A. Rogers: We haven't, but we haven't looked closely for them.

4

Infection of Salmonid Fish Gills by Aquatic Amebas (Amoebida: Thecamoebidae)

THOMAS K. SAWYER
GLENN L. HOFFMAN
JOHN G. HNATH
and JOHN F. CONRAD

Recently we had the opportunity to study tissue sections of gills of fingerling salmonid fish that were infected with a previously unrecognized and undescribed species of ameba. Fish from three different hatcheries in Michigan, Washington, and Oregon had amebas situated between the gill lamellae but not within the tissue, while one fish from a fourth hatchery (in Oregon) had tissue infection. Diseased fish were lethargic or moribund when examined, and it is likely that bacteria on the gills provided food which favored the growth of otherwise free-living aquatic amebas.

Our findings are similar to those of Chatton (1, 2), who found *Amoeba mucicola* (= *Vahlkampfia*) and *Trichodina labrorum* in the mucus of diseased marine labrid fish, *Symphodus melops* and *S. tinca,* and proposed that temporary conditions favored the growth and reproduction of otherwise "free-living" aquatic amebas. Kubota and Kamata (3) reported on an unidentified ameba from gills of salmon (*Oncorhynchus rhodorus*) in Japan that were suffering from bacterial furunculosis, but they did not mention histopathological examination.

The purpose of this report is to document our findings and to identify the ameba as an undetermined species of the genus *Thecamoeba* Fromentel, 1874.

143

AMEBIASIS IN SALMONIDS

One whole fingerling rainbow trout, *Salmo gairdneri*, and one intact gill that had been preserved in 10% formalin and stored at the Grayling, Michigan, hatchery were processed for histological examination at the Oxford, Maryland, laboratory. Tissues were embedded in paraffin, sectioned at 6 microns, and stained with either Heidenhain iron hematoxylin and eosin or the Feulgen reagent with fast-green counterstain. Sections of gill tissue of chinook, *O. tshawytscha*, and silver or coho salmon, *O. kisutch*, previously stained with Heidenhain iron hematoxylin and eosin, had been prepared during a period of fish mortality at the Alsea and North Nehalem hatcheries in Oregon. Wet mount preparations of gills from the Oregon and Michigan fish were examined microscopically to note the gross morphology and pattern of locomotion of living amebas.

Serial sections of gills from the fingerling rainbow trout contained amebas which were located externally between the gill lamellae (Figs. 4.1–4.4) but not

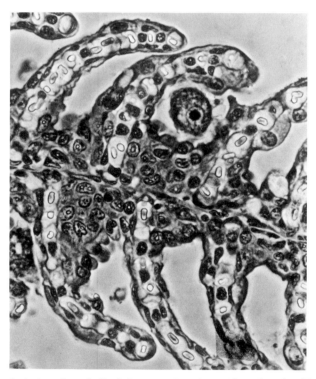

Fig. 4.1. Histological section of gill of silver or coho salmon (*Oncorhynchus kisutch*). Note scalloped appearance of ectoplasm of amebas due to plane of sectioning through wrinkles and folds; also note cellular hyperplasia between gill lamellae. Hematoxylin and eosin (H&E); phase contrast X560.

within the tissue. Some gill lamellae were short and abnormally wide (Figs. 4.1, 4.2), and others had cellular hyperplasia at the junction of the lamella and the gill filament (Fig. 4.1). The mortality at the Michigan hatchery probably was caused by respiratory impairment and asphyxiation due to large numbers of amebas on the gill surfaces. Microorganisms other than amebas were not found in the tissue sections of trout gills. Specific pathological responses to amebic infection could not be determined with certainty because other conditions are known to cause similar tissue responses.

Sections of gills from silver or coho salmon from the Alsea hatchery in Oregon also had amebas between the lamellae but not within the tissue and had the same microscopic features as tissue from trout.

One chinook salmon fingerling from the North Nehalem hatchery in Oregon had amebas on the gills and in the tissue of the gill filaments. Infected tissue was necrotic, vacuolated, and hyperplastic (Fig. 4.5). Developing miracidia of the trematode *Cardicola* (= *Sanguinicola*) were present in the gills, and filamentous strands of mucus formed a web (Fig. 4.6) which acted as a cementing substance

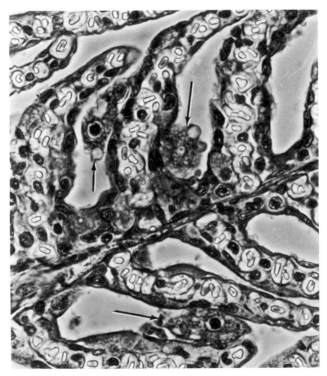

Fig. 4.2. Histological section of gill of coho salmon. Note presence of three amebas between gill lamellae and thickened abnormal lamellae. H&E; phase contrast ×560.

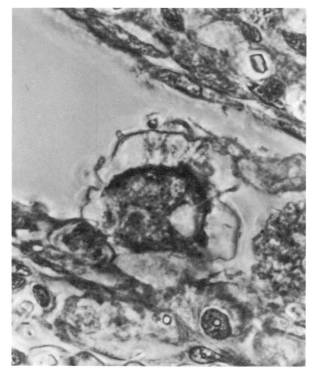

Fig. 4.3.

Figs. 4.3, 4.4. Histological sections of gill of coho salmon. Note scallops or indentations in thickened ectoplasm and irregular nuclear membrane in Figure 4.4. H&E; phase contrast ×1400.

that distorted the positioning of more normal lamellae along the branchial axis. Numerous unidentified rod-shaped bacteria, which probably served as food organisms for the amebas, were present in the mucus between the lamellae (Fig. 4.6). The presence of bacteria, immature trematodes, and mucus accumulation, in addition to intercellular amebas, suggested that amebic infection was secondary to primary helminthic and bacterial infection. Because of the multiple infection it was not possible to attribute the severe pathological response solely to tissue invasion by amebas. The histological appearances of the gills were similar to those of acute bacterial gill disease as described by Wood and Yasutake (6).

The generic identification of the gill amebas was made on the basis of their appearance in tissue sections and their gross appearance in wet mounts. The scalloped or indented areas in the pseudopodia (Figs. 4.1, 4.3, 4.4) were interpreted to be artifacts caused by sectioning through thick and wrinkled ectoplasm. Earlier observations of living amebas showed that they were lobose, flattened, and

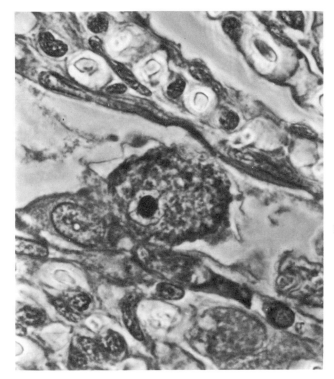

Fig. 4.4.

oval, and moved slowly without the formation of explosive or eruptive hyaline pseudopodia which characterize other genera of more active and deformable amebas. The amebas described here were assigned to the genus *Thecamoeba* on the basis of their slow rate of locomotion, broad hyaline pseudopodia, and thick folded or wrinkled ectoplasm as described by Schaeffer (5). The thick-walled de-formable nuclear membrane and large dense nucleolus (Figs. 4.1, 4.2, 4.4, 4.5) are also characteristic of several known species of *Thecamoeba* redescribed by Page (4).

SIGNIFICANCE OF AMEBAS

Conditions which led to amebic infection of the gills are not known at present because in all cases the fish hosts were lethargic or moribund when examined. The reports of Chatton (1, 2), Kubota and Kamata (3), and the present authors all in-clude accounts of bacterial infection in association with the amebas. It is there-fore presumed that invasion by the amebas is a secondary response to other causes which support bacterial growth. Bacteria, in turn, provide the food source

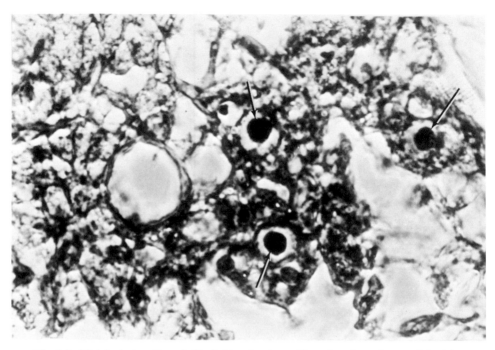

Fig. 4.5. Histological section of gill of chinook salmon (*Oncorhynchus tshawytscha*) with amebas, *Thecamoeba* sp., within the tissue. Note three large nucleoli of amebas within tissue and vacuolated hyperplastic features of tissue. H&E; phase contrast ×1400.

which favors growth and reproduction of otherwise free-living protozoans. Chatton (1, 2) reported that amebas were numerous on fish gills and resembled an epithelial sheet. He concluded that the amebas probably were "opportunists" and temporarily found growth conditions which favored their reproduction. Our observations on salmonid fish agree with this conclusion. The cause-and-effect relationship of the findings of Kubota and Kamata (3) is more difficult to interpret, since they reported only a single specimen of an ameba in gills of trout which were suffering from bacterial furunculosis. The etiology of amebic gill disease, therefore, must remain speculative at present. Experimental infections of aquarium fish with known species of amebas and bacteria probably would yield valuable information on host response and tissue lesions which we cannot interpret with natural infections.

The discovery of amebas between the gill lamellae, but not within the tissues, originally led us to believe that mortalities were due only to asphyxiation caused by large numbers of amebas on the outer surfaces of the gills. The fourth and last group of slides that were available to us (from the North Nehalem, Oreg., hatchery) however, contained evidence that amebas could penetrate the tissue and

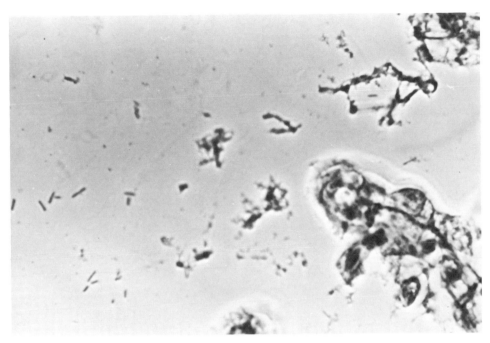

Fig. 4.6. Mucous web and associated bacteria in gill section of chinook salmon. H&E; phase contrast ×1400.

cause considerable tissue damage in addition to having a smothering effect. Concurrent infection by trematode miracidia in these tissues, and the presence of bacteria, suggested that perhaps the severity of amebic infection was related to stress from other causes. Our observations with fish that were selected for study because of their overt signs of respiratory distress suggest that new studies on asymptomatic fish are needed to determine whether the amebas are present when fish are not stressed by other causes.

The identification of the amebas illustrated in this report is limited to the generic designation, *Thecamoeba* Fromentel, 1874. Our identification is provisional and is proposed here in order to provide a generic name for the organism found in salmonid fish and to provide the basis by which other workers may be able to identify amebas found in gills of different fish species. Our studies were limited by the fact that living amebas were not available for examination when the work was initiated. However, because of the excellent response we received from other investigators (see Acknowledgment), adequate material was available to support our choice of the genus *Thecamoeba*. The identification of the gill amebas to genus and species will be given in a detailed taxonomic manuscript that is now in preparation.

Acknowledgment. We gratefully acknowledge the excellent cooperation of the following individuals: W. T. Yasutake, Bureau of Sport Fisheries and Wildlife Fish Disease Laboratory, Seattle, Washington, for additional gill sections of infected silver and chinook salmon; James W. Wood, Washington Department of Fisheries, Seattle, Washington, for additional information on motility patterns of gill amebas from chinook salmon at the Washougal Hatchery, Camas, Washington; Dr. Fred P. Meyer, Bureau of Sport Fisheries and Wildlife, Fish Farming Experimental Station, Stuttgart, Arkansas, for information on motility of amebas from non-salmonid pond fish; Dr. Fred C. Page, Culture Centre of Algae and Protozoa, Cambridge, England, who gave us the photographs and typescript of his comparative studies of *Thecamoeba* prior to publication.

REFERENCES

1. Chatton, E.   Une Amibe, *Amoeba mucicola,* n. sp., parasite des branchies des labres, associée à une trichodine. *C. r. séances Soc. Biol. 67:* 690–692. 1909.
2. Chatton, E.   Protozoaires parasites des branchies des labres, *Amoeba mucicola* Chatton, *Trichodina labrorum* n. sp. *Arch. zool. exp. gen. 5:* 239–266. 1910.
3. Kubota, S., and Kamata, T.   An amoeba observed on the gill of amago. *Fish Pathol. (Japan) 5*(2): 155. 1971.
4. Page, F. C.   A comparative study of five freshwater and marine species of Thecamoebidae. *Trans. Amer. Microscop. Soc. 90*(2): 157–173. 1971.
5. Schaeffer, A. A.   *Taxonomy of the Amebas.* Carnegie Inst. Wash., Publ. No. 345. 1926.
6. Wood, E. M., and Yasutake, W. T.   Histopathology of fish. V. Gill disease. *Progr. Fish-Cult. 19*(1): 7–13. 1957.

DISCUSSION OF INFECTION OF SALMONID FISH GILLS BY AQUATIC AMEBAS

Question: The ameba photos were very good. Was that phase contrast with new methylene blue, or what were you using?

T. K. Sawyer: If you use phase contrast, you can create a lot of artifacts that look much better. That was phase contrast and those were simply different filters. The green photos were made with the green filter, and the idea was to emphasize the nucleus and the pseudopodia.

5

Lesions due to Internal Helminths of Freshwater Fishes

GLENN L. HOFFMAN

Helminths are very common in freshwater fishes. Very few lesions have been attributed to intestinal forms. *Crepidostomum farionis* has been reported as an enteric pathogen and I have observed intestinal hemorrhage and death caused by, or associated with, the spined nematode *Spinitectus* sp.

Histozoic helminths, particularly migrating forms, cause greater damage, although cellular responses are usually less pronounced in fishes than in homeotherms. In severe cases hyperemia, hemorrhage, cellular infiltration, hyperplasia, fibrosis, calcification, and necrosis are seen. In some cases there is practically no host response.

After encystment and fibrotic encapsulation, many larval helminths produce no further obvious damage except pressure on adjacent host tissues (16). The most comprehensive work on fish response to infective agents is that of Reichenbach-Klinke (31).

Herein are reviewed selected examples of lesions caused by trematodes, cestodes, nematodes, and acanthocephalans of freshwater fishes.

GENERAL CONSIDERATIONS

The extent of the host's cellular reaction is dependent on the number of invasive elements, length and place of migratory phase, and probably host and parasite species differences. Migrating larvae of trematodes (cercariae), cestodes

151

(plerocercoids), and nematodes produce the most serious reactions: leukocytosis, fibrosis, and more rarely hemorrhage, hyperemia, and necrosis. Continual migrators, such as plerocercoids of *Proteocephalus ambloplitis*, *Philonema* spp., and larvae of *Contracaecum* spp. produce peritonitis which results in fibrosis and extensive adhesions. Larvae that migrate rapidly to a final site, and then grow considerably, produce less severe damage but cause a rather significant granuloma or connective tissue encapsulation. Those helminths, such as certain metacercariae, which produce cysts of parasite origin tend to elicit less host encapsulation. Those which grow little and produce a cyst of parasite origin usually cause the least response.

Several metacercariae of the *Neascus* (black grub) type and *Apophallus* spp. stimulate local melanin pigment cell proliferation following connective tissue encapsulation.

Rapid invasion by large numbers of cercariae produce extensive hemorrhage, hyperemia, necrosis, and even death if present in sufficient numbers (9, 14, 17, 34).

RECOGNITION OF HELMINTHS IN TISSUE SECTIONS

Definitive identification of fish helminths can best be made using living material followed by permanent *in toto* preparations (15). In some cases formalin-preserved material is satisfactory. However, helminthic lesions are often found in the course of histopathological studies and it becomes necessary to attempt identification. The main criteria for identifying the general types are listed in Table 5.1. Unless the section happens to include unusually specific structures of some parasites (suckers, spines, papillae, etc.) the genus and species can rarely be identified. The photos in the text illustrate sections of various types of helminths.

Identification of veterinary metazoans in histological sections has recently been reviewed by Chitwood and Lichtenfels (6) and is useful for comparison.

ADULT TREMATODES

Adult trematodes are found frequently in the intestine and more rarely in the stomach, esophagus, mouth, urinary system, biliary system, ovaries, circulatory system, and gas bladder. Except for *Sanguinicola* (*Cardicola*) spp. and *C. farionis* no one has reported any lesions due to adult trematodes in freshwater fishes.

Adult trematodes are more easily identified *in toto* than in sections. In sections, a trematode, except for *Sanguinicola* spp., can be identified as a trematode if the section includes portions of suckers, gonads, and intestine.

1. Sanguinicola davisi **Wales, 1958** (*blood fluke*)

The adults (Fig. 5.1) live in the gill arch blood vessels of trouts in the western United States and cause no apparent damage. Eggs which are produced become

Table 5.1. Diagnostic Characteristics of Internal Helminths in Sections[a]

	Shape	Approximate size of cross section in microns	Cuticle	Internal parasite tissue	Gut	Attachment organs	Miscellaneous
Trematodes	Usually flattened	20–1000	Thin	Parenchyma containing muscle	Pharynx, esophagus, *ceca*	*Anterior sucker, Ventral sucker*	Monogenea in urinary system have no suckers. Eggs, vitellaria, gonads in adults.
Cestodes	Usually flattened	100–1000	Thin, sometimes peudociliated	Parenchyma containing muscle	*None*	Scolex with *suckers,* grooves, or rarely hooks	*Calcareous corpuscles* of larvae may be seen if not removed by acid solutions. Oncospheres in adults.
Nematodes	*Cylindrical*	20–500	Usually thicker than flatworms	*Longitudinal musculature* appearing as a ring	*Esophagus, intestine*	None, Spinitectus and Gnathostoma spined	Eggs or *larvae* in uterus of female adults.
Acanthocephalans	*Cylindrical* or slightly flattened	20–1020	Usually thicker than flatworms	Nuclei few but large	*None*	*Spined proboscis*	Eggs in uterus of female adults.

[a]The most helpful characteristics are in italics.

153

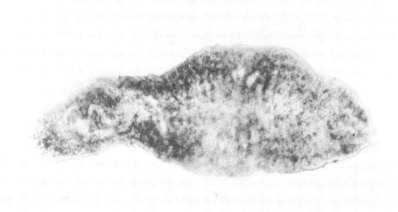

Fig. 5.1. *Sanguinicola* sp., living adult from blacknose dace (*Rhinichthys atratulus*). Note that there are no typical trematode suckers. ×100.

trapped and encapsulated in the gill capillaries, where they become miracidia. No great harm is done unless there are massive numbers. The greatest damage occurs when miracidia migrate out of the gills.

This is most easily diagnosed in a wet mount by recognizing the single large eye-spot of the miracidium. Lesions consist of blocked capillaries and hemorrhages after the miracidium leaves the host (Figs. 5.2, 5.3).

2. Sanguinicola inermis *Plehn, 1905*

This blood fluke is a serious pathogen of carp in Europe. The lesions are similar to those of *Sanguinicola davisi* except that eggs are also trapped in visceral organs because the adults are not restricted to the gill arch blood vessels. Histological examination of the gills reveals capillaries plugged with eggs, necrosis of ischemic areas, and finally after the miracidia leave, hemorrhage followed by septic necrosis; similar lesions occurred in the kidneys of two-year-old carp in the Soviet Union (30).

3. Crepidostomum farionis *(Müller, 1784) Niccol, 1909*

This is reported to have caused intestinal inflammation, but no detailed studies are available (7, 28).

METACERCARIAE

Certain cercariae are able to penetrate fish, develop to metacercariae, and remain until they are eaten by the proper final host or until they die of senility.

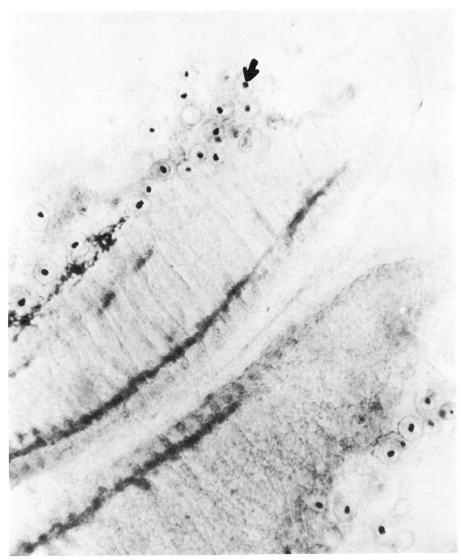

Fig. 5.2. Miracidia of *Sanguinicola* sp. in gills of blacknose dace. Note single large, black eye-spot in each. ×100.

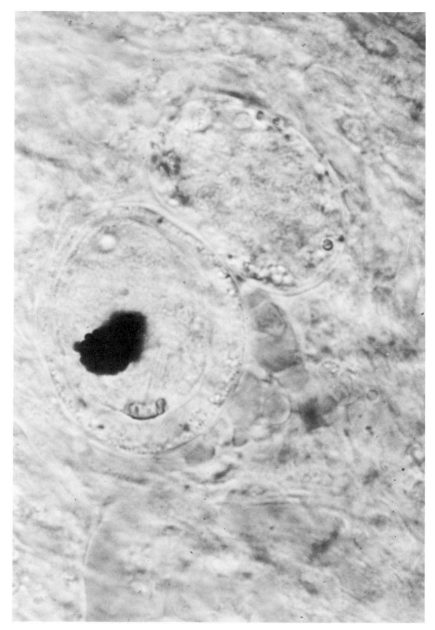

Fig. 5.3. Miracidia of *Sanguinicola davisi* in gills of rainbow trout (*Salmo gairdneri*). Note single large, black eye-spot. (Courtesy of J. Warren, BSFW, Genoa, Wis.) ×430.

Some cercariae are able to penetrate only one species of fish, while others lack host specificity. Many will develop only in certain organs. In general, the greatest damage is done during cercarial migration to target organs. If large numbers invade simultaneously, the fish may die. Tissue response is greatest before the parasites become localized and encysted. Melanin pigmentation of cysts occurs in some cases, and tissue necrosis has occurred in at least one case.

Most metacercariae can be recognized if the section includes suckers or caeca of the parasite. Specific identification is usually possible with *in toto* preparations.

1. Diplostomulum baeri eucaliae *Hoffman and Hundley, 1957*

The cercariae of this strigeid penetrate the brook stickleback, *Eucalia inconstans*, and migrate to the brain, where they tend to localize in the choroid plexus. As they accumulate and grow in this organ it becomes hyperplastic. The resultant "tumor-like" structure (Figs. 5.4, 5.5) extends posterolaterally from the optic

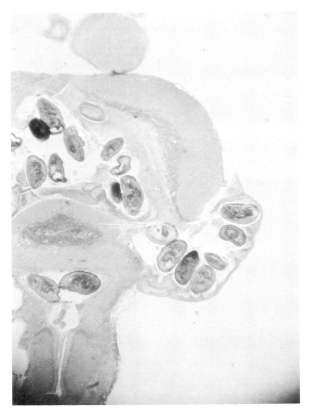

Fig. 5.4. *Diplostomulum baerieucaliae* in frontal section of brain of experimentally infected brook stickleback. Note tumor-like structure on right containing metacercariae. "Tumor" is composed of hyperplastic peripheral epithelium and internal macrophages. (Hoffman photo, courtesy of *Journal of Parasitology*.) ×32.

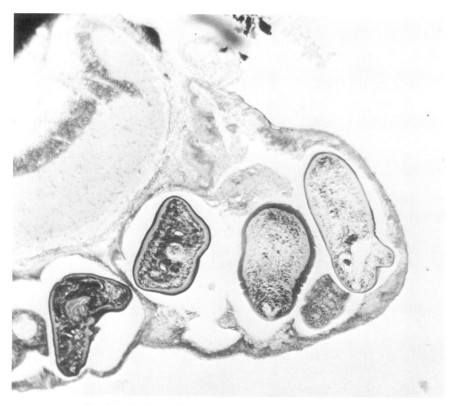

Fig. 5.5. Similar to Figure 5.4 at higher magnification. ×100.

lobes and consists of a substantial amount of columnar epithelium plus cells which appear to be macrophages surrounding the worms (19).

2. Diplostomulum flexicaudum (*Cort and Brooks, 1928*) *Van Haitsma, 1939* (*eye fluke*). (*This is synonymous with or nearly identical to* Diplostomulum spathaceum *of Europe.*)

Normally the cercaria of this species penetrates the eye lens of many fishes, grows, and becomes the occupant of the hole it makes in the lens. Frequently there is not much tissue reaction. Ashton, Brown, and Easty (3), however, demonstrated marked proliferation of lens epithelium adjacent to the parasites (Fig. 5.6). Heavily infected lenses become opaque and the fish is blinded. Other species of *Diplostomulum* are found elsewhere, including in the vitreous chamber of the eye.

Larson (25) found an unusual type of *Diplostomulum flexicaudum.* The cercariae localize in the lens, but as they grow, the lens herniates, forming a dorsally located cyst containing the metacercariae (Fig. 5.7). The hernia (cyst) possesses

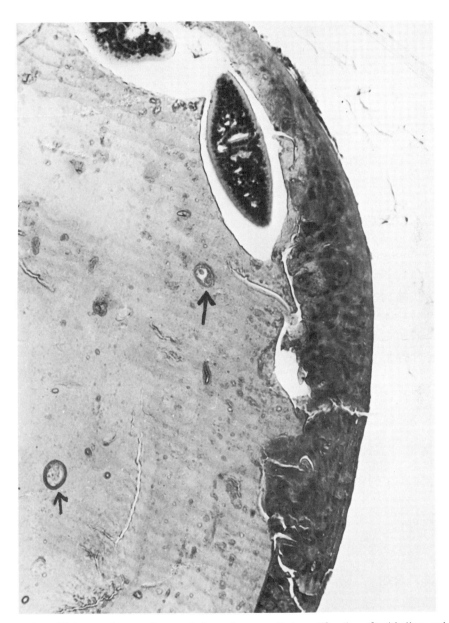

Fig. 5.6. *Diplostomulum spathaceum* in lens of guppy. Note proliferation of epithelium and two small vesicles (arrows). (Courtesy of Dr. N. Ashton and Institute of Ophthalmology, University of London, and *Journal of Small Animal Practice*.) ×160.

Fig. 5.7. Herniation of the lens of black bullhead (*Ictalurus melas*) caused by *Diplostomulum flexicaudum* (?) (Courtesy of Dr. O. Larson and *Journal of Parasitology.*) ×80.

the same tissues as the lens; the outer cuticular capsule and its underlying epithelium are continuous with the lens. Internal to the epithelium of the hernia is a layer of lens fibers having typical degenerating nuclei. The inner portion of the lens contains metacercariae in a fine granular matrix which is the remainder of the lens fibers after exposure to the parasites. Ashton, Brown, and Easty (3) reported less spectacular lens herniation in experimentally infected trout.

3. Diplostomulum *sp. of Mueller, 1972*

Szidat and Nani (35) reported a severe epizootic of diplostomiasis of the Argentine fish, *Basilichthys microlepidotus.* There were many specimens of *Diplos-*

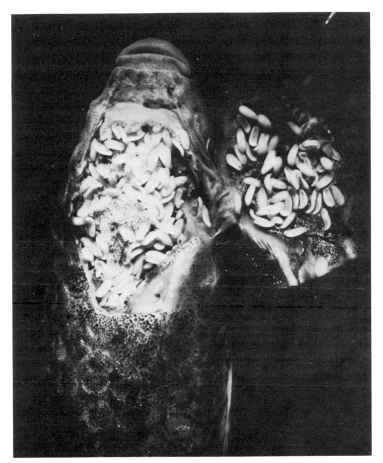

Fig. 5.8. Fish, *Orestias* sp., with deformed head due to *Diplostomulum* sp. Roof of cranium opened to show parasites. (Courtesy of Dr. J. F. Mueller and *Journal of Parasitology.*)

tomulum in the brains of the diseased fish. Parasites were in the ventricles, optic lobes, cerebellum, and in the optic chiasma. The fish were nearly paralyzed. Mueller (29) reported severely misshapen heads of the Peruvian fish, *Orestias* sp., caused by massive cranial invasion by *Diplostomulum* sp. (Fig. 5.8).

4. Posthodiplostomulum minimum (*MacCullum, 1921; Dubois, 1936*) *Hoffman, 1958* (*white grub*)

This very common strigeid metacercaria is seen as a white bladder-like cyst in the viscera of many species of fishes. Experimentally, fish can be killed with the cercariae (13), but the slower accumulation of the cercariae in nature probably does not kill fish. The parasite cysts become encapsulated by a thin connective tissue host cyst (Figs. 5.9, 5.10) (13, 33).

A very unusual case was reported by Hoffman and Hutcheson (20). Many striped bass fingerlings (*Morone saxatilis*) were killed by large numbers of *Posthodiplostomulum minimum* invading the body and head musculature, thus producing marked exophthalmos and extensive swelling of the body musculature. It was assumed that the parasite had different tissue affinities and elicited unusual responses in a fish unrelated to the usual host.

A most unusual case in a related form, *Ornithodiplostomum ptychocheilus,* was observed by Hoffman (14). Experimental infection produced so many metacercariae that when they grew to maximum size their accumulated mass caused the body wall to rupture, expelling many larvae. Surprisingly, the lesion healed and the fish recovered (Fig. 5.11).

5. Black-spot Neascus (*black grub*)

Neascus is a larval genus containing metacercariae of *Uvulifer* spp., *Crassiphiala* spp., *Ornithodiplostomum* spp., and *Posthodiplostomulum* spp. If the adult is unknown, the metacercaria is known as a *Neascus* sp. (15).

At least four species of strigeid metacercariae cause the formation of pigmented host cysts in the skin and muscle of North American freshwater fishes (15). Two of these, *Crassiphiala bulboglossa* in the skin, and *Uvulifer ambloplitis* in the

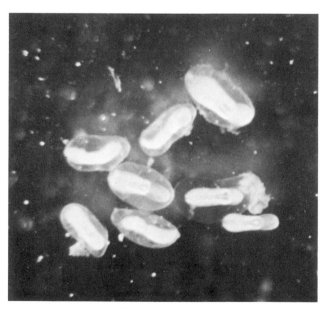

Fig. 5.9. Cysts of the white grub, *Posthodiplostomulum minimum;* photograph taken through dissection microscope. X20.

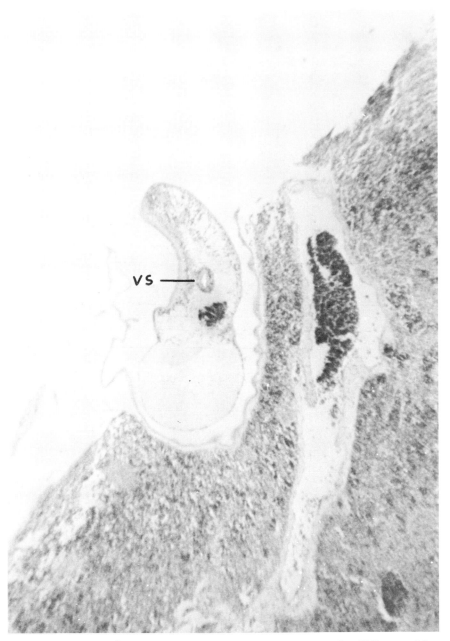

Fig. 5.10. White grub, *P. minimum,* in liver. Section shows ventral sucker (VS), cupped fore-body and bulbous hindbody. Inner thin cyst wall is of parasite origin covered by thin con-nective tissue capsule. ×150.

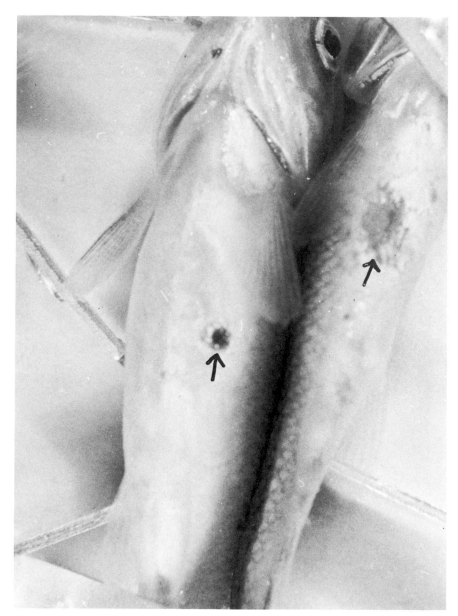

Fig. 5.11. Two fathead minnows (*Pimephales promelas*) 40 days post-infection with a large number of cercariae of *Ornithodiplostomum ptychocheilus*. Note large dark scars where the body wall had burst and healed. (Hoffman photo, courtesy of *Journal of Parasitology*.)

musculature, have been studied (12, 21–23). These parasites produce a parasite cyst around which is formed a connective tissue capsule overlaid with melanophores (Figs. 5.12, 5.13). Related parasites and cysts are found in Europe, Africa, and South America.

6. Neogogatea kentuckiensis (*Cable, 1935*) *Hoffman and Dunbar, 1963*

The small (275 micron) cyst of this strigeid appears to be innocuous, but migrating cercariae cause considerable damage. Two-week-old rainbow trout were killed in

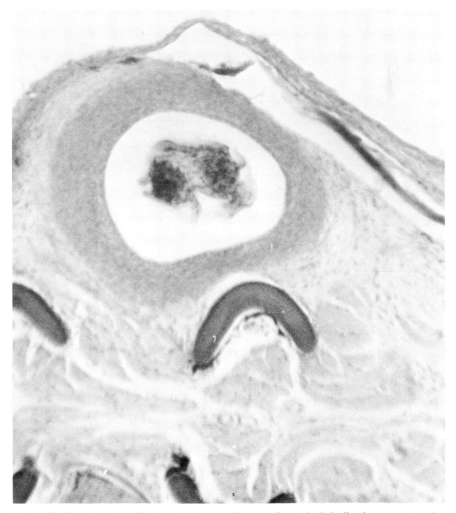

Fig. 5.12. Experimental infection, black-spot *Neascus, Crassiphiala bulboglossa*, in skin of *Fundulus* sp. Note thick connective tissue cyst. Melanin accumulation has not yet occurred. ×150.

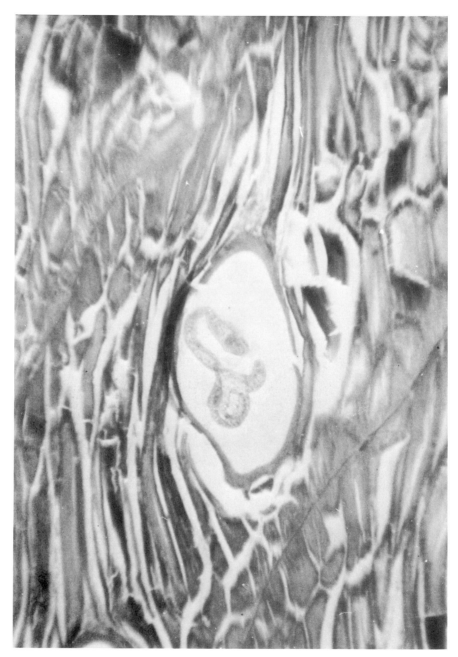

Fig. 5.13. Experimental black-spot *Neascus, Uvulifer ambloplitis* in muscle of bluegill (*Lepomis macrochirus*). Note wide forebody and smaller, bulbous hindbody. Connective tissue cyst not very thick. Melanin accumulation has not yet occurred. ×150.

2.5 hours when exposed to 30 cercariae each. Several species of fishes were exposed to about 50 cercariae per fish; within 30 minutes ecchymoses could be seen in the skin and muscle. Histological examination revealed hemorrhage and muscle necrosis around the cercariae as early as one hour post-infection (similar to Fig. 5.1) (18).

7. Bucephalus polymorphus *Baer, 1827*

In 1966, larvae caused high mortality of cyprinid fish in the Seine River near Paris, France. A similar situation occurred in the Wda River, Poland, about the same time.

Afflicted fish rub their bellies and sides on the river bottom. The mouth and bases of the caudal and anal fins have marked congestion and hemorrhage. Some fish are exophthalmic with numerous opaque areas in the cornea. Many cysts containing the metacercariae are present in these regions. Septic necrosis of fins contributes to the disease.

Microscopically, the cysts are found in many parts of the fish, but tissue reaction (inflammation) is marked in the mouth (Fig. 5.14). There is less reaction elsewhere. Migrating cercariae cause muscle necrosis (Fig. 5.15). In some cases metacercariae are very numerous in the cornea and retina with retinal hemorrhages (10, 24).

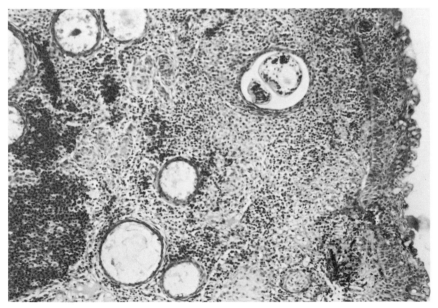

Fig. 5.14. *Bucephalus polymorphus* in buccal skin of gardon (*Rutilis rutilis*). Acute phase showing extensive inflammation. (Courtesy of Dr. P. de Kinkelin.) ×140.

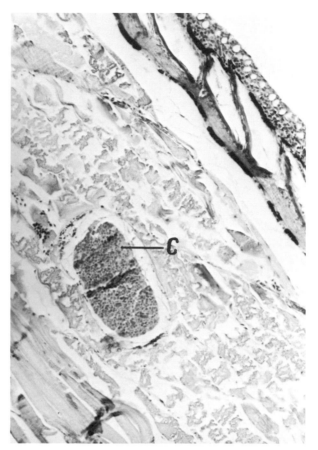

Fig. 5.15. Cercaria (C) of *Bucephalus polymorphus* in muscle of trout fry (experimental infection). Note muscle necrosis. (Courtesy of Dr. P. de Kinkelin.) ×140.

8. Ascocotyle tenuicollis *Price, 1935*

In 1961, the author received some moribund mosquitofish (*Gambusia affinis*) from a warm spring pond near Salt Lake City, Utah. Disease signs included loss of vigor and appetite, immobility at the surface, erratic swimming, and apparent paralysis.

Cysts about 200 microns in diameter, containing the heterophyid metacercariae of *Ascocotyle tenuicollis*, were found under the endothelium in the bulbus arteriosus; in some cases they were very numerous and occluded the lumen of the bulbus. In one case, one cyst in the distal end of the bulbus was seen to be positioned so as to occlude blood flow (Fig. 5.16). Sogandares-Bernal and Lumsden (32) have studied the cysts of the closely related *A. leighi* in *Cyprinodon variega-*

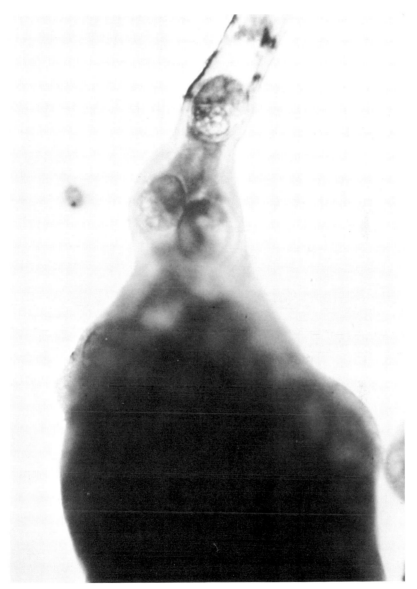

Fig. 5.16. Metacercariae of *Ascocotyle tenuicollis* occluding bulbus arteriosus of mosquito-fish (*Gambusia affinis*). ×28.

tus and *Mollienesia latipinna*, where growth of the cysts, including fibrosis, often results in partial occlusion of the lumen of the bulbus.

CESTODES

Very little damage has been attributed to adult cestodes in the intestine and pyloric caeca of North American freshwater fishes. *Corallobothrium* of catfish is considered pathogenic but no detailed studies are available, and *Eubothrium salvelini* reportedly causes reduced weight gain of salmon (L. Margolis, FRBC, Nanaimo, B.C., Canada, personal communication). *Bothriocephalus gowkongensis* of cyprinids in Asia and Europe is a serious pathogen.

Some larval tapeworms (plerocercoids), however, produce severe damage in fish, particularly those larvae which do not encyst and continue to migrate. Plerocercoids can best be recognized as such when alive, when the spectacular calcareous corpuscles are visible. The calcareous corpuscles are usually not visible in histological sections and identification is difficult unless the section includes the recognizable scolices of certain species. Generic, but not specific, identification is usually possible with intact plerocercoids.

1. Proteocephalus ambloplitis (*Leidy, 1887*) *Benedict, 1900* (*bass tapeworm*)

The plerocercoid causes extensive fibrosis in the viscera, particularly the gonads of smallmouth and largemouth bass (*Micropterus* spp.). In severe cases the viscera may become a solid mass of fibrous adhesions (Fig. 5.17).

2. Diphyllobothrium *spp.*

Some species of *Diphyllobothrium* produce little damage in fish but at least two are severely pathogenic.

Diphyllobothrium sebago in American trout and landlocked salmon often does not encyst, and migrating larvae may penetrate vital organs (27); this may kill trout fingerlings (Fig. 5.18) (17).

D. dendriticum caused serious epizootics in *Salmo trutta* in Ireland and England during the forties. The fish had shown "plastic" peritonitis. Bloodstained ascitic fluid was present in 25% of the fish examined, and edematous granulation tissue containing blood extravasations was present in 80%. Such tissue often bound the stomach and pyloric caeca into a large tumor-like mass. Marked pallor of flesh and gills suggested severe anemia (11).

3. Triaenophorus *spp.*

These are related to *Diphyllobothrium* spp. but can be recognized by the presence of two pairs of trident hooks on the scolex. *Triaenophorus crassus* is encapsulated in the musculature (Figs. 5.19, 5.20) and *T. nodulosus* is encapsulated in the viscera. Both may become large and unsightly; *T. nodulosus* is considered a serious pathogen in Europe.

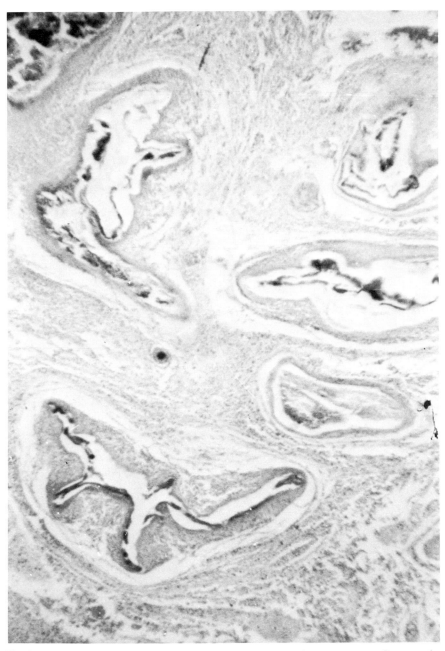

Fig. 5.17. Fibrotic mass containing remains of plerocercoids of bass tapeworm (*Proteocephalus ambloplitis*) from smallmouth brood bass (*Micropterus dolomieui*). ×52.

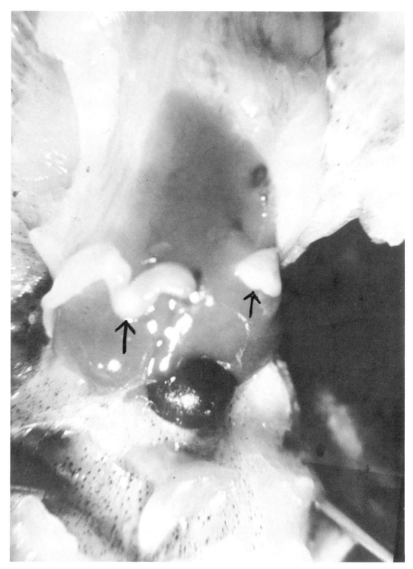

Fig. 5.18. *Diphyllobothrium sebago* plerocercoid (arrows) migrating through liver of Atlantic salmon fingerling. (Courtesy of Roger Dexter, U.S. Fish and Wildlife Service, East Orland, Maine.)

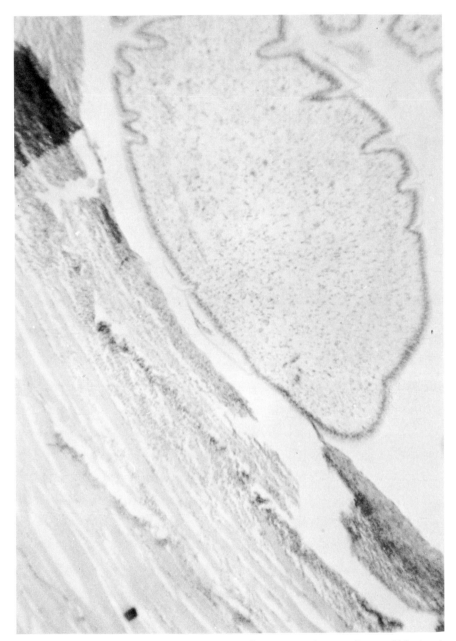

Fig. 5.19. Encapsulated plerocercoid of *Triaenophorus crassus* in musculature of lake trout (*Salvelinus namaycush*) fingerling. ×52.

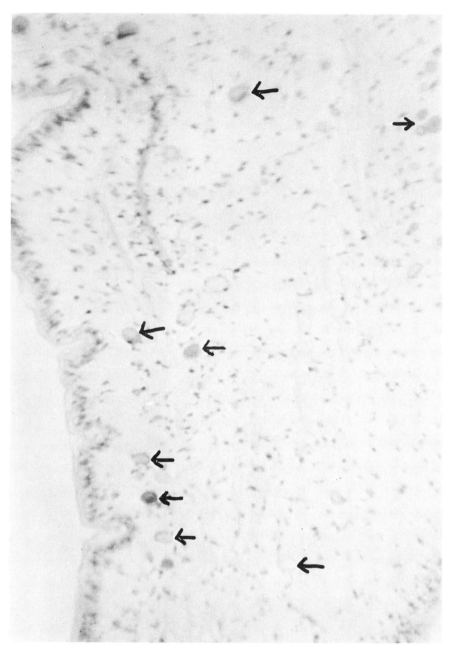

Fig. 5.20. Higher magnification of section of *T. crassus* showing calcareous corpuscles (arrows). ×150.

4. Ligula *and* Schistocephalus

These plerocercoids become almost adult in the visceral cavity of fish. Their tremendous size may burst the body wall of small fishes. Short of this, the larvae cause compression of abdominal organs, extensive proliferation of fibrous connective tissue, and almost complete obliteration of the gonads; death is common (Figs. 5.21, 5.22). In addition, there are pituitary changes and extreme reduction of gonad size (1, 2).

NEMATODES

Little is known of the damaging effects of adult intestinal nematodes of fish. Adults and larvae in the viscera and eyes can produce much damage, however. In histological section, nematodes can often be recognized as such, but specific identification can be made only with *in toto* specimens. Larval nematodes apparently produce little damage unless extremely numerous.

1. Philonema agubernaculum *Simon and Simon, 1936*

In severe cases, landlocked salmon infested with this parasite may become extremely emaciated and sexually impotent. Adult worms may be free in the body cavity or encysted beneath the serosa of the viscera or body wall. The cysts,

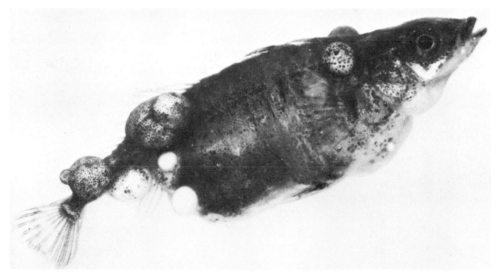

Fig. 5.21. *Gasterosteus aculeatus* infected with plerocercoids of *Schistocephalus solidus* and cysts of *Glugea anomala.* Note enlarged abdomen due to *S. solidus.* (Courtesy of Dr. E. El-kan, Watford General Hospital, Watford, England.)

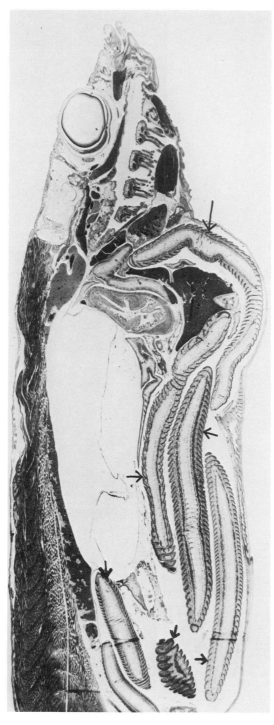

Fig. 5.22. Section through *G. aculeatus* heavily infected with plerocercoids of *S. solidus*. Arrows indicate parasites. (Courtesy of Dr. C. Arme, The Queen's University of Belfast, Belfast, Ireland.)

about 3 cm in diameter, may be spherical or flattened; enclosed worms are dead and in different stages of disintegration. Free worms may be dead or alive (Fig. 5.23) and many microscopic larvae are present. The visceral adhesions may be so severe that normal spawning or manual stripping is impossible (Fig. 5.24).

2. *Other* Philometra *spp.*

Large viviparous nematodes are also found in the cheek galleries, body cavity, and fins of fish. Recently a spectacular exophthalmos-producing form has been found in the eye of bluegill sunfish (T. Wellborn, Mississippi State College, College Station, Miss., personal communication). *Philometra nodulosa* in the "cheek galleries" of *Catostomus commersoni* is fairly common (Fig. 5.25).

3. Hepaticola petruschewskii *Schulman, 1948* (Capillaria eupomitis *Ghittino, 1961*)

This has been reported from the liver of *Lepomis gibbosus, S. gairdneri,* and other fish in Europe. The adults are found in the liver, which is enlarged, anemic, and yellow. White, grey, and black nodules containing parasites and typical capillarid eggs are present (Fig. 5.26) (8).

4. Spinitectus *sp.*

Moribund bluegill (*L. macrochirus*) have been encountered which contained many spined *Spinitectus* sp. in the inflamed intestine. Some of the parasites had burrowed into the mucosa. Eggs must have become trapped in fish tissue because many were lodged in the gill lamellae (Fig. 5.27).

ACANTHOCEPHALANS

The insertion of the spiny proboscis into the intestinal lining of fish destroys small amounts of mucosa and connective tissue. In some instances there appears to be no marked pathogenicity, but with others there is rather severe local reaction surrounding the proboscis and the intestine may be perforated, resulting in peritonitis. Bauer and Nikol'skaya (4) describe leukocytosis, hyperemia, and hyperplasia of connective tissue in *Coregonus* caused by *Echinorhynchus salmonis*. Bullock (5) reported damage to the intestinal epithelium, connective tissue hyperplasia, and a mucous layer interposed between *Acanthocephalus jacksoni* and the epithelium of the hosts, *Salvelinus* and *Salmo* (Fig. 5.28). He also described the cellular repair of wounds caused by withdrawn probosces.

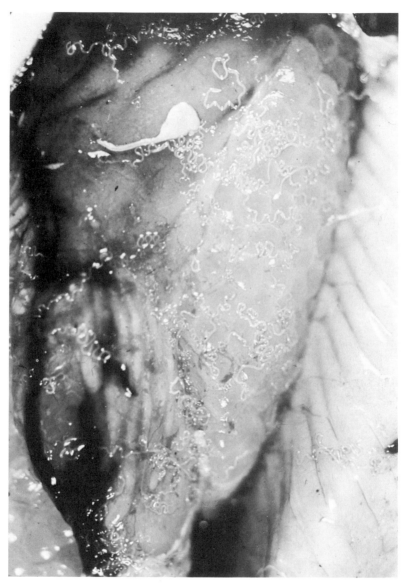

Fig. 5.23. *Philonema agubernaculum* in ovary and other viscera of brook trout (*Salvelinus fontinalis*). (Courtesy of Dr. M. C. Meyer, University of Maine, Orono.)

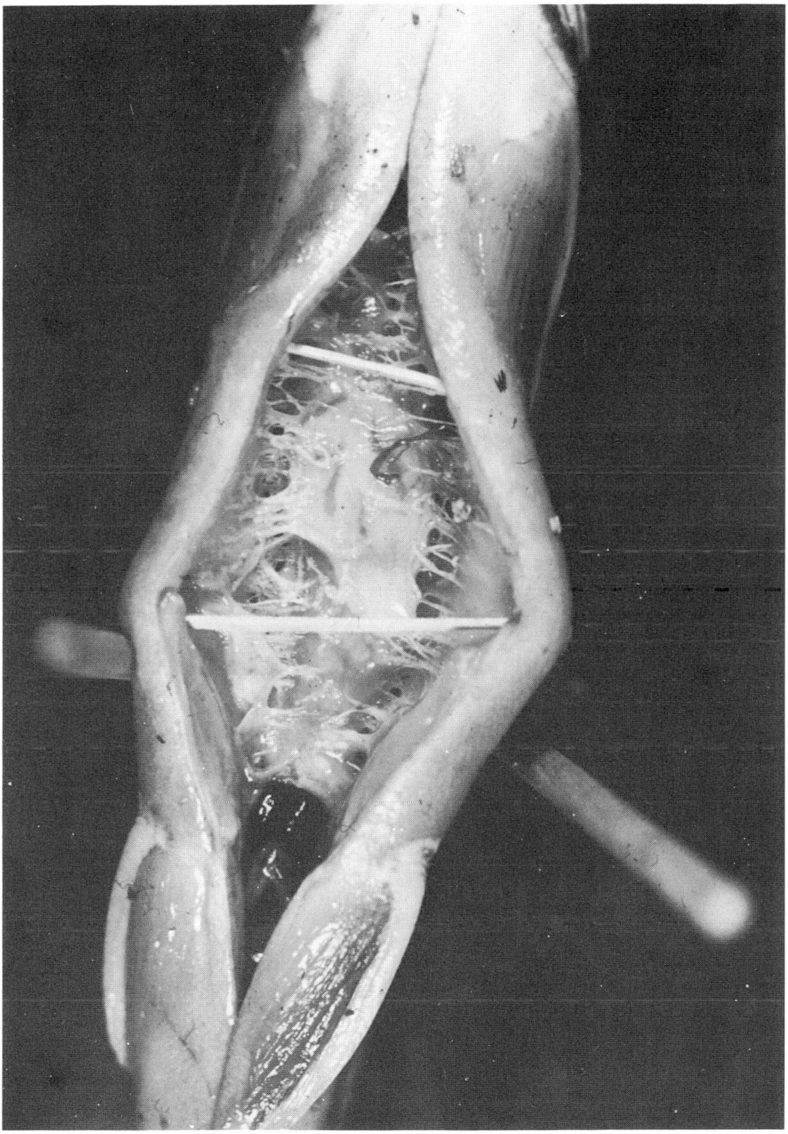

Fig. 5.24. Same as Figure 5.23, but a later stage showing the mass of adhesions. (Courtesy of Dr. M. C. Meyer, University of Maine, Orono.)

Fig. 5.25. *Philometra nodulosa* in "cheek galleries" of *Catostomus commersoni.*

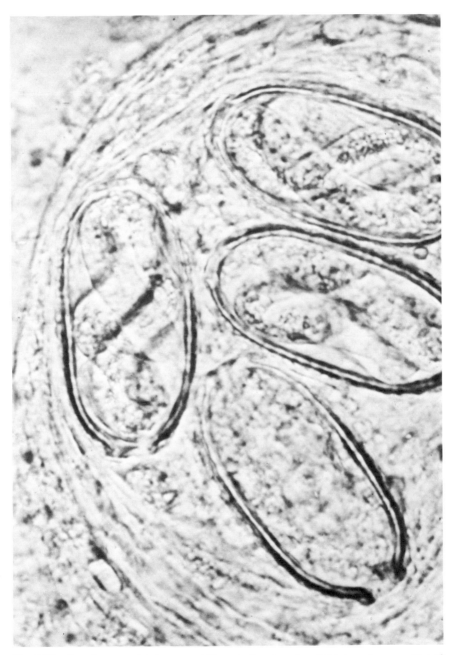

Fig. 5.26. Granuloma containing eggs of *Hepaticola petruschewskii* in teased preparation of liver of *Lepomis gibbosus*. (Courtesy of Dr. P. Ghittino, Instituto Zooprofilattico Sperimentale del Piemonte e della Liguria, Turin, Italy.) X468.

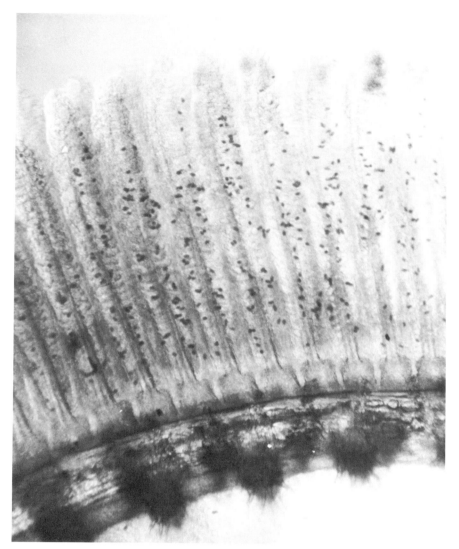

Fig. 5.27. Eggs of *Spinitectus* sp. (black dots) in gill lamellae of bluegill (*Lepomis macrochirus*). Eggs appear black because of opacity; photograph taken through bright field microscope. ×52.

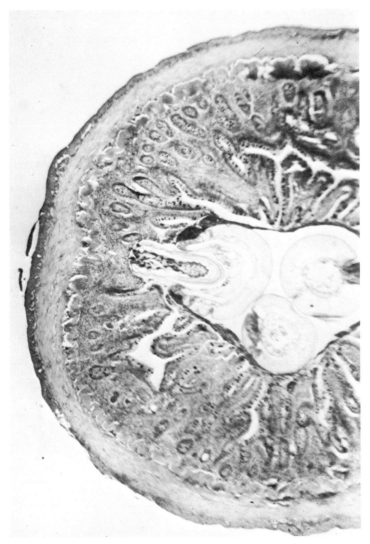

Fig. 5.28. *Acanthocephalus jacksoni.* Longitudinal section through proboscis partially embedded in intestine of brook trout. Note destruction of mucosa. (Courtesy of Dr. W. Bullock, University of New Hampshire, Durham, and *Journal of Morphology.*) ×60.

REFERENCES

1. Arme, C. Effects of the plerocercoid larva of a pseudophylidian cestode, *Ligula intestinalis,* on the pituitary gland and gonads of its host. *Biol. Bull. (Woods Hole) 134:* 15. 1968.

2. Arme, C., and Owen, R. W. Infections of the three-spined stickleback, *Gasterosteus aculeatus* L., with the plerocercoid larvae of *Schistocephalus solidus* (Müller, 1776). with special reference to pathological effects. *Parasitology 57:* 301. 1967.

3. Ashton, N., Brown, N., and Easty, D. Trematode cataract in freshwater fish. *J. Small Anim. Pract. 10:* 471. 1969.

4. Bauer, O. N., and Nikol'skaya, N. P. Dynamics of the parasitofauna of the whitefish, *Coregonus lavaretus,* from Lake Ladoga and its epizootic importance, p. 224. In *Parasites and Diseases of Fish.,* ed. G. K. Petrushevski, *Bull. State Sci. Res. Inst. Lake River Fish. 42.* 1957.

5. Bullock, W. L. Intestinal histology of some salmonid fishes with particular reference to the histopathology of acanthocephalan infections. *J. Morphol. 112:* 23. 1963.

6. Chitwood, M. B., and Lichtenfels, J. R. Identification of parasitic metazoa in tissue sections. *Exp. Parasitol. 32:* 407. 1972.

7. Davis, H. S. Care and diseases of trout. *U.S. Dept. Commerce, Bur. Fish. Inv. Rep.* 35 pp. 1937.

8. Ghittino, P. Piscicoltura e Ittiopatologia. *Ittiopatologia, Edizione Rivista de zootecnia. 2:* 420. 1970.

9. Ginetsinskaya, T. A. The life cycles of fish helminths and the biology of their larval stages, p. 140. In *Parasitology of Fishes,* ed. by V. A. Dogiel, G. K. Petrushevski, and Yu. I. Polyanski. (Transl.: Edinburgh, Oliver and Boyd, 1961. Reprint: Jersey City, TFH Publications,).

10. Grabda, E., and Grabda, J. Masowa inwazja metacerkarii *Bucephalus polymorphus* Baer, 1827 W Oku Leszcza—*Abramis brama* (L.). [Mass incidence of *Bucephalus polymorphus* Baer, 1827 metacercariae in the eye of *Abramis brama* (L.).] *Wiad. parazytol. 13.* 1967.

11. Hickey, M. D., and Harris, J. R. Progress of the *Diphyllobothrium* epizootic at Poulaphouca Reservoir, Co. Wicklow, Ireland. *J. Helminthol. 22:* 13. 1947.

12. Hoffman, G. L. The life cycle of *Crassiphiala bulboglossa* (Trematoda: Strigeoidea), development of the metacercaria and cyst, and effect on the fish hosts. *J. Parasitol. 42:* 435. 1956.

13. Hoffman, G. L. Experimental studies on the cercaria and metacercaria of a strigeoid trematode, *Posthodiplostomum minimum. Exp. Parasitol. 7:* 23. 1958.

14. Hoffman, G. L. Studies on the life-cycle of *Ornithodiplostomum ptychocheilus* (Faust), (Trematoda: Strigeoidea) and the "self cure" of infected fish. *J. Parasitol. 44:* 416. 1958.

15. Hoffman, G. L. *Parasites of North American Freshwater Fishes.* 486 pp. Berkeley and Los Angeles, Univ. Calif. Press, 1967.

16. Hoffman, G. L.   Helminths and leeches affecting laboratory fishes, pp. 645–779. In *Parasites of Laboratory Animals,* ed. R. Flynn. 884 pp. Ames, Iowa State Univ. Press, 1973.

17. Hoffman, G. L., and Dunbar, C. E.   Mortality of eastern brook trout caused by plerocercoids (Cestoda: Pseudophyllidea: Diphyllobothriidae) in the heart and viscera. *J. Parasitol. 47:* 399. 1961.

18. Hoffman, G. L. and Dunbar, C. E.   Studies on *Neogogatea kentuckiensis* (Cable, 1935) n. comb. (Trematoda: Strigeoidea: Cyathocotylidae). *J. Parasitol. 49:* 737. 1963.

19. Hoffman, G. L., and Hoyme, J. B.   The experimental histopathology of the "tumor" on the brain of the stickleback caused by *Diplostomum baeri eucaliae* Hoffman and Hundley, 1957 (Trematoda: Strigeoidea). *J. Parasitol. 44:* 374. 1958.

20. Hoffman, G. L., and Hutcheson, J. A.   Unusual pathogenicity of a common metacercaria of fish. *J. Wildlife Dis. 6:* 109. 1970.

21. Hoffman, G. L., and Putz, R. E.   The black-spot (*Uvulifer ambloplitis:* Trematoda: Strigeoidea) of centrarchid fishes. *Trans. Amer. Fish. Soc. 94:* 143. 1965.

22. Hunter, G. W., III, and Hamilton, J. M.   Studies on host-parasite reactions to larval parasites. IV. The cyst of *Uvulifer ambloplitis* (Hughes). *Trans. Amer. Microscop. Soc. 60:* 498. 1941.

23. Hunter, G. W., III, and Hunter, W. S.   Studies on host-parasite reactions. V. The integumentary type of strigeid cyst. *Trans. Amer. Microscop. Soc. 61:* 134. 1942.

24. de Kinkelin, P., Tuffery, G., Leynaud, G., and Arrignon, J.   Étude épizootiologique de la bucéphalose larvaire *A Bucephalus polymorphus* (Baer, 1827) dans le peuplement piscicole du bassin de la Seine. *Rech. vet. (Paris) 1:* 77. 1968.

25. Larson, O. R.   *Diplostomulum* (Trematoda: Strigeoidea) associated with herniations of bullhead lenses. *J. Parasitol. 51:* 224. 1965.

26. Meyer, M. C.   Notes on *Philonema agubernaculum* and other related dracunculoids infecting salmonids. Sobretiro del libro homenaje al Doctor Eduardo Caballero y Caballero. *Caballero Jubilee Volume* 487. 1960.

27. Meyer, M. C., and Vik, R.   Observations on *Diphyllobothrium sebago* plerocercoids in the fish hosts. *Proc. Helminthol. Soc. Wash. 35:* 92. 1968.

28. Mitchum, D.   Diseases and Parasites of fish. *Wyoming Game and Fish Commission FW-3-R-12:* 6. 1965.

29. Mueller, J. F.   Cranial deformation in a fish resulting from intracranial parasitism by strigeid metacercariae. *J. Parasitol. 58:* 183. 1972.

30. Naumova, A. M.   Some forms of *Sanguinicola* infection of carp and its control. *Tr. vserossiyskogo nauch.-issled. inst. prudovogo ryb. khoz.* [Works All-Russian Inst. Pond Fish Cult. Res.] *10:* 153. 1961.

31. Reichenbach-Klinke, H.-H.   Untersuchungen über die bei Fischen durch Parasiten hervorgerufenen Zysten und deren Wirkung auf den Wirtskörper. *Z. Fisch. Hilfswiss. 3:* 565; *4:* 1. 1954–55.

32. Sogandares-Bernal, F., and Lumsden, R. D.   The heterophyid trematode *As-*

cocotyle (A.) leighi Burton, 1956, from the hearts of certain poicilid and cyprinodont fishes. *Z. Parasitenk. 24:* 3. 1964.

33. Spall, R. D., and Summerfelt, R. C.   Life cycle of the white grub, *Posthodiplostomum minimum* (MacCullum, 1921: Trematoda, Diplostomitidae), and observations on host-parasite relationships of the metacercaria in fish, p. 218. In *A Symposium on Diseases of Fishes and Shellfishes,* ed. S. F. Snieszko. Amer. Fish. Soc., Spec. Publ. No. 5. Washington, D.C., 1970.

34. Styczyńska-Jurewicz, E.   Expansion of cercariae of *Diplostomum spathaceum* Rud. 1819, a common parasite of fishes, in the littoral zone of the lake. *Pol. arch. hydrobiol. 19:* 105. 1959.

35. Szidat, L., and Nani, A.   Diplostomiasis cerebralis del pejerrey. Una grave epizootia que afecta a la economia nacional producida por larvas de trematodes que destruyen el cerebro de los pejerreyes. *Rev. Inst. nac. Invest. Cienc. Natur. 1:* 324. 1951.

DISCUSSION OF LESIONS DUE TO INTERNAL HELMINTHS

D. E. Hinton: We have been exposing channel catfish to methyl mercury and studying enzyme levels in liver and kidney homogenates. Some of our fish have been infected with parasites, and I wonder if there are any data that exist on the enzyme levels of organs in response to parasitic infection.

G. L. Hoffman: This is out of my field. I don't recall seeing any such titles in respect to parasitology, but hazily in the background of my memory are some similar things on mammalian work.

P. H. Cahn: There are very few reports on enzyme levels in fish in general, other than trout and maybe goldfish. I think you might find a bit of datum in the book *Fish in Research* by O. W. Neuhaus and J. E. Halver (1969). Also, such information might be found in the book *Chemical Biology of Fish.*

D. E. Hinton: The things that I am interested in are the early enzymes like aminopeptidase, of which the levels go up when there is scarring. I thought that maybe this enzyme might have been studied in relation to scar formation around the parasites.

H. Evans: I wonder if Dr. Hoffman can say anything about why certain species always seem to be more heavily parasitized than others? It seems to be the same species that are heavily infected even though there are five or six types of fish in the same area.

G. L. Hoffman: There is sometimes great host specificity in these infections and sometimes not. When there is, the parasites tend to seek out their own specific host. The host specificity goes all the way from no host specificity to very strict one-host species specificity.

Question: I wonder if one can distinguish a trematode egg from say a copepod egg in a histological section of fish tissue?

G. L. Hoffman: I think you have hit upon very difficult ground. We have been looking at some sections containing eggs and diagnosis is not easy. The miricidium with the large eye spot is easy, but if you had a trematode egg, any of hundreds of them, diagnosis would be very difficult, and sometimes it would be difficult to separate a trematode egg from a nematode egg. Dr. Ghittino from Italy has been working on one that causes damage in trout and sunfish. It is a *Capillaria* worm where the egg has a specific shape. Like *Capillaria hepatica* it has barrel-shaped eggs with opercular plugs at each end, so in tissue section that one is easy. Those are exceptions rather than rules.

6

Crustacean Parasites of Marine Fishes

FREDERICK G. SMITH

INTRODUCTION: THE CLASS CRUSTACEA

The class Crustacea includes all those arthropods that are mandibulate and have two pairs of antennae (2). Crustaceans are an important part of the food chain for most fishes and for man. They are important parasites of the skin and gills of marine fishes. They are among the largest fish parasites and can cause considerable damage to their hosts. They have been considered to be involved in the spread of lymphocystis disease (15), ichthyophonus (12), and to open the way for other secondary microbial infections. The biology of these parasites and a discussion of the direct injuries they cause follows. Structure rather than taxonomy will be emphasized.

Biology of the Branchiura

Within the Crustacea are four subclasses that have members parasitic on marine fishes. The first subclass to be considered here, Branchiura, has fewer than 150 species. All are parasitic on the skin of fishes (occasionally on amphibians) but may also invade the branchial cavity (11). These parasites are dorsoventrally flattened and are often referred to as fish lice. The carapace forms a wide shield over the head and along the thoracic segments (Fig. 6.1A). There is a pair of sessile, compound eyes. The first antennae and second maxillae have claws for gripping the host. A distinctive feature of the subclass (except in the freshwater genus *Dolops*) is the modification of the first maxillae into stalks that are tipped with suckers. These aid the movement of the parasite over the surface of the host. The

189

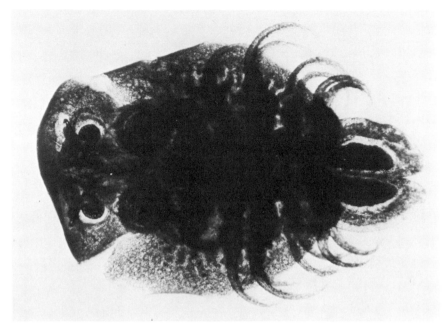

Fig. 6.1A.

Figs. 6.1A-D. Examples from each of the four subclasses of crustacean parasites of marine fish. *Argulus chesapeakensis* (A), *Ergasilus* sp. (B), *Chonchoderma virgatum* (C) and *Olencira praegustator* (D).

mouth is cone-shaped and equipped with a pre-oral sting. The sting is said to inject a toxin produced by a gland at its base (11). These parasites can swim from host to host and drop free of the host to lay their eggs. Most are less than 5 mm in length but can overwhelm a small fish, particularly if the parasite is present in large numbers.

Biology of the Copepoda

The subclass Copepoda contains about 5000 species worldwide, most of which are free-living. Copepods parasitic on marine fish can be divided into two groups, the cyclopids and the caligids. These two groups have distinct differences in mouth parts and life history (11). The cyclopids have small, pore-like mouths. The caligids have tube mouths armed with rasping mandibles. The cyclopids usually have a direct life cycle, while the caligids often depend on intermediate hosts and larvae with specialized frontal filaments to secure them to these hosts. Few animal groups have undergone such amazing parasitic adaptations as have the copepods. Some closely resemble their free-living relatives, but the more evolved species have developed great claws, projections of the carapace, **anterior segments** separated from the trunk by long thin "necks," interlocking "hands" at the end of long "arms," and even tethers which are inserted into the host at one end while

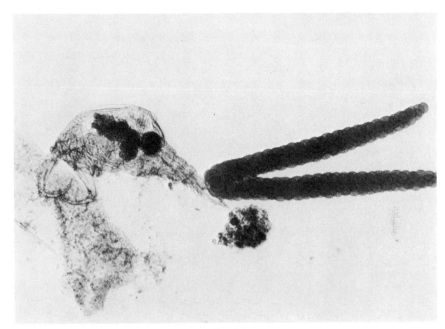

Fig. 6.1B.

the parasite dangles from the other end. A few are nearly featureless sacs deeply
embedded in the host tissues.

Biology of the Cirripedia

The Cirripedia are the barnacles. Kabata describes one parasitic barnacle and
one genus of commensal barnacle that causes damage to fish (11). All are stalked
barnacles. This stalk is a derivative of the first antennae. These barnacles retain
their feeding structures (cirri) and alimentary tract but have only vestiges of shell
plates (2). The parasitic barnacle, *Anelasma squalicola* (Loven), has absorptive
dendritic processes emanating from the embedded portion of the stalk. The commensal barnacles (*Chonchoderma* spp.) sometimes attach to marine fish. They
apparently do not receive nourishment from the host, but there is tissue damage
associated with the attachment (Fig. 6.1C).

Biology of the Malacostraca

The Malacostraca are the "higher" crustaceans. Parasites are found in the orders Amphipoda and Isopoda of this subclass. There are few parasitic Amphipoda
and they can be considered here as essentially the same as the parasitic isopods.
Isopods are usually large parasites, 1 to 4 cm in length. They have chitinous
plates over the dorsum of the body that may cover the seven pairs of legs
(peraeopods). The peraeopods may be prehensile appendages or swimming ap-

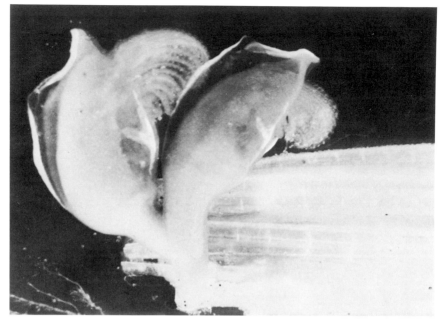

Fig. 6.1C.

Fig. 6.1D.

pendages (17). The mouth parts are biting or sucking structures in those isopods parasitic on marine fish. The female carries the developing young in a ventral brood pouch (marsupium). Some of the isopods are parasitic only in the juvenile stages and swim free of the host as adults. The majority are parasitic throughout their life (11, 17).

Parasite-Host Relationships

All crustacean parasites are involved with their hosts in three ways. Their first need is to establish and maintain contact with their host. They must attach, however loosely or securely, in order to begin their parasitic life. Most have evolved morphological "improvements" to aid them to this end. Many of the lesions seen are caused strictly by the parasite's attachment activity.

The second need is to feed, at the host's expense. The mouth parts tend to be of the biting-chewing kind or of the tube (sucking) kind in these parasites. Some have abandoned such primitive feeding structures entirely and absorb food directly through their body wall.

The third need is to reproduce. The previous activities provide the necessary energy sources for this function.

There is tissue damage in the host caused by one or a combination of these three activities, no matter which parasite is involved. The host in turn reacts to the presence of the parasite. The lesion ultimately seen by the pathologist is then a mixture of parasite damage and host reaction.

LESIONS ASSOCIATED WITH MAINTAINING CONTACT

Mere Presence

A part or all of the parasite's life must be spent in contact with the host on which it intends to feed. The parasite can be detrimental to the host simply by being there. The normal functioning of host structures can easily be disturbed, especially the fins, opercula (Fig. 6.2A), mouth (Fig. 6.1D), and lateral line canal (4). Pressure atrophy can often be seen in the tissues surrounding the larger crustacean parasites (Fig. 6.2B).

Attachment Structures

Host tissue damage results when the parasites utilize their own specialized attachment structures. The usual adaptations are prehensile structures, suckers, anchors inserted into or around the host tissues, and finally, entrance of the entire parasite into the host tissues. Some examples of each follow.

Prehensile Structures—Isopods. Many of the isopods depend entirely on prehensile peraeopods in order to attach to the host. These claws dig into the host tissues (Fig. 6.2A). The result is usually a localized destruction of the epidermis and an inflammatory response around the attachment. Mucus secretion may in-

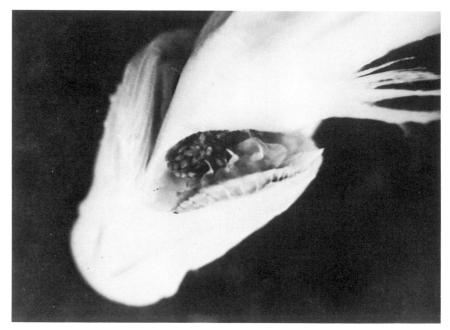

Fig. 6.2A.

Fig. 6.2. Prehensile attachment of *Lironeca ovalis* (A). The lesion which results (B). Attachment structures of two caligid copepods: *Naobranchia* sp. (C) and *Lernaeenicus radiatus* (D).

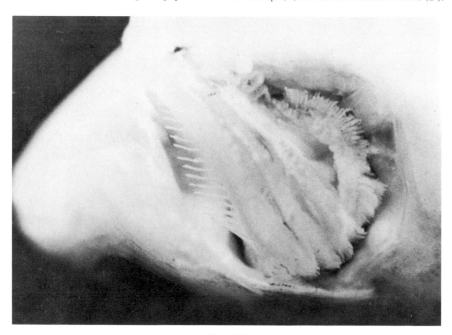

Fig. 6.2B.

Fig. 6.2C.

crease as epithelial mucous cells increase in number peripheral to the wound. Scaleless areas such as the fins, branchial cavity, or oral cavity are usually selected by these parasites. When the parasites attach in the branchial cavity, exuberant production of epithelial tissue can be stimulated. This may significantly reduce the effective respiratory area of the gills (Fig. 6.2B).

Prehensile Structures–Copepods. Some copepods, such as *Ergasilus* spp. and *Caligus* spp., have their second antennae modified into a strong claw. This is used to attach the parasite to the host (Fig. 6.1B). On the gills, proliferating tissue stimulated by the presence of the parasite may cover the respiratory surfaces. A few of these parasites on one host may be no problem at all, but a heavy infestation can damage so much of the respiratory tissue that it kills the host fish.

Prehensile attachment structures lend themselves to easy movement of the parasite. Many copepods and isopods make frequent shifts in position on the host and can cause a series of wounds by so doing.

Suckers. Suckers or sucker-like attachment structures are found in branchiurans (Fig. 6.1A) and in some caligid copepod parasites. These parasites are usually quite mobile but appear to cause little damage to the host with the sucker structures. The presence of the parasite may stimulate an increase in mucus production.

Fig. 6.2D.

Anchors and Entrance into Host. The final two categories of attachment are anchors and entrance of the complete parasite into the host. These are merely degrees of the same trend in parasitic evolution. Anchors are structures used by the parasite to secure a part of its body to the host, varying from the small frontal filament utilized by caligid copepods to nearly complete entrance of the parasite into the host, as in *Sphyrion* and *Lernaeenicus* spp. (Figs. 6.2D, 6.3A). Complete entrance into the host is known in only a few copepods and isopods.

Anchors and Entrance—Typical Lesion. Mechanical injury along the path of entrance of the anchor and encapsulation of this part of the parasite by the host is often seen. Between the connective tissue fibers of this capsule, one finds large (7 to 15 microns), nonphagocytic cells containing many distinct eosinophilic granules in the cytoplasm. These cells have a small dense nucleus which does not appear to be lobulate. These eosinophilic granulocytes presumably enter the tissues from the numerous capillaries that are present in the connective tissue adjacent to the parasites. Pressure caused by the presence of the parasites can lead to deformation or destruction of nearby tissues and organs.

Anchors—Clavellina and Barnacles. Around the attachment of the commensal barnacle, *Chonchoderma* sp. (Fig. 6.1C), and the frontal filament anchor (bulla)

Fig. 6.3A.

Fig. 6.3. Attachment of *Lernaeenicus radiatus*. The neck of the parasite is seen to the top (A); Hematoxylin and eosin (H&E); ×40. Host tissue adjacent to parasite (B); H&E; ×100. Damage resulting from the attachment and feeding of *Argulus chesapeakensis*. The epidermis has been penetrated at the bottom of this section (C); H&E; ×40. (D); H&E; ×100.

of the caligid copepods is found a connective tissue capsule. Epidermis may cover the attachment or be incomplete over the base of the stalk (1).

Anchors–Cephalothoracic. The cephalothoracic anchors found in copepods such as *Lernaeenicus radiatus* (Figs. 6.3A, 6.3B) and *Sphyrion lumpi* (16) are typically destructive attachments. Although the parasite is encapsulated where it enters the host, its movements continually aggravate the wound. Secondary infection of this wound by opportunistic microbial agents is seen in many cases. The area of necrotic tissue caused by the insertion and movement of the parasite can make the meat of an otherwise valuable fish all but worthless, and so these parasites are costly even if they do not kill the host.

Entrance. Very few of the crustacean parasites enter completely into the host tissue for attachment. *Artystone trysibia*, a freshwater isopod, is an example of one that does. It forms a blind sac by burrowing into the host at the base of a fin. The presence of the parasite causes atrophy of adjacent muscles and, to a lesser extent, the viscera. Inflammation with obvious swelling is observed initially as the parasite enters the host, but subsides by the 30th day of infestation (9).

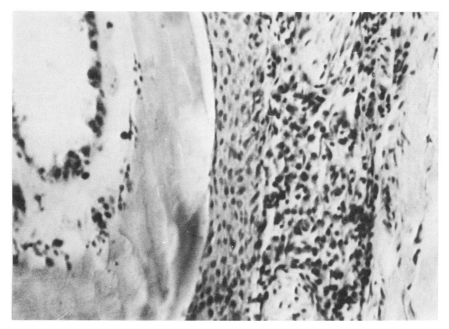

Fig. 6.3B.

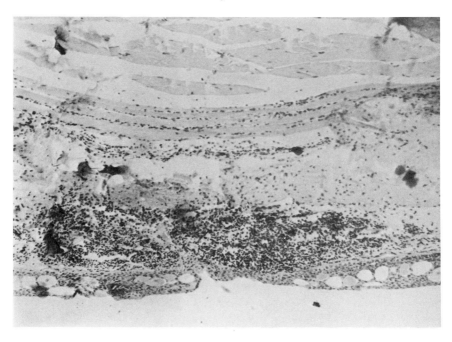

Fig. 6.3C.

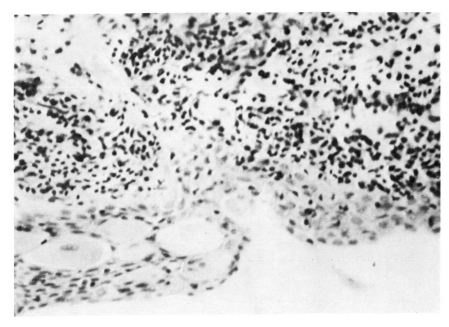

Fig. 6.3D.

LESIONS ASSOCIATED WITH PARASITE FEEDING

Grazing

The feeding activities of many of the crustacean parasites involve the shredding of the host's epidermis or branchial epithelium and ingestion of the debris thus produced. The parasites often move about as they feed. These activities also (1) stimulate mucus production, (2) stimulate epidermal proliferation, and (3) stimulate dilation of dermal capillaries. The products of the host's reactions may become part of the food utilized by the parasites. These parasites tend to feed in a zone around themselves.

Argulus spp. are typical of this group of parasites. They use an accessory feeding structure, the pre-oral sting, and their legs to abrade the host epidermis (11). Mucous cells increase in number in the epidermis peripheral to the wound. Mucus production increases and there are the signs of inflammation in the dermis beneath the wound (Figs. 6.3C, 6.3D).

External Digestion

External digestion is reported in ergasilid copepods and in *Argulus* spp. (11). These parasites secrete products which digest the host tissues and thus enable the parasites to ingest material which could not otherwise be taken in through their small mouths. The digestive secretions apparently cause a significant amount of damage to the host's tissues.

Blood

Direct ingestion of the host's blood is reported in the gnathid isopods. The juvenile stages of these parasites engorge themselves. The adults are free-living and do not feed (17). Copepods such as *S. lumpi* and *Lernaeenicus* spp. are known to take in blood from the engorged capillaries and from the tissue spaces that are found around the anchor of the parasites (11). The cumulative effect of three or four of these parasites can so weaken, waste, and disfigure a fish that it loses its commercial value.

Direct Absorption

Only one crustacean parasite of marine fish is known to absorb nutrition directly from the host through absorptive processes. *A. squalicola*, the barnacle parasitic on sharks, apparently obtains nutrition directly from the host through dendritic processes extending from the base of its attachment stalk (7).

LESIONS ASSOCIATED WITH REPRODUCTION OF PARASITES

There are a few instances where damage to the host is related directly to reproductive activities of the parasites. A marked increase in the size of the parasite may be seen with the development of egg strings (Figs. 6.1B, 6.2C, 6.3A) or with the development of a marsupium full of juvenile isopods (Fig. 6.2A). This can significantly increase the pressure atrophy caused by the presence of the parasites. The long egg strings seen on *L. radiatus* add to the hydrodynamic resistance the host must overcome in swimming and indirectly aggravate the wound at the site of entrance.

Argulus is an example of a species of parasite that drops free of the host to lay its eggs. This will probably carry the parasite away from the individual it originally parasitized and eventually lead it to another individual. This reproduction-related activity increases the chance that the parasite will serve as a vector for microbial parasites such as hematozoans. This has not been proven.

There are other even less direct effects of reproductive activity of the parasite, for example those due to changes in attachment or in feeding that relate to maturation of the parasite. An example might be *Phrixocephalus cincinnatus*. It enters the choroid layer of the eye of the host as a juvenile form. Later, as it matures it inserts its trunk back through the chambers of the eye and out through the cornea (10). The advantage gained by this is apparently that the egg strings are outside the host and can be released easily, but the host's eye is damaged.

SUMMARY

Most lesions are related to attachment, feeding and/or reproductive activity of the parasite. The effects are usually localized; pressure atrophy often accompanies the presence of the larger parasites. The host response typically is increased mucus production, inflammation, and encapsulation of those portions of the parasite that enter the host. The lesions and wasting may lead to economic losses in commercial species of fish.

REFERENCES

1. Balakrishnan, K. P. Observations on the occurrence of *Choncoderma virgatum* (Spengler) (Cirripedia) on *Diodon hystrix* Linnaeus (Pisces). *Crustaceana* *16*(1): 101–103. 1969.
2. Barnes, R. D. *Invertebrate Zoology*. 632 pp. Philadelphia, Saunders, 1963.
3. Causey, D. Parasitic copepods of Texas coastal fishes. *Texas U. Inst. Mar. Sci. 3*(1): 7–16. 1953.
4. Cressey, R.F., and Collette, B. B. Copepods and needlefishes: A study in host-parasite relationships. *Fish. Bull. 68*(3): 347–432. 1970.
5. Green, J. *The Biology of Crustacea*. 180 pp. Chicago, Quadrangle Books, 1963.
6. Hastings, R. W. The barnacle, *Chonchoderma virgatum* (Spengler), in association with the isopod, *Neurocila acuminata* Schioedte and Meinert, and the orange filefish, *Alutera schoepfi* (Walbaum). *Crustaceana 22*(3): 273–278. 1972.
7. Hickling, C. F. On the small deep-sea shark *Etmopterus spinax* L. and its cirripede parasite, *Anelasma squalicola* (Loven). *J. Linn. Soc. London,* Zool. *45:* 17–24. 1963.
8. Hoffman, G. L. *Parasites of North American Freshwater Fishes.* 486 pp. Berkeley and Los Angeles, Univ. Calif. Press, 1967.
9. Huizinga, H. W. Pathobiology of *Artystone trysibia* Schioedte (Isopoda: Cymothoidae), an endoparasitic isopod of South American freshwater fishes. *Wildlife Dis. 8*(3): 225–232. 1972.
10. Kabata, Z. *Phrixocephalus cincinnatus* Wilson, 1908 (Copepods, Lernaeoceridae): Morphology, metamorphosis and host-parasite relationship. *J. Fish. Res. Board Can. 26*(4): 921–934. 1969.
11. Kabata, Z. *Crustacea as Enemies of Fishes,* book 1, 171 pp. In *Diseases of Fishes,* ed. S. F. Snieszko and H. R. Axelrod. Jersey City, T.F.H. Publications, 1970.
12. Mann, H. Copepoda and Isopoda as parasites of marine fishes, pp. 177–189. In *A Symposium on Diseases of Fishes and Shellfishes,* ed. S. F. Snieszko. Amer. Fish. Soc., Spec. Publ. No. 5. Washington, D.C., 1970.
13. Menzies, R. J., and Frankenberg, D. *Handbook of the Common Marine Isopod Crustacea of Georgia.* 93 pp. Athens, Univ. Georgia Press, 1966.

14. Miner, R. W. *Field Book of Seashore Life.* 888 pp. New York, Putnam, 1950.

15. Nigrelli, R. F. Virus and tumors in fishes. *Ann. N. Y. Acad. Sci. 54:* 1076–1092. 1952.

16. Nigrelli, R. F., and Firth, F. E. On *Sphyrion lumpi* (Kroyer) a copepod parasite on the redfish, *Sebastes marinus* (Linnaeus), with special reference to the host-parasite relationships. *Zoologica (New York) 24*(1): 1–10 and plates I–IV. 1939.

17. Schultz, George A. *How to Know the Marine Isopod Crustaceans.* 359 pp. Dubuque, Iowa, W. C. Brown, 1969.

18. Sindermann, C. J. *Principal Diseases of Marine Fish and Shellfish.* 369 pp. New York and London, Academic Press, 1970.

19. Wilson, C. B. The copepods of the Woods Hole region, Massachusetts. *U. S. Nat. Mus. Bull. 158:* 1–635. 1932.

DISCUSSION OF CRUSTACEAN PARASITES OF MARINE FISH

V. H. Logan: Recently we obtained an ocean sunfish, *Mola mola,* which has rather unusual skin in that it has denticles just beneath the epidermis and also a greatly thickened collagenous dermis, and on this particular specimen there were two crustacean parasites. We haven't identified them yet, but they had gone through the dermis. You mentioned that crustaceans were often found in scaled areas. Have you ever run across any which have gone through very tough skin such as this, and if so was it associated with the feeding by the crustaceans?

F. G. Smith: No, I have not seen any marine crustacean that carried the feeding to the extent that it actually penetrated completely through the epidermis. Some of the parasites are covered by the hyperplastic response of the epithelium, but they have not actually entered within the host.

V. H. Logan: There was one position on the ventral surface of the fish I mentioned where the parasite had gone right through 4 to 5 cm of this type of tissue.

L. T. Hunt: I have seen toadfish which had a rather heavy parasite infestation around the eyes so that the cornea had become opaque. I wondered if this could have been done by an *Argulus* sp. Could you comment on it?

F. G. Smith: I believe that is certainly within the realm of what *Argulus* could do. I don't think it is typical to see that at all. It is not typical in those marine fish which we find in our Georgia coastal area with *Argulus* infection. The pre-oral sting is used freely by the parasites and they have a rather active feeding behavior; they use those swimming legs freely, so they can be quite damaging. I don't believe they select the eye. It would probably be a chance occurrence in this case. There are some copepod parasites that prefer the areas adjacent to the eye, but not *Argulus,* though.

H. W. Huizinga: In general, with crustaceans do repeated exposures stimulate an immune response that might be functional in preventing subsequent infections?

F. G. Smith: I will have to say I don't know. There are some comments in the literature about the resistance of different ages of fish and the ability to accept new parasites. I think copepods are studied most in this regard, but I don't know of specific studies of immunological response.

7

Parasites in Tissue Sections:
Recognition and Reaction

G. E. COSGROVE

During the course of histological or histopathological examinations of the tissues and organs of fish it is a common occurrence to encounter portions of zooparasites. In many instances the remainder of the fish has been discarded, so a return to the carcass to dissect out the parasite for identification is not possible. Therefore, if a tentative or more detailed opinion on the identity of the parasite is desired, it must be attained by studying the available slide preparations.

In fish the problem is especially complex because of the tremendous number of species of parasites that are known to occur. Most of the thoroughly studied fish species have extensive parasite faunas, and there are many other fishes that have been studied little if at all. An idea of the complexity of fish parasitology can be gained by a look at Yamaguti's (1958-63) massive *Systema Helminthum* (23), where, in Volume 1, 366 text pages are required to describe fish Digenea; in Volume 2, Cestoda, 150 pages for fish parasites; in Volume 3, Nematoda, 74 pages; Volume 4, Monogenea and Aspidogastrea, 318 pages; and Volume 5, Acanthocephala, is not divided by host, but approximately a third of the more than 150 text pages deal with fish parasites. Yamaguti's volume *Parasitic Copepoda and Branchiura of Fishes* (24) has 334 text pages. The aquatic media in which fish live apparently favor the completion of parasite cycles and simplify survival problems of parasitic species.

Here we will deal with some of the questions of identification that the histopathologist must answer in making diagnoses on fish tissues.

205

PROBLEMS IN ZOOPARASITE IDENTIFICATION

Is a parasite or parasite by-product present in the tissue?

Considerable difficulty is often encountered in answering this preliminary question. First, pseudoparasites of various kinds have to be differentiated from true parasites. Pseudoparasites may be present originally in the fish tissue or may be introduced during subsequent processing. There are also nonzoological parasites, such as viruses, bacteria, and plants, that occur in fish tissues with or without lesions. Furthermore, the reaction of the host to a parasite or some other pathogen often obscures the etiological agent by such processes as inflammation, hemorrhage, encapsulation, granuloma formation, foreign-body reaction, fibrosis, scarring, calcification, metaplasia, or neoplasia. Experience and familiarity with the various forms of tissue parasites are the greatest aids in solving this and subsequent problems. Helpful techniques include deeper cuts in the block if available, and sometimes the use of special stains or electron microscopy. Many of the considerations below are also important factors in determining the actual presence of a zooparasite.

Is the morphology of the parasite so adequately represented that a diagnosis of its type can be made?

The first step here is an attempt to determine the major zoological affinity of the parasite. Is it protozoan or metazoan? If it is metazoan, can it be identified as a trematode, cestode, nematode, arthropod, mollusc, or as belonging to another major category? This step and the subsequent steps toward genus or species identification require various degrees of familiarity with the morphological characteristics of the members of the various phyla, classes, orders, etc., in the parasite fauna. The degree of familiarity, i.e., skill as a parasite morphologist, will determine at what level of identification we are forced to stop. Since most pathologists are not expert parasitologists, we probably will do well to determine the major grouping of a tissue parasite (e.g., trematode). Certainly, if we were to see the whole parasite dissected out and prepared suitably, diagnosis to this level would usually be easy. However, in tissue preparations we often have only a small fragment of the parasite. If this fragment contains some relatively characteristic structure or portion of a structure, diagnosis is greatly simplified.

The second step involves more processes of elimination. The portion of parasite in tissue may be from any stage in the life cycle—adult, larva or nymph, ovum, cyst, etc. This considerably complicates diagnosis in some ways, since our range of familiarity must be extended to these stages as well as the adult stage. Often larvae and nymphs are more difficult to identify than adults of the same species even when one has the whole specimen. Ova and cysts, however, can be very helpful when they are found in tissues, since they are small enough for much more of their total structure to be represented in a tissue cut. The level of success in identifying a parasite type depends on the examiner's familiarity with parasites and their stages and on the suitability and adequacy of the material in section.

Can the condition of the parasite in the tissue be determined?

So far we have assumed that the parasite in the tissue was alive or very freshly dead and nonautolyzed at the time of sampling. However, anyone who examines tissues for parasites frequently encounters deteriorated parasites, and this complicates diagnosis. For one thing, the parasite has lost many of its characteristics, perhaps leaving only some telltale persistent remnants, or nothing but a host reaction. Another complication is that dead parasites often produce more violent host reactions than living ones, and this tends to obscure the remaining diagnostic features.

What are the sources of helpful information on the identity of zooparasites in fish tissues?

If possible, consultation with specialists in fish pathology or with specialists in parasite taxonomy who are also experienced in looking at tissue lesions would be a desirable step. Many of the major aquatic biology laboratories have such people, and others can be identified by perusal of appropriate literature. Such persons and institutions often have reference collections of typical lesions. The development of registries of comparative pathology, such as those at the Smithsonian Institution and the Armed Forces Institute of Pathology in Washington, D.C., has been very helpful.

In recent years there have appeared a number of good texts on fish diseases, which are excellent sources of information on the pathology of fish parasites (1, 5, 8, 16, 18-20). Reichenbach-Klinke and Elkan include much parasitology in their text on lower vertebrate diseases (15). Some of the more parasitologically oriented texts which are valuable for the pathology included are listed in the attached references (2, 3, 7, 9, 14).

More elaborate descriptions of helminths in tissues are generally found in texts of human tropical medicine, such as Marcial-Rojas (12), or texts of veterinary medicine, such as Smith and Jones (17). Three valuable articles on the recognition of helminths in tissues are those of Hopps and Price (10), Margolis (13) on fish nematodes with a review of fish parasitic pathology, and Williams, McVicar, and Ralph (22), concerning the fish alimentary canal as a site for parasites. The anatomy of the various helminths likely to be encountered is described in texts of parasitology, in Hyman's texts on the invertebrates (11), and more specifically in Chitwood and Chitwood for nematodes (4), Dawes for trematodes (6), and Wardle and McLeod for cestodes (21).

SOME TYPES OF ZOOPARASITES FOUND IN TISSUE SECTIONS

Protozoans

The protozoans found in tissue sections may represent freely motile, surface-inhabiting forms such as amebas, ciliates, or flagellates, which may or may not cause epithelial damage by their activities, feeding, or structural characteristics (Figs. 7.1-7.4). Some motile forms can invade tissues at times. In general, however, the most pathogenic protozoans are the sporozoans. These form cysts in tissues or cells, resulting in enlargement, inflammation, or hyperplasia, as can be seen with microsporidians and myxosporidians (Figs. 7.5–7.7). There are also blood-inhabiting protozoans, such as haemosporidians and trypanosomes, which are not easily seen in tissue sections.

Trematodes: Monogenea

These trematodes are usually surface or gill parasites and have well-developed attachment structures, such as hooks, clamps, and suckers, which are often partly visible in section (Figs. 7.8–7.10) and may be uniquely adapted to the attachment site. The parasite often remains attached through the process of tissue fixation, and the attachment sites vary from relatively undamaged (Figs. 7.8–7.10) to badly scarred and inflamed areas with distorted gill or epithelial anatomy. The internal structure is rather complicated, with variable genital and alimentary development similar to that seen in Digenea (Fig. 7.11).

Trematodes: Digenea

Larval forms of these parasites are frequently encountered in the tissues of fish. They are usually terminal larval stages, so the trematode morphology is often obvious, with suckers, cuticle, genital primordia, alimentary canal, etc. (Figs. 7.12–7.14). However, some of the strigeid larvae are relatively featureless and resemble larval tapeworms (Fig. 7.15). The larva may be encapsulated in a cyst (Figs. 7.13, 7.14) and may cause marked tissue reaction (Fig. 7.12) or may be free, with no obvious reaction (Fig. 7.15). Adults may be encysted in tissues with or without inflammatory reaction (Fig. 7.16). They are also commonly found in hollow viscera, such as the alimentary and biliary tracts (Figs. 7.17–7.19), where there may or may not be damage at the attachment sites. The degree of damage is partially related to the permanence of attachment. Adults have complex internal genital-alimentary anatomy seen to some degree in sections, and portions of suckers are often seen.

Cestodes

In fish, cestodes are most frequently encountered in larval forms that vary from a loosely structured, partially fluid-filled sac (Fig. 7.20) to a dense, solid immature worm (Fig. 7.21). Unless a portion of the scolex is present (Fig. 7.22), the worm is relatively featureless. The scolex with inverted or everted suckers or holdfasts is very prominent. Sometimes immature worms are found in the alimentary tract, apparently shortly after release from an intermediate host (Fig. 7.23). Immature worms in tissue are often responsible for an encapsulation or inflammatory reaction (Fig. 7.24). Adult worms are much easier to identify, because of the segmentation and development of genital structures in each proglottid (Fig. 7.25). The caryophyllids, however, are not segmented, and they resemble trematodes in tissue except that they never have a ventral sucker or an alimentary tract (Fig. 7.26). The attachment sites of adult cestodes may be much damaged, with ulceration, inflammation, and scarring (Fig. 7.26).

Nematodes

Sectioned in the proper plane, the long, slender nematode shape can be seen in a longitudinal cut (Figs. 7.27, 7.28); cross sections are usually rounded (Figs. 7.29, 7.30). The external cuticle is generally obvious and may bear alae, ridges, or spines. Internally, parts of intestinal and genital tracts are often encountered (Figs. 7.29, 7.30). The lateral chords and body-wall muscle cells vary in different genera but usually are present to some degree. There may be a pronounced tissue reaction of encapsulation around the parasite, especially when it is degenerating (Figs. 7.27, 7.31).

Acanthocephalans

This group of pathogenic fish parasites is characterized anatomically by a spiny proboscis, the lack of an alimentary canal, well-developed gonadal structures with separate sexes, and a thick, layered body covering (Figs. 7.32–7.34). The larvae occur in cysts in tissue, and reaction may be minimal (Fig. 7.34) unless the worm dies. Adults are usually parasites of the alimentary canal, and the attachment sites of the very damaging proboscis are the seat of prominent lesions.

Copepods

These are arthropods and have the more complex anatomy of that group. Striated muscles are often seen, and the chitinous surface and appendages may be obvious (Fig. 7.35) except in some highly modified forms. Copepods are usually gill and surface parasites and vary from freely moving to immovably anchored forms. The anchoring appendages are often extremely complex and deeply penetrating, with concomitant severe tissue damage. If they do remain at one site for a time, tissue damage occurs (Figs. 7.36–7.38).

Acknowledgment. Research sponsored by the U.S. Atomic Energy Commission under contract with the Union Carbide Corporation.

REFERENCES

1. Amlacher, E. *Textbook of Fish Diseases,* transl. D. A. Conroy and R. L. Herman. 302 pp. Jersey City, T.F.H. Publications, 1970.
2. Baer, J. G. *Ecology of Animal Parasites.* 224 pp. Urbana, Univ. Illinois Press, 1952.
3. Cheng, T. G. *The Biology of Animal Parasites.* 727 pp. Philadelphia, Saunders, 1964.

4. Chitwood, B. G., and Chitwood, M. B. *An Introduction to Nematology.* 213 pp. Published by the authors, 1950.
5. Davis, H. S. *Culture and Diseases of Game Fishes.* 332 pp. Berkeley, Univ. Calif. Press, 1961.
6. Dawes, B. *The Trematoda.* 644 pp. Cambridge, Cambridge Univ. Press, 1956.
7. Dogiel, V. A. 1964. *General Parasitology,* transl. Z. Kabata, 516 pp. Edinburgh, Oliver and Boyd, 1962.
8. Goldstein, R. *Diseases of Aquarium Fishes.* 126 pp. Jersey City, T.F.H. Publications, 1971.
9. Hoffman, G. L. *Parasites of North American Freshwater Fishes.* 486 pp. Berkeley and Los Angeles, Univ. Calif. Press, 1967.
10. Hopps, H. C., and Price, D. L. Introduction. Parasitic disease–general considerations, including ecology and geographic distribution, pp. 1–54. In *Pathology of Protozoal and Helminthic Diseases,* ed. R. A. Marcial-Rojas. Baltimore, Williams & Wilkins, 1971.
11. Hyman, L. H. *The Invertebrates.* Vol. 2, *Platyhelminthes and Rhynchocoela,* 550 pp. Vol. 3, *Acanthocephala, Aschelminthes and Entroprocta,* 572 pp. 5 vols. New York, McGraw-Hill, 1940–59.
12. Marcial-Rojas, R. A., ed. *Pathology of Protozoal and Helminthic Diseases.* 1010 pp. Baltimore, Williams & Wilkins, 1971.
13. Margolis, L. Nematode diseases of marine fishes, pp. 190–208. In *A Symposium on Diseases of Fishes and Shellfishes,* ed. S. F. Snieszko, Amer. Fish. Soc., Spec. Publ. No. 5. Washington, D.C., 1970.
14. Noble, E. R., and Noble, G. A. *Parasitology.* 617 pp. Philadelphia, Lea & Febiger, 1971.
15. Reichenbach-Klinke, H.-H., and Elkan, E. *The Principal Diseases of Lower Vertebrates.* 600 pp. London and New York, Academic Press, 1965.
16. Sindermann, C. J. *Principal Diseases of Marine Fish and Shellfish.* 369 pp. New York and London, Academic Press, 1970.
17. Smith, H. A., and Jones, T. C. *Veterinary Pathology.* 1192 pp. Philadelphia, Lea & Febiger, 1966.
18. Snieszko, S. F., ed. *A Symposium on Diseases of Fishes and Shellfishes.* 526 pp. Amer. Fish. Soc., Spec. Publ. No. 5. Washington, D.C., 1970.
19. Snieszko, S. F., and Axelrod, H. R., eds. *Diseases of Fishes.* Book 1, Z. Kabata, *Crustacea as Enemies of Fishes,* 171 pp. Book 3, S. Sarig, *The Prevention and Treatment of Diseases of Warmwater Fishes under Subtropical Conditions with Special Emphasis on Intensive Fish Farming,* 127 pp. Jersey City, T.F.H. Publications, 1971.
20. Van Duijn, C., Jr. *Diseases of Fishes.* 309 pp. London, Iliffe Books, 1967.
21. Wardle, R. A., and McLeod, J. A. *The Zoology of Tapeworms.* 780 pp. Minneapolis, Univ. Minn. Press, 1952.
22. Williams, H. H., McVicar, A., and Ralph, R. The alimentary canal of fish as an environment for helminth parasites, pp. 43–77. In *Aspects of Fish Parasitology,* ed. A. E. R. Taylor and R. Muller. (*Symp. Brit. Soc. Parasitol.* 8.) Oxford, Blackwell, 1970.

23. Yamaguti, S. *Systema Helminthum*. Vol. 1, *The Digenetic Trematodes of Vertebrates*, 1575 pp. Vol. 2, *The Cestodes of Vertebrates*, 860 pp. Vol. 3, *The Nematodes of Vertebrates*, 1261 pp. Vol. 4, *Monogenea and Aspidocotylea*, 699 pp. Vol. 5, *Acanthocephala*, 423 pp. New York, Wiley, Interscience, 1958–63.
24. Yamaguti, S. *Parasitic Copepoda and Branchiura of Fishes*. 1104 pp. New York, Wiley, Interscience, 1963.

DISCUSSION OF PARASITES IN TISSUE SECTIONS

M. M. Sigel: I am fascinated by the variation in the presence or absence of the host response to the obvious foreign body. You have shown us beautiful examples of this phenomenon. I would like to ask you or any others in the audience to try to explain this lack of reaction. It is said that even invertebrates recognize foreignness, and the aggregation of cells in sponges and coelenterates is governed by the principle of recognition of self and nonself. Here in fishes you have examples of major infestation in vital tissues with absence of host reaction.

G. E. Cosgrove: The capsule that forms around the parasite is apparently relatively permeable to some substances but not to others and this may have something to do with the phenomenon. The parasite can be present in viable form and the host often doesn't seem to recognize that any foreign body is there, but when the parasites die, then the reaction starts. Others here may like to say something about that from the immunological viewpoint.

K. Balogh: As a human pathologist one cannot help ask the same questions. Perhaps I could add some answers to your question. One of course is that the reaction depends on whether the parasite is dead or alive. The other would be the length of time that has passed since the parasite entered the organism. Another possibility might be the endocrine status of the animal. In humans, for instance, you can ward off the connective tissue response by giving corticosteroid hormones. Furthermore, we haven't heard anything about the nutritional status and the immunological status of these fish. These are all factors that influence very markedly the response of tissue in human and other vertebrates.

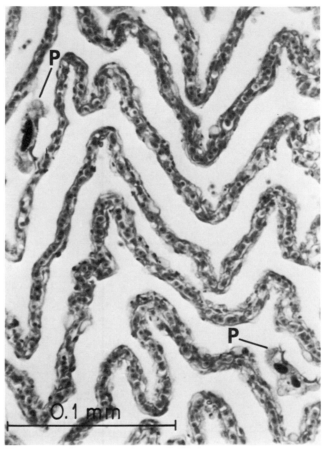

Fig. 7.1. Section from the gill of a puffer, showing two trichodinid ciliates (P) on side view. The concave attaching disc is well shown, as are portions of the dark-staining nucleus. No tissue damage is evident.

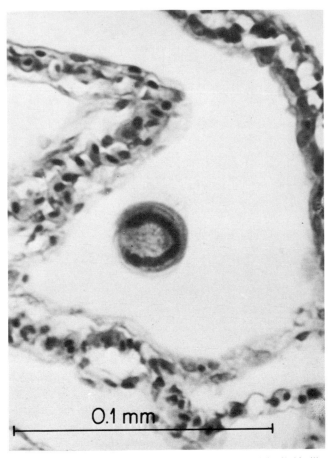

Fig. 7.2. Section from the gill of an American eel, containing a trichodinid ciliate in surface view. The horseshoe-shaped nucleus is well shown. No obvious tissue damage is seen.

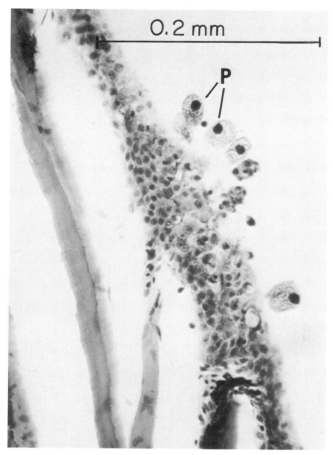

Fig. 7.3. Section of skin from an aquarium-maintained *Brachydanio*. The fishes had fuzzy greyish patches on skin and gills and mortality was high. There are many flagellates (*Costia?*) (P) on and in the skin, which is inflamed and hyperplastic.

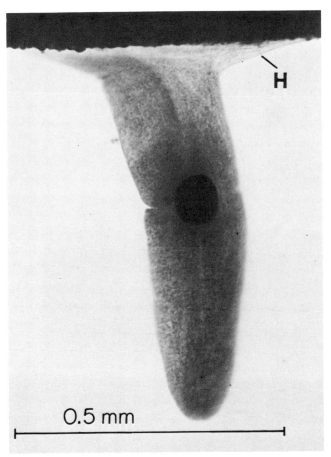

Fig. 7.4. Gill filament of *Fundulus* with an attached dinoflagellate (*Oodinium*). Note the foot-like holdfast (H).

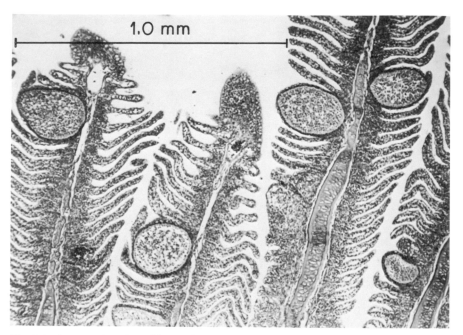

Fig. 7.5. Section of gill from *Hypentelium,* showing four cysts of myxosporidian protozoans. The invaded filaments are distorted. There are other thickened, fused gill lesions that may be the result of parasite invasion.

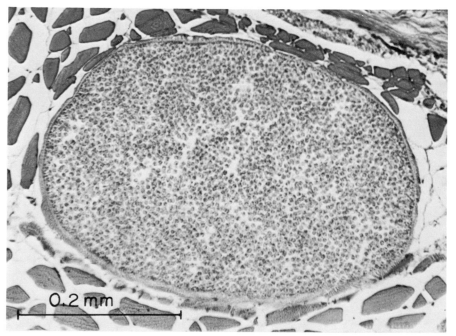

Fig. 7.6. Section of body-wall muscle from a mullet, showing a large myxosporidian cyst. There is no apparent surrounding inflammation.

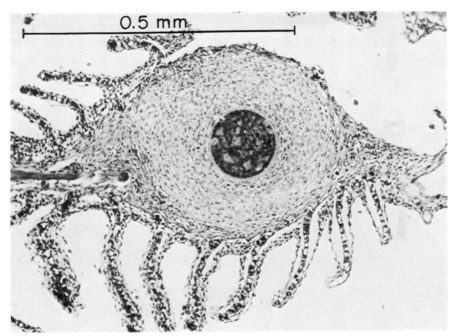

Fig. 7.7. Section of gill from a catfish, showing a central sporozoan (?) surrounded by a broad reaction zone of granulomatous tissue.

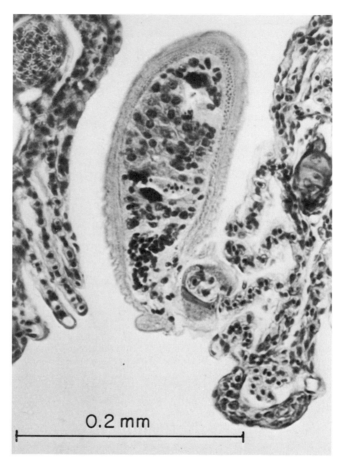

Fig. 7.8. Section of gill from a needlefish, showing an attached monogenetic trematode. *Ancyrocephalus*. The opisthaptor hooks are holding a gill lamella, which appears relatively undamaged.

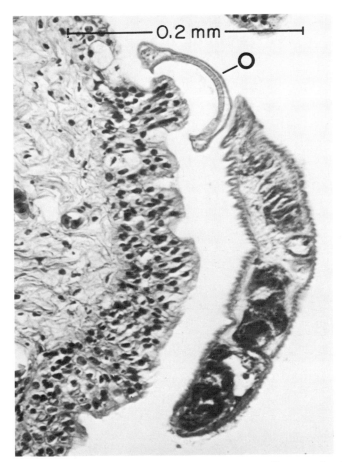

Fig. 7.9. Section of nasal mucosa of a South African clawed frog, *Xenopus*, showing a monogenetic trematode, *Gyrdicotylus*, attached by the concave hooked opisthaptor (O). The mucosa appears pinched but otherwise undamaged.

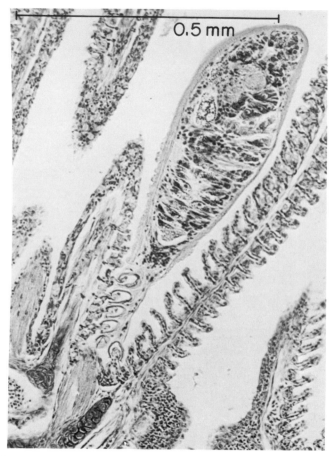

Fig. 7.10. Section from the gill of a needlefish, showing an attached monogenetic trematode, *Nudaciraxine*. This is a monocotylid, and the small clamp-like posterior suckers each attach to a separate gill lamella.

Fig. 7.11. Whole mount of a monocotylid monogenetic trematode. Note the elongated posterior opisthaptor (O) with many small clamp-like suckers. Note also the complex viscera composed chiefly of gonads and accessory gonadal structure.

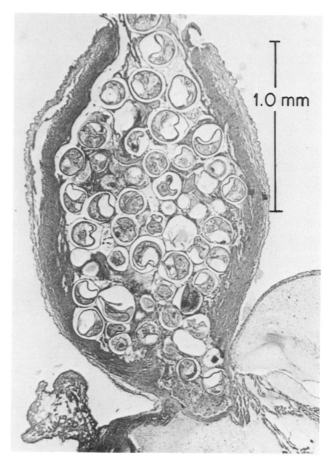

Fig. 7.12. Mass of encysted larval trematodes (*Ascocotyle* sp.) in the bulbus arteriosis of the heart of a green molly.

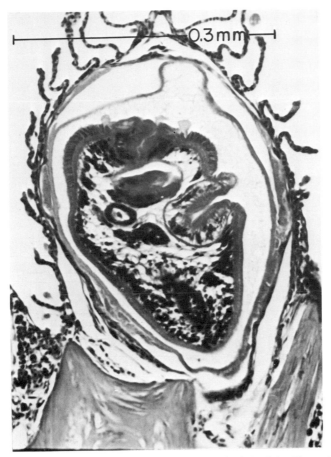

Fig. 7.13. Larval digenetic trematode in a cyst in the gill of a flyingfish. The suckers and portions of the alimentary canal are visible.

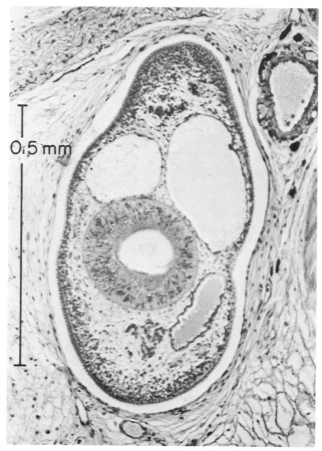

Fig. 7.14. Immature digenetic trematode in a thin-walled cyst in the connective tissue of *Umbra*. The large ventral sucker and branches of alimentary and genital tracts are easily seen.

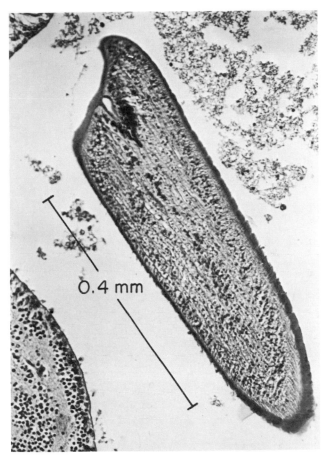

Fig. 7.15. Larval strigeid trematode in the ventricle of the brain of *Umbra*. It is relatively featureless in the plane of cut and difficult to differentiate from a larval cestode.

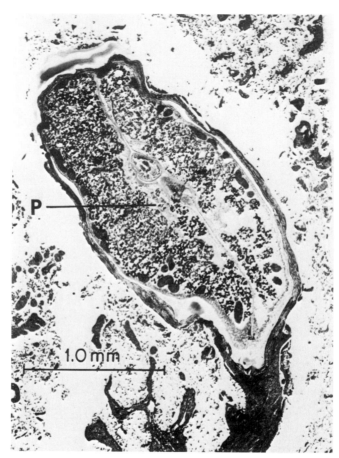

Fig. 7.16. Portion of a didymozoid trematode (P) in a fold of the stomach mucosa of *Euthynnus*. The chief feature is the abundance and complexity of female genital structures and contained ova.

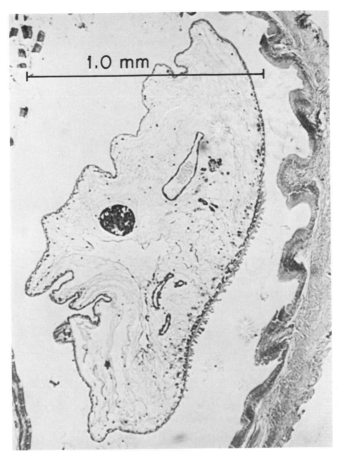

Fig. 7.17. Digenetic trematode in the gallbladder of a freshwater catfish. Branches of the alimentary canal and one gonad are present. This is a very weakly muscled and loosely structured worm.

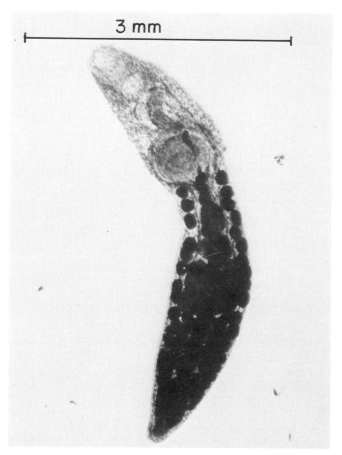

Fig. 7.18. Whole mount of a digenetic trematode, *Bucephalopsis* sp., from the intestine of *Strongylura.* The complexity of internal structure is obvious.

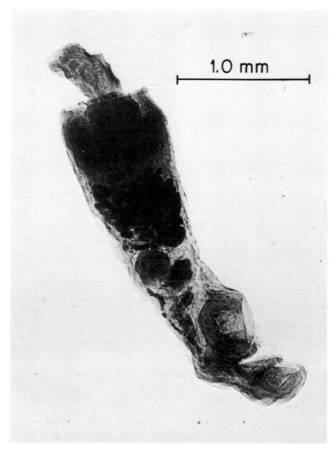

Fig. 7.19. Whole mount of an adult hemiurid trematode from the intestine of a marine fish, again showing the complexity of internal structure.

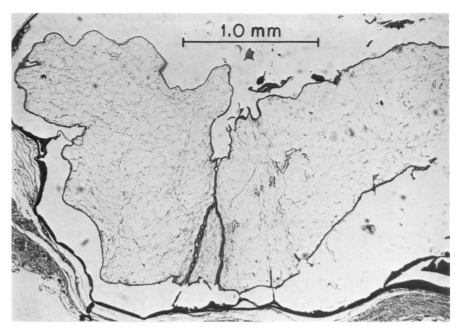

Fig. 7.20. Larval cestode in a cyst in the serosa of an ocean fish. The interior is filled with loose, watery tissue, and no organs can be seen.

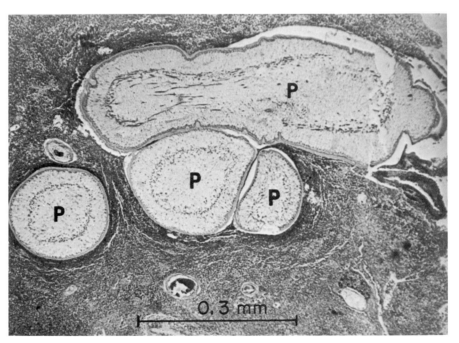

Fig. 7.21. Portions of larval cestode, *Proteocephalus* sp. (P), in the liver of a smallmouth bass. The interior shows no prominent structures. The muscle bundles are seen in thin bands.

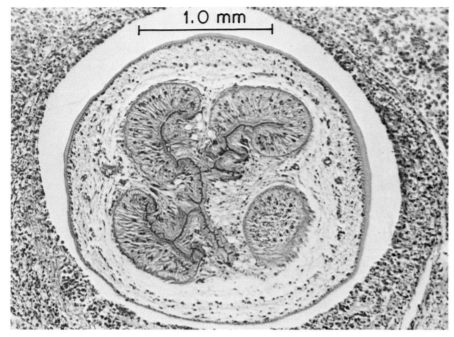

Fig. 7.22. Invaginated scolex of a larval cestode, *Proteocephalus* sp., in the liver of a small-mouth bass. The four muscular suckers are evident.

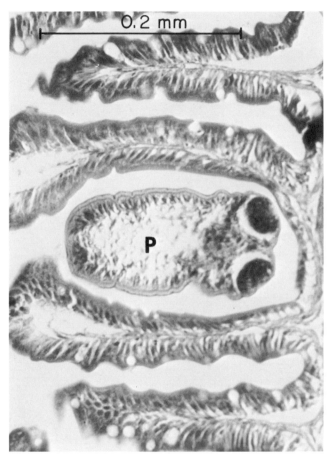

Fig. 7.23. Very immature cestode (P), probably just released by digestion from a cyst in an intermediate host, in the intestine of a silverside. Note the prominent suckers and the lack of segmentation.

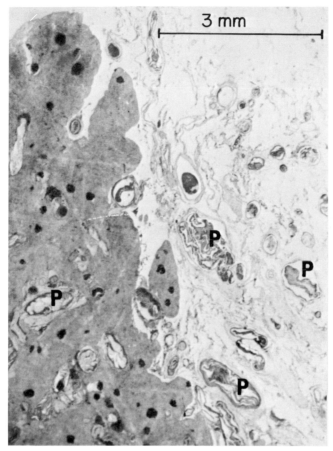

Fig. 7.24. Liver and adjacent serosa with fibrous adhesions from a smallmouth bass, containing cysts with larval *Proteocephalus* (P). Most of the worms are dead and degenerated, which has resulted in inflammation, granuloma formation, scarring, and adhesions.

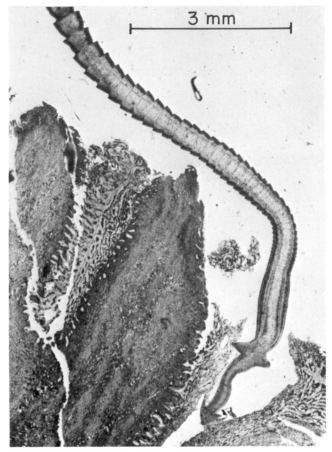

Fig. 7.25. Mature, reproducing tapeworm, *Marsipometra* sp., attached to the intestine of *Polyodon* by the anvil-shaped scolex. The segmented strobila is free in the lumen.

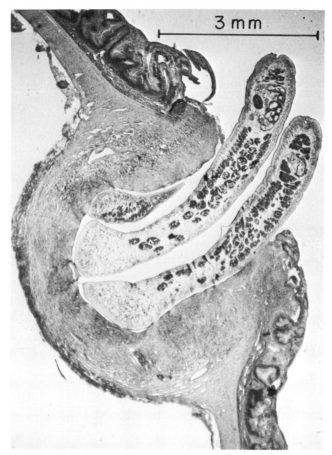

Fig. 7.26. Three individual caryophyllid cestodes, *Hunterella nodulosa,* in a deep, pouch-like lesion in the stomach of a sucker. Note the relatively plain, expanded scolex and the non-segmented character of the body, with an abundant content of genital organs. There is no alimentary tract, which distinguishes them from trematodes.

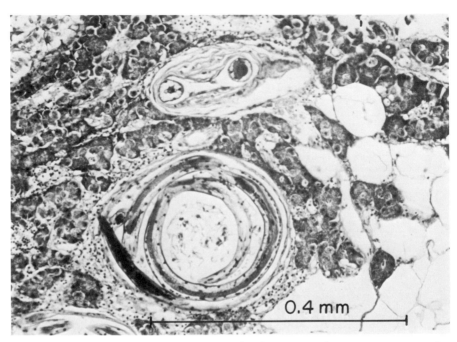

Fig. 7.27. Section of pancreas from a bluegill, showing two granulomatous areas surrounding larval nematodes, which do not appear degenerated.

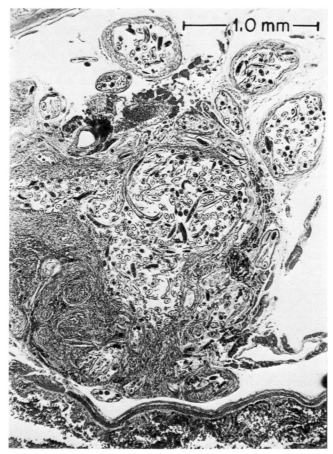

Fig. 7.28. Pancreas and intestinal ceca of another bluegill, showing widespread areas of encapsulated larval nematodes of the same type as in Figure 7.27.

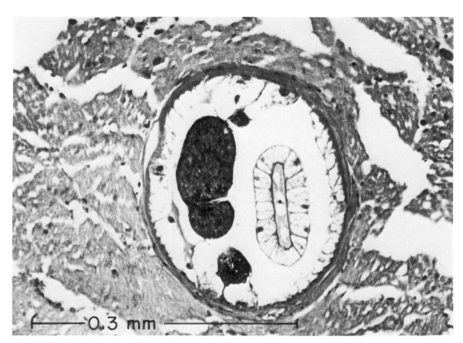

Fig. 7.29. Cross section of a larval nematode from the stomach wall of a paddlefish. The encysted nematode shows alimentary tract, gonadal primordia, lateral chords, and body-wall muscle cells. No host inflammatory reaction is present.

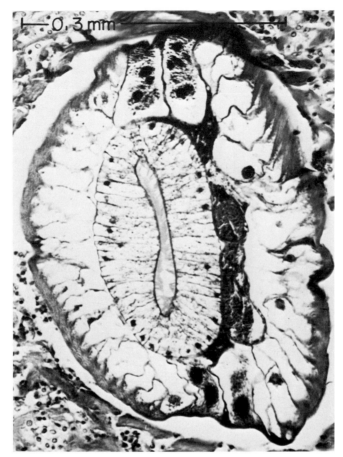

Fig. 7.30. Section from a different level of a larval nematode from the fish in Figure 7.29. In this case there is inflammatory exudate in the surrounding host tissue.

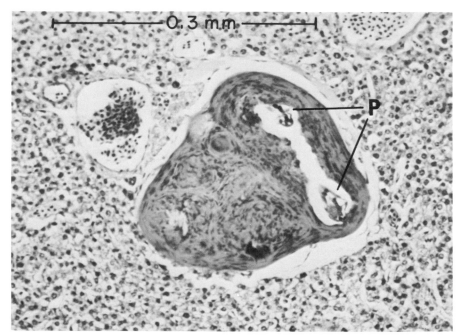

Fig. 7.31. Section of liver from *Percina,* showing a degenerating larval nematode (P) in a dense, granulomatous reaction.

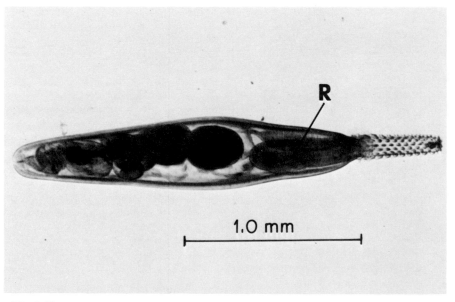

Fig. 7.32. Whole mount of a male acanthocephalan (*Echinorhynchus?*) from the intestine of a bluegill. Note the everted spiny proboscis, the proboscis receptacle (R), and the male gonads and accessory structures.

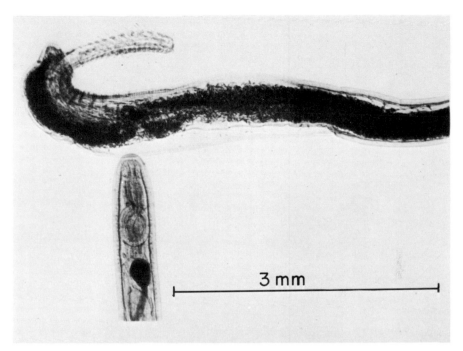

Fig. 7.33. Whole mount of a female acanthocephalan (*Leptorhynchoides*) from the intestine of a largemouth bass. The worm is filled with embryonated ova.

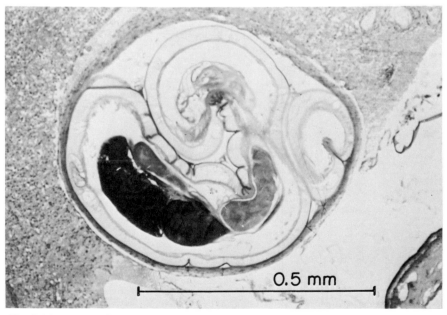

Fig. 7.34. Section of liver from *Fundulus,* showing an encapsulated larval acanthocephalan. Note the thick, multilayered body wall and the gonadal primordia.

241

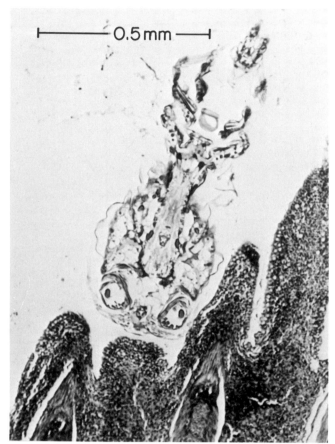

Fig. 7.35. Section of gill from *Catostomus,* showing an argulid copepod. Note the complex structure, appendages, and eye-spots. The attachment site is somewhat thickened and deformed.

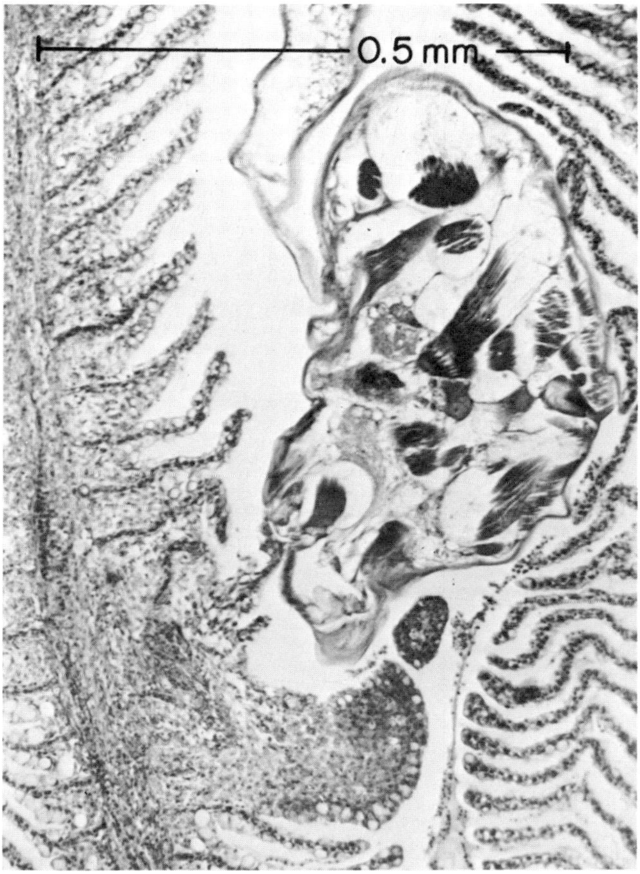

Fig. 7.36. Section of gill from *Spheroides*, showing an attached parasitic copepod. Muscle bundles are evident. There is considerable inflammation and distortion at the attachment site.

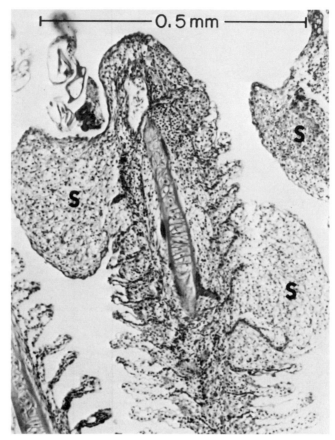

Fig. 7.37. Section of gill from a sea bass, showing three attachment sites (S) of parasitic copepods, with one parasite *in situ*. There is deformation, inflammation, and nodular reaction.

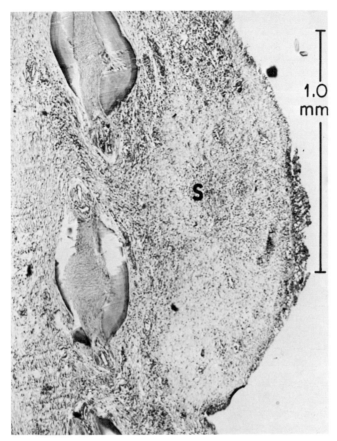

Fig. 7.38. Section of skin from a fin of *Chilomycteris,* showing the attachment site (S) of a copepod, *Tucca.* There is a dome-shaped, nodular, inflammatory, and scarred lesion, with surface ulceration.

8

Fish Viral Diseases: Clinical, Histopathological, and Comparative Aspects

WILLIAM T. YASUTAKE

The most recent comprehensive reviews of viral diseases of fishes are by Wolf (72) and Schaperclaus (53). They reported that four fish viruses had been isolated: an orphan virus, the causative agent of lymphocystis, infectious pancreatic necrosis (IPN), and viral hemorrhagic septicemia (VHS). Five additional viruses, the etiological agents of stomato-papilloma of eel, epitheliocystis, infectious hematopoietic necrosis (IHN), spring viremia of carp (SVC), and channel catfish virus disease (CCVD), have since been isolated and described (74). There are, however, many more fish diseases suspected to be of viral origin. Moreover, conflicting opinions concerning the etiology of several diseases were expressed by various investigators at the recent symposium on the Major Communicable Fish Diseases in Europe and Their Control (Amsterdam, The Netherlands, April, 1972): "Swim-bladder Inflammation of Carp" (BI) (7, 8, 11, 30), "Ulcerative Dermal Necrosis of Salmonids" (UDN) (40, 47), and "Infectious Dropsy of Carp" (IDC) (24, 58). With the exception of the acute form of IDC, which is apparently the same as SVC (17), it is apparent that further investigation is necessary to confirm the viral etiological nature of these and other diseases.

The present paper will summarize the current literature and describe the clinical, histopathological, and comparative aspects of fish diseases presently known to be of viral etiology. This includes lymphocystis, IPN, VHS, IHN, and CCVD.

The orphan (12), spring viremia of carp (17), stomato-papilloma of eel (44,

247

74), and epitheliocystis (25) viruses will not be included in this presentation. Orphan virus, also known as the grunt fin agent (GFA), was isolated and studied electron microscopically but all the work was with tissue culture and no histopathological *in vivo* study has been reported. Fijan et al. (17) recently isolated and identified a virus, *Rhabdovirus carpio*, which they suggested is the etiological agent for the acute form of IDC, namely spring viremia of carp (SVC). Although they established the etiological role of the virus by fulfilling the Rivers' postulate, most of their studies were also with tissue cultures. Pfitzner and Schubert (44) isolated a virus from juvenile eels with stomato-papilloma, commonly known as "cauliflower disease." Wolf and Quimby (personal communication) later confirmed Pfitzner and her colleague's work. Here again, as with the SVC study, much of their investigation was carried out with tissue culture, and no specific histopathological work has been correlated with their findings. Hoffman et al. (25) have investigated epitheliocystis disease of bluegill and isolated an agent in tissue culture. Although histopathological and electron microscopic studies were conducted, the relation of the agent to the disease is still somewhat obscure (74). Rivers' postulate has yet to be fulfilled.

LYMPHOCYSTIS DISEASE VIRUS

Lymphocystis disease virus (LDV) is the etiological agent of a common benign disease found in many fishes (33, 34, 37). It is considered the oldest known fish virus (72), since it was first recorded by Weissenberg in 1914 (67). It was not until 52 years later that Wolf, Gravell, and Malsberger (81) isolated and propagated the virus in centrarchid fish cell lines. Wolf noted interesting historical aspects of the LDV and tissue culture studies in his comprehensive review (72). An annotated bibliography on the disease has been reported by Nigrelli and Ruggieri (41). More recently McCosker and Nigrelli (34) recorded lymphocystis disease in four new species of fish. Recent electron microscopic studies of LDV were done by several investigators (26, 38, 91).

Clinical Pathology

Lymphocystis disease is a nonlethal infection resulting in neoplastic-like growths or flat patches on various parts of the body. These usually occur on the external body surface but have been reported in internal tissues (41). The infection apparently seldom causes death, but depending on the size and location of the lesion, swimming behavior may be greatly affected (72). It is probable that infected fish are more vulnerable to predation.

Microscopic Pathology

The histopathological picture of mature lymphocystis cells is so characteristic (Fig. 8.1) that it is relatively easy to identify the LDV (72). Wolf noted that his-

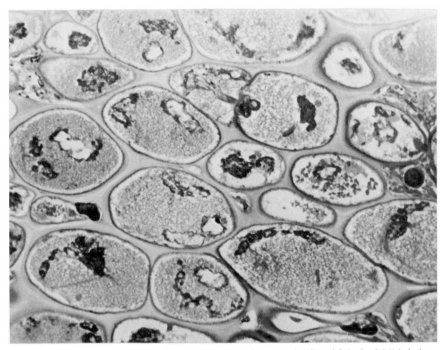

Fig. 8.1. Mature lymphocystis cells. Small nodule from caudal fin of 2-inch cichlid *Apistro-gramma ramirezi.* Note the presence of cytoplasmic inclusions. Hematoxylin and eosin (H&E); X100.

tological diagnosis is a more expedient method for diagnosing the infection than attempting to isolate the slow-growing virus.

The virus infects cells of the fibroblastic series and precipitates extensive changes, particularly an increase in the size of the cells. The increase of the infected cells may be as much as 100,000-fold or more (14). The affected areas may consist of one or many hypertrophic lymphocystis cells.

Nigrelli and Ruggieri (41) in their review gave a detailed histopathological report of the virus infection. They stated that the following characteristics may be seen in infected cells: hyaline capsule, enlarged nucleus often in various stages of necrosis, one to several nucleoli, granular cytoplasm, and single or clustered intracytoplasmic inclusions. Most of these characteristics are readily seen with routine histological technique. Only a mild inflammatory reaction apparently occurs in the infected area (41).

INFECTIOUS PANCREATIC NECROSIS

Infectious pancreatic necrosis (IPN) is a widespread fish viral disease and consequently has been extensively researched. Since it was first reported in the United

States (85), the disease has been diagnosed in several European countries, including France (9, 79), Denmark (62), Sweden, Italy, and Scotland (55). The latest report of IPN was from Japan (50–52).

IPN is usually a disease of young trout, but the virus has also been found in yearling and adult carriers (3, 73). Recently the etiological agent was isolated from Atlantic salmon fry (35) and from asymptomatic fingerling and adult coho salmon (*Oncorhynchus kisutch*) (J. L. Fryer, personal communication; 76).

Latest information from the biochemical and electron microscopic studies reported by Kelly and Loh (27) seem to indicate that the IPN virus is composed of single-stranded RNA, and therefore is neither a reovirus (13, 39) nor a picornavirus (36) but may represent a new group of viruses. Numerous other reports covering the morphological, biochemical, and immunological aspects of the virus have been recorded (10, 31, 51, 63, 64, 77–80, 83).

Clinical Pathology

The first noticeable external sign of an acute epizootic of IPN is a characteristic "corkscrew" spiralling or whirling along the long axis of the body in the swimming behavior of fish, and a sudden increase in mortality, particularly in the larger and healthier fish. Other clinical signs seen frequently are exophthalmos, ascites, external darkening, and hemorrhaging at the base of the ventral fins.

Internally, the liver and spleen are usually pale. The digestive tract is void of food and often has a clear or opaque mucoid plug in the stomach and anterior intestine. Petechiation may also occur in the cecal and pancreatic tissue areas (43, 77).

Microscopic Pathology

Histopathologically, the pancreas appears to be the primary tissue involved in IPN (56, 85); however, later reports indicate more extensive involvement of other tissues (52, 79, 86, 89). Frank necrosis of pancreatic acinar cells is usually accompanied by intracytoplasmic inclusions, pyknosis, and karyorrhexis (Fig. 8.2). In terminal cases, pathological changes in the kidney, particularly in the hematopoietic tissues, have been observed. Both Wolf and Quimby (79) and Sano (52) have reported finding catarrhal gastroenteritis, characterized by the desquamation of the mucous membrane, in their experimentally infected fish. Sano (52) also observed partial necrosis in the liver in some of his specimens. Etiological aspects of hyaline degeneration of the skeletal muscle reported by most investigators are not yet understood. It has occasionally been observed in fish which are not infected with IPN (72, 86, 88).

VIRAL HEMORRHAGIC SEPTICEMIA

Viral hemorrhagic septicemia (VHS) or Egtved disease, as it is commonly known, is a virulent virus disease which has been enzootic in trout farms through-

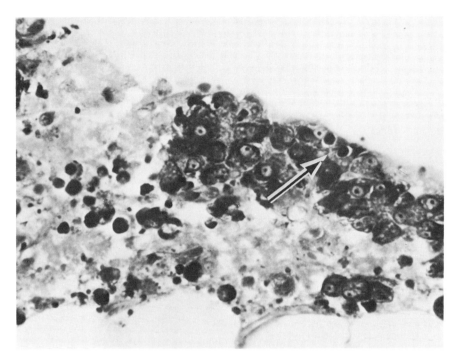

Fig. 8.2. IPN. Rainbow trout pancreas showing extensive necrosis. Several intracytoplasmic inclusions can be seen (arrow). May-Grünwald Giemsa; X700.

out Europe. The disease apparently was first recorded over 30 years ago and to date has not been reported outside Europe. The latest thorough review is by Ghittino (23). Although it is chiefly a disease of rainbow trout, an epizootic occurred in brown trout (*Salmo trutta*) (20) and there have been scattered reports of possible VHS epizootics occurring in other species (23).

During the last several years there have been studies covering various aspects of the disease and its etiological agent. Most of these works have dealt with the morphological (28, 54, 90, 92) and immunological aspects (59–65). A number of studies of the histopathology of VHS have appeared since Wolf's 1966 review: Ghittino (19–22), Yasutake and Rasmussen (88), and Yasutake (86).

Clinical Pathology

VHS outbreaks have been reported in summer months but more serious epizootics usually occur during late winter or early spring when the water temperature is lower than 8°C. Table-market-size fish seem to be most vulnerable, although the infection has been found on rare occasions in fry and brood trout (23).

Ghittino (23) agreed with Wolf's (72) and Yasutake's (86) premise that the three forms of the disease earlier reported by Klinger (29) and Ghittino (18) are different stages rather than different forms of the disease. These stages are acute, chronic, and nervous or latent. The acute stage is seen during the early period of an epizootic and mortality rate is high. The fish are usually characterized by dark coloration, unilateral exophthalmos, anemia, and hemorrhaging of eyes and at bases of pectoral fins. The chronic stage usually follows the acute state and mortality is generally moderate. Extensive bilateral exophthalmos, severe anemia, intense darkening, and occasional dropsy may be observed. Hemorrhagic conditions which usually occur in the acute stage may not always occur in the chronic stage. In the nervous stage, mortality is usually low and the clinical behavior changes noticeably. This is apparently the terminal stage, where lethargy is replaced by rapid spiral, circular, and erratic swimming behavior. During this last stage fish are occasionally seen with retracted abdominal walls.

Gross internal lesions of the acute stage are many punctiform extravasations in the skeletal muscles and throughout the visceral tissue. There may or may not be hemorrhaging in the chronic stage, but the kidney is often swollen, somewhat corrugated, and greyish. No external, internal, or microscopic lesions have yet been reported in fish in the nervous stage (23).

Microscopic Pathology

In the skeletal musculature, hemorrhage usually occurs in the form of a massive infiltration of erythrocytes between the muscle bundles and fibers with no apparent damage to the muscle tissue (Fig. 8.3). In the chronic stage the extravasation may occur to a lesser degree or may not even be present.

Distended and blood-engorged sinusoids are seen in livers, which appear grossly hemorrhagic. These hepatic tissues frequently are accompanied by focal necrotic changes such as cytoplasmic vaculation, pyknosis, karyorrhexis, and karyolysis. Ghittino (23) further observed that similar tissue changes occur in the kidney and spleen. Swollen kidneys frequently have involvement of both the renal and hematopoietic elements. In the acute stage, leukopenia may be observed in the hematopoietic areas, whereas mononuclear lymphoid hyperplasia appears to predominate in the chronic stage.

In an experimental histopathological study, Yasutake and Rasmussen (88) found that the kidney appears to be the initial target tissue and subsequent tissue changes in the spleen, skeletal muscle, liver, pancreas, and adrenal cortex indicate progressive stages of VHS. Although the histological alterations were similar to those in epizootic specimens, they observed that the degree of severity was noticeably less. The massive hemorrhage generally associated with VHS epizootics was replaced by scattered isolated petechiae. On the 17th day after virus exposure, the kidney hematopoietic tissue had obvious degenerative and necrotic changes (Fig. 8.4). Leukopenia and melanocyte destruction were also evident. Hepatocytes exhibited focal degeneration and necrosis (Fig. 8.5). By the fourth week after exposure other tissues, such as pancreatic acinar and adrenal cortical tissues, displayed incipient cellular changes.

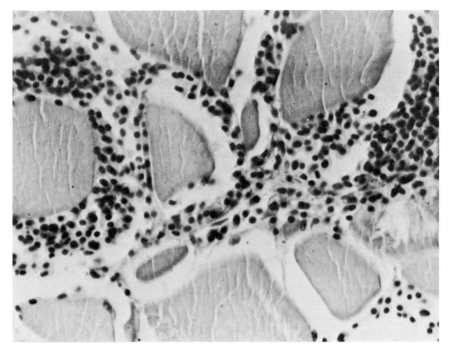

Fig. 8.3. VHS. Rainbow trout striated muscle with extravasation. (Specimen contributed by P. Ghittino.) H&E; X750.

INFECTIOUS HEMATOPOIETIC NECROSIS

Infectious hematopoietic necrosis (IHN) is a viral disease found primarily in juvenile trout and salmon. Amend et al. (5) in their comprehensive review of IHN noted that the evidence to date indicates that IHN is very similar in most respects to sockeye salmon virus disease (SSVD) and chinook salmon virus disease (CSVD). Most of the recent work substantiates the striking similarities clinically, histopathologically (4, 86), morphologically, biochemically, physiologically (1, 2, 69–71), and serologically (32). Therefore, as proposed by Amend, Yasutake, and Mead (4), the term IHN in this report will encompass all three: IHN, SSVD, and CSVD. IHN is apparently enzootic in the western Canadian and United States coastal areas. It has been reported in several midwestern states; however, transportation of infected eggs and fish from the western states was evidently responsible for these epizootics (5, 46).

Clinical Pathology

IHN has seldom been observed at water temperatures of 15°C or higher. Sudden increase in mortality of the larger fish is usually the initial sign of IHN infection. Pale gills, dark coloration, exophthalmos, ascites, petechiae in the buccal

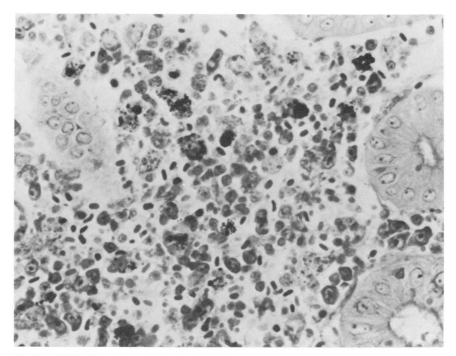

Fig. 8.4. VHS. Experimentally induced. Rainbow trout kidney hematopoietic tissue show-ing degeneration and necrosis. May-Grünwald Giemsa; X700.

cavity, fecal casts, hemorrhagic area in the skeletal muscle in the dorsal fin area and bases of fins are the clinical signs seen in IHN-infected fish. Internally, the gross lesions are pale liver, kidney, and spleen, and some petechiation of the visceral areas. Frequently the survivors of an epizootic have varying degrees of scoliosis (4, 42, 48, 49).

Microscopic Pathology

Histopathological analyses of chinook and sockeye salmon and rainbow trout from IHN epizootics have shown striking similarities. In all three species there is extensive involvement of kidney, spleen, pancreas, and the granular cells of the intestinal tract. Hepatic parenchymal cells are also involved in severely affected fish (86).

The hematopoietic tissue of the kidney and the splenic tissue is usually most markedly involved. The kidney lesions often consist of extensive degeneration and necrosis (Fig. 8.6). Necrosis may be so severe that the affected tissue may consist primarily of necrotic detritus. Granular cells in the area of the stratum compactum and stratum granulosum are also usually affected (Fig. 8.7). Pleomorphic intracytoplasmic inclusions frequently occur in the pancreas (Fig.

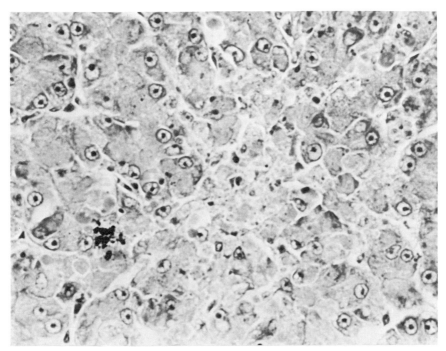

Fig. 8.5. VHS. Experimentally induced. Rainbow trout liver with focal degeneration and necrosis. H&E; ×600.

8.8) but these are not considered to be pathognomonic. Fish with terminal infection may exhibit focal degeneration and necrosis in the liver (Fig. 8.9). Areas of grossly visible petechiation and punctate hemorrhaging, histologically also have hyperemia. Many moribund fish have sloughing of the mucous membrane of the intestine. Amend, Yasutake, and Mead (4) hypothesized that this may be responsible for the fecal casts observed clinically in the diseased fish.

Histopathogenesis studies by Yasutake, Parisot, and Klontz (89) and Yasutake and Amend (87) substantiate the fact that kidney is the target tissue. In the latter study, a very close correlation was found between histopathological changes and virus concentration. All of the experiments showed the cytotropic nature of the virus for the kidney and splenic hematopoietic elements, with minimal effect on the renal, adrenal, and corpuscles of Stannius tissues. The earliest change seen was the focal concentration of macrophages in the kidney, followed by eventual involvement of the pancreas, liver, and the intestinal wall granular cells (87). Subtle change was observed in the hematopoietic tissue three days after virus exposure. There was an apparent increase in macrophages and decrease in the undifferentiated "blast" cells. In infected fathead minnow (FHM) cells, the earliest cytopathic effect was also observed on the third day.

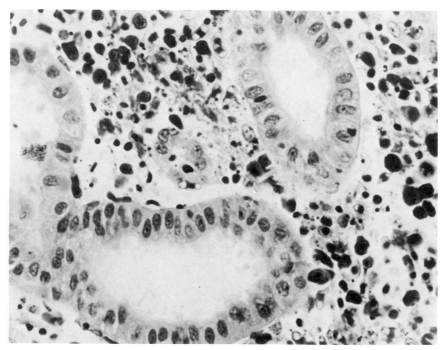

Fig. 8.6. IHN. Sockeye salmon kidney with degenerative and necrotic hematopoietic tissue.
H&E; ×1000.

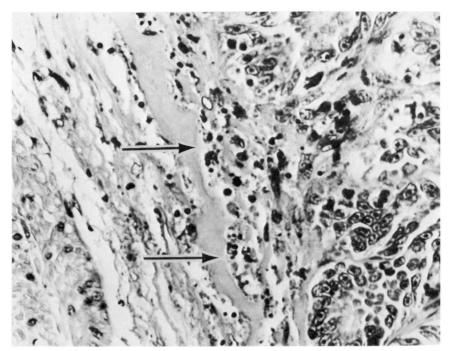

Fig. 8.7. IHN. Rainbow trout stomach wall with extensively necrotic granular cells (arrows). H&E; ×700.

Watson, Guenther, and Royce (66) in their study of IHN observed hemato-pathological changes. These changes included degenerating leukocytes and thrombocytes, extracellular basophilic granules, and bi-lobed erythrocytes. Wood and Yasutake (84) also reported observing bi-lobed red blood cells in the peripheral blood smears. Preliminary unpublished analyses of peripheral blood smears and anterior kidney imprints taken from recent IHN epizootics by the author showed extensive hematological changes which were somewhat similar to those reported by Watson, Guenther, and Royce (66) and Wood and Yasutake (84).

CHANNEL CATFISH VIRUS DISEASE

Channel catfish virus disease (CCVD) is an acute hemorrhagic disease of channel catfish fingerlings. The etiological agent, along with that of SVC, is the latest fish virus to be isolated and characterized. A virus had been suspected of causing some of the catfish epizootics in the past; however, Fijan (15) was first to isolate the agent. Fijan, Wellborn, and Naftel (16) in a later report gave a more detailed description of the clinical manifestations and viral etiology of CCVD. Wolf and

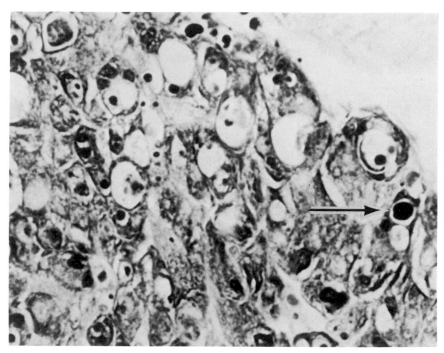

Fig. 8.8. IHN. Sockeye salmon pancreas showing necrosis and many intracytoplasmic inclusions. May-Grünwald Giemsa; ×1500.

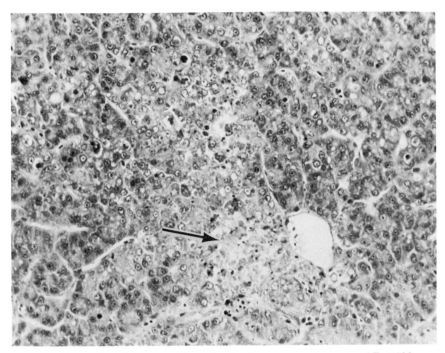

Fig. 8.9. IHN. Rainbow trout liver showing focal necrosis (arrow). H&E; X400.

Darlington (75) described additional characteristics of the virus using plaque assay methods and light and electron microscopy. Their studies indicated that CCV has the essential properties of a herpes virus. Tissue distribution of the virus in catfish infected experimentally was reported by Plumb (45). The most recent work on the disease is the histopathological study of experimental CCVD by Wolf, Herman, and Carlson (82).

Clinical Pathology

The first indication of CCVD is a sudden increase in the mortality of fingerlings (16, 68). Epizootics generally occur during the summer, often when the water temperature reaches 20°C and above. Spiralling or corkscrew swimming, much like that associated with IPN, and "stargazing" vertical swimming are often observed. The latter behavior is considered the most typical clinical behavior of CCVD-infected fish (68). Other external signs included hemorrhages on the fins and abdominal areas, pale or hemorrhagic gills, and mono- and bilateral exophthalmos. Internally, hemorrhagic muscle, kidney, spleen, and liver may be seen. Ascites and a stomach distended with yellowish mucoid material are also often associated with CCVD.

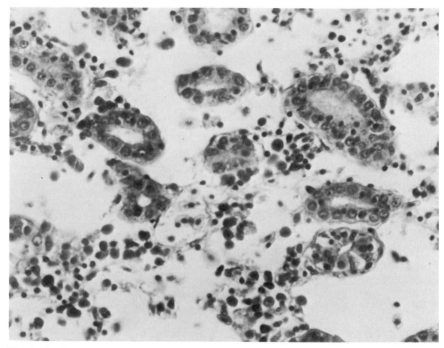

Fig. 8.10. CCVD. Experimentally induced. Catfish kidney showing edema and degenerative and necrotic hematopoietic tissue. (Specimen contributed by K. Wolf.) H&E; ×750.

Fig. 8.11. CCVD. Experimentally induced. Catfish skeletal dorsal muscle with extravasation. (Specimen contributed by K. Wolf.) H&E; X400.

Microscopic Pathology

The only reported histopathological study of CCVD is that of Wolf, Herman, and Carlson (82) in catfish which were injected intramuscularly with CCV. Natural epizootic specimens have not been histologically described. Acuteness of CCVD was well demonstrated by Wolf, Herman, and Carlson (82). The juvenile catfish were in terminal stages of the disease 48 to 72 hours after exposure. General systemic blood extravasation and extensive necrosis in kidney, liver, and alimentary tract were observed. As in the salmonid virus diseases previously described, the hematopoietic tissues and not the renal elements were most markedly involved. Wolf, Herman, and Carlson (82) also observed edema (Fig. 8.10) and numerous macrophages in the kidney. Skeletal muscle focal extravasation of blood (Fig. 8.11) occurred with some necrosis, but the latter tissue change was not considered to be a specific CCVD-associated histopathological characteristic. Edema and necrosis were present in liver and in the mucous and submucous membranes of the digestive tract. Sloughing of intestinal epithelium and hyperemia of the submucosa were also noted (Fig. 8.12). The other tissues apparently showed no atypical changes.

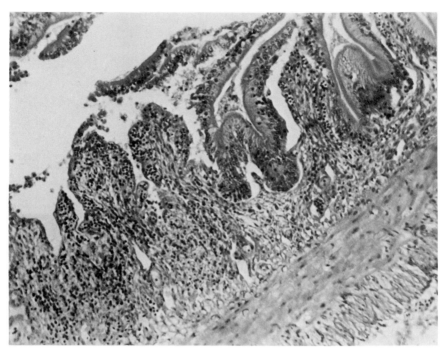

Fig. 8.12. CCVD. Experimentally induced. Catfish intestine showing extensive hyperemia and degenerative changes in the mucous membrane and submucosa. (Specimen contributed by K. Wolf.) H&E; X350.

SUMMARY

Similarities have been found in the cytotropic pattern and histopathological changes in the diseases of known viral etiology discussed in this report. Lymphocystis disease is the exception.

Most of the investigations indicated that in IPN, VHS, IHN, and CCVD, the hematopoietic tissue of the kidney is involved to some degree in the pathogenesis of the diseases. In VHS and IHN the spleen also has changes. In IHN the massive renal necrosis occurring in the terminal cases is usually so extensive that the hematopoietic tissue may be completely obliterated and replaced by detritus. A similar observation was made in catfish experimentally infected with CCV (82). The kidney may have severe changes in VHS but even fish in terminal stages often do not exhibit the massive necrosis seen in IHN. In fish severely infected with IPN, these tissue changes are also frequently found, but they resemble early stages of IHN. Generally, the renal and other nonhematopoietic elements of the kidney in all these diseases are involved only in the most severely infected fish.

Further similarities have been found in VHS, IHN, and CCVD. Hemorrhagic manifestations are associated with epizootics of all three diseases. Although extensive hyperemia is almost always associated with epizootics as well as with experimentally induced CCVD, it does not seem to apply to VHS and IHN. In histopathogenesis studies of both VHS and IHN, hyperemia is noticeably lacking in the experimental fish (87, 88). Liver involvement is also associated in VHS, IHN, and CCVD. The similarities in histopathological changes in IHN and VHS are not too surprising, since the IHN and VHS viruses are morphologically similar and have rhabdovirus characteristics. Wolf, Herman, and Carlson (82) observed that while CCV differs in nucleic acid composition and apparently belongs to an entirely different group of viruses, it appears to cause histopathological changes usually associated with VHS and IHN. They further noted that the most noticeable difference is the absence of pancreatic involvement in CCVD. The pancreas, as well as the kidney, is usually involved in all salmonid virus diseases (IPN, VHS, and IHN).

There are many more fish diseases of possible viral etiology which need to be studied further (37). The histopathological aspects of the newly described SVC (17) have not been well defined. Hematopathological characteristics of viral diseases need to be investigated. One study should be noted here: Angiolelli and Rio (6) recently transmitted the IPN virus to Swiss albino mice. This is apparently the first time that a virus which has been isolated from a poikilotherm has been transmitted to a homeotherm.

Acknowledgment. The author gratefully acknowledges the invaluable technical assistance of Dennis E. Crouch.

REFERENCES

1. Amend, D. F., and Chambers, V. C. Morphology of certain viruses of salmonid fishes. I. *In vitro* studies of some viruses causing hematopoietic necrosis. *J. Fish. Res. Board Can. 27:* 1285. 1970.
2. Amend, D. F., and Chambers, V. C. Morphology of certain viruses of salmonid fishes. II. *In vivo* studies of infectious hematopoietic necrosis virus. *J. Fish. Res. Board Can. 27:* 1385. 1970.
3. Amend, D. F., and Wedemeyer, G. Approved procedure for determining absence of infectious pancreatic necrosis (IPN) virus in certain fish and fish products. *U. S. Bur. Sport Fish. Wildlife, Fish Dis. Leafl. 27.* 4 pp. 1970.
4. Amend, D. F., Yasutake, W. T., and Mead, R. W. A hematopoietic virus disease of rainbow trout and sockeye salmon. *Trans. Amer. Fish. Soc. 98:* 796. 1969.
5. Amend, D. F., Yasutake, W. T., Fryer, J. L., Pilcher, K. S., and Wingfield, W. H. Panel review on epizootiology of infectious hematopoietic necrosis (IHN) virus in salmonids. In *Symposium on the Major Communicable Fish Diseases in Europe and Their Control,* Working document no. C6879, p. 9. FAO (Food Agr. Organ. U. N.), Rome, in press, 1972.

6. Angiolelli, R. F., and Rio, G. J.   The Swiss/ICR (Ha) albino mouse as an experimental host for infectious pancreatic necrosis virus of trout. *J. Fish Biol. 3:* 139. 1971.

7. Antychowicz, J.   Experience paper on swim-bladder inflammation of cyprinids.   In *Symposium on the Major Communicable Fish Diseases in Europe and Their Control,* Working document no. C7182, p. 7. FAO (Food Agr. Organ. U. N.), Rome, in press, 1972.

8. Arshaniza, N. M., and Bauer, O. N.   Experience paper on epizootiology, diagnosis and prophylaxis of swim-bladder inflammation of cyprinids. In *Symposium on the Major Communicable Fish Diseases in Europe and Their Control,* Working document no. C6460. FAO (Food Agr. Organ. U. N.), Rome, in press, 1972.

9. Besse, P., and de Kinkelin, P.   Sur l'existence en France de la necrose pancreatique de la truite arc-en-ciel (*Salmo gairdneri*). *Bull. Acad. vet. Fr. 38:* 185. 1965.

10. Billi, J. L., and Wolf, K.   Quantitative comparison of peritoneal washes and feces for detecting infectious pancreatic necrosis (IPN) virus in carrier brook trout. *J. Fish. Res. Board Can. 26:* 1459. 1969.

11. Braun, F.   Experience paper on swim-bladder inflammation of carps. In *Symposium on the Major Communicable Fish Diseases in Europe and Their Control,* Working document no. C6894. FAO (Food Agr. Organ. U. N.), Rome, in press, 1972.

12. Clem, L. W., Sigel, M. M., and Friis, R. R.   An orphan virus isolated in marine fish cell tissue culture. *Ann. N. Y. Acad. Sci. 125:* 343. 1965.

13. Cohen, J., and Scherrer, R.   Structure de la capside du virus de la necrose pancreatique infectieuse (NPI) de la truite. *C. r. hebd. séances Acad. Sci. (Paris) 274:* 1222, 1972.

14. Dunbar, C. E., and Wolf, K.   The cytological courses of experimental lymphcystis in the bluegill. *J. Infec. Dis. 116:* 466. 1966.

15. Fijan, N. N.   Progress report on acute mortality of channel catfish fingerlings caused by a virus. *Bull. Off. int. Épizoot. 69:* 1169. 1968.

16. Fijan, N. N., Wellborn, T. L., Jr., and Naftel, J. P.   An acute viral disease of channel catfish. *U. S. Bur. Sport Fish. Wildlife, Tech. Pap. 43.* 11 pp. 1970.

17. Fijan, N. N., Petrinec, Z., Sulimanovic, D., and Zwillenberg, L. O.   Isolation of the viral causative agent from the acute form of infectious dropsy of carp. *Vet. arh. 41:* 125. 1971.

18. Ghittino, P.   Viral hemorrhagic septicemia (VHS) in rainbow trout in Italy. *Ann. N. Y. Acad. Sci. 126:* 468. 1965.

19. Ghittino, P.   La Setticemia emorragica virale (SEV) dell trota iridea di allevamento. *Riv. ital. piscic. ittiopat. 2:* 90. 1967.

20. Ghittino, P.   Grave enzoozia di setticemia emorragica virale in trote fario di allevamento (*Salmo trutta*). *Riv. ital. piscic. ittiopat. 3:* 17. 1968.

21. Ghittino, P.   Septicemie hemorragique virale de la truite arc-en-ciel, pp. 19–37. In *Les Maladies contagieuses des poissons inclusés dans le Code Zoosanitaire international de l'O.I.E.* Paris, Off. int. Épizoot., 1968.

22. Ghittino, P. *Piscicoltura e Ittiopatologia.* Vol. 2—Ittiopatologia, p. 420, Ed. Riv. Zooteonia, Sesto S. Giov. Milan, 1970.

23. Ghittino, P. Review of panel 1. Viral hemorrhagic septicemia (VHS). In *Symposium on the Major Communicable Fish Diseases in Europe and Their Control,* Working document no. C6459, p. 15. FAO (Food Agr. Organ. U. N.), Rome, in press, 1972.

24. Havelka, J. Experience paper on infectious dropsy of carp. In *Symposium on the Major Communicable Fish Diseases in Europe and Their Control,* Working document no. C6896, p. 7. FAO (Food Agr. Organ. U. N.), Rome, in press, 1972.

25. Hoffman, G. L., Dunbar, C. E., Wolf, K., and Zwillenberg, L. O. Epitheliocystis, a new infectious disease of the bluegill (*Lepomis macrochirus*). *Antonie van Leeuwenhoek J. Microbiol. Serol. 35:* 146. 1969.

26. Howse, H. D., and Christmas, J. Y. Observations on the ultrastructure of lymphocystis virus in the Atlantic croaker *Micropogon undulatus* (Linnaeus). *Virology 44:* 211. 1971.

27. Kelly, R. K., and Loh, P. C. Some properties of infectious pancreatic necrosis virus and its RNA. *Abstr. Annu. Meet. Amer. Soc. Microbiol.,* p. 208 (V139). 1972.

28. de Kinkelin, P. Properties *in vitro* of the virus of Egtved. In *Symposium on the Major Communicable Fish Diseases in Europe and Their Control,* Working document no. C6898, p. 5. FAO (Food Agr. Organ. U. N.), Rome, in press, 1972.

29. Klinger, K. Forellenfutterung und "neue Krankheit." Infektiose Nierenschivellung und Leberdegeneration der Regenbogenforelle (INuL). *Allg. Fischerei-Ztg. 83:* 12, 1958.

30. Liebmann, H. Panel review of swim-bladder inflammation of carps. In *Symposium on the Major Communicable Fish Diseases in Europe and Their Control,* Working document no. C6881, p. 3. FAO (Food Agr. Organ. U. N.), Rome, in press, 1972.

31. Lightner, D., and Post, G. Morphological characteristics of infectious pancreatic necrosis virus in trout pancreatic tissue. *J. Fish. Res. Board Can. 26:* 2247. 1969.

32. McCain, B. B., Fryer, J. L., and Pilcher, K. S. Antigenic relationship in a group of three viruses of salmonid fish by cross neutralization. *Proc. Soc. Exp. Biol. Med. 137:* 1042. 1971.

33. McCosker, J. E. A behavioral correlate for the passage of lymphocystis disease in three blennioid fishes. *Copeia 1969:* 636. 1969.

34. McCosker, J. E., and Nigrelli, R. F. New records of lymphocystis disease in four eastern Pacific fish species. *J. Fish. Res. Board Can. 28:* 1908. 1971.

35. MacKelvie, R. M., and Artsob, H. Infectious pancreatic necrosis in young salmonids of the Canadian Maritime Provinces. *J. Fish Res. Board Can. 26:* 3259. 1969.

36. Malsberger, R. G., and Cerini, C. P. Characteristics of infectious pancreatic necrosis virus. *J. Bacteriol. 86:* 1283. 1963.

37. Mawdesley-Thomas, L. E.   Research into fish diseases. *Nature (London) 235:* 17. 1972

38. Midlige, F. H., Jr., and Malsberger, R. G.   *In vitro* morphology and maturation of lymphocystis virus. *J. Virol. 2:* 830. 1968.

39. Moss, L. H., III, and Gravell, M.   Ultrastructure and sequential development of infectious pancreatic necrosis virus. *J. Virol. 3:* 52. 1969.

40. Murphy, T.   Panel review on ulcerative dermal necrosis (UDN) of salmonids. In *Symposium on the Major Communicable Fish Diseases in Europe and Their Control,* Working document no. C6883, p. 9. FAO (Food Agr. Organ. U. N.), Rome, in press, 1972.

41. Nigrelli, R. F., and Ruggieri, G. D.   Studies on virus diseases of fishes. Spontaneous and experimentally induced cellular hypertrophy (lymphocystis disease) in fishes of the New York Aquarium, with a report of new cases and an annotated bibliography (1874–1965). *Zoologica (New York) 50:* 83. 1965.

42. Parisot, T. J.   An interim report on Sacramento River chinook disease: A virus-like disease of chinook salmon. *Progr. Fish-Cult. 24:* 51. 1962.

43. Parisot, T. J., Yasutake, W. T., and Klontz, G. W.   Virus diseases of the Salmonidae in western United States. I. Etiology and Epizootiology. *Ann. N. Y. Acad. Sci. 126:* 502. 1965.

44. Pfitzner, I., and Schubert, G.   Ein Virus aus dem Blut mit Blumenkohlkrankheit behafterter Aale. *Z. Naturforsch.,* Sect. B *24:* 790. 1969.

45. Plumb, J. A.   Tissue distribution of channel catfish virus. *J. Wildlife Dis. 7:* 213. 1971.

46. Plumb, J. A.   A virus-caused epizootic of rainbow trout (*Salmo gairdneri*) in Minnesota. *Trans. Amer. Fish. Soc. 101:* 121. 1972.

47. Reichenbach-Klinke, H.-H.   Experience paper: Investigations on ulcerative dermal necrosis (UDN) in the Alps. In *Symposium on the Major Communicable Fish Diseases in Europe and Their Control,* Working document no C6888, p. 5. FAO (Food Agr. Organ. U. N.), Rome, in press, 1972.

48. Ross, A. J., Pelnar, J., and Rucker, R. R.   A virus-like disease of chinook salmon. *Trans. Amer. Fish. Soc. 89:* 160. 1960.

49. Rucker, R. R., Whipple, W. J., Parvin, J. R., and Evans, C. A.   A contagious disease of salmon possibly of virus origin. *U. S. Fish Wildlife Serv., Fish. Bull. 76:* 35. 1953.

50. Sano, T.   Etiology and histopathology of hexamitiasis and an IPN-like disease of rainbow trout. *J. Tokyo Univ. Fish. 56:* 23. 1970.

51. Sano, T.   Studies on viral diseases of Japanese fishes. I. Infectious pancreatic necrosis in rainbow trout: First isolation from epizootic in Japan. *Bull. Jap. Soc. Sci. Fish. 37:* 495. 1971.

52. Sano, T.   Studies on viral diseases of Japanese fishes. II. Infectious pancreatic necrosis of rainbow trout: Pathogenicity of the isolants. *Bull. Jap. Soc. Sci. Fish. 37:* 499. 1971.

53. Schäperclaus, W.   Virusinfektionen bei Fischen, pp. 106–114. In *Handbuch der Virusinfektionen bei Tieren,* ed. H. Rohrer. Vol. 2. Jena, Gustav Fischer Verlag, 1969.

54. Scherrer, R.   Abstract of an experience paper on morphology and ultrastruc-

ture of the virus of Egtved. In *Symposium on the Major Communicable Fish Diseases in Europe and Their Control*, Working document no. C6895, p. 2. FAO (Food Agr. Organ. U. N.), Rome, in press, 1972.

55. Scherrer, R.   Panel review on infectious pancreatic necrosis of salmonids. In *Symposium on the Major Commjnicable Fish Diseases in Europe and Their Control*, Working document no. C7179, p. 12.   FAO (Food Agr. Organ. U. N.), Rome, in press, 1972.

56. Snieszko, S. F., Wood, E. M., and Yasutake, W. T.   Infectious pancreatic necrosis in trout.   *A.M.A. Arch. Pathol. 63:* 229. 1957.

57. Sonstegard, R. A., and McDermott, L. A.   Infectious pancreatic necrosis of salmonids in Ontario.   *J. Fish. Res. Board Can. 28:* 1350. 1971.

58. Tomašec, I. I.   Panel review on infectious dropsy of cyprinids. In *Symposium on the Major Communicable Fish Diseases in Europe and Their Control*, Working document no. C6880, p. 8.   FAO (Food Agr. Organ. U. N.), Rome, in press, 1972.

59. Vestergard Jørgensen, P. E.   Serological identification of Egtved virus (virus of viral hemorrhagic septicemia of rainbow trout). A preliminary report. *Bull. Off. int. Epizoot. 69:* 985. 1968.

60. Vestergard Jørgensen, P. E.   Egtved virus: Antigenic variation in 76 virus isolates examined in neutralization tests and by means of the fluorescent antibody technique. In *Diseases of Fish*, ed. L. E. Mawdesley-Thomas. (Symp. Zool. Soc. London, No. 30.) London and New York, Academic Press, 1972.

61. Vestergard Jørgensen, P. E.   Experience paper: Diagnostic methods and serological studies on the virus of VHS. In *Symposium on the Major Communicable Fish Diseases in Europe and Their Control*, Working document no. C6892, p. 5. FAO (Food Agr. Organ. U. N.), Rome, in press, 1972.

62. Vestergard Jørgensen, P. E., and Bregnballe, F.   Infectious pancreatic necrosis in rainbow trout (*Salmo gairdneri*) in Denmark. *Nord. vet. med. 21:* 142. 1969.

63. Vestergard Jørgensen, P. E., and Grauballe, P. C.   Problems in the serological typing of IPN virus. *Acta vet. scand. 12:* 145. 1971.

64. Vestergard Jørgensen, P. E., and Kehlet, N. P.   Infectious pancreatic necrosis (IPN) viruses in Danish rainbow trout: Their serological and pathogenic properties. *Nord. vet. med. 23:* 568. 1971.

65. Vestergard Jørgensen, P. E., and Meyling, A.   Egtved virus: Demonstration of virus antigen by the fluorescent antibody technique in tissues of rainbow trout affected by viral hemorrhagic septicemia and in cell cultures infected with Egtved virus. *Arch. gesamte Virusforsch. 36:* 115. 1972.

66. Watson, M. E., Guenther, R. W., and Royce, R. D.   Hematology of healthy and virus-diseased sockeye salmon, *Oncorhynchus nerka. Zoologica (New York) 41:*27. 1956.

67. Weissenberg, R.   Uber infektiose Zellhypertrophie bei Fischen (Lymphocystiserkrankung). *Sitzungsber. kgl. preuss. Akad. Wiss. 30:* 792. 1914.

68. Wellborn, T. L., Jr., Fijan, N. N., and Naftel, J. P.   Channel catfish virus disease. *U. S. Bur. Sport Fish. Wildlife, Fish Dis. Leafl. 18.* 3 pp. 1969.

69. Wingfield, W. H., and Chan, L. D.   Studies on the Sacramento River chinook

disease and its causative agent, pp. 307–318. In *A Symposium on Diseases of Fishes and Shellfishes,* ed. S. F. Snieszko. Amer. Fish. Soc., Spec. Publ. No. 5. Washington, D.C., 1970.

70. Wingfield, W. H., Fryer, J. L., and Pilcher, K. S.   Properties of the sockeye salmon virus (Oregon strain). *Proc. Soc. Expt. Biol. Med. 130:* 1055. 1969.

71. Wingfield, W. H., Nims, L., Fryer, J. L., and Pilcher, K. S.   Species specificity of the sockeye salmon virus (Oregon strain) and its cytopathic effects in salmonid cell lines, pp. 319–326. In *A Symposium on Diseases of Fishes and Shellfishes,* ed. S. F. Snieszko. Amer. Fish. Soc., Spec. Publ. No. 5. Washington, D.C., 1970.

72. Wolf, K.   The fish viruses, pp. 35–101. In *Advances in Virus Research,* ed. K. M. Smith and M. A. Lauffer. Vol. 12. New York, Academic Press, 1966.

73. Wolf, K.   Infectious pancreatic necrosis (IPN) of salmonid fishes. *U. S. Bur. Sport Fish. Wildlife, Fish Dis. Leafl. 1.* 4 pp. 1966.

74. Wolf, K.   Advances in fish virology: A review, 1966–1972, pp. 305–327. In *Diseases of Fish,* ed. L. E. Mawdesley-Thomas. (Symp. Zool. Soc. London, No. 30.) London and New York, Academic Press, 1972.

75. Wolf, K., and Darlington, R. W.   Channel catfish virus: A new herpesvirus of ictalurid fish. *J. Virol. 8:* 525. 1971.

76. Wolf, K., and Pettijohn, L. L.   Infectious pancreatic necrosis virus isolated from coho salmon fingerlings. *Progr. Fish-Cult. 32:* 17. 1970.

77. Wolf, K., and Quimby, M. C.   Infectious pancreatic necrosis (IPN): Its diagnosis, identification, detection, and control. *Riv. ital. piscic. ittiopat. 2*(4): 76. 1967.

78. Wolf, K., and Quimby, M. C.   Infectious pancreatic necrosis: Clinical and immune response of adult trouts to inoculation with live virus. *J. Fish. Res. Board Can. 26:* 2511. 1969.

79. Wolf, K., and Quimby, M. C.   Salmonid viruses: Infectious pancreatic necrosis virus, morphology, pathology, and serology of first European isolations. *Arch. gesamte Virusforsch. 34:* 144. 1971.

80. Wolf, K., and Vestergard Jørgensen, P. E.   Salmonid viruses: Double infection of RTG-2 cells with Egtved and infectious pancreatic necrosis viruses. *Arch. gesamte Virusforsch. 29:* 337. 1970.

81. Wolf, K., Gravell, M., and Malsberger, R. G.   Lymphocystis virus: Isolation and propagation in centrarchid fish cell lines. *Science (Wash., D.C.) 151:* 1004. 1966.

82. Wolf, K., Herman, R. L., and Carlson, C. P.   Fish viruses: Histopathologic changes associated with experimental channel catfish virus disease. *J. Fish. Res. Board Can. 29:* 149. 1972.

83. Wolf, K., Quimby, M. C., and Carlson, C. P.   Infectious pancreatic necrosis virus: Lyophilization and subsequent stability in storage at 4 C. *Appl. Microbiol. 17:* 623. 1969.

84. Wood, E. M., and Yasutake, W. T.   Histopathologic changes of a virus-like disease of sockeye salmon. *Trans. Amer. Microscop. Soc. 75:* 85. 1956.

85. Wood, E. M., Snieszko, S. F., and Yasutake, W. T.   Infectious pancreatic necrosis in brook trout. *A.M.A. Arch. Pathol. 60:* 26. 1955.

86. Yasutake, W. T.   Comparative histopathology of epizootic salmonid virus diseases, pp. 341–350.   In *A Symposium on Diseases of Fishes and Shellfishes,* ed. S. F. Snieszko.   Amer. Fish. Soc., Spec. Publ. No. 5.   Washington, D.C., 1970.

87. Yasutake, W. T., and Amend, D. F.   Some aspects of the pathogenesis of infectious hematopoietic necrosis.   *J. Fish Biol. 4:* 261.   1972.

88. Yasutake, W. T., and Rasmussen, C. J.   Histopathogenesis of experimentally induced viral hemorrhagic septicemia in fingerling rainbow trout (*Salmo gairdneri*).   *Bull. Off. int. Épizoot. 69:* 977.   1968.

89. Yasutake, W. T., Parisot, T. J., and Klontz, G. W.   Virus diseases of the Salmonidae in western United States.   II. Aspects of pathogenesis.   *Ann. N. Y. Acad. Sci. 126:* 520.   1965.

90. Zwillenberg, L. O.   Abstract: Morphological ultrastructure and classification of Egtved virus.   In *Symposium on the Major Communicable Fish Diseases of Europe and Their Control,* Working document no. C7660, p. 2.   FAO (Food Agr. Organ. U. N.), Rome, in press, 1972.

91. Zwillenberg, L. O., and Wolf, K.   Ultrastructure of lymphocystis virus.   *J. Virol. 2:* 393.   1968.

92. Zwillenberg, L. O., and Zwillenberg, H. L.   Transmission and recurrence problems in viral hemorrhagic septicemia of rainbow trout.   *Bull. Off. int. Épizoot. 69:* 969.   1968.

DISCUSSION OF FISH VIRAL DISEASES

Question: I am interested in the latency phenomena that you talk about with IHN and IPN viruses.   Does the virus disappear from the tissue?   Can you recover a latent form of the virus, or does the virus assume some sort of mask prototype?

W. T. Yasutake: If I may, I would like to refer that question to Dr. Wolf.

K. E. Wolf: No, as far as we know, virus is generally recoverable through all stages of infection.   While I have this opportunity I would like to call the audience's attention to the work of Dr. Yasutake.   The quality of his work with viral hemorrhagic septicemia exceeds that of anyone else because his group did use specific pathogen-free fishes, they used culture-grown virus, and they knew that the effects resulted from the viral infection and only the virus.   In contrast, prior work was with farm-raised fishes that came out of the ponds, detailed microbiology was not done, and in my personal observations of epizootics in Denmark, the work that Yasutake has described is certainly in agreement with farm epizootics where the virology was known.

Question: Do you think you have learned enough to make specific diagnosis using only tissue sections without doing tissue cultures for any of these viruses?

W. T. Yasutake: Answer to that would be a qualified yes.   Qualified because, even if we may be reasonably certain that a given specimen is histopathologically IHN or IPN positive, we would still consider it to be only presumptively positive until it has been confirmed by virological tests. It has been the general policy of our laboratory not to give out definitive diagnostic reports on any suspected viral disease material until both the histopathological and virological tests are completed. Please let me clarify—if you were to histologically examine specimens from a terminal stage of IHN or IPN, it could be difficult to distinguish one disease from another. However, if enough samples are examined from an epizootic, one would expect to see various stages of the disease. In the case of IHN, for instance, the intermediate stage will very likely exhibit dramatic changes in the kidney hematopoietic tissue, while there may only be moderate degenerative changes in the pancreatic tissue. In case of IPN, since pancreatic tissue seems to be the target tissue, the reverse would be true. In fish older than approximately three months, the absence or presence of granular cell necrosis—these cells are normally found in the wall of the digestive tract of three-month-old salmonids—would give you a clue as to which disease the fish might have. As I mentioned in my presentation, in IHN-infected fish these cells would be involved, while in IPN-infected specimens these granular cells would exhibit no abnormal changes. With VHS one may encounter more of a problem, particularly in fish younger than three months old. This is because, with the exception of granular cell involvement, histopathological changes associated with IHN are very similar to those of VHS. Since VHS is yet to be found in the United States, we have had limited opportunity to examine fish with this disease. Therefore, I am not sure whether we can, only by histological means, determine the difference between these two diseases. In fish with experimentally induced VHS, we have found that the hemorrhagic areas are not always present and kidney hematopoietic tissue does not seem to be as extensively involved as in IHN.

K. E. Wolf: I think I can agree with Yasutake on this, but there has arisen an unfortunate misconception that viruses are mutually exclusive, and they are not. The Danes have found both VHS and IPN in the same fish. This is something that histopathological examination cannot distinguish. I dare say with what is happening now, and man's interference in spreading fish from one place to another, that we are going to find the same fish with IHN and IPN. Both viruses will be found to occur within the same animal. Virology would then provide this answer. It is really part of a team approach. I don't think one approach, microbiology or histopathology, is self-sufficient. Working together, then, we know a more complete story.

Question: From work with human and animal viruses I find it very difficult to believe that North American fish have only five viruses. I would like to ask either you or Dr. Wolf, in what percentage of the material that is submitted for diagnosis, in which you have strong evidence that viral diseases are involved, are you actually able to identify one of these five diseases? To put it another way, do you think that these really constitute the bulk of our fish viral diseases or are we just scratching the surface?

K. E. Wolf: I believe we haven't even scratched the surface yet. There are more viruses being worked on. Dave Beckwith is characterizing a myxovirus isolated from a centrarchid fish. We have eight viruses isolated to date and the French wrote in the last couple of weeks that they have isolated a virus from an esocid fish, possibly the lymphosarcoma virus. I don't know that anyone can answer the question of how prevalent the viruses are, but additional fish viruses are being described at the rate of one or two a year.

R. Walker: In the lymphocystis lesions which you showed you suggested that the basophilic cytoplasmic inclusion body was where the virus was located. Actually the basophilic material is "viroplasm" including the viral DNA not yet packaged as virions. The virus particles are completed at the surface of this viroplasm, and if the mature particles ever aggregate and crystallize it must be in other parts of the cytoplasm where there is space enough. In the bluegill, for instance, where the viroplasm in the giant cells is relatively compact and localized, crystal arrays of virus may be seen about a month after infection. In the walleye, however, even after a year, with a much larger host cell and greater virion multiplicity, there is never crystallization, since the lacy inclusion extends through almost all of the cytoplasm, and the mature virions must stay in the narrow interstices.

The lymphocystis viruses are all about 200 nm in diameter, indistinguishable in form and size; but almost surely there are several families not easily transferrable to other orders of fishes. I once thought that the characteristic differences in lymphocystis cells in bluegills, walleyes, and flatfishes were host-specific responses. Twice, now, I have managed to get bluegill lymphocystis virus into walleyes. The host cell response was recognizably like that of the bluegill disease. Thus the differences in cell response are virus-specific: rate of cell growth, limit of cell size, and laciness of viroplasmic inclusion.

As to how many fish viruses there are, quite aside from these subdivisions of a group (e.g., lymphocystis), as a visualist I put some faith in structure. When we find a consistent correlation between virus-like particles and a certain type of lesion (e.g., C-type particles in dermal sarcoma or epidermal hyperplasia in walleye, or PCDV [polyhedral cytoplasmic deoxyribo-virus] in cod red blood cells) I am willing to say, not just virus-like particles, but virus.

PART II
Diseases of a Species: Channel Catfish

9

The Pathology of the
Major Diseases of Catfish

FRED P. MEYER

The commercial production of channel catfish is a very young industry. Since its start in the early 1960s, acreages have climbed from 250 acres in 1960 to upwards of 50,000 acres in 1972. This explosive growth far overtaxed available technical assistance and has occurred faster than the necessary basic research could be completed. As a consequence, many areas, including disease control, have not been adequately investigated.

Much of the disease-control work at the Fish Farming Experimental Station in Stuttgart, Arkansas, is directly involved with diagnostic service. Gross signs, environmental conditions, identifiable stresses, and macroscopic and microscopic examinations of fresh preparations are coupled with bacterial isolations to provide the basis for diagnosis and treatment. Histopathology is used but, unfortunately, only when necessary to make a diagnosis or as time permits. This paper will be directed toward the clinical and gross signs of significant diseases of channel catfish.

VIRAL DISEASES

One viral disease of catfish is known at the present time. Channel catfish virus disease (CCVD) causes massive mortalities in young channel catfish. Epizootics occur most commonly in young-of-the-year animals at water temperatures above 30°C. Although outbreaks have occurred in at least five states, the occurrence of

275

CCVD is sporadic. Epizootics appear only when proper conditions of stress, temperature, and susceptible fish are present. The disease is highly contagious and usually runs its course in 7 to 10 days. Losses approach 95 to 100%. Survivors are generally unthrifty and may have poor growth rates (J. Gratzek, personal communication).

Characteristics of CCVD include various combinations of the following external signs: (1) hemorrhagic areas on fins, eyes, and abdomen; (2) distention of the abdomen with ascites; (3) pale or hemorrhagic gills; and (4) exophthalmia on one or both sides.

Many infected fish have no internal indication of disease other than pale, enlarged kidneys. Others exhibit one or more of the following signs: (1) hemorragic areas in the musculature, liver, kidneys, and spleen, which is often pale, red, and enlarged; (2) stomach distended with a mucoid secretion; and (3) a yellowish exudate in the abdominal cavity (ascites).

Behavioral signs include swimming in spirals, listlessness, and floating vertically with the head up (2).

Positive diagnosis is dependent upon isolation and serological identification of the virus. Tissue culture isolation, histopathological examination, and electron microscopy provide presumptive diagnosis with a high probability of accuracy.

While CCVD alone kills experimentally infected fish in the laboratory, most natural infections of CCVD have had accompanying bacterial infections. Associated bacterial agents may include *Aeromonas, Pseudomonas,* or myxobacteria. Clinical signs will vary with the particular bacterium involved and may mask the presence of the viral disease (2).

BACTERIAL DISEASES

Most infectious diseases of catfish are caused by four genera of bacteria: *Aeromonas, Pseudomonas, Chondrococcus,* and *Edwardsiella.* While other organisms serve as pathogens, the incidence of such infections is uncommon (1, 8).

Aeromonas liquefaciens, the most common bacterial pathogen, is the cause of bacterial hemorrhagic septicemia in catfish. The disease is endemic throughout catfish-producing areas of the country and affects most other species of fish. Many species of fish from natural waters as well as amphibians serve as reservoir hosts (4).

Incidence patterns of disease on fish farms and observations on kills in natural waters suggest that stress plays an important role in the suceptibility of fish to *A. liquefaciens* and other bacterial pathogens (7, 9).

A thorough discussion of contributing factors and physiological changes associated with *A. liquefaciens* infections may be found in Bullock, Conroy, and Snieszko (1).

Infected fish may exhibit a great diversity of signs. Characteristics of infection vary according to the locations of lesions. Four forms are known. These include: (1) True septicemia with high levels of bacteria in circulating blood. External lesions may be absent, loss rates are exceedingly high, and the course of the disease is very rapid in such instances. (2) Focal lesions in liver, kidney, muscle tissue, or within the cranium. Impaired kidney function results in dropsy or exophthalmia, and fish may exhibit erratic, convulsive swimming behavior due to brain damage. Loss rates are low to moderate. (3) Cutaneous lesions involving dermal and subcutaneous layers of the skin (Fig. 9.1) or ulcers which penetrate deeply into muscle tissue. Capillaries and small blood vessels become hyperemic with hemorrhaging in and around lesions. Visceral organs are conspicuously hyperemic. Loss rates range from moderate to high. (4) Asymptomatic carrier fish which exhibit no signs of disease and have no losses unless stressed.

Any stress such as low oxygen, high temperature, poor water conditions, or handling may induce epizootics. On fish farms, a 10-to-14-day incubation period is common.

Many strains of *A. liquefaciens* are known and great differences in virulence are apparent in cases observed on fish farms. Highly virulent strains may kill entire populations within 48 hours following moderate stress without the usual external signs of disease being present (3). Strains of low virulence induce a chronic form of disease accompanied by localized gross lesions and a lingering illness. In such cases, losses occur over extended periods before reaching epizootic proportions (Fig. 9.2).

Pseudomonas fluorescens and other pseudomonads cause a chronic form of disease in catfish. Infected fish usually have large cutaneous or ulcerous lesions with well-defined borders over the body (Fig. 9.3). Loss of pigmentation is common within the lesions. Hemorrhage and inflammation are confined to the lesions and do not extend into surrounding tissue, contrary to cases of *A. liquefaciens* infections. Septicemia usually develops but death results only in advanced cases. Infected individuals tolerate extensive tissue damage by *P. fluorescens* and skeletal elements may be exposed in ulcerous lesions on fish which are still feeding. Loss rates are generally low, although over 50% of the fish may have lesions.

Fig. 9.1. Lesions on channel catfish associated with *Aeromonas liquefaciens* infection.

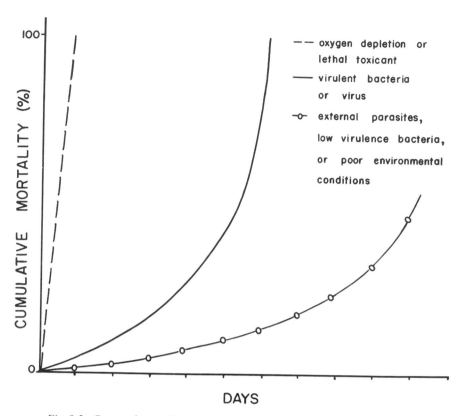

Fig. 9.2. Curves of mortality rates associated with various etiological agents.

Fig. 9.3. Channel catfish with typical lesions caused by *Pseudomonas fluorescens.*

Secondary invasions by fungi and facultative bacteria are common contributing factors in mortalities associated with *Pseudomonas* infections.

Chondrococcus columnaris and other myxobacteria constitute a significant problem whenever fish are crowded or held under less than optimal environmental conditions, particularly during summer months. Infections are especially common in tank and raceway culture systems. Lesions due to myxobacteria are usually limited to the mucous membranes, skin, fins, or gills (Fig. 9.4). Gross cutaneous lesions with accompanying loss of pigmentation are characteristic of columnaris disease. Fibrous connective tissue elements of the skin remain intact and crater-like ulcers are not observed in *C. columnaris* infections. Septicemia develops in advanced cases, with death occurring soon thereafter.

In lesions, myxobacteria may be most readily observed at the live-dead tissue interface. Seldom can they be found in the center of lesions. Because of the highly proteolytic nature of myxobacteria, secondary bacterial invasion is rare but fungi are common. Observers must take care not to overlook the myxobacteria which are the primary etiological agent and usual cause of death.

Myxobacterial disease is highly contagious and quickly spreads through a population if not controlled. Losses are high in untreated fish.

Edwardsiella tarda is the etiological agent of emphysematous putrefactive disease of catfish (EPDC) (8). An enteric bacterium, the organism causes large, gas-filled, malodorous, necrotic lesions in muscle tissue (Fig. 9.5). There is a striking resemblance to gangrene of humans but it lacks the dark bluish-green color of that condition. Tissue surrounding the lesion is invaded by bacteria, with advancing necrosis of tissue. While bacteria are readily isolated from the blood or kidney, a true septicemia often fails to develop. A marked inflammatory response is lacking despite extensive tissue damage associated with *E. tarda* infections. The disease is first evident as small cutaneous lesions, measuring 3 to 5 mm in diameter. While the lesions may resemble catfish-spine puncture wounds, it appears

Fig. 9.4. Lesions on black bullheads caused by myxobacteria.

Fig. 9.5. Gas-filled, necrotic lesions on channel catfish typical of *Edwardsiella tarda* infections.

that these openings develop after a fistula has formed from deep within the muscle.

The course of EPDC is slow. Fish with large lesions continue to feed. Death occurs when vital functions fail, usually because of a breakdown in kidney or liver function. Concurrent infections with *Aeromonas* or *Pseudomonas* are common. The presence of these organisms greatly speeds the loss rate and may mask the signs of EPDC. EPDC is primarily a disease of fish 38 cm or larger, occurring when water temperatures are above 30°C and when high levels of organic fertility are present in pond waters.

Incidence rates in ponds are seldom higher than 5%. However, if infected fish are harvested and confined in holding tanks, the disease quickly spreads and loss rates may approach 50%.

PARASITIC DISEASES

External signs induced by parasitism are extremely nonspecific. Most external parasites cause the same generalized signs, and affected catfish may show any of, or combinations of, the following conditions: (1) emaciation, (2) excess mucus,

(3) erosion of fins, (4) clubbed gills, (5) abrasions, (6) petechiae, (7) anemia, (8) listlessness, (9) erratic swimming, and (10) failure to feed.

Small fish are most affected by parasitism and may be killed by excessive numbers of parasites. Newly hatched fry may die before they are able to feed, occasionally within minutes after hatching. Small fish may fail to feed because of parasitism, and death then may result from starvation.

Parasitized postlarval and fingerling fish often have no lesions and usually exhibit a slow, continuous loss rate that increases with time. Daily loss rates of 1 to 5% are common and may continue for several weeks or more. This is in contrast to normal loss patterns associated with bacterial infections (Fig. 9.2).

Primary agents in external parasitic disease are the protozoans *Trichodina*, *Chilodonella*, *Ichthyophthirius*, *Ambiphyra* (= *Scyphidia*), *Costia*, and *Trichophrya* and monogeneans of the genus *Cleidodiscus* (6).

Ichthyophthirius deserves additional comment because of the unusual lesions associated with its presence. Trophozoites of *Ichthyophthirius* develop in the cutaneous layers of the skin. There they may be observed in cavities within and beneath epithelial tissue. Whether they actively destroy and consume epithelial cells or merely feed on body fluids is uncertain. As the trophozoites grow, visible pustules of about 0.5 mm, each containing an organism, are apparent over the body, in the fins, and in gill tissue. Severely infected fish may have thousands of pustules over the body.

Matured trophozoites leave the fish and undergo multiple fission to form infective stages called tomites. The penetration of tomites is exceedingly irritating and fish under attack will twitch, rub themselves on the bottom, and have frayed fins and excess mucus.

Fish infected with ichthyophthiriasis become emaciated, listless, refuse to feed, and become highly anemic. Hematocrit values of 6 to 12 are common, compared to the normal range of 30 to 34.

Completion of the developmental cycle requires 52 hours under near-ideal conditions of 21° to 24°C. Epizootic disease may occur 7 to 10 days after initial exposure (5). Loss rates are up to 75% if infected fish are left untreated.

Among internal protozoans, sporozoans of the genus *Henneguya* occur commonly on channel catfish. Although spores appear morphologically similar (Fig. 9.6), certain tissue sites are preferred by particular forms or strains. Gall bladder, adipose tissue, cutaneous tissue, and two gill forms have been observed in channel catfish. One gill form develops spores within gill lamellae (Fig. 9.7), the other between lamellae (Fig. 9.8).

While cutaneous lesions due to *Henneguya* infections disfigure infected fish, loss rates are generally low and the fish often effect a full recovery. The interlamellar form of *Henneguya* induces the greatest histological change and may cause severe losses. This form induces gross changes in the gill tissue with exten-

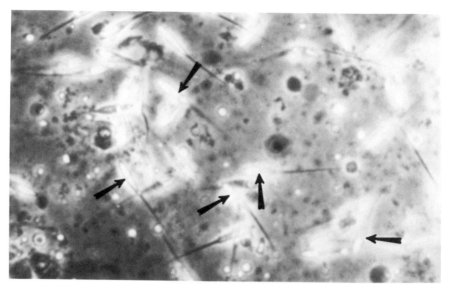

Fig. 9.6. *Henneguya* spores from intralamellar cyst in gill tissue of channel catfish.

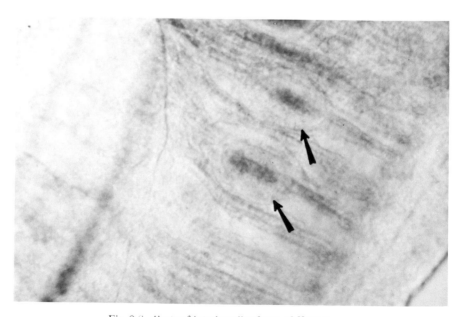

Fig. 9.7. Cysts of intralamellar form of *Henneguya*.

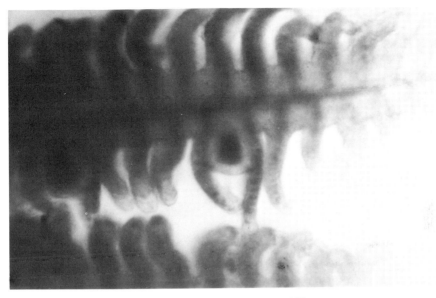

Fig. 9.8. Cyst of interlamellar form of *Henneguya*.

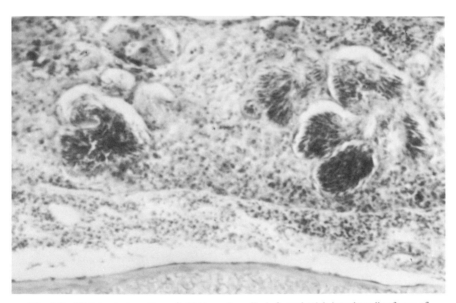

Fig. 9.9. Histological section of gill tissue heavily infected with interlamellar form of *Henneguya*.

sive hyperplasia. Lamellae fuse and lose all resemblance to normal tissue (Fig. 9.9). Vascularization is lost and the resulting tissue consists of a mass of epithelial cells, fibrocytes, and spores. Loss of respiratory surface approaches 90% or more. Heavily infected fish have signs of anoxia and general weakness. Loss rates are high following even mild stress conditions.

Parasites of many other groups occur on and in catfishes, including Digenea, Cestoda, Nematoda, Acanthocephala, Hirudinea, and Copepoda. Only under conditions of extreme parasitism or unique cultural conditions are these likely to cause problems. Internal metazoan parasites have not proved of economic significance to date and no major problems have been associated with their presence.

NUTRITIONAL DISEASE

The nutritional requirements of channel catfish have not been well defined. While supplemental rations are adequate under pond conditions, these have proved unsuitable under cage, tank, or raceway culture conditions in which no natural feed is available.

A condition named "broken-back syndrome" has appeared in channel catfish maintained on incomplete diets. The syndrome is typified by melanosis, cataracts, and fractures of the spinal column. Fractures occur most frequently in the first

Fig. 9.10. Broken-back syndrome of channel catfish. Arrows point to areas of fractures and to cataracts.

five caudal vertebrae. Each fracture is accompanied by loss of control over melanophores in the area, and a well-demarcated light band surrounding the body is evident (Fig. 9.10).

Mineralization of vertebrae is not complete in affected fish and is probably the contributing factor in the spinal weakness. Localization of the fractures in the vicinity of the first caudal vertebrae is coincident with the locus of greatest stress on the vertebral axis.

The cause of broken-back syndrome is generally considered to be nutritional. Researchers do not agree beyond this point. T. Lovell of Auburn University considers it to be a manifestation of an ascorbic acid deficiency. W. H. Hastings of the Fish Farming Experimental Station attributes it to a calcium-phosphorus imbalance which may be aggravated by an ascorbic acid deficiency.

Broken-back syndrome may occur eight or more weeks after the start of confinement, depending upon the inadequacy of the diet. The incidence in lots fed strictly supplemental rations may reach 75% or more. Feeding highly fortified catfish diets or trout feed will prevent its occurrence.

REFERENCES

1. Bullock, G. L., Conroy, D. A., and Snieszko, S. F. Bacterial diseases of fishes, pp. 60–87. In *Diseases of Fishes,* ed. S. F. Snieszko and H. R. Axelrod. 151 pp. Jersey City, T.F.H. Publications, 1971.
2. Fijan, N. N., Wellborn, T. L., Jr., and Naftel, J. P. An acute viral disease of channel catfish. *U. S. Bur. Sport Fish. Wildlife, Tech. Pap. 43.* 11 pp. 1970.
3. Lewis, W. M., and Bender, M. Heavy mortality of golden shiners during harvest due to a bacterium of the genus *Aeromonas. Progr. Fish-Cult. 22*(1): 11–14. 1960.
4. Meyer, F. P. Field treatments of *Aeromonas liquefaciens* infections in golden shiners. *Progr. Fish-Cult. 26*(1): 33–35. 1964.
5. Meyer, F. P. Parasites of freshwater fishes. II. Protozoa. 3. *Ichthyophthirius multifiliis. U. S. Bur. Sport Fish. Wildlife, Fish Dis. Leafl. 2.* 4 pp. 1966.
6. Meyer, F. P. Parasites of freshwater fishes. IV. Miscellaneous. 6. Parasites of catfishes. *U. S. Bur. Sport Fish. Wildlife, Fish. Dis. Leafl. 5.* 7 pp. 1966.
7. Meyer, F. P. Seasonal fluctuations in the incidence of disease on fish farms, pp. 21–29. In *A Symposium on Diseases of Fishes and Shellfishes,* ed. S. F. Snieszko. Amer. Fish. Soc., Spec. Publ. No. 5. Washington, D.C., 1970.
8. Meyer, F. P., and Bullock, G. L. *Edwardsiella tarda,* a new pathogen of channel catfish (*Ictalurus punctatus*). *Appl. Microbiol. 25*: 155–156. 1973.
9. Wedemeyer, G. The role of stress in the disease resistance of fishes, pp. 30–35. In *A Symposium on Diseases of Fishes and Shellfishes,* ed. S. F. Snieszko. Amer. Fish. Soc., Spec. Publ. No. 5. Washington, D.C., 1970.

DISCUSSION OF THE PATHOLOGY OF THE MAJOR DISEASES OF CATFISH

S. F. Snieszko: I am very reluctant to take part in the discussion from the floor, but Fred Meyer always stimulates me to do so. For quite a few years I've worked in the field of fish diseases. Last year I was invited to write a little history of the subject. I approached it from the point of view of an epidemiologist. To me, fish are a natural for the epidemiologists. You have three things: a host, disease agents, and the environment. Fish are animals in which effects of the environment play a tremendous role in their survival.

People like Fred Meyer and Paul Osborne, and probably others, have daily contact with spontaneous fish diseases. Such persons can usually go around a pond at a particular season of the year at a given location, and can predict from the existing conditions what is going to happen within the next few days.

Another intriguing thing from the epidemiologist's point of view is the control of fish disease. You see, we are developing a number of different compounds, you can call them drugs, for the control of disease. It is sometimes very difficult to explain to the general public what is the role of the drug. I try to explain it this way: If you have a fire, the fire department can help, but the fire department cannot prevent the outbreak of the fire. What is needed is prevention and an understanding of the balance between the environment, the host, and the potential pathogen. If you understand this balance, you can, in most instances, prevent the outbreak of fish disease.

10

Channel Catfish Virus Disease

JOHN A. PLUMB
and JOHN L. GAINES, JR.

Channel catfish virus disease (CCVD) was first reported in 1968 by Fijan (2) and has now been diagnosed in 23 epizootics from nine southern states (5). The etiological agent is a highly communicable herpes virus with a DNA nucleoprotein and measures approximately 100 mµ in diameter (11). The channel catfish (*Ictalurus punctatus*) is the primary host and the virus may cause over 90% mortality among susceptible fry and fingerlings throughout the summer months. The mortality rate depends upon the condition of the fish, water temperature, and probably other environmental factors. Fijan, Wellborn, and Naftel (3) described the clinical signs of CCVD in infected fish. Available evidence indicates that the virus causes a viremia affecting most if not all organs and tissues of infected fish.

Little quantitative information is available concerning recovery of various viruses from organs of infected fish. K. E. Wolf (personal communication) determined the amount of infectious pancreatic necrosis (IPN) virus present in the various organs of naturally infected rainbow trout (*Salmo gairdneri*). Klontz, Yasutake, and Parisot (4) reported the recovery on a daily basis of Sacramento River chinook disease virus from whole fish but individual organs were not assayed. Plumb (7) reported the sequential recovery of CCV from several internal organs of artificially infected catfish.

The histopathological changes of certain viral diseases of trout have been studied (1, 12, 14, 15). Wolf, Herman, and Carlson (13) reported the histopathological changes associated with CCV in experimentally infected fish. The purpose

287

of this paper is to describe the sequential development of histopathological changes and virus recovery from selected organs of catfish fingerlings experimentally infected with CCV.

METHODS AND MATERIALS

Cell cultures

Monolayer cultures of brown bullhead (BB) cells, in 16×125 mm culture tubes, were used in the isolation of CCV. This cell line was developed by R. G. Malsberger and C. P. Cerini at Lehigh University, Bethlehem, Pennsylvania. The culture medium utilized was Eagle's minimum essential medium in Earl's balanced salt solution, supplemented with 10% fetal bovine serum, 100 IU penicillin G, 100 μg streptomycin, and 25 μg Kanomycin per ml.

Virus

The CCV was from the original isolate made in 1968 (2) and was designated channel catfish virus Auburn$_1$.* It has been maintained for four years in successive passages of brown bullhead cells. Virus was harvested from infected cell cultures and the titer determined by the method of Reed and Muench (9). Serial 10-fold dilutions of the virus were made in Hank's balanced salt solution (HBSS), and triplicate BB cultures were inoculated with 0.1 ml of each dilution. Titrations are expressed as the 50% endpoint of cell culture infectious doses ($CCID_{50}$) per 0.1 ml of media.

Fish

Two hundred three-month-old channel catfish fingerlings weighing 3 to 5 grams each were anesthetized in 20 μg/ml quinaldine sulfate. Each fish was injected intraperitoneally with 0.1 ml of HBSS containing 3.1×10^4 $CCID_{50}$ of CCV. At the time of virus injection three uninfected control fish were examined for the presence of CCV. Inoculated fish were held in eight 40-liter aquaria at 30°C. Oxygen was supplied by bubbling air into the water. The water was neither filtered nor replaced. The visceral organs were removed from each fish and homogenized with a mortar and pestle, diluted 1:10 with HBSS and filtered through a .45 micron membrane. Triplicate BB cultures were each inoculated with 0.1 ml of the filtrate from each fish. Three control fish were also prepared for histological examination.

Histopathology

At 6-hour intervals for 96 hours post-injection (PI) three fish were selected and

* The virus was given the "Auburn$_1$" notation because it was first isolated at Auburn University, Auburn, Alabama, but the isolate was not from Auburn University fish.

killed by severing the spinal column. Moribund fish were used whenever possible.

The following organs and tissues were removed and placed in 10% formalin: (1) a flap of ventral tissue where injection had been made, (2) liver, (3) spleen, (4) intestine, (5) posterior kidney, (6) heart, (7) gills, and (8) brain. The formalin was changed after 12 hours, and the tissues allowed to fix for another 12 hours. All tissues were then processed in an Autotechnicon using ethanol and xylene, and were embedded in Paraplast. Sections were cut at a thickness of 6 microns, stained with Harris hematoxylin and eosin, cleared in xylene, and mounted in Permount.

Virus assay

At each 24-hour interval for 168 hours three infected fish were randomly selected and killed. The posterior kidney, liver, intestine, brain, spleen, and a blood sample were collected from each fish. The three spleens were pooled but the other organs were individually measured volumetrically and were then homogenized with a mortar and pestle. The homogenates and the blood were diluted with HBSS, filtered, and further serially diluted in 10-fold steps to 10^{-5} and titrated as previously described.

RESULTS

A total of 69 fish was examined in both portions of the experiment; 49 of these were examined histologically. The remaining inoculated fish died during the study. Virus was isolated from one of three kidneys at 24 hours PI. All three kidneys were positive at 48 to 144 hours PI (Fig. 10.1). At 168 hours PI only two of three specimens were positive. A peak CCV titer of $10^{5.25}$ in the kidneys was reached at 72 hours PI. At 168 hours PI the titer had dropped to $10^{2.0}$ (Fig. 10.1).

The posterior kidney had an increase in the number of lymphoid cells 6 hours after injection (Figs. 10.3–10.5). This increase continued and reached a peak at 36 hours PI (Fig. 10.4). Hemorrhage was first observed 18 hours PI and at this time there was some necrosis of the epithelial cells of the proximal tubules indicated by the presence of pyknotic nuclei. Necrosis of hematopoietic tissue occurred at 48 hours PI, but became massive at later stages (Fig. 10.5). The amount of hemorrhage increased (Fig. 10.5) and deposits of hemosiderin were observed 36 hours PI. The period of time from 42 hours PI to 96 hours PI was marked by a gradual decrease in the number of lymphoid cells present.

Virus recovery from the liver followed a pattern similar to that of the kidney (Fig. 10.1). One liver sample was CCV positive at 24 hours PI, two were positive at 48 hours PI, and all three were positive at the other sampling periods up to 168 hours PI, when CCV was isolated from only two of three fish. A peak CCV titer of $10^{4.5}$ in the liver was reached at 120 hours PI. Necrosis of the liver devel-

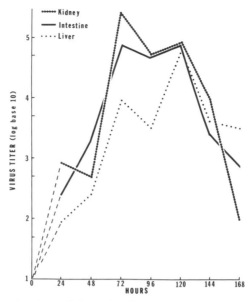

Fig. 10.1. Post-injection titers of channel catfish virus in kidney, liver, and intestine of artificially infected channel catfish fingerlings.

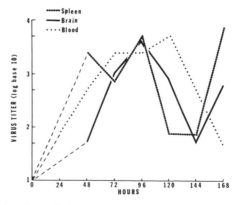

Fig. 10.2. Post-injection titers of channel catfish virus in blood, brain, and spleen of artificially infected channel catfish fingerlings.

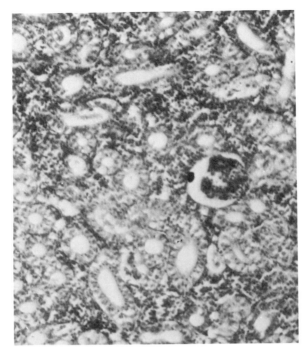

Fig. 10.3. Normal channel catfish kidney. Harris hematoxylin and eosin (H&E); ×100.

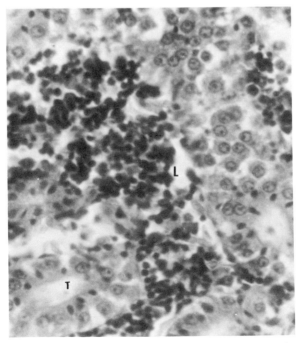

Fig. 10.4. Kidney of CCV-diseased channel catfish 36 hours PI. Note the presence of lymphocytes (L) but normal tubules (T). H&E; ×450.

291

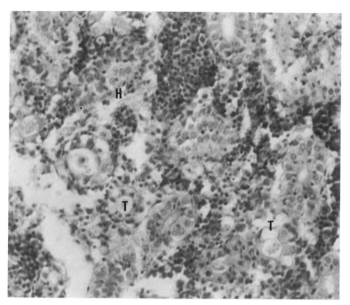

Figure 10.5. Kidney tissue of CCV-infected channel catfish 96 hours PI with necrosis of hematopoietic tissue (H) and tubules (T). H&E; X200.

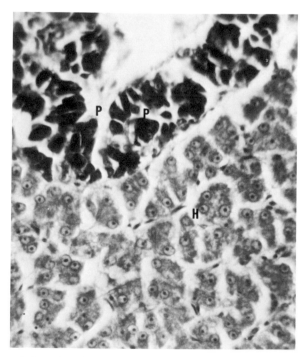

Fig. 10.6. Normal channel catfish liver with hepatic cells (H) and pancreatic cells (P). H&E; X450.

292

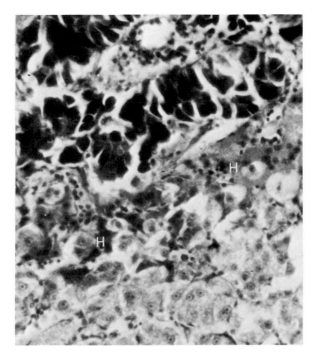

Fig. 10.7. Liver from CCV-diseased channel catfish 72 hours PI with necrosis of hepatic cells (H) adjacent to normal pancreatic tissue. H&E; X450.

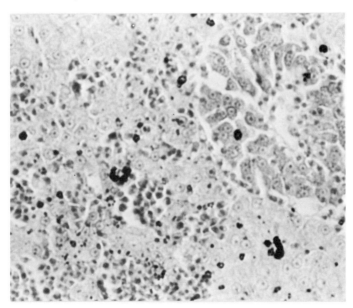

Fig. 10.8. Liver from CCV-diseased channel catfish 96 hours PI with hemorrhage. H&E; X450.

293

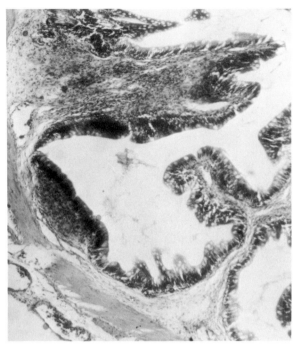

Fig. 10.9. Normal gastrointestinal tract of channel catfish. H&E; ×100.

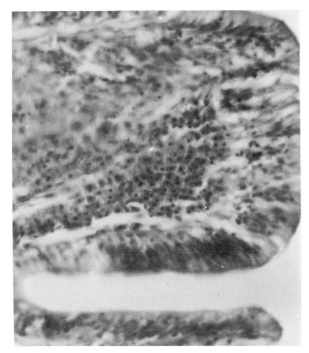

Fig. 10.10. Gastrointestinal tract of CCV-diseased channel catfish 72 hours PI. Massive hemorrhage. H&E; ×200.

oped more slowly than in the posterior kidney (Figs. 10.6-10.8). Pyknotic nuclei were first observed in the liver epithelial cells 18 hours PI, and focal necrosis was present at 36 hours PI. Extra vascular erythrocytes, indicating hemorrhage, were not observed in the liver until 36 hours PI. By 72 hours PI there was extensive necrosis and karyolysis of the liver epithelium (Fig. 10.7) and generalized hemorrhage by 96 hours (Fig. 10.8). Necrosis was particularly evident throughout the study in the liver epithelium surrounding the acinar pancreatic cells but the acinar cells were seldom affected. Edema was present in the terminal stages of the study.

Two samples of intestine contained CCV at 24 and 48 hours PI, but virus was present in all later samples up to 168 hours (Fig. 10.1). The peak virus titer was present in the intestine at 72 hours PI, when it reached $10^{4.75}$. Sections of the gastrointestinal tract (Figs. 10.9, 10.10) were hemorrhagic at 18 hours PI. This was particularly severe in the submucosa. These hemorrhages extended into the villi and were massive by 72 hours PI (Fig. 10.10). There was no evidence of mucosal sloughing, but edema was present.

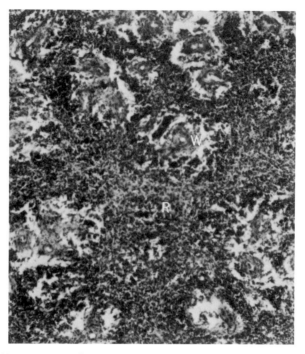

Fig. 10.11. Normal spleen of channel catfish showing white pulp (W) and red pulp (R). H&E; ×200.

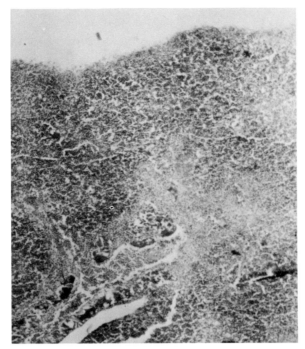

Fig. 10.12. Spleen of CCV-diseased channel catfish 48 hours PI. There is a lack of clear differentiation between white and red pulp. H&E; ×100.

The initial virus assay of spleen samples was made at 48 hours PI, at which time the titer was $10^{3.4}$ (Fig. 10.2). The titer reached a peak at 96 hours ($10^{3.5}$), followed by a decline and then another increase in titer at 168 hours. The spleens of infected fish (Figs. 10.11, 10.12) were filled with erythrocytes from 18 hours PI until 168 hours PI. At 48 hours PI it was difficult to differentiate between white and red pulp (Fig. 10.12).

Cardiac tissue was necrotic and edematous 96 hours after infection (Figs. 10.13, 10.14); however, the heart was not assayed for virus.

Virus was not detected in the brain at 24 hours PI. Only one specimen was positive at 48 hours (Fig. 10.2). All three samples were positive for virus 96 hours PI, at which time the peak titer was reached. Lesions were not observed in sections of the brains, gills, or muscles.

Two of three blood samples contained CCV at 24 hours PI and all three samples had positive titers at 48 hours PI (Fig. 10.2). All other blood samples were positive except the three samples assayed at 168 hours PI. The peak titer of the blood was $10^{3.5}$ at 120 hours PI.

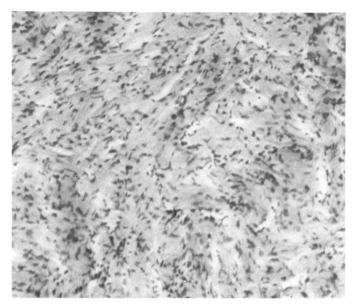

Fig. 10.13. Normal cardiac tissue of channel catfish. H&E; ×100.

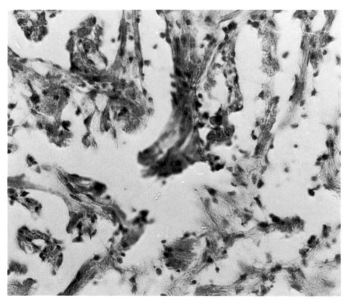

Fig. 10.14. Cardiac tissue of CCV-diseased channel catfish 96 hours PI. Necrotic myocardial cells. H&E; ×450.

SUMMARY

In artificially infected channel catfish, CCVD is an acute condition, marked by a rapid onset, short duration, and a quickly developing viremia. The disease follows a similar course during natural epizootics. Plumb (8) reported an epizootic in which 100% of 8,000 three-week-old fry died three days after the appearance of clinical signs. Many epizootics have resulted in over 90% mortality.

Histologically CCVD is characterized by necrosis and hemorrhage. Our observations essentially agree with those of Wolf, Herman, and Carlson (13); histopathological changes were most severe in the posterior kidney, liver, gastrointestinal tract, and spleen.

The posterior kidney of the channel catfish appears to be the organ most rapidly and most seriously affected (7, 13). In this study the first signs of injury appeared 18 hours PI as necrotic tubular epithelial cells in the kidney and an increased number of lymphoid cells. Virus was isolated from one kidney at 24 hours PI. Maximal injury to the kidney occurred 48 to 72 hours PI, which corresponds to the peak virus titer. The very early and major role of the kidney in the development of CCVD is further supported by the appearance in electron photomicrographs of a greater number of mature virus particles in kidney cells than in cells of other organs (8). The relationship between virus titer and histopathological changes was also observed in the liver, spleen, and gastrointestinal tract but the peak titers lagged behind the presence of maximal pathological changes.

The results indicate that the pathogenesis of CCVD in artificially infected fish conforms to the following sequence: the kidney is the initial organ in which CCV replication takes place and is followed in close succession, or concurrently, by the spleen. After virus replication in the kidney, a viremia is established which transports the virus to the intestine, liver, heart, and brain. The maximal virus titers in all organs or tissues occurred between 72 and 120 hours PI. This was followed by a gradual decline in titer. The study was terminated 168 hours PI and at this time some tissues were negative for CCV, whereas others had low virus titers. In a case history of CCVD at Auburn University, virus could not be isolated from surviving fish 10 days after the epizootic started (8). At the termination of the current study, the decrease in virus level in the infected catfish may have been approaching a carrier or dormant state, as previously suggested (6, 10). A carrier state for CCV in adult channel catfish has been investigated, but this condition has not been confirmed in spite of intensive study (5, 6, 8).

Histopathological changes were not observed in the gills, brain, or skeletal muscle. Wolf, Herman, and Carlson (13) reported no pathological changes in brain tissues; however, they did observe focal hemorrhage and some necrosis of muscles. Plumb (7) reported a very low level of virus in muscle tissue; thus little cellular injury should occur.

Virus has previously been reported in brain homogenates (7). In the present study the virus titer in the brain was not as high as that in the kidney, liver, or intestine, but it was very close to that in the blood and spleen. Since there were no observable lesions in the brain it is suspected that the virus titer in the brain reflects the level of virus in the blood. In the electron microscopic study (8), definitive virions could not be seen in brain tissues of moribund channel catfish 36 hours after infection; thus the central nervous system's role in CCVD is still unclear. However, erratic swimming (5, 10) was frequently associated with the disease 48 to 72 hours after artificial infection. This correlates closely with the isolation of virus from the brain, thus indicating central nervous system involvement.

Although the hosts are different, and the viruses differ in their classification and nucleic acid composition, there are some similarities between the histopathological changes caused by CCV in catfish and those caused by infectious hematopoietic necrosis (IHN) virus (1, 14) and IPN virus (12, 14) of North American salmonids. With CCV and the salmonid viruses the hematopoietic tissue of the kidney and spleen is damaged and necrosis occurs in epithelial liver tissue. A major difference between CCV and IHN and IPN is the slight involvement of the pancreatic tissue in catfish.

REFERENCES

1. Amend, D. F., Yasutake, W. T., and Mead, R. W.   A hematopoietic virus disease of rainbow trout and sockeye salmon. *Trans. Amer. Fish. Soc. 98*(4): 796–804. 1969.
2. Fijan, N. N.   Progress report on acute mortality of channel catfish fingerlings caused by a virus. *Bull. Off. int. Épizoot. 69*(7–8): 1167–1168. 1968.
3. Fijan, N. N. Wellborn, T. L., Jr., and Naftel, J. P.   An acute viral disease of channel catfish. *U. S. Bur. Sport Fish. Wildlife, Tech. Pap. 43.* 11 pp. 1970.
4. Klontz, G. W., Yasutake, W. T., and Parisot, T. J.   Virus diseases of the Salmonidae in western United States. III. Immunopathological aspects. *Ann. N. Y. Acad. Sci. 126:* 531–542. 1965.
5. Plumb, J. A.   Channel catfish virus disease in southern United States. *Proc. Annu. Conf. Southeast. Ass. Game Fish Comm. 25:* 489–493. 1971.
6. Plumb, J. A.   Channel catfish virus research at Auburn University. *Auburn Univ. Agr. Exp. Sta., Progr. Rep. 95.* 4 pp. 1971.
7. Plumb, J. A.   Tissue distribution of channel catfish virus. *J. Wildlife Dis. 7:* 213–216. 1971.
8. Plumb, J. A.   Some biological aspects of channel catfish virus disease. Ph.D. thesis, Auburn Univ., Auburn, Ala. 132 pp. 1972.
9. Reed, L. J., and Muench, H.   A simple method of estimating fifty percent endpoints. *Amer. J. Hyg. 27:* 493–497. 1938.
10. Wellborn, T. L., Jr., Fijan, N. N., and Naftel, J. P.   Channel catfish virus disease. *U. S. Bur. Sport Fish. Wildlife, Fish Dis. Leafl. 18.* 3 pp. 1969.
11. Wolf, K., and Darlington, R. W.   Channel catfish virus: A new herpes virus of ictalurid fish. *J. Virol. 8*(4): 525–533. 1971.

12. Wolf, K., and Quimby, M. C.   Salmonid viruses: Infectious pancreatic necrosis virus. *Archiv. gesamte Virusforsch. 34:* 144–156. 1971.
13. Wolf, K., Herman, R. L., and Carlson, C. P.   Fish viruses: Histopathologic changes associated with experimental channel catfish virus disease. *J. Fish. Res. Board Can. 29:* 149–150. 1972.
14. Yasutake, W. T.   Comparative histopathology of epizootic salmonid virus diseases, pp. 341–350. In *A Symposium on Diseases of Fishes and Shellfishes,* ed. S. F. Snieszko. Amer. Fish. Soc., Spec. Publ. No. 5. Washington, D.C., 1970.
15. Yasutake, W. T., Parisot, T. J., and Klontz, G. W.   Virus diseases of the Salmonidae in western United States. II. Aspects of pathogenesis. *Ann. N. Y. Acad. Sci. 126:* 520–530. 1965.

DISCUSSION OF CHANNEL CATFISH VIRUS DISEASE

M. M. Sigel: I couldn't help notice the distinctions between this type of infection and the herpetic infection in mammals. For example there is total absence of involvement of dermal tissues, which is a characteristic site of infection in birds and in mammals. Is this indeed a herpes virus? Have you done any antigenic studies?

J. A. Plumb: We have not done a great many antigenic studies with it. Dr. Wolf has characterized the virus, with Dr. Darlington. They have tentatively put it into the herpes virus group. Maybe Dr. Wolf would like to clarify this statement because he is the one that actually did the characterization.

K. E. Wolf: We did labelled precursor uptake studies with tritium-labelled thymidine, uridine, and leucine. At about four hours post-infection there is very rapid uptake of thymidine, the uridine uptake declines markedly, as does protein synthesis. This is presumptive evidence. Morphologically it is a herpes virus. Since that time, Goodhart in Chicago has found the guanine/cytosine ratio and it is exactly like that of one of the horse herpes viruses. We have done no antigenic comparisons. We have antiserum prepared against this if there is anyone interested in doing cross-neutralizations with this. I don't think John Plumb was aware of the g/c ratios that have been done, and Goodhart confirms its herpes virus identity.

Question: Two short questions: What about temperature requirements for this virus? Obviously it multiplies in the tissues of a cold-blooded animal. Do you know if this same virus will replicate in mammalian cells, and, conversely, will ordinary herpes multiply in the tissues of a catfish?

J. A. Plumb: Again, Dr. Wolf has done much of the work, and tried to infect several mammalian homeothermic cell lines and was unsuccessful. The optimum temperature is between 25° and 30°C in fish and in cell culture.

K. E. Wolf: We used 14 different cell lines, titrating virus immediately post-infection and then again after the incubation time appropriate for the cell line. We used mammalian, avian, reptilian, amphibian, and fish cells and this is the most host-specific virus that we have in fishes. It will only grow, to my knowledge, in cells from an ictalurid fish. Regarding temperature, we did get replication as low as 10°C, but with plaque and phase studies this was a 2- to 10-fold increase at the most. It replicated all the way through 33°C, well above the tolerance temperature of the brown bullhead cell line that we have used. The virus replicates so rapidly there that the cells will not sustain themselves in continuous passage, but it does replicate up to 33°C but not at 37°C. To my knowledge, very little has been done in fish cell lines compared to what has been done with mammalian cells and mammalian herpes viruses, but again I think this is quite a host- or cell-specific group.

Comment: We had some success in growing human herpes virus in turtle cells. You said you have not recovered virus from normal fish and this is interesting because herpes virus is notoriously known to exist in a latent form in mammals. However if you were to look for herpes virus in human beings you wouldn't ordinarily find it, but you would find that about 90% of human blood would have antibodies to herpes virus. I wonder if you have studied antibodies or serum of your catfish. Do they have antibodies to this virus?

J. A. Plumb: Yes, we have. Just about 100% of the adult fish which we know to have been associated with CCV epizootics, either directly or having produced virus-diseased fish, will have a high antibody titer. We can go to other populations of catfish on which we have no known history of CCV and find no antibodies whatsoever. This is on a neutralization index basis. We have done some serological work with it as far as immunity is concerned and we can create the normal immune response in adult channel catfish. One thing interesting about it is that when we sampled a group of brood stock over a period of one year there was no significant change in the antibody levels.

Question: Regarding the reservoir of the virus, do the recovered fish, even though they have antibodies, still shed virus?

J. A. Plumb: They do not so far as we can detect. At least with our detection methods we can't find it and this has been the big problem with this virus, trying to determine which populations are potentially reservoirs and which are not. We have been using the indirect method by determining which populations have antibodies and which have not. Of course this is not 100% foolproof.

PART III
Lesions of Organ Systems

11

Gill Lesions in Freshwater Teleosts

L A F A Y E T T E   L .   E L L E R

INTRODUCTION

The gills of fishes are located on each side of the head beneath a gill-covering operculum and are composed of finger-like filaments attached to a cartilaginous gill bar. Numerous, delicate, leaf-like structures, the lamellae, project from each filament and these consist of minute capillaries covered by a single layer of thin epithelial cells (Fig. 11.1). The epithelium forms a barrier between the fish's blood and the surrounding water. Gaseous exchange needed to sustain life takes place through this barrier and any thickening induced by physical, chemical or biological agents hinders the respiratory, secretory, and excretory function of this organ. Since 1910, investigators have reported specific, and often distinctive, morphological or histological changes in gill tissue caused by one or more of the above agents.

Plehn (58) suggested and Burrows (12) later concluded that a chemical irritant in the water was responsible for marked gill lesions in fishes. In other studies, a wide variety of pathological changes in the gills of trout, *Salmo gairdneri* and *S. clarki*, of bluegill, *Lepomis macrochirus*, and of goldfish, *Carassius auratus*, have been attributed to exposure to acute or chronic levels of pesticides (14–17, 25, 26, 43, 48, 49, 72, 79). Gill damage has also been described in bluegills, goldfish, or trout after exposure to heavy metals (2, 4, 13, 41, 46, 47, 64–67), to

305

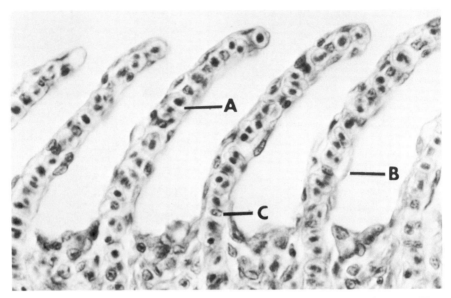

Fig. 11.1. Typical delicate leaf-like structures (lamellae) project from a gill filament. The lamellae were magnified 425× to demonstrate nucleated blood cells within the capillaries (A), a single layer of thin epithelial cells surrounding the capillaries (B), and the so-called pilaster supporting cells (C).

organic toxicants (9, 45, 51), to an organic solvent (7), to gases (57, 60, 61, 80), and to wood-fiber waste (67). Bullock, Conroy, and Snieszko (10), Davis (20, 21, 23), Fish (27), Fish and Rucker (29), Pacha and Ordal (55), and Wood and Yasutake (81) described well-defined and specific changes in the gills of fishes affected by gram-negative myxobacteria. Other organisms such as protozoans, monogenetic and digenetic trematodes, and fungi attached to or on the gills, encysted in the lamellae, or present within the vascular system are also responsible for gill lesions (1, 6, 22–24, 28, 32–34, 36, 38, 39, 41, 44, 56, 63, 80, 81).

Furthermore, fish food may cause gill lesions such as those described in fish fed diets containing crude or crystalline aflatoxins (5), and diets deficient in ascorbic acid or vitamin C (37), pantothenic acid (62, 76, 77, 81), or folic acid (68). Several authors have reviewed the histopathology of gill disease (33, 81). The ultrastructure of the secondary lamellae of the gills has been described (40, 52).

PHYSICAL AND CHEMICAL AGENTS

The first reference to a pathological change induced by an irritant in gill tissue was made by Osburn (54) in 1910. In silver salmon fingerlings with shortened gill covers he found cuboidal or columnar epithelial cells two to three cells deep instead of a single flattened layer. He attributed the proliferation of gill epithelium and specific clubbing of filaments as an adaptive measure to protect the gill filaments from continual irritation caused by the lack of an adequate external gill cover.

Plehn (58) was first to suggest that a chemical in the water was responsible for the appearance of gill lesions in fishes. She reported that a marked hyperplasia of gill epithelium may cause the filaments to grow together in a solid mass and thus impair gas exchange. She mentioned that the severe injury may cause afflicted fish to suffocate.

Wales and Evins (74) concluded that foreign matter in hatchery water, such as diatoms, small algae forms, bacteria, and protozoans, induced mechanical injury to the gills of certain strains of hatchery fish.

Accumulated Nitrogenous Wastes

Wolf (77) failed to transmit gill disease to healthy hatchery trout even though he fed them gills from fish with myxobacterial infections, held diseased fish in close contact with healthy fish, and introduced bacteria in the water supply. Hence, he presumed that a chemical irritant from excretory products of the fish themselves caused the respiratory epithelium to proliferate. Both Borg (8) and Burrows (12) supported Wolf's inference. Borg stated that it is almost certain that myxobacteria are ever present in hatchery waters and that gill disease is precipitated by crowding, which results in oxygen deficiency and water pollution by nitrogenous products excreted by fish. Burrows, studying the effects of accumulated excretory products on hatchery-reared salmonids, concluded that gill lesions resulted from exposures to ammonium hydroxide concentrations as low as 0.3 ppm and as high as 0.7 ppm. Hyperplasia of gill epithelium resulted from a continuous exposure to the lowest concentration for six weeks. An intermediate exposure to 0.5 ppm caused marked hyperplasia, and at the highest concentration, adjacent lamellae became extensively fused. However, Rucker, Johnson, and Kaydas (62) found no evidence of gill damage in blueback (sockeye) salmon, *Oncorhynchus nerka*, when the gills were irritated by ammonium chloride.

Ammonia water solutions also affected the gills of carp (30) and young trout (59). Flis (30), studying the effects of ammonia water on carp, found that 15 to 20 mg per liter of ammonia, expressed as NH_3, was lethal. This acute concentration caused marked deterioration in organs in direct contact with the solution, such as skin, gills, and intestine. Prolonged exposures to sublethal concentrations were more harmful than short-term exposures and caused an increase in the production of mucus. However, NH_3 concentrations of 1.75 to 3.0 mg per liter in free-flowing water and 0.25 to 0.75 mg per liter (60) in static water caused a 60% mortality in trout fry. NH_3 concentrations of 0.27 mg per liter caused inflammatory lesions in tissues, lumps in the gills, and a sharp decrease in the number of erythrocytes.

Pesticides

In 1961, the Bureau of Sport Fisheries and Wildlife, Fish-Pesticide Research Laboratory, then located at Denver, Colorado, initiated a series of laboratory and field studies designed to investigate the histopathological effects of selected pesticides on fish tissues. During 1961–63 Wood (79) evaluated microscopically the morphological and histochemical alterations in these tissues. In short-term studies designed to cause rapid pesticide effects, he found moderate gill edema in rainbow trout surviving exposures of 7.5 to 17.5 µg per liter of heptachlor for two weeks. Exposure of this species to 1300 µg per liter of parathion for 11 days caused thickened lamellae with swollen epithelial cells, whereas exposure to 0.005 µg per liter of toxaphene for the same interval caused minimal distortion of individual lamellae. Trout exposed to 0.075 µg per liter of malathion for 4 or 11 successive days had gill lesions with slightly edematous lamellae; the edema increased progressively with exposure until the epithelium separated from capillaries in individual lamellae. The respiratory epithelia of some exposed fish were ruptured at various points, thereby exposing the capillaries to water.

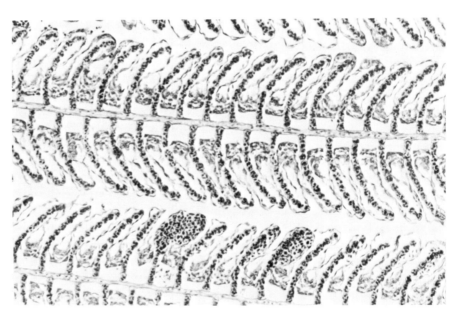

Fig. 11.2. Swollen, edematous lamellae and clavate-globate lamellae packed with erythrocytes were present in the gill of a bluegill treated with 4.0 mg per liter sodium arsenite for 21 days. ×125.

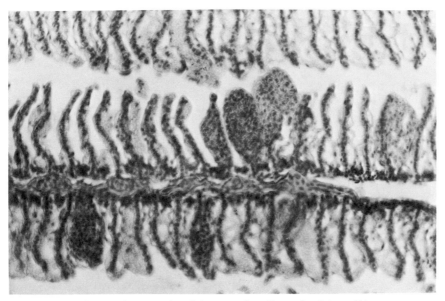

Fig. 11.3. Gill of a bluegill exposed to 3.0 mg per liter diuron for 3 days. Edema was present within many lamellae and some lamellae were distended by rounded masses of blood. ×125.

In other pesticide studies, Christie and Battle (14) found a lethal concentration of 6.0 ppm of the sodium salt of 3-trifluoromethyl-4-nitrophenol (TFM) induced edema of lamellae and vasodilation of arterioles and capillaries of the gill filaments in both larval lamprey, *Entosphenus lamottei*, and rainbow trout. In trout, the vasodilation was accompanied by increased mucus secretion.

Cope (15) reported proliferation of gill epithelium and hemorrhagic lamellae in bluegills exposed to dichlobenil for 4 days. After 63 days the lesions were sharply defined, blood vessels of filaments were engorged, and lamellae were fused. Gill lesions have also been observed in fish exposed to other herbicides. In bluegills exposed to 4.0 mg per liter of sodium arsenite (35) for 21 days, the gill lamellae became swollen and edematous, whereas others were described as clavate-globate lamellae packed with erythrocytes (Fig. 11.2). Similar gill damage was found in bluegills exposed to 3.0 mg per liter of diuron (48) for 3 days (Fig. 11.3). However, rapidly multiplying epithelial cells "blanketed" or caused adjacent lamellae to fuse in fish exposed to diuron for 21 days (Fig. 11.4). In contrast, adjacent lamellae and filaments of redear sunfish, *L. microlophus*, were extensively fused in the early stages of contact with 0.3 mg per liter of endothal (Hydrothol 191) (25) (Fig. 11.5). These fish apparently acclimated to the herbicide after 14 days and tissue alterations were reversed with a gradual return to normal (Fig. 11.6).

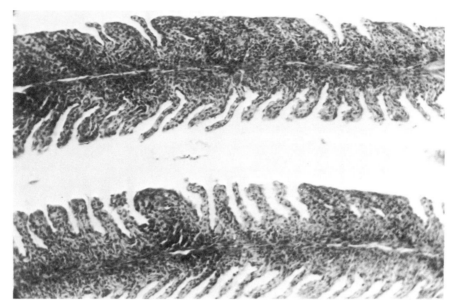

Fig. 11.4. Gill of bluegill exposed to 3.0 mg per liter diuron for 21 days. Rapidly multiplying epithelial cells blanketed or fused adjacent lamellae. ×125.

Matton and LaHam (49) described pseudogill damage in rainbow trout exposed to 50 mg per liter of trichlorofon (Dylox) for 10 hours. The parallel arrangement of cell rows was disrupted and the epithelial cells were elongated and distended with swollen nuclei. Striking gill lesions were present in goldfish exposed to mirex for 56 days (72). Exposure to 0.1 mg per liter of mirex caused proteinaceous fluids to separate the respiratory epithelium from capillaries in individual lamellae (Fig. 11.7). In contrast, the gill damage in fish exposed to 1.0 mg per liter consisted of hyperplasia of gill epithelium, accumulation of hemorrhagic exudates in the branchial cavity, and lamellae congested with blood (Fig. 11.8). Monthly one-hour exposures of cutthroat trout to 0.01 mg per liter of endrin for 11 months and 0.04 mg per liter the 12th month caused striking gill lesions (26). Proteinaceous fluids dissociated the respiratory epithelium from central capillaries of individual lamellae (Fig. 11.9). However, a concentration of 0.04 mg per liter of methoxychlor (43) had a different effect on bluegills. A glycoprotein material circulated in the branchial blood vessels (Fig. 11.10) and in some instances plugged the capillaries in individual lamellae (Fig. 11.11). Similar observations were made on bluegills exposed to 1.0, 5.0, and 10.0 mg per liter of 2,4-D (17).

Fig. 11.5. Gill of a bluegill treated with 0.3 mg per liter Hydrothol 191 for 7 days. Adjacent lamellae and filaments were extensively fused. ×125.

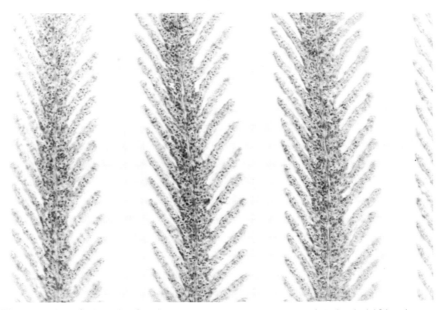

Fig. 11.6. Gill of a bluegill after 21 days' exposure to same level of Hydrothol 191 as in Figure 11.5. The spatial arrangement of filaments and lamellae was similar to that found in the gills of a typical bluegill control. ×125.

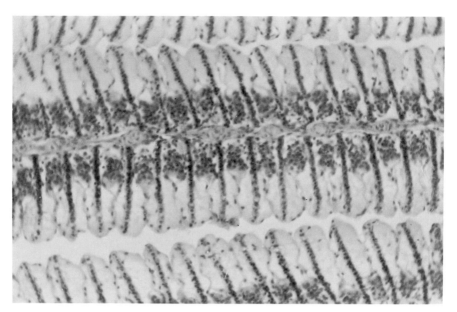

Fig. 11.7. Proteinaceous fluid lifted and ballooned respiratory epithelium from capillaries of individual lamellae in gills of goldfish treated with 0.1 mg per liter mirex for 56 days. ×125.

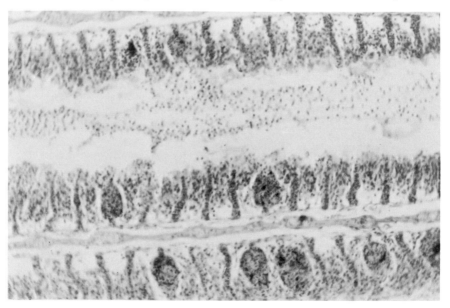

Fig. 11.8. Gill of goldfish treated with 1.0 mg per liter mirex for 56 days. Note epithelial hyperplasia along the longitudinal axes of filaments, clavate-globate lamellae congested with blood, and hemorrhagic exudate in the branchial cavity. ×125.

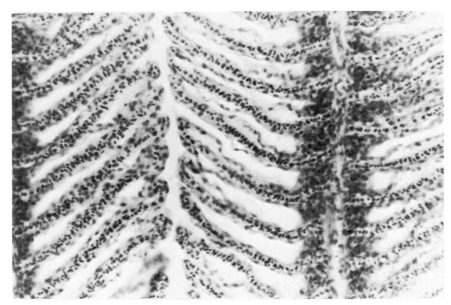

Fig. 11.9. Gill of a cutthroat trout exposed to 0.01 mg per liter endrin for 11 months, then to 0.04 mg per liter endrin the 12th month. Proteinaceous fluids lift respiratory epithelium from capillaries in individual lamellae. ×125.

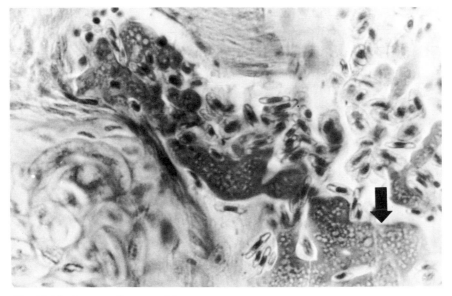

Fig. 11.10. Large confluent, multivacuolated masses of glycoprotein material (arrow) were present within the lumen of a branchial blood vessel after exposure to 0.04 mg per liter methoxychlor for 7 days. ×425.

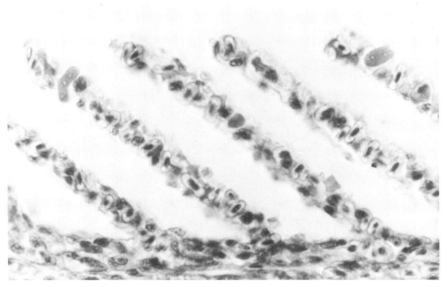

Fig. 11.11. Glycoprotein material is shown plugging capillaries of individual lamellae. ×425.

Heavy Metals

Carpenter (13) and Jones (42) observed copious secretions of mucus on the gills of minnows, *Phoxinus phoxinus,* and on those of sticklebacks, *Gasterosteus aculeatus,* which had been killed by high concentrations of zinc. They presumed that the abundant mucus mechanically disrupted gill function and caused asphyxiation of the fish. Lloyd (46) and Schweiger (64), however, suggested that heavy metals may form insoluble metal-protein complexes and that the toxic action of these complexes is confined to the epithelial cells of gill lamellae.

Schweiger (64) found that exposure of carp, *Cyprinus carpio,* to toxic solutions of cobalt and manganese caused the gill epithelial cells to become swollen, to separate from the pilaster cells, and finally to slough off. Lloyd (46) was unable to see coagulated mucus on the gill of rainbow trout killed by zinc poisoning. Parry (in 46) made a histological study of Lloyd's fish and confirmed his findings. No mucus was present in the gill chamber, but exposure to 20 ppm of zinc caused a breakdown of gill epithelium within 2.5 hours. Exposure to 4 ppm resulted in swollen gill lamellae before death, and exposure to 3 ppm for two days caused no detectable change in the gills. Cusick (18) also observed a decrease of mucous cells and thinner epithelium in the guppy, *Poecilia reticulata* (*Lebistes reticulatus*), after exposure to zinc in diluted water at pH 6. He found that the epithelium was more likely to be damaged when the water lacked calcium and magnesium because these metals compete with zinc for adsorption-desorption sites at the epithelial barrier. In other studies, Lloyd (47) found that pathological conditions in the gills of trout exposed to toxic concentrations of zinc, copper, and lead were similar to those described by Schweiger. Skidmore (66) concluded that water containing 40 ppm of zinc sulfate caused respiratory distress to trout after an hour or more and that gill epithelium was damaged when hatched rainbow trout are killed rapidly by zinc sulfate solutions. The gill damage was reported in a later paper. Skidmore and Tovell (67) found that initial changes in the gill tissue of 8 to 12 gram rainbow trout exposed to 40 ppm of zinc sulfate solution were typical of an acute inflammatory reaction. The epithelium covering the secondary lamellae lifted away in a continuous sheet from the pillar cell system, thus increasing the diffusion distance from water to blood. The central lamellar spaces were markedly decreased in size. Granulocytes appeared in large numbers within the lamellar blood spaces and beneath the raised epithelium. Finally the lamellar blood circulation became stagnant, terminating in respiratory collapse and the death of fish.

Iron salts also cause severe gill lesions. Ashley (4) reported that Cruz found gill lesions in goldfish exposed to 5, 10, 50, and 100 mg per liter of ferrous or ferric chlorides or sulfates dissolved in distilled water. The iron salts, at repeated low-level exposures or at single exposures at the high concentrations caused epithelial hyperplasia, capillary congestion, hypersecretion of mucus, and inflammation. The respiratory epithelium was destroyed and gill filaments and lamellae were blocked by muco-ferruginous precipitates. Gill destruction was aggravated by lowering the pH of the water to less than 5.0.

Organic Toxicants

Gill epithelium in bluegills exposed to 6.5 and 13.5 mg per liter of alkyl benzene sulfonate (ABS) (45) was two to three times thicker than normal. The cell walls and the cell mass lying between lamellae were also thickened. The gill damage was especially apparent in fish exposed to the higher concentration for 35 days. More recently, gill lesions were described in rainbow trout exposed to a mixture of the detergent (ABS) and 0.8 mg per liter of zinc (9), and to solutions of hard water containing 6.5 to 9.3 mg per liter of phenol (51). The detergent caused swelling and thickening of filaments, destruction of the epithelial walls of the secondary lamellae, and fusion of the tips of pillar cells. Phenol at the lower concentration caused gill alterations similar to those described by Brown, Mitrovic, and Stark (9). However, in fish surviving 7 days' exposure to the highest concentration, the epithelial walls of secondary lamellae were acutely inflamed and filaments were partially destroyed. Hematomas occurred on some filaments and the distal ends of filaments were extensively damaged.

Gases and Organic Solvents

Rucker and Hodgeboom (61) attributed gas-bubble disease in fishes to an excess of free nitrogen gas in water supplies. The disease affects many organs, including the gills (57, 60). In a microscopic examination of gills from affected fish, Renfro (60) found branchial arterioles completely filled with gas bubbles. Pauley and Nakatani (57) reported swollen edematous lamellae on individual filaments of salmon fingerlings afflicted with gas-bubble disease. Both Renfro and Pauley and Nakatani inferred that gas emboli may occlude the blood vessels, produce anoxia, and thereby cause necrosis of gills. Wood (80) also found swollen edematous lamellae in fish exposed to hydrogen sulfide.

Benville, Smith, and Shanks (7) also described edema within gill lamellae, and hypertrophy and hyperplasia of lamellar epithelium, in trout and salmon fed a diet containing 17.7% dimethyl sulfoxide. Immersion in 4% dimethyl sulfoxide caused lamellae to swell and fuse, and necrotic epithelial cells with pyknotic nuclei were sloughed from the lamellae.

Wood-Fiber Wastes

Smith, Kramer, and Oseid (69) reported that holding walleye fingerlings, *Stizostedion vitreum vitreum*, in aqueous solutions containing suspended conifergroundwood fibers at a concentration of 150 ppm for 193 days caused a 38% reduction in the number of mucus-secreting cells on the lamellae and on the interlamellar spaces of the gills.

MICROORGANISMS

Bacteria

Most investigators (10, 19, 29, 81) believe bacterial gill disease to be principally a myxobacterial infection which is preceded by unfavorable environmental conditions. The typical pathogenic myxobacterium, a long, thin, gram-negative rod, infects freshwater fish in ponds, rivers, or reservoirs and often causes severe epizootics during summer when water levels drop and the temperature rises.

Taxonomically, the organism belongs to the family Cytophagaceae, genus *Cytophaga*, or the family Myxococcaceae, genus *Chondrococcus*, and is the cause of columnaris disease. The bacterium is not a true tissue invader, but lodges and grows on the gill epithelium.

Columnaris Disease. Davis (19-21, 23), Fish and Rucker (29), Ordal and Rucker (53), and Pacha and Ordal (55) have shown that *Chondrococcus columnaris* or *Cytophaga columnaris* often damages gill tissue extensively in freshwater fish. Davis (19) first proposed the name *Bacillus columnaris* for the filamentous rod-shaped bacterium that appeared abundantly in grossly visible, localized gill lesions. In 1944, Ordal and Rucker (53) isolated a myxobacterium from the gills of salmonid fishes. Because they found swarming, fruiting bodies in both fresh and cultured material they diagnosed the organism as *Chondrococcus columnaris*. Garnjobst (31) isolated a myxobacterium with nonfruiting bodies and termed the organism *Cytophaga columnaris.* The myxobacterium isolated by Ordal and by Garnjobst closely resembled *C. columnaris* in size, shape, and characteristic movements.

Davis (23) reported the appearance of localized grey spots on the gill surrounded by a red tinge as the first indication of gill infection by *C. columnaris* disease. When examined in microscopic sections, the gill lesions associated with *C. columnaris* frequently start with hyperplasia of lamellar epithelium at the distal ends of the filaments. Later, the lesions extend downward toward the base and at the same time spread laterally. Epithelial cells in the immediate vicinity of the lesions become strongly vacuolated, but the characteristic proliferation and thickening of gill tissue associated with a continuous irritation is almost lacking. In heavy infections, the bacteria's advance over the epithelium may destroy entire lamellae and break down the filaments. The blood vessels supplying the gills become greatly congested.

Fish and Rucker (29), however, described gross gill lesions resulting from *C. columnaris* as dry infarcts which often unilaterally involved a part or all of the gill tissue. A bright hemorrhagic area at the confluence of the branchiostegal rays often accompanied the infection of the gills. Following observation of preparations made from the affected gills, they described a marked proliferation of the epithelium of the lamellae and gill rakers. In well-advanced cases, the epithelial hyperplasia was followed by sloughing and disintegration of lamellae and eventual necrosis of the central cartilaginous structure. The authors presumed that the gill tissue of fish reacts to *C. columnaris* in a manner typical of a continuous irritation.

Pacha and Ordal (55) observed limited or no gross gill injury at time of death in young salmonids naturally infected with strains of *C. columnaris* of high virulence. However, in slides prepared from gill tissue of young salmon experimentally infected with strains of *C. columnaris* of high virulence they observed a marked congestion of blood vessels supplying the gills, dissociation of surface epithelium of lamellae from the capillary bed, and scattered areas of hemorrhage. They concluded that the grossly visible lesions in fish infected with *C. columnaris* must be used with caution to estimate the incidence of the disease in the population, since infected fish often die before gross external manifestations of the disease appear. Depending on water temperature, gross lesions may be more common in infections resulting from strains of *C. columnaris* of lower virulence.

All studies indicated that the anatomo-pathologic changes in gills infected with *C. columnaris* were undoubtedly severe enough to lead to respiratory insufficiency and eventually contribute to the death of the fish.

Western-Type Bacterial Gill Disease. Other types of bacteria have been described (27, 81) from gill lesions. In gill infections of hatchery trout from three western states Fish (27) found gram-negative bacteria which differed from the typical filamentous myxobacterium associated with columnaris disease. In stained smears from heavily infected gill tissue, he observed two separate morphological types of gram-negative rods. The first measured 1.6 × 4.8 × 0.25 microns, the second 1.64 × 4.0 × 0.5 microns. Organisms were usually paired and seldom formed long chains. Progressive pathological changes of the gills occurred in fish infected by the organisms. In an early stage, lesions consisted of actively proliferating epithelium along the longitudinal axis of the filaments as well as along that of lamellae. When rapidly multiplying, the cells caused fusion of the distal margins of adjacent lamellae. In a more advanced stage, the interlamellar space of the filaments was partially or completely filled with a solid block of epithelial tissue and blanketed the greater part of the respiratory surface. In an extreme state, the lamellae became completely overgrown and the epithelium of one filament completely fused with that of a bordering filament. Fish (27) implied that the lesions resulted from one or both organisms; however, he acknowledged that he was unable to determine whether the organisms were responsible for the disease condition.

Wood and Yasutake (81) also found high concentrations of gram-negative short rod-shaped organisms in fish affected with gill disease and, by association, considered them the causative agent of the disease.

Bacterial Plaques. Burrows (11) and Wood and Yasutake (81) described plaque-like structures accompanied by hyperplasia of gill epithelium as an early developmental feature in bacterial disease. Burrows described the "plaques" as oval or flat structures on the gill epithelium, whereas Wood described the structures as single globose cells and projecting from the lamellae. Burrows indicated that bacteria projected outward from the plaques but Wood stated the plaques were often filled with intensely basophilic granules that did not resemble myxobacteria. However, both authors agreed the plaques either disappeared or were obscured by other cell-types as the hyperplasia developed and, at this point, typical filamentous bacteria appeared and increased in numbers.

Fungi

Davis (22), Dunkerly (24), Jirovec (41), Leger (44), and Pauley (56) have reported the presence of the parasite *Dermocystidium* on the gills of fish. Cysts containing the parasites were found on the gills of brown trout, *S. trutta,* on the gills of the pike, *Esox lucius* (41), and on the gills of adult salmon, *O. tshawytscha* (22).

The early workers identified the parasite as a protozoan and Davis (22) placed the organism in the order Haplosporidia. However, Pauley (56) identified the parasite as a fungus belonging to the genus *Dermocystidium.* He found *Dermocystidium* colonies in the gills of salmon, *O. tshawytscha,* held in spawning channels at Priest Rapids Dam, Washington. Grossly, the gill lesions appeared as small white spots on or in the filaments. In sections made from the affected tissue, the cysts along the filaments were enclosed in a thin, clear capsule, varied in size, and contained developmental stages of *Dermocystidium*. A subacute inflammatory reaction and well-developed granulation tissue surrounded the cysts. Hypertrophy and hyperplasia of gill epithelium were present and in many instances, adjacent lamellae were blanketed by an accumulation of macrophages, fibroblasts, and epithelial cells in interfilamentous spaces. The dense connective tissue of the gill and gill arches was edematous. The principal cause of death, according to Pauley, was anoxia resulting from the subacute inflammation and granulation of gill tissue. Allen et al. (1) also reported heavy mortalities among both adult and juvenile Columbia River chinook salmon infected with *Dermocystidium*. The disease evoked the same gill lesions as those described by Pauley.

Two Italian workers, Ghittino (34) and Grimaldi (36), reported heavy losses among bleak, *Alburnus alborella,* carp, and tench, *Tinca tinca,* infected with fungi belonging to the genus *Branchiomyces*. Ghittino found fungi circulating in the gill capillaries of carp and tench whereas Grimaldi observed numerous fungal elements along the gill arches and longitudinal axes of gill filaments. The fungi obstructed the flow of blood, caused gill hemorrhage and necrosis, and were responsible for the subsequent asphyxiation of afflicted fishes.

Protozoans

A variety of protozoans commonly found in fresh water have been reported to cause specific and distinctive changes in gills (22, 28, 32-34, 39, 80, 81).

Fish (28) inferred that an infection by the ectoparasite *Costia necatrix* may cause gill epithelium to proliferate and thus induce gill lesions comparable to those found in the early stages of Western bacterial gill disease. Ghittino (33) also found that gill disease arose with frequency in fishes affected by *Costia* and *Ichthyophthirius,* and hypothesized that the pathogenesis of gill disease may be related to the presence of protozoans.

Microsporidians also have an adverse effect on the gills of hatchery fish. They encyst in the gill and cause lamellae to thicken or fuse (80, 81).

Davis (22), Ghittino (32), and Hoffman et al. (39) have reported gill damage in freshwater fish infected by myxosporidians. Davis found *Henneguya* sp. in the gill cartilage of the white crappie, *Pomoxis annularis.* He also described *Chloromyxum externum* attached to gill epithelium or lying in the mucous coat surrounding the gills of the pearl minnow, *Margariscus margarita,* and the blacknose dace, *Rhinichthys atratulus. Myxosoma endovasa* was found in the lamellar capillaries of the smallmouth buffalo, *Ictiobus bubalus.* He presumed that a heavy infection by *C. externum* may severely injure gill epithelium, and sporulating trophozoites of *M. endovasa* may eventually block or stop the movement of blood in the capillaries.

Ghittino (32) and Hoffman et al. (39) also described myxosoma in the gills of freshwater fishes. Hoffman et al. found clear zones of liquefaction around encysted trophozoites and spores of *M. cartilaginis* n. sp. in the gill arches and filaments of bluegills. On the other hand Ghittino found *Lentospora* (*Myxosoma*) *cabeda* encysted in the middle of the thin sheet of connective tissue in the gill lamellae or in the proximity of the gill arch of the cyprinid *Leuciscus cephalus cabeda.* He inferred that the protozoans affecting the Po Basin fish caused a reduction and atrophy of secondary lamellae.

In various acute and chronic studies of pesticides, L. L. Eller (unpublished) observed numerous protozoans in, or attached to, gills. Because the tissues were fixed, either no identification or only tentative identification of the parasites was made. Gill lesions in the test fishes were characterized by thickened and fused lamellae around encysted parasites (Fig. 11.12). Also, there was marked hyperplasia of surface epithelial cells or an increase in the number of mucus-secreting cells at the site of parasitic attachment to the gills (Figs. 11.13, 11.14).

Trematodes

Trematodes are referred to as microorganisms only in the broad sense of the word. Monogenetic or digenetic trematodes attached to the gills, encysted in gill tissue, or present within gill vessels may cause severe gill damage (6, 23, 38, 63, 73, 81).

Monogenetic Trematodes. Two monogenetic trematodes, *Dactylogyrus vasator* and *D. solidus,* caused mortality of carp reared in southern Russian ponds

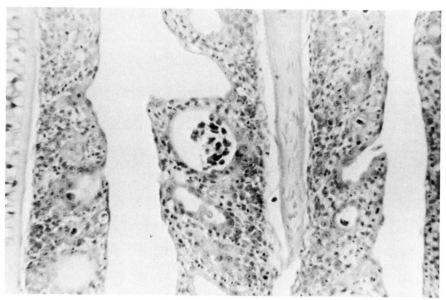

Fig. 11. 12. Gill section of a cutthroat trout reared in a tank for 8 months. Note the hyperplasia of gill epithelium and the fusion of adjacent lamellae. Unidentified protozoans are encysted by fused lamellae. ×125.

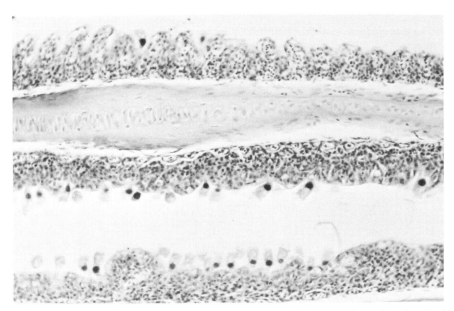

Fig. 11.13. Unidentified protozoans attached to the gill tissue of a goldfish induced marked hyperplasia of gill epithelium. ×125.

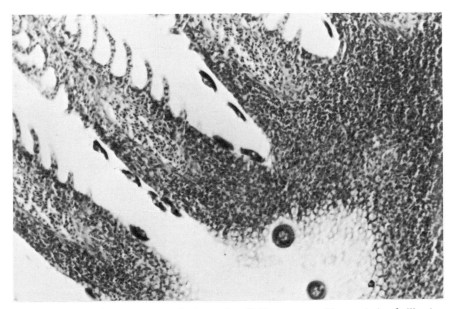

Fig. 11.14. Ciliated protozoans at the base of a gill filament caused hyperplasia of gill epithelium and an apparent increase in mucus-secreting cells. ×125.

(6). Each species caused severe losses of fry and death of individual adults. *D. vasator* localized at the very top of gill lamellae, whereas *D. solidus* attached itself to the middle of the gill. In both instances, they caused marked epithelial outgrowth. In addition to the epithelial hyperplasia, *D. solidus* caused many epithelial cells to degenerate into secretory cells. Bauer (6) indicated that the copious mucus secreted by the cells was enough to impair the respiratory functions of the gill.

Digenetic Trematodes. Severe epizootics in fish are caused by the digenetic blood fluke *Sanguinicola*, which may be localized in the gill blood vessels. Davis (23) briefly recorded the presence of a large number of blood flukes in the gill blood vessels of fingerling cutthroat trout and yearling rainbow trout. More recently, Hoffman and Surber (38) summarized Davis' notes on the blood fluke *Sanguinicola davisi.* They described the location and developmental stages of the parasite and stated that heavy mortalities resulted from the damage done to the gills by the presence of developing miracidians.

Schäperclaus (63) indicated that large numbers of *S. inermis* eggs found in the gill capillaries of carp brought about thrombosis and caused death.

Wales (73), however, was unable to show experimentally the degree of respiratory inhibition in two subspecies of rainbow trout heavily infected with the eggs of *S. davisi* or *S. klamathensis.* He inferred that large numbers of emerging miracidians may cause severe blood loss leading to the death of fishes. However, digenetic trematodes also attach themselves to the surface of the gills and cause gill lesions. Wood and Yasutake (81) observed a marked hyperplasia of epithelial cells around parasites they presumed to be metacercariae of *Nanophyteus salmicola*, a diagenetic trematode.

In various pesticide studies, especially those in which bluegills were used as test animals, Eller (unpublished) observed trematodiasis of gill tissue. No effort was made to determine if the trematodes were monogenetic or digenetic because only fixed tissue was available. In most instances, the trematodes caused only mechanical injury to gill tissue, which was represented by a mild hyperplasia of lamellar epithelium and of epithelial cells along the longitudinal axes of filaments (Fig. 11.15).

"NUTRITIONAL GILL DISEASE"

Wolf (76) produced a hyperplasia of gill epithelium by feeding trout a diet deficient in pantothenic acid, and introduced the concept "nutritional gill disease." In the same year, Tunison et al. (71) found that adding pantothenic acid to the diet corrected the characteristic gill epithelial cell hyperplasia in fish fed a pantothenic acid-deficient diet. Later, Wolf (77) found characteristic gill lesions in brown trout fingerlings fed a pantothenic acid-deficient diet and inferred that the diet increased the susceptibility of the respiratory epithelium to chemical irritation. Subsequently, Rucker, Johnson, and Kaydas (62) were able to produce gill

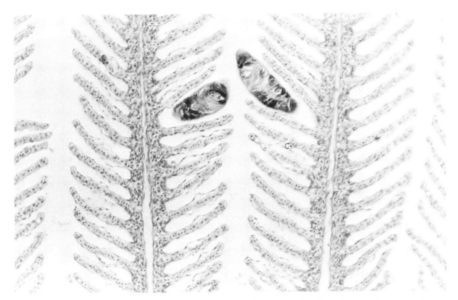

Fig. 11.15. Two trematodes present between lamellae caused only minimal tissue reaction represented by a slight hyperplasia of gill epithelium along the longitudinal axes of filaments. ×125.

disease under controlled conditions using Wolf's 1951 pantothenic acid-deficient diet.

Wood and Yasutake (81) described histopathological changes in the gill associated with nutritional gill disease. The authors inferred that shortened, swollen lamellae with very little structural distortion and hyperplasia of basal epithelium, distal fusion of filaments, and complete fusion of adjacent filaments are present in fish fed a nutritionally deficient diet.

On the other hand, Ghittino (33) hypothesized that dusty, dry feeds rather than pantothenic acid deficiencies produce gill disease. In his study, fish developed gill disease although they were fed a diet containing adequate B-complex ingredients.

Halver, Ashley, and Smith (37), studying the ascorbic acid requirements in coho salmon and rainbow trout, found distorted and twisted cartilage of gill filaments in fish fed a diet containing 5 mg ascorbic acid per 100 grams of diet for 24 weeks. The incidence and severity of gill damage increased in fish deprived of vitamin C for 12 to 14 weeks. In contrast, both the gills and blood in coho salmon fed a folic-acid deficient diet were pale and anemic when compared with those of control fish (68).

Trout that were force-fed aflatoxins, a broad spectrum carcinogen, developed acute aflatoxicosis characterized by severe gill edema, hemorrhagic necrosis of liver, and hemorrhagic visceral fat. Most fish fed crude aflatoxin at 1 to 5 mg per kg of body weight or crystalline aflatoxin B_1 at 0.1 to 0.5 mg per kg of body weight died within 3 to 6 days. The survivors were moribund by the 10th day (5).

"HEMORRHAGIC GILL DISEASE"

According to Wood and Yasutake (81), Snieszko used the term "hemorrhagic gill disease" to describe gross gill lesions characterized by minute hemorrhages in the gill filaments. Wolf (75) presumed that similar gill conditions in fishes were blood clots. However, in a microscopic examination of affected tissue, Wood and Yasutake (81) found no true hemorrhages. The gill capillaries were not ruptured, but were distended by rounded masses of blood. The blood appeared to remain in circulation, but pushed the intact respiratory epithelium outward and gave the lamellae their characteristic clavate-globate appearance. More recently, Wood (79) found clavate-globate lamellae packed with erythrocytes in fish exposed to Dead X, a coal-tar naphtha. A number of other investigators (2, 4, 15, 35, 48, 72) also found similar lesions in fishes exposed to pesticides. A better term is probably "aneurysmal gill disease."

GILL NECROSIS OF UNKNOWN ETIOLOGY

Gill necrosis of uncertain etiology was found in carp from many farm ponds in Poland (50). The course of the disease was usually mild, but could be severe. In the mild form, only an anemic discoloration of the tips or ends of lamellae were present. In the severe form, the gill lamellae became necrotic and even whole sections of gill tissue disintegrated. The pathological changes resembled to a certain degree those found in gills infected by the fungus *Branchiomyces sanguinis*. However, the thickening of lamellae present in fish infected with fungi is lacking in gill necrosis. Moreover, fungal disease occurs only in the summer and autumn, whereas gill necrosis is present the year round.

CONCLUSIONS

The early as well as the more recent fishery research workers identified the nature of gill lesions, outlined topographic distribution, and correlated their findings with functional impairment of the organ. They often arrived at a presumptive diagnosis, but rarely made specific diagnoses because clinical studies were seldom included in their experiments. The most notable exceptions were fishery personnel interested in experimental studies on infections and dietary deficiencies. But even in this area investigators disagreed about the causative organism or agent producing specific gill lesions.

The criteria set forth by Wood (80) to differentiate histologically the bacterial from the nutritional gill disease help to identify each disease condition. In bacterial lesions, the lamellae are frequently long, twisted in an abnormal position, and contorted, and are often fused. Epithelial hyperplasia frequently starts from the lamellar epithelium and is often present at the distal ends of filaments. Fusion of filaments resulting from the hyperplasia usually begins at the distal end of filaments, but frequently small islands of hyperplasia are scattered in a sporadic fashion along the filaments. In contrast, with nutritional lesions the lamellae are short, often swollen, clubbed-shaped, and have little or no structural distortion. Filaments are fused by the proliferation of cells at the base of lamellae and the longitudinal axes of filaments. The hyperplasia usually starts at the distal ends of filaments, steadily progresses toward the proximal segment, and filaments become completely fused as hyperplasia advances toward the gill arches. Gill lesions are more prevalent in the summer months when water temperatures are elevated, the water levels drop, and waters are rich in ambient organic substances.

Gill damage is easily detected in pesticide studies designed to measure acute toxicity within one to two weeks. But, in long-term, subacute studies, gill damage is subtle and is not always apparent or observed. The most consistent lesions take the form of swollen edematous lamellae and clavate-globate lamellae congested with blood and may be specific tissue reactions to toxic substances in water or food, or may be secondary effects of other dysfunctions. Wood (80) has pointed out that a layer of edema within the lamellae swells the lamellar epithelium to a nonfunctional state. Hence, this pathological condition inhibiting the normal ventilatory function eventually contributes to the death of fish. Pesticide exposure may also lower the fish's potential to resist infections. Trout exposed to 0.005 μg per liter of toxaphene for 11 days developed secondary gill changes characterized by the appearance of large protozoans (79).

The manner in which gill changes occur is often an accurate indicator of the causative agent, e.g., bacteria, diet, or chemical. However, various agents may produce gill lesions simultaneously. Extensive damage from a specific agent may overshadow or mask gill injury produced by a second or third source. And, in fish with large areas of gill necrosis, death may be related to asphyxiation, partial or complete loss of secretory or excretory function, or to a loss of plasma electrolytes or proteins from open gill lesions.

Gill alterations such as hyperplasia and hypertrophy of gill epithelium, edema within lamellae, clavate-globate lamellae congested with blood, hemorrhage, and necrosis represent basic physiological problems. Such changes occur singly, or in combination, in fish diseases or toxicosis and are often directly related to disorders in gill functions which ultimately may affect physiological parameters (e.g., reproduction) or cause the death of fish. However, gill lesions are seldom present in the absence of other systemic changes. For example, in "nutritional gill disease" liver damage usually takes the form of degeneration and regeneration of liver parenchyma and cytopathological changes. In "bacterial gill disease" gram-negative myxobacteria often cause lesions in the skin and muscle. Thus, gill damage correlated with other systemic changes often identifies the causative agent or agents producing gill lesions. This knowledge allows fishery management to use corrective measures to check or retard the spread of gill disease within a population, especially hatchery fish, and in turn, helps to maintain a viable, dynamic sports fishery and freshwater fish population.

REFERENCES

1. Allen, R. L., Meekin, T. K., Pauley, G. B., and Fujihara, M. P.   Mortality among chinook salmon associated with the fungus *Dermocystidium.   J. Fish. Res. Board Can. 25:* 2467–2475. 1968.

2. Amend, D. F., Yasutake, W. T., and Morgan, R.   Some factors influencing susceptibility of rainbow trout to the acute toxicity of an ethyl mercury phosphate formulation (Timsan). *Trans. Amer. Fish. Soc. 98:* 419–426. 1969.

3. Ashley, L. M.   Histopathology of rainbow trout aflatoxicosis, pp. 105–120. In *Trout Hepatoma Research Conference Papers,* ed. J. E. Halver and I. A. Mitchell. *U. S. Fish Wildlife Serv., Res. Rep. 70.* 1967.

4. Ashley, L. M.   Action of iron salts in solution on goldfish. *Progr. Fish-Cult. 32:* 109. 1970.

5. Ashley, L. M.   Pathology of fish fed aflatoxins and other antimetabolites, pp. 366–379. In *A Symposium on Diseases of Fishes and Shellfishes,* ed. S. F. Snieszko. Amer. Fish. Soc., Spec. Publ. No. 5. 1970.

6. Bauer, O. N.   Parasites of freshwater fish and the biological basis for their control. *Bull. State Sci. Res. Inst. Lake River Fish. 49* (English transl., U. S. Dep. Commerce, Off. Tech. Serv., No. 61-31056, 236 pp., 1962). 1959.

7. Benville, P. E., Jr., Smith, C. E., and Shanks, W. E.   Some toxic effects of dimethyl sulfoxide in salmon and trout. *Toxicol. Appl. Pharmacol. 12:* 156–178. 1968.

8. Borg, A. F.   Studies on myxobacteria associated with disease in salmonid fishes. *Wildlife Dis. 8:* 1–85. 1960.

9. Brown, V. M., Mitrovic, V. V., and Stark, G. T. C.   Effects of chronic exposure to zinc on toxicity of a mixture of detergent and zinc. *Water Res. 2:* 255–263. 1968.

10. Bullock, G. L., Conroy, D. A., and Snieszko, S. F.   Bacterial diseases of fishes, pp. 60–87. In *Diseases of Fishes,* ed. S. F. Snieszko and H. R. Axelrod, Jersey City, T.F.H. Publications, 1971.

11. Burrows, R. E.   Lecture notes of Leavenworth in-training school of U. S. Fish and Wildlife Service. Unpublished. 1949.

12. Burrows, R. E.   Effects of accumulated excretory products on hatchery-reared salmonids. *U. S. Fish Wildlife Serv., Res. Rep. 66:* 1–12. 1964.

13. Carpenter, K. E.   The lethal action of soluble metallic salts on fishes. *Brit. J. Exp. Biol. 4:* 378–390. 1927.

14. Christie, R. M., and Battle, H. I.   Histological effects of 3-trifluoromethyl-4-nitrophenol (TFM) on larval lamprey and trout. *Can. J. Zool. 41:* 51–61. 1963.

15. Cope, O. B. Some responses of freshwater fishes to herbicides. *Proc. S. Weed Conf. 18:* 439–445. 1965.
16. Cope, O. B. Contamination of the freshwater ecosystem by pesticides. *J. Appl. Ecol. 3*(suppl.): 33–44. 1966.
17. Cope, O. B., Wood, E. M., and Wallen, G. H. Some chronic effects of 2,4-D on the bluegill (*Lepomis macrochirus*). *Trans. Amer. Fish. Soc. 99:* 1–12. 1970.
18. Cusick, C. J. Mucous cells response of the guppy to heavy metals. Thesis, Univ. Cincinnati, 143 pp. *Diss. Abstr.* 1967.
19. Davis, H. S. A new bacterial disease of freshwater fishes. *Bull. Bur. Fish., Wash. 38:* 261. 1922.
20. Davis, H. S. A new gill disease of trout. *Trans. Amer. Fish. Soc. 56:* 156–160. 1926.
21. Davis, H. S. Further observations on the gill disease of trout. *Trans. Amer. Fish. Soc. 57:* 210–212. 1927.
22. Davis, H. S. Studies of the protozoan parasites of freshwater fishes. *U. S. Fish Wildlife Serv., Fish. Bull. 41:* 1–29.
23. Davis, H. S. *Culture and Diseases of Game Fishes.* 332 pp. Berkeley, Univ. Calif. Press, 1953.
24. Dunkerly, J. S. *Dermocystidium pusula* Pérez parasitic in *Trutta fario*. *Zool. Anz. 44:* 179–182. 1914.
25. Eller, L. L. Pathology in redear sunfish exposed to Hydrothol 191. *Trans. Amer. Fish. Soc. 98:* 52–59. 1969.
26. Eller, L. L. Histopathologic lesions in cutthroat trout (*Salmo clarki*) exposed chronically to the insecticide endrin. *Amer. J. Pathol. 64:* 321–336. 1971.
27. Fish, F. F. A western type of bacterial gill disease. *Trans. Amer. Fish. Soc. 65:* 85–87. 1935.
28. Fish, F. F. Notes on *Costia necatrix*. *Trans. Amer. Fish. Soc. 70:* 441–445. 1941.
29. Fish, F. F., and Rucker, R. R. Columnaris as a disease of cold water fishes. *Trans. Amer. Fish. Soc. 73:* 32–36. 1943.
30. Flis, J. Anatomicohistopathological changes induced in carp (*Cyprinus carpio* L.) by ammonia water. I. Effects of toxic concentrations. II. Effects of subtoxic concentrations. *Acta hydrobiol. 10:* 205–224, 222–238. 1968.
31. Garnjobst, L. *Cytophaga columnaris* (Davis) in pure culture: A myxobacterium pathogenic to fish. *J. Bacteriol. 49:* 113–128. 1945.
32. Ghittino, P. Lentosporiosi branchiale in cavedeni (*Leuciscus cephalus cabeda*) pescati nelle acque del bacino del Po in Piedmonte. *Riv. parassitol. 23:* 241–248. 1962.
33. Ghittino, P. Eziologia e lesioni anatomopathologiche della malattia branchiale (MB) della trotelline in Italia. *Riv. ital. piscic. ittiopat. 2*(2): 24–29. 1967.
34. Ghittino, P. La piscicoltura in Europa. *Riv. ital. piscic. ittiopat. 1*(2): 23–46. 1967.
35. Gilderhus, P. A. Some effects of sublethal concentrations of sodium arsenite

on bluegills and the aquatic environment. *Trans. Amer. Fish. Soc. 95:* 289–296. 1966.

36. Grimaldi, E.   Heavy mortalities inside the populations of bleak (*Alburnus alborella*) in lakes of North Italy caused by a gill infection due to the fungi of the genus *Branchiomyces*. *Riv. ital. piscic. ittiopat. 6*(1): 11–14. 1971.

37. Halver, J. E., Ashley, L. M., and Smith, R. R.   Ascorbic acid requirements of coho salmon and rainbow trout. *Trans. Amer. Fish. Soc. 98:* 762–771. 1969.

38. Hoffman, G. L., and Surber, E. W.   Notes on *Sanguinicola davisi* (Trematoda: Sanguinicolidae) in the gill of trout. *J. Parasitol. 47:* 512–514. 1960.

39. Hoffman, G. L., Putz, R. E., and Dunbar, C. E.   Studies on *Myxosoma cartilaginis* n. sp. (Protozoa: Myxosporidae) of centrarchid fish and a synopsis of the *Myxosoma* of North American freshwater fishes. *J. Protozool. 12:* 319–332. 1965.

40. Hughes, G. M., and Grimstone, A. V.   The fine structures of the gills of *Gadus pollachius*. *Quart. J. Microsc. Sci. 106:* 343–353. 1965.

41. Jirovec, O.   *Dermocystidium vejdovskyi* n. sp. ein neuer Parasit des Hechtes, nebst einer Bemerkung uber *Dermocystidium daphniae* (Rühberg). *Arch. Protistenk. 92:* 137–146. 1939.

42. Jones, J. R. E.   The relation between the electrolytic solution pressures of the metals and their toxicity to the stickleback (*Gasterosteus aculeatus* L.) *J. Exp. Biol. 16:* 425–437. 1939.

43. Kennedy, H. D., Eller, L. L., and Walsh, D. F.   Chronic effects of methoxychlor on bluegills and aquatic invertebrates. *U. S. Bur. Sport Fish. Wildlife, Tech. Pap. 53:* 1–18. 1970.

44. Leger, L.   Sur un nouveau protiste du genre *Dermocystidium* parasite de la truite. *C. r. hebd. séances Acad. Sci. (Paris) 158:* 807–809. 1914.

45. Lemke, A. E., and Mount, D. I.   Some effects of alkyl benzene sulfonate on the bluegill, *Lepomis macrochirus*. *Trans. Amer. Fish. Soc. 92:* 372–379. 1963.

46. Lloyd, R.   The toxicity of zinc sulphate to rainbow trout. *Ann. Appl. Biol. 48:* 84–94. 1960.

47. Lloyd, R.   Factors which affect the tolerance of fish to heavy metal poisoning. *Third Seminar Biol. Probl. Water Pollut.* Cincinnati. 1962.

48. McCraren, J. P., Cope, O. B., and Eller, L. L.   Some chronic effects of diuron on bluegills. *Weed Sci. 17:* 497–504. 1969.

49. Matton, P., and LaHam, Q. N.   Effect of the organophosphate Dylox on rainbow trout larvae. *J. Fish. Res. Board Can. 26:* 2193–2200. 1969.

50. Miacynski, T. B.   Viral diseases and diseases of uncertain etiology in fish in Poland. *Ann. N. Y. Acad. Sci. 126:* 621–628. 1965.

51. Mitrovic, V. V., Brown, V. M., Shurben, D. G., and Berryman, M. H.   Some pathological effects of sub-acute and acute poisoning of rainbow trout by phenol in hard water. *Water Res. 2:* 249–254. 1968.

52. Newstead, J. D.   Fine structure of the respiratory lamellae of teleostean gills. *Z. Zellforsch. mikrosk. Anat. 79:* 396–428. 1967.

53. Ordal, E. J., and Rucker, R. R.   Pathogenic myxobacteria. *Proc. Soc. Exp. Biol. Med. 56:* 15–18. 1944.

54. Osburn, R. C.   The effects of exposure on gill filaments of fishes. *Trans. Amer. Fish. Soc. 40:* 371–376. 1910.

55. Pacha, R. E., and Ordal, E. J. Epidemiology of columnaris disease in salmon. *Bacteriol. Proc. 63.* 3. 1963.
56. Pauley, G. B. Prespawning adult salmon mortality associated with a fungus of the genus *Dermocystidium. J. Fish. Res. Board Can. 24:* 843–848. 1967.
57. Pauley, G. B., and Nakatani, R. E. Histopathology of "gas-bubble" disease in salmon fingerlings. *J. Fish. Res. Board Can. 24:* 867–871. 1967.
58. Plehn, M. *Praktikum der Fischkrankheiten,* p. 179. Stuttgart, E. Schweizerbart, 1924.
59. Reichenbach-Klinke, H.-H. Untersuchungen über die Einwirkung des Ammoniakgehalts auf den Fischorganismus [Investigations on the influence of the ammonia content on fish organisms]. *Archiv. Fischereiwiss. 17:* 122–132. 1967.
60. Renfro, W. C. Gas-bubble mortality of fishes in Galveston Bay, Texas. *Trans. Amer. Fish. Soc. 92:* 320–322. 1963.
61. Rucker, R. R., and Hodgeboom, K. Observations on gas-bubble disease. *Progr. Fish-Cult. 15:* 24–26. 1953.
62. Rucker, R. R., Johnson, H. E., and Kaydas, G. M. An interim report on gill disease. *Progr. Fish-Cult. 14:* 10–14. 1952.
63. Schäperclaus, W. *Fischkrankheiten.* 3d ed. 708 pp. Berlin, Akademie Verlag, 1954.
64. Schweiger, G. Die toxikologische Einwirkung von Schwermetallsalzen auf Fische und Fischnahrtiere. *Arch. Fischereiwiss. 8:* 54–78. 1957.
65. Skidmore, J. F. Toxicity of zinc compounds to aquatic animals with special reference to fish. *Quart. Rev. Biol. 39:* 227–248. 1964.
66. Skidmore, J. F. Respiration and osmoregulation in rainbow trout with gills damaged by zinc sulphate. *J. Exp. Biol. 52:* 481–494. 1970.
67. Skidmore, J. F., and Tovell, P. W. A. Toxic effects of zinc sulphate on the gills of rainbow trout. *Water Res. 6:* 217–230. 1972.
68. Smith, C. E., and Halver, J. E. Folic acid anemia in coho salmon. *J. Fish. Res. Board Can. 26:* 111–114. 1969.
69. Smith, L. L., Jr., Kramer, R. H., and Oseid, D. M. Long-term effects of conifer-groundwood paper fiber on walleyes. *Trans. Amer. Fish. Soc. 95:* 60–70. 1966.
70. Snieszko, S. F. Nutritional (dietary) gill disease and other less known gill diseases of freshwater fishes. *U. S. Fish Wildlife Serv., Fish. Leafl. 463,* 2 pp. 1958.
71. Tunison, A. V., Phillips, A. M., Jr., Schaffer, H. B., Maxwell, J. M., Brockway, D. R., and McCay, C. M. *Rept. 13, N.Y. Cons. Dept. Fish. Res. Bull. 6,* 21 pp., 1944.
72. Van Valin, C. C., Andrews, A. K., and Eller, L. L. Some effects of mirex on two warm-water fishes. *Trans. Amer. Fish. Soc. 97:* 185–196. 1968.
73. Wales, J. H. Two new blood fluke parasites in trout. *Calif. Fish Game 44:* 125–136. 1958.
74. Wales, J. H., and Evins, D. Sestonosis, a gill irritation in trout. *Calif. Fish Game 23:* 144–146. 1937.
75. Wolf, L. E. Blood clots in gill of trout. *Trans. Amer. Fish. Soc. 66:* 369–371. 1937.
76. Wolf, L. E. *Annual Report, 1943,* pp. 111–112. N. Y. Conserv. Dep. 1944.

77. Wolf, L. E.   Dietary gill disease of trout. *N. Y. Conserv. Dep., Fish Res. Bull. 7:* 1–30. 1945.
78. Wolf, L. E.   Diet experiments with trout. *Progr. Fish-Cult. 13:* 17–24. 1951.
79. Wood, E. M.   The pathology of pesticide toxicity in fish. Unpublished.
80. Wood, E. M.   Definitive diagnosis of fish mortalities. *J. Water Pollut. Contr. Fed. 32:* 994–999. 1960.
81. Wood, E. M., and Yasutake, W. T.   Histopathology of fish. V. Gill disease. *Progr. Fish-Cult. 19:* 7–13. 1957.

DISCUSSION OF GILL LESIONS IN FRESHWATER TELEOSTS

Comment: On another occasion you mentioned that you disagreed with a presentation in which it was suggested that separation of the lamellar epithelium from the basement membrane was artifactual. Certainly after seeing your slides I have no question that you are correct in the cases of the cyclodienes and a couple of organophosphates. The thing that strikes me is that in my experience separation of the gill lamellar epithelium is one of the earliest signs, if not the earliest, of autolysis that I have seen. I was thinking in terms of people being presented with fish that are dead; they will see this, and the very distinct proteinaceous material that you have seen under the epithelium is missing in this case, and I think it can be very deceptive. I think people should be aware of this.

L. L. Eller: I agree with you, and one of the things we do in all of our experiments is run control fish. Actually, I am comparing a control fish with a treated fish, so I believe that these results are valid.

Comment: I was very much impressed with Louis Wolf's experiments on Eastern fish with gill disease. You recall that in his experiment he attributed disease in his fish to their being put on a pantothenic acid-deficient diet, but the actual cause of the lesion was due to toxic metabolites released by other fish in the system, and these metabolites were associated with this lesion. This proliferative lesion was hypertrophy of the adrenals. He followed it and attributed the proliferation to a combination of factors, not just a single deficiency. There was a toxic metabolite, the deficiency, and the action of some stress on the adrenal which probably produced excessive corticosteroids. I think that all of these parameters should be followed in all of the gill proliferations that occur in fish.

12

Some Lesions in the Heart of Trout

ROGER LEE HERMAN

The presence of parasitic helminths in the heart of fishes is common and these animals may cause extensive damage, as demonstrated by several authors in this volume. References in the literature to heart lesions caused by other pathogens seem to be rare. Lymphocystis cells have been reported in the heart of naturally infected walleye (*Stizostedion vitreum vitreum*) (2), and Wolf produced the lesions in artificially infected bluegill (*Lepomis macrochirus*) (10). Ghittino reported hemorrhages in the heart of trout infected with viral hemorrhagic septicemia (4). Wood and Yasutake found myocarditis in trout having bacterial kidney disease (*Corynebacterium* sp.) (11); epicarditis is also common with this disease. Herman and Putz reported the occurrence of a microsporidian in the heart of a channel catfish (5). Overall, it would seem the heart of fishes is little affected by disease. The following cases extend this rather short list and perhaps will focus more attention on the fish heart in disease.

SPECIFIC DISEASES

Furunculosis, the disease caused by *Aeromonas salmonicida* of fish, and hepatoma of rainbow trout (*Salmo gairdneri*) are two of the most frequently studied diseases of fishes. Despite this, effects of these diseases on the heart appear to have escaped note.

McCraw (8) did not mention the heart in his review of the pathological effects of *A. salmonicida*. Mawdesley-Thomas (9) found no heart lesions in goldfish suf-

331

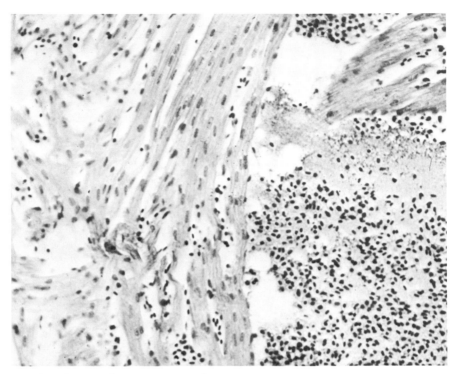

Fig. 12.1. Section of the spongy layer of the ventricle of a rainbow trout. Hematoxylin and eosin (H&E); ×125.

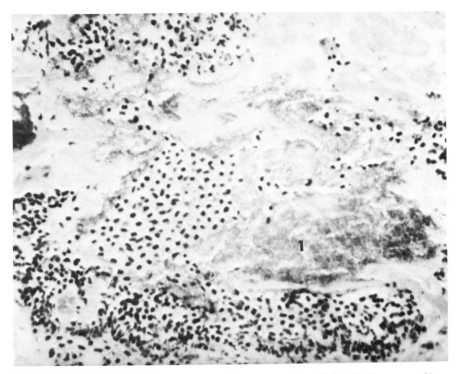

Fig. 12.2. Myocarditis in brown trout due to *Aeromonas salmonicida* infection: mass of bacteria (1). Gram; ×375.

fering from furunculosis. Klontz, Yasutake, and Ross (7) did not even examine the heart in their studies.

A. salmonicida can cause myocarditis (Fig. 12.2). The appearance of the lesions supports the finding by Klontz (6) of a leukocytic toxin. The mass of bacteria causes some vascular stasis and necrosis of the cardiac muscle, although the latter is not extensive. The inflammatory response appears to be directed toward the tissue necrosis. A layer of lymphocytes is present outside the areas of stasis. Macrophages can be found throughout the ventricle except around the masses of bacteria.

The cases reported here were from fish suffering chronic infections, or recovering. Past studies have generally been carried out on more or less acute diseases, which may explain the lack of reports of heart lesions.

Hepatoma of rainbow trout generates metastases easily. In an unusual case, Ashley and Halver (1) reported metastasis to nearly every organ. However, they did not report any in the heart.

Hearts from large rainbow trout with advanced hepatoma and chronic kidney disease were examined. In addition to myocarditis and pericarditis (Fig. 12.3),

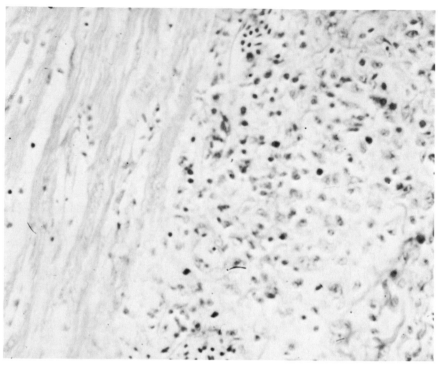

Fig. 12.3. Pericarditis in rainbow trout due to *Corynebacterium* sp. infection. H&E; ×400.

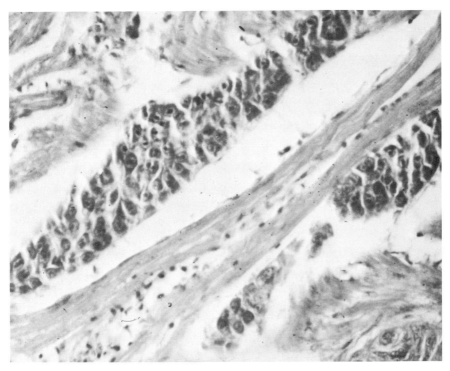

Fig. 12.4. Metastatic hepatoma in ventricular wall of rainbow trout. H&E; X400.

several fish had metastatic tumors in the ventricular wall. The majority of foci were of normal-appearing hepatocytes (Fig. 12.4) but occasionally abortive bile ducts were seen. The growths did not invade the myocardium but did appear to be attached and covered by an endothelial layer. No tissue reaction to the tumor cells was seen.

Examples of emboli can be found in various fish tissues fairly readily. In some geographical areas parasite and gas emboli are all too familiar. Thrombi, on the other hand, seem to be rare. Cohen (3) described extensive thrombosis in the dorsal aorta of two aquarium fishes.

The thrombus reported here (Fig. 12.5) was found at the base of the bulbus arteriosus of an emaciated male brook trout. The fish had exhibited signs of a wasting disease for some time. When sacrificed, the animal was found to be infected by a nonoxidative *Pseudomonas* sp. The gross appearance of the heart was normal.

The thrombus was circular with indistinct layering (Fig. 12.6). Liquefaction had begun in the center. Macrophages filled with cell debris or pigment were numerous. The attachment was not evident in the sections available.

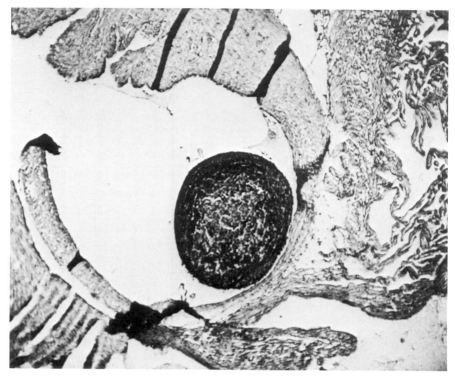

Fig. 12.5. Thrombus in bulbus arteriosus of brook trout. H&E; ×40.

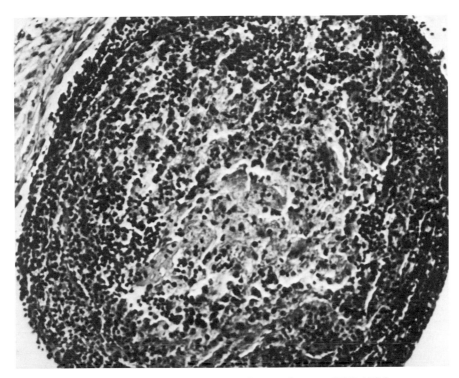

Fig. 12.6. Thrombus showing liquefaction of center. H&E; ×125.

Another blood lesion associated with the heart is epicardial hematopoiesis. This has been seen by several pathologists but does not seem to be described in the literature. A possible reason is that there seems to be no pathological cause for this extra hematopoiesis; it is not compensatory for loss of hematopoietic tissue elsewhere.

Grossly the heart appears to be encased in a large blood clot. Sections, however, show generally healthy blood cells, mostly red cells, present in active hematopoietic tissue in the epicardium (Fig. 12.7). The hematopoietic tissue does not appear to penetrate, to any great extent, into the myocardium but the normal structure of the epicardium is lost in many areas.

Lesions such as those described here are difficult to note on gross examination. It is very likely that we miss many interesting lesions because we discard "normal" hearts from our fishes. One wonders whether much of the "normal mortality" seen in hatcheries might not be due to some form of coronary artery disease.

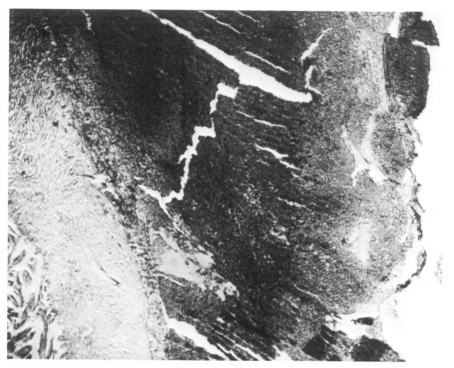

Fig. 12.7. Extraordinary hematopoiesis on surface of heart of rainbow trout. Giemsa; X375.

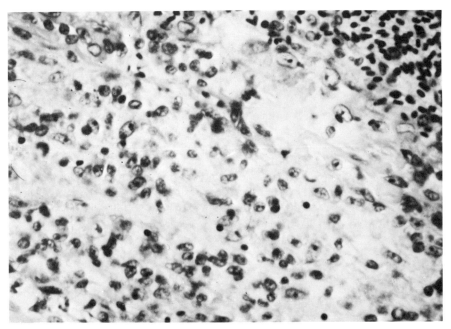

Fig. 12.8. Epicardial area of heart shown in Figure 12.7. H&E; X600.

REFERENCES

1. Ashley, L. M., and Halver, J. E.   Multiple metastasis of rainbow trout hepatoma. *Trans. Amer. Fish. Soc. 92:* 365. 1963.
2. Bangham, R. V., and Hunter, G. W., III.   Studies on fish parasites of Lake Erie: Distribution studies. *Zoologica (New York) 24:* 383. 1939.
3. Cohen, S.   Thrombosis of the aorta in a small aquarium fish. *Drum Croak. 48:* 9. 1968
4. Ghittino, P.   "L'Ipertrofia renale e degenerazione epatica infettiva" della trota iridea di allevamento (*Salmo gairdneri*).   Caratteristiche cliniche, eziologiche ed anatomo-isto-patologiche. *Vet. ital. 13:* 457. 1962.
5. Herman, R. L., and Putz, R. E.   A microsporidian (Protozoa: Cnidospora) in channel catfish (*Ictalurus punctatus*). *J. Wildlife Dis. 6:* 173. 1970
6. Klontz, G. W.   Immunopathology, p. 11. In *Progress in Sport Fishery Research, 1965. U. S. Bur. Sport Fish. Wildlife, Resour. Publ. 17.* 1966.
7. Klontz, G. W., Yasutake, W. T., and Ross, A. J.   Bacterial diseases of the Salmonidae in the western United States: Pathogenesis of furunculosis in rainbow trout. *Amer. J. Vet. Res. 27:* 1455. 1966.

8. McCraw, B. M. Furunculosis of fish. *U. S. Fish Wildlife Serv., Spec. Sci. Rep., Fish. 84.* 1952.

9. Mawdesley-Thomas, L. E. Furunculosis in the goldfish *Carassius auratus* (L.). *J. Fish Biol. 1:* 19. 1969.

10. Wolf, K. The fish viruses, p. 35. In *Advances in Virus Research,* ed. K. M. Smith and M. A. Lauffer. Vol. 12. New York, Academic Press, 1966.

11. Wood, E. M., and Yasutake, W. T. Histopathology of kidney disease in fish. *Amer. J. Pathol. 32:* 845. 1956.

DISCUSSION OF SOME LESIONS IN THE HEART OF TROUT

R. Walker: This is with respect to the lymphocystis. I can't conceive of this number of lymphocystis cells in the heart unless they were put in experimentally.

R. L. Herman: I thought I said this was an experimental infection.

R. Walker: Yes, but the question is whether it was put into the blood-vascular system? It was not subcutaneous or intraperitoneal, I hope.

K. E. Wolf: Intraperitoneal? No, more direct. We were trying experimental infections and having failed with many other routes, went directly into the heart. This was an experimental introduction and it "took" in two places. It "took" in the skin at the perforation of the skin itself, and secondarily and quite surprisingly, it "took" in the epicardium. To further confuse the issue I am sure, because I did aspirate blood and introduced virus directly into the vascular system, those are the only two places that contained lesions.

R. Walker: The other question that I would like to ask is about the great big mass in the epicardium, the last slide you showed there, with static blood in the middle. You didn't show us a high magnification of the stuff which you said was hematopoietic tissue. Could this not be invading phagocytic cells?

R. L. Herman: No, these weren't. This was normal hematopoietic tissue. I know it has been observed before by several quite competent pathologists, and this is what they considered it to be. I realize that I didn't show you a higher magnification, mainly because I didn't have it.

M. M. Sigel: Several years ago, Bob Mathewson at the Lerner Marine Laboratory and I made an observation of myocardial infarctions in the muscle of fish hearts following decompression of fish. These were fish brought in from great depths. They managed to survive, say four or five days, then proceeded to die. Prior to death we managed to obtain a few electrocardiograms on them and observed typical inversions which one sees in the case of human occlusive heart disease. Of course fish do not have coronary blood vessels as far as I know. I am not a fish pathologist or a fish histologist, so I am really commenting on my own observation, yet asking for advice and comments. These definitely had electrophysiological changes in the heart. They also had histological changes compatible with anoxia and local heart damage and yet we still do not know the mechanism of it, except maybe caisson disease in fish. I would like to have a comment as to whether anyone has seen this before, either in freshwater or marine fishes.

R. L. Herman: I haven't seen it.

L. M. Ashley: I haven't seen infarction in fish hearts as yet, but I would like to say that fish do have coronary arteries, and Dr. Olin of Chicago has made a fairly good study of a series of mature returning-to-spawn steelhead trout and found quite a bit of coronary artery occlusion or partial occlusion in these fish.

R. Walker: I have a question. You speak of coronary arteries, which I have seen myself in every dogfish I open up, but in the literature I have not been able to find anything about coronary veins. Do you know whether the blood passes directly back into the heart chamber or are there veins returning elsewhere?

R. L. Herman: Lagler, Bardach, and Miller refer to coronary veins in their book, *Ichthyology*. They can be seen in sections, at least on the surface, of the heart.

L. E. Mawdesley-Thomas: As a general rule, as one goes down the phylogenetic chain one is less inclined to come across spontaneous coronary occlusion. When one thinks about coronary occlusion, say in rats and mice, we can produce those only with pretty heroic measures. They don't occur spontaneously and if I remember rightly they are not all that common in the higher animals, although cases of them are definitely recorded in some of the older animals.

R. J. Roberts: There is one reference that you probably haven't seen. It is in reference to some New Zealanders who I think were trying to get money to work on fish as a model for coronary artery disease. They did quite extensive studies on brown trout in New Zealand with metastatic deposition of calcium within the coronary vessels. In our department there is quite a strong fish physiology program, and I am told by those persons that there is a direct feedback of aerated blood from the gills directly to the coronary vessels. The blood that passes through the gills and gets aerated goes into the body's generalized low pressure system, through the whole body, and takes a long time to get back to be aerated by the gills. As far as the other things in the heart are concerned, we've certainly seen those. What you call hematopoietic tissue, we've always thought were organizing red thrombi and possibly the hematopoietic tissue which you did occasionally see was in fact being set up there because there was so much degeneration of red blood cells that it wasn't going to be allowed to go to waste, very much like organizing red thrombi. We also see a lot of parasitic lesions within the pericardium and in the heart in the pallon, which is a corigonid fish of Loch Lomond; some of these are reported. The New Zealand work is reported and if you want slides of other things, I can certainly get them for you.

R. L. Herman: I am well aware that parasites are quite common in the heart. Regarding some of these other things, I know I have been guilty of, on occasion, discarding hearts because they look perfectly normal. Yet in most of these fish I was looking at the heart for some other reason and just happened to find the particular items mentioned. My question at this point is, do we really not have as many lesions in the heart as it would appear, or do we throw away a lot of potential information because there are no gross lesions?

K. E. Wolf: In regard to the coronary blood supply, the whole system can be nicely demonstrated by latex injection of the afferent vessels. It comes out very beautifully, and then the musculature can be digested away with pepsin. Then you have the latex casting and there are plastics available for more sophisticated tracing of this. The other comment concerns some of the Danish work, where again the heart is the prime site for fluorescence microscopy of viral hemorrhagic septicemia. It's not as sensitive as virological detection and comparative studies. They found it about 75% as sensitive, but it was the site of the most specific and the most brilliant fluorescence for this specific viral antigen.

R. L. Herman: Dr. P. Ghittino has reported hemorrhages in the heart with viral hemorrhagic septicemia.

C. J. Dawe: There is a difference between metastasis and tumor embolism. In a metastasis there has to be some evidence that the change of the location of the cells has been established and growing. Tumor embolism can occur as a terminal event from handling a big trout with a swollen belly. It is possible to squeeze some of the cells out into the circulation where you may see them. This is a distinction that has to be made. There is another, in that normal liver cells can be squeezed out and will embolize to lungs in mice, for example, and presumably it could happen in a trout.

R. L. Herman: This is why I indicated what appeared to me to be the endothelial lining which had covered at least some of the foci. I was able to trace the endothelium away from the metastatic liver cells themselves so that it appeared that the liver cells had grown under the lining, or possibly it could be an embolus which was then overgrown by the endothelial cells.

13

Some Diseases of Muscle

LIONEL E. MAWDESLEY-THOMAS

Diseases of muscle in most animal species are often poorly documented. The lack of a definite etiology in many of the myopathies seems to discourage interest and investigation. The close association of muscle with the nervous system has also appeared to inhibit anything but the most general of comments. As in all other systemic pathology, a rational consideration of the reaction of muscle to various stimuli shows a response which is similar to the other systems. Although only little is known, or appreciated, about the response of muscle in the poikilothermic vertebrate, diseases of muscle can be considered under several main headings. These headings, of necessity, are incomplete, and as more diseases of muscle are documented the deficiencies will be rectified. The subjects to be considered are (1) general pathology, (2) congenital conditions, (3) bacterial diseases, (4) parasitic diseases, (5) viral diseases, (6) myopathies, and (7) tumors of muscle.

GENERAL PATHOLOGY

The ways in which skeletal muscle can react in response to injury are limited. Many different etiologies can, therefore, provoke a similar morphological reaction. This is as true in the poikilothermic vertebrate as in the homeotherm.

Degeneration

The best-known degeneration is probably Zenker's degeneration. This is a primary necrobiosis of skeletal muscle, and is associated with a waxy or vitreous

343

degeneration affecting a particular area of muscle fibers. This degeneration is not associated with any of the regular sequences of myophagia, nor is there any evidence of regeneration. The etiology of this type of degeneration is unknown, but a simple toxic phenomenon is now considered to be improbable.

In other types of degeneration, a more definite pathogenesis occurs, from cloudy swelling to granular or hydropic degeneration. Any or all of these changes may be seen in or around inflammatory foci. Fat may be found in constantly active muscle fibers. Fat may also be found stored in muscle under certain physiological conditions, such as in premigratory salmonids. Excessive accumulation of fatty globules can also be associated with injury to muscle fibers.

Degenerative changes are seen in muscle following injury (5). The changes range from minimal swelling of fibers to complete loss and their replacement by loose connective tissue elements. Muscle degeneration proceeds for several weeks following the injury. The muscle fibers become smaller and less distinct, the bundle arrangement is lost, and the connective tissue elements proliferate. The structure of the myofibrils remains until the degeneration is almost complete. These myofibrils are useful markers for identifying skeletal muscle when little more than an eosinophilic blob of sarcoplasm remains (Fig. 13.1). In many areas

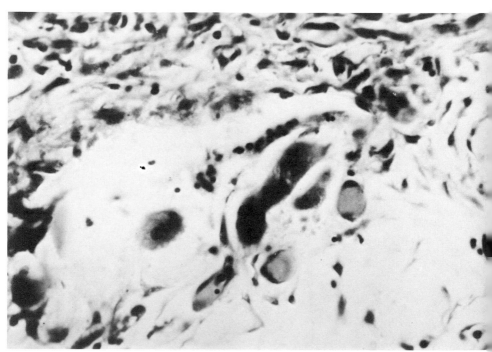

Fig. 13.1. Section of degenerating skeletal muscle showing muscle remnants. Hematoxylin and eosin (H&E); ×500.

of degeneration, muscle giant cells are seen. These consist of irregularly shaped areas of sarcoplasm containing several nuclei.

Regeneration

Although the central nervous system in poikilothermic vertebrates has reparative powers far in excess of those in the higher vertebrates, this power is not manifested by the skeletal musculature. It has often been considered that the fish muscle is incapable of regeneration; this is untrue. Fish muscle is capable of regeneration although to an extremely limited extent. The regenerative processes are similar to those seen in higher vertebrates and include sarcolemmal sprouting and nuclear reduplication. In areas of regenerating muscle, a sarcolemmal tube is seen containing many nuclei closely aligned within the tube (Fig. 13.2). The sarcolemmal tube is usually tapered toward each end, but should not be mistaken for a young or immature fibroblast, since both cell types are frequently seen in areas of muscle damage, particularly following trauma (Fig. 13.3).

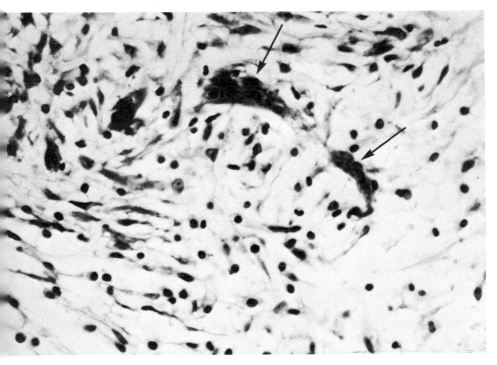

Fig. 13.2. Regenerating muscle fiber showing reduplication and alignment of sarcolemmal nuclei. H&E; X500.

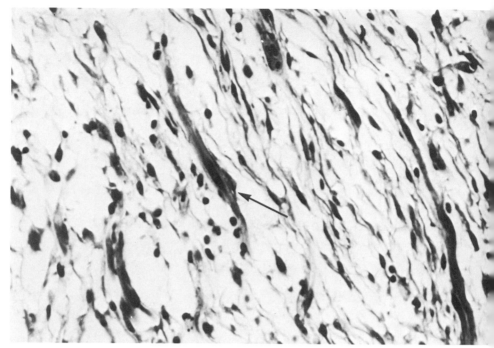

Fig. 13.3. Spindle-shaped regenerating muscle fiber. Sarcolemmal nuclei seen. Note surrounding loosely knit connective tissue. H&E; ×500.

Atrophy

Only a few of the simple forms of atrophy have been investigated in the fish. These include atrophy associated with starvation, seen in rainbow trout which have become blind and in eels having a severe degree of stomato-papillomatosis, in which the neoplastic tissues prevent feeding. In nutritional experiments in which fish have been fed deficient diets, muscle atrophy has also been reported.

CONGENITAL CONDITIONS

In young trout fry a high incidence of congenital anomalies has been recorded. Associated with these congenital anomalies, which were primarily of the osseous system, were many secondary congenital anomalies of skeletal muscle ranging from a complete aplasia to a hyperplasia seen in the near-monster type of deformity. The lesions were considered to be secondary, as the muscle in the unaffected myotomes was within normal limits.

Congenital atrophy of muscle has been noted in fish which have severe congenital defects of the vertebral column.

Acquired atrophies have occurred in fish with deformed spines due to *Myxosoma cerebralis* or a mycobacterial infection. A further simple atrophy is due to pressure and this can be seen in skeletal muscle adjacent to expanding lesions associated with parasitic cysts, bacterial infections, granulomas, and neoplastic conditions. As in the higher vertebrates, it is probable there may occur a senile atrophy, particularly in aquarium fish, and a neurogenic atrophy; however, these conditions have not yet been documented. Although there are many causes of simple atrophy, the morphological picture is essentially similar. There is variation in the diameter of the muscle fibers, the atrophic fibers appearing smaller and less well stained. The fibers appear shrunken and no longer fill the endomysial sheaths. As the fibers further atrophy, the sarcolemmal nuclei and connective tissue elements in and around the muscle fibers and bundles appear more prominent. Degenerative changes may also affect some fibers. The morphological features of degeneration and atrophy do not usually pose a problem of diagnosis.

BACTERIAL DISEASES

The true acute suppurative condition of higher animals has no exact counterpart in the poikilothermic vertebrate. In many conditions, while a polymorphonuclear leukocyte response is detected, it does not seem to play an important part in the cellular response to an infectious agent. Often much necrotic tissue is seen but there is no pus (dead polymorphonuclear leukocytes). In areas where pus is to be expected, a histological examination reveals little more than necrotic tissue associated with essentially a "chronic" inflammatory cell reaction. A typical bacterial response occurs in furunculosis, a condition seen in many fish species and due to *Aeromonas salmonicida.* In this infection, there is often marked necrosis of the muscle fibers and their replacement by loose connective tissue in which many cells, primarily of the "chronic" inflammatory type, are seen (Fig. 13.4). At the edge of some infections there is evidence of swelling of the muscle fibers, with some sarcolemmal nuclei proliferation, together with some increase in cellular infiltration around both the individual muscle fibers and the larger muscle bundles. Often muscle fibers become surrounded by this cellular reaction and ultimately degenerate and disintegrate. Where the lesion is more active, then actual muscle necrosis occurs (3).

Such changes appear to be nonspecific, as they have been recorded in other species with other types of infections (8). Many of the changes described in muscle, particularly those associated with bacterial infections, are affected by temperature. However, much more documentation of disease processes, throughout a range of temperatures, is required before many of these reactions can be fully explained.

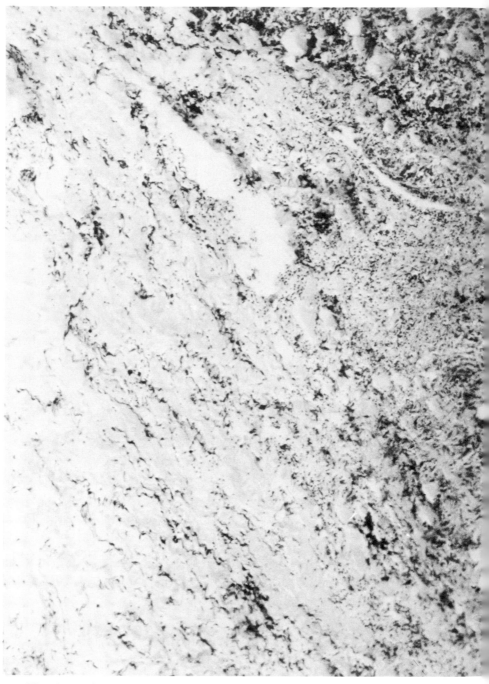

Fig. 13.4. Inflammatory reaction has destroyed most of the skeletal muscle; only the occasional muscle fiber is recognizable (top right). H&E; ×100.

PARASITIC DISEASES

Although much is known, and has been written, about the parasites of fish, little is appreciated at a pathological level as to their exact method of causing tissue damage or, in some cases, as to the lack of tissue change. Kabata (2) discussed in some detail the changes caused by parasitic crustaceans. This account would have been more valuable to the pathologist had the text been illustrated by photomicrographs showing the changes at a cellular level. The reaction of the host to its parasitic invader has attracted much attention over the past few years. If this subject is to be fully understood, then a multidisciplinary approach must be followed. This is no longer the absolute field of the parasitologist. The help of the morphologist and the immunologist is required. Although only a few examples of parasitic diseases, as affecting muscle, are given, some principles may be recognized. The reaction seen in skeletal muscle in parasitic infestations seems to be related to the general ecological requirement of the parasite. It is this overriding ecological consideration which dictates to some extent the host or tissue response.

In the case of *Carassius auratus* infested by *Lernea cyprinacea,* the anchoring antlers which develop on the anterior end of the parasite and penetrate deeply into the subcutaneous tissue and muscle provoke the marked fibroblastic response. This response helps the antlers to attach this copepod more firmly to its host. The parasitic antlers, in this instance, act as foreign bodies, and the marked fibroblastic response results (Fig. 13.5). This reaction is in complete contradistinction to *Cryptocotyle lingua,* which, when found in skeletal muscle, provokes no response from its immediate environment (Fig. 13.6). The type of reaction found must therefore be related to the overall ecological patterns of the parasites; the means whereby they are achieved are not, as yet, completely understood. In the instance mentioned, the metacercaria of the *C. lingua* has persuaded the host that it is "self" and that no reaction has occurred. This possibly takes place through some immunological reaction dictated by the parasite. In the case of *L. cyprinacea* it is in the parasite's best interest not to provoke any immune response, as a marked fibroblastic response is the type of response required. Various other parasites such as *Stephanostomum buccatuna* provoke an intermediate response. Much research is still required to solve the many factors which govern the host-parasite relationship. In a discipline where taxonomy has been all-important, it is interesting to see the part of the host and its reaction being upgraded.

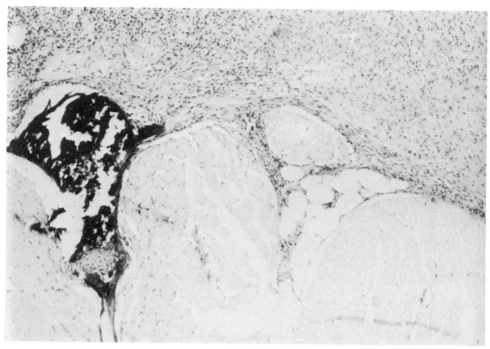

Fig. 13.5. Marked fibroblastic response extending deep into the dorsal musculature and due to *Lernea cyprinacea*. Note muscle bundle isolated by fibroblastic response. H&E; X80.

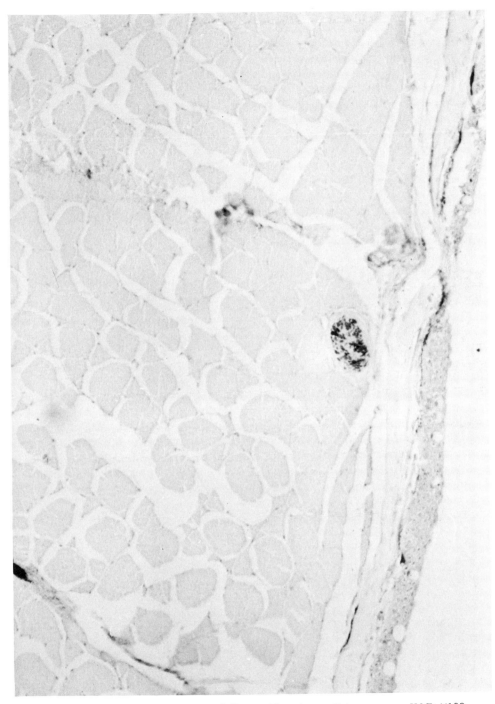

Fig. 13.6. Metacercaria of *Cryptocotyle lingua*. There is no cellular response. H&E; ×100.

VIRAL DISEASES

General comment, only, can be made on the lesions seen in muscle of fish infected with viruses. In several viral diseases, viral hemorrhagic septicemia of rainbow trout and spring viremia of carp, the increased fragility of the capillaries gives rise to petechial hemorrhages in the skeletal muscle. These lesions appear as areas of capillary congestion and localized hemorrhage associated with some degenerative change in the surrounding muscle.

MYOPATHIES

By definition, a myopathy is a condition which affects primarily the muscle fiber, as distinct from its connective tissue surroundings and its nerve supply. Little is known about myopathies in fish, although there is some evidence of nutritional myopathies being induced in the salmonids when they are fed deficient diets. Such work is being undertaken by the Western Fish Disease Laboratory. The myopathy described in the present paper is of unknown etiology.

Nodular Lymphocytic Myositis

This is the name given to a condition described on three occasions in fish in the British Isles. Two cases have been seen by the author, one in an eel (*Anguilla anguilla*) and the other in a tench (*Tinca tinca*). The third case was seen in a cyprinid fish recorded by R. J. Roberts (personal communication). In all three instances the fish presented a lump, which on initial observation was suggestive of a neoplasm of fibrous or muscle tissue (Fig. 13.7). On macroscopical examination the lumps appeared to be neoplastic, arising in or from skeletal muscle. The lesions appeared to be encapsulated, and connective tissue elements transversed the mass (Fig. 13.9). On histological examination the lesions were clearly seen to be non-neoplastic. The distinctive histological findings may be summarized: (1) The

Fig. 13.7. Figures 13.7 through 13.14 are of cases of nodular lymphocytic myositis. Lateral musculature of eel (*Anguilla anguilla*), showing apparent tumor.

Fig. 13.8. Lateral view of tench (*Tinca tinca*), showing ventral swelling.

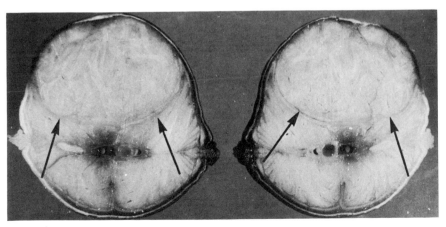

Fig. 13.9. Transverse section of eel from Figure 13.7, showing muscle lesion.

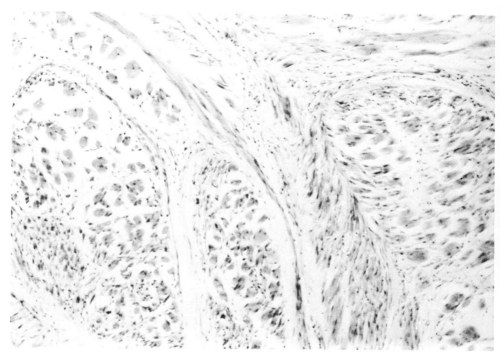

Fig. 13.10. Atrophy of majority of muscle fibers. H&E; X80.

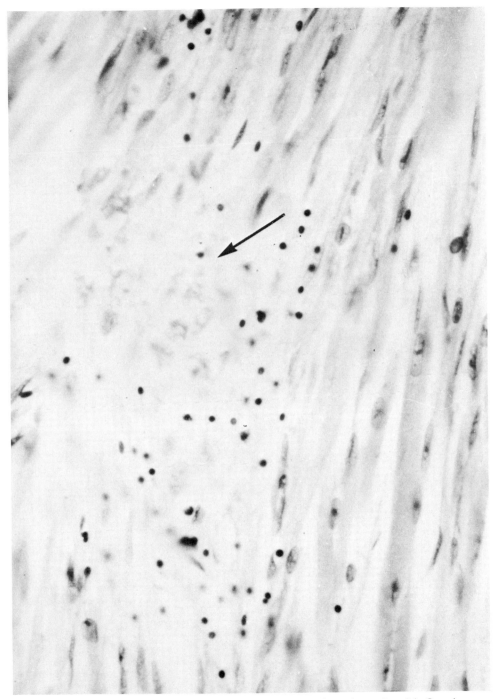

Fig. 13.11. Degenerate muscle fibers with marked swelling of sarcolemmal nuclei. Occasional lymphocyte is seen. H&E; X720.

355

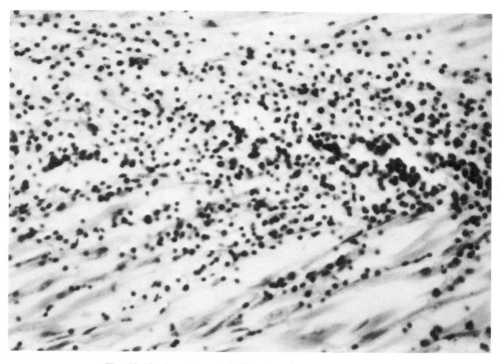

Fig. 13.12.   Lymphocytic infiltration of muscle.   H&E; X500.

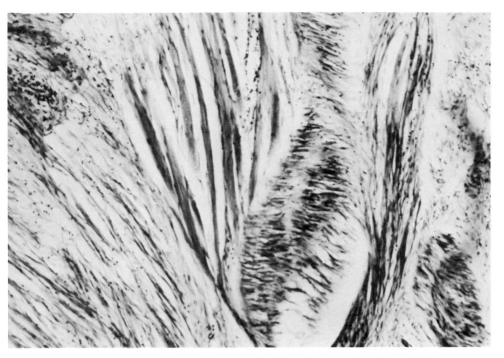

Fig. 13.13. Marked increase in connective tissue elements. Van Gieson; X80.

muscle bundles were edematous. (2) Marked atrophic change was seen in many of the muscle fibers (Fig. 13.10). (3) There was minimal muscle regeneration. (4) There was a vacuolar degenerative change affecting muscle fibers associated with sarcolemmal nuclei proliferation (Fig. 13.11). (5) There was a variable degree of lymphocytic infiltration (Fig. 13.12). (6) Marked increase in connective tissue elements was noted (Fig. 13.13). (7) There was marked increase in reticulin fibers in the epimysium and perimysium (Fig. 13.14). At the present time the remaining tissues of the fish are being examined to see if any systemic lesions are present. As the fish were received fixed in formalin, it was not possible to make comment on blood cell counts or serum chemistry.

There are many inflammatory lesions of animal muscle of unknown etiology, and these have been well summarized (1). In the previously described instance, Gram, Ziehl-Neelsen, and Giemsa stains were negative and no organisms were seen. There were no parasitic metacercariae seen in the many sections examined. The vacuolar degeneration of the muscle fiber was similar to that seen in man, associated with systemic lupus erythematosus (7). Although it is unlikely that a single area of nodular myositis could be considered part of a generalized collagen disorder, at this stage of the investigation all the differential diagnoses must be respected.

Fig. 13.14. Marked increase in reticulin fibers seen around the muscle fibers. Van Gieson; ×720.

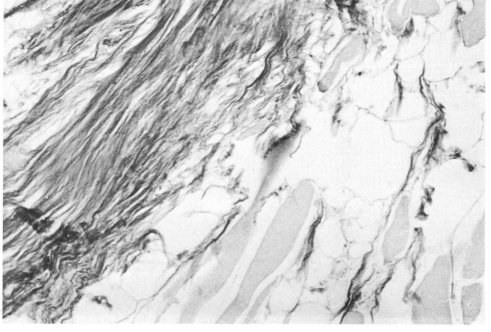

Fig. 13.15. Rhabdomyoma. Nuclear detail is lost due to autolysis. Van Gieson; ×80.

TUMORS

Muscle is of three main types, skeletal, smooth, and cardiac. Tumors of skeletal and smooth muscle have been recorded. No primary cardiac tumors have yet been documented.

Rhabdomyoma

This is a tumor of skeletal or striped muscle. These are not common tumors in any animal species but have been described in several species of fish (4). These tumors are characterized by muscle fibers running in all directions. The fibers are of variable diameter, but often much enlarged. There is usually a marked increase in the amounts of connective tissue (Fig. 13.15). Four rhabdomyomas have been seen in this laboratory, two in rainbow trout (*Salmo gairdneri*), one in a herring (*Clupea harengus*), and the fourth in an unnamed fish from Rhodesia.

Leiomyoma

This is a tumor of smooth or unstriated muscle. It is possibly more common than its skeletal counterpart (4) and those associated with the gastrointestinal

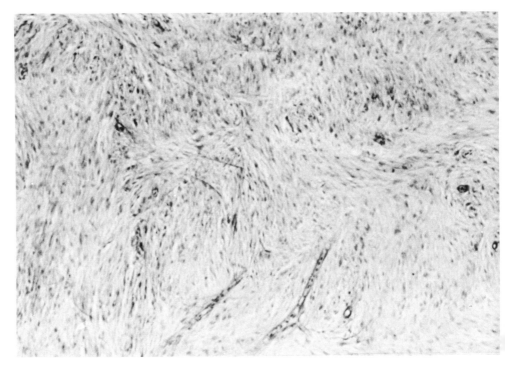

Fig. 13.16. Leiomyoma. Note prominent capillaries. H&E; ×80.

tract. The leiomyoma presents difficulties in its diagnosis, as the spindle-shaped cells can be confused with fibroblasts. If the nuclei are aligned, some pseudo-palisading can be seen. Only a single case of a leiomyoma, that in a goldfish (*C. auratus*), has been observed in this laboratory (Fig. 13.16).

This brief review of some of the conditions that can affect the musculature of fish has emphasized how little is known of these conditions and how even less is understood. This organ system presents many challenges to the researcher who may be tempted to fill some of the gaps in our knowledge.

REFERENCES

1. Innes, J. R. M., and Saunders, L. Z. *Comparative Neuropathology*, pp. 210–220. New York and London, Academic Press, 1962.
2. Kabata, Z. *Crustacea as Enemies of Fishes*, book 1. In *Diseases of Fishes*, ed. S. F. Snieszko and H. R. Axelrod. Jersey City, T.F.H. Publications, 1970.
3. Mawdesley-Thomas, L. E. Furunculosis in the goldfish *Carassius auratus* (L.). *J. Fish Biol. 1:* 19–23. 1969.
4. Mawdesley-Thomas, L. E. Some tumours of fish, pp. 191–283. In *Diseases of Fish*, ed. L. E. Mawdesley-Thomas. (Symp. Zool. Soc. London, No. 30.) London and New York, Academic Press, 1972.

5. Mawdesley-Thomas, L. E., and Bucke, D.   Tissue repair in a poikilothermic vertebrate: A preliminary study. *J. Fish Biol. 5:* 115–119. 1973.

6. Mawdesley-Thomas, L. E., and Jolly, D. W.   Diseases of fish. II. The goldfish (*Carassius auratus*). *J. Small Anim. Pract. 8:* 33–54. 1967.

7. Pearson, C. M., and Yamazaki, J. N.   Vacuolar myopathy in systemic lupus erythematosus. *Amer. J. Clin. Pathol. 29:* 455–463. 1958.

8. Thorpe, J. E., and Roberts, R. J.   An aeromonad epidemic in brown trout (*Salmo trutta* L.). *J. Fish Biol. 4:* 441–451. 1972.

DISCUSSION OF SOME DISEASES OF MUSCLE

M. M. Sigel: I was fascinated with your presentation and slides. I would like to make several comments concerning the etiology of these lesions. While this is extremely speculative, I cannot help but comment that the lesions you have just shown resemble in some way the Coxsackie virus infection in mice.

L. E. Mawdesley-Thomas: I have just been talking with Dr. Roberts, who has undertaken some ultrastructure studies on these lesions and he has not been able to show any virus particles.

M. M. Sigel: You mention that this condition could be an autoimmune one, and you also mentioned lupus erythematosus. We have never seen any evidence of this type of etiology or even immediate type of hypersensitivity in fish, although we are still searching for it. In one or two instances immunization of fish with antigens containing complete Freund's adjuvant, tubercle bacilli, and mineral oil, by the intramuscular route, has led to muscle lesions similar to yours.

L. E. Mawdesley-Thomas: This is an interesting piece of information, of which we had no previous knowledge. Dr. Roberts and I thought initially that this lesion was neoplastic and although we have searched the literature thoroughly we have not come up with any interesting diagnoses. The nearest condition we have found is that in horses known as an eosinophilic granuloma. There are, of course, many interesting myopathies that are seen in animal species. We have looked at all these and do not think that this particular muscle lesion had anything in common with any previously described lesions.

A. H. Walsh: Paul Yevitch described something that I have seen in a number of fish, and that is numerous vacuoles within muscle bundles. In longitudinal section they seem to almost interrupt the bundles in some places. Of course mine have always been captive fish and I believe yours were all wild fish. I had assumed that this change resulted from prolonged captivity and was associated with some degenerative change. Are you familiar with this type of thing and have you any thoughts on it?

L. E. Mawdesley-Thomas: No. These were wild fish. The only thing I could find in the literature was one case of a young boy of 15 who had systemic lupus erythematosus and had exactly the same changes in the muscle that I have just described. I suppose, as Roger Lee Herman was saying, you tend to think that certain structures don't have many lesions in them. This is primarily because one doesn't look at them thoroughly. I think the central nervous system is a good example of this. I must say that I have only recently started to look at muscle in a new light but I don't obviously recall seeing this. I am sure that I shall go back home tomorrow and see vacuolated muscle fibers for the rest of my life.

W. E. Ribelin: In looking at parasitized fish I have been impressed with the lack of extensive eosinophilic response to the parasites such as we see in mammals, including man. There is some degree, but certainly it is much less, and I wondered if Dr. Sigel would comment on the reason for this and what he considered to be a typical allergic response in muscle to foreign antigens.

M. M. Sigel: Unfortunately my answer is very simple. I haven't done the work that you are asking for an explanation of. I am just beginning to study the lymphocytic response and I can say that in some respects the lymphocytic behavior in fish resembles that of mammals, but in other respects it is quite different. I must emphasize this particular point. The lymphocytes of both sharks and teleosts seem to be incapable of recognizing histocompatibility antigens. This is extremely strange in view of the recent theory that recognition of histocompatibility antigens is a primordial early type of recognition and is a response to various viral, bacterial, and proteinaceous antigens. They do react to fibrinohemagglutinins but do not seem to react against alloantigens, and this is surprising considering that fish do reject allografts. As Hildeman shows, the rejection is a chronic slow process, about 40 days in the shark, and yet we don't seem to get the type of cell that one associates with recognition of alloantigens. So I am sort of evading your question because I haven't worked on eosinophils. I cannot tell you anything about eosinophils except that they exist. In the thymus of fish we find lymphocytes that produce antibody on the one hand, which is strange because in higher species lymphocytes of the thymus do not produce antibody, and on the other hand these lymphocytes of fish thymus also respond to antigenic stimulation with a blastogenic reaction. That is as far as I can go. I would like to indicate again that the mucus of fish, both unimmunized and immunized, contains antibodies which are produced locally at some as yet undetermined site. This antibody is not derived from the serum or the blood because it has been demonstrated by using a radioactive antibody placed into the circulation. This antibody can be recovered from the circulation but not from the surface slime, nor from the mucus. Perhaps in certain critical circumstances you do find lymphocytes in the integument, but according to Dr. Ashley and some other speakers, under normal circumstances lymphocytes are not found in the epidermis. One does see granular cells and it has been suggested that these might be associated with antibody formation.

L. E. Mawdesley-Thomas: I wonder if I could ask my medical colleague if he would like to say something about the similarity of these muscle lesions to collagen disease in man.

K. Balogh: Since you have asked, I will say that I think that it is a possibility but the best I can say at a guess is that if this is collagen disease one must examine all other organs, as it would seem to be unusual that a systemic disease would produce such a localized response at only one given site. This condition, if seen in man, would be called myositis proliferans, which is just to give it a name. It is a benign lesion thought to be somewhere between reactive hyperplasia and neoplasia. When it is found in man the surgeons excise the lesion and that is all. Perhaps in man it is related to trauma but in your muscle lesion no hemosiderin was seen around it to suggest a traumatic etiology. Nevertheless, one does not usually see this degree of inflammatory response in myositis proliferans so there may be a lot more to this diagnosis. A possible viral etiology cannot be ruled out.

R. J. Roberts: One of the previous speakers was asking about the vacuolation seen in muscle fibers. A good place to see these in large numbers is in extrinsic eye muscles of migrating Atlantic salmon as they are returning from the sea. I think that they are probably age-related but they certainly are extremely marked.

S. F. Snieszko: My remarks are about the antibody in the mucus which you have mentioned. Quite a long time ago attempts were made to immunize against some enteric diseases by oral vaccination and it was explained that the antibody was being produced in the mucous membrane of the intestinal tract. Interesting experiments were made showing the presence of antibodies in the slime of the fish infested with parasites. Therefore, since fish are covered with this type of mucous membrane, I would not be at all surprised if in this mucous membrane local immunity could take place.

H.-H. Reichenbach-Klinke: I wish to add that we also have found antibodies in the mucus of fish. For instance, in carp with infectious ascites we found higher levels of antibodies in infected carp than in the healthy ones.

R. J. Roberts: Someone was asking about lymphocytes in the skin. The epithelium covering the lesion in the fish we discussed, a cyprinid, was heavily invaded with lymphocytes. It is uncommon for us to get the mucus in the desquamating cells to stay intact. It just so happened that in one section we could, and the mucus itself was loaded with lymphocytes. I cannot explain this but it is certainly a most striking example of lymphocytes within the epidermis and actually migrating through it.

14

Histopathology of Teleost
Kidney Diseases

R . A . B E N D E L E , J R .
and G . W . K L O N T Z

Morphologically and physiologically the mesonephric kidney of higher bony fishes is composed of three distinct systems: endocrine, hematopoietic, and excretory. The endocrine portion includes the nonencapsulated adrenal cortical (interrenal) and chromaffin tissues in the anterior kidney, and the encapsulated corpuscles of Stannius in the posterior kidney (15). The hematopoietic tissue is located primarily in the anterior and mid-kidney with some being present in the intertubular spaces of the posterior kidney. This tissue serves as the primary blood-forming organ in teleosts (3). As in all vertebrates, the excretory portion of the kidney is composed of nephrons, the individually functional excretory units of the posterior kidney. There is extreme variability in the complexity of nephrons in different teleost species, related to their evolutionary development in diverse habitats. These variations range from the typical freshwater teleost nephron, which is composed of glomerulus, neck segment, first proximal segment, second proximal segment, intermediate segment, distal segment, and collecting ducts, to that of the aglomerular marine teleosts, which have only the second proximal segment and collecting ducts (13).

Lesions developing in the teleost kidney may involve one or all of the three tissue systems. For example, tissue destruction can vary from selective necrosis of hematopoietic tissue to necrosis and/or displacement of all normal tissue by proliferative lesions such as neoplasms and granulomatous inflammation.

365

This paper constitutes a review of the literature of diseases that primarily affect the teleost kidney. Emphasis has been placed upon articles that contain specific information concerning histopathological findings in the various diseases discussed. No attempt was made to include all reports concerning any specific disease. The diseases are classified for discussion according to general taxonomic groupings of the causative agents (e.g., viral, bacterial, etc.).

VIRAL DISEASES

Infectious Hematopoietic Necrosis (IHN)

IHN is an acute viral disease of rainbow trout (*Salmo gairdneri*) and sockeye salmon (*Oncorhynchus nerka*) (1). Fry and fingerlings are most severely affected, although sockeye up to three years of age are susceptible. Gross lesions include widespread petechial and ecchymotic hemorrhages in the body musculature, serosal surfaces, fat depots, and meninges. Advanced cases may have exophthalmia, ascites, and edematous, friable viscera. Histologically there is necrosis of the renal hematopoietic tissue, which apparently is the target tissue of the virus. This lesion develops early in the disease and results in anemia and leukopenia. Despite the necrosis of hematopoietic tissue the nephronal elements are relatively unaffected until the terminal stages of the disease. Necrosis of the liver, spleen, pancreas, and granular cells of the alimentary tract are other salient features of the infection; however, the hematopoietic lesions appear to be the primary cause of death.

Chinook Salmon Virus Disease (CSVD)

CSVD has been reported as a spontaneous disease only in chinook salmon (*O. tshawytscha*). Young salmon are acutely infected, and gross lesions include exophthalmia, ascites, and, reportedly, a well-defined area of hemorrhage in the hypaxial muscles between the head and the dorsal fin (46). The gills and viscera are pale, probably because of severe anemia associated with involvement of the hematopoietic tissue. Histologically the most prominent lesion is massive necrosis of the hematopoietic tissue of the kidney and spleen. In their pathogenesis study, Yasutake, Parisot, and Klontz (46) observed vague changes in hematopoietic cells within 24 hours post-inoculation (PI) and degenerative nuclear changes such as pyknosis and karyorrhexis by 36 hours PI. Hematopoietic necrosis progressed rapidly to involve the entire renal and splenic blood-forming tissues and resulted in death within about 120 hours PI. As in IHN, the nephrons in the affected kidneys remained essentially unchanged. Microscopic lesions occurred in the pancreas and eosinophilic granular cells of the alimentary tract, but again these were of less physiological significance than those of the hematopoietic tissue. One observation of particular interest was the consistent finding of complete necrosis of the adrenal cortical tissue. This specific lesion has not been reported in histological descriptions of other piscine viral diseases which affect the kidney, but if it occurs in others it would definitely contribute to rapid death because of alteration of adrenocorticoid function.

Sockeye Salmon Virus Disease (SSVD)

Although this disease has been reported from several sources as occurring only in sockeye salmon, it is characterized by lesions which are very similar to those produced in IHN and CSVD (1, 46). Grossly there are ecchymotic hemorrhages at the base of the fins, and petechial hemorrhages in the alimentary tract. The gills and viscera are pale and ascitic fluid is often present in the body cavity. As in IHN and CSVD, the hematopoietic tissue is necrotic by 48 to 72 hours following exposure to the virus. Other histological lesions include necrosis of the pancreas, spleen, and intestinal granular cells. It is probable that SSVD, CSVD, and IHN are due to variants of the same virus.

Viral Hemorrhagic Septicemia (VHS)

VHS is a disease of rainbow trout that at present occurs only in Europe. It affects fingerlings and market-size fish while generally sparing fry and brood fish. Clinical signs are variable; external color change, exophthalmia, and ascites, as well as nervous signs without gross tissue changes have been described (2, 10, 22). Internal lesions include widespread hemorrhages in acute cases and renal swelling in chronic cases. Histological lesions have been described in detail from spontaneous and experimentally produced cases (10, 44). In both kinds of cases severe kidney lesions involving necrosis of hematopoietic tissue, necrosis and sloughing of tubular epithelium, and glomerular edema were observed. Marked hyperplasia of lymphoid cells without necrosis occurred in the kidney in chronic cases (10). Other prominent histological changes include degeneration and necrosis of the liver, spleen, and skeletal muscle.

Channel Catfish Virus Disease (CCVD)

CCVD is an acute disease of channel catfish (*Ictalurus punctatus*) fingerlings (9, 21). The etiological agent has been described and classified as a herpes virus by Wolf and Darlington (34). The clinical signs include erratic, frenzied swimming, exophthalmia, ascites, and petechial hemorrhages in the fins and musculature. Recently a similar disease was produced in channel catfish fingerlings by passage of a bacteria-free filtrate prepared from the viscera of blue catfish (*I. furcatus*) fingerlings obtained in a spontaneous epizootic (5). Wolf, Herman, and Carlson (35) reported the histopathology of experimental CCVD in which they described marked necrosis of the kidney with edema and extensive necrosis of

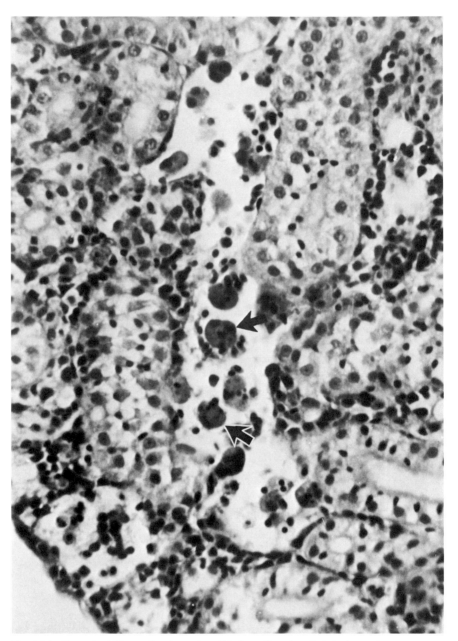

Fig. 14.1. Posterior kidney of a channel catfish fingerling that died during a virologically confirmed epizootic of CCVD. Note the large macrophages (arrows) containing **erythrocytic** debris in the hematic sinusoids. Hematoxylin and eosin (H&E); ×430.

the hematopoietic tissue. Numerous macrophages were also present in the kidney. Other lesions included focal hepatic necrosis and edema, intermuscular hemorrhage, and submucosal edema in the alimentary tract. Bendele (unpublished observation) has found, in both spontaneous and experimental cases, numerous macrophages laden with erythrocytic debris in the vascular sinusoids of the kidney and coagulation necrosis of renal hematopoietic tissue and renal tubular epithelium.

BACTERIAL DISEASES

Furunculosis

Furunculosis has been reported in a variety of teleost species (17). The disease was first described and has been most frequently reported in salmonids; thus the causative gram-negative, nonmotile bacterium was classified as *Aeromonas salmonicida*. The organisms gain entry into the host either orally or through cutaneous abrasions. The disease develops as a bacteremia with resultant spread of the infectious agent to all tissues of the body. The more virulent strains of *A. salmonicida* resist phagocytosis and thus rapidly overwhelm the host's defensive mechanisms. Gross lesions vary according to the stage of the disease process encountered. In peracute cases splenomegaly is usually the only noticeable change (16), while in acute cases there might be petechial and ecchymotic hemorrhages in the fins and body musculature and a hemorrhagic discharge from the cloaca (28). The infection persists in a subacute or chronic state in some animals to produce fluid-filled "furuncles" and cutaneous ulcerations (2, 17).

Klontz, Yasutake, and Ross (16) reported the microscopic lesions associated with an acute experimental infection in rainbow trout. The most significant finding was the change produced in the hematopoietic tissue. Initially, by 24 hours PI, there was an increase in the number of macrophages, neutrophils, and small lymphocytes. However, by 32 to 40 hours PI the leukopoietic and erythropoietic elements of the kidney had decreased markedly, and by 48 to 56 hours PI hematopoiesis in the anterior and mid-kidney had virtually ceased. The cause of the hematopoietic tissue destruction and phagocytosis inhibition was found to be a water-soluble leukocytolytic endotoxin produced by *A. salmonicida*. Their experimental findings were similar to those seen in the naturally occurring disease in salmonids.

Corynebacterial Kidney Disease (KD)

KD is a subacute-to-chronic systemic infection by a gram-positive diplobacillus currently classified in the genus *Corynebacterium*. A relatively acute form of the infection has been reported in members of the genus *Oncorhynchus*, which Wood

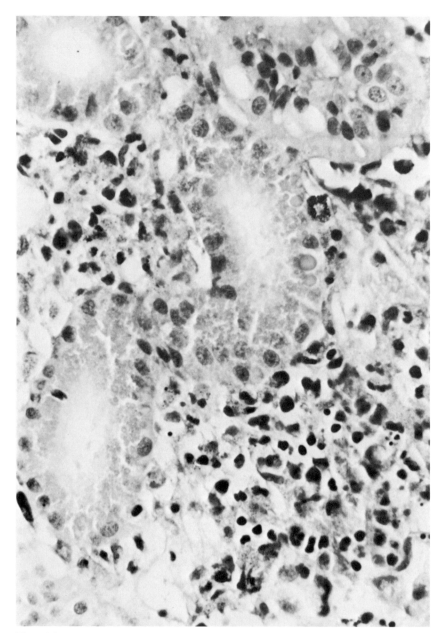

Fig. 14.2. Posterior kidney of a rainbow trout with corynebacterial kidney disease. Note the large hyalin droplets in the tubular epithelium, the pyknotic nuclei in the intertubular hematopoietic tissue, and the causative bacteria seen as dark stippling in the cytoplasm of macrophages. McCallum-Goodpasture; ×430.

and Yasutake (37) interpreted as a lower resistance in salmon as compared with trout. Gross lesions are not striking, usually consisting of a swollen and slightly pale kidney. Occasionally there is swelling and paleness of the liver and spleen. The detailed histopathology of KD was described by Wood and Yasutake (37). Microscopically the disease is characterized by granuloma formation in almost every tissue of the body. The hematopoietic tissue of the kidney is apparently the first tissue infected. Yasutake (43) reported that in test-inoculated fish there is hyperplasia of hemoblastic cells and decreased lymphocytes in the kidney at the end of one week PI. Foci of macrophages containing phagocytized bacteria also were evident at that time. These same lesions developed in test-fed fish but were not present until the fifth week PI. The infection involves all renal components, resulting in necrosis with replacement of the normal tissue by granulomatous tissue. This lesion progresses to cause death due to renal insufficiency. The development of granulomatous lesions throughout the viscera and in the gills, skeletal muscle, and brain also contributes to the fish's demise.

Mycobacteriosis

Piscine tuberculosis has been reported in marine, freshwater, and aquarium fishes (2). In the past the disease has been of economic importance in the salmon industry (41), but it has been controlled since the late 1950s by the initiation of feeding pasteurized instead of raw salmon viscera to hatchery fish. The disease is still of importance in aquarium fishes (2). According to different authors the clinical signs vary from none to skin ulceration, exophthalmia, emaciation, swimming incoordination, stuntedness, and lack of development of secondary sexual characteristics (2, 6, 41). Microscopic lesions have been well described by Amlacher (2) and Parisot and Wood (20). Conroy (6) has reviewed the reported histopathology.

In general the microscopic lesions are similar from all species of teleosts reported. The tubercular lesions result from the development of multiple foci of caseation necrosis surrounded by proliferative inflammation which progressively replaces the normal parenchymal tissue. Acid-fast bacilli can routinely be demonstrated in the reticulo-endothelial cells in and around the tubercles. In advanced cases developing granulomas may be found in almost every tissue of the body, and necrosis of kidney tubules is a constant finding (2). The causative organisms are rarely found free in blood plasma, but are spread throughout the system, engulfed in macrophages which apparently are enzymatically incapable of destroying them.

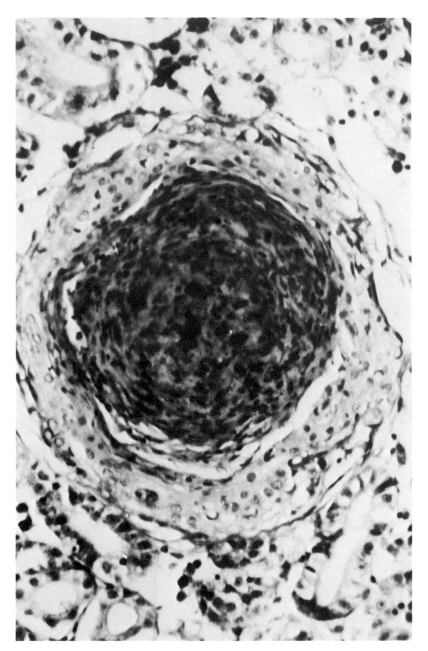

Fig. 14.3. Posterior kidney of a common pompano (*Trachinotus carolinus*) with mycobacteriosis. Note the prominent zone of epithelioid cells surrounding the central core of cellular debris. Acid-fast bacteria were abundant with the central core. H&E; ×430.

FUNGAL DISEASES

Ichthyophonosis (Ichthyosporidiosis)

Ichthyophonosis is a chronic disease of marine, freshwater, and aquarium fishes caused by a phycomycete classified as *Ichthyophonus hoferi*. This is by far the most common and best-described systemic fungal disease of fish. The biology of the organism and development of lesions in the host have been reported (2, 7, 23, 26).

The parasite gains entrance to the body via the alimentary canal and germinates in the stomach, from which ameboid stages enter the bloodstream by migrating into the vasculature of the gastric wall. The organisms are then transported throughout the body in the circulatory system and continue their development in various organs and tissue. The most heavily parasitized organs are those receiving the richest blood supply (i.e., liver, kidney, heart, and spleen), but any organ of the body can be involved in advanced cases. The developing organisms are phagocytized but apparently are not readily destroyed by macrophage lysosomal enzymes. As the pathogenic agents overwhelm the macrophages in newly invaded tissue, a zone of leukocytes surrounds them and renewed phagocytosis occurs. These areas become the centers of granulomas as reticulo-endothelial cells and fibroblasts surround the nidi. The developing plasmodia produce local tissue necrosis and die within the developing granulomas. In the kidney, as in other organs, recurrent episodes of necrosis with accompanying proliferative inflammation occur until the normal tissue has been replaced by granulomatous and fibrous elements. Histologically the granulomas appear like those produced in other granulomatous diseases when observed in tissue sections stained with hematoxylin and eosin. For differential diagnosis a periodic acid-Schiff (PAS) stain is helpful because it allows detection of the PAS-positive organisms in the granulomas and in free macrophages in the hematopoietic tissue of affected kidneys. Many mycobacterial granulomas also contain PAS-positive material, making an acid-fast stain essential for differential diagnosis in some cases.

Other Fungal Diseases

Two other systemic fungal agents affecting the kidney of teleosts have been reported. Wood, Yasutake, and Lehman (39) described a budding, yeast-like fungus resembling the blastomycetes in the kidneys of freshwater trout from the eastern United States. The organism produced coagulation necrosis with resultant granuloma formation. The primary damage to the kidney appeared to be necrosis of the hematopoietic tissue, while necrosis of the nephrons appeared to be secondary to more extensive disease. The authors discussed the relationship of the fungus to bacterial kidney disease, and the possibility that the feed was the source of the infectious agent. The economic impact of the disease was not known.

The other fungal disease was reported by Plehn (in 23) as a renal disease of

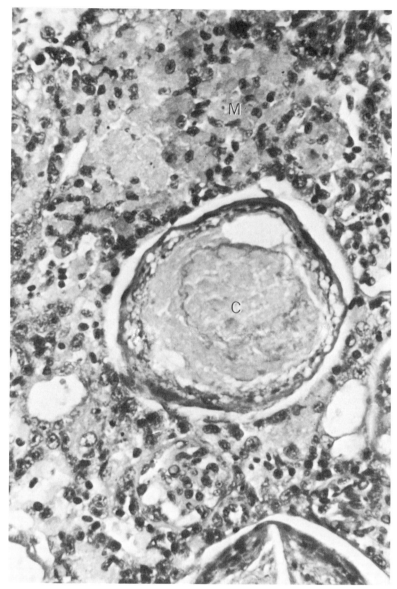

Fig. 14.4. Granulomatous inflammation in the posterior kidney of a goldfish (*Carassius carassius*) with ichthyophonosis. Note large degenerating cyst (C) and aggregate of large foamy macrophages (M). Cyst and macrophage cytoplasm were strongly periodic acid-Schiff-positive. H&E; X430.

carp caused by *Nephromyces piscium.* The same disease was observed by Reichen-bach-Klinke and Elkan (23), who classified the etiological agent as a mold in the family Aspergillaceae and described it as *Penicillium piscium.*

NEOPLASIA

There are few documentations of renal neoplasms in teleosts. Schlumberger and Lucké (25) did an extensive literature review of fish neoplasia and reported only nine neoplasms of renal origin. These included two adenocarcinomas, two adenomas, one fibrosarcoma, and four lymphosarcomas. Since that time Stolk (29, 30) has reported a renal carcinoma and an adenocarcinoma. Ashley (4) has produced renal neoplasms in rainbow trout using dimethylnitrosamine and I^{131}, and Helmboldt and Wyand (11) reported a nephroblastoma in a striped bass (*Morone saxatilis*). The latter authors compared the tumors with Wilms' tumor in man. Both described primitive glomeruli, anomalous renal tubules, and fibrous stroma. Helmboldt and Wyand stated that approximately 90% of the tumor mass was cartilage, whereas Ashley did not mention cartilage in the experimental tumors. Several cases of spontaneous lymphoid neoplasia have also been reported during the last 15 years. The majority of these tumors appear to have originated in the kidney, but some are possibly of subcutaneous origin (24), while others are possibly of thymic origin (8).

The most thoroughly studied lymphoid neoplasms are those described in the northern pike (*Esox lucius*) by Mulcahy (18, 19). The neoplastic cell type was described as being a hemocytoblastic or hematopoietic reticular cell with abundant cytoplasm and a large nucleus containing a single moderately large nucleolus. Mitotic figures were moderately abundant in some areas of the tumor and rare in others. Necrosis of neoplastic tissues with associated phagocytosis of the debris was common, but subsequent fibrosis of the necrotic areas did not occur. In the kidney there was active invasion and destruction of the nephrons. Similar renal destruction was reported by Smith (27) in a malignant lymphoma with concurrent leukemia described in a cutthroat trout (*S. clarki*).

PARASITIC DISEASES

Protozoans

Protozoans, especially members of the subphylum Cnidospora, are common parasites of both marine and freshwater fishes. An estimate of the annual economic loss of fish production due to these organisms is extremely difficult because the parasites are present in the host species in varying numbers, and only on rare occasions have they been reported as the primary cause of epizootics.

Several species of protozoans have been reported as occurring in the kidney of

teleosts. Many of these have been incidental findings, but a few have been described as causing significant tissue damage and death of the host.

Superclass Mastigophora
  Order: Protomonadina
    Genus: *Cryptobia*

Two species of *Cryptobia*, *Cryptobia borreli* and *C. cyprini*, have been reported
in the blood of teleosts. Wales and Wolf (32) reported finding *C. borreli* in several
species of freshwater teleosts in California. They described the infection in yearling and adult rainbow trout and yearling king salmon (*O. tshawytscha*), in which
they observed the flagellates in the parenchyma of the kidney. The extent and the
type of renal lesions, if any, were not described.

Subphylum Cnidospora
  Class: Myxosporidea
    Ceratomyxa shasta

Wales and Wolf (32) described this parasite as causing severe losses in rainbow
trout at one hatchery in California. The source of the infection was found to be
fish in Crystal Lake, from which the hatchery drew its water supply. Diseased
fish had exophthalmia and ascites. In microscopic preparations, the causative organisms were found throughout the viscera, but again the type of lesion was not
described.

Myxidium menteri

Yasutake and Wood (45) described the histopathology of *Myxidium menteri*
infection in salmonids of the Pacific Northwest. They reported finding both
trophozoites and spores in the renal tubules and adjacent hematopoietic tissue.
Degeneration of renal tubular epithelium was present in extensive infections.

Chloromyxum majori

In the same report, Yasutake and Wood (45) described the occurrence of another coelozoic myxosporidian, *Chloromyxum majori*, in the kidneys of rainbow
trout. A similar parasite was mentioned as having been found in the kidneys of
chinook salmon. The organisms were located primarily in the glomerular tufts,
although some were found in the hematopoietic tissue. The authors felt that
losses of released hatchery salmonids due to these parasites could be significant
because of the tubular degeneration and glomerular damage that resulted from
the observed infections.

Bendele (unpublished) has observed a myxosporidian of undetermined classification in the renal tubules of channel catfish. The infection was of moderate severity and had produced minimal changes in the tubular epithelium.

Other myxosporidians that have been reported as occurring in the kidneys of
freshwater teleosts include *Myxobolus pfeifferi* (2), *Myxidium americanum* (14),
Mitraspora elongata (14), and *Hoferellus cyprini* (14).

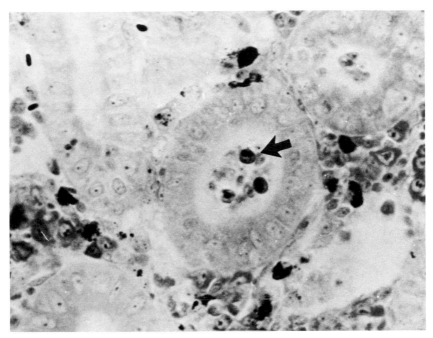

Fig. 14.5. Coelozoic myxosporidian (arrow) in the tubules of the posterior kidney of a channel catfish. Giemsa; ×430.

Subphylum Cnidospora
Class: Microsporidea

Two members of the class Microsporidea have been described as occurring incidentally in the kidneys of teleosts. These organisms produce cysts which cause pressure necrosis of the surrounding tissue but little or no inflammatory reaction. Summerfelt (31) reported *Plistophora ovariae* in the golden shiner (*Notemigonus crysoleucas*) as occurring primarily in ovarian tissue, but frequently it was found in the kidney when the infection was extensive. Amlacher (2) mentions that *Glugea pseudotumefaciens* might be found in the kidney; however, no lesions were described.

Trematodes

Damage to the kidney of teleosts occurs when cercariae of various species enter the fish and migrate through the tissues. Most cercariae encyst in the tissues following the migratory period (14) and cause tissue destruction due to pressure necrosis as the organism continues a short period of growth and stimulates fibroplasia. Inflammation is not prominent; usually the organism is surrounded by a fibrous tissue capsule which contains a few lymphocytes and melanophores that have migrated into the area. The metacercariae remain in this encysted state until ingested by the final host.

The Sanguinicolidae are specialized digenetic trematodes, the adult form of which lives in the circulatory system. The parasites produce ova which are often trapped in the vasculature of the host fish's kidney, where they become encapsulated in fibrous cysts and degenerate.

Cestodes

Cestode larvae, plerocercoids, behave similarly to the trematode cercariae in that they migrate through the host fish tissues and often become encysted in the visceral organs where they produce pressure necrosis and replacement of normal parenchymal tissue by fibrous tissue. As with the metacercariae, there is very little inflammation associated with the larval cysts, but the larvae die and the cysts become filled with necrotic debris. Old lesions in the kidney can resemble the mature lesions of some of the granulomatous diseases previously discussed. Generally plerocercoids and metacercariae can be differentiated on the basis that all but very young metacercariae have suckers, which plerocercoids lack, and many plerocercoids have calcarious concretions which are lacking in metacercarial cysts (14).

Nematode Larvae

The larvae of some species of nematodes migrate extensively in fish tissues. They produce damage primarily by direct cellular destruction and hemorrhage in the path through which they move. These organisms often become encysted in fibrous capsules similar to the two platyhelminths described above. The kidney can be damaged by these parasites, but it seems to be less vulnerable to invasion than are the other visceral organs, especially the liver.

MISCELLANEOUS RENAL DISEASES

Nephrocalcinosis

Nephrocalcinosis is a disease of unknown etiology which has been reported in rainbow trout in Europe and North America (12). It is primarily a chronic degenerative disease of the kidney, although microscopic lesions are sometimes present in the stomach. Advanced cases can be recognized grossly by whitish streaks and spots in the kidney. Microscopically, there are dilation of renal tubules and degeneration of tubular epithelium due to pressure. Mineral-laden tubular casts which are histochemically positive for calcium salts are usually present. The occurrence of the disease has been associated with dietary constituents and water chemicals; however, no strict correlation has been found with either.

Visceral Granuloma

Visceral granuloma is primarily a disease of brook trout (*Salvelinus fontinalis*) which is classified with nephrocalcinosis and is considered by some to be the same disease with different manifestations. The disease was first described histologically by Wood and Yasutake (36). Herman (12) described it as often occurring concomitantly with corynebacterial kidney disease and believes that it is the same disease that Wood, Yasutake, and Lehman (39) reported as a mycotic granulomatous disease in brook trout. In advanced cases there is granuloma formation in the kidney, gastric mucosa, and visceral adipose tissue. The kidney is often swollen and may contain whitish streaks and spots. Histologically, the lesions are composed of macrophages, fibroblasts, Langhans' giant cells, and deposits of calcium salts. The development of the lesions is suspected to be associated with dietary constituents, especially addition of cottonseed meal. Water chemicals have also been suggested as contributory factors, but this has been less well substantiated than in nephrocalcinosis.

Sulfonamide Toxicity

Wood et al. (38, 40) have reported acute and chronic sulfonamide toxicity in salmonids being treated for bacterial infections. Acute toxicity was observed in young fall chinook which received a single overdose of sulfamethazine. Mortalities occurred 24 hours following administration of the drug and the rate continued high for four days. Grossly, the affected animals had distended stomachs with marked constriction of the pylorus. Microscopically there were necrosis of arterioles in the viscera, minimal degenerative changes in the renal tubular epithelium, and sulfonamide crystals in the kidney. Experimental attempts to reproduce the disease failed.

Chronic kidney lesions were produced in fish that were fed sulfamerazine a few days each month for two years to control endemic furunculosis. No gross lesions were associated with the disease, but the problem was discovered when the fish failed to spawn. Histologically there was severe degeneration of renal tubular epithelium which in hematoxylin and eosin-stained preparations appeared as white or yellowish opaque, amorphous masses bounded by basement membranes. The necrotic tubular epithelium and eosinophilic globular masses in the hematopoietic tissue both stained positively for hemoglobin. Degeneration of renal tubular epithelium and formation of tubular casts of cellular debris were produced after 26 weeks of experimental therapy. Globular masses of hemoglobin were evident in some cases after 34 weeks of experimental therapy, but hemoglobic tubular nephrosis was not produced experimentally. Sulfonamide crystals were not observed in either the spontaneous or experimental cases.

Acknowledgment. This is a contribution of a cooperative project between the Texas Parks and Wildlife Department and the Department of Veterinary Pathology, College of Veterinary Medicine and the Texas Agricultural Experiment Station, Texas A&M University; supported by Texas Pittman-Robertson Project W-93R.

REFERENCES

1. Amend, D. F., and Yasutake, W. T. A hematopoietic virus disease of rainbow trout and sockeye salmon. *Trans. Amer. Fish. Soc. 98*(4): 796–804.
2. Amlacher, E. *Textbook of Fish Diseases,* transl. D. A. Conroy and R. L. Herman. Jersey City, T.F.H. Publications, 1970.
3. Andrew, W. *Comparative Hematology.* New York and London, Grune & Stratton, 1965.
4. Ashley, L. M. Renal neoplasms of rainbow trout. *Bull. Wildlife Dis. Ass. 3:*86. 1967.
5. Bendele, R. A., and Klontz, G. W. A viral disease of blue catfish fingerlings. *J. Wildlife Dis.* In preparation.
6. Conroy, D. A. Piscine tuberculosis in the sea water environment, pp. 273–278. In *A Symposium on Diseases of Fishes and Shellfishes,* ed. S. F. Snieszko. Amer. Fish. Soc., Spec. Publ. No. 5. Washington, D.C., 1970.
7. Dorier, A., and Degrange, C. L'Evolution de l'Ichthyospiridium (*Ichthyophonus hoferi*) (Plehn and Mulsow) chez les salmonides d'elevage (truite arc-enciel et saumon de fontaine). *Trav. Lab. Hydrobiol. Piscicult. Univ. Grenoble, 51-52.* 1960–61.
8. Dunbar, C. E. Lymphosarcoma of possible thymic origin in salmonid fishes. *Nat. Cancer Inst. Monogr. 31:* 167–171. 1969.
9. Fijan, N. N., Wellborn, T. L., Jr., and Naftel, J. P. An acute viral disease of channel catfish. *U.S. Bur. Sport Fish. Wildlife, Tech. Pap. 43,* 11 pp. 1970.
10. Ghittino, P. Viral hemorrhagic septicemia (VHS) in rainbow trout in Italy. *Ann. N. Y. Acad. Sci. 126:* 468–478. 1965.
11. Helmboldt, C. F., and Wyand, D. S. Nephroblastoma in a striped bass. *J. Wildlife Dis. 7:* 162–165. 1971.
12. Herman, R. L. Visceral granuloma and nephrocalcinosis. *U.S. Bur. Sport Fish. Wildlife, Fish Dis. Leafl. 32.* 1971.
13. Hickman, C. P., and Trump, B. J. The kidney, pp. 91–239. In *Fish Physiology,* ed. W. S. Hoar and D. J. Randall, vol. 1. New York and London, Academic Press, 1969–70.
14. Hoffman, G. L. *Parasites of North American Freshwater Fishes.* 486 pp. Berkeley and Los Angeles, Univ. Calif. Press, 1967.
15. Jones, I. C., Chan, D. K. O., Henderson, I. W., and Ball, J. N. The adrenocortical steroids, adrenocorticotropin and the corpuscles of Stannius, pp. 321–376.

In *Fish Physiology*, ed. W. S. Hoar and D. J. Randall, vol. 2. New York and London, Academic Press, 1969–70.

16. Klontz, G. W., Yasutake, W. T., and Ross, A. J. Bacterial diseases of the Salmonidae in the western United States: Pathogenesis of furunculosis in rainbow trout. *Amer. J. Vet. Res. 27:* 1455–1460. 1966.

17. Mawdesley-Thomas, L. E. Furunculosis in the goldfish *Carassius auratus* (L.). *J. Fish Biol. 1:* 19–23. 1969.

18. Mulcahy, M. F. Lymphosarcoma in the pike *Esox Lucius* L. (Pisces; Esocidae) in Ireland. *Proc. Roy. Irish Acad.*, Sect. B 63: 103–129. 1963.

19. Mulcahy, M. F., Winqvist, G., and Dawe, C. J. The neoplastic cell type in lymphoreticular neoplasms of the northern pike, *Esox lucius* L. *Cancer Res. 30:* 2712–2717. 1970.

20. Parisot, T. J., and Wood, E. M. A comparative study of the causative agent of a myxobacterial disease of salmonid fishes. II. A description of the histopathology of the disease in chinook salmon (*Oncorhynchus tshawytscha*) and a comparison of the stain-characteristics of the fish disease with leprosy and human tuberculosis. *Amer. Rev. Resp. Dis. 82:* 212–222. 1960.

21. Plumb, J. A. Some biological aspects of channel catfish virus disease. Ph.D. thesis, Auburn Univ., Auburn, Ala. 1972.

22. Rasmussen, C. J. A biological study of the Egtved disease (INUL). *Ann. N. Y. Acad. Sci. 126:* 427–460. 1965.

23. Reichenbach-Klinke, H.-H., and Elkan, E. *The Principal Diseases of Lower Vertebrates.* London and New York, Academic Press, 1965.

24. Schlumberger, H. G. Tumors characteristic for certain animal species: A review. *Cancer Res. 17:* 823–832. 1957.

25. Schlumberger, H. G., and Lucké, B. Tumors of fishes, amphibians, and reptiles. *Cancer Res. 8:* 657–712. 1948.

26. Sindermann, C. J., and Scattergood, L. W. Diseases of fishes of the western North Atlantic. II. Ichthyosporidium disease of the sea herring (*Clupea harengus*). *Maine Dep. Sea Shore Fish., Res. Bull. 19:* 1–40. 1954.

27. Smith, C. E. An undifferentiated hematopoietic neoplasm with manifestations of leukemia in a cutthroat trout (*Salmo clarki*). *J. Fish. Res. Bd. Canada 28:* 112–113, 1971.

28. Snieszko, S. F. *U. S. Bur. Sport Fish. Wildlife, Fish Dis. Leafl. 17.* 1969.

29. Stolk, A. Tumors of fishes. XII. Carcinoma of the kidneys in the characid, *Thayeria obliqua* (Eigenmann). *Proc. Kon. Ned. Akad. Wetensch.*, Ser. C 60: 31–40. 1957.

30. Stolk, A. Tumors of fishes. XV. Renal adenocarcinoma in the cyprinid, *Barbus tetrazona* (Bleeker). *Proc. Kon. Ned. Akad. Wetensch.*, Ser. C 60: 196–211. 1957.

31. Summerfelt, R. C. A new microsporidian parasite from the golden shiner, *Notemigonus crysoleucas. Trans. Amer. Fish. Soc. 93*(1): 6–10. 1964.

32. Wales, J. H., and Wolf, H. Three protozoan diseases of trout in California. *Calif. Fish Game 41*(2): 183–187. 1955.

33. Wellings, S. R. Neoplasia and primitive vertebrate phylogeny: Echinoderms,

prevertebrates, and fishes—a review. *Nat. Cancer Inst. Monogr. 31:* 59–128. 1969.

34. Wolf, K., and Darlington, R. W. Channel catfish virus: A new herpes virus of ictalurid fish. *J. Virol. 8:* 525–533. 1971.

35. Wolf, K., Herman, R. L., and Carlson, C. P. Fish viruses: Histopathologic changes associated with experimental channel catfish virus disease. *J. Fish. Res. Board Can. 29*(2): 149–150. 1972.

36. Wood, E. M., and Yasutake, W. T. Histopathology of fish. IV. A granuloma of brook trout. *Progr. Fish-Cult. 18*(3): 108–112. 1956.

37. Wood, E. M., and Yasutake, W. T. Histopathology of kidney disease in fish. *Am. J. Pathol. 32:* 845–852. 1956.

38. Wood, E. M., Yasutake, W. T., and Johnson, H. E. Acute sulfamethazine toxicity in young salmon. *Progr. Fish-Cult. 19*(2): 64–67. 1957.

39. Wood, E. M., Yasutake, W. T., and Lehman, W. L. A mycosis-like granuloma of fish. *J. Infec. Dis. 97:* 262–267. 1955.

40. Wood, E. M., Yasutake, W. T., and Snieszko, S. F. Sulfonamide toxicity in brook trout. *Trans. Amer. Fish. Soc. 84:* 155–160. 1955.

41. Wood, J. W., and Ordal, E. J. Tuberculosis in Pacific salmon and steelhead trout. *Oreg. Fish Comm. Contrib. 25:* 1–38. 1958.

42. Yasutake, W. T. Comparative histopathology of epizootic salmonid virus diseases, pp. 341–350. In *A Symposium on Diseases of Fishes and Shellfishes,* ed. S. F. Snieszko. Amer. Fish. Soc., Spec. Publ. No. 5. Washington, D.C., 1970.

43. Yasutake, W. T. Histopathology, p. 68. In *Progress in Sport Fish. Research, 1969. U. S. Bur. Sport Fish. Wildlife, Resour. Publ. 88.* 1970.

44. Yasutake, W. T., and Rasmussen, C. J. Histopathogenesis of experimentally induced viral hemorrhagic septicemia in fingerling rainbow trout (*Salmo gairdneri*). *Bull. Off. int. Épizoot. 69*(7–8): 977–984. 1968.

45. Yasutake, W. T., and Wood, E. M. Some myxosporidia found in Pacific Northwest salmonids. *J. Parasitol. 43*(6): 633–642. 1957.

46. Yasutake, W. T., Parisot, T. J., and Klontz, G. W. Virus diseases of the Salmonidae in western United States. II. Aspects of pathogenesis. *Ann. N. Y. Acad. Sci. 126:* 520–530. 1965.

15

Ophthalmic Pathology of Fishes

T H O M A S   W .   D U K E S

The eye is an organ that has all too frequently been neglected during disease investigations in spite of its availability for examination. A great deal more is known about ophthalmic pathology in mammals than in fish. Since the eyes of all vertebrates are essentially the same, much of the information applies to fish. Very little has been done in ophthalmic pathology of fishes *per se*. The following compilation is based to some extent on personal experience and to a large extent on the literature. Since fish disease papers are relatively few in number and scattered far and wide in many publications of various kinds, and since many descriptions of eye disease are in papers dealing with systemic diseases, this cannot be a comprehensive treatise on the subject. Frequently the description published is "eyes affected frequently resulting in blindness," and very few descriptions of the lesions are available.

The general pathological changes occurring in other organs apply to the eye but certain factors are peculiar to that organ. The circulation of intraocular fluids, for one, is peculiar to the eye. Most pathological changes are disastrous to the transparency and thereby the function of the eye. The avascularity of some ocular tissues (cornea and lens) makes them prone to degeneration and also unresponsive in the inflammatory reaction to infection, whereas the rich vascular network of the uvea makes the eye susceptible to involvement in systemic diseases.

The eyes are organs of great structural and functional complexity. The combination of a dense fibrous sclera (through which fixatives permeate slowly) and a delicate retinal tissue with a high metabolic rate (which must be fixed rapidly for best results) makes handling difficult. This problem is compounded by the deli-

383

cacy of fish tissue in general. Under these circumstances, several important considerations bear repeating. First, the eye must be removed rapidly at necropsy (or surgery) and must receive prompt fixation. Rapid removal of the adnexa, when in large quantity, will facilitate fixation but this is generally not necessary with fish since the globe fills the orbit. Secondly, although rapid removal is necessary it must be done carefully to avoid producing artifacts. The choice of fixatives is important since rapid penetration is necessary. Bouin's or Zenker's fixatives are best for routine use. It is unnecessary and even harmful to cut holes in the globe or inject fixatives into it. The technique for enucleation and fixation as described by Saunders and Jubb (26) can be modified slightly for fish.

Saunders' text from Yost's *Handbook* (25) and his chapter "The Eye and Ear" in Jubb and Kennedy's *Pathology of Domestic Animals* (13) are invaluable reading for the study of ophthalmic pathology of fishes even though they deal with our domestic species. *Ophthalmic Pathology* by Hogan and Zimmerman (11) is also an excellent source of information on the pathological changes of the eye and invaluable in the study of comparative ophthalmic pathology.

The clinical examination of the eye can reveal much important information. The eye is normally kept level when a fish is rotated on the body axis. One should also note if the eyes are sunken or protruded, and one should describe changes seen with accuracy since, for example, corneal opacity and lens opacity can be confused by the unwary observer. Examination can be done while the fish is under anesthesia or immediately after its death, using an ophthalmoscope or just a hand lens and flashlight. A dissecting microscope is very useful for examination, or when trimming the eye for processing after fixation, in order to make accurate gross descriptions.

In view of the marked variation in the normal anatomy of fishes, as each species has adapted to its own peculiar way of life (see, e.g., Fig. 15.1), I refer you to the texts of Walls (32), Prince (22), and Duke-Elder (6) for further information and will mention only a few examples here. A thorough knowledge of the normal anatomy is essential to ophthalmic pathology and probably more important in fishes than in other species, since, compared to mammals, there are so many species of fishes in many different environments.

Some fishes have developed patterns of camouflage such as skin spots on the dorsal part of the cornea, as in *Epinephelus guttatus,* to prevent predators from seeing their prominent eyes. Others have developed tubular eyes (*Argyropelecus olfersi*), or four eyes (*Bathylychnops exilis*), or shields to protect the eye as in *Selar crumenophthalmus.* Most persons are, no doubt, familiar with the eye migration of **flatfishes.** The eyeball of the *Anableps* of South America is adapted to seeing both below and above the water simultaneously and for that purpose has two corneas and two retinas in each globe.

In general there are the usual three layers of the eye: connective tissue, vascular tissue, and nervous tissue (Fig. 15.2). The lens of fishes is spherical, usually

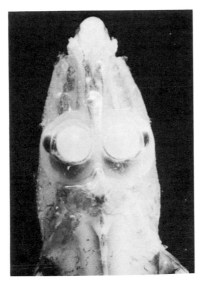

Fig. 15.1. Dorsally oriented eyes of a new species of marine fishes of genus *Dolichopteryx*. (Photo by permission of C. Cruchy, Assistant Curator, National Museum of Canada.)

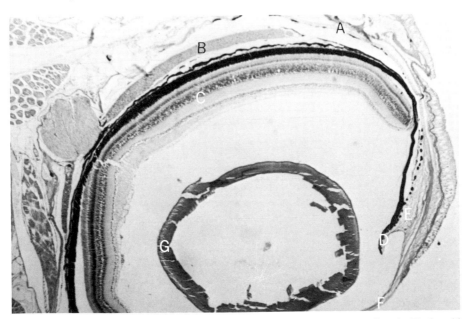

Fig. 15.2. Teleost eye: (A) scleral cartilage (part of outer connective tissue layer); (B) choroid gland (part of middle vascular layer); (C) retina (inner nervous layer); (D) iris (part of middle vascular layer); (E) annular ligament; (F) cornea (part of outer connective tissue layer); (G) lens.

occupies a large part of the inside of the globe, and is relatively fixed in shape and tends to protrude through the pupil. In the posterior uvea is a rete mirabile arrangement of blood vessels composing the choroid gland. Oxygen secretion and blood pressure regulation are functions suggested for this gland. In most teleosts a richly vascular pigmented falciform process extends into the vitreous. This process is suggestive of the pecten of birds and is probably nutritive in function. The scleral cartilage is less extensive than in birds in that there is less cartilage and more fibrous connective tissue around the optic nerve and adjacent to the limbus.

MALFORMATIONS

Pigmentation of the underside of some flatfishes is associated with improper migration of the eye, and in some individuals of a species the wrong eye migrates, making taxonomic identification more challenging. The snub-nose malformation seen in some fishes can be severe enough to alter the normal ocular structures. Cyclopia could result in severe cases. There are numerous malformed eyes that are "normal" for certain species or strains (e.g., telescope-eye goldfish).

EXOPHTHALMOS

Exophthalmos (pop-eye) is the most frequently reported change in the fish eye, but can be due to many causes and is really not a very specific entity. In very few cases were the lesions specifically described. It has been seen in fish affected with various infectious diseases, larval trematodes encysted in the orbit (18), infectious pancreatic necrosis, infectious hemorrhagic necrosis, viral hemorrhagic septicemia, ichthyosporidium, and various bacterial diseases (e.g., corynebacterial kidney disease (15), tuberculosis, aeromoniasis, pseudomoniasis, flavobacteriosis, and vibriosis). Hormonal problems have also been suggested (testosterone and thyroid hormone) (31). Mechanical injury and gas bubbles in the eye or blows to the head could also produce exophthalmos. In some of these cases the eye can be completely destroyed and the fish survive.

Fluke metacercariae can produce exophthalmos. Frequently they are found subretinally. In one of the cases I have seen a fluke was evident behind the globe in the orbital tissue in a fish with exophthalmos. Another case had extensive fluid behind the globe for no known reason but, in view of the following, trematodes are suspect. The larval trematode *Cryptocotyle lingua* has produced exophthalmos in Atlantic herring (29), causing blindness. Millemann and Knapp (18) described exophthalmos and damage to the retina and cornea due to *Nanophyetus salmincola*, the "salmon poisoning" trematode. Orbital hemorrhages were seen. They found few parasites in the eyes and optic nerves of their fish. They postulated that the exophthalmos may be due to edema resulting from kidney damage by the parasite, as it occurs in other diseases affecting the kidney, such as bacterial kidney disease, viral hemorrhagic septicemia, and Sacramento River chinook disease.

Exophthalmos has also been seen in infectious pancreatic necrosis and infectious hematopoietic necrosis, and numerous punctiform extravasations were seen in the periocular connective tissues (34). In Ghittino's (8) classification of the acute form of viral hemorrhagic septicemia there was darkening color, unilateral exophthalmos, hemorrhaging into the eyes, and heavy mortality. In the chronic form there was extensive bilateral exophthalmos. Periocular connective tissue hemorrhages are probably the cause of the eye protrusion in such cases, although simple fluid accumulation in retrobulbar tissues may be significant in some.

Aeromonas, pseudomonas, flavobacterium, and vibrio infections frequently are associated with exophthalmos. These are usually cases of a bacterial panophthalmitis or hemorrhage from a septicemia. Kluge (14) described an exophthalmos produced in mollies by a flavobacterium inducing granulomas in the optic nerve, orbit, and retina. About 80% of the fish had unilateral or bilateral exophthalmos. Lesions were characterized by a central mass of macrophages surrounded by a zone of lymphocytes one or two cells thick which in turn was surrounded by connective tissue. Lesions were found in various stages of development with the center frequently having undergone coagulation necrosis extending to the fibrous connective tissue.

Acid-fast bacteria can be demonstrated in smears from the eyes of fish affected with mycobacteriosis. Nigrelli and Vogel (19) cited the eye as an organ involved, as did Amlacher (3). The typical granulomatous reaction seen in the rest of the body has been seen histologically. Besse (cited by Amlacher, 3) divided tuberculosis into five types, one of which was an exophthalmos, in *Brachydanio*. He observed opacity of the cornea. One must keep in mind the similarities of tuberculosis and nocardiosis when confronted with this type of lesion.

Rock and Nelson (23) described blindness in varying degrees of exophthalmos in *Aeromonas liquefaciens*-affected catfish. In an experiment known to me, involving an inoculation of tumor tissue into fishes, *A. liquifaciens* was isolated from protruding eyes seen in the experimental sunfish. The unilateral eye lesion was the only change until the fish was in-extremis. The eye was disoriented internally and had many inflammatory cells and some exudate. The retina was completely detached and mostly destroyed. The choroidal gland was greatly engorged with blood and inflammatory cells were numerous. The inflammation also involved the cornea and extraglobal tissues. The disease spread to other fish. In these initially there was marked vascular engorgement with hemorrhage in the uvea and then infiltration of inflammatory cells and necrosis. The cornea became edematous, then ulcerated and there was proteinaceous exudate in the anterior, posterior, and vitreous chambers. The choroid was thickened by fluid and the retina became detached locally. Globoid cells were evident in the lens.

Williamson (33) was able to isolate 22 different strains of bacteria from infected eyes of marine fish but concluded that none of the organisms was specific for gas-bubble disease. An exophthalmos due to nitrogen gas bubbles associated with over-aeration was described by Marsh and Gorham (17). Could changes in hydrostatic pressure as a fish is moved from deep water to shallow water also be involved? Atlantic cod, *Gadus morhua,* held in captivity often develop unilateral or bilateral exophthalmos characterized by the accumulation of gas bubbles in the eye. There was some preliminary work done on pop-eyed cod by Dehadrai in 1966 (5). He suggested that the cause was a malfunctioning of the choroid gland-pseudobranch complex that is rich in carbonic anhydrase and is involved in gas secretion in the choroid gland of cod. The mechanism is like that in the teleost swim bladder. The choroid gland of the exophthalmic eye of cod was hypertrophic and formed a spongy, dark mass of red tissue around the retina. Histologically, vessels were seen to be dilated. Grossly, in specimens seen by this author, the cornea was greatly enlarged and thin, with the anterior chamber greatly increased in size. There were large cystic spaces in the choroid. Histologically in these eyes there were accumulations of reticulo-endothelial cells and some macrophages containing brownish pigment. Vascular walls of the choroid gland were thickened. The retinas were detached and there were some inflammatory cells in the vitreous. Hemorrhage was evident in anterior parts of the eye.

CATARACT

Cataract (white eye, opaque eye) is the second most frequently described ophthalmic condition but again specific pathological descriptions are lacking in most cases. Care must be taken to avoid confusing disease of the cornea and disease of the lens. Opaque eyes were seen associated with riboflavin-deficient diets by Phillips et al. (21) and there was a species variation of incidence. Corneal vascularization, cloudy lens, ulceration, and photophobia were evident in riboflavin-deficient fish (10). Feeding thioacetamide for 12 months to induce hepatoma resulted in cataracts that were irreversible after withdrawal of the carcinogen (24). Allison (1, 2) was able to induce the disease using ultraviolet light, as has been done in other animals. There has been an increase in cataracts in lake trout with the increased demands of hatchery production. The reason is probably increased light (ultraviolet) exposure of the fish raised in shallow water of raceways as opposed to their natural deep water environment of low light intensity. The lens capsule was thickened with minimal epithelial proliferation in sections of eyes examined by this author. Occasional inflammatory cells were present in the various eye chambers. The work of Steucke et al. (30) is suggested reading for anyone interested in this area.

Parasitic cataracts are commonly seen. The trematode parasites of Strigeidae are frequently found in the lens or other areas of the eye (Fig. 15.3). The metacercaria of one species, *Diplostomum flexicaudum,* has a wide distribution. It has

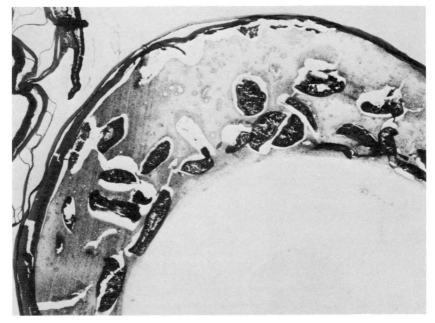

Fig. 15.3. Numerous fluke metacercariae in the lens of a common white sucker.

been found in Lake of the Woods in 16 species of fishes, in Lake Huron in 20 species, in Lake Ontario in 21 species, and in Lake Erie in 20 species (A. Dechtia-renko, personal communication). The metacercariae were found in the lens. It may be that the site (i.e., the eye) is especially prone to being pecked at by birds, thus increasing the parasites' chance for survival. When these parasites occur in low numbers, they can be seen, with careful examination with the naked eye, hand lens, or ophthalmoscope, as small white lines. More severely affected eyes were diffusely opaque. Histologically there was liquefaction of the lens at the periphery initially, with no apparent host reaction to the parasites unless second-ary ocular injury occurred. Globoid cells were seen on some occasions in the lens. A detailed description of the lesions was published by Ashton, Brown, and Easty (4).

OTHER PARASITIC DISEASES OF THE EYE

In addition to the aforementioned fluke-induced cataract, the eye is affected by several other parasites. Hall and Iversen (9) described a myxosporidian, *Hen-neguya lagodon*, in *Lagodon rhomboides*, the Florida pinfish. Cysts occurred in tissues surrounding the eyes, often forming conspicuous external bulges. Pflug-felder (20) described *Glugea pseudotumifaciens* in cells of connective tissue. Nod-ules were formed in ovary, liver, spleen, kidney, central nervous system, and eye.

Elkan (7) described a *Dermocystidium* (microsporidian) in two species of stickle-back. Cylindrical cysts covered the whole body of the fish, including the cornea of the eye, and extended into the orbital tissues. Spores had a large inclusion body but no lid. Perch or other fish living in the same area were not affected, and the parasite may be identical to *Dermocystidium cuticulare* found by Sheer (27). Alex Dechtiarenko of the Ontario Ministry of Natural Resources has seen a myxo-sporidian, *Myxosoma scleroperca*, in perch, which appears similar to the above-mentioned cases (personal communication). The large myxosporidial cysts were present in the scleral cartilage and adjacent periocular tissues (Fig. 15.4). Four or five cysts were frequently found in one eye. Although there was no reaction to the cysts, degenerative changes were evident in the lens and the retina was de-tached secondarily.

Baudouin and Wilson, cited by Sindermann (28), have described a copepod, *Lernaeenicus sprattae*, that occurs embedded in the eye, or occasionally in dorsal body muscle of sprat and sardines in Europe. Mann (16) also described this para-site. No ocular lesions were described. A crustacean, *Artystone trysibia*, was de-scribed recently from the orbit of a South American fish (12).

Lymphocystis can involve the cornea, especially in severe cases, as can *Ichthy-ophthirius multifiliis*. Lymphocytis cells have been found in the sclera and as retrobulbar masses (A. Lawler, personal communication). The "Ich" parasites were found under the corneal epithelium at the outer edge of the corneal lamina propria (Fig. 15.5).

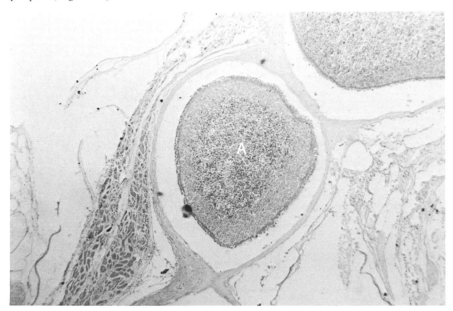

Fig. 15.4. *Myxosoma scleroperca* cysts in the scleral cartilage of a yellow perch (A).

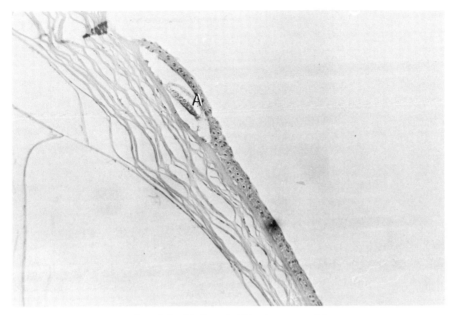

Fig. 15.5. *Ichthyophthirius* in cornea (A).

ENDOPHTHALMOS

This can be seen as an artifact after death but has also been associated with emaciation and with certain hemoprotozoans.

MISCELLANEOUS CONDITIONS

Trauma

Injuries can lead to hemorrhage and dislocation of the lens.

Neoplasia

Melanosarcoma with loss of the eyes has been described. A fibrosarcoma was seen below the eye of one fish caught commercially in Ontario. One wonders if such tumors as lymphosarcoma can affect the eye in fish affected by this neoplasm. No pathological descriptions are available.

Fungus

Saprolegnia fungi frequently attack the eyes but are opportunists in already damaged eyes. Chemicals and trauma are frequent causes of initial damage. Fungal hyphae are frequently found during histological examination of corneal lesions and may extend to the lens and other tissues. This infection can spread to the brain. Many inflammatory cells and edema along with hyphae were evident in the cornea.

Table 15.1. Diseases of Fishes' Eyes

Malformation
    1. cyclopia
    2. abnormal eye migration in flatfish
    3. "normal" eyes of certain species, e.g., goldfish varieties

Degeneration
    1. cataract
        i   secondary to infection of bacteria and parasites
        ii ultraviolet light
        iii carcinogenic chemicals
        iv riboflavin deficiency

    2. exophthalmos
        i   gas bubble disease
        ii hormones
        iii secondary to inflammation (kidney and eye)

Inflammation
    1. bacterial
        i   tuberculosis } proliferation
        ii flavobacteria

        iii aeromonas
        iv pseudomonas } necrosis and hemorrhage
        v   vibrio

    2. viral
        infectious hematopoietic necrosis
        viral hemorrhagic septicemia
        infectious pancreatic necrosis
        Sacramento River chinook disease

    3. parasitic
        i   protozoan
            microsporidian
            myxosporidian
            ichthyophthirius
        ii crustacean
            Artystone trysibia
            Lernaeenicus sprattae
        iii trematode
            Cryptocotyle lingua
            various members of **Strigeidae**
            Nanophyetus salmincola
        iv cestode
            probably seen in future

    4. fungi
        ichthyosporidium
        saprolegnia

Table 15.1 (*cont.*)

Hyperplasia & Neoplasia
 lymphocystis
 melanosarcoma
 fibrosarcoma
 probably many more both primary and secondary tumors

SUMMARY

Very little is known about the diseases of the fish's eye, since descriptions are rare, and when the eye's involvement is described it is only in general terms. Exophthalmos and cataract are the most commonly reported conditions. Parasitic conditions have been described frequently, as they have been for other body systems of the fish.

Acknowledgments. The specimens submitted to the author by Drs. J. Budd, A. Dechtiarenko, and D. R. MacKelvie are appreciated. The author would be interested in corresponding further with anyone who would be interested in contributing to a museum of ocular lesions.

REFERENCES

1. Allison, L. N. Cataract among hatchery-reared lake trout. *Progr. Fish-Cult. 24:* 155. 1962.
2. Allison, L. N. Cataract in hatchery lake trout. *Trans. Amer. Fish. Soc. 92:* 34–38. 1963.
3. Amlacher, E. *Textbook of Fish Diseases.* transl. D. A. Conroy and R. L. Herman. 302 pp. Jersey City, T.F.H. Publications, 1970.
4. Ashton, N., Brown, N., and Easty, D. Trematode cataract in freshwater fish. *J. Small Anim. Pract. 10:* 471–478. 1969.
5. Dehadrai, P. V. Mechanism of gaseous exophthalmia in the Atlantic cod, *Gadus morhua* L. *J. Fish. Res. Board Can. 23:* 909–914. 1966.
6. Duke-Elder, S. *System of Ophthalmology.* Vol. 1, *The Eye in Evolution.* St. Louis, Mosby, 1958.
7. Elkan, E. *Dermocystidium gasterostei* n. sp. a parasite of *Gasterosteus aculeatus* L. and *Gasterosteus pungitius* L. *Nature (London) 196:* 958–960. 1962.
8. Ghittino, P. Viral hemorrhagic septicemia (VHS) in rainbow trout in Italy. *Ann. N. Y. Acad. Sci. 126:* 468–478. 1965.
9. Hall, D. L., and Iversen, E. S. *Henneguya lagodon,* a new species of myxosporidian parasitizing the pinfish *Lagodon rhomboides. Bull. Mar. Sci. 17:* 274–279. 1967.
10. Halver, J. E. Ph.D. thesis, Univ. Wash., Seattle, 1953.
11. Hogan, M. J., and Zimmerman, L. E. *Ophthalmic Pathology.* Philadelphia, Saunders, 1962.
12. Huizinga, H. W. Pathobiology of *Artystone trysibia* Schioedte (Isopoda:

Cymothoidae), an endoparasitic isopod of South American freshwater fishes. *J. Wildlife Dis. 8:* 225–232. 1972.

13. Jubb, K. V. F., and Kennedy, P. C. *Pathology of Domestic Animals,* pp. 427–474. New York, Academic Press, 1963.

14. Kluge, J. P. A granulomatous disease of fish produced by flavobacteria. *Pathol. Vet. 2:* 545–552. 1965.

15. MacLean, D. G., and Yoder, W. G. Kidney disease among Michigan salmon in 1967. *Progr. Fish-Cult. 32:* 26–30. 1970.

16. Mann, H. Copepoda and Isopoda as parasites of marine fishes, pp. 177–189. In *A Symposium on Diseases of Fishes and Shellfishes,* ed. S. F. Snieszko. Amer. Fish. Soc., Spec. Publ. No. 5. Washington, D.C., 1970.

17. Marsh, M. C., and Gorham, F. P. The gas disease in fishes. *Rep. U. S. Comm. Fish., 1904,* pp. 343–376. 1905.

18. Millemann, R. E., and Knapp, S. E. Pathogenicity of the "salmon poisoning" trematode *Nanophyetus salmincola* to fish, pp. 209–217. In *A Symposium on Diseases of Fishes and Shellfishes,* ed. S. F. Snieszko. Amer. Fish. Soc., Spec. Publ. No. 5. Washington, D.C., 1970.

19. Nigrelli, R. F., and Vogel, H. Spontaneous tuberculosis in fishes and other cold-blooded vertebrates with special reference to *Mycobacterium fortuitum* from fish and human lesions. *Zoologica (New York) 48:* 131–143. 1963.

20. Pflugfelder, O. Ein neuer Fischparasit aus der Gruppe der Mickrosporidien. *Aquarien Terrarien 5.* 1952.

21. Phillips, A. M., Jr., Podoliak, H. A., Brockway, D. R., and Balzer, G. C. The nutrition of trout. Cortland Hatchery Report 26 for the year 1956. *N. Y. Conserv. Dep. Fish. Res. Bull. 21.* 93 pp. 1956.

22. Prince, J. H. *Comparative Anatomy of the Eye.* Springfield, Thomas, 1956.

23. Rock, L. F., and Nelson, H. M. Channel catfish and gizzard shad mortality caused by *Aeromonas liquefaciens. Progr. Fish-Cult. 27:* 138–141. 1965.

24. Sallmann, L. von, Halver, J. E., Collins, E., and Grimes, P. Thioacetamide-induced cataract with invasive proliferation of the lens epithelium in rainbow trout. *Cancer Res. 26:* 1819–1825, 1966.

25. Saunders, L. Z. *Pathology of the Eye of Domestic Animals.* Berlin, Paul Parey, 1968.

26. Saunders, L. Z., and Jubb, K. V. Notes on the technique for post mortem examination of the eye. *Can. Vet. J. 2:* 123–129. 1961.

27. Sheer, D. Die Fischparasiten der Haplosporidiengattung Dermocystidium. *Z. Fisch. 6:* 127–134. 1957.

28. Sindermann, C. J. *Principle Diseases of Marine Fish and Shellfish,* p. 71. 369 pp. New York and London, Academic Press, 1970.

29. Sindermann, C. J., and Rosenfield, H. Diseases of fishes of the western North Atlantic. III. Mortalities of sea herring (*Clupea harengus*) caused by larval trematode invasion. *Maine Dep. Sea Shore Fish., Res. Bull. 21.* 16 pp. 1954.

30. Steucke, E. W., Allison, L. N., Piper, R. G., Robertson, R., and Bowen, J. T. Effects of light and diet on the incidence of cataract in hatchery-reared lake trout. *Progr. Fish-Cult. 30:* 220–226. 1968.

31. Van Duijn, C., Jr. Diseases of the eye, pp. 179–188. In his *Diseases of Fishes*. 2d ed. 309 pp. London, Iliffe Books, 1967.
32. Walls, G. L. *The Vertebrate Eye and Its Adaptive Radiation*. 1942. Reprint: New York, Hafner, 1967.
33. Williamson, J. *Bacteriological Investigation of the Cause of Bulging Eye in Certain Marine Food Fishes*, p. 64. Aberdeen, Scotland, Press and Journal Office, 1927.
34. Yasutake, W. T. Comparative histopathology of epizootic salmonid virus diseases, pp. 341–350. In *A Symposium on Diseases of Fishes and Shellfishes*, ed. S. F. Snieszko. Amer. Fish. Soc., Spec. Publ. No. 5. Washington, D.C., 1970.

DISCUSSION OF OPHTHALMIC PATHOLOGY OF FISHES

H. E. Evans: This excellent outline just gave me some ideas on malformation; one thinks immediately of bubble eye in the goldfish. Did you ever see those very fancy goldfish that look as though the entire head is composed of two eyes? Another interesting thing that I think needs confirmation is the old work of Stockard on the lithium- and magnesium-affected embryos. Stockard in 1910 or 1911, around that time, using lithium and magnesium salts produced these cyclopic fish in the genus *Fundulus*, I believe they were. I don't think it has ever been reproduced. I also remember a Japanese worker who produced microphthalmia by hatching zebra fish eggs under higher than normal temperature (i.e., stress) and he had something like 15% microphthalmia, very tiny eyes, in these zebra fish. And another thing that one thinks of are these benthic forms that have pelagic larvae, that gradually lose their eyes, and likewise the cave-forms that, when the eggs are swept out of the caves and develop in the light, will develop eyes. If they go back in the cave ophthalmic degeneration occurs. It is an interesting natural shift. The question I would like to raise concerns the mention that Dr. Roberts made of vacuolization in the external ocular muscles. Do you know anything about that? I had never heard of that before.

T. W. Dukes: It is seen quite regularly in other animals. I've seen it on occasion in fish, but I think it is just a nonspecific degenerative change. I'm not surprised to see it or hear about it.

R. Walker: This is sort of a reinforcement of what Dr. Evans has just said. The telescope-eyed goldfish is normal in its first season and it only later becomes abnormal. In regard to the catfish-shark telescope eyes, not the deep sea ones which are functional: in the former the telescope eye is nonfunctional in the sense that it is a distended eyeball; the lens does not grow further after its normal period of growth, so this is a genetically related anomaly. Also regarding cyclopia, not only experimentally, but in a hatchery: I was very kindly given great quantities of abnormal embryos from one of the New York state hatcheries and a high percentage had all degrees of cyclopia.

L. E. Mawdesley-Thomas: I should like to thank Dr. Dukes for focusing on these eyes for a short while. I think there are many important points in looking at the eye as an index of toxicity. We certainly have found this in mammals, particularly in relation to the pesticides. Because the lens is an avascular structure the eye is often a very good structure to assess toxicity. I think some of us would do quite well in pesticide evaluation if we did in fact look at these eyes more clearly. I think that the proliferation we sometimes see is in the lens epithelium; I don't think that we actually saw it within the lens where one encounters the effects of fluke infestation. But there is this proliferation in the lens, and I think von Sallmann reported this with thioacetamide in 1966. He inferred that this was malignant. He called it invasive. I don't think this is the case at all. It is a proliferation of the lens epithelium and it is quite nonspecific in my opinion. It can be induced by parasites, it can be produced by nutritional deficiencies, and it can also be produced by potassium permanganate. So again, I think we ought to be very careful before we call it "invasive"; it's an epithelial proliferation. I don't believe it is a true neoplasm.

T. W. Dukes: I agree.

P. H. Cahn: I just want to set the blind cave-fish story straight. I was going to suggest that perhaps genetic abnormalities be included as well. The blind cave-fish eyes, according to the genetic strain, will deteriorate no matter whether they are reared in the dark or in the light. There are five or six different caves with blind fish various distances away from the rivers where the normal eye strain is present. This is a strict genetic effect, not determined by the environment at all. My doctoral dissertation was on the development of the eye in *Astyanax mexicanis* and *A. jordanae*. The Cheeka cave fish, which is the *jordanae* strain, does have in many cases a small eye when the embryo hatches. The lens fibers, however, never form normal protein fibers so that the lens never forms a typical transparent lens. Now there are variations on this, depending on how pure your strains are. The original strain Breiter and Gresser (Gresser was the ophthalmologist) brought back, but since then many, many aquaria have been selling these as tropical fish and the strain is no longer pure. I can tell you where to get a pure strain, though, from Dr. Chatagleau at Brown University. She has been keeping the strain going for about 15 years now, if you are interested in this.

D. L. DeGiusti: I merely want to add one parasite that you don't have in your list. Many of the trematode parasites really are incidental inhabitants of the eye because they are migratory forms in the larval stages. There are a number of other forms that under certain circumstances can migrate and it has been found in human medicine that there are a number of parasites that may end up in the eye. In some recent experiences in doing a large series of examinations of freshwater fish from Lake Michigan and also from the South Bay area over a number of years, I have been impressed with the number of times that we've found immature acanthocephalids in the posterior chamber behind the lens. I was impressed by the fact that these appear to be free in the chamber but there is nevertheless evidence of host reaction. I think many of us who are parasitologists and have had occasion to look at so many specimens many times relegate the eye to a rather unimportant part of our examination. We seem to focus on some of the other more popular areas. I think that it is quite possible that as some of the fish populations change, and some disappear and others take over the niche of some of those that have disappeared, some parasites are going to be present in tremendous numbers, especially some of the digestive-tract parasites. I think there is some evidence to show that there is a certain natural population control of parasites present and that many of the parasitic forms present will not develop to maturity, and also these forms have a tendency to wander and migrate. In fact some of the acanthocephalid migrations of these immature forms occur from the digestive tract out into other tissues and probably these got lost in the eye. I think that these could be added to your list.

T. W. Dukes: This list was purposely not complete. I didn't know about that particular case. I thought I would stimulate some people if I didn't do it completely.

G. L. Hoffman: To continue Dr. DeGiusti's discussions, under experimental conditions we can do the same thing. At least in two experimental studies of trematode life cycles I put mammoth dosages into the fish and in one case the target organ was the brain and in another case the target organ was the kidney. In these cases under these unusual mammoth infections there were trematodes in the eyes that wouldn't have been there otherwise.

Question: We are dealing with a fish off Southern California, the white croaker, which has a great many anomalies and we are trying to see what the causation is. If you think that pesticides are affecting the eye more than other organs, would it be wise to examine eyes, instead of liver or other tissues?

L. E. Mawdesley-Thomas: I am not certain. We have just started to work in regard to pesticides with the poikilothermic animals in relation to the lens. I always feel that the clinician can tell you more than the pathologist if he has a good camera. You can take a picture of the lens and you can see whether you have a peripheral opacity, you can see whether the opacity is spreading down the suture lines, whether it's anterior lens, posterior lens, or mid-lens. The problem with the eyes, of course, is that in processing you have to induce so much artifact in them it doesn't really matter what you do with them. It is very difficult to get an artifact-free eye, so if in doubt this is one case where you believe the clinician and not the pathologist. The only such case, I think.

W. E. Ribelin: In answer to the question regarding pesticides, we have worked on a number of pesticides, and examined a number of eyes, and we have seen no changes whatsoever. The behavior of the fish did not indicate that there was any eye involvement. My suggestion would be that if somebody indicated that there were lesions in the eye because of pesticides, I would be reluctant to believe him.

Another question: you listed a number of possibilities as causes of exophthalmos, but I was disturbed by the fact that most of the things that you listed were those that I would have expected to produce bilateral exophthalmos, yet in at least 50% of the cases we see this is unilateral; the other eye appears to be perfectly normal. We have cultured a number of these unilateral cases and have isolated no organisms. We have examined these eyes microscopically and have seen no abnormalities, but we have frequently seen a great increase in the amount of acidic mucopolysaccharide in the ground substance behind the eye. Our impression is that whatever the change is, it is not in the eye itself, but it is pushing the eye forward. I can't explain it any more beyond that.

T. W. Dukes: That's why I think we need to look at it a little more closely.

W. E. Ribelin: Now another question. When we were speaking of *M. cerebralis* infection the darkening of the affected fish was mentioned and I commented that the darkening in myxosoma infection, with many systemic diseases, and in many cases of blindness, was probably due to irritation of the nerves so that the chromatophores were stimulated, rather than destruction of the nerves and lack of enervation. I suggested this because of the fact that when these same dark fish had been anesthetized or killed very quickly they then became blanched. To support this hypothesis, I have been told that if fish are blind because of damage to the eye proper when they die they do not become pale, but they remain dark. Do you know whether this is correct?

T. W. Dukes: I have heard that too but I don't know.

P. H. Cahn: You asked if blind fish pale when they die. They do not pale, they remain dark. I have seen schooling fish in the wild that have become blind and can be spotted easily because they are darker and they trail behind. If they are then removed to captivity, they die shortly thereafter and they remain dark. I have also seen this under aquarium conditions in some of the characins and goldfish and many other species. Blind fish are dark once they are blind and they remain dark.

Comment: I don't believe this is always the case. In hatchery rainbow trout whenever we use the whitefish meal in our diet instead of herring meal we end up with lens cataracts, and quite often the case is that the fish turn light instead of dark. I think this is referred to in the literature as "white blindness."

16

Melanin-Containing Cells of Teleost Fish and Their Relation to Disease

RONALD J. ROBERTS

THE MELANIN-CONTAINING CELLS

The number and widespread distribution of melanin-containing cells in teleost fish is one of the most obvious and disconcerting problems facing the mammalian histopathologist when examining fish tissues for the first time.

Traditionally, the term *melanin* is used to describe the yellow to dark brown pigment of the melanosomes of integumentary pigment cells. Recently this definition has been widened to include all biological polycyclic polymers which have a high molecular weight and a yellow to dark brown color, provided they are insoluble in the majority of solvents (4). The latter definition will be used in the present paper, as it encompasses ceroid and the other lipofuscins and allows a more coherent view of the similarities which exist between the integumentary melanophore system and the cells of the "melanin-macrophage centers" which are a feature of the hematopoietic tissues of all teleosts.

Mammalian integumental melanin-producing cells originate embryonically in the neural crest ectoderm. In the mature animal the major localization is in the epidermis, where melanin is manufactured within the clear dendritic cells of the basal layer, the melanocytes, and transferred to the fibrous malpighian cells which constitute the major component of all vertebrate epidermes (6). It is also found normally in the meninges, eye, choroid, and adrenals. In pathological conditions melanin-containing cells are also found, in mammals, within leukocytes of heavily

399

pigmented species, in metastatic localization of melanomas, in the cardiac and hepatic tissue in the brown atrophy conditions, and in toxic conditions such as phenothiazine poisoning (28). Nowhere in the Mammalia is there the diversity of melanization found in the lower vertebrates, and especially in the teleost fish.

In teleosts and amphibians, integumentary melanin-producing cells are again derived from neural crest ectoderm, although it is believed that they can also arise from other cells of the embryonic brain (16, 17). The principal sites of melanin-containing cells in normal fish are: (1) the stratum spongiosum of the dermis, (2) the hypodermis, (3) the hematopoietic tissue of the spleen, kidney, and liver, and (4) small foci along blood and lymph vessels. Classification of the melanin-containing cells of vertebrates has been a subject of considerable confusion, but the generally accepted nomenclature agreed upon at the Sixth International Pigment Conference, Sofia, is that of Fitzpatrick et al. (1966) (6). Unfortunately these definitions do not include a suitable definition for the melanin-macrophage center cells of teleosts. These latter cells have been defined as large cells found frequently in discrete groups in hematopoietic and some other soft tissues of teleost fish; they are periodic acid-Schiff (PAS)-, Schmorl's-, and Ziehl-Neelsen-positive and generally yellow-black in color (5).

Melanophores of fish are asteroid cells in the stratum spongiosum of the dermis. They are derived from melanocytes and contain large numbers of melanosomes, or mature melanin granules. Fish are capable of adjusting the disposition of these under nervous or humoral control, and hence controlling the contribution made by melanin pigments to the total color of the fish (Fig. 16.1). The rate of pigment cell replacement is apparently quite high (8) and melanin from effete melanophores may be engulfed by dermal macrophages which migrate through the epidermis to release them into the surface mucus (Fig. 16.2).

Melanophores are only one component of the integumentary pigment system of the teleost, which comprises also the iridophores with their reflective plates of guanine, and xanthophores and erythrophores, which contain carotenoids as their pigment (7).

Melanocytes are found mainly in the deeper layers of the stratum spongiosum and in the hypodermis, and are more dendritic than asteroid. They are DOPA- and tyrosinase-positive, indicating that they are the cells responsible for synthesis of melanin in the melanosomes. They are also found in small groups at various levels of the circulatory system, especially in association with the larger veins and lymphatics, which, coupled with their dendritic morphology, has suggested to de Sousa (personal communication) that in this site they may represent a primitive analogue of the peripheral lymphoid nodules of higher species (mammals and birds).

The cells of the melanin-macrophage centers are a striking feature of all teleosts. In the Isospondyli (Clupeiformes), the lower teleosts, they are distributed apparently at random throughout the interstitial hematopoietic tissue of the kidney, the white pulp of the spleen, and the periportal tissue of the liver (Fig. 16.3).

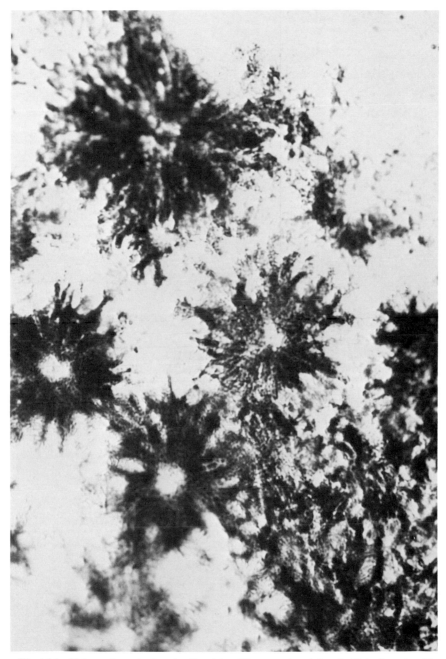

Fig. 16.1. Melanophores in dermis of a plaice (*Pleuronectes platessa*). Note the asteroid shape. Hematoxylin and eosin (H&E); ×1000.

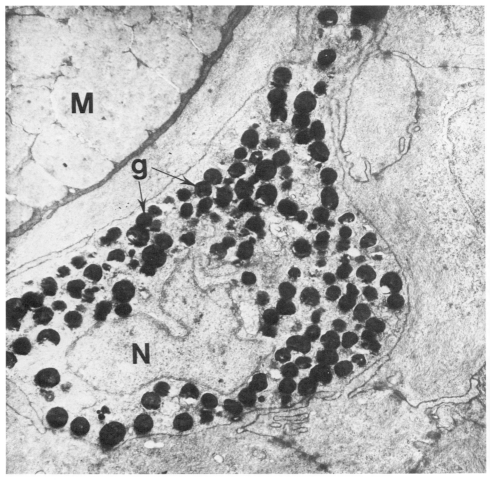

Fig. 16.2. Melanin-bearing macrophage migrating through epidermis of a plaice, to release its granules on the surface. M = Mucous cell. g = Melanin granules. N = Nucleus of macrophage. ×12,300.

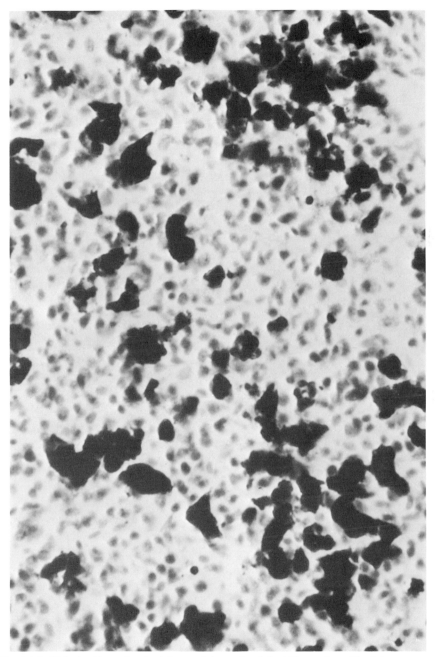

Fig. 16.3. Melanin (visceral melanin)-containing cells of the kidney of an old rainbow trout (*Salmo gairdneri*). There is no focal aggregation, as occurs in higher teleosts, but the pigment is almost all very dark. H&E; ×1000.

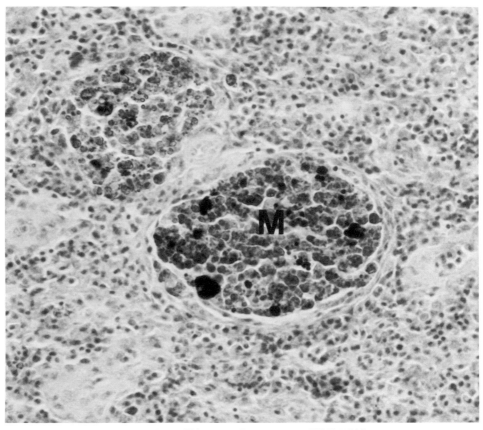

Fig. 16.4A. *Trisopterus luscus* spleen. H&E; ×500.

Figs. 16.4A–D. Different types of melanin-macrophage centers in hematopoietic tissues of a variety of teleosts, showing the focal and often capsulated morphology. M = Melanin-macrophage. L = Lymphoid follicle.

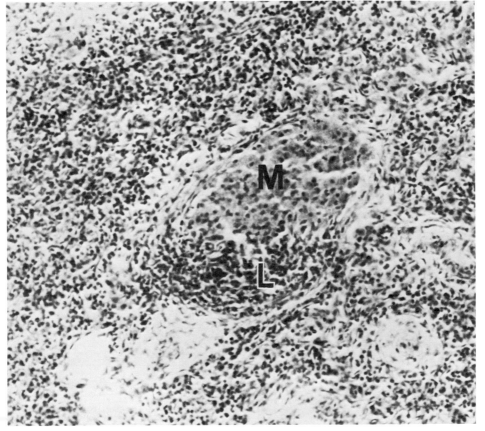

Fig. 16.4B. *Rhombus maximus* spleen. H&E; X500.

The degree of melanization increases with age, but at all ages the cells are very heavily laden with dark brown melanin, and little in the way of morphology or histochemistry is possible without peroxide-bleaching of the dense pigment.

In higher teleosts the amount of dark pigment present under normal circumstances is often very small with only occasional cells in any one section showing it, but this is variable between species (Fig. 16.4).

The morphology of the melanin-macrophage centers in the higher teleosts is much more defined. They are usually nodular with a delicate argyrophilic capsule and in many species are closely applied to vascular channels. In the turbot (*Rhombus maximus*), especially, they are also frequently seen in close association with clusters of lymphocytes.

Mackmull and Michels (12) were the first to describe these centers. They demonstrated in the cunner (*Tautogolabrus adspersus*), by means of intraperitone-

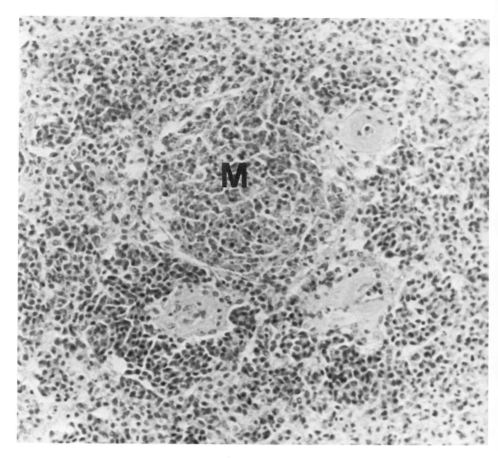

Fig. 16.4C. *Trigla gurnardus* spleen. H&E; ×500.

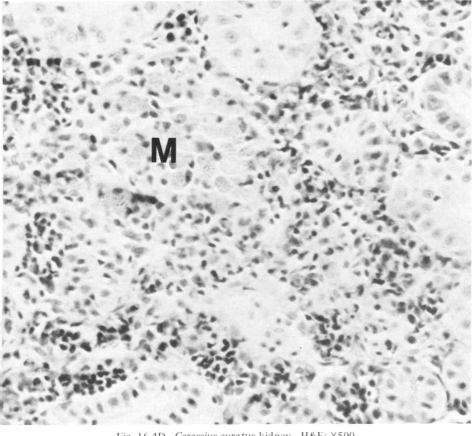

Fig. 16.4D. *Carassius auratus* kidney. H&E; X500.

al injection of carbon particles, that circulating macrophages homed specifically on these sites. Further studies on adsorption of carbon from the peritoneal cavity in a variety of species have shown that the process is similar in a wide variety of teleosts (5). Ellis (unpublished) has also carried out transfer experiments with radio-isotopically labelled cells which suggest that a small proportion of lymphocytes circulate through the melanin-macrophage centers. These centers may therefore represent the primitive nonspecific analogue of the avian or mammalian germinal center (29, 30).

Melanin-macrophage center cells are ultrastructurally very complex (Fig. 16.5). They have indented nuclei and large numbers of membrane-bound vacuoles containing a variety of materials (Figs. 16.6, 16.7). The pigment granules appear to be contained in groups in such vacuoles, suggesting that they may be phagocytosed, but the question of whether melanin-macrophages are melanogenic or

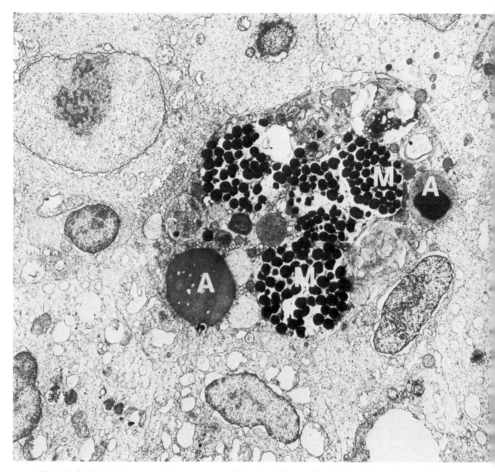

Fig. 16.5. Melanin-macrophage center cell in the kidney of a plaice. Note the membrane-bound vesicles containing dark amorphous material (A) presumed to be phagocytosed, and the membrane-bound clusters of melanin granules (M). ×7800.

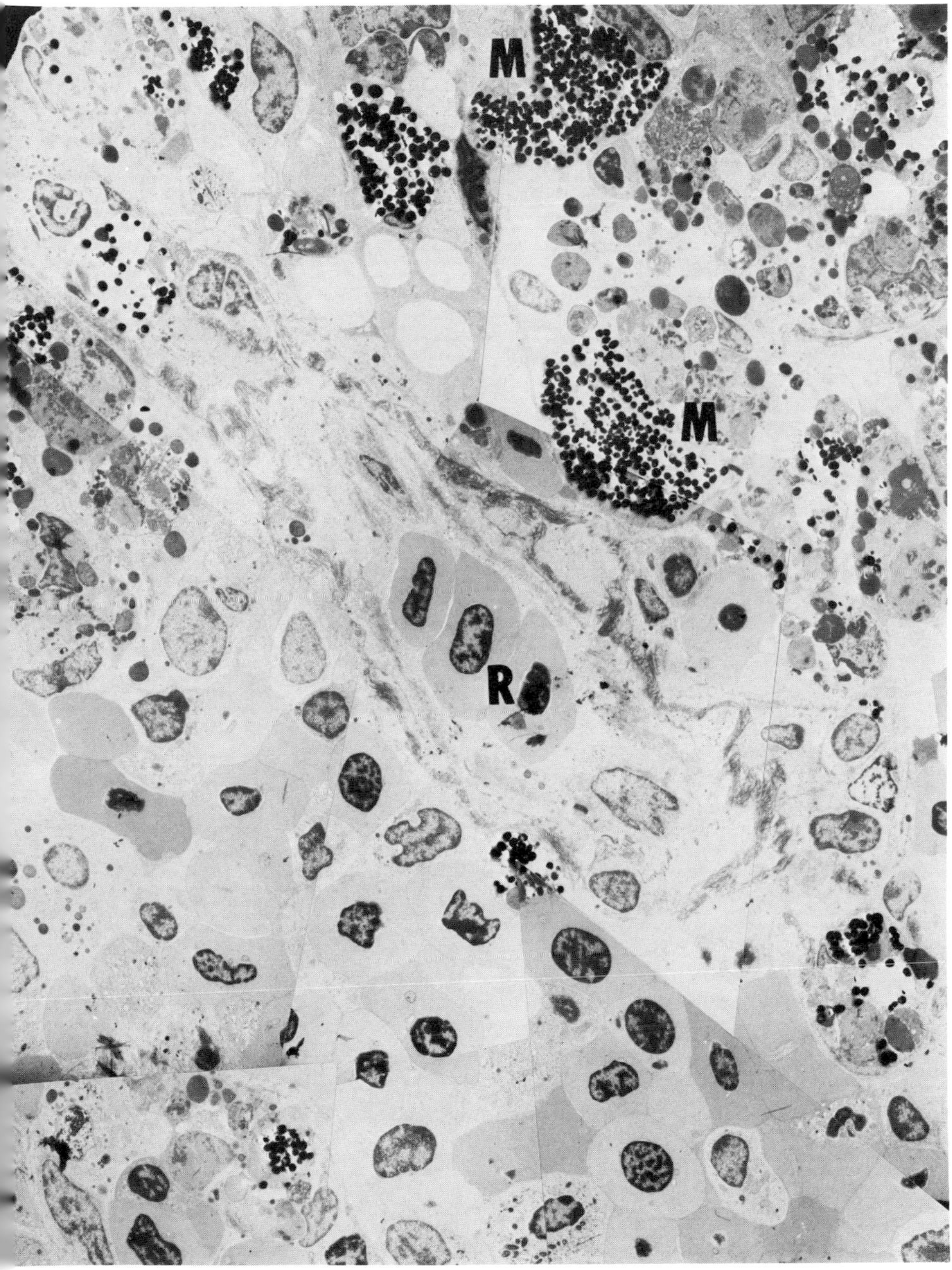

Fig. 16.6. Low-power electron microscope mosaic of a melanin-macrophage center adjacent to a splenic vessel. R = erythrocytes. M = Melanin-macrophage.

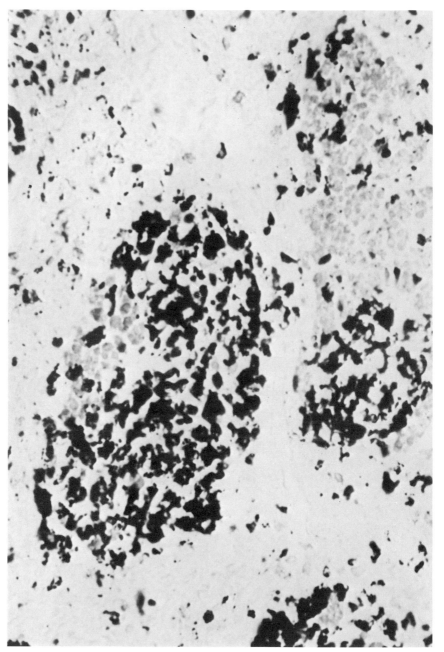

Fig. 16.7. Carbon-laden macrophages within melanin-macrophage centers of a turbot (*Rhombus maximus*) 7 days after injection of colloidal carbon intraperitoneally. Periodic acid-Schiff (PAS); ×500.

merely phagocytose melanin has still to be resolved. Certainly the amount of melanin contained within them bears little relation to the degree of pigmentation of the skin. Coalfish (*Gadus virens*), which have very heavy integumentary pigmentation, have very small amounts of black melanin in their melanin-macrophage cells, whereas pseudo-albino plaice (*Pleuronectes platessa*) reared under marine farm conditions have even more black pigment in their melanin-macrophages than their wild, normally pigmented, cousins. Ellis (personal communication) has shown that in tissue culture melanin-containing cells of salmonid kidney assume a dendritic form, suggesting the possibility of a neural crest origin for these cells as well as the other melanin-containing cells.

Melanin-macrophages frequently stain Perls'-positive, indicating that they can phagocytose breakdown products of hemoglobin. They may or may not contain granules of black pigment but the yellow-brown pigment, unstained in hematoxylin and eosin sections, is always present. It stains positively with Schmorl's stain, PAS, and prolonged Ziehl-Neelsen stain, indicating that chemically it too is of the melanin series (lipofuscin or ceroid).

MELANIN-CONTAINING CELLS OF TELEOST FISH AND DISEASE PROCESSES

The following definitions are used in this section:
A melanocyte is a cell which synthesizes a specialized melanin-containing organelle, the melanosome.
A melanophore is a type of melanocyte which participates with other chromatophores in the rapid color changes of animals by intracellular displacement of melanosomes.
A melanin-macrophage is a large cell found frequently in discrete groups within the hematopoietic and some other soft tissues of teleost fish. It is PAS- and Schmorl's-positive, actively phagocytic, and generally yellow-brown or black in color. The degree of pigmentation depends on the species, age, and state of health of the fish.

Melanophores and Melanocytes

Since the melanophores are under nervous or humoral control, any disease processes affecting such centers will have an effect on the pigment cells. Thus, in whirling disease, *Myxosoma cerebralis* infection of rainbow trout (*Salmo gairdneri*), there is compression damage to nervous tissue due to necrosis of cartilages of the head and vertebrae. This often results in the loss of control of posterior chromatophores and intense blackening of the tail area, which may be a nervous effect. In the saithe or coalfish (*G. virens*), which is susceptible to cataracts of nutritional origin under present conditions of intensive culture, the affected fish in a group can be readily distinguished clinically by their light green color which in normal dark fish is mediated by an optic reflex to match the environment. Skin

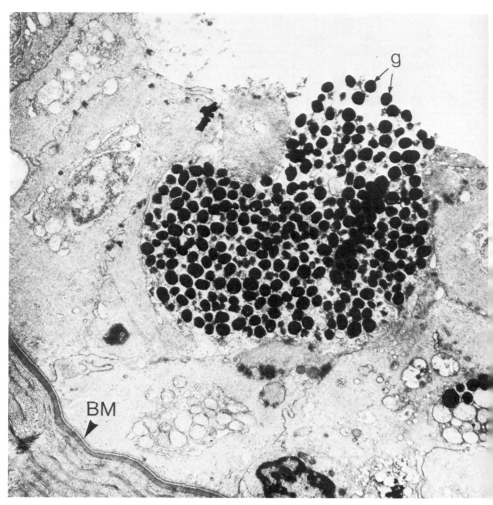

Fig. 16.8. Melanin granules being voided at surface of epithelium of a plaice by a macrophage. BM = Basement Membrane. g = Melanin granules. ×1230.

sections of fish affected by these two conditions demonstrate the features of melanophore activity which are expected. The melanosomes are fully dispersed in whirling disease and closely aggregated in the blind saithe.

Other examples of melanophore-effects associated with systemic disease are numerous; indeed, loss of control of melanophores with consequent alteration of skin color would appear to be one of the best clinical indications of disease within a fish population. Intermedin, an octopeptide derived from the pars intermedia of the pituitary, and ACTH, which contains a similar peptide moiety, produce rapid dispersion of melanin granules in many species. Thus in fish under stress high levels of ACTH may be responsible for pigmentary changes (3).

Melanomas, tumors of the melanocyte and melanophore cell series, are relatively common in fish and a great deal of work on melanomas and the genetics of their occurrence, especially in the platy/swordtail hybrid, has been carried out (8). This work will be discussed in Chapter 39 of this volume, so it will not be described here.

Melanophores play a part in the development of most skin lesions by virtue of their presence immediately below the relatively delicate epidermis, where they are vulnerable to traumatic damage of many kinds. When the skin is wounded, by predators, or in the process of tagging, for instance (23), the melanosomes released from the damaged pigment cells are engulfed relatively rapidly, and macrophages laden with such granules can then be seen in considerable numbers, migrating through the epidermis of the healing lesion and dehiscing, on the surface (Fig. 16.8) (23).

In certain ulcerative conditions, notably ulcerative dermal necrosis of salmon (*S. salar*) and furunculosis of Cyprinidae, melanocytes grow into the epithelialized scar tissue as it heals, and develop into melanophores. Although initially they are a lighter brown than the mature melanophores nearby, they often become extremely numerous so that the healing lesion appears black (Fig. 16.9) (14, 21).

The metacercariae of certain digenean parasites, which encyst in the skin and muscle of teleost fish, stimulate production of black spots which are visible to the naked eye. Noteworthy among these are *Cryptocotyle lingua* (Fig. 16.10), whose pathogenesis has been described (13, 25), and *Uvulifer ambloplitis*. As with most digeneans the metacercariae of these parasites stimulate the production of a fibrous host capsule around the parasitic cyst. Unlike most vertebrate cysts, however, these have melanocytes as a major component and histological studies have shown that these melanin-containing cells arise from both the melanocytes of the stratum spongiosum and from foci in the perivascular connective tissue. The precise nature of the melanocyte-stimulating factor is not known, but it appears to be a specific product of certain digeneans and can exert its effect on melanocytes at some distance from the cyst as it induces melanization of metacercariae in unpigmented sites such as the ventral surface of pleuronectid fish and

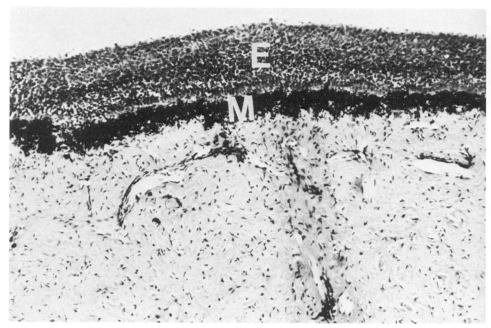

Fig. 16.9. Melanocyte invasion of a healing UDN lesion in a salmon (*Salmo salar*). E = Epidermis. M = Melanocytes. H&E; ×150.

the center of the cornea in species with such large eyes as cod (*G. callarias*) and salmon (*S. salar*).

Occasionally the density of infection with *C. lingua* is such that not only does the parasitic cyst become surrounded by melanocytes, but there is general proliferation of melanin-containing cells over the whole body surface, producing completely blackened fish. This condition has been recorded in the cod (*G. callarias*) (10) and the flounder (*Platichthys flesus*) (15). The latter paper draws attention to the similarity between this condition and melanosis induced by X-irradiation (24).

Melanin-Macrophage Centers

The melanin-macrophage centers should possibly be considered a component of the reticulo-endothelial system and hence part of the defensive system of the fish against microbial attack. Experimentally it has been found that they are capable of concentrating circulating *Salmonella* organisms, as well as carbon particles and hemosiderin. In the parasitic infestation of roach (*Rutilis rutilis*) caused by *Myxobolus pseudo-dispar*, the spores of the organism localize specifically in the melanin-macrophage tissue of spleen and kidney, and in affected roach the degree of melanization of such cells is higher than in uninfected fish (Fig. 16.11)

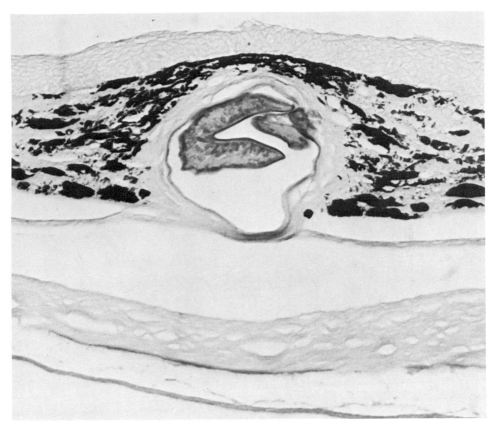

Fig. 16.10. Melanocytes surrounding the cyst of a developing metacercaria of *Cryptocotyle lingua* in the center of the cornea of an adult cod (*Gadus callarias*). PAS; X500.

(R. J. Roberts and M. Halliday, unpublished observations). This observation further enhances the evidence that these centers are functionally distinct environments from the hematopoietic tissue in general.

In the aeromonad diseases of salmonid fish, the melanin-macrophages play a specific part in the pathogenesis. This has been described for furunculosis (*Aeromonas salmonicida* infection) in rainbow trout (*S. gairdneri*) (11) and for aeromoniasis (*A. liquefaciens* group) in brown trout (*S. trutta*) (26). In aeromonad infections the hematopoietic tissue is selectively attacked by bacterial products and the resultant necrosis affects the melanin-macrophages as well. Prior to the onset of severe necrosis some melanin-macrophages are seen moving into the vessels of the spleen and kidney and can be detected in blood smears. They can also be seen at the site of the lesion in the skin (Fig. 16.12).

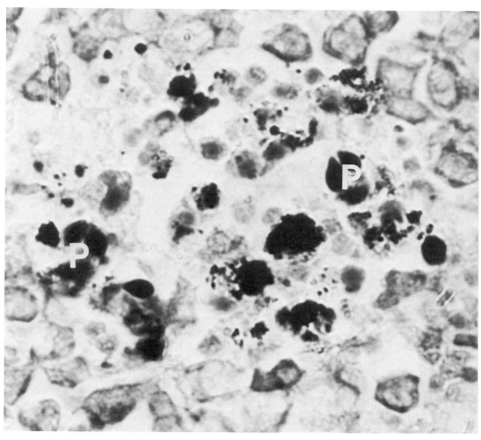

Fig. 16.11A. Specific localization of *Myxobolus pseudo-despar* within the melanin-macro-phage centers of a roach (*Rutilis rutilis*). Note the increased melanization compared with normal. P = Parasites. Giemsa; ×1500.

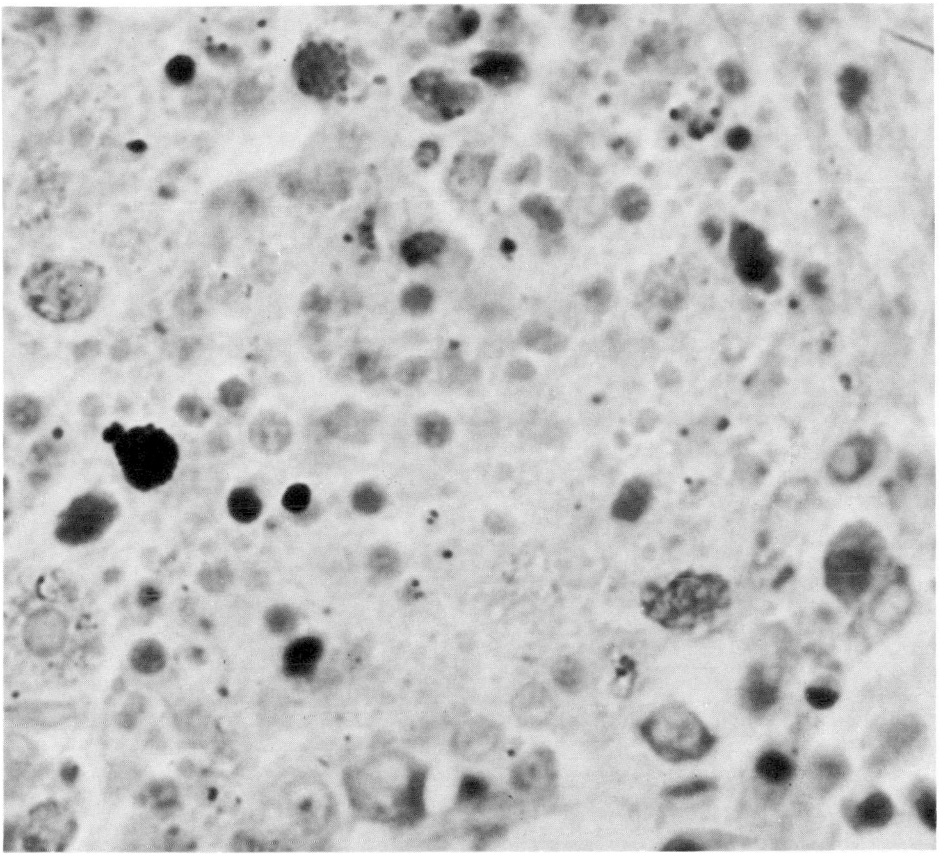

Fig. 16.11B. Normal melanin-macrophage center, roach, with relatively smaller amounts of black pigment. Giemsa; ×1500.

In chronic skin lesions associated with bacteria, where there is extensive granu-lation, numbers of macrophages with foamy cytoplasm and dark melanin pigment are often seen (Fig. 16.13). These may have acquired their melanin from damaged melanophores, but they are morphologically similar to the melanin-containing cells of the spleen and kidney, and like them are PAS- and Schmorl's-positive. It seems possible that these are cells from the melanin-macrophage system which have passed out via the circulation to the site of the lesion.

Vibriosis, sometimes referred to as the furunculosis of marine fish, is caused by *Vibrio anguillarum* and does not usually produce the acute necrosis of hema-topoietic tissue characteristic of aeromonad infections. However, the extreme anemia produced by the vibrio (1) is reflected in the melanin-macrophage system by an increase in the amount of Perls'-positive material resulting from hemoglobin breakdown (Fig. 16.14).

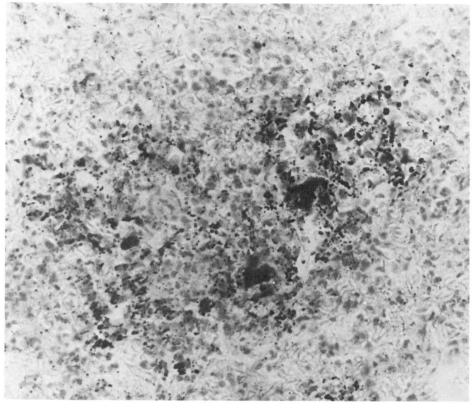

Fig. 16.12A. Acute aeromoniasis in an eel (*Anguilla anguilla*) showing destruction of melanin center in the spleen. H&E; X500.

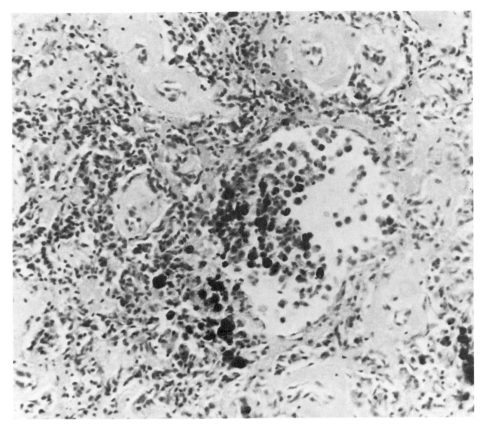

Fig. 16.12B. Acute furunculosis in a brown trout (*Salmo trutta*) showing melanocytes moving from the hematopoietic tissue into the splenic vessels. H&E; ×500.

EPILOGUE

Van Woert, Prasad, and Borg (27) have shown the close chemical similarity which exists between the classical melanosome-related integumentary melanins and the pigmentary deposits occurring in ageing processes and certain diseases, which latter Edelstein (4) described as visceral melanins. Their findings showed that these various polymers of melanin were identical in their electon spin-resonance (indicative of free radical characteristics) and almost all of their spectral characteristics. The only point of divergence was a slight variation in the infrared absorption between DOPA (integumental) melanin and the other compounds.

Lipofuscin (Edelstein's liponeuromelanin), a visceral melanin which is a major component of all cells of the melanin-macrophage centers, is generally considered

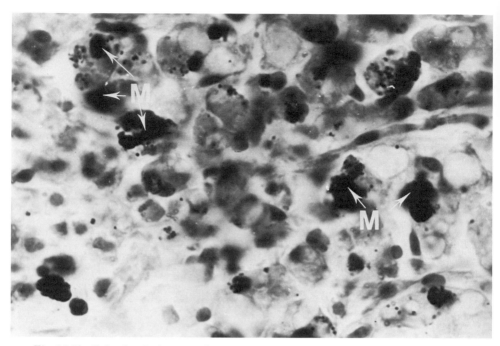

Fig. 16.13. Cells of melanin-macrophage type in the dermis beneath a chronic skin ulcer in a Dover sole (*Solea solea*). These cells are PAS-, Ziehl-Neelsen-, and Schmorl's-positive and almost certainly arise from melanin-macrophage centers. M = Melanin. H&E; ×760.

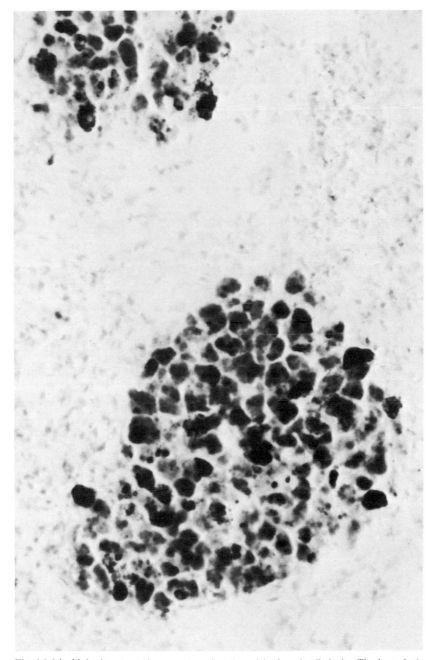

Fig. 16.14. Melanin-macrophage center of plaice with chronic vibriosis. The hemolytic anemia has resulted in massive hemosiderin deposits in the centers. Perls' stain; ×1000.

to be an ageing pigment consisting of "indigestible residues of lipid metabolism lying in cytoplasmic vacuoles derived from lysosomes" (2). The variations in the degree of darkness of the pigment between species may be a function of the degree of oxidation of the specific lipofuscin present. The histochemical reactions of both the black pigment and the lighter ones, namely being positive to prolonged hydrogen peroxide bleaching and Schmorl's ferrocyanide reaction but negative to DOPA, coupled with failure to observe the typical premelanosomes of integumentary melanocytes in the electron microscope, suggest that the black granules as well as the yellow material are stages in the oxidation of lipid residues to lipofuscin (visceral melanin).

Lipid metabolism pathways in fish are as yet ill-defined, although there are well-recognized problems associated with excessive lipid levels in cultured fish (19, 20). Some pigment is present in melanin-macrophage centers in larval fish, but amounts increase with maturity and especially with old age.

It has been shown that the melanin-macrophage centers are homing sites for carbon-laden macrophages (5, 12), and their accumulation of hemosiderin in hemolytic anemias suggests that a main function of the centers is as a repository for materials which are either metabolically inert, or required for recycling.

The acid-fast lipofuscin-type pigment ceroid is commonly associated with metabolic disorders in laboratory animals, and its histochemistry and histology have been described in a variety of disparate disease conditions (31). It is suggested that fish, with their high content of unsaturated fatty acids, are particularly susceptible to formation of ceroid (32). Ceroid is found extensively in the liver in viral infections of young salmon. Wood and Yasutake (31) worked predominantly with salmonids, and in these lower teleosts the cells which comprise melanin-macrophage centers in higher teleosts are distributed throughout the hematopoietic tissue and these fishes' pigment is almost entirely in the very black, presumably completely oxidized, state. Consequently any relationship between these cells and the ceroid-containing cells which these authors described from pathological conditions is inapparent. However, when viewed across the species from a phylogenetic point of view, it seems possible that many of their ceroid-containing cells were intermediate stages in the development of black melanin cells.

Hatchery-reared fish have much higher levels of triglycerides in both liver and extrahepatic tissues than wild stocks (18). This will result in greater amounts of lipid residues for disposal in the melanin-macrophage centers and provides a convincing explanation for the considerably higher levels of pigmentation of such centers in hatchery-reared plaice when compared with wild stock. It also accounts for the rapid build-up of ceroid, an early stage in the oxidation of lipid residues to lipofuscin (visceral melanin), in hepatic lesions (32).

Edelstein suggests a number of potential biological functions for melanin compounds apart from direct pigmentation (4). Since melanin has a capacity for binding aromatic and cyclic compounds and cations it may selectively take up harmful compounds. In view of the high concentration of melanin in the spleen and kidney of teleosts, studies on the levels of environmental pollutants and carcinogens in fish should take special cognizance of skin and of these two tissues. The free-radical characteristic of melanin and its precursors, and the NADH oxidation of melanin with resultant hydrogen peroxide generation, are both bactericidal properties. This may explain the observation that melanins are found in macrophages, possibly of melano-macrophage center origin, associated with both furunculosis and longstanding bacterial ulceration.

In this review a number of new concepts have been suggested, especially with reference to melanin-macrophage centers. A number of points of importance have still to be resolved. Notably these are the embryonic origin of the melanin-macrophage cell, and the relationship between the centers and the vascular and lymphatic systems, to which they often appear to be closely applied.

Acknowledgment. I would like to thank Dr. M. A. B. de Sousa, Mr. A. E. Ellis, and Professor J. A. Milne for helpful discussion on the concepts of the melanin-macrophage center; Mr. R. B. Stewart for photographic assistance; Messrs. I. H. MacRae and A. I. Wilson for painstaking histological preparations. Many of the exotic species examined were supplied by Dr. E. Egidius of the Bergen Aquarium and marine-farmed species by Mr. M. Cheetham.

The work was largely funded by the Natural Environment Research Council, The Nuffield Foundation, and the Atlantic Salmon Research Trust.

REFERENCES

1. Anderson, J. I. W., and Conroy, D. A. Vibrio disease in marine fishes. In *A Symposium on Diseases of Fishes and Shellfishes,* ed. S. F. Snieszko. Amer. Fish. Soc., Spec. Publ. No. 5. Washington, D.C., 1970.
2. Cappell, D. F., and Anderson, J. R. *Muir's Textbook of Pathology.* 9th ed. London, Arnold, 1971.
3. Dixon, A. F. B. A.C.T.H. and control of melanophores in teleost fish. *Biochem. Biophys. Acta 19:* 392. 1956.
4. Edelstein, L. M. Melanin : A unique biopolymer. In *Pathobiology Annual,* ed. H. L. Ioachim. Butterworth, London, 1971.
5. Ellis, A. E., Munro, A. L. S., and Roberts, R. J. A comparative study of the spleen and splenic phagocytosis in some teleost fish, birds and mammals. *J. Fish. Biol.* 1974 (in press).
6. Fitzpatrick, T. B., Queveda, W. C., Levene, A. L., McGovern, V. J., Mishima, Y., and Oettle, A. G. Terminology of vertebrate melanin containing cells. *Science 152 (Wash. D.C.):* 88–89. 1966.
7. Fujii, R. Chromatophores and pigments, pp. 307–344. In *Fish Physiology,* ed. W. S. Hoar and D. J. Randall, vol. 3. New York and London, Academic Press, 1969–70.

8. Gordon, M. *Pigment Cell Biology.* New York, Academic Press, 1959.

9. Hoffman, G. L., and Putz, R. E. The black-spot (*Uvulifer ambloplitis:* Trematoda: Strigeoidea) of centrarchid fishes. *Trans. Amer. Fish. Soc. 94:* 143–151. 1965.

10. Hsiao, S. C. T. Melanosis in the common cod (*Gadus callarias* L.) associated with trematode infection. *Biol. Bull. (Woods Hole) 80:* 37–44. 1941.

11. Klontz, G. W., Yasutake, W. T., and Ross, A. J. Bacterial diseases of the Salmonidae in the western United States: Pathogenesis of furunculosis in rainbow trout. *Amer. J. Vet. Res. 27:* 1455–1460. 1966.

12. Mackmull, G., and Michels, N. A. Absorption of colloidal carbon from the peritoneal cavity in the teleost *Tautogolabrus adspersus. Amer. J. Anat. 51:* 4–47. 1932.

13. McQueen, A., Mackenzie, K., Roberts, R. J., and Young, H. Studies on the skin of plaice (*Pleuronectes platessa*). III. The effect of temperature on the inflammatory response to the metacercariae of *Cryptocotyle lingua* (Digenea: Heterophyidae) *J. Fish Biol. 5:* 388–399. 1973.

14. Mawdesley-Thomas, L. E. Furunculosis in the goldfish *Carassius auratus* (L.). *J. Fish Biol. 1:* 19–23. 1969.

15. Mawdesley-Thomas, L. E., and Young, P. C. Cutaneous melanosis in a flounder (*Platichthys flesus*). *Vet. Rec. 81:* 384–385. 1967.

16. Newth, D. R. Experiments on the neural crest of the lamprey embryo. *J. Exp. Biol. 28:* 248–261. 1951.

17. Oppenheimer, J. M. Atypical pigment cell differentiation in embryonic teleostean grafts and isolates. *Proc. Nat. Acad. Sci. U.S.A. 35:* 709–712. 1949.

18. Owen, J. M. The influence of dietary fatty acids on the lipids of plaice. *Proc. Meet. Aquat. Biochem. 3:* 12. Aberdeen Univ., Scotland, 1971. (Private circulation.)

19. Rasmussen, C. J. Lipoid leverdegeneration hos regnbueorreder. *Ferskvandsfiskeribladet 59:* 64–69. 1961.

20. Roberts, R. J. Lateral lipidosis in intensively-farmed plaice. *Vet. Rec. 87:* 402–404. 1970.

21. Roberts, R. J. Ulcerative dermal necrosis (U.D.N.) of salmon. *Symp. Zool. Soc. London 30:* 53–88. 1972.

22. Roberts, R. J., Young, H., and Milne, J. A. Studies on the skin of plaice (*Pleuronectes platessa*). I. The structure and ultrastructure of normal plaice skin. *J. Fish. Biol. 4:* 87–98. 1972.

23. Roberts, R. J., McQueen, A., Shearer, W. M., and Young, H. The histopathology of salmon tagging. I. The tagging lesion in newly tagged parr. *J. Fish Biol. 5:* 407–420. 1973.

24. Smith, G. M. Eruption of corial melanophores and general cutaneous melanosis in goldfish following X-ray. *Amer. J. Cancer 16:* 863–870. 1935.

25. Stunkard, H. W. The life history of *Cryptocotyle lingua* with notes on the physiology of the metacercariae. *J. Morphol. Physiol. 50:* 143–191. 1929.

26. Thorpe, J. E., and Roberts, R. J. An aeromonad epidemic in brown trout (*Salmo trutta* L.). *J. Fish Biol. 4:* 441–451. 1972.

27. Van Woert, M. H., Prasad, K. M., and Borg, D. C.   Spectroscopic studies of *substantia nigra* pigment in human subjects. *J. Neurochem. 14:* 107–118. 1967.

28. Wasserman, H. P.   Leukocytes and melanin pigmentation. *J. Invest. Dermatol. 45:* 104–109. 1965.

29. White, R. G.   Functional recognition of immunologically competent cells by means of the fluorescent antibody technique, pp. 6–16. In *The Immunologically Competent Cell,* ed. G. E. W. Wolstenhome, and J. Knight. London, Churchill, 1963.

30. White. R. G.   Recognition mechanisms in the chicken spleen, pp. 24–34. In *The Immune Response and Its Suppression,* ed. E. Sorkin. Basel, Karger, 1969.

31. Wood, E. M., and Yasutake, W. T.   Ceroid of fish. *Amer. J. Pathol. 32:* 591–603. 1956.

32. Yasutake, W. T., Parisot, T. J., and Klontz, G. W.   Virus diseases of the Salmonidae in western United States. II. Aspects of pathogenesis. *Ann. N. Y. Acad. Sci. 126:* 520–530. 1965.

DISCUSSION OF MELANIN-CONTAINING CELLS OF TELEOST FISH AND THEIR RELATION TO DISEASE

R. F. Nigrelli: May I ask your interpretation of those melanin centers. I think you implied that the colloidal carbon was picked up elsewhere and was brought there; now, how about the pigmentation? Are you implying that the lipid by-products were picked up elsewhere and were brought there for maturation into melanin? May I ask the same question with respect to the parasitic lesions, specifically the one in the middle of the cornea. You said something was migrating in. Is it macrophages which have come, and become pigmented in contact with the stimulus, or have already pigmented cells migrated in and settled?

R. J. Roberts: I'm sure that in parasitic lesions they are pigmented cells either from the perivascular or the intermyotomal connective tissue. You can follow their migration progressively. These are melanocytes, melanin-containing, true melanocyte cells, or at least I think this is what they are. We have an associate, a rather well-known mammalian immunologist, and she has an idea, which I am just not in a position to comment on, that these melanin cells which come into such lesions, but are also found normally in small foci down the length of blood vessels and in certain other sites, may be the sort of primitive, early precursor of what eventually develops into the lymph node in higher animals. These cells are reticular, they are dendritic cells, and they come from the neural crest. There is a cell in the mammalian lymph node which also is a dendritic cell of neural crest origin but doesn't have melanin in it. These may be the primitive analogues of this cell and the presence of melanin is accidental. They simply haven't evolved sufficiently to get rid of it. As far as the melanin centers are concerned, I don't know whether the lipid is carried there by macrophages or reaches the site through the circulation. I suspect it is probably carried by macrophages and then sits there in the same way as experimentally injected carbon is removed from the circulation.

R. F. Nigrelli: I am really asking, where does the chemical shift from the lipid precursors of the melanin occur? Is that happening elsewhere and is it the latent cell which happens to settle there, or is it in this particular center that the stimulus comes?

R. J. Roberts: I am sorry, I am not a biochemist. This is a completely new concept; I am just trying to rationalize all the information which I have. Really, I don't know.

T. G. Bell: We have recently done some studies which might shed some light on the question about the pigmentation of the cornea in the parasitized eye you demonstrate. We used a laser beam, which as you know is a very intense beam of light, to irradiate steelhead trout and some salmon. By using a medium, in this case saline or water, to immerse the trout we were able to pass the beam through the surface layers doing very little damage whatsoever and then observe the effects on various cells which pick up the energy. Of course the pigment cells pick up quite a bit of energy. As we go from a lower energy level to a higher energy level (we are working in terms of about 0.8 joules per square centimeter up through 3 joules per centimeter squared) we observe a number of phenomena. One very interesting thing is that we are able at the lower levels to damage the melanophore, the mature cell, so that it can no longer transport pigment granules. If we do this and observe the fish for over a year's period we note that as long as the melanophore has not been eradicated, that is, it hasn't been blasted apart, there is no re-migration. In fact, these damaged melanophores will stay *in situ* and they are very noticeable because of course they are relaxed, and they are just lying lazily there with their granules out in their tips and nothing seems to happen. If, however, we increase the intensity and actually blast these cells so that the melanophores are degraded and removed then we notice that very small cells will come in. There is an intense pigmentation some two to three weeks after the blast and over a four- or five-month period mature melanophores then appear in that site. We believe that's the response to migration of what you call the melanocyte. If we do enough damage to actually kill tissue then we see a very complex phenomenon that is difficult to interpret. We see macrophages, we see inflammatory response, and we see migration of melanocytes into the area with the deposition of connective tissue. One sees a very complex phenomenon happening that we have not yet been able to interpret. But it is interesting that if you damage the melanophore so that it can no longer control itself in terms of how the fish wants to appear, that is, light or dark, nothing further happens. As long as the damaged melanophores are there and alive, there is no stimulus for migration.

R. F. Nigrelli: I feel a little bit confused about what you are trying to define. You've got the melanophore, skin form, then you've got macrophages containing melanin granules, then you speak of the other cells, the dendritic staining cells. Now what about the hemosiderin thing?

R. J. Roberts: In regard to the hemosiderin, I think that the cells of the melanin-macrophage centers of a hematopoietic tissue pick up the lipid metabolic material and take it through melanin, possibly as part of their metabolic functions. I think they also take up hemosiderin when it is released. They also seem to have an affinity for certain parasites and particulate material such as colloidal carbon either as it passes through the area, in the circulation, or is transported to the center by macrophages.

They could be specific so that one macrophage cell may only deal with hemosiderin and another may only deal with melanin; however, I don't think so because one can see melano-macrophages with melanin in them which also have lots of hemosiderin.

R. F. Nigrelli: But you do believe that these are all part of the melanin-producing, melanin-containing system?

R. J. Roberts: I think so.

R. F. Nigrelli: The melanin cells that are around parasites such as *Cryptocotyle*, are those melano-macrophages?

R. J. Roberts: I don't think so. I think they are melanocytes.

R. F. Nigrelli: Suppose that parasite got deeper into the flesh, you wouldn't get any melanocytes there?

R. J. Roberts: Yes, you do; in such cases melanocytes migrate from the foci around adjacent blood vessels. Melanophores are the pigment cells that are immediately subepidermal. Melanophore, by definition, is the one that contributes to the pigmentation of the body. Melanocytes are found in various sites in the fish tissues, such as along blood vessels, in the lower dermis, and in the hypodermis and peritoneum.

R. F. Nigrelli: Without melanin?

R. J. Roberts: No, they have melanin in them.

R. F. Nigrelli: What about the *Cryptocotyle* if they get into the flesh?

R. J. Roberts: The lesion is populated with melanocytes from these sites, either from the hypodermis coming down or from around the peritoneum, which is another site where we get lots of them. I think these are cells of the true melanocyte series, containing DOPA-type melanin rather than visceral melanin, which are just not mature melanophores. There are a lot of them and they are located all over the body. In our completely unpigmented fishes on marine fish farms (this isn't an albinism, it's a cultural type-characteristic) they have no melanin in the skin at all, but they still have lots of these melanin-containing melanocytes along blood vessels and in the hypodermis. There they are not contributing to the pigmentation.

R. F. Nigrelli: I want to call your attention to one very early reference by George W. Hunter II, where he suggests that the melanin production is due to a DOPA that has been released by the parasite, and that is the way he accounts for the production of melanin.

R. J. Roberts: I don't think this is true because, for instance in the case of the parasite in the middle of the cornea, there are no melanin cells of precursors in the cornea and you can see, if you do serial kills of infected fish over a period of time, that the melanin-containing cells moving in do move in from these specific sites. I don't think it is stimulation of DOPA-deficient cells, or developing cells.

17

Some Skin Lesions of Fishes

JOHN L. GAINES, JR.
and WILMER A. ROGERS

The integument of the fish is its outermost defense against the surrounding environment. The skin is composed of three layers. The distal layer, the epidermis, is a derivative of the ectoderm; the middle layer, the dermis (cutis or corium), is a derivative of the mesoderm; the basal hypoderm is also a derivative of the mesoderm.

The skin may contain scales of various types, or it may be scaleless. When there are scales present they are embedded in the dermis and extend toward the surface of the fish where only the epidermis covers them. Scaleless fish have an epidermis that extends from a basal layer of columnar epithelium to a distal layer of squamoid epithelium.

The epidermis may contain neuromasts, mucus-secreting cells, taste buds, and in some fishes, modified club cells, the schreckstoffzellen (24-26). The dermal layer is composed of either a loose (stratum laxum) and compact (stratum compactum) connective tissue, or a solitary compact connective tissue. Melanophores and iridophores are located within the dermis. Thickness and structure of both the epidermis and the dermis may vary seasonally, with age, and with location on the body.

Because the skin is generally the first area to come into contact with pathogens, it is important to know what reaction the fish host will have, and also, for diagnostic purposes, which lesions are pathognomonic. The skin lesions discussed herein will be those commonly seen in fish culture.

429

SPECIFIC SKIN LESIONS

Viruses

Several viruses (infectious pancreatic necrosis, IPN; viral hemorrhagic septicemia, VHS) which affect the salmonids have been reported to turn the skin dark (21, 22, 28, 41, 43, 45, 46).

Infectious hematopoietic necrosis (IHN) in chinook salmon is characterized by a dull red area in the epithelium anterior to the dorsal fin. This patch is a subdermal hemorrhage due to erythrocyte infiltration of the myotomes and occurs subsequent to kidney damage. IHN is also reported to cause hemorrhages at the bases of fins (46).

Lymphocystis, a well-studied oncogenic viral disease, is characterized by hypertrophied dermal fibroblasts which produce wart-like lesions on the surface of the skin. These giant cells contain Feulgen-positive cytoplasmic inclusions (37, 38). This disease is not particularly harmful to the fish, although it may produce large unsightly lesions. Nigrelli and Ruggieri (19) have published a list of lymphocystis-susceptible fish.

Dropsy of carp (also called carp rubella) is now considered by many Europeans to be of viral etiology (7, 10, 11, 16, 32, 36). This disease takes four individual forms and the external clinical signs vary with the form. The latent form has no external clinical signs. The ascitic form is characterized by an edema of

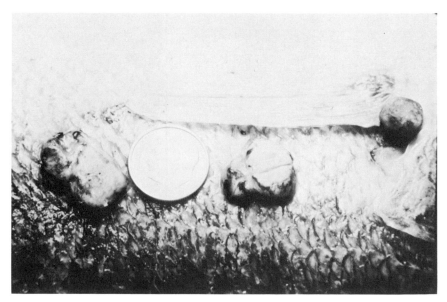

Fig. 17.1. Lesion caused by lymphocystis virus in the walleye (*Stizostedion vitreum vitreum*).

the dermis. The connective tissue fibers are separated and there may be some evidence of hemorrhage in this area. The scales stand away from the body of the fish (lepidorthosis) and may break through the epidermis covering these scales. The epidermis may have areas of focal necrosis. Both the subacute and chronic forms of viral carp dropsy are characterized by ulcers of the epidermis and edema in the dermis. Separation of the connective tissue fibers of the dermis similar to that in the acute form is observed.

Cauliflower disease of eels (stomato-papilloma) (42), another oncogenic viral disease, is seen frequently in European and Asian waters (17). This disease is characterized by hyperplasia of the skin epithelium. This hyperplastic tissue may or may not be pigmented. The resultant tumor consists of fibro-epithelium that most commonly is seen on the upper and lower jaws, as well as on the fins and lateral areas of the fish.

The highly virulent channel catfish virus disease (CCVD) is characterized by hemorrhages around the vent and paired fins (9, 40). Occasionally there is accompanying hyperemia in the dorsal and anal fins. Plumb and Gaines have discussed this disease in Chapter 10 of this volume.

Bacteria

Wolke has discussed in Chapter 2 of this volume skin lesions associated with the Pseudomonadales, the Mycobacteria, and *Corynebacterium* sp.

Some members of the Myxobacteria are injurious to the skin of fish. *Chondrococcus columnaris* frequently attacks fish (33). The most commonly seen clinical signs of this infection are whitish areas on the lateral surfaces of fish. Frequently, the fins are frayed or missing. There is some mild hyperplasia and edema of the epidermis around these fin lesions. The area within the lesions is filled with bacteria and necrotic epithelial cells. Often the lesion extends into the underlying musculature.

Cytophaga psychrophila (3), the etiological agent of coldwater peduncle disease, produces similar lesions in the Salmonidae.

Fungi

Wolke has discussed *Saprolegnia* sp. and *Ichthyophonus* sp. infections in Chapter 2 of this volume.

Fijan (8) reported that *Phialophora* sp. caused mortalities in channel catfish (*Ictalurus punctatus*). Ulcers ranging in size from 2 to 15 mm were present on the ventrum of the fish. Neither the edges of the ulcers nor the exposed muscular tissue appeared to be inflamed.

Carmichael (5) also reported a *Phialophora*-like fungus from trout. The only external clinical signs were swellings of the head. These swellings broke down, forming ulcers. The lesions were characterized by monocyte and lymphocyte in-

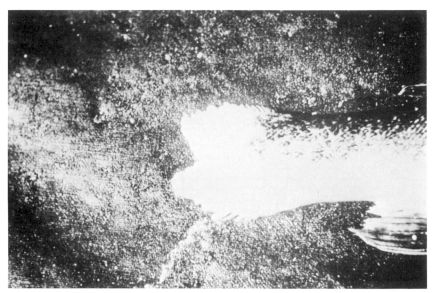

Fig. 17.2. Erosion of caudal fin and caudal peduncle by *Cytophaga psychrophila.*

Fig. 17.3. Nodular lesions in ventral epithelium due to fungus infection of channel catfish (*Ictalurus punctatus*). Note the hemorrhagic cloaca.

filtration, indicating a chronic granuloma. Carmichael described this fungus as *Exophiala salmonis.*

Protozoans

Rogers and Gaines have discussed skin lesions associated with the protozoans in Chapter 3 of this volume.

Platyhelminths

Monogenea. Members of the genus *Gyrodactylus* may, on occasion, cause superficial lesions of the epidermis. The gross clinical signs may include an opacity of the skin with some hyperemia. The organism both attaches to and feeds on the epidermis, creating sites of focal necrosis. Infestation may be so severe as to cause small wounds, allowing secondary invasion by bacteria and/or fungi.

The *Gyrodactylus* sp. infestation causes an increase in production of mucus. This excessive mucus apparently disturbs the respiratory function of the skin. Reports of mortalities due to *Gyrodactylus* sp. are not uncommon in the literature (12).

Digenea. The "black-spot" disease caused by invasion of the epidermis by *Diplostomulum* sp. is often seen. The black spots are due to melanophore infiltration of the dermis in response to the presence of the metacercarial form of this worm.

Hoffman has discussed this disease in greater detail in Chapter 5 of this volume.

Nematodes

Occasionally small blister-like lesions are seen on channel catfish (*I. punctatus*) in the southeastern United States. These lesions are due to larvae of *Contracaecum* sp., the adult host of which is commonly found in water birds. Grossly, lesions consist of small whitish nodules approximately 3 mm or less in diameter. Histologically, there is little damage. The worms are located in the dermis, but no cyst walls can be seen microscopically.

Annelida

The only members of the Annelida causing skin lesions of fish are the leeches (class Hirudinea).

Acanthobdella peledina damages the skin of the salmonids, causing the appearance of small round wounds. When present in great numbers these leeches can cause complete destruction of the fins. *Cystobranchus* sp. have been reported to completely cover gills of *I. punctatus* (14) and have been observed by Rogers to cause severe erosion of epithelium of the isthmus region of bass (*Micropterus* sp.) in a stream population.

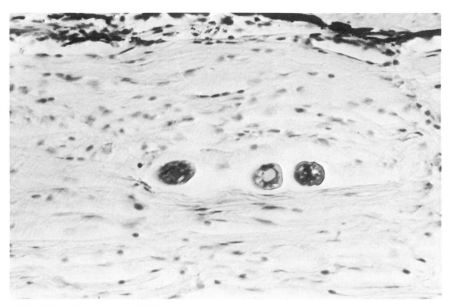

Fig. 17.4. Cross section of *Contracaecum* sp. (Nematoda) in the dermis of the speckled bullhead, *Ictalurus nebulosus.*

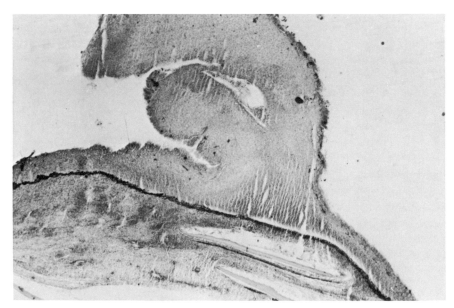

Fig. 17.5. Hyperplastic response of epidermis due to *Lernaea cyprinacea.* Note the scales.

Crustaceans

Argulus sp. damages the epithelium by repeatedly inserting its stylet into the epidermal cells. Ulceration can become quite extensive, and there may be hyperplasia of the epithelium around the ulcer. The number of mucous cells may increase significantly. The epithelial cells beneath the parasite undergo compression atrophy, and those being fed upon are hollowed-out and become necrotic. There may be hemorrhages in the connective tissue. Scales may become loose in the pockets because of damage to the dermal cells. The fish host reacts with a copious flow of mucus. There is a gradual influx of lymphocytes into the area surrounding the ulcer and the host sets up a severe inflammatory response to the toxins released by feeding *Argulus* sp. (34).

Lernaea cyprinacea forms swellings and hematomas on the body of *Carassius carassius*. At and around the point of penetration of the parasite, the scales of the host are destroyed (35). Similar damage to the skin and scales of *Abramis brama* is caused by *Tracheliastes maculatus* (34). Lesions caused by marine crustaceans are discussed by Smith in Chapter 6 of this volume.

Mollusks

The glochidia of some freshwater clams may parasitize the skin of fishes. Small whitish nodules may be seen in the skin of the host. After the attachment of the mollusk, there is considerable hyperplasia of the epithelium by the host. The epidermis grows around and over the glochidium, completely enveloping it.

Dietary Effects

The nutritional needs and effects of diets on cultured fish have, until recently, been rarely studied.

Dupree (6) reported that lack of panthothenic acid in the diet caused an erosion of the fins and a discoloration of the skin. He also found that hemorrhages at the axilla of the fins and on the skin were eliminated by injecting menadione (synthetic vitamin K) into previously deficient fish.

Halver, Ashley, and Smith (13) discussed the role of ascorbic acid (vitamin C) in wound-healing. The amount of healing three weeks after incision was commensurate with the level of vitamin C in the diet. Lovell (18) noted that an ascorbic acid deficiency produced skin depigmentation in fish along with either lordosis or scoliosis.

Lack of biotin causes "blue-slime disease" of some trouts (17). This disease is characterized by excessive production of mucus, which then sloughs off, giving the fish a patchy appearance.

Miscellaneous Skin Diseases

Agalaides and Bernardini (1) discussed the clinical signs and treatment for the "ulcer-like" skin disease of electric eels. The initial lesion is approximately 1 cm in diameter and consists of a whitish patch on the body or fins. These authors note that it is grossly similar to common fungus diseases of tropical fish. The lesion increases in size and others form and enlarge, until death occurs. Examination of a biopsy sample showed nothing but necrotic epidermis and mucus. Epitheliocystis was first reported by Hoffman et al. (15) from the bluegill sunfish (*Lepomis macrochirus*). This disease is of uncertain etiology (44). Both a virus and *Bedsonia* were isolated. The observed white cysts were found to be elongate, located in the epithelium, and varied from 15 to 85 microns in size. Histologically, the epitheliocystis cells are enlarged with an extremely large basophilic inclusion body. The nucleus is eccentric because of this inclusion body. There is a proliferation of the epithelium. The disease appears to be infectious and chronic.

In studying various types of fish diabetes, Yohote (47) injected carp with hydrocortisone. The skin of injected fish became rough after two or three days, and ichthyophthiriasis was often observed. Yohote suggested that the excessive administration of hydrocortisone may result in a disturbance of the mucous metabolism of the fish, and thus provide a site for skin infection.

Ulcerative dermal necrosis (UDN), reported first from Ireland (4), is an acute ulcerative condition of the cephalic area of some salmonids. The characteristic clinical sign is a whitish area on the head epithelium. These lesions rapidly ulcerate and secondary infection by *Saprolegnia parasitica* occurs (30). Roberts et al. (31) described these lesions as ranging from small oval roughened areas of skin through shallow ulcers with hemorrhagic margins to extensive deep ulcers covering most of the head. They also have pointed out that control of the *S. parasitica* infection is most important in preventing mortalities (29, 31). If the fungus was successfully combatted, healing followed. Characteristically, there developed a covering of cuboidal epithelium over the collagen, which eventually organized itself into a normal epithelial covering (30).

Neoplasms of fish skin and the effects of various chemicals on fish skin are discussed by other authors elsewhere in this volume.

Mechanical Causes

Routine procedures of fish culture often cause skin lesions. Most of these lesions are of the abrasion variety and are due to rough handling, seining, or transportation of too many fish in a container. These lesions are caused by trauma to the epidermis and result in loss of scales and hemorrhages in the scale pockets. Generally speaking, there is usually little damage to the dermis in scaled fish. However, in scaleless fish, the abrasion lesions may expose the underlying musculature.

Behavioral characteristics of the particular species may lead to mechanical damage. The male largemouth bass (*Micropterus salmoides*) prepares a spawning bed using his fins. After mating he stands guard over the developing eggs and

Fig. 17.6. Erosion of epithelium and fin rays of the caudal fin due to spawning activities of *Micropterus salmoides.*

fans them to prevent silt accumulation. This often leads to abrasion lesions along the ventral margin of the caudal peduncle and caudal fin. These lesions are characterized by an irregular area of necrosis in the epidermis, some surrounding hyperemia, and loss of scales. Frequently, myxobacteria are isolated from these lesions, or can be seen in histological preparations.

In the southern United States, pairs of channel catfish are placed in pens to spawn. Because the behavioral pattern is for the male fish to chase the female away after spawning, the female occasionally is injured, for there is relatively little space in which to hide. The male frequently bites the female on the sides of the body.

It is not uncommon to find the majority of females at spawning time with lesions due to abrasion or bites. These lesions are superficial, with necrosis limited to cells of the epidermis. There are occasionally small hemorrhages in the dermis. Older females that have been used for brood stock for a number of years usually have large scars on the sides of their bodies from wounds inflicted in this manner.

SUMMARY

As can be seen, there are a vast number of causes of skin lesions; we have discussed here only a few of them. In many cases there is little, if any, host reaction. In other cases, there is inflammation, **hyperemia**, increased mucus production, and leukocyte infiltration of the wound. These defense mechanisms may occur separately or together.

Trauma to the fish may have varied consequences. Roberts discusses in Chapter 20 of this volume wound-healing in relation to temperature. Environmental conditions undoubtedly contribute to the success or failure of the fish to maintain or repair its epithelial covering. Wedemeyer (39) discussed the stress phenomenon with regard to disease. Parry (23) has pointed out that osmotic problems may result from injury to the integument. Black (2) suggested that excessive exercise of salmonids may cause a loss of scales, and a consequent osmotic problem.

All too often the initial lesion is compounded by a secondary invader: bacterial lesions are invaded by fungi or lesions made by arthropods may become sites for superficial bacterial infections. The feeding upon the skin of some parasites may transmit other pathogens which can rapidly become systemic. This is seen with *Aeromonas hydrophila* infections being transmitted by leeches and copepods. *Argulus* sp. has been reported to transmit viral dropsy of carp and the blood protozoan parasite, *Trypanosoma* sp. (34).

Since the skin of the fish is vulnerable to so many sources of lesions, it is easy to see the importance of maintaining an uninjured integument. A normal integument may serve another function. O'Rourke (20) has reported that the skin mucus may function in antibody response.

The complete integrity of the skin of the fish is its first line of defense against disease. Thus it is important that more research be done in this area.

Acknowledgment. Supported jointly by Southeastern Cooperative Fish Disease Project (in part Sport Restoration funds) and AID/csd-2780.

REFERENCES

1. Agalaides, E., and Bernardini, J. A cure for the ulcer-like skin disease of the electric eel. *Nature (London) 201:* 102–103. 1964.
2. Black, E. C. Alterations in the blood level of lactic acid in certain salmonid fishes following muscular activity. III. Sockeye salmon, *Oncorhynchus nerka.* *J. Fish. Res. Board Can. 14*(6): 807–814. 1957.
3. Bullock, G. L., and Snieszko, S. F. Fin rot, coldwater disease, and peduncle disease of salmonid fishes. *U. S. Bur. Sport Fish. Wildlife, Fish Dis. Leafl. 26.* 4 pp. 1970.
4. Carbery, J. T. Ulcerative dermal necrosis of salmonids in Ireland. *Symp. Zool. Soc. London 24:* 39–49. 1969.
5. Carmichael, J. W. Cerebral mycetoma of trout due to a *Phialophora*-like fungus. *Sabouraudia 5*(2): 120–123. 1966.
6. Dupree, H. K. Vitamins essential for growth of channel catfish. *U. S. Bur. Sport Fish. Wildlife, Tech. Pap. 7.* 12 pp. 1966.

7. Fijan, N. N. Experimental transmission of infectious dropsy of carp. *Bull. Off. int. Épizoot. 65*(5): 731–738. 1966.
8. Fijan, N. N. Systemic mycosis in channel catfish. *Bull. Wildlife Dis. Ass. 5:* 109–110. 1969.
9. Fijan, N. N., Wellborn, T. L., Jr., and Naftel, J. P. An acute viral disease of channel catfish. *U. S. Bur. Sport Fish. Wildlife, Tech. Pap. 43.* 11 pp. 1970.
10. Fijan, N. N., Petrinec, Z., Sulimanovic, D., and Zwillenberg, L. O. Isolation of the viral causative agent from the acute form of infectious dropsy of carp. *Vet. arh. 41* (5–6): 125–138. 1971.
11. Goncharov, G. D. Rubella, a viral fish disease. *Ann. N. Y. Acad. Sci. 126:* 598–600. 1965.
12. Guseva, A. V. Parasitic crayfish producing red pest phenomena in various fish. *Konsul. Coll. Pap. Inst. Freshw. Fish, Leningrad 1–2:* 33–35. 1940.
13. Halver, J. E., Ashley, L. M., and Smith, R. R. Ascorbic acid requirements of coho salmon and rainbow trout. *Trans. Amer. Fish. Soc. 98* (4): 762–771. 1969.
14. Hoffman, G. L. *Parasites of North American Freshwater Fishes.* 486 pp. Berkeley and Los Angeles, Univ. Calif. Press, 1967.
15. Hoffman, G. L., Dunbar, C. E., Wolf, K., and Zwillenberg, L. O. Epitheliocystis, a new infectious disease of the bluegill (*Lepomis macrochirus*). *Antonie van Leeuwenhoek J. Microbiol. Serol. 35.* 146–158. 1969.
16. Kocylowski, B. The role of virus in septicemia of carp (*Cyprinus carpio*) and pox of carp: Influence of environment on infection. *Ann. N. Y. Acad. Sci. 126:* 616–619. 1965.
17. Koops, H., Mann, H., Pfitzner, I., Schmid, O. J., and Schubert, G. The cauliflower disease of eels, pp. 341–350. In *A Symposium on Diseases of Fishes and Shellfishes,* ed. S. F. Snieszko. Amer. Fish. Soc., Spec. Publ. No. 5. Washington, D.C., 1970.
18. Lovell, R. T. Essentiality of vitamin C in feeds for intensively fed caged channel catfish. *J. Nutr. 103*(1): 134–138. 1973.
19. Nigrelli, R. F., and Ruggieri, G. D. Studies on virus diseases of fishes: Spontaneous and experimentally induced cellular hypertrophy (lymphocystis disease) in fishes of the New York Aquarium, with a report of new cases and an annotated bibliography (1874–1965). *Zoologica (New York) 50*(2): 83–96. 1965.
20. O'Rourke, F. J. Serological relationships in the genus *Gadus. Nature (London) 183:* 1, 192. 1961.
21. Parisot, T. J. Sacramento River chinook disease. *U. S. Bur. Sport Fish. Wildlife, Fish Dis. Leafl. 502* 2 pp. 1963.
22. Parisot, T. J., Yasutake, W. T., and Klontz, G. W. Virus diseases of the Salmonidae in western United States. I. Etiology and epizootiology. *Ann. N. Y. Acad. Sci. 126:* 502–519. 1965.
23. Parry, G. Osmotic and ionic changes in blood and muscle of migrating salmonids. *J. Exp. Biol. 38:* 411–427. 1961.
24. Pfeiffer, W. Über die Verbreitung der Schrechreak bei Fischen. *Naturwissenschaften 41:* 23. 1960.

25. Pfeiffer, W.   The fright reaction of fish. *Biol. Rev. Cambridge Phil. Soc. 37:* 495–511. 1962.
26. Pfeiffer, W.   The fright reaction in North American fish. *Can. J. Zool. 41:* 69–77. 1963.
27. Phillips, A. M., Brockway, D. R., and Rogers, E. O.   Biotin and brown trout: The tale of a vitamin. *Progr. Fish-Cult. 12:* 67–71. 1950.
28. Rasmussen, C. J.   A biological study of the Egtved disease (Inul). *Ann. N. Y. Acad. Sci. 126:* 427–460. 1965.
29. Roberts, R. J.   U.D.N.–The present state of our knowledge. *Riv. ital. piscic. ittiopat. 6*(3): 63–66. 1971.
30. Roberts, R. J., Ball, H. J., Munro, A. L. S., and Shearer, W. M.   Studies on ulcerative dermal necrosis of salmonids. III. The healing process in fish maintained under experimental conditions. *J. Fish Biol. 3:* 221–224. 1971.
31. Roberts, R. J., Shearer, W. M., Munro, A. L. S., and Elson, K. G.   Studies on ulcerative dermal necrosis of salmonids. II. The sequential pathology of the lesions. *J. Fish Biol. 2:* 373–378. 1970.
32. Schäperclaus, W.   Etiology of infectious carp dropsy. *Ann. N. Y. Acad. Sci. 126:* 587–597. 1965.
33. Snieszko, S. F., and Ross, A. J.   Columnaris disease of fishes. *U. S. Bur. Sport Fish. Wildlife, Fish Dis. Leafl. 16.* 1969.
34. Stolyarov, V. P.   Parasitic fauna of carp of Rospha fish nursery and its commercial importance. *Trudy Kevin ob. est. 63*(3): 345–350. 1934.
35. Stolyarov, V. P.   Observation of the cycle of development of *Lernea cyprincea* and its pathogenic effect on the skin tissue of fish. *Trudy Kevin ob. est. 65*(2): 239–254.
36. Tomašec, I. I., and Fijan, N. N.   The etiology of infectious dropsy of carp. *Ann. N. Y. Acad. Sci. 126:* 606–615. 1965.
37. Walker, R.   The capsule of virus-induced lymphocystis cells of fish. *Amer. Zool. 3:* 490. 1963.
38. Walker, R.   Viral RNA and cytoplasmic RNA in lymphocystis cells of fish. *Ann. N. Y. Acad. Sci. 126:* 386–395. 1965.
39. Wedemeyer, G.   The role of stress in the disease resistance of fish, pp. 30–35. In *A Symposium on Diseases of Fishes and Shellfishes,* ed. S. F. Snieszko. Amer. Fish. Soc., Spec. Publ. No. 5. Washington, D.C., 1970.
40. Wellborn, T. L., Jr., Fijan, N. N., and Naftel, J. P.   Channel catfish virus disease. *U. S. Bur. Sport Fish. Wildlife, Fish Dis. Leafl. 18.* 3 pp. 1971.
41. Wolf, K.   Viral hemorrhagic septicemia of trout. *U. S. Bur. Sport Fish. Wildlife, Fish Dis. Leafl. 6.* 4 pp. 1966.
42. Wolf, K.   Advances in fish virology: A review, 1966–1971, pp. 305–331. In *Diseases of Fish,* ed. L. E. Mawdesley-Thomas. (Symp. Zool. Soc. London, No. 30.) London and New York, Academic Press, 1972.
43. Wolf, K., and Quimby, M. C.   Infectious pancreatic necrosis (IPN): Its diagnosis, identification, detection, and control. *Riv. ital. piscic. ittiopat. 2*(4): 76–80. 1967.
44. Wolke, R. E., Wyand, D. S., and Khairallah, L. H.   A light and electron micro-

scopic study of epitheliocystis disease in the gills of Connecticut striped bass (*Morone saxatilis*) and white perch (*Morone americanus*). *J. Comp. Pathol. 80:* 559–563. 1970.

45. Yasutake, W. T.   Comparative histopathology of epizootic salmonid virus diseases, pp. 341–350. In *A Symposium on Diseases of Fishes and Shellfishes,* ed. S. F. Snieszko. Amer. Fish. Soc., Spec. Publ. No. 5. Washington, D.C., 1970.

46. Yasutake, W. T., Parisot, T. J., and Klontz, G. W.   Virus diseases of the Salmonidae in western United States. II. Aspects of pathogenesis. *Ann. N. Y. Acad. Sci. 126:* 520–530. 1965.

47. Yohote, M.   Sekohe disease, spontaneous diabetes in carp, *Cyprinus carpio,* found in fish farms. V. Hydrocortisone diabetes in carp. *Bull. Freshwater Fish. Res. Lab. Tokyo 20*(2): 161–169. 1970.

18

The Pathology of the
Liver and Spleen in
Naturally Stressed Atlantic Menhaden

PHYLLIS H. CAHN

Massive kills involving primarily the Atlantic menhaden (*Brevoortia tyrannus*), a member of the herring family (Clupeidae), have occurred yearly during the summer in the New York area and in many other regions of the North and South Atlantic. This problem first received attention almost 20 years ago when the dying fish were described as "spinners" because of loss of coordinated movement. The hemorrhages present in gills, eyes, and brain (optic lobes) of the moribund fish were considered signs of stress. It was noted that the waters in which these fish were dying were characterized by "markedly varying salinities and organic pollution to a degree where shellfishing is prohibited" (54). Even at that time, before pollution studies had become common, the roles of chemical and physical imbalances in the environment of the fish were mentioned as causal factors in the kills.

Menhaden are a commercially valuable species; they are used as chum for sports fishing, fish protein concentrate made of menhaden homogenates is fed to poultry, and more recently menhaden are being used as feed in fish farming. There has been a substantial decline in the menhaden catch during the last 15 years, and many people have speculated about the relative roles of overfishing, estuarine pollution, and the regional changes in ocean temperature in this decline (24, 33, 42). The overall problem associated with the menhaden kills and the depleted fishery

443

prompted new menhaden programs in many laboratories, including a Federal Menhaden and Estuarine Fisheries Laboratory in Beaufort, North Carolina, and also, in recent years, at Gulf Breeze, Florida. Since then much has been learned about the basic biology and life history of these fish (13, 22, 28, 29, 38, 39), although many aspects, such as the histology of normal liver, spleen, and other organs, have not been described. Despite these efforts, it may still be lamented that "probably no other clupeid is as well known as the menhaden for mortalities about which so little is known" (43).

Menhaden use estuaries as nursery grounds; they spawn in oceanic waters all along the Continental Shelf from the Carolinas as far north as Maine. Young larvae enter the estuaries, where they remain in shallow, brackish waters until after metamorphosis. Decreasing water temperatures seem to trigger migration to warmer, offshore waters. The fish undertake extensive migrations, and in the course of their lives encounter waters of varying chemical and physical properties. They are subjected to changes in temperature, salinity, oxygen, organics, and, especially in estuaries, to competition for space and food, and to predator pressure. These, as well as parasites and disease, are all possible factors in weakening these fish (39, 43). Other anadromous species are subjected to similar environmental pressures but at present massive kills of other species seem to be much better understood. For example, cyclic kills of Atlantic herring (*Clupea harengus harengus*) have been ascribed to an epizootic fungus (*Ichthyophonus hoferi*) (43); winter die-offs of alewives (*Alosa pseudoharengus*) appear to result from cold-induced osmoregulatory failure (12, 45); and red tides contaminated with dinoflagellate toxins kill many different inshore species (35). The different kills often have similar clinical signs: shock and stress are always involved, also erratic swimming indicative of nervous system involvement. But menhaden kills in particular have defied satisfactory explanation. That a single disease is the primary factor seems unlikely because of the extensive geographical range of the fish killed yearly. In the Chesapeake Bay area, menhaden kills are associated with oxygen and temperature changes, but proof of causal relationship is lacking (43).

Most fish, especially schooling species, exhibit marked signs of stress when netted and handled. The trauma, even in very hardy nonschooling types such as the goldfish (*Carassius auratus*), produces rapid "asphyxiation hyperglycemia" (10), and other changes of a slower nature. Unless one is familiar with the normal, unstressed, and possibly cyclic changes in a species, it is difficult to recognize environmentally induced effects. As far as menhaden and other herring are concerned, little is known of cyclic biochemical and histological changes, except in regard to lipids, where seasonal changes in storage concentrations occur (14). The problem of acquiring knowledge of these effects is further complicated by the very rapid deterioration of clupeids after death (6).

This paper reports an initial study of the histopathology of menhaden liver and spleen, part of our continuing interest in menhaden and pollution (9, 46). Of par-

ticular interest is the possible relationship between any lesions found and the annual menhaden kills.

STUDIES ON LIVE-CAUGHT FISHES

Three series of fish (designated A, B, and C) were collected by gill netting from
two bays in western Long Island Sound, New York (Table 18.1). The fish were
alive when removed from the water from 15 minutes to one hour after the nets
were set. Twenty-nine fish were anesthetized in MS-222 and immediately dissected. The visceral mass, including liver, pyloric ceca, stomach, intestine, spleen, pancreas and associated mesentery, was removed. The liver and spleen were separated
from the remaining organs and fixed separately. The rest of the visceral mass was
also fixed immediately.

Bouin's fixative was used in most cases. In several instances either ice-cold picro-
alcoholic formalin, Hollande's-Bouin's, or formalin alone was used. There appeared
little in the way of fixation differences with the stains used (Harris' hematoxylin
and eosin, and Masson's trichrome).

After dissection, the fish were measured, sexed, and aged. All were found to
be sexually mature. Standard lengths ranged from 22.5 to 32.5 cm. Table 18.2
gives specific liver and spleen sizes for the 13 fish examined microscopically to
date.

The liver and spleen were examined for gross lesions after 24 to 48 hours of
fixation.

For histology a peripheral and a central region were processed for each liver
and spleen. Cross sections were cut at 5 to 7 microns. In some spleens a third region, below the central, was processed. An effort was made to process the same
region of each fish as nearly as possible. This was somewhat more difficult for the

Table 18.1. Age Distribution of Menhaden, *Brevoortia tyrannus,* Sampled for Gross Lesions
of Liver and Spleen, from Two Bays of Western Long Island Sound, New York

Series	Date	Site	Sex	2	2+	3	3+	4	4+	Total
				Number of fish, by age class[a]						
A	4/16/72	Oyster Bay	M	1	3	2	2	0	0	8
			F	0	0	0	2	0	0	2
B	4/19/72	Manhasset	M	0	0	0	3	0	1	4
		Bay	F	0	0	0	3	0	3	6
C	6/20/72	Manhasset	M	0	0	0	1	0	0	1
		Bay	F	0	2	4	2	0	0	8
										29

[a]Based on scale measurement method of June and Roithmayr (25).

livers than for the spleens because the liver shapes varied a great deal from fish to fish.

RESULTS

All livers were intact and had no gross lesions, although slight differences in color were apparent. Some of the livers were very pale, possibly because of different proportions of zoo- and phytoplankton in the diets of the fish. In general, the females had slightly heavier livers, although mean body lengths were similar (Table 18.2). On dissection, the centro-lobular regions of many of the livers were thickened and rugose, with especially large portal vessels and bile ducts. The peripheral areas, however, were smooth, soft, and more regular in outline.

Histologically, normal liver areas were more commonly seen in sections from perpiheral regions, although some central areas also showed normal features. These characteristics, a poorly defined lobular organization and two-cell-layered, anastomosing, parenchymal sheets, were similar to those described for trout (53). The typical cytoplasmic granulation and vacuolation of parenchymal cells varied in different fish but seemed to be fairly uniform in the same fish. Thus in some there was much cytoplasmic granulation, fewer vacuoles, basophilic cytoplasm, and poorly defined cell boundaries (Fig. 18.1). In others there was little granulation, much vacuolation, acidophilic cytoplasm, and well-defined cell boundaries (Fig. 18.2). Reticular cells and fibers that lined the ducts and blood vessels were of moderate thickness, with occasional larger, Kupffer-type cells present. Some pigment deposits, not tested as yet for specific type of pigment, were seen along the duct and blood vessel linings. Also, occasional macrophages with pigment within were observed in the parenchyma.

Hemorrhagic areas were frequently seen in the livers, especially in sections of central regions (Table 18.3). In the vicinity of these areas the parenchymal cells were of irregular shape and size, often with pyknotic nuclei, sparse cytoplasmic granulation, many vacuoles, and dilated and engorged sinusoids (Fig. 18.3). In some of the congested regions there were swollen meshworks of red blood cells, fibroblasts, and pale-staining fluid and fibrinous masses, with broken-down blood. Hypertrophy of sinusoidal and duct endothelium, and increased pigmentation-density were common in these livers. Five of the 13 livers contained small masses of muscle, some of which were enclosed by what appeared to be a cuticle. These could be either fish cardiac muscle or invertebrate muscle from a parasite, the two muscle types closely resembling each other (5).

No gross lesions were apparent in 10 of the 12 spleens; two were enlarged, however. In one of the enlarged spleens brownish nodules were found on the surface. In smears and in histological sections the nodules were found to consist of parasite eggs, plus additional types of tissue, described in the next paragraph. The

Table 18.2. Size and Liver Weight of Menhaden, *Brevoortia tyrannus*, Sampled for Liver and Spleen Histology, from Fish Listed in Table 18.1

Series	Date	Fish	Fork length[a] (cm)	Sex	Age class[b]	Liver weight[c] (grams)
A	4/16/72	1	28.0	M	2+	16.5
		2	29.0	M	3	10.0
		3	22.5	F	3+	11.0
		4	28.0	M	3+	9.0
B	4/19/72	1	30.5	F	4+	14.6
		2	31.0	F	3+	12.4
		3	25.8	M	4+	9.0
		4	30.5	M	3+	10.4
		5	32.5	F	4+	20.4
C	6/20/72	1	28.6	F	2+	9.0
		2	29.4	M	3+	6.5
		3	27.9	F	2+	13.0
		4	29.5	F	3	21.0

[a] Mean fork length is about the same for males and females (28.8 cm and 28.9 cm respectively).

[b] Mean age is the same for males and females (3.4 years).

[c] This is based on weight after 48 hours in Technicon Dehydrant solution. The mean liver weight is 10.2 grams for males and 14.4 grams for females.

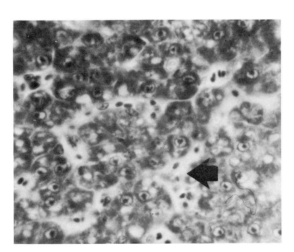

Fig. 18.1. Section from peripheral region of series B#2, menhaden liver with much basophilic cytoplasmic granulation, few vacuoles, and poorly defined cell boundaries. Sinusoids (arrow) are relatively empty in this view. In most other sections of this liver they were dilated and engorged. Hematoxylin and eosin (H&E); X900.

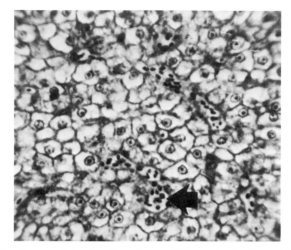

Fig. 18.2. Section from peripheral region of series A#1, menhaden liver with little acidophilic cytoplasmic granulation, many vacuoles and well-defined cell boundaries. Sinusoids (arrow) have more blood than in Figure 18.1, but are not as dilated or engorged in this view as in other sections of this liver. H&E; X600.

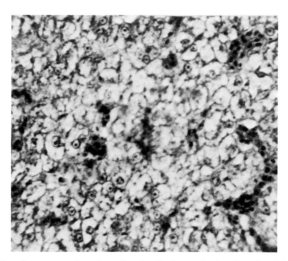

Fig. 18.3. Section from central region of series C#2, menhaden liver in which parenchymal cells are of irregular shape and size, some with pyknotic nuclei, and sinusoids are dilated and engorged. H&E; X900.

Table 18.3. Appearance of Sinusoids and Blood Vessels of Menhaden Liver and Spleen as Seen in Histological Section

Series	Fish	Liver		Spleen	
		Peripheral	Central	Peripheral	Central
A	1	++	++	+	++
	2	(++)	(++)	++	(+++)
	3	+	++	−	−
	4	+	(++)	(++)	(+++)
B	1	(++)	(+++)	+	++
	2	++	(+++)	+	++
	3	+	(++)	−	−
	4	++	(+++)	++	(+++)
	5	+	(+++)	+	+++
C	1	++	(+++)	(++)	++
	2	+	+++	(+++)	(+++)
	3	(+)	(+)	(+)	++
	4	(++)	(+++)	−	−

+ Sinusoids and blood vessels of moderate size, with loosely packed blood cells.

(+) Same as above but with eosinophilic fluid within blood vessels, and fewer blood cells.

++ Sinusoids dilated and congested with blood cells; blood vessels are engorged with blood.

(++) Same as above, but with eosinophilic fluid within blood vessels, and fewer blood cells.

+++ Sinusoids dilated and congested with blood cells, blood vessels are engorged with blood, and many hemorrhagic areas present.

(+++) Same as above, but with eosinophilic and yellow fluid within blood vessels and in hemorrhagic areas, and lower density of blood cells.

− Not preserved.

other enlarged spleen had no external abnormalities, but in section it was found to contain many hemorrhagic areas.

In menhaden, typical splenic structure was similar to that described for other fish. In particular, there was a lack of clear separation of red and white pulp, and no distinct cortex and medulla (16, 31, 44, 57), although peripheral areas showed these regions more distinctly. A common feature of the white pulp areas was the presence of reticular cell swirls surrounded by lymphocytes and similar to mammalian splenic lymphoid nodules (Fig. 18.4). These cells usually contained chromophobic cytoplasm and elongate nuclei, and were usually surrounded by a thin collagenous capsular-like area. A small blood vessel was often found in the center of the swirl. Few lymphocytes were found in red pulp areas (Fig. 18.5). Moderate pigmentation was seen around blood vessels and in the occasional macrophages. Also, a thin splenic capsule of collagenous fibers was present.

In atypical sections of the spleen, especially in central areas, there were many engorged sinusoids and blood vessels, and the red pulp was hyperemic and contained

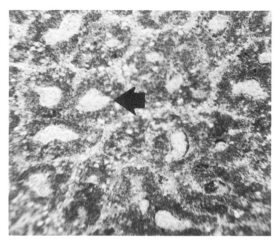

Fig. 18.4. Section from central region of series B#5, menhaden spleen. Numerous reticular cell swirls (arrow) surrounded by lymphocytes are found in white pulp area. H&E; ×100.

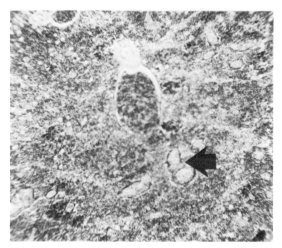

Fig. 18.5. Section from peripheral region of series B#5, menhaden spleen with few reticular cell swirls (a double one at arrow), and few lymphocytes. View is of a red pulp area. H&E; ×100.

many masses of broken-down blood cells (Table 18.3). Blood vessel walls were especially thick and had some endothelial hypertrophy (Fig. 18.6). Pigmentation was greatly increased in the vicinity of the engorged blood vessels. The nature of the pigment is not determined as yet. Also many pigmented macrophages were present (Fig. 18.7). Few lymphocytes were found in the white pulp; also very few reticular cell swirls. In the spleen that contained eggs, the eggs were part of a parasite as yet unidentified, but probably a crustacean. The presence of the two-

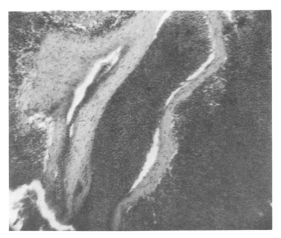

Fig. 18.6. Section from central region of series A#2, menhaden spleen with thickened and engorged artery adjacent to hyperemic red pulp. H&E; ×200.

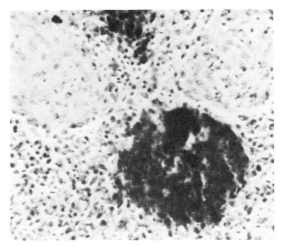

Fig. 18.7. Section from central region of series C#3, menhaden spleen with large, heavily pigmented macrophages. Few lymphocytes are present around reticular cell swirls. H&E; ×600.

layered cuticle (Fig. 18.8), within which were the mature and immature eggs and the masses of striated muscle (Figs. 18.9, 18.10), rules out parasites from other invertebrate phyla known to lack striated muscle (5). The splenic cells adjacent to the parasite were congested, and some fish-type blood cells were also found around eggs and muscle of the parasite (Fig. 18.10). An additional structure within the cuticle of the parasite resembles a germinal organ, with peripherally located ova in the outer epithelium (Fig. 18.11).

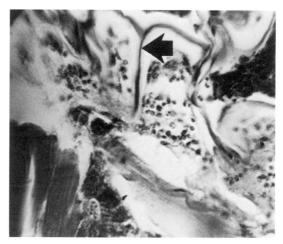

Fig. 18.8. Section from region posterior to the central area of series A#2, menhaden spleen with cuticle of parasite (arrow). Other parasite tissues are not clearly distinguishable in this view. No splenic cells are visible. H&E; ×600.

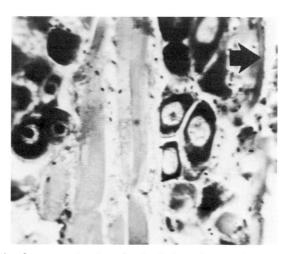

Fig. 18.9. Section from central region of series A#2 menhaden spleen. Eggs and striated muscle of parasite are visible. Note the large, centrally located nucleolus of several of the eggs; also part of cuticle (arrow). H&E; ×600.

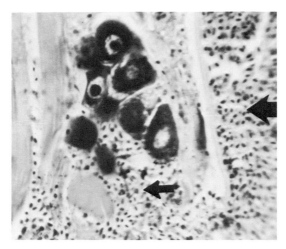

Fig. 18.10. Section in vicinity of that shown in Figure 18.9, with congested splenic tissue (large arrow) adjacent to parasite, blood cells (small arrow) within cuticle. H&E; ×600.

Fig. 18.11. Section of parasite in vicinity of that shown in Figures 18.8–18.10. Large, mature eggs lie at the top edge of the photo and there is present an unidentified main mass that resembles a hollow germinal tissue. Small eggs lie near arrow. Debris in the cavity is not recognizable. H&E; ×600.

SUMMARY

All 13 of the fish examined histologically had signs of stress in their liver and spleen structure. Without more complete data on the typical cyclic histology of these organs in menhaden it is difficult to evaluate all of the observations described. Histological studies of the liver and spleen of feral fish, and especially of marine forms, are rare in the literature. The liver is an organ that is highly susceptible to damage by virtue of its detoxifying role and active metabolic functions. It is possible, therefore, that localized lesions are normally present in many fishes. The only evidence for this in the literature is one study on hatchery-reared cutthroat trout (*Salmo clarki*), where it is stated that "progressive degenerative changes were present in all groups, including controls, but the incidence of liver damage was four times as severe in the endrin-treated fish" (18). Despite all of the recent pollution work, few investigators have examined in any depth the normal histological picture.

It is difficult to say with confidence whether the hemorrhagic areas seen commonly in the liver and spleen were the result of the stress of capture, are normal to fish of the age and at the time of year studied, or represent disease. In humans who have died of circulatory collapse, it is known that erythrocyte accumulations are found in the liver (36). Although the menhaden used in this study were alive following capture, they no doubt suffered severe respiratory and circulatory stress prior to the anesthetizing and dissection. Therefore some localized liver and possibly splenic hemorrhagic areas may have been expected. But it appears unlikely that the massive hemorrhagic areas seen, with the engorged sinusoids and areas of blood breakdown, are the result solely of the stress of capture.

Hemorrhagic livers with enlarged and engorged sinusoids may be characteristic of dietary deficiencies, tumors, viral infections, and pesticide toxicity (1, 19, 21, 55). Other common changes associated with these include bile duct connective tissue hyperplasia, irregularly sized and shaped parenchymal cells and nuclei, and parenchymal necroses. These histopathological changes also resemble some of the changes that occur in spawning fishes (40, 47–49) and even some of the deteriorative changes in senile fish (40). Fish spleen lesions associated with fungal, bacterial, and viral diseases may include areas congested with erythrocytes, leukopenia, and necroses of the hematopoietic regions (1, 2, 34, 41). These also resemble, to a certain extent, the histological changes seen in spawning and migrating animals and in fish stressed by prolonged periods in darkness (37, 40, 47, 49), except that in the latter congestion and hemorrhages are less frequent. An unfortunate multiplicity of explanations then emerges for the hemorrhagic areas and associated changes observed in this menhaden series.

For the variations from individual to individual of degree of vacuolization, cytoplasmic granulation, and basophilia found in the liver, fewer explanations present themselves. These may represent agonal change associated with the period of struggle after the fish has been trapped by the gill net and before it has been anesthetized. Such rapid changes have been described in association with asphyxiation hyperglycemia in other fish (10, 30). Another possibility is that they represent periods of degeneration and regeneration of the liver, such as occur in trout with pesticide poisoning (18). A final possibility is that they represent a normal variability of unknown cause. Normal cyclic changes in liver and muscle glycogen and lipid have been described for several different species. The changes are generally associated with migration and spawning (10, 23, 30, 48, 50). Abnormal factors such as dietary deficiencies, starvation, toxins, thermal stress, senility, and chronic pesticide exposure may also produce glucose, glycogen, and lipid changes (7, 14, 17, 21). To distinguish normal from aberrant, it is necessary to examine age, seasonal, hormonal, sexual, dietary, genetic, and other internal and external influences on the biology of a species. To date, this has been accomplished for but a handful of fishes, and not for menhaden and other herring.

Herring which are known to be feeding heavily will decompose more rapidly when removed from the water than nonfeeding individuals. The rapid decomposition was ascribed to a softening of the wall of the digestive tract from hypersecretion of digestive enzymes (6). The rapid deterioration noted for the menhaden tissue may be related, although menhaden livers were found to have only trace amounts of proteases. Even amylases and lipases are low (11). The very high metabolic rate of menhaden, and such associated physiological attributes as high red blood cell count, high hemoglobin levels, and large amounts of dark muscle, may all be factors contributing to rapid decomposition (7, 15, 20).

A number of tissue-invading crustacean parasites are known for fishes (27, 32, 43, 51). The characteristics of the organism found in the spleen of 1 of the 13 menhaden examined histologically appears to be that of a copepod, possibly of the genus *Lernanthropus* or *Lernaecocera*. The former, especially the species associated with menhaden, *Lernanthropus brevoortiae*, is characterized by dark brown egg tubes (56). The brown nodules seen grossly on the splenic surface of the parasitized menhaden contained eggs and may have been the egg tubes. This copepod species, however, is not known to be a tissue-invading one; it is typically a gill parasite. *Lernaecocera*, and in particular *Lernaecocera branchialis*, penetrates heart tissue and feeds on the host's blood but has not been previously described in menhaden (32). There was much fish blood present within the parasite. It is possible that a new species of this copepod that invades the spleen was the organism found here. Both of the above-named copepod genera are morphologically modified. No structures resembling appendages were seen, although serial sections of the menhaden spleen with parasites were not available.

Additional verification of the arthropod nature of the parasite found in the menhaden spleen was the two-layered cuticle that surrounded the eggs and muscle. Such a cuticle is unlike that of any of the nonarthropods known to parasitize fish (5). The striated muscle within the cuticle was also arthropod-like and although there was a resemblance to fish cardiac muscle, the surrounding cuticle makes it evident that this tissue is not of fish origin.

A superficial examination of the eggs seen in the menhaden spleen might indicate a resemblance to fish eggs. More careful study shows otherwise. Herring and other fish oocytes of that size and cytoplasmic density typically contain several small nucleoli, located almost in contact with the nuclear membrane, rather than the one large nucleolus seen here (3, 4, 8). Also, typical fish eggs are surrounded by follicle cells, as well as zonal cells. These cells are lacking in the eggs of many invertebrates and were lacking in the eggs of the splenic parasite.

The overall picture, from the minimal histopathology described in this report, is indicative of stressed fish. Are some of the stressed fish also showing early signs of disease? There is no doubt that stress lowers resistance (52). Further studies are needed to determine if any disease is developing. Are old-age changes playing a role? Although the recorded deaths include juvenile as well as adult fish, some authors have noted degenerative changes in liver, kidney, gills, and thyroid which were indicative of senility (R. F. Nigrelli, personal communication). If these fish are in poor condition during the spring following migration, spawning, and winter depletions, the additional stresses imposed by high summer temperatures, lowered oxygen, pollution, and increased predator pressures may be too severe for recovery and survival. Certainly, their existence during the summer may be marginal, creating perhaps the basis for a dramatic fish kill due to relatively slight but somewhat synchronized additional pressures.

Acknowledgment. Special thanks are extended to Mrs. Ethel Hafter Atz for her fine histological work, numerous suggestions, and critical reading of the manuscript. L. L. Eller, Bureau of Sport Fisheries and Wildlife, was kind enough to examine some of the histological sections and made very useful comments. Douglas Clarke, graduate student, Marine Science Department, Long Island University, helped in the fish collecting and carried out the scale analyses for ageing. Dr. R. F. Nigrelli, New York Aquarium, was consulted on various aspects of this work. The C. W. Post College Council Research Fund supported part of this work.

REFERENCES

1. Amend, D. F., and Chambers, V. C. Morphology of certain viruses of salmonid fishes. I. In vitro studies of some viruses causing hematopoietic necrosis. *J. Fish. Res. Board Can. 27:* 1285. 1970.
2. Amend, D. F., Yasutake, W. T., and Mead, R. W. A hematopoietic virus disease of rainbow trout and sockeye salmon. *Trans. Amer. Fish. Soc. 98:* 796. 1969.
3. Anderson, E. The formation of the primary envelope during oocyte differentiation in teleosts. *J. Cell Biol. 35:* 193. 1967.

4. Anderson, E. Cortical alveoli formation and vitellogenesis during oocyte differentiation in the pipefish, *Syngnathus fuscus,* and the killifish, *Fundulus heteroclitus. J. Morphol. 125:* 23. 1968.

5. Andrew, W. *Textbook of Comparative Histology.* New York, Oxford Univ. Press, 1959.

6. Battle, H. I. Digestion and digestive enzymes in the herring, *Clupea harengus. J. Biol. Board Can. 1:* 145. 1935.

7. Bilinski, E. Lipid catabolism in fish muscle. In *Fish in Research,* ed. O. W. Neuhaus and J. E. Halver. New York and London, Academic Press, 1969.

8. Bowers, A. B., and Holliday, F. G. T. Histological changes in the gonad associated with the reproductive cycle of the herring, *Clupea harengus. Mar. Res. Scot. 5:* 3. 1961.

9. Cahn, P. H., Siler, W., and Fujiya, M. Sensory detection of environmental changes by fish. In *Responses of Fish to Environmental Changes,* ed. W. Chavin. Springfield, Ill., Charles C. Thomas, in press.

10. Chavin, W., and Young, J. E. Factors in the determination of normal serum glucose levels of goldfish, *Carassius auratus. Comp. Biochem. Physiol. 33:* 629. 1970.

11. Chesley, L. C. The concentration of proteases, amylase, and lipase in certain marine fishes. *Biol. Bull. (Woods Hole) 66:* 133. 1934.

12. Colby, P. Alewife dieoffs: Why do they occur? *Limnos 4:* 18. 1971.

13. Dahlberg, M. A systematic review of the North American species of menhaden, genus *Brevoortia.* Ph.D. thesis, Tulane Univ., New Orleans, La., 1966.

14. Dahlberg, M. Fat cycles and condition factors of two species of menhaden, *Brevoortia* (Clupeidae), and natural hybrids from Indian River of Florida. *Amer. Midland Natur. 82:* 117. 1969.

15. Dawson, A. B. The relative numbers of immature erythrocytes in the circulating blood of several species of marine fishes. *Biol. Bull. (Woods Hole) 64:* 33. 1933.

16. Dawson, A. B. The hemopoietic response in the catfish, *Ameiurus nebulosus,* to chronic lead poisoning. *Biol. Bull. (Woods Hole) 68:* 335. 1935.

17. Dean, J. M., and Berlin, J. D. Alterations in hepatocyte function of thermally acclimated rainbow trout, *Salmo gairdneri. Comp. Biochem. Physiol. 29:* 307. 1969.

18. Eller, L. L. Histopathologic lesions in cutthroat trout, *Salmo clarki,* exposed chronically to the insecticide endrin. *Amer. J. Pathol. 64:* 321. 1971.

19. Grant, B. F., and Mehrle, P. M. Chronic endrin poisoning in goldfish, *Carassius auratus. J. Fish. Res. Board Can. 27:* 2225. 1970.

20. Hall, F. G., Gray, I. E., and Lepkovsky, S. The influence of asphyxiation on the blood constituents of marine fishes. *J. Biol. Chem. 67:* 549. 1926.

21. Halver, J. E. The role of ascorbic acid in fish disease and tissue repair. *Bull. Jap. Soc. Sci. Fish. 38:* 79. 1972.

22. Higham, J. R., and Nicholson, W. R. Sexual maturation and spawning of Atlantic menhaden. *Fish. Bull. 63:* 255. 1964.

23. Hochachka, P. W. Intermediary metabolism in fishes. In *Fish Physiology,*

ed. W. S. Hoar and D. J. Randall, vol. 1. 6 vols. New York and London, Academic Press, 1969–70.

24. Jensen, A. C. Regional changes in ocean temperature and fish distribution and abundance. *Trans. Northeast Fish Wildlife Conf. 1972.*

25. June, F., and Roithmayr, C. Determination of age of Atlantic menhaden from their scales. *Fish. Bull. 60:* 323. 1959.

26. Kott, E. Differences between the livers of spawning male and female sea lamprey (*Petromyzon marinus*). *Can. J. Zool. 48:* 745. 1970.

27. Kroger, R. L., and Guthrie, J. F. Incidence of the parasitic isopod, *Olencira praegustator*, in juvenile Atlantic menhaden. *Copeia 2:* 370. 1972.

28. Lewis, R. M. The effect of minimum temperature on the survival of larval Atlantic menhaden, *Brevoortia tyrannus*. *Trans. Amer. Fish. Soc. 94:* 409. 1965.

29. Lewis, R. M. Effects of salinity and temperature on survival and development of larval Atlantic menhaden, *Brevoortia tyrannus*. *Trans. Amer. Fish. Soc. 95:* 423. 1966.

30. Mackay, W., and Beatty, D. D. Plasma glucose levels of the white sucker, *Catastomus commersonii*, and the northern pike, *Esox lucius*. *Can. J. Zool. 46:* 797. 1968.

31. Mackmull, G., and Michels, N. A. Absorption of colloidal carbon from the peritoneal cavity in the teleost *Tautogolabrus adspersus*. *Amer. J. Anat. 51:* 3. 1932.

32. Mann, H. Copepoda and Isopoda as parasites of marine fishes. In *A Symposium on Diseases of Fishes and Shellfishes,* ed. S. F. Snieszko. Amer. Fish. Soc., Spec. Publ. No. 5. Washington, D.C., 1970.

33. Nicholson, W. Changes in catch and effort in Atlantic menhaden purse seine fishery, 1940–68. *Fish. Bull. 69:* 765. 1971.

34. Nigrelli, R. F., and Vogel, H. Spontaneous tuberculosis in fishes and in other cold-blooded vertebrates with special reference to *Mycobacterium fortuitum* Cruz from fish and human lesions. *Zoologica (New York) 48:* 131. 1963.

35. Oppenheimer, C. H. On marine fish diseases. In *Fish as Food,* ed. G. Borgstrom, vol. 2. 6 vols. New York, Academic Press, 1961–65.

36. Rappaport, A. M. Acinar units and the pathophysiology of the liver. In *The Liver: Morphology, Biochemistry, Physiology,* ed. C. Rouiller, vol. 1. 2 vols. New York, Academic Press, 1963–64.

37. Rasquin, P., and Rosenbloom, L. Endocrine imbalance and tissue hyperplasia in teleosts maintained in darkness. *Bull. Amer. Mus. Natur. Hist. 104:* 365. 1954.

38. Reintjes, J. W. Synopsis of biological data on the Atlantic menhaden, *Brevoortia tyrannus*. *U. S. Fish Wildlife Serv., Circ. 320.* 1969.

39. Reintjes, J. W., and Pacheco, A. L. The relation of menhaden to estuaries. Amer. Fish. Soc., Spec. Publ. No. 3:50. 1966.

40. Robertson, O. K., and Wexler, B. C. Histological changes in the organs and tissues of senile castrated kokanee salmon, *Oncorhynchus nerka*. *Gen. Comp. Endocrinol. 2:* 458. 1962.

41. Ruggieri, G. D., Nigrelli, R. F., Powles, P. M., and Garnett, D. G. Epizootics in yellowtail flounder, *Limanda ferruginea*, in the western North Atlantic caused by *Ichthophonus*, an ubiquitous parasitic fungus. *Zoologica (New York) 55:* 57. 1970.

42. Schaaf, W. E., and Huntsman, G. R. Effects of fishing on the Atlantic menhaden stock 1955–1969. *Trans. Amer. Fish. Soc. 101:* 290. 1972.

43. Sindermann, C. J. *Principal Diseases of Marine Fish and Shellfish.* New York and London, Academic Press, 1970.

44. Squicciarini, P. J. A histological and histopathological study of the induced inflammatory response in the brown bullhead catfish, *Ictalurus nebulosus*. Ph.D. thesis, New York Univ., New York, N.Y., 1970.

45. Stanley, J. G., and Colby, P. J. Effects of temperature on electrolyte balance and osmoregulation in the alewife, *Alosa pseudoharengus*, in fresh and sea water. *Trans. Amer. Fish. Soc. 100:* 624. 1971.

46. Stott, M. Some aspects of the biology of the Long Island Atlantic menhaden, *Brevoortia tyrannus*. M.Sc. thesis, Long Island Univ., Greenvale, N.Y., 1970.

47. Tamura, E., and Honma, Y. Histological changes in the organs and tissues of the gobiid fishes throughout the life span. III. Hemopoietic organs in the ice-goby, *Leucopsarion petersi*. *Bull. Jap. Soc. Sci. Fish. 36:* 661. 1970.

48. Tamura, E., and Honma, Y. Histological changes in the organs and tissues of the gobiid fishes through the life span. IV. Digestive organs of the ice-goby. *Bull. Jap. Soc. Sci. Fish. 37:* 831. 1971.

49. Tamura, E., and Honma, Y. Histological observations on another dealfish, *Trachipterus ishikawai*, caught off the coast of Sado Island in the Japan Sea. *Annu. Rep. Sado Mar. Biol. Sta. Niigata Univ. 2:* 11. 1972.

50. Todd, W. R., Laastuen, L. E., and Thomas, A. E. Effect of amino acid imbalance on liver glycogen levels in young salmon. *Comp. Biochem. Physiol. 23:* 431. 1967.

51. Turner, W., and Roe, R. B. Occurrence of the parasitic isopod, *Olencira praegustator* in the yellowfin menhaden, *Brevoortia smithi*. *Trans. Amer. Fish. Soc. 96:* 357. 1967.

52. Wedemeyer, G. The role of stress in the disease resistance of fishes. In *A Symposium on Diseases of Fishes and Shellfishes*, ed. S. F. Snieszko. Amer. Fish. Soc., Spec. Publ. No. 5. Washington, D.C., 1970.

53. Weinreb, E. L., and Bilstad, N. M. Histology of the digestive tract and adjacent structures of the rainbow trout, *Salmo gairdneri irideus*. *Copeia 3:* 194. 1955.

54. Westman, J. R., and Nigrelli, R. F. Preliminary studies of menhaden and their mass mortalities in Long Island and New Jersey waters. *N. Y. Fish Game J. 2:* 142. 1955.

55. Wolf, K., Herman, R. L., and Carlson, C. P. Fish viruses: Histopathologic changes associated with experimental channel catfish virus disease. *J. Fish. Res. Board Can. 29:* 149. 1972.

56. Yamaguti, S. *Parasitic Copepoda and Branchiura of Fishes.* New York, Wiley, Interscience, 1963.

57. Yoffey, G.   A contribution to the study of the comparative histology and physiology of the spleen, with reference chiefly to its cellular constituents. I. In fishes. *J. Anat. 63:* 314. 1929.

DISCUSSION OF THE PATHOLOGY OF THE LIVER AND SPLEEN IN NATURALLY STRESSED ATLANTIC MENHADEN

K. Balogh: In human pathology beginners will often contaminate tissue with "float-ons" from unclean scalpel and scissors. Is it possible that some of the muscle masses in the liver and spleen and eggs in the spleen of the male fish were a result of contamination?

P. H. Cahn: This is unlikely, since extreme care was taken with each piece of tissue. What appears more probable is that the muscle and eggs were part of a parasite lodged in these organs; the presence of a cuticle around most of the foreign masses adds credence to this theory.

PART IV

Chemical and Physical Agents of Disease

19

Radiation-Induced Hematopoietic Lesions in Fish

G . E . C O S G R O V E
B . G . B L A Y L O C K
G . U . U L R I K S O N
and P . H . C O H A N

Fish radiobiology has not been studied comprehensively, but more work has been done on fish than on other poikilotherms. There have been recent reviews of fish radiobiology by Cosgrove and Blaylock (10), Donaldson and Foster (11), Egami, Hyodo-Taguchi, and Etoh (16), and Ulrikson (54). This paper will deal principally with radiation effects on the hematopoietic tissues of fish, omitting reference to such other aspects as LD_{50}, gonadal effects, growth and developmental effects, etc. Experimental studies utilizing radiation exposures in the dose range for hematopoietic effects in several species of fish will be presented, and much of the literature on such studies will be included in the references. In preparing this paper we gained some familiarity with the literature on blood cells and sites of hematopoiesis in fish, and we felt that many of these references should be included here for essential background information.

Our personal experience with changes in the hematopoietic organs of irradiated fish is a by-product of several different experiments (Table 19.1), which were performed at different times, with different radiation sources, and under different holding conditions. The only constant is the histopathology, which was all done in one laboratory by one individual. A brief summary of the experimental procedure follows.

463

Table 19.1. Summary of Experimental Groups of Irradiated Fish

Species	Year	Place	Sex	Radiation dose (rads)	Radiation factors	Temperature (°C)	Duration of study (days)
Gambusia affinis (Mosquitofish)	1967-70	ORNL[a]	M, F	750-6000	Acute ^{60}Co gamma	15, 25	36
Gambusia affinis (Mosquitofish)	1970-71	ORNL	M, F	336-9216	Chronic ^{60}Co gamma (0.5-5.43 rad/hr)	15, 25	128
Ictalurus punctatus (Channel catfish)	1972	ORNL	M, F	500-2500	Acute ^{60}Co gamma	25	41
Lepomis macrochirus (Bluegill)	1968	UM[b]	M, F	1000-3000	Acute ^{60}Co gamma	20	12
Xiphophorus maculatus (Swordtail)	9172	CSEC[c]	M, F	2496 (estimated)	Acute ^{137}Ce gamma	23	42
Poecilia reticulata (Guppy)	1972	CSEC	M, F	"	"	"	"
Gambusia affinis (Mosquitofish)	1972	CSEC	M, F	"	"	"	"
Brachydanio rerro	1972	CSEC	M, F	"	"	"	"
Capoeta tetrazona	1972	CSEC	M, F	"	"	"	"
Tanichthys albonubes	1972	CSEC	M, F	"	"	"	"

[a]Ecological Sciences Division, Oak Ridge National Laboratory, Oak Ridge, Tennessee.
[b]University of Michigan Facilities, Ann Arbor, Michigan.
[c]Cooperative Science Education Center, Oak Ridge, Tennessee.

464

In the experiments conducted at Oak Ridge National Laboratory on mature mosquitofish (*Gambusia affinis*), the fish were collected at 2 to 3 cm in size from local creeks and ponds. In most experiments, "wild" fish were used; in one, however, F_1 offspring of wild fish were used; they had been held in laboratory tanks until they attained maturity (Table 19.1). All fish were acclimated to the laboratory at 15° or 25°C for at least two weeks before the experiments.

Irradiation was performed with a Gammacell 200 (Atomic Energy Commission Limited of Canada) containing ^{60}Co. For the acute studies, dose rates of approximately 360 rad/min were delivered to fish in groups of five in 100 ml of water in a plastic container. Doses were checked with Toshiba fluoroglass dosimeters. For the chronic studies, plastic boxes were arranged in the source room at three distances from the 30-Ci^{60} source. Radiation doses were measured by exposing Toshiba fluoroglass dosimeters (Type FGD-3B) in the water-filled boxes for 86 hours. The calculated dose rates ranged from 0.5 to 5.43 rad/hr. During irradiation, boxes at each dose were maintained at either 15° or 25°C ($\pm$ 1°C), with four fish per box. The fish were irradiated for 23.5 hours each day, with the other half hour used for observation, cleaning, and feeding. The chronic experiment lasted 128 days.

After acute irradiation, the fish were returned to the appropriate environmental chambers, checked daily, and fed at least every other day. At selected times, up to 36 days after the acute dose and 128 days after chronic irradiation, fish were removed for histopathological examination; also, some fish that died were examined histologically.

In the experiments on young channel catfish (*Ictalurus punctatus*), fish approximately 3 inches long were obtained from the Frankfort National Fish Hatchery, U.S. Department of the Interior, Frankfort, Kentucky. They were acclimated for at least two weeks in laboratory tanks at 25°C and then irradiated individually in plastic containers with acute doses of ^{60}Co gamma radiation from a Gammacell at a dose rate of about 305 rad/min, with total doses of 500 to 2500 rads. They were then returned to the laboratory tanks and maintained until they died or were killed.

The adult bluegills (*Lepomis macrochirus*) used in the study at the University of Michigan were obtained from Sugarloaf Lake, Washtenaw County, Michigan, and were held at a fish hatchery in Saline, Michigan, in large metal holding tanks. After acclimation, they were transported by special container to the University of Michigan, where they were given 1000 or 3000 rads of whole-body radiation from a 6000-Ci^{60}Co source at a dose rate of approximately 160 rad/min. They were then returned to the outdoor holding tanks. Temperature varied from about 13.5° to 20°C during the 12-day period of sampling. These fish were part of a more extensive study on LD$_{50}$, radiation sterilization, and blood and serum protein effects (54).

In the experiment at the Cooperative Science Education Center, six small species of aquarium-maintained fish were used. They were acclimated in balanced five-gallon aquaria for several weeks at 23°C and then irradiated individually in small plastic bags in a Cesi-Radiator (American Nuclear Corporation) with ^{137}Ce gamma rays at a dose rate of about 1248 rad/min. They were then returned to the aquaria and sampled at weekly intervals for seven weeks.

In most cases the small fish were fixed whole in Bouin's fixative, with a slit in the abdominal wall for better penetration. Larger fish were dissected, and their major viscera were preserved. Bouin's fixative produced decalcification in 7 to 10 days so the small fish could be sectioned whole in desired planes with a razor blade. Tissues were processed according to the usual procedure and stained with hematoxylin and eosin.

EFFECTS OF RADIATION

Tissue sampling in the *Gambusia* experiment was more thorough than in the others. Findings were similar in all species, however. In the species examined, the chief site of hematopoiesis is the head kidney. Acute doses of 750 rads caused only slight depression of hematopoiesis in male *Gambusia* maintained at 25°C, and no depression in fish held at 15°C. After 1500 rads, effects in both sexes were mild and relatively late; more damage was seen in females at 15°C than at 25°C, while the reverse was true in males. At 2800 rads, kidney hematopoiesis was equally affected in both sexes, with slight depression in 8- and 16-day samples and moderate depression in 26- and 36-day samples. There was some disparity between the two temperature groups, similar to that seen at 1500 rads. Depression of kidney hematopoiesis at 5800 rads was rapid and complete, the fish at 25°C being affected more quickly than those held at 15°C. The spleens of control fish had leukocyte accumulation and some hematopoiesis. The spleen was more sensitive to radiation than the kidney, with atrophy as early as 2 days after 750 rads and more severe responses after higher doses. No sex or temperature effect was noted for spleen damage.

In the first chronic radiation experiment, where doses of 5.43 rad/hr were accumulated in *Gambusia* for 37 days, there was no demonstrable damage to the hematopoietic organs. In the second chronic experiment, where doses as high as 3.0 rad/hr were accumulated for as long as 128 days to a total of more than 9000 rads, some fish in the two higher dose groups (3.0 and 1.5 rad/hr) had hematopoietic atrophy of a relatively mild degree in kidney and spleen in the later days of the experiment. Other fish with equal total doses, however, did not have hematopoietic atrophy.

In the experiment with channel catfish, the initial dose of 2500 rads killed all the fish by 13 days, and severe hematopoietic atrophy was seen in all the samples, including the earliest at day 7 (Figs. 19.1, 19.2). The radiation dose was then varied from 500 to 2000 rads at 500-rad intervals. Severe hematopoietic atrophy in kidney, spleen, and thymus was found in all the fish sampled after 500 to 2000

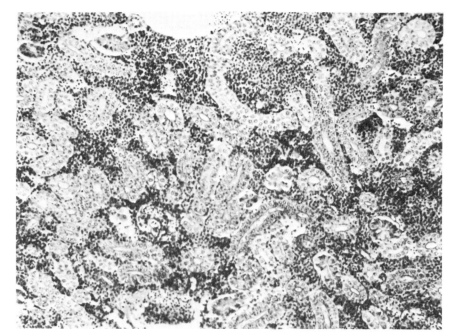

Fig. 19.1. Kidney, unirradiated catfish. The interstitial tissue between the tubules is packed with nucleated hematopoietic cells.

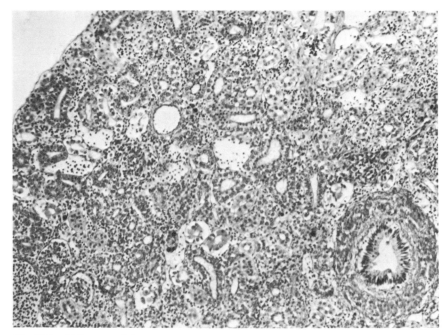

Fig. 19.2. Kidney, catfish 7 days after 2500 rads. The interstitial tissues are packed with nucleated erythrocytes, but there are very few hematopoietic cells.

467

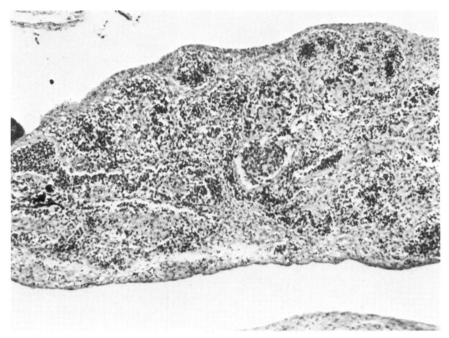

Fig. 19.3. Spleen, unirradiated catfish. The follicles are moderately cellular, and the sinusoids are packed with erythrocytes.

rads (Figs. 19.3, 19.4), persisting until the last sampling at 32 days in the 1000-rad group. (The 2000-rad group all died well before 30 days.) However, in the 500-rad group, hematopoietic recovery was seen in samples taken after 29 days.

In the bluegill study, limited tissue samplings of fish that received 1000 rads indicated hematopoietic atrophy in the kidney by 3 days, which persisted until the end of the 13-day sampling period. Kidney findings were similar in the 3000-rad group. In addition, the spleen was sampled in the latter group and had necrosis and hematopoietic cell debris at 1 day, disappearance of debris and hematopoietic cells at 3 days, and persistent atrophy thereafter.

In the study of six species of small aquarium fish given 2500 rads followed by weekly samplings, radiation effects were observed in hematopoietic organs only in the 7-day sample. Normal hematopoiesis was restored by 14 days, except for persistent thymic damage in the sampled *Brachydanio* (Figs. 19.5, 19.6). These findings seemed to indicate some unsolved dosimetry problems, so two more groups of fish were exposed, at two and three times the original dose. Tissues from these fish showed severe hematopoietic atrophy in kidney and spleen during the three-week sampling period.

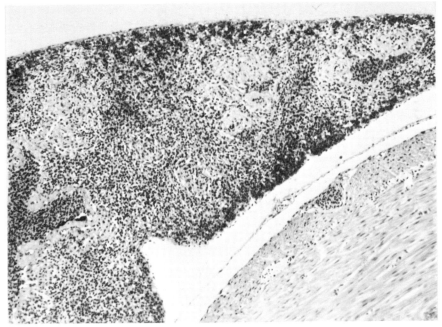

Fig. 19.4. Spleen, catfish 7 days after 2500 rads. The follicles contain no lymphocytes and are dense and compact. The sinusoids are packed with erythrocytes.

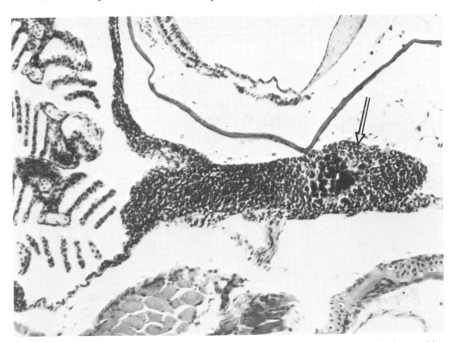

Fig. 19.5. Thymus, unirradiated *Brachydanio rerro*. The background stroma is obscured by dense collections of lymphocytes.

469

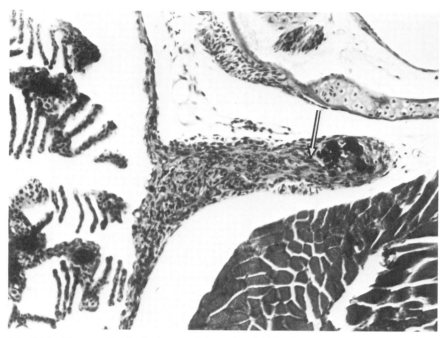

Fig. 19.6. Thymus, *Brachydanio rerro* 7 days after 2496 rads. Most lymphocytes are gone and the stromal background is exposed.

SUMMARY

Table 19.2 lists various studies on the direct hematopoietic effects of radiation. With the exception of *Myxine* and *Petromyzon*, all the fish listed in the table are teleosts (bony fishes). In these, opinion is rather uniform that the head kidney is the chief site of hematopoiesis and has early and rapid depletion of hematopoietic cells in proportion to the dose of radiation, with recovery from sublethal doses beginning in a few weeks. Depression of blood cells in the circulation reportedly lags somewhat behind the loss of cells in the irradiated head kidney. The spleen and thymus likewise are radiosensitive sites of hematopoiesis, but they are thought to be relatively unimportant in the bony fishes. Radiation effects on hematopoietic organs in our experiments on several species of teleosts were similar to those previously reported in the literature.

The study using the hagfish (*Myxine*) and the lamprey (*Petromyzon*) is of special interest because it shows the point in the vertebrate phylogenetic scale where hematopoietic cells change from very radio resistant (*Myxine*) to relatively radiosensitive (*Petromyzon*) (24).

The temperature at which fish are held after irradiation is very important in

Table 19.2. Studies on Hematopoietic Effects of Radiation in Fish[a]

Author(s)	Year	Reference number	Organism
Aoki	1963	2	*Carassius*
Aoki	1966	3	*Carassius*
Blaylock & Mitchell	1969	5	*Gambusia*
Bonham et al.	1948	6	Salmon fingerling
Egami	1969	13	*Oryzias*
Ellinger	1940	18	*Carassius*
Engel et al.	1966	19	*Lagodon*
Finstad et al.	1969	24	*Myxine, Petromyzon*
Hevesy et al.	1964	27	*Tinca*
Nakatani & Foster	1963	34	Rainbow trout
Preston	1959	38	Plaice
Ray	1970	40	*Campostoma*
Shechmeister et al.	1962	50	*Carassius*
Sletten et al.	1964	51	*Tinca*
Watson et al.	1963	55	*Carassius*
Welander et al.	1948	57	Salmon larvae
Welander et al.	1949	58	Rainbow trout

[a]Reviews and special articles are not included. Other articles are listed in the References.

determining the degree of hematopoietic damage. In general, cold is radioprotective, but if the temperature is too low (e.g., 4°C) it not only markedly slows the damage, but also prolongs or prevents the regenerative sequelae in irradiated cell populations (2, 5, 10, 13, 16, 27, 51).

Chemical protection studies are much used in higher vertebrates, but apparently few studies have been made of hematopoietic protection in fish. Egami (14) and Egami and Etoh (15), using cysteamine and reserpine injections prior to irradiation, noted definite protective effects.

Administration of chronic or fractionated radiation doses is much less effective than acute irradiation in inducing hematopoietic damage, even though massive doses may be accumulated (5, 10, 16). In a study by Nakatani and Foster (34), trout fed $^{90}Sr-^{90}Y$ showed definite hematopoietic as well as growth and mortality effects proportional to dose.

Some studies indicate that fish with post-irradiation hematopoietic damage are more susceptible to pathogens, e.g., *Aeromonas* or *Gyrodactylus* invasion in irradiated carp (50, 55). However, irradiated plaice are still able to develop leukocytosis in response to bacteremia (38). Depression of ^{59}Fe incorporation and of [^{3}H]thymidine uptake in irradiated kidneys of the tench (*Tinca*) are reported by Hevesy, Lockner, and Sletten (27) and Sletten, Lockner, and Hevesy (51).

Table 19.3 lists 39 articles dealing with fish hematology and indicates the nature of the articles. There is a great deal of variation in the hematopoietic organs of different fish, which is related to their phylogenetic standing and anatomical and physiological peculiarities. As new species are used for research in hematopoietic radiobiology, their peculiarities will become apparent.

Table 19.3. Articles on Fish Hematology

Author(s)	Year	Reference number	Fish	Comment
Andrew	1959	1	–	Textbook
Babudieri	1930	4	50 species	
Boyar	1962	7	*Clupea*	
Bradley	1937	8	3 species	
Catton	1951	9	5 species	
Downey	1909	12	*Polyodon*	
Eisler	1965	17	15 species	
Fey	1963	20	*Carassius*	
Fey	1965	21	Several species	Erythrocyte study
Fey	1966	22	Several species	Granulocyte study
Fey	1966	23	Several species	Other leukocytes
George	1941	25	–	Leukocyte study
Hafter	1952	26	*Astyanax*	Thymus changes with age
Hunn	1960	28	–	Bibliography
Jakowska	1956	29	11 species	Review
Jordan	1938	30	–	Review of phylogenetic levels
Kelényi & Németh	1969	31	3 species	Eosinophils
Loewenthal	1928	32	–	Leukocytes
Loewenthal	1930	33	5 species	Leukocytes
Papermaster et al.	1964	35	–	Review of phylogenetic levels
Patt and Patt	1969	36	–	Textbook
Piavis and Hiatt	1971	37	*Petromyzon*	
Rabalais	1938	39	3 species	
Reznikoff & Reznikoff	1936	41	*Mustelus*	Experimental
Romer	1962	42	–	Textbook
Sabnis & Rangnekar	1962	43	*Ophiocephalus*	
Saunders	1966-68	44–48	Many marine species	
Selye	1965	49	–	Mast cells
Slicher	1961	52	*Fundulus*	Experimental
Smith et al.	1967	53	*Lepomis*	
Weinreb	1958	56	Rainbow trout	Experimental
Werzberg	1911	59	16 species	Phylogenetic levels
Wintrobe	1933	60	–	Erythrocytes
Yoffey	1929	61	–	Spleen phylogenetic levels
Yokoyama	1960	62	*Perca*	

REFERENCES

1. Andrew, W. *Textbook of Comparative Histology*. New York, Oxford Univ. Press, 1959.
2. Aoki, K. The effects of whole body X-irradiation on the hematopoietic tissue in the goldfish, *Carassius auratus*. *Zool. Mag. 72:* 283–288. 1963.
3. Aoki, K. Effect of temperature on changes in number of hematopoietic cells and mitosis in the head kidney in the X-irradiated goldfish. *Jap. J. Ichthyol. 14:* 85–90. 1966.
4. Babudieri, B. Studi di ematologica comparata. *Haematologica 11:* 199–255. 1930.
5. Blaylock, B. G., and Mitchell, T. J. The effect of temperature on the dose response of *Gambusia affinis affinis* from two natural populations. *Radiat. Res. 40:* 503–511. 1969.
6. Bonham, K., Donaldson, L. R., Foster, R. F., Welander, A. D., and Seymour, A. H. The effect of X-ray on mortality, weight, length, and counts of erythrocytes and hematopoietic cells in fingerling chinook salmon, *Oncorhynchus tshawytscha* Walbaum. *Growth 12:* 107–121. 1948.
7. Boyar, H. C. Blood cell types and differential cell counts in Atlantic herring, *Clupea harengus harengus*. *Copeia 2:* 463–464. 1962.
8. Bradley, B. Observations on the comparative anatomy of blood. *Med. J. Aust. 2:* 992–999. 1937.
9. Catton, W. T. Blood cell formation in certain teleost fishes. *Blood J. Hematol. 6:* 39–60. 1951.
10. Cosgrove, G. E., and Blaylock, B. G. Acute and chronic irradiation effects in mosquito fish at 15° or 25°C. In *Proceedings of the Third National Symposium on Radioecology*, ed. D. J. Nelson. U. S. At. Energy Comm. (USAEC-DTIE, Oak Ridge, Tenn.), 1972.
11. Donaldson, L. R., and Foster, R. F. Effects of radiation on aquatic organisms. *Nat. Acad. Sci., Nat. Res. Counc. Publ. 551:* 96–102. 1957.
12. Downey, H. The lymphatic tissue of the kidney of *Polyodon spathula*. *Folia haematol. (Leipzig) 8:* 415–463. 1909.
13. Egami, N. Kinetics of recovery from injury after whole-body x-irradiation of the fish, *Oryzias latipes* at different temperatures. *Radiat. Res. 37:* 192–201. 1969.
14. Egami, N. Temperature effect on protective action by cysteamine against X-rays in the fish, *Oryzias latipes*. *Int. J. Radiat. Biol. 15:* 393–394. 1969.
15. Egami, N., and Etoh, H. Dose-survival time relationship and protective action of reserpine against X-irradiation in fish, *Oryzias latipes*. *Annot. zool. Jap. 35:* 188–198. 1962.
16. Egami, N., Hyodo-Taguchi, Y., and Etoh, H. Recovery from radiation effects on organized cell population in fish at different temperatures. *Proc. Int. Conf. Radiat. Biol. Cancer, Kyoto, 1966:* 117–123. 1967.
17. Eisler, R. Erythrocyte counts and hemoglobin content in nine species of marine teleosts. *Chesapeake Sci. 6:* 119–120. 1965.

18. Ellinger, F. The goldfish as a new biologic test object in experimental radiation therapy. *Radiology 35:* 563–574. 1940.
19. Engel, D. W., Angelovic, J. W., and Davis, E. M. Effects of acute gamma irradiation on the blood constituents of pinfish, *Lagodon rhomboides. Chesapeake Sci. 7:* 90–94. 1966.
20. Fey, F. Untersuchungen zur vergleichenden Hämatologie niederer Wirbeltiere. *Folia haematol. (Leipzig) 81:* 21–29. 1963.
21. Fey, F. Vergleichende Hämozytologie niederer Vertebraten. I. Erythrozyten. *Folia haematol. (Leipgiz) 84:* 271–282. 1965.
22. Fey, F. Vergleichende Hämozytologie niederer Vertebraten III. Granulozyten. *Folia haematol. (Leipzig) 86:* 1–20. 1966.
23. Fey, F. Vergleichende Hämozytologie niederer Vertebraten IV. Monozyten-Plasmozyten-Lymphozyten. *Folia haematol. (Leipzig) 86:* 133–147. 1966.
24. Finstad, J., Fänge, R., and Good, R. A. The development of lymphoid systems: Immune response and radiation sensitivity in lower vertebrates. *Advan. Exp. Med. Biol. 5:* 21–31. 1969.
25. George, W. C. Comparative hematology and the functions of the leucocytes. *Quart. Rev. Biol. 16:* 426–439. 1941.
26. Hafter, E. Histological age changes in the thymus of the teleost, *Astyanax. J. Morphol. 90:* 555–574. 1952.
27. Hevesy, G. V., Lockner, D., and Sletten, K. Über die Strahlensensibilität extramedullarer Hämopoese. *Med. Welt 10:* 455–460. 1964.
28. Hunn, J. B. The chemistry of fish blood, a bibliography. *Wildlife Dis. 7:* 1–27. 1960.
29. Jakowska, S. Morphologie et nomenclature des cellules du sang des teleosteens. *Rev. hematol. 11:* 519–539. 1956.
30. Jordan, H. E. Comparative hematology. In *Handbook of Hematology,* ed. H. Downey. New York, Hoeber, 1938.
31. Kelényi, G., and Németh, Á. Comparative histochemistry and electron microscopy of the eosinophil leucocytes of vertebrates. *Acta biol. Acad. Sci. Hung. 20:* 405–422. 1969.
32. Loewenthal, N. Étude sur les globules blancs du sang. *Arch. anat. histol. embryol. 8:* 223–306. 1928.
33. Loewenthal, N. Nouvelles observations sur les globules blancs du sang: Chez les animaux vertebrés. *Arch. anat. histol. embryol. 11:* 245–332. 1930.
34. Nakatani, R. E., and Foster, R. F. Effect of chronic feeding of Sr^{90}–Y^{90} on rainbow trout. In *Radioecology,* ed. V. Schultz, and A. W. Klement, Jr. New York, Reinhold, and AIBS, Washington, D.C., 1963.
35. Papermaster, B. W., Condie, R. M., Finstad, J., and Good, R. A. Significance of the thymus in the evolution of the lymphoid tissue and acquired immunity. In *The Thymus in Immunobiology,* ed. R. A. Good and A. E. Gabrielsen. New York, Hoeber, 1964.
36. Patt, D. I., and Patt, G. R. *Comparative Vertebrate Histology.* New York, Harper & Row, 1969.

37. Piavis, G. W., and Hiatt, J. L.   Blood cell lineage in the sea lamprey, *Petromyzon marinus. Copeia 4:* 722–728. 1971.

38. Preston, A.   Leucocytosis in response to bacteraemia as a feature of the acute radiation syndrome in the plaice. *Nature (London) 183:* 832–833. 1959.

39. Rabalais, R.   Observations on the blood of certain reptiles, pisces, mollusca, and one amphibian of the Grand Isle region. *Proc. Acad. Sci. 4:* 142–148. 1938.

40. Ray, D. L.   Effects of ionizing radiation on the blood count in the stone roller. *J. Tenn. Acad. Sci. 45:* 25. 1970.

41. Reznikoff, P., and Reznikoff, D. G.   Hematological studies in dogfish (*Mustelus canis*). *Biol. Bull. (Woods Hole) 66:* 115–123. 1936.

42. Romer, A. S.   *The Vertebrate Body.* Philadelphia, Saunders, 1962.

43. Sabnis, P. B., and Rangnekar, P. V.   Blood cell function in the freshwater teleost, *Ophiocephalus punctatus* (Bloch). *J. Anim. Morphol. Physiol. 9:* 124–130. 1962.

44. Saunders, D. C.   Differential blood cell counts of 121 species of marine fishes of Puerto Rico. *Trans. Amer. Microsc. Soc. 85:* 427–449. 1966.

45. Saunders, D. C.   Elasmobranch blood cells. *Copeia 2:* 348–351. 1966.

46. Saunders, D. C.   Neutrophils and Arneth counts from some Red Sea fishes. *Copeia 3:* 681–683. 1967.

47. Saunders, D. C.   Differential blood counts of 50 species of fishes from the Red Sea. *Copeia 3:* 491–498. 1968.

48. Saunders, D. C.   Variations in thrombocytes and small lymphocytes found in the circulating blood of marine fishes. *Trans. Amer. Microsc. Soc. 87:* 39–43. 1968.

49. Selye, H.   Comparative anatomy, chap. 5. In *The Mast Cells.* Washington, D.C., Butterworth, 1965.

50. Shechmeister, I. L., Watson, L. J., Cole, V. W., and Jackson, L. L.   The effect of X-irradiation on goldfish. I. The effect of X-irradiation on survival and susceptibility of the goldfish, *Carassius auratus* to infection by *Aeromonas salmonicida* and *Gyrodactylus* spp. *Radiat. Res. 16:* 89–97. 1962.

51. Sletten, K., Lockner, D., and Hevesy, G.   Radiosensitivity of haemopoiesis in fish. I. Studies at 18°C. *Int. J. Radiat. Biol. 8:* 317–328. 1964.

52. Slicher, A. M.   Endocrinological and hematological studies in *Fundulus heteroclitus* (Linn.). *Bull. Bingham Oceanogr. Collect., Yale Univ. 17:* 3–54. 1961.

53. Smith, A. M., Potter, M., and Merchant, E. B.   Antibody-forming cells in the pronephros of the teleost. *J. Immunol. 99:* 876–882. 1967.

54. Ulrikson, G. U.   Use and effects of cobalt-60 for sterilization of bluegills (*Lepomis macrochirus*). Ph.D. thesis, Univ. Michigan, Ann Arbor, Mich., 1969.

55. Watson, L. J., Shechmeister, I. L., and Jackson, L. L.   The effect of X-irradiation on goldfish. II. The effect of total-body X-irradiation on the hematology of *Carassius auratus. Physiol. Zool. 36:* 370–382. 1963.

56. Weinreb, E. L.   Studies on the histology and histopathology of the rainbow trout, *Salmo gairdneri irideus.* I. Hematology under normal and experi-

mental conditions of inflammation. *Zoologica (New York) 43:* 145–149.
1958.

57. Welander, A. D., Donaldson, L. R., Foster, R. F., Bonham, K., and Seymour,
A. H.   The effects of roentgen rays on the embryos and larvae of the chinook
salmon. *Growth 12:* 203–242. 1948.
58. Welander, A. D., Donaldson, L. R., Foster, R. F., Bonham, K., Seymour,
A. H., and Lowman, F. G.   The effects of roentgen rays on adult rainbow
trout. Rep. Univ. Wash. Appl. Fish. Lab. *17.* 1949.
59. Werzberg, A.   Studien zur vergleichenden Hämozytologie einiger poikilo-
thermer Vertebraten. *Folia haematol. (Leipzig) 11:* 17–218. 1911.
60. Wintrobe, M. M.   Variations in the size and hemoglobin content of erythrocytes in the blood of various vertebrates. *Folia haematol. (Leipzig) 51:*
32–49. 1933.
61. Yoffey, J. A.   A contribution to the study of the comparative histology and
physiology of the spleen, with reference chiefly to its cellular constituents.
I. In fishes. *J. Anat. 63:* 314–344, 1929.
62. Yokoyama, H. O.   Studies on the origin, development, and seasonal variations in the blood cells of the perch, *Perca flavescens. Wildlife Dis. 6:* 1–103.
1960.

DISCUSSION OF RADIATION-INDUCED HEMATOPOIETIC LESIONS IN FISH

Question: You mentioned that there had been a number of radio-contaminated
ponds around the Oak Ridge area. Have you examined the fish from these contaminated ponds? Have you seen similar hematopoietic inhibition in those fish?

G. E. Cosgrove: Originally we examined fish from those areas. We found that
most of the fish that were exposed to low levels of radiation did not develop hematopoietic damage. They had sterility or interference with breeding, but rather
massive doses of radiation accumulated at the slow rate found in a naturally contaminated pond didn't result in hematopoietic damage. Blaylock gave some of
these fish chronic radiation exposures in the laboratory, and again even massive
doses of 6000 to 8000 rads accumulated over a long enough period did not hurt
the kidney hematopoietic tissue. This will be in the article in the Proceedings of
the Third National Radioecology Symposium, which is due to be released soon.

Question: I wondered if hormone treatment was administered to any fish
prior to radiation to see if it reduced the problems?

G. E. Cosgrove: We haven't modified any experimental conditions except
temperature. We found that fish held at 15° had less hematopoietic damage than
those held at 25°C.

20

The Effects of Temperature on
Diseases and Their Histopathological
Manifestations in Fish

RONALD J. ROBERTS

The evolution of a constant body temperature by the species now recognized as
homeotherms, the birds and the mammals, has removed one of the major environmental factors in the epizootiology of their infectious diseases. The germ theory
of disease, such an advance on the "evil vapors" thought to be responsible for the
plagues of the Middle Ages, is now recognized to be an oversimplification, and un-
acceptable even for mammals (8), since it fails to take account of the ubiquity of
potential pathogens in the environment and the variations in susceptibility of
hosts.

This variability of susceptibility is greatly enhanced in the lower vertebrates,
the poikilotherms or ectotherms, whose body temperature is a reflection of the
ambient temperature of their environment. Their interactions with their microorganisms is dominated by the temperature at which these episodes take place
and are almost always modified by changes in that temperature.

Alterations in temperature may enhance or retard the rate of multiplication of
microorganisms, increase or decrease the amount of dissolved oxygen in the water,
raise or lower the hosts' metabolic rate with consequent changes in excreted metabolites in the water, or, most important, it may alter the rate at which the bodies'
defensive mechanisms act and antibody formation takes place.

The teleost in normal health has a balance, at a given temperature, with the po-

477

tential pathogens in its environment. When changes occur in ambient temperature it is forced to reorient its defensive mechanisms to deal with the new situation.

TEMPERATURE EFFECTS ON BACTERIAL DISEASES

Teleosts are among the most successfully adapted groups of animals, with climatic adaptation allowing them as a group to inhabit waters ranging in temperature from $-2°C$ around the polar ice caps to maxima in excess of $35°C$ in the equatorial regions. However, each species has an optimum range above and below which it cannot survive. As the temperature approaches the upper limits of this range bacteria which are normally nonpathogenic are enabled to become so. This pathogenicity may be due to the microorganisms being able to multiply more quickly at these temperatures or to the hosts' defenses being lowered by the temperature stress. Usually it is a combination of both.

One of the best examples of this interrelationship is the condition of Pacific salmonids known as columnaris disease (12). The optimum growth temperature for the organism *Chondrococcus columnaris* is $25°$ to $32°C$ (14). At $20°C$ the organism can still multiply sufficiently rapidly to invade the tissues of salmon, which at this temperature are becoming heat-stressed, although in the absence of *C. columnaris* the fish are still able to survive.

This relationship between high temperature stress and bacterial invasion is also exemplified in Scottish experience with marine fish culture in heated power-station effluents (R. J. Roberts and C. D. Anderson, unpublished observations). Plaice (*Pleuronectes platessa*) and other flatfish can be grown rapidly to market size at temperatures of $12°$ to $16°C$, but above that temperature there occurs invasion by *Vibrio* spp. These produce a characteristic "red mouth and eye" lesion which spreads, especially if the temperature rises further, to all of the stock. This infection can be kept in check by feeding oxytetracycline at therapeutic levels but this is not to be recommended as a standard procedure. Presumably the antibiotic tips the balance of the host-parasite reaction back in favor of the host.

Vibriosis and columnaris are part of a group of infections caused by gram-negative bacilli whose pathogeneses are often closely related to temperature. Others include furunculosis (*Aeromonas salmonicida*), aeromoniasis (*A. liquefaciens* and *punctata* group), and pseudomoniasis (*Pseudomonas fluorescens*). G. W. Klontz (personal communication) has shown that there are several pathogenic strains of *A. salmonicida* capable of causing furunculosis and that they have different ranges of optimum pathogenicity, most being in the range $12°$ to $20°C$. One strain is particularly pathogenic between $5°$ and $7°C$. There are fewer gram-positive organisms responsible for fish diseases, but epizootics of bacterial kidney disease, also known as Dee disease, caused by *Corynebacterium* spp. in adult salmon (*Salmo salar*), have been shown by Smith (30) to be closely correlated with environmental temperature. There was also a relationship between temperature and pathological findings. At low temperatures ($<9°C$) lesions consisted mainly of the development of pseudo-diphtheritic membranes over the abdominal viscera, whereas at higher temperatures the lesions were generally necrotizing foci within parenchymatous tissues. In agreement with the findings of Wolf and Dunbar (35) she found that at low temperatures losses were minimal but in those years when early summer temperatures rose rapidly epizootics of fatal disease occurred readily.

Saprolegniasis of salmonid fish, usually caused by an aquatic fungus, *Saprolegnia parasitica*, has an inverse correlation with temperature. *Saprolegnia* zoospores are more numerous at cold water temperatures (34), and many pathogenic strains have a sexual stage which occurs at low temperature (L. G. Willoughby, personal communication). Salmon with skin lesions such as those of ulcerative dermal necrosis (UDN) are therefore very vulnerable to *Saprolegnia* infection in winter when skin lesions also heal more slowly (25).

TEMPERATURE AND PARASITIC DISEASES

The relationship between degree of skin parasitism and temperature has been thoroughly explored both in the Soviet Union (7) and the United States (24) and strong correlations between optimum temperature for multiplication of parasites and outbreaks of disease have been defined. Thus *Chilodonella cyprini*, whose optimum temperature is 5° to 10°C, is not a problem in Russian carp farms in summer but appears when temperatures are falling in autumn. Similarly ichthyophthiriasis is not normally of significance in Scottish trout farms, where temperatures rarely if ever approach that parasite's optimum of 21° to 24°C (C. Sommerville, personal communication), but on similar farms in southern England, where such temperatures are more likely, it can be responsible for regular summer mortality (P. Yonge, personal communication). It never occurs in Britain with such severity as in the channel catfish (*Ictalurus punctatus*) and golden shiner (*Notemigonus crysoleucas*) farms of the subtropical southern states of the United States; there Meyer (24) described it as occurring regularly over nine months of the year.

VIRAL DISEASES AND TEMPERATURE

Developments in fish virus research have been considerable since the isolation of infectious pancreatic necrosis (IPN) virus of salmonids by Wolf and co-workers in 1960. Now there are three highly significant viruses recognized in salmonid culture: IPN virus, IHN virus (3), and VHS virus (9), a major pathogenic virus from catfish culture (channel catfish virus, CCV), and at least one from extensive carp culture (*Rhabdovirus carpei*) (10). Isolation of these agents in tissue culture is well documented (36) and each requires specific conditions of temperature for optimum demonstration of cytopathogenic effects. However, *in vivo* they often require different temperature ranges for optimum utilization of the protein synthetic pathways of host cells in order to produce their own specific nucleic acids and capsid proteins. Viral hemorrhagic septicemia virus, which is an endotheliotropic rhabdovirus specifically attacking older trout and therefore of considerable economic importance, is generally restricted in its pathological effects to temperatures below 8°C (15).

Attempts to control IHN virus, another rhabdovirus, by elevating water temperature above the optimum for the virus have shown some success (1). It was found that when the water temperature of sockeye salmon fingerlings (*Oncorhynchus nerka*) was raised to 18°C (optimum for the disease organisms being 15°C) within 24 hours of infection and held there for four to six days the disease did not recur unless the fish were reinfected later. However, this subsequent susceptibility, coupled with the risk of producing a carrier state, precludes the routine use of this therapy.

Infectious pancreatic necrosis virus, which is currently classified as a reovirus (20), can be controlled to some extent by lowering environmental temperature to below 5°C (13). This suggests the possibility that despite their negative effects on growth rates the cold water temperatures of Canada and Northern Europe may be beneficial in terms of disease management.

TEMPERATURE AND THE DEFENSE MECHANISMS OF THE TELEOST

The Skin

The outermost defense of the teleost fish is the nonkeratinized mucigenic epithelium. Abrasions and wounds constitute the major route of infection of many of the pathogenic bacteria and fungi, including vibriosis (4), furunculosis (20), Dee disease (30), and saprolegniasis (26). This emphasizes the evolutionary significance of rapid healing of such wounds, and Roberts and his co-workers (27, 28) have investigated the effects of temperature on the rate of healing of natural and surgically inflicted ulcers in salmon (*S. salar*) and plaice (*P. platessa*). The results of these investigations showed considerable differences between the rates of healing and density of the connective tissue in such wounds. At 4°C healing was very slow with little cellular inflammatory response below the epidermis. Although epithelial healing was slow it was still relatively rapid compared with that of the underlying connective tissue. The latter had very little fibrosis, as if the major requirement, integumental integrity, was receiving priority. At 14°C there was rapid epithelialization and fibrosis (Fig. 20.1). These findings would appear

---

Figs. 20.1A, B. Surgical wound in plaice skin after 30 days. (A) At 4°C ambient temperature; (B) at 14°C ambient temperature. Note the irregular surface of the epithelium at the lower temperature, and the complete lack of orderly repair of the stratum reticulare of the dermis compared with the higher temperature. Hematoxylin and eosin (H&E); ×250.

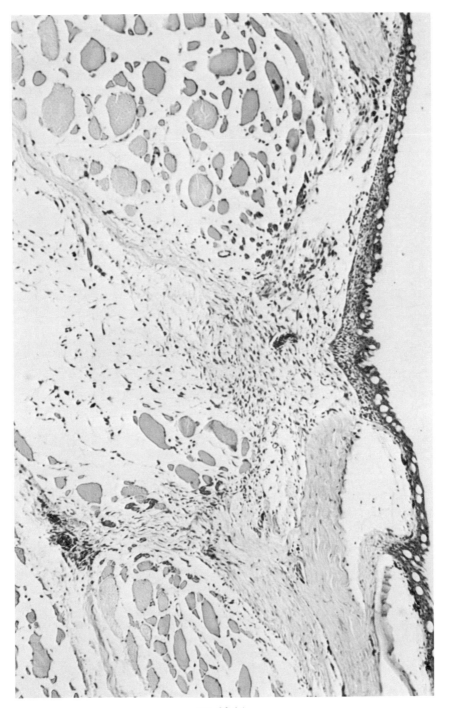

Fig. 20.1A.

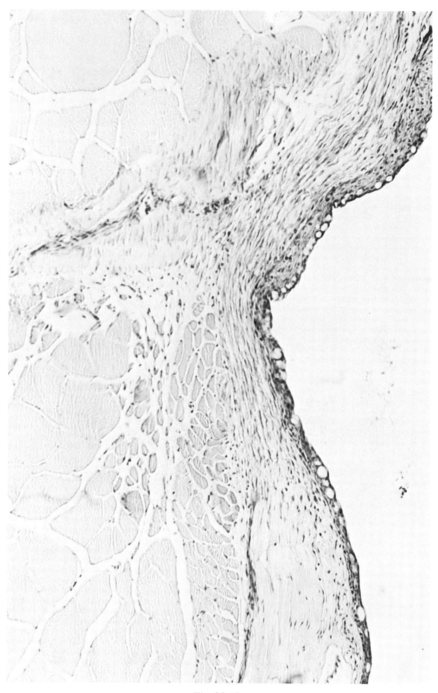

Fig. 20.1B.

to have ecological significance in so far as the multiplication of most pathogens increases greatly over the range 4° to 14°C. At the low temperature relatively slow healing rates are not of major significance since most bacteria cannot multiply sufficiently rapidly to take advantage of the breach, whereas at higher temperatures it is of prime importance for the host to seal up the lesion as quickly as possible and prevent access by the potentially rapidly-growing microorganism.

There are a great many "cold water" myxobacterial diseases of teleost skin. Anderson and Conroy (4) have summarized these well as regards the properties of the bacteria, but relatively little is known of their pathogenesis. Wolke (personal communication) and Roberts and Mace (unpublished observations) have studied the histopathology of these conditions in salmonids and plaice (*P. platessa*) and the initial lesion in all cases is an extreme hyperplasia of malphigian cells of the epidermis of the extremities, the fins, and the caudal peduncle. Eventually the hyperplastic epidermis sloughs and is invaded by myxobacteria. Whether the myxobacteria play a part in the earlier stages is not known, but the organisms are not obvious histologically. A similar, but more localized, hyperplastic lesion occurs at the site of invasion by cercariae of *Cryptocotyle lingua* when the host is held at low temperatures (21). It is possible that in all of these "cold water" hyperplasias the initial lesion is traumatic (Fig. 20.2).

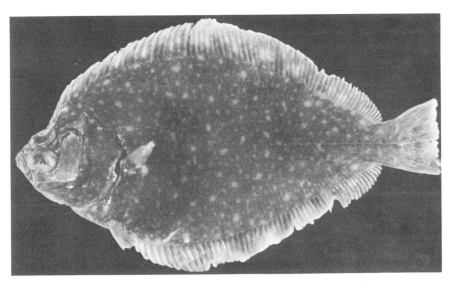

Fig. 20.2A. Plaice having earliest observed signs, swelling of fin ray epithelium. Temperature 4°C. ×1.50.

Figs. 20.2A–C. Epithelial hyperplasia associated with cold temperatures in cultured plaice.

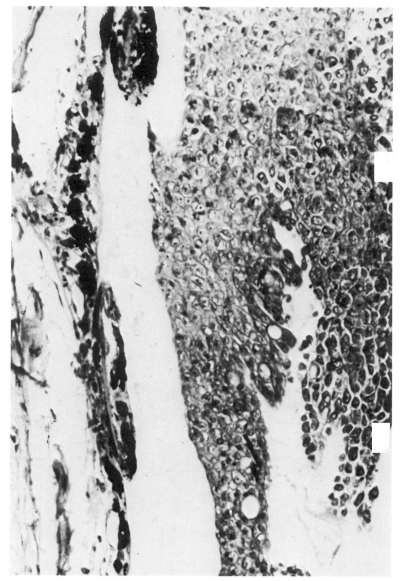

Fig. 20.2B. Later stage with hyperplastic epithelium about to slough from dermis, where melanophores are swollen and fragmented. H&E; ×300.

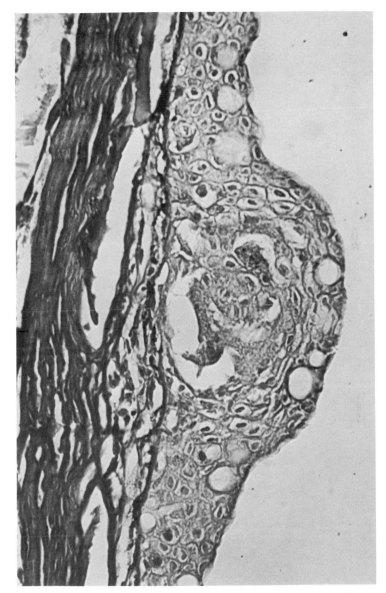

Fig. 20.2C. Hyperplasia at site of entry of *Cryptocotyle lingua* cercariae at 5°C. Masson; X350.

The Inflammatory Response within Tissue

The effect of temperature on the inflammatory response of rainbow trout (*S. gairdneri*) tissues to *staphylococci,* Freund's adjuvant, and burning, was investigated by Finn and Nielsen (11). They found that the effect of low temperature was to delay the appearance and development of phenomena such as macrophage responses and fibroplasia so that the net effect was a halving of this activity for a drop of temperature of 10°C. Roberts et al. (28) confirmed these findings in their studies on the development of the tagging lesion in salmon parr (*S. salar*) held at different temperatures (Fig. 20.3). One exception to these findings, however, was that the latter workers observed sarcoplasmic budding and basophilic myodegeneration, albeit only occasionally, in those fish held at 14°C, whereas Finn and Nielsen's series did not show this feature. Mawdesley-Thomas and Bucke (22) also showed well-substantiated evidence of fibrillar regeneration in goldfish (*Carassius auratus*) held at 19°C, although unfortunately they did not have fish held at lower temperatures for comparison. All agreed, however, that the major reparative effect is not regeneration of muscle, but its replacement with fibrous granulation tissue.

The rate of the inflammatory response to encystment of metacercariae of digenetic parasites has been studied by Hoffman and Putz (18) and by McQueen et al. (21). Hoffman and Putz studied the metacercariae of the digenean *Uvulifer ambloplitus,* a parasite of centrarchid fish. Their experiments in the bluegill sunfish (*Lepomis macrochirus*) showed that there was complete inhibition of cellular response at 13°C, but that development at 24°C was twice as rapid as at 21°C. McQueen et al. working with wild juvenile plaice (*P. platessa*) also used a digenean which stimulates a host reaction involving melanocytes, *C. lingua.* Their experiments, in a temperate marine fish, were carried out in the range 5° to 14°C, but although the nine-degree differential more than halved the rate of development of the host capsule, a response qualitatively similar to that at 14°C was eventually obtained at 5°C.

The Fixed Macrophage System

The internal defensive system, the fixed macrophages of the reticulo-endothelial system, is as yet poorly defined in fish. Ferguson, Roberts, and Stuart (unpublished) have carried out preliminary vital staining experiments to define the system at various temperatures in higher and lower teleosts, and these studies suggest that the activity of this protective system is also inhibited at lower temperatures. Further studies are in progress to define the rate of depression and ascertain that it applies equally to the uptake of pathogens.

Circulating Antibodies

The effect of temperature on antibody production in poikilothermic animals has been investigated extensively by a number of workers and is reviewed by

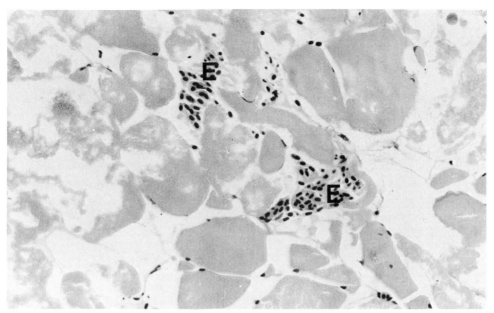

Fig. 20.3A. Muscle with only myofibrillar degeneration and hemorrhage (E) at 4°C. H&E; ×700.

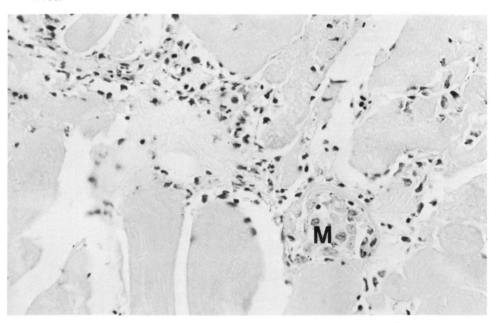

Fig. 20.3B. Myophagia (M) and polymorph reaction in similar situation at 12°C. H&E; ×700.

Figs. 20.3A–D. Histological response to salmon tagging at different temperatures. M = myophagic cells; E = erythrocytes; F = fibrous granulation tissue.

487

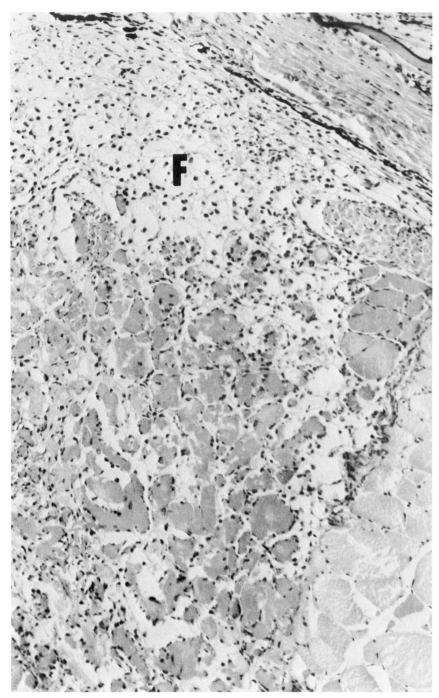

Fig. 20.3C. Poorly developed fibrous granulation tissue (F) around tagging wound after 31 days at 4°C. H&E; ×500.

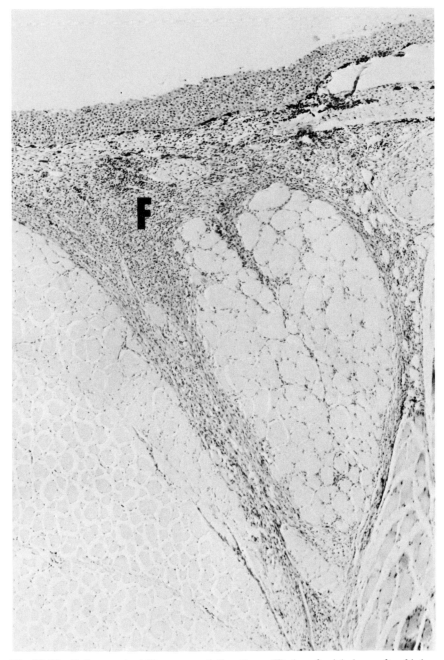

Fig. 20.3D. Fully organized fibrous granulation tissue (F) along fascial planes after 31 days at 12°C. H&E; ×250.

489

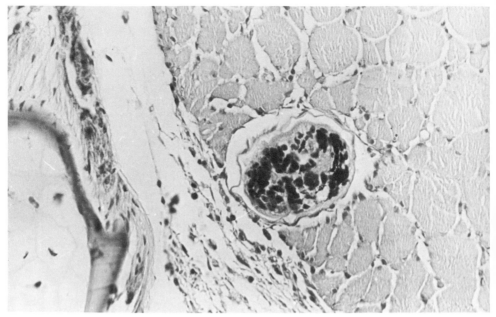

Fig. 20.4A.

Figs. 20.4A, B. Response to metacercariae of *Cryptocotyle lingua* within muscle of young plaice. (A) No host capsule and poorly developed parasite cyst at 5°C, 28 days post-infection. H&E; ×425. (B) Development of host response consisting of a cellular zone and fibrous capsule with melanocytes at 14°C, 28 days post-infection. PAS; ×500.

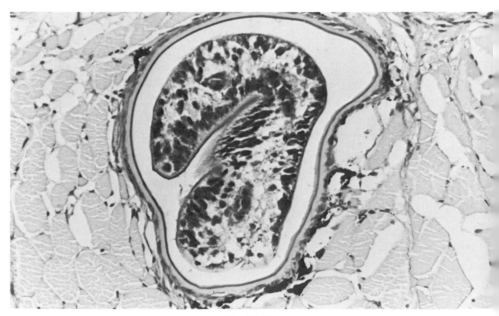

Fig. 20.4B.

490

Hildemann (17) and Snieszko (31). It is generally agreed that the cold-blooded vertebrate's ability to produce an immune response is closely related to the temperature at which it is held. Temperatures in excess of 20°C are generally necessary to produce a response in any way comparable, in its rate of production, with that of mammals. The classic work of Metchnikoff (23), subsequently confirmed by Evans and Cowles (9), showed that reptiles require even higher temperatures to allow comparable reactions.

Antibodies are produced at low temperatures, but unless adjuvants are used the rate is so slow that many months may elapse before measurable levels are obtained. It would appear that, at low temperatures, circulating antibody plays a relatively insignificant part in maintaining the balance between teleost host and pathogen.

Interferons

Since viruses are incapable of independent replication, the mechanism by which temperature controls the severity of viral diseases of fish must be intimately related to the temperature effect on host cells. Cell metabolism is slower at lower temperatures so it might be expected that as temperature and host metabolic rate increased, so would viral numbers. However in VHS, where the optimum temperature for disease is very low, it must be assumed that temperature-dependent host defense mechanisms, such as interferon, which controls virion maturation, must be coming into action at higher temperatures. Gravell and Malsberger (16) have provided some evidence that fish cells can produce an interferon-like substance, but there are no details of the relationship between temperature and its production.

Circulating Leukocytes

Evidence of the effect of temperature change on the *in vivo* phagocytic ability of fish leukocytes is lacking, although Yokoyama (37) studied the seasonal changes in perch blood, which may have been related to hormonal or temperature effects.

The best example, albeit from an invertebrate poikilotherm, of the effect of temperature on the balance between blood-borne defenses and the rate of pathogen multiplication is the detailed study by Cornick, Stewart, and co-workers (6, 32, 33) on Gaffkaemia of lobsters (*Homarus americanus*). This is a highly fatal disease of lobsters, which can be caused by infections with as few as five microorganisms. Once the integument has been breached the defensive mechanisms are bactericidal and agglutinating serum components and phagocytic hemocytes. The mean time to death is directly related to temperature and varies from 2 days at 20°C, when massive bacterial infection is possible due to rapid multiplication of the organism *Gaffkya homari,* to 172 days at 3°C.

EPILOGUE

The effects of temperature are important to all aspects of the physiology of the teleosts, and control the rate of feeding, the ability to escape from predators, oxygen requirements, and many other factors. The strategic control by temperature of the balance in the continuous and closely meshed power struggle between the teleost and its hostile environmental pathogens is one of the most significant factors in its ectothermic existence.

REFERENCES

1. Amend, D. F.   Control of infectious hematopoietic necrosis virus disease by elevating the water temperature. *J. Fish. Res. Board Can. 27:* 265–270. 1970.

2. Amend, D. F.   Myxobacterial infections of salmonids: Prevention and treatment. In *A Symposium on Diseases of Fishes and Shellfishes,* ed. S. F. Snieszko. Amer. Fish. Soc., Spec. Publ. No. 5. Washington, D.C., 1970.

3. Amend, D. F., Yasutake, W. T., and Mead, R. W.   A hematopoietic virus disease of rainbow trout and sockeye salmon. *Trans. Amer. Fish. Soc. 98:* 796–804. 1969.

4. Anderson, J. I. W., and Conroy, D. A.   The pathogenic myxobacteria, with special reference to fish diseases. *J. Appl. Bacteriol. 32:* 30–39. 1969.

5. Anderson, J. I. W., and Conroy, D. A.   Vibrio disease in marine fishes, pp. 266–272. In *A Symposium on Diseases of Fishes and Shellfishes,* ed. S. F. Snieszko. Amer. Fish. Soc., Spec. Publ. No. 5. Washington, D.C., 1970.

6. Cornick, J. W., and Stewart, J. E.   Interaction of the pathogen *Gaffkya homari* with natural defense mechanisms of *Homarus americanus. J. Fish. Res. Board Can. 25:* 695–708. 1968.

7. Dogiel, V. A., Petrushevskii, G. K., and Polyanski, Y. I.   *Parasitology of Fishes,* transl. Z. Kabata. Jersey City, T.F.H. Publications, 1958.

8. Dubos, R. J.   Second thoughts on the germ theory. *Sci. Amer. 192:* 31–35. 1954.

9. Evans, E. E., and Cowles, R. B.   Effect of temperature on antibody synthesis in the reptile *Dipsosaurus dorsalis. Proc. Soc. Exp. Biol. Med. 101:* 482–483. 1959.

10. Fijan, N.   Viral diseases of carp. *Symp. Zool. Soc. London 30:* 39–51. 1972.

11. Finn, J. P., and Nielson, N. O.   The effect of temperature variation on the inflammatory response of rainbow trout. *J. Pathol. 105:* 257–268. 1971.

12. Fish, F. F., and Rucker, R. R.   Columnaris as a disease of coldwater fishes. *Trans. Amer. Fish. Soc. 73:* 32–36. 1943.

13. Frantsi, C., and Savan, M.   Infectious pancreatic necrosis virus: Temperature and age factors in mortality. *J. Wildlife Dis. 7:* 249–255. 1971.

14. Garnjobst, L.   *Cytophaga columnaris* (Davis) in pure culture: A myxobacterium pathogenic to fish. *J. Bacteriol. 49:* 113–128. 1945.

15. Ghittino, P.   Review of viral hemorrhagic septicemia. Paper presented to

E.I.F.A.C. *Symposium on Major Communicable Diseases of Fish*. Amsterdam, 1972.

16. Gravell, M., and Malsberger, R. G.   A permanent cell line from the fathead minnow (*Pimephales promelas*). *Ann. N. Y. Acad. Sci. 126:* 555-565. 1965.

17. Hildemann, W. H.   Immunogenetic studies of poikilothermic animals. *Amer. Natur. 46:* 195-204. 1962.

18. Hoffman, G. L., and Putz, R. E.   The black-spot (*Uvulifer ambloplitis:* Trem+toda: Strigeoidea) of centrarchid fishes. *Trans. Amer. Fish. Soc. 94:* 143-151. 1965.

19. Jensen, M. H.   Research on the virus of Egtved disease. *Ann. N. Y. Acad. Sci. 126:* 422-426. 1965.

20. McCraw, B. M.   Furunculosis of fish. *U. S. Fish Wildlife Serv., Spec. Sci. Rep., Fish. 84.* 1952.

21. McQueen, A., MacKenzie, K., Roberts, R. J., and Young, H.   Studies on the skin of plaice (*Pleuronectes platessa*). III. The effects of temperature on the inflammatory response to the metacercariae of *Cryptocotyle lingua* (Digenea: Heterophyidae). *J. Fish. Biol. 5:* 241-247. 1973.

22. Mawdesley-Thomas, L. E., and Bucke, D.   Tissue repair in a poikilothermic vertebrate: *Carassius auratus*. A preliminary study. *J. Fish Biol. 5:* 201-210. 1973.

23. Metchnikoff, E.   *L'Immunité dans les maladies infectieuses,* pp. 346-363. Paris, Masson, 1904.

24. Meyer, F. P.   Seasonal influence on the fluctuation of disease on fish farms. In *A Symposium on Diseases of Fishes and Shellfishes,* ed. S. F. Snieszko. Amer. Fish. Soc., Spec. Publ. No. 5. Washington, D.C., 1970.

25. Roberts, R. J.   Ulcerative dermal necrosis (UDN) of salmon (*Salmo salar*). *Symp. Zool. Soc. London 30:* 53-88. 1972.

26. Roberts, R. J., Shearer, W. M., Munro, A. L. S., and Elson, K. G. R.   Studies on ulcerative dermal necrosis of salmonids. II. The sequential pathology of the lesions. *J. Fish Biol. 2:* 373-378. 1970.

27. Roberts, R. J., Ball, H. J., Munro, A. L. S., and Shearer, W. M.   Studies on ulcerative dermal necrosis of salmonids. III. The healing process in fish maintained under experimental conditions. *J. Fish Biol. 3:* 221-224. 1971.

28. Roberts, R. J., McQueen, A., Shearer, W. M., and Young, H.   The histopathology of salmon tagging. I. The tagging lesion in newly tagged parr. *J. Fish Biol. 5:* 407-420. 1973.

29. Scherrer, R.   Review of infectious pancreatic necrosis. Paper presented to E.I.F.A.C. *Symposium on Major Communicable Diseases of Fish.* Amsterdam, 1972.

30. Smith, I. W.   The occurrence and pathology of the Dee disease. *Scot. Dep. Agr. Fish., Freshwater Salmon Fish. Res. Rep. 34:* 3-10. 1964.

31. Snieszko, S. F.   Immunization of fishes—a review. *J. Wildlife Dis. 6:* 24-30. 1970.

32. Stewart, J. E., Cornick, J. W., and Zwicker, B. M.   Influence of temperature on Gaffkaemia, a bacterial disease of the lobster *Homarus americanus*. *J. Fish. Res. Board Can. 26:* 2503-2510. 1969.

33. Stewart, J. E., Dockrill, A., and Cornick, J. W.   Effectiveness of the integument and gastric fluid as barriers against transmission of *Gaffkya homari* to the lobster *Homarus americanus J. Fish. Res. Board Can. 26:* 1–14. 1969.
34. Waterhouse, G. H.   Some water moulds of the Hogsmill River collected from 1937–39. *Trans. Brit. Mycol. Soc. 25:* 3-5–325. 1942.
35. Wolf, K., and Dunbar, C. E.   Methods of infecting trout with kidney disease and some effects of temperature on experimental infections. *U. S. Fish Wildlife Serv., Spec. Sci. Rep. Fish. 286:* 3–8. 1959.
36. Wolf, K., and Quimby, M. C.   Fish cell and tissue culture, pp. 253–301. In *Fish Physiology,* ed. W. S. Hoar and D. J. Randall, vol. 3. New York and London, Academic Press, 1969–70.
37. Yokoyama, H. O.   Ph.D. thesis. Quoted by J. P. Finn in *Vet. Bull. (U.K.) 40:* 873–886. 1970.

DISCUSSION OF THE EFFECTS OF TEMPERATURE ON DISEASES AND THEIR HISTOPATHOLOGICAL MANIFESTATIONS IN FISH

L. E. Mawdesley-Thomas: I was very interested, Dr. Roberts, to see these various experiments that you've carried out. I noted that the response was not primarily neutrophilic. We were looking primarily at something that I would call a more chronic response. Have you done any experiments where you have produced an "acute" response rather than a chronic one, as we so often see in the homeothermic counterpart?

R. J. Roberts: The function of the neutrophil leukocyte in fish I wouldn't even like to speculate about, having little experience with fish hematology. We do see neutrophils in salmon-tagging lesions. I can't say I've seen them playing a tremendous part in anything else, but I think they do more than just come out and watch the ball game. At low temperatures we don't see them until about 7 days and they stay until 21 days. At high temperatures we get them within 1 day and they stay for about 4 days, but they never seem to be particularly active or in large numbers and I certainly don't consider them a major factor in the histological response, certainly not to traumatic lesions. I have formed a similar impression from routine diagnostic experience. I haven't seen anything like the response in bacterial diseases that one would expect in many such infections in higher animals.

M. M. Sigel: I would like to comment about effective temperature in climates which I consider subtropical, let's say, when the difference may be between 20°C in the winter time and 30°C in the summer. I agree with you that lower temperature slows down metabolic processes. We've shown this in terms of reduced phagocytosis or reduced clearance of antigen. We've also shown it in terms of inhibition of antibody production but in this case it is only inhibition of the primary response, because once the fish has been primed initially, the secondary response does take place quite readily even when the temperature is lowered. I would also like to point out that many of our fishes have cold agglutinins, in fact the predominant antibody in the gar and in several other fishes is a cold antibody which has its optimal reactivity at 4°C. Whether this is by design or accident, I don't know, but certainly these fishes have an advantage at lower temperatures. So things were very simple until it was discovered that in the same fishes the secretory mucus antibody is not a cold agglutinin. It doesn't make any sense at all, because the mucus should be really endowed with a special capacity to withstand or react at lower temperatures, yet we find that the serum antibody does react optimally at, say 15°C, whereas the mucus antibody has an optimum at higher temperature. So I would like to caution that we cannot extrapolate in all directions from England, Scotland, Ireland, and Miami. We have to consider these all individually; perhaps some phenomena, some responses and part of some cells may be enhanced by low temperature, others by high temperatures.

R. J. Roberts: I would certainly like to agree with this. I don't know whether it was Dr. Sigel who said that there are something like 2000-odd species of teleost that we know of. The scope for variation is wide, to say the least; I would agree with you in the production of a mucus antibody which is different from serum antibody. Our experience is in plaice. We don't know how the antibody gets to the mucus but they do have a most peculiar epithelial cell which may be involved. It looks like a secretory cell but certainly does not have much endoplasmic reticulum.

T. G. Bell: We have been very interested in wound healing in salmon, and particularly steelhead trout because of the obvious benefits that we might derive in comparing these to mammalian systems, particularly with regard to chromatophores, melanophores, etc. You make allusion to the fact that when fibroblastic proliferation occurred you saw some migration of pigment cells. I would like to ask you two questions in this regard. How far into the tissue, depending of course on the depth of the wound and the depth of proliferation of the connective tissue, have you seen pigment cell migration? The second question is, have you ever been able to wound, or injure by infection or whatever means you might use, such that six to eight months later you still see an area of altered pigmentation?

R. J. Roberts: First question—I am going to talk about melanin cells later. Second, we have seen returning salmon, salmon that have been in Greenland for two years, with tag lesions, and in looking at these, the subepithelial connective tissue seems to be a replacement fibrosis. The first change is that there are tremendous numbers of these eosinophil granule cells which I tend to agree with Dr. Ashley are almost certainly mast cells. They are very similar to the ones you get in the submucosa of the fishes' gut. Tremendous numbers of these cells occur. We have seen these in salmon at sea. I have never seen them in healing wounds in salmon in fresh water. The other feature is the large numbers of melanocytes. I don't call them melanophores. The melanophore is a cell which is directly affecting pigmentation of the fish, and these things aren't, so I think that probably melanocytes is the term. In my book there are types of melanin-containing cells other than melanophores, and one of them is the melanin-containing macrophage and the other one is a melanosome-containing, melanin-producing, cell. In chronic skin lesions we frequently see melanin-containing melanophores. But certainly we get numerous melanocytes into the depths of the tissue and they are there three years later.

P. P. Yevich: I just want to make a few comments, a word of caution. Our experience has been mostly with the invertebrates and fishes from power plant environments where, as the temperature goes up above 27°C, millions and millions will all die at one time. We did studies in the laboratory, taking the temperature all the way from 20°C and taking it up to 27°C, and we found out that the first response is what we would call the typical amebacytic response from what would be the blood cells of these animals. However, when one goes into the field one doesn't get the same type of response because of fluctuating temperatures. What happens in the field is one thing and what is going to happen in the laboratory may be another thing. We must be very careful in extrapolating each stress experiment in the laboratory into what is going to occur in the field.

R. J. Roberts: I certainly agree with this. What I didn't mention was that the plaice experiments, the surgical wounding and parasite-infection experiments and some other labeling experiments, were done at fixed constant temperatures. The salmon experiments, since tagging is a process which is done on a fish which is then going to go into the river, were carried out in spring, summer, and winter. So in fact this was the mean temperature, using river water, and fish impounded in the river. The variation wasn't more than two or three degrees but we did feel it important to look at this phenomenon in terms of the fish in the river.

K. Balogh: I don't know anything about wound healing in fish, but in mammals and man temperature influences the rate of wound healing. One of the factors is vascularization of the wound and there are others directly related to this, namely, vasospasm and vasodilation, all within limits depending upon temperature.

R. J. Roberts: Yes, but nevertheless, the body temperatures in these animals is not in terms of 10 degrees below normal fixed temperatures.

K. Balogh: I can't answer the question, but my impression is that it is considered among clinicians that if it is winter time it takes much longer for a wound to heal, comparable to what it takes in the summer.

R. J. Roberts: Certainly our salmon agree!

21

Lesions Associated with
Chronic Exposure to Ammonia

CHARLIE E. SMITH
and ROBERT G. PIPER

It is well documented that ammonia is toxic to teleost fishes (1, 3, 9, 17, 27). Wuhrmann and Woker (29) and Downing and Merkens (7) demonstrated that ammonia toxicity is determined by the amount of un-ionized ammonia (NH_3, NH_4OH) present in solution rather than the ionized form (NH_4^+). The degree of dissociation is controlled primarily by pH and temperature. Other variables such as carbon dioxide (18), dissolved oxygen tension (16, 20), and salinity (12) also affect toxicity.

Ammonia is probably one of the most common pollutants discharged into river systems (9, 16, 19). It is also present in waters and aquaria in which fish are cultured intensively (2, 5, 13).

It has been demonstrated that exposure of fish to ammonia can result in pathological changes in gill tissue (4, 5, 10, 14, 22). Flis (10) found cellular degeneration and hemorrhage in internal organs of carp exposed to lethal and sublethal ammonia concentrations. Reichenbach-Klinke (22) observed congestion in liver sinusoids and irreversible anemia in trout fry exposed to ammonia. He also found that fry were more sensitive to ammonia than larger trout.

Ammonia is the main form of nitrogen excreted by teleost fishes. Smith (23) found that ammonia accounted for 80% of the total nitrogen excreted by some freshwater fish. Burrows (5) experimentally demonstrated that concentrations of urea exceeding maximum levels encountered by chinook salmon in rearing ponds had no effect on gill epithelium. He therefore concluded that ammonia was the

497

toxic excretory product of salmonids, and not urea. He found that prolonged exposure to an ammonia concentration of 0.3 ppm for a six-week period resulted in reduced growth and decreased stamina as well as hyperplasia of gill epithelium.

Rainbow trout reared in hatcheries under crowded conditions or in reused water encounter ammonia which results from the accumulation of excretory products. Larmoyeux and Piper (15) reported that ammonia concentrations are often in excess of those reported by Burrows (5) to be detrimental to chinook salmon.

At the Bozeman, Montana, Fish Cultural Development Center, experiments were conducted to determine: (1) at what level ammonia becomes limiting for growth of rainbow trout, and (2) if degenerative tissue changes can be correlated with reduced growth and increased ammonia concentrations.

This report describes histopathological changes in tissues of trout exposed chronically to metabolic ammonia over a 12-month period.

MATERIALS AND METHODS

When fish are fed at a standard rate, ammonia production and oxygen utilization can be correlated with size and weight of fish. As long as aquarium fish loads, temperature, and water inflow are constant, ammonia levels can be closely regulated. In the spring of 1970 six 4-foot-diameter circular fiberglas tanks, each having a capacity of 188 gallons, were set up in duplicate to give metabolic ammonia concentrations of approximately 0.5, 1.0, and 1.5 ppm as total ammonia. In order to maintain these levels it was necessary to have two experimental variables: numbers of fish and water inflow. In each of tanks #1 and #2 were placed 4200 rainbow trout averaging 2.3 grams. Water flow was constant at 4.0 gpm and ammonia concentrations were approximately 0.5 ppm. Fish in tanks #1 and #2 served as controls. Tanks #3 and #4 also held 4200 trout of the same size, but water flow was only 2.0 gpm. Ammonia was estimated at 1.0 ppm. In each of tanks #5 and #6, which also received 2 gpm water inflow, were placed 6500 fingerlings weighing 2.3 grams each. The ammonia level for tanks #5 and #6 was estimated to be 1.5 ppm.

Fish were fed a standard pelleted trout ration (6) and fish load was determined by using a loading factor (21). Factors of 2, 4, and 6 based on fish length were used in tanks #1 and #2, #3 and #4, and #5 and #6, respectively. According to this method, factor × length of fish × gallon per minute inflow = desired pounds of fish. Fish were weighed biweekly and excess fish were removed to maintain the desired size and weight. This procedure resulted in a constant quantity of food being fed to each tank for the duration of the experiment.

In order to insure adequate aeration and constant flow, water was pumped under a pressure of 30 psi through Bell and Gossett flow regulators. Water temperature was constant at $10^{\pm 1}°C$. Total water hardness as $CaCO_3$ was 200 ppm and pH was 7.75.

Water was analyzed for ammonia and oxygen biweekly, ammonia by direct nesslerization (8) and oxygen with a Yellowsprings Instrument Company oxygen meter. Carbon dioxide and pH were determined bimonthly, carbon dioxide by potentiometric titration (8) and pH with a Beckman pH meter. At three different times throughout the experiment, water was analyzed for ammonia, oxygen, pH, and CO_2 every hour over a 14-hour period.

At the end of four months 10 fish were randomly taken from each tank, giving a total of 20 fish taken at each ammonia concentration. Gills were the only tissues sampled from these fish. After six months, five fish from tanks #5 and #6 having clinical signs and five controls were killed. Internal organs, gills, brain, and thymus were preserved. At nine months gill samples were taken from 10 randomly selected fish in each tank. An additional five fish from each tank were killed, and gills as well as internal organs, thymus, and brain were preserved. Random samples were taken from tanks #1 to #4, but samples from tanks #5 and #6 were selected from fish having clinical signs. Two weeks later, fish in tank #5 were placed in a normal environment. The ammonia level was dropped from an average of 1.5 ppm to 0.3 ppm by increasing water flow to 10 gpm. At the end of 45 days' recovery, and a total of 12 months on experimentation, five fish were killed and samples preserved for histological examination. At the same time, 14 fish were selected from tank #6 in which the ammonia level was maintained at 1.5 ppm. Internal organs as well as brain, gills, and thymus were preserved from seven fish. Gills and livers were the only organs preserved from the remaining seven fish.

All tissues were preserved in Bouin's solution and processed using standard histological technique. Sections were cut at 5 microns and stained with hematoxylin and eosin.

RESULTS

Previous data collected at the Bozeman FCDC demonstrated that ammonia concentrations were at their lowest level in the morning prior to feeding. Values subsequently increased after feeding and were at their peak at 6:00 to 9:00 p.m. Average values could be obtained if samples were taken at 2:00 to 3:00 p.m. Oxygen concentrations varied inversely with ammonia and therefore were highest in the morning prior to feeding and lowest at 6:00 to 9:00 p.m.

The 99% confidence intervals for the average ammonia and oxygen concentrations are presented in Table 21.1, along with the calculated amount of un-ionized ammonia. Ammonia concentrations were slightly elevated above the estimated levels of 0.5, 1.0, and 1.5 ppm.

When compared with controls, growth of trout was not affected after four months' exposure to 1.0 and 1.5 ppm ammonia. There was, however, a significant reduction in growth after 6 and 12 months for fish reared in 1.6 ppm (P

Table 21.1. Average Ammonia Nitrogen and Oxygen Concentrations in Tanks #1–#6 over a 9½-Month Period, and the Calculated Un-ionized Ammonia

Tank no.	Total ammonia[a] (ppm)	Un-ionized[b] ammonia (ppm)	Corrected[c] un-ionized ammonia (ppm)	Oxygen[a] (ppm)
1	$.64^{\pm.06}$	0.013	.0066	$7.45^{\pm.35}$
2	$.59^{\pm.07}$	0.012	.0061	$7.41^{\pm.36}$
3	$1.17^{\pm.123}$	0.024	.0121	$6.62^{\pm.32}$
4	$1.20^{\pm.112}$	0.025	.0125	$6.43^{\pm.34}$
5	$1.60^{\pm.173}$	0.033	.0166	$5.88^{\pm.38}$
6	$1.59^{\pm.187}$	0.033	.0165	$5.80^{\pm.38}$

[a] $\pm 99\%$ Confidence interval.
[b] Calculated from Burrows (5), temp. $10°C$, pH 7.75.
[c] Calculated from Trussell (26), temp. $10°C$, pH 7.75.

$< .05$). At the end of the experiment, fish maintained in 1.2 ppm ammonia weighed 9% less than controls. However, this was not statistically significant ($P > .01$).

Statistical treatment of mortality data by analysis of variance revealed that after nine months there was no significant difference in percent mortality between the six groups. However, during the 12th month, fish in tank #6 became severely infected with bacterial gill disease. The infection resulted in severe mortality. Fish in tank #5, which had been exposed to 1.6 ppm ammonia for 9½ months, then placed in a normal environment, never became infected.

Grossly, all fish appeared normal after four months. Histologically, fish sampled from the experimental groups and controls after four months had mild-to-moderate scattered fusion of gill lamellae. When compared with gills of control fish, only mild scattered hypertrophy of gill epithelium could be correlated with increased ammonia concentrations (Figs. 21.1, 21.2).

After six months of experimentation, a few lethargic and emaciated fish were apparent in tanks #5 and #6. Gill filaments were usually swollen and extended posteriorly beyond the opercula (Fig. 21.3). Fish having these signs were more prevalent after 9 and 12 months. At necropsy, a few fish had pale diffuse areas in their livers. The number of fish with gross liver changes increased with exposure time.

Histologically, gills from lethargic fish sampled at 6, 9, and 12 months had severe pathological changes. In many filaments, severe hyperplasia of gill epithelium resulted in extensive fusion of lamellae, and occasionally, of filaments (Figs. 21.4 and 21.5). Fused lamellae were usually more common at tips of filaments than at their bases and quite often the tissue was edematous (Fig. 21.6). Examination of edematous tissue under high-power magnification revealed cellular degeneration and a mild inflammatory response. In regions where severe hyperplasia was absent, hypertrophy of gill epithelium was common (Fig. 21.7).

Blood-filled aneurysms were also apparent in most sections of gill tissue. In fish sampled at 9 and 12 months, aneurysms often contained blood that was liquefied and an inflammatory response accompanied by degeneration and necrosis was sometimes seen (Figs. 21.8–21.10).

Necrotic lesions were found in the liver of one of the eight fish maintained in the highest ammonia concentration for six months. Liver cell nuclei were pyknotic and cell cytoplasm was dense and somewhat eosinophilic (Fig. 21.11). Incipient focal areas of liver cell degeneration were seen in livers of four fish. When compared with controls, liver cells of fish maintained in the highest ammonia concentration lacked typical glycogen vacuolation. The remaining tissues, which included brain, spleen, pancreas, intestine, interrenal cells, stomach, thyroid, and thymus, compared favorably with those of controls.

Histological examination of tissues from fish held in tanks #1 to #4 for 9 and 12 months revealed that all tissues, with the exception of gills, were quite normal. Mild hyperplasia and hypertrophy of gill epithelium and a few fused lamellae were sometimes seen. In fish from tanks #5 and #6 necrotic lesions were found in only one of the five livers examined at 9 months. The remaining four, however, had

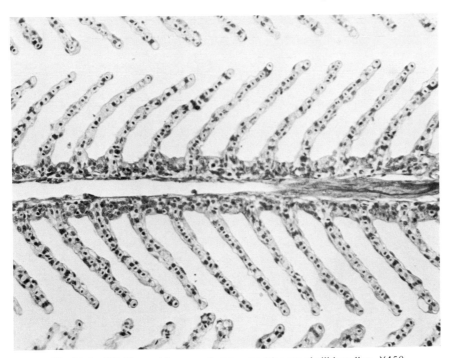

Fig. 21.1. Gill filament from control trout with normal gill lamellae. X450.

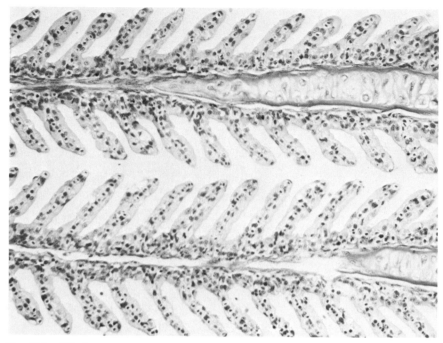

Fig. 21.2. Gills from trout exposed to 1.6 ppm ammonia for 4 months. While most lamellae were normal, some showed hypertrophy of lamellar epithelium, as shown in the figure. ×450.

Fig. 21.3. Trout on left had been exposed to 1.6 ppm ammonia for 12 months. Gill filaments are swollen and protrude beyond edge of opercle. Control trout is shown on the right.

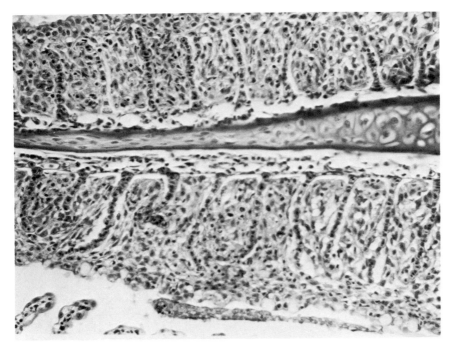

Figure 21.4. Severe hyperplasia of gill epithelium has resulted in fusion of lamellae. Note that epithelium has proliferated beyond tips of lamellae. 1.6 ppm ammonia, 6 months. ×450.

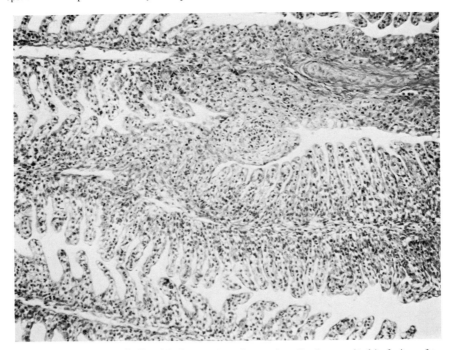

Fig. 21.5. Hyperplasia of gill epithelium at tips of some lamellae has resulted in fusion of two filaments. Note hypertrophied epithelial cells on the majority of gill lamellae. 1.6 ppm ammonia, 6 months. ×320.

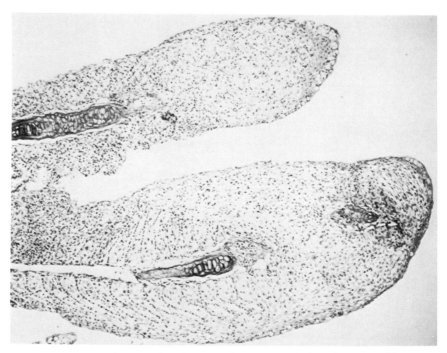

Fig. 21.6. Severe proliferation of epithelium and consequent fusion of lamellae. Note severe edema which has resulted in swelling of tip of filaments. 1.6 ppm ammonia, 9 months. X200.

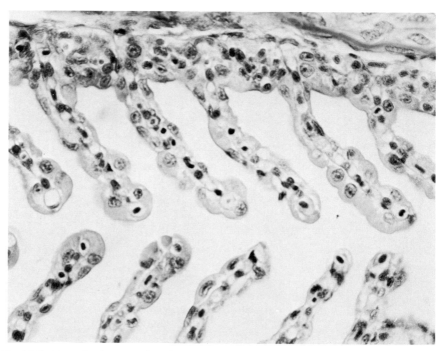

Fig. 21.7. Extensive hypertrophy of epithelium on gill lamellae. 1.6 ppm ammonia, 9 months. X1250.

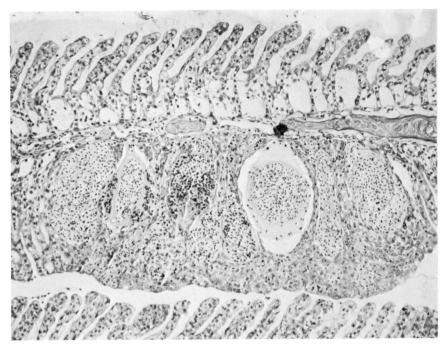

Fig. 21.8. Fusions of gill lamellae in which several aneurysms are present. Note swollen epithelial cells and edema at bases of lamellae on opposite side of filament. 1.6 ppm ammonia, 12 months. ×320.

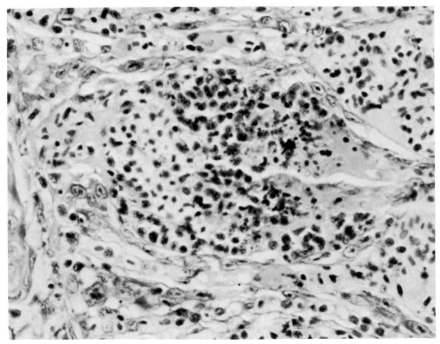

Fig. 21.9. Higher-power view of Figure 21.8, showing leukocytic infiltration in gill aneurysm containing liquefied blood. ×1250.

505

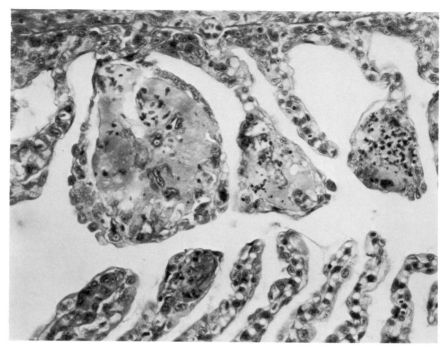

Fig. 21.10. High-power view of aneurysms. Largest aneurysm contains liquefied blood and epithelioid cells as well as a few erythrocytes and cell debris. Cell debris is abundant in aneurysm at right of figure. ×700.

some areas of cell degeneration which consisted mainly of scattered necrotic cells and some cytoplasmic vacuolation. Cytoplasmic degeneration of liver cells around central veins was also seen in a few livers.

Other changes that were apparent in fish maintained in the highest ammonia concentration for 9 and 12 months were reduction of splenic lymphoid tissue and mild necrosis and sloughing of intestinal mucosa (Fig. 21.12). Lesions were found in livers of all 13 fish sampled at 12 months. Focal necrosis of liver cells was found in 6 of 13 livers examined (Figs. 21.13, 21.14). Small focal areas in which sinusoids were dilated and individual liver cells were undergoing necrosis were seen in the other seven. Moderate vacuolation which appeared to be fatty metamorphosis was found in two livers.

Examination of tissues from fish placed on recovery for 45 days revealed that tissues were essentially normal.

DISCUSSION AND SUMMARY

Products of catabolism are excreted from animals by diffusion and by active processes of elimination. In no group of animals is nitrogenous excretion limited

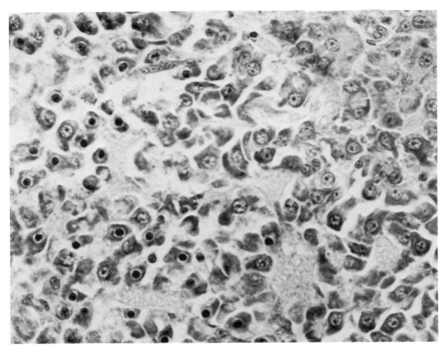

Fig. 21.11. Focal area of liver cell degeneration. Note cells with pyknotic nuclei. 1.6 ppm ammonia, 6 months. ×1250.

to one product. Animals which excrete nitrogen primarily in the form of ammonia are called ammonotelic, ureotelic when urea is the principle product, and urico telic when the main product is uric acid. Ammonia is a substance to which cells of all phylogenetic levels of animal life are accustomed. Despite its presence in living protoplasm, ammonia can produce deleterious effects which are well known to students of many areas of biology and medicine. These harmful effects are believed to arise from the action of ammonia at intracellular sites and may become manifested (1) when normal detoxification processes are impaired as by disease, (2) when ammonia is introduced too rapidly, (3) when the quantities of ammonia are excessive, or (4) when the form of ammonia introduced is highly toxic (28).

Trussell (26) recently reported that Table I of Burrows (5) was not based on accurate ionization constants for aqueous ammonia; thus, it does not contain accurate percentages of un-ionized ammonia for temperatures and pH's indicated. The un-ionized ammonia values in Table 21.1 are calculated from Table I of Burrows for ease of comparison with his data. The corrected un-ionized ammonia values for our data are also given in our Table 21.1.

The primary pathological changes we observed were found in gills and livers of trout exposed to 1.6 ppm (0.033 un-ionized) ammonia. That gill tissue is extremely sensitive to ammonia has been demonstrated by previous investigators (4, 5, 10,

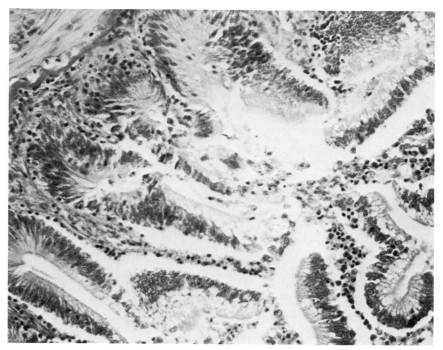

Fig. 21.12. Intestine of trout exposed to 1.6 ppm ammonia for 12 months. Note separation of mucosa from tunica propria and sloughing of epithelial cells into lumen. X450.

14, 22). Contrary to the findings of Burrows (5), however, who reported extensive gill hyperplasia in salmon exposed to 0.30 (0.006 un-ionized) ppm ammonia, we did not find significant pathological changes in gill tissue of trout until ammonia concentrations exceeded 1.2 (0.025 un-ionized) ppm. Bullock (4) was also unable to demonstrate hyperplasia of gill epithelium of trout exposed to 1.0 ppm for one month and then for 2.5 ppm for an additional month (approximately 0.008 and 0.020 ppm un-ionized, respectively, when calculated from Burrows (5)). He did, however, observe aneurysms in gill capillaries typical of those we found.

After 9½ months there was no significant increase (P > .01) in percent mortality between our experimental fish and controls. However, a severe bacterial gill disease which resulted in a 75% mortality occurred in fish in tank #6 which had been maintained in an ammonia concentration of 1.6 ppm for 12 months. Burrows (5) postulated that continuous exposure to ammonia is a precursor of bacterial gill disease in salmon. More recently, Bullock (4) stated that "bacterial gill disease is primarily an environmental disease and secondarily, a bacterial disease of fingerling salmonids."

Growth of fish fed an unrestricted diet is readily affected by reduced oxygen levels. However, fish fed a restricted amount of food have reduced growth only at levels of oxygen well below saturation (25). In our experiment, fish were fed a

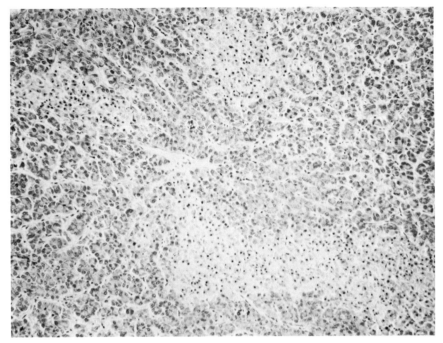

Fig. 21.13. Liver section from trout exposed to 1.6 ppm ammonia for 12 months, showing focal areas of liver cell necrosis. ×320.

restricted amount of food. Average oxygen levels ranged from 7.4 ppm in control tanks to 5.8 ppm in tanks having the highest ammonia concentration. In a previous report from the Bozeman Center, Piper (21) demonstrated that growth of rainbow trout was not retarded until the average oxygen concentration dropped below 4.9 ppm.

Burrows (5) demonstrated that the growth of salmon was reduced after six weeks' exposure to 0.3 ppm ammonia (0.006 ppm un-ionized). Our results are that growth of trout was not significantly reduced until average ammonia concentrations reached 1.6 ppm (0.033 un-ionized) and then only after continuous exposure for six months.

Kawamoto (13) reported that after 91 days carp grew poorly when exposed to an ammonia concentration of 0.3 ppm for 58 days and 1.2 ppm for the remaining 33 days. The facts that the pH of his solutions was only 6.4 to 6.5 and that control fish only had a 0.39 gram average increase in weight compared to a 0.03 gram average decrease in weight for test fish suggest that some other factor(s) than ammonia were growth-limiting.

Brockway (2) recommended that ammonia concentrations in trout-rearing ponds not exceed 0.3 ppm as total ammonia. He cites an instance in which an unexplained mortality occurred among trout in the last pond of a series of five

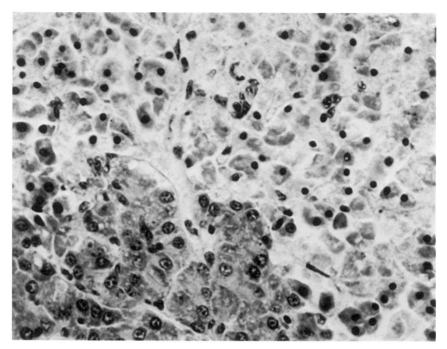

Fig. 21.14. Higher-power view of Figure 21.13, showing necrotic liver cells. Unaffected cells are present at lower left. ×1250.

when the water temperature was greater than 15.5°C and the ammonia concentration was 0.9 ppm. However, neither the oxygen content of the water nor its pH was given.

Brockway (2) also reported that when total ammonia concentrations increased to 1 ppm the oxygen content of trout blood decreased to one-seventh of its normal value and the CO_2 content increased about 15%. He suggested that the hemoglobin lost its ability to unite with oxygen and to liberate CO_2. Contrary to this finding, Fromm and Gillette (11) demonstrated that ammonia has no effect on the ability of oxygen to combine with hemoglobin. They suggest, however, that increased oxygen usage and CO_2 production may have given rise to alterations in blood gas content similar to those reported by Brockway (2).

Spotte (24) stated that "in general, the concentration of total ammonia in solution should not be allowed to exceed 0.1 ppm." Contrary to this belief, we have shown that in rearing rainbow trout it is not necessary to attempt to maintain ammonia concentrations this low as long as oxygen levels are kept at 5.0 ppm or greater. Indeed it becomes impractical to rear rainbow trout at such a low ammonia concentration.

A subsequent experiment of six months' duration (unpublished data) compared growth of trout reared in water with an average ammonia and oxygen content of 0.60 and 8.0 ppm, respectively, to that of trout reared in water with ammonia and oxygen contents of 0.3 and 8.0 ppm, respectively. Histological examination of gills revealed that there was no difference between the two groups. Neither was there any significant difference in growth.

REFERENCES

1. Ball, I. R.   The relative susceptibilities of some species of freshwater fish to poison. I. Ammonia. *Water Res. 1:* 767. 1967.
2. Brockway, D. R.   Metabolic products and their effects. *Progr. Fish-Cult. 12:* 127. 1950.
3. Brown, V. M., Jordan, D. H. M., and Tiller, B. A.   The acute toxicity to rainbow trout of fluctuating concentrations of mixtures of ammonia, phenol and zinc. *J. Fish Biol. 1:* 1. 1969.
4. Bullock, G. L.   Studies on selected myxobacteria pathogenic for fishes and on bacterial gill disease in hatchery-reared salmonids. *U. S. Bur. Sport Fish. Wildlife, Tech. Pap. 60:* 1. 1972.
5. Burrows, R. E.   Effects of accumulated excretory products on hatchery-reared salmonids. *U. S. Fish Wildlife Serv., Res. Rep. 66:* 1. 1964.
6. Buterbaugh, G. L., and Willoughby, H.   A feeding guide for brook, brown, and rainbow trout. *Progr. Fish-Cult. 29:* 210. 1967.
7. Downing, K. M., and Merkens, J. C.   The influence of dissolved oxygen concentration on the toxicity of un-ionized ammonia to rainbow trout (*Salmo gairdneri* Richardson). *Ann. Appl. Biol. 43:* 243. 1955.
8. Ellis, M. M., Westfall, B. A., and Ellis, M. D.   Determination of water quality. *U. S. Fish Wildlife Serv., Res. Rep. 9:* 1. 1948.
9. European Inland Fisheries Advisory Commission.   Water quality criteria for European freshwater fish: Report on ammonia and inland fisheries. *Eur. Inland Fish. Advis. Comm., Tech. Pap. 11:* 1. 1970.
10. Flis, J.   Anatomicohistopathological changes induced in carp (*Cyprinus carpio* L.) by ammonia water. I. Effects of toxic concentrations. II. Effects of subtoxic concentrations. *Acta hydrobiol. 10:* 225. 1968.
11. Fromm, P. O., and Gillette, J. R.   Effect of ambient ammonia on blood ammonia and nitrogen excretion of rainbow trout (*Salmo gairdneri*). *Comp. Biochem. Physiol. 26:* 887. 1968.
12. Herbert, D. W. M., and Shurben, D. S.   The susceptibility of salmonid fish to poisons under estuarine conditions. II. Ammonium chloride. *Int. J. Air Water Pollut. 9:* 89. 1965.
13. Kawamoto, N. Y.   The influence of excretory substances of fishes on their own growth. *Progr. Fish-Cult. 23:* 70. 1961.
14. Kuhn, O., and Koecke, H. U.   Histologische und cytologische Veränderungen der Fischkieme nach Einwirkung im Wasser enthaltener schädigender Substanzen. *Z. Zellforsch. mikrosk. Anat. 43:* 611. 1956.
15. Larmoyeux, J. D., and Piper, R. G.   The effects of water reuse on rainbow trout in hatcheries. *Progr. Fish-Cult. 35:* 2. 1973.
16. Lloyd, R.   Effect of dissolved oxygen concentrations on the toxicity of sev-

eral poisons to rainbow trout (*Salmo gairdneri* Richardson). *J. Exp. Biol. 38:* 278. 1961.

17. Lloyd, R.   The toxicity of ammonia to rainbow trout (*Salmo gairdneri* Richardson). *Water Waste Treat. J. 8:* 278. 1961.

18. Lloyd, R., and Herbert, D. W. M.   The influence of carbon dioxide on the toxicity of un-ionized ammonia to rainbow trout (*Salmo gairdneri* Richardson). *Ann. Appl. Biol. 48:* 399. 1960.

19. Lloyd, R., and Orr, L. D.   The diuretic response by rainbow trout to sublethal concentrations of ammonia. *Water Res. 3:* 335. 1969.

20. Merkens, J. C., and Downing, K. M.   The effect of tension of dissolved oxygen on the toxicity of un-ionized ammonia to several species of fish. *Ann. Appl. Biol. 45:* 521. 1957.

21. Piper, R. G.   Know the carrying capacity of your farm. *Amer. Fishes U. S. Trout News 15:* 4. 1970.

22. Reichenbach-Klinke, H.-H.   Untersuchungen über die Einwirkung des Ammoniakgehalts auf den Fischorganismus. *Arch. Fischerei. wiss. 17:* 122. 1967.

23. Smith, H. W.   The excretion of ammonia and urea by the gills of fish. *J. Biol. Chem. 81:* 727. 1929.

24. Spotte, S. H.   Toxic metabolites, pp. 102–108. In *Fish and Invertebrate Culture*. New York, Wiley, 1970.

25. Sprague, J. B.   Measurement of pollutant toxicity to fish. III. Sublethal effects and "safe" concentrations. *Water Res. 5:* 245. 1971.

26. Trussell, R. P.   The percent un-ionized ammonia in aqueous ammonia solutions at different pH levels and temperatures. *J. Fish. Res. Board Can. 29:* 1505. 1972.

27. Vamos, R.   Ammonia poisoning in carp. *Acta Biol. (Szeged) 9:* 291. 1963.

28. Visek, W. J.   Some aspects of ammonia toxicity in animal cells. *J. Dairy Sci. 51:* 286. 1968.

29. Wuhrmann, K., and Woker, H.   Experimentelle Untersuchungen über die Ammoniak–und Blausäurevergiftung. *Schweiz. Z. Hydrol. 11:* 210. 1948.

DISCUSSION OF LESIONS ASSOCIATED WITH CHRONIC EXPOSURE TO AMMONIA

Question: What was the percentage of dietary protein?

C. E. Smith: Approximately 40%.

Question: Did you find any lesions in the brain or in the kidney?

C. E. Smith: No, nothing that I couldn't find in the controls. There were no significant lesions in any of the other organs. With ammonia in higher concentrations, we do find hemorrhages in the thymuses of these fish, but this later work is not completed; this is just a gross observation.

Question: I realize the importance of this work but think you ought to consider a possible synergistic effect of the lower oxygen and higher ammonia levels. You did say that when you tried a study of that type you didn't get any effects on growth, but did you by any chance look at any of the tissues?

C. E. Smith: Yes, I looked at the gill tissue only, but did not find any significant changes after six months' exposure to 0.3, 0.6, and 0.75 ppm ammonia.

Question: One more procedural question: How difficult is it to keep the pH levels stable without adding any buffers when you are changing your ammonia concentrations? Did you buffer your solutions continually?

C. E. Smith: No, our pH's remained quite constant. We have fairly hard water and at such low ammonia levels we do not have problems with the pH changing.

M. M. Sigel: All along we have been rather impressed with the hardiness of the shark to various biological and chemical insults, but apparently ammonia does get the best of the shark. An incident occurred accidentally. We placed our sharks in a tank to maintain them in a laboratory which also housed chickens, mice, rabbits, and other animals. Apparently the amount of urea generated by the urine and feces of these other animals was picked up by the air conditioning, succeeding in dissolving enough ammonia in the water to really hurt our sharks. These sharks were kept in the tanks about two months and at about six weeks we noticed lesions in the skin, the sharks lost their appetite, and became very docile. We carried out considerable studies on the blood plasma, on other tissue, and on proteins from these animals and found no major changes. The only thing we could demonstrate was the increased amount of ammonia. Do keep in mind that the shark uses urea as an osmotic balancing system, and whether this played a role in our situation, I cannot say.

C. J. Dawe: I think those gill epithelial lesions are extremely interesting, especially with respect to the possibility that such a hyperplasia might have a promotional effect in the presence of some other carcinogen, which, of course, you are not concerned with. I wonder about the reversibility of that lesion if you removed the ammonia.

C. E. Smith: We took fish from the highest level of ammonia after 9½ months and put them in fresh water where the ammonia concentration was approximately 0.2 ppm. We could find no degenerative changes after 2½ months. I feel the changes probably disappear more rapidly than this. We did study the recovery of these fish and they definitely recover. Incidentally, we also determined stamina performances and found that fish maintained in the highest concentration of ammonia performed much more poorly than those in the fresh water.

A. D. Bradford: Would you comment on your technique of determining ammonia. Did you have any trouble with that in highly alkaline water?

C. E. Smith: No. We determined the ammonia by direct nesslerization, using Rochelle salts to eliminate magnesium, and obtained good consistent results. We do not have interfering substances such as sulfates, sulfides, or sulfur dioxide in our water.

Question: Your table shows ionized and un-ionized ammonia. In looking at the table it seemed to me that there was very little difference between the groups in the un-ionized ammonia; that the major differences were in the ionized ammonia. Do you attribute the effects that you observed to the ionized?

C. E. Smith: No, according to the literature, the toxic portion is the un-ionized, and it is in extremely low concentrations that it is toxic.

Question: There were very small differences in the un-ionized portion as illustrated in your table. Were the differences you observed in the histopathological effects similarly related to those small differences observed in the un-ionized ammonia?

C. E. Smith: No.

T. E. Murchison: I notice you point out that some of the blood in your aneurysms showed degenerative changes. To me as a pathologist that means a thrombosis. Did you feel there was thrombosis present, and if so, might that not have been the initial lesion before the aneurysm?

C. E. Smith: I don't know for sure. Quite commonly we find aneurysms that have normal-appearing blood cells and thromboses are not apparent. Occasionally, we can find aneurysms that contain a few degenerating erythrocytes. I assume that the degeneration is due to improper circulation or stagnation of the blood.

22

The Pathology of Pesticide Poisoning

A. H. WALSH
and WILLIAM E. RIBELIN

The toxicity to fish of that group of agricultural chemicals known as pesticides*
has been well documented. The reader is referred to Johnson's review (20) should
clarification of this point be desired. Further evidence of the toxicity of these
compounds is provided by the numerous reports cited in Tables 22.1 through 22.5
which tabulate the tissue changes observed in fish exposed to several pesticides.
Despite the known toxicity of these compounds, their incrimination in fish kills
has often been based upon a history of pesticide exposure or upon chemical analysis of water or of fish tissue. Though all of these factors suggest a causal relationship between pesticide and fish death, such information is not in itself diagnostic.
Conversely, it is not unusual for pesticides to kill fish under circumstances not
suggestive of pesticide toxicity. In either case the diagnostic value of specific lesions indicative of pesticide toxicity in general or of a specific pesticide or of a
pesticide family is self-evident.

STUDIES BY THE AUTHORS

Studies were conducted in our laboratory utilizing a flowing water system in
which temperature was maintained at $12.5 \pm 2.0°$ C. Oxygenation was maintained

---

* The report of the President's Science Advisory Committee, "Use of Pesticides," contains
this definition, "The term pesticide broadly includes compounds intended for a variety of
purposes. They are used to control insects, mites, ticks, fungi, nematodes, rodents, pest birds,
predatory animals, rough fish, plant diseases, and weeds; and also to act as regulators of plant
growth, as defoliants, and as desiccants . . ."

515

Table 22.1. Lesions Reported in Fish Following Exposure to Chlorinated Hydrocarbon Insecticides

	None	Gill	Liver	Kidney	Gut	Brain	Endocrine	Vessels	Miscellaneous
DDT									
Lake trout					Tract of fry distended by air (6)				Swim bladder of fry distended by air (6)
Coho salmon				Degeneration and deposits distal tubules (5)					Nose erosion (5)
Chinook salmon	(5)								
Cutthroat trout	(1)								
Rainbow trout	(38)		Hepatoma (17)						
Brown trout			Nuclear hypertrophy and cytoplasmic vacuolization (23)	Degeneration tubular epithelium and debris in lumina (23)	Submucosal vacuolization, epithelial degeneration (23)		Adrenal cortical necrosis (23)		
Guppy			Severe necrosis (23)				Adrenal cortical necrosis (23)		Spleen shrunken (23)
Asian species			Degeneration, hypertrophy and necrosis of hepatocytes (28)	Degeneration of tubule epithelium (28)	Submucosal vacuolization epithelial degeneration and loss of goblet cells (28)				

Eel					ATPase inhibition (19)		Degranulation of ϵ cells of pituitary (DDD) (4)		
MIREX									
Cutthroat trout		Fused lamellae (37)[a]							
Goldfish		Edema and aneurysms of lamellae (37)							Epithelium of distend gall bladder flattened (37)
Bluegill	(37)								
LINDANE									
Rainbow trout			Focal necrosis (38)	Disintegration of convoluted tubules (38)					
METHOXYCHLOR									
Rainbow trout			Nonspecific degeneration (38)						
Bluegill			Hepatocyte shrinkage and granulation plus loss of radial orientation of cords (22)			Vascular congestion (22)		Eosinophilic globules plugging blood vessels (22)	

[a]Considered pathognomic by original author.

by constant aeration. Pesticide dissolved in acetone was delivered by gravity either into the incoming water or directly into the aquaria. The latter technique was necessary with atrazine and 2,4-D, which both required very high concentrations of pesticide to elicit evidence of toxicity. Table 22.6 depicts the physical and chemical properties of the water used.

All pesticide levels were determined by water analyses performed by chemists at the Wisconsin Alumni Research Foundation (WARF) laboratories. Table 22.7 lists these pesticide levels for each study. The desired pesticide level was that which would kill exposed fish in 30 days. Since the longest exposure period for which a published LC_{50} value was available was 96 hours, it was necessary to estimate the 30-day figure for each pesticide.

Coho salmon (*Oncorhynchus kisutch*) and lake trout (*Salvelinus namaycush*) obtained from Wisconsin hatcheries were used in all studies. These fish were from 6 to 18 months of age and ranged from 8.9 to 25.5 cm in length. This variation was impossible to avoid since these fish are hatched only once a year. Following acclimation in our laboratory, randomly selected males and females of both species were exposed to each of the seven pesticides listed in Table 22.7. Appropriate controls were maintained for all studies.

Exposure to pesticide was continued until death occurred or was imminent. At that time body weight and length were recorded, a complete autopsy performed and the liver, spleen, and right eye weighed. Portions of all organs and tissues were fixed in buffered formalin, and suitable sections prepared for microscopic examination. Approximately one-half of each fish was frozen, and selected fish from each exposure group were analyzed for pesticide content by chemists at the WARF laboratories. The results of these analyses are presented in Table 22.8.

No significant changes in organ weights were noted in any of these studies. Physical and behavioral changes observed during life are reported in Table 22.9. Those gross and microscopic tissue changes considered pertinent because of their relationship to the earlier literature or their possible diagnostic value are recorded in Table 22.10.

Comparison of the changes observed in coho salmon and lake trout in our laboratory with changes observed in numerous other fish species under widely varying experimental conditions is obviously highly assumptive. However, such assumptions are necessary if any attempt is to be made to arrive at conclusions which may offer assistance for those interested in the diagnosis of pesticide toxicity in fish. For this reason, results which are contradictory to previous reports are discussed, as well as those in which agreement exists. It is hoped this will shed new light on some areas, stimulate further studies into others, or perhaps bring about the re-evaluation of data in others.

Nonspecific Tissue Changes

The majority of changes observed in this study were of a nonspecific nature and are, therefore, of limited diagnostic value. These general changes and several

Table 22.2. Lesions Reported in Fish Following Exposure to Organophosphate and Carbamate Insecticides

	None	Gill	Liver	Kidney	Fat	Brain	Fin
PARATHION							
Rainbow trout		Marked epithelial hyperplasia (38)	Degeneration (38)	Protein-like material in Bowman's space and collecting tubules (33)			
Bluegill & White crappie							Extreme extension of pectoral fins in life (3)
MALATHION							
Rainbow trout		Edema and epithelial separation (38)	Transient unspecified lesions (38)				
Cutthroat trout	(1)						
Bluegill	(21)						Extreme extension of pectoral fins in life. Reddish discoloration base of dorsal fins (12)
CARBARYL							
Rainbow trout	Unspecified (26)	Unspecified (26)			Unspecified lesions of visceral fat (26)		
Spot						Sporozoon parasite (26)	

Table 22.3. Lesions Reported in Fish Following Exposure to Cyclodiene Insecticides

	None	Gill	Liver	Kidney	Ovary	Endocrine	Blood
TOXAPHENE							
Rainbow trout		Edema (38)	Parenchymal cell necrosis and disruption of radial orientation of cords (38)				
Spot		Thickening of lamellar epithelium (25)	Degeneration (25)				
HEPTACHLOR							
Rainbow trout		Edema and patchy congestion (38)	Heavy bile pigment deposits (38)				
Cutthroat trout		Edema and patchy congestion (2)	Degeneration (2)				
Bluegills	(8)		Hepatocyte shrinkage with loss of lipid and glycogen, disruption of radial orientation of cords (2)				Enlarged erythrocytes (2)

ENDRIN

Rainbow trout							
Cutthroat trout	Edema and separation of epithelium (14)	Degeneration (38)	Pigment, inflammation, severe morphological change. Pre-neoplastic? (14)	Yellow pigment in tubules (38)	Hyperplasia of germinal layer and involution of some ova (14)		Islet cell hyperplasia (14)
Spot	(20)						
Guppy		Fatty infiltration (30)					
Not designated				Vacuolated cells in glomeruli (31)			
Goldfish		Reduced cytoplasmic vacuolization (16)				Reduced thyroid follicular cell height (16)	

DIELDRIN

	Hepatocyte pleomorphism, cytoplasmic vacuoles (29)	

Table 22.4. Lesions Reported in Fish Following Exposure to Phenoxyacetate Herbicides

	None	Gill	Liver	Testis	Brain	Vessels
2,4-D						
Bluegill			Hepatocyte shrinkage and loss of glycogen. Distortion of radial cords. Bizarre hepatocytes (11)		Vascular congestion (11)	PAS + globular masses (11)
KUROSAL						
Bluegill	(38)					
KURON						
Bluegill			Hepatocyte shrinkage and loss of glycogen. Distortion of radical cords (38)	Stimulation of spermatogenesis followed by exhaustion atrophy (38)		
DICHLOBENIL						
Bluegill		Vascular engorgement with lamellar-aneurysms and fusion (9)	Hepatocyte karyolysis, fibrosis, and adenomatous change (10)[a]			
DIURON						
Bluegill		Lamellar aneurysms, hemorrhage and hyperplasia of epithelium progressing to fusion of lamellae (27)				

[a]Study included two other centrarchid species plus the yellow perch.

findings which apparently represent the normal, but which might be mistaken for lesions of toxicity when controls are not available, must be carefully evaluated.

Hyperplasia of gill lamellar epithelium has been cited as a finding suggestive of toxicity in several fish species following exposure to several pesticides (13, 25, 27, 37, 38). Examination of Table 22.10 reveals that this condition is actually more prevalent among controls than among exposed fish in this study. Similar lesions were also observed in apparently healthy coho salmon and lake trout taken directly from hatchery raceways. The descriptions of bacterial gill disease (34, 39) and nutritional gill disease are quite suggestive of the gill changes ascribed to pesticide toxicity in the reports previously mentioned. With these facts in mind one must conclude that such changes are of limited diagnostic value.

Gill lamellar telangiectasis, reported as toxic gill disease, lamellar aneurysms, hemorrhagic gill disease, and hemorrhagic globes, has been frequently suggested as a diagnostic lesion of fish exposed to toxins (9, 15, 27, 35, 37, 39). Examination of Table 22.10 reveals that this lesion was present in a number of controls as well as in fish exposed to pesticides. Exposure of two groups of coho salmon and lake trout for 30 days to acetone levels of 50 and 500 ppm did not produce this lesion. This indicates that lamellar telangiectasis seen in pesticide control fish did not result from acetone exposure. As with epithelial hyperplasia of the gill lamellae, the diagnostic value of lamellar telangiectasis becomes suspect in the light of these findings.

An additional gill change frequently reported in fish pesticide literature is edema with epithelial separation (2, 7, 14, 37, 38). This lesion was not observed in fish examined in our laboratory following exposure to pesticides. It was observed that the gill lamellar epithelium separates from the underlying endothelium soon after death. This autolytic change is easily distinguished from true lamellar edema by the presence of proteinaceous edema fluid in those fish manifesting the latter condition.

King (23) noted that guppies (*Poecilia reticulata = Lebistes reticulatus*) exposed to DDT had "shrunken" spleens. Examination of Table 22.10 reveals that small pale spleens were grossly evident in 25% or more of lake trout exposed to either DDT, endosulfan, or dieldrin. Examination of relative spleen weights and microscopic evidence reveals that there is a weight loss and a marked difference in the morphology of spleens in both coho salmon and lake trout exposed to any of the seven pesticides used in these studies. It should be noted that this weight loss was not statistically significant because of the wide variation in the weights of spleens from control animals and the small numbers of fish per group. The microscopic change was in all cases a marked reduction in the number of lymphocytes in the spleens of exposed fish. A similar change in the spleens of fish exposed to ammonia has been reported by C. E. Smith and R. G. Piper (see Chapter 21 of this volume). They suggest that this is a response to stress.

Liver changes, important in toxicity studies in higher vertebrates, were minimal and diagnostically unimportant in these studies. Periportal necrosis and

Table 22.5. Lesions Reported in Fish Following Exposure to Miscellaneous Pesticides

	Gill	Liver	Muscle	Pancreas	Gonad	Vessels	Miscellaneous
			HYDROTHOL 191				
Redear sunfish	Reversible epithelial hyperplasia with lamellar and filament fusions (13)	Inflammation, pigmented swollen hepatocytes progressing to bizarre cells and distorted cords. Pre-neoplasic? (13)			Development of ova-like cells in testes (13)	Spherical purple-red masses within vessels (13)	
			SODIUM ARSENITE				
Bluegill	Lamellar aneurisms (15)	Fatty infiltration and focal necrosis (15)			Cytoplasmic clumping and karyolysis of ova (15)	Endothelial separation and subendothelial myositis (vasculitis?) (15)	
			DALAPON				
Carp				Various changes of acinar cells from submicroscopic degeneration to acute necrosis of organ (33)			

Species	NaTA	TEPA	TFM
Carp	Increased number of mucous cells progressing to lamellar epithelial necrosis (32). Degenerative atrophy of myotomes (32)		
Guppy		Testicular atrophy and hypospermia (36)	
Rainbow trout			Reddening of pharyngeal area with heavy mucus secretion upon gills. Lamellar edema and increased mucous cell activity (7). Reddening (7)
Lamprey			Reddening and swelling of pharyngeal area with heavy mucus secretion upon gills. Lamellar edema and increased mucous cell activity (7). Edema of myotomes (7). Reddening of cloaca. Increased activity of epidermal mucous cells (7)

Table 22.6. Chemical Properties of Water Used in Pesticide Studies
(Quantities expressed in ppm)

	Control aquarium	Madison Well No. 1[a]	Madison Well No. 2[a]	Madison Well No. 3[a]	Madison Well No. 4[a]
Ammonia	0.25				
Copper	0.036				
Calcium		60	64	48	60
Bicarbonate		335	350	340	335
Magnesium		0.04	0.04	0.04	0.04
Oxygen	10.5				
DDE	0.000010				
DDD	0.000010				
DDT	0.000020[b]				
PCB established	0.000120[b]				
BHC	0.000018[b]				
pH	7.2				

[a]Each of these wells contributed to water supply at some time.
[b]Value questionable, near limit of detection.

changes in hepatocyte architecture are discussed under DDT. All other changes seen in the liver were not considered to be of diagnostic significance, and will not be discussed. However, a photograph depicting the most severe example of fatty change observed in the livers of any fish in these studies is included (Fig. 22.6).

Two rather striking features which apparently represent the normal structure of fish kidney were apparent in this study. The lumina of many kidney tubules of lake trout and coho salmon contain a dense proteinaceous material. This precipitate was present equally in both exposed fish and controls. Mention is made of this material to alert the reader to it and to point out the confusion such a finding could create in the absence of control fish. Similarly, the epithelium of the small distal portion of the convoluted tubule in lake trout frequently contains large cytoplasmic vacuoles. These are equally prominent in controls and in exposed fish, and their significance is unknown.

Hyperemia of varying degrees was evident in the brains of some coho salmon and lake trout exposed to several pesticides (see Table 22.10). Only in the case of 2,4-D was this change sufficiently striking to suggest that it might have diagnostic value. This latter observation agrees with the findings of Cope, Wood, and Wallen (11) in bluegills (*Lepomis macrochirus*). Gross and microscopic evidence of hyperemia seen in the brain of fish following exposure to the other pesticides reported in Table 22.10 was not of sufficient magnitude to be diagnostically important without having control fish available for comparison. The presence of eosinophilic globules, which appeared to be plugging blood vessels, was suggested as the mechanism of vascular stasis in the 2,4-D exposed bluegills previously mentioned. Similar globules have been reported in bluegills exposed to methoxychlor (22) as well as 2,4-D and in redear sunfish (*L. microlophus*) exposed to the herbicide Hydrothol 191 (13). These three compounds do not appear to be related chemically and no similar globules have been described in other fish species exposed to any of these compounds. This evidence suggests that formation of eosinophilic globules may be a response common to these fish, all of which belong to the family Centrarchidae, rather than to the compounds in question. Hinton, Snipes, and Kendall (18) have suggested these globules are artifacts and of no diagnostic importance.

Physical and Behavioral Changes Observed During Life

A number of changes were noted in living fish during exposure to various pesticides. Examination of Table 22.9 reveals that many of these changes would be difficult to assess under any circumstances other than those of a controlled laboratory experiment. Changes of possible diagnostic value under field conditions were evident with fish exposed to two pesticides, carbaryl (Sevin) and atrazine.

Coho salmon and lake trout exposed to carbaryl were frequently observed to develop scoliosis and patches of intense black pigmentation near the site of spinal deviation. These same fish when stimulated by either increased light, or sound, or movement near the aquarium would swim erratically and at some of these times appear to momentarily lose equilibrium.

Lake trout exposed to atrazine developed a syndrome characterized by intense black pigmentation of the skin, exophthalmos, ascites, and a preference for the water surface rather than deeper levels. All other lake trout in these experiments remained in the deepest one-third of the aquaria almost constantly. Lake trout exposed to atrazine were without exception close to the water surface if not partially above it during their last one or two days of life. Similar behavioral changes were noted in coho salmon exposed to atrazine. However, the only evidence of color change in cohos was a tendency for those areas of the skin which are normally green to become iridescent.

Specific Tissue Changes

Specific diagnostic lesions were observed only in fish exposed to the insecticide carbaryl. Lesions suggestive of atrazine, 2,4-D, and organophosphate poisoning were also noted. The following discussion is limited to these more or less specific changes and to any evidence coming out of our work which either supported or contradicted earlier reports.

DDT. Buhler, Rasmusson, and Shanks (5) reported extensive erosions of the epithelium and deeper tissues of the premaxillary region of coho salmon exposed to DDT. Our results indicate this lesion is not confined to cohos exposed to DDT or even to fish exposed to pesticide. It would appear from the results presented in Table 22.10 that this erosive lesion may, under the conditions of our experiments, be a manifestation of confinement rather than toxicity.

Periportal necrosis was observed in the livers of two coho salmon exposed to DDT. Though the low incidence makes the importance of this finding difficult to assess, this finding does agree with King's and Mathur's reports of DDT-induced hepatocellular necrosis (23, 28). It is not possible to determine if the changes observed by these two authors were actually necrosis or autolysis. In our study autolysis can be eliminated as a factor since the two fish in question were both sacrificed and tissues placed in fixative less than five minutes after death. It is also important to consider the DDT levels in those studies in which liver necrosis has occurred. King and Mathur were both involved in acute toxicity studies and therefore exposed fish to theoretical levels of up to 10 ppm of DDT. In our study, though the assayed level in aquarium water at which the two fish in question died was only 0.0152 ppm, it was in fact the highest DDT level to which any of our fish were exposed. It is reasonable to conclude on the basis of our own low level studies and those of Buhler, Rasmusson, and Shanks (5), Allison et al. (1), and Wood (38), all of whom utilized low DDT levels, that liver necrosis is not a lesion of chronic low level DDT toxicity in fish. However, hepatocellular necrosis may be a lesion of acute DDT toxicity in fish.

A subtle change in the basic liver architecture was also observed in the two coho salmon in which periportal necrosis was noted. This change has been reported previously for fish exposed to methoxychlor (22), toxaphene (38), heptachlor (8), endrin (14), 2,4-D (11), Kuron (38), Hydrothol 191 (13), and possibly for

Table 22.7. Theoretical and Reported Pesticide Levels for Water during Exposures
(Quantities expressed in ppm)

	DDT	Carbaryl	Malathion	Endosulfan	Dieldrin	2,4-D	Atrazine
96 hr LC$_{50}$[a]	0.0032	3.2	0.101	0.0012	0.013	600.0	4.5
Estimated 30 day LC$_{50}$	0.0017	1.0	0.060	0.0007[b]	0.007[b]	80.0	4.0
1st analysis	0.0005	0.89	0.060	0.00034[c]	0.0033[c]	1.03	1.5
Adjusted input to:	0.005	2.0[b]	0.060			400.0[e]	4.0
2nd analysis	0.00237	2.6[c]	0.042			133.0	3.3
Adjusted input to:	0.005		0.180[b]			1200.0[b]	8.0[b]
3rd analysis	0.00085		0.178[c]			430.0[c]	N.D.
Adjusted input to:	0.009[d]						
4th analysis	0.00179						
Adjusted input to:	0.0156[d,b]						
5th analysis	0.0152[c]						

N.D. = Not determined.

[a] Supplied by R. A. Schoettger, Fish Pesticide Research Laboratory, Columbia, Missouri.

[b] Theoretical pesticide level at termination.

[c] Reported pesticide level at termination.

[d] Upward adjustment 3 days after previous adjustment.

[e] Upward adjustment 5 days after experiment began.

Table 22.8. Pesticide Levels in Selected Fish and in Water Samples Taken at the Termination of the Corresponding Study

	DDT	Carbaryl	Malathion	Endosulfan	Dieldrin	2,4-D	Atrazine
Water concentration ppm	0.0152	2.6	0.178	0.00034	0.0033	430.0	8.0[a]
Lake trout							
Tissue concentration ppm (treated)	6.94	9.3	1.31	0.60	4.34	25.0	2.9
Tissue concentration ppm (control)	0.113	0.5	<0.02	<0.005	0.068	00.10	<0.3
Coho salmon							
Tissue concentration ppm (treated)	7.17	10.4	5.22	0.54	2.15	25.4	13.0
Tissue concentration ppm (control)	0.134	<0.5	<0.02	<0.005	<0.005	0.01	0.37

[a]Theoretical value. Actual value not determined.

dieldrin (29) and DDT (28). The importance of the reports which state that the basic structure of the hepatic muralia is altered by DDT and dieldrin is questioned, since the morphological picture described by all of these authors is indistinguishable from that which is seen in autolyzed fish liver. Since autolysis is rapid, even in refrigerated fish. care must be taken in evaluating the tissues of any fish which has died more than a few minutes before fixation was commenced. In addition, tissues to be fixed must be exposed to adequate fixative and they must be small enough to allow rapid penetration of that fixative.

Infiltration by lymphocytes of the lamina propria of either the intestine or the pyloric ceca or both was evident in 7 of the 23 fish exposed to DDT. This change has not been reported previously, though changes in the intestinal submucosa have been noted by two investigators using much higher DDT levels than were used in these studies (23, 28).

Degeneration of kidney tubules following DDT exposure has been reported by three authors in several fish species (5, 23, 28). Though similar changes were not present in the kidneys of the fish in this study the frequency with which this finding has been made suggests the change is real. Unfortunately the complication of autolysis clouds the significance of the findings in two of these studies (23, 28). In one of these studies (23) adrenal cortical changes which are indistinguishable from autolysis are reported in two species of fish.

Any attempt to interpolate the findings of several studies, including our own, in order to define a set of lesions which could be considered even suggestive of DDT poisoning seems futile. At best, with the data on hand, one can only state that the lesions produced in fish exposed to DDT are nonspecific, variable, and generally confined to liver, kidney, and intestine.

Carbaryl (Sevin). As noted previously, fish exposed to carbaryl develop a syndrome which may have diagnostic value. In addition, these same fish develop several lesions which also appear to have diagnostic value. These include hemorrhages within the muscle adjacent to the vertebral column and near the site at which scoliosis and skin darkening were evident (scoliosis and the areas of skin discoloration did not persist after death), atrophy of the small band of muscle which runs parallel to the lateral line, myxomatous degeneration of fat, and vacuoles within the optic tectum or lateral geniculate body.

Scoliosis, muscle atrophy, and fat degeneration have been described in fish on a vitamin E-deficient diet (see Chapter 32 of this volume). Since the fish in our studies did not eat for a prolonged period, the possibility that a vitamin E deficiency existed and caused these lesions must be considered. However, Lowe has reported lesions of visceral fat in rainbow trout (*Salmo gairdneri*) exposed to carbaryl (26). Unfortunately no details describing the lesion are given, and E. M. Wood, who interpreted the lesion, reports that a fire has destroyed his records (personal communication). Also, feed was withheld from controls during that period of the experiments in which the exposed fish did not eat. The lesion mentioned by Wood and the absence of similar changes in starved controls suggest that these lesions are indicative of carbaryl toxicity.

Changes in the lateral line muscle of fish exposed to carbaryl were not always evident in tissue slices stained by the standard hematoxylin and eosin method. They were evident in most tissue slices stained by the hematoxylin-basic fuchsin-picric acid method of Lie et al. (24) which detects early anoxic lesions. Future investigations may show that carbaryl in some way interferes with selenium/vitamin E metabolism and can therefore produce lesions which mimic vitamin E deficiency. However, the data from this study indicate that any or all of the above lesions may well be a direct result of carbaryl exposure.

The brain lesion seen in coho salmon and lake trout exposed to carbaryl has not, to our knowledge, been reported as a lesion of vitamin E deficiency or of any other disease in fish. It is similar to a lesion of the vagal roots observed by J. M. King in rats exposed to carbaryl (personal communication). The lesion in fish consists of large vacuoles (8 to 20 microns in diameter) in the molecular layer of the optic tectum of coho salmon and slightly smaller vacuoles (8 to 16 microns in diameter) within the lateral geniculate body of lake trout. Attempts to identify the nature of the material which had created these vacuoles was not rewarding. They did not stain with Bodian's method for nerve fibers, Luxol fast blue for myelin, oil red O for fat (with frozen sections) nor did they show evidence of a positive periodic acid-Schiff (PAS) reaction.

Carbaryl, at the levels tested, appears to have produced an array of lesions which are diagnostic in the two fish species examined. Further work may indicate that the brain lesion is pathognomonic. At this point it seems safe to conclude that the presence of the brain lesion coupled with the muscle and fat lesions indicates carbaryl poisoning as the probable cause of death.

Malathion. In this study, no lesion of any significance was observed in fish exposed to malathion. However, subcutaneous hemorrhages at the base of the pectoral fin were observed in two lake trout exposed to malathion. This change is mentioned, not on its own merits, but in connection with the report of Eaton (12) that a similar change was observed in bluegills exposed to malathion. It would appear worthwhile to alert other investigators to this readily discernible change. The presence of this lesion combined with the extreme extension of the pectoral fins noted by Eaton (12), and also observed in bluegill and white crappie (*Pomoxis annularis*) exposed to parathion (3), may be suggestive of organophosphate toxicity. Additional substantiation of such toxicity can be obtained by blood cholinesterase determinations.

Endosulfan (Thiodan). Hyperemia of the intestine and brain is the only change observed in fish exposed to endosulfan which warrants discussion.

Intestinal hyperemia was observed in fish exposed to several pesticides but was most striking following exposure to endosulfan. Unfortunately the importance of intestinal hyperemia is minimized not only by this lack of specificity as a lesion of pesticide toxicity but by its frequent occurrence in fish with viral and bacterial infections. Similarly, hyperemia of the brain was observed in many exposed fish in our studies. Though the frequency of this change was highest in fish ex-

Table 22.9. Physical and Behavioral Changes Observed during Pesticide Exposure

	DDT		Carbaryl		Malathion		Endosulfan		Dieldrin		2,4-D		Atrazine	
	E	C	E	C	E	C	E	C	E	C	E	C	E	C
Appetite stimulated	+	–	–	–	–	–	–	–	–	–	–	–	–	–
Appetite depressed	–	–	+	–	+	–	+	–	+	–	+	–	+	–
Equilibrium disturbed	–	–	+	–	–	–	–	–	–	–	–	–	–	–
Posture altered	–	–	+	–	–	–	–	–	–	–	–	–	–	–
Response to stimuli increased	+	–	+	–	–	–	+	–	+	–	+	–	–	–
Activity increased	+	–	–	–	–	–	+	–	+	–	–	–	–	–
Activity decreased	–	–	–	–	+	–	–	–	–	–	–	–	–	–
Pigmentation altered	–	–	+	–	–	–	–	–	–	–	–	–	+	–
Water depth selection altered	–	–	–	–	–	–	–	–	–	–	–	–	+	–
Exophthalmos	–	–	–	–	–	–	–	–	–	–	–	–	+	–
Ascites	–	–	–	–	–	–	–	–	–	–	–	–	+	–

E = Exposed
C = Control

Table 22.10. Incidence of Tissue Changes Observed in Lake Trout and Coho Salmon Following Exposure to Several Pesticides

		DDT		CARBARYL		MALATHION		ENDOSULFAN		DIELDRIN		2,4-D		ATRAZINE	
		Exposed	Control	Exposed	Control	Exposed	Control	Exposed	Control	Exposed	Control	Exposed	Control	Exposed	Control
SKIN:															
Erosion premaxillary region	G	0/10	0/6	0/14	0/5	0/6	0/6	0/12	0/6	0/7	0/6			0/9	0/6
		7/13	4/6	7/14	1/6	3/8	3/5	5/13	1/6	3/10	1/6			1/9	0/5
Hemorrhage base of dorsal fin	G					2/6	0/6								
						0/8	0/5								
SKIN & GILL:															
Covered with mucoid slime	G													9/9	0/6
														9/9	0/5
GILL:															
Hyperplasia of lamellar epithelium	M	4/6	5/6	5/6	4/5	4/6	5/5	4/6	4/6	2/6	4/6	4/6	4/6	6/6	6/6
		3/6	3/6	0/6	0/6	4/6	2/5	0/6	4/6	4/6	3/6	1/6	2/5	4/6	3/5
Telangiectasia of lamellae	M			3/6	0/5	0/6	0/5	2/6	0/6	2/6	3/6	1/6	2/6	6/6	2/6
				0/6	0/6	2/6	0/5	0/6	0/6	3/6	1/6	0/6	0/5	2/6	2/5
Hypertrophy of lamellar epithelial cells	M					0/6	0/5								
						4/6	0/5								
EYE:															
Hemorrhage anterior chamber	G			6/14	0/5									0/6	0/6
				0/14	0/6									5/9	0/5
Exophthalmos	G														
MUSCLE:															
Hemorrhage near vertebrae	G			5/14	0/5										
				2/14	0/6										
Atrophy near lateral line	M			4/6	1/5										
				5/6	1/6										
FAT:															
Edema of myotomes	G													4/9	0/6
														3/9	0/5
Myxomatous degeneration	M	4/6	0/6	4/6	0/5										
		6/6	0/6	6/6	0/6										
SPLEEN:															
Pale and atrophic	G	3/10	0/6					3/12	0/6	3/7	0/6			1/9	0/6
		0/13	0/6					1/13	0/6	0/10	0/6			0/9	0/5
LIVER:															
Reduced cellularity, increased connect. tissue	M	4/5	1/5	5/6	0/5	6/6	1/6	5/6	0/5	4/5	1/6	4/6	1/6	6/6	0/6
		5/6	0/5	4/6	0/6	4/6	2/4	3/6	0/6	4/6	1/6	3/6	0/5	5/6	1/5
Hyperemia	G	4/10	0/6							6/7	0/6	6/7	0/6		
		2/13	0/6							5/10	0/6	5/9	0/5		
Petechia or discolored areas	G	4/10	0/6					7/12	0/6	3/7	0/6				
		4/13	0/6					6/13	0/6	3/10	0/6				
Fatty change	M	6/6	0/6	6/6	0/5	5/6	3/6	5/6	0/5	6/6	0/6	5/6	3/6		
		6/6	0/6	6/5	0/6	3/6	0/5	4/6	0/6	5/6	0/6	3/6	0/5		
Congestion of sinusoids and veins	M									4/6	0/6	3/6	1/6		
										2/6	0/6	4/6	0/5		
Periportal necrosis	M	0/6	0/6												
		2/6	0/6												
Change in hepatocyte architecture	M	0/6	0/6												
		2/6	0/6												
Prominent deposits of glycogen	M					0/6	0/6								
						2/6	3/5								

BILE:	Pink or red color	G	3/10 2/13	0/6 0/6					3/12 0/13	0/6 0/6	2/7 0/10	0/6 0/6	2/7 2/9	0/6 0/5		
	Colorless or absent	G	0/10 0/13	0/6 1/6	4/14 3/14	0/5 0/6	2/6 7/8	0/6 0/5								
GALL BLADDER:	Alteration of epithelium	M					0/6 4/6	0/6 0/5								
STOMACH & ABDOMEN:	Distended with thick mucus	G													3/9 3/9	0/6 0/5
STOMACH:	Edema	G													2/9 2/9	0/6 0/5
	Edema	M													2/6 3/6	2/6 2/5
PYLORIC CECA:	Edema	G													1/9 5/9	0/6 0/5
INTESTINE:	Hyperemia	G	2/10 4/13	0/6 0/6			2/6 3/8	0/6 0/5	9/12 12/13	0/6 0/6	4/7 8/10	0/6 0/6			1/9 3/9	0/6 0/5
	Hyperemia	M									3/6 3/6	0/6 0/6	3/6 3/6	0/6 0/5		
	Flaccid and injected	G											5/7 6/9	0/6 0/5		
	Edema	G													1/9 3/9	0/6 0/5
	Edema	M													2/6 3/6	2/6 2/5
	Lymphocytic infiltrate	M	3/10 4/13	0/6 0/6												
SWIM BLADDER:	Edema	G													2/9 3/9	0/6 0/5
URETERS & URIN. BLAD.:	Edema	G													5/9 1/9	0/6 0/5
KIDNEY:	Precipitate in tubules	M	Present in all fish examined													
	Vacuolization of distal tubules	M	Present in all coho salmon examined													
ADRENAL:	Hyperplasia of cortical tissue	M									0/6 4/6	0/6 0/6				
BRAIN:	Hyperemia or hemorrhage	G	7/10 7/13	0/6 0/6			1/6 2/8	0/6 0/5	10/12 10/13	1/6 0/6	5/7 6/10	1/6 0/6	5/7 5/9	0/6 0/5		
	Hyperemia or hemorrhage	M							5/6 6/6	5/6 4/6	3/6 2/6	1/6 0/6	5/6 5/6	0/6 0/5		
	Vacuolization of opt. tectum or lateral geniculate	M			5/6 6/6	0/5 0/6										

G observed during necropsy.
M observed during microscopic examination.

The top figure in each block represents lake trout, the bottom figure coho salmon.
Blank spaces indicate no change was evident in exposed or control fish.

posed to endosulfan, the degree of change was minimal. Interpretation of the change in any situation but that of a controlled experiment would be difficult if not impossible to assess.

Based on the data generated by this study, diagnosis of endosulfan toxicity in fish must depend entirely upon historical and toxicological evidence. No reports of endosulfan-induced lesions in fish were found in reviewing the literature.

Dieldrin. Hyperemia of the intestine and brain was evident in coho salmon and lake trout exposed to dieldrin. As with endosulfan, these changes were minimal and nonspecific. Adrenal cortical hyperplasia was evident in four out of six exposed coho salmon. Though the degree of hyperplasia was moderate to marked, it may represent a response to stress rather than being diagnostic of dieldrin toxicity.

Mathur's (29) work on the effects of dieldrin upon the liver of several Asian species of fish mentions hepatocyte pleomorphism and cytoplasmic vacuolization. Vacuoles were present in the cytoplasm of hepatocytes in both coho salmon and lake trout in our study. Though they undoubtedly represented minimal fatty change, in our opinion such vacuoles are of no diagnostic importance. The hepatocyte pleomorphism described by Mathur suggests the possibility that dieldrin is causing extensive hepatocellular damage. However, he reported dieldrin levels of from 5 to 50 ppm or 385 to 3850 times the reported 96-hr LC_{50} (0.013 ppm; see Table 22.7). With such levels it must be assumed death was rapid and very possibly occurred before lesions could develop. No mention is made as to the time of death or the method of handling tissues. It is very possible that the liver changes reported by Mathur are those of advanced autolysis. Consideration of this single report (no others were discovered) and of our own data indicates that diagnosis of dieldrin poisoning in fish on the basis of morphological change is not possible.

2,4-D. The only lesion of consequence observed in coho salmon and lake trout exposed to 2,4-D was a very striking degree of brain hyperemia. This agrees with the single report in which the effects of 2,4-D upon fish tissues is discussed (11). The significance of the PAS-positive globular masses described in this same report were discussed previously. The liver changes described in bluegills exposed to 2,4-D (11) were not observed in coho salmon and lake trout in our study. Since very similar liver changes have been reported in bluegills exposed to two herbicides related to 2,4-D (10, 38) (Kuron and dichlobenil) it appears that these lesions have some diagnostic value in at least that species.

The hyperemia and flaccidity observed in the intestine of fish of both species exposed to 2,4-D was unique among compounds in our studies. However, this change has not been reported in other studies with 2,4-D or related phenoxyacetate herbicides. The diagnostic value of this change is further reduced by its similarity to changes seen in several infectious diseases.

Marked vascular congestion of the brain appears to be the only change which can be considered to have diagnostic value in determining 2,4-D toxicity in coho salmon and lake trout. This change in combination with the liver changes and PAS positive globules described by Cope, Wood, and Wallen (11) appears to have considerable value in diagnosing 2,4-D toxicity in the bluegill.

Atrazine. All changes observed in fish exposed to atrazine appear to be related to tissue fluid accumulation. Though variation did occur in the specific sites in which fluid accumulated, all atrazine-exposed fish were afflicted. Table 22.10 lists the organs affected. The marked blackening of exposed lake trout was probably a result of blindness. The mechanism for this is not completely evident but may be related to increased intra-orbital pressure. That such an increase was present in at least some fish is substantiated by the observation of exophthalmos in a number of exposed fish. Whether the iridescent green discoloration of coho salmon exposed to atrazine is a phenomenon related to the blackening of lake trout is only speculative. The alteration of depth selection by all fish exposed to atrazine was probably not voluntary. The most likely cause would appear to be distention of the swim bladder due to a reduction in the fish's ability to remove gas from that organ. This could be due to a mucous film slowing gas resorption or to direct obstruction of the pneumatic duct due to edema of the esophagus. Since generalized edema can result from bacterial infection, culturing of abdominal and orbital fluid as well as material from the kidney was attempted. No organisms of any kind grew on nutrient agar, trypticase soy agar, or furunculosis agar. Tissue slices stained with the Brown-Brenn stain for detection of bacteria in tissue were also negative.

The finding of fish swimming at the water's surface, having superficial pigment changes, marked evidence of edema, and no evidence of pathogenic bacteria would appear to be quite suggestive of atrazine toxicity. Certainly, the above evidence plus a history of recent use of the compound would appear to be diagnostic.

CONCLUSIONS

Attempts to analyze the data from our own studies and those reviewed in Tables 22.1 through 22.5 in an effort to identify characteristic lesions of any group or class of pesticides have been futile. To substantiate the suggestion of similarity in the response of fish to the organophosphates will require a considerable amount of additional evidence. At best, our present knowledge of fish pathology appears to offer the pathologist no more than a minimal ability to aid others in the determination of cause in cases of pesticide poisoning of fish. This role is limited to either eliminating other causes of fish death, such as infectious disease, suggesting the possibility of a pesticide or of pesticides in general, or to confirming the suspicious of the chemist. In all cases, with the possible exceptions of carbaryl and atrazine, the pathologist must have either historical or analytical evidence to support his case.

Acknowledgment. This study was supported by the University of Wisconsin-Madison Sea Grant Program.

REFERENCES

1. Allison, D. B., Kallman, B. J., Cope, O. B., and Van Valin, C. C.   Some chronic effects of DDT on cutthroat trout. *U. S. Fish Wildlife Serv., Res. Rep. 64:* 1–30. 1964.
2. Andrews, A. K., Van Valin, C. C. and Stebbings, B. E.   Some effects of Heptachlor on bluegills (*Lepomis macrochirus*). *Trans. Amer. Fish. Soc. 95:* 297–309. 1966.
3. Auburn University Agricultural Experiment Station and Alabama Department of Conservation.   The principal parasites of fresh-water fish causing severe losses in Alabama waters in 1960–61. *Auburn Univ. Agr. Exp. Sta., Ala. Dep. Cons., Job 30:* 11–14. 1962.
4. Ball, J. N., and Baker, B. I.   The pituitary gland: Anatomy and histophysiology, p. 23. In *Fish Physiology*, ed. W. S. Hoar and D. J. Randall, vol. 2. New York and London, Academic Press, 1969-70.
5. Buhler, D. R., Rasmusson, M. E., and Shanks, W. E.   Chronic oral DDT toxicity in juvenile coho and chinook salmon. *Toxicol. Appl. Pharmacol. 14:* 535–555. 1969.
6. Burdick, G. E., Harris, E. J., Dean, H. J., Walker, T. M., Skea, J., and Colby, D. The accumulation of DDT in lake trout and the effect on reproduction. *Trans. Amer. Fish. Soc. 93:* 127–136. 1964.
7. Christie, R. M., and Battle, H. I.   Histological effects of 3-trifluoromethyl-4-nitrophenol (TFM) on larval lamprey and trout. *Can. J. Zool. 41:* 51–61. 1963.
8. Cope, O. B.   Sport fishery investigations in pesticide-wildlife studies. *U. S. Fish Wildlife Serv., Circ.* 199: 31. 1963.
9. Cope, O. B.   Contamination of the freshwater ecosystem by pesticides. *J. Appl. Ecol. 3* (suppl.): 33–44. 1966.
10. Cope, O. B., McCraren, J. P., and Eller, L. L.   Effects of dichlobenil on two fishpond environments. *Weed Sci. 17:* 158-165. 1969.
11. Cope, O. B., Wood, E. M., and Wallen, G. H.   Some chronic effects of 2,4-D on the bluegill (*Lepomis macrochirus*). *Trans. Amer. Fish. Soc. 99:* 1–12. 1970.
12. Eaton, J. G.   Chronic malathion toxicity to the bluegill (*Lepomis macrochirus*, Rafinesque). *Water Res. 4:* 673–684. 1970.
13. Eller, L. L.   Pathology in redear sunfish exposed to Hydrothol 191. *Trans. Amer. Fish. Soc. 98:*52–59, 1969.
14. Eller, L. L.   Histopathologic lesions in cutthroat trout (*Salmo clarki*) exposed chronically to the insecticide endrin. *Amer. J. Pathol. 64:* 321–336. 1971.
15. Gilderhus, P. A.   Some effects of sublethal concentrations of sodium arsenite on bluegills and the aquatic environment. *Trans. Amer. Fish. Soc. 95:* 289–296. 1966.
16. Grant, B. F., and Mehrle, P. M.   Chronic endrin poisoning in goldfish, *Carassius auratus. J. Fish. Res. Board Can. 27:* 2225–2232. 1970.
17. Halver, J. E., Johnson, C. L. and Ashley, L. M.   Dietary carcinogens induce fish hepatoma. *Fed. Proc. 21:* 390. 1962.
18. Hinton, D. E., Snipes, R. L. and Kendall, M. W.   Morphology and enzyme

histochemistry in the liver of largemouth bass (*Micropterus salmoides*). *J. Fish. Res. Board Can. 29:* 531–534. 1972.

19. Janicki, R. H., and Kinter, W. B. DDT: Disrupted osmoregulatory events in the intestine of the eel. *Science (Wash., D.C.) 173:* 1146–1148. 1971.

20. Johnson, D. W. Pesticides and fishes—a review of selected literature. *Trans. Amer. Fish. Soc. 97:* 398–424. 1968.

21. Kennedy, H. D., and Walsh, D. F. Effects of malathion on two warm-water fishes and aquatic invertebrates in ponds. *U. S. Bur. Sport Fish. Wildlife, Tech. Pap. 55:* 1–13. 1970.

22. Kennedy, H. D., Eller, L. L., and Walsh, D. F. Chronic effects of methoxychlor on bluegills and aquatic invertebrates. *U. S. Bur. Sport Fish. Wildlife, Tech. Pap. 53:* 1–18. 1970.

23. King, S. F. Some effects of DDT on the guppy and the brown trout. *U. S. Fish Wildlife Serv., Spec. Sci. Rep., Fish. 399:* 1–22. 1962.

24. Lie, J. T., Holley, K. E. Kampa, W. R. and Titus, J. L. New histochemical method for morphologic diagnosis of early stages of myocardial ischemia. *Mayo Clin. Proc. 46:* 319–327. 1971.

25. Lowe, J. I. Chronic exposure of spot, *Leiostomus xanthurus*, to sublethal concentrations of toxaphene in seawater. *Trans. Amer. Fish. Soc. 93:* 396–399. 1964.

26. Lowe, J. I. Effects of prolonged exposure to Sevin on an estuarine fish, *Leiostomus xanthurus*, Lacépède. *Bull. Environ. Contam. Toxicol. 2:* 147–155. 1967.

27. McCraren, J. P., Cope, O. B. and Eller, L. L. Some chronic effects of diuron on bluegills. *Weed Sci. 17:* 497–504. 1969.

28. Mathur, D. S. Studies on the histopathologic changes induced by DDT in liver, kidney and intestine of certain fishes. *Experientia 18:* 506–509. 1962.

29. Mathur, D. S. Histopathological changes in the liver of certain fishes induced by dieldrin. *Sci. Cult. 31:* 258–259. 1965.

30. Mount, D. I. Chronic effects of endrin on bluntnose minnows and guppies. *U. S. Fish Wildlife Serv., Res. Rep. 58:* 1–38. 1962.

31. Mount, D. I., and Putnicki, G. J. Summary report of the 1963 Mississippi River fishkill. *N. Amer. Wildlife Natur. Resour. Conf. Trans. 31.* 1966.

32. Schulz, D. Research into the side effects of the herbicide NaTA$_2$ (sodium trichloroacetate) on the carp. *Zentralbl. Veterinaermed.,* Reihe A, *17:* 230–251. 1970.

33. Schulz, D. Light microscopic, biochemical and electron microscopic changes on the exocrine pancreas of the carp caused by the herbicide Dowpon. *Z. angew. Zool. 58:* 63–97. 1971.

34. Snieszko, S. F. Bacterial gill disease of freshwater fishes. *U. S. Bur. Sport Fish. Wildlife, Fish Dis. Leafl. 19.* 1970.

35. Snieszko, S. F. Nutritional (dietary) gill disease and other less known gill diseases of freshwater fishes. *U. S. Bur. Sport Fish. Wildlife, Fish Dis. Leafl. 23.* 1970.

36. Stock, J. N., and Cope, O. B. Some effects of TEPA, an insect chemosterilant, on the guppy, *Poecilia reticulata. Trans. Amer. Fish. Soc. 98:* 280–287. 1969.

37. Van Valin, C. C., Andrews, A. K., and Eller, L. L.   Some effects of mirex on two warm-water fishes. *Trans. Amer. Fish. Soc. 97:* 185–196. 1968.
38. Wood, E. M.   The pathology of pesticide toxicity in fish. Unpublished.
39. Wood, E. M., and Yasutake, W. T.   Histopathology of fish. V. Gill disease. *Progr. Fish-Cult. 19:* 7–13. 1957.

DISCUSSION OF THE PATHOLOGY OF PESTICIDE POISONING

Comment: In certain marine fish, like the croakers, I have observed that there are a tremendous number of mitoses in the white blood cells in the region of the intestinal lamina propria.

L. M. Ashley: My experience is that in the lamina propria you frequently find a light infiltration of lymphocytes and perhaps a few other leukocytes, and occasionally you will find a heavy infiltration possibly due to some infectious condition. We know that lymphocytes eventually migrate through the mucosa and possibly carry out their immune antibody functions in that area, perhaps more than in any other areas, so mitotic figures would be fairly normal in that area.

L. E. Mawdesley-Thomas: I am very interested to see the changes in the central nervous system because with these changes, as Dr. King has said, one is struck with the similarity between various species. In many of the experiments that we have done in higher animals with these pesticides we see these brain lesions. We see the vacuolation that you've described and we see much swelling of the white fibers. Now, like you, we haven't been able to stain these vacuoles, and I believe that these most likely are edema fluid. The big problem is, is it intracellular or extracellular edema, because one of the great arguments going on at the moment is that so many of these pesticides are thought to interfere with, or uncouple, the oxidative phosphorylation.   It would seem that you are getting the same sort of thing in the fish brain here that we see in dogs and in rats.

J. M. King: I happened to work with Sevin for a few years and in pigs saw hypermetria. It would be interesting to know if fish could show overstepping movements. I don't know how they would manifest this. Do your fish have nervous signs?

A. H. Walsh: The fish exposed in Sevin were allowed to die, or were moribund when killed. As death approached, exposure to light was the thing that seemed to affect them. They would go into rather strange gyrations and in some cases would bend into a U-shape, just hold it like that for several seconds, and then relax and appear to have died. Frequently there would be no activity for a couple of minutes, then they would be back up and swimming around. So it may be similar.

J. M. King: You might call that hypermetria in fish, somehow. In these pigs that have it after a long period of time, about 60 days on Sevin at low levels, the only lesion found would be vacuolization of the ventral nucleus of the vagus.

Question: Did you indicate what doses were used and what levels are toxic? Did you indicate what the minimal doses are?

A. H. Walsh: I didn't. This is extremely complex. Because we wanted reasonably long exposures, we hoped that we could kill these fish within 30 to 60 days, and we made exposures at sublethal levels that we interpreted from the literature. The only references that we could find were 96-hr LC_{50}'s. The interpretations that we made were perhaps valid, but the difficulty lay in achieving the desired levels. Levels were achieved by periodic analysis of water and subsequent alteration of dosage rate. Typically we found that the level that existed was considerably under what we had put in. We had to keep increasing the levels as we received the reports. In the case of Sevin, there were several different groups; the highest exposure group eventually received over 10 ppm. We started with somewhere in the neighborhood of 200 ppb and those fish developed a remarkable resistance.

Question: Is there anything known about synergistic action if there is more than one of these compounds? Do you or anyone else in the audience know, are fish useful for the detection of minute amounts of pesticides?

A. H. Walsh: Well, there have been multiple exposures, and recently there has been some work in which dieldrin and DDT appeared to be antagonistic. It seemed to take higher levels of dieldrin, I believe it was, to kill fish if they had been exposed to DDT previously. However, when the order is reversed the effect is synergistic or at least additive. Fish brain cholinesterase levels have been used as a means of monitoring for organophosphate pesticides. Weiss, I think, first suggested that, but other people have claimed it is useless.

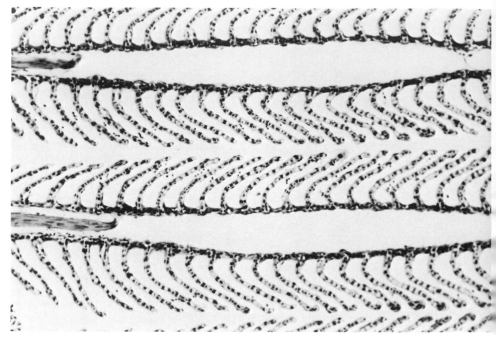

Fig. 22.1. Gill lamellae (normal). Note flat epithelial surface and constant lamellar width. Control coho salmon in 2,4-D study. Hematoxylin and eosin (H&E); ×100.

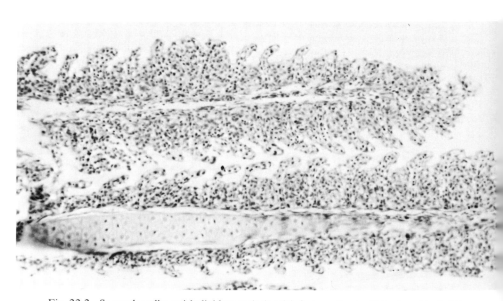

Fig. 22.2. Severe lamellar epithelial hyperplasia with fusion. Control lake trout in 2,4-D study. H&E; ×100.

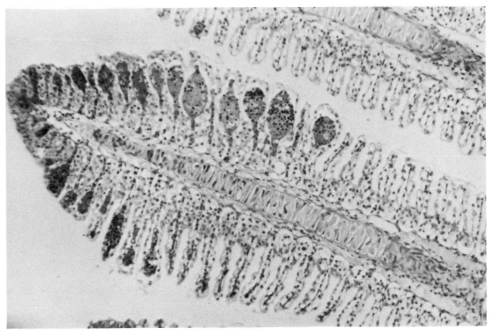

Fig. 22.3. Lamellar telangiectasis. Some of the enlarged capillaries are thrombosed, while others contain what appears to be normal blood. Dieldrin-exposed coho salmon. H&E; ×100.

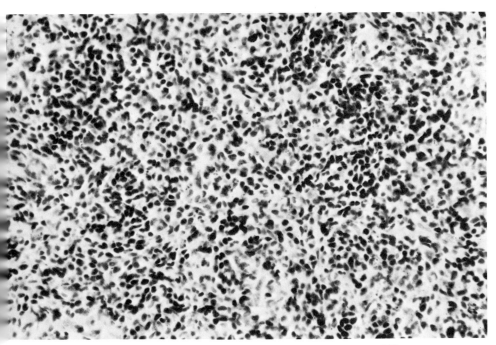

Fig. 22.4. Spleen. Control lake trout in DDT study. H&E; ×250.

543

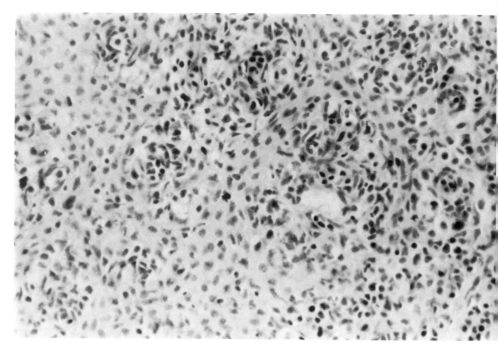

Fig. 22.5. Spleen with reduced cellularity and apparent increase in connective tissue. DDT-exposed lake trout. H&E; ×250.

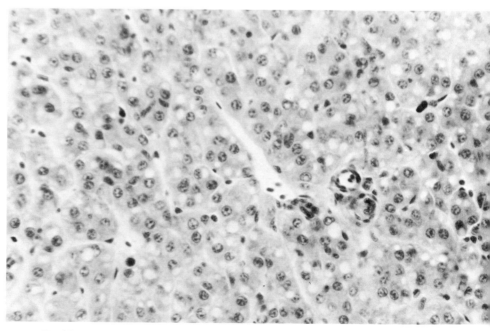

Fig. 22.6. Randomly distributed lipid vacuoles in hepatocyte cytoplasm. The extent of fatty change in this photograph typifies the most severe examples of this lesion seen in these studies. Endosulfan-exposed lake trout. H&E; ×250.

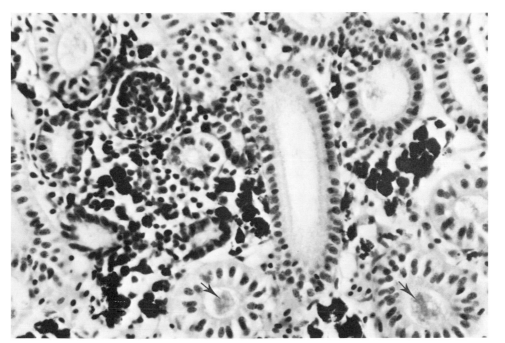

Fig. 22.7. Precipitate in lumina of proximal convoluted tubules. Control lake trout in DDT study. H&E; ×250.

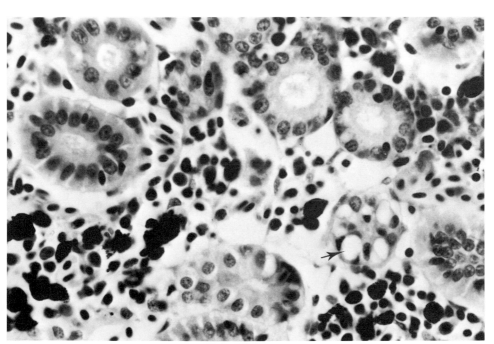

Fig. 22.8. Large intracytoplasmic vacuoles in epithelial cells of distal convoluted tubules. Control coho salmon in endosulfan study. H&E; ×420.

545

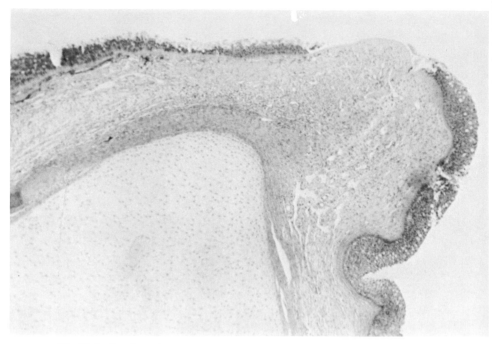

Fig. 22.9. Small erosion, premaxillary region. Coho salmon control. H&E; ×40.

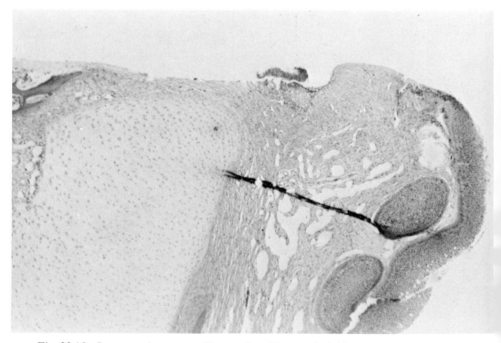

Fig. 22.10. Severe erosion, premaxillary region. Note marked thinning of dermis nearly exposing bone and cartilage. Coho salmon control. H&E; ×40.

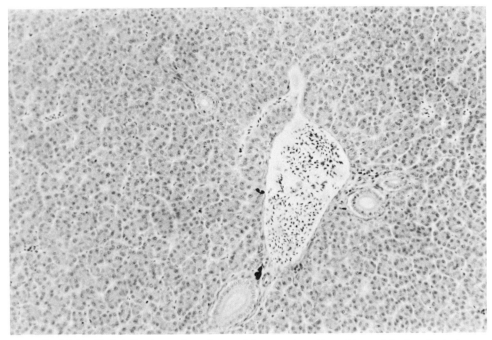

Fig. 22.11. Well-defined muralia and normal hepatocytes adjacent to portal vein. Control coho salmon in DDT study. H&E; ×100.

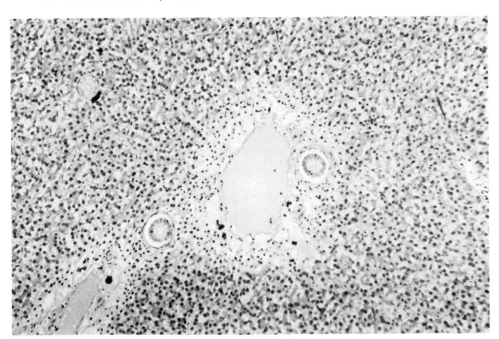

Fig. 22.12. Evidence of liver architectural pattern is lost, many hepatocytes contain pyknotic nuclei, and there is marked necrosis of hepatocytes adjacent to portal vein. DDT-exposed coho salmon. H&E; ×100.

547

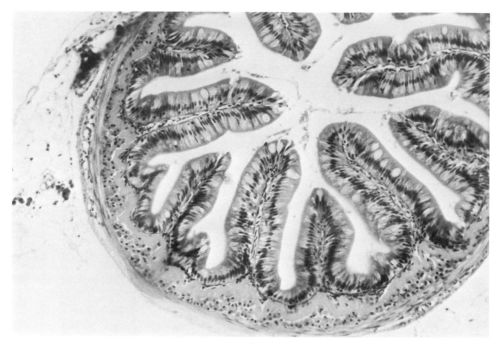

Fig. 22.13. Pyloric cecum. Control coho salmon in DDT study. H&E; ×100.

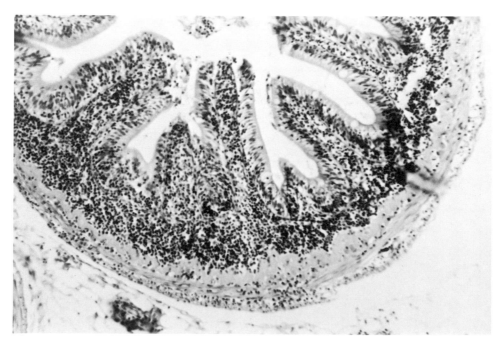

Fig. 22.14. Lymphocytic infiltrate, lamina propria of pyloric cecum. DDT-exposed coho salmon. H&E; ×100.

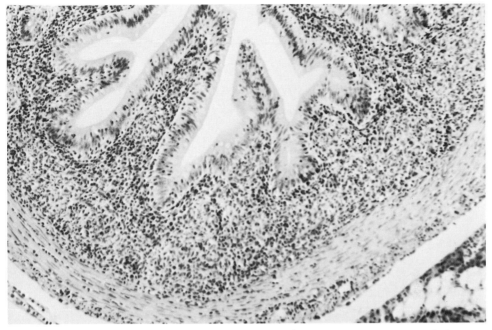

Fig. 22.15. Lymphocytic infiltrate, lamina propria of pyloric cecum. DDT-exposed lake trout. H&E, ×100.

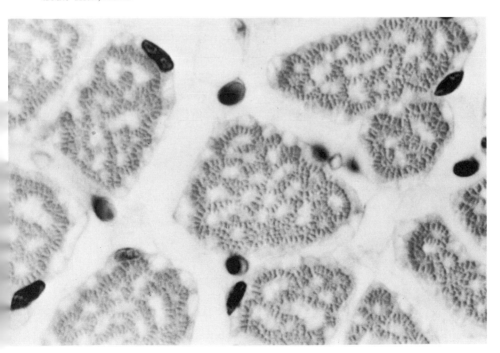

Fig. 22.16. Small normal muscle bundles near lateral line. Note radial arrangement of myofibrils about vacuoles. Control coho salmon in carbaryl study. H&E; ×1025.

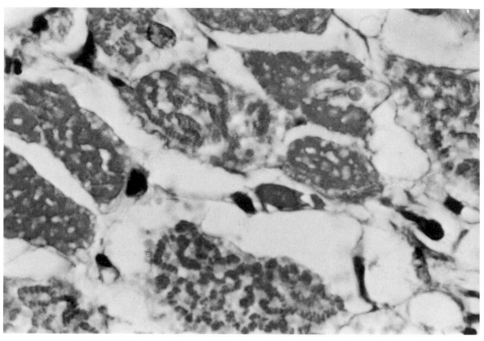

Fig. 22.17. Hyaline degeneration of muscle bundles near lateral line. Largest bundles have very early change. Medium-sized bundles have more marked hyalinization and condensation. A markedly atrophic bundle is located just below and to the right of center. Carbaryl-exposed coho salmon. H&E; ×1025.

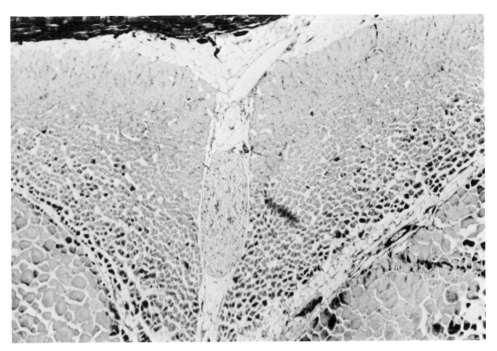

Fig. 22.18. Band of normal muscle adjacent to lateral line. Note small but rather constant size of bundles. Only a few of the bundles in the deeper portion of the muscle have taken the dark fuchsin stain. Control coho salmon in carbaryl study. Hematoxylin-basic fuchsin-picric acid (HBFP); ×40.

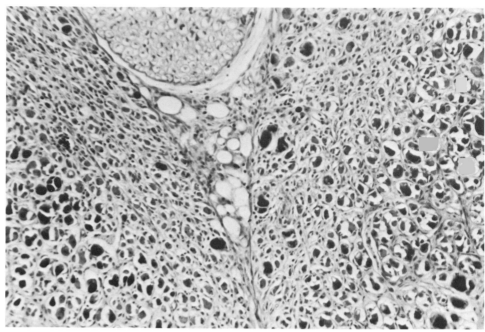

Fig. 22.19. Markedly atrophic bundles, lateral line muscle. Note that the very small irregular bundles do not accept the dark fuchsin stain. Carbaryl-exposed coho salmon. HBFP; X100.

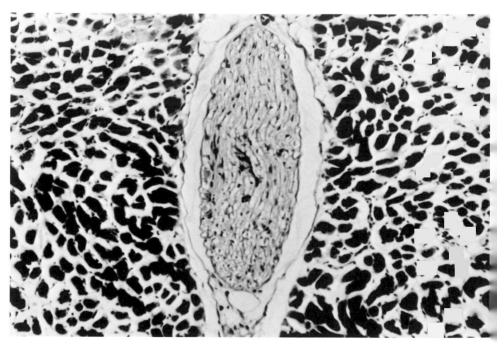

Fig. 22.20. Dark-staining lateral line muscle bundles indicative of early atrophic change. Carbaryl-exposed coho salmon. HBFP; X100.

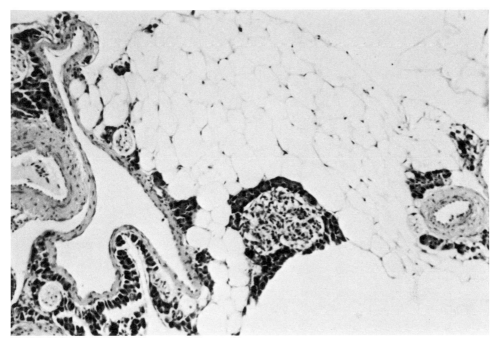

Fig. 22.21. Normal fat adjacent to pancreatic tissue. Control coho salmon in carbaryl study. H&E; ×100.

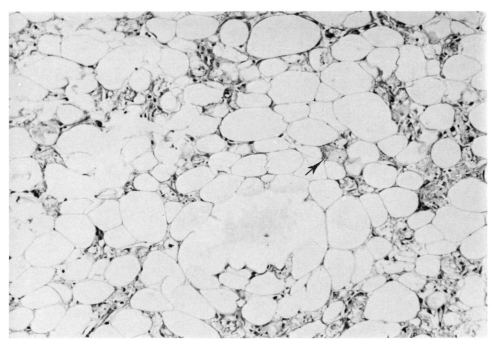

Fig. 22.22. Degenerated and normal fat near pancreas. Carbaryl-exposed coho salmon. H&E; ×100.

553

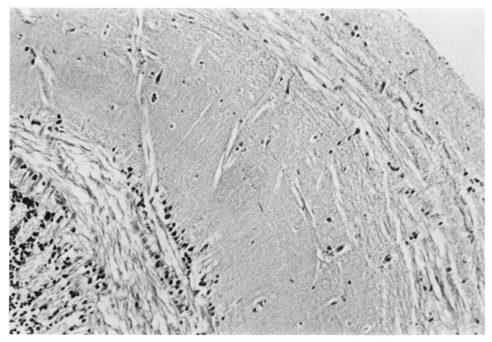

Fig. 22.23. Optic tectum. Control coho salmon in carbaryl study. H&E; ×100.

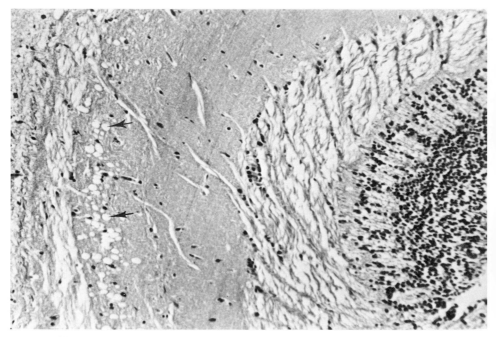

Fig. 22.24. Vacuoles (arrows), optic tectum. Carbaryl-exposed coho salmon. H&E; ×100.

554

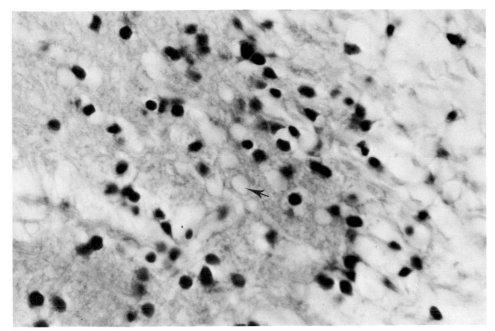

Fig. 22.25. Vacuoles (arrow), lateral geniculate body. Carbaryl-exposed lake trout. H&E; ×400.

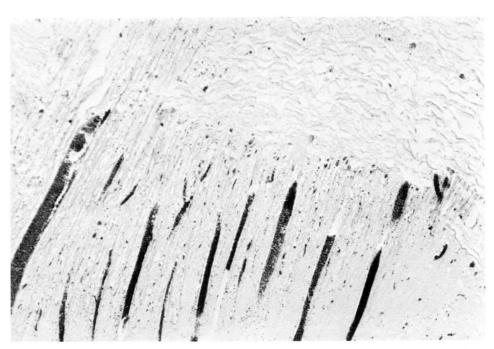

Fig. 22.26. Marked congestion, medulla oblongata. Coho salmon exposed to 2,4-D. H&E; ×40.

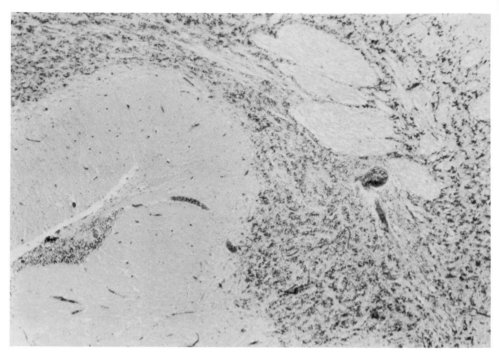

Fig. 22.27. Moderate congestion, cerebellum. Lake trout exposed to 2,4-D. H&E; ×40.

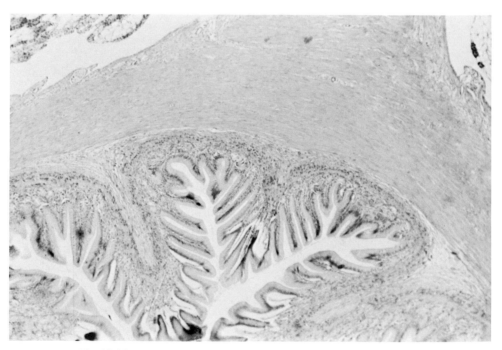

Fig. 22.28. Stomach, control coho salmon in atrazine study. H&E; ×40.

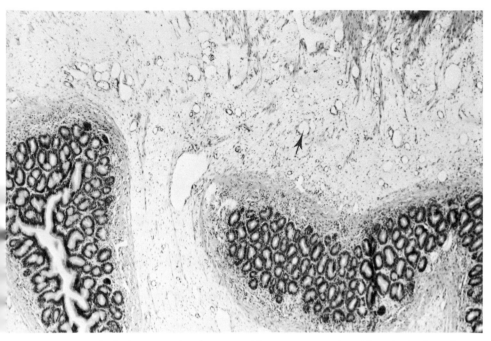

Fig. 22.29. Marked edema, gastric submucosa. Note numerous enlarged lymphatics (arrow). Atrazine-exposed coho salmon. H&E; ×40.

23

Histopathological Effects of Pesticides and Related Chemicals on the Livers of Fishes

JOHN A. COUCH

Evidence for the accumulation of pesticides in aquatic ecosystems is abundant (26). Nontarget species such as fishes from salt and fresh water have been monitored for pesticide contamination (15, 16). Certain pesticides, e.g., organochlorines and their metabolites, accumulate in wild fish, particularly in liver and fatty tissues (7).

Results of controlled laboratory exposures of fishes to pesticides and related chemicals reveal that the liver is often the organ with highest pesticide concentrations (7, 14, 15), and greatest damage or impairment (8, 12). This information, combined with the general knowledge that the liver of vertebrates is a chief metabolic and detoxication organ, suggests that a review of the histopathology of the livers of fishes in reference to pesticide exposure would be of value.

REVIEW OF PESTICIDE-RELATED LIVER LESIONS

Considerable bioassay and toxicological research concerning effects of pesticides on fishes has been reported. Experimental pesticide-induced acute and chronic mortalities have been well documented for many fresh- and saltwater species (26). However, of over 900 commercial pesticide formulations in general use (26), fewer than 30 have been reported to have been tested in the laboratory for histological effects on the livers of fishes (Table 23.1).

Table 23.1. Pesticides and Related Chemicals That Have Induced Nonspecific or
Specific* Liver Changes in Fishes (see text for details)

Organochlorines	Organophosphates	Carbamates	Other
Insecticides	Insecticides	Insecticide	Lampreycide
Chlordane	Abate	Sevin*	TFM (3-trifluoromethyl-
DDT	Dursban		4-nitrophenol)
Endrin*	Dylox		
Heptachlor	Malathion		Herbicide
Lindane*	Parathion		Hydrothol 191 (N,N
Methoxychlor*			dimethyl-alkylamine salt
Mirex			of endothal)
Telodrin			
Toxaphene			
Herbicides			
Dichlobenil			
Dowicide G			
2,4-D*			
Silvex			
Industrial chemicals			
Polychlorinated biphenyls			
(Aroclor 1248)			
(Aroclor 1254)*			

Even though many species of fishes are inadvertently exposed to pesticides
every year, fewer than 20 species have been reported to have been examined for
liver changes following exposures to pesticides under controlled conditions (Table
23.2).

The following is an attempt to summarize available results of controlled field
and laboratory research. Included are recent results from the author's laboratory
concerning the pathogenic effects of pesticides and certain related chemicals on
the livers of estuarine and marine fishes.

The significance of microscopic effects reported by different authors should
be determined in relation to the concentration of pesticides and the methods of
exposure of fishes. Information has been included, when available, on the types
of exposure (e.g., bath, food, flowing water, ponds, aquaria, tanks) as well as on
the concentration of pesticide and the duration of exposure. Lethal concentration data (LC_{50}; LC_{100}) for specific pesticides and fishes are given when cited in
relevant works.

Discussions of pesticides and their effects are placed under the following major chemical groupings: (1) organochlorines, (2) organophosphates, (3) carbamates, (4) other chemicals.

Table 23.2. Fishes Examined for Liver Lesions Following Exposure to
Pesticide or Related Chemicals

Common name	Scientific name	Chemical and source data
Freshwater species		
Bluegill	*Lepomis macrochirus*	Abate (11), heptachlor (1), methoxychlor (16), mirex (27), dichlobenil (Casoron) (4), 2,4-D (5, 11), silvex (29)
Brook lamprey	*Entosphenus lamottei*	TFM (2)
Brown trout	*Salmo trutta*	DDT (17)
Bluntnose minnow	*Pimephales notatus*	Endrin (25)
Cutthroat trout	*Salmo clarki*	Endrin (12)
Goldfish	*Carassius auratus*	Mirex (27)
Guppy	*Poecilia reticulata (Lebistes reticulatus)*	DDT (17), Dowicide G (6)
Lake trout	*Salvelinus namaycush*	Aroclor 1248 (11), chlordane (11)
Rainbow trout	*Salmo gairdneri*	DDT (29), endrin (29), heptachlor (3, 29), malathion (3, 29), methoxychlor (3, 29), parathion (29), Toxaphene (29), TFM (2)
Redear sunfish	*Lepomis microlophus*	Hydrothol 191 (10)
Marine species		
Pinfish	*Lagodon rhomboides*	Mirex (21)
Sheepshead minnow	*Cyprinodon variegatus*	Dursban (Lowe, Wood)
Spot	*Leiostomus xanthurus*	Aroclor 1254, endrin (19), Sevin (Lowe), Telodrin (Lowe), 2,4-D (Lowe)

ORGANOCHLORINES

Organochlorine Insecticides

*Chlordane.** Eller (11) examined lake trout† that were exposed to 1.2 to 12 ppm of chlordane for one year (from March 1970 to March 1971). He found that early in the exposure period both control and exposed fish had liver damage consisting of focal areas of parenchymal cell vacuolation and degeneration. From April through June the incidence and severity of degeneration in the liver increased in the chlordane-exposed fish to a level about twice as severe as that in control trout. About 80% of the exposed fish had degenerative changes.

---

* Common names of pesticides are used here. Chemical names or structural formulas of many pesticides can be found references 13, 24, and 26.

† All fishes examined in this and subsequent summaries were killed and fixed for histological examination; i.e., fish were survivors of experimental exposures.

DDT. King (17) found liver lesions in brown trout fry and adult guppies exposed in aerated aquaria for 14 days to 0.00032 to 3.2 ppm DDT. In the trout fry, both control and experimental fish had many small vacuoles in hepatic cells. This may have been related to resorption of fatty yolk by the young trout. Guppies in 0.32 ppm DDT for one day presented entire liver sections with severe vacuolation and necrosis.

Wood (29) examined rainbow trout exposed to 5 ppb DDT in tanks for 14 days (LC_{50} 14 days = 5 ppb). He found no signs of liver changes.

Endrin. Mount (25) found lipid deposits in hepatocytes of bluntnose minnows exposed for 291 days to 0.4 ppm or more of endrin in a continuous flow freshwater system. Wild fish did not have extensive lipid deposits but control fish did. Mount attributed the lipid change in the liver of exposed fish and control fish to high lipid content of the artificial diet.

Wood (in 19) found no liver changes in spot, an estuarine fish, exposed to sublethal concentrations of endrin in flowing sea water. However, in spot surviving near-lethal concentration (0.075 ppb) exposures he found focal necrosis and inflammation in the liver as well as loss of glycogen and lipid.

Rainbow trout surviving exposure to 0.269 ppb endrin in tanks (LC_{50} 7 days = 0.269 ppb) had severe, nonspecific degenerative liver lesions (29).

The most detailed report available on endrin-induced changes in the liver of fishes is that of Eller (12). He found that cellular changes occurred in the livers of cutthroat trout following water or food exposures of 0.01 ppm or 0.01 mg/kg respectively of endrin. Certain of the induced changes resembled prehepatomatous lesions: (1) liver cord disarray, (2) presence of mitotic cells in liver, (3) binucleate cells, (4) swollen cells, (5) pleomorphic cells, (6) bizarre cells with enlarged nuclei, (7) acidophilic, pigmented cells, and (8) intrazonal and periportal inflammatory foci. However, no fully developed hepatoma occurred. Fish exposed to lower levels of endrin also showed certain of the above changes, but most had lesions that were intermediate in severity between those in fish exposed to higher levels and those of the unexposed controls. Eller believed the above degenerative changes in the liver suggested nutritional deficiency enhanced by endrin exposure.

Heptachlor. Bluegills exposed to 0.050 ppm and 0.037 ppm heptachlor in ponds developed severe degenerative liver lesions (1). After 14 days' exposure, lesions consisted of variation in staining intensity, early necrotic change, and loss of glycogen and fat. Exposures to lower concentrations produced no liver changes. Bluegills fed 25 mg of heptachlor per kg of body weight in small ponds had vague liver changes (1) consisting of loss of liver cord pattern, cellular shrinkage, and loss of glycogen and fat.

Wood (in 3; 29) reported that rainbow trout exposed to 7.5 to 17.5 ppb heptachlor for 14 days (LC_{50} 14 days = 7.5 ppb) in tanks had severe liver changes consisting of deposition of bile pigment in parenchymal cells and degeneration of liver tissue. The changes were too nonspecific to be used to identify heptachlor as the cause of the changes.

Lindane (BHC). Wood (in 3; 29) found lesions in the livers of rainbow trout surviving exposure to 15 to 23 ppb lindane for 7 days (LC_{50} 7 days = 15 ppb). The lesions were focal, necrotic areas mainly associated with the portal triads. Fish having signs of toxicity during exposures had liver lesions of an "early coagulative type." Cellular detail in these lesions was obliterated. Wood believed that these lesions were specific for lindane in comparison to more general lesions produced by exposures of fish to other insecticides.

Methoxychlor. Rainbow trout exposed to 10.0 ppb methoxychlor in ponds for one week (LC_{50} 7 days = 10.0 ppb) had only nonspecific degenerative changes in the liver (3, 29). These changes indicated damage caused by a toxic substance, but were not specific enough to identify methoxychlor as the toxic agent.

Bluegills exposed to 0.01 ppm or 0.04 ppm methoxychlor in ponds for 13 weeks exhibited variation in liver condition over a period of time (16). After 3 days at 0.01 ppm or 14 days at 0.04 ppm, nonspecific degenerative changes characterized by some liver parenchymal shrinkage, increased cytoplasmic granularity, and partial loss of liver cord orientation occurred. By day 56 of exposure, these vague changes were not obvious. At day 1 of the 0.04 ppm exposure, minute eosinophilic globules appeared in blood vessels of the liver of all exposed fish. By day 3, these globules had coalesced to form spherical masses of variable sizes in the liver blood capillaries. By day 56 the spherical masses (possibly precipitated serum proteins (16)) had disappeared.

Mirex. Bluegills exposed to 0.0013 ppm or 1.0 ppm mirex in ponds had no liver changes (27).

Pinfish fed approximately 20 ppm mirex for five months in flowing sea water had no liver changes (21).

Goldfish exposed to 1.0 ppm or 0.1 ppm mirex underwent little change in liver structure (27). However, Van Valin, Andrews, and Eller (27) did find foci of acidfast bacteria in the livers of exposed fish and stated that the stress of the pesticide challenge in the presence of mycobacterial infection contributed to higher mortality in the exposed as compared to control fish.

Telodrin. J. I. Lowe (personal communication) reported that of several pesticides tested on estuarine and marine fishes, Telodrin was one of the more toxic. Wood examined the spot which Lowe had exposed to 0.01 ppb Telodrin (sublethal level) for five months in flowing sea water. He found minimal degenerative changes in the livers of surviving fish. These changes consisted of scattered eosinophilic globules (remains of necrotic liver cells) adjacent to the intrahepatic pancreatic acinar tissues.

Toxaphene. Rainbow trout that survived exposure to 0.005 ppb toxaphene for seven days (LC_{50} 7 days = 0.005 ppb) had extensive liver damage, according to Wood (29). Parenchymal cell necrosis and disruption of liver cord structure were striking, but neither together nor alone were these signs sufficient for identification of toxaphene as the toxic agent.

Organochlorine Herbicides

Dichlobenil (Casoron). Cope, McCraren, and Eller (4) studied changes in the livers of bluegills exposed to single treatments of 10 ppm, 20 ppm, and 40 ppm of dichlobenil in ponds. Livers of exposed fish had an increase in connective tissue, and early adenomatous change. Also present was abundant nuclear pyknosis, hepatocyte karyolysis, and focal and massive necrosis. All exposed bluegills had these lesions through 59 days. Livers of fish exposed to 10 ppm dichlobenil returned to normal by 59 days, but those treated with 20 ppm and 40 ppm continued to have the lesions through 112 days.

Dowicide G (Sodium pentachlorophenate). Guppies were exposed to 0.5 ppm of this herbicide for 180 days in aerated aquaria by Crandall and Goodnight (6). Fish examined following 20 to 30 days of exposure had enlarged liver sinusoids and enlarged, hyperchromic hepatocyte nuclei. Controls were normal. At 60 days, the exposed fish possessed less liver fat than controls, but were histologically similar to controls. At 88 to 100 days, one fish had a necrotic liver and at 131 days, one had a "fatty" liver. At 180 days, two surviving fish had abnormally compact parenchyma with few visible sinusoids and their liver parenchyma tissues appeared "coagulated."

2,4-D. Bluegills were exposed in ponds for 112 days to single treatments of 0.1 ppm to 10.0 ppm 2,4-D by Cope, Wood, and Wallen (5). Liver sections from fish exposed 1 to 14 days had glycogen loss, irregular staining, and periodic acid–Schiff–positive deposits in liver sinusoids. These signs were not found in fish exposed longer than 112 days. The authors considered that the glycogen loss in the fish from early exposure was possibly related to the appearance of the PAS-positive deposits in the liver sinusoids and to similar deposits found throughout the vascular system of the exposed fish. These deposits appeared globular or spherical and ranged in diameter from 1 to 50 microns. Their PAS-positive material was also diastase-resistant, iron-negative (Prussian blue reaction), was not acidfast, and was gram-negative. PAS-positive bodies in the liver sinusoids provided a possible clue to the origin of the PAS bodies elsewhere. The authors suggested that the concomitant losses of glycogen from the liver and the appearance of the PAS-positive vascular deposits were highly specific signs of 2,4-D toxicity.

In an unrelated experiment, Eller (11) found histological evidence of effects of 2,4-D on liver carbohydrate metabolism in bluegills. In exposed, moribund fish he found abnormal PAS-positive material in the nuclei of hepatocytes along with large clear intranuclear vacuoles. This, with other evidence, suggested a 2,4-D-induced hyperglycemic state. This state was only transitory, however, because in fish exposed for long periods the pathological liver changes disappeared.

Lowe (personal communication) exposed spot to 1.0 ppm of 2,4-D for 30 days in flowing sea water. I have examined livers of both control and exposed fish. In only one of five exposed spot was there a significant departure from normal. This fish had moderate-to-heavy congestion of the liver sinusoids and large lytic cavities in the liver parenchyma. The cavities may have been the result of tissue instability during the tissue processing, but the congestion seen in the sinusoids appeared to be a genuine pathological condition.

Silvex (Kuron). Wood (29) examined bluegills exposed to 1.0 ppm, 3.0 ppm, and 10.0 ppm silvex in ponds. In exposed fish he found generalized, degenerative liver changes consisting of glycogen and lipid loss, staining variability, cell shrinkage, and liver cord disorientation.

Polychlorinated Biphenyls (PCB'S)

These chemicals have not been used extensively as pesticides, but are listed in Pimentel's review (26) of ecological effects of pesticides on nontarget species. Several polychlorinated biphenyls have been found in water, sediments, and animal tissues from around the world (14, 28). The apparent ubiquity of PCB's in the natural environment has led to considerable effort to learn of their possible toxic effects on many animal species (26, 28), including fishes (11, 14).

Chemically the PCB's are chlorinated biphenyls and thus share some characteristics, such as fatty and liver tissue affinity and relative long life (persistence) in the environment, with certain organochlorine pesticides, e.g., DDT.

To date, no published reports exist concerning effects of PCB's on livers of fishes. However, the following information is from work recently completed by Eller (11) at the U.S. Bureau of Sports Fisheries and Wildlife, Fish Pesticide Laboratory, Columbia, Missouri, and from work recently completed by several investigators at the U.S. Environmental Protection Agency, Gulf Breeze, Florida, Laboratory.

Two PCB's, Aroclor 1248 and Aroclor 1254, have been tested on fishes at the above laboratories.

Aroclor 1248. Lake trout exposed to 1.2 to 12.0 ppm Aroclor 1248 for one year (March 1970 to March 1971), and examined by Eller (11), had early, progressive, degenerative liver changes. Control fish also had some similar lesions initially. The changes were (1) focal degenerative regions of the liver, (2) cytoplasmic vacuolation, and (3) pleomorphism of parenchymal cells. As the exposure period progressed, the liver lesions of exposed fish increased in severity. From April through June, 80% of exposed fish examined had liver lesions two to three times more severe than any found in control fish. By August all fish exposed to high levels of Aroclor 1248 had extensive liver parenchymal cell vacuolation.

The final effects of this exposure are yet to be reported.

Aroclor 1254. Hansen et al. (14) at the Gulf Breeze Laboratory studied the chronic toxicity, uptake, and retention of Aroclor 1254 in two estuarine fishes, spot and pinfish. They determined the relative uptake of Aroclor 1254 in six different tissues. The liver concentrated the greatest relative amount of this PCB. Lowe and Hansen (personal communication) supplied me with fish samples for

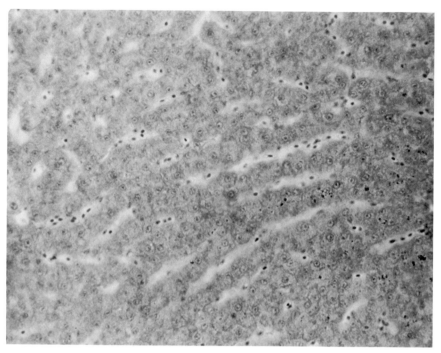

Fig. 23.1. Normal liver parenchyma of spot. Note liver cords, 1 to 2 cells thick, and sinusoids in tubulo-sinusoidal pattern. X450.

pathology from Aroclor 1254 chronic exposure experiments. Also, I have exposed spot to Aroclor 1254 in order to acquire tissue for pathology. The following is a report on liver changes in spot associated with Aroclor 1254 exposures.

Spot from wild populations in Pensacola Bay, Florida, and from control tanks were used to establish histological and cytological patterns in normal liver, and were directly compared to exposed fish.

Normal spot possess a tubulo-sinusoidal liver (9) containing disseminated pancreatic tissue (Figs. 23.1-23.6). The pancreas follows the course of the portal vein and bile duct through the liver parenchyma. In wild and control fish the liver parenchymal cells are arranged in cords (or muralia) 1 to 2 cells thick (Figs. 23.1, 23.2). Liver parenchymal cells of wild spot are usually laden with glycogen (heavily PAS-positive, diastase-labile), whereas those of fish held for one week or longer under control or experimental exposure conditions lose most of the detectable glycogen. Apparently these fish do poorly on artificial diets. This fact possibly introduces a nutritional variable into any evaluation of effects of toxic substances. Wild spot have very little fat in their livers, as demonstrated by oil red O treatment of frozen sections.

Juvenile and adult spot were exposed to 5.0 ppb Aroclor 1254 in flowing sea

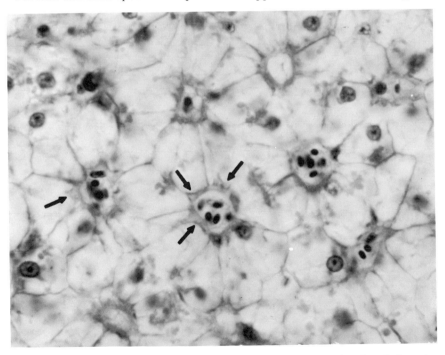

Fig. 23.2. Cross section of normal liver parenchyma of spot demonstrating the tubular nature of sinusoids and their relationship to parenchymal cells. Note space of Disse (arrows). X1000.

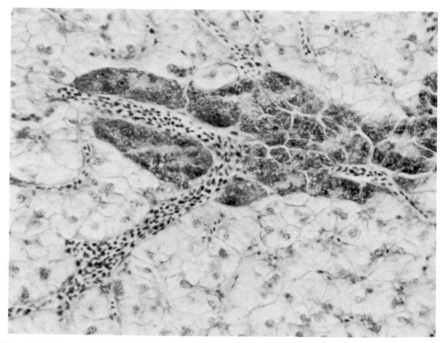

Fig. 23.3. Normal liver parenchyma, pancreatic acinar tissue, and branches of the portal vein in spot. X450.

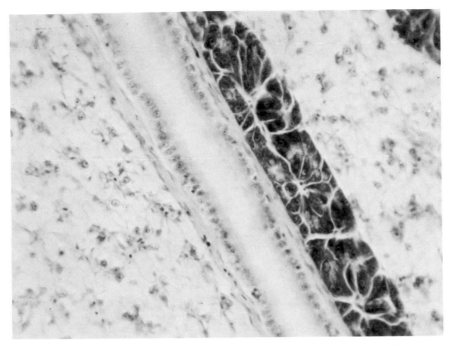

Fig. 23.4. Longitudinal section of normal bile duct and parallel pancreatic acinar tissue in liver of spot. X450.

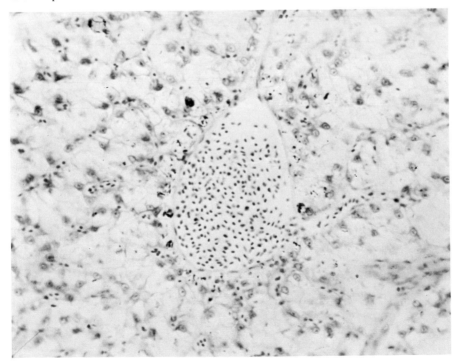

Fig. 23.5. Central vein and branches in normal liver of spot. Note that lumen of vein is only partially filled with red blood cells. X450.

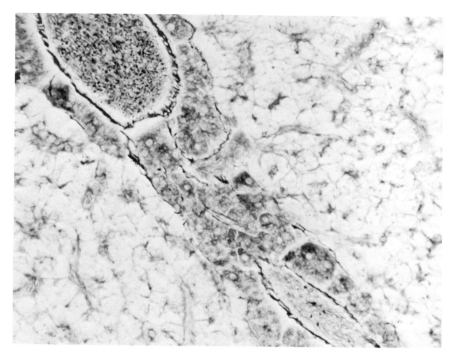

Fig. 23.6. Normal reticulin pattern of portal vein, adjacent pancreatic acinar tissue, and liver parenchyma. Lillie's silver oxide method; ×450.

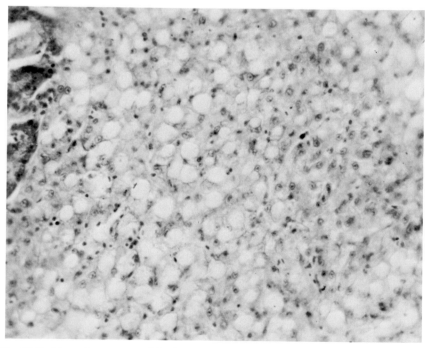

Fig. 23.7. Liver of spot exposed for 2 weeks to 5 ppb Aroclor 1254. Note extensive vacuolation of parenchymal cells characteristic of intermediate pathological response. ×450.

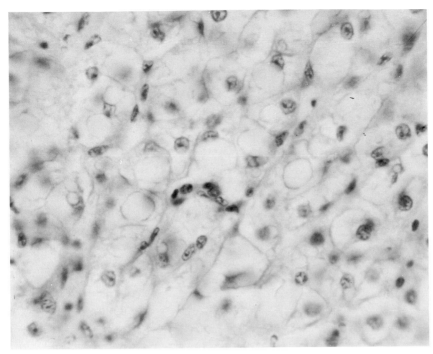

Fig. 23.8. Large, smooth-edged vacuoles in liver of spot (enlarged from Figure 23.7), ×1000.

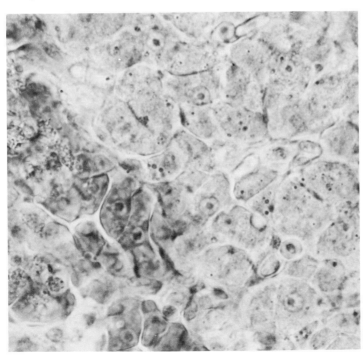

Fig. 23.9. Frozen section of control, normal spot liver treated with oil red O. Note lack of large lipid deposits. ×1000.

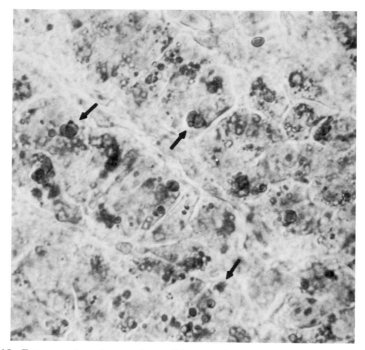

Fig. 23.10. Frozen section of exposed spot liver treated with oil red O. Note extensive lipid deposits which are oil red O-positive. Arrows indicate parenchymal cells. ×1000.

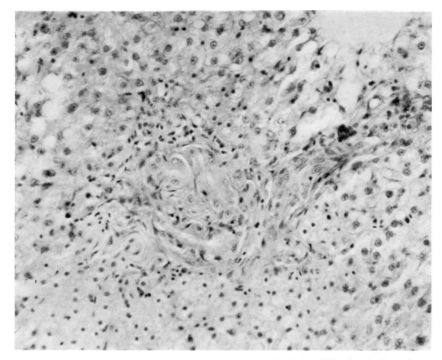

Fig. 23.11. Focus of early fibrosis and cholangiolar epithelial proliferation in liver of spot exposed to Aroclor 1254 for 2 weeks. X450.

water for from 14 to 56 days. After one week's exposure, considerable glycogen depletion had occurred in livers from both control and exposed spot, but there were no significant morphological differences between the two groups.

Following two weeks' exposure, relative differences in histological patterns of exposed vs. control spot livers were found. Parenchymal cell vacuolation in exposed livers was two to three times as great as that in control livers (Figs. 23.1, 23.7, 23.8). Moderately large (15 to 20 microns), smooth-edged vacuoles in hepatic cells indicated fatty accumulation in the exposed spot. Oil red O staining of frozen sections from these fish confirmed that the content of the vacuoles was lipid (Figs. 23.9, 23.10). One fish had abnormal fibrotic, cholangiolar epithelial proliferative foci in the parenchyma (Fig. 23.11).

Usually, following the third week of exposure to 5.0 ppb, cumulative mortality reached 50% or greater (14). During this period, surviving fish that were examined demonstrated fatty change, as indicated by extensive vacuolation in liver parenchymal cells (Fig. 23.12). Also, in some, pancreatic acinar tissue had undergone severe degeneration, consisting of vacuolation and necrosis (Fig. 23.12). Moribund fish had the most striking changes in liver tissues. These changes consisted of focal necrosis, sinusoidal congestion, extreme fatty change, and occurrence of PAS-positive, diastase-resistant, amorphous inclusions (probably ceroid)

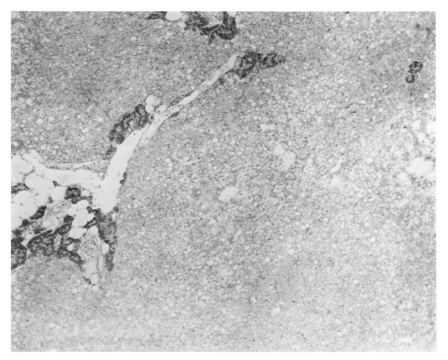

Fig. 23.12. Liver from spot exposed for 3 weeks to 5 ppb of Aroclor 1254. Note extensive vacuolation of parenchyma and degeneration of pancreatic acinar tissue characteristic of advanced pathological response. X100.

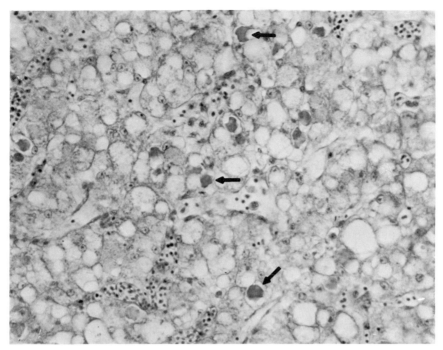

Fig. 23.13. Parenchyma of liver from moribund spot exposed to 5 ppb Aroclor 1254 for 3 weeks. Note congestion of sinusoids, vacuolation of cells, and presence of PAS-positive, diastase-resistant, intracellular inclusions (arrows). Hematoxylin and PAS method; X450.

in parenchymal cells (Figs. 23.13, 23.14). A few moribund fish also had extensive infiltrates of lymphocytes in and around the degenerate pancreatic acinar tissues of the liver.

Control fish examined during the exposures had light-to-moderate parenchymal cell vacuolation but none of the other signs described above. Vacuoles in liver cells of controls were usually much smaller than those in exposed fish.

The great extent of the fatty change as indicated by oil red O retention in frozen sections and extensive vacuolation in paraffin sections (Figs. 23.12–23.14) and the occurrence of PAS-positive amorphous bodies in parenchymal cells of the liver of moribund spot are indications, possibly specific, for Aroclor 1254 toxicity. These two changes, in combination, have not been reported for fish exposed to other toxic compounds.

ORGANOPHOSPHATES

Organophosphate Insecticides

Abate. Bluegills exposed to 1 lb of Abate per acre in ponds for 63 days had liver alterations, according to Eller (11). The changes were (1) atrophy and stain-

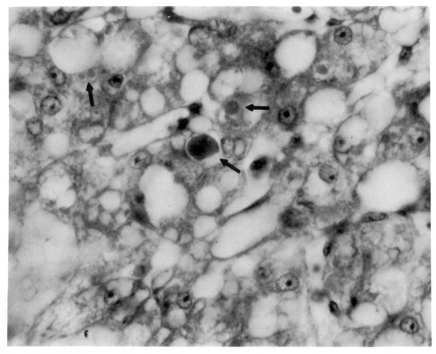

Fig. 23.14. Higher magnification of liver parenchyma from spot shown in Figure 22.13. Note varying sizes of PAS-positive inclusions (arrows) and vacuoles. Hematoxylin and PAS method; ×1000.

ing variability of liver parenchymal cells, (2) liver cord distortion, (3) massive foci of edema, (4) hyperemia, and (5) necrosis of both liver parenchyma and pancreatic tissue.

Dursban. Lowe (personal communication) exposed sheepshead minnows to 5 to 10 ppb Dursban in flowing sea water for five months. These control and exposed fish were examined by Wood and by me for lesions. Both of us found extensive fatty change (Figs. 23.15, 23.16) in the livers of exposed fish. Wood suggested that these changes may have been due not to a direct effect of Dursban, but to a secondary effect of starvation caused by a change in food habits (personal communication). I found vascular stasis in the livers of several sheepshead minnows that survived the exposure (Fig. 23.17). This condition was not apparent in any control fish.

None of these changes was considered specific for Dursban.

Dylox. Matton and LaHam (22) exposed rainbow trout to 10 to 100 ppm Dylox for 16 hours. They found vacuolation of liver cells and suggested that the cause was tissue hypoxia. No other liver changes were reported.

Malathion. Wood (in 3; 29) found degenerative lesions of an undescribed nature in livers of rainbow trout exposed to sublethal 0.6 ppm and 1.0 ppm malathion concentrations for up to 30 days in pond exposures. These lesions disappeared after 30 days.

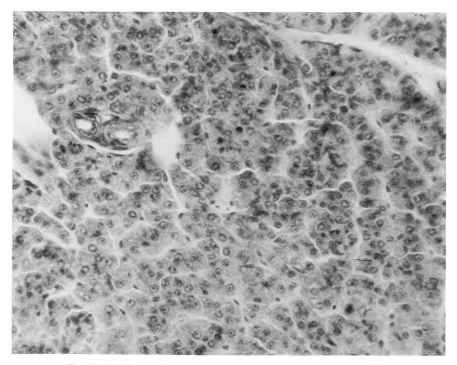

Fig. 23.15. Normal liver parenchyma of sheepshead minnow. ×450.

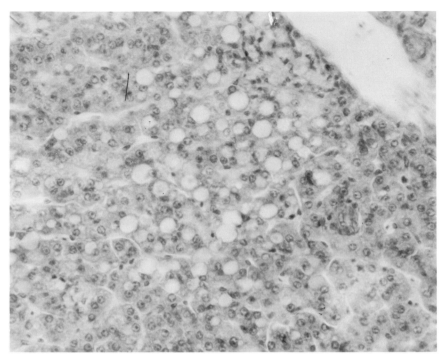

Fig. 23.16. Region of parenchymal cell vacuolation in liver of sheepshead minnow exposed to Dursban insecticide for 5 months. ×450.

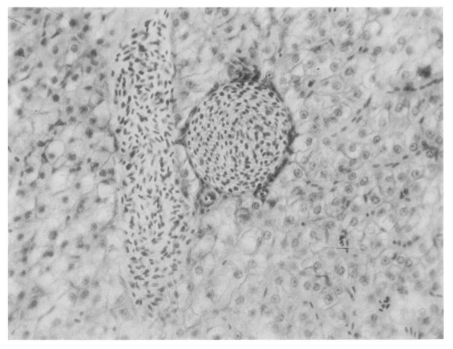

Fig. 23.17. Stasis in central vein of liver of sheepshead minnow exposed to Dursban. Compare with normal condition of central vein in spot in Figure 23.5. ×450.

Parathion. Rainbow trout exposed in ponds to 950 ppb parathion for 7 days (LC_{50} 7 days = 950 ppb) had nonspecific liver changes. Wood found liver parenchymal cell swelling and liver sinusoid congestion. He thought these changes were probably secondary to either gill or kidney damage which he found in the exposed fish (29).

CARBAMATES

Carbamate Insecticide

Sevin (carbaryl). The only carbamate pesticide tested for possible liver effects was Sevin. Lowe (20) exposed spot to 0.1 ppm Sevin for five months (LC_{50} 12 days = 1.0 ppm) in flowing sea water. Wood (in 20) reported that he was unable to find changes in liver tissues of exposed fish. I have recently examined fish that Lowe exposed to Sevin and have found a possible change in the intrahepatic pancreatic tissue in the liver. Four out of five exposed spot which were examined had clusters of large vacuoles in the deep periportal pancreatic acinar tissue (Fig. 23.18). The vacuoles appeared to be intracellular, having caused hypertrophy of the acinar cells. They did not appear to be hydropic in nature, but could have

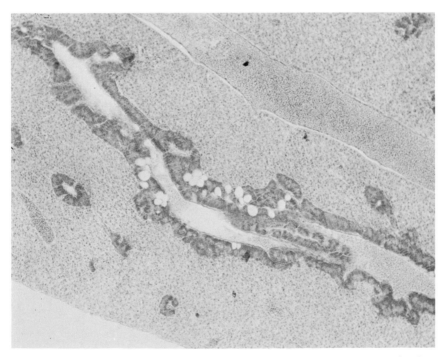

Fig. 23.18. Foci of vacuolation (possible fatty change) in deep periportal pancreatic acinar tissue in spot liver. Fish was exposed to 0.1 ppm Sevin for 5 months. ×100.

contained lipids, which were extracted during tissue processing. Control fish did not have these vacuoles and I have not found them in other pesticide-exposed fishes or seen them described in reports in the literature.

OTHER CHEMICALS

Lampreycides

TFM (3-trifluoromethyl-4-nitrophenol). TFM selectively kills lamprey larvae at low concentrations (LC_{100} for 8 hours = 0.75 ppm), but is relatively nontoxic to rainbow trout, according to Christie and Battle (2). Wild lamprey larvae and rainbow trout were exposed to 0.75 ppm, 3.00 ppm, and 6.00 ppm by these authors and examined for liver lesions. At all three concentrations the brook lamprey livers became excessively red in color, indicating considerable stasis in the superficial hepatic vessels. Vasodilation was found involving the hepatic sinusoids. Liver vascular/cellular ratios were greater in lampreys exposed to all three concentrations than in control lampreys or rainbow trout. Rainbow trout had no liver vascular or cytological effects. The authors suggested that the toxic effect of TFM was perhaps associated with a direct effect on the vascular endothelium (in gills as well as liver), giving rise to increased permeability of vascular membranes and to loss of plasma.

Herbicides

Hydrothol 191 (N,N-dimethylalkylamine salt of endothal). Eller (10) studied redear sunfish that had been exposed to 0.3 ppm to 1.50 ppm Hydrothol 191 in ponds (LC_{50} 96 hours = 125 ppm). He sampled these fish over a period of 56 days following single, initial applications of the herbicide. Liver structure had considerable change over this period in different fish samples. At sublethal doses of 0.03 ppm and 0.30 ppm, between 7 to 14 days' exposure the liver showed small lymphocyte infiltrates, small aggregates of pigmented liver cells, and occasional swollen liver cells. At 0.3 ppm after 28 days' exposure, fish livers had chronic changes consisting of many pleomorphic cells, hypertrophic bizarre cells, large masses of pigmented cells containing hemosiderin and lipofuchsins, and liver cord distortion. By 56 days of exposure, liver structure had returned to a condition similar to controls. Because of marked variation among replicate samples taken simultaneously, Eller believed that these changes could not be associated unequivocally with Hydrothol 191 exposure.

CRITICAL EVALUATION

The liver, gills, kidney, gonads, and brain have usually been the organs of choice for histological studies of pesticide-induced changes in fishes. Although the present review is restricted to pesticide-induced changes in the livers of fishes, it also serves as a representative index to the available or published histological works on fishes experimentally exposed to pesticides and related chemicals.

Except for the work of Eller (4, 10-12) and Wood (in 3, 19; 29), few detailed investigations have been reported. Most studies providing data on liver lesions have involved freshwater fishes, particularly the rainbow trout and the bluegill (see Table 23.2). Of special concern is the paucity of published studies on effects of commercial biocides on estuarine and marine fishes. Information in this regard is presently to be found for only three species (Table 23.2) (18-21), and this information is far from conclusive.

Most liver lesions in fishes which have been exposed to pesticides have been general or nonspecific. Specific syndromes produced in the liver as responses to particular pesticides have been few in number. This may reflect the lack of detailed work and the relatively small number of pesticides and fish species tested. The following are worthy of emphasis. Cutthroat trout exposed to different concentrations of endrin (12) had a large spectrum of lesions constituting a prehepatomatous syndrome. The severity of the lesions was related to concentrations of endrin. Early necrotic, coagulative lesions were associated with the portal triads of rainbow trout exposed to critical levels of lindane (BHC) (3, 29). Bluegills exposed to methoxychlor had unique, eosinophilic globular masses in the liver vascular system (16). These globules increased in number and size up to several days' exposure and then disappeared. The similar occurrence of PAS-positive vascular deposits in liver vessels of bluegills was related to abnormal glycogen metabolism following 2,4-D exposure (5). Extensive fatty change, necrosis, and deposition of PAS-positive amorphous inclusions in liver cells appear to be characteristic of PCB (Aroclor) exposures in spot. Foci of medium-to-large vacuoles in the pancreatic acinar tissue in the livers of spot were associated with Sevin exposure.

The most commonly encountered nonspecific liver lesion reported for fish following pesticide exposure was fatty change. Exposure of fishes to the following pesticides and chemicals produced liver parenchymal cell vacuolation or oil red O-positive frozen liver sections interpreted here as probably the result of abnormal accumulation of lipid in the liver: chlordane, DDT, endrin, Dowicide G, Aroclor 1248, Aroclor 1254, Dursban, Dylox. This list includes both organochlorines and organophosphates. In certain of these cases (DDT, endrin, Aroclor 1254, Dursban) nutritional factors, as well as pesticide exposure, were suspected in the onset of fatty change.

Chemicals from each of the representative major classes of commercial biocides (e.g., organochlorines, organophosphates, carbamates, etc.) have been tested for effects on livers of fishes. No completely characteristic trend of histopathologic effects has been reported for any of the given classes of chemicals. That is, no described liver histopathological syndromes are presently known for positive identification of particular classes of chemicals toxic to fishes. Pesticides within the same major group, such as DDT and endrin, both organochlorines, may produce different or noncomparable signs in livers of fishes. Thus, even they are difficult to diagnose on histopathology alone.

It is pertinent to note, at this point, that the information available does demonstrate unequivocally that liver damage occurs in both acutely lethal and chronic sublethal exposures of fishes to certain pesticides.

From the above brief evaluation it is obvious that considerable histological and cytological investigation is needed to further define and characterize effects of pesticides on the livers of fishes. Particularly needed are studies of the possible interaction of variables such as nutrition and pesticides and their effects on such organs as the liver. Mawdesley-Thomas (23) recently stated: "Following the use of the more persistent biocides, much concern has been expressed in recent years as to their long term effects on wild species. The long term effects of sublethal doses of even DDT are ill-defined and insufficiently documented and further study is required." Unfortunately, even the histopathology of acute or lethal pesticide poisoning is unknown or incomplete for most wild species, including fishes.

In future studies, emphasis should be placed on histochemistry and electron microscopy of pesticide-related lethal and chronic sublethal changes in order to approach more closely actual mechanisms of pesticide-induced injury in fishes.

Acknowledgment. I thank Jack Lowe and Dave Hansen for providing fish tissues from their experimental exposures. L. L. Eller and E. M. Wood were very cooperative in supplying information. Darryl Christinsen prepared some of the fish tissue used in the Aroclor 1254 study. Pat Borthwick aided in design and construction for experimental exposures of fish and in collection of fish.

Use of trade names of pesticides and related chemicals does not constitute endorsement of these products by the U.S. Environmental Protection Agency.

Conribution number 152, Gulf Breeze Environmental Research Laboratory.

REFERENCES

1. Andrews, A. K., Van Valin, C. C., and Stebbings, B. E.   Some effects of heptachlor on bluegills (*Lepomis macrochirus*). *Trans. Amer. Fish. Soc. 95:* 297. 1966.
2. Christie, R. M., and Battle, H. I.   Histological effects of 3-trifluoromethyl-4-nitrophenol (TFM) on larval lamprey and trout. *Can. J. Zool. 41:* 51. 1963.
3. Cope, O. B.   Contamination of the freshwater ecosystem by pesticides. *J. Appl. Ecol. 3*(suppl.): 33. 1966.
4. Cope, O. B., McCraren, J. P., and Eller, L. L.   Effects of dichlobenil on two fishpond environments. *Weed Sci. 17:* 158. 1969.
5. Cope, O. B., Wood, E. M., and Wallen, G. H.   Some chronic effects of 2,4-D on the bluegill (*Lepomis macrochirus*). *Trans. Amer. Fish. Soc. 99:* 1. 1970.
6. Crandall, C. A., and Goodnight, C. J.   The effects of sublethal concentrations of several toxicants to the common guppy, *Lebistes reticulatus*.   *Trans. Amer. Microsc. Soc. 82:* 59. 1963.

7. Duke, T. W., and Wilson, A. J., Jr. Chlorinated hydrocarbons in livers of fishes from the northeastern Pacific Ocean. *Pestic. Monit. J. 5:* 228. 1971.

8. Eisler, R., and Edmunds, P. H. Effects of endrin on blood and tissue chemistry of a marine fish. *Trans. Amer. Fish. Soc. 95:* 153. 1966.

9. Elias, H., and Bengelsdorf, H. The structure of the liver of vertebrates. *Acta anat. 14:* 24. 1952.

10. Eller, L. L. Pathology in redear sunfish exposed to Hydrothol 191. *Trans. Amer. Fish. Soc. 98:* 52. 1969.

11. Eller, L. L. Annual reports. *U. S. Bur. Sport Fish. Wildlife, Fish Pestic. Lab.,* Columbia, Mo. Also unpublished reports, cited with permission of Eller. 1970, 1971.

12. Eller, L. L. Histopathologic lesions in cutthroat trout (*Salmo clarki*) exposed chronically to the insecticide endrin. *Amer. J. Pathol. 64:* 321. 1971.

13. Frear, D. H., ed. *Pesticide Index.* 4th ed. State College, Pa., College Sci. Publishers, 1969.

14. Hansen, D. J., Parrish, P. R., Lowe, J. I., Wilson, A. J., Jr. and Wilson, P. D. Chronic toxicity, uptake, and retention of Aroclor 1254 in two estuarine fishes. *Bull. Environ. Contam. Toxicol. 6:* 113. 1971.

15. Johnson, D. W. Pesticides and fishes—a review of selected literature. *Trans. Amer. Fish. Soc. 97:* 398. 1968.

16. Kennedy, H. D., Eller, L. L., and Walsh, D. F. Chronic effects of methoxychlor on bluegills and aquatic invertebrates. *U. S. Bur. Sport Fish. Wildlife, Tech, Pap. 53.* 18 pp. 1970.

17. King, S. F. Some effects of DDT on the guppy and the brown trout. *U. S. Fish Wildlife Serv., Spec. Sci. Rep., Fish. 399.* 20 pp. 1962.

18. Lowe, J. I. Chronic exposure of spot, *Leiostomus xanthurus,* to sublethal concentrations of toxaphene in seawater. *Trans. Amer. Fish. Soc. 93:* 396. 1964.

19. Lowe, J. I. Some effects of endrin on estuarine fishes. *Proc. Annu. Conf. Southeast. Ass. Game Fish Comm. 19:* 271. 1965.

20. Lowe, J. I. Effects of prolonged exposure to Sevin on an estuarine fish, *Leiostomus xanthurus,* Lacépède. *Bull. Environ. Contam. Toxicol. 2:* 147. 1967.

21. Lowe, J. I., Parrish, P. R., Wilson, A. J., Jr., Wilson, P. D., and Duke, T. W. Effects of mirex on selected estuarine organisms. *N. Amer. Wildlife Natur. Resour. Conf. Trans. 36.* 1971.

22. Matton, P., and LaHam, Q. N. Effect of the organophosphate Dylox on rainbow trout larvae. *J. Fish. Res. Board Can. 26:* 2193. 1969.

23. Mawdesley-Thomas, L. E. Research into fish diseases. *Nature (London) 235:* 17. 1972.

24. Menzie, C. M. Metabolism of pesticides. *U. S. Fish Wildlife Serv., Spec. Sci. Rep., Wildlife 127.* 487 pp. 1969.

25. Mount, D. E. Chronic effects of endrin on bluntnose minnows and guppies. *U. S. Fish Wildlife Serv., Res. Rep. 58.* 38 pp. 1962.

26. Pimentel, D. Ecological effects of pesticides on non-target species. Exec. Off. President, Off. Sci. Technol. U. S. Government Printing Off., Washington, D.C., 1971.

27. Van Valin, C. C., Andrews, A. K., and Eller, L. L. Some effects of mirex on two warm-water fishes. *Trans. Amer. Fish Soc. 97:* 185. 1968.

28. Vos, J. G. Toxicology of PCB's for mammals and for birds. *Environ. Health Perspect. 1:* 105. 1972.

29. Wood, E. M. The pathology of pesticide toxicity in fish. Unpublished.

DISCUSSION OF HISTOPATHOLOGICAL EFFECTS OF PESTICIDES AND RELATED CHEMICALS ON THE LIVERS OF FISHES

C. J. Dawe: This kind of work has been needed for a long time and you are just getting into the studies. I wonder how the situation will be for long-term study, particularly keeping in mind the idea of looking for neoplasms, either in the liver or elsewhere?

J. A. Couch: The problem of estuarine fish that we chose to work with is that most of them are not amenable to culture and to maintenance as satisfactorily as many of the freshwater species. You can keep fish three months or so and think you are doing everything right and then lose them overnight. That is the problem we face. For example, dietary needs are not even known for most of the estuarine fishes as compared to the cultured fishes such as the rainbow trout. As long as you try hard, I think you can maintain spot for long-term sublethal exposures that might lead to neoplastic involvement. It is still a pioneering field as far as concerns maintenance of any of the very fastidious marine organisms.

Question: You mentioned fin rot. I believe it took place only in the experimental fish.

J. A. Couch: Right; I didn't go into detail. The most striking effect grossly to the fish exposed to PCB's was that in the control tank you could maintain the fish for weeks and have a very low mortality, no fin rot, and the fish appeared well, whereas in those fish exposed to PCB I would say that the primary cause of death was a tremendous induced fin rot concurrent with exposure to PCB's. By the second or third week of exposure, you might lose up to 90% of your fish with fin rot disease. After seeing this repeated several times I can only believe that it is related to the PCB action somehow on the mucous or protective coating of the fish.

Question: Did you notice any damage to the hematopoietic system, particularly the thymus?

J. A. Couch: I haven't looked at the thymus in that much detail.

24

Cellular Effects of
Mercury on Fish Kidney Tubules

BENJAMIN F. TRUMP
RAYMOND T. JONES
and SOMPHONG SAHAPHONG

Relatively little is known about the mechanisms of action of mercury on the fish kidney or indeed on any cell or tissue in fish or in mammals. The majority of the reported studies have examined the concentrations of mercury in fish tissues. The purpose of this paper is to consider present knowledge concerning the effects of various types of mercurial compounds on the structure and function of the fish kidney and on fish kidney tubules and to put this information in the context of the general reaction of cells to injury at the cellular and subcellular levels. There are a number of implications in these studies for possible sites of the toxic actions of mercury as well as other toxins on the kidney.

Fish kidneys accumulate high concentrations of mercury when fish are exposed to either organic or inorganic mercurials (10, 11, 16). They accumulate high levels especially when the mercurial is an organic one or when the mercury is given with food (1).

Since we cannot discuss all classes of fish and since knowledge on both normal and abnormal fish physiology is most thoroughly developed for the teleosts (2-5, 7, 12, 17-24), we will confine our discussion to that group. In general, it is usual to classify the teleosts as being either stenohaline or euryhaline; the stenohaline group can be either freshwater or marine. It is also convenient to classify either group into glomerular, those having renal corpuscles, or aglomerular, those not

585

possessing renal corpuscles. Aglomerular fish can be freshwater, marine, or euryhaline, although most known species are marine.

The study of both normal and abnormal fish kidney function has a number of values to biology and medicine. These include methods for tracing the process of vertebrate evolution both at the cellular and subcellular levels. Certain specialized forms such as aglomerular fish continue to provide methods for evaluating functions of specific nephron segments. The circumstance of homologies that exist between certain areas of the fish nephron and the mammalian nephron and the fact that simplified *in vitro* systems can be utilized to examine relationships between structure and function in such systems also demonstrate the value of these studies in biomedical science.

The study of fish renal physiology has also contributed materially to our understanding of kidney structure and function in general, including elucidation of the role of tubular secretion in renal physiology and the role of the glomerulus, which has been made possible particularly through studies of aglomerular forms. Through the use of isolated fish nephron segments, it has been possible to do many studies on cell injury in the nephron and structural-functional correlations in kidney tubules under a variety of physiological conditions. In this paper we will show how studies of the effects of mercury on the fish can not only contribute to understanding the problems of mercury toxicity, but also to understanding the problem of a mechanism of mercury action on cells.

KIDNEY FUNCTION

The function of the kidney in freshwater teleosts can be summarized as follows. These fish are hyperosmotic regulators living, as they do, in very hypotonic environments. In these forms the kidney serves as a means of water excretion and must conserve filtered electrolytes, implying powerful ion pumps and a low water permeability of the tubules. Sodium and chloride are almost completely reabsorbed. The relatively high glomerular filtration rate (GFR) can change markedly, and urine flow is roughly proportional to the GFR. The role of the freshwater teleost kidney in divalent ion excretion is not well established, but it seems to be relatively inactive in that regard, and this may be an important limiting step in adaptation of such fish to marine environments. Organic anion and cation transport systems such as those for p-amino hippuric acid (PAH) and phenol red or chlorphenol red are much less well developed than in marine forms.

Marine teleosts are hypoosmotic regulators living in a hypertonic surrounding and in these forms the principal function of the kidney seems to be the excretion of magnesium and sulfate. This, however, also implies active pumps for reabsorption of other filtered components such as chloride and potassium. The glomerular filtration rates are generally less than in freshwater forms and urine flow is related more to tubular activity. These fish also have well-developed anion and cation pumps, although it should be kept in mind that the main work of such a kidney is reabsorption of sodium, potassium, and chloride.

In euryhaline fish the kidney is characterized functionally by the capability of adapting to either hypoosmotic or hyperosmotic regulation. In general, the glomerular filtration rates are higher in fresh than in sea water, although the mechanism of control for GFR is unknown and probably involves change in blood flow, with the possibility of glomerular intermittency. In fresh water, the tubules stop secreting magnesium and sulfates and alter their water permeability.

The significance of the kidney in fish physiology can thus be summarized as follows:

1. In freshwater fish the kidney principally functions as an organ for water excretion, based primarily on filtration at the glomerulus followed by solute reabsorption. It should be noted, however, that this function implies the presence of suitable cellular machinery to reabsorb filtered ions and cellular components which are relatively impermeable to water.

2. In marine forms the principal function of the kidney seems to be the excretion of divalent cations and anions such as magnesium and sulfate. In glomerular marine forms, water, univalent ions, and other filtered components must also be conserved, which again implies active transport mechanisms for ion regulation.

3. In the cartilaginous sharks, skates, and rays, the function can be considered as a combination of (1) and (2) above because of the different problems of ion regulation that exist in these forms. Therefore, it is possible to generalize that divalent ion excretion and water excretion are the principal functions of the kidney while univalent ion regulation and nitrogenous end-product excretion are principally functions of the gill. The gut is also active in the latter function, and in certain forms, especially the cartilaginous fish, other excreting systems such as the rectal salt gland also participate.

Because of the toxic effects of mercury on a variety of membrane functions and because membrane functions are inherent to most of the functions of the kidney, as mentioned above, there are many possible ways in which mercury-cell interactions can interfere with kidney function in fish.

KIDNEY STRUCTURE IN RELATION TO FUNCTION

Teleost fish kidneys consist of nephrons embedded in an abundant interstitial tissue which contains well-developed hematopoietic cells (Fig. 24.1). The loosely coiled nephrons converge to form a collecting duct system which drains into the so-called archinephric duct. The following segments typically exist in the teleost nephron, although differences exist among various types of functional classes, as noted below: (1) the renal corpuscle, (2) the neck segment, (3) the first proximal segment, (4) the second proximal segment, which may have a modification of its terminal part into a third proximal segment, (5) the intermediate segment, (6) the

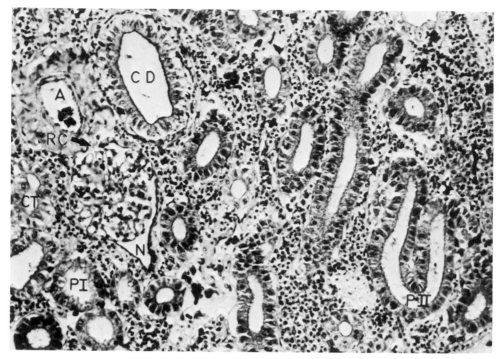

Fig. 24.1. Light micrograph of hogchoker kidney showing renal corpuscle (RC), arteriole (A), neck (N), first proximal segment (PI), second proximal segment (PII), small collecting duct or collecting tubule (CT), and collecting duct (CD). Mason trichrome; ×300.

distal segment, (7) the collecting tubule, and (8) the collecting duct system (Fig. 24.2).

Renal Corpuscle

The renal corpuscle is composed of the glomerulus plus Bowman's capsule and varies in structure in different fish. In general, in freshwater fish the glomerulus is larger and better developed, with thinner capillary walls, while in marine glomerular teleosts it is smaller, more avascular, and has thicker walls. The structure resembles that of mammals though it has somewhat better developed mesangial regions. The mesangial region in marine forms is quite well developed, with processes from mesangial cells encircling the capillaries and thickening the capillary wall. In pauciglomerular forms such as the goosefish, many glomeruli are obsolescent, resembling those seen in end-stage mammalian kidney disease. In aglomerular forms, of course, no glomeruli are present, having disappeared apparently by obsolescence during development.

Neck Segment

The neck segment is of variable length, but usually is quite short and is characterized by a cuboidal or flattened epithelium possessing numerous long cilia and

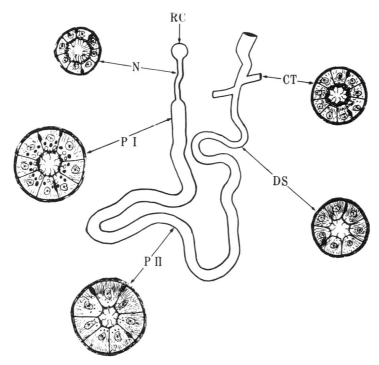

Fig. 24.2. Diagram illustrating schematically the nephron segments in a typical euryhaline teleost. This particular diagram was made from a three-dimensional reconstruction of the southern flounder (*Paralichthys lethostigma*). Note the characteristic morphology of each region. Note the renal corpuscle (RC), neck segment (N), first proximal segment (PI), second proximal segment (PII), distal segment (DS), and collecting tubule (CT). (From C. P. Hickman and B. F. Trump, The Kidney, in *Fish Physiology,* Vol. 1, W. S. Hoar and D. J. Randall, eds., Academic Press, Inc., 1969. Used by permission.)

prominent apical mucous granules. The function of the neck segment is uncertain, although it is speculated that ciliary action is of some importance in propelling fluid along the tubule, particularly because of the low filtration pressures which probably exist in most fish.

First Proximal Segment

This segment is very similar in structure and function to the mammalian proximal convoluted tubule. The cells are cuboidal or low columnar with a well-developed brush border, apical tubules and vacuoles, a well-developed lysosome system, and numerous mitochondria. The cells are joined by junctional complexes and at the base there are elaborate infoldings and interdigitations. The segment is seen only in glomerular fish and is active in phagocytosis and pinocytosis of materials that pass through the glomerulus. This tubule probably also functions in glucose, sodium, and chloride reabsorption and is capable of active secretion of organic anions such as PAH, Diodrast, and chlorphenol red. It is doubtful if this section is active in divalent ion transport since it is equally prominent in freshwater fish, which are not active in this process.

Second Proximal Segment

This is the predominant segment in teleost fish and sometimes has a slight modification at its termination, forming a third segment. In this region the brush border is less well developed than in the first segment, but the mitochondria are much more numerous. The cells are tall columnar in the second and lower in the third and there is only a moderately developed lysosome system. This segment is not active in phagocytosis and pinocytosis, but presumably functions in organic anion and cation secretion and in divalent cation transport.

Intermediate Segment

This segment, known only in freshwater fish, is of variable length and composed of cuboidal or low columnar epithelium. The structure of the cell somewhat resembles that of the neck in that numerous clumps of cilia are present, extending from the cell apices. In some species, abundant mucous granules are also present in the apex. Although the function of this segment is not clear, it is thought to assist in propelling urine along the tubule.

Distal Tubule

The distal tubule resembles that of amphibians, birds, and mammals, being composed of columnar cells with elongate, numerous mitochondria arranged perpendicular to the basement membrane and parallel to the membranes of the basilar labyrinth. Its lysosome system and microvilli are poorly developed. This segment is believed to be very active in sodium and chloride reabsorption, removing in some species the last traces of these ions from the filtrate. In this regard it seems that it must possess a low and variable water permeability.

Collecting Tubules and Ducts

The collecting tubules and ducts are simpler cells, although collecting tubules have numerous mitochondria sometimes clustered in the cell apex with often very prominent mitochondrial enzyme activity. Few microvilli and apical mucous granules also characterize this segment. It probably also functions in sodium and chloride reabsorption and, in this regard, the numerous mitochondria may well be important.

Some comment on the variations among segments is in order. This seems clearly related to the function and adaptation of the particular species. Freshwater fish typically possess all of the segments outlined above, with open thin-walled glomerular capillaries. Marine teleosts typically lack the intermediate segment and the distal segment and have a very well developed second segment, the terminal part of which is modified and often referred to as the third proximal segment. This modification is probably related to the divalent ion excretion and to the active accumulating ability for phenol red and related compounds that marine teleost nephrons exhibit. Marine aglomerular forms that have been studied lack not only the glomerulus but also the neck, the first proximal segment, the intermediate segment, and the distal tubule. The nephrons are, therefore, composed of segments resembling the second and/or third proximal segment along with the collecting duct system.

IN VITRO NEPHRON SYSTEM

Many of our studies have been done *in vitro* on isolated nephrons prepared from various species of flatfish, which is a system originally described by Forster (6) using *Pseudopleuronectes americanus.* We have used various species: *Parophrys vetulus* in the Puget Sound area; *Paralichthys lethostigma* in Beaufort, North Carolina; and *Trinectes maculatus* in the Chesapeake Bay area at the present time. These nephron segments can be easily isolated and maintained for long periods of time in buffered, aerated salt solutions. By adding various colored compounds, which are actively transported by the kidney tubules, it is possible to readily assay visually the functional status of the tubules in terms of organic anion or cation transport. It has been usual to use the dye chlorphenol red, which is an organic anion which is actively transported from the bath to the lumen and concentrated in the lumen, to which it imparts a magenta color. Concentration ratios as high as 6,000:1, lumen to medium, have been observed by microspectrophotometry in this system (13). The ends of the tubules seal off and thus it seems the dye concentrations can be maintained. It is also possible to note the progress of transport as a function of time and to quantify this by using similar organic anions, such as Diodrast labeled with ^{131}I.

A variety of organic anions are transported by the system, although the substances transported by this system *in vivo* are not known. It may well function in substrate transport and probably is also related to organic cation transport, such as that involved in the excretion of trimethylamine oxide (TMAO), which is carried on to some extent by the kidney. The transport is active and dependent upon ATP synthesis, since a variety of inhibitors of respiration or oxidative phosphorylation inhibit the process. It is known to have two stages, the first stage from the bath or peritubular compartment to the tubular cell itself, and the second from the cell to the tubular lumen. The first stage is dependent upon potassium and the second on calcium. In the absence of calcium, dye accumulates in the cell rather than in the lumen and correlated ultrastructural studies reveal massive changes in the cell apex, including modification of the cell junctions when flounder kidney tubules are isolated in calcium-deficient media.

REACTIONS OF CELLS TO INJURY

How cells react to injurious stimulus is the key to considering not only the effects of mercury but also the effects of any noxious substance on cells. A useful visualization of the effects of injury on cells (25) is shown in Figure 24.3. Let us

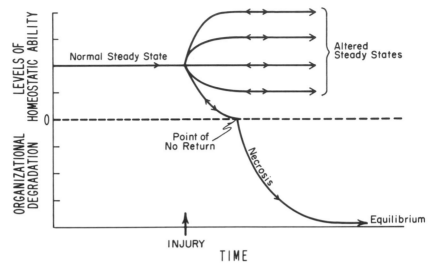

Fig. 24.3. Diagram showing a conceptualization of the effects of injury on a cell; both lethal and sublethal injuries are shown. The cell is depicted in a normal steady state at a normal level of homeostatic ability. Following lethal injury the cell approaches a "point-of-no-return" indicated by zero homeostatic ability, following which it undergoes necrosis and approaches equilibrium. If the injury is removed prior to this point, reversibility can occur. Also shown are several new or altered steady states representing continued response to sublethal injury. (From B. F. Trump and F. L. Ginn, The Pathogenesis of Subcellular Reaction to Lethal Injury, in *Methods and Achievements in Experimental Pathology,* Vol. 4, E. Bajusz, and G. Jasmin, eds., Karger, 1969. Used by permission.)

first consider an acute lethal injury, that is, one which is followed by the death of the cell. Following a lethal injury to the cell two phases can immediately be arrived at on the basis of logic. These two phases are a point or phase prior to the time the cell has lost the ability to recover if the injurious stimulus is removed and the phase when it cannot recover even if the stimulus is removed. The point separating the two is often called the point-of-no-return or the point of cell death. The changes prior to this time are reversible, those after this time are irreversible. The irreversible phase is often referred to as necrosis and involves a variety of

Fig. 24.4. This series of diagrams shows the reaction to injury by a flounder kidney tubule cell from the second proximal segment. These diagrams represent a series of intracellular compartment changes leading from control (stage 1) to necrotic cell (stage 5). Stage 1 represents a normal cell. AV, autophagic vacuole; BB, brush border; BI, membranes of basilar labyrinth; BM, basement membrane; Ci, cilium; Go, Golgi apparatus; JC, junctional complex; L, secondary lysosome; Mb, microbodies; MvB, multivesicular bodies; NP, nuclear pore; and free arrow, polysomes. Stage 2 consists of dilatation of endoplasmic reticulum (ER) and nuclear envelope (NE). Stage 3 shows enlargement of cell sap and contraction of mitochondrial inner compartments. (From F. L. Ginn, J. D. Shelburne, and B. F. Trump, *American Journal of Pathology 53:* 1041, 1968. Used by permission.)

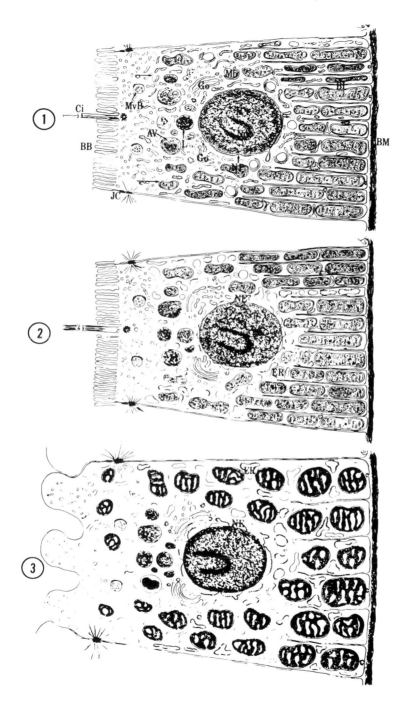

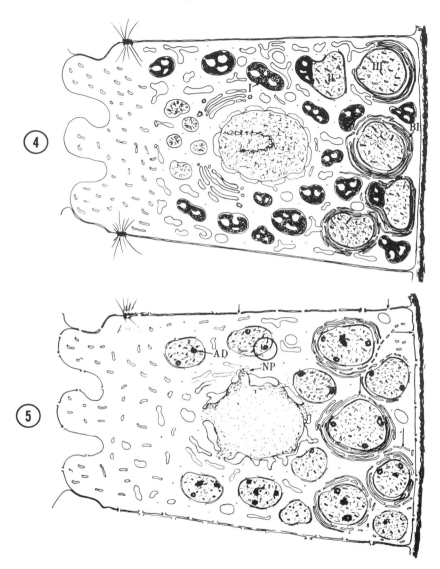

Fig. 24.5. Stage 4 exhibits contraction of some mitochondria (I); others (II) have both condensed and swollen portions; still others show high amplitude swelling (III). Polysomes are
detached from the endoplasmic reticulum. In stage 5 two types of densities are seen within
the mitochondrial matrix; flocculent densities (AD) and calcific deposits (as shown in cir-
cled area). Karolysis of the nucleus occurs with extrusion of nuclear contents through nuclear pores (NP). Interruptions are seen in the plasma membrane and basilar infoldings (free
arrows). (From F. L. Ginn, J. D. Shelburne, and B. F. Trump, *American Journal of Pathology 53:* 1041, 1968. Used by permission.)

processes, including autolytic breakdown due to lysosomal enzymes and other factors such as low pH. Changes prior to the point-of-no-return often involve such changes as loss of cell volume regulation, with cell swelling, vacuolization, fatty accumulation, increased numbers of autophagic vacuoles, and so on. These are known not to be lethal to the cell but to be compatible with continued survival if the stimulus is removed. Changes after this point are of a different type and involve many membrane systems, especially the mitochondria, which undergo denaturation and show calcium accumulation and swelling. We can also infer that other injuries, even if continued, do not result in the death of the cell, but allow the cell to continue its existence, though in some altered form or altered steady state. Hypertrophy, many types of fatty change, and atrophy are examples of this type of alteration to a cell which, though injured, is able to continue its existence.

In the flounder nephron cell as well as in all other cells, mammalian and otherwise, that we have studied, it is convenient to recognize a sequence of changes that occur following application of a lethal injury at the cellular and subcellular levels (7) (Figs. 24.4, 24.5). It is remarkable how similar these changes are with various types of injuries in various types of cells, though the initial interactions may vary. For example, mercury binds to some sulfhydryl (SH) groups on membrane proteins, whereas carbon tetrachloride or some of the insecticides are metabolized to free radicals inducing membrane changes or anoxia resulting in limitations of the supply of ATP following cessation of mitochondrial function.

Stages 2 and 3 are reversible stages of cell injury and seem to be compatible with continued survival. However, stage 5, though a completely necrotic cell, cannot initially be differentiated by light microscopy using hematoxylin and eosin stained sections of tissue fixed in formaldehyde. A cell can be in this necrotic stage for several hours, perhaps eight or more, without showing any discernible change under light microscopy. This is why the electron microscope, as well as associated biochemical techniques, has found such wide applicability in the study of cell reactions to injury. Although in electron microscopy the sampling problem has to be contended with, enough is now known to permit the study of toxic effects using electron microscopy and related techniques. Visualization of organelle changes by electron microscopy permits many predictions concerning functional alterations and presence or absence of irreversible cell injury.

IN VITRO EFFECTS OF MERCURY

Using the previously described in vitro system, we have studied the effects of methylmercuric chloride, parachloromercuribenzenesulfonate (PCMBS), and mercuric chloride on the function and structure of isolated fish kidney tubules (17, 18). Function was measured by observing active transport of chlorphenol red by the tubules at serial time intervals. The degree of intraluminal dye accumulation was

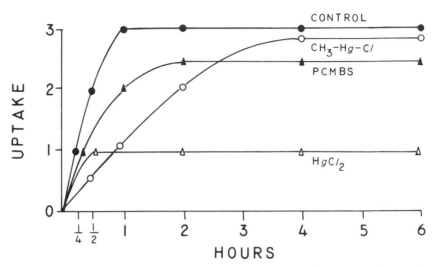

Fig. 24.6. Graph showing the effects of mercuric chloride, PCMBS, and methyl mercuric chloride, all at a concentration of 10^{-5} M on chlorphenol red uptake by flounder kidney tubules. The time is plotted along the abscissa and dye uptake is plotted along the ordinate. The three levels indicated should be regarded as logarithmic increments because of the known response of the eye to variations in color.

given as follows: 1+, coloration just detectable; 2+, intermediate coloration; 3+, intense or maximal concentration.

In this isolated cell system inorganic mercuric chloride was more toxic than the organic mercurials, PCMBS and methylmercuric chloride (Fig. 24.6). Complete loss of function was seen at 10^{-3} M and 10^{-4} M concentrations of all mercurials studied. Using the organic mercurials at 10^{-6} M, no change in intraluminal dye accumulation was observed. However, mercuric chloride at this concentration impaired dye transport.

Studies of the progress of subcellular change by electron microscopy, using the various mercurials, showed progression of structural alterations which generally correlated with the functional changes shown in Figure 24.4. The progression of change through the various stages discussed above is illustrated in Table 24.1. Note that at 10^{-3} M all of the compounds produced stage 5 change within 30 minutes, which is characteristic of agents that damage cells by direct interaction with the plasma membrane. On the other hand, with 10^{-4} and 10^{-5} M concentrations, differences in the rate of change with the various compounds could be observed. Examples of these changes are shown in Figures 24.7 through 24.10. Figure 24.7 shows a good example of stage 3 changes with marked dilation of endoplasmic reticulum, condensation of mitochondria, and swelling of cell sap. Note also the irregular appearance of the nuclei and that the lysosomes remain intact. In Figure 24.8 a slightly more advanced stage, stage 4, is shown, in which many of the

Table 24.1. Stages of Cell Injury of Isolated Flounder Kidney Tubules
after Exposure to Various Mercurials

Mercurial	Concentration (moles)	Stage of cell injury, at various hours:				
		½	1	2	4	6
PCMBS	10^{-5}	1	1	2	2	2
HgCl$_2$		2	3	4	4	5
Me Hg-Cl		2	3	3	3	3
PCMBS	10^{-4}	2	3	5	5	5
HgCl$_2$		4	4	5	5	5
Me Hg-Cl		5	5	5	5	5
PCMBS	10^{-3}	5	5	5	5	5
HgCl$_2$		5	5	5	5	5
Me Hg-Cl		5	5	5	5	5

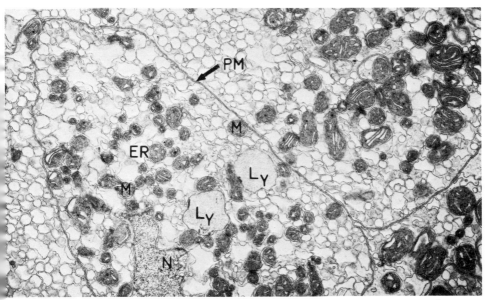

Fig. 24.7. Portion of flounder kidney tubule treated with methyl mercuric chloride, 10^{-5}M, for 1 hour. Note the typical stage 3 changes with condensation of mitochondria (M), dilatation of endoplasmic reticulum (ER), and swelling of cell sap. The lateral cell membranes (PM) are clearly seen. Note the irregularity of the nucleus (N), and the two intact lysosomes (Ly). ×14,700.

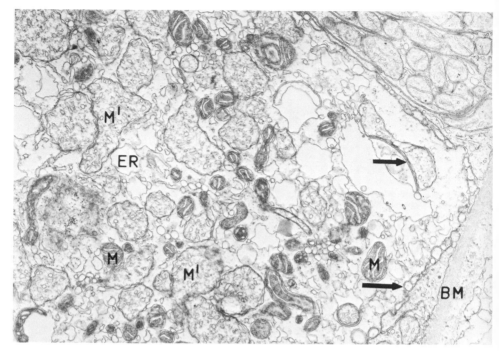

Fig. 24.8. Cell from kidney tubule treated with methyl mercuric chloride 10^{-5} M for 2 hours. Note the typical stage 4 changes. Some of the mitochondria (M) are condensed, while most mitochondria (M′) show high amplitude swelling. The ER is dilated, the polysomes are scattered, and cell membranes near the base of the cell are becoming irregular (free arrows). A portion of basement membrane (BM) can be seen at the lower right. ×13,800.

mitochondria are swollen, while others remain condensed. The marked cell swelling, dispersion of polysomes, and general clearing of the mitochondrial matrix are also apparent. Note too the clear appearance of the cell sap because of general cell swelling. Stage 5 changes are seen in Figure 24.9, in which the mitochondria are massively swollen and show flocculent densities. In this case, however, no calcifications were present, presumably because the accumulation system had been inhibited, perhaps by penetration of the methyl mercury. On the other hand, in Figure 24.10, stage 5 changes with intramitochondrial calcium deposits are shown. The calcifications seen under these conditions suggest that the increased calcium entering the cell through the damaged cell membrane was accumulated by the mitochondria, the mercury probably remaining largely bound at the cell membrane. We studied the general characteristics of calcium uptake on tubules treated *in vitro* and in Figure 24.11 show the rates of uptake of ^{45}Ca/mg protein as a function of time. In other experiments, we also investigated the direct effect of mercury on calcium uptake by isolated mitochondria from rat kidney in calcium-loading media and noted that as the concentration of mercurial was increased the uptake

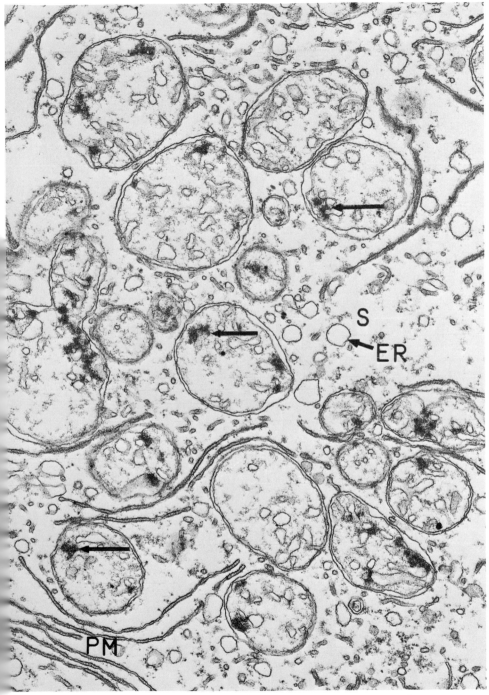

Fig. 24.9. Portion of kidney tubule treated with methyl mercuric chloride 10^{-4} M for 4 hours. Note the typical stage 5 changes with high amplitude swelling of all mitochondria which show flocculent densities (free arrows) within the matrix. Note the irregularities of the cell membranes of the basal labyrinth (PM), enlargement of the cell sap (S), and fragments of vesicles representing dilated endoplasmic reticulum (ER). ×30,000.

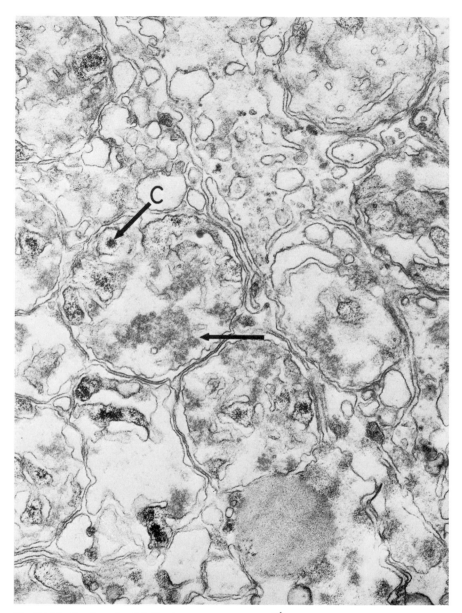

Fig. 24.10. Portion of cell following treatment with 10^{-4} M mercuric chloride for 4 hours. Note the stage 5 change showing high amplitude swelling of mitochondria with both flocculent densities (free arrow) and calcific deposits (C). Vesicles in the cytoplasm represent fragments of endoplasmic reticulum. X40,000.

CALCIUM UPTAKE (Ca⁴⁵) BY FLOUNDER KIDNEY TUBULES

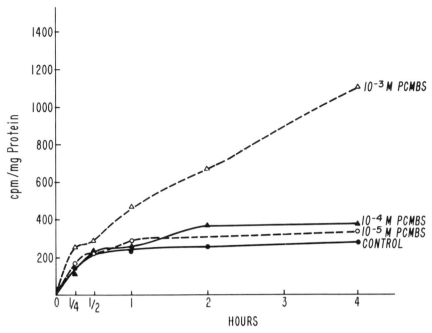

Fig. 24.11. Graph showing calcium uptake by flounder kidney tubules exposed to various concentrations of PCMBS. The tubules were incubated in Forster's medium to which $^{45}CaCl_2$ (0.26 nc/50 ml) was added. The total calcium concentration in the medium was 1.5 mm per liter. The tubules were removed from the medium after incubation for the stated time intervals, collected on Millipore filters, washed, and transferred in 1 N NaOH. Aliquots of this were taken for protein analysis and other aliquots were added to liquid scintillation fluid for liquid scintillation counting. (From S. Sahaphong and B. F. Trump, *American Journal of Pathology 63:* 277, 1971. Used by permission.)

was inhibited (Fig. 24.12). The apparent disparity between these two sets of data is explained as follows.

Mercury-damaged cells may or may not show dystrophic calcification exemplified by mitochondrial calcium phosphate precipitates, depending on the mercury concentration. Mercury is toxic to the accumulating system of the mitochondrial inner membrane and, if exposed to the mitochondria as shown above, inhibits uptake. On the other hand, mercury-damaged cells, both in the rat and in the fish, commonly show mitochondrial calcification. This occurs at low or intermediate concentrations, especially of nonpenetrating mercurials such as PCMBS, but is apparently inhibited at higher concentrations. This suggests that at the higher concentrations mercury probably enters the cell, is bound to the mitochondrial

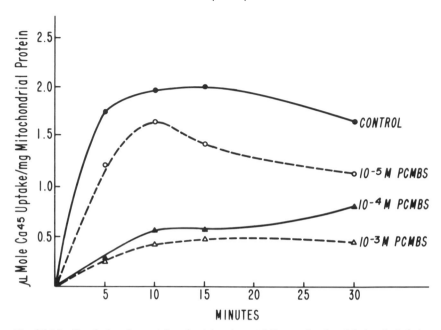

Fig. 24.12. Graph showing uptake of calcium by rat kidney mitochondria incubated at 30°C in control calcium-loading condition or in the same condition with the addition of various concentrations of PCMBS. The incubation medium contained the following final concentrations: 4mM $NaH_2PO_4 \cdot H_2O$; 10mM tris malate; 10mM succinate; 10mM $MgCl_2 \cdot 6H_2O$; 4mM $CaCl_2$; 3mM ATP; 80mM NaCl and the pH was adjusted to 7.02. To determine calcium uptake, a small (12.3 nc) $^{45}CaCl_2$ was added to the medium.

transport sites, and inhibits the calcium uptake. Mitochondrial calcification does not entirely correlate with total calcium uptake by the kidney tubules, probably indicating that other calcium-binding sites occur in damaged tissues, possibly involving calcium-binding sites in denatured proteins. It has been known for many years that necrotic tissue has a greater affinity for calcium binding than does normal tissue.

IN VIVO EFFECTS OF MERCURY

Everything we have discussed so far has been on the fish nephron model system that Forster had originally described and that we and others have used for various physiological and pathological studies. We are currently exposing hog-chokers (*T. maculatus*) to concentrations of mercury mimicking those that were mentioned in the isolated system but are using still lower concentrations. The

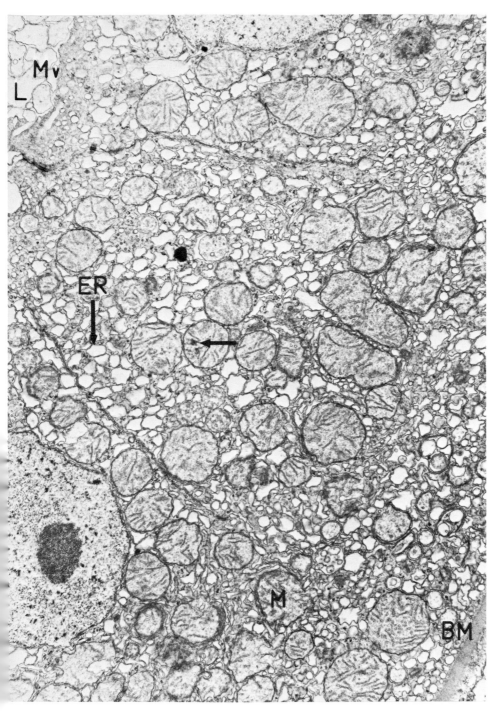

Fig. 24.13. Second proximal segment from a hogchoker which had been maintained in sea water containing 10^{-4} M $HgCl_2$ for 2 hours. The lumen (L) is at the upper left, the basement membrane (BM) at the lower right. Note the distortion of the microvilli (Mv). The endoplasmic reticulum (ER) is generally dilated and the mitochondria (M) show beginning swelling with early flocculent densities (free arrow) in one mitochondrion. ×14,000.

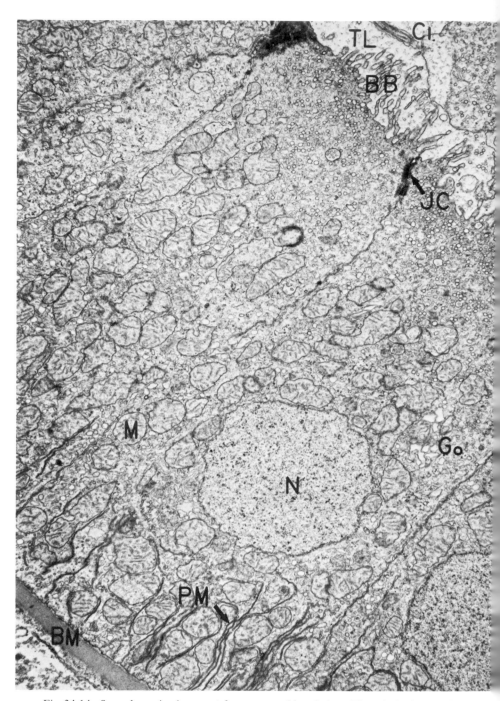

Fig. 24.14. Second proximal segment from a normal hogchoker. The tubular lumen (TL) is at the top, the basement membrane (BM) at the lower left. Note the cilium (Ci) in the tubular lumen. The brush border (BB) consists of a few microvilli. Note the orientation of the organelles, including the nucleus (N), the mitochondria (M), the Golgi apparatus (Go), the basement membrane (BM) and the complex plasma membrane (PM) of the basilar labyrinths. Junctional complexes (JC) can be seen near the lumen. ×12,000.

results of preliminary studies are as follows: in the second segment of the nephron from a fish that had been in 10^{-4}M (20 ppm) mercuric chloride for about two hours, the cells have already gone into stage 2 cell injury, implying once again a loss of cell volume control consistent with the action of mercury at the cell membrane (Fig. 24.13). This can be compared with the appearance of a normal kidney (Fig. 24.14).

We have done a few experiments in which we have tried to reproduce, in the hogchoker, the classic lesion of mercuric chloride poisoning in rat (9). Doses of 4 and 16 mg/kg body weight of mercuric chloride given to a rat produce a characteristic necrosis of the pars recta of proximal tubules in the outer stripe of the outer medulla. This reaction reaches the maximum in about 24 hours, and if the dose is withdrawn it is followed by regeneration. In the present experiment the hogchoker was injected with 16 mg/kg body weight of mercuric chloride, the same dose we used in the rat. It was associated in the hogchoker, as it was in the rat, with a selective necrosis which apparently does not involve all regions of the nephron but seems to involve the second segment, and probably the first as well. However, the collecting tubules seem to be unaltered (Fig. 24.15). In control

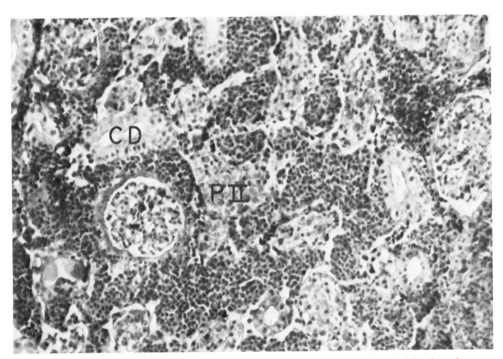

Fig. 24.15. Light micrograph of the kidney of a hogchoker 96 hours after the injection of 16 mg/kg of $HgCl_2$ into the peritoneal cavity. Note the extensive necrosis involving principally the second proximal segments (PII). Other tubules, principally collecting ducts (CD), do not show necrosis. Hematoxylin and eosin (H&E); ×300.

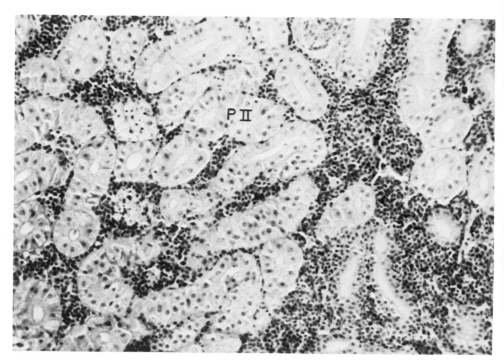

Fig. 24.16. Light micrograph of a hogchoker kidney 96 hours after the injection of distilled water intraperitoneally in an amount equivalent to that used as a vehicle for the HgCl₂ in Figure 24.15. Note the preservation of the tubules, most of which are second proximal segments (PII). H&E; ×300.

fish injected with 1 ml distilled water intraperitoneally, the same amount used for the mercuric chloride injections, no alteration was seen (Fig. 24.16). These are preliminary experiments, but do seem to indicate that, as in the rat, the fish may have localized lesions after exposure to mercury *in vivo*. That implies selective concentration of the mercurial in certain segments or some other factor induced by the mercury, since tubules incubated in mercury-containing compounds *in vitro* seem to have more uniform reaction. Whether or not mercury might be actively transported, for example, by the divalent pump that transports magnesium and calcium has not been determined.

SUMMARY

Figure 24.17 summarizes our hypothesis regarding the effects of mercury on cells and in this case on the fish kidney tubule. We visualize the important effect of mercury to be a binding with SH groups on surface membrane proteins. This may have a variety of effects of course, including inhibition of ATPase. One of the most important effects, we feel, is to induce leak with leak-in of sodium and

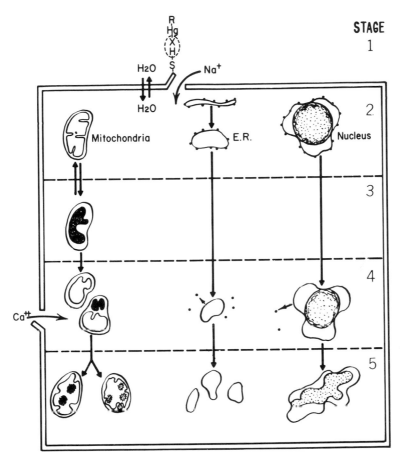

Fig. 24.17. Summary diagram showing our hypothesis of the effects of mercury on flounder tubule cells. Mercury binding to SH groups of the cell surface membrane increases the permeability to the membrane to cations. Na^+ and water enter the cell dilating the endoplasmic reticulum (ER) and nuclear envelope, and increasing the volume of the cell. These changes are characteristic of stage 2. In stage 3 the mitochondria contract and the cell sap enlarges along with the previous dilatational changes. The stretching of the cell membrane during stages 2 and 3 may cause a secondary leak permitting other cations, such as Ca^{++}, to enter the cell. As the result of Ca^{++} entering the cell, the mitochondria swell and calcification occurs if the mitochondrial transport system has not been inhibited within the matrix. Stages 2 and 3 are believed to be reversible stages; stage 4, a transitional stage; and stage 5 is the final stage or the stage of cell necrosis. (From S. Sahaphong and B. F. Trump, *American Journal of Pathology 63*: 277, 1971. Used by permission.)

leak-out of potassium with subsequent volume shifts in the cell, including dilation of the endoplasmic reticulum (ER). Perhaps even the effects on mitochondria are mediated this same way since high concentrations of sodium are known to in-hibit mitochondrial respiration (10). Subsequently, if the mitochondria are not damaged sufficiently or do not "see" the mercury, calcium enters through a still leaky membrane. However, the calcium pumps may already be inhibited. Thus the mitochondria commonly show calcification and this, of course, is the basis of one important type of nephrocalcinosis, the deposition of calcium in mitochon-dria in kidney or in some other organs. Therefore, we tend to agree with the Roth-stein (15) idea. Our experiments with mercury, in light of our experiments with other compounds in the fish nephron and other cells, imply strongly to us that the important action is at the cell surface membrane and that a permeability change rather than a classic Peters (14) type of biochemical lesion is probably the important factor. Studies of the basic mechanism of mercurial action are obvious-ly very difficult. This is probably due to the fact that mercury has such a high af-finity for binding to SH groups and since virtually all proteins have SH groups and their conformations are dependent upon these SH groups. Thus at some con-centration mercury will inhibit the function of virtually any protein. Consequent-ly, it seems more consistent with our data to think of the important lesion as be-ing an interaction involving cell membrane and primarily affecting membrane permeability.

REFERENCES

1. Bäckström, J. Distribution studies of mercuric pesticides in quail and some fresh-water fishes. *Acta pharmacol. toxicol.* 27(Suppl. 3). 1969.
2. Bulger, R. E., and Trump, B. F. Effects of fixatives on tubular ultrastructure of the aglomerular midshipman, *Porichthys notatus,* and the glomerular flounder, *Parophrys vetulus. J. Histochem. Cytochem. 13:* 719. 1965.
3. Bulger, R. E., and Trump, B. F. Renal morphology of the English sole (*Parophrys vetulus*). *Amer. J. Anat. 123:* 195. 1968.
4. Bulger, R. E., and Trump, B. F. Ca^{2+} and K^+ ion effects on ultrastructure of isolated flounder kidney tubules. *J. Ultrastruct. Res. 28:* 301. 1969.
5. Bulger, R. E., and Trump, B. F. A mechanism for rapid transport of colloid-al particles by flounder renal epithelium. *J. Morphol. 127:* 205. 1969.
6. Forster, R. P. Use of thin kidney slices and isolated renal tubules for direct study of cellular transport kinetics. *Science (Wash., D.C.) 108:* 65. 1948.
7. Ginn, F. L., Shelburne, J. D., and Trump, B. F. Disorders of cell volume reg-ulation. I. Effects of inhibition of plasma membrane adenosine triphospha-tese with ouabain. *Amer. J. Pathol. 53:* 1041. 1968.
8. Gómez-Puyou, A., Sandoval, F., Peña, A., Chávez, E., and Tuena, M. Effect of Na^+ and K^+ on mitochondrial respiratory control, oxygen uptake, and ade-nosine triphosphatase activity. *J. Biol. Chem. 244:* 5339. 1969.
9. Gritzka, T. L., and Trump, B. F. Renal tubular lesions caused by mercuric

chloride. Electron microscopic observations: Degeneration of the pars recta. *Amer. J. Pathol. 52:* 1225. 1968.

10. Haga, Y., Haga, H., Hagino, T., and Kariya, T. Studies on the post-mortem identification of the pollutant in fish killed by water pollution. XII. Acute poisoning with mercury. *Bull. Jap. Soc. Sci. Fish. 36:* 225. 1970.

11. Hannerz, L. Experimental investigations on the accumulation of mercury in water organisms. *Rep. Inst. Freshwater Res. Drottningholm 48:* 120. 1968.

12. Hickman, C. P., and Trump, B. F. The kidney, p. 91. In *Fish Physiology,* ed. W. S. Hoar and D. J. Randall, vol. 1. New York and London, Academic Press, 1969-70.

13. Kinter, W. B. Chlorphenol red influx and efflux: Microspectrophotometry of flounder kidney tubules. *Amer. J. Physiol. 211:* 1152. 1966.

14. Peters, R. A. The biochemical lesion and its historical development. *Brit. Med. Bull. 25:* 223. 1969.

15. Rothstein, A. Sulfhydryl groups in membrane structure and function, p. 1. In *Current Topics in Membranes and Transport,* ed. F. Bronner and A. Klein-zeller, vol. 1. New York and London, Academic Press, 1970.

16. Rucker, R. R., and Amend, D. F. Absorption and retention of organic mer-curials by rainbow trout and chinook and sockeye salmon. *Progr. Fish-Cult. 31:* 197. 1969.

17. Sahaphong, S. The role of cell membrane sulfhydryl groups in pathogenesis of cell death. Ph.D. thesis Duke Univ., Durham, N.C., 1972.

18. Sahaphong, S., and Trump, B. F. Studies of cellular injury in isolated flounder kidney tubules. V. Effects of inhibiting sulfhydryl groups of plasma membrane with the organic mercurials PCMB (parachloromercuribenzo-ate) and PCMBS (parachloromercuribenzenesulfonate). *Amer. J. Pathol. 63:* 277. 1971.

19. Shelburne, J. D., and Trump, B. F. Inhibition of protein synthesis in flounder kidney tubules. *Fed. Proc. 27:* 410. 1969.

20. Trump, B. F., and Bulger, R. E. Studies of cellular injury in isolated floun-der tubules. I. Correlation between morphology and function of control tubules and observations of autophagocytosis and mechanical cell damage. *Lab. Invest. 16:* 453. 1967.

21. Trump, B. F., and Bulger, R. E. Studies of cellular injury in isolated floun-der tubules. III. Light microscopic and functional changes due to cyanide. *Lab. Invest. 18:* 721. 1968.

22. Trump, B. F., and Bulger, R. E. Studies of cellular injury in isolated floun-der tubules. IV. Electron microscopic observations of changes during the phase of altered homeostasis in tubules treated with cyanide. *Lab. Invest. 18:* 731. 1968.

23. Trump, B. F., and Bulger, R. E. Experimental modification of lateral and basilar plasma membranes and extracellular compartments in the flounder nephron. *Fed. Proc. 30:* 22. 1971.

24. Trump, B. F., and Ginn, F. L. Studies of cellular injury in isolated flounder tubules. II. Cellular swelling in high potassium media. *Lab. Invest. 18:* 341. 1968.

25. Trump, B. F., and Ginn, F. L.   The pathogenesis of subcellular reaction to lethal injury. p. 1. In *Methods and Achievements in Experimental Pathology,* ed. E. Bajusz and G. Jasmin, vol. 4. Basel, Karger, 1969.

DISCUSSION OF CELLULAR EFFECTS OF MERCURY ON FISH KIDNEY TUBULES

A. Stein: We've seen *in vivo* in mammalian systems this type of what you have classified as stage 3 and stage 4 change. This will appear as indicated if you take serial biopsies in your experimental situation. We are also impressed that if you continue the experiment, and continue to give the dose, at the end of the third or fourth day all of your ultrastructural changes have disappeared.

B. F. Trump: This is in what animal?

A. Stein: We've seen this in a rat; we've seen this in a monkey.

B. F. Trump: Could you give the dose of the mercury?

A. Stein: This happened to be with chlorinated hydrocarbons. I just raise a question that the classic pharmacological approach still holds here, that we have to be certain of a time-dose response and that the degree of adaptability is something very surprising.

B. F. Trump: I didn't have time to comment on that and of course my comments were oversimplified in some ways. The important issue that I was presenting was that following application of an injury that kills the cells, the cells commonly go through a series of stages like this, 1, 2, 3, 4, 5. The initial changes vary with initial interaction depending on whether it attacks the membrane or whether it inhibits ATP synthesis. Now something that just puts the cells into the third stage or the second stage would not be a lethal injury, but left in there for a long time it would be a sublethal injury. We know of many compounds including chlorinated hydrocarbons, phenobarbital, and others that do induce a type of what you might call sublethal injury by inducing endoplasmic reticulum (ER) synthesis and drug metabolizing sequences that are capable of detoxifying the compound. Even though the cell type may be quite different, it still undergoes hypertrophy in general in the process. The liver gets larger, heavier; the cells are larger; the ER is much more abundant. Also, obviously you have to keep the time relations in mind. If in the rat, for example, if you give a dose of 4 mg of mercury, it will not kill the rat, it will just kill this one segment of the nephron. The cells become necrotic by day 1; they begin to slough, but the adjacent cells at the end that aren't affected re-enter the mitotic cycle. Kidney tubules in general are in G zero; they re-enter the cycle, cover the area, and then undergo differentiation over a period of about two weeks, after which the tubular continuity is re-established. Following this, the tubules are then more resistant to mercury; they do adapt to mercury and now a larger dose is required. Obviously all these principles have to be kept in mind.

R. J. Roberts: About two years ago I was involved in a considerable amount of electron microscopy of necrotizing cells in Atlantic salmon in the disease known as ulcerative dermal necrosis. One of the features that we were regularly finding in these cells was the myelin figures which you discussed. Another feature was what we called coated-vesicles which could occasionally be mistaken for virus particles. Do you believe that these myelin figures are in fact degeneration of mitochondria? In some of our cells we seemed to find a lot of very intact mitochondria and yet we also encountered myelin figures.

B. F. Trump: The myelin figures were originally described by Rudolf Virchow, who noted that myelin, as well as any cell, when it underwent autolysis in aqueous media would give rise to worm-like things that grew out; you could see them under the light microscope. If you cut these in sections they are laminated and are composed chiefly of phospholipid bilayers and of course myelin itself is a modified sort of thing where the Schwann cell is wrapping around the axon and the membranes are coming in apposition. Now any phospholipid structure therefore can yield myelin forms (mitochondria, ER, Golgi apparatus, etc.). Now if we look at a cell about the only place you see them in the normal cells is in the lysosomes where various kinds of lipid debris accumulate and the reason presumably that we see them in the lysosomes is that they have been phagocytized. They are phagocytized debris, either other cells, food organisms, or autophagocytized organelles, such as mitochondria, which we know in most cells can get into the lysosome by the process of budding into that space and pinching off. This whole thing deteriorates after adding hydrolases and may do so even in part independent of hydrolases. Autophagocytosis as well as heterophagocytosis gives rise to myelin forms and in many kinds of sublethal injury we will see a lot more of the autophagic vacuoles; these often give rise to inclusions visible by light microscopy. For example pictures of livers with biphenols show large PAS-positive inclusions; almost certainly those inclusions will turn out to be heterophagic or autophagic bodies of this type, full of degenerating organelles. When the whole cell undergoes necrosis after a long period of time, perhaps a week, most of the organelles by then seem to be involved and now we can see huge myelin figures by light microscopy or electron microscopy in the cell. Normally they are seen in the lysosome system. In sublethal injury where we have more lysosomes being formed for one reason or another, they will still be making myelin figures inside of those. The figures can form from any organelle when the whole cell undergoes necrosis or autolysis. Eventually they begin to form and apparently all the organelles participate in their formation.

Question: It appears from what has gone on so far in the discussion that since the rat takes in the mercury by eating or drinking whereas the fish lives in the water that may contain the mercury, we really don't know whether the kidney lesion is what kills the fish. Is that not correct?

B. F. Trump: That is correct. I don't think we know very much about the important effects of mercury in intact fish. We are in the process of trying to start working on this now. Up until now we have been working on the *in vitro* system.

Of course marine animals drinking sea water can absorb mercury in that way or from eating other animals in the food chain. You can also have a direct effect of mercury on the gill if the concentration is high enough. In some of our preliminary experiments where we have raised the concentration in the sea water to 200 ppm, which is associated with the rapid death of the tubules when used *in vitro*, associated with this there was rapid death of the fish and changes in the gill resembling those seen in the isolated kidney tubules.

25

Cadmium-Induced Histopathological Changes in Goldfish

ROBERT TAFANELLI
and ROBERT C. SUMMERFELT

In 1968 the United States used approximately one-half the world production of cadmium, a relatively rare element with an abundance in the earth's crust of 0.5 grams per ton (30). Forecasts of cadmium uses in the United States indicate a demand of 21.2 to 39 million pounds compared with 13.3 million pounds in 1968 (30). The major industrial use has been for electroplating, but a faster rate of increase is occurring in the manufacture of polyvinylchloride, paints, and nickel-cadmium energy cells. Expanding uses of cadmium have caused concern for the health peril from environmental contamination.

Contamination of water and crop soils from the production or utilization of cadmium in manufacturing processes creates public health hazards of considerable magnitude. Cadmium exhibits a pronounced tendency to accumulate in the body, with a very long biological half-life (23). "Itai-itai" disease, a rheumatoid ailment responsible to date for about 100 human deaths in Japan, was associated with chronic contamination of rice fields with Jintsu River water containing mine effluents high in cadmium particles (23). "Itai-itai" was the manifestation of chronic cadmium poisoning from consumption of cadmium-contaminated rice. A voluminous review by Friberg, Piscator, and Nordberg (23) shows cadmium associated with hypertension, emphysema, renal tubule damage, liver dysfunction, and cancer.

613

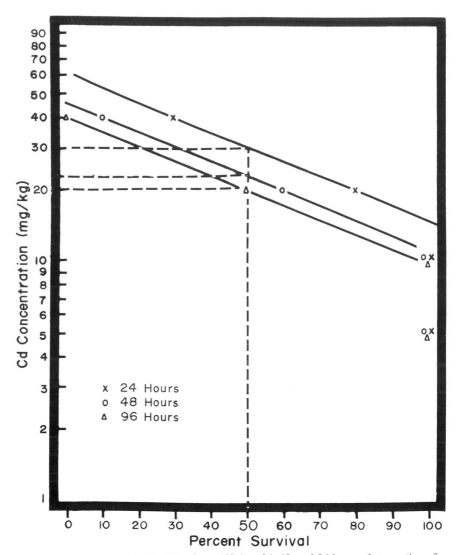

Fig. 25.1. Cadmium chloride LD$_{50}$ for goldfish at 24, 48, and 96 hours. Intersection of dashed lines with survival line (solid) indicates LD$_{50}$ concentrations.

Cadmium generally occurs in surface waters in concentrations of less than one part per billion. However, in Japan cadmium was undetectable in solutions in some samples of river water polluted with cadmium wastes (23). In Sweden, 500 meters downstream from the effluent of an industry discharging cadmium, 4 ppb as Cd was found in the water and 80 ppm in the mud (dry weight) (23). In the North Canadian River, Oklahoma, a concentration of 2.8 ppm Cd was found in a water sample immediately downstream from a major industrial effluent, but 358 ppm (ash weight) was found in a mud sample from the receiving arm of a reservoir 250 miles downstream from the source (22). Aquatic life is potentially able to magnify residues through trophic relationships to levels in fish tissue which would represent a public health hazard. The biological magnification of organochlorine insecticides in aquatic ecosystems has resulted in accumulation of residue levels in predators one million times their concentration in water. DDT concentrations in Lake Michigan water are 1 to 5 parts per trillion, while residues of 5 to 10 parts per million have been reported in coho salmon (*Oncorhynchus kisutch*) (51). The impact of cadmium on fish and other aquatic life is largely unknown. Cadmium has potential for a devastating effect on the reproductive success and general well-being of aquatic life. However, our knowledge of the impact of heavy metals on fish is largely based on short-term toxicity studies.

The present report describes a series of studies by the authors on (1) the LD_{50} of cadmium chloride for 24, 48, and 96 hours, (2) the effect of cadmium on the gonadal weight, (3) cadmium residues in the gonads, liver, kidney, and muscle, and (4) the relationship between histopathological changes in the gonads, liver, and kidney and cadmium residues. Emphasis is placed on dose-response studies to relate specific quantities of the metal to histopathological effects.

ACUTE TOXICITY

Median Lethal Dose (LD_{50})

The LD_{50} of intraperitoneal (IP) injections of $CdCl_2$ to the goldfish was 30.0, 23.0, and 20.0 mg/kg wet weight at 24, 48, and 96 hours, respectively, using standard graphical procedures (Fig. 25.1) (51). The maximum dose which did not produce mortality in 96 hours was 10 mg/kg. Observations of goldfish receiving 10 mg/kg indicated that mortality of about < 3% occurred over 10 to 20 days. Goldfish did survive a total dose of 37.5 mg/kg $CdCl_2$ when administered over five weeks at levels of 7.5 mg/kg per injection, whereas a single dose of 37.5 mg/kg would be expected to kill about 90% of the fish in 96 hours, or about 50% of the fish in 5 hours (Fig. 25.1). Gross examination of the gonads gave no indication of swelling, or discoloration as observed in the mammalian testis (48).

LD_{50} values of cadmium were not found in the literature for fish or other vertebrates. Injections (IP) of 3.5 to 7.5 mg/kg body weight as $CdCl_2$ were sublethal to a variety of mammals (rats, mice, rabbits, hamsters, and guinea pigs), although a single subcutaneous injection of 7.5 mg/kg produced necrotic lesions in the testis (12, 13, 27, 36, 43, 45, 47, 48). The route of administration affects the lethal dose. Cadmium administered subcutaneously and intravenously is lethal to rabbits at 18 and 5 mg/kg, respectively (56).

Median Tolerance Limits (TL_m)

In solution, the concentration of cadmium salts lethal to fish is generally less than the LD_{50} reported above. Toxicity of solutions of heavy metals to fish is generally explained by the "coagulation-film anoxia theory." Solutions of heavy metals generally suffocate fish by precipitating or coagulating mucoproteins on the gill epithelium, which thus interferes with oxygen exchange, secretion of waste products, and osmoregulation (5). The lethal concentration is inversely proportional to the oxygen concentration of the water (55), solution pressure (34), and water hardness (33). The cause of death is apparently due to precipitation of mucoproteins on the gills; thus TL_m is directly affected by the number of fish per unit volume of water (10). There is also variation in tolerance due to species and age differences (11). In general, young fish are less tolerant than adults, larvae less tolerant than young fish, and eggs more tolerant than adults. Anions responsible for water hardness precipitate cadmium and other heavy metals. Thus, the TL_m of various fish species for cadmium is dependent upon water hardness, and values vary 10- to 100-fold from soft to hard water, depending upon the species involved (19, 34, 49). Pickering and Henderson studied the toxicity of several heavy metals, including cadmium, on fish in both soft (total hardness 20 mg per liter) and hard (total hardness 360 mg per liter) water (49). The 24-hour TL_m values of cadmium for fathead minnows (*Pimephales promelas*) were approximately 1 and 78 mg per liter in soft and hard water, respectively, and 7.8 and 88.6 mg per liter in soft and hard water, respectively, for green sunfish (*Lepomis cyanellus*). In soft water, 24-hour TL_m values of cadmium for bluegills (*L. macrochirus*), goldfish, and guppies (*Poecilia reticulata* = *Lebistes reticulatus*) were 4.6, 3.5, and 3.4 mg per liter, respectively. The 96-hour TL_m of cadmium for goldfish was 2.3 mg per liter. The concentration of cadmium at which the average survival time of large sticklebacks (*Gasterosteus aculeatus*) was 1, 2, and 4 days was 7.0, 3.0, and 0.7 ppm, respectively (34). Thomas found that 6 ppm cadmium nitrate killed mummichogs (*Fundulus heteroclitus*) in 36 hours (52).

EFFECTS ON GONADAL WEIGHT

Relative gonadal weight, i.e., gonadal weight as a percentage of total body weight, is a widely utilized expression of the degree of gonadal maturity, general-

Table 25.1. Effects of (IP Injections) CdCl₂ on Goldfish Gonadal Weight
Expressed as a Percentage of Total Body Weight

	Males W/Cd		Males WO/Cd		Females W/Cd		Females WO/Cd	
	WO/ HCG	W/ HCG[a]	WO/ HCG	W/ HCG[a]	WO/ HCG	W/ HCG[a]	WO/ HCG	W/ HCG
	Fish receiving a single IP injection of 7.5 mg/kg CdCl₂							
$\overline{X}$	2.0	1.7	2.2	2.6	5.3	2.8	6.4	6.6
N	18	11	12	15	5	10	9	9
	Fish receiving single IP injections of 10 mg/kg CdCl₂							
$\overline{X}$	1.7	1.2	1.7	1.9	5.7	3.9	4.8	5.1
N	45	40	57	52	42	54	53	52

[a]Fish received single injections of human chorionic gonadotropin (HCG).

ly called gonadal-somatic index and abbreviated as GSI. The effect of cadmium injections on the GSI of goldfish was influenced by the level of gonadal activity, as indicated by comparison of fish with and without injections of human chorionic gonadotropin (HCG) (Table 25.1). The decreased GSI values observed in the cadmium-treated fish were associated with increased uptake of cadmium and pathological changes as shown by a decrease in the stage of gonadal maturation and increased frequency of histopathological changes such as occurrence of focal granulomas.

Group mean GSI of male goldfish without human chorionic gonadotropin (WO/HCG) varied from 1.7 to 2.2, when temperature was 21°C with a 12-hour photoperiod; male fish stimulated by exogenous hormone (W/HCG) had group mean GSI values of 1.9 to 2.6 (Table 25.1). The observed differences in the mean groups W/ and WO/HCG were nonsignificant (P > .05). Male goldfish given IP injections of 7.5 to 10.0 mg/kg CdCl₂ (i.e., 4.6 to 6.1 mg/kg as Cd) had smaller averages (Table 25.1). Testicular activation with HCG affected the observed dose-response, as seen by comparing the difference between control groups (WO/Cd, but W/HCG) and groups of male fish receiving cadmium and HCG. Differences observed (Table 25.1) between the mean GSI of males receiving cadmium and HCG (1.7 and 1.2, respectively) and the mean GSI of the control groups receiving HCG (2.6 and 1.9, respectively) were highly significant (P < .01).

Relative gonadal weight of female goldfish was also increased by injecting HCG, and, as with males, cadmium injections had a greater effect on female fish stimulated with HCG (Tables 25.1, 25.2). The difference between group means for female fish receiving HCG and cadmium ($\overline{X}$ = 2.8 and 3.9) compared with fe-

Table 25.2. Cadmium Residues in Organs of Goldfish[a] Given Single (S.I.)
or Multiple Injections (M.I.) of Cadmium with or without Injections of Human
Chorionic Gonadotropin (HCG)

| Group | Days and number of Cd injections[b] in parentheses | | | | | | | | Group mean |
	13 (1)	31 (2)	44 (3)	86 (4)	122 (6)	159 (8)	215 (10)	615 (12)	
Liver									
Control	0.0	–	4.9	0.0	5.7	1.9	1.5	1.9	2.3
S.I.	74.9	111.3	94.1	107.1	92.6	38.6	12.3	–	75.8
M.I.	87.5	154.1	–	199.7	241.7	143.9	159.9	–	164.5
S.I. + HCG	105.3	103.5	–	139.6	71.6	34.9	33.1	–	81.3
M.I. + HCG	65.9	113.2	–	214.6	312.4	223.8	300.0	165.4	199.3
Kidney									
Control	0.0	0.0	0.0	0.0	0.0	0.0	0.0	25.3	3.2
S.I.	86.1	82.1	65.7	–	72.5	109.2	80.3	–	82.6
M.I.	88.1	149.5	337.2	221.1	425.1	325.1	447.0	–	284.7
S.I. + HCG	108.0	84.7	154.1	–	113.1	93.9	118.8	366.4	148.4
M.I. + HCG	66.3	253.7	384.1	–	395.1	211.3	385.7	923.4	374.2
Ovary									
Control	19.5	0.0	1.3	0.0	0.0	0.0	0.0	0.0	2.6
S.I.	4.4	9.4	4.7	–	0.0	2.7	21.2	–	7.1
M.I.	–	11.7	101.5	52.5	33.5	46.0	3.3	–	41.4
S.I. + HCG	–	0.0	14.2	20.5	5.3	29.8	1.8	7.3	11.3
M.I. + HCG	–	19.3	–	25.0	32.7	144.3	35.1	68.6	54.2
Testis									
Control	0.0	0.0	0.0	–	0.0	–	2.7	4.2	1.2
S.I.	78.1	–	47.2	–	0.0	11.3	0.0	–	27.3
M.I.	–	0.0	138.0	0.0	108.7	17.1	70.4	–	55.7
S.I. + HCG	–	–	0.9	–	0.0	–	0.0	21.8	22.7
M.I. + HCG	–	42.6	18.1	–	–	–	20.6	–	27.1
Muscle									
Control	0.0	0.0	0.0	0.0	0.0	0.0	0.0	0.0	0.0
S.I.	1.7	0.0	0.0	0.0	2.1	0.0	0.0	–	0.5
M.I.	0.0	0.0	0.0	0.0	0.0	0.0	0.0	–	0.0
S.I. + HCG	2.1	0.0	1.5	2.1	0.0	0.0	0.9	1.3	0.9
M.I. + HCG	0.0	0.0	0.0	0.6	4.3	0.0	0.0	0.0	0.6

[a] Residue analysis of liver, kidney, and muscle was of a composite of 10 fish; analysis of ovary and testis was of a composite of organs from 3 to 8 fish.

[b] Injections were 10 mg/kg wet weight $CdCl_2$, or 6.1 mg/kg as Cd; residues are expressed as mg of Cd/kg dry weight.

males receiving cadmium but not HCG (X = 5.3 and 5.7) (Table 25.1) was highly significant (P < .01).

Gonadal development has been inhibited—occasionally complete gonadal degeneration has occurred—in fish held in 2 to 5 ppm lead nitrate for four months (16). The "Itai-itai" victims were mostly postmenopausal women with several children (23). The suggestion is that pregnancy, lactation, or hormonal factors were predisposing conditions. The present study shows that hormonal stimulation of gonadal activity was a predisposing factor affecting the toxicity of cadmium to goldfish gonads.

CADMIUM RESIDUES

Cadmium residues were determined in gonads, liver, kidney, and muscle of goldfish injected with single and multiple doses of 6.1 mg/kg as Cd over a period from 0 to 615 days (Table 25.2). Residues, reported as mg/kg dry weight, for liver, kidney, and muscle are composites of male and female organs of 10 fish. Ovaries and testes were analyzed separately, and each composite was made up of 3 to 8 fish. Organ residue levels of cadmium were determined by atomic absorption spectrophotometry. Samples dried to constant weight (±0.1 mg) in 20 ml beakers at 100°C in a drying oven were ashed in a muffle furnace at 550° to 575°C in the same beakers in which they were dried. Residual weight (±0.1 mg) after ignition was the ash weight. Cadmium in the ash was put into solution by dissolving it in 5 ml of 2 N nitric acid. The cadmium in the sample solution was converted to mg/kg cadmium of the dried weight of the organ. Reliable results were not obtained with the testis because the amount of tissue yielded from some males was insufficient to weigh with precision.

Most determinations of cadmium residues in organs of the control fish had concentrations below the lowest detectable limit, i.e., 0.1 mg/kg (Table 25.2). The spontaneous occurrence of concentrations as high as 19.5 mg/kg in the ovaries of the control fish and 25.3 mg/kg in the kidney of the control fish in single composite samples is unexplainable. Cadmium residues in organs of goldfish exposed to single or multiple injections of $CdCl_2$ were so much greater than residues occurring in control fish as to leave no doubt that these concentrations were associated with the experimental procedures (Table 25.2). Liver and testis of the controls most often had the highest residues. Group means of cadmium residue concentrations in the controls were always significantly different from the mean concentration of cadmium in other organs, except for muscle. Cadmium was never found in the muscle of control fish and only rarely detected in muscle of fish receiving injections of cadmium. Highest cadmium concentration in muscle of injected fish was 1.3 mg/kg 615 days after a single cadmium injection and 6.5 mg/kg over a year after termination of 12 cadmium injections. Residues in several organs

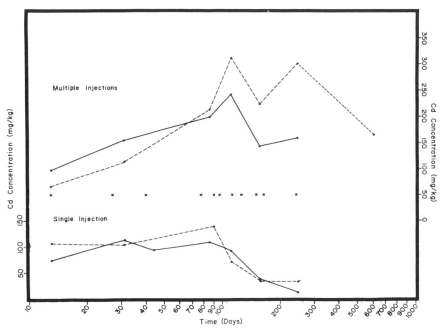

Fig. 25.2. Cadmium residues of the dry weight of the liver of goldfish receiving single or multiple injections of 6.1 mg/kg as Cd (* injection dates; — fish W/HCG; - - fish WO/HCG).

were higher in groups receiving injections of HCG, supporting the initial hypothesis that cadmium uptake would be affected by metabolic activation with HCG.

Liver

Cadmium residues in livers of goldfish exposed to single or multiple injections of $CdCl_2$ were of an order of magnitude greater than the residues in the control fish. Highest cadmium residues were observed in livers of goldfish receiving multiple injections, and higher residues occurred in groups receiving cadmium and HCG compared with their matched group receiving cadmium but not HCG. The 81.3 mg/kg dry weight cadmium residue in the singly-injected group receiving HCG was not, however, statistically greater than the mean of 75.8 mg/kg for the group receiving only a single cadmium injection but no HCG. By contrast, the means for the two groups receiving multiple injections was significantly greater than the two groups receiving a single injection.

Livers of the two groups receiving multiple cadmium injections had a significantly ($P < .01$) higher cadmium residue than livers of fish which had received a single injection. The group means of the two groups receiving multiple injections, with and without HCG, were not significantly different. The group receiving HCG had lower cadmium residues through 31 days, but larger residues from 86 to 215 days.

The liver of groups receiving a single cadmium injection with and without HCG had similar temporal variations in cadmium residues (Table 25.2, Fig. 25.2). Decreases in liver residues of cadmium between 86 and 215 days in the two groups receiving a single injection indicate a gradual clearance from the liver (Fig. 25.2). Gunn, Gould, and Anderson found that liver tissues had a decrease in cadmium content in the first 20 days after injection (27). On the other hand, the cadmium levels in the liver of dogs after a single oral dose remained essentially constant (17).

In dogs, the liver, because of its greater mass, contained the greatest total quantity of cadmium (17). Usually, the liver and kidney will contain 50 to 75% of the total body cadmium burden (23). Oral administration of cadmium to dogs revealed that it is highly concentrated in the liver and kidney (18). Although most of the cadmium was excreted, a diet of 10 ppm per day for one year resulted in 80 ppm in the kidney and 40 ppm in the liver. The liver of rats injected with cadmium contained more total cadmium than the kidney because of the larger organ weight, but the kidney had a higher concentration of cadmium per unit weight of organ (4, 15). Pathological effects of cadmium on organs, especially the kidney, liver, and lungs, were varied but there was some relationship between occurrence of sarcomas and tumors with experimental exposure to cadmium (21).

Kidney

Cadmium residues in kidney tissues averaged higher than in liver tissues, for

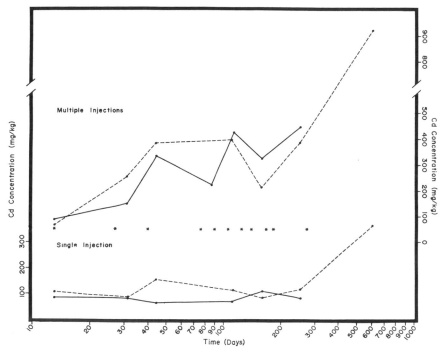

Fig. 25.3. Cadmium residues of the dry weight of kidney of goldfish receiving single or multiple injections of 6.1 mg/kg as Cd (* injection dates; —— fish W/HCG; - - fish WO/HCG).

the same treatment. Because of the larger mass, however, the liver contained a greater percentage of total body burden than the kidney. Fish receiving a single injection of cadmium, without HCG, had a residue of 86.1 mg/kg 13 days after injection and this was retained for up to 215 days. The 366.4 mg/kg recorded in the composite at 615 days after a single injection of cadmium in the group also receiving an injection of HCG can be explained only by assuming a redistribution of cadmium from other organs to the kidney, as this group did not receive additional cadmium injections. The mean cadmium residue in the group receiving a single injection of cadmium and HCG (148.4 ppm) was significantly different from the mean (82.6 ppm) of the group receiving cadmium but not HCG.

Group means of residues in the kidneys of two groups receiving multiple injections were significantly different ($P < .01$) from the mean of the group receiving a single injection. The former showed a distinct upward slope through 122 days (Fig. 25.3), but considerable fluctuation occurred throughout. The difference in the mean concentration of cadmium in the group receiving HCG and multiple cadmium injections and the other group receiving multiple injections of cadmium but without injections of HCG was not significant ($P > .05$).

Large residues of cadmium were found in the kidney of rats (18, 54) and mice (6) after a single cadmium injection. Only a small turnover of cadmium was indicated in mammals (15). Gunn and Gould observed that the cadmium content of the kidney cortex increased sharply while the content of the medulla increased slowly (24). They also found that the cadmium residue increased more slowly in young rats, suggesting a relationship between cadmium retention and the number of nephrons present. Cadmium accumulation in the liver, kidney, intestine (6), and adrenals (54) has been noted after a single cadmium injection. Other investigators have noted that the kidney has the highest cadmium concentration per unit weight of organ although the liver has the greatest total amount of cadmium (4). In our experiments, kidneys of goldfish also had higher relative concentrations than the liver.

Lucis, Lynk, and Lucis found that after a single injection of cadmium chloride, the concentration of cadmium in blood cells, liver, and kidney increased for 336 hours (42). It has also been observed that cadmium levels in the blood of rats receiving a single injection of cadmium increased rapidly within 24 hours (54).

Gonads

The sex of goldfish could not be determined before sampling, which made it difficult to accumulate sufficient gonadal tissue for residue analysis of both sexes on all sample dates. This problem was especially true for males receiving multiple cadmium injections and HCG because testicular atrophy made difficult the accumulation of enough testicular tissue for a composite analysis (Table 25.1).

Cadmium residues of both sexes receiving a single injection had minor fluctuations but no conspicuous trend. The larger mean residue in ovaries of fish receiving a single injection of cadmium but no HCG compared with the group receiving a single injection of cadmium and HCG (7.1 to 11.3 mg/kg, respectively) suggested that ovarian uptake of cadmium was greater in the more active ovary, but the difference between the two means was not significant (P > .05).

The groups receiving multiple cadmium injections had much larger means (41.4 and 54.2) than the groups receiving only a single injection (7.1 and 11.3 mg/kg). Differences in the means of the two groups receiving multiple injections and the means of the two groups receiving single injections were significant (P < .05). In the groups receiving multiple injections, as in the groups receiving single injections, cadmium residue was higher in the group receiving injections of HCG; however, the difference was nonsignificant (P > .05).

The inability to obtain a sufficient sample of testicular tissue resulted in many missing residue determinations and large variations in residue values obtained. Since the dry weight of the organ is the divisor for calculation of Cd per kg of organ weight (i.e., mg/kg), the very small dry weights obtained for testis caused large fluctuations in residues because of a difference of a few tenths of a milligram in testis weight. Also, testes could not be found in some fish, especially those which had received multiple cadmium injections.

Groups receiving a single injection of cadmium had testicular residues averaging 22.7 and 27.3 mg/kg for the groups with and without injections of HCG, respectively. The difference between these means was nonsignificant. Thus, the testis was the only case where cadmium residues were higher in the group not receiving HCG injections. A trend suggesting a gradual decrease in cadmium residue level occurred in the group receiving single cadmium injections and no HCG but this trend was not verified by the group receiving HCG. A greater frequency of high values (> 70.0 mg/kg) was noted in the group receiving multiple cadmium injections but no HCG than in fish receiving a single injection of cadmium and HCG. However, in the latter group, testes were often so small (i.e., nearly destroyed) that they could not be found. Since the testes of the multiple-injected group had atrophied to such a degree that no tissue could be collected, data are lacking in the groups where concentrations were probably maximum.

In mammals several organs have higher residues of cadmium than the testis. Parizek observed, after a single cadmium injection, a 100-fold higher concentration of cadmium in the liver compared to the testis (48). This ratio is somewhat higher than our experiments with goldfish, which had 15 times more cadmium in the liver than in the testis.

HISTOLOGY

Observations on the histology of goldfish gonads, liver, and kidney were made to determine the extent of pathological changes occurring after single and repeated injections of 10 mg/kg cadmium chloride.

Histological preparation included fixation in Bouin's solution for a minimum of four days, dehydration to 70% isopropyl alcohol, and embedding in paraffin (31). The blocks were sectioned at 7.5 microns and affixed to glass slides with an albumin-glycerin solution, stained with Mallory's triple connective tissue stain, or hematoxylin and eosin, using Permount as a mounting medium. Four slides were made of each gonad. Two slides were made of each of three randomly selected kidney and liver tissue samples from each group.

Testis

Associated with the reduction in relative testis weight (Table 25.1), changes in spermatogenesis were observed in histological sections. Quantitation of cadmium effects on goldfish spermatogenesis was obtained by giving various stages a numerical rating. Spermatogenesis was divided into eight stages, determined by the degree of maturity of the germ cells according to characteristics described by Ansan (3). The percentage frequency of occurrence of histopathological changes was computed to assess the effects of cadmium.

Comparison of the histopathological conditions of fish sacrificed after receiving one or more cadmium injections showed that fish receiving multiple cadmium injections had greater frequency of histopathological changes than those receiving single injections. Especially obvious were the changes observed after six or seven injections. These differences were quantified by averaging the stages of spermatogenic development (Table 25.3).

The mean spermatogenic development index of the control group not receiving cadmium injections was significantly higher than all experimental groups receiving cadmium injections (P < .01). The mean index of the group receiving a single cadmium injection and no HCG was larger than that of the group receiving a single injection and HCG. The effect of cadmium was greater in the testis stimulated with HCG than in that of the group without HCG. Also, the higher cadmium residue level occurring in the fish receiving HCG compared with the group without HCG (Table 25.3). Groups receiving multiple injections had a lower mean index of spermatogenic development than the groups receiving a single injection. However, the difference between the mean index value of the two groups receiving a multiple injection was not significantly different (P > .05) from the group receiving the single cadmium injection and injections of HCG.

A single intraperitoneal injection of 10 mg/kg cadmium chloride produced histopathological changes in 40% of the males. Groups receiving up to 12 cadmium injections had the same types of pathological changes as fish injected once, but the frequency of occurrence and size of area affected increased as the number of cadmium injections increased. After five injections, nearly 100% of the fish were affected. The most obvious histopathological change was a sharp increase in the number of macrophages which contained numerous small granules, apparently derived from phagocytosis of cellular debris. Occasionally, the controls also had

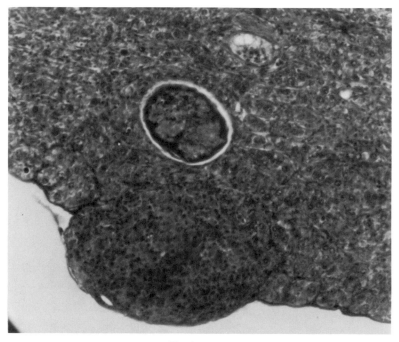

Fig. 25.4A.

Figs. 25.4A, B. Photomicrograph of testis from goldfish receiving: (A) 3 injections of 10 mg/kg cadmium chloride showing a focal granuloma protruding from surface of organ; (B) 12 injections of 10 mg/kg cadmium chloride showing nearly complete destruction of the organ and only a few germ cells.

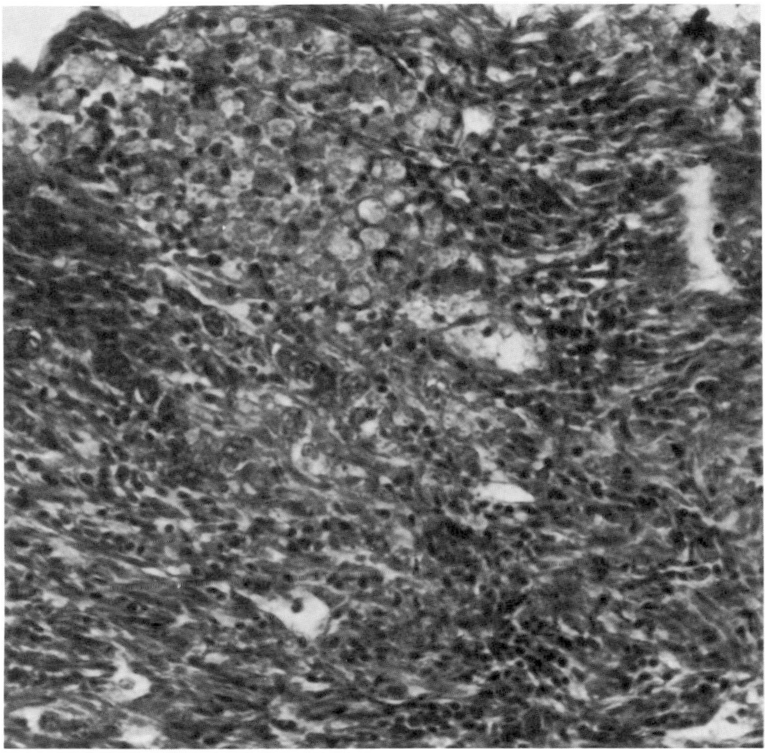

Fig. 25.4B.

small focal accumulations of macrophages, but usually these cells were diffusely distributed in small numbers throughout the organ. In severely damaged organs, occurring in fish receiving multiple injections of cadmium and HCG, macrophages were aggregated to form small granulomas. Often, granulomas were seen at the surface of the testis, forming a protruding growth (Fig. 25.4A). These granulomas contained numerous macrophages, which appeared to be smaller than those found in the interior of the organ, and many small mononuclear inflammatory cells. The granules were, as was the remainder of the testis, not birefringent with polarized light, negative with Perls' stain for iron, and negative with sodium rhodizonate stain, which produces a colored precipitate at an acid pH in the presence of cadmium. The presence of glycogen, fibrin, or collagen in the macrophages was indicated by a positive periodic acid-Schiff (PAS) reaction. A unique lesion consisting of a focal area containing some macrophages and necrotic debris circumscribed by fibrous connective tissue was seen in one slide (Fig. 25.4A).

Table 25.3. Effects of Single and Multiple Injections of CdCl$_2$, with or without Injections of Human Chorionic Gonadotropin (HCG), on Spermatogenic Development of Goldfish

	0 (1)	31 (2)	44 (3)	86 (4)	122 (6)	159 (8)	215 (10)	615 (12)	Group mean
Single }	5.5 (2)	7.3 (2)	7.5 (2)	3.4 (5)	4.5 (2)	4.0 (4)	2.9 (7)	---	4.3 (24)
Multiple }	4.5 (2)	7.0 (1)	4.0 (2)	0.0 (3)	1.3 (4)	2.0 (2)	0.0 (1)	---	2.2 (15)
Single + HCG }	4.0 (2)	4.5 (2)	1.0 (2)	0.0 (1)	3.0 (2)	3.7 (3)	1.0 (3)	5.0 (1)	2.8 (16)
Multiple + HCG }	---	6.0 (1)	3.3 (3)	3.0 (3)	0.0 (1)	1.0 (3)	0.3 (4)	0.0 (1)	1.8 (16)
Control	6.0 (2)	7.5 (2)	5.7 (3)	4.5 (2)	7.0 (3)	1.0 (1)	3.0 (5)	3.0 (2)	4.8 (20)

Days and number of Cd injections in parentheses[a]

[a]Tabular data is the average stage of spermatogenetic development, and values in ( ) represent the number of fish examined.

Degeneration of the germinal epithelium occurred after a single cadmium injection, and after multiple injections the entire seminiferous tubule was damaged. When damage was intense, primary germ cells appeared condensed, darkened, and finally separated from the basement membrane, leaving only a shell of the seminiferous tubule (Fig. 25.5B). The nucleus and cytoplasm of the primary germ cells became darker and appeared to take up more orange G, whereas normal tissue took up more acid fuchsin at this stage, indicating a change in the tissue from acidic to basic. The loss of primary germ cells resulted in a depletion of the number of seminiferous tubules, as in Figure 25.4B, which were replaced with connective tissue and mononuclear inflammatory cells. This depletion occurred first in the interior of the organ, leaving seminiferous tubules only at the periphery (Fig. 25.5A). A nearly complete denudation of the seminiferous tubules occurred after nine or more cadmium injections (Fig. 25.5B). These histopathological changes were never observed in testes of fish which had not received cadmium.

Parizek noted that single subcutaneous injections of 7.5 mg/kg cadmium chloride per kg of body weight induced irreversible necrosis of testicular tissue in laboratory rats (47). Testicular necrosis and atrophy in mammals has been induced with injections of 5 to 10 mg/kg cadmium chloride (13, 14, 25-28, 35, 44-46, 48). Although cadmium injections resulted in testicular degeneration in rats, the interstitial cells were not damaged and full hormone production was unimpaired. Given a sufficient dose, proliferation of the germinal epithelium was rare (1).

Pronounced histopathological changes occurred in spermatogenic epithelium of rabbits 24 hours after a single subcutaneous injection (12). Nuclei of spermatogonia, spermatocytes, and spermatids were disrupted and a general disarrangement occurred in the regular succession of cells. A single injection of 1.1 mg/kg cadmium chloride in rats damaged the germinal epithelium and caused a complete denudation of seminiferous tubules except for an occasional Sertoli cell (44). The damage was said to be similar to that of vitamin E deficiency in rats. Parizek produced testicular necrosis in rats with a single subcutaneous injection of 3.7 mg/kg cadmium chloride (48). Regeneration of interstitial tissue occurred below the tunica albuginea and hormone production resumed, but the tubules did not regenerate. Even two years after a single subcutaneous injection of 1.2 mg/kg of cadmium chloride, Allanson and Deanesley reported, the germinal epithelium from the tubule was absent, apparently replaced by an amorphous mass of nonfatty material; however, these rats had regained androgenic activity by 266 days (1). Tubule regeneration could occur with doses of less than 1.2 mg/kg of cadmium chloride, but none occurred at larger dosages. At doses of 0.45 mg/kg of cadmium chloride, damage to germinal epithelium was irregular and regeneration was the rule. Kar and Kamboj described the testis of the rat as completely necrotic and the seminiferous epithelium as debris after a single injection of 2.5 mg/kg of cadmium chloride (38).

The effects of cadmium on the mammalian testis were assumed to result from circulatory failure in the testes causing a destruction of the tubules (13, 46, 53) or from a direct and apparently specific toxic effect on the germinal epithelium (48). Similar histopathological effects of cadmium were observed in mice, rabbits, goats, and monkeys (44), although an effective dose was not the same for all species. The frog, opossum, and rooster have been reported insensitive to subcutaneous injections of cadmium chloride (13). Domestic fowl injected subcutaneously with cadmium chloride contained less cadmium in the testes 40 minutes after injection than did rats treated the same way (32). However, upon analysis of various cell components of fowl testis for cadmium, some cell fractions had higher concentrations than corresponding cell fractions of rats. In other investigations, testicular damage was not induced in domestic fowl even with intratesticular injections (20, 29). Lofts and Murton reported that cadmium injections had little or no effect on the resting or regressive avian testis, but the germinal epithelium was affected when spermatogenic activity was high (41). They suggested that cadmium may only damage the gonads under conditions of spermatogenic activity.

The mode of action of cadmium in the body has not been determined; however, it has been suggested that cadmium can replace zinc; and cadmium damage can be prevented by simultaneous injections of large quantities of zinc (26, 38, 47, 48). A difference in accumulation of zinc and cadmium in the nuclear frac-

Fig. 25.5A.

Figs. 25.5A–C. Photomicrographs of testes from goldfish receiving: (A) 6 injections of 10 mg/kg cadmium chloride, showing partial destruction of the organ and germ cells remaining only at periphery (top); (B) 6 injections of 10 mg/kg cadmium chloride, showing condensation and separation of germinal cells from connective tissue network; (C) section of testis of goldfish which had received 12 injections of 10 mg/kg cadmium, showing almost complete destruction of the germ cells.

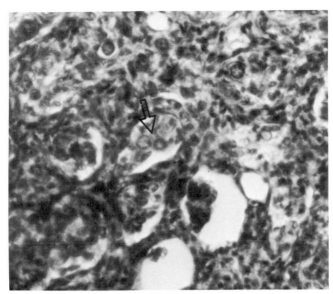

Fig. 25.5B.

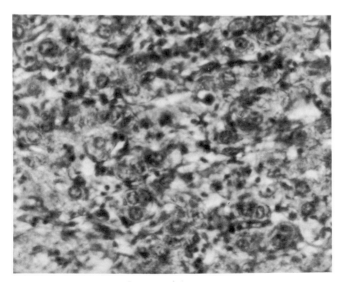

Fig. 25.5C.

Table 25.4. Percentage Frequency Occurrence of Oocyte Stages in Ovaries of Goldfish by Treatment. Cd Levels Represent Cumulative Amounts Given During the Course of the Experiment

Day	Treatment	Stage						
		1	2	3	4	5	6	7
0	Control + HCG	1	3	74	9	3	1	7
13	Control + HCG	7	8	73	12	0	0	0
	10 mg/kg	12	9	74	5	0	0	0
31	Control + HCG	12	6	80	2	0	0	0
	10 mg/kg	3	4	91	2	0	0	0
	20 mg/kg	8	15	71	5	1	0	0
	10 mg/kg + HCG	4	7	88	1	0	0	0
	20 mg/kg + HCG	3	5	88	4	0	0	0
44	Control + HCG	13	15	66	6	0	0	0
	10 mg/kg	8	14	77	1	0	0	0
	30 mg/kg	29	14	53	8	0	0	0
	10 mg/kg + HCG	6	13	69	4	1	0	3
	30 mg/kg + HCG	10	15	71	5	0	0	0
86	Control + HCG	8	10	74	6	0	0	0
	10 mg/kg	8	9	76	5	2	0	0
	40 mg/kg	0	3	97	0	0	0	0
	10 mg/kg + HCG	0	2	82	0	3	0	3
	40 mg/kg + HCG	5	10	88	2	0	0	0
122	Control + HCG	8	10	80	2	0	0	0
	10 mg/kg	6	3	91	0	0	0	0
	60 mg/kg	4	8	88	0	0	0	0
	10 mg/kg + HCG	7	10	83	0	0	0	0
	60 mg/kg + HCG	9	8	79	4	0	0	0
159	Control + HCG	10	10	66	5	2	1	6
	10 mg/kg	4	5	90	2	0	0	0
	80 mg/kg	5	3	89	2	0	0	0
	10 mg/kg + HCG	7	5	85	3	0	0	0
	80 mg/kg + HCG	10	3	87	0	0	0	0
215	Control + HCG	7	7	70	5	4	2	5
	10 mg/kg	11	11	76	2	0	0	0
	100 mg/kg	7	5	84	2	0	0	2
	10 mg/kg + HCG	10	5	76	7	2	0	0
	100 mg/kg + HCG	26	5	69	0	0	0	0
615	Control + HCG	9	12	63	8	3	0	5
	10 mg/kg + HCG	4	8	65	12	2	0	9
	120 mg/kg + HCG	11	10	77	1	0	0	1

tion suggests that cadmium can replace zinc but does not respond metabolically as zinc does (15). Johnson, Sigman, and Miller also observed high quantities of cadmium in the nuclear fraction of the testis of rats injected with cadmium, but quantities were also high in the supernatant (32). In the fowl testis, quantities of cadmium were high only in the supernatant.

Ovary

Quantification of the effects of cadmium on goldfish oogenesis was accomplished by determining the mean developmental stage. This was accomplished by recognizing the seven stages of oogenesis as Braekevelt and McMillan have done for the stickleback (*Culaea* = *Eucalia inconstans*) (8). The developmental stage of the ovary was determined by characterizing the abundance of the stage of oogenesis of 100 random ova from each fish and the number of ova of each developmental stage reported as a percent of the total. The normal ovary of adult fish has primary oocytes (stages 1, 2, and 3) throughout the year, but secondary oocytes (stages 4 to 7) are present only at spawning.

Ova development was examined on nine occasions from 0 to 615 days. In all groups of controls, single, and multiple cadmium-injected groups, with and without HCG, stage 3 ova were most abundant (Table 25.4). Stages 1 through 4 composed 89 to 100% of all developmental stages. Generally, the control fish had development to stage 7 ova. Fish receiving cadmium injections had a lower frequency of occurrence of stages 5, 6, and 7 than the controls. The group receiving a single injection of cadmium and stimulated with hormone was more similar to the controls than the two groups receiving multiple injections of cadmium. The frequency of occurrence of oocyte stages 5 to 7 in the group receiving multiple injections of cadmium and hormone was 0% at all sample dates except for 1% occurrence at 615 days. The groups receiving multiple cadmium injections failed to develop ova beyond stage 4 with the following exceptions. Stage 5 oocytes were found in the group receiving only cadmium at 31 days and stage 7 oocytes at 215 days (1 out of 5 fish) and 615 days (1 out of 8 fish).

The groups receiving multiple cadmium injections had approximately 10% more stage 3 ova than the controls. Average values for stages 1 and 2 were usually around 10%, but stage 1 ova varied from 0 to 29% (group receiving only multiple cadmium injections) with individual values up to 47% (the group receiving only cadmium injections) when nests of ova appeared throughout the ovary.

Also, only once did the mean number of stage 7 ova exceed 7% of the total number of ova in an ovary, although in surface area the stage 7 ova occupied 70 to 80% of the ovary in the controls. Stage 7 ova occasionally constituted 10 to 15% of the ova in individual fish, but in one control fish were as high as 28%.

Little damage occurred to the ovary of mature rats after cadmium injections (37). In prepubertal rats, the ovary was almost destroyed by subcutaneous injec-

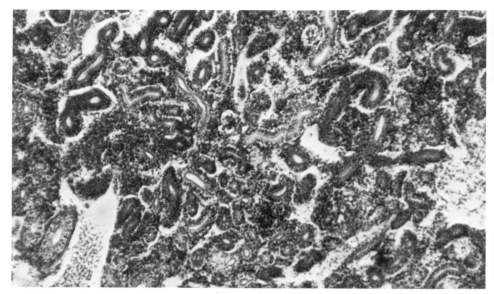

Fig. 25.6A.

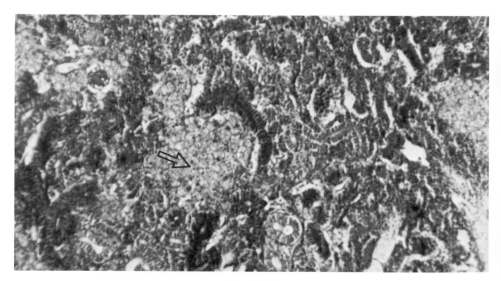

Fig. 25.6B.

Figs. 25.6A, B. Photomicrographs of kidney from (A) control goldfish, and kidney section of (B) goldfish after 5 injections of 10 mg/kg $CdCl_2$. The latter had numerous granulomas, one of which is illustrated here (arrow). X315.

tion of cadmium chloride but later regenerated (39). However, Kar found destruction of the "germinal elements" 18 hours after intra-ovarian injections of guinea pigs with 1.25 mg/kg of cadmium chloride, and total loss of the histological integrity of the ovary by 15 to 90 days (35). The goldfish ovary never lost "histological integrity" but it was affected, as shown by a decrease in relative weight (GSI), and a decreased frequency of mature oocytes.

Kidney

The kidney of normal freshwater fish consists of glomeruli, first and second proximal segments, intermediate and distal segments, collecting tubules, and interstitial hematopoietic tissue. Most of these structures can be seen in any section through a goldfish kidney (Fig. 25.6A). In goldfish not exposed to cadmium, macrophages were common in the interstitial space but rarely aggregated into focal granulomas. The size, shape, and staining characteristics of these cells were very similar to the macrophages found in the testis. A considerable degree of pathological change was noted in the kidney of cadmium-treated fish, especially after multiple injections; single injections also produced obvious changes.

The types of pathological changes in kidneys of cadmium-injected fish were similar to changes which occasionally appeared in control fish, but the frequency of occurrence and intensity of these effects were higher in the cadmium-injected fish. Macrophages were more abundant in cadmium-injected fish than in controls and were usually aggregated to form focal granulomas (Fig. 25.6B). Usually granulomas were in the interstitial areas, but occasionally they were observed in the tubules (Fig. 25.7A).

Renal lesions have been observed in rats after cadmium injections, the intensity of renal damage being related to the dose of cadmium and the cadmium concentration in the kidney (7). In rats the damage consisted of severe tubular atrophy such as that which occurred in a few severely affected goldfish kidneys after 10 injections of $CdCl_2$ (Fig. 25.7C).

Because of similarity in size, shape, and characteristics of hematopoietic and mononuclear inflammatory tissue, it was not possible to distinguish the degree of inflammation in the kidney. To determine the relationship between quantity of cadmium chloride injected and degree of damage in the kidney, observed effects were ranked using the terms low, moderate, or heavy damage (Table 25.5). The extent of tissue damage was classed as low if the damage area was less than 10% of the tissue, moderate if approximately 10 to 50%, and heavy if over 40%. Little damage occurred in fish receiving a single cadmium injection with or without HCG. The degree of damage increased with increasing dosage (Table 25.5).

Selective staining of kidney tissue with Perls', PAS, and sodium rhodizonate stains produce the same results as in the testis, namely, negative for iron and cadmium and positive for the group, glycogen, fibrin, and collagen.

Changes in metabolism, excretion, growth, homeostasis, and other physiologi-

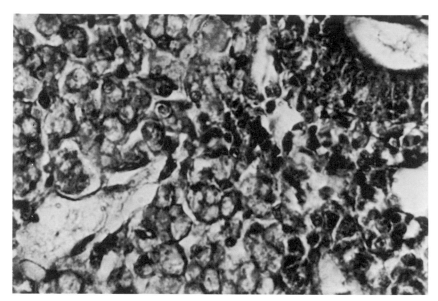

Fig. 25.7A.

Figs. 25.7A–C. Photomicrographs of kidney from goldfish (A) receiving 6 injections of 10 mg/kg CdCl$_2$, showing macrophages in the kidney tubule, X900; (B) receiving 10 injections of 10 mg/kg CdCl$_2$ showing extensive masses of macrophages, X315; and (C) receiving 12 injections of 10 mg/kg CdCl$_2$, showing markedly dilated atrophic tubules, X315.

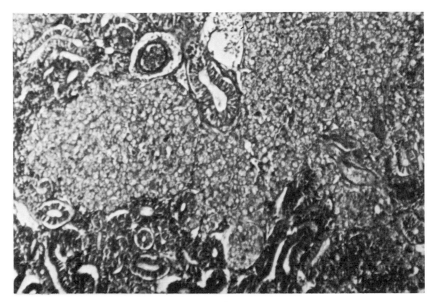

Fig. 25.7B.

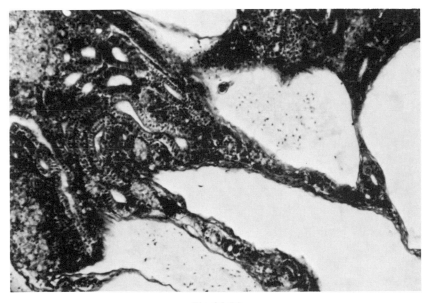

Fig. 25.7C.

Table 25.5. Relative Effects of IP Injections of CdCl$_2$ on Goldfish Kidneys

mg/kg CdCl$_2$ injected	Levels of tissue damage		
	Low	Moderate	Heavy
20	100	0	0
30	100	0	0
40	45	55	0
60	17	83	0
100	0	83	17
120	0	66	34

cal functions were not determined in this study. The osmoregulatory and hematopoietic activity of the kidney must have been affected in the most severely affected fish, which had only a small area of normal tissue remaining.

Liver

The goldfish liver is composed of a mass of hepatic cells which are many-sided with a centrally located nucleus and nucleolus (Fig. 25.8A). Occasionally, blood vessels are seen throughout the tissue.

Although the cadmium content in the liver reached high levels in injected fish (Table 25.2), no adverse histological effects were observed. On some occasions, macrophages, usually forming focal granulomas, were visible and appeared to be identical to those found in the kidney (Fig. 25.8B). Granulomas occurred in fish given multiple injections of **cadmium** but never occupied more than a minor area of the tissue section.

The same selective stains (Perls', PAS, and sodium rhodizonate) used on other organs were negative for iron and cadmium and positive for glycogen, fibrin, and collagen. The histochemical stain did not give a positive test for cadmium even though concentrations in excess of 300 ppm were determined with an atomic absorption spectrophotometer.

In general, the histological changes in the testis, liver, and kidney were similar in that the macrophages aggregated to form focal granulomas. A conspicuous increase in macrophages in treated fish as compared with controls strongly suggests damage resulting from cadmium injections. Specific changes in each organ, such as sloughing of germinal epithelium and replacement by fibroblasts in the testes, and formation of tubular atrophy in kidneys, are further evidence.

Figs. 25.8A, B. Photomicrographs of (A) normal liver from goldfish, and (B) a granuloma in section of liver of goldfish after 6 injections of 10 mg/kg CdCl$_2$. ×315.

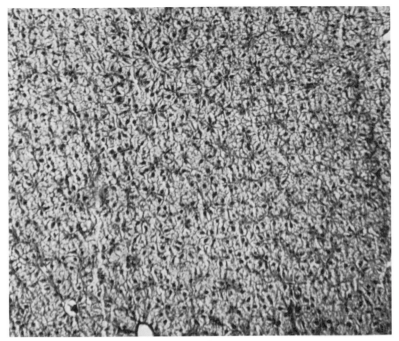

Fig. 25.8A.

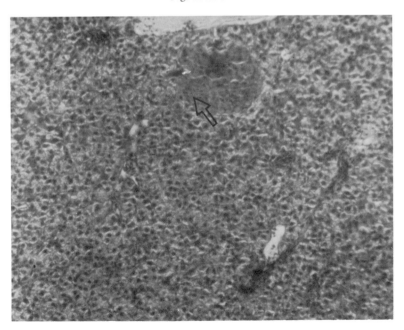

Fig. 25.8B.

639

SUMMARY AND CONCLUSIONS

The LD_{50} of intraperitoneal injections of cadmium chloride for 24 hours was 30.0 ppm cadmium chloride, 23.0 ppm for 48 hours, and 20.0 ppm for 96 hours. Relatively small doses of cadmium (10 mg/kg) were lethal to some goldfish.

Quantities of cadmium chloride ranging from 7.5 to 10.0 mg/kg in either single or repeated intraperitoneal injections did not alter the physical appearance or behavior of goldfish. However, relative gonadal weight, tissue residues, and histopathological changes indicate numerous detrimental effects.

The gonadal-somatic index, GSI, which is the gonadal weight expressed as a percentage of total body weight, of cadmium-injected goldfish was always lower than control groups. The GSI of multiple-injected cadmium groups was lower than the GSI of single-injected cadmium groups.

Higher concentrations of cadmium were found in the kidney and liver than in the muscle and gonads. Because of its larger mass, the liver contains the largest quantity of cadmium, but the kidney accumulates the greatest concentration. Quantities of cadmium over 400 ppm occurred in the kidney; the liver contained up to 300 ppm; and the ovary contained less than 100 ppm. Quantities of cadmium in the testis were too variable to establish any pattern. Very little cadmium was found in muscle tissue, especially after single cadmium injections. The largest quantity was 6.5 ppm, found after multiple injections. Higher concentrations occurred in fish receiving multiple injections than occurred in fish receiving single injections.

Maximum cadmium residues appeared in the liver 90 days after a single injection; then the quantity of residue decreased in several samples, but the highest residues were found after 615 days. After multiple cadmium injections, residues of 200 to 300 ppm were reached by about 90 days and maintained to about 215 days. Single injections of cadmium chloride produced cadmium residues of about 100 ppm in kidney. Quantities of cadmium occurring in the kidney after multiple injections generally ranged from 300 to 400 ppm, but at 615 days the quantity was 923.4 ppm. Cadmium residues in the ovary fluctuated greatly but quantities of 5 to 15 ppm were common after a single cadmium chloride injection, and cadmium residues of 20 to 40 ppm were common after multiple cadmium chloride injections.

Histopathological damage to the testis is mainly limited to periods of active spermatogenesis. Some destruction of the germinal epithelium occurred in the testis after a single injection of 10 mg/kg of cadmium chloride. Occasionally, focal granulomas composed of macrophages and mononuclear inflammatory cells were noted. The testes of most fish were able to develop normally after single cadmium injections. Effects of cadmium on germinal epithelium of males was much more severe after multiple cadmium injections; destruction of the germinal epithelium was common and only a few fish were able to produce sperm.

The only histological change noted in the ovary was retardation of development of ova. Development of mature ova was slowed immediately after a single injection of cadmium and remained inhibited from multiple cadmium injections throughout the test period.

In the kidney, a slightly higher frequency of small focal granulomas was produced in singly-injected fish than in the controls. Multiple cadmium injections produced extensive focal granulomas and smaller granulomas which were circumscribed with fibrous connective tissue. On rare occasions, tubular atrophy was extensive, leaving very little normal kidney tissue.

The liver had greater tolerance to cadmium than other organs did. No histological change was observed after a single cadmium injection, but some focal granulomas appeared after multiple cadmium injections. On rare occasions, the granulomas occupied a considerable area of the liver and some hepatic cells appeared altered with apparent loss of nuclei. Muscle tissue was not examined histologically because of its very low level of cadmium residues.

The significance of this study lies in its comparative value and the implications that cadmium may have serious effects on osmoregulation, hematopoiesis, and gametogenesis. Continuous exposure to sublethal doses results in accumulation of large residues in several organs. Histopathological changes in the kidney and testis, and inhibition of ova production are all caused by the accumulation of the metal. Potential effects of cadmium on fishes could be: (1) reduced fecundity, which may drastically reduce diversity of the ichthyofauna and community interrelationships; (2) destruction of vital organs, which could also render members of the species much more vulnerable to disease and alter their survival under stress from other environmental changes. The presence of cadmium in the flesh of fish suggests that biological magnification through the food chain can facilitate transfer of cadmium to man. If observations of histopathological effects of cadmium on fish are indicative of the effects on man, the undesirability of additional cadmium pollution of aquatic ecosystems is self-evident.

Acknowledgment. This study was largely sponsored by the Oklahoma Department of Wildlife Conservation, the Oklahoma State University, and the Bureau of Sport Fisheries and Wildlife, U.S. Department of the Interior. Some financial support was provided by the Department of Zoology and the Reservoir Research Program. For the latter, we extend our thanks to Dr. T. C. Dorris. Gratitude is extended to Dr. B. C. Ward for assistance in analysis of histopathological changes, to Dr. M. C. Warner for histological preparations, and to Dr. S. Burks for assistance with atomic absorption spectrophotometry.

REFERENCES

1. Allanson, M., and Deanesley, M.   Observations on cadmium damage and repair in the rat testes and the effects on the pituitary gonadotrophs. *J. Endocrinol. 24:* 453–462. 1962.

2. American Public Health Association. *Standard Methods for the Examination of Water and Waste water.* 13th ed. 874 pp. Washington, D.C., Amer. Pub. Health Ass., 1971.

3. Ansan, S.   Clinical changes in the testicular activity of the lake chub, *Cousesius plumbeus* (Agassiz). *Can. J. Zool. 44*(22): 149–159. 1966.

4. Anwar, R. A., Hoppert, C. A., and Byerrum, R. U.   Toxicity studies on cadmium and hexavalent chromium. *Water Sewage Works 107*(2): 465–466. 1960.

5. Belding, D. L.   Toxicity experiments with fish in reference to trade waste pollution. *Trans. Amer. Fish. Soc. 57:* 100–119. 1927.

6. Berlin, M., and Ullberg, S.   The fate of cadmium[109] in the mouse. *Arch. Environ. Health 7:* 686–693. 1963.

7. Bonnell, J. A., Ross, J. H., and King, E.   Renal lesions in experimental cadmium poisoning. *Brit. J. Ind. Med. 17:* 69–80. 1960.

8. Braekevelt, C. R., and McMillan, D. B.   Cyclic changes in the ovary of the brook stickleback, *Eucalia inconstans* (Kirtland). *J. Morphol. 123*(4): 373–395. 1967.

9. Byerrum, R. U., Anwar, R. A. and Hoppert, C. A.   Toxicity of small quantities of cadmium and chromium in drinking water administered to dogs during a 4 year period. *J. Amer. Water Works Ass. 52*(1): 651–652. 1960.

10. Cairns, J., Jr., and Scheier, A.   The effects of temperature and hardness of water upon toxicity of zinc to the common bluegill. *Notulae natur. (Philadelphia) 299:* 1957.

11. Cairns, J., Jr., and Scheier, A.   A comparison of the sensitivity to certain chemicals of adult zebra danios and zebra danio eggs with that of adult bluegill sunfish. *Notulae natur. (Philadelphia) 381:* 1965.

12. Cameron, E., and Foster, C. L.   Observations on the histological effects of sub-lethal doses of cadmium chloride in the rabbit. I. The effect on the testis. *J. Anat. 97*(2): 269–280. 1963.

13. Chiquoine, A.   Observations of the early events of cadmium necrosis of the testis. *Anat. Rec. 149:* 23–36. 1964.

14. Chiquoine, A., and Suntzeff, V.   Sensitivity of mammals to cadmium necrosis of the testis. *J. Reprod. Fert. 10:* 455–457. 1965.

15. Cotzias, G. C., Gorg, D. C., and Selleck, B.   Virtual absence of turnover in cadmium metabolism: Cadmium[109] studies in the mouse. *Amer. J. Physiol. 201*(5): 927–930. 1961.

16. Crandall, C. A., and Goodnight, C. J.   The effects of sublethal concentrations of several toxicants to the common guppy, *Lebistes reticulatus. Trans. Amer. Microsc. Soc. 82:* 59–73. 1963.

17. Decker, C. F., Byerrum, R. U., and Hoppert, C. A.   A study of the distribution and retention of cadmium-115 in the albino rat. *Arch. Biochem. Biophys. 66*(1): 140–145. 1957.

18. Decker, C. F., Hoppert, C. A., and Byerrum, R. U.   Report on toxicity studies of cadmium and chromium. *J. Amer. Water Works Ass.* 48(2): 1279–1280. 1956.
19. Doudoroff, P., and Katz, M.   Critical review of literature on the toxicity of industrial wastes and their components to fish. II. The metals as salts. *Sewage Ind. Wastes 25:* 802–839. 1953.
20. Erickson, A. E., and Pincus, G.   Insensitivity of fowl testis to cadmium. *J. Reprod. Fert. 7:* 379–382. 1964.
21. Favino, A., and Nazari, G.   Renal lesions induced by a single subcutaneous cadmium chloride injection in rats. *Lav. umano 19*(8): 367–372. 1967.
22. Frank, R. H.   Trace metal pollution of the lower North Canadian River basin. Ph.D. thesis, Univ. Oklahoma, Norman, Okla. 150 pp., 1969.
23. Friberg, L., Piscator, M., and Nordberg, G.   *Cadmium in the Environment.* 166 pp. Cleveland, Ohio, Chemical Rubber Co., 1971.
24. Gunn, S. A., and Gould, T. C.   Selective accumulation of cadmium[115] by cortex of rat kidney. *Proc. Soc. Exp. Biol. Med. 96:* 820–823. 1957.
25. Gunn, S. A., Gould, T. C., and Anderson, W. A. D.   Zinc protection against cadmium injury to rat testis. *Arch. Pathol. 71:* 274–281. 1961.
26. Gunn, S. A., Gould, T. C., and Anderson, W. A. D.   The selective injurious response of testicular and epididymal blood vessels to cadmium and its prevention by zinc. *Amer. J. Pathol. 42*(2): 685–694. 1963.
27. Gunn, S. A., Gould, T. C., and Anderson, W. A. D.   Loss of selective injurious vascular response to cadmium in regenerated blood vessels of testes. *Amer. J. Pathol. 48*(2): 959–969. 1966.
28. Gupta, R. K., Barnes, G. W., and Skelton, F. R.   Light microscope and immunopathologic observations on cadmium chloride induced injury in mature rat testis. *Amer. J. Pathol. 51*(1): 191–205. 1967.
29. Guthrie, J.   Histological effects of intra-testicular injections of cadmium chloride in domestic fowl. *Brit. J. Cancer 18:* 255. 1964.
30. Heindl, R. A.   Cadmium, pp. 515–526. In *Mineral Facts and Problems.* 1970 ed. *U. S. Bur. Mines, Bull. 650.* 1970.
31. Humason, G.   *Animal Tissue Techniques.* 569 pp. 2d ed. San Francisco, W. H. Freeman, 1967.
32. Johnson, A. D., Sigman, M. B., and Miller, W. J.   Early actions of cadmium in the rat and domestic fowl testis. *J. Reprod. Fert. 23:* 201–213. 1970.
33. Jones, J. R. E.   The relative toxicity of salts of lead, zinc and copper to the stickleback and the effect of calcium on the toxicity of lead and zinc salts. *J. Exp. Biol. 15:* 394–407. 1938.
34. Jones, J. R. E.   The relation between the electrolytic solution pressures of the metals and their toxicity to the stickleback (*Gasterosteus aculeatus*). *J. Exp. Biol. 16:* 425–437. 1939.
35. Kar, A. B.   Chemical sterilization of female guinea pigs. *Indian J. Exp. Biol.* 3(1): 50–52. 1965.
36. Kar, A. B., and Das, R. P.   Testicular changes in rats after treatment with cadmium chloride. *Acta biol. med. ger. 5:* 153–173. 1960.

37. Kar, A. B., and Das, R. P.   Effects of cadmium chloride on fertility of rats. *Indian J. Vet. Sci. Anim. Husb. 32:* 210. 1962.
38. Kar, A. B., and Kamboj, V. P.   Cadmium damage of the rat testis and its prevention. *Indian J. Exp. Biol. 3*(1): 45–49. 1965.
39. Kar, A. B., Das, R. P., and Karkum, J. N.   Ovarian changes in prepubertal rats after treatment with cadmium chloride. *Acta biol. med. ger. 3:* 372–399. 1959.
40. Kar, A. B., Chowdhury, A. R., Goswami, A., and Kamboj, V. P.   Intertesticular distribution of cadmium in rats. *Indian J. Exp. Biol. 3*(2): 139–141. 1965.
41. Lofts, B., and Murton, R. K.   The effects of cadmium on the avian testis. *J. Reprod. Fert. 13:* 155–164. 1966.
42. Lucis, O. J., Lynk, M. E., and Lucis, R.   Turnover of cadmium[109] in rats. *Arch. Environ. Health 16:* 788–793. 1968.
43. Mason, K. E., Young, J. O. and Brown, J. A.   Effectiveness of selenium and zinc in protecting against cadmium-induced injury of the rat testis. *Anat. Rec. 148:* 309 (abstr.). 1964.
44. Mason, K. E., Brown, J. A., Young, J. O., and Nesbit, R. R.   Cadmium-induced injury of the rat testis. *Anat. Rec. 149:* 135–148. 1964.
45. Meek, E. S.   Cellular changes induced by cadmium in mouse testis and liver. *Brit. J. Exp. Pathol. 40:* 503–506. 1959.
46. Niemi, M., and Kormano, M.   An angiographic study of cadmium-induced vascular lesions in the testis and epididymis of the rat. *Acta pathol. microbiol. scand. 63:* 513–521. 1965.
47. Parizek, J.   The destruction effect of cadmium ion on testicular tissue and its prevention by zinc. *J. Endocrinol. 15:* 56–63. 1957.
48. Parizek, J.   Sterilization of the male by cadmium salts. *J. Reprod. Fert. 1:* 294–309. 1960.
49. Pickering, Q. H., and Henderson, C.   The acute toxicity of some heavy metals to different species of warmwater fishes. *Air Water Pollut. 10*(6/7): 453–463. 1966.
50. Pickford, G., and Atz, J. W.   *The Physiology of the Pituitary Gland of Fishes.* 613 pp. New York, N. Y. Zool. Soc., 1957.
51. Reinert, R. E.   Pesticide concentrations in Great Lakes fish. *Pestic. Monit. J. 3:* 233–240. 1970.
52. Thomas, A.   Effects of certain metallic salts upon fishes. *Trans. Amer. Fish. Soc. 44:* 120–124. 1915.
53. Waites, G. M. H., and Setchell, B. P.   Changes in blood flow and vascular permeability of the testis, epididymis and accessory reproductive organs of the rat after the administration of cadmium chloride. *J. Endocrinol. 34:* 329–342. 1966.
54. Walsh, J. J., and Burch, G. E.   The rate of disappearance from plasma and subsequent distribution of radiocadmium (Cd[115]) in normal dogs. *J. Lab. Clin. Med. 54:* 59–65. 1969.

55. Westfall, B. A.   Coagulation film anoxia of fishes. *Ecology 26:* 283–287. 1945.

56. Wilson, R. H., DeEds, F., and Cox, A. J.   Effects of continued cadmium feeding. *J. Pharmacol. Exp. Ther. 71:* 222–235. 1941.

26

Lesions due to Drugs

H.-H. REICHENBACH-KLINKE

With multiplication and intensification of fish production the use of medicaments is mounting from year to year. Not only does the total quantity of medication increase, the number of drugs also increases. Along with the more intensive medication, the possibility of accumulation of residues is greater than ever before. The International Office of Epizootics has therefore recommended cessation of all medication four or even six weeks before sale of fish to the human consumer. But what sort of residues are these? Residues of pesticides, metals, etc., are found, but to a lesser degree than those of drugs (mercury, copper, malachite, Masoten, etc.). Fish themselves do not seem to be harmed. It was our desire to see if significant histopathological damage does not exist. During the last five years we have therefore tested a number of common drugs over a long time in order to see if the application of drugs is followed by cellular alterations.

We have begun to study the effects of some drugs used frequently in fish cultivation and we will present these findings here. The experiments are performed in 50-liter tanks with small carp, trout, and gudgeons.

MALACHITE GREEN

Malachite green is a drug used all over the world in all types of ectoparasitism and is frequently used as a disinfectant. Histological sections contained slight inflammation of epithelium in the gut, gills, and skin, and slight dilation of the kid-

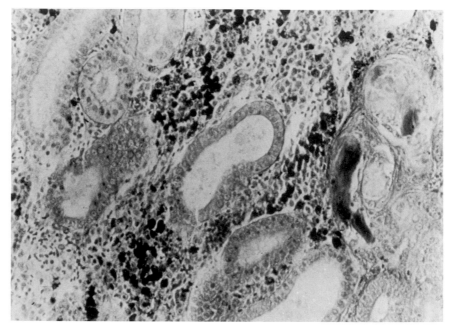

Fig. 26.1. Section through the kidney of a carp fingerling treated with malachite green. Note pigmentous degeneration and deposits around the tubules. In the center it is evident that the epithelium is lower; the mass of the cell is diminished in favor of the nuclei.

ney tubules' lumina and alteration of the nucleus-to-cytoplasm ratio, favoring the nuclei.

A very significant effect of malachite green is the blocking of intestinal enzymes: experiences with whitefish showed that up to 10 milliunits of trypsin and up to 100 SE (Somogy Units) of alpha amylase disappeared after contamination with dissolved malachite green. This is a diminution of 70%! It is not clear whether this effect is caused by inactivation of the enzymes or by a chemical binding, but it is often seen: the consumption of food stops after medication with malachite green. When the treatment is pursued several times, the growth rate is significantly lowered.

COPPER SULFATE

Copper sulfate is used against molds and algae. We could recognize the following lesions in fish exposed to copper sulfate: dilation of the kidney tubules, renal necroses around the tubules, destruction of hematopoietic tissues, increased liver fat, copper residues in gills, muscles, and liver, and enzyme inhibition as mentioned above.

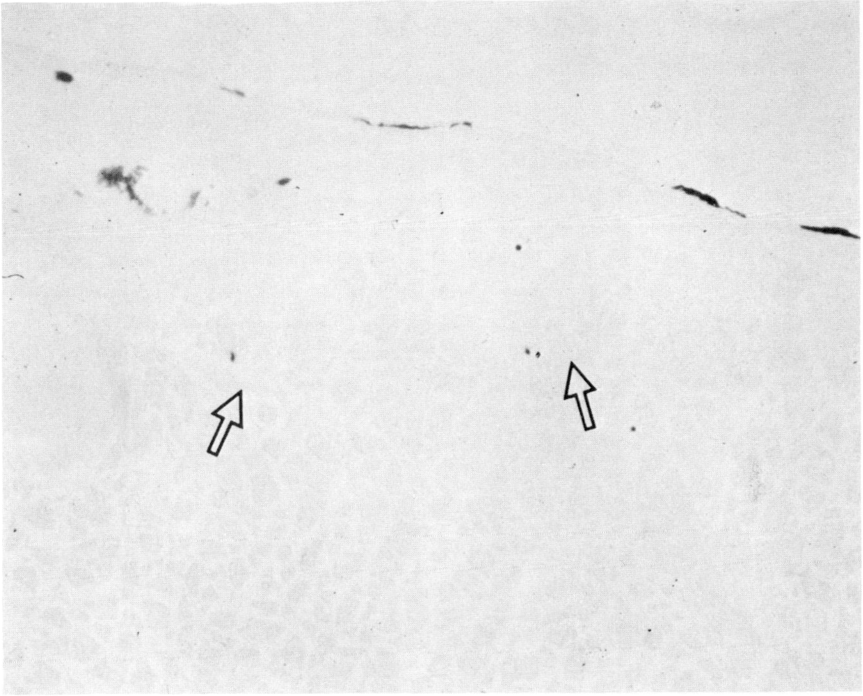

Fig. 26.2. Section through posterior part of the muscles of a carp treated with calomel. The mercury residues are marked by white arrows. They are situated within the muscle substance, rarely in the intercellular space. The black deposits in the upper part are melanocytes in the skin.

MERCURIALS

There are legal limits for the contents of mercury in all sorts of fish foods. In fish usually the limit is 0.5 ppm Hg. Chemicals with mercury are removed from trade as much as possible and others with the same effect but without this toxic metal are sought.

THIABENDAZOLE

This vermicide can hardly be dissolved in water. It is a drug of great efficacy but it often has undesired side effects, e.g., bloody infiltration in the kidney and liver. The intestine and the gills did not contain any detectable alterations.

NEGUVON, MASOTEN

The two drugs have an effect similar to the chlorinated hydrocarbon insecticides. They are damaging to the nervous system. We see a swelling of the non-

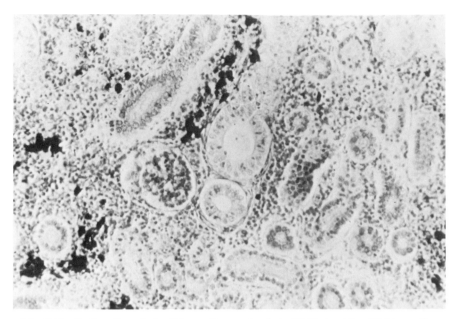

Fig. 26.3. Section through the kidney of a carp treated with Emtrysidina (Gabbrocol). (Gabbrocol is produced by Farmitalia, Milan, Italy.) Pigment deposits occur in the tissue but note greater damage in the epithelium.

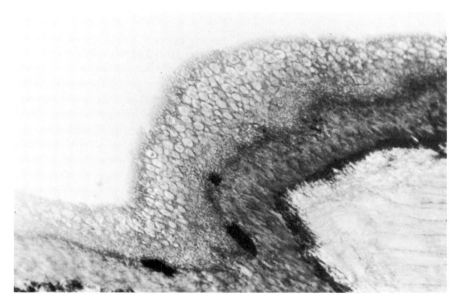

Fig. 26.4. Section through the skin of a carp treated with Emtrysidina. Great masses of slime cells are present because of the irritation of Emtrysidina. Inflammation is absent.

650

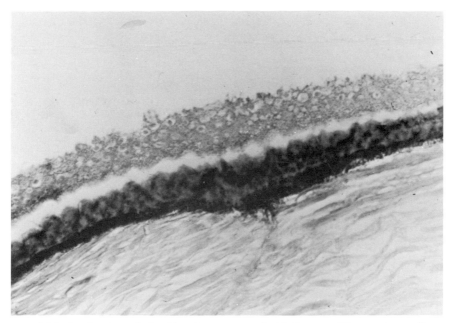

Fig. 26.5. Section through the skin of a carp treated with Hexa-ex. (Hexa-ex is a medicament of Zoomedica Frickhinger, Planegg near Munich, Germany.) This is a chemical used in treatment of tropical fish. The skin is partially destroyed, but will regenerate.

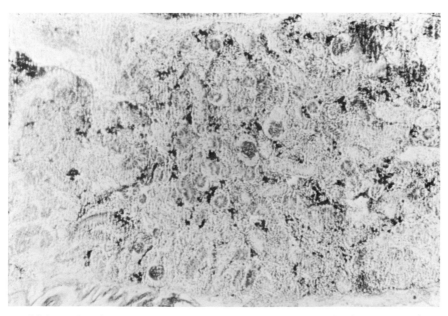

Fig. 26.6. Section through the kidney of a carp treated with thiabendazole. A greater degeneration of the intertubular tissue occurs here. Some tubules are filled with deposits. The damage will require prolonged regeneration.

651

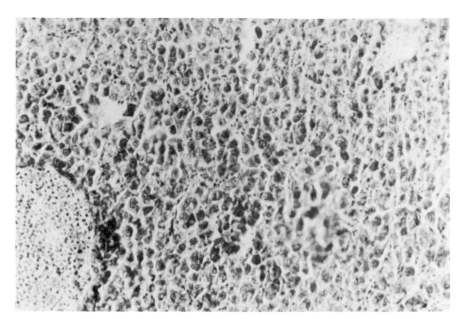

Fig. 26.7. Section through the liver of a carp treated with thiabendazole. The cells of the liver are somewhat enlarged, and the intercellular spaces also. Note the filling of the blood vessel at left.

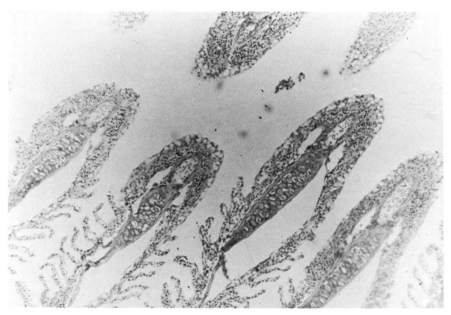

Fig. 26.8. Section through the gills of a trout treated with 32 mg per liter of Bradophen. (Bradophen is a chemical produced by Ciba AG, Basle, Switzerland.) It has a disinfectant effect. The use in fish hatcheries has certain limits, which are evinced as damage in the gill tissues. The 32 mg per liter is a very high concentration, at which destruction of the gill epithelium and appearance of slime cells are prominent.

652

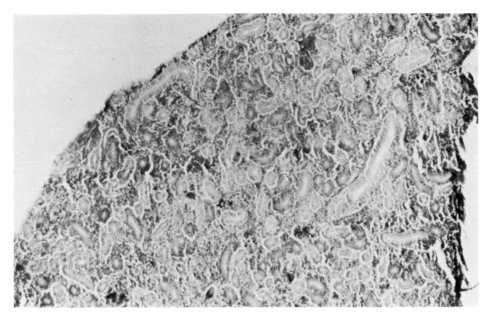

Fig. 26.9. Section through the kidney of a carp treated with Neguvon. Damage is not seen in the tissues. Tubules are normal.

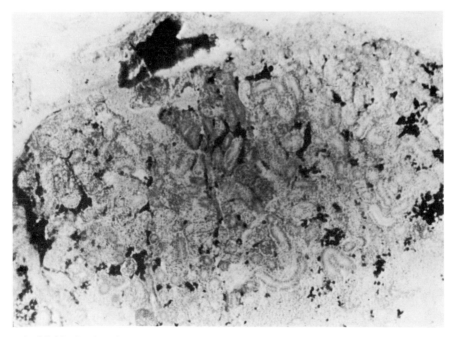

Fig. 26.10. Section through the kidney of a carp treated with Yomesan, an anthelminthic. Here great degeneration in the intertubular tissue, combined with pigment deposits, occurs.

653

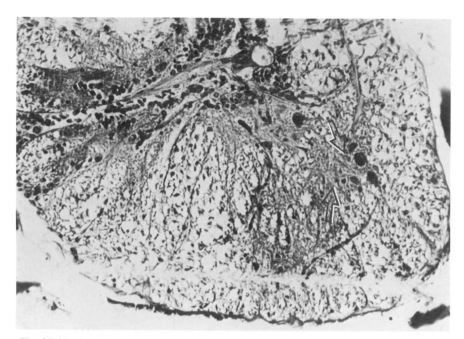

Fig. 26.11. Section through the spine of a carp treated with Dipterex. The large nerve cells are normally surrounded by whitish lipoidal substances. In some cells swelling of these lipoid substances is seen. In other cells the nucleus is not cut, but the swelling of the lipoid substance can be recognized.

staining surroundings of the nerve nuclei. This seems to be due to the lipids inhibiting certain lipophile chemicals and therefore enlarging. We often saw this swelling in the brain and the medulla.

METHYLENE BLUE

Experiences with methylene blue have shown that the number of erythrocytes in fish is significantly increased. We have seen this in repeated tests. We believe that the helpful effects of methylene blue are due to this special behavior and in a lesser degree to its disinfectant properties. We therefore give methylene blue in convalescence in order to strengthen the fish.

SULFONAMIDES AND ANTIBIOTICS

Sulfonamides are very often used. We have seen severe damage of the kidneys and do not recommend the prolonged use of such drugs.

Antibiotics are dissipated very soon after application. Here the danger consists not in tissue damage but in the favoring of certain human-pathogenic bacteria. It is known that tetracyclines can cause resistance in coliform bacteria. The so-called resistance factor which is transmitted from the common coliform bacteria to salmonellae and shigellae is evolving. Besides this, some cases of human allergies are known, not only to penicillin but also to streptomycin and rarely bacitracin. Streptomycin is often used in fish culture, so this matter should be considered. Recently in the United States resistance has also been shown to the sulfonamide furazolidone.

SUMMARY

Most of the medicaments used in fish cultivation can lead to residues, alterations in the kidney and liver, and the inhibition of intestinal enzymes. If these medicaments are used over a long time, residues (copper, chlorinated hydrocarbons) can be transmitted to man. We therefore recommend use of these drugs, except methylene blue, only in urgent cases. The medication should not be repeated in less than two weeks, and therapy should cease one month before consumption of the fish. In addition to the danger of residues, fish can be harmed by damage, mostly to the kidney, when the therapy is repeated too many times. Dangers also arise when metals (copper) are left in the ponds, eventually affecting the microfauna and the plants. It seems that medicaments like methylene blue, vitamins, etc., should be used more than they are at present in order to replace drugs with cell-damaging effects.

REFERENCES

European Inland Fisheries Advisory Commission and U.S. Bureau of Sport Fisheries and Wildlife. Report of the 1970 workshop on fish-feed technology and nutrition. *U. S. Bur. Sport Fish. Wildlife, Resour. Publ. 102.* 1972.

Reichenbach-Klinke, H.-H. Enzymuntersuchungen an Fischen. I. Die Enzymaktivität und ihre Abhängigkeit von pH, Temperatur und Wasserchemismus. *Arch. Fischereiwiss. 20:* 169–177. 1969.

Reichenbach-Klinke, H.-H. Medikament-Spätschäden bei Fischen. *Wasser Abwasser-Forsch. 5:* 84–89. 1972.

Schulz, D. Studien über Nebenwirkungen des Herbizids NaTA (Na-Trichloracetat) auf Karpfen. *Zentralbl. Veterinaermed.,* Reihe A *17:* 230–251. 1970.

Schulz, D. Durch das Herbizid DOWPON bedingte lichtmikroskopische, biochemische und elektronenmikroskopische Veränderungen am exokrinen Pankreas des Karpfens. *Z. angew. Zool. 58:* 63–97. 1971.

DISCUSSION OF LESIONS DUE TO DRUGS

F. P. Meyer: In Australia they are feeding methylene blue in the diet for bacteriocidal treatment. Is this the manner of treatment that you were prescribing with methylene blue?

H.-H. Reichenbach-Klinke: Yes, methylene blue we can try, but not anti-biotics. This is a question that should be discussed, although fish can become accustomed to this drug.

F. P. Meyer: You feel, then, that it is the increased antibacterial resistance rather than a true chemotherapy that we find with methylene blue?

H.-H. Reichenbach-Klinke: Chemotherapy with methylene blue should be recommended but it must be restricted, not too many doses.

G. Phipps: I was wondering if you had had any contact with MS-222, the anesthetic?

H.-H. Reichenbach-Klinke: Yes, we have used MS-222. All the fish were unharmed during the experiment.

27

Chemically Induced Lesions in Estuarine or Marine Teleosts

GEORGE R. GARDNER

Chemically induced and spontaneous lesions as observed in certain estuarine or marine teleosts are described in this paper, and the results of continuing investigations with the adult euryhaline teleost *Fundulus heteroclitus* (common mummichog) exposed to cadmium and copper, and preliminary exposures to mercury, silver, zinc, and the chlorinated pesticide methoxychlor are included. The preliminary experimentation reported herein includes the toxic effects of Texas-Louisiana crude oil and the saltwater soluble and insoluble fractions of the whole crude to the adult marine teleost *Menidia menidia* (Atlantic silverside). Spontaneous lesions were observed in adult *Brevoortia tyrannus* (Atlantic menhaden) obtained from Narragansett Bay and from the site of a menhaden "fish kill."

Degeneration of anterior lateral line and olfactory sensory structure in *Fundulus,* following short-term exposures to sublethal levels of copper, has been documented by Gardner and LaRoche (8). Current observations demonstrate the vulnerability of these perceptive structures to artificial stress from metals other than copper, to other chemical toxicants, and to an undefined stress in the natural marine environment. Neurosensory vulnerability has been emphasized to demonstrate the potential impact that neurotropic pollutants may have on vital behavioral and/or physiological responses compatible with survival of the teleost.

657

METHODS OF STUDY

A total of 768 adult common mummichog and 48 adult Atlantic silversides obtained from local Rhode Island waters served as experimental organisms.

These test organisms were held in laboratory facilities for an acclimation period of at least seven days prior to their use in experiments. During the test period, organisms were maintained on a prepared diet of chopped clams and a commercial dog food meal. Unless otherwise specified, the preliminary exposure studies reported herein were carried out in 1-gallon glass jars, at a temperature of 20°C and 20% salinity. All toxicants were added to solution following the introduction of test organisms to their respective jars.

Metals

Preliminary studies were conducted separately using reagent grade chloride salts of five metals: silver at 5 mg per liter, cadmium at 65 mg per liter, copper at 15 mg per liter, mercury at 1 mg per liter, and zinc at 70 mg per liter. These studies were designed to determine the effects of each metal on the gross anatomy of the gills. The 10 animals in each experimental group were individually removed from the toxic medium for fixation when signs of distress were displayed, or after 48 hours of exposure. Following transection of the trunk near the pectoral fins, the gill arches were individually excised and stained in alcian blue for five minutes. The stained gills were then mounted in glycerin in hanging drop slides, cover-slipped, and sealed with Vaseline for subsequent examination. The remaining tissues of those organisms were prepared for routine histological examination.

These initial investigations provided evidence of histological change, prompting additional investigations with copper and cadmium previously reported in the literature (7, 8, 10, 11, 14); however, continuing investigations with cadmium and copper were carried out for the current report as follows:

Cadmium. Three hundred *Fundulus* were exposed to 5 mg per liter of cadmium for periods as long as one year. Twenty-five test and 25 control organisms were removed for histological examination at 30-day intervals. The exposure was conducted in a closed aquarium system having a total volume of approximately 1800 liters. The salt water within the system was recirculated continuously, and organic wastes were partially removed by the daily operation of a "foam column." The water was changed twice during the year-long test period. The cadmium concentration in the medium was monitored on a weekly schedule by atomic absorption analysis. Mortality in the cadmium-exposure group was negligible during the test period, but was high in the control group after a period of four months because of a mechanical malfunction in the aquarium system.

Copper. With the knowledge that copper induces lesions in lateral line and olfactory organs of *Fundulus* (8), further investigations were conducted to determine the ability of these neutral tissues to regenerate following exposure to the metal. Twenty-four adult *Fundulus* were exposed to 5 mg per liter of the metal for 24 hours and then removed to an uncontaminated saltwater medium in a 45-liter recovery tank. Twelve adults were then removed from the recovery tank after two weeks, and the remaining 12 after four weeks. The fish were offered food during the period of recovery.

Mercury and Silver. Acute exposure studies utilizing 72 adult *Fundulus* were conducted with the heavy metals mercury and silver for preliminary histological evaluation. The initial test concentrations of mercury used were 0.25, 0.50, 1.0, and 5.0 mg per liter, while those for silver were 0.05, 0.25, 0.5, 1.0, 5.0, and 20.0 mg per liter. Six *Fundulus* were exposed to each metal concentration. The organisms were removed when visibly stressed or after 96 hours of exposure.

Petroleum

Precursory studies utilizing 48 adult *Menidia* were designed to study the effects of Texas-Louisiana crude oil, and the saltwater soluble and insoluble components of the whole crude oil. The separation of the crude oil into its water soluble and insoluble fractions was accomplished with a specially designed glass column that permitted rapid mixing and aeration of approximately 40 liters of sea water and approximately 1 liter of the crude oil. After 10 minutes of mixing, a sufficient period of settling (10 to 20 minutes) was allowed for separation of the two components. These two components were then drawn off for experimental purposes.

The studies with *Menidia* were conducted in fiberglass tanks measuring 8' X 4' X 6''. For testing purposes, each of these containers received a maximum of 170 liters of salt water and combined petroleum product. The test container received 150 liters of salt water (28% salinity) in the segment of the study utilizing the saltwater soluble fraction of crude oil. Following the addition of test organisms, 19 liters of the water soluble fraction of crude oil was added, bringing the total volume of each of the media to 170 liters. The symbolic soluble oil concentration was approximately 0.167 ml per liter.

Saltwater insoluble crude oil was introduced directly to 170 liters of fresh sea water in the test container after the addition of test fish. A symbolic saltwater insoluble crude oil concentration of approximately 0.58 mg per liter was achieved by the addition of 100 ml of that fraction. Whole crude oil was added directly to 170 liters of sea water for a test concentration of approximately 0.14 mg per liter. These studies with *Menidia* were conducted for a period of seven days (168 hr).

Pesticide

Twelve adult *Fundulus* surviving 96-hour exposures to the chlorinated hydrocarbon methoxychlor were evaluated for histological change. Test concentrations of the compound in these bioassays were 1.1, 5.2, and 25.2 mg per liter.

Menhaden

Thirty adult menhaden (*Brevoortia tyrannus*) were collected from three different sites. Thirteen moribund or stressed adults were collected by dip net from the "discharge stone quarry," or effluent of the Northeastern Utilities Company nuclear power generating plant located at Millstone Point, Connecticut. Field investigations were conducted on two dates, May 19 (8 adults), and June 13 (5 adults), 1972, during the progress of a continuing fish kill first reported on or about April 28, 1972. Four so-called "crazy" or "spinning" menhaden were collected by dip net within five miles of the city of Providence, Rhode Island, near Gaspee Point in Narragansett Bay. Thirteen control fish were collected by dip net during a commercial purse seine operation in Narragansett Bay. The live or moribund fish collected from these sites were immediately immersed in Dietrich's fixative. Five to 10 minutes later excess tissue had been selectively trimmed away to insure rapid penetration of the fixative.

Dietrich's fixative was also used exclusively with experimental fish. These live fish were immersed in the fixative immediately upon removal from test containers. Tissue preparations were cut at 6 microns and stained with Harris' hematoxylin and eosin. Stained blood and tissue preparations followed the procedure of Gardner and Yevich (9).

RESULTS

Gross Anatomy of Gills

Concentrations of silver, cadmium, copper, mercury, and zinc considered to be acutely toxic to *Fundulus* elicited a heavy gill-mucus response. Due to excessive mucus accumulations the respiratory archetype was not always retained, but rather, concentrated accumulations of mucus partially collapsed the lamellar framework. The heavy concentrations of mucus did not occur uniformly across any one gill arch, or cause a complete collapse of the respiratory structure. Mucus accumulations were lesser in animals exposed to cadmium and mercury than in those exposed to silver, copper, and zinc. Apical areas of many gill filaments were necrotic following exposures to cadmium and mercury and, therefore, the cartilaginous filament rods were denuded and exposed.

Metals

The metals mercury and silver, like copper (7, 8, 14), were neurotoxic. Lesions were present in the olfactory and lateral line systems of *Fundulus* (Figs. 27.1–27.8) following exposures to these metals. There are, however, distinguishing differences in the damage resulting from each of these metals. Cadmium and zinc exposures failed to elicit morphological anomalies in these neurosensory structures.

Copper. Studies designed to investigate the regenerative ability of lateral line and olfactory epithelium of *Fundulus* after a brief exposure to copper were insuf-

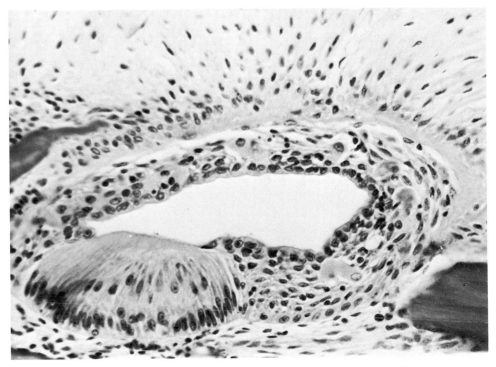

Fig. 27.1. Mandibular canal and neuromast, *Fundulus*, control. X130.

ficient in scope to permit a sound conclusion. However, cystic formations were occasionally observed in areas where chemoreceptive sites could normally be identified prior to treatment. A complete review of the histopathological effects of copper on *Fundulus* and *Menidia* may be found in "Copper induced lesions in estuarine teleosts" (8).

Mercury. Mercury levels of 0.5 mg per liter or higher caused severe cytoplasmic and nuclear degeneration of all cellular elements comprising the lateral line canals (cephalic extension) of *Fundulus.* The necrocytosis encompassed the secretory cells of the canal lining, the squamous epithelium comprising the canal walls, and the canals' investment of secretory and mucous cells. Neurosensory hillocks located within these canals were severely necrotic in most cases.

Severe degenerative changes in *Fundulus* olfactory organs also accompanied mercury exposures of 0.5 mg per liter or more. Various degrees of cellular degeneration were identifiable in neurosensory cells of these organs. However, no evidence of hyperplasia or widespread necrosis, such as that observed following copper exposures, could be associated with the sustentacular cells. The degree of morphological alteration to the neurosensory cells was generally uniform throughout the organ, except basally, where the lesion had progressed further. The epithelial lining of olfactory pits was also necrotic.

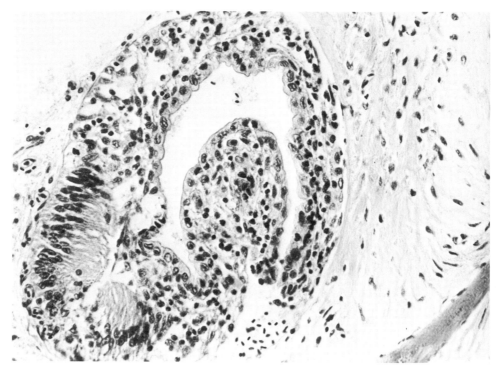

Fig. 27.2. Mandibular canal and neuromast, *Fundulus,* after exposure to 0.5 mg per liter copper. ×130.

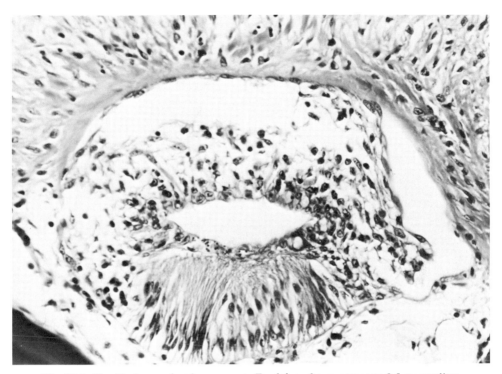

Fig. 27.3. Mandibular canal and neuromast, *Fundulus,* after exposure to 0.5 mg per liter mercury. ×130.

Silver. Silver, like mercury and copper, exerts a toxic effect within the canals of the cephalic lateral line extension of *Fundulus* (Fig. 27.4). The change induced by silver was most similar to those observed following copper exposures. The epithelium of canal walls was necrotic, although no evidence of damage was discernible in other anatomical structures of the canal. The sensory units within these canals were not affected. Granular leukocytes were observed in the canal lumina, in the canal walls, and in peripheral connective tissues in several cases.

The epithelial lining of the olfactory pit and the sustentacular epithelium of the olfactory organs were affected, as indicated by widespread cellular degeneration (Fig. 27.8). Cellular debris from degenerating sustentacular cells was sloughed into olfactory lumina, denuding the sensory units of the organ. The sensory organs were usually apically necrotic in these cases. Although all specimens exposed to silver did not have these changes, the change could be observed at all metal concentrations studied. In spite of the small number of animals tested, the occurrence of the lesion in the lateral line and olfactory organs seemed to be an "all or none" reaction. The condition was always severe if present, regardless of toxicant concentration.

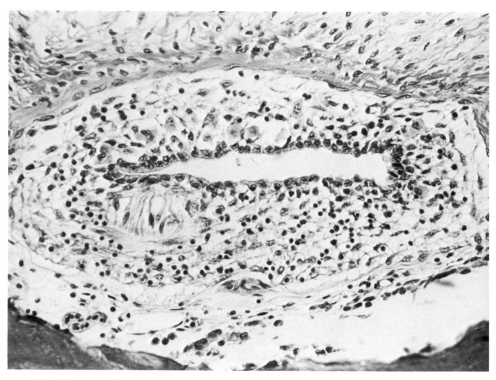

Fig. 27.4. Mandibular canal and neuromast, *Fundulus,* after exposure to 0.5 mg per liter silver. ×130.

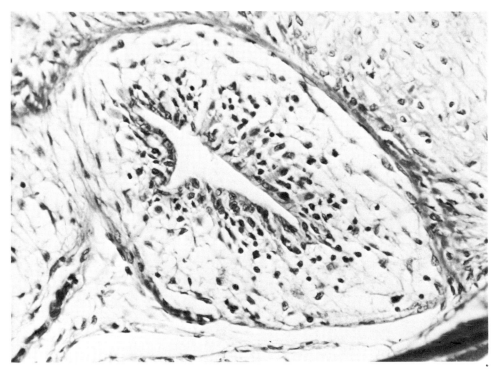

Fig. 27.5. Mandibular canal, *Fundulus,* after exposure to 25.2 mg per liter methoxychlor. X130.

Cadmium. No identifiable lesions were associated with the intestine, the kidney, or circulating blood cells of *Fundulus* exposed to 5 mg per liter of cadmium at any time during the year-long test; these tissues in *Fundulus* are known to be altered by higher levels of cadmium (11). However, subtle alterations were associated with the thyroid gland. The thyroid of several animals was hyperplastic following three months of continuous exposure. The hyperplasia was indicated by a marked numerical increase of follicles. The condition was evident through the eighth month of continuous exposure, but regressed with exposures extending beyond eight months. Approximately 10% of the specimens examined in the third and eighth months had the thyroid condition; the proportion rose to nearly 80% during the seventh month (September). Because of the early loss of control organisms, it could not be determined whether the hyperplasia was due to the toxic properties of cadmium or was a natural phenomenon.

Although morphological changes could not be detected in the cellular elements of the peripheral blood by light microscopy, examination of these elements by a specially modified coulter counter adapted to a multichannel analyzer did indicate the presence of discrete alterations (W. A. Curby, Sias Research Laboratories, Brooks Hospital, Brookline, Mass., personal communication). Characterized by

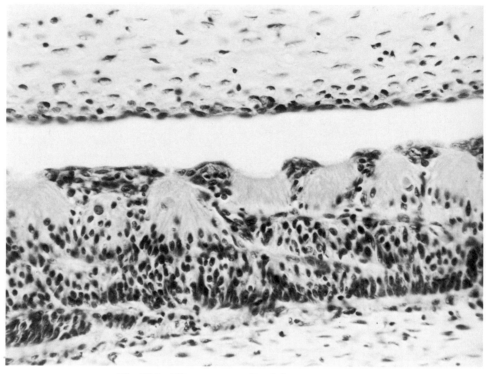

Fig. 27.6. Olfactory organ, *Fundulus*, control. X130.

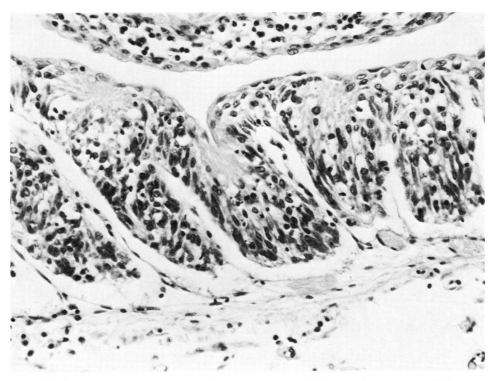

Fig. 27.7. Olfactory organ, *Fundulus,* after exposure to 0.5 mg per liter mercury. ×130.

numerical shifts in the populations of individual cell lines and changes in cell size and shape, these alterations were primarily associated with the red blood cell population.

Pesticide

The highest concentration of methoxychlor tested (25.2 mg per liter) caused lesions in the lateral line canals of *Fundulus* (Fig. 27.5). Canal epithelium was necrotic, while other elements were not visibly affected. The change gave an appearance of increased cellularity, while swelling reduced the radius of canal lumina. No evidence of damage to the mechanoreceptors appeared in the limited number of fish examined.

Petroleum

Texas-Louisiana crude oil and the saltwater soluble and insoluble fractions induced lesions in the olfactory organs of *M. menidia* (Figs. 27.9, 27.10, 27.14–27.17). Whole crude oil promoted hyperplasia of the olfactory sustentacular, or supporting epithelium. The increased cellularity resulted in the formation of "nodules" that protruded into the olfactory lumina (Fig. 27.10). These protru-

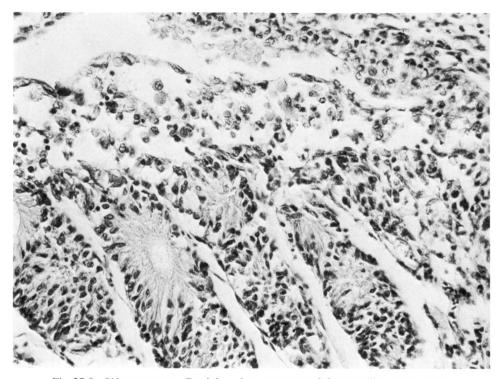

Fig. 27.8. Olfactory organ, *Fundulus,* after exposure to 0.5 mg per liter silver. ✕130.

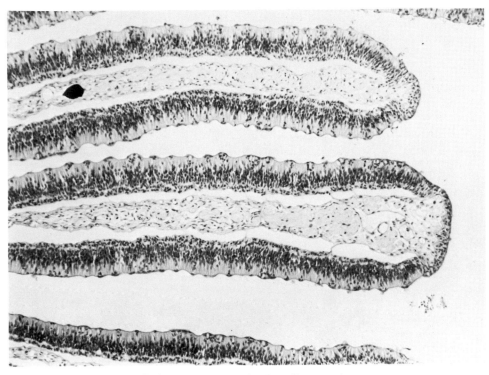

Fig. 27.9. Olfactory lamellae, *Menidia*, control. X33.

sions either reduced or eliminated the surface area of the sensory epithelium exposed to the aquatic environment. Wide areas of the olfactory mucosa underwent severe cellular degeneration. The necrocytosis encompassed both neurosensory and sustentacular epithelium. No damage was apparent in constituents of the submucosa.

Histological evaluation of the effects of whole crude oil has indicated that it may produce a degeneration of the ventricular myocardium (Fig. 27.11) and pseudobranch secretory cells (Figs. 27.12, 27.13). The ventricle of the heart in one case was observed to have large foci of necrotic myocardium. Marked cytoplasmic clearing in swollen secretory cells encompassed a sizable portion of the pseudobranch. The vascular system of the pseudobranch, however, was not noticeably influenced.

Saltwater insoluble Texas-Louisiana crude oil induced lesions in the olfactory organ of *M. Menidia* similar to that observed following exposure to whole crude oil; hyperplasia of sustentacular epithelium with "nodule" formation, and wide areas of necrosis (Figs. 27.14, 27.15). The saltwater insoluble petroleum additionally caused vasodilation in the submucosa, which was not apparent in *Menidia* after exposures to whole crude oil in a comparable time period.

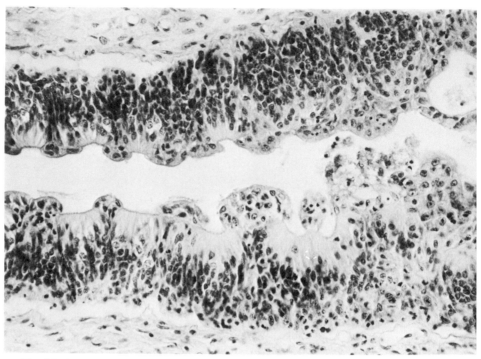

Fig. 27.10. Olfactory lamellae, *Menidia,* after exposure to 0.14 mg per liter crude oil. Note hyperplasia of sustentacular cells. ×140.

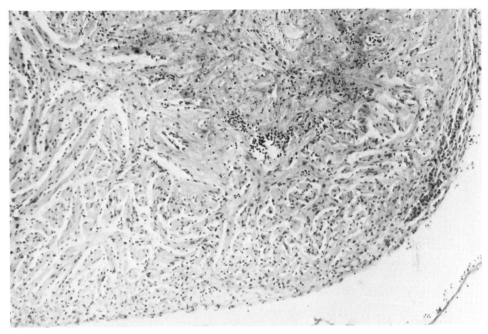

Fig. 27.11. Myocardial necrosis ventricle, *Menidia*, after exposure to 0.14 mg per liter crude oil. X130.

Saltwater soluble Texas-Louisiana crude oil induced olfactory lesions in *M. menidia* different from those observed following exposure to whole crude oil or to the saltwater insoluble fraction. Epithelial metaplasia occurred, whereby the sensory epithelium of the organ was replaced (Figs. 27.16, 27.17). Replacement of neurosensory, sustentacular, and mucus cells by a less differentiated cell type, possibly in a transitional state morphologically, had apparent basal cell derivation. These neoplastic cells were orientated vertically rather than on a longitudinal plane. Small, isolated groups of cells, recognizable as cellular components of the original sensory mucosa, could be observed in random locations engulfed or overgrown by the replacement epithelium. Numerous mitotic figures were present with the advent of metaplasia.

Refractile rods of an unknown composition were evident throughout the newly generated replacement epithelium. These elongated, sometimes "wavy" rods (approximately 15 X 1 microns) were located extracellularly. The rods, which had an affinity for eosin, were either in conglomerates or scattered randomly in the replacement epithelium. The occurrence of these rods in presence of the cellular transition suggests that they are remnants of cellular components representing the

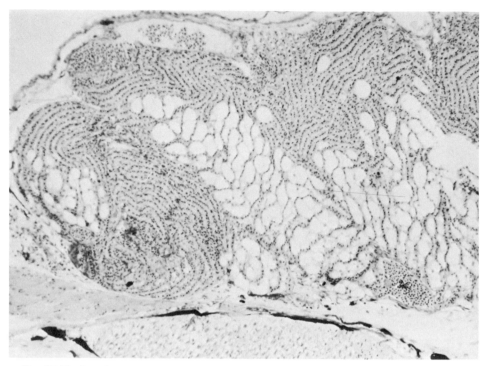

Fig. 27.12. Pseudobranch, *Menidia*, after exposure to 0.14 mg per liter crude oil. Note vacuolation of organ. X35.

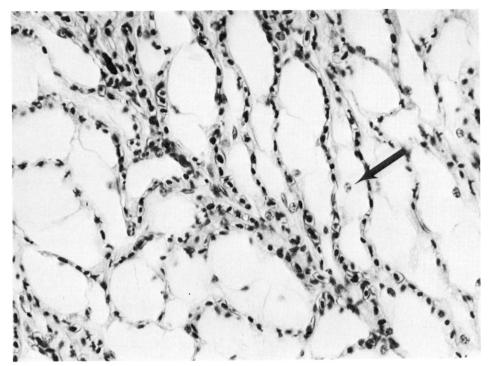

Fig. 27.13. Vacuolated secretory cells of pseudobranch, *Menidia,* as in Figure 27.12. Note nuclei (arrow). ×140.

original sensory mucosa. Epithelial metaplasia generally prevailed over the apical one half, or more, of each olfactory lamella, while the basal extremities were usually free from the cellular transition. Limited hyperplasia and cytoplasmic degeneration could be observed in the neurosensory and sustentacular cells located in the basal extremities of these olfactory lamellae.

During the extensive holding period prior to exposure, the test fish displayed schooling patterns. At the onset of exposure, however, and throughout the entire test period, general disorientation was marked by the lack of an ability to maintain schooling patterns.

Menhaden

Adult menhaden (*B. tyrannus*) collected from a "discharge quarry" which receives the Millstone Point, Connecticut, nuclear generating station effluent generally displayed erratic swimming patterns associated with an apparent loss of equilibrium. These fish were observed swimming through the water in a "corkscrew" fashion, on their sides in large or small circular patterns, or swimming upright in circular patterns with their heads above the water surface, and their mouths open.

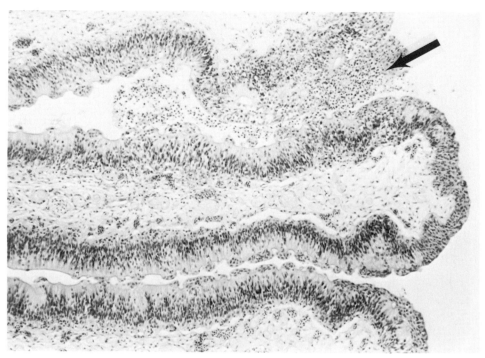

Fig. 27.14. Olfactory lamellae, *Menidia,* after exposure to 0.58 mg per liter of a water insoluble crude oil fraction. Note dilation and congestion of vasculature in submucosa. Arrow
indicates cellular debris in lumen. ×35.

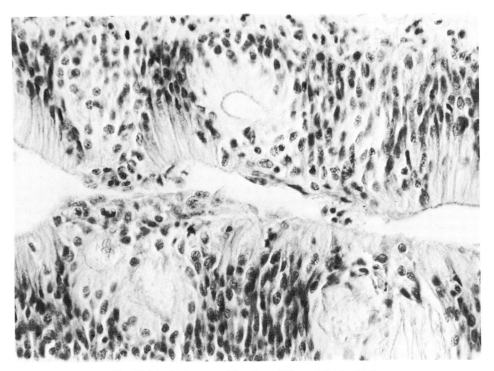

Fig. 27.15. Higher magnification of Figure 27.14. ×140.

Extreme irritability was evident with slight mechanical stimuli. However, following stimulation, the fish often submerged to swim away or accelerate in a
rather normal fashion. The length of time that a fish would spend swimming after stimulation could not be evaluated with certainty, but a considerable amount
of time elapsed before affected fish reappeared.

The eyes of many fish appeared bulged (exophthalmic) and hemorrhagic. Upon
transection of the head, midway between the olfactory organs and the eyes,
hemorrhage was indicated by darkly-colored connective tissue about the cephalic
sinuses (Fig. 27.18). Transection at the level of the membranous labyrinth also
indicated severe tissue alteration, as evidenced by dark coloration of the endolymph, which had a gel consistency.

The microscopic examination of tissues revealed lesions to be associated with
the following sensory areas: the lateral line canals (cephalic extension), cephalic
sinuses, the olfactory organs, and the membranous labyrinth or internal ear.

Anatomical change associated with the cephalic extension of the lateral line
was primarily confined to the epithelium of the canal walls which were necrotic
(Fig. 27.19). Degeneration of connective tissues adjacent to these canals occurred

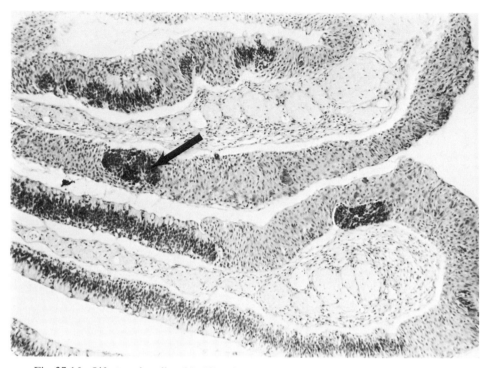

Fig. 27.16. Olfactory lamellae, *Menidia,* after exposure to 0.17 mg per liter of a water soluble crude oil fraction. Note sharp demarcation of metaplastic and sensory epithelium, and remnants of sensory epithelium (arrow). X35.

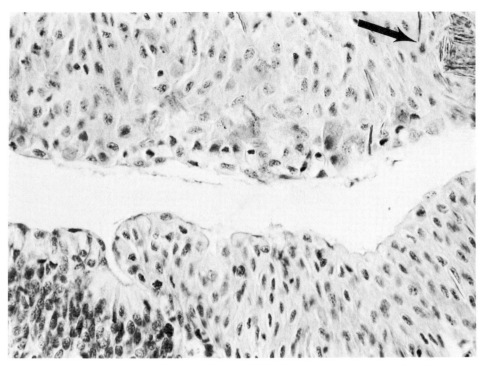

Fig. 27.17. Higher magnification of Figure 27.16. Note elongated, extracellular rods (arrow). X140.

in some cases, and was accompanied by an inflammatory response as indicated by the presence of granular leukocytes. Alterations were observed in mechanoreceptors (neuromasts), but these changes were not consistent. The lateral line canals and cephalic sinuses were often filled with red blood cells and proteinaceous debris.

Lesions in olfactory organs involved the sensory epithelium and the epithelial lining of the olfactory lumina (Figs. 27.20, 27.21). The necrotic olfactory mucosa was usually accompanied by an inflammatory response marked by the presence of granular leukocytes similar to those observed in the membranous labyrinth and other affected tissues (Fig. 27.22). Connective tissues adjacent to the basal extremities of the olfactory organs and in close proximity to the olfactory nerves were hemorrhagic. Vasculature in the submucosa of olfactory folds was dilated and congested in a majority of specimens examined.

Endolymphatic ducts of the membranous labyrinth, the perilymphatic space, and adjacent connective tissues of all specimens examined were congested; cellular debris and granular leukocytes were also associated with the lesion (Figs.

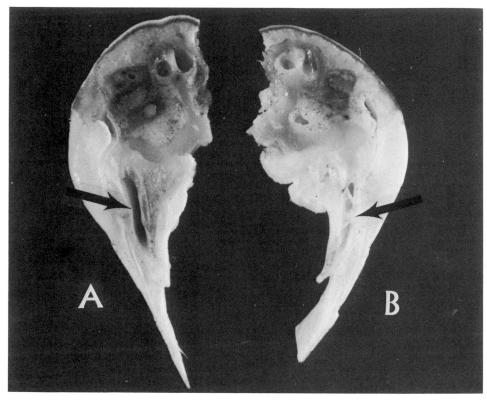

Fig. 27.18. Transverse section posterior to olfactory organs, *Brevoortia*. Compare cephalic sinus of Millstone specimen (A) to control (B) (arrows). ×4.

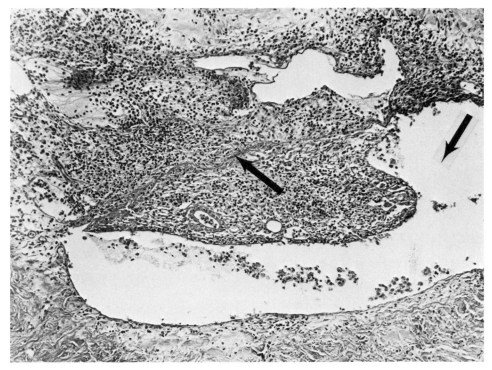

Fig. 27.19. Lateral line canal (cephalic), longitudinal section of a Millstone menhaden. Note canal wall and lumen (arrows). ×130.

27.23–27.27). Cellular debris was indicative of the severe morphological deterioration of the membranous labyrinth proper, sensory maculae, secretory cells, and innervative tissues (Figs. 27.28, 27.29). A generally widespread hemorrhagic condition, or vascular leakage, existed in the proximity of cranial nerve bundles. Dilation of the vasculature had become very extreme in most cases. The granular leukocytes (tissue eosinophils) respondent to the above degenerative changes contained large, spherical granules having an affinity for eosin. Numerous granular leukocytes, having a similar morphological appearance, had invaded a majority of the cranial nerves (Fig. 27.30).

The "crazy" or "spinning" menhaden captured near Gaspee Point in Narragansett Bay displayed erratic swimming patterns and symptoms of equilabratory dysfunction similar to those observed in menhaden from Millstone Point. Morphological alterations in "crazy" menhaden were not unlike those observed in specimens from Millstone Point, with the exception of the olfactory organs, which were not visibly affected in the limited number of specimens. Exophthalmos, noted in specimens from Millstone Point, was not evident in the "spinning" men-

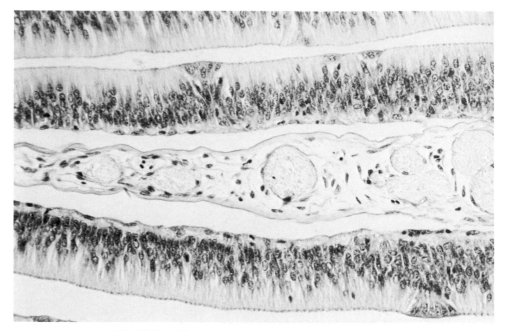

Fig. 27.20. Olfactory lamellae, *Brevoortia*, control. X130.

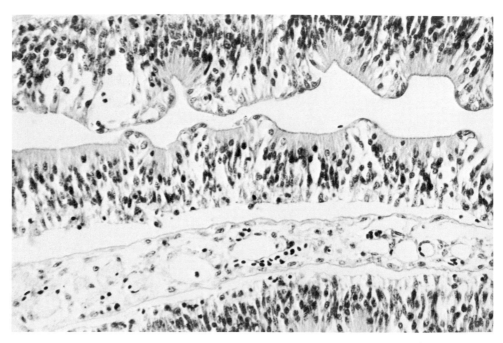

Fig. 27.21. Olfactory lamellae, *Brevoortia*, Millstone Point specimen. X130.

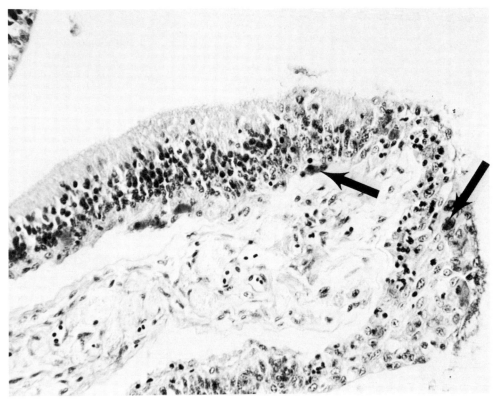

Fig. 27.22. Apex of olfactory lamellae, *Brevoortia*, Millstone Point specimen. Note granular leukocytes (arrows). ×160.

haden from Gaspee Point. The phenomenon of exophthalmos has been attractive to sea gulls, which display an apparent preference for eyes of the disabled menhaden.

Evidence of viral or other microorganisms was lacking in current tissue preparations. No morphological alterations were associated with other major tissues of these fish, including their gills.

CONCLUSIONS

Sensory organ systems of some teleosts have demonstrated vulnerability to the heavy metals, copper, mercury, silver, the pesticide methoxychlor, crude oil, pulp mill effluent, and adverse physicochemical conditions in the natural marine environment. These facts serve to indicate that many of the chemical wastes discharged into the aquatic environment may be exerting similar neurotoxic effects within the sensory organ systems of the teleost and perhaps other fauna. These neuro-

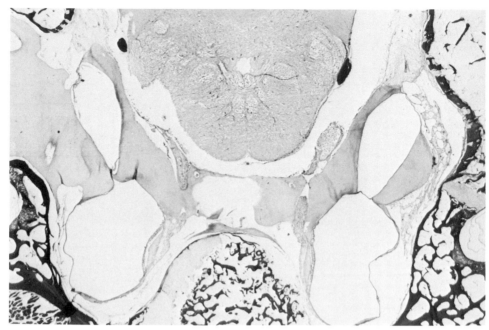

Fig. 27.23. Membranous labyrinth, *Brevoortia*, control. ×3.25.

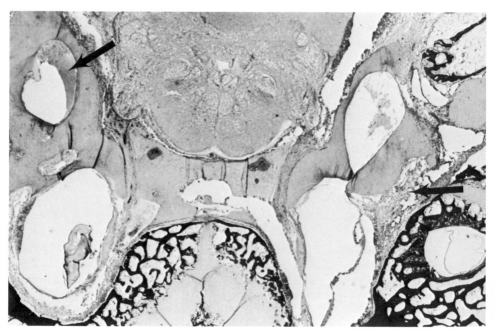

Fig. 27.24. Membranous labyrinth, *Brevoortia*, Millstone Point specimen. Note congestion in endolymph and perilymph (arrows). ×3.25.

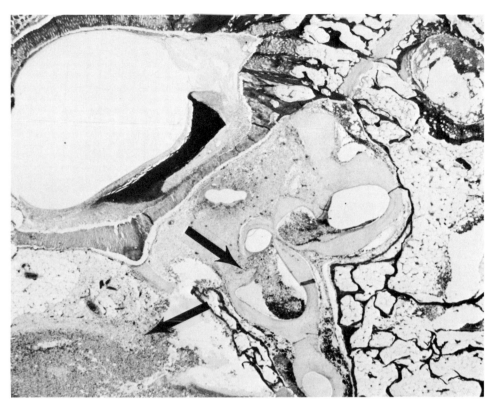

Fig. 27.25. Membranous labyrinth, *Brevoortia,* Millstone Point specimen. Arrows indicate degeneration of labyrinth and hemorrhage in connective tissues. ×4.

toxic effects are significant even if they do not cause permanent neurological damages, for a temporary disability that prevents an organism from relating to a viable environment for only moments can be disastrous. Disablement of sensory perception in some organisms can, therefore, make them much more susceptible to enemies and predation, disease, or other hazards due to an inability to relate to, or cope with, a viable environment.

Sensory organ systems constitute the means by which the teleost and other organisms maintain harmony with their environment. Environmental unity established via lateral line and olfactory sense organs was essentially nullified in *Fundulus* and *Menidia* by the neurotropic effects of copper, mercury, silver, methoxychlor, or crude oil. Evidence of disrupted harmony between the organism and the environment due to physicochemical influences may not always be as apparent as it was in the case of "spinning" menhaden, but rather may go virtually unnoticed until the species has been endangered. The lethal influences of some chemical wastes are therefore subtle by lack of a clear definition of their effects. Subtle effects of neurotropic chemicals exerted either continuously or intermittently

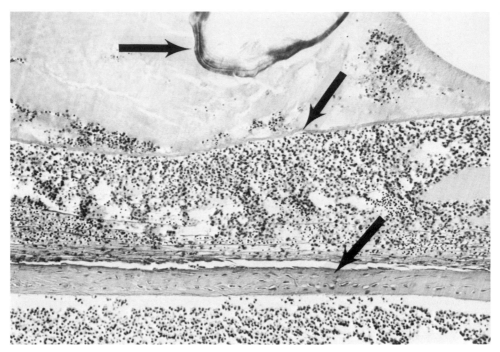

Fig. 27.26. Membranous labyrinth, *Brevoortia,* Millstone Point specimen. Arrows indicate (top to bottom) otolith, membranous labyrinth, bony labyrinth. Note cellular infiltration composed of granular leukocytes. ×40.

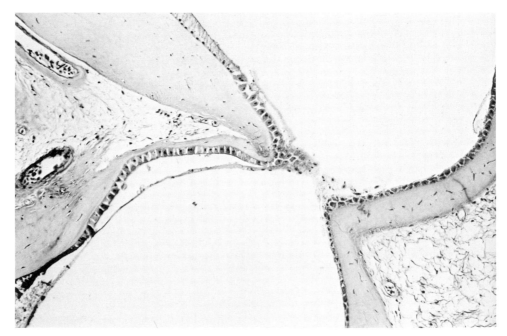

Fig. 27.27. Membranous labyrinth, *Brevoortia,* control. ×33.

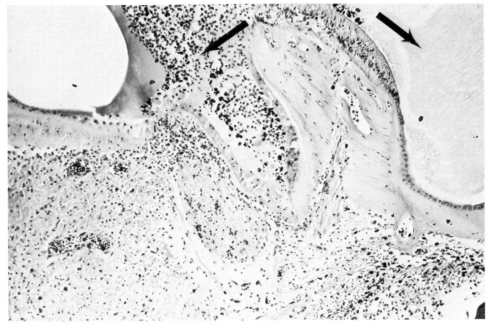

Fig. 27.28. Membranous labyrinth, *Brevoortia*, Millstone Point specimen. Lumen indicated by arrow. ×33.

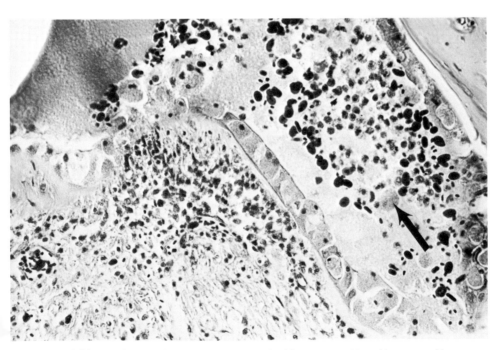

Fig. 27.29. Membranous labyrinth as in Figure 27.28. Lumen indicated by arrow. Note degeneration of sensory maculae. ×130.

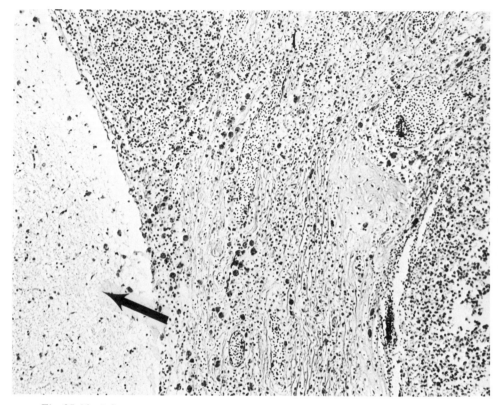

Fig. 27.30. Inflammatory response in nerve tissue, *Brevoortia*, Millstone Point specimen. Brain tissue indicated by arrow. X40.

can best be illustrated by considering the impact that a loss of olfactory sensations could have on salmon during migration and home-stream orientation. Olfaction, essential to successful salmon migrations and home-stream orientation (12), can be impaired in Atlantic salmon (*Salmo salar*) by pulp mill effluents (unpublished observations). Effluents of the pulp-paper industry caused lesions in olfactory organs of fingerling and juvenile Atlantic salmon following exposures both in the laboratory and in a natural location. Therefore, the gradual decline of a once-flourishing Atlantic salmon fishery may conceivably be linked to the presence of chemical wastes, such as pulp mill effluents, which have subtly reduced the olfactory acuity of the fish and consequently their ability to migrate and orient to home streams.

The behavior of fish during migration, reproduction, schooling, feeding, and other activities compatible with survival is dependent upon correlated sensory perceptions to locate their social partners, enemy, and prey. The feeding behavior of *Fundulus*, for example, may be seriously disrupted by reducing or eliminating anterior lateral line and olfactory sensory acuity with copper (7, 8). Altered behavioral and physiological expressions which have been documented during the course of toxicant exposures in fresh water (1, 3, 5, 13, 15-17, 21) and in sea water (2, 8) strongly suggest impairment of teleostean perceptive efficiency. For example, the olfactory response of two species of salmon (*Onchorhyncus nerka* and *O. kisutch*) and rainbow trout (*S. gairdneri*) to food extracts and some amino acids can be completely inhibited by solutions of copper and mercury (13). The sensitivity of olfactory stimulation to chemicals in these salmonids and the lesions associated with the olfactory organs in *Fundulus, Menidia,* and *S. salar* provide convincing evidence that olfaction and other sensations can be highly vulnerable to water pollution.

Lesions of a spontaneous nature in menhaden, as herein reported, present a unique situation whereby the morphological change in specimens from two geographical locations was similar, while the existing environmental conditions were quite different. Olfactory and lateral line lesions, coupled with equilibratory dysfunction in menhaden surviving at the Millstone Point fish kill and "spinning" menhaden from Gaspee Point, convincingly illustrate the vulnerability of the teleostean sensory system to stress in a graphic environment.

Currently, the genesis of lesions which have been described for the menhaden is purely speculative. Based on current research reported by Gardner and LaRoche (8) and Hara (13), lateral line and olfactory lesions may be a response linked to an external contact with a toxic substance or substances rather than to assimilation following internal contact. Laboratory investigations must be conducted, however, before the precise route of intoxication can be determined.

"Crazy" or "spinning" menhaden are terms used in reference to adult menhaden exhibiting symptoms of extreme irritability linked to frenetic contortions that are followed by loss of equilibrium and ultimate death (18). Observations of such behavior are commonplace in Chesapeake Bay and the coastal waters of New

Jersey and New York during May and June (18). No definite explanations exist
for the phenomenon to date; however, water pollution and/or virus have been suggested as causes (18). Similarity of lesions in "spinning" menhaden from Gaspee
Point and in menhaden from the Millstone Point fish kill strongly suggests that
the causes of the anomalies in both instances may be related in origin.

The occurrence of "spinning" menhaden has been known since the turn of the
century. Heavy metals or other pollutants such as textile dyes may be suspect,
as they would represent substances used in the dominant industry during that era.
Pesticides and petroleum products would appear to be eliminated as single causative agents. Experienced menhaden fishermen have related to the author that
"spinners" are observed in coastal regions and in the reaches of the bays, such as
Narragansett, but have never been observed in the open ocean, indicating that a
triggering mechanism for the "spinning" behavior exists in near-coastal environments.

Inculpating certain toxicants does not necessarily imply that the neurotic response in menhaden was elicited by the water quality in the immediate vicinity
of the visibly stressed fish. Possibly, a residual toxic burden may have been previously assumed by the menhaden before entering the heated effluent at Millstone Point or the waters near Gaspee Point. The sensational lethal response at
Millstone Point, however, may have been greatly accelerated by the extremely altered environment which either additively or synergistically contributed to an
original toxic exposure.

Realistically, intoxication of the menhaden must also be evaluated in terms of
their diet and their method of feeding. Traveling in large schools, the menhaden
frequent and feed within a narrow coastal zone in the Gulf of Maine (4). During feeding they may pass from 24 to 28 liters of sea water per minute across the
pharyngeal sieve, which very efficiently entraps planktonic organisms and other
particulates. Metals such as silver, discharged as soluble wastes into freshwater
streams, readily adsorb on suspended particulates that can be removed from the
dissolved state by planktonic organisms comprising the diet of the menhaden in
an estuarine environment (19). Coastal waters of Connecticut and Rhode Island, where "spinners" have been observed and where specimens were collected
for the present report, are known to have abnormally high levels of silver (19; and
W. H. Oldaker, Northeast Water Quality Management Center, Needham Heights,
Mass., personal communication) and copper (D. Hallett, Central and Southern
Florida Flood Control District, West Palm Beach, Fla., personal communication).
Based on the foregoing, the equilibratory dysfunction and other sensory organ
impairments in "spinning" menhaden could then relate to the magnification of a
toxic element through the lower level of the food chain, or the response might be
imposed upon them after filtering large volumes of sea water containing contaminated particulates. A combination of the above, coupled with the habitation of
an extensive coastal environment, may then be significant contributing factors to
the phenomenon of "spinning" menhaden.

Chemical wastes cause sensational fish kills in the United States, statistical reports on which are compiled annually by the Environmental Protection Agency. Among these wastes are heavy metals which in the past have generally been believed to be lethal to fish by their tendency to elicit a heavy gill mucus response that causes hypoxia, while the absence of these secretions allegedly allows internal penetration by the toxicant (6). A great deal of attention has lately been focused on the morphological changes in the gills; however, numerous appraisals of respiratory tissues by light microscopy at the National Marine Water Quality Laboratory (NMWQL) have indicated that many of the heavy metals and many other chemical wastes rarely induce lesions in gill tissue elements. "Ballooning," or detachment and lifting of the respiratory epithelium, for example, has been cited as a lesion on numerous occasions as a result of disease and pollutant exposure, and "ballooning" has emerged as a nonspecific response. Respiratory "ballooning" encountered in research at the NMWQL has been considered artifactural because the condition has been encountered as often in the untreated as in the treated fish. Plausibly, the frequent occurrence of "ballooning" and other reponses can be related to tissue-processing techniques.

The respiratory epithelium of *Menidia,* as previously mentioned, was not affected by toxicants used during the present investigations; however, crude oil did alter the pseudobranch. Lesions involving the secretory elements of the pseudobranch and the ventricle of the heart of *Menidia* may be of more than cursory significance, since the research at the NMWQL has indicated that vascular changes occur consistently in other marine species exposed to crude oil. The transitional or metaplastic change in the olfactory organs of *Menidia* following exposure to the saltwater soluble crude oil fraction signifies that the component may be carcinogenic to fish and, therefore, necessitates further exploration.

Sensory dysfunction has also served to indicate that water quality criteria designed to permit the survival of all stages of aquatic fauna (20) should no longer be derived exclusively from the results of short-term acute and long-term chronic bioassays. Such criteria, if they are to be achieved economically and if they are to withstand the changes of time, may be strengthened by incorporating adaptable interdisciplinary scientific approaches. Preservation of the aquatic environment by scientific research that can more fully aid the assessment and the prediction of the impact of a pollutant, as well as other man-made environmental modifications, needs to be accelerated. Obviously, histopathology can and must play a major role in that determination.

REFERENCES

1. Anderson, J. M. Effect of sublethal DDT on the lateral line of brook trout, *Salvelinus fontinalis. J. Fish. Res. Board Can.* 25(12): 2677–2682. 1968.
2. Atema, J., Boyland, D. B., and Todd, J. H. Importance of chemical signals in stimulation of marine organism behavior. Effects of altered environmental

chemistry on animal communication. *Amer. Chem. Soc., Abstr.,* 162d Nat. Meeting, Section on Water, Air, and Waste Chemistry. No. 8. 1971.

3. Bahr, T. G.   Responses of trout to cyanide and hypoxia: Electrophysiological effects. *Amer. Chem. Soc., Abstr.,* 162d Nat. Meeting, Section on Water, Air, and Waste Chemistry. No. 8. 1971.

4. Bigelow, H. B., and Schroeder, W. C.   Fishes of the Gulf of Maine. *U. S. Fish Wildlife Serv., Fish. Bull. 74.* 1953.

5. Calventi, I. D.   Copper poisoning in the snail *Helix pomatia* and its effect on mucous secretion. *Ann. N. Y. Acad. Sci. 118:* 1015–1120. 1965.

6. Doudoroff, P., and Katz, M.   Critical review of literature on the toxicity of industrial wastes and their components to fish. II. The metals as salts. *Sewage Ind. Wastes 25*(7): 802–839. 1953.

7. Eisler, R. E., and Gardner, G. R.   Acute toxicology to an estuarine teleost of mixtures of cadmium, copper, and zinc salts. *J. Fish Biol. 5:* 131–142. 1973.

8. Gardner, G. R., and LaRoche, G.   Copper-induced lesions in estuarine teleosts. *J. Fish. Res. Board Can. 30:* 363–368. 1973.

9. Gardner, G. R., and Yevich, P. P.   Studies on the blood morphology of three estuarine cyprinodontiform fishes. *J. Fish. Res. Board Can. 26:* 433–447. 1969.

10. Gardner, G. R., and Yevich, P. P.   Toxicological effects of cadmium on *Fundulus heteroclitus* under various oxygen, pH, salinity and temperature regimes. *Amer. Zool. 9:* 1096(abstr.). 1969.

11. Gardner, G. R., and Yevich, P. P.   Histological and hematological responses of an estuarine teleost to cadmium. *J. Fish. Res. Board Can. 27:* 2185–2196. 1970.

12. Hara, T. J.   An electrophysiological basis for olfactory discrimination in homing salmon: A review. *J. Fish. Res. Board Can. 27*(3): 565–586. 1970.

13. Hara, T. J.   Electrical responses of the olfactory bulb of Pacific salmon *Oncorhynchus nerka* and *Oncorhynchus kisutch. J. Fish. Res. Board Can. 29*(9): 1351–1355. 1972.

14. LaRoche, G., Gardner, G. R., Eisler, R. E., Jackim, E. H., Yevich, P. P., and Zaroogian, G. E.   Analysis of toxic responses in marine poikilotherms. *Amer. Chem. Soc., Abstr.,* 162d Nat. Meeting, Section on Water, Air, and Waste Chemistry. No. 8. 1971.

15. Mount, D. I.   Chronic toxicity of copper to the fathead minnow (*Pimephales promelas,* Rafinesque). *Water Res. 2:* 215–223. 1968.

16. Mount, D. I., and Stephan, C. E.   Chronic toxicity of copper to the fathead minnow (*Pimephales promelas*) in soft water. *J. Fish. Res. Board Can. 26:* 2449–2457. 1969.

17. Ozaki, H., Uematsu, K., and Tanaka, K.   Survival and growth of goldfish and carp in dilute solutions of copper sulfate. *Jap. J. Ichthyol. 17*(4): 166–172. 1970.

18. Sindermann, C. J.   *Principal Diseases of Marine Fish and Shellfish.* New York and London, Academic Press, 1970.

19. Turekian, K. K.   Rivers, tributaries, and estuaries. In *Impingement of Man on the Oceans,* ed. D. Hood. New York, Wiley, 1971.

20. U. S. Dep. Interior, Federal Water Pollution Control Administration, Committee Report. Water quality criteria. 1968.

21. Weir, P. A., and Hine, C. H. Effects of various metals on behavior of conditioned goldfish. *Arch. Environ. Health 20*(1): 45–51. 1970.

DISCUSSION OF CHEMICALLY INDUCED LESIONS IN ESTUARINE OR MARINE TELEOSTS

P. H. Cahn: Were these fish killed during May, June, or July?

G. R. Gardner: The fish kill at Millstone Point started in April and was continuous at least through mid-June.

P. H. Cahn: In other words, the fish were about in their spawning stage in the middle of April. Did you by any chance get a peek at gonads to see whether they had spawned or not spawned?

G. R. Gardner: They had spawned.

P. H. Cahn: The problems that you have brought up have been worrying persons like Dr. Nigrelli, Dr. Cindamon, and many other people for the past 25 or 30 years. No one has been able to shed much light on what is going on. The lateral line seems to respond to many of the pollutants very rapidly. We found in some of the neurophysiological studies done on the lateral line that the fish can be swimming around and looking fairly normal and feeding well, not spinning as yet, but the lateral line nerve will no longer have any activity. Two or three days later the spinning will occur and the fish will eventually die. I hope that some of the fish pathologists will become more interested in this problem and give us a hand so the menhaden kills can cease.

Question: There was such a rapid degeneration of the neuromasts and the olfactory cells, I was wondering if you noted similar effects on taste buds, say on the lips?

G. R. Gardner: No, I haven't, either in them, nor in the free neuromasts in the epidermis. They don't seem to be affected; I don't know why.

H. W. Huizinga: Have you ruled out the possibility of the Bohr effect, that is, increase in environmental CO_2 which might cause unloading of oxygen and might contribute to the die-off in addition to the sensory effects? It is well known with some species of freshwater fishes that if you have an increase of environmental CO_2 it will cause an unloading of oxygen.

G. R. Gardner: In the experimental situations water quality was monitored and oxygen was at saturation. At Millstone Point the water was saturated with oxygen, although temperature was an additional factor there, but it was not in the case of the "spinning" menhaden from a different location. Therefore, oxygen was sufficient in all situations; however, I don't know to what extent CO_2 might have been a factor, especially in the marine environment.

Question: Did you work on *Fundulus?* Was that your test organism?

G. R. Gardner: Yes, *Fundulus heteroclitus* and the Atlantic silverside (*Menidia menidia*) were the experimental organisms.

Question: I wondered what was the logic behind that choice of organism?

G. R. Gardner: Well, we use *Fundulus* extensively in laboratory experimentation, because there is a lot known about the animal and it is easily accessible. We also use *Menidia* extensively because it provides a much more sensitive species than *Fundulus.*

R. G. Gammon: It seems that *Fundulus* is one of the most adaptable osmoregulative fishes and also can support a lot of chemical and thermal changes. If you seek to find subtle effects in the higher trophic web, it would be better to work with other species.

G. R. Gardner: That is right.

K. Balogh: I was very much interested in your presentation because in people we have ototoxic drugs which selectively affect the vestibular labyrinth or the cochlea, or both, and it is apparently true in mammals, in which selective destruction of the sensory epithelial cells occurs. I know about a group in Stockholm, Sweden, who have used the lateral line organ in—I forgot which fish they used— and they tested dihydrostreptomycin in experiments comparable to human dosage. They found that the sensory epithelium was selectively destroyed and, if I remember correctly, they had no inflammatory changes whatsoever. It was purely a degenerative change. The epithelial cells gradually degenerated and fell off and there was no regeneration whatsoever. And, this was not accompanied by any inflammatory or hemorrhagic changes such as you have shown. I wondered, therefore, if there might not be some other factor involved. Also, I should add that their changes were much more subtle and I think chronologically theirs were also experiments of a much more chronic type.

P. H. Cahn: I just want to go back to the temperature and bore effect and CO_2 point for a moment. Were these fish hanging around the thermal effluent all winter, presumably the fish that were involved in the kill? Do you know if the menhaden involved in the kill in the vicinity of the power plant were nonmigrating species?

G. R. Gardner: I don't know that. From the reports I've heard they were migratory.

P. H. Cahn: The menhaden are extremely sensitive to high CO_2, low oxygen, temperature changes, salinity changes, stresses of all kinds—they scare when you look at them. Also, I wondered if you had gill-netted these fish because I have gill-netted all of mine and they are as hemorrhagic as can be. This may be the stress of gill netting. You certainly don't get hyperplastic lateral line, neuromast changes, and such that rapidly. Also, remember that these fish are swimming in and out of estuaries from North Carolina up through Rhode Island and they do accumulate tremendous quantities of toxic materials, so this could be a chronic condition.

Question: I would like to ask very briefly, Is there any indication of specific lesions so that you think you might in the future be able to identify specific poisons?

G. R. Gardner: I don't know of any at this point; however, more work needs to be done with these goals in mind.

28

Skeletal Anomalies in Marine Teleosts

Physical anomalies in both marine and freshwater fishes are well documented. Dawson (5-7) has presented extensive bibliographies on terata in natural populations. With few exceptions the literature on such anomalies is restricted to one or a few aberrant individuals and does not deal with anomalous populations. When sizable numbers of aberrant individuals are reported, observations are generally based on the examination of many thousands, or in some cases, tens of thousands of specimens (16, 21).

Another body of literature exists on anomalies encountered by experimental and inland fisheries biologists. For the most part, reported observations consist of descriptions of congenitally deformed specimens, individuals which could probably not long survive the rigors of the wild.

The primary concern in this paper is not the occasional aberrant fish observed from wild populations nor the congenitally deformed laboratory novelty, but rather the less well understood phenomenon where high frequencies of deformed fish are reported from wild populations. Such cases are not well documented and, when closely observed, can usually be traced to some unusual environmental (19, 43) or populational event (17, 41).

The species to be described is the barred sand bass (*Paralabrax nebulifer*). Barred sand bass from Southern California are known to have a high frequency of skeletal anomalies (38).

Specimens were either captured by the author or obtained from various museums in California. In addition, 27 small live barred sand bass from the Scripps Institution of Oceanography aquarium were utilized in the analysis.

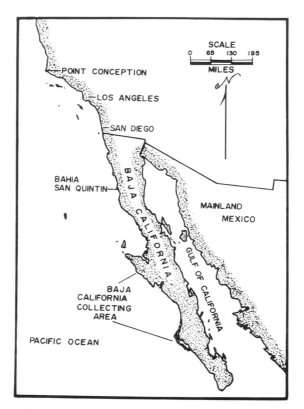

Fig. 28.1. Map of Southern and Baja California. The Baja California collecting area is the entire zone between the two lines.

All barred sand bass were examined for the presence of internal and external physical anomalies. Examination included the fins, gill rakers, and general appearance. Lesions, tumors, and ectoparasites, if present, were recorded. The soft tissues of several hundred specimens were digested by immersing the previously fleshed carcass in boiling water for approximately five minutes.

Anomalies encountered were arbitrarily scored for degree of deformity. A structure was assigned a "0" if normal, a "1" if mildly anomalous, and "2" if it deviated greatly from the norm of Mexican specimens, which are here considered to be a control population.

In the following sections reference will be made to specific localities in Southern and Baja California. These localities are shown in Figures 28.1 and 28.2.

All reference to length refers to standard length, defined as extending from the anterior notch between the premaxillaries to the end of the hypural plate.

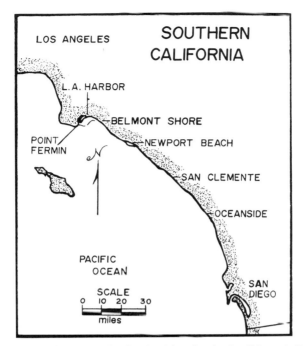

Fig. 28.2. Map of Southern California with collecting localities as indicated.

RESULTS OF SURVEYS

Reports are often difficult to follow when a large amount of new data is presented in compact form. To partially obviate this problem there will be posed specific questions and answers.

What kinds of anomalies are found in barred sand bass?

Principal deformities encountered were all related to calcified skeletal structures. These anomalies involved the gill rakers (Fig. 28.3A, B, C), bones of the opercular series (Fig. 28.4), snubnosedness (Fig. 28.5), cranial asymmetries (Fig. 28.6A, B), various fin anomalies (Fig. 28.7A, B), and deformed vertebral columns (Fig. 28.8A, B). The latter were always confirmed by dissection or digestion. The inclusion of fin anomalies as being skeletal is perhaps debatable. Fins are part of the appendicular firm skeleton and are here considered to be a part of the skeleton proper.

Of these anomalies, which are likely to be caused by ectoparasites and which are likely to be of viral or bacterial origin?

To date, over 1,000 barred sand bass have been examined. None has been observed with large ectoparasites capable of producing easily visible damage, although Turner (36) reported finding the gill isopod *Lironeca vulgaris* on barred

Fig. 28.3A. Normal gill rakers. Note the long, straight gill rakers.

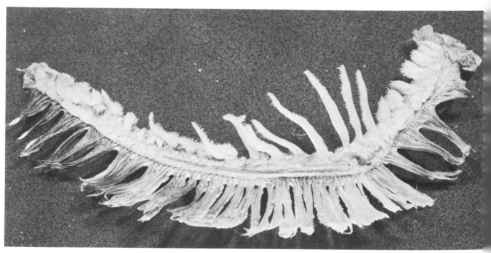

Fig. 28.3B. Mildly deformed gill rakers. A slight bending of the gill rakers is evident when compared to Figure 28.3A.

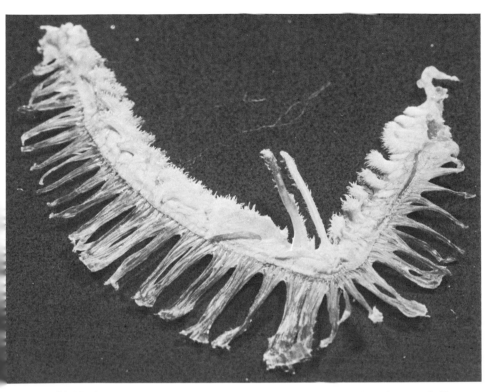

Fig. 28.3C. Severely deformed gill rakers. Only two rakers are straight, as in normal gill rakers. Other rakers, normally straight, are severely bent and in contact with the underlying arch.

sand bass and assumed that some of the damaged gill rakers may have been produced by this parasite. No degenerative changes normally ascribed to bacterial or viral infection have been observed. The only exception may be certain fin anomalies which might be caused by fin rot. However, none of the fins examined appears to be infected with fin rot disease as is commonly found on other species of fish from certain localities in Southern California (44).

What is the overall frequency of external physical anomalies in barred sand bass from Southern and Baja California?

In this context only gross differences between these two areas are of interest. Data are presented in Table 28.1. In all cases differences in the frequency of anomalies between Southern California and Baja California barred sand bass are significantly different (P < .005), Southern California barred sand bass always possessing more anomalies than Mexican barred sand bass do.

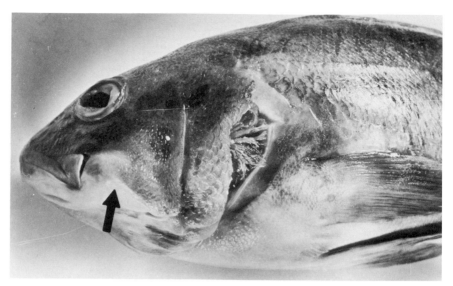

Fig. 28.4. Deformed opercular bones. This specimen also has severely deformed gill rakers and a calcified knob on the ceratohyal (arrow). Compare to Figure 28.5, where the operculum is normal.

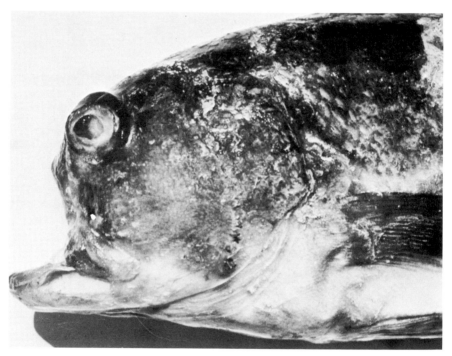

Fig. 28.5. Snubnosed barred sand bass. Mouth parts are nonfunctional. The mouth itself is reduced to a small aperture. Gill rakers are also severely deformed. Compare to Figure 28.4, where the snout and mouth parts are normal.

Table 28.1. Overall Frequency of External Physical Anomalies in Barred Sand Bass

	Total number of specimens examined	Gill rakers[a]					
		Normal	%	Mildly deformed	%	Severely deformed	%
Southern California	487	253	52.0	85	17.5	149	30.5
Baja California	348	344	98.9	4	1.1	0	0.0

	Ventral fins					
	Normal	%	Mildly deformed	%	Severely deformed	%
Southern California	408	83.8	54	11.1	25	5.1
Baja California	347	99.7	1	0.3	0	0.0

	Other anomalies[b]					
	Normal	%	Mild	%	Severe	%
Southern California	439	90.1	35	7.2	13	2.7
Baja California	346	99.4	2	0.6	0	0.0

[a] For both gill rakers and ventral fins the most deformed side of a bilateral character was used to assign that character to the level of deformity as used here. For instance, if a set of gill rakers had one arch mildly deformed and the other severely deformed then, for the purpose of this analysis, that specimen was considered to have severely deformed gill rakers.

[b] Other anomalies include all fin anomalies (excluding ventral fins), deformed opercula, etc.

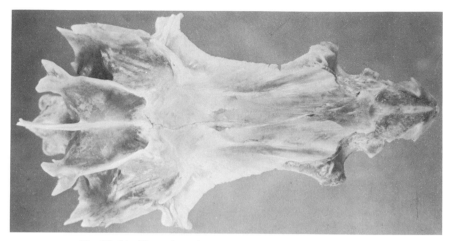

Fig. 28.6A. Normal cranium. Note perfect symmetry of parts.

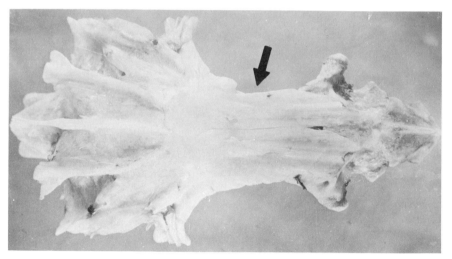

Fig. 28.6B. Asymmetric cranium. A small piece of the cranium is missing (arrow). The cranium is visibly asymmetrical, being twisted to the left.

Is there an association among the external anomalies?

The most prevalent form of anomaly in Southern California barred sand bass is gill raker deformities. To answer the above question the samples were divided into fish with normal, mildly, and severely deformed gill rakers; and a similar division was made for the other anomalies. From Table 28.2 it can be seen that not only do barred sand bass with deformed gill rakers account for the bulk of the deformities, but the frequency and severity of associated anomalies also increase with increasing gill raker deformity.

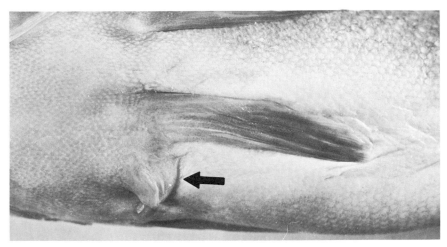

Fig. 28.7A. Ventral fin deformity. Bottom ventral fin (arrow) is badly deformed, while the other is normal. This "asymmetry" of ventral fins, where one is normal and the other deformed, was encountered four times in barred sand bass from Southern California. The appearance of these fins is similar to that produced when fins are clipped for tagging studies and regenerated. As far as can be determined, no agency or individual has used such a tagging procedure on barred sand bass.

Fig. 28.7B. Mildly deformed ventral fins. Both ventral fins have "wavy" rays. Compare to the normal ventral fin in Figure 28.7A.

Of the 253 remaining Southern California barred sand bass which did not have anomalous gill rakers, only 6 with other deformities were found. Two specimens were encountered with mildly deformed ventral fins and no other anomalies. Of the four remaining individuals, one specimen was mildly snub-nosed (a condition that may be congenital) (18, 39). Another had visibly asymmetrical opercular bones, and the remaining specimen had a regenerated scale pattern on the left side. From these data, I would conclude that a very strong association exists between deformed gill rakers and the other external anomalies in barred sand bass.

Is there an association between deformed gill rakers and internal skeletal anomalies?

Data from Southern California were obtained from 155 digested barred sand bass, the first series of specimens being collected from that area in 1968 and 1969. From the results presented in Table 28.3 it can be seen that only one fish had an internal anomaly not associated with deformed gill rakers. The concurrence of vertebral and cranial deformities with deformed gill rakers is virtually perfect. As with the previous data on external anomalies, the frequency of internal anomalies increases with increasing gill raker deformity.

For comparison, the first 72 Mexican barred sand bass collected in 1969 were digested. Only three specimens with one mildly deformed gill arch apiece were encountered, and another three specimens were found with slightly asymmetric crania. There was no association between these anomalies.

Are these anomalies congenital?

This question is difficult, if not impossible, to answer directly. I have not reared sand bass in the laboratory and, therefore, have not seen the progression of events leading to the various deformities.

An indirect method available to examine this question is the study of cohorts. Cohorts in this case are defined as fish spawned during the same time period regardless of the size or age of the fish at the time of capture.

The assumption of this cohort analysis is as follows: If the deformities are congenital, more anomalies should be encountered in young-of-the-year fish than in adults, since we might expect selection to eliminate the most severely deformed individuals. If, on the other hand, the frequency of anomalies is lower in juveniles than in adults hatched during the same time period we might infer that the anomalies are developmental and not congenital (developmental is here taken to mean deformities which appear after hatching as opposed to congenital deformities which are present at hatching).

The largest group of young-of-the-year fish available were spawned during the time period 1957–1959. There were 32 specimens in this group, none with deformities. Coincidentally, the group of adult fish most likely to have been spawned contemporarily was also composed of 32 individuals (average age 10.8 years, mean length 329 mm). These adults had 34.4 and 39.9% mildly and severely deformed gill rakers, respectively.

Another large group of adults, mean age 8.6 years, was spawned sometime be-

Table 28.2. Association of External Anomalies in Southern California Barred Sand Bass with the Degree of Gill Raker Deformity

Gill rakers,[a] bilateral assignment	Numbers of specimens	%	Ventral fins				Other anomalies[b]			
			Mildly deformed	%	Severely deformed	%	Mild	%	Severe	%
Normal	253	52.0	2	0.41	0	0.00	3	0.61	1	0.21
Mildly deformed	85	17.5	17	3.49	4	0.82	8	1.64	2	0.41
Severely deformed	149	30.5	39	8.00	21	4.31	25	4.13	9	1.85
Totals	487	100.0	58	11.91	25	5.13	36	7.39	12	2.46

a See note a, Table 28.1.
b See note b, Table 28.1.

Table 28.3. Association of Internal Skeletal Anomalies and the Degree of Gill Raker Deformity in Barred Sand Bass from Southern California

Gill rakers[a] bilateral assignment	Number of specimens	%	Vertebral deformities	%	Cranial deformities	%
Normal	40	25.8	0	0.0	1	0.6
Mildly deformed	43	27.7	3	1.9	7	4.5
Severely deformed	72	46.5	12	7.7	34	21.9
Totals	155	100.0	15	9.7	42	27.1

a See note a, Table 28.1.

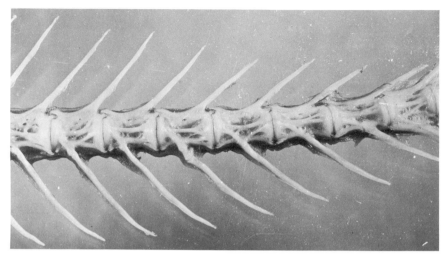

Fig. 28.8A. Normal section of vertebral column. Vertebral segments are of normal length, and neural and hemal spines are straight.

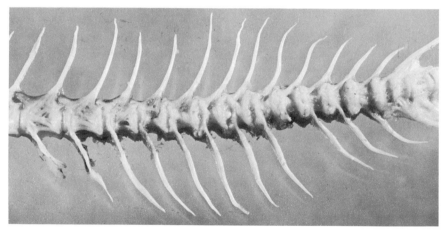

Fig. 28.8B. Badly deformed section of vertebral column. Vertebral segments are shortened and heavily calcified. Missing hemal spine was originally present, but, as in many specimens with this type of deformity, was weak at the base and broke off when handled.

tween 1959 and 1961. The frequency of mildly deformed gill rakers was 25.1%, severely deformed 42.9%. Nine young-of-the-year were available from this time period. Again, no deformities were present. Alternatively, 24 specimens ranging in size from 103.7 to 170.5 mm (mean age about 3 years) were available. The frequency of mildly deformed gill rakers was 2.1%, a great deal lower than 25.1 and 42.9%, respectively, for the adult population spawned during the same time period.

From the above data it seems reasonable to conclude that these anomalies are not congenital.

Are the anomalies increasing in frequency and severity with age?

If these anomalies are developmental, then, logically, they must be increasing both in frequency and severity with age.

Figure 28.9 presents data on the frequency of gill raker anomalies in barred sand bass from Southern California. Data from all collections made between 1967 and 1971 have been combined. From these data it would appear that gill raker anomalies increase both in frequency and severity with age, as do the other related deformities which are closely associated with deformed gill rakers.

Is there any indication that the frequency of gill raker anomaly within a given size-class of fish has been changing with time?

In this case we are interested in determining if fish in a given size-class (i.e., 200 to 249.9 mm) have more or fewer anomalies now than the same size-class did several years ago. Adequate samples have not been taken continuously within a given area long enough to supply a definitive answer. The only data which can be used to answer this question are from three separate localities (Table 28.4). Los Angeles and San Diego collections are composed entirely of barred sand bass in the size-class 200 to 249.9 mm. San Clemente barred sand bass, on the other

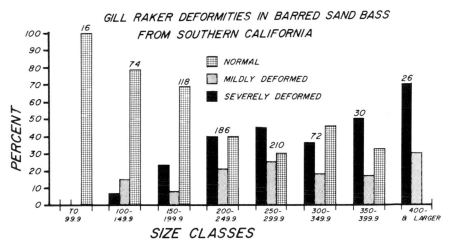

Fig. 28.9. Bar graph of the incidence of normal, mildly deformed, and severely deformed gill rakers in barred sand bass from Southern California. With increasing size (age), expressed in standard length (mm), the percentage of normal gill rakers decreases while the percentage of deformed gill rakers increases. All specimens utilized in this figure were captured between 1967 and 1971, inclusive. Sample sizes for each size class are as indicated. The percentage of severely and mildly deformed and normal gill rakers respectively, are as follows (size classes first, percentages second): To 99.9 mm, 0.0, 0.0, 100.0; 100–149.9 mm, 6.8, 14,9, 78.3; 150–199.9 mm, 22.9, 8.5, 68.6; 200–249.9 mm, 39.2, 21.0, 39.8; 250–299.9 mm, 45.2, 24.8, 30.0; 300–349.9 mm, 36.1, 18.0, 46.0; 350–399.9 mm, 50.0, 16.7, 32.3; 400 and larger, 69.2, 30.8, 0.0.

Table 28.4. Time Series and Locality Analysis of Severely Deformed Gill Rakers in
Southern California Barred Sand Bass in the Size-Class 200-249.9

Year and locality of collection	Number of arches examined	Number of severely deformed arches	Frequency of severely deformed arches
Los Angeles (1967-68)	72	22	30.6
San Clemente (1971)	60	29	48.3
San Diego (1969)	34	15	44.1

hand, include specimens ranging in size from 188 to 240 mm, which were arbitrarily assigned to the 200 to 249.9 mm size-class to obtain a single large sample. Such a procedure may tend to bias results, but it should bias them in such a way as to underestimate the frequency of severely deformed gill rakers since, as was previously demonstrated, the frequency of severely deformed gill rakers increases with increasing size.

It would appear that the frequency of severely deformed gill rakers has been increasing with time in this size-class. However, these changes are not statistically significant. The important thing to note is that there has been no apparent decrease in gill raker deformities, even though these collections cover a four-year period.

Is there any difference in the frequency of gill raker deformity between Los Angeles and San Diego?

Up until this point Southern California barred sand bass have been treated as if they belong to one large interbreeding population. This may not be true. There is evidence that barred sand bass are virtually nonmigratory; thus the amount of mixing between Los Angeles and San Diego populations may be minimal (45). Data for the frequency of gill raker anomalies from these two areas are presented in Tables 28.5 and 28.6. From these two tables it would appear that the frequency of gill raker deformity per size-class is roughly similar. The exceptions are most interesting since they would seem to indicate that deformities begin appearing in smaller fish in the area around Los Angeles compared to fish in the area around San Diego, but that the eventual equilibrium of the frequency of gill raker deformity, if such exists, is comparable for the two localities.

CONCLUSIONS

The main points emerging from the previously presented data are: (1) a wide range of skeletal anomalies exist in barred sand bass from Southern California, (2) these anomalies are present in a high frequency in Southern California, but not in Baja California, (3) the anomalies in barred sand bass are restricted to structures which contain considerable amounts of calcium, (4) there appears to be an excellent association between the presence of gill raker anomalies and both

Table 28.5. Gill Raker Deformities in Barred Sand Bass from San Diego[a]
(By size-class)

Size-class	Number of rakers examined	Number of deformities		Percentage		
		Mild	Severe	Normal	Mild	Severe
0-49.9	0	–	–	–	–	–
50-99.9	2	0	0	100.0	0	0
100-149.9	8	0	0	100.0	0	0
150-199.9	38	1	1	94.8	2.6	2.6
200-249.9	52	13	32	13.5	25.0	61.5
250-299.9	138	34	59	32.6	24.6	42.8
300-349.9	30	8	14	26.6	26.7	46.7
350-399.9	16	4	7	31.2	25.0	43.8
400-499.9	20	8	12	0.0	40.0	60.0

[a]Only specimens captured from 1967 to 1971 were utilized in this table.

Table 28.6. Gill Raker Deformities in Barred Sand Bass from Los Angeles[a]
(By size-class)

Size-class	Number of rakers examined	Deformities		Percentage		
		Mild	Severe	Normal	Mild	Severe
0-49.9	4	0	0	100	0	0
50-99.9	10	0	0	100	0	0
100-149.9	66	11	5	75.7	16.7	7.6
150-199.9	70	9	26	50.0	12.9	37.1
200-249.9	134	26	41	50.0	19.4	30.6
250-299.9	72	18	36	25.0	25.0	50.0
300-349.9	42	5	12	59.5	11.9	28.6
350-399.9	14	1	8	35.9	7.1	57.1
400 up	6	0	6	0	0	100.1

[a]Only specimens captured from 1967 to 1971 were utilized in this table.

internal and external anomalies, (5) the anomalies do not appear to be congenital, (6) the anomalies increase in both frequency and severity with increasing age (size), (7) the frequency of these anomalies does not appear to be decreasing with time within a given size-class, (8) the anomalies, or the unique combination of them, have apparently never been attributed to marine pathogens or parasites, and (9) the anomalies are not restricted to a limited area but may be found in a high frequency over the entire Southern California continental shelf.

The remaining questions, then, are "What are the origins of these anomalies and how are they maintained in the population at such a seemingly high frequency?"

As far as origins are concerned, most investigators would probably agree that the previously described anomalies result from a metabolic instability directly concerned with, or closely linked to, the metabolism, transport, or deposition of calcium. Factors previously known to yield abnormal calcified structures include five basic categories: nutritional deficiencies, various pathogens, late-onset genetic disorders, various populational phenomena, and finally, various categories of toxicants.

It seems doubtful that barred sand bass suffer from a nutritional deficiency. Analyses of stomach contents have failed to show a deficiency in either quality, quantity, or diversity of food.

A pathogenic origin for these anomalies cannot be eliminated; however, an extensive literature search has failed to uncover any disease which can produce the wide range of skeletal disorders observed in barred sand bass. There is also the possibility that several diseases, or a disease made more virulent by the presence of an environmental pollutant, may be acting in conjunction to cause these anomalies. Some ubiquitous pollutants have been shown to increase the susceptibility of animals to infection (33).

Late-onset genetic disorders are well documented in man, but not well documented in marine vertebrates. It seems peculiar that a high incidence of anomalies should exist in waters off Southern California and virtually none off Baja California. If these anomalies are indeed genetic one would expect to find a much higher frequency in Baja California barred sand bass. Almost 200 fish from Baja California over 3 years of age have been examined, the oldest being in its 15th year, yet the frequency of even mildly anomalous individuals is very low.

The introduction of an exotic species into a previously unoccupied water mass and its subsequent rapid proliferation may temporarily yield a population with a high frequency of anomalies. Whitney (41) studied such a case in the Salton Sea of California. In 1950 and 1951, 67 biardiella (*Biardiella icistius*) were introduced from San Felipe, Baja California, to the Salton Sea (8). Explosive population growth ensued and it was estimated that there were millions of biardiella within a few years. The 1952 year-class of fish had between 13 and 23% anomalies. Whitney drew no conclusions as to whether the anomalies were genetic or environmental in origin, but they were most certainly congenital. Whitney (41) stated

"The stress of competition with the younger more abundant 1953 year-class evidently led to a reduction of abnormalities in the 1952 year-class to about 2.5 percent in 1954." No evidence has been found which would indicate that the frequency of abnormalities in barred sand bass is decreasing.

There is some evidence indicating that a population explosion of barred sand bass occurred in Southern California sometime between 1957 and 1959 (12). If we first assume the anomalies in barred sand bass to be congenital, and second assume that a population explosion did occur, and, last, assume that the explosion has been waning, then a frequency of anomalies similar to those reported would be predicted, providing that selection did not cull all of the aberrant individuals. However, as previously stated, the deformities do not appear to be congenital. Recall that young-of-the-year spawned during the hypothetical population explosion were not deformed while adults hatched during the same time period were.

Intense fishing pressure on adult barred sand bass might increase juvenile recruitment which might, in turn, allow some congenitally deformed individuals to reach maturity. The assumption of this argument is again that there is a congenital origin. There is apparently no evidence that would support a congenital origin for these anomalies.

An environmental origin of physical anomalies is documented in fish but only poorly. Hubbs (19) attributed the high incidence of vertebral deformities found in mosquitofish (*Gambusia affinis*) inhabiting warm springs in Texas primarily to the elevated water temperature of the springs themselves. Several other conditions, in addition to elevated water temperatures, may apparently likewise lead to various anomalies (13, 25). None of the previously reported causes for anomalies appears to be applicable to barred sand bass.

Most of the agents previously known to produce anomalies in fishes would appear not to be applicable to the case in question. As alternative possibilities they must not be ignored. The only remaining possibility of those already listed is the most difficult to investigate: the induction of skeletal anomalies by a ubiquitous pollutant or pollutants that interfere with calcium metabolism. Such agents include various heavy metals and chlorinated hydrocarbons. Chlorinated phenolic compounds, particularly DDT and its derivatives, polychlorinated biphenyls, or PCB's, are thought to have similar actions (15, 27, 28, 31).

Both have been implicated in calcium upsets, particularly in birds. Among other effects, such agents reduce the amount of mobilized calcium (26, 29) and perhaps interfere with carbonic anhydrase activity (2), an enzyme thought to be important in bone metabolism (24).

High concentrations of pesticides are to be expected in Southern California marine waters and organisms. Roughly 20% of the pesticides produced in the United States are applied to California crops (4, 37), and much of that eventually finds its way into the ocean. The largest producer of DDT in the United States is situated in the Los Angeles basin and, until relatively recently, one sewage outfall situated adjacent to the Los Angeles Harbor (White's Point) was discharging an estimated 97 kg per day DDT and 100 kg per day PCB's (32). Fairly extensive survey work is now being conducted on pesticide residues in Southern California marine fishes by various agencies and individuals. Risebrough et al. (31) conducted a survey of such residues and found that the highest values were in fish taken from waters adjacent to Los Angeles. DDT and its metabolite concentrations have been reported in livers of some fish near the White's Point outfall as consisting of up to 1026 ppm with a mean concentration for 71 samples of 318.2 ppm (9).

Heavy metals are also known to interfere with calcium metabolism. Among the more ubiquitous are cadmium (23), mercury (11, 22), and lead (10). The latter possibly competes for sites normally occupied by other divalent ions, such as calcium (20). While the concentrations of these elements in marine fishes from Southern California are not well documented, their presence should certainly be suspected from the high concentrations found in various marine sediments (14).

If these anomalies are intimately associated with the accumulation of toxicants that, when concentrated, produce metabolic instabilities, then similar anomalies should be observable in other marine teleosts from the same locality. To date, two additional species have been examined, California grunion (*Leuresthes tenuis*) and barred surfperch (*Amphistichus argenteus*). Results for these two species in many respects closely parallel those for barred sand bass. In all three species the most prevalent forms of anomalies are those of the gill rakers, the anomalies appear to increase in frequency with age, and they are virtually restricted to fishes from Southern California. Furthermore, there appears to be an excellent association between these skeletal deformities and elevated levels of bilateral asymmetry. The latter, with statistical procedures being used. is being examined in our laboratory as a possible measure of environmental stress (40).

Again, it should be stressed that the causative mechanisms producing skeletal anomalies in these marine teleosts are unknown. If they are caused by the accumulation of toxicants, then serious research should be initiated to determine the toxicant involved, the threshold dosages, and the actual mechanisms of metabolic interference.

Finally, the mere existence in an otherwise "natural" environment of deformities such as those described here would seem to indicate that the environment is far from healthy. If abnormal individuals are not being effectively eliminated, then perhaps other serious ecological problems exist which have as yet not been discovered.

REFERENCES

1. Anas, R. E., and Wilson, A. J. Residues in fish, wildlife and estuaries. *Pestic. Monit. J. 3:* 198. 1970.
2. Bitman, J., Cecil, H. C., and Fries, G. F. DDT-induced inhibition of avian shell gland carbonic anhydrase: A mechanism for thin eggshells. *Science (Wash., D.C.) 168:* 594. 1970.

3. Burnett, R.   DDT residues: Distribution of concentrations in *Emerita analoga* (Stimpson) along coastal California. *Science (Wash., D.C.) 174:* 606. 1971.

4. California, State of.   Report of special committee on public policy regarding agricultural chemicals. State of California, Sacramento, Calif., 15 June 1960.

5. Dawson, C. E.   A bibliography of anomalies of fishes. *Gulf Res. Rep. 1:* 308. 1964.

6. Dawson, C. E.   A bibliography of anomalies of fishes. Supplement 1. *Gulf Res. Rep. 2:* 169. 1966.

7. Dawson, C. E.   A bibliography of anomalies of fishes. Supplement 2. *Gulf Res. Rep. 3(2):* 215. 1971.

8. Douglas, P. A.   Survival of some fishes recently introduced into the Salton Sea, California. *Calif. Fish Game 39:* 264. 1953.

9. Duke, T. W., and Wilson, A. J.   Chlorinated hydrocarbons in livers of fishes from the northeastern Pacific Ocean. *Pestic. Monit. J. 5:* 228. 1971.

10. Ferm, V. H., and Carpenter, S. J.   Developmental malformation from the administration of lead salts. *Exp. Mol. Pathol. 7:* 208. 1967.

11. Fimbreite, N., Fyfe, R. W., and Keith, J. A.   Mercury contamination of Canadian prairie seed-eaters and their avian predators. *Can. Field Natur. 84:* 269. 1970.

12. Frey, H. W., ed.   *California's Living Marine Resources and Their Utilization.* 148 pp. *Calif. Dep. Fish Game, Fish Bull.* 1971.

13. Gabriel, M. L.   Factors affecting the number and form of vertebrae in *Fundulus heteroclitus. J. Exp. Zool. 95:* 105. 1944.

14. Galloway, J. N.   Man's alteration of the natural geochemical cycle of selected trace metals. Ph.D. thesis, Univ. Calif., San Diego, 1972.

15. Gustafson, C. G.   PCB's—prevalent and persistent. *Environ. Sci. Technol. 4:* 814. 1970.

16. Hansen, D. J.   Vertebral anomaly in *Micropogon undulatus. Quart. J. Fla. Acad. Sci. 31:* 207. 1969.

17. Hendricks, L. J.   The striped mullet, *Mugil cephalus* Linnaeus, pp. 95–104. In *The Ecology of the Salton Sea, California, in Relation to the Sportfishery,* ed. B. W. Walker. *Calif. Dep. Fish Game, Fish Bull. 113.* 1961.

18. Hickey, C. L., Jr.   Common abnormalities in fishes, their causes and effects. *N. Y. Ocean Sci. Lab., Tech. Rep. 13.* 1972.

19. Hubbs, C.   High incidence of vertebral deformities in two natural populations of fishes inhabiting warm springs. *Ecology 40:* 154. 1959.

20. Kehoe, R. A.   The metabolism of lead in man in health and disease. *Advan. Water Poll. Res. 3:* 153. 1961.

21. Kroger, R. L., and Guthrie, J. F.   Incidence of crooked vertebral columns in juvenile Atlantic menhaden, *Brevoortia tyrannus. Chesapeake Sci. 12:* 276. 1971.

22. Lehner, P. N., and Egbert, A.   Dieldrin and eggshell thickness in ducks. *Nature (London) 224:* 1218. 1969.

23. McCaull, J.   Building a shorter life. *Environment (St. Louis) 13:* 2. 1971.

24. Minkin, C., and Jennings, J. M.   Carbonic anhydrase and bone remodeling:

Sulfonamide inhibition of bone resorption in organ culture. *Science (Wash., D.C.) 176:* 1031. 1972.

25. Mottley, C. McC. The number of vertebrae in trout (*Salmo*). *J. Biol. Board Can. 3:* 169. 1937.

26. Peakall, D. B. p,p'-DDT: Effect on calcium metabolism and concentrations of estradiol in the blood. *Science (Wash., D.C.) 168:* 592. 1970.

27. Peakall, D. B., and Lincer, J. L. Polychlorinated biphenyls, another long-life widespread chemical in the environment. *BioScience 20:* 958. 1970.

28. Pichirallo, J. PCB's: Leaks of toxic substances raises issue of effects, regulation. *Science (Wash., D.C.) 173:* 899. 1971.

29. Porter, R., and Wiemeyer, S. Dieldrin and DDT: Effects on sparrow hawk eggshells and reproduction. *Science (Wash., D.C.) 165:* 199. 1970.

30. Risebrough, R. W., Menzel, D. B., Martin, D. J., and Olcott, H. S. DDT residues in Pacific sea birds: A persistent insecticide in marine food chains. *Nature (London) 216:* 1. 1967.

31. Risebrough, R. W., Menzel, D. B., Martin, D. J., and Olcott, H. S. DDT residues in Pacific marine fish. Unpublished.

32. Schmidt, T. T., Risebrough, R. W., and Gress, R. Input of polychlorinated biphenyls into California coastal waters from urban sewage outfalls. *Bull. Environ. Contam. Toxicol. 6:* 235. 1971.

33. Sclye, H., Tuchweber, B., and Bertoc, L. Effect of lead acetate on the susceptibility of rats to bacterial endotoxins. *J. Bacteriol. 91:* 884. 1966.

34. Shaw, S. B. Chlorinated hydrocarbon pesticides in California sea otters and harbor seals. *Calif. Fish Game 57:* 290. 1971.

35. Shaw, S. B. DDT residues in eight California marine fishes. *Calif. Fish Game 58:* 22. 1972.

36. Turner, C. H. Aspects of fish deformities. Testimony presented to an emergency hearing of the House Committee on Fisheries and Oceanography, Santa Ana, Calif., 30 April 1970.

37. United States. Report of the President's Science Advisory Committee. Use of pesticides. U.S. Government Printing Office, Washington, D.C. 1963.

38. Valentine, D. W., and Bridges, K. W. High incidence of deformities in the serranid fish, *Paralabrax nebulifer*, from southern California. *Copeia 3:* 637. 1969.

39. Valentine, D. W., and Samollow, P. A snubnosed kelp bass, *Paralabrax clathratus*, from Alijos Rocks, Baja California. *Calif. Fish Game 59:* 148. 1973.

40. Valentine, D. W., Soulé, M. E., and Samollow, P. Asymmetry: A possible indicator of environmental stress. *U. S. Nat. Mar. Fish. Serv., Fish. Bull. 71:* 357. 1973.

41. Whitney, R. R. The bairdiella, *Bairdiella icistius* (Jordan and Gilbert), pp. 105–151. In *The Ecology of the Salton Sea, California, in Relation to the Sportfishery*, ed. B. W. Walker. *Calif. Dep. Fish Game, Fish Bull. 113.* 1961.

42. Wolman, A. A., and Wilson, A. J., Jr. Occurrence of pesticides in whales. *Pestic. Monit. J. 4:* 8. 1970.

43. Wunder, W. Missbildungen beim Kabeljau (*Gadus morhua*) verursacht durch Wirbelsäulenverkürzung. *Helgolaender wiss. Meeresunters. 22:* 201. 1971.

44. Young, P. H.   Some effects of sewer effluents on marine life. *Calif. Fish and Game 50:* 33. 1964.
45. Young, P. H.   The California partyboat fishery, 1947–1967. *Calif. Dep. Fish Game, Fish Bull. 145.* 91 pp. 1969.

DISCUSSION OF SKELETAL ANOMALIES IN MARINE TELEOSTS

Question: What would be the feasibility of capturing barred sand bass off Baja California, tagging them, liberating them off the coast of Southern California, and seeing what changes occur after liberation?

D. W. Valentine: The chances of releasing a tagged fish in any marine open water area and hoping to recover it four or five years later is undoubtedly very small. The barred sand bass population in Southern California is probably composed of 20 or 30 million fish, as a rough estimate. Of this number roughly half a million are taken by sport fishermen annually; the idea is, of course, feasible, but I don't think any agency would fund this type of project, given the rather small probability of success.

Question: Are barred sand bass nonmigratory and would they be found near where they are liberated?

D. W. Valentine: Barred sand bass are thought to be nonmigratory, according to the California Department of Fish and Game. If we, for instance, tagged a large number of barred sand bass near a rocky area, one of their favorite haunts, they would move toward the rock-sand ecotonal area and disperse. Unfortunately, fishermen also know of the barred sand bass's habitat preferences. Fishing pressure would, therefore, be intense and the probability of recovery of a given individual several years after release very small. This same possibility has been voiced by others but, again, I doubt whether any agency would fund this type of research.

Question: Regarding pesticide levels in tissues, do they correlate with the lesions that you find?

D. W. Valentine: The problem here is that you can, if so desired, correlate any increasing function with deformity levels. Unfortunately, correlations are not causations.

Question: You don't get any exceptions? You don't find that the fish without the lesions also have high pesticide levels?

D. W. Valentine: The basic problem you are referring to is one of a time-frame reference. The lesions obviously don't appear overnight, so that by the time you analyze deformed adults for pesticide burden it may not reflect the pesticide burden present at the time the deformities were instigated. There is a 100-fold increase in chlorinated hydrocarbon body burdens (DDT and derivatives and polychlorinated biphenyls) from Baja California to the Los Angeles area. I would say that chlorinated hydrocarbons are a chief suspect as one class of possible deformity-producing agents. Another class is the heavy metals.

Comment: A little introspective comment. Among the people who are most guilty of heavy-metal pollution are pathologists. We dump our mercurials down the sink; and we recently stopped doing this at our laboratories after the safety people made a little examination of how much was going in. They figured on the basis of the procurement figure of mercurials that something like 4000 pounds of mercury were being dumped in yearly just from our laboratories, so we have now started the habit of collecting our mercurials and putting them in a bottle and the safety people come and pick that up and take it somewhere, but we don't know where.

D. W. Valentine: Probably to the New York Bight.

Question: How far will these fish migrate?

D. W. Valentine: The longest distance that a barred sand bass has been shown to migrate was 40 miles over a two-year period. This was the longest distance recorded for all fish tagged. A reasonable estimate for the entire population is on the order of a mile or two. It is 100 miles between Los Angeles and San Diego, and these fish have been shown to be relatively nonmigratory, so I think it reasonable to use 50-mile quadrants in this type of work.

F. P. Meyer: Bill Lewis found that fluorine would produce many anomalies in fishes' gill rakers. Is there a difference in the fluoridation rate in the area that you are in and the Mexican area?

D. W. Valentine: There is probably a difference between Baja California and Southern California; Baja California is virtually uninhabited in the areas where my samples were collected. I don't know anything about fluorine concentrations in sea water. This is one possibility that I hadn't considered.

Comment: There might be one other explanation, in that there might be better survival in one geographical area than the other of fish with developmental anomalies. In many of these anatomical phenomena things like anomalies form at a very early stage. These don't happen later on in the life of a fish. The absolute numbers of anomalous fish are set at a very early stage when the egg is just developing. I think it is something that we have to keep in mind, that there are these developmental factors that change with temperature, they are temperature dependent. They also affect survival and in some areas for some reason or other you might have a better survival of deformed fish in one area than you do in another because of predatory factors, or something of this nature. I was wondering if there might be some explanation of this.

D. W. Valentine: You are talking about the survival of congenitally deformed individuals. I think my data indicate that the deformities are developmental, not congenital. Further, I can think of no mechanism that would favor the survival of deformed individuals over normal.

Comment: I admire your diligence in having dissected so many fish. I would have used an X-ray machine. There is a small do-it-yourself X-ray machine that costs about $2500 and is called a Faxitron and is widely used in human pathological laboratories to pick up calcification, say, in a surgical specimen. You don't have to invest in that equipment, you probably would have access to somebody's. What I am really asking is, did you examine histologically these bones and did you examine other organs?

D. W. Valentine: In a word, no. That is obviously the next step. I have acquired an enormous amount of beneficial input from this symposium along these lines. I knew that eventually I would have to begin histological investigations, but for a population biologist, it is getting a little far afield. I have discussed the possibility of sending properly preserved specimens to various qualified histologists for examination. Perhaps this effort can commence in the near future.

Question: I was wondering, is there a fairly good incidence of dead fish of this species washed up on the beach?

D. W. Valentine: The incidence of moribund fishes along the beaches in Southern California is very low. Any dead or dying fish would probably be rapidly consumed by predators. We have a fair number of chronically hungry sharks in Southern California that will eat virtually anything that will get in their mouths. There may be periods when massive mortalities occur, but I think that if such a die-off occurred, it would be taken care of by the ever-present large predators.

PART V
Nutritional Disease

29

Nutritional Deficiencies in Intensively Cultured Catfish

RICHARD T. LOVELL

Catfish farming is the largest freshwater fishculture industry in the United States today. An estimated 54 million pounds of catfish were harvested from intensively fed culture systems in 1970 (20); yet nutritional deficiencies have not been considered as major problems. One explanation for this is that most of the production thus far has been from "conventional" pond culture. A general description of conventional pond culture is a situation where 1500 to 2000 fingerling fish per acre are stocked in a nonflowing earthen pond, fed a commercial feed to appetite capacity, and harvested five to seven months later at an average weight of one to two pounds. In conventional pond culture the commercial feeds are supplemented by the natural food from the pond. The earlier catfish feeds were not fortified with vitamins, yet satisfactory production was achieved because the natural food supplied nutrients deficient in the processed feeds. Hastings (9) and Prather and Lovell (26) have shown that the addition of a complex, though not complete, vitamin package to feeds for pond-cultured catfish increased production by 15 and 19%, respectively. Currently, commercial catfish feeds contain a fairly sophisticated vitamin supplement, although most of them do not contain all of the vitamins necessary to make them nutritionally complete diets.

As the culture environment deviates from the conventional pond system to more intensive or artificial cultures, the availability of natural food diminishes and the nutritional adequacy of the prepared feed becomes more critical. Several types of culture systems are emerging which show practical potential for growing

721

catfish under highly concentrated conditions. There are raceways of many de-
signs with water which "flows one way" or recirculates, aeration and filtration devices for ponds, suspended cages; and the list continues. It is when fish-culturists
attempt to use the nutritionally incomplete, supplemental-type feeds to grow catfish in artificial or unconventional pond cultures that nutritional deficiencies become manifest. On numerous occasions catfish have been brought to the Cooperative Parasite and Disease Laboratory at Auburn University, Auburn, Alabama, with
disease signs but without evidence of pathogen infestation. It was usually determined that the fish came from a modified culture system with limited natural food
and were intensively fed a nutritionally incomplete diet.

VITAMINS

Deficiency signs for several nutrients have been demonstrated experimentally
in catfish. While at Auburn University, Dupree (2) demonstrated clinical deficiency signs due to lack of a number of vitamins in channel catfish fingerlings.
Later at the Warmwater Fish Cultural Laboratory of the U.S. Bureau of Sport
Fisheries and Wildlife he determined quantitative requirements for vitamins A and
E. He used purified nutrients and fed the fish in aquaria with flowing water. Table
29.1 summarizes his results. He was unable to demonstrate a dietary need for ascorbic acid (vitamin C), biotin, inositol, and para-aminobenzoic acid by channel
catfish fingerlings. Jewell, Schneberger, and Ross (12) demonstrated that channel
catfish required vitamin D.

A study was conducted at Auburn University in 1971 to determine the essentiality of vitamin C in high-performance diets for channel catfish grown to harvestable size with limited access to natural aquatic food (17). This investigation was
prompted by the many occasions when catfish were brought to the Cooperative
Fish Disease Laboratory with signs of nutritional deficiency. In most cases, examination of the culture system and the feed the fish had received indicated that
vitamin C might be deficient. In this experiment, 1600 channel catfish fingerlings
were stocked in 1-m^3 suspended cages at a rate of 400 fish per cage and fed intensively for 180 days. Half of the fish were fed a practical-type diet that was nutritionally sufficient except for being low in vitamin C. The others received vitamin
C supplement. At the end of the feeding period the fish receiving supplemental
vitamin C had significantly superior weight gains, feed conversion ratios, and rate
of survival. Table 29.2 compares the responses of the fish fed the two diets.
Growth response of the fish fed the vitamin C-supplemented diet was excellent,
so apparently the diet was nutritionally adequate. Mortality among the vitamin
C-deficient fish was caused primarily by infestations of *Aeromonas liquefaciens.*

Forty-five percent of the fish on the vitamin C-deficient diet had visually detectable deformities, which included scoliosis, lordosis, and depigmented areas
on the backs. In severely deformed fish the vertebral column was separated or
severely eroded, with pronounced atrophy of the spinal cord. In less severely de-

Table 29.1. Responses of Channel Catfish Fingerlings to Purified Diets
Deficient in Various Vitamins[a]

Vitamins tested	Deficiency signs	Requirement (per kg diet)
Pyridoxine	Erratic swimming, tetany, reduced growth, mortality	n.d.[b]
Panthothenic acid	"Flabby" body tissues, "mummy-textured" skin, mucus on gills, clubbed gills, erosion of lower jaw and fins, reduced growth, mortality	n.d.
Riboflavin	Opaque lens of eye, reduced growth, mortality	n.d.
Thiamine	Reduced growth, lethargy, poor equilibrium	n.d.
Folic acid	Lethargy, reduced food consumption, reduced growth, mortality	n.d.
Nicotinic acid	Tetany, reduced growth, lethargy, mortality	n.d.
B_{12}	Reduced weight gain	n.d.
Choline	Hemorrhagic areas in kidney, enlarged liver, reduced growth	n.d.
A	Reduced weight gain, protruding and opaque eyes, fluid in body cavity, mortality	1,000-2,000 units as vitamin A acetate
K	Hemorrhages on body surface	n.d.
E	Mortality, reduced growth, lethargy, reduced pigmentation, fluid in body cavity	30 IU
C	None	–
Biotin	None	–
Inositol	None	–
Para-aminobenzoic acid	None	–

[a] From Dupree (2, 3, 4).
[b] n.d. means not determined.

formed fish there were enlarged, spongy vertebrae, and hemivertebrae were often found. Many fish had internal hemorrhagic areas along the spinal column but appeared normal externally. Figures 29.1 and 29.2 show a photograph and radiographs of catfish with deformed spinal columns.

None of the fish had swimming irregularities or tetany. Histological examination of gill filaments indicated normal development. No external lesions could be attributed to diet and no tissue damage, other than areas along the spinal column, was detected by visual examination. Liver, anterior kidney, and blood analyses all reflected the differences in content of vitamin C in the diet.

Monthly sampling indicated that differences in weight or physical conformation between fish fed the two diets were not manifested until after the 12th week of the feeding period, or until the fish weighed 100 to 180 grams.

Studies by Japanese workers (11) showed that carp can synthesize ascorbic

Table 29.2. Weight Gain, Feed Conversion Ratio (g feed/g gain), Survival and
Body Deformation in Caged Channel Catfish Fed Diets with or without
Supplemental Vitamin C for 180 Days

Supplemental vitamin C	Average wt gain (g)	Feed conversion ratio	Survival (%)	Deformed fish (%)
Yes	531.2	1.29	98.0	3.9
No	331.4	1.88	77.8	45.0

Fig. 29.1. Top. Channel catfish weighing approximately 400 grams fed a vitamin C-deficient diet for 180 days, showing scoliosis and lordosis.

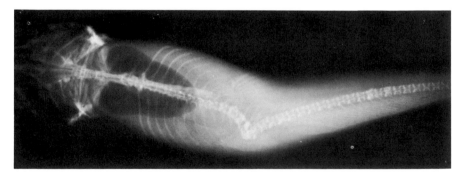

Fig. 29.2. Radiograph of channel catfish weighing approximately 400 grams fed a vitamin C-deficient diet for 180 days, showing severe dislocation of spinal column.

acid but not in quantities sufficient to support rapid growth. This is probably
the situation with channel catfish. Dupree (2) did not demonstrate a vitamin C
deficiency in channel catfish fingerlings, perhaps because the fish in his study did
not grow as rapidly under the artificial conditions as those fed the practical-type
diets in cages.

Spinal damage in fish has been reported from other causes. Vitamin E deficiency in diets of carp caused lordosis (30). Trout fed tryptophan-free diets developed spinal deformities (6). Exposure to sublethal levels of pesticides caused vertebral injuries in golden shiners (22), and bullheads (23). Primbs and Sinnhuber
(27) presented data in support of their contention that excessive levels of vitamin
A in diets of young trout interfere with vitamin C metabolism, thus creating the
need for dietary supplementation of the vitamin.

MINERALS

Mineral deficiencies in practical catfish culture have not been identified as a
problem; however, when diets containing low quantities of animal by-products
with no mineral supplements are fed intensively to catfish, mineral deficiencies
could possibly occur. Fish absorb minerals dissolved in the water as well as those
of dietary origin. This has been demonstrated in trout at the Cortland Fish Hatchery Laboratory, Cortland, New York (25). Dissolved phosphorus was not absorbed as effectively as calcium from the water (24). Dietary calcium deficiency
probably is not as much of a potential problem as is phosphorus deficiency because of the relatively high concentration of dissolved calcium in most water and

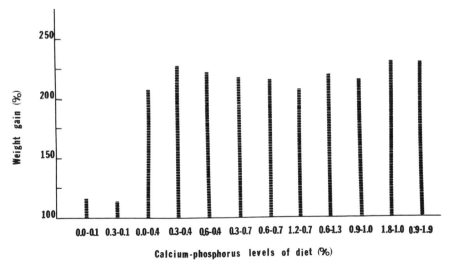

Fig. 29.3. Weight increases of channel catfish fingerlings in a controlled aquatic environment
fed semipurified diets containing a wide range of percentages of calcium and phosphorus.

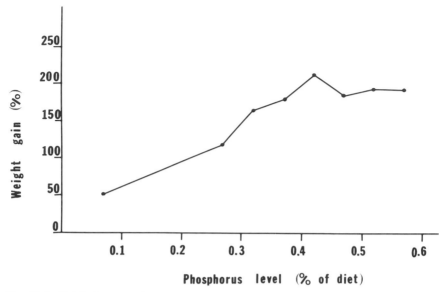

Fig. 29.4. Weight increase of channel catfish fingerlings in a controlled aquatic environment fed semipurified diets containing various percentages of phosphorus.

the relative ease with which it is absorbed by fish to meet metabolic needs.

Dietary calcium and phosphorus requirements for channel catfish fingerlings were studied by Lovell (15), in controlled environments with highly purified diets. A series of 10- and 12-week feeding trials was conducted in water at 27°C which contained 14 ppm of calcium ion and 2.6 ppm of phosphorus. Figure 29.3 shows that addition of calcium to the diet made very little difference in growth rate of the fish; however, increasing the phosphorus level from 0.2 to 0.4% of the diet made a dramatic improvement in growth rate. A subsequent study was conducted to refine the knowledge regarding phosphorus of channel catfish. Figure 29.4 indicates that the minimum percentage of phosphorus in the diet for satisfactory growth appears to be slightly above 0.4. Gross examination of the fish revealed no signs of phosphorus deficiency other than decreased growth rate and increased mortality. A study is in progress to determine minimum phosphorus requirements in practical feeds for catfish grown to harvestable size.

ESSENTIAL FATTY ACIDS

Experiments on essential fatty acid requirements of trout have revealed a need for omega-3 fatty acids or the linolenic series instead of the omega-6 or linoleic series which is required by warm-blooded animals (1, 13). Specific fatty acid requirements of channel catfish have not been delineated; however, Dupree (5) and Lovell (16) found that the substitution of marine fish oils, which contain relatively high amounts of omega-3 fatty acids, for plant oils in catfish diets improved growth rates of the fish. Conversely, Stickney and Andrews (28) found that beef tallow triglycerides, which contained no omega-3 fatty acids, provided as much growth as an equal amount of menhaden oil triglyceride and more growth than several plant triglycerides in channel catfish diets. They also presented data to indicate that the omega-3 or linolenic series had no unique nutritional importance to catfish (29).

The available data are inconclusive on specific fatty acid requirements of channel catfish, although essential fatty acids probably play an important role in catfish nutrition. Commercial catfish feeds usually contain a minimum of 12% fishmeal, plus additional animal by-products, which probably insures them against serious fatty acid deficiencies.

PROTEIN

Channel catfish have essential amino acid requirements that are qualitatively similar to the rat and to salmonid fish. Dupree and Halver (7) found that fingerling channel catfish fed diets deficient in either arginine, histidine, leucine, isoleucine, lysine, methionine, phenylalanine, threonine, tryptophan, or valine failed to grow until the limiting amino acids were added to the diet. Quantitative requirements of essential amino acids have been determined for salmonids but only lysine has been tentatively evaluated for catfish. Dupree (3) reported the minimum lysine requirements, in a 30% protein diet, to be between 1.25 and 1.75% of the total diet. A feeding trial conducted at Auburn University indicated that 1.37% was the minimum level of lysine for channel catfish fingerlings (14).

Dietary protein requirements of channel catfish are much higher than those of warm-blooded animals. Hastings and Dupree (10) fed channel catfish practical-type diets containing 10 to 50% protein in aquaria and in conventional pond culture. In aquaria growth increased linearly with protein up to 40% dietary protein, but in ponds where the fish had access to natural aquatic food, weight gains were linear with protein levels up to about 28%. The fish on the 10% protein diet actually lost weight in the aquaria and those on the 25% protein diet gained only 12.8% as much as those on the 40% protein diet. Lovell (18) found that channel catfish grown from fingerlings to harvestable size in suspended cages, where access to natural food is negligible, had maximum weight gains from practical-type diets containing 40% protein. Commercial catfish feeds for conventional pond culture contain from 25 to 33% protein. Protein levels for catfish in unconventional cultures without natural food should probably contain 35 to 40% protein.

Adverse effects of amino acid imbalance or protein excess in catfish have not been studied in depth. One hazard that fish-culturists may be confronted with, which terrestrial animal feeders aren't, is the possibility of unabsorbed dietary nitrogen causing ammonia toxicity. Digested protein which is not synthesized into body protein by catfish is excreted primarily as ammonia into the water. In several types of intensive catfish culture, ammonia accumulation in the water is the primary factor that limits the productive capacity of the system.

CONCLUSION

The nutritional needs of catfish are similar to those of higher animals. Demonstrated exceptions are the higher quantitative protein requirement, the dietary need for vitamin C, the use of dissolved minerals, and possibly the essentiality of specific fatty acids.

REFERENCES

1. Castell, J. D., Sinnhuber, R. O., Lee, D. J., and Wales, J. H.   Essential fatty acids in the diet of rainbow trout: Physiological symptoms of EFA deficiency. *J. Nutr. 102:* 87. 1972.

2. Dupree, H. K.   Vitamins essential for growth of channel catfish. *U. S. Bur. Sport Fish. Wildlife, Tech. Pap. 7.* 12 pp. 1966.

3. Dupree, H. K.   Vitamin E requirement of channel catfish, pp. 220–221. In *Progress in Sport Fisheries Research 1968. U. S. Bur. Sport Fish. Wildlife, Resour. Publ. 77.* 1969.

4. Dupree, H. K.   Dietary requirement of vitamin A acetate and beta carotene, pp. 148–149. In *Progress in Sport Fisheries Research 1969. U. S. Bur. Sport Fish. Wildlife, Resour. Publ. 88.* 1970.

5. Dupree, H. K.   Fish oil and corn oil in the diet of channel catfish, pp. 191–192. In *Progress in Sport Fisheries Research 1970. U. S. Bur. Sport Fish. Wildlife.* 1970.

6. Dupree, H. K.   Lysine requirement of channel catfish. In *Progress in Sport Fisheries Research. U. S. Bur. Sport Fish. Wildlife, Resour. Publ. 107.* 1970.

7. Dupree, H. K., and Halver, J. E.   Amino acids essential for growth of channel catfish. *Trans. Amer. Fish. Soc. 99:* 90. 1970.

8. Halver, J. E., and Shanks, W. E.   The nutrition of salmonid fishes. VIII. Indispensable amino acids for sockeye salmon. *J. Nutr. 72:* 340. 1960.

9. Hastings, W. H.   Formula feeds for channel catfish. *Progr. Fish-Cult. 31*(4): 187. 1969.

10. Hastings, W. H., and Dupree, H. K.   Practical diets for channel catfish, pp. 190–191. In *Progress in Sport Fisheries Research 1969. U. S. Bur. Sport Fish. Wildlife, Resour. Publ. 77.* 1969.

11. Ikeda, S., and Sato, M.   Biochemical studies on L-ascorbic acid synthesis by carp. *Bull. Jap. Soc. Sci. Fish. 30:* 365. 1964.

12. Jewell, M. E., Schneberger, E., and Ross, J. A.   The vitamin requirements of goldfish and channel catfish. *Trans. Amer. Fish. Soc. 63:* 338. 1933.

13. Lee, D. J., Roehm, J. N., Yu, T. C., and Sinnhuber, R. O.   Effect of omega-3 fatty acids on the growth rate of rainbow trout. *J. Nutr. 92:* 93. 1967.

14. Lovell, R. T.   Quantitative requirement of lysine in semipurified diet for channel catfish. *Auburn Univ. Agr. Exp. Sta., Fish. Res. Annu. Rep.* vol. 1, pt. 1. 1969.

15. Lovell, R. T.   Dietary calcium and phosphorus requirements of channel catfish fingerlings fed semipurified diets in controlled water. *Auburn Univ. Agr. Exp. Sta., Fish. Res. Annu. Rep.* vol. 1, pt. 1. 1970.

16. Lovell, R. T.   Catfish waste in practical diets for catfish. *Auburn Univ. Agr. Exp. Sta., Fish. Res. Annu. Rep.* vol. 1, pt. 1. 1971.

17. Lovell, R. T.   Essentiality of vitamin C in feeds for intensively fed caged channel catfish. *J. Nutr. 103:* 134. 1973.

18. Lovell, R. T.   Protein requirements of cage-cultured channel catfish. *Proc. Annu. Conf. Southeast. Ass. Game Fish Comm. 26.* Accepted for publication in 1973.

19. McCann, J. A., and Jasper, R. L.   Vertebral damage to bluegills exposed to acutely toxic levels of pesticides. *Trans. Amer. Fish. Soc. 101:* 317. 1972.

20. Madewell, C. E.   Historical development of catfish farming, pp. 7–14.   In *Producing and Marketing Catfish in Tennessee Valley. Tenn. Valley Author. Bull. Y-38.* 1971.

21. Matton, P., and LaHam, Q. N.   Effect of the organophosphate Dylox on rainbow trout larvae. *J. Fish. Res. Board Can. 26:* 2193. 1969.

22. Meyer, F. P.   A new control for the anchor parasite, *Lernea cyprinacea. Progr. Fish-Cult. 28:* 33. 1966.

23. Mount, D. I., and Boyle, H. W.   Parathion-use of blood concentration to diagnose mortality of fish. *Environ. Sci. Technol. 3:* 1183. 1969.

24. Phillips, A. M., Jr., Lovelace, F. E., Brockway, D. R., and Balzer, G. C.   Cortland hatchery report 22 for the year 1953. *N. Y. Conserv. Dep., Fish. Res. Bull. 17.* 1953.

25. Phillips, A. M., Jr., Podoliak, H. A., Brockway, D. R., and Balzer, G. C.   Cortland hatchery report 26 for the year 1956. *N. Y. Conserv. Dep., Fish. Res. Bull. 21.* 1956.

26. Prather, E. E., and Lovell, R. T.   Effect of vitamin fortification of Auburn No. 2 fish feed. *Proc. Annu. Conf. Southeast. Ass. Game Fish Comm. 25:* 479. 1971.

27. Primbs, E. R. J., and Sinnhuber, R. O.   Evidence for non-essentiality of ascorbic acid in the diet of rainbow trout. *Progr. Fish-Cult. 33*(3): 141. 1971.

28. Stickney, R. R., and Andrews, J. W.   Combined effects of dietary lipids and environmental temperature on growth, metabolism and body composition of channel catfish. *J. Nutr. 101:* 1703. 1971.

29. Stickney, R. R., and Andrews, J. W.   Effects of dietary lipids on growth, food conversion, lipid and fatty acid composition of channel catfish. *J. Nutr. 102:* 249. 1972.

30. Watanabe, T., Takashima, F., Ogina, C., and Hibuja, T.   Requirements of young carp for alpha-tocopherol. *Bull. Jap. Soc. Sci. Fish. 36*(9): 972. 1970.

DISCUSSION OF NUTRITIONAL DEFICIENCIES IN INTENSIVELY CULTURED CATFISH

R. E. Wolke: What happens if we feed an excess of phosphorus to fish, and what about hypervitaminosis?

R. T. Lovell: These are among the questions yet to be answered.

W. E. Ribelin: A comment and then a question. In one of the radiographs you showed, your comments were directed at the irregular spacing between the vertebrae in vitamin C deficiency, but I was also impressed with what appeared to be a series of exostoses on the transverse processes of the vertebrae. To my knowledge, the occurrence of exostoses in the absence of other changes has not been described in vitamin C deficiency in fish, and I wondered if this was merely my imagination or if this was really a true occurrence. There are areas of the world in which exostoses occur in rather epidemic form, for example in barbels in the Mosel River, and I think it has been described in the North Sea. If it can be related to some cause of this sort we would at least be on our way to an explanation. Were these really exostoses or was it something else?

R. T. Lovell: We have no evidence that this was what it was. We removed the flesh from some of the fish and found only hemorrhages in the area you describe.

K. Balogh: May I make a comment regarding this question? In human pathology as well as in animals if you have vitamin C deficiency you get periosteal new bone formation—reactive new bone formation. It's very common in children and in older people who are on a vitamin C-deficient diet to get this kind of new bone formation, and I don't think it is a neoplasm or exostosis, it just doesn't look that way to me. It looks very much like old hemorrhage.

Comment: That is what I thought it was too. I was going to ask the same question. I think it is probably subperiosteal hemorrhage. It shows my ignorance about the way bone is developed in the fish, but in that particular area is it a cartilaginous or a bony area?

R. T. Lovell: Which area are you talking about, the vertebral column or the transverse processes?

Comment: The vertebral column where the ribs join the vertebrae; we think if they are going to grow that this would be the point at which the cartilage would proliferate.

R. T. Lovell: There is cartilage in the area to which you refer. There is also bone development in this area in a growing fish such as the one in the radiograph. Collagen or cartilage forms the basis for the skeleton of teleost fishes.

W. E. Ribelin: The situations in which I have seen most of the exostoses have been on these transverse processes in the red snapper, and in these fish the processes are bony. Also I would like to direct a question at any one of the three previous speakers or anyone else in the audience who would like to tackle it. That is, other than simple starvation, what nutritional deficiencies have been recognized in wild fishes?

R. T. Lovell: When you study nutritional deficiencies in fish you have a unique animal because fish will live for a long time at zero intake of nutrients. Quite often when we stock fish in the spring we have fish left over, or perhaps we are holding a few in reserve, and we place them in a cage or raceway and inadvertently feed them absolutely nothing. I have observed, even in the summer, fish fed absolutely nothing living for several months, and they even seem to be fairly resistant to disease. On several occasions we have held fish over the winter in raceways without feeding and they survive. In fish the stress of growth is quite important in demonstrating nutrient deficiencies. I have never examined wild fish so I really don't know what nutritional deficiencies may be recognized. Of course the diet of wild fish is pretty much carnivorous, and you have in live aquatic prey a pretty good blend of the essential nutrients.

L. M. Ashley: In this connection I think it would be interesting to refer to the experiments done by Norman Reiners of the High Sierra Aquatic Experiment Station in California. He planted, more than 20 years ago, some brook trout fry in a small mountain lake at a little more than 11,000 feet elevation. Each year he collected samples from that population. The lake had previously had no fish in it, and these fish had very little to eat other than a few insect nymphs and larvae and they were pretty well starved most of the time. After 18 to 20 years, these fish averaged about six inches in length and still lived. They apparently had never spawned successfully and I examined tissues from many of these old brook trout. The ovary and testis usually were somewhat atrophic. Dr. Reiners did recover some live ones and packed them in a backpack of water down the mountain to his laboratory at 7,000 feet elevation. He got them to eat brine shrimp and was able to spawn one of the females with hatchery males. The lake males were sterile, apparently, and the attempts to spawn this one female with hatchery males were mostly unsuccessful. There were no normal viable fish hatched. I thought that was rather interesting as an example of starved fish. They lived all right, but they didn't grow.

J. M. King: I have to agree with Dr. Ribelin in this lesion underneath the bone. Blood is not radiopaque; therefore it wouldn't have shown up if it were just blood. Any bone that forms in an area of blood or whatever else outside of the pre-existing bone as an inflammatory response or response to injury should be called an exostosis.

30

Intestinal Histology of *Fundulus heteroclitus* with Observations on the Effects of Starvation

ROBERT H. CIULLO

Although basically similar to that of the higher vertebrates, the digestive tract of the teleost is generally simpler. The works of previous investigators on the morphology and physiology of the alimentary canal support this view (4). Through the years, the cyprinodontiform fish *Fundulus heteroclitus* (common mummichog) has been used as an experimental animal in biology, particularly in pharmacology, embryology, and physiology. Therefore, it is surprising to find few references to the anatomy and histology of the digestive system. The complete absence of a stomach in the mummichog, both structurally and physiologically, was clearly demonstrated by Babkin and Bowie (1). This study was essentially a physiological investigation, and little histological information was provided. Other common teleosts which lack a stomach are carp, goldfish, molly, mosquitofish, and guppy.

F. heteroclitus is recognized for its ready availability and universal presence in suitable habitats along the coast of North America from the Gulf of St. Lawrence to the Mantanzan River in northeastern Florida. The present study is concerned with the histology of the digestive tube of this fish and the effects of starvation on the histological pattern of this portion of the alimentary tract.

Fish were collected by a minnow trap from a tidal saltwater marsh area of Great Bay, New Hampshire, and transported to a marine cold room and maintained in an aerated aquarium containing 50% sea water at a temperature of 12°C. Small populations of male and female fish were maintained as needed under the following conditions: (1) 48 hours without feeding were allowed for clearing of the gut lumen: these 2-day starved fish represent the normal fish; (2) starvation for periods of four, six, and eight days prior to being killed: the sequence of two, four, six, and eight days of starvation constitutes the starved-fish series referred to in this paper. Over 90 fish were used for this study.

The fish used ranged from 65 to 85 mm in total length. Each fish was killed by severing the vertebral column just back of the skull. A dorsolateral incision was made on one side from the upper edge of the operculum to behind the anus. This approach exposed the digestive tract from the mouth to the anus. The digestive tube, which includes that region from the esophagus to the rectum, was then removed. The digestive tube was divided into three sections. The first section contained the esophagus, the transition zone, and the anterior intestine. The second section comprised the middle intestine. The third section contained the posterior intestine and the rectum. Each of the three sections was immediately dropped into ice-cold fixative.

Tissue processing involved the fixation of the series of intestinal sections in each of the following fixatives: Bouin's, 10% neutral buffered formalin (NBF), Helly's, 85% ethyl alcohol, and 1% formalin-calcium. Appropriate washing was used for each fixative. A typical paraffin-embedding technique was employed for the first four fixatives and the digestive tube was sectioned serially (7 microns) in cross section on a rotary microtome. The intestinal sections fixed in 1% formalin-calcium were sectioned (10 to 25 microns) in cross section on a clinical freezing microtome.

Following appropriate fixation, embedding, and sectioning, a number of different histological and histochemical techniques were employed. The histological staining techniques included Ehrlich's hematoxylin and eosin, safranin and fast green, Gomori's trichrome, Mallory's phosphotungstic acid hematoxylin (MPH).

Histochemical procedures employed: buffered azure-eosinate as outlined by Lillie (19), periodic acid-Schiff (PAS) for polysaccharides (13), alcian blue for acid mucopolysaccharides as outlined by Barka and Anderson (3), aldehyde-fuchsin as modified by Cameron and Steele (11), and Baker's acid hematin test for phospholipids (13). Alkaline phosphatase distribution was determined using a modified Gomori technique (7, 8). Oil red O was used for lipids as outlined in Humason (15).

NORMAL STRUCTURE OF THE DIGESTIVE TUBE

The digestive tube of *F. heteroclitus* exhibits basic histological similarities and topographically distinctive regions. It is essential that the basic histology of the digestive tube be considered in detail first; this histological information forms the basis for consideration of the effects of starvation on this region. Of the fish examined, the 2-day starved fish are more consistent in this respect from fish to fish. Consequently, these fish are used as the normal fish for the description of the histological composition of the esophagus, transition zone, intestine, and rectum.

The external morphology of the digestive tube reveals a remarkably short esophagus that originates at the posterior end of the pharynx and joins the intestine at its anterior end. There is no distinct external line of demarcation at the junction of the esophagus with the intestine, but a narrow transition zone microscopically is present here. Three sections are present, as listed previously.

The anterior region of the first intestinal section displays a noticeable swelling, which is very evident in well-fed fish. Nevertheless, there is no distinct intestinal bulb as has been reported for some other stomachless fishes. This section tapers as it proceeds posteriorly, dorsally, and slightly to the left. The posterior end of the section forms a loop around the posterior end of the liver. It then extends anteriorly and dorsally along the left aspect of the visceral cavity to form the second intestinal section. This section forms a sharp ventrally directed loop at the level of the postesophageal region. It then extends posteriorly as a straight tube to the anus, to form the third intestinal section. There is a discernible external indentation between the posterior end of the intestine and the anterior end of the rectum.

The internal morphology of the digestive tube reveals an esophagus that exhibits distinct, straight, longitudinal folds which extend its entire length. These folds increase in height towards the brief transition zone, from their anterior origin with the pharyngeal mucosa. The longitudinal folds end abruptly at the beginning of the transition zone. The esophageal folds are thin, moderate in height, and display a broad ribbon-like form.

In the brief transition zone, the mucosal folds are thinner, higher, and show a narrower form. These folds produce a distinct zone between the esophagus and the intestine. The longitudinal pattern of the folds in the esophagus is continuous with the folds of this zone, but changes abruptly to an irregular winding pattern.

The folds of the transition zone are continuous with the mucosal folds of the anterior intestine. Here, the folds are broader and show a compact zigzag pattern. This pattern is found in about one-quarter of the anterior intestine. The folds in the remaining portion of the anterior intestine are shorter and exhibit a winding, but less zigzag pattern. The form and pattern of the folds in this region continue throughout the middle and posterior intestine. However, in the posterior intestine the folds become thicker, broader, and more plate-like, and gradually become oriented in a longitudinal direction toward the ileo-rectal junction. At the junction of the posterior intestine with the rectum, there is a band of thick and broad mucosal folds which constitute a distinct zone of demarcation between these two regions.

The rectal mucosa is thrown into pyramidal-shaped folds which are longitudinally oriented. The folds are thick, moderately high, and broad in form. In the anal region, the pattern of the mucosal folds becomes more irregular.

Esophagus

Mucosa. A large number (40 to 46) of distinct longitudinal folds extend the entire length of the esophagus (Fig. 30.1). A differentiation exists between major and minor folds. The mucosa is lined with a type of stratified epithelium. Two basic cell types are present in this epithelial layer: the basal and superficial epithelial cell, and the saccular mucous cell. In addition to the epithelial cell types, lymphocytic wandering cells and granular cells are present in varying numbers. Rodlet cells, such as those to be described for the intestine and the rectum, are not found in the esophagus.

The basal epithelial cells are small, polygonal in shape and tightly packed together (Fig. 30.2). The cell boundaries are not clearly visible in most cases. The cytoplasm is lightly granular and characteristically basophilic. The nuclei of these cells are oval to angular in shape and relatively large. The nucleus contains an irregular chromatin network, but no distinct nucleolus is visible.

The superficial epithelial cells are present in many regions of the epithelium. In most regions, these cells are flattened upon the surface of the saccular mucous cells. The cell boundaries are more distinct and the cytoplasm less basophilic than those of the basal epithelial cells. The nuclear characteristics are similar to those of the basal cells. In some regions of the epithelium, particularly at the tips and

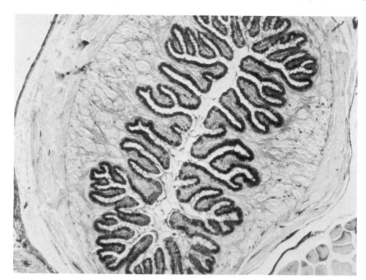

Fig. 30.1. Cross section of the esophagus. Note the arrangement of the longitudinal folds and the dark-staining mucous cells. Note also the bundles of skeletal muscle scattered throughout the submucosa. NBF, PAS; X40.

the sides of the large folds, the superficial epithelial cells are enlarged and bulge out into the lumen.

The most prominent and distinctive feature of the epithelium is the presence of numerous large saccular mucous cells. These cells are abundant at the base and on the sides of the larger mucosal folds, but are fewer in number at the tips of the folds. Many of the smaller folds show the tips covered with mucous cells (Fig. 30.3). In some regions of the epithelium, the outer membrane of the mucous cells is directly exposed to the lumen of the esophagus. However, in most regions the mucous cells are capped by flattened superficial epithelial cells. The mucous cells disappear suddenly and completely at the transition zone (Fig. 30.4). A few granular cells are found scattered throughout the epithelium.

Many of the mucous cells occupy almost the entire thickness of the epithelium. The compactness of the basal epithelial cells and the flattening of the superficial ones are due to the large size of the mucous cells, as well as to their abundance. The characteristic size and shape of these cells is markedly different from the typical goblet cells of the epithelium in the transition zone, the intestine, or the rectum. A flattened crescent-shaped nucleus is pressed against the cell boundary at the base of the mucous cell. The nucleus shows a dense-staining chromatin material. The mucus of these cells stains intensely with alcian blue and aldehyde fuchsin; it is also PAS-positive.

The epithelium rests upon a thin but prominent basement membrane. This basement lamina is composed chiefly of collagenous connective tissue fibers. Interspersed among these fibers are a few markedly flattened fibroblasts and elastic

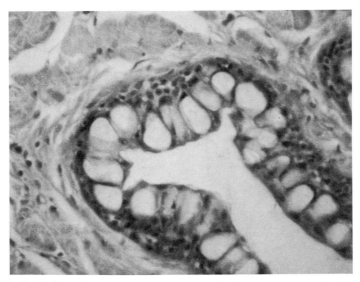

Fig. 30.2. Epithelium of the esophagus at the base of a fold. Note the small, dark-staining basal cells and the large saccular mucous cells. NBF, hematoxylin and eosin; ×400.

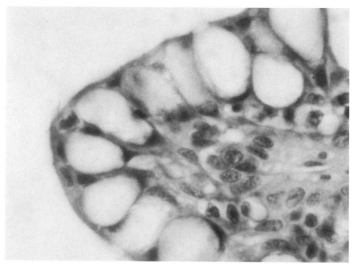

Fig. 30.3. View of the tip of an esophageal fold. Note the mucous cells covering the tip of the fold and the flattened crescent-shaped nucleus at the base of these cells. NBF, hematoxylin and eosin; ×1000.

Fig. 30.4. Junction of the esophagus and the transition zone. Note the sudden disappearance of the mucous cells and their complete absence in the epithelium of the transition zone. Note also the presence of a few goblet cells in the transitional zone epithelium. Helly's, trichrome; ×400.

fibers. The basement membrane stains clearly with fast green, aldehyde fuchsin, trichrome, and in hematoxylin and eosin preparations; it is distinctly PAS-positive.

With the exception of the granular cells, no alkaline phosphatase activity is detectable in the esophageal epithelium of the starved-fish series (Fig. 30.5).

The epithelium of the esophagus is devoid of neutral lipids, except for a few lipid droplets scattered throughout it (Table 30.1). The numerous large, saccular, mucous cells of the epithelium are visible as nonstained clear areas (Fig. 30.6).

The esophagus in the starved-fish series has a limited phospholipid reaction: the nuclei of the saccular mucous cells, the vascular and nervous elements, and the granules of the granular cells. What appear to be positive phospholipid granules of varying sizes are scattered throughout the cytoplasm of the epithelial cells in this region (Fig. 30.7).

Submucosa. The submucosa includes neither a stratum compactum nor a muscularis mucosae and is basically similar to that of the transition zone, the intestine, and the rectum. In the esophagus, irregularly arranged bundles of skeletal muscle are scattered throughout the connective tissue of the submucosa, in the core and at the base of the mucosal folds (Fig. 30.1). The bundles of skeletal muscle increase in number and become oriented in a longitudinal direction as the circular layer of the muscularis is approached. This is evident particularly on the lateral aspects of the esophagus. It is very difficult to distinguish a definite layer of longitudinal skeletal muscle because of the presence of a considerable amount of connective tissue. Therefore, the bundles of skeletal muscle are included as a component of the submucosa. A few granular cells are found in the subepithelial region of the submucosa.

Intense alkaline phosphatase reaction is present throughout the submucosa of the esophagus in the 2- and 4-day starved fish (Fig. 30.5). A reduction in this enzymatic activity occurs in the 6- and 8-day starved fish (Fig. 30.8).

In distinct contrast to the epithelium, the underlying connective tissue of the submucosa is heavily laden with neutral lipid substances. This is particularly true within the mucosal folds and at the base of the folds. Neutral lipids are also present in both heavy and light concentrations in the connective tissue which surrounds the scattered bundles of striated muscle fibers in the submucosa. The neutral lipids of the submucosa are diffuse in appearance due to the presence of masses of minute lipid droplets (Table 30.1).

Muscularis. With the longitudinal skeletal muscle as a component of the submucosa, the muscularis is composed of a single relatively thick layer of circular muscle. This skeletal muscle layer is interspersed with a small amount of connective tissue. The individual muscle fibers are of varying width, but tend to be narrow.

A very light concentration of neutral lipids is noted in the fine connective tissue between the muscle fibers.

Serosa. The esophagus is covered by an inner thin layer of areolar connective

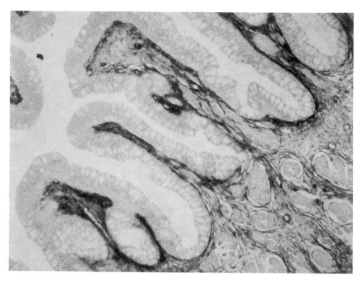

Fig. 30.5. Alkaline phosphatase reaction in the esophagus of a 2-day starved fish. Note the absence of enzyme activity in the epithelium as compared to the intense activity in the submucosa. Ethyl alcohol; X100.

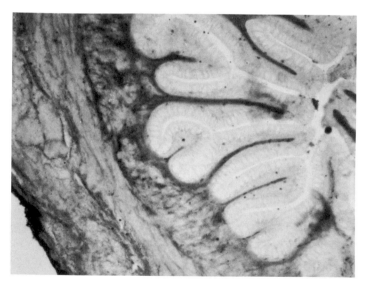

Fig. 30.6. Cross section of the esophagus showing the epithelium devoid of neutral lipids, with the exception of a few lipid droplets scattered throughout the layer. Note the non-stained mucous cells. Note also the heavy concentration of lipid substances in the submucosa. Oil red O; X100.

Table 30.1. Neutral Lipid Concentration in the Epithelium and Submucosa of the Digestive Tube of Starved Fish as Indicated by the Presence of Lipid Droplets in These Regions Following Oil Red O Technique

	Esophagus	Transition zone	Anterior intestine	Middle intestine	Posterior intestine	Rectum
Epithelium						
2-day	–	+	+++	++	+	+
4-day	–	+	+++	++	+	++
6-day	–	+	+	+	+	+
8-day	–	+	–	–	+	+
Submucosa						
2-day	+++	+++	+++	++	+	++
4-day	+++	+++	+++	++	+	++
6-day	+++	+++	++	+	+	+
8-day	+++	+++	+	+	+	+

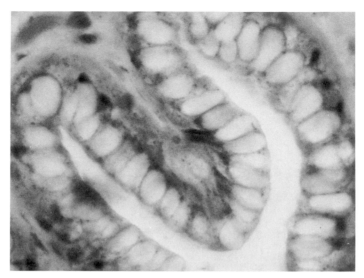

Fig. 30.7. Esophageal fold. Note the phospholipid reaction in the nuclei of the mucous cells. Note also the phospholipid granules scattered throughout the cytoplasm of the epithelial cells. Acid hematin; ×400.

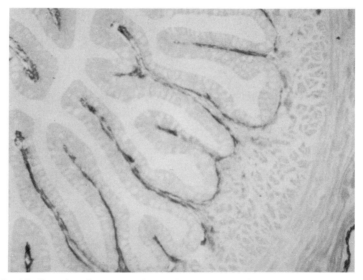

Fig. 30.8. Alkaline phosphatase reaction in the esophagus of an 8-day starved fish. Note the further reduction of enzyme activity in the submucosa. Ethyl alcohol; ×100.

tissue and an outer layer of squamous epithelium, except for the anterior portion. Here, the esophagus is attached to the surrounding tissues by fibrous connective tissue.

When present, the serosa has a light concentration of neutral lipids in its connective tissue.

Transition Zone

Mucosa. In this short region between the esophagus and the intestine, the straight longitudinal folds of the esophageal mucosa join with the more irregular mucosal folds of the intestine. The irregular pattern of mucosal folds in the transition zone gradually changes to the zigzag arrangement characteristic of the anterior intestine (Fig. 30.9). The mucosa is lined with simple columnar epithelium. Typical goblet cells are present throughout this layer, a few in the anterior portion of the transition zone and an increased concentration towards its junction with the anterior intestine. In addition to the basic epithelial columnar cells, lymphocytic wandering cells and granular cells are present in varying numbers. Rodlet cells, such as those to be described for the intestine and the rectum, are not found in the transition zone.

The columnar cells are typically cylindrical in shape. They are shorter and not tightly packed together as are the taller absorptive cells of the simple epithelium in the intestine and the rectum (Fig. 30.10). The cell boundaries are more clearly defined than in the intestinal epithelium.

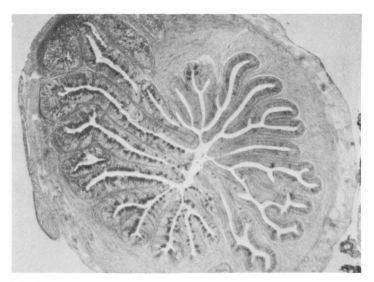

Fig. 30.9. Cross section at the junction of the anterior intestine and the transition zone. Note the irregular mucosal folds of the transition zone to the right and the arrangement of the folds of the anterior intestine to the left. Note also the dark stained goblet cells in both of these regions. NBF, PAS; ×40.

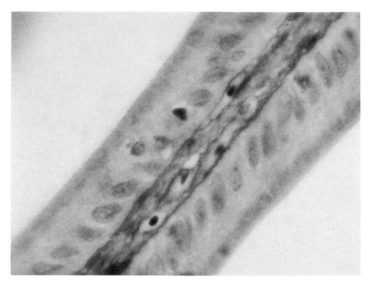

Fig. 30.10. Portion of a transition zone fold showing the simple columnar appearance of the epithelium. Note the diffuse PAS-positive material in the sub-border region of the columnar cells. NBF, PAS; ×100.

The free border of the columnar epithelium is not stained with alcian blue nor with the PAS reagent. This characteristic is in distinct contrast to the free border of the intestinal and the rectal epithelium. However, a diffuse PAS-positive reaction occurs in the sub-border region of the columnar cells and clearly differentiates it from the supranuclear region. The sub-border region also stains with aldehyde fuchsin, but not with alcian blue. The cytoplasm of the sub-border region is more heavily granulated than the supranuclear region. The cytoplasm of both regions is slightly vacuolated. The differentiation of the sub-border region from the supranuclear region in the transition zone is in contrast to the nondifferentiation of these two regions in the intestinal and rectal epithelium. The infranuclear region of the columnar cells is clearly visible. The cytoplasm is lightly granular and slightly vacuolated. The nuclei are elongated and ovoid in shape. The nuclear boundaries are distinct. One or two nucleoli are present in the finely dispersed chromatin material.

The saccular mucous cells of the esophagus are absent from the transition zone epithelium. The typical goblet cells of the intestine and the rectum are present in the epithelium, particularly as the junction of the transitional zone with the anterior intestine is approached. The change from the transition zone epithelium to that of the anterior intestine is gradual; the change from the esophageal epithelium to that of the transition zone is sudden (Fig. 30.11; see also Fig. 30.4). The goblet cells give a PAS-positive reaction; they also stain intensely with alcian blue and aldehyde fuchsin. A few granular cells are found scattered throughout

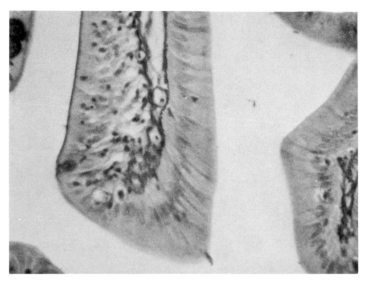

Fig. 30.11. Mucosal fold showing the junction of the transition zone and the anterior intestine. Note the gradual change from the transition zone epithelium to the right to that of the anterior intestine to the left. Note also the stained free border of the anterior intestine. NBF, PAS; ×400.

the epithelium of the transition zone. Immediately beneath the epithelium is a distinct basement membrane similar to that described for the esophagus.

With the exception of the granular cells, no alkaline phosphatase activity is detectable in the epithelium of the transition zone in the starved-fish series (Fig. 30.12).

The transition zone displays a pattern of neutral lipid distribution and concentration similar to that of the esophagus. A difference is noted in the tips of some of the mucosal folds in the starved-fish series. In these folds, moderate-to-heavy concentrations of lipid droplets of varying sizes are located at the base of the epithelial layer (Table 30.1).

The distribution of phospholipid-staining components in the transition zone in the starved-fish series is similar to that of the esophagus. In the transition zone, the phospholipid granules are mainly concentrated in the supranuclear region of the columnar cells.

Submucosa. The submucosa of the transition zone includes neither a stratum compactum nor a muscularis mucosae, and is similar to that of the esophagus. It is thicker in the region between the base of the mucosal folds and the muscularis than that of the esophagus. This thickness is due to an increase in connective tissue separating the irregularly arranged bundles of longitudinal skeletal muscle that are scattered throughout the submucosa. As the junction of the transition zone with the anterior intestine is approached, the longitudinal muscle disappears. A

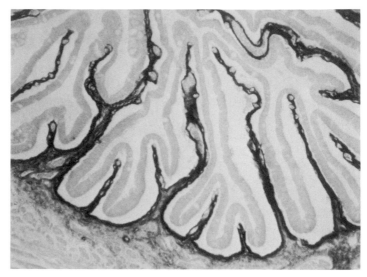

Fig. 30.12. Alkaline phosphatase reaction in the transition zone of a 2-day starved fish. Note the absence of enzyme activity in the epithelium as compared to the intense activity mainly in the subepithelial region of the submucosa. Ethyl alcohol; X100.

few granular cells are found in the submucosa. Individual skeletal muscle fibers are also present in this stratum.

Intense alkaline phosphatase activity is detectable, mainly in the subepithelial region of the submucosa, in the starved-fish series.

Muscularis. The muscularis consists of a single circular layer of skeletal muscle. This layer is continuous with the striated muscularis of the esophagus and it is present throughout the entire length of the transition zone. At the junction of the transition zone with the anterior intestine the circular layer increases in thickness. This is due to an increase in the width of the individual muscle fibers, as well as to an increase in the number of fibers. In my opinion, the increased thickening of the muscularis at this point does not constitute a muscular sphincter. If a valve-like structure does exist here, then its effect is due chiefly to the physical narrowness of the transition zone as compared to the beginning of the anterior intestine. The striated muscle fibers continue a short distance into the anterior intestine.

Serosa. A thin serosa is present in the transition zone. It consists of a very thin layer of areolar connective tissue and an outer mesothelium. The simple squamous cells of the mesothelium are thin and flattened.

Intestine and Rectum

Mucosa. In *F. heteroclitus* the arrangement, shape, form, and height of the mucosal folds present a pattern by which the three intestinal sections and the rec-

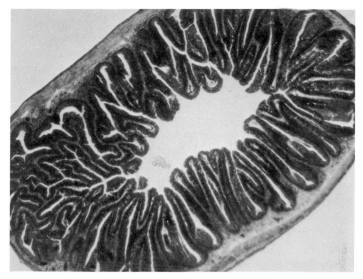

Fig. 30.13. Cross section of the anterior intestine of a 2-day starved fish. Note the complex array of mucosal folds. Bouin's, trichrome; X40.

tum can be distinguished one from the other. The mucous membrane or mucosa is thrown into clearly visible convolutional folds. The anterior intestine displays a complex array of these mucosal folds (Fig. 30.13). This pattern is less complex in the middle and posterior intestine, as is shown by the increase in luminal space between the folds (Fig. 30.14). The mucosal folds of the posterior intestine and the rectum are broader than those of the two preceding intestinal sections. The luminal surface of the epithelium commonly shows depressions lined by epithelial cells which give a notched or indented appearance to the surface of the mucosal folds. The degree to which the luminal surface of the epithelium in these regions shows pit-like depressions also aids in their recognition. More of these indentations are present in the anterior intestine than in the middle intestine. Fewer are commonly found in the posterior intestine and the rectum. They are not present in the epithelium of the esophagus nor in the transition zone. Two basic cell types are present in this epithelial layer: the absorptive or columnar cell and the goblet cell. In addition to the basic epithelial cell types, lymphocytic wandering cells, rodlet cells, and granular cells are present in varying numbers and in a patterned distribution.

The simple columnar epithelium of the transition zone is replaced in the anterior intestine by a taller and more crowded columnar epithelium. These "absorptive cells" are irregularly-shaped, cylindrical forms, wide at the luminal surface and tapering toward their base. The shape is particularly evident at the tips of the folds where the cells are not closely packed together. The sides and base

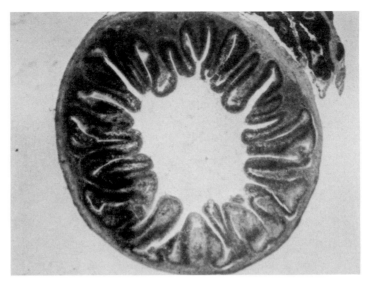

Fig. 30.14. Cross section of the posterior intestine of a 2-day starved fish. Note the less complex array of mucosal folds and the broad form of these folds. Bouin's, trichrome. X40.

of the folds are lined with closely packed columnar cells. Cell boundaries are distinctly visible at the tips and upper sides of the folds.

The free border of the absorptive cells exhibits three distinct layers: a thin superficial layer, a wide middle layer, and a narrow basal layer. In the anterior intestine the free border is clearly delimited, but it becomes thickened and its boundary with the sub-border region less distinct as the anal region is approached. The superficial layer stains intensely, the middle layer lightly and it appears striated, while the basal layer is dense in its staining quality. The free border is clearly demonstrated by staining with either hematoxylin and eosin or with fast green and safranin. The most spectacular demonstration of the free border is obtained with aldehyde fuchsin, particularly the superficial layer, which stains a deep purple. A PAS-positive reaction intensely stains all three layers of the free border, especially the superficial layer, while MPH strongly stains the basal layer. In many of the mucosal folds, MPH also intensely stains the superficial layer. This layer also stains clearly with alcian blue, especially following Helly's fixation. Gomori's trichrome differentially stains the free border green, particularly the basal layer. With the buffered azure-eosinate technique, the free border is unstained from pH 3.5 to 5.5, while at pH 6 and 6.6, it is clearly light blue.

The sub-border and supranuclear regions of the absorptive cells are not separately discernible. The cytoplasm in this area appears lightly granular and slightly vacuolated; it stains lightly in aldehyde fuchsin and in hematoxylin and safranin preparations. Trichrome decidedly stains this area green. A very light but distinct

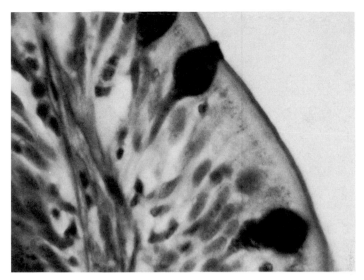

Fig. 30.15. Anterior intestinal epithelium of a 2-day starved fish. Note the band of granular PAS-positive material dividing the sub-border and supranuclear regions. Note also the PAS-positive reaction of the free border and the goblet cells. NBF, PAS; ×1000.

PAS-positive reaction is present in the cytoplasm of this area as well as in the infranuclear region. A band of granular PAS-positive material divides the sub-border and supranuclear regions, mainly in the posterior intestine and the rectum (Fig. 30.15). Buffered azure-eosinate stains this area light pink from pH 3.5 to 5.5; it is distinctly blue at pH 6 and 6.6. The infranuclear region of the absorptive cells is indistinguishable at the base, but is discernible at the sides and tips of the folds. This is due to the basal position of the absorptive cell nucleus with the concomitant reduction in the width of this region. The compactness of the absorptive cells, coupled with the presence and the distribution of nonabsorptive cells, adds a masking effect to this region. The cytoplasm of the infranuclear region is slightly vacuolated and less granular than the sub-border and supranuclear regions, but has similar staining reactions.

The nuclei of the absorptive cells are elongated and ovoid in shape. Many of the nuclei are tapered toward the basal end of the cells. The nuclear boundary is distinct. The finely dispersed chromatin granules have one or two definite clumps that represent the nucleoli. The nuclei are in a basal position at the bottom and along the sides of the folds, but are centrally located at the tips of the folds. The basal orientation of the nuclei results in a reduction in size of the infranuclear region. In the posterior intestine and in the rectum of some fish, numerous large vacuoles which represent the remains of digestive activity displace many of the nuclei toward the base of the absorptive cells, thereby completely obscuring the infranuclear region. These vacuoles are densely packed into the sub-border and supranuclear regions. Their outline is distinct and many of the cavities contain granular clusters. These vacuoles are few at the base of the folds, but gradually increase in concentration along the sides and at the tips of the folds.

Large spherical and oval cells showing various stages of mitotic activity are present in the epithelial tissue, particularly at the base of the folds. Cell boundaries are distinct. The cytoplasm is homogeneous and appears clear in some of the cells. The chromatin material is coarse and stains intensely.

Typical goblet cells become a prominent component of the intestinal and rectal epithelium, and they increase in concentration as the anal region is approached. A few goblet cells are present in the base and at the tips of the mucosal folds, whereas the major concentrations of these cells are found lining the sides of the folds. The goblet cells are sandwiched between the absorptive cells. The extrusion of mucus is visible at the apices of many cells and in the luminal space between the mucosal folds. Fully developed cells are found at all levels of the folds. Immature goblet cells are spherical in shape and appear to be restricted to the basal and lower region of the folds. The goblet cell contents stain intensely with alcian blue and aldehyde fuchsin; they are also PAS-positive.

Lymphocytic wandering cells are present in the epithelial and submucosal tissues. These cells have a typically large nucleus surrounded by a thin band of cytoplasm. The cytoplasm is basophilic and gives a slight PAS-positive reaction.

The epithelium of the intestine and the rectum rests upon a thin but distinct basement membrane similar to that described for the esophagus.

Submucosa. The epithelium of the mucosal folds rests upon a thin core of connective tissue. This single layer of connective tissue represents the lamina propria and the submucosa of the intestine of the higher vertebrates. It is a highly vascular layer composed of areolar connective tissue. Connective tissue cells, such as fibroblasts and others not specifically identified, are located in a stroma of collagenous and elastic fibers. The collagenous fibers stain green with fast green and with trichrome, and light pink in hematoxylin and eosin preparations. They are distinctly PAS-positive. The elastic fibers stain purple with aldehyde fuchsin. In addition, certain other cells, such as lymphocytic wandering cells and granular cells are present in the submucosa throughout the digestive tube. Aggregations of adipose cells are also dispersed throughout this stratum. Neither a stratum compactum nor a muscularis mucosae is present.

Muscularis. A muscularis envelops the submucosa and is present throughout the intestine and the rectum. It is composed of an inner circular and an outer longitudinal layer, both of smooth muscle. The inner layer is about twice the width of the outer layer. The smooth muscle fibers are long and relatively thick with prominent long slender tapering nuclei. The chromatin granules are scattered throughout the center of the nucleus. The smooth muscle fibers are supported in a stroma of fine collagenous and elastic connective tissue fibers. The myenteric plexus of Auerbach is present between the two muscle layers throughout most of the intestine. The presence of the ileo-rectal valve is indicated by some thickening of the inner circular layer, but the bulk of the valve core consists of connective tissue.

Serosa. The intestine and the rectum are enclosed by a serosa similar to that described for the transition zone.

CHANGES DUE TO STARVATION

Generally, the histological composition of the intestine and the rectum in the 4-, 6-, and 8-day starved fish is similar to the same regions in the fish starved for two days. A few differences are noted. In the 4-day starved fish, the anterior region of the first intestinal section continues to show a large and well-defined lumen, whereas in the posterior region of the section and in the middle and posterior intestine the lumen is very narrow and sometimes only slightly visible. Here, some of the opposite mucosal folds abut each other. The superficial layer of the free border stains clearly with alcian blue, especially following Helly's fixation. The rodlet cells and the granular cells have individual variations in concentration and distribution throughout the intestine and the rectum in the starved fish series. The large vacuoles in the posterior intestine of some of the 2-day starved fish are no longer visible. These vacuoles are not present in the posterior intestine or the rectum in either the 6-day or the 8-day starved fish. The cytoplasm in the sub-border and supranuclear regions of the absorptive cells is highly vacuolated. In the 8-day starved fish there is a heavier concentration of goblet cells in the anterior intestine than had been present in the 2-, 4-, or 6-day starved fish. The middle and posterior intestine shows no change in goblet cell concentration.

Alkaline Phosphatase

The intensity of alkaline phosphatase activity is indicated by the amount of black sulfide present in the free border and in the submucosa of the intestine and the rectum following the Gomori technique.

Data on the distribution and the intensity of phosphatase activity in these regions in the starved-fish series (Figs. 30.16, 30.17) are presented (Table 30.2).

Granular cells with markedly positive phosphatase activity are present in the epithelium of the intestine and the rectum. Fewer granular cells are noted as one follows the intestine posteriorly to the anal region. Throughout the digestive tube in these fish, the goblet cells and the rodlet cells give a negative alkaline phosphatase reaction.

Neutral Lipids

In the starved-fish series, the free border of the absorptive cells is devoid of lipids while the lipid droplets occupy the sub-border, the supranuclear, and the infranuclear regions. Lipid droplets are evident throughout the lumen of the di-

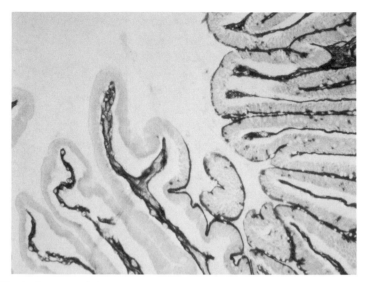

Fig. 30.16. Junction of the transition zone and the anterior intestine. Note the sudden appearance of alkaline phosphatase reaction in the free border of the intestine and the granular cells in the epithelium. Note also the intense enzyme activity in the submucosa of both regions. Ethyl alcohol; ×100.

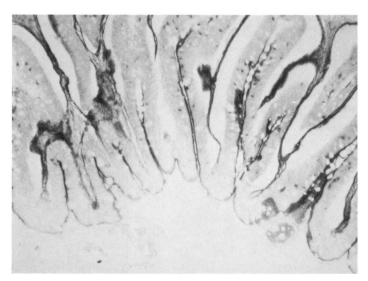

Fig. 30.17. Alkaline phosphatase reaction in the posterior portion of the middle intestine of a 6-day starved fish. Note the weak enzyme activity in the free border as compared with Figure 30.16. Ethyl alcohol; ×100.

Table 30.2. Phosphatase Activity in the Free Border and the Submucosa of the Intestine and the Rectum of Starved Fish as Indicated by the Amount of Black Sulfide Present in These Regions Following the Gomori Technique

	Anterior intestine	Middle intestine		Posterior intestine	Rectum
		Anterior	Posterior		
Free border					
Experimental					
2-day	++	++	+	+	+
4-day	++	++	+	+	+
6-day	++	+	−	+	+
8-day	++	+	+	+	+
Control	−	−	−	−	−
Submucosa					
Experimental					
2-day	++	+	+	++	+
4-day	++	+	+	++	+
6-day	++	+	+	++	+
8-day	++	+	+	++	+
Control	−	−	−	−	−

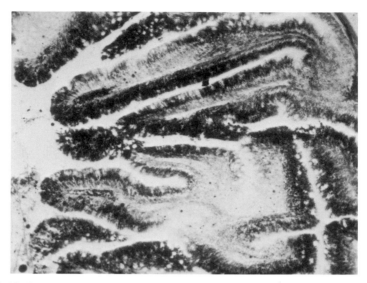

Fig. 30.18. Neutral lipid distribution and concentration in the anterior intestine of a 2-day starved fish. Note the heavy concentration of lipid droplets in the epithelium. Note also the heavy concentration of lipids in the submucosa at the tips of the folds. Oil red O. X100.

gestive tube, particularly in the intestine and the rectum. Many of them are in contact with the luminal surface of the free border. Throughout the digestive tube in these fish the goblet cells are visible as unstained clear areas.

Data on the distribution and the concentration of lipids in the epithelium and in the submucosa of the digestive tube in the starved-fish series are presented (Table 30.1).

The anterior intestine of the 2-day starved fish contains a heavy concentration of lipid droplets of varying sizes in the epithelium at the tips of the mucosal folds and at the sides of most of the folds (Fig. 30.18). The infranuclear regions of the absorptive cells become more clearly visible toward the base of the mucosal folds because of a reduction in the concentration of lipid droplets. However, even at the base of the mucosal folds the absorptive cells contain lipids in the sub-border region, and particularly in the supranuclear region of these cells.

In the tips of the mucosal folds, the submucosa of the anterior intestine contains a heavy concentration of lipids. Most of the larger lipid droplets are present in the upper part of the folds. Fewer droplets are found at the base of the mucosal folds. The lipids of the submucosa between the base of the mucosal folds and the muscularis are diffuse in appearance. The muscularis and serosa are devoid of lipids in both the anterior and the middle intestine, except for a few lipid droplets scattered throughout them. A clear line of demarcation exists between the lipids of the submucosa and the inner circular layer of the muscularis in the anterior intestine.

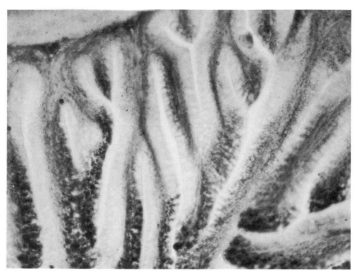

Fig. 30.19. Neutral lipid distribution and concentration in the middle intestine of a 2-day starved fish. Note the lighter concentration of lipid droplets in the epithelium as compared with Figure 30.18. Note also the lipids in the submucosa at the tips of some of the folds. Oil red O; ×100.

The middle intestine of the 2-day starved fish has a lighter concentration of lipids in the epithelium at the tips of the mucosal folds, as compared with the anterior intestine (Fig. 30.19). The epithelium at the base of some of the mucosal folds contains a light concentration of small lipid droplets. However, most of the folds are devoid of lipids in this region or they have a few large lipid droplets scattered throughout them. Most of the epithelium at the sides of the mucosal folds has a light concentration of lipids to none at all. The epithelium at the sides of some of the mucosal folds and the upper sides of others displays a heavy concentration of lipids.

The lipids in the submucosa of the middle intestine between the base of the mucosal folds and the muscularis have a diffuse appearance. The submucosa at the tips of the mucosal folds presents a heavy concentration of lipid droplets of varying sizes. A lighter concentration of smaller lipid droplets is found in the middle and at the base of the mucosal folds.

The epithelium of the mucosal folds of the posterior intestine in the 2-day starved fish is almost devoid of lipids. A light concentration of lipid droplets is found scattered throughout the tips of most of the mucosal folds (Fig. 30.20). A few droplets of varying sizes are present elsewhere throughout this layer.

In the posterior intestine, the submucosa in the tips of many of the mucosal folds contains a heavier concentration of slightly larger lipid droplets than is present in the middle and at the base of the folds. The submucosa between the base

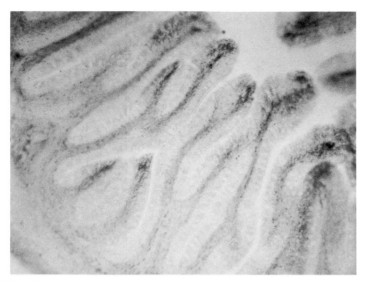

Fig. 30.20. Neutral lipid distribution and concentration in the posterior intestine of a 2-day starved fish. Note that the epithelium is almost devoid of lipids. Note also the heavy concentration of lipid droplets in the submucosa at the tips of the folds. Oil red O; ×100.

of the mucosal folds and the muscularis is similar to that of the middle intestine. The muscularis and the serosa have a very light concentration of lipids.

The rectum of the 2-day starved fish has a pattern of lipid distribution similar to that of the posterior intestine. However, only a few lipid droplets are scattered in the epithelium at the tips of the mucosal folds (Fig. 30.21). In the rectum, the submucosa at the tips of the folds and between the base of the folds and the muscularis contains a heavier concentration of lipids than is present in the posterior intestine. In the muscularis, the outer longitudinal layer has a heavy concentration of lipids. These lipids form a ragged line of demarcation between the outer and the inner layers of the muscularis.

Lipid distribution and concentration in the intestine and the rectum of the 4-day starved fish is similar to that of the 2-day starved fish. However, many of the mucosal folds of the rectum have a moderate concentration of lipids at the tips of the folds in both the epithelium and the submucosa.

The anterior intestine of the 6-day starved fish has a distinct decrease in the concentration of lipids. Only a few lipid droplets are observed scattered throughout the epithelium of the mucosal folds. At the tips of a few of the folds a light concentration of lipids is present, mostly in the sub-border and the supranuclear region of the absorptive cells. Otherwise, the absorptive cells are devoid of lipids.

The submucosa of the anterior intestine has a decrease in lipids in many of the mucosal folds from the tips of the middle of the folds, then an increase in lipid content toward the base of the mucosal folds. The lipids of the submucosa be-

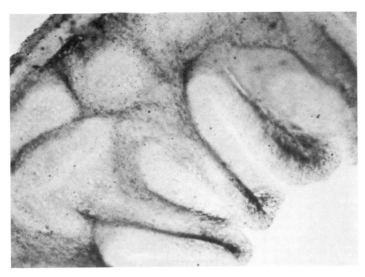

Fig. 30.21. Neutral lipid distribution and concentration in the rectum of a 2-day starved fish. Note that the epithelium is almost devoid of lipids. Note also the heavier concentration of lipid droplets in the submucosa at the tips of the folds as compared with Figure 30.20. Oil red O; ×100.

tween the base of the mucosal folds and the muscularis have a heavy diffuse appearance. A difference in the concentration of lipids is also noted in the muscularis. The inner circular layer contains a lighter concentration of lipid droplets, while the outer longitudinal layer has a heavier concentration of lipids. A few lipid droplets are observed scattered throughout the serosa.

The middle intestine of the 6-day starved fish also has a sharp decrease in the concentration of lipids. The epithelium of most of the mucosal folds is clear of lipids (Fig. 30.22). The submucosa contains a light concentration of lipids at the tips and in the middle of most of the mucosal folds. A heavier concentration of lipids is noted at the base of the folds. The muscularis and the serosa of the middle intestine are similar to those of the 2-day starved fish.

With the exception of what appears to be a lighter concentration of lipids throughout the submucosa of the posterior intestine and rectum of the 6-day starved fish, these two portions of the digestive tube are similar to those of the 2-day starved fish.

The epithelium of the anterior intestine and the middle intestine in the 8-day starved fish is devoid of lipids (Fig. 30.23). Throughout the submucosa of these regions, a very light concentration of lipids is observed. The muscularis in both intestinal sections exhibits a distribution of lipids similar to that noted for the 6-day starved fish. However, a very light concentration of lipids is present.

The posterior intestine and the rectum of the 8-day starved fish have a lipid distribution and concentration similar to that of the 6-day starved fish.

Fig. 30.22. Neutral lipid distribution and concentration in the middle intestine of a 6-day starved fish. Note the sharp decrease in the concentration of lipids as compared with Figure 30.19. Oil red O; X100.

Fig. 30.23. Neutral lipid distribution and concentration in the anterior intestine of an 8-day starved fish. Note that the epithelium is devoid of lipids. Note also that a light concentration of lipid droplets is present throughout the submucosa. Oil red O; X100.

Phospholipids

In the 2-day starved fish, the free border of the absorptive cells in the intestine and the rectum stains differentially, that is, the superficial and the basal layer are phospholipid-positive while the middle layer is negative. A negative phospholipid sub-border region displays a distinct clear zone between the free border and the supranuclear region. The most prominent display of phospholipid granules of varying sizes occurs in the supranuclear and infranuclear regions of the intestine and the rectum (Fig. 30.24). The concentration of granules is most intense beneath the sub-border region; it is gradually reduced as the nuclei are approached and then is intense again in the infranuclear region. At the base of the mucosal folds, the concentration of phospholipids in the supranuclear region is not as dense as it is along the sides and at the tips of the folds. The basal position of the nuclei at the bottom of the folds results in a size reduction of the infranuclear region and consequently a less intense concentration of phospholipid granules. The submucosa has distinct staining components: the vascular elements particularly at the tips of the folds, the nervous elements, and the granular cells. Some of the rodlet cells in the intestine and the rectum have intense phospholipid reaction.

In viewing tissue sections of comparable thickness there appears to be a reduction in the concentration of phospholipids in the supranuclear and infranuclear regions, from the anterior intestine to the anal region in the 2-day starved fish

Fig. 30.24. Portion of a mucosal fold in the anterior intestine of a 2-day starved fish. Note the prominent display of phospholipids in the supranuclear and the infranuclear regions. Note also the negative phospholipid sub-border region between the free border and the intense concentration of phospholipids in the upper portion of the supranuclear region. Acid hematin; X400.

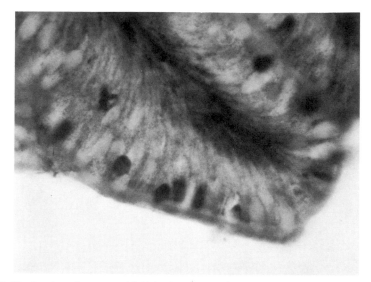

Fig. 30.25. Portion of a mucosal fold in the rectum of a 2-day starved fish. Note the reduction in the concentration of phospholipids in the supranuclear and the infranuclear regions. Note also the markedly positive phospholipid reaction of the rodlet cells in the epithelium and the vascular elements in the submucosa. Acid hematin; X400.

(Fig. 30.25). Otherwise, the middle intestine, the posterior intestine, and the rectum are similar in phospholipid distribution to the anterior intestine. There is no change in the phospholipid pattern of the intestine and the rectum in the 4-, 6-, and 8-day starved fish.

In *F. heteroclitus* the concentration of rodlet cells ranges from a few in each of the three intestinal sections and throughout the rectum to heavy concentrations in the posterior intestine. These cells were found in all the fish examined and they appear to be most abundant in the middle intestine. The rodlet cell in the epithelium of the intestine and the rectum is elongate and oval in shape with a finely granular cytoplasm (Fig. 30.26). These cells are located between the absorptive cells but within the free border adjacent to the sub-border and supranuclear regions. The cytological description of rodlet cells in *F. heteroclitus* is as follows: a prominent cell boundary, rodlets within chambers surrounding a central core, a large oval basal nucleus, and a stoma.

The rodlets are clearly shown in fish fixed in Bouin's or in 10% neutral buffered formalin. They stain green with trichrome, bright red with PAS, green in fast green and safranin, a brilliant purple with aldehyde fuchsin, and light red with hematoxylin and eosin. The rodlets show no evidence of alkaline phosphatase activity, nor do they stain with alcian blue. Some of the rodlet cells stain markedly with Baker's acid hematin technique.

The granular cells are common to the wall of the digestive tract, particularly

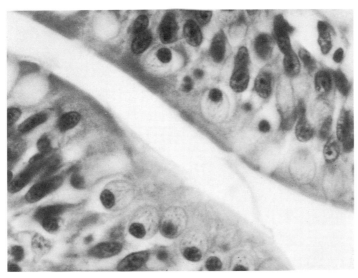

30.26. Posterior intestinal epithelium of a 2-day starved fish. Note the oval shaped rodlet cells with well-defined cell boundaries within the free border. Note also the large spherical nuclei at the base of these cells and the distinct rodlets radiating towards the tips of the cells. NBF, trichrome; X1000.

in the submucosa, although they are found sparingly in the basal part of the epithelium. They are irregular in shape and contain numerous minute and coarse cytoplasmic granules (Fig. 30.27). Cell boundaries are not always well defined. The nucleus is oval to angular in shape and eccentrically located. The most spectacular demonstration of the granular cells is found in fish fixed with 10% neutral buffered formalin and stained with trichrome. Here, the granules stain a dark red against a light green background. Bouin's fixation coupled with trichrome, and MPH following Helly's fixation, readily demonstrate the granular cells of the submucosa, but those of the epithelium could be distinguished only with difficulty. In the epithelium these cells are masked by the presence of nonabsorptive cells and the nuclei of the absorptive cells. The granules in these cells stain green with fast green, pink with hematoxylin and eosin, red with PAS, and a light purple with aldehyde fuchsin. Strong alkaline phosphatase activity is detectable in the granular cells, and they give a markedly intense Baker's acid hematin test for phospholipids.

SUMMARY

The digestive tube of *F. heteroclitus* consists of the esophagus, the intestine, and the rectum. As reported by Babkin and Bowie (1) for *F. heteroclitus* and by Schacht (21), Hale (14), and Bullock (10) for other cyprinodontiform fishes,

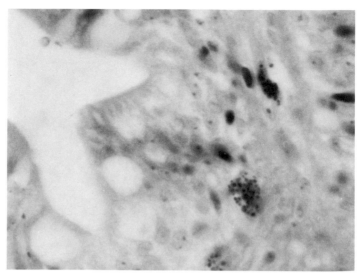

30.27. Granular cells in the epithelium and the submucosa of the posterior intestine of a 2-day starved fish. The two cells towards the bottom of the photograph are in the basal portion of the epithelium. The cell above them is in the submucosa. NBF, trichrome; ×1000.

there is no stomach. Schacht (21) and Bullock (10) recognized that there is a transition zone between the esophagus and the intestine and that this region has histological characteristics that properly differentiate it as a separate portion of the digestive tube.

Beginning with the anterior intestine, the lumen of the digestive tube is lined with characteristic absorptive cells. Bullock (9, 10) and Al-Hussaini (17) described the cytoplasm of these cells as divided into four regions: the free border, the sub-border, the supranuclear region, and the infranuclear region. With the exception of the fused appearance of the sub-border and the supranuclear regions in the absorptive cells of *F. heteroclitus*, these regions can be distinguished throughout the intestine and the rectum.

As indicated by Al-Hussaini (17) for the cyprinid absorptive cell, the free border is built up of three principal layers: the superficial layer, the canal layer, and the granular layer. Bullock (9, 10), in salmonid fishes and in *Gambusia affinis* respectively, reported that only two of the three layers could be definitely identified: the canal or microvilli region and the basal granular layer. Chaicharn and Bullock (12) also made a similar observation on the free border in the white sucker (*Catostomus commersoni*). Hale (14) distinguished terminal bars and the various regions of the striated border of columnar absorbing cells in the guppy. In *F. heteroclitus*, this border displays a differential staining pattern with the staining techniques employed. The variability in staining of the free border suggests a difference in the chemical structure of the three layers and/or differences in the physiological state of the free border at the time of fixation.

Alkaline phosphatase activity is abundant in the free border of the absorptive cells in the species of cyprinids studied by Al-Hussaini (17). Bullock (10) reported alkaline phosphatase activity in the free border of the intestine and in the anterior portion of the rectum in *G. affinis*. He noted that it gradually fades away in the mid-rectum and is completely absent in the posterior rectum and the anal canal. In the salmonids, Bullock (9) detected phosphatase activity in the free border of the absorptive cells in the intestinal epithelium.

In the starved-fish series, alkaline phosphatase reaction is present in the free border of the intestine and the rectum. It is most intense in the anterior intestine and in the anterior portion of the middle intestine. Caudally from this point a gradual decrease in phosphatase activity occurs into the rectum, where some of the mucosal folds do not have this reaction at all. The superficial layer and the granular layer appear more intense in phosphatase activity than the middle striated layer. Al-Hussaini (17) noted that the superficial layer appeared jet black, the canal and the granular layer paler, and the rest of the cytoplasm showed no appreciable coloration.

The most striking concentration of alkaline phosphatase activity is found in the connective tissue of the submucosa throughout the digestive tube. In the starved-fish series, this phosphatase activity first appears to diminish from the anterior intestine to the posterior portion of the middle intestine, then to increase in the posterior intestine; a gradual reduction in phosphatase activity occurs from the posterior intestine to the anal region.

Al-Hussaini (17) held that phosphatase activity is also seen in the subepithelial connective tissue in the cyprinids. With the salmonids, Bullock (9) remarked that the network of the lamina propria often exhibited marked alkaline phosphatase activity. In some of his fish, the entire lamina was affected, while in other fish this phosphatase activity appeared limited, either to the stroma or to the nuclei. He further noted that a strong reaction occurred in a somewhat condensed subepithelial region of the lamina propria. On the other hand, Chaicharn and Bullock (12) found that in the lamina propria of the white sucker the connective tissue elements are usually negative, with the exception of those immediately underneath the epithelium, which are occasionally positive. In accordance with the suggestion of Moog and Wenger (20) and Weinreb and Bilstad (24), the close association between neutral mucopolysaccharides and the sites of alkaline phosphatase activity may indicate heavy concentrations of these substances in the connective tissue of the submucosa in *F. heteroclitus*.

The enzyme, alkaline phosphatase, may be directly related to the process of absorption in biological systems. The detection of this enzyme in the free border of the intestine and the rectum suggests a close relationship between the luminal-digested foodstuffs which are in direct contact with the free border and this site

of phosphatase activity. The high concentration of alkaline phosphatase throughout the submucosa of the digestive tube may also indicate the involvement of this
enzyme in the absorption of digested foodstuffs, from the absorptive cells into
the fluid systems of the body proper. Al-Hussaini (17) offered a similar interpretation.

Fish were examined each month from July through October to ascertain possible seasonal distribution of alkaline phosphatase activity, particularly that of
the submucosa. The results were negative. Of course, this finding does not take
into account the possible reduction of phosphatase activity during the winter
months when these fish live buried in the mud of deeper holes and creeks.

The neutral lipid series of starved fish produced some interesting as well as supporting evidence as to the regions of secretory and/or absorptive activity in the
digestive tube. In this series, the starved fish have a marked change in the appearance of the absorptive cells. A spectacular decrease in the concentration of lipid
droplets occurs in these cells in the anterior and middle intestine of the 6-day
starved fish. This reduction in lipids continues through the 8-day starvation period. Throughout the starved-fish series, the absorptive cells in the posterior intestine and the rectum are almost devoid of lipids.

In contrast to neutral lipids, there is no change in the phospholipid pattern of
the intestine and the rectum in the 4-, 6-, and 8-day starved fish. Reduction in
the concentration of phospholipids appears to occur in the supranuclear and infranuclear regions, from the anterior intestine to the anal region in the 2-day starved
fish.

The rodlet cells deserve special mention because of their enigmatic nature.
These cells have been observed by many investigators in different fishes and amphibians, and have sometimes been considered to be sporozoan parasites (2, 14,
18, 22). They are generally reported from the intestinal mucosa, but are not exclusively limited to this region. In *F. heteroclitus,* the rodlet cells are found in the
epithelium of the intestine and the rectum in the starved-fish series. None was observed in the esophagus and the transition zone. They appear to be identical with
the "pear-shaped" cells of Al-Hussaini (16, 17) and of Bishop and Odense (5); they
are similar to the "rodlet cells" described by Bullock (9, 10) and Chaicharn and
Bullock (12). These cells also fit the general description given the bodies found
among the columnar cells of the intestinal epithelium by Hale (14). Vickers' (23)
second cell-type of those variably present in the epithelial lining of the intestine
of the goldfish, *Carassius auratus,* unquestionably fits the description of a rodlet
cell. With the staining techniques used, the rodlets are similar to those reported
in *G. affinis* (10) and in the salmonids (9).

It should be noted, in conjunction with the description of the staining quali-
ties of the rodlet cells, that although the majority of them give a characteristic
staining reaction with a given technique, some of these cells show variability in
staining from fish to fish, within the same fish, and even within a single tissue section. For example, the rodlet cells generally stain green with trichrome but some

of them may stain completely red in the same tissue section. This variability in staining quality may be indicative of different physiological states of the same cell and/or different species of rodlet cells. The failure of the rodlets to give a PAS-positive reaction in the cod (5) and the staining of some, but not all, of the rodlet cells with acid hematin in *F. heteroclitus* further emphasize a difference between these cells.

Empty rodlet cells were observed in *F. heteroclitus*, but none were seen discharging rodlets or cellular contents into the lumen of the intestine or the rectum. Bullock (9) mentioned seeing the extruding of rods from several cells in the American eel. He also stated that such extrusion was not seen in the salmonid and that this could be attributed to the much smaller number of rodlet cells. In *F. heteroclitus*, this is not the case, as the rodlet cells are generally quite plentiful.

Another controversial cell-type described by many investigators as present in the digestive tract of fishes is the large granular cell. No specific function has been attributed to these cells (6, 12, 17). Weinreb and Bilstad (24) reported that the granules of the granular cells appeared to have a protein core surrounded by a lipid-phospholipid shell and a trace of nonacid mucopolysaccharides. The evidence with *F. heteroclitus* would tend to support their view.

In the starved-fish series the granular cells are found in the epithelium and the submucosa throughout the digestive tube. They were present in all the fish examined and were most abundant in the rectum. Except for their staining reaction with buffered azure-eosinate, these cells are similar to the granular cells described by Bullock (10) in *G. affinis* and by Chaicharn and Bullock (12) in the white sucker.

The granular cells in *F. heteroclitus* give constant and reproducible staining results as compared to those studied by Bullock (9) in salmonid fishes.

Buffered azure-eosinate was used at varying pH's to stain the granules. In *F. heteroclitus*, the granules of the epithelial and the submucosal granular cells stain a light pink from pH 3.5 to 5.5. At pH 6 and pH 6.6, the granules in both regions were unstained. No intermediate forms were found. In *G. affinis*, Bullock (10) stated that the granules of the epithelial granular cells stained intensely red at pH 4, while the granules of the cells in the submucosa were unstained. At pH 6, the granules of the submucosal granular cells stained dark blue; those of the epithelium were unstained. In the white sucker, Chaicharn and Bullock (12) reported that the granules of the granular cells stained light pink with azure-eosinate at pH 4 and light blue at pH 5. The evidence suggests that in *F. heteroclitus* the granular cells in the epithelium and the submucosa are similar and it would tend to support the past assumption of Bolton (6) that the granular cells of the submucosa give rise to those in the epithelium.

More than a passing mention should be made concerning the band of PAS-positive material which appears at the boundary between the sub-border and the supranuclear regions in the absorptive cells. Buffered azure-eosinate stains this area light pink from pH 3.5 to 5.5; it is distinctly blue at pH 6 and 6.6. In well-fed fish, Bullock (10) mentioned a similar band of PAS-positive material in the absorptive cells. No specific region of the intestinal tube was indicated by him except in a caption of a figure in which this band was found in the epithelium of the anterior intestine. The granular layer is present mainly in the posterior intestine and the rectum of *F. heteroclitus*. It was present in the starved-fish series. Moreover, this layer is found mainly in those regions of the digestive tube thought to be associated with secretory and/or absorptive activity. Therefore, it is tempting to suggest that the presence or absence of this band of PAS-positive granules is somehow coupled with these functions. However, much more evidence is needed before such a conclusion can be offered.

Note: The material of this study has been accepted in partial fulfillment of a doctoral dissertation by the University of New Hampshire.

REFERENCES

1. Babkin, B. P., and Bowie, D. J. The digestive system and its function in *Fundulus heteroclitus*. *Biol. Bull. (Woods Hole)* 54: 254–277. 1928.
2. Bannister, L. H. Is *Rhabdosporasa thelohani* (Laguesse) a sporozoan parasite or a tissue cell of lower vertebrates? *Parasitology 56:* 633–638. 1966.
3. Barka, T., and Anderson, P. J. *Histochemistry: Theory, Practice, and Bibliography*. 660 pp. New York, Harper & Row, Hoeber Med. Div., 1963.
4. Barrington, E. J. W. The alimentary canal and digestion, pp. 109–161. In *The Physiology of Fishes*, ed. M. E. Brown. Vol. 1. New York and London Academic Press, 1957.
5. Bishop, C., and Odense, P. H. Morphology of the digestive tract of the cod, *Gadus morhua*. *J. Fish. Res. Board Can. 23:* 1607–1615. 1966.
6. Bolton, L. L. Basophilic (mast) cells in the alimentary canal of salmonid fishes. *J. Morphol. 54:* 549–591. 1933.
7. Bullock, W. L. Phosphatases in experimental *Trichinella spiralis* infections in the rat. *Exp. Parasitol. 2:* 150–162. 1953.
8. Bullock, W. L. Histochemical studies on the Acanthocephala. III. Comparative histochemistry of alkaline glycerophosphatase. *Exp. Parasitol. 7:* 51–68. 1958.
9. Bullock, W. L. Intestinal histology of some salmonid fishes with particular reference to the histopathology of acanthocephalan infections. *J. Morphol. 112:* 23–44. 1963.
10. Bullock, W. L. The intestinal histology of the mosquitofish, *Gambusia affinis* (Baird and Girard). *Acta zool. (Stockholm) 48:* 1–17. 1967.
11. Cameron, M. L., and Steele, J. E. Simplified aldehyde fuchsin staining of neurosecretory cells. *Stain Technol. 34:* 265–266. 1959.
12. Chaicharn, A., and Bullock, W. L. The histopathology of acanthocephalan infections in suckers with observations on the intestinal histology of two species of catostomid fishes. *Acta zool. (Stockholm) 48:* 19–42. 1967.
13. Davenport, H. A. *Histological and Histochemical Techniques*. 401 pp. Philadelphia, Saunders, 1960.

14. Hale, P. A. The morphology and histology of the digestive systems of the freshwater teleosts, *Poecilia reticulata* and *Gasterosteus aculeatus*. *J. Zool. (London) 146:* 132–149. 1965.

15. Humason, G. L. *Animal Tissue Techniques.* 468 pp. San Francisco, W. H. Freeman, 1962.

16. Hussaini, A. H. al-. On the functional morphology of the alimentary tract of some fish in relation to differences in their feeding habits. I. Anatomy and histology. *Quart. J. Microsc. Sci. 90:* 109–139. 1949.

17. Hussaini, A. H. al-. On the functional morphology of the alimentary tract of some fish in relation to differences in their feeding habits. II. Cytology and physiology. *Quart. J. Microsc. Sci. 90:* 323–354. 1949.

18. Laguesse, E. Sur le pancreas du crénilabre et particulierement sur le pancreas intrahepatique. *Rev. biol. Nord 7:* 343–363. 1895.

19. Lillie, R. D. *Histopathologic Technic.* 300 pp. Philadelphia, Blakiston, 1948.

20. Moog, F., and Wenger, E. L. The occurrence of a neutral mucopolysaccharide at sites of high alkaline phosphatase activity. *Amer. J. Anat. 90:* 339–372. 1952.

21. Schacht, H. Ueber den Vorderdarm der Cyprinodonten. *Z. mikrosk.-anat. Forsch. 26:* 534–546. 1931.

22. Thélohan, P. Sur quelques coccidies nouvelles, parasites des poissons. *J. anat. physiol. (Paris) 28:* 151–171. 1892.

23. Vickers, T. A study of the intestinal epithelium of the goldfish *Carassius auratus:* Its normal structure, the dynamics of cell replacement, and the changes induced by salts of cobalt and manganese. *Quart. J. Microsc. Sci. 103:* 93–110. 1962.

24. Weinreb, E. L., and Bilstad, N. M. Histology of the digestive tract and adjacent structures of the rainbow trout, *Salmo gairdneri irideus*. *Copeia 3:* 194–204. 1955.

31

Ascorbic Acid Deficiency in Rainbow Trout and Coho Salmon and Effects on Wound Healing

LAURENCE M. ASHLEY
J. E. HALVER
and R. R. SMITH

Few animal species are known to require dietary vitamin C. The ability of most animals to synthesize ascorbic acid is well documented, but those that lack this ability must regularly ingest the vitamin for good growth and good health. Kitamura (9) cited the work of Kedo, Ikeda, and Fujimura (8), Ikeda, Sato, and Kimura (6, 7), and Ikeda and Sato (4, 5), who analyzed various fish tissues for ascorbic acid content. These authors also found by enzyme analysis that the path of ascorbate synthesis in carp is almost the same as that in mice but the rate is much slower.

Kitamura (9) examined by chemical analysis and histochemistry the L-gulonolactone oxidase activity which converts L-gulonolactone to ascorbic acid. At 37°C this activity was significant for mouse and rat but was lacking in guinea pig. Activity in carp was comparatively slight but consistently present. In rainbow trout the activity was either very slight or absent. Hatchery fish fed vitamin E-enriched diets to activate the enzyme had no significant activity, and wild rainbow trout that had lived in a river more than six months had no detectable activity.

Kitamura (9) described the histochemical localization of L-gulonolactone oxidase activity in tissues of several vertebrate species determined by Nitro B T staining. L-Gulonolactone oxidase activity was strong in the mouse but was weak or negative in rainbow trout. These results, in addition to those described below for fish fed diets lacking L-ascorbic acid (C_1), show that rainbow trout require dietary C_1 for normal growth.

Spinal curvatures have been reported periodically for hatchery salmonids since the appearance of a paper by Kitamura et al. (10). These authors showed that L-ascorbic acid was needed by salmonids after rainbow trout (*Salmo gairdneri*) developed scoliosis and lordosis when fed low ascorbic acid diets for 16 to 24 weeks. Poston (11) reported lordosis and scoliosis in brook trout (*Salvelinus fontinalis*) fed similar deficient diets for 34 weeks.

Halver, DeLong, and Mertz (3), Halver and Shanks (1), and Shanks, Gahimer, and Halver (12) observed scoliosis among tryptophan-deficient sockeye salmon (*Oncorhynchus nerka*) and rainbow trout but did not report any lesions in the anomalous fish. Kitamura (9) compared scoliosis histopathologically for tryptophan-deficient and for ascorbic acid-deficient rainbow trout. Scoliosis appeared in one to three weeks in tryptophan-deficient and in five to six weeks in ascorbic acid-deficient fish. The anomalies of the former group consisted of typical scoliotic vertebral columns in which the centrums remained attached, but the disease in the vitamin C-deficient fish resulted in displaced centrums which in severe cases became completely separated and were set at various angles to one another. When tryptophan was restored to the diet, all fish recovered within two weeks whether or not ascorbic acid was included in the diet. Deformed ascorbic acid-deficient fish placed on recovery diet remained scoliotic indefinitely.

Halver, Ashley, and Smith (2) described lordosis and scoliosis and other anomalies in rainbow trout and coho salmon (*O. kisutch*) reared on vitamin C-deficient diets for 24 to 30 weeks. Controls fed a complete test diet including 100 mg L-ascorbic acid per 100 grams of dry diet remained normal and grew more rapidly than the deficient fish (Fig. 31.1). Gross examination of the gills in deficient fish revealed distortion of gill filaments. Histological examination later showed these gills had twisted, hyperplastic filamentar cartilages (Fig. 31.2). Control fish had uniformly straight filamentar cartilages (Fig. 31.3). Histological examination also showed that some scleral cartilages were deformed by a mottled pattern of hyperplasia, not found in controls (Figs. 31.4, 31.5). Stained sagittal sections of vertebrae with severe lordosis revealed a dramatic anomaly of the spinal column in which the spinal axis was deflected anterodorsally for approximately 120 degrees. This anomaly was accompanied by focal hemorrhage, atrophy of the spinal cord, and distortion of intervertebral discs (Fig. 31.6).

CONFIRMATORY EXPERIMENTS

Long-term confirmatory experiments on rainbow trout and coho salmon were conducted at the Hagerman, Idaho, Field Station. The 15°C spring water there provides an optimum growing environment for young salmonids. Replicate lots

Fig. 31.1. Coho salmon control (middle), showing scoliosis (above), and showing lordosis (below), fed a test diet in which ascorbic acid was lacking. (Courtesy of *Transactions of the American Fisheries Society* and authors J. E. Halver, L. M. Ashley, and R. R. Smith.) X1.

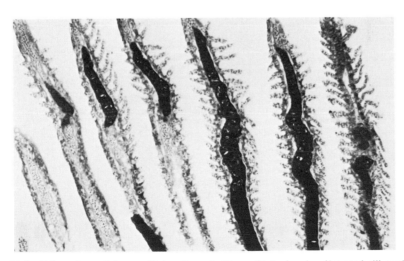

Fig. 31.2. Coho salmon fed same diet as those in Figure 31.1, showing distorted gill cartilages in filaments. (Courtesy of *Transactions of the American Fisheries Society* and authors J. E. Halver, L. M. Ashley, and R. R. Smith.) Giemsa; X176.

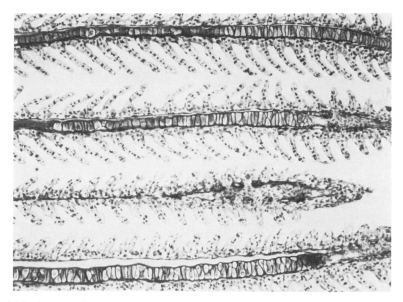

Fig. 31.3. Section of coho salmon gill showing healthy filamentar cartilages. Fed complete test diet. Hematoxylin and eosin (H&E); ×280.

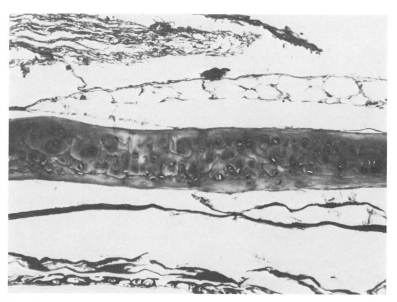

Fig. 31.4. Mottled hyperplasia of scleral (eye) cartilage in coho salmon fed diet lacking ascorbic acid. H&E; ×280.

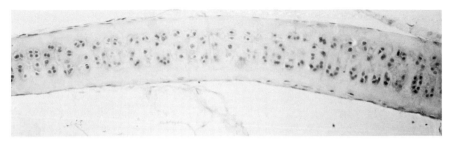

Fig. 31.5. Healthy scleral cartilage from coho salmon control. H&E; ×280.

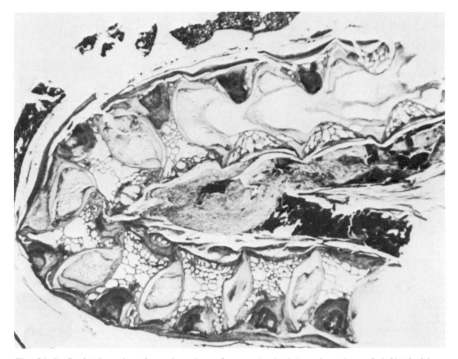

Fig. 31.6. Sagittal section through region of severe lordosis in coho salmon fed diet lacking vitamin C. Note displaced vertebral centrums, distorted intervertebral discs, compressed spinal cord, and surrounding hemorrhage. Flexion of vertebral column is approximately 120 degrees. (Courtesy of *Transactions of the American Fisheries Society* and authors J. E. Halver, L. M. Ashley, and R. R. Smith.) H&E; × 8.

of 200 fish with average weight of 0.4 grams for the salmon and 0.3 grams for the trout were fed diets containing 0, 5, 10, 20, 40, and 100 mg of L-ascorbic acid per 100 grams of dry diet. The 100 mg-treated group served as controls. Rearing and feeding methods were those published by Halver, Ashley, and Smith (2). Tissues of deformed and moribund fish were preserved for histological examination by Bouin's fixation. After thorough washing in several changes of 70% ethanol, these were dehydrated, cleared, and paraffinized in an Autotechnicon. Alternate 6-micron sections were stained with hematoxylin and eosin and with either Mallory-Heidenhain, Giemsa, or Gomori stains.

After 24 weeks on test, wound repair experiments were performed under mild anesthesia (1:25,000 MS-222 *Sandoz*) on 10 fish from each diet treatment. A 1-cm skin incision was made at two sites per fish. The first was between the dorsal fin and the lateral line and extended about ½ cm into the underlying muscle. The second was through the abdominal midline midway between the pectoral girdle and the anus. Wounds were promptly closed with a single chromic acid-treated gut suture. Wounded fish were continued on the same diets fed formerly for three additional weeks, after which all survivors were sacrificed. Tissues from deficient and control fish and from the fish wounds were resected and processed as described above.

RESULTS AND SUMMARY

Acute lordosis or scoliosis appeared in most coho salmon and rainbow trout fed no vitamin C for more than 20 weeks. These fish also had distorted hyperplastic gill cartilages, hyperplastic, mottled sclerotic cartilages, and occasional hemorrhages of the gas bladder (Fig. 31.7), fin, mouth, skin (Fig. 31.8), and thymus tissues. In one fish hemorrhages were also found around the optic nerve, choroid gland, and thyroid gland (Fig. 31.9). Some fish fed 5 or 10 mg vitamin C per 100 grams of diet also had scoliosis or lordosis. Sections through spinal curvatures sometimes contained displacement of adjacent portions of kidney and skeletal muscle in addition to the severe vertebral dislocations described above (Fig. 31.10). Moderate-to-severe changes were sometimes observed in skull and jaw cartilages and in developing bone and teeth (Figs. 31.11, 31.12). One fish had severely vacuolated epithelial cells and pyknotic nuclei in the macula of the internal ear (Fig. 31.13).

Although this syndrome is not identical to that of scurvy, the two appear to have at least one common biochemical defect, i.e., a failure to hydroxylate enough proline for needed collagen formation in the development of connective tissue, cartilage, and bone. This deficiency may even affect the integrity of cell membranes to permit frequent petechial and at times massive hemorrhages within the body. To date, inflammatory change in salmonid joints has not been identified but experiments now in progress may eventually demonstrate this sign of the scurvy syndrome.

Wound-repair studies from the different ascorbic acid diets help determine the minimum requirement of vitamin C for maximum wound repair besides showing the kind and degree of pathological change in the various diet groups. Wound repair in guinea pigs as reported by Wolbach (13) may be compared with that ob-

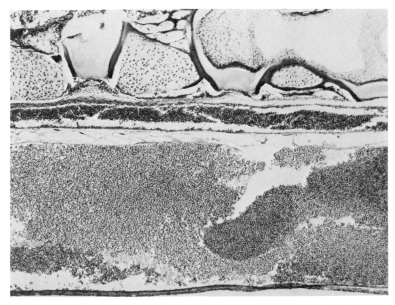

Fig. 31.7. Hemorrhage within gas bladder of trout lacking vitamin C in diet. Note aorta containing blood and vertebral column above gas bladder. H&E; ×110.

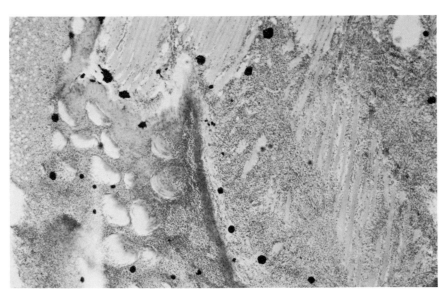

Fig. 31.8. Hemorrhage of scales, skin, and hypodermal musculature in rainbow trout receiving no ascorbic acid in diet. ×110.

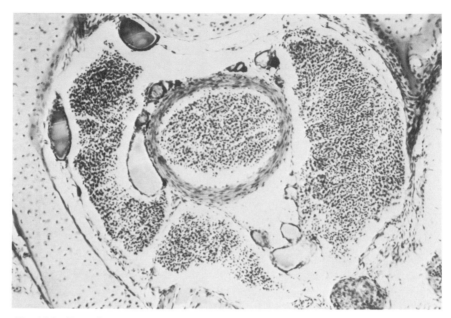

Fig. 31.9. Trout from same lot as that shown in Figure 31.8, showing hemorrhage around thyroid follicles. H&E; ×280.

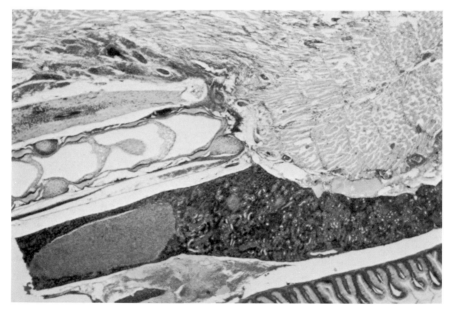

Fig. 31.10. Compression of trout kidney by displaced musculature caused by spinal curvature. There was hemorrhage around spinal cord and there was also displacement of the vertebrae. H&E; ×44.

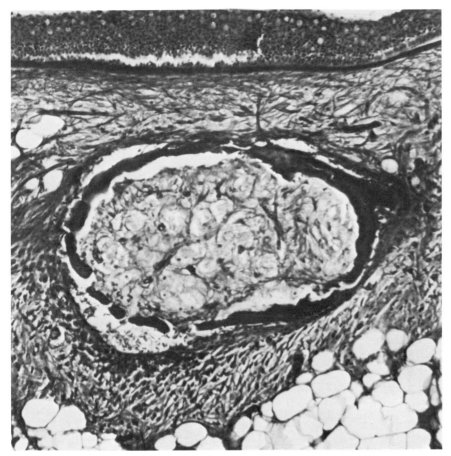

Fig. 31.11. Coho salmon receiving no vitamin C in diet, showing hyperplasia of dental pulp and breaks in dentine (black layer). Osteoclasts are not evident. Giemsa; ×270.

served in salmonids. Wolbach found guinea pig wounds from ascorbic acid-deficient animals failed to develop collagen after nine days while controls produced an abundance of collagen in that time. Salmon and trout controls, after three weeks, had many delicate collagen fibers, but those given no ascorbic acid had little or no collagen in the wounds (Figs. 31.14–31.16). Wounds of fish unprotected by ascorbic acid were gaping or were plugged by poorly organized blood clots in the case of dorsolateral wounds and by visceral tissues and blood clots in the case of belly wounds (Figs. 31.16, 31.17). Wounds frequently became infected during seepage of water into the peritoneal cavity, often resulting in death. All wounded trout fed the vitamin C-deficient diet died but all wounded salmon on the same ration survived for at least three weeks. Wound repair was generally poor in trout

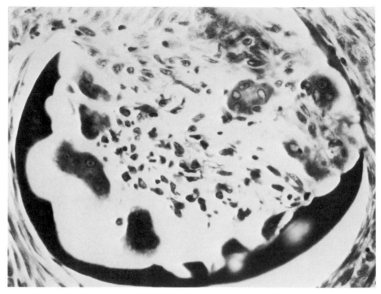

Fig. 31.12. Coho salmon control showing intact dentine, dental pulp, and peripherally placed osteoclasts. Giemsa; ×875.

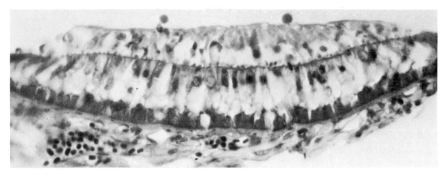

Fig. 31.13. Severe vacuolation and cell distortion of neuroepithelial cells of macula in rainbow trout whose diet lacked ascorbic acid. Note basement membrane supporting row of low columnar supporting cells above which are abnormal vacuoles and nuclei of neuroepithelial cells. An otolithic membrane lies above these layers. H&E; ×875.

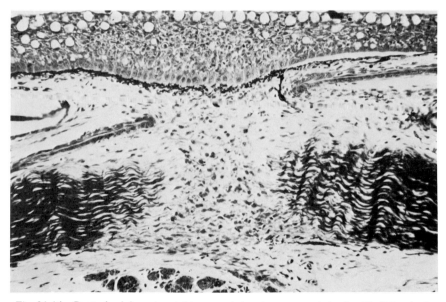

Fig. 31.14. Control rainbow trout skin wound showing regenerated subepithelial melanin, two regenerating scales surrounded by osteoblasts in vascular layer, and the cut ends of dense collagenous dermal layer, between which is granulation tissue containing delicate regenerating collagenic fibers. Epidermal thickening above wound is typical of salmonid wound repair. This precedes repair of dense dermal collagen. Mallory-Heidenhain (MH); ×350.

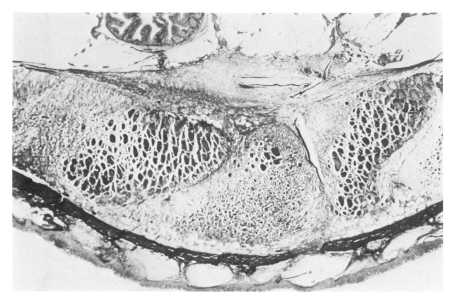

Fig. 31.15. Section of belly wound of trout fed 5 mg ascorbic acid per 100 grams of dry diet. Note edema of scale pockets above healed epidermis, muscle atrophy, scales within wound, and visceral plug where scales appear at inner portion of wound. MH; ×44.

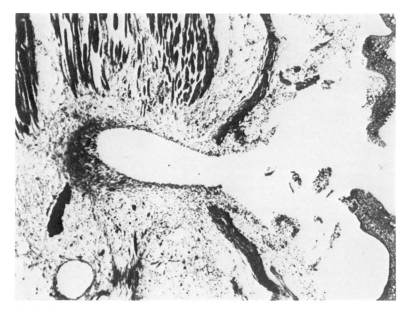

Fig. 31.16. Section through gaping wound of trout fed no vitamin C. Such wounds admit water into tissues and often result in death. MH; ×32.

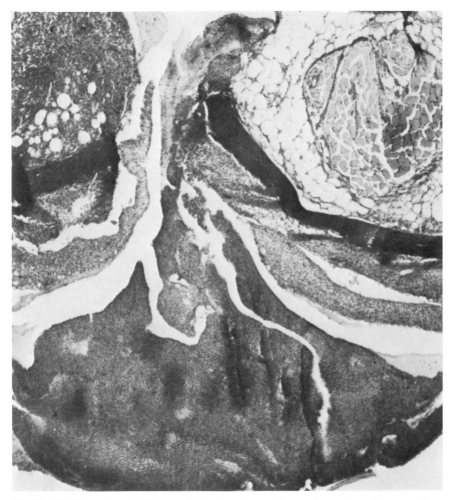

Fig. 31.17. Coho salmon belly wound showing depressed wound margins and no wound repair. A large blood clot partially closes the wound externally. Diet lacked vitamin C. (Courtesy of *Transactions of the American Fisheries Society* and authors J. E. Halver, L. M. Ashley, and R. R. Smith.) H&E; ×120.

fed vitamin C at the 5 or 10 mg levels, while salmon fed these levels repaired wounds somewhat better. Both species of salmonids repaired wounds nearly as well as controls when fed 40 mg or more of ascorbic acid per 100 grams of diet.

Traumatic change due to wounding included loss of scales and melanin adjacent to the wound, and atrophy of significant amounts of skeletal muscle. Sometimes inflammation occurred and healing was impaired. Foreign body giant cells were occasionally present within such wounds (Fig. 31.18). Granulation tissue could usually be seen but the amount in a given wound appeared to vary in proportion to the amount of trauma, skin, or scales in a wound (Fig. 31.19).

Coho fed 5 mg and rainbow fed 10 mg ascorbic acid diets had well-healed epidermis and partially repaired dermis and skeletal muscle by the 21st post-operative day (Figs. 31.20, 31.21). The dense dermal collagen layer in these wounds was represented by a rather highly cellular pro-collagen.

Our finding that epidermal repair is completed first in the healing of salmonid skin incisions is of special significance in view of the fact that dermal healing in mammalian skin either precedes or occurs concomitantly with epidermal repair. Replacement of melanin, scales, deep muscle, and fascia in trout appears to occur concurrently with repair of the dermis. This precedence of epidermal over dermal repair may be significant in wound protection of fish and probably other aquatic organisms from contamination by water-borne infectious organisms.

Large trout (300 to 500 grams) intubated with 14_1C and 3_4H labeled L-ascorbic acid had rapid fixation of labeled material wherever collagen or cartilage was being formed (Fig. 31.22). Radioautographs of tissue sections from these trout were prepared three days after intubation and showed prompt fixation of ascorbate in all tissues active in metabolism of this vitamin.

Analysis of urine from the intubated trout showed rapid conversion of vitamin C_1 into ascorbate-2-sulfate (vitamin C_2). Urine and tissue metabolites had $^{14}C/^3H$

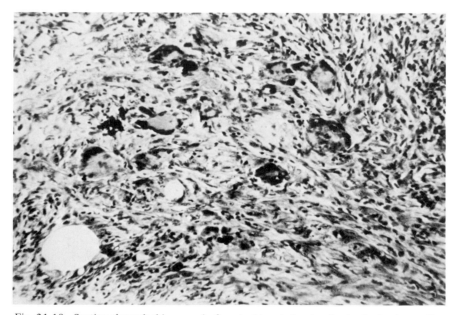

Fig. 31.18. Section through skin wound of control trout showing foreign body giant cells. These cells may arise near embedded scales or bits of epidermis displaced during wounding. H&E; X450.

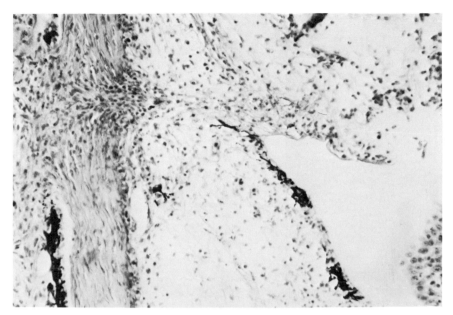

Fig. 31.19. Section through healing wound of coho salmon fed 10 mg ascorbic acid per 100 grams of dry diet. Note fragment of epidermis (lower right), cellular granulation tissue (center) with regenerating melanin. Healing dense collagen layer of dermis (left) with regenerating deep melanin layer. H&E; X450.

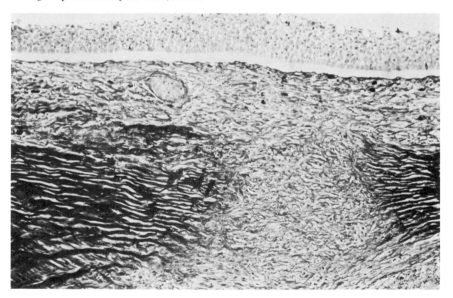

Fig. 31.20. Regeneration of dense dermal collagen layer showing very fibrous granulation tissue between cut ends of old dermal collagen layer (black). Epidermis remains swollen above wound area. MH; X280.

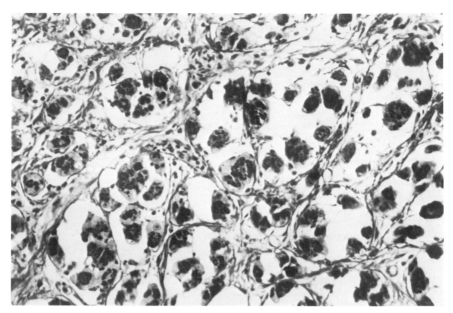

Fig. 31.21. Atrophic skeletal muscle with regenerating muscle fibers (black) within old, degenerate fibers (grey). Trout fed 10 mg vitamin C per 100 grams of dry diet. MH; ×560.

Fig. 31.22. Radioautograph of 3- to 4-year old rainbow trout showing $^{14}C/^{3}H$ labeled sites for binding of labeled ascorbic acid. Major sites are skin, pituitary, kidney, liver, and spleen, with lesser amounts in ovarian stroma, gill support cartilage, skull, vertebrae, and fins. ×1/4.

ratios identical to or greater than the $^{14}C/^{3}H$ ratio of dose material. Thus, during metabolism little C-1 decarboxylation had occurred. This is in direct contrast to a major metabolic pathway in guinea pig tissue and more closely resembles the metabolic pathway in man. Rainbow trout may be an important model for the study of vitamin C, in fact, a better model than the test guinea pig commonly used today.

REFERENCES

1. Halver, J. E., and Shanks, W. E. The nutrition of salmonid fishes. VIII. Indispensable amino acids for sockeye salmon. *J. Nutr. 72:* 340–349. 1960.
2. Halver, J. E., Ashley, L. M., and Smith, R. R. Ascorbic acid requirements of

coho salmon and rainbow trout. *Trans. Amer. Fish. Soc. 98:* 762–771. 1969.

3. Halver, J. E., DeLong, D. C., and Mertz, E. T.   The nutrition of salmonid fishes. V. Classification of essential amino acids for chinook salmon. *J. Nutr. 63:* 95–105. 1957.

4. Ikeda, S., and Sato, M.   Biochemical studies on L-ascorbic acid in aquatic animals. III. Biosynthesis of L-ascorbic acid by carp. *Bull. Jap. Soc. Sci. Fish. 30:* 365–369. 1964.

5. Ikeda, S., and Sato, M.   Biochemical studies on L-ascorbic acid in aquatic animals. IV. Metabolism of L-ascorbic acid-1-^{14}C in carp. *Bull. Jap. Soc. Sci. Fish. 31:* 814–817. 1965.

6. Ikeda, S., Sato, M., and Kimura, R.   Biochemical studies on L-ascorbic acid in aquatic animals. I. An improved method for assessment. *Bull. Jap. Soc. Sci. Fish. 29:* 757–764. 1963.

7. Ikeda, S., Sato, M., and Kimura, R.   Biochemical studies on L-ascorbic acid in aquatic animals. II. Distribution in various parts of fish. *Bull. Jap. Soc. Sci. Fish. 29:* 765–770. 1963.

8. Kedo, S., Ikeda, S., and Fujimura, K.   Discussion of measurement of L-ascorbic acid by Roe's method. On minimization of measuring time. *J. Jap. Soc. Food Nutr. 13:* 242–245. 1960.

9. Kitamura, S.   Summary on the hypovitaminosis C of rainbow trout, *Salmo gairdneri. Fish Pathol. (Japan) 3:* 73–92. 1969.

10. Kitamura, S., Ohara, S., Suwa, T., and Nakagawa, K.   Studies on vitamin requirements of rainbow trout, *Salmo gairdneri.* I. On the ascorbic acid. *Bull. Jap. Soc. Sci. Fish. 31:* 818–826. 1965.

11. Poston, H. A.   Effect of dietary L-ascorbic acid on immature brook trout. *N. Y. Conserv. Dep., Fish. Res. Bull. 30:* 46–51. 1967.

12. Shanks, W. E., Gahimer, G. D., and Halver, J. E.   The indispensable amino acids for rainbow trout. *Progr. Fish-Cult. 24:* 68–73. 1962.

13. Wolbach, S. B.   Controlled formation of collagen and reticulum: A study of the source of intercellular substance in recovery from experimental scorbutus. *Amer. J. Pathol. (suppl.) 9:* 689–699. 1933.

DISCUSSION OF ASCORBIC ACID DEFICIENCY IN RAINBOW TROUT AND COHO SALMON

Comment: I was very much intrigued with the elegant autoradiograph of the fish, and have a few questions. The people in Sweden who started this technique on mammals in Stockholm at the Veterinary School found that there was a deceptive concentration of radioactivity following injections of various compounds into animals if you forgot about the vascularity of tissues. I just wonder if the high uptake in the fishes' spleen and kidneys and liver was not perhaps related to the congested tissue. The second question was, "Was there any uptake around the adrenal glands and the Stannius body?"

L. M. Ashley: I don't recall that there was any uptake in adrenal or the Stannius body, although we do have several other sections more laterally. This was a mid-sagittal section. We do have many other sections from these fish and I would have to recheck those because this work was done by one of my colleagues and I am not quite familiar with what all those sections did show. Blood in kidney, spleen, and liver could influence the amount of radioactivity there, but much less so in the highly reactive skin.

Comment: The reason I ask is because the adrenal cortex is known to have a very high concentration of ascorbic acid.

L. M. Ashley: Yes, it probably showed some of the tritiated ascorbate.

Comment: And the other reason is because it is not known what the Stannius bodies are functionally.

32

Nutritional Myopathy in Fish

JOHN M. KING

Three outbreaks of nutritional myopathy and steatitis usually associated in domestic animals with a vitamin E/selenium-responsive disease are briefly described as they occurred in young hatchery-raised rainbow trout. All three outbreaks were successfully treated by dietary manipulations. A brief discussion as to the probable cause and their mechanism as well as some comparison to the domestic animal diseases is given. No attempt at detailed research was made in these cases, as they appear to fit the usual picture one sees in the common domestic animals with nutritional myopathy and steatitis (2). One can assume this relationship on the basis of the idea that there are more similarities between fish and other animals than there are differences. The concept is strengthened by the favorable response of affected fish to dietary improvements.

All three of the outbreaks involved hatchery-raised rainbow trout (*Salmo gairdneri*) fingerlings from 10 to 100 grams, and occurred in Pennsylvania (PA.), Missouri (MO.), and Venezuela (S.A.). The affected fry in Venezuela were hatched from eggs obtained from the state of Washington. The fry in PA. and MO. were fed a commercially available fish diet exclusively, but the diet of the South American fry was described as containing fish flour 30%, meat 40%, soya 9%, 21 pellets 10%, corn flour and rye 9%, salt and cumin 2%.

Changing the diet to a different commercial feed in the PA. fish and removal of the excessive cod-liver oil from the feed of the MO. fish corrected their problems. The S.A. fish were apparently successfully treated by the addition of 2% cod-liver oil to the diet.

787

All three outbreaks were first observed in March, April, and May.

The clinical signs in the smallest fry were general listlessness, slight spinning, some imbalance, and death. The larger fish (MO. and S.A.) had irregular swimming habits (upside-down swimming, etc.), decreased activity, downstream crowding, and anorexia.

Clinical signs in the PA. and MO. fish lasted only a few days before death, while the S.A. fish were deformed but did not die.

No significant gross lesions were found on or in the smallest fry (PA.) or in the MO. fish, but the larger fish had an overall weight loss and many additionally had a definite constriction in the body just cranial to the tail. In some instances this gave the tail a permanently deformed curvature. The lack of normal musculature, seen microscopically, was the apparent reason for this stricture.

A few other gross sporadic lesions were found on the larger fish, such as head region depigmentation spots in the MO. fish; and both the MO. and S.A. fish had a few cases of gill disease and furunculosis.

The fishes' abdomens were opened and the entire carcass fixed in aqueous formalin. Hematoxylin and eosin sections were made by cutting some fish in sagittal sections and others in cross sections in order to see as many organs and tissues as possible *in situ*. Histologically, the disease-related lesions were limited to somatic body muscles and depot fat.

Fig. 32.1. Fish from case #3 showing gross deformities associated with muscular dystrophy.

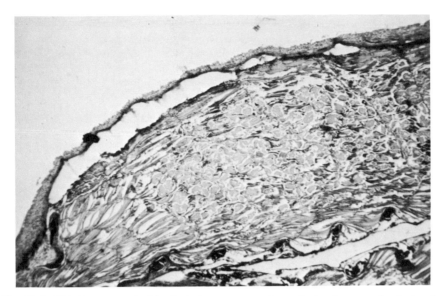

Fig. 32.2. Fish from case #3. Histological appearance of muscle showing muscular dystrophy.

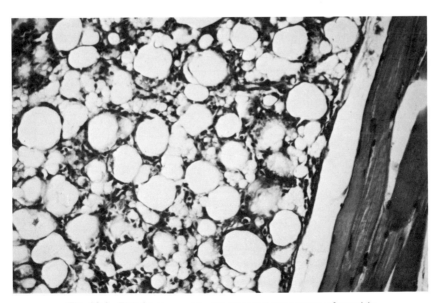

Fig. 32.3. Fish from case #1. Histological appearance of steatitis.

Muscular dystrophy was recognized by the bilateral presence of swollen, hyalinized, and in many instances mineralized degenerate muscle fibers. Some muscles had well-marked atrophy of individual fibers and groups of fibers, plus varying degrees of sarcolemmal (satellite) cell proliferation as an attempt at regeneration. In any one muscle bundle, a single fiber only may have been involved, as seen on cross or longitudinal section.

Steatitis (nutritional fat necrosis) was recognized by the presence of focal accumulations of chronic inflammatory cells and fibrosis with degenerate fat cells in the scattered fat-depot areas. No acid-fast pigment was present. These lesions had a tendency to be more concentrated dorsally along both sides of the midline and along the lateral line, with the lesions being more diffusely scattered in the abdominal fat depots. This lesion of steatitis was seen only in the MO. fish and was not seen in the PA. or the S.A. fish.

SUMMARY

The considered cause of the disease in the MO. fish is the excessively high level of cod-liver oil in the commercial feed, for when this was decreased but not eliminated from the diet no more losses occurred. It has been shown experimentally that excess cod-liver oil can cause the disease in experimental animals (1). In the PA. fish the feed was considered rancid from age, and new but otherwise similar feed prevented further losses. Increased rancidity of fats has been proven to be causative of nutritional myopathy and steatitis (3). The S.A. fish are not as easily understood, as they were treated with cod-liver oil to cure the disease. This may be explained in part by the fact that cod-liver oil enhances the fat transport into the blood, and since fish meal intended for animal use may have a tendency to get rancid before use, the added nonrancid cod-liver oil may have allowed the increased absorption of vitamin E from the feed and even added its own content of vitamin E.

The caudal body muscles apparently were the major muscles involved because of their greater functional state, even though other striated muscles, such as the heart, must necessarily be active at all times. This fits well with the disease as seen at the New York State Veterinary College, Cornell University, in which beef calves running free with their dams often have massive nutritional myopathy of heart and leg muscles but minimal lesions in the diaphragm, tongue, and muscles of deglutition. Conversely, veal calves raised in individual crates and fed a vitamin E or selenium-deficient milk replacer often have major muscle lesions in the muscles of deglutition and sucking such as the diaphragm, intercostal, tongue, labial, and laryngeal muscles, with few if any lesions in the leg muscles or heart.

Steatitis is not a factor in cattle or sheep cases, but it is a common lesion seen in cats and pigs as a result of being fed high levels of, or exclusively, fish products.

Lesions of the liver, as in pigs with hepatosis dietetica, a vitamin E/selenium-responsive disease, were not seen nor were lesions of the pancreas, such as are seen in baby chicks with a selenium deficiency. Encephalomalacic lesions present in chicks with a vitamin E deficiency likewise were not seen. Leiomyometaplasia of the bowel as seen in dogs was not found in these fish.

No attempt to evaluate the blood picture for anemia was made in these cases nor were the red blood cell fragility tests utilized.

The other suspected causes of these vitamin E/selenium-responsive diseases, such as the anti-vitamin E factors that develop in spoiled feeds, were not investigated.

REFERENCES

1. Maynard, L. A., and Loosli, J. K. *Animal Nutrition.* 6th ed. New York, McGraw-Hill, 1969.
2. Schwartz, K. Development and status of experimental work on factor 3-selenium. *Fed. Proc. 20(2)*, pt. 1: 666. 1961.
3. Sinnhuber, R. O., Lee, D. J., Wales, J. H., and Ayres, J. L. Dietary factors and hepatoma in rainbow trout (*Salmo gairdneri*). II. Co-carcinogenesis by cyclopropenoid fatty acids and the effect of gossypol and altered lipids on aflatoxin-induced liver cancer. *J. Nat. Cancer Inst. 41:* 1293. 1968.

DISCUSSION OF NUTRITIONAL MYOPATHY IN FISH

Question: What is a satellite cell?

J. M. King: To me it is a sarcolemmal cell. I always call it a sarcolemmal nucleus cell, one of the paramysial cells that's increasing just to regenerate the muscle. Incidentally, if I had a lamb with this disease it could have massive Zenker's degeneration in the muscle with mineralization, and if you would give it six to eight weeks regeneration would be completely resolved and essentially normal muscles would result. Animal muscle can really regenerate surprisingly well.

R. J. Roberts: I am very struck by your presentation. We certainly see plenty of this in Atlantic salmon. In Scotland we've also considered it to be classic white muscle disease based upon our experience in pigs, but we have never taken it any further than that. But the point I would like to ask you about is, have you seen any muscle regeneration in the fish tissues? We certainly see plenty of this in higher animals, but although I have seen it, and certainly Dr. Mawdesley-Thomas has seen it, Peter Finn says he hasn't seen it. It certainly doesn't seem to be a tremendous feature in our experience to get regeneration of muscle fibers in this disease or in any other disease in fish.

J. M. King: I have not seen it but I don't know why you would not. We tell fisheries biologists it is white muscle disease and they'd better take the cod-liver oil out of the diet, and lo and behold, they take the cod-liver oil out of the diet, and the fish get better. They might even add a bit of vitamin E if the original cod-liver oil was rancid. It also depends on how much of the unsaturated fats are in the other fat fractions of their diet. I don't wish to go into that.

Question: Were the bone changes due to vitamin E deficiency?

J. M. King: I had no reason to think that they weren't associated with the muscle lesion. I think they are a secondary atrophic type of bone lesion due to the marked muscle damage.

Comment: The only way that I can tell the difference between a satellite cell and a sarcolemmal nucleus is at the ultrastructure level. I don't think one can do it with any degree of certainty at the light microscope level, in my experience.

R. F. Nigrelli: I just want to ask if any of this type of disease has been found in feral fish? Have any of them been brought in to you? The reason I ask is because a number of years ago I got a number of pickerel, I think they were, from Lake Cuyahoga that had this disease occurring naturally.

J. M. King: No, sir. These are the only outbreaks I have had: Pennsylvania, Missouri, and New York State, plus one from Venezuela.

Question: I have one question for you. Did you see any "brown bowel" as we sometimes see in Scotty dogs associated with the disease of vitamin D deficiency?

J. M. King: No, I did not see it. I looked for it, but I did not see it.

33

Visceral Granuloma and Nephrocalcinosis of Trout

MARSHA L. LANDOLT

The brook trout (*Salvelinus fontinalis*) and the rainbow trout (*Salmo gairdneri*) are two extensively cultured native North American fishes that are subject to diet-related diseases which affect primarily the kidneys and stomach. Known respectively as visceral granuloma and nephrocalcinosis or nephrolithiasis, these are chronic, inflammatory diseases that generally do not result in high mortality unless the fishes are under stress (5). For this reason, the disease may pass unnoticed. Both diseases are restricted to cultured fishes.

VISCERAL GRANULOMA

Described originally as a neurilemmoma (14), and subsequently as a mycosis-like granuloma (12), visceral granuloma is an inflammatory disease which was thought to be infectious (11), but from which no organism has ever been isolated. The name visceral granuloma was proposed by Snieszko (9) when no infective agent could be demonstrated.

Grossly, the disease first appears as small papillary lesions which can be felt on the dorsal surface of the stomach. These lesions proliferate and become visible. As the disease progresses, greyish-white streaks and spots, which are composed of semifluid calcium deposits, appear in the kidneys (Fig. 33.1). Frequently the entire kidney is swollen. The granulomatous growths spread through the mesen-

793

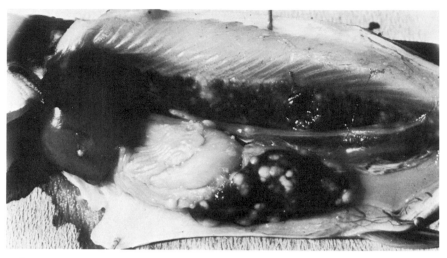

Fig. 33.1. Stomach, spleen, and kidney of brook trout affected with visceral granuloma.

teries and visceral fat in most cases, and in extreme cases there may be a similar involvement of the spleen and liver.

Histologically, visceral granuloma begins in the wall of the stomach as an inflammatory response with distinct foci of leukocytes. This inflammatory response is generally followed by the appearance of Langhans-type giant cells. These cells, which contain many nuclei arranged at the periphery of the cell, are thought to be formed either by fusion or by amitotic division of mononuclear phagocytes, and they are characteristic of tuberculosis in higher animals. Frequently, the giant cells contain concentric deposits of amorphous material which resemble the Schaumann bodies seen in diseases such as sarcoidosis. These laminar concretions, which also occur extracellularly, are sometimes multilobed and resemble fungi. The giant cells and concretions are gradually walled off by connective tissue, macrophages, and epithelioid cells, and assume an increasingly tubercle-like appearance (Fig. 33.2). Very often, several of these granulomatous centers will coalesce to form a single large mass. Eosinophilic cells may be associated with these centers. The disease progresses in a similar manner in the other affected organs. In the kidneys, the granulomas may be accompanied by tubular dilation and degeneration, the formation of tubular casts, and in extreme cases, the destruction of most of the functional kidney tissue.

The concretions and casts stain positively with the McManus periodic acid-Schiff's reagent, and are variably positive within a given section with Dahl's stain for calcium. Despite the resemblance of visceral granuloma to tuberculosis, a Ziehl-Neelsen stain does not reveal the presence of acid-fast bacteria.

Visceral granuloma has been shown to be a diet-related disease (3) and a strong but not complete correlation has been demonstrated between the incidence of visceral granuloma and the presence of cottonseed meal in the diet (3). This disease

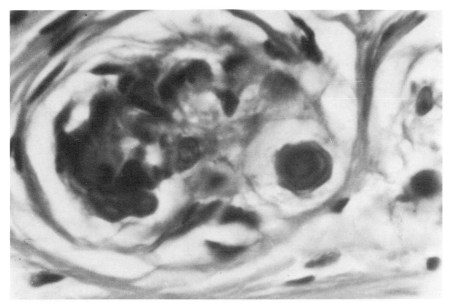

Fig. 33.2. Granuloma in stomach wall of fish with visceral granuloma. Note the laminated concretion. ×280.

resembles sarcoidosis, which is considered by Israel and Sones (6) to be a hypersensitivity reaction to some unknown widespread excitant. No relationship has yet been shown to exist between the presence of the disease and total or various concentrations of dietary magnesium or calcium. Water hardness also has not been implicated. Some correlation has been suggested, however, with total dietary phosphorus (3).

Of sixty-six 20-cm yearling brook trout obtained in January 1971 from the White Sulphur Spring NFH brood stock, 56.3% had visceral granuloma. The incidence was similar in males and females. A second group of fifty 20-cm yearling brook trout was examined in January 1972. These fish were of the same strain as the previous lot, they were maintained at the same hatchery (10) and were fed diets SD4-25 (1971 and 1972) and PR6-25 (1971 and 1972) which had the same formulation specifications (7), but less than 1% of the fish were affected. The explanation for such a fluctuation has yet to be found.

NEPHROCALCINOSIS

The incidence of nephrocalcinosis, like that of visceral granuloma, fluctuates greatly. The cause of the disease is unknown, although it is suspected to be nutritional. The disease has been referred to informally as nephrolithiasis, urinary calculi, and nephrocalcinosis; the latter name is the most widely used.

Grossly, nephrocalcinosis is seen in the kidneys of rainbow trout as prominent

Fig. 33.3. Mineral deposits in kidney of rainbow trout with nephrocalcinosis.

white streaks or spots (Fig. 33.3). Upon cutting, this white material, which is thought to be calcium phosphate (2, 13), appears cheesy and gritty in texture. Listlessness, loss of appetite, and darkening of the skin color (2) similar to that reported in fish that were fed linseed meal (1) may accompany the disease. The affected trout also may have pale gills, exophthalmia, ascites, and cardiac hypertrophy. While there is gastric involvement, the stomach lesions are generally not visible macroscopically. Wunder (13) reports a higher incidence of nephrocalcinosis among males than females.

Histologically, the formation of granulomas in the stomach appears to be identical to that in visceral granuloma. The gastric areas that are primarily affected are the serosa, the muscularis externa, and the connective tissue separating the circular and longitudinal muscles. The sequence of giant cell, inclusion body, and granuloma formation is that seen in visceral granuloma; however, there are fewer granulomatous centers, they are smaller, and they do not tend to coalesce into the large papillary masses seen in visceral granuloma. In contrast, the pathological changes seen in the kidneys are quite distinct. While granulomas do occasionally form in the kidneys and while there are some laminated concretions formed in the parenchyma, the sites primarily affected are the convoluted tubules and the ureters. Early in the course of the disease some of the tubules become dilated, with casts occurring in the lumen (Fig. 33.4). These casts are comprised of material that looks more like caseous necrosis than mineral deposits. The casts ex-

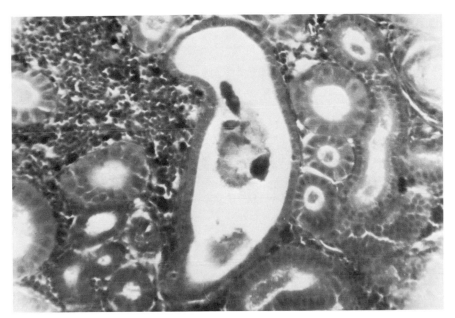

Fig. 33.4. Early nephrocalcinosis. Parenchyma is normal and only one tubule is dilated and contains casts. ×66.

tend throughout the tubules and into the ureters. As the disease progresses, the nuclei of the tubular epithelial cells become pyknotic, the cytoplasm vacuolated, and the cells are eventually sloughed into the lumen. In the kidneys, there is only a mild inflammatory response (4), but in the late stages of the disease the normal parenchymal tissue may be almost completely replaced by connective tissue, causing periglomerular fibrosis (Fig. 33.5). Surprisingly, the kidneys apparently do not cease to function, and in the absence of undue stress, mortality is low.

The material within the tubules generally stains negatively with the periodic acid-Schiff's reagent, and it is variably positive when stained by Dahl's method for calcium. As in the previous disease, the Ziehl-Neelsen stain reveals no acid-fast organisms.

Little work has been done on the etiology of nephrocalcinosis, although it has been speculated that it is just a species modification of visceral granuloma (3). Water hardness may play a role. Workers in France (2) found that after changing food suppliers there was a marked reduction in the incidence of the disease, which suggests that handling and storage of food may be a key factor. Smith, Holway, and Hammer (8) described pathological changes associated with sulfamerazine toxicity in cutthroat trout (*S. clarki*) that resemble some of those seen in nephrocalcinosis. Similar changes also occur in brook trout suffering from sulfamerazine toxicity (8). While isolated cases of urolithiasis have been reported in several

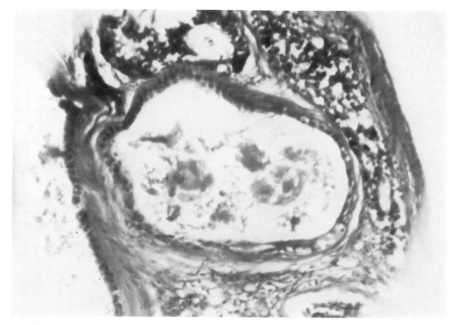

Fig. 33.5. Late nephrocalcinosis. Note fibrosis of parenchyma and necrosis of tubules. ×70.

species of wild fish, these cases have not been shown to be comparable to either of these diseases.

CONCLUSION

Even though they generally do not produce high mortality in hatchery fish, both nephrocalcinosis and visceral granuloma are important not only because of the potential information that the study of these diseases might yield but also because of the effect these diseases may have on hatchery-reared fish once they are released into the wild. Just as study of hepatoma in rainbow trout contributed to the understanding of the cause of hepatoma in higher vertebrates, so too might an understanding of these diseases produce information about other renal disorders. Similarly, further study of the role played by nutrition in fish diseases and of the importance of other physical factors on fish health may provide valuable ecological information.

REFERENCES

1. Almy, L. H., and Robinson, R. K. Toxic action of ingested linseed meal on trout. *J. Biol. Chem. 43:* 97. 1920.
2. Besse, P., de Kinkelin, P., and Levaditi, J. C. La Néphrocalcinose de la truite

arc-en-ciel (*Salmo irideus*, Gibbons, 1855). *Bull. Off. int. Épizoot. 69:* 1391. 1968.

3. Dunbar, C. E., and Herman, R. L.   Visceral granuloma in brook trout (*Salvelinus fontinalis*). *J. Nutr. 101:* 1445. 1971.

4. Finn, J. P., and Nielson, N. O.   The inflammatory response of rainbow trout. *J. Fish Biol. 3:* 463. 1971.

5. Herman, R. L.   Visceral granuloma and nephrocalcinosis. *U. S. Bur. Sport Fish. Wildlife, Fish. Dis. Leafl. 32.* 1971.

6. Israel, H. L., and Sones, M.   Sarcoidosis. *Advan. Tuberc. Res. 11:* 214. 1961.

7. Orme, L. E.   Trout feed formulation and development, pp. 187–189. *In* Report on the 1970 Workshop on Fish-Feed Technology and Nutrition. *U. S. Bur. Sport Fish. Wildlife, Resour. Publ. 102.* 1972.

8. Smith, C. E., Holway, J. E., and Hammer, G. L.   Sulfamerazine toxicity in cutthroat trout broodfish (*Salmo clarki*). *J. Fish Biol. 5:* 97. 1973.

9. Snieszko, S. F.   Hepatoma and visceral granuloma in trouts. *N. Y. Fish Game J. 8:* 145. 1961.

10. Warren, J. W.   Toxicity tests of erythromycin thiocyanate in rainbow trout. *Progr. Fish-Cult. 25:* 88. 1963.

11. Wood, E. M., and Yasutake, W. T.   Histopathology of fish. IV. A granuloma of brook trout. *Progr. Fish-Cult. 18:* 108. 1956.

12. Wood, E. M., Yasutake, W. T., and Lehman, W. L.   A mycosis-like granuloma of fish. *J. Infec. Dis. 97:* 262. 1955.

13. Wunder, W.   Eigenartige Veränderungen an der Niere und die Ausbildung einer Nierenzyste bei der Regenbogenforelle. *Allg. Fischerei-Ztg. 92:* n.p. 1967.

14. Young, G. A., and Olafson, P.   Neurilemmomas in a family of brook trout. *Am. J. Pathol. 20:* 413. 1944.

DISCUSSION OF VISCERAL GRANULOMA AND NEPHROCALCINOSIS OF TROUT

Question: I wonder what the age group of the experimental trout was with the small earliest lesions. Were they young animals?

M. L. Landolt: Yes, the ones I used were yearlings.

Question: Did you find any evidence of any parasite burdens, particularly nematodes in the alimentary tract?

M. L. Landolt: No. Dr. Herman and Mr. Dunbar followed the course of visceral granuloma rather closely from the very earliest stages of the disease with no evidence of parasites.

I was going to say that the trouble with visceral granuloma and nephrocalcinosis is that you don't know which fish have it because the fish don't look sick. You know the hatchery men don't appreciate your sampling their fish just in the hopes that you'll find it, so what we really get is a poor representation.

K. E. Wolf: Just to amplify an answer to the second question; this study occurred under laboratory conditions from protected water supplies. The animals used began as eggs brought in, and were some of the highest quality production fish obtainable. This is a specific-pathogen-free station, so I think we can say the likelihood of parasites being involved is minimal or almost to the vanishing point.

Comment: This is the most interesting disease that I know of in fish or other animals. The concentric rings similar to Schaumann bodies in human sarcoidosis are no less fascinating. If you look at these under polarized light there are birefringent bodies included in these and in the giant cells. With respect to the nephrocalcinosis, I wanted to ask if there is any sex difference?

M. L. Landolt: It is reported to be predominant in males.

Comment: When exposed to very low doses of chloroform in the atmosphere, male mice, particularly those of the C3H strain, develop a severe nephrocalcinosis which is often fatal. The thought just occurred to me that perhaps something that might account for these variable factors which we see would be components of the cottonseed meal which is soluble in chloroform. I am not thinking of chloroform specifically, but chloroform or related compounds and perhaps the storage of food in certain places. Who knows, freon is closely related, and is found in refrigerators. This might be something that could account for this disease.

Comment: I can't help but think of calciphylaxis described in mice in the work with stress where the mast cell is the mediator. This leads to deposition of calcium. I wonder if you couldn't consider mast cells as mediators of this response in these fishes. I think fluoroscopy would show which fishes had the lesion. Study the mast cells. There are some mast cell depletors that could be used to prevent the further deposition or further progression.

Comment: I was very interested in your comments about the Schaumann-like body here. Of course, you can see these in the lungs of man in conditions other than sarcoid. Some of these other conditions have an allergic background. Nephrocalcinosis is very interesting when you consider some of the very common conditions one encounters in laboratory rats which are also bred under nearly ideal conditions. It is a very common condition. It is what we call progressive glomerular nephrosis and also renal periarteritis. Some people would suggest that this could be an allergic response to something that you are feeding. We are thus getting away from a truly infectious etiology rather to a possibly modified allergic response.

M. L. Landolt: This does not appear to be in connection with an allergic response. We do find that you have a better chance of detecting or finding nephrocalcinosis and granuloma at particular times of the year. At our own station we find in late winter and early spring that fish in the raceways begin to show the condition known as "blue slime." The latter is just a hyperplasia of the goblet cells in the epidermis; that is a good time to look for nephrocalcinosis. It has been suggested that "blue slime" may be related to biotin deficiency, but you can't count on it.

G. L. Hoffman: There was one important economic sidelight to this. You may have noticed that the nephrocalcinosis on the kidney looks very much like worms, and when fishermen catch these fish and see these things that look like worms they throw the fish away. So it is a significant economic loss.

A. H. Walsh: I have seen this condition in a number of lake trout and it is very typical of visceral granuloma. The thing that bothers me is that one sees the concretions, but in addition I have seen in a few cases some PAS-positive and methenamine-staining bodies which seem to be budding. They are reminiscent to me of *Blastomyces dermatitidis*.

M. L. Landolt: I think that's why this condition was at one time described as a mycosis-like granuloma. These budding concretions, or whatever, look like fungal hyphae, and there was some error.

L. L. Eller: I have seen many similar lesions in other fish besides trout, specifically guppies. I have never found them to take a positive PAS or a methenamine stain. Thus I have actually eliminated in my own mind the idea of these being anything but calcium deposits because in the calcium stains I have done on these fish deposits they are always positive. To answer one of the other questions about the age of fish, these lesions also occur in large trout. I have examined many a large trout and the larger the fish becomes, the more granular the kidneys become, so they occur in all ages. In lake trout I have found the predominance of these lesions is in winter months, and in the summer months and autumn you won't find them. I can't explain why it would be, but I do know this happens. I just got through doing an experimental study on lake trout from Wyoming and the lesions were present.

M. L. Landolt: I think there is some question as to whether or not these lesions can regress, because as you said, you can find them in winter and when you go back in a few months they cannot be found. Something is happening to them.

G. Migaki: From a comparative histological standpoint, we have seen similar lesions in cattle and from sections we identified the organism as a colorless alga. Since we don't know the etiology of these granulomas I would just like to throw this out as a possible cause. I had a chance to look at these slides quite some time ago and at that time we ran a number of different special stains for many different organisms, but were unable to demonstrate an etiological agent. I know that Dr. Hoffman has described an infection by the alga *Chlorella,* which is a blue-green alga causing infection in bluegills. I don't know the histological appearance of it, but in cattle we have similar concentric laminations which resemble tubercle-like granulomas, and in those we have demonstrated an alga organism.

Comment: A number of years ago I went on a nine-month-long wild-goose chase with a cell culture approach to the visceral granuloma problem. We had long hyphal-like elements extend out several millimeters in the culture and that was my first introduction to myelin. We took time-interval micrographs of myelin and it performed beautifully, just like a mycotic organism, but as far as we are concerned an organ-type culture was completely negative.

PART VI
Neoplasia

34

Neoplasia in Fish

LIONEL E. MAWDESLEY-THOMAS

The study of the causes of things must be preceded by the study of
things caused.

J. Hughlings Jackson (1835–1911)

INTRODUCTION

When reviewing the progress of fish pathology in this century, Snieszko (1972)
stated that "anyone expecting to find there is a wealth of publications on fish
pathology more than 100 years old will be disappointed," and with few exceptions, this statement applies to the documentation of fish tumors. This also gives
some indication that the study of fish pathology is a young science. This is at
first a surprising fact, for one would have expected this science to have been
studied since the seventeenth century, following the invention of the earliest microscopes. Nevertheless, the specialities of comparative and veterinary pathology
have long lagged behind medical pathology. Although John Hunter (1728–1793),
the famous London surgeon, was the first English comparative pathologist, the
subject has been seriously neglected until this century. For while histology has
been studied since the advent of the microscope, the concept of disease at a cellular level was not appreciated until the middle of the nineteenth century. Rudolf
Virchow (1821–1902) published his now famous work on *Cellular Pathology* in
1858. Virchow was a medical man, and his new approach to disease was applied
only to man. The veterinarian might have been expected to follow suit, but it

805

must be remembered that the veterinarian, until this century, was concerned more with horses than with any other species. Much time had to elapse before the subject of animal pathology was considered in any detail, and then on an extremely limited basis, mainly confined to the horse. Still more time had to elapse before the more exotic species were considered. The lower vertebrates have had to wait the longest. Interest in comparative pathology has now gained much momentum, and one cannot write on this subject without mentioning the names of Schlumberger, the American medical pathologist, who added so much to the field of comparative pathology, and Innes, the veterinary pathologist from Cambridge, England, who, with Schlumberger, laid the foundation for much of the current work in comparative pathology. The field of pathology is a specialized one and until recently the majority of pathologists were either medically or veterinary qualified, for it was only in those two degree courses that any undergraduate teaching in disease processes was given. This is no longer strictly true, and in the field of fish pathology fishery biologists are receiving fundamental training in some of the more important disease processes. It is against such a background that pathology of fish tumors is studied.

GENERAL CONSIDERATIONS

At first sight, the study of fish tumors might seem to be unrewarding for the comparative pathologist, but further investigation shows the relevance of such a project, and how it can facilitate the establishment of a further link in the study of comparative pathology. Of far more significance in the study of neoplasia in the poikilothermic vertebrate is its significance in relation to the further basic understanding of neoplasia in general, and in particular in relation to the homeothermic vertebrates, specifically man.

Over the years, many viral-induced "neoplasms" have been documented, and these lesions are now considered under the heading of viral infections. Lymphocystis disease is the best example of this type of lesion. Theoretically, if an etiological agent, or agents, were found for all tumors, then the subject of neoplasia per se would disappear as an entity, for a neoplasm is essentially a lesion of unknown etiology. The study of fish tumors can shed some light on the part played by such conditions as geographical location, genetic factors, environmental factors, phylogenetic factors (including enzymatic or immunological considerations), oncogenic viruses, and trauma. The liver cell tumor, seen in some members of the Salmonidae when exposed to extremely low doses of aflatoxin B_1 (ppb), shows the extreme sensitivity of such a system. Stanton (1965) stated that *"the high sensitivity of small fish to a known carcinogen, their poikilothermic physiology and the ease with which their aquatic environment can be controlled are particular advantages in studies on carcinogenesis."* These are but a few reasons to show that while the documentation of tumors in fish is a worthwhile scientific entity in itself, it should be seen, as well, in the general context of neoplasia as a possible property of all life.

Dawe (1969b) in an excellent paper on the problems of oncogeny in relation to phylogeny raised many interesting questions, including the problems associated with "the phylogenetic point of neoplasm." Over the years this point was fixed within the class Pisces (Tentschländer, 1920), but more recently this point has been moved further down the phylogenetic tree (Howell, 1969; Jones, 1969; Pauley, 1969; Sparks, 1969). It is probable that as more information on neoplasia becomes available, the phylogenetic point of neoplastic transformation may recede further. Neoplasia may ultimately be considered a property of life. The hydra will have become a neoplasm with tentacles!

As comparative pathology is the study of as many phyla as possible, it was considered to be a useful procedure to update the taxonomic exercise carried out by Schlumberger and Lucké (1948) and to include in this paper the taxonomic distribution of tumor-bearing fish within the Chondrichthyes and Osteichthyes classes of fish. The present-day pattern might, therefore, be appreciated more readily, and it might prove to be a useful exercise to help in the understanding of the possible epidemiology and geographical distribution of neoplasia in fish.

DEFINITIONS

It is useful to define the two scientific words associated within this symposium in general and in relation to this paper in particular.

"Pathology" is essentially the study of disease, but disease, per se, does not exist; rather, it represents the response by a host to a noxious agent, whether it be physical, chemical, biological, or unknown. The response of a biological system to any known injurious agent is variable, and it is this variation which presents many of the problems that confront the pathologist. This is frequently seen in the response of the host to a tumor which is rapidly growing, as opposed to one which is slow growing.

The word "neoplasm," as defined by the Shorter Oxford English Dictionary, is a combination of Greek and French words, and was first used in 1864 as describing "a new formation of tissue in some part of the body: a tumor." In this paper the word "tumor" will be used in its specific sense, and will not refer in general to a swelling which could have a non-neoplastic etiology. A brief survey of the literature shows that there are a variety of definitions which have been given by various authorities, but the working definition to which most pathologists would subscribe is that given by Willis (1967): "A tumor is an abnormal mass of tissue, the growth of which exceeds and is uncoordinated with that of the normal tissue and persists in the same excessive manner after cessation of the stimuli which evoked the change." This definition implies that a neoplasm is essentially a proliferative lesion, and care must be taken to distinguish it from other proliferative lesions, as seen in the repair and inflammatory processes and in some of the more exotic hyperplastic conditions. This condition is particularly well illustrated by the case of thyroid hyperplasia in fish. The differential diagnosis in these cases can be extremely difficult, and many histological sections, using special stains, may have to be studied to ensure a definitive diagnosis.

A neoplasm is delineated by its distinctive characteristic of proliferation, which is progressive, and uncoordinated with the other tissues in the particular biological system in which it is found.

CLASSIFICATION

Few classifications can be either absolute or complete, but it is essential to try to formulate one which will cover the majority of tumors. A useful classification is one based on the anatomical or histological type of tissue from which the tumor arises.

Classification of Tumors
(modified after Willis, 1967)

i	Tumors of epithelial tissue	Consist of papillomas, adenomas, or carcinomas.
ii	Tumors of nonhematopoietic mesenchymal tissue	Consist of fibromas, lipomas, chondromas, osteomas, angiomas, leiomyomas, rhabdomyomas, etc. Malignant tumors are described as sarcomas, being prefixed by the name of the type of tissue from which they have arisen.
iii	Tumors of hematopoietic tissue	Consist of tumors of lymphatic or other hematopoietic tissue.
iv	Tumors of neural tissue	Consist of tumors arising from the central or peripheral nervous system, e.g., neurilemmomas and ganglioneuromas.
v	Special classes of tumors	Consist of tumors arising from pigment cells, including the melanomas, the erythrophoromas, etc., teratomas, and embryonic tumors.

It must be remembered that a tumor is designated by the predominate tissue in the tumor, for all tumors have a mesenchymal supportive stroma and contain blood vessels, but these elements should not be considered as prime-movers when classifying a tumor.

This classification includes all known types of neoplasia in fish. This list is longer than its mammalian counterpart, from which it was derived, as many of the pigmented tumors are specific to fish.

BENIGN AND MALIGNANT TUMORS

While the definition of a tumor may be difficult, there is a further complication, since another subdivision has to be made, as to whether the tumor is a simple noninvasive, innocent or benign tumor, or an invasive, malignant one. This is an extremely important point to establish, since the status of the tumor is vital when considering the prognosis or life span of the biological system. This aspect is confused in man, where much more is known about the behavior of tumors, but even more confusion exists in comparative pathology, where far fewer facts are known about the general biology of the tumors encountered. The terms "benign" and "malignant," although now part of the accepted parlance of pathology, initially did not represent a pathological but rather a clinical distinction. The terms were used by the medical clinician to indicate a clinical prognosis. Now they have, through usage, come to have pathological overtones. Like all scientific terms, they are meaningless unless they are defined precisely (Mawdesley-Thomas, 1970). In few cases in animals can a tumor be studied by biopsy over a period of time culminating in a full and thorough necropsy, such as can be done in man. It is inadvisable to relate tumors in animals to their apparent counterparts in man, as they may not have any true human counterpart, as is the case with certain pigment-cell tumors. Furthermore, even if they are similar histologically, their biological behavior may be different. As so little is known about the biological behavior of fish tumors, it is extremely unwise to assume that they are anything more than analogous to those tumors seen in man. As every experimentalist is aware, "only man is like man." Wellings (1969b), in his excellent review on neoplasia in fish, considers fish tumors to be both analogous and homologous. In the present state of knowledge, there is insufficient evidence to consider them as anything more than analogous. Studies of neoplasia in the rat, particularly tumors of mammary tissue, have shown that it is only by an appreciation of the total biological behavior of a neoplasm that a correct designation in this context can be made. Morphological criteria are far from absolute in comparative pathology. There can be only one absolute criterion of malignancy, and that is of invasion, either local or distant. The line of demarcation between hyperplasia and neoplasia is far less easily defined.

The subject of neoplasia in fish has been extensively reviewed and annotated over the past years. The initial stimulus to this subject was the first review article on "Tumors of Fishes, Amphibians, and Reptiles" by Schlumberger and Lucké (1948). In the last few years the subject has attracted more attention, and the once-scattered literature has been brought together and critically reviewed (Wellings, 1969b; Dawe, 1969a; Mawdesley-Thomas, 1969, 1971a, 1972b). It would be pointless to repeat the contents of these articles. This paper will concentrate on some of the problems posed by the study of neoplasia in this poikilothermic vertebrate group, together with some of the practical difficulties of making an exact diagnosis.

ETIOLOGICAL CONSIDERATIONS

It is often only a function of time before a particular tumor in a particular species is placed in its proper perspective. Nowhere is this more true than in the case of the central nervous system, which usually results in a total failure to examine the system. It is thought that tumors of this system are rare, but it will not be until the brains of tens of thousands of specimens of any species have been exam-

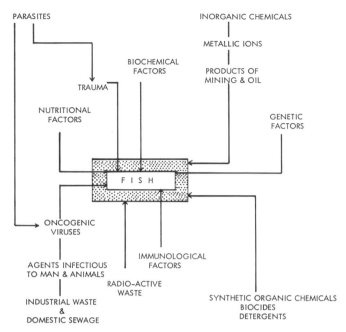

Fig. 34.1. Possible etiologies of neoplasia in fish.

ined that their true incidence will be appreciated (Mawdesley-Thomas and Newman, 1972). Harshbarger (1973) was the first to record an olfactory neuroepithelioma in a bloater (*Caregonus hoyi*). The central nervous system illustrates another interesting difference between the poikilothermic vertebrate and its higher counterparts. This system is capable of much regeneration and repair in the poikilotherm, and one wonders what relationship exists between this property and neoplastic transformation. The incidence of neoplasia in the central nervous system is completely unknown at the present time.

The varying incidence of tumors of pigment cells is extremely interesting, considering the widespread distribution and variation of the chemical moieties of pigments found in fish. These tumors have shed much interesting light on the genetic basis of neoplasia. The study of neoplasia in animals, while of interest in relation to man, has, on occasion, provided a vital link to a potential human hazard. This is exemplified by the aflatoxin story in which Halver and Ashley were the leading protagonists.

GEOGRAPHICAL DISTRIBUTION

Epidemiological studies of both human and animal disease have shown that in some instances there is a distinct geographical distribution of a particular disease, examples being the distribution of carcinoma of the liver in the Bantu tribes in

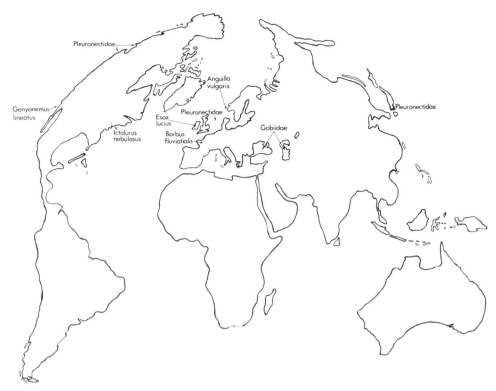

Fig. 34.2. Geographical distribution of some fish species with specific tumors.

Africa and Burkitt's lymphoma in Central Africa. Documentation already exists to show that certain tumors of fish, particularly those which can be seen on the external surfaces of the body, are to be found within a particular, and often highly specific, geographical location. Examples of this are seen in the papillomas of the Pleuronectidae off the west coast of America (Chuinard et al., 1964), the lymphosarcomas in the Esocidae in Ireland (Mulcahy, 1970), the stomato-papillomas in the Anguillidae in the North and Baltic seas (Deys, 1969). When considering any etiology, one is often faced with a multifactorial problem. Such is the case with the etiology of some of these fish tumors. The geographical location of any given tumor is often very helpful in the assessment of priorities in relation to etiology. Local factors must, in all probability, be important irrespective of whether they are genetic or environmental. In the case of the lymphosarcomas in the Esocidae in Ireland, it would be interesting to see what, if any, was the relationship between this condition, Marek's disease in poultry, and Burkitt's lymphoma in man. Such a comparative approach would be of the utmost value in the establishment of possible oncogenic agents which are common to the animal kingdom, but which may present variations on a theme according to which particular animal species is affected.

GENETIC FACTORS

The genetic basis of disease in man has only just begun to be appreciated in the past few years. While geneticists have been associated with animal and plant husbandry, seldom have they been interested in the genetic basis of disease. Tumors of pigment cells, particularly the melanomas and melanosarcomas, have proved to be useful animal models in which to study the genetic basis of neoplasia. Work still continues on this tumor type, particularly in the smaller tropical fish species. Recent workers (Siciliano, Perlmutter, and Clark, 1971) have shown the effect of sex on the development of melanomas in xiphophoran fish. Male sex hormones appeared to augment the melanotic process. Other workers (Vielkind, Vielkind, and Anders, 1971) have shown, also in xiphophoran fish, that amelanotic melanomas appear to show a higher degree of malignancy than their melanotic counterparts. It was suggested that this was associated with their higher DNA content. Several tumors have been described as "species specific." These include the melanomas already mentioned, together with the neurilemmomas seen in the goldfish and the snapper fish. The geographical distribution of the papillomas in the Pleuronectidae and the lymphosarcomas in the Esocidae has already been mentioned, but the possibility of a common genetic pool cannot be overlooked as an etiological possibility.

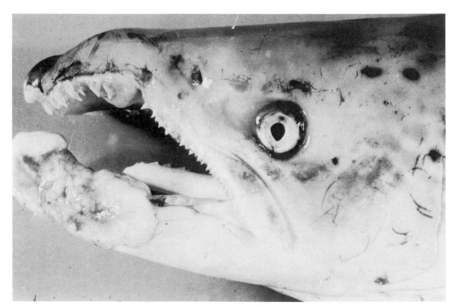

Fig. 34.3. Squamous cell carcinomas affecting the upper and lower mandible of an Atlantic salmon (*Salmo salar*). (Courtesy of Dr. R. J. Roberts.)

Fig. 34.4A. Adenocarcinoma of the thyroid in a roach (*Rutilus rutilus*).

Fig. 34.4B. Adenocarcinoma of the thyroid in a roach (*Rutilus rutilus*), showing invasion of the gill filaments.

ENVIRONMENTAL FACTORS

As the poikilothermic vertebrate is so intimately associated with its environment, it is affected by the many physical and chemical changes which occur within that particular environment. Water pollution, particularly of the lakes, rivers, and estuarine and coastal waters, presents a real and immediate hazard to their respective flora and fauna. A not-so-obvious risk is the potential carcinogenic hazard which pollution may bring in its wake. Skin and mouth tumors have been re-

Fig. 34.5. Stickleback with tumor on posterior ventral aspect.

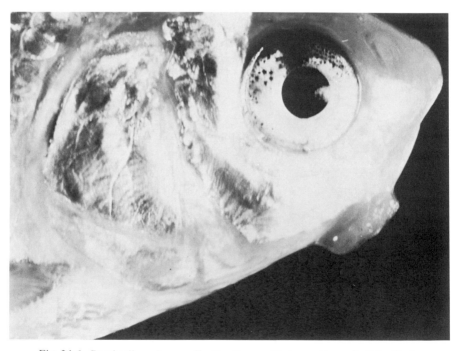

Fig. 34.6. Basal cell carcinoma affecting the maxilla in a golden orfe (*Idus idus*).

Fig. 34.7. Squamous cell carcinoma of the upper maxilla of *Parabasogigas crassus.*

ported in fish from polluted waters (Lucké and Schlumberger, 1941; Russell and Kotin, 1957; Cooper and Keller, 1969). The presence of chemical carcinogens in water has been established (Hueper, 1942; Hueper and Ruchhoft, 1954). The potential hazards of biocides, detergents, polychlorinated biphenyls, and like compounds have still to be evaluated. The relationship between these compounds and neoplasia represents a difficult problem and one which will not readily be resolved. One of the main problems is the paucity of fish caught every year with tumors that are available for scientific investigation. The problems of biological concentration of biocides, particularly at predator pinnacles, must also be studied further (Mawdesley-Thomas and Leahy, 1967), together with the effect of these compounds on many of the migratory species, particularly the Salmonidae.

PHYLOGENETIC FACTORS

Enzymatic Factors

Within the class of Pisces, the largest phylum in the animal kingdom, it is not surprising that there are biochemical and enzymatic differences between and

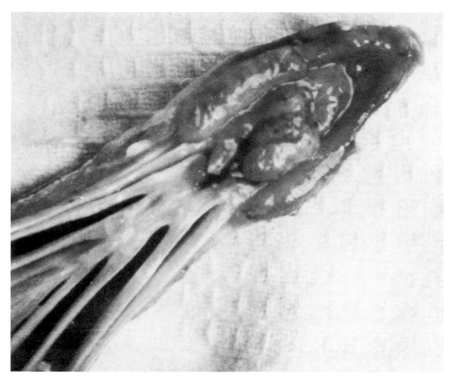

Fig. 34.8. Lymphosarcoma of the mandible in a pike (*Esox lucius*). (Courtesy of Dr. M. F. Mulcahy.)

within the various species and subspecies. The presence or absence of a particular enzyme system will determine a specific metabolic pathway in relation to various foods and other exogenous compounds. In some instances, particularly in relation to potentially carcinogenic substances, it is important to establish whether a proximate carcinogen is formed or not. It has already been shown that enzymatic differences occur between subspecies of the Salmonidae (Mawdesley-Thomas and Barry, 1970). It is such thinking that will ultimately explain the difference in incidence of liver tumors between rainbow and brown trout when fed aflatoxin. The presence or absence of certain enzyme or iso-enzyme systems is seen in various species and subspecies, according to the genetic make-up of the species. With all these etiological considerations associated with neoplasia, there is seldom a single factor acting at a single time, but it is more a problem of multifactorial interaction.

Immunological Factors

The relationship between phylogenic position and neoplastic transformation is thought to be closely associated with the presence or absence of a lymphoid

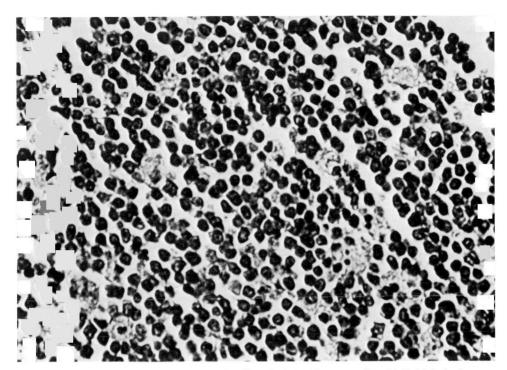

Fig. 34.9. Lymphosarcoma in the pike (*Esox lucius*). (Courtesy of Dr. M. F. Mulcahy.) Hematoxylin and eosin (H&E); ×55.

system, upon which the immune response is dependent. Whether the immunological response in fish with tumors is altered or absent needs further investigation. Some tumors have been transplanted successfully, as in the case of the carcinomas described by Lucké and Schlumberger (1941) in which auto- and homo- transplants showed continued growth (Good and Papermaster, 1964). The involution of the lymphoid system is age-related, and this could account for the fact that neoplasia is more common in the older animal. This is a subject which is still ill-understood, and little work in this field has been undertaken in fish, although the immune response, particularly in the Salmonidae, has been studied in relation to various infectious agents (Klontz, 1972; Dorson, 1972).

ONCOGENIC VIRUSES

The increasing importance of oncogenic viruses in neoplastic disease in animals has now been realized. This subject has recently been reviewed (Wolf, 1972; Mawdesley-Thomas, 1972a). The role of viruses in the etiology of such diseases as Burkitt's lymphoma, Marek's disease, and lymphosarcoma in fish has already been established in part. There can be little doubt that the viral etiology of many

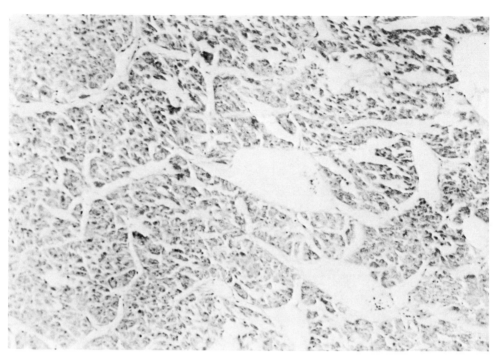

Fig. 34.10. Malignant liver cell tumor in a rainbow trout (*Salmo gairdneri*). The normal histological pattern is completely distorted. H&E; ×80.

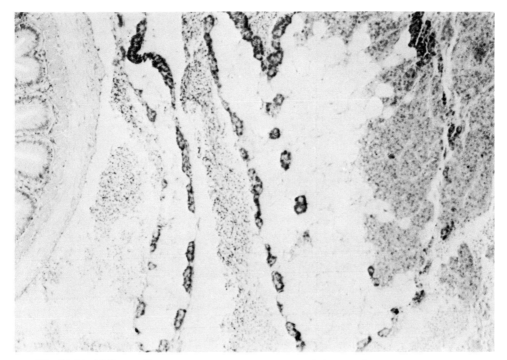

Fig. 34.11. Malignant liver cell tumor in a rainbow trout (*Salmo gairdneri*), showing invasion of the pancreas and omental fat. H&E; ×80.

other tumors will become established over the next decade. Viral diseases can be transmitted through the agencies of water, other fish, and parasites.

TRAUMA

In many animals, local trauma can give rise to various pathological conditions, including neoplastic transformation. The fact that many species of fish whose habitat is on the sea or river bed, or which are bottom feeders, have buccal and skin neoplasms suggests that trauma, possibly coupled with chemical agencies found on the sea or river beds, may be an etiological factor in neoplasia (Mawdesley-Thomas and Fraser, 1972). It is also thought that once the epithelium has been damaged it may be more sensitive to chemical carcinogens or oncogenic viruses.

CELL TYPE

The histological classification of tumors has always appeared to be the most logical one. The distribution of certain tumor cell types throughout the animal kingdom reveals many interesting facts; not least is that, in fish, the predominant

Fig. 34.12. Leiomyoma in a goldfish (*Carassius auratus*).

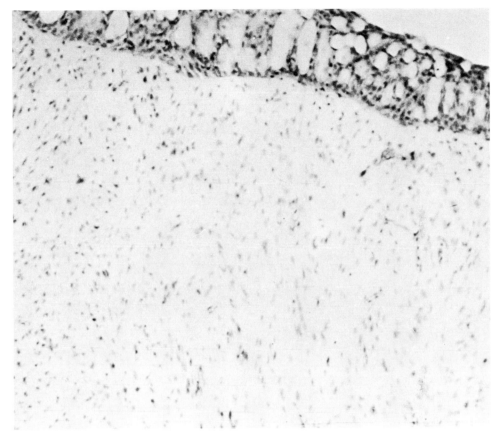

Fig. 34.13. Leiomyoma in a goldfish (*Carassius auratus*). The smooth muscle cells are clearly visible and extend up to the basal cells of the epidermis. H&E; ×150.

tumors of this vertebrate class are the tumors of mesenchymal origin, the lipoma, the fibroma, osteoma, together with their malignant counterparts. The epithelial tumor, which is the most common type of tumor seen in man, is feared because of the tendency to metastasize early in its growth. This is in contrast to epithelial tumors in the lower phyla, where metastasis is distinctly uncommon.

TAXONOMIC DISTRIBUTION

Little can be added to the comments of Schlumberger and Lucké (1948), who first described a taxonomic distribution. The incidence of tumors is far higher in the bony fishes than in cartilaginous fishes. However, this difference may be over-emphasized when the sample sizes are considered. Of the bony fishes, six families would appear to show a preponderance of tumors, namely the Salmonidae, Cypri-

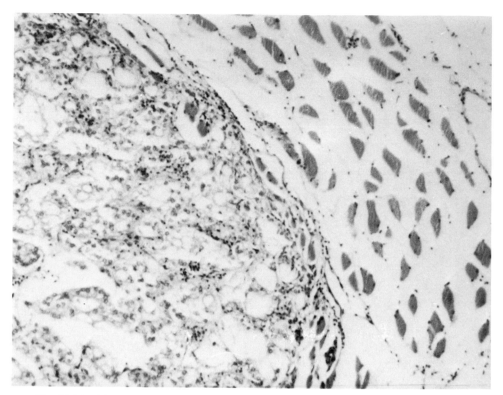

Fig. 34.14. Adenocarcinoma of the thyroid. There is infiltration of the surrounding skeletal muscle fibers. H&E; ×140.

nidae, Gadidae, Bothidae, Pleuronectidae, and the Poeciliidae. This distribution may again be more apparent than real, as these six species constitute major food species and the sample size would be larger than for most other species. It must also be remembered that about 50% of the world's fish catch is caught from approximately 1% of the ocean surface. In relation to the number of fish caught, there is a distinct impression that tumors are more common in freshwater fish than in marine fish.

TAXONOMIC DISTRIBUTION OF NEOPLASIA IN FISH

1.   **CLASS CHONDRICHTHYES–CARTILAGINOUS FISHES**

1.1.   ORDER SQUALIFORMES

1.1.1.   *FAMILY CARCHARHINIDAE–REQUIEM SHARKS*

Prionace glauca	Adenoma, liver	Schroeders, 1908
Carcharhinus milberti	Reticulum cell sarcoma	Harshbarger, 1973
Carcharhinus leucas	Fibrosarcoma	Harshbarger, 1973

1.1.2.   *FAMILY SCYLIORHINIDAE–CAT SHARKS*

Scyliorhinus caniculus	Odontoma	Ladreyt, 1929
Scyliorhinus caniculus	Chondroma, right flank	Thomas, 1933d
Scyliorhinus caniculus	Osteoma, trunk	Thomas, 1933d
Scyliorhinus caniculus	Epidermoid carcinoma, oral	Stolk, 1956c

1.1.3.   *FAMILY SQUALIDAE–DOGFISH SHARKS*

Squalus fernandinus	Thyroid tumor	Cameron & Vincent, 1915
Squalus fernandinus	Chondroma, lumbar vertebrae	Takahashi, 1929
Squalus acanthias	Fibroepithelial polyps, oral	Weilings, 1969b

1.1.4.   *FAMILY RAJIDAE–SKATES*

Raja clavata	Malignant melanoma, head	Johnstone, 1910-11
Raja clavata	Malignant melanoma, head	Johnstone, 1911-12
Raja clavata	Melanomas	Haddow & Blake 1933
Raja macrorhynchus	Fibrosarcoma	Drew, 1912
Raja maculata	Hemangioma	Drew, 1912
Raja batis	Malignant melanoma, posterior fin	Johnstone, 1911-12
Raja batis	Malignant melanoma	Johnstone, 1913

2.   **CLASS OSTEICHTHYES–BONY FISHES**

2.1   ORDER ELOPIFORMES

2.1.1.   *FAMILY ELOPIDAE–TARPONS*

| Elops saurus | Chondroma, subcutaneous | Surbeck, 1921 |

(continued)

Tumors included in this table are considered to be spontaneous. Induced tumors have not been included.

Various amendments have been made to the names to bring them into line with current designation.

2.2.   ORDER ANGUILLIFORMES

2.2.1.   *FAMILY ANGUILLIDAE—FRESHWATER EELS*

Anguilla anguilla	Adenocarcinoma, kidney	Schmey, 1911
Anguilla anguilla	Fibrosarcoma, coelom	Wolff, 1912
Anguilla anguilla	Fibrosarcoma, coelom	Plehn, 1924
Anguilla anguilla	Adenocarcinoma	Plehn, 1924
Anguilla anguilla	Papilloma	Thomas & Oxner, 1930
Anguilla anguilla	Papilloma	Christiansen & Jensen, 1947
Anguilla anguilla	Papilloma	Schäperclaus, 1953
Anguilla anguilla	Papilloma	Lümann & Mann, 1956
Anguilla anguilla	Papilloma	Mattheis, 1964
Anguilla anguilla	Papilloma, oral	Deys, 1969
Anguilla anguilla	Papilloma	Mann et al., 1970

2.2.2.   *FAMILY CONGRIDAE—CONGER EELS*

Conger conger	Hemangioepithelioma	Drew, 1912
Conger conger	Fibrosarcoma, subcutaneous	Johnstone, 1920
Conger conger	Lymphosarcoma, kidney	Williams, 1931

2.2.3.   *FAMILY ELECTROPHORIDAE—ELECTRIC EELS*

Electrophorus electricus	Papilloma, trunk	Coates et al., 1938

2.2.4.   *FAMILY MURAENIDAE—MORAYS*

Muraena helena	Adenocarcinoma, oral	Ladreyt, 1935

2.3.   ORDER CLUPEIFORMES

2.3.1.   *FAMILY CLUPEIDAE—HERRINGS*

Clupea harengus harengus	Lymphosarcoma	Johnstone 1926
Clupea harengus harengus	Rhabdomyoma	Williams, 1931
Clupea harengus harengus	Leiomyoma (?)	Thomas, 1933a
Clupea harengus	Rhabdomyoma	Mawdesley-Thomas, 1972b
Sardina pilchardus	Fibroma	Johnstone, 1911-12
Sardina pilchardus	Fibroma	Johnstone, 1924-25
Sardina pilchardus	Fibroma	Biavati & Mancini, 1967

2.4.   ORDER SALMONIFORMES

2.4.1.   *FAMILY SALMONIDAE—SALMONS AND TROUTS*

Oncorhynchus tshawytscha	Fibroameloblastoma	Schlumberger & Katz, 1956
Oncorhynchus keta	Fibrosarcoma, body cell	Kazama, 1922
Oncorhynchus keta	Fibrosarcoma, body cell	Takahashi, 1929

2.4.1. *FAMILY SALMONIDAE–SALMONS AND TROUTS* (cont.)

Oncorhynchus keta	Fibrosarcoma, body cell	Takahashi, 1929
Oncorhynchus keta	Lymphosarcoma	Honma & Hirosaki, 1966
Oncorhynchus gorbuscha	Fibrosarcoma, body cell	Takahashi, 1929
Oncorhynchus kisutch	Fibroma, back	Milleman, 1968
Oncorhynchus kisutch	Fibroma	Milleman, 1968
Oncorhynchus kisutch	Lymphosarcoma, stomach	Ashley et al., 1969
Oncorhynchus kisutch	Osteogenic sarcoma	Harshbarger, 1973
Oncorhynchus rhodurus	Hepatoma	Harshbarger, 1973
Oncorhynchus rhodurus	Polyps, stomach	Harshbarger, 1973
Oncorhynchus masou ishikawae	Hepatoma	Harshbarger, 1973
Oncorhynchus nerka	Rhabdomyosarcoma	Harshbarger, 1973
Salmo salar	Thyroid tumor (?)	Gilruth, 1902
Salmo salar	Thyroid tumor (?)	Wilkie, 1891
Salmo salar	Lymphosarcoma, kidney	Haddow & Blake, 1933
Salmo salar	Squamous cell carcinoma, oral	Roberts, 1972
Salmo spp.	Thyroid tumor (?)	Plehn, 1902
Salmo gairdneri	Thyroid tumor (?)	Gilruth, 1902
Salmo gairdneri	Leiomyoma, stomach	Plehn, 1906
Salmo gairdneri	Adenoma, thyroid	Leger, 1925
Salmo gairdneri	Fibrosarcoma	Leger, 1925
Salmo gairdneri	Adenoma, liver	Haddow & Blake, 1933
Salmo gairdneri	Liver cell tumor	Scolari, 1953
Salmo gairdneri	Thyroid hyperplasia	Robertson & Chaney, 1953
Salmo gairdneri	Liver cell tumor	Nigrelli, 1954
Salmo gairdneri	Liver cell tumor	Nigrelli & Jakowska, 1955
Salmo gairdneri	Liver cell tumor	Cudkowicz & Scolari, 1955
Salmo gairdneri	Leiomyoma, oral	Kubota, 1955b
Salmo gairdneri	Liver cell tumor	Honma & Shirai, 1959
Salmo gairdneri	Cholangiocystadenoma	Honma & Shirai, 1959
Salmo gairdneri	**Cystadenoma**, liver	Honma & Shirai, 1959
Salmo gairdneri	Rhabdomyoma	Mawdesley-Thomas, 1969
Salmo gairdneri	Liver cell tumor	Levaditi et al., 1960
Salmo gairdneri	Rhabdomyoma	Mawdesley-Thomas & Jolly, 1968
Salmo gairdneri	Fibrosarcoma, trunk	Mawdesley-Thomas, **1971a**
Salmo trutta	Fibroma, subcutaneous	Eberth, 1878
Salmo trutta	Thyroid tumor (?)	Bonnet, 1883
Salmo trutta	Thyroid tumor	Ayson, 1896, 1898, 1902
Salmo trutta	Leiomyoma, stomach	Pesce, 1907a
Salmo trutta	Adenocarcinoma, thyroid	Smith, 1909
Salmo trutta	Adenoma, liver	Plehn, 1909
Salmo trutta	Odontoma	Plehn, 1915

(continued)

2.4.1.   *FAMILY SALMONIDAE–SALMONS AND TROUTS* (cont.)

Salmo trutta	Papilloma, skin	Thomas, 1932e
Salmo trutta	Fibroma, coelom	Kreyberg, 1937
Salmo trutta	Adenoma, gill	Sarkar & Dutta Chaudhuri, 1964
Salmo mykis	Adenoma, gut	Thomas, 1931b
Salmo clarki	Rhabdomyoma, trunk	Adami, 1908
Salmo spp.	Adenocarcinoma, thyroid	Gilruth, 1902
Salmo spp.	Thyroid tumor (?)	Pick, 1905
Salmo spp.	Adenocarcinoma, thyroid	Jaboulay, 1908a,b
Salmo spp.	Thyroid tumor (?)	Marine & Lenhart, 1910a
Salmo spp.	Thyroid tumor (?)	Gaylord & Marsh, 1912a,
Salmo spp.	Thyroid tumor (?)	Peyron & Thomas, 1930
Salmo spp.	Erythrophoroma, skin	Thomas, 1931a
Salvelinus namaycush	Lymphosarcoma, kidney	Ehlinger, 1963
Salvelinus namaycush	Lymphosarcoma	Dunbar, 1969
Salvelinus namaycush	Fibroma	Broughton & Choquette, 1971
Salvelinus fontinalis	Thyroid tumor (?)	Scott, 1891
Salvelinus fontinalis	Sarcoma, trunk	Plehn, 1906
Salvelinus fontinalis	Osteoma	Thomas, 1932b
Salvelinus fontinalis	Lymphosarcoma	Dunbar, 1969
Salvelinus fontinalis × S. miyabe	Fibrosarcoma	Harshbarger, 1973
Hucho hucho	Fibrosarcoma, liver	Plehn, 1909
Coregonus hoyi	Olfactory neuroepithelioma	Harshbarger, 1973

2.4.2.   *FAMILY PLECOGLOSSIDAE–JAPANESE FISHES*

Plecoglossus altevelis	Lipoma, subcutaneous	Takahashi, 1929
Plecoglossus altivelis	Myxoma	Honma, 1965
Plecoglossus altivelis	Lymphosarcoma, ovary	Honma, 1966
Plecoglossus altivelis	Adrenal, tumor	Honma, 1966
Plecoglossus altivelis	Hemangioendothelioma	Honma, 1966

2.4.3.   *FAMILY OSMERIDAE–SMELTS*

Osmerus eperlanus	Squamous cell carcinoma, oral	Breslauer, 1915–16
Osmerus eperlanus	Rhabdomyoma, trunk	Bergman, 1921
Hypomesus olidus	Sarcoma	Hoshina, 1950

2.4.4.   *FAMILY ESOCIDAE–PIKES*

Esox lucius	Osteosarcoma, fin	Walgren, 1876b
Esox lucius	Osteoma, mandible	Bland-Sutton, 1885
Esox lucius	Fibrosarcoma, trunk	Ohlmacher, 1898
Esox lucius	Fibroma, trunk	Plehn, 1906
Esox lucius	Osteoma, fin	Plehn, 1906
Esox lucius	Fibrosarcoma, kidney	Plehn, 1906
Esox lucius	Thyroid tumor (?)	Marine & Lenhart, 1910

2.4.4.   *FAMILY ESOCIDAE–PIKES* (cont.)

Esox lucius	Lipoma, subcutaneous	Bergman, 1921
Esox lucius	Adenocarcinoma, ovary	Haddow & Blake, 1933
Esox lucius	Lymphosarcoma, subcutaneous	Haddow & Blake, 1933
Esox lucius	Lymphosarcoma, kidney	Nigrelli, 1947
Esox lucius	Lymphosarcoma, general	Mulcahy, 1963
Esox lucius	Lymphosarcoma, general	Mulcahy & O'Rourke, 1964a,b
Esox lucius	Sarcoma	Ljungberg & Lange, 1968

2.5.   ORDER CYPRINIFORMES

2.5.1.   *FAMILY CHARACIDAE–CHARACINS*

Astyanax mexicanus	Lymphosarcoma, head	Nigrelli, 1947
Thayeria obliqua	Adenocarcinoma, kidney	Stolk, 1957a
Phenecogrammus interruptus	Myxoma, skin	Stolk, 1958a
Pristella riddlei	Sarcomas	Wessing, 1959
Pristella riddlei	Sarcomas	Wessing & von Bargen, 1959
Anoptichthys jordani	Melanoma, eye	Stolk, 1958e,g
Ctenobrycon spilurus	Guanophoroma	Stolk, 1959c

2.5.2.   *FAMILY CYPRINIDAE–MINNOWS AND CARPS*

Cyprinus carpio	Fibroma, coelom	Crisp, 1854
Cyprinus carpio	Fibroma, coelom	Gervais, 1876
Cyprinus carpio	Squamous cell carcinoma, skin	Dauwe & Pennemann, 1904
Cyprinus carpio	Squamous cell carcinoma	Bashford et al., 1905
Cyprinus carpio	Squamous cell carcinoma, operculum	Fiebiger, 1909a
Cyprinus carpio	Osteoma, skull	Fiebiger, 1909b
Cyprinus carpio	Fibroma, coelom	Ronca, 1914
Cyprinus carpio	Neurilemmoma	Harshbarger, 1973
Carassius carassius	Fibroma, coelom	Plehn, 1906
Carassius carassius	Fibrosarcoma, testis	Plehn, 1906
Carassius carassius	Chondroma, skull	Mulsow, 1915
Carassius carassius	Fibroma, ovary	Freudenthal, 1928
Carassius carassius	Papilloma, skin	Takahashi, 1929
Carassius auratus	Fibrosarcoma, fin	Bland-Sutton, 1885
Carassius auratus	Carcinoma, generalized	Ceretto, 1968
Carassius auratus	Fibrosarcoma, urinary tract	Semer, 1888
Carassius auratus	Transitional cell carcinoma, urinary bladder	Plehn, 1909
Carassius auratus	Fibroma, orbit	Guglianetti, 1910
Carassius auratus	Fibrosarcoma, skin	Schamberg & Lucké, 1922

(continued)

2.5.2.   *FAMILY CYPRINIDAE–MINNOWS AND CARPS* (cont.)

Carassius auratus	Fibroma, subcutaneous	Wago, 1922
Carassius auratus	Fibrosarcoma, subcutaneous	Johnstone, 1923
Carassius auratus	Lymphosarcoma, kidney	Plehn, 1924
Carassius auratus	Fibrosarcoma, subcutaneous	Roffo, 1924
Carassius auratus	Papilloma, skin (?)	Sagawa, 1925
Carassius auratus	Fibroma, skin	Sagawa, 1925
Carassius auratus	Fibroma, subcutaneous	Eguchi & Oota, 1926
Carassius auratus	Fibrosarcoma, fin	Dominguez, 1928
Carassius auratus	Fibrosarcoma, skin	Montpellier & Dieuziede, 1932
Carassius auratus	Neurofibroma, subcutaneous	Picchi, 1933
Carassius auratus	Leiomyoma	Schlumberger, 1949
Carassius auratus	Fibrosarcoma, subcutaneous	Lucké et al., 1948
Carassius auratus	Neurilemmomas	Schlumberger, 1951
Carassius auratus	Neurilemmomas	Schlumberger, 1952
Carassius auratus	Melanoma, orbit	Mawdesley-Thomas, 1972b
Carassius auratus	Neurilemmomas	Mawdesley-Thomas, 1972b
Leuciscus idus	Fibrosarcoma, trunk	Plehn, 1906
Leuciscus idus	Squamous cell carcinoma	Mawdesley-Thomas, 1972b
Leuciscus leudiscus	Lipoma, coelom	Mawdesley-Thomas, 1972b
Rutilus rutilus	Adenocarcinoma, thyroid	Mawdesley-Thomas, 1972b
Chondrostoma nasus	Fibrosarcoma, trunk	Plehn, 1906
Chondrostoma soetta	Squamous cell carcinoma, lip	Mazzarelli, 1910
Abramis brama	Fibroma, coelom	Plehn, 1906
Abramis brama	Lipoma, subcutaneous	Mawdesley-Thomas & Bucke, 1968
Alburnus alburnus	Leiomyoma, trunk	Plehn, 1906
Rasbora daniconius	Fibroma, dorsal fin	Smith et al., 1936
Rasbora lateristriata	Thyroid tumor (?)	Smith et al., 1936
Rasbora lateristriata	Lymphosarcoma, coelom.	Smith et al., 1936
Rasbora lateristriata	Thyroid tumor (?)	Smith & Coates, 1937
Rasbora lateristriata	Lymphosarcoma	Smith et al., 1936
Danio albolineatus	Thyroid tumor (?)	Klemm, 1927
Barbus barbus	Squamous cell carcinoma, lip	Keysselitz, 1908
Barbus barbus	Squamous cell carcinoma, lip	Clunet, 1910
Barbus barbus	Chondroma, mandible	Surbeck, 1921
Barbus barbus	Thyroid tumor (?)	Schreitmüller, 1924
Barbus tetrazona	Adenocarcinoma, kidney	Stolk, 1957d
Gobio gobio	Squamous cell carcinoma	Mawdesley-Thomas & Bucke, 1967b
Gobio spp.	Papilloma, skin	Schroeders, 1908
Mesogobius migroratatus	Papilloma, skin	Anitschkow & Pavlowsky, 1923
Proterorhinus marmaratus	Papilloma, skin	Anitschkow & Pavlowsky, 1923

2.5.2. *FAMILY CYPRINIDAE–MINNOWS AND CARPS* (cont.)

Phoxinus phoxinus	Fibrosarcoma, tail	Bugnion, 1875
Phoxinus phoxinus	Fibrosarcoma, trunk	Plehn, 1906
Phoxinus phoxinus	Chondroma, mandible	André, 1927
Tinca tinca	Myxoma, orbit	Plehn, 1906
Tinca tinca	Squamous cell carcinoma, lip	Fiebiger, 1909a
Tinca tinca	Rhabdomyoma, trunk	Kolmer, 1928
Tanichthys albonubes	Thyroid tumor (?)	Stolk, 1956b
Brachydanio rerio	Melanosarcoma	Stolk, 1953e
Brachydanio rerio	Liver cell tumors	Stanton, 1965

2.5.3. *FAMILY ANOSTOMIDAE*

Chilodus punctatus	Hemangioma	Stolk, 1958b

2.5.4. *FAMILY BAGRIDAE–BAGRID CATFISHES*

Mystus seenghala	Leiomyoma	Sarkar et al., 1955
Mystus seenghala	Pituitary tumor	Sathyanesan, 1962
Mystus vittatus	Kidney tumor	Sathyanesan, 1966

2.5.5. *FAMILY SILURIDAE– OLD WORLD CATFISHES*

Wallago attu	Osteogenic fibroma	Sarkar & Dutta-Chaudhuri, 1958

2.5.6. *FAMILY POECILIIDAE–LIVEBEARERS*

Xiphophorus maculatus X X. helleri	Melanoma, skin	Haüssler, 1928
Xiphophorus maculatus X X. helleri	Melanoma, skin	Kosswig, 1929a
Xiphophorus maculatus X X. helleri	Melanoma, skin	Reed & Gordon, 1931
Xiphophorus maculatus X X. helleri	Melanoma, skin	Haüssler, 1934
Xiphophorus maculatus X X. helleri	Erythrophoroma, skin	Smith et al., 1936
Xiphophorus maculatus X X. helleri	Melanoma, skin	Gordon, 1937
Xiphophorus maculatus X X. helleri	Melanoma, eye	Levine & Gordon, 1946
Xiphophorus maculatus X X. helleri	Xanthoerythrophoroma	Nigrelli et al., 1951
Xiphophorus helleri	Fibrosarcoma, eye	Jahnel, 1939
Xiphophorus helleri	Squamous cell carcinoma	Stolk, 1953c
Xiphophorus helleri	Adenoma, thyroid	Stolk, 1955b
Xiphophorus helleri	Teratoma	Hisaoka, 1963
Xiphophorus maculatus	Adenoma, kidney	Jahnel, 1939

(continued)

2.5.6.   *FAMILY POECILIIDAE—LIVEBEARERS* (cont.)

Xiphophorus maculatus	Melanosarcoma, eye	Levine & Gordon, 1946
Xiphophorus maculatus	Erythrophoroma	Ghadially & Whiteley, 1951
Xiphophorus maculatus	Thyroid tumor (?)	Baker et al., 1955
Xiphophorus maculatus	Xanthoerythrophoroma	Ermin, 1953
Xiphophorus maculatus	Fibrosarcoma, head	Stolk, 1954
Xiphophorus maculatus	Teratoma, ovary	Stolk, 1959a
Xiphophorus pygmaeus	Melanoma, eye	Levine & Gordon, 1946
Xiphophorus variatus	Thyroid tumor (?)	Aronowitz et al., 1951
Xiphophorus variatus	Squamous cell carcinoma, head	Aronowitz et al., 1951
Xiphophorus variatus	Thyroid hyperplasia	Aronowitz et al., 1951
Xiphophorus variatus	Thyroid tumor (?)	MacIntyre, 1960
X. variatus xiphidium	Melanoma, skin	MacIntyre & Baker-Cohen, 1961
X. variatus xiphidium	Thyroid tumor (?)	MacIntyre & Baker-Cohen, 1961
Xiphophorus montezumae	Thyroid tumor (?)	Gorbman & Gordon, 1951
Xiphophorus montezumae	Thyroid tumor (?)	Berg et al., 1953
Xiphophorus spp.	Erythromelanoma	Nigrelli et al., 1950
Xiphophorus spp.	Adenocarcinoma, pancreas	Nigrelli & Gordon, 1951
Xiphophorus spp.	Renal tumor (?)	Baker & Gordon, 1953
Xiphophorus spp.	Renal tumor (?)	Baker et al., 1954
Xiphophorus spp.	Melanosarcomas	Weissenfels et al., 1970
Xiphophorus spp.	Melanoma	Vielkind et al., 1971
Xiphophorus spp.	Melanoma	Siciliano et al., 1971
Heteradandria formosa	Thyroid tumor (?)	Smith et al., 1936
Mollienesia velifera	Adenocarcinoma, coelom	Raabe, 1939
Mollienesia velifera	Pituitary chromophobe adenoma	Stolk, 1958d
Poecilia reticulata	Teratoma, ovary	Stolk, 1953a
Poecilia reticulata	Pituitary chromophobe adenoma	Stolk, 1953b
Poecilia reticulata	Carcinoma, pharynx	Stolk, 1953d
Poecilia reticulata	Teratoma	Stolk, 1955a
Poecilia reticulata	Thyroid adenoma	Stolk, 1955b
Poecilia reticulata	Adenoma (?) Carcinoma (?)	Vivien & Ruhland-Gaiser, 1954
Poecilia reticulata	Fibroma, heart	Stolk, 1957c
Poecilia reticulata	Fibroma, gut	Stolk, 1957g
Poecilia reticulata	Sarcoma, undifferentiated	Wessing, 1959
Poecilia reticulata	Sarcoma, generalized	Wessing & von Bargen, 1959
Poecilia reticulata	Teratoma	Hisaoka, 1961
Poecilia reticulata	Thyroid tumor (?)	Woodhead & Ellett, 1967
Poecilia reticulata × P. sphenops	Melanoma	Ghadially & Gordon, 1957
Poecilia reticulata × P. sphenops	Melanoma, skin	Stolk, 1958f,g
Poecilobrycon harrisoni	Anal epithelioma	Harshbarger, 1973

2.5.7.   *FAMILY ICTALURIDAE–FRESHWATER CATFISHES*

Ictalurus catus	Squamous cell carcinoma	McFarland, 1901
Ictalurus catus	Squamous cell carcinoma	Lucké & Schlumberger, 1941
Ictalurus catus	Adenoma, kidney	Schlumberger & Lucké, 1948
Ictalurus nebulosus	Liver cell tumor	Dawe et al., 1964
Ictalurus nebulosus	Papilloma, skin	Steeves, 1969
Ictalurus natalis	Papilloma, skin	Harshbarger, 1973
Ictalurus natalis	Papilloma, skin	Harshbarger, 1973
Ictalurus sp.	Papilloma, skin	Harshbarger, 1973

2.5.8.   *FAMILY CLARIIDAE–AIRBREATHING CATFISHES*

Clarias dumerilii	Thyroid tumor (?)	Schreitmüller, 1924

2.5.9.   *FAMILY CALLICHTHYIDAE*

Corydoras julii	Melanoma, eye	Cohen, 1965

2.5.10.   *FAMILY CATOSTOMIDAE–SUCKERS*

Catostomus commersoni	Papilloma, skin	Schlumberger & Lucké, 1948
Catostomus commersoni	Cholangiosarcoma	Dawe et al., 1964

2.6.   ORDER LOPHIIFORMES

2.6.1.   *FAMILY LOPHIIDAE–GOOSEFISHES*

Lophius piscatorius	Melanoma, skin	Ingleby, 1929

2.6.2   *FAMILY LINOPHRYNIDAE*

Acentrophyrne longidens	Fibrocarcinoma	Nigrelli, 1946–47

2.7.   ORDER GADIFORMES

2.7.1.   *FAMILY GADIDAE–CODFISHES*

Gadus morhua	Fibroma, stomach	Hunter, 1782
Gadus morhua	Fibroma, subcutaneous	Bland-Sutton, 1885
Gadus morhua	Fibroma, stomach	Bland-Sutton, 1885
Gadus morhua	Osteoma, maxilla	Bland-Sutton, 1885
Gadus morhua	Osteoma, vertebra	Bland-Sutton, 1885
Gadus morhua	Sarcoma, swim bladder	Bashford & Murray, 1904a
Gadus morhua	Hemangioma, pectoral region	Murray, 1908
Gadus morhua	Osteosarcoma, operculum	Murray, 1908
Gadus morhua	Fibroma, esophagus	Williamson, 1911

(continued)

2.7.1.   *FAMILY GADIDAE—CODFISHES* (cont.)

Gadus morhua	Fibrosarcoma, subcutaneous	Johnstone, 1911–12
Gadus morhua	Osteoma, vertebra	Williamson, 1911
Gadus morhua	Fibroma, orbit	Johnstone, 1914a,b
Gadus morhua	Fibrosarcoma, trunk	Johnstone, 1915
Gadus morhua	Fibrosarcoma, oral	Johnstone, 1920
Gadus morhua	Fibroma, stomach	Johnstone, 1923–25, 1924–25
Gadus morhua	Hemangioma, swim bladder	Johnstone, 1923–25, 1924–25
Gadus morhua	Ganglioneuroma, trunk	Thomas, 1927b
Gadus morhua	Fibrosarcoma, subcutaneous	Thomas, 1927a
Gadus morhua	Fibrosarcoma, ovary	Thomas, 1927a
Gadus morhua	Osteoma, maxilla	Williams, 1929
Gadus morhua	Fibrosarcoma, trunk	Williams, 1931
Gadus morhua	Osteosarcoma, pectoral fin	Thomas, 1932b
Gadus morhua	Fibroma, gut	Thomas, 1933c
Gadus morhua	Lymphosarcoma, orbit	Wolke & Wyand, 1969
Gadus morhua	Melanosarcoma	Mawdesley-Thomas, 1971a
Gadus macrocephalus	Adenoma, pectoral gland	Takahashi, 1929
Gadus macrocephalus	Adenoma, parabranchial	Takahashi, 1929
Gadus macrocephalus	Adenoma, parabranchial body	Wellings, 1969b
Gadus macrocephalus	Neurofibroma, head	Wellings, 1969b
Gadus macrocephalus	Neurofibroma	Wellings, 1969b
Gadus virens	Fibroma	Lawrence, 1895
Gadus virens	Fibroma, oral	Fiebiger, 1909a
Gadus virens	Rhabdomyoma, gut	Fiebiger, 1909c
Gadus virens	Fibrosarcoma, skin	Fiebiger, 1912
Gadus virens	Fibrosarcoma, subcutaneous	Johnstone, 1926
Gadus virens	Hemangioma, trunk	Johnstone, 1926
Gadus virens	Fibrosarcoma, mandible	Johnstone, 1926
Gadus virens	Osteosarcoma, vertebra	Williams, 1929
Gadus virens	Squamous cell carcinoma	Williams, 1929
Gadus virens	Chondroma, head	Thomas, 1932d
Gadus virens	Lipoma, liver	Thomas, 1933b
Melanogrammus aeglefinus	Melanoma, skin	Prince, 1891
Melanogrammus aeglefinus	Fibroma, subcutaneous	Johnstone, 1910–11, 1911–12
Melanogrammus aeglefinus	Fibrosarcoma, head	Johnstone, 1922a,b
Melanogrammus aeglefinus	Fibroma, subcutaneous	Johnstone, 1923–25, 1924, 1924–25
Melanogrammus aeglefinus	Adamantinoma, maxilla	Thomas, 1926
Melanogrammus aeglefinus	Fibroma, trunk	Mawdesley-Thomas, 1971a
Merlangus merlangus	Squamous cell carcinoma, oral	Johnstone, 1923–25, 1924, 1924–25
Merlangus merlangus	Hamartoma, gut	Labbé, 1930
Merlangus merlangus	Fibroma	Mawdesley-Thomas, 1971a

2.7.1.   *FAMILY GADIDAE–CODFISHES* (cont.)

Merluccius merluccius	Hemangioma, gut	Johnstone, 1926
Molva molva	**Adenoma, ovary**	Johnstone, 1915
Molva molva	Fibrosarcoma, subcutaneous	Johnstone, 1923
Molva molva	Hemangioma, trunk	Johnstone, 1923–25, 1924, 1924–25
Theragra chalcogramma	Adenoma, parabranchial body	Takahashi, 1929
Theragra chalcogramma	Squamous cell carcinoma, oral	Takahashi, 1929
Theragra chalcogramma	Fibroma, trunk	Takahashi, 1929
Theragra chalcogramma	Fibrosarcoma, trunk	Takahashi, 1929
Theragra chalcogramma	Fibrosarcoma, subcutaneous	Takahashi, 1929
Theragra chalcogramma	Osteoma, fin	Takahashi, 1929
Theragra chalcogramma	Melanoma, skin	Takahashi, 1929
Theragra chalcogramma	Sarcoma	Nishikawa, 1954

2.7.2.   *FAMILY ZOARCIDAE–EELPOUTS*

Zoarces viviparus	Melanoma, skin	Bergman, 1921

2.7.3.   *FAMILY BROTULIDAE*

Parabassogigas crassus	Squamous cell carcinoma of muscle	Mawdesley Thomas, 1971a

2.8.   ORDER CYPRINODONTIFORMES

2.8.1.   *FAMILY CYPRINODONTIDAE–KILLIFISHES*

Jordanella floridae	Thyroid tumor (?)	Schreitmüller, 1924
Epiplatys chaperi	Thyroid tumor (?)	Klemm, 1927
Cyprinodon variegatus	Thyroid adenoma	Nigrelli, 1952b,c
Cyprinodon variegatus	Ameloblastoma, jaw	Stolk, 1957k
Fundulus heteroclitus	Thyroid adenoma	Nigrelli, 1952b,c
Anatolichthys sp.	Carcinoma of orbit	Ermin, 1954
Girardinus falcutus	Thyroid tumor (?)	MacIntyre, 1960
Nothobranchius guentheri	Erythrophoroma	Stolk, 1959b
Rivulus xanthonotus	Xanthophoroma	Stolk, 1959d
Various spp.	Sarcomas	Breider, 1939

2.9.   ORDER GASTEROSTEIFORMES

2.9.1.   *FAMILY GASTEROSTEIDAE–STICKLEBACKS*

Gasterosteus aculeatus	Hemangioma, head	Plehn, 1906
Gasterosteus aculeatus	Fibroma, tail	Mawdesley-Thomas, 1972b
Pungitius pungitius	Hemangioma, eye	Johnstone, 1915
Spinachia spinachia	Squamous cell carcinoma, skin	Murray, 1908

(continued)

2.10.   ORDER PERCIFORMES

2.10.1.   *FAMILY CENTRARCHIDAE–SUNFISHES*

Lepomis megalotis	Thyroid hyperplasia	Schlumberger, 1955
Micropterus salmoides	Melanoma	Erdman, 1968a
Micropterus salmoides	Lipoma	Mawdesley-Thomas, 1972b
Pomoxis nigromaculatus	Lipoma	Harshbarger, 1973

2.10.2.   *FAMILY CALLIONYMIDAE–DRAGONETS*

Callionymus lyra	Lipoma	Williams, 1929

2.10.3.   *FAMILY BLENNIIDAE–COMBTOOTH BLENNIES*

Blennius spp.	Xanthoma, skin	Schroeders, 1908

2.10.4.   *FAMILY ANABANTIDAE–CLIMBING PERCHES*

Anabas testudineus	Papilloma, skin	Fiebiger, 1909a
Anabas testudineus	Papilloma, skin	Nigrelli, 1952a
Anabas testudineus	Papilloma, skin	Sarkar & Dutta-Chaudhuri, 1953
Colias labius	Papilloma, skin	Nigrelli, 1952a
Colis labiosa	Squamous cell carcinoma, skin	Stolk, 1956h
Betta anabantoides	Adenocarcinoma, pharyngeal gland	Stolk, 1962

2.10.5.   *FAMILY SCOMBRIDAE–MACKERELS AND TUNAS*

Scomber scombrus	Hemangioma, trunk	Johnstone, 1923–25, 1924, 1924–25
Scomber scombrus	Hamartoma, pineal	Charlton, 1929
Scomber colias	Melanosarcoma, skin	Takahashi, 1929
Euthynnus alletteratus	Erythrophoroma, skin	Thomas, 1931a
Trachurus trachurus	Lipoma, trunk	Anadon, 1956

2.10.6.   *FAMILY TRICHIURIDAE–CUTLASSFISHES*

Lepidopus spp.	Osteoma, fin	Gervais, 1875
Menidea beryllina	Melanoma, skin	Nigrelli & Gordon, 1944

2.10.7.   *FAMILY PERCICHTHYIDAE–TEMPERATE BASSES*

Morone saxatilis	Nephroblastoma	Helmboldt & Wyand, 1971

2.10.8.   *FAMILY SERRANIDAE–SEA BASSES*

Serranus scrila	Thyroid tumor (?)	Marsh & Vonwiller, 1916
Serranus cabrilla	Thyroid tumor (?)	Marsh & Vonwiller, 1916

2.10.8.   *FAMILY SERRANIDAE—SEA BASSES* (cont.)

Lateolabrax japonicus	Fibrosarcoma, subcutaneous	Takahashi, 1929
Lateolabrax japonicus	Fibrosarcoma, pharynx	Takahashi, 1929
Epinephelus guaza	Melanoma	Dollfus et al., 1938

2.10.9.   *FAMILY LUTJANIDAE—SNAPPERS*

Lutianus griseus	Neurofibroma	Lucké, 1942
Lutianus griseus	Neurofibroma	Harshbarger, 1973
Lutianus apodus	Neurofibroma	Lucké, 1942
Lutianus jocu	Neurofibroma	Lucké, 1942

2.10.10. *FAMILY SPARIDAE—PORGIES*

Chrysophrys major	Osteomas	Kazama, 1924
Chrysophrys major	Osteoma	Sagawa, 1925
Chrysophrys major	Adenocarcinoma, coelom	Takahashi, 1929
Chrysophrys major	Osteoma	Takahashi, 1929
Chrysophrys major	Osteoma	Schlumberger & Lucké, 1948
Sparus auratus	Neuroepithelioma, olfactory plate	Thomas, 1932c
Archosargus probatocephalus	Guanophoroma, skin	Mawdesley-Thomas, 1972b

2.10.11. *FAMILY GOBIIDAE—GOBIES*

Bathygobius soporator	Squamous cell carcinoma	Tavolga, 1951
Acanthogobius flavimanus	Papilloma (?)	Oota, 1952
Acanthogobius flavimanus	Papilloma, skin	Nishikawa, 1954
Acanthogobius flavimanus	Sarcoma, undifferentiated	Nishikawa, 1955a
Acanthogobius flavimanus	Papilloma, skin	Oota, 1952
Acanthogobius flavimanus	Papilloma, skin	Imai & Fujiwara, 1959
Acanthogobius flavimanus	Papilloma, skin	Kimura et al., 1967a
Acanthogobius flavimanus	Papilloma, skin	Harshbarger, 1973

2.10.12. *FAMILY TRIGLIDAE—SEAROBINS*

Lepidotrigla alata	Fibrosarcoma, subcutaneous	Takahashi, 1929
Chelidonichthys kumu	Allophoroma, subcutaneous	Takahashi, 1929

2.10.13. *FAMILY CICHLIDAE—CICHLIDS*

Aequidens maronii	Malignant lymphoma	Harshbarger, 1973
Cichlasoma tetracanthus	Squamous cell carcinoma, skin	Puente-Duany, 1930
Hemichromis bimaculatus	Osteochondroma	Nigrelli & Gordon, 1946
Etroplus maculatus	Squamous cell carcinoma	Stolk, 1960b
Cichlasoma biocellatum	Thyroid tumor (?)	Stolk, 1956d
Haplochromis multicolor	Adenoma, pharyngeal gland	Stolk, 1957i
Pterophyllum scalare	Melanoma	Stolk, 1960a

(continued)

2.10.13. *FAMILY CICHLIDAE–CICHLIDS* (cont.)

Pterophyllum eimekei	Melanoma	Mawdesley-Thomas, 1971a

2.10.14. *FAMILY LABRIDAE–WRASSES*

Platyglossus bivattatus	Papilloma	Lucké, 1937–38
Labrus mixtus	Rhabdomyoma	Ladreyt, 1930
Tautogolabrus	Papilloma	Harshbarger, 1973

2.10.15. *FAMILY ECHENEIDAE–REMORAS*

Echeneis naucrates	Thyroid tumor (?)	Schlumberger & Lucké, 1948

2.10.16. *FAMILY PERCIDAE–PERCHES*

Perca flavescens	Testicular tumor	Budd & Schroder, 1969
Stizostedion vitreum	Fibroma & fibrosarcoma	Walker, 1958
Perca fluviatilis	Rhabdomyoma	Finkelstein & Dancheno-Ryzchkova, 1965
Perca fluviatilis	Malignant Schwannoma (?)	Finkelstein & Dancheno-Ryzchkova, 1965

2.10.17. *FAMILY POMATOMIDAE–BLUEFISHES*

Pomatomus saltatrix	Lymphangioepithelioma	Harshbarger, 1973

2.10.18. *FAMILY KYPHOSIDAE–SEA CHUBS*

Boops boops	Thyroid tumor (?)	Johnstone, 1923–25, 1924, 1924–25

2.10.19. *FAMILY CHAETODONTIDAE–BUTTERFLYFISHES*

Chaetodon sp.	Osteomas	Bell, 1793
Angelichthys isabelita	Adenocarcinoma, thyroid	Nigrelli, 1952b,c

2.10.20. *FAMILY SCIAENIDAE–DRUMS*

Sciaenidae spp.	Osteomas	Chabanaud, 1926
Pogonias chromis	Squamous cell carcinoma, mouth	Beatti, 1916
Pogonias chromis	Fibrosarcoma, subcutaneous	Beatti, 1916
Pogonias chromis	Osteoma, vertebra	Beatti, 1916
Micropogon undulatus	Odontoma, mouth	Roffo, 1925
Micropogon undulatus	Sarcoma, subcutaneous	Roffo, 1926
Micropogon opercularis	Osteoma	Bertullo & Traibel, 1955
Genyonemus lineatus	Papilloma	Russell & Kotin, 1957
Genyonemus lineatus	Papilloma	Harshbarger, 1973

2.10.21.   *FAMILY EPHIPPIDAE—SPADEFISHES*

Chaetodipterus faber	Osteoma, vertebrae	Schlumberger & Lucké, 1948

2.10.22.   *FAMILY STICHAEIDAE—PRICKLEBACKS*

Lumpenus sagitta	Neurofibroma	McArn & Wellings, 1967

2.10.23.   *FAMILY SCORPAENIDAE—SCORPIONFISHES*

Scorpaena inermis	Fibroma, subcutaneous	Takahashi, 1929
Scorpaena porcus	Fibrosarcoma, subcutaneous	Schroeders, 1908
Sebastes diploproa	Lipoma	Harshbarger, 1973
Sebastes crameri	Thyroid carcinoma	Harshbarger, 1973

2.10.24.   *FAMILY HEXAGRAMMIDAE—GREENLINGS*

Hexagrammos otakii	Guanophoroma, skin	Takahashi, 1929

2.10.25.   *FAMILY COTTIDAE—SCULPINS*

Myoxocephalus octo- decemspinosus	Teratocarcinoma	Harshbarger, 1973
Myoxocephalus octo- decemspinosus	Renal cystadenoma	Harshbarger, 1973

2.11.   ORDER PLEURONECTIFORMES

2.11.1.   *FAMILY BOTHIDAE—LEFTEYE FLOUNDERS*

Scophthalmus maeoticus	Osteoma, vertebra	Schroeders, 1908
Scophthalmus maeoticus	Myxoma, head	Schroeders, 1908
Scophthalmus maeoticus	Myxoma, trunk	Schroeders, 1908
Scophthalmus maeoticus	Fibrosarcoma, subcutaneous	Schroeders, 1908
Scophthalmus maximus	Fibrosarcoma, subcutaneous	Johnstone, 1923
Scophthalmus maximus	Fibroma, dorsal fin	Johnstone, 1924
Scophthalmus maximus	Rhabdomyoma, trunk	Young, 1923–25
Schopthalmus maximus	Fibrosarcoma, trunk	Johnstone, 1927
Scophthalmus maximus	Myxoma, trunk	Williams, 1929
Lepidorhombus whiffia- gonis	Ganglioneuroma	Haddow & Blake, 1933
Paralichthys olivaceus	Lipoma, trunk	Kazama, 1924
Paralichthys olivaceus	Osteoma, vertebra	Takahashi, 1929

2.11.2.   *FAMILY PLEURONECTIDAE—RIGHTEYE FLOUNDERS*

Hippoglossus hippoglossus	Papilloma, snout	Johnstone, 1911–12
Hippoglossus hippoglossus	Fibroma, coelom	Johnstone, 1913
Hippoglossus hippoglossus	Fibroma, trunk	Johnstone, 1914a,b

(continued)

2.11.2. *FAMILY PLEURONECTIDAE–RIGHTEYE FLOUNDERS* (cont.)

Hippoglossus hippoglossus	Melanoma, skin	Johnstone, 1915
Hippoglossus hippoglossus	Fibroma, subcutaneous	Johnstone, 1926
Hippoglossus hippoglossus	Fibrosarcoma, trunk	Johnstone, 1926
Hippoglossus hippoglossus	Lipoma, trunk	Williams, 1929
Hippoglossus hippoglossus	Rhabdomyoma, trunk	Thomas, 1932a
Pleuronectes platessa	Myxoma, trunk	McIntosh, 1908
Pleuronectes platessa	Fibrosarcoma, subcutaneous	Drew, 1912
Pleuronectes platessa	Lipoma, trunk	Bergman, 1921
Pleuronectes platessa	Fibroma, fin	Johnstone, 1922a,b
Pleuronectes platessa	Melanoma, skin	Johnstone, 1923–25, 1924–25
Pleuronectes platessa	Papilloma, skin	Johnstone, 1923–25, 1924–25
Pleuronectes platessa	Hemangioma, trunk	Johnstone, 1923–25, 1924–25
Pleuronectes platessa	Fibroma, head	Johnstone, 1926
Pleuronectes platessa	Papilloma, skin	Sandeman, 1893a
Pleuronectes platessa	Papilloma, skin	Wellings et al., 1963
Pleuronectes platessa	Papilloma, skin	Wellings & Chuinard,
Pleuronectes platessa	Papilloma, skin	Chuinard et al., 1964, 1966
Pleuronectes platessa	Papilloma, skin	Wellings et al., 1965, 1966, 1967
Platichthys flesus	Papilloma, skin	Sandeman, 1893a
Platichthus flesus	Lymphosarcoma, orbit	Johnstone, 1911–12
Platichthys stellatus	Papilloma, skin	Wellings et al., 1966
Platichthys stellatus	Papilloma, skin	McArn et al., 1968
Psettichthys melanostictus	Papilloma, skin	Ketchen, 1953
Psettichthys melanostictus	Papilloma, skin	Wellings et al., 1965
Psettichthys melanostictus	Papilloma, skin	Nigrelli et al., 1965
Psettichthys melanostictus	Papilloma, skin	McArn et al., 1968
Limanda limanda	Papilloma, skin	Johnstone, 1923–25, 1924–25
Limanda herzensteiri	Papilloma, skin	Kimura et al., 1967b
Pseudopleuronectes ameri-canus	Erythrophoroma	Smith, 1934
Pseudopleuronectes yoko-hamae	Ganglioneuroma	Takahashi, 1929
Pseudopleuronectes herzen-steiri	Papilloma, skin	Kimura et al., 1967
Isopsetta isolepis	Papilloma, skin	McArn et al., 1968
Microstomus pacificus	Papilloma, skin	Young, 1964
Microstomus pacificus	Papilloma, skin	Wellings, 1969b
Microstomus pacificus	Papilloma, skin	Harshbarger, 1973
Parophyrs vetulus	Papilloma, skin	Pacis, 1932
Parophyrs vetulus	Papilloma, skin	Good, 1940
Parophyrs vetulus	Papilloma, skin	Wellings et al., 1966
Parophyrs vetulus	Papilloma, skin	McArn et al., 1968

2.11.2.   *FAMILY PLEURONECTIDAE–RIGHTEYE FLOUNDERS* (cont.)

Parophrys vetulus	Papilloma, skin	Cooper & Keller, 1969
Hippoglossoides elassodon	Papilloma, skin	Wellings et al., 1964
Hippoglossoides elassodon	Papilloma, skin	Wellings et al., 1964
Hippoglossoides dubius	Papilloma, skin	Kimura et al., 1967b
Hippoglossus stenolepis	Fibroma, trunk	Wellings, 1969b
Hippoglossus stenolepis	Fibroma, mandible	Wellings, 1969b
Hippoglossus stenolepis	Fibrolipoma, tail	Wellings, 1969b
Hippoglossus stenolepis	Lipo-osteoma	Wellings, 1969b
Hippoglossus stenolepis	Fibro-osteoma	Wellings, 1969b
Lepidopsetta bilineata	Papilloma, skin	Nigrelli et al., 1965
Lepidopsetta bilineata	Papilloma, skin	Wellings, 1969b
Glyptocephalus zachirus	Papilloma, skin	Wellings et al., 1965
Glyptocephalus stelleri	Papilloma, skin	Honma & Kon, 1968
Glyptocephalus cynoglossus	Papilloma, skin	Honma & Kon, 1968

2.11.3.   *FAMILY SOLEIDAE–SOLES*

Solea solea	Myxoma, coelom	Johnstone, 1926
Solea solea	Papilloma, skin	Thomas, 1930

2.12.   ORDER TETRAODONTIFORMES

2.12.1.   *FAMILY BALISTIDAE–TRIGGERFISHES AND FILEFISHES*

Aluterus schoepfi	Osteoma	Schlumberger & Lucké, 1948

REFERENCES

This annotated bibliography lists the majority of references to neoplasia in fish. An earlier version appeared in Diseases of Fish *(L. E. Mawdesley-Thomas, ed.),* Symp. zool. Soc. Lond. *No. 30 (London and New York: Academic Press, 1972) and is used with permission.*

Adami, J. G. 1908. On a giant-celled rhabdomyosarcoma from the trout. *Montreal med. J. 37:* 163–165.

Aldrovandi, U. 1613. *De piscibus.* Bologna. (Concerning fish.)

Amlacher, E. 1961. *Taschenbuch der Fischkrankheiten.* Gustav Fischer Verlag. Jena Rev. 11, 286. (Textbook of fish diseases.)

Anadon, E. 1956. Nota sobre un tumor en *Trachurus trachurus* L. *Investigación pesq. 5:* 13–15. (Note on a tumor in *Trachurus trachurus* L.)

Anders, A., and Klinke, K. 1965. Untersuchungen über die erbbedingte Aminosäurenkonzentration, Farbenmanifestation und Tumorbildung bei lebendgebärenden Zahnkarpfen (Poeciliidae). *Z. VererbLehre 96:* 49–65. (Studies on the hereditary amino acid concentration, color manifestation, and tumor formation in viviparous "tooth carp.")

Anders, F. 1967. Tumour formation in platyfish-swordtail hybrids as a problem of gene regulation. *Experientia 23:* 1–10.

André, E. 1927. Sur un chondrome du vairon. *Suisse Pêche Piscic. 28:* 177–178. (On a chondroma in the minnow.)

André, E. 1939. Myome chez un poisson. *Bull. fr. Piscic.* No. 118. (Myoma in a fish.)

Anitschkow, N., and Pavlowsky, E. N. 1923. Über die Hautpapillome bei *Gobius* und ihre Beziehung zur normalen Struktur der Fischhaut. *Z. Krebsforsch. 20:* 128–147. (On the skin papilloma in the *Gobius* and its relation to the normal structure of the fish skin.)

Anonymous. 1964. Hepatomas in trout. *Nutr. Rev. 22:* 208–210.

Anonymous. 1968. *Neoplasia of Invertebrate and Primitive Vertebrate Animals.* A symposium sponsored by the Smithsonian Institution and the National Cancer Institute, Washington, D.C.

Aronowitz, O., Nigrelli, R. F., and Gordon, M. 1951. A spontaneous epithelioma in the platyfish, *Xiphophorus (Platypoecilus) variatus. Zoologica, N.Y. 36:* 239–241.

Ashley, L. M. 1965. Histopathology of rainbow trout aflatoxicosis. *Res. Rep. U.S. Fish. Wildl. Serv.* No. 70: 103–120.

Ashley, L. M. 1967. Renal neoplasms in rainbow trout. *Bull. Wildl. Dis. Ass. 3:* 86 (Abstract).

Ashley, L. M. 1969. Experimental fish neoplasia. In *Fish in Research:* 23–43. (Neuhaus, O. W., and Halver, J. E., eds.). New York and London: Academic Press.

Ashley, L. M. 1970. Pathology of fish fed aflatoxins and other antimetabolites. (Snieszko, S. F., ed.). *Spec. Publs Am. Fish. Soc.* No. 5: 366–379.

Ashley, L. M., and Halver, J. E. 1961. Hepatomagenesis in rainbow trout. *Fedn Proc. Fedn Am. Socs exp. Biol. 20:* 290 (Abstract).

Ashley, L. M., and Halver, J. E. 1963. Multiple metastasis of rainbow trout hepatoma. *Trans. Am. Fish. Soc. 92:* 365–371.

Ashley, L. M., and Halver, J. E. 1968. Dimethylnitrosamine-induced hepatic cell carcinoma in rainbow trout. *J. natn. Cancer Inst. 41:* 531–552.

Ashley, L. M., Halver, J. E., and Johnson, C. L. 1962. Histopathology of induced trout hepatoma. *Fedn Proc. Fedn Am. Socs exp. Biol. 21:* 304 (Abstract).

Ashley, L. M., Halver, J. E., and Wellings, S. R. 1969. Case reports of three teleost neoplasms. *Natn. Cancer Inst. Monogr.* No. 31: 157–166.

Ashley, L. M., Halver, J. E., and Wogan, G. N. 1964. Hepatoma and aflatoxicosis in trout. *Fedn Proc. Fedn Am. Socs exp. Biol. 23:* 105 (Abstract).

Ashley, L. M., Halver, J. E., Gardner, W. K., Jr., and Wogan, G. N. 1965. Crystalline aflatoxins cause trout hepatoma. *Fedn Proc. Fedn Am. Socs exp. Biol. 24:* 627 (Abstract).

Ayson. 1896. Carcinoma of the thyroid gland in *Salmo levensis.* (Cited by Schmey, M., 1911.)

Ayson. 1898. Carcinoma of the thyroid gland in *Salmo levensis.* (Cited by Schmey, M., 1911.)

Ayson. 1902. Carcinoma of the thyroid gland in *Salmo levensis.* (Cited by Schmey, M., 1911.)

Baker, K. F. 1958. Heterotopic thyroid tissue in fish. *J. Morph. 103:* 91-129.

Baker, K. F., and Gordon, M. 1953. Preliminary studies of the differential susceptibility of various strains of the platyfish to a kidney tumor. *Genetics, N.Y. 38:* 655 (Abstract).

Baker, K. F., Berg, O., Nigrelli, R. F., Gorbman, A., and Gordon, M. 1954. Thyroid cell origin of spontaneous adenocarcinomas of the kidneys in fishes. *Proc. Am. Ass. Cancer Res. 1:* 3 (Abstract).

Baker, K. F., Berg, O., Gorbman, A., Nigrelli, R. F., and Gordon, M. 1955. Functional thyroid tumors in the kidneys of platyfish. *Cancer Res. 15:* 118-123.

Barcellos, B. N. 1962. Anomalias do esqueleto da corvina. *Ciênc. Cult. Maracaibo 14:* 111-113. (Anomalies of the skeleton of the sea bass.)

Barnard, K. H. 1948. Further notes on South African marine fishes. *Ann. S. Afr. Mus. 36:* 341-406.

Bashford, E. F. 1904-5. The zoological distribution of cancer. *Scient. Rep. imp. Cancer Res. Fund 1:* 3-11.

Bashford, E. F., and Murray, J. A. 1904a. Spindle cell sarcoma of the swim bladder in a cod (*Gadus morhua*, Linnaeus). (Cited by Schmey, M., 1911.)

Bashford, E. F., and Murray, J. A. 1904b. Abdominal carcinoma in *Trigla gunardus*, Linnaeus. (Cited by Schmey, M., 1911.)

Bashford, E. F., Murray, J. A., and Cramer, W. 1905. Transplantation of malignant new growths. *Scient. Rep. imp Cancer Res. Fund 2:* 13-17.

Bean, T. H. 1907. Translation into English of part of *Handbuch der Fischkrankheiten* by Hofer, B., 1904. *Rep. Forest Fish Game Commn, N.Y. St. 12.* (Textbook of fish diseases.)

Beatti, M. 1916. Geschwülste bei Tieren. *Z. Krebsforsch. 15:* 452-491. (Tumors in animals.)

Becher, H. 1929. Über die Entwicklung der Farbstoffzellen in der Haut der Knockenfische. *Verh. anat. Ges. Jena 38:* 164-181. (Development of pigment cells in the skin of Teleostae.)

Bell, W. 1793. Description of a species of *Chaetodon*, called by the Malays "Ecan bonna." *Phil. Trans. R. Soc. 83:* 7-9.

Berg, O., and Gorbman, A. 1954. Iodine utilization by tumorous thyroid tissue of the swordtail, *Xiphophorus montezumae*. *Cancer Res. 14:* 232-236.

Berg, O., and Gordon, M. 1953. Thyroid drugs that control growth of goiters in Xiphophorin fishes. *Proc. Am. Ass. Cancer Res. 1:* 5.

Berg, O., Edgar, M., and Gordon, M. 1953. Progressive growth stages in the development of spontaneous thyroid tumors in inbred swordtails, *Xiphophorus montezumae*. *Cancer Res. 13:* 1-8.

Berg, O., Gordon, M., and Gorbman, A. 1954. Comparative effects of thyroidal stimulants and inhibitors on normal and tumorous thyroids in Xiphophorin fishes. *Cancer Res. 14:* 527-533.

Bergman, A. M. 1921. Einige Geschwülste bei Fischen: Rhabdomyom, Lipome und Melanom. *Z. Krebsforsch. 18:* 292-302. (Some tumors in fish: rhabdomyoma, lipoma, and melanoma.)

Bertullo, V. H., and Bellagamba, C. J. 1964. Neoplasmas en los peces de las costas uruguayas. II. Lipofibroma en corvina. *Revta Inst. Invest. pesq. 1:* 261-

264. (Neoplasms in fish of the Uruguayan coastal waters. II. Lipofibroma in the sea bass.)

Bertullo, V. H., and Traibel, R. M. 1955. Neoplasma de los peces de las costas uruguayas. 1. Osteoma de la costilla pleural de la corvina (*Micropogon opercularis*). *An. Fac. Vet. Urug.* No. 3: 55–59. (Neoplasm in fish of the Uruguayan coastal waters.) 1. Osteoma of the pleural rib of the sea bass (*Micropogon opercularis.*)

Besse, P., Levaditi, J. C., Destombes, P., and Nazimoff, O. 1959. Reins polykystiques observes cheq der Cyprinidés d'un étarg de l'Eure. *Bull. Acad. vét. Fr. 32:* 421–426. (Polycystic kidneys observed in Cyprinids in a pond in the Eure.)

Besse, P., Levaditi, J. C., Vibert, R., and Nazimoff, O. 1960. Sur l'existence de tumerus hépatiques primitives chez la truite arc-en-ciel (*Salmo irideus*). *C. r. hebd. Séanc. Acad. Sci., Paris 251:* 482–483. (On the existence of primitive hepatic tumors in the rainbow trout (*Salmo irideus*).)

Besse, P., Levaditi, J. C., Doublet-Normand, A.-M., and de Kinkelin, P. 1966. Incidence de l'Hepatome dans les piscicultures françaises. *Bull. Off. int. Épizoot. 65:* 1071–1076. (The incidence of hepatoma in fish farms in France.)

Biavati, S. T., and Mancini, L. 1967. Un caso di fibroma in sardina *Pilchardus sardina. Nuova Vet. 43:* 11–14. (A case of fibroma in the sardine.)

Biesele, J. J. 1943. Diplochromosomes in a goldfish tumor. *Cancer Res. 3:* 411–412.

Blaehser, S. 1961. *Contribution à l'étude des tumeurs de la fibre musculaire striée chez les animaux.* Thesis, Université de Paris. (Contribution to the study of tumors in the striated muscular fiber in animals.)

Bland-Sutton, J. 1885. Tumours in animals. *J. Anat. Physiol., Lond. 19:* 415–475. (Many tumors described which have subsequently been lost. Useful early work.)

Bonnet, R. 1883. Studien zur Physiologie und Pathologie der Fische. *Bayer. Fisch. Z. 6:* 79. (Studies on physiology and pathology of fish.)

Bonser, G. M. 1967. Factors concerned in the location of human and experimental tumours. *Br. med. J. (2):* 655–660. (Sensitivity of the trout liver to aflatoxin is stressed.)

Borcca, M. I. 1909. Sur l'origine du coeur des cellules vasculaires migratrices et des cellules pigmentaires chez les téléostéens. *C. r. hebd. Séanc. Acad. Sci., Paris 149:* 688–689.

Breider, H. 1938. Die genetischen, histologischen und cytologischen Grundlagen der Geschuulstbildung nach Kreuzung verschiedener Rassen und Arten lebendgebärender Zahnkarpfen. *Z. Zellforsch. mikrosk. Anat. 28:* 784–828. (The genetic, histological, and cytological etiology of tumor formation after crossing different strains and species of viviparous dental carp.)

Breider, H. 1939. Über die pigmentbildung in den Zellen von Sarkomen albinotischer und nichtalbinotischer Gattungsbastarde lebendgebärender Zahnkarpfen. *Z. wiss. Zool.* (A) *152:* 107–128. (Pigment formation in the cells of sarcoma in albino and nonalbino genus hybrids of viviparous dental carp.)

Breider, H. 1956. Farbgene und Melanosarkomhaufigkeit. *Zool. Anz. 156:* 129–140. (Color genes and frequency of melanosarcoma.)

Breider, H., and Schmidt, E. 1951. Melanosarkome durch Artkreuzung und Spontantumoren bei Fischen. *Strahlentherapie 84:* 498–523. (Melanosarcoma by crossing of breed and spontaneous tumors in fish.)

Breslauer, T. 1915-16. Zur Kenntnis der Epidermoidalgeschwülste von Kaltblütern. *Arch. mikrosk. Anat. EntwMech. 87:* 200–262. (On the knowledge of epidermoidal tumors of cold-blooded animals.)

Brooks, R. E., McArn, G., and Wellings, S. R. 1969. Ultrastructural observations on an unidentified cell type found in epidermal tumours of Flounders. *J. natn. Cancer Inst. 43:* 97–109.

Broughton, E., and Choquette, L. P. E. 1971. Subcutaneous fibroma in lake trout (*Salvelinus namaycush*) in Quebec. *J. Fish. Res. Bd Can. 28:* 448–449.

Budd, J., and Schroder, J. D. 1969. Testicular tumors of yellow perch, *Perca flavescens* (Mitchill). *Bull. Wildl. Dis. Ass. 5:* 315–318.

Bugnion, E. 1875. Ein Fall von Sarcoma beim Fische. *Dt. Z. Tiermed. Vergl. Path. 1:* 132–134. (A case of sarcoma in the fish.)

Bukirev. A. I., and Pushkin, Z. M. 1957. [Some abnormalities in fish.] *Probl. Ichthyol. 9:* 147. (In Russian.)

Buniva, M. F. 1802. Sur la physiologie et la pathologie des poisson. *Memorie Acad. Sci. Torino 12:* 78–121. (Fish physiology and pathology.)

Burwash, F. M. 1929. The iodine content of the thyroid of two species of elasmobranchs and one species of teleost. *Contr. Can. Biol. Fish. 4:* 117–120.

Cameron, A. T., and Vincent, S. 1915. Notes on an enlarged thyroid occurring in an elasmobranch fish (*Squalus suckleyi*). *J. med. Res. 27:* 251–256.

Ceretto, F. 1968. Carcinoma di tipo psammomatoso in *Carassius auratus*. *Riv. ital. Piscis. Ittiopat.* (A.) *3:* 37–40. (Carcinoma of the psammoma type in the goldfish.)

Chabanaud, P. 1926. Fréquence, symétrie et constance specifique d'hyperostoses externes chez divers poissons de la famille des sciaenides. *C. r. hebd. Séanc. Acad. Sci., Paris 182:* 1647–1649. (Frequency, symmetry, and specific persistence of external hyperstoses in various fish of the Sciaenide family.)

Charlton, H. H. 1929. A tumor of the pineal organ with cartilage formation in the mackerel, *Scomber scombrus*. *Anat. Rec. 43:* 271–276.

Chavin, W. 1956a. Thyroid distribution and function in the goldfish, *Carassius auratus* L. *J. exp. Zool. 133:* 259–279.

Chavin, W. 1956b. Thyroid distribution and function in the goldfish, *Carassius auratus* L., as determined by the uptake of tracer doses of radio-iodine. *Anat. Rec. 124:* 272 (Abstract).

Chavin, W. 1956c. Thyroid follicles in the head kidney of the goldfish, *Carassius auratus* L. *Zoologica, N.Y. 41:* 101–104.

Christiansen, M., and Jensen, A. J. C. 1947. On a recent and frequently occurring tumor disease in eel. *Rep. Dan. biol. Stn* No. 50: 31–44.

Chuinard, R. G., Berkson, H., and Wellings, S. R. 1966. Surface tumors of starry flounder and English sole from Puget Sound, Washington. *Fedn Proc. Fedn Am. Socs exp. Biol. 25:* 661 (Abstract).

Chuinard, R. G., Wellings, S. R., Bern, H. A., and Nishioka, R. S. 1964. Epidermal papillomas in pleuronectid fishes from the San Juan Islands, Washington, *Fedn Proc. Fedn Am. Socs exp. Biol. 23:* 337 (Abstract).

Clunet, J. 1910. *Recherches experimentales sur les tumeurs malignes.* Paris: G. Steinheil. (Experimental research on malignant tumors.)

Coates, C. W., Cox, R. T., and Smith, G. M. 1938. Papilloma of the skin occurring in an electric eel, *Electrophorus electricus* L. *Zoologica, N.Y. 23:* 247–251.

Coates, J. A., Potts, T. J., and Wilcke, H. L. 1967. Interim hepatoma research report. *Res. Rep. U.S. Fish. Wildl. Serv.* No. 70: 34–38.

Codegone, M. L., Provana, A., and Ghittino, P. 1968. Evolution of the early hepatoma in rainbow trout. *Tumori 54:* 419–426.

Cohen, S. 1965. Malignant melanoma of the eye of a catfish *Corydoras julii. Copeia 1965:* 382–383.

Cole, F. J., and Eales, N. B. 1917. The history of comparative anatomy. A statistical analysis of the literature. *Sci. Prog., Lond. 11:* 578–590.

Conroy, D. A. 1965. Anormalidades patologicas en los peces marinos de la zona de Mar del Plata (Argentina). *Revta Inst. Invest. pesq. 1:* 341–343. (Pathological abnormalities in the seawater fish of the Mar del Plata zone (Argentina).)

Conroy, D. A. 1967. Thyroid tumour in Argentine pearl fish. *Br. Ichthyol. Soc. Newsletter 1967* (Dec.): 7–8.

Cooper, R. C., and Keller, C. A. 1969. Epizootiology of papillomas in English sole, *Parophrys vetulus. Natn. Cancer Inst. Monogr.* No. 31: 173–186.

Cramer, W. 1932. The comparative study of cancer. *Cancer Res. 7:* 241–257.

Crisp, E. 1854. Large fungoid tumour in a carp. *Trans. path. Soc. Lond. 5:* 347–348.

Cudkowicz, G., and Scolari, C. 1955. Un tumore primitive epatico a diffusione epizootica nella trota iridea di allevamento (*Salmo irideus*). *Tumori 41:* 524–537. (A primitive hepatic tumor, with epizootic distributions in the bred rainbow trout.)

Cuvier, Baron G. L. C. F. D., and Valenciennes, A. 1831. *Histoire naturelle des poissons 8:* 249. (22 volumes–1828–49). Paris. (Natural history of fish.)

Daniel, P. M., and Prichard, M. M. L. 1967. Further studies on mammary tumours induced in rats by 7,12-Dimethylbenz (α) anthracine (DMBA). *Int. J. Cancer 2:* 163–177.

Dauwe, F., and Pennemann, G. 1904. Contributions à l'étude du cancer chez les poissons. *Annls Soc. méd. Gand. 84:* 41–52. (Contributions to the study of cancer in fish.)

Dawe, C. J. 1969a. Neoplasms of blood cell origin in poikilothermic animals: A review. *Natn. Cancer Inst. Monogr.* No. 32: 7–28.

Dawe, C. J. 1969b. Phylogeny and oncogeny. *Natn. Cancer Inst. Monogr.* No. 31: 1–39.

Dawe, C. J., and Harshbarger, J. C. (eds.) 1968. Neoplasms and related disorders of invertebrate and lower vertebrate animals. *Natn. Cancer Inst. Monogr.* No. 31.

Dawe, C. J., Stanton, M. F., and Schwartz, F. J. 1964. Hepatic neoplasms in native bottom-feeding fish of Deep Creek Lake, Maryland. *Cancer Res. 24:* 1194–1201.

Dean, B. (Assisted by Gudger, E. W., and Henn, A. W.) 1923. A bibliography of fishes. 3 vols. (1916–23), 546–550. American Museum Natural History. (A most useful reference.)

Deys, B. F. 1969. Papillomas in the Atlantic eel, *Anguilla vulgaris. Natn. Cancer Inst. Monogr.* no. 31: 187–194.

Dinulesco, G., and Vasilescu, C. 1939. Thyroid cancer disease in two specimens of rainbow trout (*Salmo gairdneri irideus*). *Z. Fisch. 37:* 689.

Dollar, A. M., Katz, M., Tripple, M. F., and Simon, R. C. 1963. Trout hepatoma. *Res. Fish. Univ. Wash. Coll. (Sch.) Fish.* No. 139: 23–25.

Dollar, A. M., Smuckler, E. A., and Simon, R. C. 1967. Etiology and epidermiology of trout hepatoma. *Res. Rep. U.S. Fish. Wildl. Serv.* No. 70: 1–17.

Dollfus, R. P., Timon-David, J., and Mosinger, M. 1938. À propos des tumeurs mélaniques des poissons. *Bull. Ass. fr. Étude Cancer 27:* 37–50. (On melanotic tumors of fish.)

Dominguez, A. G. 1928. Fibroblastic sarcoma in a goldfish. *Clin. Med. Surg. 35:* 256–257.

Dorson, M. 1972. Some characteristics of antibodies in the primary immune response in rainbow trout. In *Diseases of Fish* (Mawdesley-Thomas, L. E., ed.) *Symp. zool. Soc. Lond.* No. 30: 129–140. London and New York: Academic Press.

Drew, G. H. 1910. Some notes on parasitic and other diseases of fish. 2nd series. *Parasitology 3:* 54–62.

Drew, G. H. 1912. Some cases of new growths in fish. *J. mar. biol. Ass. U.K. 9:* 281–287.

Duerst, J. U. 1941. *Die Urachen der Entstehung des Kropfes.* Bern: Huber. (Causes of goiter formation.)

Dunbar, C. E. 1969. Lymphosarcoma of possible thymus origin in salmonid fishes. *Natn. Cancer Inst. Monogr.* No. 31: 167–171.

Duncan, T. E., and Harkin, J. C. 1968. Ultrastructure of spontaneous goldfish tumors previously classified as neurofibromas. *Am. J. Path. 52:* 33a.

Duncan, T. E., and Harkin, J. C. 1969. Electron microscopic studies of goldfish tumors previously termed neurofibromas and schwannomas. *Am. J. Path. 55:* 191–202.

Dupont, A., and Vandaele, R. 1959. Un cas de tumeur mélanique chez un poisson albinos, *Protopterus annecteus,* Owen du Congo. *Bull. Soc. r. Zool. Anvers 8:* 252–253. (A melanotic tumor in an albino fish, *Protopterus annecteus.*)

Eberth, C. J. 1878. Fibrosarcom der Kopfhaut einer Forelle. *Virchows Arch. path. Anat. Physiol. 72:* 107–108. (Fibrosarcoma in the scalp of a trout.)

Ebins, K. 1936. On the growth of *Evynnis cardinalis* (Lacep.). *J. imp. Fish. Inst., Tokyo 31:* 69–78.

Eguchi, S., and Oota, J. 1926. [Of a tumor in a fish.] *Aichi Igakkwai Zasshi. 33* (*Biol. Abstr.* 5: Item 20406, 1931) (In Japanese).

Ehlinger, N. F. 1963. Kidney disease in lake trout complicated by lymphosarcoma. *Progve Fish Cult. 25:* 3–7.

Elwin, M. C. 1957. Pathological melanosis in an intergenic hybrid. *Nature, Lond. 179:* 1254–1255.

Erdman, D. S. 1968a. Melanotic tumours in *Micropterus salmoides* (Personal communication).

Erdman, D. S. 1968b. Ovarian tumours in *Coryphaena hippurus* (Personal communication).

Ermin, R. 1953. *Platypoecilus maculatus* var. *fuliginosus* da Ksantoiritroforoma Tesekkülü Hakkinda. *Instanb. Üniv. Fen Fak. Mecm.* (B) *18:* 301–314. (On a case of xanthoerythrophoroma formation in *Platypoecilus maculatus* var. *fuliginosus.*)

Ermin, R. 1954. Bir Anatolichthys Melezinde Tesekkül Eden Göz Tümörü Hakkinda. *Instanb. Üniv. Fen Fak. Mecm.* (B) *19:* 203–211. (On an ocular tumor with exophthalmia in an interspecific hybrid of anatolichthys.)

Falk, H. L. 1967. Potential hepatocarcinogens for fish. *Res. Rep. U.S. Fish Wildl. Serv.* No. 70: 175–177, 182–192.

Fiebiger, J. 1909a. Über Hautgeschwülste bei Fischen nebst Bemerkungen über die Pockenfankheit der Karpfen. *Z. Krebsforsch. 7:* 165–179. (On skin tumors in fish together with remarks on fish pox disease in carp.)

Fiebiger, J. 1909b. Ein Osteochondrom bei einem Karpfen. *Z. Krebsforsch. 7:* 371–381. (An osteochondroma in a carp.)

Fiebiger, J. 1909c. Ein Rhabdomyom bein einem Kabljau. *Z. Krebsforsch. 7:* 382–388. (A rhabdomyoma in a codfish.)

Fiebiger, J. 1912. Bösartige Neubildung (fibrosarkom) bei einem Seefisch. *Ost. Fisch-Ztg. 9:* 308. (Malignant formation (fibrosarcoma) in a saltwater fish.)

Finkelstein, E. A. 1944. [Development of tumors in invertebrates and lower vertebrates.] *Adv. mod. Biol. 17:* 324–339 (In Russian).

Finkelstein, E. A. 1960. [Tumors of fish.] *Arkh. Patol. 22:* 56–91 (In Russian—a most useful review paper).

Finkelstein, E. A. 1962. [On some aspects of tumor distribution in the classes of fishes.] *Progr. recent Biol. 53:* 2 (In Russian).

Finkelstein, E. A., and Danchenko-Ryzchkova, L. K. 1965. [Neurinoma in the perch *Perca fluviatilis.*] *Arkh. Patol. 27:* 81–84 (In Russian).

Ford, E. 1930. Some abnormal fishes received at the Plymouth laboratory. *J. mar. biol. Ass. U.K. 17:* 53–64.

Freudenthal, P. 1928. Fibrom (Spindelzellensarkom?) im Ovarium einer Karausche (*Carassius vulgaris*). *Z. Krebsforsch. 26:* 414–417. (Fibroma (spindle cell sarcoma) in the ovary of the crucian carp (*Carassius vulgaris*).)

Gaillard, C. 1923. *Recherches sur les poisson representés dans quelques tombeaux Egyptien de l'ancien Empire.* Memoires publiés par les Membres de l'Institut Français d'Archeologie Orientale du Caire p. 51. (Research on the fish represented in some Egyptian tombs of the Ancient Empire.)

Gardner, L. W., and Wachowski, H. E. 1951. The thyroid gland and its function in cold-blooded vertebrates. *Q. Rev. Biol. 26:* 123–128.

Gaylord, H. R. 1909. An epidemic of cancer of the thyroid in brook trout in a fish hatchery. *J. Am. med. Ass. 52:* 411.

Gaylord, H. R. 1910. An epidemic of carcinoma of the thyroid gland among fish. *J. Am. med. Ass. 54:* 227.

Gaylord, H. R. 1916. Further observations on so-called carcinoma of the thyroid in fish. *J. Cancer Res. 1:* 197–204.

Gaylord, H. R., and Marsh, M. C. 1912a. Relation of feeding to thyroid hyperplasia in Salmonidae. *Z. Krebsforsch. 12:* 436–438.

Gaylord, H. R., and Marsh, M. C. 1912b. Carcinoma of the thyroid in the salmonoid fishes. *Bull. U.S. Fish Commn* (published 1914) *32:* 363–524.

Gervais, P. 1875. De l'hyperostose chez l'homme et chez les animaux. *J. de Zool. 4:* 272–284, 445–465. (Hyperostosis in man and in animals.)

Gervais, P. 1876. Carpe atteinte d'une énorme tumeur fibreuse de l'abdomen. *J. de Zool. 5:* 466. (Carp suffering from an enormous fibrous tumor in the abdomen.)

Gessner, C. 1558. *Historiae Animalium Liber IV, qui est de Piscium et Aquatilium Animantium Natura.* Zurich: Tiguri. (Animal History Book IV, on fish and living aquatic creatures.)

Ghadially, F. N. 1966. Trauma and melanoma production. *Nature, Lond. 211:* 1199.

Ghadially, F. N., and Gordon, M. 1957. A localized melanoma in a hybrid fish *Lebistes* X *Mollienesia. Cancer Res. 17:* 597–599.

Ghadially, F. N., and Whitelcy, H. J. 1951. An invasive red-pigmented tumour (erythrophoroma) in a red male platyfish (*Platypoecilus maculatus* var. *rubra*). *Br. J. Cancer 5:* 405–408.

Ghadially, F. N., and Whiteley, H. J. 1952. Hormonally induced epithelial hyperplasia in the goldfish (*Carassius auratus*). *Br. J. Cancer 6:* 246–248.

Ghittino, P. 1963. Caso di epatoma nel salmerino di allevamento (*Salvelinus fontinalis*). *Atti Soc. ital. Sci. vet. 17:* 574–579. (Case of hepatoma in a small bred brook char (*Salvelinus fontinalis*).)

Ghittino, P., and Ceretto, F. 1961. Studio istologico ed eziopatogenetico dell' epatoma della trota iridea di allevamento (*Salmo gairdneri*). *Atti Soc. ital. Sci. vet. 15:* 579–585. (Histopathological study of the hepatoma in the bred rainbow trout.)

Ghittino, P., and Ceretto, F. 1962. Studio sulla eziopatogenesi dell'epatoma della trota iridea di allevamento. *Tumori 48:* 393–409. (Study on the pathogenesis of the hepatoma of the bred rainbow trout.)

Ghittino, P., Provana, A., and Codegone, M. L. 1967a. Experimental dietary hepatoma in rainbow trout. The role of cottonseed meals and other diets. *Cancro 20:* 3–24.

Ghittino, P., Dalforna, S., Provana, A., and Codegone, M. L. 1967b. Aspetti istologici di tumore tiroidea in una trota iridea di laboratoria. *Riv. ital. Piscic. Ittiopat.* (A) *2:* 30–31. (Histological aspects of thyroid tumor in laboratory-reared rainbow trout.)

Gilruth, J. A. 1902. Epithelioma affecting the branchial arches of salmon and trout. *Rep. Dep. Agric. N.Z. Vet. Div. 1901/1902:* 312–315.

Golden, T., and Stout, A. P. 1941. Smooth muscle tumours of the gastro-intestinal tract and retro-peritoneal tissues. *Surg. Gynecol. Obstet. 73:* 784–810.

Good, H. V. 1940. *A Study of an Epithelial Tumor of* Parophyrus vetulus. Master's dissertation, University of Washington. (Cited by Wellings, 1969.)

Good, R. A., and Finstad, J. 1967. The phylogenetic development of immune responses and the germinal center system. In *Germinal Centers in Immune Responses:* 4–27. Berlin: Springer Verlag.

Good, R. A., and Papermaster, B. W. 1964. Ontogeny and phylogeny of adaptive immunity. *Adv. Immun. 4:* 1–115.

Goodrich, H. B., Hill, G. A., and Arrick, M. S. 1941. The chemical identification of gene-controlled pigments in *Platypoecilus* and *Xiphophorus* and comparisons with other tropical fish. *Genetics, N.Y. 26:* 573–586.

Gorbman, A. 1964. Comparative pathology of the thyroid. In *The Thyroid.* International Academy of Pathology Monograph. Chapter 2: 32–48. (Beach Hazard, J., and Smith, D. E., eds.). Baltimore: Williams and Wilkins Co.

Gorbman, A., and Gordon, M. 1951. Spontaneous thyroidal tumours in the swordtail, *Xiphophorus montezumae. Cancer Res. 11:* 184–187.

Gordon, M. 1937. The production of spontaneous melanotic neoplasms in fishes by selective matings. II. Neoplasms with macromelanophores only. III. Neoplasms in day old fish. *Am. J. Cancer 30:* 362–375.

Gordon, M. 1946. Genetics of ocular-tumor development in fishes (preliminary report). *J. natn. Cancer Inst. 7:* 87–92.

Gordon, M. 1948. Effects of five primary genes on the site of melanomas in fishes and the influence of two color genes on their pigmentation. *Spec. Publs N.Y. Acad. Sci. 4:* 216–268.

Gordon, M. 1950. Heredity of pigmented tumours in fish. *Endeavour 9:* 26–34.

Gordon, M. 1951. The variable expressivity of a pigment cell gene from zero effect to melanotic tumor induction. *Cancer Res. 11:* 676–686.

Gordon, M., and Lansing, W. 1943. Cutaneous melanophore eruptions in young fish during stages preceding melanotic tumor formation. *J. Morph. 73:* 231–245.

Gordon, M., and Nigrelli, R. F. 1950. The effect of two linked color genes upon the atypical growth of erythrophores and macromelanophores to form erythromelanomas in four generations of hybrid fishes. *Cancer Res. 10:* 220 (Abstract).

Gordon, M., and Smith, G. M. 1938a. Progressive growth stages of a heritable melanotic neoplastic disease in fishes from the day of birth. *Am. J. Cancer 34:* 255–272.

Gordon, M., and Smith, G. M. 1938b. The production of a melanotic neoplastic disease in fishes by selective matings. *Am. J. Cancer 34:* 543–565.

Grafflin, A. L. 1937. Cyst formation in the glomerular tufts of certain fish kidneys. *Biol. Bull. mar. biol. Lab., Woods Hole 72:* 247–257.

Greenberg, S. S., and Kopac, M. J. 1960. The amino acids of xiphophorin fishes and their tumorous hybrids. *Anat. Rec. 137:* 360 (Abstract).

Greenberg, S. S., and Kopac, M. J. 1963. Studies of gene action and melanogenic enzyme activity in melanomatous fishes. *Ann. N.Y. Acad. Sci. 100:* 887–923.

Greenberg, S. S., Kopac, M. J., and Gordon, M. 1956a. Tissue culture studies of fish melanomas. *Anat. Rec. 124:* 488.

Greenberg, S. S., Kopac, M. J., and Gordon, M. 1956b. Cytology and cytochemistry of melanoma cells. *Ann. N.Y. Acad. Sci. 67:* 55–122.

Gudenatsch, J. F. 1910. The structure, distribution and variation of the thyroid gland in fish. *J. Am. med. Ass. 54:* 227.

Gudenatsch, J. F. 1911a. The thyroid gland of teleosts. *J. Morph. 21:* 709–782.

Gudenatsch, J. F. 1911b. The relationship between the normal and pathological thyroid gland of fish. *Johns Hopkins Hops. Bull. 22:* 152–155.

Gudger, E. W. 1934. The five great naturalists of the sixteenth century: Belon, Rondelet, Salviani, Gessner and Aldrovandi. A chapter in the history of ichthyology. *Isis 22:* 21–40.

Gudger, E. W. 1936. The beginnings of fish teratology, 1555–1642. *Scient. Mon., N.Y. 43:* 252–261.

Guglianetti, L. 1910. Fibroma dell'orbita in un ciprino. *Archo Ottal. 17:* 289–297. (Orbital fibroma in a cyprinid.)

Gunther, A. 1860. *Catalogue of the Acanthopterygiian Fishes in the British Museum 2:* 345–347. London: Brit. Mus. (Nat. Hist.).

Guseva, V. V. 1963. [Data on the investigation of fish tumors. Tumors of the pike-perch.] *Papers Leningr. Vet. High Sch.* No. 25 (In Russian).

Haddow, A., and Blake, I. 1933. Neoplasms in fish: A report of six cases with a summary of the literature. *J. Path. Bact. 36:* 41–47.

Halver, J. E. 1965a. Aflatoxicosis and rainbow trout hepatoma. In *Mycotoxins in Foodstuffs:* 209–234. (Wogan, G. N., ed.). Cambridge, Mass: M.I.T. Press.

Halver, J. E. 1965b. Hepatomas in fish. In *Primary Hepatomas:* 103–112. (Burdette, W. J., ed.) Salt Lake City, Utah: University of Utah Press.

Halver, J. E. 1967. Crystalline aflatoxin and other vectors for trout hepatoma. *Res. Rep. U.S. Fish Wildl. Serv.* No. 70: 78–102.

Halver, J. E. 1968. Aflatoxicosis and trout hepatoma. *Bull. Off. int. Épizoot. 69:* 1249–1278.

Halver, J. E. 1969. Aflatoxicosis and trout hepatoma. In *Aflatoxin, Scientific Background, Control and Implications:* 265–306. (Goldblatt, L. A., ed.). New York and London: Academic Press.

Halver, J. E., and Mitchell, I. A. (eds.) 1967. Trout Hepatoma Research Conference Papers. *Res. Rep. U.S. Fish. Wildl. Serv.* No. 70: 1–199. (To date, the most comprehensive report in the field.)

Halver, J. E., Ashley, L. M., and Smith, R. R. 1969. Aflatoxins and neoplasia in Coho salmon. *Natn. Cancer Inst. Monogr.* No. 31: 141–149.

Halver, J. E., Johnson, C. L., and Ashley, L. M. 1962. Dietary carcinogens induce fish hepatoma. *Fedn Proc. Fedn Am. Socs exp. Biol. 21:* 390 (Abstract).

Halver, J. E., LaRoche, G., and Ashley, L. M. 1964. Experimental hepatocellular carcinoma in rainbow trout. *Proc. Int. Congr. Nutr.* No. 6: 603. Edinburgh, 1963.

Halver, J. E., Ashley, L. M., Smith, C. E., and Wogan, G. N. 1967. Early acute aflatoxicosis stimulates rainbow trout hepatomagenesis. *Toxic appl. Pharmac. 10:* 398 (Abstract).

Halver, J. E., Ashley, L. M., Smith, R. R., and Wogan, G. N. 1968. Age and sensitivity of trout to aflatoxin B_1. *Fedn Proc. Fedn Socs exp. Biol. 27:* 552 (Abstract).

Hamre, C., and Nicholas, M. S. 1926. Exophthalmia in trout fry. *Proc. Soc. exp. Biol. Med. 26:* 63–65.

Harold, E. S., and Innes, K. F. 1922. *The Shrimp and Associated Organisms of San Francisco Bay.* Steinhart Aquarium, Calif. Acad. Sci., Golden Gate Park. San Francisco.

Harshbarger, J. C. 1973. *Activities Report. Registry of Tumors in Lower Ani-*

mals, Apr. 1972–*Mar.* 1973. Mus. Nat. Hist., Smithsonian Institution, Washington, D.C. (This registry includes many tumors of fishes.)

Harshbarger, J. C., and Bane, C. W. 1969. Case report of fibrolipoma in a rockfish, *Sebastodes diploproa*. *Natn. Cancer Inst. Monogr.* No. 31: 219–222.

Haüssler, G. 1928. Über Melanombildungen bei Bastarden von *Xiphophorus hellerii* und *Platypoecilus maculatus* var. *rubra*. *Klin. Wschr. 7:* 1561–1562. (On melanoma formations in hybrids of *Xiphophorus helleri* and *Platypoecilus maculatus* var. *rubra*.)

Haüssler, G. 1934. Über die Melanome der *Xiphophorus Platypoecilus* Bastarde. *Z. Krebsforsch. 40:* 280–292. (On melanomas of the *Xiphophorus-Platypoecilus* hybrids.)

Helmboldt, C. F., and Wyand, D. S. 1971. Nephroblastoma in a striped bass. *J. Wildl. Dis. 7:* 162–165.

Hess, W. N. 1937. Production of nutritional cataract in trout. *Proc. Soc. exp. Biol. Med. 37:* 306–309.

Hisaoka, K. K. 1961. Congenital teratomata in the guppy, *Lebistes reticulatus*. *J. Morph. 109:* 93–100.

Hisaoka, K. K. 1963. Congenital teratoma in the swordtail, *Xiphophorus helleri*. *Copeia 1963:* 189–191.

Hofer, B. 1894. Carcinoma of the thyroid in the lake trout. (Cited by Schmey, M., 1911.)

Hofer, B. 1898. Melanoma (pectoral and abdominal fin) in the tench (*Tinca tinca*, Linnaeus). (Cited by Schmey, M., 1911.)

Hofer, B. 1904a. A cystosarcoma in a char (*Salvelinus fontinalis*, Mitchill). (Cited by Schmey, M., 1911.)

Hofer, B. 1904b. *Handbuch der Fischkrankheiten.* Munich. (Handbook of fish diseases.) (See Bean, T. H., 1907.)

Hoffman, G. L., and Hoyme, J. B. 1958. The experimental histopathology of the "tumor" on the brain of the stickleback caused by *Diplostomum baeri eucaliae* Hoffman and Hundley, 1957 (Trematoda: Strigeoidea). *J. Parasit. 44.* 374-378.

Honma, Y. 1965. A case of the myxoma developed in the head of the salmonoid fish, the ayu, *Plecoglossus altevelis* Temminck et Schlegel. *Bull. Jap. Soc. scient. Fish. 31:* 192–197.

Honma, Y. 1966. Studies on the endocrine glands of the salmonoid fish, the ayu, *Plecoglossus altivelis* Temminck et Schlegel. VI. Effect of artificially controlled light on the endocrines of the pond-cultured fish. *Bull. Jap. Soc. scient. Fish. 32:* 32–40. (Brief description on the lymphosarcoma in the ovary, haemangioendothelioma, and adrenal neoplasia.)

Honma, Y., and Hirosaki, Y. 1966. [Histopathology on the tumors and endocrine glands of the immature chum salmon, *Oncorhynchus keta*, reared in the Enoshima aquarium.] *Jap. J. Ichthyol. 14:* 74–83 (In Japanese).

Honma, Y., and Kon, T. 1968. A case of the epidermal papilloma in the witch flounder from the Sea of Japan. *Bull. Jap. Soc. scient. Fish. 34:* 1–5.

Honma, Y., and Shirai, K. 1959. Cystoma found in the liver of rainbow trout (*Salmo gairdneri irideus* Gibbons). *Bull. Jap. Soc. scient. Fish. 24:* 966–970.

Hoshina, T. 1950. [A case of fibroblastic sarcoma developed in *Hypomesus olidus* (Pallas).] *Jap. J. Ichthyol. 1:* 53–56 (In Japanese).

Hoshina, T. 1952. [Four cases of tumorous growths in fish.] *Jap. J. Ichthyol. 2:* 81–88 (In Japanese).

Howell, J. H. 1969. *Accession No. 89. Registry of Tumors of Lower Animals.* The Smithsonian Institution, Washington, D.C.

Hsiao, S. C. T. 1941. Melanosis in the common cod, *Gadus callarias* L., associated with trematode infection. *Biol. Bull. mar. biol. Lab. Woods Hole 80:* 37–44.

Hueper, W. C. 1942. *Occupational Tumours and Allied Diseases:* 5 and 33. Springfield, Illinois: C C Thomas.

Hueper, W. C., and Payne, W. W. 1961. Observations on the occurrence of hepatomas in rainbow trout. *J. natn. Cancer Inst. 27:* 1123–1143. (A key reference.)

Hueper, W. C., and Ruchhoft, C. C. 1954. Carcinogenic studies on adsorbates of industrially polluted raw and finished water supplies. *A.M.A. Archs ind. Hyg. 9:* 488–495.

Hunter, J. 1782. An account of the organ of hearing in fish. *Phil. Trans. R. Soc. 72:* 379–383.

Ichikawa, R. 1954. Studies on the abnormalities of scales in the tumour appearing on the skin of Japanese common goby. *Jap. J. Ichthyol. 3:* 188–192.

Imai, T., and Fujiwara, N. 1959. An electron microscopic study of a papilloma-like hyperplastic growth in a goby, *Acanthogobius flavimanus. Kyushu J. med. sci. 10:* 135–147.

Ingleby, H. 1929. Melanotic tumor in *Lophius piscatorius. Archs Path. 8:* 1016–1021.

Iwashita, M. 1955. On the tumour of gobies. *Collecting Breed., Tokyo 17:* 50.

Jaboulay, M. 1908a. Poissons atteints de goitres malins héréditaires et contagieux. *J. Méd. Chir. prat. 79:* 239–240. (Fish suffering from malignant hereditary and contagious goiters.)

Jaboulay, M. 1908b. Poissons atteints de goitres malins héréditaires et contagieux. *Lyon méd. 110:* 335–336. (Fish suffering from malignant, hereditary and contagious goiters.)

Jackson, E. W., Wolf, H., and Sinnhuber, R. O. 1968. The relationship of hepatoma in rainbow trout to aflatoxin contamination and cottonseed meal. *Cancer Res. 28:* 987–991.

Jahnel, J. 1939. Über einige Geschwülste bei Fischen, ein Beitrag zur Erblichkeitsfrage von Tumoren. *Wien. tierärztl. Mschr. 26:* 325–333. (On some tumors in fish, a contribution on the question of the heredity of tumors.)

Johnstone, J. 1910–11. Internal parasites and diseased conditions of fishes. *Proc. Trans. Lpool biol. Soc. 25:* 88–122.

Johnstone, J. 1911–12. Internal parasites and diseased conditions of fishes. *Proc. Trans. Lpool biol. Soc. 26:* 103–144.

Johnstone, J. 1913. Diseased conditions in fishes. *Proc. Trans. Lpool biol. Soc. 27:* 196–218.

Johnstone, J. 1914a. Internal parasites and diseased conditions in fishes. *Proc. Trans. Lpool biol. Soc. 28:* 127–142.

Johnstone, J. 1914b. Diseased and abnormal conditions of marine fishes. *Rep. Lancs Sea-Fish. Labs 23:* 18–56.

Johnstone, J. 1915. Diseased and abnormal conditions of marine fishes. *Proc. Trans. Lpool biol. Soc. 29:* 80–113.

Johnstone, J. 1920. On certain parasites, diseased and abnormal conditions in fishes. *Proc. Trans. Lpool biol. Soc. 34:* 120–129.

Johnstone, J. 1922a. Diseases and parasites of fishes. *Proc. Trans. Lpool biol. Soc. 36:* 287–301.

Johnstone, J. 1922b. On some malignant tumours in fishes. *Rep. Lancs. Sea-Fish. Labs 31:* 87–99.

Johnstone, J. 1923. On some malignant tumours in fishes. *Proc. Trans. Lpool biol. Soc. 37:* 145–157.

Johnstone, J. 1923–25. Malignant tumours in fishes. *J. mar. biol. Ass. U.K.* (N.S.) *13:* 447–471.

Johnstone, J. 1924. Diseased conditions in fishes. *Proc. Trans. Lpool biol. Soc. 38:* 183–213.

Johnstone, J. 1924–25. Malignant tumours in fishes. *Proc. Trans. Lpool biol. Soc. 39:* 169–200.

Johnstone, J. 1926. Malignant and other tumours in marine fishes. *Proc. Trans. Lpool biol. Soc. 40:* 75–98.

Johnstone, J. 1927. Diseased conditions in fishes. *Proc. Trans. Lpool biol. Soc. 41:* 162–167.

Jones, J. C. 1969. Hemocytes and the problems of tumors in insects. *Natn. Cancer Inst. Monogr.* No. 31: 481–485.

Kazama, Y. 1922. On a spindle cell sarcoma in a salmon. *Gann 16:* 12–13.

Kazama, Y. 1924. Einige Geschwülste bei Fischen (*Pagrus major* et *Paralichthys olivaceus*). *Gann 18:* 35–37. (Some tumors in fishes (*Pagrus major* et *Paralichthys olivaceus*).)

Ketchen, K. S. 1953. Tumorous infection in sand soles of Northern Hecate Strait (British Columbia). *Report on the Survey of Hecate Strait in July,* 1953. Manuscript, 3 pp.

Keysselitz, G. 1908. Über ein Epithelioma der Barben. *Arch. Protistenk. 11:* 326–333. (On an epithelioma in the barbel.)

Kimura, I., Miyake, T., and Ito, Y. 1967a. [Studies on tumors in fishes. II. Papillomatous growths of skin in the goby, *Acanthogobius flavimanus.*] *Proc. Jap. Cancer Ass.* 26th Annual Meeting, 154 (In Japanese).

Kimura, I., Sugiyama, T., and Ito, Y. 1967b. Papillomatous growth in sole from Wakasa Bay area. *Proc. Soc. exp. Biol. Med. 125:* 175–177.

Klemm, E. 1927. Über die Schilddrüsengeschwülste bei Aquarienfischen. *Mikrokosmos 20:* 184–187. (On the thyroid glandular tumors of aquarium fishes.)

Klontz, G. W. 1972. Haematological techniques and the immune response in rainbow trout. In *Diseases of Fish.* (Mawdesley-Thomas, L. E., ed.) *Symp. zool. Soc. Lond.* No. 30: 89–100. London and New York: Academic Press.

Kolmer, W. 1928. Partieller Riesenwuchs in Verbindung mit grossem Rhabdomyon bei enier Schleie, *Tinca tinca. Virchows Arch. path. Anat. Physiol. 268:* 574–575. (Particular giant growth in connection with a large rhabdomyoma in a tench, *Tinca tinca.*)

Konnerth, A. 1966. Tilly bones. *Oceanus 12:* 6–9.

Kosswig, C. 1929a. Melanotische Geschwülstbildungen bei Fischbastarden. *Munch. med. Wschr. 76:* 1070. (Melanotic tumor formations in fish hybrids.)

Kosswig, C. 1929b. Zur Frage der Geschwülstbildungen bei Gattunsbastarden der Zahnkarpfen, *Xiphophorus und Platypoecilus. Z. indukt. Abstamm.-u. VerebLehre 52:* 114–120. (On the question of tumor formations in genus hybrids of the tooth carp.)

Kosswig, C. 1931. Über Geschwülstbildungen bei Fischbastarden. *Z. indukt. Abstamm.-u. VerebLehre 59:* 61–76. (On tumor formations in fish hybrids.)

Kraybill, H. F., and Shimkin, M. B. 1964. Carcinogenesis related to foods contaminated by processing and fungal metabolites. *Adv. Cancer Res. 8:* 191-248. Useful review article.)

Kreyberg, L. 1937. An intra-abdominal fibroma in a brown trout. *Am. J. Cancer 30:* 112-114.

Kubota, S. S. 1955a. Notes on liver cell carcinoma found on the rainbow trout, *Salmo irideus* Gibbons, *Rep. Fac. Fish. prefect. Univ. Mie 2:* 27-32.

Kubota, S. S. 1955b. [A case of leiomyoma found in rainbow trout *Salmo irideus* Gibbons.] *Bull. Jap. Soc. scient. Fish. 20:* 1060-1062 (In Japanese).

Labbé, A. 1930. Une tumeur complex chez un merlan. *Bull. Ass. fr. Étude Cancer 19:* 138-158. (A complex tumor in a whiting.)

Ladreyt, F. 1929. Sur un odontome cutane chez un *Scyllium catulus. Bull. Inst. océanogr. Monaco* No. 539: 1-4. (On a cutaneous odontoma in a *Scyllium catulus.*)

Ladreyt, F. 1930. Sur un rhabdomyosarcome chez un *Labrus mixtus. Bull. Inst. océanogr. Monaco* No. 550: 1-4. (On a rhabdomyosarcoma in a *Labrus mixtus.*)

Ladreyt, F. 1935. Sur un epithelioma de la muqueuse palatine chez une murène (*Muraena helena*). *Bull. Inst. océanogr. Monaco* No. 677: 1-16. (On an epithelioma of the palatine mucous membrane in a marine eel.)

LaRoche, G., Halver, J. E., Johnson, C. L., and Ashley, L. M. 1962. Hepatoma inducing agents in trout diets. *Fedn Proc. Fedn Am. Socs exp. Biol. 21:* 300 (Abstract).

Lawrence, G. 1895. Note on a tumour found attached to the stomach of a Saithe. *Rep. Fishery Bd Scotl. 13:* 236.

Lee, D. J., Wales, J. H., Sinnhuber, R. O., Ayres, J. L., and Roehm, J. N. 1967. A comparison of cyclopropenes and other possible promoting agents for Aflatoxin induced hepatoma in rainbow trout. *Fedn Proc. Fedn Am. Socs exp. Biol. 26:* 322 (Abstract).

Leger, L. 1925. Tumeurs observés chez les salmonides d'élévage. *C. r. Ass. fr. Avanc. Sci. 49:* 395-396. (Tumors observed in the bred salmonids.)

Levaditi, J. C., Besse, P., Vibert, R., Destombes, P., Guillon, J.-C., Nazimoff, O., and Normand, A. M. 1963a. Apparition d'hépatomes malins dans les élévages de truites arc-en-ciel (*Salmo gairdneri*). Aspects géographiques et histologiques: facteurs génétiques et nutritionnels. *Presse méd. 71:* 2743-2746. (Appearance of malignant hepatomas in hatchery rainbow trout (*Salmo gairdneri*). Geographic and histological aspects: genetic and nutritional factors.)

Levaditi, J. C., Besse, P., Vibert, R., Guillon, J.-C., and Nazimoff, O. 1963b. Particularités actuelles de l'hepatomé de la truite arc-en-ciel d'élévage. (*Salmo irideus*). *C. r. hebd. Séanc. Acad. Sci., Paris 257:* 1739-1741. (Actual peculiarities of hepatoma in the breeding rainbow trout.)

Levaditi, J. C., Besse, P., Vibert, R., and Nazimoff, O. 1960. Sur les critères histopathologiques et biologiques de malignité propres aux tumeurs épithéliales hépatiques des salmonides. *C. r. hebd. Séanc. Acad. Sci., Paris 251:* 603-610. (On the histopathological and biological criteria of malignity peculiar to the epithelial hepatic tumors in salmonids.

Levine, M., and Gordon, M. 1946. Ocular tumours with exophthalmia in xiphophorin fishes. *Cancer Res. 6:* 197-204.

Levy, B. M. 1962. Experimental induction of tumor-like lesions of the notochord of fish. *Cancer Res. 22:* 441-442.

Li, M. H., and Baldwin, F. M. 1944. Testicular tumors in the teleost. (*Xipho-*

phorus helleri) receiving sesame oil. *Proc. Soc. exp. Biol. Med. 57:* 165–167.

Ljungberg, O., and Lange, J. 1968. Skin tumors of northern pike (*Esox lucius L.*). I. Sarcoma in a Baltic pike population. *Bull. Off. int. Épizoot. 69:* 1007–1022.

Loeb, L. 1910. Demonstration of tumors of fish. *J. Am. med. Ass. 54:* 228.

Loewenthal, W. 1907a. An epithelioma in a carp (*Cyprinus carpio*, Linnaeus). (Cited by Schmey, M., 1911.)

Loewenthal, W. 1907b. Einschlüssartige Zell- und Kernveranderungen in der Karpfenpocke. *Z. Krebsforsch. 5:* 197–204.

Lombard, C. 1962. *Cancérologie comparée:* 25, 49–52, 144–147. Paris: G. Doin et Cie. (Comparative cancerology.)

Lotlikar, P. D., Miller, E. C., Miller, J. A., and Halver, J. E. 1967. Metabolism of the carcinogen 2-acetylaminofluorene by rainbow trout. *Proc. Soc. exp. Biol. Med. 124:* 160–163.

Lucké, B. 1937–38. Studies on tumors in cold-blooded vertebrates. *A. Rep. Tortugas Lab. 1937–1938:* 92–94.

Lucké, B. 1942. Tumors of the nerve sheaths in fish of the snapper family (Lutianidae). *Archs Path. 34:* 133–150.

Lucké, B., and Schlumberger, H. G. 1941. Transplantable epithelioma of the lip and mouth of catfish. I. Pathology. Transplantation to anterior chamber of eye and into cornea. *J. exp. Med. 74:* 397–408.

Lucké, B., and Schlumberger, H. G. 1942. Common neoplasms in fish, amphibians and reptiles. *J. tech. Meth. Bull. int. Ass. med. Mus. 22:* 4–9.

Lucké, B., and Schlumberger, H. G. 1949. Neoplasia in cold-blooded vertebrates. *Physiol. Rev. 29:* 91–126. (An essential reference.)

Lucké, B., Schlumberger, H. G., and Breedis, C. 1948. A common mesenchymal tumor of the corium of goldfish, *Carassius auratus. Cancer Res. 8:* 473–493.

Lümann, M., and Mann, H. 1956. Beobachtungen über die Blumenkohl Krankheit der Aale. *Arch. Fisch Wiss. 3:* 229–239. (Observations on "cauliflower" disease in eels.)

McArn, G., and Wellings, S. R. 1967. Neurofibroma in a teleost fish, *Lumpenus sagitta. J. Fish. Res. Bd Can. 24:* 2007–2009.

McArn, G., Chuinard, R. G., Miller, B. S., Brooks, R. E., and Wellings, S. R. 1968. Pathology of skin tumors found on English sole and starry flounder from Puget Sound, Washington. *J. natn. Cancer Inst. 41:* 229–242.

McFarland, J. 1901. Epithelioma of the mouth and skin of a catfish. *Proc. path. Soc. Philad. 4:* 79–81.

McGregor, E. A. 1963. Publications on fish parasites and diseases, 330 B.C.–A.D. 1923. *Spec. scient. Rep. U.S. Fish Wildl. Serv.* No. 474: 84.

McIntosh, W. C. 1884–1885. Multiple tumours in plaice and common flounders. *Rep. Fishery Bd Scotl. 3:* 66–67.

McIntosh, W. C. 1885a. Further remarks on the multiple tumours of common flounders, etc. *Rep. Fishery Bd Scotl. 4:* 214–215.

McIntosh, W. C. 1885b. On the spawning of certain marine fishes. *Ann. Mag. nat. Hist.* (5) *15:* 429–437.

McIntosh, W. C. 1908. On a tumour in a plaice. *Ann. Mag. nat. Hist.* (8) *1:* 373–387.

MacIntyre, P. A. 1960. Tumors of the thyroid gland in teleost fishes. *Zoologica, N.Y. 45:* 161–170.

MacIntyre, P. A., and Baker-Cohen, K. F. 1961. Melanoma, renal thyroid tumor and reticulo-endothelial hyperplasia in a non-hybrid platyfish. *Zoologica, N.Y. 46:* 125–131.

Mann, H. 1962. Beobachtungen über Krankheiten und Parasiten an Elbfischen. *Fischwirt 10:* 300–308. (Observations on diseases and parasites in "Elbfish.")

Mann, H. K. H., Pfitzner, I., Schmid, O. J., and Schubert, G. 1970. The cauliflower disease of eels. *Spec. Publs Am. Fish. Soc.* No. 5: 291–295.

Marine, D. 1914. Further observations and experiments on goitre in brook trout. *J. exp. Med. 19:* 70–88.

Marine, D., and Lenhart, C. H. 1910a. On the occurrence of goitre (active thyroid hyperplasia) in fish. *Bull. Johns Hopkins Hosp. 21:* 95–98.

Marine, D., and Lenhart, C. H. 1910b. Observations and experiments on the so-called thyroid carcinoma of brook trout (*Salvelinus fontinalis*) and its relation to ordinary goitre. *J. exp. Med. 12:* 311–327.

Marine, D., and Lenhart, C. H. 1911. Further observations and experiments on the so-called thyroid carcinoma of the brook trout (*Salvelinus fontinalis*) and its relation to endemic goitre. *J. exp. Med. 13:* 455–475. (A definitive paper on the fish thyroid.)

Marsh, M. C. 1903. Epithelioma in trout. *Wash. med. Ann. 2:* 59.

Marsh, M. C. 1911. Thyroid tumor in salmonoids. *Trans. Am. Fish. Soc. 40:* 377–392.

Marsh, M. C., and Vonwiller, P. 1916. Thyroid tumour in the sea bass (*Serranus*). *J. Cancer Res. 1:* 183–196.

Mattheis, T. 1964. Fälle von Zystenbildung und Geschwülsten bei Aalen (*Anguilla vulgaris*). *Z. Fisch. N. F. 12:* 709–715. (Cases of cyst formation and tumors in eels (*Anguilla vulgaris*).)

Mawdesley-Thomas, L. E. 1967. Fish pathology. *Proc. Br. Coarse Fish Conf.* No. 3: 27–29.

Mawdesley-Thomas, M. E. 1968. Fish and their environment. *Instn publ. Hlth Engrs J. 67:* 96–105.

Mawdesley-Thomas, L. E. 1969. Neoplasia in fish—A bibliography. *J. Fish. Biol. 1:* 187–207.

Mawdesley-Thomas, L. E. 1970. Significance of liver tumour induction in animals. In *Metabolic Aspects of Food Safety:* 481–531. (Roe, F. J. C., ed.) Oxford: Blackwell.

Mawdesley-Thomas, L. E. 1971a. Neoplasia in fish—A review. *Adv. Pathobiol, 1:* 88–170.

Mawdesley-Thomas, L. E. 1971b. Toxic chemicals—The risk to fish. *New Scient. 49:* 74–75.

Mawdesley-Thomas, L. E. 1972a. Research into fish diseases. *Nature, Lond., 235:* 17–19.

Mawdesley-Thomas, L. E. 1972b. Some tumours of fish. In *Diseases of Fish.* (Mawdesley-Thomas, L. E., ed.) *Symp. zool. Soc. Lond.* No. 30: 191–284. London and New York: Academic Press.

Mawdesley-Thomas, L. E., and Barry, D. H. 1970. Acid and alkaline phosphatase activity in the liver of brown and rainbow trout. *Nature, Lond. 227:* 738–739.

Mawdesley-Thomas, L. E., and Bucke, D. 1967a. Fish pox in the roach (*Rutilus rutilus* L.). *Vet. Rec. 81:* 56.

Mawdesley-Thomas, L. E., and Bucke, D. 1967b. Squamous cell carcinoma in a gudgeon (*Gobio* L.). *Pathologia veterinaria 4:* 484–489.

Mawdesley-Thomas, L. E., and Bucke, D. 1968. A lipoma in a bream (*Abramis brama* L.). *Vet. Rec. 82:* 673–674.

Mawdesley-Thomas, L. E., and Fraser, W. D. 1972. The conservation of fish. *Br. vet. J. 128:* 337–346.

Mawdesley-Thomas, L. E., and Jolly, D. W. 1967. Diseases of fish. II. The goldfish (*Carassius auratus*). *J. small Anim. Pract. 8:* 33–54.

Mawdesley-Thomas, L. E., and Jolly, D. W. 1968. Diseases of fish. III. The trout. *J. small Animl Pract. 9:* 167–188.

Mawdesley-Thomas, L. E., and Leahy, J. S. 1967. Organochlorine pesticide residues in pike. *Progve Fish Cult. 29:* 64.

Mawdesley-Thomas, L. E., and Newman, A. J. 1972. Tumours of rat brain. *Abstr. Path. Soc. Gt Br. Ire.* No. 125.

Mawdesley-Thomas, L. E., and Young, P. C. 1967. Cutaneous melanosis in a flounder (*Platichthys flesus*). *Vet. Rec. 81:* 384.

Mazzarelli. 1910. Epithelioma of the mouth of *Chondrostoma soetta.* (Cited by Thomas, L., 1931.)

Milleman, R. E. 1968. (Cited by Wellings, S. R., 1969.)

Montpellier, J., and Dieuzeide, R. 1932. Sur une production tumeurs cutanées du cyprin (*Carassius auratus*). *Bull. Ass. fr. Étude Cancer 21:* 295–306. (Cutaneous tumors in the goldfish.)

Montpellier, J., and Dieuzeide, R. 1934. Tumeurs mélaniques de la peau du cyprin. *Bull. Stn Agric. Pêche Castiglione 1934:* 97–103. (Melanotic tumors of the skin in carp.)

Mukoyama. 1917-18. [About a new tumor of the goldfish.] *Gann 2* (In Japanese).

Mulcahy, M. F. 1963. Lymphosarcoma in the pike, *Esox lucius* L. (Pisces; Esocidae) in Ireland. *Proc. R. Ir. Acad.* (B) *63:* 103–129.

Mulcahy, M. F. 1970. The thymus gland and lymphosarcoma in the pike, *Esox lucius* L., in Ireland. *Proc. Int. Symp. Comp. Leukaemia Res. Bibliotheca Haemat.,* No. 4: 600–609.

Mulcahy, M. F., and O'Leary, A. 1970. Cell-free transmission of lymphosarcoma in the northern pike, *Esox lucius* L. (Pisces, Esocidae). *Experientia 26:* 891.

Mulcahy, M. F., and O'Rourke, F. J. 1964a. Lymphosarcoma in the pike (*Esox lucius* L.) in Ireland. *Life Sciences 3:* 719–720.

Mulcahy, M. F., and O'Rourke, F. J. 1964b. Cancerous pike in Ireland. *Ir. Nat. 14:* 312–315.

Müller, F. W. 1926. Über Schilddrüsendewächse bei Kaltblütern. *Virchows Arch. path. Anat. Physiol. 260:* 405–427. (Thyroid gland growths in cold-blooded animals.)

Mulsow, K. 1915. Chondroma on top of head of three carp. (Cited by Thomas, L., 1932b).

Murray, J. A. 1908. The zoological distribution of cancer. *Scient. Rep. Invest. imp. Cancer Res. Fund 3:* 52–60.

Nicholson, G. W. 1926. *The Nature of Tumour Formation.* Erasmus Wilson Lectures, 1925. Cambridge: Heffer.

Nigrelli, R. F. 1938. Fish parasites and fish diseases. I. Tumors. *Trans. N.Y. Acad. Sci.* (11) *1:* 4-7.

Nigrelli, R. F. 1943. Causes of diseases and death of fishes in captivity. *Zoologica, N.Y. 28:* 203-216.

Nigrelli, R. F. 1946. Studies on the marine resources of southern New England. V. Parasites and diseases of the ocean pout, *Macrozoarces americanus.*—(IV) On a fibro-epithelial growth on the snout. *Bull. Bingham oceanogr. Coll. 9:* 218-221.

Nigrelli, R. F. 1946-47. Spontaneous neoplasms in fishes. II. Fibro-carcinoma-like growth in the stomach of *Borophryne apagon* Regan, a deep-sea ceratioid fish. *Zoologica, N.Y. 31:* 183-184.

Nigrelli, R. F. 1947. Spontaneous neoplasms in fishes. III. Lymphosarcoma in *Astyanax* and *Esox. Zoologica, N.Y. 32:* 101-108.

Nigrelli, R. F. 1948. Hyperplastic epidermal disease in the bluegill sunfish, *Lepomis macrochirus* Rafinesque. *Zoologica, N.Y. 33:* 133-137.

Nigrelli, R. F. 1951. Lip tumours in fishes kept in captivity. *Cancer Res. 2:* 272 (Abstract).

Nigrelli, R. F. 1952a. Virus and tumors in fishes. *Ann. N.Y. Acad. Sci. 54:* 1076-1092.

Nigrelli, R. F. 1952b. Spontaneous neoplasms in fishes. VI. Thyroid tumors in marine fishes. *Cancer Res. 12:* 286.

Nigrelli, R. F. 1952c. Spontaneous neoplasms in fishes. VI. Thyroid tumors in marine fishes. *Zoologica, N.Y. 37:* 185-189.

Nigrelli, R. F. 1954. Tumors and other atypical cell growths in temperate freshwater fishes of North America. *Trans. Am. Fish. Soc. 83:* 262-296. (A useful review paper.)

Nigrelli, R. F., and Gordon, M. 1944. A melanotic tumor in the silverside, *Menidia beryllina peninsulae* (Good and Bean). *Zoologica, N.Y. 29:* 45-47.

Nigrelli, R. F., and Gordon, M. 1946. Spontaneous neoplasms in fishes. I. Osteochondroma in the jewelfish, *Hemichromis bimaculatus. Zoologica, N.Y. 31:* 89-92.

Nigrelli, R. F., and Gordon, M. 1951. Spontaneous neoplasms in fishes. V. Acina: adenocarcinoma of the pancreas in a hybrid platyfish. *Zoologica, N.Y. 36:* 121-125.

Nigrelli, R. F., and Jakowska, S. 1953. Spontaneous neoplasms in fish. VII. A spermatocytoma and renal melanoma in an African lungfish, *Protopterus annectens* (Owen). *Zoologica, N.Y. 38:* 109-112.

Nigrelli, R. F., and Jakowska, S. 1955. Spontaneous neoplasms in fish. IX. Hepatomas in rainbow trout, *Salmo gairdneri. Proc. Am. Ass. Cancer Res. 2:* 38 (Abstract).

Nigrelli, R. F., and Jakowska, S. 1961. Fatty degeneration, regenerative hyperplasia and neoplasia in the livers of rainbow trout, *Salmo gairdneri. Zoologica, N.Y. 46:* 49-55.

Nigrelli, R. F., and Smith, G. M. 1940. A papillary cystic disease affecting the barbels of *Ameiurus* sp. *Zoologica, N.Y. 25:* 89-96.

Nigrelli, R. F., Jakowska, S., and Gordon, M. 1950. Histological and cytological observations on hereditary erythromelanomas in platyfish-swordtail hybrids. *Cancer Res. 10:* 234 (Abstract).

Nigrelli, R. F., Jakowska, S., and Gordon, M. 1951. The invasion and cell replacement of one pigmented neoplastic growth by a second and more malignant type in experimental fishes. *Br. J. Cancer 5:* 54–68.

Nigrelli, R. F., Ketchen, K. S., and Ruggieri, G. D. 1965. Studies on virus diseases of fishes. Epizootiology of epitheliam tumors in the skin of flatfishes of the Pacific coast, with special reference to the sand sole (*Psettichthys melanostictus*) from Northern Hecate Strait, British Columbia, Canada. *Zoologica, N.Y. 50:* 115–122.

Nishikawa, S. 1954. On the tumorous growth observed in two fishes. *Collecting Breed., Tokyo 16:* 236.

Nishikawa, S. 1955a. [A case of spindle cell sarcoma developed in the Japanese common goby (*Acanthogobius flavimanus*).] *J. Shimonseki Coll. Fish. 5:* 171–174 (In Japanese).

Nishikawa, S. 1955b. [A case of fibroblastic sarcoma developed in *Theragra chalcogramma* (Pallas).] *J. Shimonoseki Coll. Fish. 4:* 666–669 (In Japanese).

Novelli, G. D. 1967. Amino acid incorporation in rat and trout liver. *Res. Rep. U.S. Fish Wildl. Serv.* No. 70: 72–77.

Ohlmacher, H. 1898. Several examples illustrating the comparative pathology of tumors. *Bull. Ohio Hosp. Epilep. 1:* 223–226.

Olearius, A. 1674. *Gottorf Museum of Arts in which are all sorts of extraordinary things/partly natural history/partly of artificial origins have been brought and prepared. Out of all four corners of the world this has been carried before one year has been described.* 2nd ed.

Oota, K. 1952. An epidemic occurrence of tumor-like hyperplasia of epidermis in a species of fish. *Acanthogobius flavimanus. Gann 43:* 264–265.

Osburn, R. C. 1925. Black tumor of the catfish. *Bull. Bur. Fish., Wash. 91:* 9–13.

Otte, E. 1964. Eine bösartige Neubildung in der Bauchhöhle eines Goldfisches (*Carassius auratus* L.). *Wein. tierärztl. Mschr. 51:* 485–488. (A malignant formation in the abdomen of a goldfish.)

Oxner, M. 1905. Über die Kolbenzellen in der Epidermis der Fische; ihre Form, Verteilung, Entstehung und Bedeutung. *Jena Z. Naturw. 40:* 589–646. (The "nodule" cells in the epidermis of fish; their form, distribution, origin, and significance.)

Pacis, M. R. 1932. *An epithelial tumor of* Parophrys vetulus. Master's dissertation, University of Washington. (Cited by Wellings, S. R., 1969b.)

Papermaster, B. W., Condie, R. M., and Good. R. A. 1962. Immune response in the California hagfish. *Nature, Lond. 196:* 355–357.

Pauley, G. B. 1969. A critical review of neoplasia and tumor-like lesions in mollusks. *Natn. Cancer Inst. Monogr.* No. 31: 509–529.

Pellegrin, J. 1901. Les poissons à gibbosité frontale. *Bull. Soc. philomath. Paris* (N.S.) *3:* 81–91. (Fish with frontal gibbosity.)

Pesce, P. 1907a. Contributo alla conoscenza dei tumori nei pesci. *Riv. mens. Pesca Idrobiol. 9:* 223–225. (Contribution to knowledge of fish tumors.)

Pesce, P. 1907b. Leiomyoma in the pylorus of a carp. (Cited by Thomas, L., 1931a.)

Petrushevski, G. K. 1957. The diseases of White Lake—"Belogo Ozera" fish. In

Parasites and Diseases of Fish: 274–277. (Petrushevski, G. K., ed.) Leningrad: Fish Industry Department of the State Planning Committee for the P.S.F.S.R.

Peyron, M. A. 1939. Sur la fréquence des tumeurs dans les divers ordres de vertébrés à sang froid et leur rareté dans les espèces venimeuses. *C. r. hebd. Séanc. Acad. Sci. Paris 209:* 261–263. (Frequency of tumors in various species of cold-blooded vertebrates and their rarity in venomous species.)

Peyron, A., and Thomas, L. 1929. Contribution à l'étude des tumeurs du revêtement branchial chez les poissons. *Bull. Ass. fr. Étude Cancer 18:* 825–837. (Contribution to the study of tumors in the branchial lining in fish.)

Peyron, A., and Thomas, L. 1930. Les tumeurs thyroidiennes des salmonides. *Bull. Ass. fr. Étude Cancer 19:* 795–819. (The thyroid tumors in salmonids.)

Phelps, R. A. 1967. Aflatoxins in feeds—A review. *Res. Rep. U.S. Fish Wildl. Serv.* No. 70: 145–159.

Picchi, L. 1933. Di un non commune tumore di un pesce (neurinoma). *Sperimentale 86:* 128–130. (On an uncommon tumor in a fish (neurinoma).)

Pick, L. 1905. Der Schilddrüsenkrebs der Salmoniden (Edelfische). *Berl. tierärztl. Wschr. 42:* 1435, 1477, 1498, 1532. (Cancer of the thyroid gland in salmonids (rarefish).)

Pick, L., and Poll, H. 1903. Über einige bemerkenswerte Tumorbildungen bei Kaltblutern. *Berl. klin. Wschr. 1903:* 23–25. (About tumor formation in animal pathology with particular reference to benign and malignant tumors of cold-blooded animals.)

Plehn, M. 1902. Bösartiger Kropf (Adenocarcinoma der Thyroidea) bei Salmoniden. *Allg. FischZtg. 27:* 117–118. (Malignant goiter (adenocarcinoma of the thyroids) in salmonids.)

Plehn, M. 1906. Über Geschwülste bei Kaltblütern. *Z. Krebsforsch. 4:* 525–564. (On tumors in cold-blooded animals.)

Plehn, M. 1909. Über einige bei Fischen beobachtete Geschwülste und Geschwülstartige Bildungen. *Ber. K. bayer. biol. VersStn 2:* 55–76. (On some tumors and growth-like formations observed in fish.)

Plehn, M. 1915. Fälle von multiplem Odontom bei der Bachforelle. *Z. Fisch. 17:* 197–200. (Cases of multiple odontomas in the stream trout.)

Plehn, M. 1924. *Praktikum der Fischkrankheiten:* 301–479. Stuttgart: E. Schweizerbart. (Practical handbook of fish diseases.) (Still a standard textbook.)

Prince, E. E. 1891. Melanosarcoma in a haddock. (Cited by Thomas, L., 1931a.)

Prince, E. E., and Steven, J. L. 1892. On two large tumours in a haddock and a cod. *Rep. Fishery Bd Scotl. 10:* 323–325.

Proewig, F. 1954. Die Beeinflussung des Wachstums bösartiger Tumoren von Zahnkarpfen. *Z. Krebsforsch. 60:* 470–472. (The influence of the growth of malignant tumors in tooth-carp.)

Puente-Duany, N. 1930. Tumoracion periocular en un pescade de rio. *Boln Liga Cáncer, Habana 5:* 240. (Periocular tumor in river fish.)

Raabe, H. 1939. Cas d'épithélioma des viscères chez le poisson *Mollienisia velifera. Archs Zool. exp. gén. 81:* 1–8. (Case of epithelioma of the viscera of the fish *Mollienisia velifera.*)

Radulescu, I. 1967. Tumori tegumentare la guvizii din Marea Neagra Tărmul Romậnesc. *Bul. Inst. Cerc. pisc. 26:* 36–40.

Radulescu, I., Vasiliu, D. G., Ilie, E., and Snieszko, S. F. 1968. Thyroid hyperplasia of the Eastern brook trout *Salvelinus fontinalis* in Romania. *Trans. Am. Fish. Soc. 97:* 486–488.

Rasquin, P., and Hafter, E. 1951. Response of a fish lymphosarcoma to mammalian ACTH. *Zoologica, N.Y. 36:* 163–169.

Rasquin, P., and Rosenbloom, L. 1954. Endocrine imbalance and tissue hyperplasia in teleosts maintained in darkness. *Bull. Am. Mus. nat. Hist. 104:* 359–426.

Rayer, P. 1843. Observations sur les maladies des poissons. Exposé succinct des principales observations faites jusqu'à ce jour sur les maladies et sur les anomalies des poissons. *Archs méd. comp. 1:* 245–308. (Observations on fish diseases. Concise report on the principal observations made up to now on disease and anomalies of fish.)

Reed, H. D., and Gordon, M. 1931. The morphology of melanotic overgrowths in hybrids of Mexican killifishes. *Am. J. Cancer 15:* 1524–1546.

Reichenbach-Klinke, H.-H. 1966. *Krankheiten und Schädigungen der Fische.* Stuttgart: Gustav Fischer. (Diseases and injuries of fish.) (A standard textbook.)

Reichenbach-Klinke, H.-H., and Elkan, E. 1965. *The Principal Diseases of Lower Vertebrates:* 152–165. London and New York: Academic Press.

Roberts, R. J. 1972. Oral carcinomata in a salmon (*Salmo salar* L.). *Vet. Rec. 91:* 199.

Robertson, O. H., and Chaney, A. L. 1953. Thyroid hyperplasia and tissue iodine content in spawning rainbow trout: a comparative study of Lake Michigan and California sea-run trout. *Physiol. Zool. 26:* 328–340.

Rodricks, J. V., Henery-Logan, K. R., Campbell, A. D., Stoloff, L., and Verrett, M. J. 1968. Isolation of new toxin from cultures of aspergillus flavus. *Nature, Lond. 217:* 668.

Roffo, A. H. 1924. Le sarcome des poissons. *Néoplasmes 3:* 231–234. (Sarcoma of fish.)

Roffo, A. H. 1925. Sobre un tumor paradentario en la corvina. *Boln Inst. Med. exp. Estud. Trat. Cáncer, B. Aires 2:* 28–42. (On a benign tumor in the sea bass.)

Roffo, A. H. 1926. Sarcomas fusocelular de corvina. *Boln Inst. Med. exp. Estud. Trat. Cáncer, B. Aires 3:* 206–207. (Fusiform sarcomas of the sea bass.)

Ronca, V. 1914. I. Tumori nei pesci. *Tumori 4:* 61–71. (Tumors in fish.)

Roth, W. 1913. *Die Krankheiten der Aquarienfische und ihre Bekämfung.* Stuttgart: Mikrokosmos Francklische Verlagshandlung. (Diseases of aquarium fish and their control.)

Roth, W. 1922. *Die Krankheiten der Aquarienfische.* Stuttgart: Francklische Verlagshandlung. (Diseases of aquarium fish.)

Rucker, R. R., Yasutake, W. T., and Wolf, H. 1961. Trout hepatoma. A preliminary report. *Progve Fish Cult. 23:* 3–7.

Russell, F. E., and Kotin, P. 1957. Squamous papilloma in the white croaker. *J. natn. Cancer Inst. 18:* 857–861.

Sagawa, E. 1925. Zur Kenntnis der Fischengeschwülste. *Gann 19:* 14–15. (On the knowledge of fish tumors.)

Sallmann, L. von., Halver, J. E., Collins, E., and Grimes, P. 1966. Thioacetamide induced cataract with invasive proliferation of the lens epithelium in rainbow trout. *Cancer Res. 26:* 1819–1825.

Salt, G. 1963. The defense reactions of insects to metazoan parasites. *Parasitology 53:* 527–642.

Sandeman, G. 1893a. On the multiple tumours in plaice and flounders. *Rep. Fishery Bd Scotl. 11:* 391–392.

Sandeman, G. 1893b. On a tumour from a tunny. *Rep. Fishery Bd Scotl. 11:* 392–394.

Sarkar, H. L., and Dutta-Chaudhuri, R. 1953. On the occurrence of an epidermal papilloma of Koi fish, *Anabas testudenius* (Bloch). *J. Indian med. Ass. 22:* 152–154.

Sarkar, H. L., and Dutta-Chaudhuri, R. 1958. On the occurrence of osteogenic fibroma on the pre-maxilla of an Indian catfish, *Wallago attu* (Bloch and Schneider). *Gann 49:* 65–68.

Sarkar, H. L., and Dutta-Chaudhuri, R. 1964. On the occurrence of adenoma in the gill apparatus of a trout, *Salmo fario. Trans. Am. microsc. Soc. 83:* 93–96.

Sarkar, H. L., Kapoor, B. G., and Dutta-Chaudhuri, R. 1955. A study of leiomyoma, a mesenchymal tumour on the fins of an Indian catfish, *Mystus (Osteobagrus) seenghala* (Sykes). *Growth 19:* 257–262.

Sathyancsan, A. G. 1962. On the basophilic tumor in the pituitary of the freshwater teleost *Mystus seenghala* (Sykes). *Sci. Cult. 28:* 432–433.

Sathyanesan, A. G. 1963. On the functional thyroid tumour in the kidney of the freshwater teleost, *Barbus stigma,* in its natural habitat. *Sci. Cult. 29:* 90–91.

Sathyanesan, A. G. 1966. The structure of the glomerular cystic tumor present in the tropical freshwater catfish, *Mystus vittatus* (Bloch). *Trans. Am. microsc. Soc. 85:* 53–57.

Scarpelli, D. G. 1967. Ultrastructural and biochemical observations on trout hepatoma. *Res. Rep. U.S. Fish Wildl. Serv.* No. 70: 60–71.

Scarpelli, D. G. 1969. Comparative aspects of neoplasia in fish and other laboratory animals. In *Fish in Research:* 45–85. (Neuhaus, O. W., and Halver, J. E., eds.) New York and London: Academic Press.

Scarpelli, D. G., Greider, M. H., and Frajola, W. J. 1963. Observations on hepatic cell hyperplasia, adenoma and hepatoma of rainbow trout (*Salmo gairdneri*). *Cancer Res. 23:* 848–857.

Schamberg, J. F., and Lucké, B. 1922. Fibrosarcoma of the skin in a goldfish (*Carassius auratus*). *J. Cancer Res. 7:* 151–161.

Schäperclaus, W. 1953. Die Blumenkohlkrankheit der Aale und anderer Fische der Ostsee. *Z. Fisch.* (N.S.) *2:* 105–124. (The cauliflower disease of eels and other fish in the Baltic Sea.)

Schäperclaus, W. 1954. *Fischkrankheiten.* Berlin: Akademie Verlag. (Fish diseases.) (A standard textbook.)

Schlumberger, H. G. 1949. Cutaneous leiomyoma of goldfish. I. Morphology and growth in tissue culture. *Am. J. Path. 25:* 287–299.

Schlumberger, H. G. 1950. Polycystic kidney (Mesonephros) in the goldfish. *Archs Path. 50:* 400–410.

Schlumberger, H. G. 1951. Limbus tumors as a manifestation of von Recklinghausen's neurofibromatosis in goldfish. *Am. J. Ophthal. 34:* 415–422.

Schlumberger, H. G. 1952. Nerve sheath tumors in an isolated goldfish population. *Cancer Res. 12:* 890–899.

Schlumberger, H. G. 1953. Comparative pathology of oral neoplasms. *Oral Surg. 6:* 1078–1094.

Schlumberger, H. G. 1954. Spontaneous hyperplasia and neoplasia in the thyroid of animals. *Brookhaven Symp. Biol.* No. 7: 169–191.

Schlumberger, H. G. 1955. Spontaneous goiter and cancer of the thyroid in animals. *Ohio J. Sci. 55:* 23–43.

Schlumberger, H. G. 1957. Tumors characteristic for certain animal species. A review. *Cancer Res. 17:* 823–832.

Schlumberger, H. G. 1958. Krankheiten der Fische, Amphibien und Reptilien. In *Pathologie der Laboratoriumstiere:* 714–761. (Cohrs, P., Jaffe, R., and Meessen, H., eds). Berlin: Springer-Verlag. (Diseases of fish, amphibians, and reptiles.)

Schlumberger, H. G., and Katz, M. 1956. Odontogenic tumors of salmon. *Cancer Res. 16:* 369–370.

Schlumberger, H. G., and Lucké, B. 1948. Tumors of fishes, amphibians, and reptiles. *Cancer Res. 8:* 657–712.

Schmey, M. 1911. Über Neubildungen bei Fischen. *Frankf. Z. Path. 6:* 230–253. (On new growths in fishes. Useful guide to early German literature.)

Schmey, M., and Pick, L. 1910. Carcinoma of the kidney in an eel (*Anguilla anguilla,* Linnaeus). (Cited by Schmey, M., 1911.)

Schreibman, M. P. 1966. Hypophysial cyst in a teleost fish. *J. exp. Zool. 162:* 57–67.

Schreibman, M. P., and Charipper, H. A. 1962. The occurrence of pituitary cysts in a particular strain of platyfish (*Xiphophorus maculatus*). *Am. Zool. 2:* 556 (Abstract).

Schreitmüller, W. 1924. Schilddrüsengeschwulst (Struma maligna) bei *Jordanella floridae* Goode et Bean. *Bl. Aquar.-u.-Terrarienk. 35:* 83.

Schroeders, V. D. 1908. [*Tumors of fishes.*] Dissertation (In Russian). (Translation in Army Med. Library, Washington, D.C.) St. Petersburg. (Cited by Schlumberger, H. G., and Lucké, B., 1948.)

Schubert, G. 1964. Elektronenmikroskopische Untersuchungen zur Pockenkrankheit des Karpfens. *Z. Naturf.* B *19:* 675–682. (Electron-microscopic studies of pox disease in carp.)

Scolari, C. 1953. Contributo alla conoscenza degli adenocarcinomi epatici della trota iridea. *Atti Soc. ital. Sci. vet. 7:* 599–605. (Contribution to the knowledge of hepatic adenocarcinoma in the rainbow trout.)

Scott, P. E. 1891. Notes on the occurrence of cancer in fish. *Trans. Proc. N.Z. Inst. 24:* 201.

Semer, E. 1888. Über Allgemeine Carcinose u. Sarkomatose und über Multiple Fibrome u. Lipoma bei den Haustieren. *Dt. Z. Tiermed. Vergl. Pathol. 14:* 245–247. (General carcinomas and sarcomas and multiple fibromas and lipomas in domestic animals.)

Siciliano, M. J., Perlmutter, A., and Clark, E. 1971. Effect of sex on the development of melanoma in hybrid fish of the genus *Xiphophorus*. *Cancer Res. 31:* 725–729.

Simon, R. C., Dollar, A. M., and Smuckler, E. A. 1967. Descriptive classification on normal and altered histology of trout livers. *Res. Rep. U.S. Fish Wildl. Serv.* No. 70: 18–28.

Sims, R. 1967. Analysis of hepato-carcinogenic fish meal lipids. *Res. Rep. U.S. Fish Wildl. Serv.* No. 70: 171–181.

Sinnhuber, R. O. 1967. Aflatoxin in cottonseed meal and liver cancer in rainbow trout. *Res. Rep. U.S. Fish Wildl. Serv.* No. 70: 48–55.

Sinnhuber, R. O., Wales, J. H., and Lee, D. J. 1966. Cyclopropenoids, co-carcinogens for aflatoxin-induced hepatoma in trout. *Fedn Proc. Fedn Am. Socs exp. Biol. 25:* 555 (Abstract).

Sinnhuber, R. O., Lee, D. J., Wales, J. H., and Ayres, J. L. 1968a. Dietary factors and hepatoma in rainbow trout (*Salmo gairdneri*). II. Co-carcinogenesis by cyclopropenoid fatty acids and the effect of gossypol and altered lipids of aflatoxin-induced liver cancer. *J. natn. Cancer Inst. 41:* 1293–1301.

Sinnhuber, R. O., Wales, J. H., Ayres, J. L., Engebrecht, R. H., and Amend, D. F. 1968b. Dietary factors and hepatoma in rainbow trout (*Salmo gairdneri*). I. Aflatoxins in vegetable protein feedstuffs. *J. natn. Cancer Inst. 41:* 711–718.

Sinnhuber, R. O., Wales, J. H., Engebrecht, R. H., Amend, D. F., Kray, W. D., Ayres, J. L., and Ashton, W. E. 1965. Aflatoxins in cottonseed meal and hepatoma in rainbow trout. *Fedn Proc. Fedn Am. Socs exp. Biol. 24:* 627 (Abstract).

Smith, G. M. 1934. A cutaneous red pigmented tumor (erythrophoroma) with metasteses in a flatfish (*Pseudopleuronectes americanus*). *Am. J. Cancer 21:* 596–599.

Smith, G. M. 1935. A hyperplastic epidermal disease in the winter flounder infected with *Cryptocotyle lingua* (Creplin). *Am. J. Cancer 25:* 108–112.

Smith, G. M., and Coates, C. W. 1937. The histological structure of the normal and hyperplastic thyroid in *Rasbora lateristriata*. *Zoologica, N.Y. 22:* 297–302.

Smith, G. M., Coates, C. W., and Strong, L. C. 1936. Neoplastic diseases in small tropical fishes. *Zoologica, N.Y. 21:* 219–224.

Smith, H. M. 1909. Case of epidemic carcinoma of thyroid in fishes. *Wash. med. Ann. 8:* 313.

Sneed, K. 1968. (Cited by Ashley, L. M., 1969.)

Snieszko, S. F. 1961. Hepatoma and visceral granuloma in trouts. *N.Y. Fish Game J. 8:* 145–149.

Snieszko, S. F. 1972. Progress in fish pathology in this century. In *Diseases of Fish.* (Mawdesley-Thomas, L. E., ed.). *Symp. zool. Soc. Lond.* No. 30: 1–16. London and New York, Academic Press.

Snieszko, S. F., Miller, J. A., and Atherton, C. R. 1966. Selected hematological and biochemical tests performed with blood and serum of adult rainbow trout (*Salmo gairdneri*) with a high incidence of hepatoma. *Ann. N.Y. Acad. Sci. 136:* 193–210.

Solomon, G., Jenson, R., and Tanner, H. 1965. Hepatic changes in rainbow trout

(*Salmo gairdneri*) fed diets containing peanut, cottonseed and soybean meals. *Am. J. vet. Res. 26:* 764–769.

Southwell, T. 1915. Notes from the Bengal Fisheries Laboratory, Indian Museum: No. 2.–On some Indian parasites of fish with a note of the carcinoma in trout. *Rec. Indian Mus. 11:* 311–330.

Southwell, T., and Prashad, B. 1918. Notes from the Bengal Fisheries Laboratory, Indian Museum: No. 5–Parasites of Indian fishes with a note on the carcinoma in the climbing perch. *Rec. Indian Mus. 15:* 341–355.

Sparks, A. K. 1969. Review of tumors and tumor-like conditions in Protozoa, Coelenterata, Platyhelminthas, Annelida, Sipunculida and Arthropoda, excluding insects. *Nat. Cancer Inst. Monogr.* No. 31: 671–682.

Stanton, M. F. 1965. Diethylnitrosamine-induced hepatic degeneration and neoplasia in the aquarium fish, *Brachydanio rerio. J. nat. Cancer Inst. 34:* 117–130.

Stanton, M. F. 1966. Hepatic neoplasms of aquarium fish exposed to *Cycas circinalis. Fedn Proc. Fedn Am. Socs exp. Biol. 25:* 661.

Starks, E. C. 1911. The osteological characters of the scombroid fishes of the families Gempylidae, Lepidopidae and Trichiuridae. *Stanford Univ. Publs* No. 5: 17–26.

Steeves, H. R. III. 1969. An epithelial papilloma of the brown bullhead, *Ictalurus nebulosus. Natn. Cancer Inst. Monogr.* No. 31: 215–218.

Stewart, H. L., and Snell, K. C. 1957. The histopathology of experimental tumours of the liver of the rat. *Acta Un. int. Cancr. 13:* 770–803.

Stewart, M. J. 1931. Precancerous lesions of the alimentary tract. *Lancet 1931 ii:* 565, 617, 669.

Stolk, A. 1953a. Tumours of fishes. I. An ovarian teratoma in the viviparous cyprinodont *Lebistes reticulatus* Peters. *Proc. K. ned. Akad. Wet.* (C) *56:* 28–33.

Stolk, A. 1953b. Tumours of fishes. II. Chromophobe adenoma of the pituitary gland in the viviparous cyprinodont *Lebistes reticulatus* Peters. *Proc. K. ned. Akad. Wet.* (C) *56:* 34–38.

Stolk, A. 1953c. Tumours of fishes. III. Carcinoma of the epidermis in the black variety of the viviparous cyprinodont *Xiphophorus hellerii* Heckel. *Proc. K. ned. Akad. Wet.* (C) *56: 143–148.*

Stolk, A. 1953d. Tumours of fishes. IV. Carcinoma of the pharynx in the viviparous cyprinodont *Lebistes reticulatus* Peters. *Proc. K. ned. Akad. Wet.* (C) *56:* 149–151.

Stolk, A. 1953e. Tumours of fishes. V. Melanoma of the skin in the cyprinid *Brachydanio rerio* (Hamilton-Buchanan). *Proc. K. ned. Akad. Wet.* (C) *56:* 152–156.

Stolk, A. 1954. Tumours of fishes. VI. Mesenchymal tumour of the skin in the viviparous cyprinodont *Xiphophorus maculatus* Günther (red variety). *Proc. K. ned. Akad. Wet.* (C) *57:* 652–658.

Stolk, A. 1955a. Tumours of fishes. VII. Congenital teratoma of the skin in the viviparous cyprinodont *Lebistes reticulatus* Peters. *Proc. K. ned. Akad. Wet.* (C) *58:* 190–194.

Stolk, A. 1955b. Hyperplasia and hyperplastic adenoma of the thyroid gland of the viviparous cyprinodonts *Xiphophorus hellerii* Heckel and *Lebistes reticula-*

tus (Peters) after thiouracil treatment. *Proc. K. ned. Akad. Wet.* (C) *58:* 313–327.

Stolk, A. 1956a. Changes in the pituitary gland of the cyprinid *Tanichthys Albonubes* Lin. with a thyroidal tumour. *Proc. K. ned. Akad. Wet.* (C) *59:* 38–49.

Stolk, A. 1956b. Tumours of fishes. VIII. Thyroidal tumour in the cyprinid *Tanichthys albonubes* Lin. *Proc. K. ned. Akad. Wet.* (C) *59:* 50–60.

Stolk, A. 1956c. Tumours of fishes. IXA and IXB. Epithelioma of the oral mucosa in the scylliid *Scylliorhinus catulus* (L.). *Proc. K. ned. Akad. Wet.* (C) *59:* 196–210.

Stolk, A. 1956d. Tumours of fishes. X. Thyroidal tumour with infiltration of the gills in the cichlid *Cichlasoma biocellatum* (Regan). *Proc. K. ned. Akad. Wet.* (C) *59:* 387–397.

Stolk, A. 1956e. Polycystic kidneys in the veiltail *Carassius auratus* var. *Japonicus Bicaudatus,* Zernecke. *Proc. K. ned. Akad. Wet.* (C) *58:* 70–73.

Stolk, A. 1956f. Changes in the pituitary gland of the cichlid *Cichlasoma biocellatum* (Regan) with thyroidal tumour. *Proc. K. ned. Akad. Wet.* (C) *59:* 494–505.

Stolk, A. 1956g. Polycystic kidneys in the characid *Moenkhausia pittieri. Proc. K. ned. Akad. Wet.* (C) *59:* 506–519.

Stolk, A. 1956h. Tumours of fishes. XI. Carcinoma of the skin in the anabantid *Colis labiosa* (Day). *Proc. K. ned. Akad. Wet.* (C) *59:* 624–633.

Stolk, A. 1957a. Tumours of fishes. XII. Carcinoma of the kidneys in the characid *Thayeria obliqua* Eigenmann. *Proc. K. ned. Akad. Wet.* (C) *60:* 31–40.

Stolk, A. 1957b. Tumours of fishes. XIII. Multiple fibromas of the skin in the malapterurid *Malapterurus electricus. Proc. K. ned. Akad. Wet.* (C) *60:* 41–52.

Stolk, A. 1957c. Tumours of fishes. XIV. Fibroma of the heart in the viviparous cyprinodont *Lebistes reticulatus* (Peters). *Proc. K. ned. Akad. Wet.* (C) *60:* 185–195.

Stolk, A. 1957d. Tumours of fishes. XV. Renal adenocarcinoma in the cyprinid *Barbus tetrazona* (Bleeker). *Proc. K. ned. Akad. Wet.* (C) *60:* 196–211.

Stolk, A. 1957e. Multiple cysts in the central nervous system and optic nerves of the cichlid, *Cichlasoma facetum. Proc. K. ned. Akad. Wet.* (C) *60:* 338–348.

Stolk A. 1957f. Cerebral cysts, abnormal pituitary gland and changes in the thyroid gland in the viviparous cyprinodont, *Lebistes reticulatus* (Peters). *Proc. K. ned. Akad. Wet.* (C) *60:* 349–363.

Stolk, A. 1957g. Tumours of fishes. XVI. Fibroma of the intestine in the viviparous cyprinodont *Lebistes reticulatus* (Peters). *Proc. K. ned. Akad. Wet.* (C) *60:* 364–375.

Stolk, A. 1957h. Pharyngeal glands of the cichlid *Haplochromis multicolor* (Hilgendorf). *Proc. K. ned. Akad. Wet.* (C) *60:* 567–577.

Stolk, A. 1957i. Tumours of fishes. XVII. Adenoma of the pharyngeal gland in the cichlid *Haplochromis multicolor* (Hilgendorf). *Proc. K. ned. Akad. Wet.* (C) *90:* 640–649.

Stolk, A. 1957j. Tumours of fishes. XVIII. Adenoma of the swim bladder in the viviparous cyprinodont *Lebistes reticulatus* (Peters). *Proc. K. ned. Akad. Wet.* (C) *60:* 650–657.

Stolk, A. 1957k. Tumours of fishes. XIX. Odontogenic tumour in the oviparous cyprinodont *Cyprinodon variegatus* Lacepede. *Proc. K. ned. Akad. Wet.* (C) *60:* 658–665.

Stolk, A. 1958a. Tumours of fishes. XX. Myxoma of the skin in characid *Phene-cogrammus interruptus* (Boulenger). *Proc. K. ned. Akad. Wet.* (C) *61:* 101–106.

Stolk, A. 1958b. Tumours of fishes. XXI. Haemangioma of the operculum in the erythrinid *Chilodus punctatus* (Müller et Troschel). *Proc. K. ned. Akad. Wet.* (C) *61:* 107–114.

Stolk, A. 1958c. Tumours of fishes. XXII. Epidermoid carcinoma of the upper lip in the characid *Ephippicharax orbicularis* (Valenciennes). *Proc. K. ned. Akad. Wet.* (C) *61:* 201–206.

Stolk, A. 1958d. Tumours of fishes. XXIIIA and XXIIIB. Some cases of chromophobe adenoma in the viviparous cyprinodont *Mollienesia velifera* Regan. *Proc. K. ned. Akad. Wet.* (C) *61:* 363–380.

Stolk, A. 1958e. Tumours of fishes. XXIV. Ocular melanoma in the characid *Anoptichthys jordani* Hubbes et Innes. *Proc. K. ned. Akad. Wet.* *61:* 382–394.

Stolk, A. 1958f. Tumours of fishes. XXV. Melanoma in the hybrid of the viviparous cyprinodont *Lebistes reticulatus* and *Mollienesia sphenops*. *Proc. K. ned. Akad. Wet.* (C) *61:* 499–514.

Stolk, A. 1958g. Some species-specific tumours in fishes. *Experientia 14:* 244.

Stolk, A. 1959a. Development of ovarian teratomas in viviparous toothcarps by pathological parthenogenesis. *Nature, Lond. 183:* 763–764.

Stolk, A. 1959b. Tumours of fishes. XXVI. Erythrophoroma in the oviparous cyprinodont *Nothobranchius guentheri* (Pfeffer). *Proc. K. ned. Akad. Wet.* (C) *62:* 59–67.

Stolk, A. 1959c. Tumours of fishes. XXVII. Guanophoroma in the characid *Ctenobrycon spilurus* (Valenciennes). *Proc. K. ned. Akad. Wet.* (C) *62:* 155–162.

Stolk, A. 1959d. Tumours of fishes. XXVIII. Xanthophoroma in the oviparous cyprinodont *Rivulus xanthonotus* Ahl. *Proc. K. ned. Akad. Wet.* (C) *62:* 163–171.

Stolk, A. 1960a. Melanoma of the skin in the black angelfish *Pterophyllum scalare* Cuvier with some theoretical considerations concerning the melanoma in extremely pigmented fishes. I and II. *Proc. K. ned. Akad. Wet.* (C) *63:* 87–118.

Stolk, A. 1960b. Tumours of fishes. XXXI. Epidermoid carcinoma in a strain of the cichlid *Etroplus maculatus* (Bloch). *Proc. K. ned. Akad. Wet.* (C) *63:* 200–219.

Stolk, A. 1960c. Histochemical analysis of three dehydrogenase systems in the renal adenocarcinoma of the cyprinodont *Aplocheilus lineatus*. *Proc. K. ned. Akad. Wet.* (C) *63:* 548–566.

Stolk, A. 1962. Tumours of fishes. XXXII. Adenoma of the pharyngeal glands in the mouthbreeding anabantid *Betta anabantoides* Bleeker. *Proc. K. ned. Akad. Wet.* (C) *65:* 469–482.

Surbeck, G. 1917. Nouvelles observations, méthode de pêche et essais d'elevage. *Bull. suisse Pêche Piscic. 10:* 149–155. (New observations, fishing methods and breeding tests.)

Surbeck, G. 1921. (Cited by Thomas, L., 1930.)

Suselack, E. 1922. Ein weiterer Fall von Schilddrüsergeschwülste bei *Lebias sophiae. Bl. Aquar. -u. Terrarienk. 33:* 201–203. (Another case of thyroid gland tumors in *Lebias sophia.*)

Takahashi, K. 1929. Studie über die Fischgeschwülste. *Z. Krebsforsch. 29:* 1–73. (All the tumors reported in the Japanese journals which follow are considered in detail in the above mentioned reference. *Gann 19:* 5–8 (1925); *Trans. Jap. path. Soc. 14:* 274–276 (1924); *Trans. Jap. path. Soc. 15:* 294 (1925); *Trans. Jap. path. Soc. 16:* 212 (1926).) (Study on fish tumors.)

Takahashi, K. 1934. Studies on tumours of fishes from Japanese waters. *Proc. Pacif. Sci. Congr. 5:* 4151–4155.

Tavolga, W. N. 1951. Epidermal fin tumors of the gobiid fish, *Bathygobius soporator. Zoologica, N.Y. 36:* 273–278.

Tentschländer, O. 1920. Beiträge zur vergleichenden Onkologie mit Berücksichtigung der Identitätsfrage. *Z. Krebsforsch. 17:* 285–407. (Contributions to comparative oncology, with consideration of the question of identity.)

Thomas, L. 1926. Epithelioma odontoblastique des maxillaires chez une morue. *Bull. Ass. fr. Étude Cancer 15:* 464–470. (Odontoblastic epithelioma in the maxilla of a cod.)

Thomas, L. 1927a. Les sarcomes fibroblastiques chez la morue. *Bull. Ass. fr. Étude Cancer 16:* 79–89. (Fibroblastic sarcomas in the cod.)

Thomas, L. 1927b. Sur un cas de ganglioneurome abdominal chez la morue. *Bull. Ass. fr. Étude Cancer 16:* 282–286. (On a case of abdominal ganglioneuroma in the cod.)

Thomas, L. 1930. Contribution à l'étude des lésions pré-cancereuses chez les poissons. Les papillomes cutanés de la sole. *Bull. Ass. fr. Étude Cancer 19:* 91–97. (Contribution to the study of precancerous lesions in fish. Cutaneous papillomas in the sole.)

Thomas, L. 1931a. Les tumeurs des poissons (étude anatomoqie et pathogénique). *Bull. Ass. fr. Étude Cancer 20:* 703–760. (Tumors of fish (an anatomical and pathological study).) (A key reference—unfortunately contains no annotated bibliography.)

Thomas, L. 1931b. Adenoma kystique de l'intestin moyen chez une truite pourpre. *Bull. Ass. fr. Étude Cancer 20:* 575–584. (Cystic adenoma of the middle intestine in a purple trout.)

Thomas, L. 1931c. La tumeur thyroidienne des salmonidés. Intérêt de ses données en pathologie générale. *Revue méd. Fr. Colon. 8:* 235–246. (Thyroid tumor in salmonids.)

Thomas, L. 1932a. Rhabdomyome chez un flet. *Bull. Ass. fr. Étude Cancer 21:* 225–233. (Rhabdomyoma in a flounder.)

Thomas, L. 1932b. Deux cas de tumeurs osseuses chez des téleosteens. *Bull. Ass. fr. Étude Cancer 21:* 280–294. (Two cases of bone tumors in the teleosts.)

Thomas, L. 1932c. Sur un cas de stiboneuroépithélioblastome chez une daurade. *Bull. Ass. fr. Étude Cancer 21:* 385–396. (A case of a neuroblastoma in a gildhead fish.)

Thomas, L. 1932d. Chondromes symetriques chez un colin. *Bull. Ass. fr. Étude Cancer 21:* 537–546. (Symmetrical chondromes in a hake.)

Thomas, L. 1932e. Papillome tegumentaire chez un truite. *Bull. Ass. fr. Étude Cancer 21:* 547–550. (Tegumentary papilloma in a trout.)

Thomas, L. 1933a. Sur un cas de léiomyome de l'estomac chez un hareng. *Bull. Ass. fr. Étude Cancer 22:* 361–376. (On a case of leiomyoma in the stomach of a herring.)

Thomas, L. 1933b. Sur un lipome abdominal chez un colin. *Bull. Ass. fr. Étude Cancer 22:* 419–435. (On an abdominal lipoma in a hake.)

Thomas, L. 1933c. Fibrome de l'intestin juxta-pyloric chez un morue. *Bull. Ass. fr. Étude Cancer 22:* 106–112. (Fibroma in the juxtapyloric intestine in a cod.)

Thomas, L. 1933d. Sur deux cas de tumeurs tegumentaires chez la rousette. *Bull. Ass. fr. Étude Cancer 22:* 306–315. (Two cases of tegumentary tumors in the lesser spotted dog-fish.)

Thomas, L., and Oxner, M. 1930. Papillomes de la lèvre inférieure chez *Anguilla vulgaris. Bull. Ass. fr. Étude Cancer 19:* 708–714. (Papillomas of the lower lip in *Anguilla vulgaris.*)

Tucker, D. W. 1953. The fishes of the genus *Bathodesmus* (Fam. Trichiuridae). *Proc. zool. Soc. Lond. 123:* 171–197.

Van Duijn, C., Jr. 1967. *Diseases of Fish.* 2nd edition. London: Iliffe Books Limited.

Vielkind, J., Vielkind, U., and Anders, F. 1971. Melanotic and amelanotic melanomas in Xiphophorin fish. *Cancer Res. 31:* 868–875.

Vincent, S., Dodds, E. C., and Dickers, F. 1924. The pancreas of teleostean fishes and the source of insulin. *Lancet 1924 ii:* 115–116.

Vincent, S., Dodds, E. C., and Dickers, F. 1925. The pancreas of teleostean fishes and the source of insulin. *Q. Jl exp. Physiol. 15:* 313–317.

Vivien, J., and Ruhland-Gaiser, M. 1954. Etude preliminaire de goitres envalissants spontanes recontres chez un cyprinodonte, *Lebistes reticulatus.* V. *Annls Endocr. 15:* 585–594. (Preliminary study of spontaneous encroaching goiters found in a cyprinodont, *Lebistes reticulatus,* V.)

Wadsworth, J. R. 1961. Neoplasia of captive zoo species. *Vet. Med. 56:* 25–26.

Wago, H. 1922. A case of a fibroblastic myxoma in a goldfish. *Gann 16:* 11–12.

Wahlgren, F. 1876a. Beiträge zur Pathologie der wilden Tiere. *Z. Tiermed. Vergl. Pathol. 2:* 232–235. (Contributions to the pathology of wild animals.)

Wahlgren, E. 1876b. Osteoid sarcoma in the anal fin of a pike. (Cited by Schmey, M., 1911.)

Wales, J. H. 1967. Degeneration and regeneration of liver parenchyma accompanying hepatomagenesis. *Res. Rep. U.S. Fish. Wildl. Serv.* No. 70: 56–59.

Wales, J. H. 1970. Hepatoma in rainbow trout. *Spec. Publs Am. Fish. Soc.* No. 5 351–365.

Wales, J. H., and Sinnhuber, R. O. 1966. An early hepatoma epizootic in rainbow trout, *Salmo gairdnerii. Calif. Fish Game 52:* 85–91.

Walker, R. 1947. Lymphocystis disease and neoplasia in fish. *Anat. Rec. 99:* 559–560.

Walker, R. 1958. Lymphocystic warts and skin tumors of walleyed pike. *Rennsselaer Rev. Graduate Stud.* No. 14: 1–5.

Weissenfels, N., Schäffer, D., and Bretthauer, R. 1970. Über die Entartung der

Makromelanophoren und den Einfluss des infiltrierenden Melanomwachstums auf die Muskulatur von Poeciliiden-Bastarden. *Virchows Arch. (Abt. B. Zellpath.) 5:* 144–158. (Studies on the degeneration of macromelanophores and the influence of infiltrating melanoma growth on the muscle system of platyfish-swordtail hybrids.)

Weissenger, R. 1922. Beitrag zur Kenntnis der Schilddrüsengeschwülste bei den Fischen. *Bl. Aquar. -u. Terrarienk. 33:* 201–203. (Contribution to the knowledge of thyroid gland tumors in fish.)

Wellings, S. R. 1969a. Environmental aspects of neoplasia in fishes. In *Fish in Research:* 3–22. (Neuhaus, O. W., and Halver, J. E., eds.) New York and London: Academic Press.

Wellings, S. R. 1969b. Neoplasia and primitive vertebrate phylogeny: Echinoderms, prevertebrates, and fishes—a review. *Natn. Cancer Inst. Monogr.* No. 31: 59–128.

Wellings, S. R. 1970. Biology of some virus diseases of marine fish. *Spec. Publs Am. Fish. Soc.* No. 5: 302–303.

Wellings, S. R., and Chuinard, R. G. 1964. Epidermal papillomas with virus-like particles in flathead sole, *Hippoglossoides elassodon. Science, N.Y. 146:* 932–934.

Wellings, S. R., Chuinard, R. G., and Bens, M. 1965. A comparative study of skin neoplasms in four species of pleuronectid fishes. *Ann. N.Y. Acad. Sci. 126:* 479–501.

Wellings, S. R., Chuinard, R. G., and Cooper, R. A. 1967. Ultrastructural studies of normal skin and epidermal papillomas of the flathead sole, *Hippoglossoides elassodon. Z. Zellforsch. mikrosk. Anat. 78:* 370–387.

Wellings, S. R., Cooper, R. A., and Chuinard, R. G. 1966. Skin tumors of pleuronectid fishes in Puget Sound, Washington. *Bull. Wildl. Dis. Ass. 2:* 68.

Wellings, S. R., Bern, H. A., Nishioka, R. S., and Graham, J. W. 1963. Epidermal papillomas in the flathead sole. *Proc. Am. Ass. Cancer Res. 4:* 71. (Abstract.)

Wellings, S. R., Chuinard, R. G., Gourley, R. T., and Cooper, R. A. 1964. Epidermal papillomas in the flathead sole, *Hippoglossoides elassodon,* with notes on the occurrence of similar neoplasms in other pleuronectids. *J. natn. Cancer Inst. 33:* 991–1004.

Wessing, A. 1959. Über einem bösartigen, virusbedingten Tumor bei tropischen Zierfischen. *Naturwissenschaften 46:* 517–518. (On a malignant tumor caused by a virus in tropical fishes.)

Wessing, A., and von Bargen, G. 1959. Untersuchungen über einem virusbedingten Tumor bei Fischen. *Arch. ges. Virusforsch. 9:* 521–536. (Studies on a tumor caused by a virus in fish.)

Wilkie. 1891. Carcinoma of the thyroid gland in two trout species (*Salvelinus fontinalis,* Mitchill, and *Salmo irideus,* Richardson). (Cited by Schmey, M., 1911.)

Williams, G. 1929. Tumourous growths in fish. *Proc. Trans. Lpool biol. Soc. 43:* 120–148.

Williams, G. 1931. On various fish tumours. *Proc. Trans. Lpool biol. Soc. 45:* 98–109.

Williamson, H. C. 1911. On diseases and abnormalities in fishes of the cod (*Ga-*

dus), flathead (*Pleuronectes*), salmon (*Salmo*), skate (*Raia*), etc. families. *Scient. Invest. Fishery Bd Scotl.* No. 11: 3-39.

Willis, R. A. 1962. *Pathology of the Tumours of Children.* London: Butterworth.

Willis, R. A. 1967. *Pathology of Tumours.* 4th ed. London: Butterworth.

Winqvist, G., Ljungberg, O., and Hellstroem, B. 1968. Skin tumours of northern pike (*Esox lucius* L.). II. Viral particles in epidermal proliferations. *Bull. Off. int. Épizoot. 69:* 1023-1031.

Wogan, G. N. 1965. Isolation, identification and some biological effects of aflatoxins. *Res. Rep. U.S. Fish Wildl. Serv.* No. 70: 121-129.

Wolf, H., and Jackson, E. W. 1963. Hepatomas in rainbow trout: Descriptive and experimental epidermiology. *Science, N.Y. 142:* 676-678.

Wolf, H., and Jackson, E. W. 1967. Hepatoma in salmonids: The role of cotton-seed products and species differences. *Res. Rep. U.S. Fish Wildl. Serv.* No. 70: 29-33.

Wolf, K. 1966. The fish viruses. *Adv. Virus Res. 12:* 35-101.

Wolf, K. 1972. Advances in fish virology: A review, 1966-1971. In *Diseases of Fish.* (Mawdesley-Thomas, L. E., ed.) *Symp. zool. Soc. Lond.* No. 30: 305-327. London and New York: Academic Press.

Wolff, B. 1912. Über ein Blastom bei einem Aal (*Anguilla vulgaris*) nebst Bemerkungen zur vergleichenden Pathologie der Geschwulste. *Virchows Arch. path. Anat. Physiol. 210:* 365-385. (On a blastoma in an eel (*Anguilla vulgaris*) together with remarks on the comparative pathology of tumors.)

Wolke, R. E., and Wyand, D. S. 1969. Ocular lymphosarcoma of an Atlantic cod. *Bull. Wildl. Dis. Ass. 5:* 401-403.

Wood, E. M., and Larson, C. P. 1961. Hepatic carcinoma in rainbow trout. *Archs Path. 71:* 471-479.

Woodhead, A. D., and Ellett, S. 1967. A note on the development of thyroid tumours in the senile guppy, *Lebistes reticulatus* (Peters). *Expl Geront. 2:* 73-77.

Woodhead, G. S. 1884-85. Caseous tumours found in the muscles of the hake. *Fishery Bd Scotl.* Nos 3 & 4: 76-78.

Worm, O. 1655. *Historia Rerum Rariorum.* Leiden. (History of rarities.)

Yasutake, W. T., and Rucker, R. R. 1967. Nutritionally induced hepatomagenesis of rainbow trout. *Res. Rep. U.S. Fish Wildl. Serv.* No. 70: 39-47.

Young, G. A., and Olafson, P. 1944. Neurilemmomas in a family of brook trout. *Am. J. Path. 20:* 413-419.

Young, M. W. 1923-25. Muscle tumours in the European turbot. *J. mar. biol. Ass. U.K. 13:* 910-913.

Young, P. H. 1964. Some effects of sewer effluents on marine life. *Calif. Fish Game 50:* 33-41.

35

Neoplasms in Feral Fishes:
Their Significance to Cancer Research

C . J . D A W E
and J . C . H A R S H B A R G E R

The furred and feathered animals have been of such great service in cancer research that one somehow feels defensive in taking the view that the fishes, the class of Vertebrata whose members are usually scaly, often slimy, and nearly always wet, should also be of interest to cancer investigators.

No special defense or justification is in fact needed. The fishes deserve attention from cancer biologists for the same reasons the mammals and birds do. Comparative oncology can exist for its own sake as long as interest burns. Interest, however, often burns brighter, as Innes and Saunders observed (23), when some benefit to man can be seen on the horizon. For this reason this paper might be divided into two parts, one dealing with aspects that appear to be of immediate practical significance to the problems of cancer in man, the other with matters that, for the moment, appear to belong to "pure" comparative oncology. In the long run, we believe that this type of distinction must be arbitrary and is apt to prove quite artificial or even misleading. We have chosen, therefore, to leave to others the decisions as to what is "practical" and what is "pure," and to center our discussion on several questions that naturally present themselves in the light of available knowledge.

Do neoplasms occur in feral fishes, and are they comparable to neoplasms in mammals and birds?

An abundance of literature, comprehensively reviewed, tabulated, and discussed by Wellings (67) and by Mawdesley-Thomas (37) answers this question affirmatively. With the exception of the central nervous system, virtually all of the major organs and cell types have been observed to give rise to neoplasms in a wide variety of teleost fishes (see Wellings (67), Table 5). While not all of the hosts were taken from a natural habitat, a sufficient portion of the tumors did occur in feral fishes to preclude debate on this question. Subsequent to the above reviews, two neoplasms of central nervous system origin (though not intracranial) have been contributed to the Registry of Tumors in Lower Animals (RTLA) at the Smithsonian Institution. One is an olfactory neuroepithelioma (Figs. 35.1–35.3) in a bloater, *Coregonus hoyi* (RTLA 257), submitted by L. N. Allison, the other a retinoblastoma (Figs. 35.4–35.6) in a croaker (RTLA 650), submitted by Michael M. Sigel.

Noteworthy is the fact that in 1968 Wellings (67) was able to collect from the literature only 14 examples of neoplasms in Chondrichthyes. Most of these were external tumors, including five melanomas. As Wellings observed, the large proportion of melanomas may only imply that surface tumors are more easily recognized than internal ones. Conversely, this also implies that visceral neoplasms in cartilaginous fishes may be awaiting discovery by some curious pathologist industrious enough to perform large numbers of necropsies on sharks and rays.

An unreported chondrichthyean neoplasm among the accessions of the Registry of Tumors in Lower Animals occurred on the left pectoral fin of a ratfish, *Hydrolagus colliei* (RTLA 416), and we have classified it as a myxosarcoma on the basis of its uniform pattern of stellate connective tissue cells enmeshed in a background of fibrils and mucinoid ground substance. Figure 35.7 shows the gross appearance of this tumor, submitted by John S. Laurie. Mitotic figures

Fig. 35.1. A bloater (*Coregonus hoyi*) with an olfactory neuroepithelioma on the snout. Arrow indicates tumor, occupying area between upper lip and eye. Skin and surface portion of tumor have been cut away by a sagittal cut, revealing tumor occupying the olfactory chamber and displacing skin and conjunctiva over the anterior portion of the eye. (RTLA Accession No. 257, contributed by L. N. Allison.)

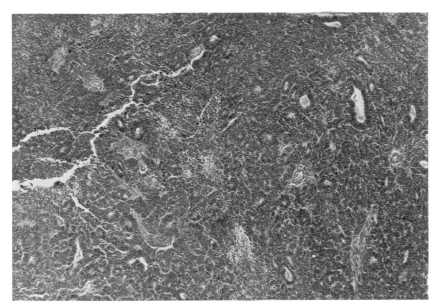

Fig. 35.2. Section of olfactory neuroepithelioma shown in Figure 35.1. Many well-developed rosettes and crypts bordered by pallisaded neoplastic neuroepithelium are present. Hematoxylin and eosin (H&E); ×48.

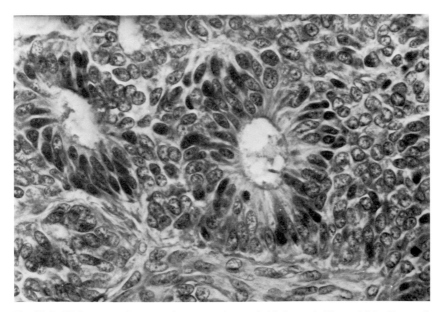

Fig. 35.3. Higher magnification of portion of same field shown in Figure 35.2. Two well-developed neuroepithelial rosettes are shown surrounded by other tumor cells that are not polarized or otherwise visibly differentiated. Olfactory "lashes" can be seen projecting into the lumens of the rosettes. Dark circumferential line adjacent to rosette lumens marks rootlets of olfactory hairs. H&E; ×480.

873

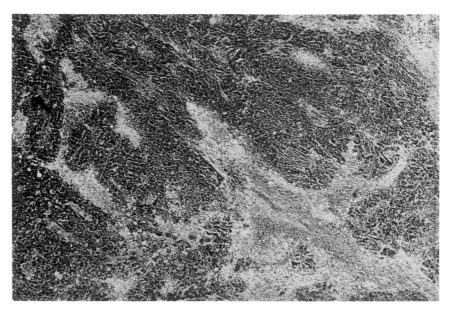

Fig. 35.4. Intraocular neuroblastoma (retinoblastoma) in a croaker. Pale areas are foci of necrosis. Tumor is composed of small, densely packed cells with little cytoplasm. (RTLA Accession No. 650, contributed by M. M. Sigel.) H&E; ×48.

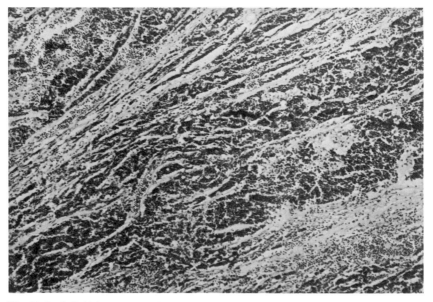

Fig. 35.5. A field from tumor shown in Figure 35.4, showing tendency of tumor cells to form columns and clusters in some areas. H&E; ×120.

874

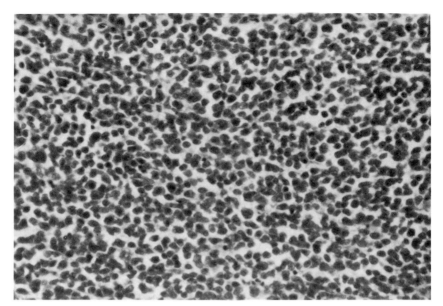

Fig. 35.6. Higher magnification of retinoblastoma shown in Figures 35.4 and 35.5. Cells have finely dispersed nuclear chromatin and scant, poorly defined cytoplasm. H&E; ×300.

Fig. 35.7. Myxosarcoma on the fin of a ratfish (*Hydrolagus colliei*). The tumor had been cut in several planes before photographing. (RTLA Accession No. 416, contributed by J. S. Laurie.)

were quite numerous in this neoplasm, suggesting that it had been growing rather rapidly, but since the complete host was not available for necropsy, the tumor's metastasizing capability remains unproven.

Regarding the comparability of neoplasms in fishes with those in mammals and birds, evidence is available to show that in their general biological and morphological features the similarities are great, but as one might expect, not complete. Words are a stumbling block on this point. It must be understood that a tumor of a particular type in catfish may not necessarily behave or look precisely like human tumors given the same name. Names cannot be substituted for a detailed knowledge of the special biological and morphological features of a particular neoplasm in a particular species. This is a principle familiar to those with broad experience in comparative oncology. For illustration, consider the nephroblastomas. In man, these tumors (sometimes designated Wilms' tumors, embryonal nephromas, or renal adenosarcomas) frequently metastasize and are often quickly lethal, particularly if untreated. In swine, nephroblastomas are common, but only rarely metastasize (63). In rabbits, nephroblastomas are relatively rare, histologically are practically identical with the counterpart in man, but have never been observed to metastasize (12). In fishes, nephroblastomas biologically seem to resemble the homologue in swine and in rabbits more than that in man. The fish nephroblastomas with which we are familiar, at least, have not metastasized. An example of one in a rainbow trout (RTLA 217) is illustrated in Figure 35.8.

Other examples where neoplasms or related conditions in fishes seem to differ from comparable conditions in man include the neurilemmomas of goldfish (51), which have a histological pattern very similar to that of neurilemmomas in man, but lack, according to electron microscopic studies (9), the basement membranes that are characteristically associated with Schwann cells. Again, the distinction between thyroid hyperplasia and thyroid carcinoma, though often difficult in man, is even more difficult in the bony fishes because the thyroid gland is not encapsulated, and hyperplastic follicles may appear to invade skeletal muscle and to surround large vessels (see 3, pp. 108-110). Still further, we may cite our own limited experience with cutaneous melanomas in catfish in the Smithsonian Registry, indicating that these growths are less prone to metastasize distantly than are melanomas of the skin in man.

Do some neoplasms in fishes occur in epizootic proportions, and if so, are these neoplasms caused by environmental carcinogens?

The hatchery-grown rainbow trout has become to the epizootiology of cancer of fishes as the chimney sweep became to the epidemiology of cancer in man. While the chimney sweeps were indentured to their masters (43), the rainbow trout were impounded in hatcheries. The trout were obliged to eat what was given them by man, including carcinogenic aflatoxins, rather than the types of food provided their forebears by the ecosystem in which they evolved. As a consequence, the trout developed hepatic cancers, much as the chimney sweeps developed scrotal cancer after exposure to man-made soot. From a feral animal the

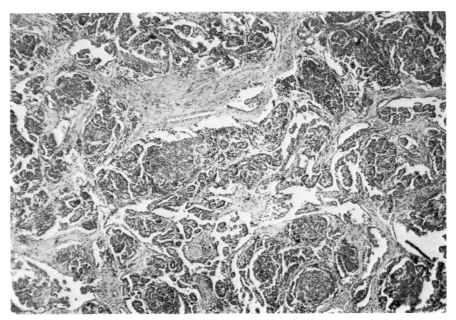

Fig. 35.8. Section of a nephroblastoma in a rainbow trout (*Salmo gairdneri*). The majority of the tumor tissue is composed of epithelial components that have undergone imperfect morphogenesis toward tubules and glomeruli. (RTLA Accession No. 217, contributed by C. E. Dunbar.) H&E; X85.

trout had become a "cultivated" animal, and after it began to manifest hepatomas, it was pressed further to become a laboratory animal. This is now all well-known history (37, 67). What seems not to be well known is that epizootics of neoplasia and closely related disorders had been identified in quite a number of feral fishes long before the recognition of epizootic trout hepatoma. A difference between the hepatoma epizootic and the others is that the etiologies of the others are still unknown. Only in the case of the trout hepatoma has a generally accepted cause been found, and so the trout remains the sole example of a fish that has served as an indicator of a proved environmental carcinogen. Can some of the other fishes serve in similar manner?

A look at other epizootic or enzootic neoplasms and related lesions in fishes may help answer this. The outstanding ones are:

1. Lymphomas in Esocidae (northern pike) in Ireland (38, 40) and in both northern pike and muskellunge in North America (41, 45, 57).

2. Cutaneous papillomas in a large number of species, including the following:

    (a) Pleuronectidae (flounders and sole) of the U.S. Pacific coast, western Gulf of Alaska, Japanese coastal waters, and the North Sea (67).

    (b) Atlantic eels (*Anguilla vulgaris*) of the Baltic Sea and northern European coasts (8).

(c) Barbels (*Barbus fluviatilis*) in the Mosel River (25).

(d) Yellowfin gobies (*Acanthogobius flavimanus*) of Japanese coastal waters (27, 42).

(e) European smelts (*Osmerus eperlanus*) of the Baltic Sea (4).

(f) Slippery dicks (*Halichoeres bivittatus*) of the Caribbean (32).

(g) White croakers (*Genyonemus lineatus*) from particular foci on the California coast (47).

(h) Cunners (*Tautogolabrus adspersus*) from a limited area in an estuary of Long Island Sound (14).

(i) Brown bullheads (*Ictalurus nebulosus*) from several areas, including the Schuylkill and Delaware rivers (34), certain lakes in Florida (13), and elsewhere (60).

(j) Atlantic salmon (*Salmo salar*) from Scandinavian and Maine coasts (69).

(k) Walleyes (*Stizostedion vitreum vitreum*) of Lake Oneida (65). These walleye lesions are nonpapillary hyperplasias, uncharacterized as to natural history.

3. Tumors of the parabranchial bodies (pseudobranchs) of Pacific cod (*Gadus macrocephalus*) (67).

4. Osteomas (possibly only exostoses) of red tai (*Pagrosomas major*) (24, 48, 64).

5. Osteomas (exostoses?) (Fig. 35.9) of Atlantic croakers (*Micropogon undulatus*) (28).

6. Neurilemmomas of snappers (Lutjanidae) off Tortugas (33).

7. Thyroid adenomas and carcinomas in trout and other salmonids, associated with enzootic and epizootic thyroid hyperplasia (35).

Fig. 35.9. Osteoma on the lateral aspect of a vertebral body of a croaker (*Micropogon undulatus*). Several bone tumors, including this one, have been found in market fish of this species after being prepared for the table. (RTLA Accession No. 218, contributed by J. P. Summerour.)

What is noteworthy about this list? There is no obvious common denominator that links either the species or the diseases together, but if one looks only at the list of fishes commonly affected by papillomas, it will be seen that the species involved are, with the exception of the Atlantic salmon, bottom-feeders and bottom-dwellers. Most are scavengers in considerable degree (eels, barbels, gobies, slippery dicks, croakers, cunners, bullheads). Only the walleyes and the Atlantic salmon are predominantly predatory.

How could one relate oral and cutaneous papillomatosis to bottom-feeding habits? Two lines of speculation occur to us. One possibility is that viruses are the etiological agents of the papillomas, and that adsorption of virus particles to bottom sediments creates a situation where bottom-feeding scavengers would be more heavily exposed than surface-feeding predators. Indeed, a once-favored but now obsolete method of concentrating viruses in the laboratory is to adsorb them upon kieselguhr (diatomaceous earth) which is composed of powdered marine sediments, deposited and compacted in earlier geologic times. Another possibility is that bottom sediments adsorb or otherwise concentrate organic chemicals that are carcinogenic and to which bottom-feeders or filter-feeders would be more intensively exposed than other fish. It is known, for example, that certain chlorinated polycyclic hydrocarbons, such as DDT, are adsorbed upon particulate matter, especially in particulates which are high in organic content (30). Carcinogenic chemicals of specific gravity higher than that of water could conceivably accumulate on bottoms through simple settling, but we know of no example where this has happened. Methyl mercury, now well known for its toxicity, can be synthesized by bacterial action on metallic mercury bottom deposits, and eventually reaches fish via food chains.

In seeking evidence that would support either or both of the above possibilities, one finds that although a viral etiology has long been suspected for the papillomas and epitheliomas, the only one of these examples from which a virus has actually been isolated, propagated, and seen by electron microscopy is the eel papilloma (70). Even there, the associated virus has not been proved to be causal, as yet. A different virus has been seen in the walleye epithelial lesion (65), and still different virus particles have been seen (54) in the lesions of carp-pox, which is a type of epithelial hyperplasia much resembling the walleye lesion. The virus in the walleye's epithelial hyperplasia is seen extracellularly, buds from the cell membrane, measures about 80 mμ in diameter, and resembles the RNA tumor viruses of birds and mammals. The virus of carp-pox is intranuclear and intracytoplasmic, measures 110 mμ when in the nucleus and 140 to 150 mμ in the cytoplasm, and has a dense, often eccentric nucleoid. It appears to belong to the herpes-virus group. In the papillomas of flounder and sole, virus-like particles as well as two types of cytoplasmic "granular bodies" have been described (68), but a virus has not been propagated in cell culture, and has not been shown to be of causal significance.

An association can be made between the epitheliomas in several of these fishes and exposure to water pollution, either industrial, domestic, or both. Croakers with papillomas were found only in an area near the outflow of sewage from the city of Los Angeles (47). Cunners with papillomas (Fig. 35.12) came from the Sakonnet River estuary in Rhode Island, downstream from the effluents of the city of Fall River (14). Catfish with papillomas and carcinomas were taken from the industrially and domestically polluted waters of the lower Delaware and Schuylkill rivers (34). The Japanese waters from which papilloma-bearing gobies were taken are adjacent to heavily populated and industrialized areas (27, 42). The papillomas of Atlantic eels are found only in the eels along the northern European and Baltic coasts, but not in eels taken from the U.S. Atlantic coast (8). Papillomas in flounders on the U.S. Pacific coast were found to be more prevalent in particular localities. Wellings (66) found a correlation between papilloma incidence and low salinity, especially in the starry flounder. Cooper and Keller (5) demonstrated a higher incidence in English sole in the northern part of San Francisco Bay than in the southern. According to them, the northern part is characterized by shallower water, lower salinity, and a higher content of industrial waste than the southern.

In short, it can be said of the oral and cutaneous papillomas of fishes that (1) they are found mainly, but not exclusively, in bottom-feeders; (2) they have a focal distribution among the fish populations in which they occur; and (3) the focality of this distribution is in most, but not all, cases associated with urbanization and industrialization.

These three characteristics seem to point toward one or more environmental oncogens. Whether these presumptive oncogens are viral, parasitic, chemical, or physical in nature cannot be stated at the moment, nor can it be said whether the causal agents are oncogenic for man. Looking at the evidence as we now know it, one can only say that it *suggests* that man is doing something to the environment that favors epithelioma development in certain kinds of fish, in certain places. There is no evidence that the papillomas and carcinomas in fishes constitute any health hazard to man, in and of themselves, but they may be indicators of health hazards to man. We need to determine more precisely just what they do indicate. In pursuing this problem, we will probably learn to take more general advantage of fishes as indicators of environmental carcinogens. Perhaps in the end we may repay the fishes for their services by removing the noxious agents from their environment as well as from our own.

The enzootic lymphomas of northern pike in Ireland (38, 40) and of northern pike and muskellunge in North America (57) present a different picture entirely from the epitheliomas just considered. The pike and muskellunge are neither bottom-feeders nor scavengers. They are fiercely predatory and even cannibalistic, they lead solitary lives except during the spawning season, and the occurrence of the lymphomas does not appear to be related to influences of man on the environment. Sonstegard (57) has found that the prevalence of the muskellunge lymphoma rises during the months following spawning and decreases again before the next spawning season. In view of this and of the external distribution of what appear to be the primary lesions, he postulated that the muskellunge lymphoma is transmitted by bites during fighting on the spawning beds. Limited evidence of subcellular transmissibility of this disease (39) gives further support to this hypothesis.

It is sometimes said that a creature's greatest strength can also be its greatest weakness. The scavenging mode of life perhaps safeguards the catfish from transmissible lymphoma while it renders it vulnerable to papillomas. The muskellunge, on the other hand, succumbs to a neoplasm perhaps transmitted through the voracious behavior that normally sustains it, while it remains free of papillomas.

In connection with the topic of the northern pike and muskellunge lymphomas, it should be noted that the epithelial hyperplasia (epithelioma?) of walleyes described by Walker (65) is another example of a proliferative disease that conceivably might be transmitted through biting. The walleye is a predatory fish well equipped with large sharp teeth, and Walker observed the lesions annually in fish taken during the spawning run. Furthermore, these lesions contain abundant virus particles resembling the C-type particles associated with avian and murine neoplasms. The situation in the walleye suggests that the predatory way of life need not exempt a fish from epidermal proliferative disease. Indeed, before assuming that feeding or fighting patterns have anything to do with this condition, it may be well to look into endocrine factors. If the walleye develops hypercorticosteroidism at spawning, as do Pacific salmon (46), then it may be that the epidermal hyperplasias are an expression of "break-through" of virally-transformed cells subsequent to steroid suppression of the thymus-dependent cell surveillance system.

Cutaneous papillomas are also common in Atlantic salmon (69), a predatory, non-bottom-feeder, and this is perhaps the most clear-cut exception to the rule that papillomas are a disease of bottom-feeders. Bluegills and perch are both insectivorous and predatory on smaller fishes, and they are also subject to epithelial hyperplasias, which in these instances have not been demonstrated to be associated with a virus.

A nonepithelial endemic tumor is the dermal fibroma or fibrosarcoma of walleyes (65). This tumor may be found alone or coexisting with either or both lymphocystis disease and the epithelial hyperplasia. It has been found to contain a virus, much like the one associated with epithelial hyperplasia, but about 20 mμ larger.

Concerning the other tumors listed earlier in this chapter, there is little if any evidence that they may be caused by environmental oncogens. As observed by Schlumberger (52), tumors that are especially common in particular species may own their prevalence to genetic factors as well as to environmental ones. Until or unless environmental factors are found to explain them, the osteomas of red tai and Atlantic croakers, the neurilemmomas of goldfish and snappers, and the parabranchial body tumors of Pacific cod may tentatively be considered to be genetically determined.

Can sporadic neoplasms in fishes be useful in disclosing environmental onco-gens?

Besides those neoplasms that occur in relatively large numbers in one or more species, there are some that have been reported in only one or a few individuals of a given species. These are of such a nature that one can see possible analogies with similar tumors in mammals, suggestive of possible etiological factors. Examples follow.

1. An olfactory neuroepithelioma in a bloater was incidentally found among a number of bloaters submitted to the Registry of Tumors in Lower Animals at the Smithsonian Institution by Dr. L. N. Allison. The specimen (RTLA 257) was taken from Lake Michigan in June 1969. The neoplasm was located over the snout (Fig. 35.1), and was presumed to be an example of another disease that was present in all of the other fish submitted. However, when histological sections were examined, the lesion was recognized as a typical neuroepithelioma arising from the olfactory neuroepithelium (Figs. 35.3 and 35.4). Such tumors are of central nervous system origin, and this one represents the first central nervous system tumor found in a fish.

The significance of this neoplasm to cancer research is that in recent years chemical carcinogens have been found that induce olfactory neuroepitheliomas in rats and hamsters (18, 56). Among these are the nitrosamines, which are particularly active in hamsters (18). Could this neuroepithelioma in a bloater have been induced by a nitrosamine? To give this question added cogency, it should be noted that nitrosamines can be formed by reactions between nitrites and secondary amines at proper pH's (31, 49). Further, nitrites can be formed by soil and water bacteria that reduce nitrates. Nitrate levels can be quite high in bodies of water such as Lake Michigan that receive run-offs from fertilized agricultural areas. Secondary amines such as trimethylamine can be introduced into waters by putrefaction of fish or breakdown of other proteinaceous animal matter. It is not difficult, therefore, to conceive of ways that a Lake Michigan bloater might have been exposed to nitrosamines. Of course, one example of an olfactory neuroepithelioma does not constitute much evidence, and more extensive investigations of bloaters in Lake Michigan should be done.

2. Two examples of multiple fibroameloblastomas involving both jaws of chinook salmon, *Oncorhynchus tshawytscha,* were reported in 1956 by Schlumberger and Katz (53). A very similar example, also in a chinook salmon (Figs. 35.10, 35.11) was submitted to the Registry of Tumors in Lower Animals by J. H. Wales in June 1969 (RTLA 248). These three specimens are fascinating in that they exhibit a neoplastic diathesis involving most of the tooth-forming tissue of each host. At this moment, it is equally tenable that these neoplasms result from genetic predisposition or from exposure to some highly tissue-specific environmental carcinogen. Both factors could be operative. In mice, multiple ameloblastomas in both jaws can be induced if newborns of the proper strain are inoculated with polyoma virus of proper strain (36, 58). Is the chinook salmon a spe-

cies peculiarly susceptible to some oncogenic virus selective for the tooth organ? While this may seem a rather farfetched question, an observation we have recently made lends some rationality to it. This observation is that among the cases of oral papillomatosis in cunners (RTLA 550–553), one example was found (RTLA 675) (Figs. 35.12–35.14) in which the histological features included multicentric foci with odontogenic activity. The observation of papillomatosis containing multiple odontogenic tumors may be different responses to a single causal agent, possibly a virus.

3. Among 12 white suckers (*Catostomus commersoni*) taken from Deep Creek Lake, Maryland, 3 were found to have cholangiomas or cholangiocarcinomas (7). These bottom-feeding fish had never been subjected to hatchery diets, suggesting that hepatic carcinogens may be present in "natural" environments. Motorboat exhausts and chlorinated hydrocarbon pesticides have been suggested as possible causes.

Can studies of neoplasms in fishes be of value in testing certain hypotheses about the origin and nature of cancer?

This question has already been partially answered by the affirmation that the generality of neoplasms of fishes have been shown to resemble closely those of birds and mammals, both biologically and morphologically. There are, however, more specific examples where studies in greater depth could be of value.

For instance, the opportunity lies open to find evidence for or against the oncogene ("infectious gene") theory of tumorigenesis (21, 22). This theory postulates that certain RNA viruses of the C type (murine and fowl leukosis viruses are examples) are transmitted vertically, like genes through the gametes and, depending on presence of genes necessary for expression of viral oncogenic action, may be capable of inducing neoplastic disease when conditions in the host are right. The oncogene theory also supposes that the quasi-gene, quasi-virus RNA moieties or their DNA complementary equivalents have experienced a long evolutionary history in which they have become an inherent part of most, if not all, vertebrate cells. It has even been suggested that such oncogenes are in some way of survival value to the animals carrying them, accounting for their widespread presence (22).

It is with regard to the concept of the ubiquity and the survival benefits of oncogenes that studies of fish neoplasms could be useful, for at present C-type viruses have been found in only one nonmammalian, nonavian species (Russell's viper, *Vipera russelli*) (73) and not at all in fishes. A possible candidate is the virus described by Walker in the hyperplastic epithelial lesion of the walleye (65), but this virus has not been antigenically characterized or analyzed so far as reverse transcriptase is concerned. If oncogenes do in fact pervade all or most vertebrate species, then it should be possible to find them and, through antigenic and nucleic acid analyses, to demonstrate their evolutionary relationships to oncogenic C-type viruses of mammals and birds. Thus fish neoplasms offer one of the pathways to find a "missing link" in the oncogene theory.

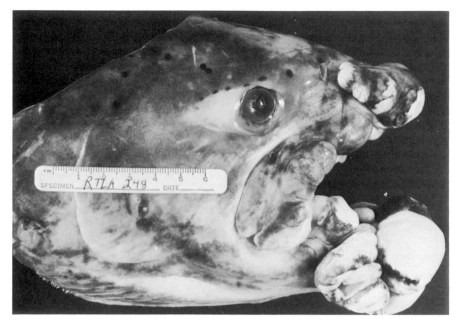

Fig. 35.10.

Figs. 35.10, 35.11. Lateral and frontal views of the head of a chinook salmon bearing multiple fibroameloblastomas on both jaws. (RTLA Accession No. 248, contributed by J. H. Wales.)

Most cancer theories can in fact be tested by studies of neoplasms in fish, but it must be acknowledged that there is no justification in using piscine neoplastic disease for experimental studies unless some advantage peculiar to a fish offers itself. For example, the concept of thymic function as a mechanism of immune surveillance against neoplasms can be and has been profitably investigated in mammals by using various experimental means to abolish thymic function, such as surgical thymectomy, thymic irradiation, treatment with anti-thymocyte serum, corticosteroid administration, and use of various chemical immunosuppressants (10, 11, 29). There is no obvious advantage in studying the effect of thymectomy on tumorigenesis in fish, if, as is the case, adequate surgical methods are available for doing the same experiment in mice. On the other hand, in the case of Pacific salmon, we are provided with an interesting "natural experiment" at each spawning season. Some species (chinook and coho salmon) have been shown to develop marked hypercorticoidism during the spawning run. These animals become lymphocyte-depleted (46) and shortly after spawning they succumb to bacterial and fungal infections which result from the combined effects of inanition and suppression of immune defense mechanisms. Theoretically, these hypercorticoid fish should carry a high probability of manifesting incipient neoplasms as a result of

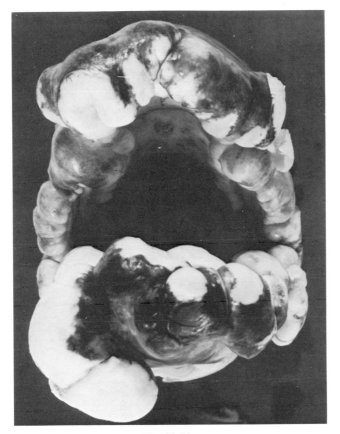

Fig. 35.11.

"escape" of aberrant cell populations from the thymus-dependent surveillance system.

The concept that neoplasms may develop in ageing cells that have "run out of program" has been elaborated upon during more than a decade (56, 57). The so-called "annual fishes" (72) would seem to offer a unique opportunity to test this concept. The annual fishes include many species native mainly to shallow puddles in the savannahs, llanos, campos, and pampas of South America and Africa. These water holes dry up, killing the fish during the dry season each year. The species are perpetuated by the hatching of fertilized ova, deposited in the mud of the pond bottom prior to the dry season and reactivated when the ponds refill during the rainy season. The complete life cycle from egg to adult and back to egg is thus completed in a single year. It can be presumed that "programming," so far as neoplasia is concerned, would need to provide protection against massive losses for only one year. What might be expected if annual fishes could be kept alive in

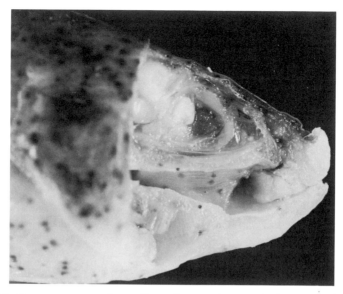

Fig. 35.12. Gross appearance of a papillary odontogenic tumor in the mouth of a cunner (*Tautogolabrus adspersus*). The pharynx and oral cavity have been exposed by a midline sagittal cut and removal of the right side of the head. The tumor is attached to the upper jaw and largely fills the oral cavity. (RTLA Accession No. 675, contributed by S. Shumway.)

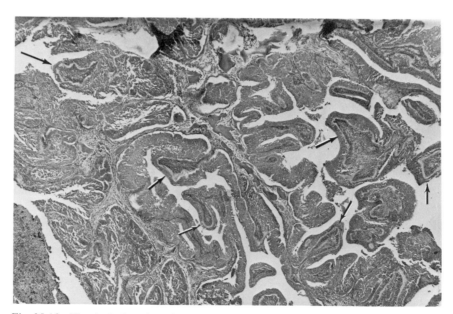

Fig. 35.13. Histological section of tumor shown in Figure 35.12. Note papillary pattern. In some papillae (arrows), structures resembling small tooth buds are present. H&E; ×48.

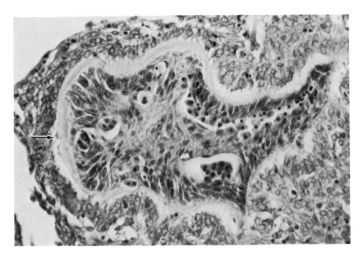

Fig. 35.14. Higher magnification of a papilla from the field shown in Figure 35.13. Note the pallisading of mesenchymal cells in the stroma of the papilla, having the features of odontoblasts. Between the pallisaded cells of the papilla and the outside ameloblastic epithelium is a zone of noncellular, amorphous, palely-staining calcific material (arrow). H&E; ×480.

the laboratory for periods greater than one year? Would this "unprogrammed" extension of the life span result in the appearance of neoplastic cell populations? From studies that have been done with wild mice kept in the laboratory beyond their "normal" life span (2), one would predict that annual fishes should develop measurably increased incidences of neoplasms after the first eight months or more of life. An interesting supplement to such a study would be a study of annual fish cells in tissue culture, to determine whether there is a correlation between normal organismal life span and the number of cell generations prior to somatic cell clone extinction. This information would be of interest in relation to the concept that cells of a given species and individual are assigned a limited number of generations after which the cell lineage must either die out or become neoplastic, depending on prevailing conditions. Much needed are studies of "spontaneous" neoplastic transformation of fish cell lines. Evidently most of the existing fish cell lines (71) are in fact "transformed," but their neoplastic potentialities have not been evaluated.

The examples above are cited only to illustrate a few of the ways in which neoplasms in fishes may be of special use in testing hypotheses about cancer. Many others can obviously be conceived.

Can neoplasms in feral fishes lead to development of laboratory systems useful in cancer research?

Much of the foregoing discussion provides an affirmative answer to this question. The conversion of the rainbow trout into a laboratory animal for use in studies of carcinogenesis has been noted. The use of fishes bearing papillomas or lymphomas in the continuing search for tumor viruses has been suggested, as has the "laboratorization" of annual fish for studies of neoplasia in relation to age and life span.

There are a number of other examples where feral fish have been or can be turned to laboratory use by cancer researchers, and some of these will be briefly mentioned. Probably the best known example of all is the use of the xiphophoran fishes in genetic studies of melanoma formation. Following the original observation by Haüssler (15) of the occurrence of melanomas in hybrid crosses of green swordtails (*Xiphophorus helleri*) with southern platyfish (*X. maculatus*), Gordon and a series of collaborators (see review by Anders, 1) systematically analyzed the genetic factors involved by classic breeding methods. It now appears clear that the pattern of macromelanophore distribution in these fish is determined by one gene, while the proliferative control of these macromelanophores is regulated by as many as five or even more modifier genes. As modifier genes are diluted out by repeated backcrossing experiments, the frequency and rapidity of appearance of melanomas increases. Recent studies by Siciliano, Perlmutter, and Clark (55) indicate that the male sex is more predisposed to melanoma development than the female, and that this influence is probably mediated by male hormones. A number of physical and chemical factors in the aquatic environment, such as ionic strength and surface tension of the water, can also influence melanoma development (44), a point that may be of special significance in considering feral fishes as indicators of environmental carcinogens.

Quite obviously, the smaller, so-called aquarium fishes offer economic advantages as candidates for laboratory animals in cancer research. Few institutions can support a trout hatchery or a set of shark cages. This was recognized by Stanton, who, following the observation that nitrosamines induce hepatomas in rainbow trout, demonstrated that the small zebra fish, *Brachydanio rerio,* also develops hepatomas in response to diethylnitrosamine (59). More recently others have reported the same is true for the guppy, *Poecilia reticulata (Lebistes reticulatus)* (26, 50). We are informed that Japanese workers are also investigating the response of the small medaka, *Oryzia latipes,* to various carcinogens. These tests have special practical significance in that the medaka has a wide range of habitats in Japan, and if found sensitive to certain carcinogens, could serve as a natural indicator of environmental contamination by carcinogens.

The guppy has also proved useful in studies of teratogenesis. Hisaoka (19) reported developmental anomalies ranging from benign teratomas to conjoined twins in guppies. He later described (20) a teratoma in a female green swordtail (*X. helleri*). In addition to the types of teratoma described by Hisaoka, Stolk found ovarian teratomas in a guppy (61) and a southern platyfish (62), and postulated that they may have been induced by a parasitic phycomycete, *Ichthyophonus hoferi*. Would it not be interesting to see if teratomas could be induced to undergo malignant change under the influence of added hormones or carcinogens of various types? In mammals, little is presently known about factors that account for marked differences in malignancy of teratomas in different anatomic sites and different age groups.

Summarizing, the opportunities for the laboratory utilization of fishes for cancer research may be considered almost limitless. For additional examples of such utilization, readers may find the brief review by Ashley of interest (3).

Can studies of neoplasms in fish be used to understand cancer in relation to evolution?

This is a complex question, not simple to answer. Of course, since fishes occupy a distinct segment of evolutionary development, the study of neoplasia in fishes as well as in all other animals should enable us eventually to draw some general conclusions about the universality and even, perhaps, about special patterns of distribution of neoplasia within the animal kingdom.

But more than this, the study of neoplasia in fishes and in the contemporary representatives of the progenitors of fishes has a special advantage in that the early vertebrates and invertebrates of most types have been thought to be strangely exempt from neoplastic disease. What could explain some "switch-on" of neoplasia at the level of vertebrate evolution? Good (10) has suggested that, whatever the activating forces and mechanisms involved, the development and continuing survival of higher vertebrates required the devising of an anti-cancer surveillance system, which we recognize today in the thymus-dependent cellular immune system. Whether neoplasia is indeed rare among invertebrates, and whether the evolutionary development of the thymus was specifically an adaptation to the need for protection against neoplasms, have been discussed elsewhere, without arriving at a satisfactory answer (6, 11). It remains important, therefore, in relation to this question to obtain data regarding the occurrence of tumors in, and the susceptibility to tumors of, animals such as the tunicates (sea squirts) and the agnathans (hagfishes and cyclostomes), where the thymus is either not recognizable at all or is only incompletely developed. And it is just as important to obtain data on neoplasms in the cartilaginous, and bony, jawed fishes, since these groups represent the animals immediately on the other side of the line where something critical *apparently* happened in evolution, resulting in increased tendency to develop neoplastic disease.

How has the evolution of new tissues or organs been related to risk of neoplastic development? For example, in the evolution of lung from swim bladder, was the more recent form of specialization bought at the expense of higher predisposition to neoplasms in the new homologue? The same can be asked about the organs and tissues, such as tongue, jaws, larynx, face, and external ears, all of which are derivatives, in later animals, of the ancestral gill arches.

Or, conversely, is predisposition to neoplasia affected when organs or tissues become vestigial? The parabranchial bodies may deserve attention in attempts to find observations pertinent to this question. For whatever it is worth, it is interesting to note that in his review, Wellings (67) was able to collect many more examples of adenoma and adenocarcinoma of parabranchial body origin than of gill origin.

Just as we do not know whether nascent organs are more prone to develop cancer than either stabilized or vestigial ones, neither do we know whether the *rate* of active evolutionary change in a tissue or organ has an effect on proneness to neoplasia. Perhaps studies of so-called living fossils such as the renowned coelacanth could tell us something about this, but some more numerous and easily caught species with particular features unchanged through many millions of years would be better suited, and more useful in comparisons with other species whose homologous features are currently undergoing a rapid rate of evolutionary change.

The fossil record of fishes is perhaps more abundantly preserved than that of any other class of vertebrates. Yet no example of a tumor-bearing fossil fish has come to our attention. Does this imply that neoplasms are modern diseases in fish, or that sufficient numbers of fossil fish have not been examined by sufficiently prepared eyes and minds to disclose the occurrence of tumors in fish of ages past? Paleoncology of fishes is a field lying completely fallow.

Might investigations of neoplasms in fishes have significance to cancer research in ways that are not presently foreseeable?

This question begs the obvious answer. "Unscheduled" discoveries in any field of science can be of key significance, and there is every reason to suppose that there will be many unscheduled discoveries in fish tumor research in the future, just as there have been in the past. Philosophically, it is interesting to consider that to some extent the motivations of the angler and of the scientific researcher are similar. Along with other things behind the irresistible urge that calls either the angler or the researcher to return again and again to his pursuits is the certain knowledge that unpredictable things happen. The angler sets out in quest of a perch and finds himself hooked to a muskellunge. He calls it luck. The researcher sets out in quest of an explanation for fish mortality and discovers a new cause of liver cancer. In the jargon of the day, he calls this serendipity. Sometimes the big fish or the big discovery slips away, just when it seems within grasp. For either the angler or the researcher there are always more fish in the sea.

REFERENCES

1. Anders, F. Tumour formation in platyfish-swordtail hybrids as a problem of gene regulation. *Experientia 23:* 1. 1967.
2. Andervont, H. B., and Dunn, T. B. Occurrence of tumors in wild house mice. *J. Nat. Cancer Inst. 28:* 1153. 1962.
3. Ashley, L. M. Experimental fish neoplasia, p. 23. In *Fish in Research*, ed. O. W. Neuhaus and J. E. Halver. New York and London, Academic Press, 1969.
4. Breslauer, T. Zur Kenntnis der Epidermoidal geschwülste von Kaltblütern. *Arch. mikrosk. Anat. Entwicklungsmech. 87:* 200. 1916.

5. Cooper, R. C., and Keller, C. A.   Epizootiology of papillomas in English sole, *Parophrys vetulus*. *Nat. Cancer Inst. Monogr. 31:* 173. 1969.

6. Dawe, C. J.   Phylogeny and oncogeny. *Nat. Cancer Inst. Monogr. 31:* 1. 1969.

7. Dawe, C. J., Stanton, M. F., and Schwartz, F. J.   Hepatic neoplasms in native bottom-feeding fish of Deep Creek Lake, Maryland. *Cancer Res. 24:* 1194. 1964.

8. Deys, B. F.   Papillomas in the Atlantic eel, *Anguilla vulgaris*. *Nat. Cancer Inst. Monogr. 31:* 187. 1969.

9. Duncan, T. E., and Harkin, J. C.   Electron microscopic studies of goldfish tumors previously termed neurofibromas and schwannomas. *Amer. J. Pathol. 55:* 191. 1969.

10. Good, R. A.   Relations between immunity and malignancy. *Proc. Nat. Acad. Sci. U.S.A. 69:* 1026. 1972.

11. Good, R. A., and Finstad, J.   Essential relationship between the lymphoid system, immunity, and malignancy. *Nat. Cancer Inst. Monogr. 31:* 41. 1969.

12. Greene, H. S. N.   The occurrence and transplantation of embryonal nephromas in the rabbit. *Cancer Res. 3:* 434. 1943.

13. Harshbarger, J. C.   Work of the Registry of Tumors in Lower Animals with emphasis on fish neoplasms. *Symp. Zool. Soc. London 30:* 285. 1972.

14. Harshbarger, J. C., Shumwah, S., and Bane, G.   Unpublished data.

15. Haüssler, G.   Über Melanombildungen bei Bastarden von *Xiphophorus helleri* und *Platypoecilus maculatus* var. *rubra*. *Klin. Wochenschr. 7:* 1561. 1928.

16. Hayflick, L.   Aging under glass. *Exp. Gerontol. 5:* 291. 1970.

17. Hayflick, L., and Moorhead, P. S.   The serial cultivation of human diploid cell strains. *Exp. Cell Res. 25:* 585. 1961.

18. Herrold, K. M.   Induction of olfactory neuroepithelial tumors in Syrian hamsters by diethylnitrosamine. *Cancer 17:* 114. 1964.

19. Hisaoka, K. K.   Congenital teratomata in the guppy, *Lebistes reticulatus*. *J. Morphol. 109:* 93. 1961.

20. Hisaoka, K. K.   Congenital teratoma in the swordtail, *Xiphophorus helleri*. *Copeia 1:* 189. 1963.

21. Huebner, R. J., and Todaro, G. J.   Oncogenes of RNA tumor viruses as determinants of cancer. *Proc. Nat. Acad. Sci. U.S.A. 64:* 1087. 1969.

22. Huebner, R. J., Sarma, P. S., Kelloff, G. J., Gilden, R. V., Meier, H., Myers, D. D., and Peters, R. L.   Immunological tolerance to RNA virus genome expressions: Significance of tolerance and prenatal expressions in embryogenesis and tumorigenesis. *Ann. N. Y. Acad. Sci. 181:* 246. 1971.

23. Innes, J. R. M., and Saunders, L. Z.   *Comparative Neuropathology*, pp. xi-xii. New York and London, Academic Press, 1962.

24. Kazama, Y.   Einige Geschwülste bei Fischen (*Pagrus major* et *Paralichthys olivaceus*). *Gann (Jap. J. Cancer Res.) 18:* 35. 1924.

25. Keysselitz, G.   Über ein Epithelioma der Barben. *Arch. Protistenk. 11:* 326. 1908.

26. Khudolei, V. V.   Induction of hepatic tumors by nitrosamines in the aquarium fish, *Lebistes reticulatus*.   *Vop. onkol.* *17*(12): 67.   1971.
27. Kimura, I., Miyake, T., and Ito, Y.   [Studies on tumors in fishes. II. Papillomatous growths of skin in the goby, *Acanthogobius flavimanus*], p. 154.   In *Proc. Jap. Cancer Ass. 26.*   1967.   [In Japanese.]
28. Landolt, M., Dawe, C. J., and Harshbarger, J. C.   Unpublished observations, filed with Accessions 218, 610, and 611, Registry of Tumors in Lower Animals, Smithsonian Inst., Washington, D.C.
29. Law, L. W.   Studies of thymic function with emphasis on the role of the thymus in oncogenesis.   *Cancer Res. 26:* 551.   1966.
30. Lichtenstein, E. P.   Pesticide residues in soils, water, and crops.   *Ann. N. Y. Acad. Sci. 160:* 155.   1969.
31. Lijinsky, W., and Epstein, S. S.   Nitrosamines as environmental carcinogens.   *Nature (London) 225:* 21.   1970.
32. Lucké, B.   Studies on tumors in cold-blooded vertebrates.   *Rep. Tortugas Lab. 1937–1938:* 92–94, 1938.
33. Lucké, B.   Tumors of the nerve sheaths in fish of the snapper family (Lutianidae).   *Arch. Pathol. 34:* 133.   1942.
34. Lucké, B., and Schlumberger, H. G.   Transplantable epithelioma of the lip and mouth of catfish. I. Pathology. Transplantation to anterior chamber of eye and into cornea.   *J. Exp. Med. 74:* 397.   1941.
35. MacIntyre, P. A.   Tumors of the thyroid gland in teleost fishes.   *Zoologica (New York) 45:* 161.   1960.
36. Main, J. H. P., and Dawe, C. J.   Tumor induction in transplanted tooth buds infected with polyoma virus.   *J. Nat. Cancer Inst. 36:* 1121.   1966.
37. Mawdesley-Thomas, L. E.   Neoplasia in fish: A review, p. 87.   In *Current Topics in Comparative Pathology,* ed. T. C. Cheng.   New York and London, Academic Press, 1971.
38. Mulcahy, M. F.   Lymphosarcoma in the pike *Esox lucius* L. (Pisces; Esocidae) in Ireland.   *Proc. Roy. Irish Acad.,* Sect. B *63:* 103.   1963.
39. Mulcahy, M. F., and O'Leary, A.   Cell-free transmission of lymphosarcoma in the northern pike, *Esox lucius* L. (Pisces; Esocidae).   *Experientia 26:* 891.   1970.
40. Mulcahy, M. F., and O'Rourke, F. J.   Cancerous pike in Ireland.   *Irish Natur. J. 14:* 312.   1964.
41. Nigrelli, R. F.   Virus and tumors in fishes.   *Ann. N. Y. Acad. Sci. 54:* 1076–1092.   1952.
42. Oota, K.   An epidemic occurrence of tumor-like hyperplasia of epidermis in a species of fish, *Acanthogobius flavimanus*.   *Gann (Jap. J. Cancer Res.) 43:* 264.   1952.
43. Potter, M.   Percivall Pott's contribution to cancer research.   *Nat. Cancer Inst. Monogr. 10:* 1.   1963.
44. Proewig, F. W.   Die Beeinflussung des Wachstums bösartiger Tumoren von Zahnkarpfen.   *Z. Krebsforsch. 60:* 470.   1954.
45. Ritchie, R. C.   Work cited by H. G. Schlumberger in *Cancer Res. 17:* 823.   1957.

46. Robertson, O. H., Krupp, M. A., Favour, C. B., Hane, S., and Thomas, S. F. Physiological changes occurring in the blood of the Pacific salmon (*Oncorhynchus tshawytscha*) accompanying sexual maturity and spawning. *Endocrinology 68:* 733. 1961.

47. Russell, F. E., and Kotin, P. Squamous papilloma in the white croaker. *J. Nat. Cancer Inst. 18:* 857. 1957.

48. Sagawa, E. Zur Kenntnis der Fischengeschwülste. *Gann (Jap. J. Cancer Res.) 19:* 14. 1925.

49. Sander, J., Brukle, G., and Schweinsberg, F. Induction of tumors by nitrite and secondary amines or amides, p. 297. In *Topics in Chemical Carcinogenesis,* ed. W. Nakahara, S. Takayama, T. Sugimura, and S. Odashima. Tokyo, Univ. Tokyo Press, 1972.

50. Sato, S., Matsushima, T., Tanaka, N., Sugimura, T., and Takashima, F. Hepatic tumors in the guppy (*Lebistes reticulatus*) induced by aflatoxin B_1, dimethylnitrosamine, and 2-acetylaminofluorene. *J. Nat. Cancer Inst. 50:* 767. 1973.

51. Schlumberger, H. G. Nerve sheath tumors in an isolated goldfish population. *Cancer Res. 12:* 890. 1952.

52. Schlumberger, H. G. Tumors characteristic for certain animal species: A review. *Cancer Res. 17:* 823. 1957.

53. Schlumberger, II. G., and Katz, M. Odontogenic tumors of salmon. *Cancer Res. 16:* 369. 1956.

54. Schubert, G. Elektronenmikroskopische Untersuchungen zur Pockenkrankheit des Karpfens. *Z. Naturforsch., Sect. B 19:* 675. 1964.

55. Siciliano, M. J., Perlmutter, A., and Clark, E. Effect of sex on the development of melanoma in hybrid fish of the genus *Xiphophorus. Cancer Res. 31:* 725. 1971.

56. Snell, K. C. Observations on olfactory neuroepitheliomas in rats following administration of N,N'-2,7-fluorenylenebisacetamide. Unpublished, 1964.

57. Sonstegard, R. Description and epizootiological studies of infectious pancreatic necrosis virus of salmonids and lymphosarcoma of *Esox masquinongy.* Ph.D. thesis, Univ. Guelph, Ontario, Can., 1971.

58. Stanley, H. R., Dawe, C. J., and Law, L. W. Oral tumors induced by polyoma virus in mice. *Oral Surg. 17:* 547, 1964.

59. Stanton, M. F. Diethylnitrosamine-induced hepatic degeneration and neoplasia in the aquarium fish, *Brachydanio rerio. J. Nat. Cancer Inst. 34:* 117. 1965.

60. Steeves, H. R. An epithelial papilloma of the brown bullhead, *Ictalurus nebulosus. Nat. Cancer Inst. Monogr. 31:* 215. 1969.

61. Stolk, A. Tumours of fishes. I. An ovarian teratoma in the viviparous cyprinodont *Lebistes reticulatus* (Peters). *Proc. Kon. Ned. Akad. Wetensch.,* Ser. C *56:* 28. 1953.

62. Stolk, A. Development of ovarian teratomas in viviparous toothcarps by pathological parthenogenesis. *Nature (London) 183:* 763. 1959.

63. Sullivan, D. J., and Anderson, W. A. Embryonal nephroma in swine. *Amer. J. Vet. Res. 20:* 324. 1959.

64. Takahashi, K.   Studie über die Fischgeschwülste. *Z. Krebsforsch. 29:* 1. 1929.
65. Walker, R.   Virus associated with epidermal hyperplasia in fish. *Nat. Cancer Inst. Monogr. 31:* 195. 1969.
66. Wellings, S. R.   Environmental aspects of neoplasia in fishes, p. 3. In *Fish in Research,* ed. O. W. Neuhaus and J. E. Halver. New York and London, Academic Press, 1969.
67. Wellings, S. R.   Neoplasia and primitive vertebrate phylogeny: Echinoderms, prevertebrates, and fishes—a review. *Nat. Cancer Inst. Monogr. 31:* 59. 1969.
68. Wellings, S. R., and Chuinard, R. G.   Epidermal papillomas with virus-like particles in flathead sole, *Hippoglossoides elassodon.* *Science (Wash., D.C.) 146:* 932. 1964.
69. Wolf, K.   The fish viruses, p. 35. In *Advances in Virus Research,* ed. K. M. Smith and M. A. Lauffer. Vol. 12. New York, Academic Press, 1966.
70. Wolf, K.   Advances in fish virology: A review, 1966–1971, p. 305. In *Diseases of Fish,* ed. L. E. Mawdesley-Thomas. (Symp. Zool. Soc. London, No. 30.) London and New York, Academic Press, 1972.
71. Wolf, K., and Quimby, M. C.   Fish cell and tissue culture, p. 253. In *Fish Physiology,* ed. W. S. Hoar and D. J. Randall, vol. 3. New York and London, Academic Press, 1969-70.
72. Wourms, J. P.   Annual fishes, p. 123. In *Methods in Developmental Biology,* ed. F. H. Wilt and N. K. Wessels. New York, Crowell, 1967.
73. Zeigel, R. F., and Clark, H. F.   Histologic and electron microscopic observations on a tumor-bearing viper: Establishment of a "C"-type virus-producing cell line. *J. Nat. Cancer Inst. 46:* 309. 1971.

36

Tumors of the Yellow Perch

JOAN BUDD
J. D. SCHRODER
and KAREN DAVEY DUKES

The tumors of yellow perch (*Perca flavescens*) have received little attention from pathologists. Nigrelli (12) stated that hyperplastic epidermal disease was common in North America in several species of fish, including perch (species not specified), and Walker (20) reported epidermal hyperplasia in yellow perch from Cassidy Lake, Michigan, and from Lake Oneida, New York.

Finkelstein and Danchenko-Ryzchkova (4) described a neurinoma in *P. fluviatilis*, a species closely related to *P. flavescens*. We reported the occurrence of testicular tumors in a population of yellow perch (2), but other tumors observed were not reported. Because of the dearth of reports concerning tumors in this species, it seems important to document the cases described herein.

TESTICULAR TUMORS

A review of naturally occurring testicular tumors in other species of fish and a preliminary report of testicular tumors of yellow perch were presented by Budd and Schroder in 1969 (2).

The yellow perch in South Bay, Lake Huron, Ontario, have been sampled each summer since 1966. By 1971, 4899 fish, of which 3579 were males, had been examined and 300 testicular tumors were identified (Table 36.1). This is 8.4% of the males and is similar to the prevalence for the first three years of sampling (7.2%).

895

Table 36.1. Prevalence of Tumors in Yellow Perch from South Bay,
Lake Huron, Ontario

Year	Number of fish examined	Number of males	Number of females[a]	Number of testicular tumors	% Males affected
1966	2239	1497	742	100	6.7
1967	911	833	78 (2)	51	6.1
1968	387	300	87 (1)	39	13.0
1969	863	561	302 (1)	60	10.7
1970	200	120	80	20	16.6
1971	499	268	231	30	11.5
Total	4899	3579	1320	300	8.4

[a]Number of tumors of the ovary in parentheses.

In 1970, yellow perch from several other lakes in the province of Ontario were sampled. Sixteen testicular tumors were obtained from 1294 males in four widely scattered locations (Table 36.2). Although we have examined testicular tumors in yellow perch from Lake Erie, none were present from the samples taken in 1970.

The testicular tumors, as described previously (2), varied in size from those barely visible to those large enough to distend the abdominal wall. Each was pale, firm, and shiny. Only a few of the larger tumors had a central necrotic area.

The first indication of a neoplasm was an outgrowth from the normal supporting tissue of the testicle. A wedge of densely packed cells arranged in a somewhat disorganized swirling manner was surrounded by normal, and apparently functional, tubules. Immediately adjacent and within the outer edges of the tumor, there were a few remaining tubules which were compressed. Spermatozoa frequently were present within these tubules, and even on the periphery of large tumors, at the testicular-tumor attachments (Fig. 36.1).

Histologically the tissue in each tumor was remarkably similar, being composed of parallel arrays of linear eosinophilic cells with central, lightly basophilic, granular nuclei, usually with rounded ends and conforming to the shape of the cells. Interspersed were cross sections of similar tissue. There were various degrees of tissue density. Mitosis was not a prominent feature.

Although sections of tumor tissue were stained with van Gieson's, Masson's trichrome, and Wilder's reticulum stains (9), the origin of the tumor cells remained in doubt. However, when tissues from normal testes and from the tumors were examined with an electron microscope, it was evident that smooth muscle cells, which were present in the supporting tissue of the tubules.in the normal testes, were the predominant cell type in the tumors.

The rate of growth of the tumor mass is unknown. There has been no evidence

Table 36.2. Testicular Tumors in Yellow Perch Collected during 1970 from
Five Locations in Ontario

Lake	Number of fish examined	Number of males	Number of testicular tumors
Ontario	865	572	2
Superior			
(Black Bay)	91	41	2
Simcoe	214	63	8
Algonquin Park			
(Opeongo and others)	435	163	4[a]
Erie			
(Wheatley)	435	340	0
(Port Dover)	209	115	0
Total	2249	1294	16

[a]Two tumor-bearing yellow perch were collected by personnel at the Fisheries Research Station, Harkness Memorial Laboratory, Lake Opeongo, Ontario, and submitted in formalin; one was from Shrew Lake, the other from Lake Opeongo.

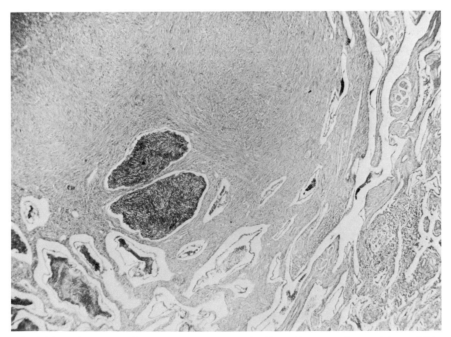

Fig. 36.1. Leiomyoma of the testicle, yellow perch. Normal regenerating testicle on right. Spermatozoa within the tumor. ×40.

of metastasis. This tumor is assumed to be benign, of smooth muscle origin, and therefore a leiomyoma.

OVARIAN TUMORS

In their reviews Schlumberger and Lucké (14), Wellings (21), and Nigrelli (12) listed tumors of the ovary from several species of fishes: a cystadenoma from a ling (*Molva molva*) (8), a fibroma in a carp (*Carassius vulgaris*) (5), an unclassified sarcoma from a cod (*Gadus morhua*) (18), and an adenoma in the goldfish (*C. auratus*) (1). Haddow and Blake (6) reported a large swelling and several smaller ones near the anterior end of the left ovary in a pike (*Esox lucius*). They considered this to be an adenocarcinoma derived from the germinal epithelium. Stolk (15, 16) described teratomas of the ovary in a guppy (*Poecilia reticulata* = *Lebistes reticulatus*) and a platyfish (*Xiphophorus maculatus*). Honma (7) in his studies of endocrine glands of the ayu (*Plecoglossus altivelis*) described a lymphosarcoma involving the ovary. Mawdesley-Thomas (11) listed in his bibliography a personal communication from Erdman (1968) reporting ovarian tumors in *Coryphaena hippurus*. Most references fail to report whether the tumor being described was within the ovary or visible on the outer surface of the ovary.

Four ovarian tumors were found in 1320 female yellow perch from South Bay (Table 36.1). Three of these tumors were within the lumen of the ovary.

Case 1

This tumor collected in June 1966 was ellipsoid, 60 mm in length and 45 mm in diameter, enclosed within the ovary and attached firmly to the stroma on one surface, but otherwise free. Except in the area of attachment of the tumor, the ovarian tissue resembled a normal, spent ovary which had remained distended. The tumor was firm, glistening, and pale pinkish on the surface. Centrally, the cut surface was yellowish and granular, with a few cavities containing an amber-colored liquid.

Case 2

A tumor collected in July 1967 resembled that described in case 1. It was a pale, ellipsoid mass, 45 × 38 mm, attached firmly within the lumen of the ovary to the anterior and dorsal stroma, but free posteriorly. This tumor was firm throughout.

Case 3

A second type of tumor, collected in July 1967, was smaller, somewhat ovoid, 25 mm in length and 15 mm in diameter, but similar in color and texture to that of case 2. It was attached to the surface of the ovary as though developing exteriorly from cortical stroma of the normal involuted ovary.

Case 4

This tumor, collected in June 1969, measured 40 × 35 mm. It was firmly attached, on all but the posterior surface, within the ovary, which extended posteriorly as a normal, spent, but distended ovary.

Only in cases 1 and 4 were the tissues suitable for microscopic study. In case 1 the tumor extended inward from the normal ovarian stroma, the walls of the ovary being the covering tissue of the tumor. The predominant cells in the tumor were arranged in swirled bands (Fig. 36.2). The cells were elongate with indistinct cytoplasmic margins giving the appearance of a fine network of fibers. In some areas of the tumor, the nuclei had a distinct outline, were basophilic, long, slender, and slightly wavy with pointed ends, but in other areas, although the cytoplasmic arrangement was similar, the nuclei contained basophilic granules, and were shorter with more rounded ends. Centrally there was cellular degeneration and necrosis. Blood vessels were present in small numbers. In case 4 the cells were arranged in a similar pattern of bands and both types of cells seen in case 1 were present throughout the tumor. There was no central necrosis.

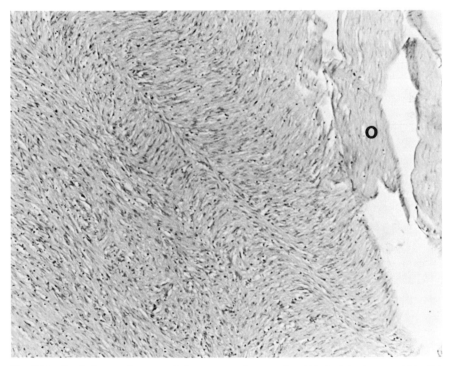

Fig. 36.2. Typical area of tumor of the ovary, yellow perch. Attached to stroma within the ovary (O). ×100.

Both tumors seemed to originate in ovarian stroma and to be of mesenchymal origin.

TUMORS OF EPITHELIAL TISSUE

Reports of tumors of epithelial tissue, including tumors of the thyroid, are numerous, and many species of fish are affected. These reports have been adequately reviewed by Schlumberger and Lucké (14), Nigrelli (12), MacIntyre (thyroid tumors) (10), and Wellings (21). References are listed also in a recent bibliography by Mawdesley-Thomas (11).

Three tumors of epithelial cell origin were observed in the yellow perch from South Bay.

1. Squamous Cell Tumor

A single, pale nodule, approximately 4 mm in diameter, slightly elevated from the surface of the lower jaw and partially covered by the free edge of the operculum, was noted on a male yellow perch caught in July 1966.

The lesion was scaleless and composed mainly of several layers of squamous epithelial cells in folds and supported by a fine connective tissue stroma. Mucous cells were present in the superficial parts of the lesion where the appearance was papillomatous (Fig. 36.3). There were scattered accumulations of inflammatory cells in all areas. The lesion extended into the subcutaneous muscle, and a small number of cells, epithelial in appearance and containing some periodic acid-Schiff-positive granules, were invading the muscle area, suggesting a squamous cell carcinoma. The extension may have been part of an inflammatory response. There was some degeneration of muscle deeper than the tumor, and here small numbers of inflammatory cells were present in the connective tissue surrounding the muscle bundles.

2. Carcinoma of the Urinary Bladder

Tumors of the urinary bladder in fish are uncommon. Plehn (13) reported a carcinoma obstructing the neck of the urinary bladder in a goldfish, and Williamson (22) noted an epithelioma of the urinary bladder in a cod (*G. callarias*).

A male yellow perch caught in July 1968 had a small nodule protruding from the body surface adjacent to the vent. The nodule was firm and lobulated, involving mainly the sinus into which the genital pore and the urinary papilla empty (3). Internally the mass extended anteriorly approximately 20 mm, involving the urinary bladder and posterior part of the testes (vas deferens). Anterior to the enlargement both testicles, which were ripe (mature), were normal in consistency, size, and color.

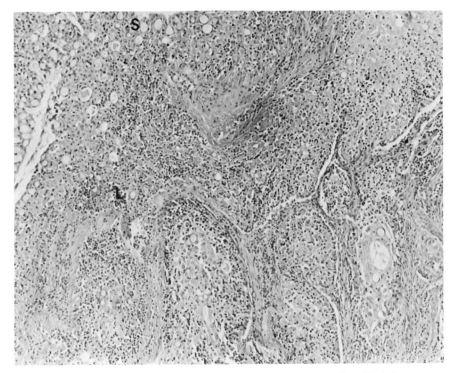

Fig. 36.3. Epithelial cell tumor of the skin, yellow perch. Tumor surface (S), inflammatory cells (L). ×100.

Microscopic examination revealed an abnormality as the columnar epithelium of the rectum changed to squamous epithelium at the anus. There was a marked increase in the thickness of the squamous epithelium, and it became papillary in appearance, with a fine supporting connective tissue stroma (Fig. 36.4). This was noticeable especially in the external parts of the tumor, but the tissue extended in similar folds along the urinary tract into the bladder, as well as along the vas deferens, and invaded the tissue adjacent to the rectum. The area of the tumor adjacent to the testes was more open and tubular in appearance. Here epithelium lined each lumen, but it was not of as many cells in thickness as that in the bladder area. There were a few spermatocytes and some evidence of degeneration and sloughing of surface epithelial cells within these tubules.

It was not evident whether the tumor had originated from transitional epithelium of the bladder, and had invaded posteriorly, or whether the tissue of origin was the squamous epithelium surrounding the urogenital sinus, and the invasion had proceeded anteriorly along the vas deferens and the urinary papilla.

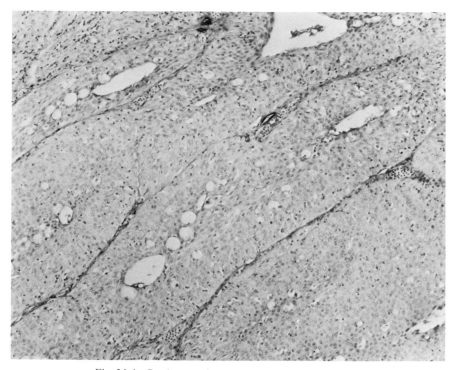

Fig. 36.4. Carcinoma of the bladder, yellow perch. ×100

3. Thyroid Carcinoma

A female yellow perch caught in October 1971 had the left operculum distended from the gills by a lobulated mass. The mass extended from the left of midline on the dorsal part of the pharynx laterally to the dorsal attachment of the operculum at about the second gill arch, and thence postero-laterally along the exterior of the branchial area, posterior to the gills and partially covered by the operculum, to about the level of the pelvic fin. The largest lobule, the most dorsal part, was about 1.5 cm in diameter.

Histologically the tumor was composed of a loosely arranged mass of cells uniform in size and staining. In some areas there was a cord-like, or acinar, arrangement (Fig. 36.5). The cells were angular, somewhat polyhedral in shape, with a large nucleus taking up more than half the cell. The scanty cytoplasm was basophilic and granular. Scattered throughout were occasional lymphocytes and single cells containing eosinophilic granules. Near a central blood vessel were small thyroid follicles with flattened epithelial cells on the periphery. There was an increase in the number of the eosinophilic granular cells adjacent to these follicles.

Although this was a highly undifferentiated tumor, the acinar grouping of cells suggested an adenocarcinoma.

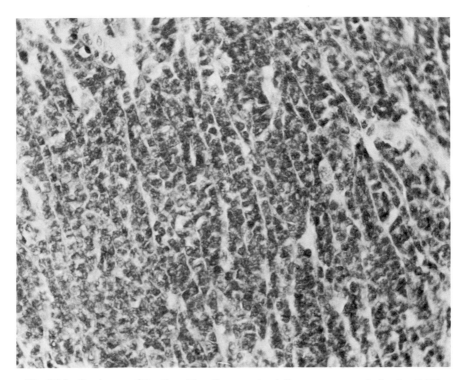

Fig. 36.5. Carcinoma of the thyroid, yellow perch. A linear arrangement of cells. X400.

GANGLIONEUROMA

Wellings (21), in a list of neural neoplasms, mentioned three reports of ganglioneuroma: one in the abdomen of a cod (19), one arising from the spinal ganglia of a plaice (*Limanda yokohamae*) (17), and one illustrated by Haddow and Blake (6), a large ganglioneuroma in the posterior of the body cavity in a flounder (*Lipidorhombus megastoma*), in which there were scattered ganglion cells in a network of nervous tissue.

A portion of a tumor removed from a yellow perch caught in Lake Erie in May 1964 was submitted in formalin. Sections from the tumor were stained with hematoxylin and eosin, hematoxylin phloxine and saffron (HPS), cresyl fast violet, and by Bielschowski's and Bodian's methods (9).

In two areas of the section there was an attachment to kidney tissue, and in the adjacent tumor were two normal collecting tubules and a glomerulus.

The tumor was composed of a network of fibers in which were large ganglion-type nerve cells (Fig. 36.6). Large neurons had a single, lightly stained nucleus, and usually a single prominent nucleolus. No mitoses were seen. The shapes of the neurons were variable. One or more processes were visible on most cells.

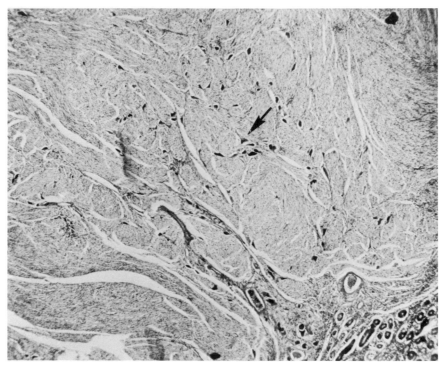

Fig. 36.6. Ganglioneuroma, yellow perch. Kidney on the lower right. Neurons scattered throughout (arrow). ×40.

With HPS stain the cytoplasm was finely granular, but in cells stained with Bielschowski's, Bodian's, or cresyl fast violet stains, Nissl's bodies were visible as clumped granules. Nerve fibers were wavy and somewhat interlaced. This tumor appeared to be a ganglioneuroma.

SUMMARY

Examination of yellow perch from several lakes in areas underlain by either Precambrian or Paleozoic bedrock indicates that the testicular tumors are not confined to populations in any specific locality or to any particular level of total hardness in the water. The presence of this tumor has been documented only since 1964, and one might postulate that the development of tumors is a recent phenomenon and thus might be related to environmental changes; however, the testicular tumors may have been present in yellow perch populations for many years, but because there has been no anatomical examination of this species (with the exception of length, weight, and sex), the tumor has been unnoticed.

Since few tumors of the ovary in fishes have been reported, the ovarian tumors in the yellow perch examined are of interest, particularly as these were mesenchymal, whereas the majority of those reported in other species were adenomatous.

Acknowledgment. The authors acknowledge the aid of directors and personnel of the Division of Fisheries Research, Ontario Department of the Lands and Forests, who provided assistance in many ways, including the provision of fish and laboratory space. Funds were provided by the Ontario Ministry of Agriculture and Food, the Canadian National Sportsman's Show, and the National Research Council of Canada. We are grateful to M. Hacking and T. Berry, for help in both the field and the laboratory, and to L. H. A. Karstad and R. G. Thomson, Department of Pathology, for advice and encouragement.

REFERENCES

1. Biesele, J. J. Diplochromosomes in a goldfish tumor. *Cancer Res. 3:* 411–412. 1943. (Cited by R. F. Nigrelli, *Trans. Amer. Fish. Soc. 83:* 262–296. 1954.)
2. Budd, J., and Schroder, J. D. Testicular tumors of yellow perch, *Perca flavescens* (Mitchill). *Bull. Wildlife Dis. Ass. 5:* 315–318. 1969.
3. Chaisson, R. B. *Laboratory Anatomy of the Perch.* Dubuque, Iowa, W C Brown, 1966.
4. Finkelstein, E. A., and Danchenko-Ryzchkova, L. K. [Neurinoma in the perch *Perca fluviatilis.*] *Arkh. patol. 27:* 81–84. 1965. [In Russian.] (*Excerpta med.* sec. 16, *14:* 4268. 1968.)
5. Freudenthal, P. Fibrom (Spindelzellensarkom?) im Ovarium einer Karausche (*Carassius vulgaris*). *Z. Krebsforsch. 26:* 414–417. 1928. (Cited by S. R. Wellings. *Nat. Cancer Inst. Monogr. 31:* 59–128. 1969.)
6. Haddow, A., and Blake, I. Neoplasms in fish: A report of six cases with a summary of the literature. *J. Pathol. Bacteriol. 36:* 41–47. 1933.
7. Honma, Y. Studies on the endocrine glands of the salmonid fish, the ayu, *Plecoglossus altivelis* Tenminck et Schlegel. VI. Effect of artificially controlled light on the endocrines of the pond-cultured fish. *Bull. Jap. Soc. Sci. Fish. 32:* 32–40. 1966.
8. Johnstone, J. Diseased and abnormal conditions of marine fishes. *Proc. Trans. Liverpool Biol. Soc. 29:* 80–113. 1915. (Cited by H. G. Schlumberger and B. Lucké. *Cancer Res. 8:* 657–712. 1948.)
9. Luna, L. G., ed. *Manual of Histologic Staining Methods of the Armed Forces Institute of Pathology.* 3d ed. New York, McGraw-Hill, Blakiston Div., 1968.
10. MacIntyre, P. A. Tumors of the thyroid gland in teleost fishes. *Zoologica (New York) 45:* 161–170. 1960.
11. Mawdesley-Thomas, L. E. Neoplasia in fish—a bibliography. *J. Fish Biol. 1:* 187–207. 1969.
12. Nigrelli, R. F. Tumors and other atypical cell growths in temperate freshwater fishes of North America. *Trans. Amer. Fish. Soc. 83:* 262–296. 1954.
13. Plehn, M. Über einige bei Fischen beobachtete Geschwülste und Geschwülstartige Bildungen. [On some tumors and growth-like formations observed in fish.] *Ber. K. Bayer. biol. Versuchs. 2:* 55–76. 1909. (Cited by S. R. Wellings. *Nat. Cancer Inst. Monogr. 31:* 59–128. 1969.)

14. Schlumberger, H. G. and Lucké, B.   Tumors of fishes, amphibians, and reptiles. *Cancer Res. 8:* 657–712. 1948.

15. Stolk, A.   Tumours of fishes. I.   An ovarian teratoma in the viviparous cyprinodont *Lebistes reticulatus* (Peters). *Proc. Kon. Ned. Akad. Wetensch.,* Ser. C *56:* 28–33. 1953. (Cited by S. R. Wellings. *Nat. Cancer Inst. Monogr. 31:* 59–128. 1969.)

16. Stolk, A.   Development of ovarian teratomas in viviparous toothcarps by pathological parthenogenesis. *Nature (London) 183:* 763–764. 1959.

17. Takahashi, K.   Studie über die Fischgeschwülste. [A Study of Fish Tumors.] *Z. Krebsforsch. 29:* 1–73. 1929. (Cited by S. R. Wellings. *Nat. Cancer Inst. Monogr. 31:* 59–128. 1969.)

18. Thomas, L.   Les Sarcomes fibroclastiques chez la morue. *Bull. Ass. fr. Étude Cancer 16:* 79–89. 1927. (Cited by S. R. Wellings. *Nat. Cancer Inst. Monogr. 31:* 59–128. 1969.)

19. Thomas, L.   Sur un cas de ganglioneurome abdominal chez la morue. *Bull. Ass. fr. Étude Cancer 16:* 282–286. 1927. (Cited by H. G. Schlumberger and B. Lucké. *Cancer Res. 8:* 657–712. 1948.)

20. Walker, R.   Epidermal hyperplasia in fish: Two types without visible virus. *Nat. Cancer Inst. Monogr. 31:* 209–213. 1969.

21. Wellings, S. R.   Neoplasia and primitive vertebrate phylogeny: Echinoderms, prevertebrates, and fishes—a review. *Nat. Cancer. Inst. Monogr. 31:* 59–128. 1969.

22. Williamson, H. C.   *Report on diseases and abnormalities of fishes (Sci. Invest. Fish. Board Scotl.).* 1911. (cited by Haddow and Blake, ref. 6).

37

Lymphosarcoma in Muskellunge (*Esox masquinongy*)

RON SONSTEGARD

In recent years, studies of the etiology and epizootiology of lymphoreticular neoplasia in man and in a variety of domestic and laboratory animals have become of paramount interest to the scientific community. Although numerous investigations dealing with these neoplasms have been made, few have dealt with the occurrence of this type of neoplasm in fish. This may be due to difficulties in recognition of the neoplasms in these animals, which, for the most part, spend their lives beyond the scrutiny of man. It is probable, however, that lymphoreticular neoplasms are a common occurrence in these animals.

Recently, Dawe (2) reviewed the occurrence of lymphoreticular neoplasia in fish and other poikilotherms. More reports have been made regarding the occurrence of lymphoreticular neoplasia in northern pike (*Esox lucius*) than in any other species of fish (3, 6–13). This paper describes the occurrence of lymphosarcoma in muskellunge (*E. masquinongy*).

SPECIMEN COLLECTION

Pound, hoop, and trap nets with a mesh at two inches were used to capture normal and tumor-bearing muskellunge (*E. masquinongy*). Tissue imprints and smears of peripheral blood were air dried, fixed in absolute methanol for 10 minutes, and air dried at 20°C. These preparations were routinely stained with Giemsa and Wright's stain for detection of morphological details of the nucleus and cytoplasm.

907

Tissues were routinely fixed in Bouin's fixative for 48 hours, washed in 70% alcohol, dehydrated, and embedded in paraffin. These preparations were routinely stained with hematoxylin and eosin (H&E). Preparations were also stained with periodic acid-Schiff stain (PAS), Mallory's trichrome, and carbol fuchsin methylene blue stain.

During the course of these investigations, normal and tumor-bearing fish were caught, tagged, and released. A number of tumor-bearing fish were also kept in laboratory tanks and kept under closed surveillance for the duration of the disease. The records of these observations, together with autopsy and histopathological examinations of diseased fish, discussions with biologists, guides, taxidermists, etc., made it possible to obtain a picture of the progression of the disease. The following is a gross and histopathological description of the disease with reference to progression of the lesion.

THE DISEASE

The external lesions of lymphosarcoma are usually large and obvious. No fish was found to have lymphosarcoma without involvement of the skin. The external lesions were found on the flank, fins, head, and gums, in decreasing order of frequency occurrence.

Flank Lesion

The most common external lesions are those on the flank of the fish, involving first the connective tissue spaces around the scales between the external muscle fascia and the overlying epithelial layer. These begin as local accumulations of a pink cloudy fluid in this region (scale pocket) and present themselves locally as a cluster of purple blisters (Figs. 37.1, 37.2). Each blister measures approximately 3 mm in diameter and 6 mm in height. The clusters are usually single, but they may be multiple, and may be found on any scaled region of the fish. The clusters are most common on the flank, dorsal to the pelvic fin.

The thin epithelial layer overlying the blisters is very fragile and breaks as a result of slight trauma. Some of the pink fluid then escapes and the scales in that region slough. The underlying connective tissues are then exposed to the aquatic environment and become pale white. The flank lesion then progressively becomes larger, gaining a characteristic size of approximately 10 cm horizontally by 12.5 cm vertically. The lesion at this time has an outer rim of purple blisters, which may be wide, narrow, or irregular in width, surrounding a flat scaleless central area of pale white connective tissue (Fig. 37.3).

Two sequelae are possible for fish with the type of lesion described above. The entire amount of involved tissue may slough, and the surrounding normal epithelium grow over the lesion site and a few scales regenerate (healed lesion). The healed lesion is grey, slightly elevated, and has a sharp outline. It has the charac-

Fig. 37.1. Early skin lesion of lymphosarcoma in muskellunge, composed of small clusters of purple blisters, several of which have broken, exposing underlying connective tissues.

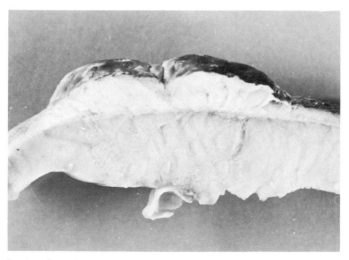

Fig. 37.2. Section through early skin lesions of lymphosarcoma, showing the size and nature of elevated purple blisters.

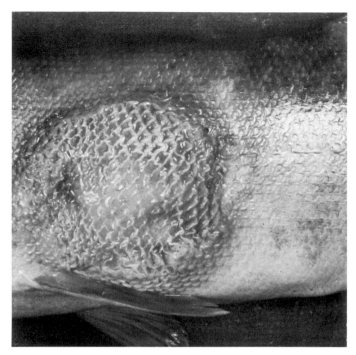

Fig. 37.3. Flank lesion of lymphosarcoma following rupture of blisters. Note the intact blisters at edge of the lesion and the central area of empty scale pockets and pale connective tissue.

teristic size, shape, and location of the flank lesion. The scales are smaller than normal, deficient in number, and irregularly arranged (Fig. 37.4).

The alternate course is the common one, and the onset of this sequel is characterized by a gradual change in the muscle immediately beneath the superficial flank lesion described above. The muscle in this area gradually loses its normal white color and assumes a pinkish hue. At the same time, it is slowly increasing in volume. These changes are observed grossly as a gradual bulging outward of the white central area of the flank lesion.

This progresses rapidly until the external muscle fascia fragments and an ulcer is formed. The terms "ulceration" and "ulcerated" are used here to describe only the external muscle fascia, and not the epidermis as described earlier (blisters). The ulcerated flank lesion is the fully developed and characteristic lesion. Externally, it has three zones: an outer rim of purple blisters, an intermediate zone of white connective tissue pitted with empty scale pockets, and a central core of protruding homogeneous cream-colored tissue (Fig. 37.5). The bulging tissue is soft and moist, and a thick creamy fluid can readily be scraped from it. The cut surface of a slice taken sagittally through the center of the flank lesion at

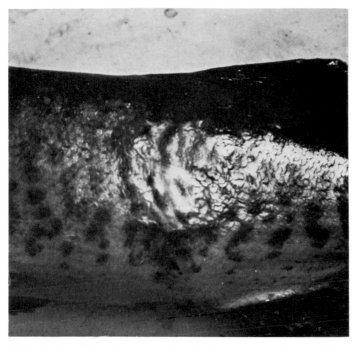

Fig. 37.4. Healed lesion of lymphosarcoma showing the characteristic size and shape of an active flank lesion. The scales are smaller than normal, deficient in number, and irregularly arranged.

this stage shows the pale homogeneous tissue to be localized and moderately well delineated from the surrounding muscle.

The microscopic changes of the flank lesion are characterized by a remarkably efficient infiltration by myriads of the neoplastic cells which will be described later. The early stages are characterized grossly by clusters of purple blisters. The connective tissue structures surrounding the attached end of each scale, which normally forms a compartment in which the scale is embedded (scale pocket), become bloated with masses of the neoplastic cells. These cells comprise the bulk of the pink opaque fluid seen grossly.

In cross section, these blisters appear as finger-like projections (Fig. 37.6). At this early stage, the epithelium is viable, but is lightly or moderately infiltrated with the neoplastic cells. The connective tissue below the blisters is moderately infiltrated; however, no neoplastic cells are found below the external muscle fascia or in the muscle.

The connective tissue spaces below the blisters gradually become more and more infiltrated with the neoplastic cells. For some time, the external muscle fascia offers a barrier to deep penetration of the infiltrating cells. However, in al-

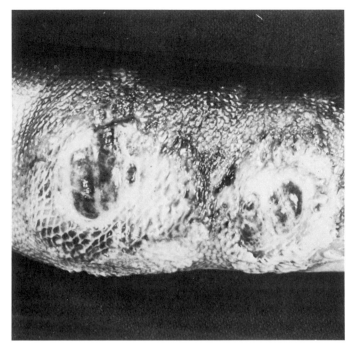

Fig. 37.5. Muskellunge with two ulcerated flank lesions of lymphosarcoma. The ulcerated flank lesion has three zones: an outer rim of purple blisters, an intermediate zone of white connective tissue pitted with empty scale pockets, and a central core of protruding cream-colored tissue.

most all cases, a gradual insinuation of the neoplastic cells takes place through the outer muscle fascia. The penetration is probably afforded by spaces in the adventitia of blood vessels and nerves which pass through the fascia.

Once the infiltrating cells have gained access to the deep side of the external muscle fascia, they spread laterally in all directions in the connective tissue spaces between the muscle septa. The neoplastic cells at this time can be found separating muscle bundles from one another by single, double, or triple rows of cells (Fig. 37.7). The cells infiltrate no further than the muscle directly beneath the external lesion. At this stage, there may be no gross evidence that the external muscle fascia has been breached.

As the lesion progresses, the spaces between the muscle bundles fill and become distended with the neoplastic cells, thus producing the gross bulging in the muscle and overlying fascia (Figs. 37.8, 37.9). It is believed that the physical tension produced by the increasing numbers of neoplastic cells accomplishes the ulceration of the external muscle fascia.

The muscle infiltration progresses until individual muscle fibers are completely surrounded by the neoplastic cells. The sarcolemma apparently is not easily in-

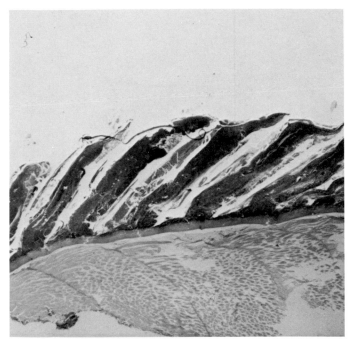

Fig. 37.6. Cross section of an early lesion of lymphosarcoma seen grossly as a cluster of purple blisters. The "finger-like" projections are composed of masses of neoplastic cells which have bloated the scale pockets. Note that no neoplastic cells are found below the external muscle fascia. Hematoxylin and eosin (H&E); X10.

filtrated, probably because no nerve or blood vessel penetrates it. However, as the infiltration of the neoplastic cells progresses, the sarcolemma of the muscle fiber breaks (Fig. 37.10). The cells then infiltrate the muscle fibers, which become more and more eosinophilic, break, and disappear. It is presumed that muscle degeneration products are carried away in solution, as no phagocytosis is apparent.

The infiltration process reaches a remarkable climax when all the muscle tissue beneath the original superficial lesion is replaced by masses of closely packed neoplastic cells. This is accomplished with no apparent alteration of the stroma except distention and expansion. No evidence of a capsule, connective tissue proliferation, inclusions, parasites, or bacteria was found. The gross changes accompanying this infiltration are localized homogenization and enlargement. The flesh changes from white to pale pink in color, from cohesive tension to brittleness, and from usual muscle dryness to excessive moistness.

Fin Lesion

The fin lesion is the most abundant type other than the flank lesion. The pelvic fin is more frequently involved than any other. More than one fin may be af-

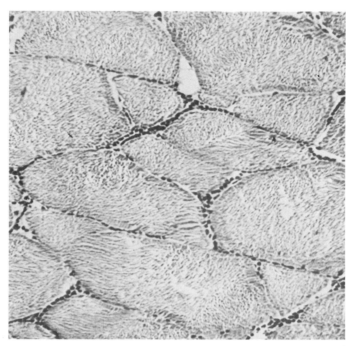

Fig. 37.7. Early stages of lymphosarcoma of the muscle, showing infiltrating cells metastasizing through the intercellular spaces between the muscle bundles. H&E; ×100.

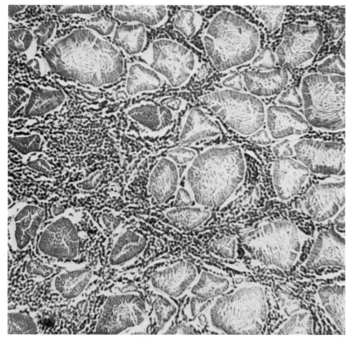

Fig. 37.8. Lymphosarcoma of the muscle, showing individual muscle fibers surrounded by masses of neoplastic cells. H&E; ×100.

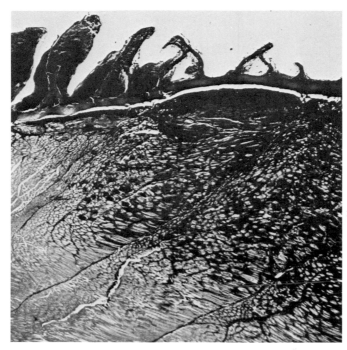

Fig. 37.9. Lymphosarcoma of the muscle, showing the infiltrating cells metastasizing into the musculature beneath the external skin lesion producing the bulging seen grossly. Note the intact bloated scale pockets at the periphery of the lesion. H&E; ×10.

fected, but single involvement is usual. The fin lesion may be found alone or in continuity with a flank lesion. The combination of a pelvic fin lesion and a flank lesion is common (Fig. 37.11).

The fin lesion usually begins at the attached edge of the fin. The fin becomes thickened and assumes a pinkish hue. Microscopically, it can be seen in the beginning as an accumulation of neoplastic cells in the connective tissue spaces between the fin rays, eventually surrounding the rays. As the lesion progresses, the external surface of the fin has a bulging, pink, quilted appearance. The peripheral edge of the fin, although perhaps not thickened, may become devitalized and slough, leaving a ragged white edge on the fin. Seen microscopically, the progression of the fin lesion is similar to that of the flank lesion.

Gum Lesion

The gum lesion may accompany other external lesions, but usually exists by itself. One or more gums may be involved. The gum may become so enlarged as to bulge into and out of the mouth. Teeth become displaced and slough. Microscopically, the thickening of the gum is characterized by the same type of infiltrating cells as discussed earlier.

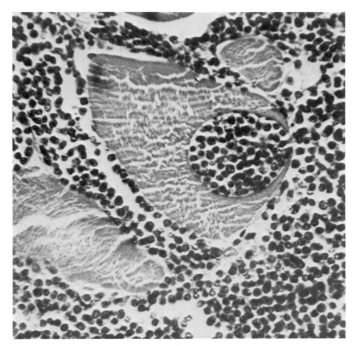

Fig. 37.10. Neoplastic cells infiltrating a muscle fiber following rupture of the sarcoma. H&E; ×400.

Fig. 37.11. Fin lesion in combination with a flank lesion of lymphosarcoma. Note that the tip of the fin has sloughed leaving a ragged white edge.

Head Lesion

The head lesion consists of a rather diffuse but circumscribed thickening of the soft tissue overlying the skull (Fig. 37.12). It has the appearance of irregular, fleshy, thick patches of tissue which are about 10 mm to 15 mm thick. The gross and microscopic appearance of the thickened tissue is the same as in the other external lesions described.

Internal Organs

It is believed that all tissues and organs may eventually become infiltrated in the late stages of the disease. However, only the kidney and spleen are commonly involved. The liver and blood may be involved in late stages of the disease, after infiltration of the kidney and spleen. The gonads are rarely infiltrated, less than 1% of the total sample being infiltrated even during the late stages of the disease (Fig. 37.13).

No fish was found to have internal organ involvement with the early subcutaneous lesions. The kidney and spleen are the first organs to be involved but usually only after an extensive nodular tumor has developed in the muscle. Grossly the kidney and spleen are indistinguishable from normal organs in the early stages of the disease and even when coexistent with a fully developed flank lesion. As these organs become infiltrated, however, there occurs a definite increase in weight and volume, which may be as much as four times the normal. The enlargement of these organs is a diffuse generalized increase in size, in contrast with the predominantly nodular nature of the muscle involvement.

The microscopic changes in the kidney and spleen are characterized by an efficient infiltration of the neoplastic cells. All stroma is eventually infiltrated and the parenchyma eventually becomes compressed and disappears. The final stage is almost indistinguishable from that in the muscle, where all parenchyma has been replaced and the stroma distended by a homogeneous mass of large round cells (Figs. 37.14, 37.15). Most fish die before this ultimate stage is reached.

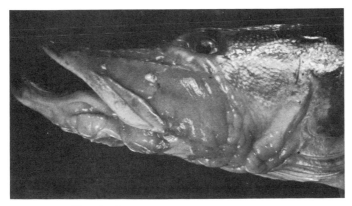

Fig. 37.12. Head lesion of lymphosarcoma.

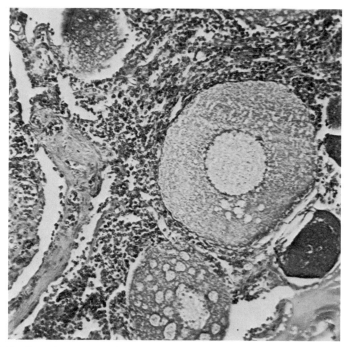

Fig. 37.13. Lymphosarcoma of the ovary, showing infiltrating cells surrounding oocytes. H&E; ×100.

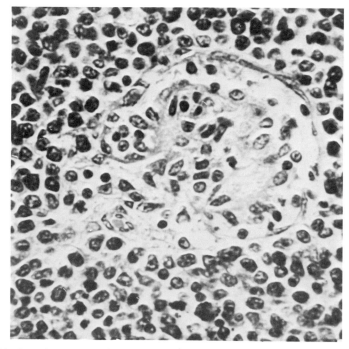

Fig. 37.14. Lymphosarcoma of the kidney, showing infiltrating cells completely surrounding the glomerulus. H&E; ×600.

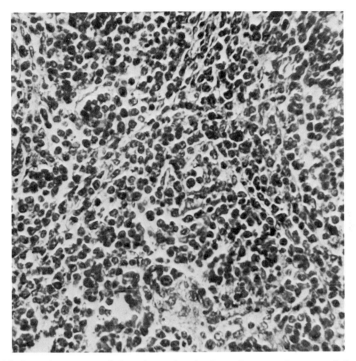

Fig. 37.15. Lymphosarcoma of the spleen, showing loss of structural aspects of the normal organ due to masses of infiltrating cells. H&E; X400.

Changes in the liver occur only in the late stages of the disease after involvement of the kidney and spleen. The change in the liver is an infiltration of neoplastic cells in the connective tissues of the portal areas around bile ducts, around central veins, and under the endothelial lining of the sinusoids (Fig. 37.16). This infiltration becomes progressively more intense until the parenchyma is destroyed, as in the other organs. Fish die before there is complete infiltration, so the liver parenchyma never becomes completely replaced, as happens in the spleen and kidney.

THE NEOPLASTIC CELL

The microscopic changes in the lesions are characterized by monotonous isomorphic masses of large blastoid cells. The infiltrating cells have the general structure of lymphocytes but are larger, being 1.5 to 2 times the diameter of normal fish lymphocytes.

The nuclei of these blastoid cells are almost as large as the cells. Typically, the cells have a prominent round or oval nucleus which has a distinct nuclear membrane. A moderate number of cells have nuclei with an acute indentation on one

Fig. 37.16. Lymphosarcoma of the liver, showing infiltrating cells around the veins, bile ducts, and sinusoids. H&E; ×100.

side and have a "bean shape" or "horseshoe" appearance. A few multinucleated cells are also observed.

The chromatin of the infiltrating cells is moderately dense and appears to be composed of a network of thick cords. Often the chromatin is clumped marginally next to the nuclear membrane and not evenly dispersed throughout the nucleus. No tumor cell nucleolus was seen in H&E, PAS, Giemsa, or Wright-stained preparations. Mitotic figures are usually present, although few in number.

The nucleus is ringed by a thin rim of cytoplasm which is structureless in H&E and PAS preparations. The cytoplasm in H&E preparations is mostly eosinophilic, although some cells are slightly basophilic. The cytoplasm of Giemsa-stained preparations of peripheral blood gives strong basophilic reaction in the cytoplasm. The cytoplasm gives a negative PAS reaction.

All infiltrating cells conform to the above description, and there is little cytological variation. One variation was cells with pyknotic nuclei (karyorrhexis), which were found in small clusters throughout the lesions. Often these cells were found at the periphery of the lesion where the epidermis had been ruptured, exposing the cells to the aquatic environment.

Smears of peripheral blood of fish with leukosarcoma revealed large numbers of cells which had the characteristics of lymphoblasts (Fig. 37.17). Frequent ex-

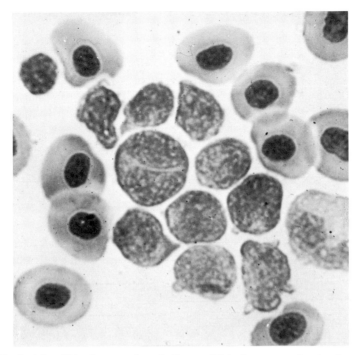

Fig. 37.17. Peripheral blood smear of muskellunge with leukosarcoma showing the morphology of the neoplastic cells. Frequent examples of division of the nucleus by transverse splitting were found. Giemsa; ×2000.

amples of division of the nucleus into two or three nuclei by transverse splitting were found. These cells are believed to be identical to those which infiltrate the tissues as described earlier.

SUMMARY

During the course of these investigations, muskellunge (*E. masquinongy*) in the Kawartha Lake region of Ontario, Canada, were captured and examined. The incidence of lymphosarcoma in these waters in the fall was as high as 16% of the catch and is the highest field incidence of a malignant tumor known in any free-living vertebrate population. The incidence may actually have been higher, since small inconspicuous lesions may have been undetected in superficial field examinations.

No fish has been found to have lymphosarcoma without involvement of the skin. The tumor is unicentric, arising in the subcutaneous tissues, forming a localized nodular tumor. The tumor metastasizes from the subcutaneous foci via intracellular spaces to involve the trunk musculature. In the late stages of the disease, the hematopoietic tissues of the spleen and kidney become infiltrated and enlarged and there may be accompanying leukosarcoma. The liver is the only other organ commonly involved, being infiltrated only after kidney and spleen infiltration. Occasionally the superficial skin lesions heal. However, the cells are malignant, and in most cases the tumor progresses to the death of the animal. Less than 1% of affected fish survive.

The external lesions of lymphosarcoma in muskellunge were found on the flank, fins, jaw, and head in descending order of occurrence. Mulcahy (6) and Haddow and Blake (3) reported the occurrence of lymphosarcoma in *E. lucius.* Both of these reports described fish with lymphosarcoma which had subcutaneous manifestations of the disease. Mulcahy (6) reported that the tumors in *E. lucius* in Ireland were found on the jaws, head, gills, and flank, in descending order of occurrence. The above descriptions of lymphosarcoma are at variance with the report of Nigrelli (11), who found no external lesions in an outbreak of lymphosarcoma in *E. lucius* in an aquarium.

The microscopic changes in the lesions are characterized by myriads of strikingly isomorphic cells, as seen by light microscopy. The neoplastic cells have the general structure of lymphocytes, but are larger, being 1.5 to 2 times the diameter of normal fish lymphocytes. The "starry sky" effect which is a characteristic of a number of lymphoreticular neoplasms in man and domestic animals was not found. The cell type from which the tumor cells arise is unknown.

One of the most striking histopathological characteristics of the syndrome is the ability of the neoplastic cells to infiltrate tissue spaces and cause atrophy without stimulating a fibroblastic or inflammatory response. No evidence of a capsule or fibroblastic proliferation was found, except that fibroblastic proliferation was found in lesions which were in the process of healing. Although the neoplasm exhibited the propensity to grow to an enormous nodular tumor accompanied by almost complete destruction of the tissue stroma, there was no evidence of an inflammatory response or phagocytosis by the tumor cells of histiocytes. The normal tissue stroma appears simply to break down in the neoplastic process and to be carried away in solution.

Despite the lack of histologic response by the host to the disease, the tumors remain remarkably localized. For example, the flank lesions may grow to enormous size without involvement of the adjacent musculature or the hematopoietic tissues. Although fascia and connective tissue barriers are partially responsible for the localization of the tumors, some humoral factors are obviously involved in controlling the growth of the tumor.

There are similar diseases (lymphomas) in humans and domestic animals which also remain remarkably localized for long periods of time. Several of these diseases respond spectacularly to thermotherapy (15, 17). It is generally believed that unusual immunological factors are involved in the retention of these tumors in the initial sites and are responsible for the rapid regression following chemotherapy (4). In view of the above, it would be of considerable interest to treat the lymphosarcoma described in this study with similar drugs. Do fish respond to chemotherapy as higher animals do? This may be an important consideration, as it may implicate hitherto unknown defense mechanisms of the host to cancer growth.

The strong epizootiological evidence of a viral etiology of the syndrome in *Esox* (14) and the report of Mulcahy and O'Leary (8) of successful cell-free transmission of the same or closely related syndrome in *E. lucius* enhance the potential attractiveness of the syndrome as an experimental subject. While demonstration of a viral etiology of the neoplasm would constitute no proof that this agent has oncogenic potential in man, it would demonstrate the oncogenic property of the virus. Therefore, it would be important evidence supporting a similar lymphosarcomatous action in man by the same or other viruses.

Of course, the question exists: Do these animals represent a potential human health hazard? Although this suggestion may seem extraordinary, one must bear in mind the successful transmission of the Rous sarcoma of fowl into poikilotherms (16), the replication of a virus associated with adenocarcinoma of frogs in cells of mammalian origin (5), and the roles that snakes are believed to play in the epizootiology of equine encephalitis (1).

It is apparent that the syndrome possesses considerable potential as a model for human cancer research. Although the relatively short life spans, the aquatic environment, and the as yet undefined host factors of fish preclude any completely realistic comparisons to human disease, the similarities and differences found may be of paramount importance to understanding basic neoplastic processes.

There are, in fact, a number of attributes both of the syndrome and of fish as experimental animals which have advantages over "higher animals." By virtue of fishes' tremendous reproductive capacity it is possible to design experiments using large numbers of animals uncomplicated by genetic variations in resistance, etc. The environment of fish may be manipulated to suit the investigator (e.g., in temperature), which cannot be done with homeotherms. The muskellunge is a cheap, large animal, a fact which facilitates hematological, biochemical and serological studies. The constant involvement of skin provides an ideal epidemiological marker for field studies, and the widespread incidence of the syndrome makes such studies profitable.

Acknowledgment. These investigations were supported by the Anna Fuller Fund, Canadian National Cancer Institute, the Canadian National Sportsman's Show, and the Ontario Ministry of Natural Resources.

REFERENCES

1. Burton, A., McLintock, J., and Rempel. J. Western equine encephalitis virus in Saskatchewan garter snakes and leopard frogs. *Science (Wash., D.C.) 154:* 1029. 1966.

2. Dawe, C. J.   Neoplasms of blood cell origin in poikilothermic animals: A review. *Nat. Cancer Inst. Monogr. 32:* 7. 1969.

3. Haddow, A., and Blake, I.   Neoplasms in fish: A report of six cases with a summary of the literature. *J. Pathol. Bacteriol. 36:* 41. 1933.

4. Lingeman, C. H.   Comparative aspects of the mastocytoses. *Nat. Cancer Inst. Monogr. 32:* 289. 1969.

5. Lunger, P. D.   Amphibia-related viruses, p. 1. In *Advances in Virus Research,* ed. K. M. Smith and M. A. Lauffer. Vol. 12. New York, Academic Press, 1966.

6. Mulcahy, M. F.   Lymphosarcoma in the pike *Esox lucius* L. (Pisces; Esocidae) in Ireland. *Proc. Roy. Irish Acad.,* Sect. B *63:* 103. 1963.

7. Mulcahy, M. F.   Lymphosarcoma in the pike *Esox lucius* L in Ireland. *Life Sci. 3:* 719. 1964.

8. Mulcahy, M. F., and O'Leary, A.   Cell-free transmission of lymphosarcoma in the northern pike, *Esox lucius* L. (Pisces; Esocidae). *Experimentia (Basel) 26:* 891. 1970.

9. Mulcahy, M. F., and O'Rourke, F. J.   Cancerous pike in Ireland. *Irish Natur. J. 14:* 312. 1964.

10. Mulcahy, M. F., Winqvist, G., and Dawe, C. J.   The neoplastic cell type in lymphoreticular neoplasms of the northern pike, *Esox lucius* L. *Cancer Res. 30:* 2712. 1970.

11. Nigrelli, R. F.   Spontaneous neoplasms in fishes. III. Lymphosarcoma in *Astyanax* and *Esox. Zoologica (New York) 32:* 101. 1947.

12. Ohlmacher, H. P.   Several examples illustrating the comparative pathology of tumors. *Bull. Ohio Hosp. Epilep. 1:* 223. 1898.

13. Schlumberger, H. G.   Tumors characteristic for certain animal species: A review. *Cancer Res. 17:* 823. 1957.

14. Sonstegard, R., Nielsen, K., and McDermott, L. A.   *Epizootiological Evidence for a Viral Etiology of Lymphosarcoma in* Esox. Int. Ass. Aquatic Anim. Med., Guelph, Ont., Canada, 1970.

15. Squire, R. A.   Burkitt's lymphoma—a comparative study. *Nat. Cancer Inst. Monogr. 32:* 297. 1969.

16. Svet-Moldavsky, G. J., Trubcheninova, L., and Ravkina, L. I.   Pathogenicity of the chicken sarcoma virus (Schmidt-Ruppin) for amphibians and reptiles. *Nature (London) 214:* 300. 1967.

17. Wright, D. H., Bell, T. M., and Williams, M. C.   Burkitt's tumor: A review of clinical features, treatment, pathology, epidemiology, entomology, and virology. *East Afr. Med. J. 44:* 51. 1967.

38

Fish Blood Changes Associated with Disease: A Hematological Study of Pike Lymphoma and Salmon Ulcerative Dermal Necrosis

MAIRE F. MULCAHY

Fish blood is increasingly studied for toxicological research, for environmental monitoring using fish, and as a possible indicator of physiological or pathological change in fishery management and disease investigations. Despite many publications in the field (28), fish hematology in health and disease is still in a fragmented and developing state, and as yet general indicative principles have not emerged. Not only are there wide variations within what is normal (37, 40, 77), but also blood values are influenced and modified by many factors (8), such as handling (30), stress (9, 10, 16), inflammation (78), metabolism (7), age (2, 41, 73), maturity (58), sex (67, 71), diet (2, 41, 64), strain (2, 26), and pollution (25, 44, 69, 70). Standardization of the methods of study was recommended in 1964 by Klontz et al. (40), to overcome some of the problems. These authors nevertheless expressed the belief at that time that because of the variation within even a single species it was not possible to produce a table of normal values which might be used with "even the remotest degree of validity." Others, including this author, hold on the other hand that such studies can be useful provided that normal blood parameters are established from a sufficiently large and representative number of control fish to reflect normal variation under the conditions of study.

The scattered literature of blood change in fish disease is varied in content and

925

objective. One of the earliest papers reviewed in 1906 the information on blood counts and hematocrits in health and disease (45). Reduction of red cell numbers, hemoglobin, and hematocrit has been found in vibriosis of marine fish (1) and juvenile chinook salmon (15), and of course in spontaneous and experimental anemias of trout and salmon (5, 34, 35, 64–66). These characters were unchanged in furunculosis (39), and in Ulcerative Dermal Necrosis (UDN) in trout (13). An increase in hematocrit on the other hand is associated with gill disease in Atlantic salmon (32) and hepatoma in rainbow trout (68), and with the onset of virus disease (unspecified) in sockeye salmon (76).

Increased white cell numbers are recorded in vibrio disease in chinook salmon (15) and in the initial stages of infectious dropsy of carp (42).

Comprehensive differential white cell counts of diseased fish have not been found in the literature, although the blood cells of virus-diseased sockeye salmon are described by Watson, Guenther, and Royce (76), basophil cell hyperplasia being the major finding. The appearance of macrophages in the blood is considered to be a feature of bacterial infections of rainbow trout (78), and is also recorded after virus inoculation in Salmonidae (76). Unusual macrophages with ingested bacteria are described by Katz in the blood of a diseased salmon fingerling (33). Experimental stressing of rainbow trout, without concomitant specific disease, produces lymphopenia, thyrombocytopenia and heterophilia (78).

Changes in the level of serum or plasma protein are recorded in a number of diseases, being reduced in UDN in trout (13), UDN and fungal infection of Atlantic salmon (47, 48), vibrio disease of chinook salmon (15), infectious dropsy in carp (23), bacterial kidney disease of brook trout (31), disease (unspecified) in rainbow trout (41), and fungus infection in sea herring (63), the level being raised only in hepatomas of rainbow trout (62, 68).

Electrophoretic separation of the protein fractions of the serum has been carried out in infectious dropsy of carp (23, 43), bacterial kidney disease (31), in UDN in salmon (47, 48) and trout (13), and hepatomas in trout (68). In hepatomas the general increase in protein level is seen in all fractions. In other diseases the albumins and globulins are affected differently, the albumin always being reduced but some globulins showing a relative or absolute increase. In infectious dropsy there is a slight rise in γ-globulin, but whether this is cause or effect is not clear, as Liebmann et al. grouped susceptibility to this disease on the basis of A/G ratio (43). In bacterial kidney disease there is an increase in the slower moving globulins (which are not classified) (31); a decrease in all but the β-globulins was found in SRC virus-infected fish by Klontz, Yasutake, and Parisot (38), while the β-1 globulin fraction also rose in UDN in trout (13). In many cases the reductions of protein level have been attributed to leakage and edema, and therefore to an indirect effect of the disease. A reduction in albumins is probably a nonspecific effect and is noted as a feature of the reaction of fish to severe stress (16). One might expect from comparative studies that a rise in a globulin fraction would represent an immune response in specific reaction to disease. However, the significance of the globulin fractions of fish blood is not known. The immune properties have variously been associated with the mammalian equivalent of the slow β- or fast γ-globulin in one species (18) and with the γ_2-globulin (55) and the β_2-globulin in others (38, 57). On the other hand, while Uhr et al. found a γ_2-globulin in goldfish (74), Hodgins, Ridgway, and Utter did not find this fraction in rainbow trout, but reported the immune globulins to be heterogeneous with respect to electrophoretic mobility and size: when compared with human baselines, the two fastest components were equivalent to the β-globulin, while the slower one acted as a fast γ or a slow β (29). The differing results may represent either a difference in experimental method or else specific differences in different species (29).

This paper documents the normal parameters of the blood of two species, the northern pike (*Esox lucius*) and the Atlantic salmon (*Salmo salar*) and presents the deviations from the normal in two very different diseases: lymphoma in pike and UDN in salmon.

BLOOD CHANGES ASSOCIATED WITH LYMPHOMA IN THE NORTHERN PIKE

Table 38.1 shows hematological values for healthy adult pike and has been discussed in a previous paper (49). It also shows the values found in pike with spontaneous lymphomas. Pike in Ireland are particularly prone to this type of tumor. It is a malignant neoplasm taking the form initially of soft tumors in the jaws or externally on the trunk or tail, and later metastasizing and invading the viscera (46). The predominant cell type is the stem cell hemocytoblast or immunoblast (53). The cause of the lymphoma is unknown but is thought to be a virus because of the high incidence and distribution (52) and because limited transmission studies have been successful (51), even though viruses have not been seen in the lesions (46, 53; L. Dmochowski, personal communication).

One expects that changes in the blood of lymphoma-bearing pike would be associated primarily with the white cells, but this is not the case, at least until a very late stage in the disease, and in fact, most parameters observed are affected.

The red:white cell ratio is reduced in the disease, which reflects more a drop in red cell count than a rise in the number of white cells. In the figures in Table 38.1 the white cell count is higher in diseased than in normal pike, but these figures are largely influenced by one fish with very advanced neoplasia, and if this fish is not considered, as shown in the table, then the white cell count is not significantly different in the two classes of fish until the terminal stages of the disease, where a leukemia develops.

Table 38.2 shows the blood values for pike with lymphoma transmitted by cell-free tumor ultrafiltrates (51). These fish were moribund and the neoplasm terminal. Leukemia is found here, in contrast to either healthy untreated pike (Table 38.1) or to control injected pike (Table 38.2) or to pike with induced granulomas (Table 38.3).

Table 38.1. Blood Values for Normal Pike and Pike with Spontaneous Lymphoma

Character	Healthy			With lymphoma		
	No.	Range	Mean	No.	Range	Mean
Hematocrit %	21	20.0–43.5	32.0	5	10.0–38.0	24.0
Red cells/mm^3	15	1,120,000–3,120,000	1,893,000	10	620,000–2,790,000	1,251,000
White cells/mm^3	15	79,000–137,000	111,500	9	83,500–225,000	132,000
				(8)	(83,500–139,500)	(101,500)
Red/white cell ratio	15	12–32	17	9	2–22	11
Lymphocytes (% total white cells)	8	63–93	79	8	55–80	70
Red cell fragility						
Partial hemolysis % NaCl	8	0.42–0.48	0.47	1	0.73	0.73
Complete hemolysis % NaCl	8	0.24–0.36	0.32	1	0.32	0.32
Hemoglobin gm/100 ml	21	5.6–15.0	8.8	5	3.0–9.8	6.4
Serum total protein gm/100 ml	32	3.9–8.38	6.34	11	2.88–6.12	4.45

Table 38.2. Blood Values in Pike with Transmitted Lymphomas[a] and Control Pike[b]

Character	Control pike			Pike with induced lymphoma		
	Range	No.	Mean	Range	No.	Mean
Hematocrit %	18.0–30.0	3	22.7	9.0–13.0	3	11.5
Red cells/mm³	1,320,000–1,620,000	3	1,440,000	600,000–840,000	3	690,000
White cells/mm³	111,000–128,500	3	117,600	140,000–175,000	3	162,500
Red cell fragility						
Partial hemolysis % NaCl	–	1	0.45	–	1	0.57
Complete hemolysis % NaCl	–	1	0.30	–	1	0.39
Hemoglobin gm/100 ml	4.9–6.7	3	6.7	1.0–2.2	3	1.7
Serum total protein gm/100 ml	–	1	7.20	2.88–3.60	3	3.12

aPike injected IP with cell-free filtrates of a spontaneous tumor. Developed lymphomas and were killed when moribund.
bControl pike injected IP with cell-free filtrates of liver and kidney from healthy pike, remained healthy, and were killed after the same intervals as the pike with transmitted tumors (51).

Table 38.3. Blood Values in Pike with Experimental Abnormalities

| Character | Pike with granulomas[a] | | Pike with thymus disorder[b] |
	Range	Number	Mean
Hematocrit %	22.5–27.0	3	25.2	25.0
Red cells/mm^3	1,010,000–1,630,000	3	1,300,000	1,840,000
White cells/mm^3	66,500 –178,000	3	112,500	132,500
Hemoglobin gm/100 ml	6.0–7.0	3	6.5	11.2
Serum total protein gm/100 ml	5.76–6.12	3	5.88	8.38

[a] Pike which developed granulomas in liver, kidney, and spleen following IP injection with cell-free filtrates of histologically normal liver and kidney from a pike with a jaw tumor. Pike killed 9-10 months post-injection.

[b] A pike, injected IP with cell-free filtrate of a spontaneous tumor, which died before lymphoma developed, and in which the only detectable abnormality was histological disruption of thymus (51).

The ratio of lymphocyte to nonlymphocyte fell in the neoplastic pike (Table 38.1).

There is a marked drop in the red cell numbers in pike with spontaneous lymphomas. This drop is in turn reflected in the lowered hematocrits and lowered hemoglobin concentrations (Table 38.1). These marked changes in red cells and hemoglobin are further emphasized in the pike with induced lymphomas (Table 38.2), which are approximately 50% of control values. Not only the number of red cells but also their nature is changed in the neoplastic fish. In fixed smears it was noticed that many circulating red cells were immature, as judged by their more rounded shape and their staining properties. In addition a greater number of "ghost" cells were observed. Osmotic fragilities were examined, using graded salt solutions, and although results from only two neoplastic pike are available for comparison with the normal, they support the impression that the red cells are more fragile in neoplastic pike.

The timing of these changes in the blood cells relative to the development of the lymphomas is not yet known. It has been found that thymic involution is associated with the lymphomas, and thymic change probably precedes the development of the tumors (50). Blood values of one injected pike, which was moribund before the lymphoma was visible but in which thymic disruption was apparent histologically, are given in Table 38.3. They all fall within the normal range.

The serum total protein levels are markedly decreased in pike with lymphomas, whether spontaneous or induced (Tables 38.1 and 38.2).

The serum was separated into fractions by electrophoresis. The normal pattern has been described (49).

On polyacrylamide gel, six major fractions were separable (Fig. 38.1). In order of increasing mobility they were:

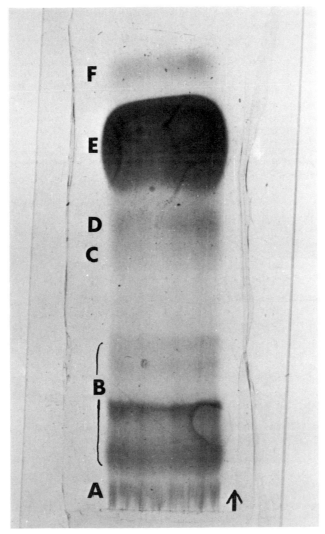

Fig. 38.1. Serum electrophoretic pattern of healthy pike (polyacrylamide gel).

A: a narrow well-defined one-component fraction comparable in mobility with human γ-globulin;

B: a complex, separable into four components, including the range of one component of bovine α- and also the β-globulin fraction;

C: a diffuse one-component fraction often confluent with D, comparable in mobility with one component of bovine α-globulin;

D: a diffuse one-component fraction often confluent with C, comparable in mobility with one of the two components of bovine albumin;

E: a dense well-defined fraction, comparable in mobility to one of the two components of bovine albumin;

F: a well-defined one-component fraction comparable in mobility with one of
the three components of bovine α-globulin.

A faint diffuse fraction bc intermediate in mobility between B and C was detectable in approximately half the sera examined.

The same fractions were also visible in pike with spontaneous lymphoma,
though the level of protein in the fractions varied with the lower total serum protein. The percentage protein in the major fractions in healthy and neoplastic pike
is shown in Table 38.4. There is no significant difference between these values
in health and in lymphoma.

The sera of pike with experimentally induced lymphomas and their controls
were also examined, as it was felt that any changes in the protein components
linked with the lymphoma would be emphasized in these fish (Table 38.4). While
the two control pike show results comparable with normal pike and with pike
with spontaneous lymphomas, the four pike with transmitted tumors showed
some differences: fraction B was relatively lower, and in two cases more than
four fractions were detectable (five in one case, seven in another), fractions E and
F were relatively higher, and in one fish the F fraction was composed of two components.

BLOOD CHANGES ASSOCIATED WITH UDN IN ATLANTIC SALMON

UDN is a disease which has caused heavy mortality in adult salmon on their return to fresh water in many European countries (14, 54, 59). The disease takes
the form of ulceration of the epidermal layers of the skin, starting in the head
region (60, 61). The ulceration probably does not cause the death of the fish
but renders the fish susceptible to secondary, especially fungal, infection (72).
It is thought to be the superinfections which bring about the death of the fish.
The cause of the disease is unknown, although there is evidence that a filtrable
agent is involved (14, 36). Diagnosis of UDN is difficult because of the variation in appearance of diseased fish in different stages of UDN and in different
river systems, ranging from very small ulcers on the head, to extensive ulceration apparently free of fungus, to complete fungal cover virtually indistinguishable from primary fungal infection.

The blood values of some healthy adult salmon in fresh water are shown in
Table 38.5. The values show considerable variation, which is perhaps less surprising
in the case of salmon than of pike, considering the wide range of environmental
stresses which the salmon experiences during its life history. A limited number of
hematocrit and hemoglobin values from salmon taken in the sea off the Irish
coast are shown in Table 38.6, and a limited number of salmon fingerlings in fresh
water were also examined (Table 38.7). The values for these young fish suggest
that red cell numbers and hemoglobin content rise and white cell numbers fall with

Table 38.4. The Percentage Protein in the Major Fractions Separated by Polyacrylamide Gel Electrophoresis from the Sera of Healthy and Neoplastic Pike

	Percent total protein						
	Healthy pike (N = 25)		Spontaneous lymphoma (N = 11)		Lymphoma transmitted by cell-free tumor filtrates (N = 4)		Control pike for transmission experiments[a] (N = 2)	
Fraction	Range	Mean	Range	Mean	Range	Mean	Range	Mean
A	3.6-11.5	6.8	2.2-11.7	7.1	4.2-17.1	7.6	1.9-12.0	7.1
B	41.1-64.1	49.6	30.7-62.7	46.8	23.3-45.6	33.9	30.5-58.9	43.8
C & D	8.7-33.2	19.5	6.2-36.9	19.7	12.9-20.7	17.0	15.4-31.3	22.8
E	8.0-34.5	21.0	10.5-33.8	21.3	6.6-50.6	31.2	19.6-20.9	22.6
F	1.2-6.9	4.0	1.2-10.5	4.3	5.9-17.8	10.7	2.4-5.6	4.0

[a]Healthy pike injected with cell-free filtrates of normal kidney and liver and killed after intervals comparable with pike with transmitted tumours.

Table 38.5. Blood Values of Healthy Adult Salmon and of UDN-infected Salmon in Fresh Water

Character	Healthy			UDN-infected		
	Range	No.	Mean	Range	No.	Mean
Hematocrit %	17.5–40.0	4	27.9			
Red cells/mm^3	800,000–1,500,000	13	1,087,000	360,000–2,150,000	44	1,024,000
White cells/mm^3	22,500–80,000	15	47,300	11,500–98,500	44	41,000
Red/white cell ratio	12.8–49.4	13	29.2	9.1–82.6	43	27.2
Lymphocytes (as percent white cells)	78–91	7	85	86–88	2	87
Fragility red cells						
Partial hemolysis % NaCl	0.57–0.73	4	0.63			
Complete hemolysis % NaCl	0.33–0.48	4	0.38			
Hemoglobin gm/100 ml	7.75–13.5	4	10.39			
Serum protein gm/100 ml	4.32–8.64	12	6.65	2.88–7.69	64	4.76

Table 38.6. Hematocrit and Hemoglobin Values for Adult Salmon in Salt Water

Character	Range	No.	Mean
Hematocrit %	52.0-58.5	10	53.7
Hemoglobin gm/100 ml	13.3-20.2	16	16.7

Table 38.7. Hematological Values of Salmon Fingerlings

Character	Number of fish	Range	Mean
Hematocrit %	3	17-23	21
Red cells/mm^3	2	900,000-920,000	910,000
White cells/mm^3	2	88,500-91,000	89,750
Red/white cell ratio	2	10.1-10.2	10.15
Lymphocytes (as percent white cells)	3	64-82	74
Hemoglobin gm/100 ml	3	4.9-7.6	6.7
Serum protein gm/100 ml	1	–	6.9

Table 38.8. Hematological Values of Salmon/Trout Hybrids

Character	Number of hybrids	Range	Mean
Hematocrit %	7	19.5-35.0	26.4
Red cells/mm^3	7	970,000-1,760,000	1,271,400
White cells/mm^3	7	105,500-134,500	118,700
Red/white cell ratio	7	9.2-14.0	10.7
Hemoglobin gm/100 ml	7	6.9-8.2	7.5
Serum protein gm/100 ml	6	5.8-8.4	7.5

age until the salmon returns to fresh water to spawn, when the hematocrit and hemoglobin again decline.

Immature salmon/trout hybrids which grow more rapidly and are more resistant to disease than the parent species (56) were available, and their blood values are given in Table 38.8. The main difference between them and salmon, which might reflect some of their hybrid vigor, appears to be the serum protein level, which is higher in the hybrid than in the parent salmon.

Blood values for salmon with UDN are compared with those of healthy salmon in Table 38.5. There is no significant difference in cellular parameters, but there is a marked drop in the serum protein levels.

This serum protein change was studied by polyacrylamide gel electrophoresis, and led to the finding that there is a progressive change in the serum electrophoretic pattern, passing through a UDN-specific phase, with an electrophoretic pattern not found in a variety of other diseases (48).

The normal electrophoretic pattern on polyacrylamide gel of salmon serum established from 15 fish is relatively constant (Fig. 38.2a). There are five major fractions, called B to F in order of increasing mobility. (Fig. 38.2a). Fractions B and C formed narrow bands, D a wide diffuse band, and E and F were sharply defined and narrow.

Three minor fractions of low mobility, called A_1, A_2, and A_3, were usually faintly visible if a sufficient quantity of serum was fractionated. Other minor fractions were only sometimes apparent: *cd* intermediate in mobility between C and D was found in 2 of the 15 salmon; and an *ef* was also found in 2.

The serum electrophoretic pattern of 64 UDN-diseased salmon was examined in detail. In contrast to the constant protein pattern visible in healthy salmon sera, the pattern in UDN-infected salmon was considerably varied. These variations appear to represent a range of change in response to the progression of UDN as indicated by the appearance of the diseased fish and by their serum protein levels.

Of the major fractions B to F, B and C remained apparently constant; fraction D tended to disappear. What happened to the E and F fractions depended on the stage of the disease. In fish where the disease had not progressed too far, as shown by only a slight reduction in serum protein, the E and more markedly the F fractions tended to show an increase (Fig. 38.2b) and an *ef* fraction was found between them (Fig. 38.2b and c). Sometimes a *cd* fraction was seen between C and D.

However, in heavily diseased fish with a low serum protein level, the E and F bands tended to disappear altogether, and there was no sign of extra fractions (Fig. 38.2d).

From these results in the series of 64 diseased salmon studied, the course of change with progressive UDN emerged, illustrated by Figure 38.2. There is a progressive reduction in the serum protein level. This is initially due to a decrease of fraction D even while fractions E and F are increased and an extra fraction develops in the *ef* and perhaps the *cd* positions (referred to as the "UDN-specific protein pattern" and found at a mean protein level of 4.37 g%). Eventually this is followed by an overall decrease in the E and F, *ef* and *cd* fractions as well, leaving only the B and C fractions.

Table 38.9 shows the range and relative values of the D, E, and F serum fractions of healthy salmon. In contrast to this, 50 out of 64 UDN-infected salmon showed a D relative value of less than 99, viz., below the normal range, and 50% of the diseased salmon showed the extra *ef* fraction of relative values up to 85. In healthy fish this fraction is absent or too faint to register in scanning.

Serum electrophoretic patterns of UDN-infected salmon from seven major Irish rivers and one Scottish river all showed comparable results, so the UDN-associated changes are general, and not just a local phenomenon.

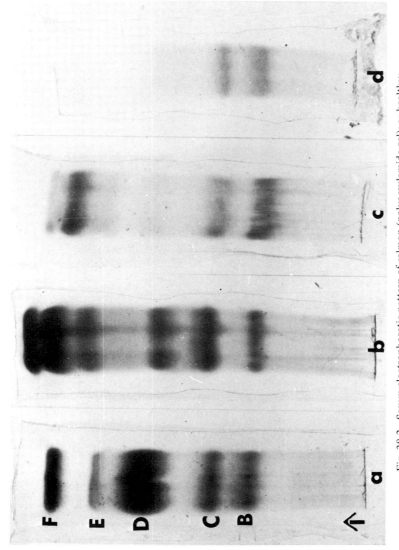

Fig. 38.2. Serum electrophoretic pattern of salmon (polyacrylamide gel): a: healthy; b, c, d: UDN-infected.

937

Table 38.9. Relative Concentration Values of Major Serum Protein Fractions
in Healthy and UDN-infected Salmon

	Relative concentration serum protein expressed as percentage of combined B and C fractions		
	D	E	F
Healthy salmon (N = 12)			
Mean	126	29	33
Range	99-149	11-45	7-57
UDN-infected salmon (N = 64)	50 out of 64 showed D value less than 99; 32 out of 64 showed an extra *ef* band of relative values up to 85.		

Serum electrophoretic patterns of salmon with simple fungal infection, salmon fingerlings with fin rot and furunculosis, and diseased trout were examined. While total serum protein levels were lower than normal in each disease, none showed changes comparable with the "UDN-specific" pattern in salmon. Even in trout, *S. trutta,* with UDN a comparable electrophoretic pattern is not seen, although there are quantitative changes.

REVIEW

A table of normal values for healthy, adult wild pike is presented, which provides baseline parameters for this species (Table 38.1). These have been discussed in a previous paper (49). In lymphoma the cellular parameters are changed, especially those of the red cell: lower red cell numbers, lower hemoglobin and hematocrit, together with increased osmotic fragility and decreased maturity of circulating cells. Similar changes are reported in the blood of mice with leukemias induced by Rauscher virus: increased osmotic fragility and autohemolysis of young and old cells precede and persist through the mouse leukemia. It was considered that the Rauscher virus had a direct effect on the red cell membrane quite apart from the leukemogenic effect (12, 21). It is possible that a similar mechanism is operating in the pike lymphoma, though it is uncertain yet whether an oncogenic virus is in fact involved. The relative numbers of the different white cells change, and the percentage of typical lymphocytes falls. The total number of white blood cells does not change until later in the disease, when it rises markedly.

The increased fragility of red cells was first noticed in fixed smears because there were relatively more "ghost" cells visible in the blood of the lymphoma-bearing pike. Such cells have been reported also by others (75, 79; D. A. Conroy, personal communication), and were considered to be due to the experimental rupture of old red cells. Experimentally the number of "ghosts" may be reduced by preparing smears differently: a small drop of blood is placed on a cover slip, another cover slip is lowered flat over it, and as the latter settles and spreads the blood the second cover slip is rapidly but gently removed by sideways movement (C. Winqvist, personal communication). Using this method of smear preparation, the number of "ghost" cells is still greater than normal in lymphoma-bearing pike.

Total serum protein was lower in lymphoma-bearing pike. Such a reduction is common in fish diseases. The lower level was reflected in all major fractions separated on polyacrylamide gel. In reports of serum proteins of amphibians, birds, and mammals with a variety of tumors, albumins have been lower than normal but an elevated globulin fraction has been found in a number of instances (4, 11, 19, 24, 27, 80, 81).

No major change in globulin level occurred in the pike with lymphoma. Minor changes in globulin level would not be detected by the electrophoretic method used. Changes were visible in the level of some serum protein fractions of four pike with induced tumors. The significance of these is not known, in view of the absence of change in spontaneous lymphoma.

The overall comparison of the blood of lymphomatous with normal pike would suggest that the stem cell type of the tumor is a hemocytoblast rather than an immunoblast. The hemocytoblast of fish is considered to be the totipotential stem cell, giving rise to all the blood cells (17, 40), and derangement of such cells could be expected to produce change in all blood cells, red and white, as occurs in the case of the lymphoma.

Normal blood values for healthy adult salmon in fresh water are given in Table 38.5. The values for hematocrit, hemoglobin, and osmotic fragility are based on too few fish to provide representative baselines, but they are included with the other parameters because of the difficulties involved in getting blood of healthy salmon from fresh water. The blood values given here agree generally with those in the literature (3, 6, 20; D. A. Conroy, personal communication). The increase in hematocrit and hemoglobin from fingerling to adult salmon in the sea, and the fall-off in these values on return to fresh water, together with the changes in white cell number, have been reported also by others (3, 6, 20). Benditt et al. (3) have found that there is compensation for the drop in hemoglobin and hematocrit in prespawning salmon, as the hemoglobin then has a higher affinity for oxygen than before.

These changes with maturity and habitat emphasize once again the variation found within what is normal for a species, and the need for baseline values for comparison to be provided under the conditions in question.

The main differences between the blood of adult pike and salmon in fresh water is the greater number of red and white cells in the pike. High red cell number is associated with high activity (22), but this generalization seems inappropriate in the case of pike and salmon.

The finding of a UDN-specific serum electrophoretic pattern provides a feasible method of diagnosis of UDN outbreaks in salmon until such time as the etiological agent of the disease is known or until a more convenient method is provided.

CONCLUSION

Changes in the blood are associated with both lymphoma in pike and UDN in salmon. They are very different, being mainly cell-associated in the former and serum-associated in the latter. A fall in total protein is found in each case, but this is probably a nonspecific effect of disease and stress, aggravated by leakage from tumors and ulcers, and perhaps by a disturbance of kidney function, as evidenced by the loss in the first instance of the lower molecular weight proteins, the albumins. Thus, provided the homeostatic flexibility of the different species is kept in mind, studies of fish blood in health and in disease may throw light on etiology, progression, or diagnosis.

Acknowledgment. I wish to thank the officers of the Inland Fisheries Trust Inc. and also Chief Fishery Inspector Dan Good, who supplied most of the fish used in these studies. The work was supported in part by a grant from the Irish Cancer Society.

REFERENCES

1. Anderson, J. I. W., and Conroy, D. A. Vibrio disease in marine fishes, pp. 266–272. In *A Symposium on Disease of Fishes and Shellfishes,* ed. S. F. Snieszko. Amer. Fish. Soc., Spec. Publ. 5. Washington, D.C., 1970.
2. Barnhart, R. A. Effects of certain variables on hematological characteristics of rainbow trout. *Trans. Amer. Fish. Soc. 98:* 3. 1969.
3. Benditt, E., et al. The blood of the Atlantic salmon during migration. *Biol. Bull. (Woods Hole) 80:* 429–440. 1941.
4. Bernfield, P., and Wan, J. Further studies on abnormal serum proteins in tumor-bearing hosts. *Proc. Soc. Exp. Biol. Med. 117:* 675–681. 1964.
5. Besse, P. L'Anémie pernicieuse des truites. *Bull. fr. piscicult. 118:* 73–83. 1958.
6. Black, E. C., Tucker, H. H., and Kirkpatrick, D. Oxygen dissociation curves of the blood of Atlantic salmon (*Salmo salar*) acclimated to summer and winter temperatures. *J. Fish. Res. Board Can. 23:* 1187–1195. 1966.
7. Booke, H. E. Blood serum protein and calcium levels in yearling brook trout. *Progr. Fish-Cult. 26:* 107–110. 1964.
8. Booke, H. E. A review of variations found in fish serum proteins. *N. Y. Fish Game J. 11*(1): 47–57. 1964.
9. Bouck, G. R., and Ball, R. C. Influence of a diurnal oxygen pulse on fish serum proteins. *Trans. Amer. Fish. Soc. 94:* 363–370. 1965.
10. Bouck, G. R., and Ball, R. C. Influence of capture methods on blood characters and mortality of rainbow trout (*Salmo gairdneri*). *Trans. Amer. Fish. Soc. 95*(2): 170–176. 1966.
11. Brenneman, M., and Rigby, P. Protein electrophoretic patterns of serum and peritoneal fluid in normal, and tumor-bearing and immune mice. *Cancer Res. 28:* 1138–1142. 1968.

12. Brodsky, I., and Benham Kahn, S.   Effect of a leukemia virus on erythropoiesis. *J. Nat. Cancer Inst. 42*(1): 39–49. 1969.
13. Carbery, J. T.   Observations on blood parameters of brown trout with U.D.N. *Res. Vet. Sci. 11:* 491–493. 1970.
14. Carbery, J. T., and Strickland, K. L.   Ulcerative dermal necrosis (U.D.N.). *Irish Vet. J. 22:* 171–175. 1968.
15. Cardwell, R. D., and Smith, L. S.   Hematological manifestations of vibriosis on juvenile chinook salmon. *Progr. Fish-Cult. 33*(4): 232–235. 1971.
16. Cardwell, R. D., Saddler, J. B., and Smith, L. S.   Hematological effects of Dennison tagging upon a juvenile pink salmon (*Oncorhynchus gorbuscha*). *Comp. Biochem. Physiol. 38*(3): 497–508.
17. Catton, W. T.   Blood cell formation in certain teleost fishes. *Blood J. Hematol. 6:* 39–60. 1951.
18. Clem, L. W., and Sigel, M. M.   Comparative immunochemical and immunological reactions in marine fishes with soluble viral and bacterial antigens. *Fed. Proc. 22*(4): 1138. 1963.
19. Deckers, C.   Electrophoretic and immunoelectrophoretic study of proteins of the rat with leucosarcoma, pp. 105–108. In *Protides of the Biological Fluids*, ed. H. Peeters. New York, Amer. Elsevier, 1963.
20. Drabkina, B. M.   Investigating the blood of mature kura salmon and their young. *Tr. soveshch. Ikhtiol. Kom. 8:* 372–379. 1958.
21. Ebert, P. S., et al.   Erythropoietic responses of mice to infection with Rauscher leukemia virus. *Cancer Res. 32:* 41–47. 1972.
22. Eisler, R.   Erythrocyte counts and hemoglobin content in species of marine teleosts. *Chesapeake Sci. 6*(2): 119–120. 1965.
23. Flemming, H.   Untersuchungen über der Bluteiweisskorpen gesunder und bauchwassersuchtkranker Karpfen. *Z. Fisch. 7:* 91–152. 1958.
24. Fletcher, O. J., and Olson, C.   Alteration of serum proteins in chickens with a lymphoid tumor. *J. Nat. Cancer Inst. 43:* 1005–1011. 1969.
25. Fujiya, M.   Use of electrophoretic serum separation in fish studies. *J. Nat. Pollut. Contr. Fed. 33:* 250–257. 1961.
26. Great Britain. Ministry of Agriculture, Fisheries and Food.   United Kingdom fish diseases, pp. 33–42. In *Annual Report.* 1971.
27. Hadji-Azimi, I.   Electrophoretic study of the serum proteins of normal and lymphoid tumor-bearing *Xenopus. Nature (London) 221:* 264–265. 1969.
28. Hawkins, R. I., and Mawdesley-Thomas, L. E.   Fish hematology—a bibliography. *J. Fish Biol. 4:* 193–232. 1972.
29. Hodgins, H. O., Ridgway, G. J., and Utter, F. M.   Electrophoretic mobility of an immune globulin from rainbow trout serum. *Nature (London) 208:* 5015, 1106–1107. 1965.
30. Houston, A. H., Madden, J. A., Woods, R. J., and Miles, H. M.   Variations in the blood and tissue chemistry of brook trout, *Salvelinus fontinalis,* subsequent to handling, anesthesia and surgery. *J. Fish. Res. Board Can. 28:* 635–642. 1971.
31. Hunn, J. B.   Some patho-physiologic effects of bacterial kidney disease in brook trout. *Proc. Soc. Exp. Biol. Med. 117:* 383–385. 1964.

32. Johansson, M.   Observations on a type of gill disease in Atlantic salmon, *Salmo salar*. *Bull. Off. int. Épizoot. 69:* 1385–1389. 1968.
33. Katz, M., Some interesting cells in the blood of a diseased silver salmon fingerling. *Copeia 4:* 295–298. 1950.
34. Kawatsu, H.   Studies on the anemia of fish. II.   Hemorrhagic anemia of rainbow trout induced by repeated bleedings. *Bull. Freshwater Fish. Res. Lab. Tokyo 18*(1): 61–66. 1968.
35. Kawatsu, H.   Studies on the anemia of fish. III.   An example of macrocytic anemia found in brook trout (*Salvelinus fontinalis*). *Bull. Freshwater Res. Lab. Tokyo 19*(2): 161–167. 1969.
36. de Kinkelin, P., and Turdu, Y. le.   L'Enzootie d'ulcerative dermal necrosis du saumon (*Salmo salar L.*).   I.   Report preliminaire. *Bull. fr. piscicult.* (in press).
37. Klontz, G. W., and Smith, L. S.   Methods of using fish as biological research subjects, pp. 323–385.   In *Methods of Animal Experimentation,* ed. W. I. Gay, vol. 3. 3 vols. New York and London, Academic Press, 1965–68.
38. Klontz, G. W., Yasutake, W. T., and Parisot, T. J.   Virus diseases of the Salmonidae in western Unived States. III.   Immunopathological aspects. *Ann. N. Y. Acad. Sci. 126:* 531–542. 1965.
39. Klontz, G. W., Yasutake, W. T., and Ross, A. J.   Bacterial diseases of the Salmonidae in the western United States: Pathogenesis of furunculosis in rainbow trout. *Am. J. Vet. Res. 27:* 1455–1460. 1966.
40. Klontz, G. W., et al.   The application of hematological techniques to fishery research. Unpublished. 13 pp. 1964.
41. Koroleva, N. V.   Variation in the content of protein in the blood serum of rainbow trout as related to age and food. *Dokl. Akad. Nauk SSSR, Biol. Sci. Sect. 148:* 1185–1186. 1963.
42. Leutelt, R.   Das weisse Blutbild des gesunden und ein infektioser Bauchwassersucht erkrankten Karpfens (*Cyprinus carpio L.*).   Dissertation, Munich. 1960. Cited by H.-H. Reichenbach-Klinke in *Bull. Off. int. Épizoot. 65:* 1039–1054. 1966.
43. Liebmann, H., et al.   Elecktrophoretische Blutuntersuchungen bei normalen und bauchwassersuchtkranken Karpfen. *Allg. Fischerei-Ztg. 85:* 502–506. 1960.
44. McKim, J. M., Christensen, G. M., and Hunt, E. P.   Changes in the blood of brook trout (*Salvelinus fontinalis*) after short term and long term exposure to copper. *J. Fish. Res. Board Can. 27*(10): 1883–1889. 1970.
45. Marsh, M. C., and Gorham, F. P.   Hemoglobin estimates and blood counts in fishes in health and disease—a review. Biol. Soc. Wash. *Science (Wash., D.C.) 23:* 666. 1906.
46. Mulcahy, M. F.   Lymphosarcoma in the pike *Esox lucius* L. in Ireland. *Proc. Roy. Irish Acad.,* Sect. B *63:* 103–129. 1963.
47. Mulcahy, M. F.   Serum protein changes in diseased Atlantic salmon. *Nature (London) 215:* 143–144. 1967.
48. Mulcahy, M. F.   Serum protein changes in U.D.N.-infected Atlantic salmon: A possible method of diagnosis. *J. Fish Biol. 1:* 333–338. 1969.
49. Mulcahy, M. F.   Blood values in the pike *Esox lucius* L. *J. Fish Biol. 2:* 203–209. 1970.

50. Mulcahy, M. F.   The thymus glands and lymphosarcoma in the pike *Esox lucius* L. (Pisces; Esocidae) in Ireland. In *Comparative Leukaemia Research* (1969), ed. R. M. Dutcher, *Bibl. Haemat. 36:* 600–609. Karger, 1970.

51. Mulcahy, M. F., and O'Leary, A.   Cell-free transmission of lymphosarcoma in the northern pike, *Esox lucius* L. (Pisces; Esocidae). *Experientia (Basel) 26:* 891. 1970.

52. Mulcahy, M. F., and O'Rourke, F. J.   Cancerous pike in Ireland. *Irish Natur. J. 14:* 312–315. 1964.

53. Mulcahy, M. F., Winqvist, G., and Dawe, C. J.   The neoplastic cell type in lymphoreticular neoplasms of the northern pike, *Esox lucius* L. *Cancer Res. 30:* 2712–2717. 1970.

54. Munro, A. L. S.   Ulcerative dermal necrosis, a disease of migratory salmonid fishes in the rivers of the British Isles. *Biol. Conserv. 2:* 2–5. 1970.

55. Papermaster, B. W., et al.   Evolution of the immune response. I. The phylogenetic development of adaptive immunologic responsiveness in vertebrates. *J. Exp. Med. 119*(1): 105. 1964.

56. Piggins, D. J.   Salmon and sea trout hybrids (1969–'70). *Annu. rep. Salmon Res. Trust Ireland 15:* 41–58. 1970.

57. Post, G.   The immune response of rainbow trout (*Salmo gairdneri*) to *Aeromonas hydrophila*. *Utah Dep. Fish Game, Inform. Bull. 63:* 7. 1963.

58. Qureshi, M. D., Hledin, R. V., Vanstone, W. E., and Anastassiadis, P. A.   Levels of constituents of glycoproteins in the sera of Pacific salmon. *J. Fish. Res. Board Can. 28*(8): 1173–1179. 1971.

59. Roberts, R. J., et al.   The pathology of ulcerative dermal necrosis of Scottish salmon. *J. Pathol. 97:* 563–565. 1969.

60. Roberts, R. J., et al.   Studies of ulcerative dermal necrosis of salmonids. I. The skin of the normal salmon head. *J. Fish Biol. 2:* 223–229. 1970.

61. Roberts, R. J., Shearer, W. M., Munro, A. L. S., and Elson, K. C. R.   Studies on ulcerative dermal necrosis of salmonids. II. The sequential pathology of the lesions. *J. Fish Biol. 2:* 373–378. 1970.

62. Scarpelli, D.G., Greider, M.H., and Frajola, W.J.   Observations on hepatic cell hyperplasia, adenoma and hepatoma of rainbow trout (*Salmo gairdneri*). *Cancer Res. 23*(6): 848–857. 1963.

63. Sindermann, C. J., and Mairs, D. F.   Serum protein changes in diseased sea herring. *Anat. Rec. 131:* 599–600. 1958.

64. Smith, C. E.   Hematological changes in coho salmon fed a folic acid deficient diet. *J. Fish. Res. Board Can. 25*(1): 151–156. 1968.

65. Smith, C. E., and Halver, J. E.   Folic acid anemia in coho salmon. *J. Fish. Res. Board Can. 26*(1): 111–114. 1969.

66. Smith, C. E., et al.   Phenylhydrazine-induced anemia in chinook salmon. *Toxicol. Appl. Pharmacol. 20:* 73–81. 1971.

67. Snieszko, S. F.   Microhematocrit values in rainbow trout, brown trout and brook trout. *Progr. Fish-Cult. 23:* 114–119. 1961.

68. Snieszko, F. S., Miller, J. A., and Atherton, C. R.   Selected hematological and biochemical tests performed with blood and serum of adult rainbow trout (*Salmo gairdneri*) with a high incidence of hepatoma. *Annals N. Y. Acad. Sci. 3:* 793–821. 1969.

69. Sprague, J. B.   Measurement of pollutant toxicity to fish. I. Bioassay methods for acute toxicity. II. Utilizing and applying bioassay results. *Water Res. 3:* 793–821. 1969.

70. Sprague, J. B.   Measure of pollutant toxicity to fish. III. Sublethal effects and "safe" concentrations. *Water Res. 5:* 245–266. 1971.

71. Steucke, E. W., and Atherton, C. R.   Use of microhematocrit values to sex largemouth bass. *Progr. Fish-Cult. 27:* 87–90. 1965.

72. Stuart, M. R., and Fuller, H. T.   Mycological aspects of diseased Atlantic salmon. *Nature (London) 217:* 90–92. 1968.

73. Tugarina, P. Ya., and Ryzhova, L. N.   Age-related features of the blood of the black Baikal grayling, *Thymallus arcticus baicalensis. Dby. J. Ichthyol. 10:* 348–357 (1970).

74. Uhr, J. W., et al.   Antibody response to bacteriophage ϕ X 174 in non-mammalian vertebrates. *Proc. Soc. Exp. Biol. Med. 111(3):* 13–15. 1962.

75. Watson, L. J., Shechmeister, I. L., and Jackson, L. L.   The hematology of goldfish, *Carassius auratus. Cytologia 28:* 118–130. 1963.

76. Watson, M. E., Guenther, R. W., and Royce, R. D.   Hematology of healthy and virus-diseased sockeye salmon, *Oncorhynchus nerka. Zoologica (New York) 41:* 27–37. 1956.

77. Wedemeyer, G., and Chatterton, K.   Some blood chemistry values for the juvenile coho salmon. *J. Fish. Res. Board Can. 28(4):* 606–608. 1971.

78. Weinreb, E. L.   Studies on the histology and histopathology of the rainbow trout, *Salmo gairdneri irideus.* I. Hematology under normal and experimental conditions of inflammation. *Zoologica (New York) 43(13):* 145–153. 1958.

79. Yuki, R.   Blood cell constituents in fish. IV. On the "nuclear shadow" found in blood smear preparation. *Bull. Jap. Soc. Sci. Fish. 26:* 490–495. 1960.

80. Zacharia, T. P., and Pollard, M.   Elevated levels of α-globulins in sera from germ-free rats with 3-methylcholanthrene induced tumors. *J. Nat. Cancer Inst. 42(1):* 35–38. 1969.

81. Zeidmann, I., et al.   Serum protein changes in neoplasia. I. Studies on mice with transplantable and induced cancers. *Arch. Pathol. 85:* 481–486. 1968.

39

Melanomas in Platy/Swordtail Hybrids

HAROLD J. SOBEL
EUGENE MARQUET
KLAUS D. KALLMAN
and GLENNA J. CORLEY

A wide variety of spontaneously occurring piscine tumors have been reported in ever-increasing frequency since the middle of the nineteenth century (33, 37, 56–58). These include both benign and malignant tumors originating in tissues from each of the primitive germ layers and including both melanomas (33, 37, 57, 58) and neoplasms arising in other chromatophores of the fish corium (guanophoroma, allophoroma (57), and erythrophoroma) (56, 58). A number of reviews have been published recently (5, 46, 52, 55, 62).

Pigmented tumors of fish are not uncommon, and the variety most frequently reported is the melanoma (33, 37, 57, 58). Haüssler (34), Kosswig (42), and Reed and Gordon (51) have described invasive melanomas which have been produced experimentally in platy/swordtail hybrids by following specific breeding regimes. Gordon and co-workers, as well as others, studied these tumors from many aspects, including genetic (4, 23–25), morphological at the level of the light microscope (29, 32, 36, 51), cytochemical and chemical (17, 31, 32), tissue culture (30–32), transplantation (40, 45), regeneration (16), and hormonal influence (54). Most of this work has been discussed by Gordon in a review (26).

Melanomas as well as benign pigmented lesions (nevi) are extremely common and important lesions of man. The human melanomas are usually exceedingly malignant but often have an unpredictable clinical course. Fish melanomas are

945

morphologically very similar to their human counterparts. Because of the peculiarities of fish and their melanomas, particularly the vast store of knowledge of this gene-determined lesion and the ease with which it can be produced, these tumors are uniquely suited for use in studies aimed at developing a better understanding of human melanomas. For this reason we have undertaken a morphological study of melanomas in platy/swordtail hybrids, including the first detailed electron microscopic study of this lesion of which we are aware. Previously a few studies have touched upon the ultrastructure of this tumor (60, 61). In this study we have compared melanomas in fish to naturally occurring human, 7,12-dimethylbenzanthracene (DMBA)-induced hamster (13, 50), and transplanted mouse melanomas (Cloudman S91) (1, 11).

REVIEW OF LITERATURE

1. Genetics

For more than 40 years it has been evident that genetic factors are of primary importance for atypical pigment cell growth in fish of the genus *Xiphophorus*. Best studied are the melanomas that arise in hybrids of green swordtail (*Xiphophorus helleri*) and southern platyfish (*X. maculatus*) (18, 20, 21, 25, 34, 42, 51). All populations of *X. maculatus* are polymorphic for a variety of sex-linked co-dominant macromelanophore factors which, within their own gene pool, give rise to specific melanophore patterns. Depending on the pigment gene, the macromelanophores may be restricted to the dorsal fin, or to the caudal peduncle, or arranged in rows or bands along the flank. Size and number of spots are also a property of the macromelanophore genes. When any of the pigment genes is introduced through hybridization into a foreign *helleri* genome, the expression of the macromelanophore gene is greatly enhanced, resulting in melanosis and melanoma. Furthermore, macromelanophores appear not only earlier during ontogeny and in larger numbers, but also in many parts of the body that were free of these pigment cells in *X. maculatus*. The degree of abnormal pigmentation is less in F_1 hybrids than in backcross hybrids to *X. helleri*. After the second backcross generation no further increase in the severity of atypical pigment cell growth is observed. Hybrids without the macromelanophore gene of *X. maculatus* have normal pigmentation.

Although the emphasis of most studies has been primarily on the *maculatus* X *helleri* system, it was soon realized that pigment cell abnormalities represent a general phenomenon that occurs in many other species combinations (2, 6, 28, 67). Of the eight known species of *Xiphophorus*, five (*helleri, maculatus, variatus, montezumae,* and *milleri*) possess macromelanophore genes. As far as is known, only the pigment genes of *X. helleri* are not enhanced after hybridization. The largest melanomas arise in hybrid combinations involving either *X. montezumae cortezi, X. helleri,* or both.

Atypical pigment cell growth may occur regardless of whether one or both parental species of a hybrid combination are polymorphic for macromelanophore genes. There is no evidence that any macromelanophore factor occurs in more than one species. Recent experiments indicate that many macromelanophore genes of *X. maculatus* are population specific; identical patterns in the eight major river systems are caused by different alleles interacting with population-specific modifier systems (22, 38). Apparently no case of an F_1 hybrid has been reported in which two macromelanophore genes, one from each parental species, are enhanced simultaneously. The closest approach to such a situation is found in the hybrids between *X. maculatus* and *X. pygmaeus*, in which the macromelanophore gene of *maculatus* and a pterinophore gene of *pygmaeus* are increased in their expressions (66).

Pigment cell abnormalities including melanoma are not only found in species crosses, but are also observed in certain interpopulation hybrids of *X. maculatus* (22, 38). The gene pool of *X. maculatus* with the greatest potential for enhancing the expression of "foreign" pigment factors is that of the Jamapa stock. Certain sex-linked spotting genes of the Dio Usumacinta and Belize rivers give rise to melanomas in F_1 and backcross hybrids to Jamapa (K. D. Kallman, unpublished data).

When the different pigment genes that are responsible for identical patterns within populations of *X. maculatus* are introduced to a common foreign genotype the resulting pigment cell abnormalities will not be the same. Especially instructive is a series of crosses in which the factors responsible for the spotted dorsal pattern of *X. maculatus* of the Rios Jamapa (Jp), Coatzacoalcos (Cp), and Hondo (Hp) populations were transferred to *X. couchianus*. The phenotypic expression of Sd^{Jp} is completely suppressed, while that of Sd^{Cp} and Sd^{Hp} is strongly enhanced, but each in its nonspecific way (67).

The genotype of the stock or population into which a pigment gene is introduced is also important for the kind of atypical cell growth. Whether Sd^{Jp} gives rise to the melanoma in the dorsal fin of F_1 hybrids depends largely upon the stock of *X. helleri* (65).

At least three situations are known where pigment cell abnormalities that have a hereditary basis develop within pure stocks. Intergenic crossovers or mutations within the macromelanophore locus not only affect the expression of *Sd* within the Jamapa stock, but also change the type of interaction of Sd^{Jp} within an X. *couchianus* gene pool (41). Mutations of modifier genes induced by X-irradiation increase the expression of *Sd* and *Sp* within the Jamapa stock (3). Apparently selection for "+" modifiers is responsible for the high incidence of the *Sc* melanoma in an inbred stock of *X. montezumae cortezi* (39).

The phenomenon of pigment cell abnormalities in *Xiphophorus* is basically a problem of gene regulation. Each pigment gene is co-adapted to its own gene pool to give rise to a normal pattern. Any change either in the pigment gene itself or in the modifier system may lead to abnormal patterns, ranging from zero effect to melanoma production. Not only the macromelanophore genes are involved, but also a number of closely linked pterinophore loci. However, the changes (sup-

pression or enhancement) in pigment cell expression of two closely linked loci are
not always parallel.

2. Anatomical Observations

It has been demonstrated that pro-pigment cells (melanoblasts) originate from
the neural tube of the hybrid embryo and after migration to their definitive anatomic location develop dendritic processes and the capability to synthesize melanin (melanocytes). This process appears to be identical in all vertebrates (36). In
the dermis as well as in other sites (nerves, deep skeletal foci, body cavities, along
blood vessels) these cells increase in size, become round and sessile, and their melanin particles become capable of movement within their cytoplasm in response to
the physiological state of the animal. In short these cells become melanophores
(16, 45). When the melanin-containing cells, particularly the older melanophores,
degenerate, it is felt that their cellular debris is phagocytosed and eliminated by
macrophages (27).

The melanoblasts are small, migratory, embryonic, actively dividing cells. On
the other hand melanocytes measure from 10 to 100 microns in diameter, depending on the length of their dendritic processes. They are young cells with frequent
mitoses and are sometimes migratory. Among melanophores, three types have
been described. The smallest adheres to the scale tissues. Its significance is not
known. Micromelanophores measuring approximately 100 microns in diameter
and rarely exceeding 300 microns are observed not only in the dermis but also in
deeper foci (especially in fish with particular genetic patterns). Micromelanophores do not become tumorous. Macromelanophores averaging 300 microns in
diameter and rarely exceeding 500 microns are confined to the dermis in normal
fish. They infiltrate inward only in hybrids (19), and they alone among the black
pigment cells are involved in melanosis and the melanotic overgrowths under consideration. Melanophores are nonmigratory, older cells derived from the melanocytes and apparently are not dividing cells, as mitoses have never been observed
(26).

Depending on the stocks and genes involved, melanotic lesions in hybrids may
be present as early as the day of birth (29). At first there is a progressive replacement of the normal corial tissues by macromelanophores (29, 51). The corium
and subcutaneous tissues, inward as far as the muscle, soon become black due to
the formation of a continuous chain of macromelanophores. Myosepta are slowly invaded from the subcutaneous tissue inward, until a generalized and continuous replacement of the connective tissue from the superficial corium to the most
central parts of the body mass occurs (29, 51). The periosteum of the skeletal
parts and the pro-cartilage may be infiltrated. In one specimen it was reported
that the meninges of the spinal cord were involved (51). Following the almost
complete infiltration of the connective tissue, the muscle fibers themselves are invaded, degenerate, and are replaced by melanophores (29, 51).

Later masses of small pigmented spindle cells (melanocytes) proliferate, commencing in the corium, where they almost completely replace the macromelano-phores. These cells are small, approximately 30 microns in length, and have short dendrites. They do not resemble the small melanophore that adheres to the scale, and these melanocytes are always associated with macromelanophores in hybrid fish. These spindle cells appear to grow rapidly and mitotic activity has been ob-served. Once they begin to grow there is tumorous development with almost complete disappearance of the melanophores, and the fish usually succumb rapid-ly (29).

Previously there was no satisfactory explanation for the reversal in frequency of macromelanophores and melanocytes during the early and late stages in the de-velopment of the melanoma. One interpretation was that the macromelanophores de-differentiated into melanocytes. It is now felt that, as the melanomatous proc-ess is intensified, melanocytes multiply rapidly but do not differentiate into ma-cromelanophores.

Transplantation (36, 40, 45) and regeneration (16) studies show that melano-phores are formed from melanocytes and that the older melanophore disintegrates and is eliminated by macrophages (16, 40, 45). Melanophores appear to be the terminal stage in melanocyte maturation in tissue culture studies (32). Melano-cytes are more active metabolically than melanophores, with a higher endogenous respiration and a three times greater ability to metabolize tyrosine (35). It has also been noted that melanocytes of man, mouse, and fish are morphologically similar by tissue culture methods (30), and that the *Xiphophorus* melanoma has the highest tyrosinase activity of any vertebrate tissue treated (10).

MATERIALS AND METHODS

Seven tumorous platy/swordtail hybrids (pedigree 2078 and 2080) were ob-tained from the genetics laboratory of the New York Zoological Society. The fish were the descendants of a tumorous stock of a platy/swordtail hybrid with an *Sd* gene of *X. maculatus* that the late Dr. M. Gordon obtained from Germany in 1948 through the courtesy of Dr. Prowig. The fish of this stock represent the 19th laboratory generation, 15 of which were obtained by sib matings and 4 by crossing a tumorous fish with a member of an inbred (15th, 17th–19th genera-tions) stock (*Cd*) of *X. helleri*. Since the identity of the *Sd* gene involved is not known, this stock will eventually be eliminated, and a stock with a known *Sd* substituted. Two fish were fixed in 10% formalin and five were anesthetized with tricaine methane sulfonate (Sandoz, Inc., New York), and small pieces of tissue were removed and fixed in veronal-acetate buffered 2% osmic acid at pH 7.2 for two hours. Material from the formalin-fixed fish was washed and similar-ly post-osmicated. The remaining material was fixed in 10% buffered formalin for light microscopy.

Sixteen human melanomas were studied. These were submitted to the surgi-cal pathology laboratory for routine study in cold 4% paraformaldehyde (44) and portions were post-fixed in osmic acid, as were the fish tumors for electron microscopy.

Tumors of six DMBA-treated Syrian hamsters (13, 50) were fixed, both directly in osmic acid, as were the fish tumors, and others directly in paraformaldehyde with portions later post-fixed in osmic acid, as were the human melanomas.

Transplanted Cloudman S91 melanomas (1, 11) from six DBA/1J female mice were fixed, as were the hamster tumors.

The formalin- and paraformaldehyde-fixed tissues were dehydrated, embedded in paraffin, and used for light microscopic study. The osmicated tissues were dehydrated with graded alcohols and propylene oxide and embedded in Araldite 502. Thin sections were cut with diamond knives and mounted on bare copper grids. The sections were stained with a saturated solution of uranyl acetate in ethyl alcohol followed by lead hydroxide (47), carbon coated for stability, and examined with an RCA EMU 3F electron microscope.

OBSERVATIONS

1. Melanoma in Platy/Swordtail Hybrid

All of the pigmented lesions studied in this work superficially appear similar; however, the large oval cells (macromelanophores) are noted only in the fish melanoma (Figs. 39.1, 39.2, 39.10, 39.11).

Gross Morphology. The fish tumors are nodular tissue masses, with smooth regular surfaces having a lobulated appearance. They are deeply pigmented (black), with occasional less well pigmented grey areas, and are mostly firm, with softer areas noted only infrequently. Often fins or other anatomic structures are infiltrated and destroyed by the tumor.

Light Microscopy. The progressive alterations in melanomas of platy/swordtail hybrids were well described by Reed and Gordon (51) more than 40 years ago. These observations were further elucidated upon by Gordon and Smith (29) and reviewed in the section dealing with anatomical observations. In well-developed melanomas like those studied in this work there is a pigmented thickening of the corium with pigmented cells infiltrating the epidermis (Figs. 39.1, 39.2) surrounding and displacing scales and extending along the horizontal and intermuscular septa to the most central portions of the body mass (Fig. 39.3). In one fish tumor, cells were noted in the meninges forming an undisturbed ring around the spinal cord without invasion of the cord (Fig. 39.4). Individual muscle fibers are surrounded by tumor cells, but appear otherwise normal. This is most marked near septa and near the corium where the tumor cells are concentrated. Also seen are foci of frank nodular tumor proliferation with remnants of destroyed fin cartilage (Fig. 39.3).

Many very large, oval, occasionally round, usually densely pigmented cells with a few short stubby processes (macromelanophores) are observed in the most superficial areas of the tumor close beneath the epidermis and in the melanotic corium (Figs. 39.1, 39.2). These cells infrequently appear stellate, with an irregularity to their shape suggesting increased numbers of the more angular dendritic processes. The cells surrounding myofibers and infiltrating through intermuscular septa are interpreted as elongated forms of this cell type.

The bulk of the tumor is composed of smaller spindle cells (melanocytes). Their nuclei are somewhat larger, often elongated, with prominent nucleoli and irregular coarse deposits of nucleoprotein. Occasional mitoses are observed. The tumor cells are usually densely pigmented, so that their nuclear details are obscured. Following bleaching of the melanin pigment, for the shortest possible time to prevent excessive disruption of tissue architecture, and prolonged staining, the nuclei of the large cells (macromelanophores) are found to be relatively small, oval, occasionally multiple, and clear with small basophilic foci. Mitoses are never observed in these cells. Vascular sinuses with a thin endothelial lining and engorged with nucleated red blood cells are seen in the tumor masses.

Electron Microscopy. With the electron microscope the tumors are found to be composed of a densely packed meshwork of cells (Figs. 39.5, 39.6) infiltrating adjacent soft tissue structures such as muscle (Figs. 39.20, 39.21) and nerve. The meshwork is caused by interdigitating dendritic processes and cell bodies and closely resembles the neuropil of the central nervous system (Fig. 39.6). The extracellular space is sparse. Cell junctions are never observed (Fig. 39.5). Occasional capillaries are noted. These are separated from the tumor by a thin basement membrane and a narrow perivascular space.

Basement membrane-like material, with small oval granular foci of similar appearance in and near it, is frequently observed between tumor cells (Figs. 39.7–39.9). Melanoma cells in these areas have prominent surface activity with vesicles containing granular material of similar density and size both near and at the surface of the cell (Figs. 39.7, 39.8).

The tumor cells vary in structure and size. The very large cells (macromelanophores) are identical to the smaller cells (melanocytes) in internal structure. They differ only in that they are round to oval with a more regular cell surface and have fewer dendritic processes and occasional multiple nuclei (Figs. 39.10, 39.11).

Most macromelanophores are packed with electron-dense, oval and elongated, homogeneous pigment granules, and contain few small relatively simple organelles. These are thought to be older, more mature cells (Fig. 39.10). Earlier, less mature macromelanophores have fewer, more clumped, less mature pigment granules and more abundant cell organelles, particularly smooth endoplastic reticulum and Golgi apparatus (Fig. 39.11). Cells of varying maturity, including transitional forms, may be observed throughout the tumor (Figs. 39.5, 39.12, 39.13).

The less mature cells (usually melanocytes) have a large, actively budding Golgi apparatus with three to five saccules or cisternae, moderate numbers of small mitochondria, and abundant smooth endoplasmic reticulum. The latter is composed of short dilated channels and vesicles and is only occasionally ribosome-studded (rough). Moderate numbers of free ribosomes are noted. Microfilaments are present, but microtubules have not been found (Figs. 39.11–39.14).

The cisternae of endoplasmic reticulum in earlier cells are often slightly distended with material of moderate electron density (Figs. 39.11–39.13) with occasional small, extremely dense foci (Figs. 39.12, 39.13). Somewhat less frequently, clumps of larger but similar electron-dense granules are noted in markedly dilated sacs of smooth endoplasmic reticulum (Figs. 39.12–39.14). These clumps of electron-dense particles appear to fuse and form the oval pigment granules (Figs. 39.12, 39.14). Other small, less electron-dense, oval-to-elongated, granular, and in some areas striated, almost crystalline foci are also observed (Figs. 39.7, 39.12, 39.13, 39.15). These seem to form the elongated granules (Figs. 39.10, 39.13, 39.15). On rare occasions small, more electron-dense deposits are noted admixed with these foci (Figs. 39.13, 39.15). Each of these distinct oval and elongated pigment granules is surrounded by a single unit membrane. The latter appears to originate from the smooth endoplasmic reticulum near the inner aspect of the Golgi apparatus (the Golgi-associated endoplasmic reticulum or GERL). As the cells mature, larger and denser granules seem to accumulate, in increasing numbers (Fig. 39.10).

Large proliferations of smooth and endoplasmic reticulum are frequently noted in melanoma cells (Fig. 39.16). On occasion these form oval myelin-like figures (Figs. 39.17, 39.18).

Although typical macrophages are never observed, there are many cells resembling melanocytes. These have large, single membrane-delimited bodies containing numbers of typical pigment granules in all stages of formation and degeneration, granular material, and myelin figures, all suggesting compound melanosomes (Fig. 39.19). These large bodies resembling compound melanosomes are also observed in elongated cells with abundant rough endoplasmic material and mitochondria that otherwise resemble fibroblasts.

In foci of tumors adjacent to muscle, apparent exocytosis of small dense particles with pinocytosis of these particles by muscle cells and deposition in the sarcoplasmic reticulum is noted (Fig. 39.21). Often this dense pigment material can be found deep in the muscle (Fig. 39.20).

2. Comparison with DMBA-Induced Hamster, Transplanted Mouse (Cloudman S91), and Human Melanomas (Table 39.1)

In a procedure like that performed by many previous workers (13, 50), the costo-vertebral spots of Syrian hamsters were painted with a single application of approximately 800 μg of DMBA, and melanomas developed in four to five months. These tumors are black, nodular lesions, measuring up to 1 cm in diameter, and are situated in the dermal collagen. They exhibit no junctional change and are composed of heavily pigmented spindle cells without cytological evidence of malignancy. Mitotic activity is not observed.

The transplanted mouse melanomas (Cloudman S91) are palpable subcutane-

Table 39.1. Summary of Comparison of Melanomas in the Fish (Platy/Swordtail Hybrid), Hamster (DMBA-induced), Mouse (Transplanted Cloudman S91) and Man (Naturally Occurring)

	Macro-melanophore	Invasive-ness	Pigment granules			Clumps of SER	RER	Lipid	Surface activity & basement membranes	Villous projections
			Oval	Crystalline	Cytolysomes					
Fish	+	+++	+++	+	±	+++	+	±	++	0
Hamster	0	+	+++	+	+	+	+++	+	++	++
Mouse	0	++	0	++	++	±	+	+++	++	+
Man	0	+ to ++	0	+++	+++	0	+	++	++	+

ous masses in the lower abdomen (near the inguinal region) of DBA/1J mice (1, 11). They were examined two to three months after transplantation and were well demarcated, firm, light grey tumors with occasional soft and darker mottled areas. The tumor cells are usually large, oval to polyhedral or spindle-shaped, with a great variation of pigmentation. Some cells have little to no pigment, and a few cells have a large amount of dark brown granular melanin pigmentation. Mitotic activity in this tumor is pronounced.

Human melanomas and nevi have been described in detail by many investigators. A good recent review of their histology can be found in the Armed Forces Institute of Pathology fascicle on tumor pathology devoted to "Melanotic Tumors of the Skin" (43). The tumors (both benign nevi and malignant melanomas) examined by us include a wide variety of these lesions.

Electron Microscopy. The fish melanoma differs from those of the hamster, the mouse, and man by the presence of macromelanophores which are absent in the other lesions. Unlike the fish melanoma, the others are composed of more loosely spaced cell nests with a more pronounced extracellular space (Fig. 39.22). Junctional change and desmosomes are seen only in the human melanoma. Although all tumors are locally infiltrating, only the fish melanoma is regularly deeply invasive and destructive.

All melanoma cells except those of the fish reveal irregular villous-like cytoplasmic projections (Fig. 39.22). The tumor cells exhibit prominent surface activity with many vesicles containing granular substances of density similar to that of the basement membrane-like material found in adjacent areas in the fish melanoma.

Microtubules and filaments are seen in all melanomas except the fish, where microtubules are never demonstrated. Pigmentation of adjacent muscle is observed only in the fish.

All melanomas are similarly composed of early, intermediate, and mature cells, as described in detail for the fish lesion. However, this distinction is least obvious in the mouse melanoma, where pigment formation is not as abundant. In all tumors the Golgi apparatus is large and active and the mitochondria small and sparse with a simple architecture. The hamster melanoma has many large, dilated channels of rough endoplasmic reticulum in early cells, as seen in actively secreting organs. The other melanomas reveal little rough endoplasmic reticulum and more somewhat-dilated sacs of smooth reticulum. Clumps of smooth reticulum, never as much as in the fish, are observed in the hamster and to a lesser extent in the mouse lesion. Cytolysomes and clumps of free ribosomes are seen in all tumors but are most frequent in those of the mouse and man.

The pigment granules of the hamster melanoma most closely resemble those of the fish tumors. The dark unit membrane-enclosed granules seem to form as they do in the fish. Groups of three or more round-to-oval granules are noted in individual membrane-enclosed units (Fig. 39.22). In older cells single large, bosselated electron-dense granules are formed. The crystalline formations, similar to those in the fish tumors, are also observed in the hamster. In the mouse and human melanomas most granules are single membrane-delimited with a fibrillar internal structure having a regular zigzag pattern (Fig. 39.23). They appear to be formed like the crystalline granules of the fish. Compound melanosomes containing the simpler pigment granules are most commonly seen in the human melanoma (Fig. 39.23). They are less abundant in the mouse and the hamster lesion, and are rare in that of the fish. Lipid-like inclusions are most frequent in the mouse lesion, less frequent in human tumors, uncommon in the hamster, and rare in the fish melanomas. Invaginations of cytoplasmic material into the nucleus, thus forming inclusions, are present in all lesions. Small vesicles resembling type-C virus particles were found only in two human melanomas.

REVIEW

One of the best-studied and most clearly understood hereditary diseases in experimental animals is melanoma in the platy/swordtail hybrid. Genetic and anatomical studies of this tumor have been discussed in detail in the review of literature. Pigment cell abnormalities in *Xiphophorus* are a problem of gene regulation of the pigment cell or its modifier systems. These alterations can occur within pure stocks of a single species either spontaneously or following external treatment such as X-irradiation (3). This suggests that similar factors might also be involved in the formation of melanomas in the human species.

The macromelanophore gene is potentially injurious. All the fish melanomas are composed in part of this distinctive cell which develops from the melanocyte (16, 45). Mitoses have never been observed in macromelanophores, and they are thought to be an end-stage cell. When the melanin-containing cells degenerate they are eliminated and are thought to be phagocytosed in part (16, 27, 40, 45). Although autophagocytosis is demonstrated in this study and by others (60), we have thus far been unable to document phagocytosis of degenerating cells and/or debris by macrophages. The failure of melanocytes to differentiate into macromelanophores is also not clearly understood. It may be caused by inadequate time for full maturation of these rapidly proliferating cells. It has been suggested that the melanocytes may be altered genetically and thus their differentiation into macromelanophores is prevented. This change may extend to proliferative capacity and life span of the melanocyte (26). This hypothesis proposes that, at least in fish, melanomas are products of a genetically controlled process which inhibits the normal differentiation of pigment cells (26).

1. Electron Microscopy of Fish Melanoma

Although the ultrastructure of melanin-forming cells (7-9, 15) and of melanomas of the mouse (12, 14, 48, 64), the hamster (14, 48, 49, 64), and man (59, 63, 64) has been studied in detail, there are only a few studies of xiphophoran melanomas existent (60, 61). These are sketchy but are in agreement with most of the work presented in this paper. It must be understood that there is considerable variability in tumor cells in the same lesion, and that variability in tumors of different species and in natural, induced, and transplanted tumors is to be expected. Nevertheless, we feel that the comparison of these lesions is of value.

Genesis of Melanin Granules. The ultrastructural observations reported in this work provide a reasonable description of a mechanism for the formation of melanin granules in the fish melanoma. Moderately electron-dense material accumulates in dilated sacs of smooth endoplasmic reticulum, usually near the inner aspect of the Golgi apparatus (GERL), and small, oval, denser foci are noted in many of these channels. Clumps of the very dense foci appear to fuse in dilated channels of smooth endoplasmic reticulum, forming the vastly more numerous mature oval granules. Infrequently, the sacs of endoplasmic reticulum appear to expand and to contain granular, almost striated areas within them. Dense foci condense on these crystalline-appearing areas, forming the infrequent elongated granules.

Ageing of Melanoma Cells. It has been possible to distinguish two broad but interrelated groups of cells within lesions. Their ultrastructure also suggests age differences. The macromelanophores are much larger, round to oval, and have fewer dendritic processes and occasional multiple nuclei, but never mitotic activity. The melanocytes are much smaller, usually elongated, and have prominent cell processes and frequent mitoses. Their internal structure, however, is identical to that of the melanophore, except that most melanophores are packed with mature pigment granules and contain a relatively simple organelle system, while very many melanocytes have fewer pigment granules and a well-defined cytoarchitecture. We believe that these observations indicate that melanophores are older and melanocytes earlier cells, although melanocytes exhibit transitional and mature forms also. Earlier melanophores are less frequently observed. The observations of Vielkind, Vielkind, and Anders (60) suggest that this interpretation is accurate, since in rapidly proliferating melanomas melanophores were found to be scarce or absent. Both Weissenfels, Schäffer, and Bretthauer (61) and the present investigators noted prominent pinocytotic activity at the surfaces of xiphophoran melanoma cells. We believe that basement membrane-like material is exocytosed by melanoma cells in these areas. Weissenfels, Schäffer, and Bretthauer (61) believe that muscle, even at a distance from the melanoma, degenerates and that there is a dystrophic effect. In the present study muscle in the region of the tumor appears well preserved, but is obviously pinocytosing dense pigment granules that are being excreted by adjacent tumor cells. The muscle is sequestering them in the sarcoplasmic reticulum.

Large proliferations of smooth endoplasmic reticulum are observed in many melanoma cells. Similar proliferations are seen in a variety of cells in which this organelle is extremely active, e.g., liver, proximal renal tubule, retina, interstitial cell of testis.

2. Comparison with Other Melanomas

Pigment granules in the hamster melanoma are very similar to those in the fish. In both human and mouse lesions the pigment granules appear to form by deposition of dense material over a fibrillar structure with a regular zigzag pattern. It is believed that the enzyme tyrosinase is found in these foci as well as in the GERL, supporting the hypothesis that the granules arise in this area. This is consistent with the morphological and histochemical evidence of Novikoff, Albala, and Biempica (48) the biochemical evidence of Seji (53), and the autoradiographic evidence of Zelickson, Hirsch, and Hartmann (68). We believe that the organization or concentration of this enzyme in the pre-melanosome differs in these animals and accounts for the differences observed. The compound melanosomes are found in cells identical to melanoma cells, suggesting their autophagic character.

SUMMARY

Melanomas in platy/swordtail hybrids were studied with the light and electron microscopes and compared with naturally occurring human, DMBA-induced hamster, and transplanted Cloudman S91 mouse melanomas.

The fish tumors are characterized by the presence of macromelanophores. They are invasive and destructive. The interrelationship of specific tumor cell types, their maturation, and the genesis of pigment granules and basement membrane-like material is discussed.

Acknowledgment. Supported in part by research grant AM-12818 from the National Institutes of Health, U.S. Public Health Service.

The authors wish to express their gratitude to Dr. Ruth Schwarz for her patient criticism of this work and to Mrs. Juanita Manning for her care and patience in typing the manuscript.

REFERENCES

1. Algire, G. H. Growth and pathology of melanoma S91 in mice of strains dba, A, and C. *J. Nat. Cancer Inst. 5:* 151. 1944.
2. Anders, A., and Klinke, K. Untersuchungen über die erbbedingte Aminosaürenkonzentration, Farbenmanifestation und Tumorbildung bei lebendgebärenden Zahnkarpfen (Poeciliidae). *Z. Vererbungsl. 96:* 49. 1965.
3. Anders, A., Anders, F., and Pursglove, D. L. X-ray induced mutations of the genetically-determined melanoma system of xiphophorin fish. *Experientia 27:* 931. 1971.
4. Anders, F. Tumour formation in platyfish-swordtail hybrids as a problem of gene regulation. *Experientia 23:* 1. 1967.
5. Ashley, L. M. Experimental fish neoplasia, p. 23. In *Fish in Research*, ed.

O. W. Neuhaus and J. E. Halver. New York and London, Academic Press, 1969.

6. Atz, J. W. Effects of hybridization on pigmentation in fishes of the genus *Xiphophorus. Zoologica (New York) 47:* 153. 1962.

7. Birbeck, M. S. C. Electron microscopy of melanocytes: the fine structure of hair-bulb premelanosomes. *Ann. N. Y. Acad. Sci. 100:* 540. 1963.

8. Birbeck, M. S. C., and Barnicot, N. A. Electron microscope studies on pigment formation in human hair follicles, p. 549. In *Pigment Cell Biology,* ed. M. Gordon. New York and London, Academic Press, 1959.

9. Charles, A., and Ingram, J. T. Electron microscope observations of the melanocyte of the human epidermis. *J. Biophys. Biochem. Cytol. 6:* 41. 1959.

10. Chavin, W. Fundamental aspects of morphological color changes in vertebrate skin. *Amer. Zool. 9:* 505. 1969.

11. Cloudman, A. M. The effect of an extra-chromosomal influence upon transplanted spontaneous tumors in mice. *Science (Wash., D.C.) 93:* 380. 1941.

12. Dalton, A. J., and Felix, M. D. Phase contrast and electron micrography of the Cloudman S91 mouse melanoma, p. 267. In *Pigment Cell Growth,* ed. M. Gordon. New York and London: Academic Press, 1953.

13. Della Porta G., Rappaport, H., Saffiotti, U., and Shubik, P. Induction of melanotic lesions during skin carcinogenesis in hamsters. *Arch. Pathol. 61:* 305. 1956.

14. Demopoulos, H. B., Kasuga, T., Channing, A.-A., and Bagdoyan, H. Comparison of ultrastructure of B-16 and S-91 mouse melanomas, and correlation with growth patterns. *Lab. Invest. 14:* 108. 1965.

15. Drochmans, P. Electron microscope studies of epidermal melanocytes, and the fine structure of melanin granules. *J. Biophys. Biochem. Cytol. 8:* 165. 1960.

16. Ermin, R., and Gordon, M. Regeneration of melanomas in fishes. *Zoologica (New York) 40:*53. 1955.

17. Fitzpatrick, T. B., Lerner, A. B., Calkins, E., and Summerson, W. H. Occurrence of tyrosinase in horse and fish melanomas. *Proc. Soc. Exp. Biol. Med. 75:* 394. 1950.

18. Gordon, M. Hereditary basis of melanosis in hybrid fishes. *Amer. J. Cancer 15:* 1495. 1931.

19. Gordon, M. Morphology of the heritable color pattern in the Mexican killifish, Platypoecilus. *Amer. J. Cancer 15:* 732. 1931.

20. Gordon, M. Effects of five primary genes on the site of melanomas in fishes and the influence of two color genes on their pigmentation. In *The Biology of Melanomas. Spec. Publ. N. Y. Acad. Sci. 4:* 216. 1948.

21. Gordon, M. Heredity of pigmented tumours in fish. *Endeavour 9:* 26. 1950.

22. Gordon, M. The variable expressivity of a pigment cell gene from zero effect to melanotic tumor induction. *Cancer Res. 11:* 676. 1951.

23. Gordon, M. The influence of the mating system upon normal and atypical pigment cell growth. *Extrait de ACTA 9:* 787. 1953.

24. Gordon, M. The genetics of fish diseases. *Trans. Amer. Fish. Soc. 83:* 229. 1954.

25. Gordon, M. A genetic concept for the origin of melanomas. *Ann. N. Y. Acad. Sci. 71:* 1213. 1958.

26. Gordon, M. The melanoma cell as an incompletely differentiated pigment cell, p. 215. In *Pigment Cell Biology,* ed. M. Gordon. New York and London, Academic Press, 1959.

27. Gordon, M., and Lansing, W. Cutaneous melanophore eruptions in young fish during stages preceding melanotic tumor formation. *J. Morph. 73:* 231. 1943.

28. Gordon, M., and Smith, G. M. The production of a melanotic neoplastic disease in fishes by selective matings. *Amer. J. Cancer 34:* 543. 1938.

29. Gordon, M., and Smith, G. M. Progressive growth stages of a heritable melanotic neoplastic disease in fishes from the day of birth. *Amer. J. Cancer 34:* 255. 1938.

30. Grand, C. G., Gordon, M., and Cameron, G. Neoplasm studies VIII. Cell types in tissue culture of fish melanotic tumors compared with mammalian melanomas. *Cancer Res. 1:* 660. 1941.

31. Greenberg, S. S., and Kopac, M. J. Studies of gene action and melanogenic enzyme activity in melanomatous fishes. *Ann. N. Y. Acad. Sci. 100:* 887. 1963.

32. Greenberg, S. S., Lopac, M. J., and Gordon, M. Cytology and cytochemistry of melanoma cells. *Ann. N. Y. Acad. Sci. 67:* 55. 1956.

33. Haddow, A., and Blake, I. Neoplasms in fish: A report of six cases with a summary of the literature. *J. Pathol. Bacteriol. 36:* 41. 1933.

34. Haüssler, G. Über Melanombildungen bei Bastarden von *Xiphophorus hellerii* und *Platypoecilus maculatus* var. *rubra. Klin. Wochenschr. 7:* 1561. 1928.

35. Humm, D. G., and Clark, E. E. The metabolism of melanomas in platyfish-swordtail hybrids. *J. Nat. Cancer Inst. 16:* 741. 1955.

36. Humm, D. G., and Young, R. S. The embryological origin of pigment cells in platyfish-swordtail hybrids. *Zoologica (New York) 41:* 1. 1956.

37. Johnstone, J. J. Malignant tumours in fish. *J. Mar. Biol. Ass. U. K. 13:* 447. 1924.

38. Kallman, K. D. Different genetic bases of identical pigment patterns in the teleost *Xiphophorus maculatus. Copeia 3:* 472. 1970.

39. Kallman, K. D. Inheritance of melanophore patterns and sex determination in the Montezuma swordtail, *Xiphophorus montezumae cortezi* Rosen. *Zoologica (New York) 56:* 77. 1971.

40. Kallman, K. D., and Gordon, M. Transplantation of potentially and definitive melanomatous fins in hybrid fishes of strain *Sd. Proc. Amer. Ass. Cancer Res. 2:* 220. 1957.

41. Kallman, K., and Schreibman, M. P. The origin and possible genetic control of new stable pigment patterns in the poeciliid fish, *Xiphophorus maculatus. J. Exp. Zool. 176:* 147. 1971.

42. Kosswig, C. Z. Über Geschwülstbildungen bei Fischbastarden. *Z. Indukt. Abstamm. -u. VererbLehre 59:* 61. 1931.

43. Lund, H. Z., and Kraus, J. M. *Melanotic Tumors of the Skin.* Armed Forces Institute of Pathology, Section 1—Fascicle 3. 1962.

44. Lynn, J. A., Martin, J. H., and Race, G. J. Recent improvements of histologic

technics for the combined light and electron microscopic examination of surgical specimens. *Amer. J. Clin. Pathol. 45:* 704. 1966.

45. Marcus, T. R., and Gordon, M. Transplantation of the Sc Melanoma in fishes.
    Zoologica (New York) 39: 123. 1954.

46. Mawdesley-Thomas, L. E. Neoplasia in fish—A bibliography. *J. Fish Biol. 1:*
    187. 1969.

47. Millonig, G. A modified procedure for lead-staining of thin sections. *J. Bio-
    phys. Biochem. Cytol. 11:* 736. 1961.

48. Novikoff, A. B., Albala, A., and Biempica, L. Ultrastructural and cytochemi-
    cal observations on B-16 and Harding-Passey mouse melanomas. The origin
    of premelanosomes and compound melanosomes. *J. Histochem. Cytochem.
    16:* 299. 1968.

49. Rappaport, H., Nakai, T., and Swift, H. The fine structure of normal and neo-
    plastic melanocytes in the Syrian hamster, with particular reference to carcin-
    ogen-induced melanotic tumors. *J. Cell Biol. 16:* 171. 1963.

50. Rappaport, H., Pietra, G., and Shubik, P. The induction of melanotic tumors
    resembling cellular blue nevi in the Syrian white hamster by cutaneous appli-
    cation of 7, 12-dimethylbenz(a)anthracene. *Cancer Res. 21:* 661. 1961.

51. Reed, H. D., and Gordon, M. The morphology of melanotic overgrowths in
    hybrids of Mexican killifishes. *Amer. J. Cancer. 15:* 1524. 1931.

52. Scarpelli, D. G. Comparative aspects of neoplasia in fish and other laboratory
    animals, p. 45. In *Fish in Research,* ed. O. W. Neuhaus and J. E. Halver. New
    York and London, Academic Press, 1969.

53. Seji, M. Subcellular tyrosinase activity and site of melanogenesis in melano-
    cytes, p. 123. In *Structure and Control of the Melanocyte,* ed. G. Della Porta
    and O. Muhlbock. New York, Springer-Verlag, 1966.

54. Siciliano, M. J., Perlmutter, A., and Clark, E. Effect of sex on the develop-
    ment of melanoma in hybrid fish of the genus *Xiphophorus. Cancer Res.
    31:* 725. 1971.

55. Siperstein, M. D., and Luby, L. J. Control of cholesterol synthesis in normal
    and malignant tissue, p. 87. In *Fish in Research,* ed. O. W. Neuhaus and J. E.
    Halver. New York and London, Academic Press, 1969.

56. Smith, G. M. A cutaneous red pigmented tumor (erythrophoroma) with me-
    tastases in a flatfish (*Pseudopleuronectes americanus*). *Amer. J. Cancer 21:*
    596. 1934.

57. Takahashi, K. Studie über die Fischgeschwülste. *Z. Krebsforsch. 29:* 1.
    1929.

58. Thomas, L. Les tumeurs des poissons (étude anatomique et pathogénique).
    Bull. Ass. fr. Étude Cancer 20: 703. 1931.

59. Toshima, S., Moore, G. E., and Sandberg, A. A. Ultrastructure of human
    melanoma in cell culture. *Cancer 21:* 202. 1968.

60. Vielkind, J., Vielkind, U., and Anders, F. Melanotic and amelanotic melano-
    mas in xiphophorin fish. *Cancer Res. 31:* 868. 1971.

61. Weissenfels, N., Schäffer, D., and Bretthauer, R. Über die Entartung der
    Makromelanophoren und den Einfluss des infiltrierenden Melanomwachstums

auf die Muskulatur von Poeciliiden-Bastarden. *Virchows Arch. Abt. B. Zell-pathol. 5:* 144. 1970.

62. Wellings, S. R. Environmental aspects of neoplasia in fishes, p. 3. In *Fish in Research,* ed. O. W. Neuhaus and J. E. Halver. New York and London, Academic Press, 1969.

63. Wellings, S. R., and Siegel, B. V. Role of Golgi apparatus in the formation of melanin granules in human malignant melanoma. *J. Ultrastruct. Res. 3:* 147. 1959.

64. Wellings, S. R., and Siegel, B. V. Electron microscopic studies of the subcellular origin and ultrastructure of melanin granules in mammalian melanomas. *Ann. N. Y. Acad. Sci. 100:* 548. 1963.

65. Zander, C. D. Physiologische und genetische Untersuchungen zur Systematik xiphophoriner Zahnkarpfen, p. 333. *Mitt. Hamburg Zool. Mus. Inst. Kosswig-Festschrift.* 1964.

66. Zander, C. D. Über die Vererbung von y-gebundenen Farbgenen des *Xiphophorus pygmaeus nigrensis* Rosen (Pisces). *Mol. Gen. Genet. 101:* 29. 1968.

67. Zander, C. D. Über die Entstehung und Veränderung von Farbmustern in der Gattung *Xiphophorus* (Pisces). *Mitt. Hamburg Zool. Mus. Inst. 66:* 241. 1969.

68. Zelickson, A. S., Hirsch, H. M., and Hartmann, J. F. Melanogenesis: An autoradiographic study at the ultrastructural level. *J. Invest. Dermatol. 43:* 327. 1964.

All illustrations show melanomas of the platy/swordtail hybrid except Figure 39.22 (DMBA-induced hamster melanoma) and Figure 39.23 (human melanoma).

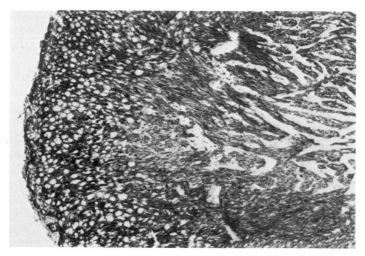

Fig. 39.1. Low magnification of melanoma nodule from platy/swordtail hybrid. Note infiltration of epithelial layer by pigmented tumor cells and pleomorphic highly pigmented tumor with many large cells (macromelanophores) in the region immediately beneath the epithelium. The deeper portion of the tumor is composed of uniform pigmented spindle cells (melanocytes). Hematoxylin and eosin (H&E); ×70.

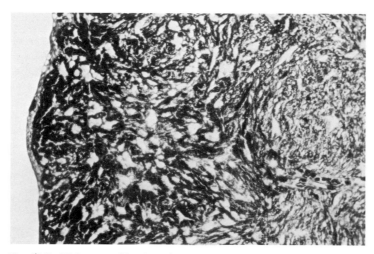

Fig. 39.2. Higher magnification of an area seen in Figure 39.1. H&E; ×175.

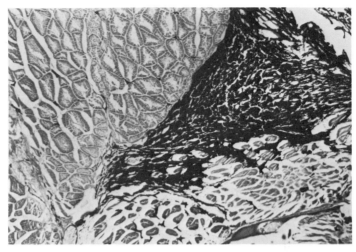

Fig. 39.3. Deeply pigmented tumor nodule near that illustrated in Figures 39.1. and 39.2. Note the infiltration of intermuscular septa with remnants of fin cartilage (lower right). Individual highly pigmented tumor cells are noted around many otherwise normal muscle fibers. H&E; X70.

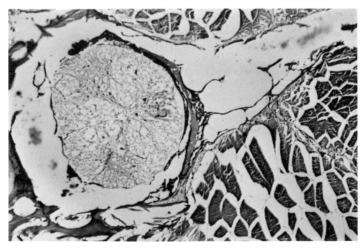

Fig. 39.4. An area deep to that pictured in Figure 39.3, illustrating infiltration by tumor of intermuscular septa and around the bony spinal column. Tumor cells are noted in the meninges surrounding the spinal cord. H&E; X70.

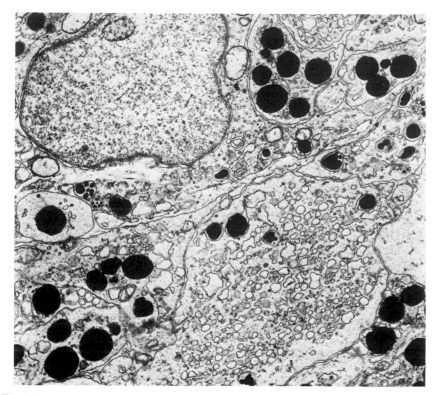

Fig. 39.5. Low-power electron micrograph of a typical area of melanoma in the platy/sword-tail hybrid. There is a densely packed meshwork of interdigitating dendritic processes and cell bodies. The cells are heterogeneous, differing in numbers of electron-dense pigment granules and abundance of cell organelles, particularly smooth endoplasmic reticulum. The extracellular space is sparse, and cell junctions are never observed. X13,500.

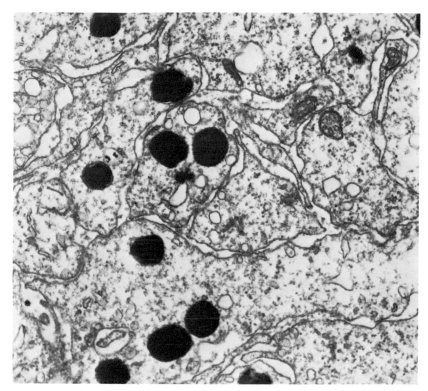

Fig. 39.6. Electron micrograph from an area adjacent to that pictured in Figure 39.5. The meshwork of dendritic processes closely resembles the neuropil of the central nervous system. X21,300.

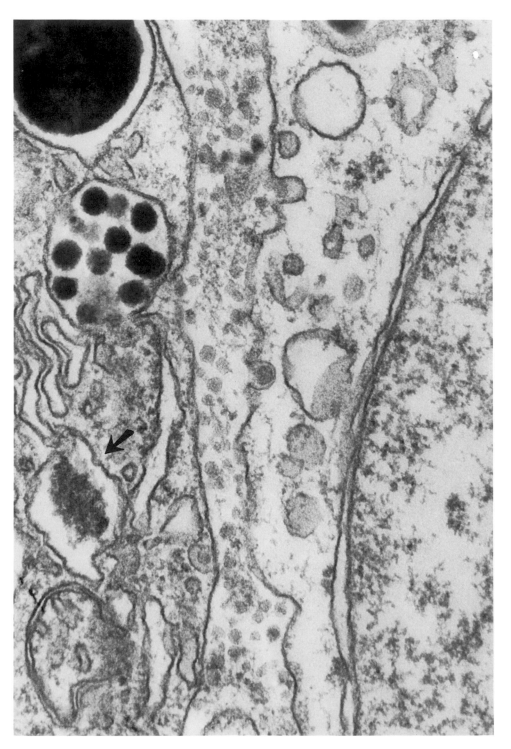

966

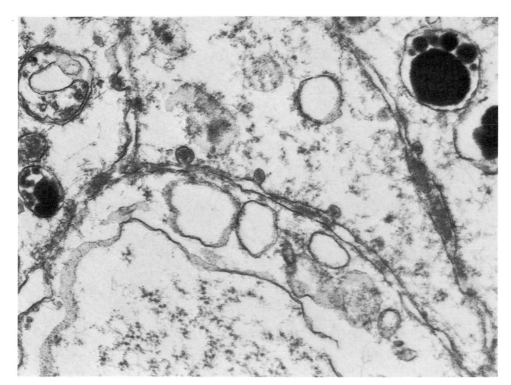

Fig. 39.8. Electron micrograph illustrating the extracellular space distended by electron-dense material, which is similar to that seen in the adjacent pinocytotic vesicles. ×53,350.

Fig. 39.7. Electron micrograph illustrating a portion of a round homogeneous electron-dense pigment granule, a nearby unit membrane enclosing many smaller but similar granules, and an elongated less dense crystal-like core (arrow). The adjacent mitochondrion does not resemble these granules. The adjacent extracellular space is distended and contains oval electron-dense foci which are identical to those near the surface of the melanoma cells and in pinocytotic vesicles. ×84,300.

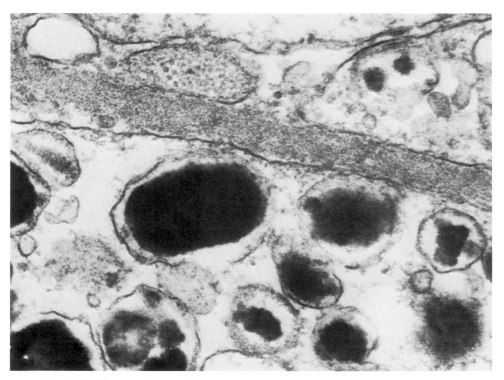

Fig. 39.9. Electron micrograph illustrating a fibrillar basement membrane between two melanoma cells. ×71,000.

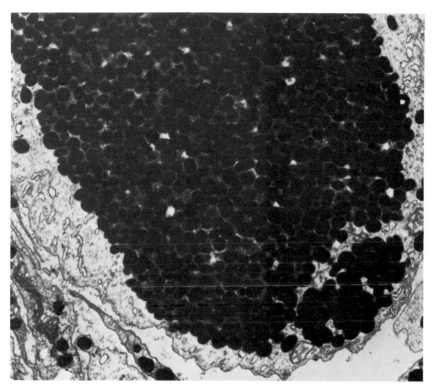

Fig. 39.10. Electron micrograph of part of an extremely large oval cell with a somewhat undulated cell surface. This cell contains few organelles and is packed with electron-dense round and elongated pigment granules. It is thought to be representative of a mature macro-melanophore. X10,500.

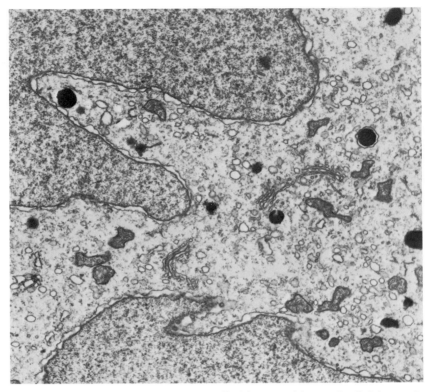

Fig. 39.11. Part of another extremely large cell with two nuclei, an active Golgi apparatus, considerable endoplasmic reticulum, and many small simple mitochondria. It contains few pigment granules and is thought to be a young macromelanophore. X13,500.

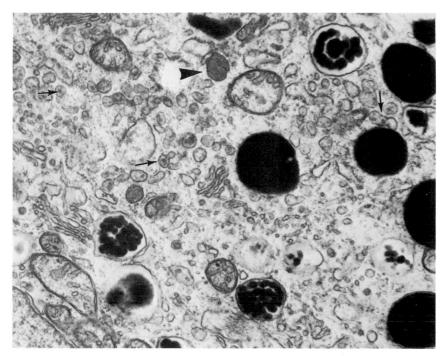

Fig. 39.12. Electron micrograph of a smaller spindle cell thought to be intermediate in age between cells illustrated in Figures 39.10 and 39.11. This cell has an active Golgi apparatus and many adjacent short dilated channels of endoplasmic reticulum, often containing electron-dense particles (arrows). Occasional unit membrane-delimited structures contain accumulations of these dense particles, some of which appear to be fusing into larger aggregates like those in the mature pigment granules. A few smaller fibrillar and less electron-dense granules are also noted (arrowhead). X27,000.

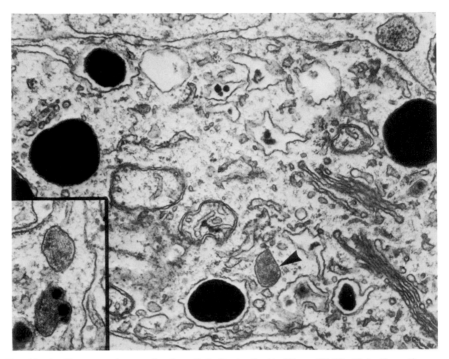

Fig. 39.13. Electron micrograph of a cell similar to that in Figure 39.12. Note the active Golgi apparatus and adjacent pigment granules forming in dilated sacs of smooth endoplasmic reticulum adjacent to the inner aspect of the Golgi apparatus (GERL). Occasionally less electron-dense fibrillar material is noted in these membrane-delimited foci (arrowhead). X27,000.
Fig. 39.13, insert. Illustrates elongated fibrillar foci in unit membrane-delimited vesicles which are thought to bud off the endoplasmic reticulum. Occasionally more electron-dense homogeneous material identical to that observed in dilated channels of endoplasmic reticulum is noted in these granules. X40,300.

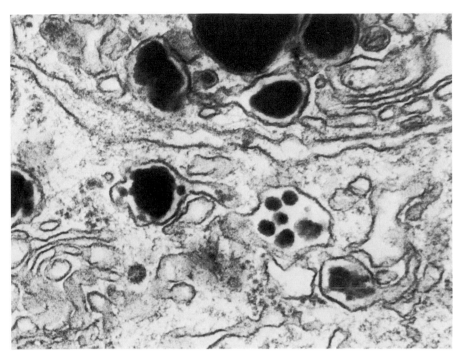

Fig. 39.14. Higher magnification illustrating small electron-dense particles in dilatations of endoplasmic reticulum with apparent fusion into large oval electron-dense pigment granules. ×64,000.

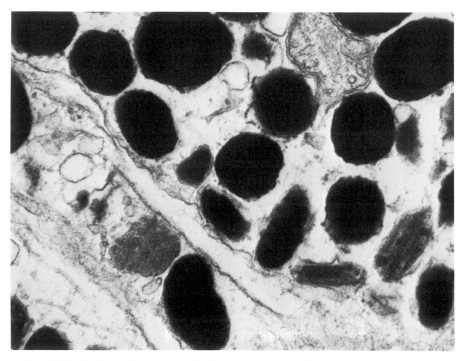

Fig. 39.15. Portions of melanoma cells illustrating large oval electron-dense granules and elongated granules of similar appearance which seem to form by deposition of electron-dense material on elongated membrane-bound fibrillar foci. X52,000.

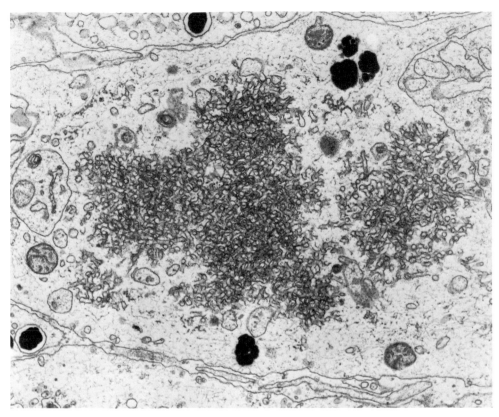

Fig. 39.16. Melanoma cell with a clump-like proliferation of smooth endoplasmic reticulum. ×17,300.

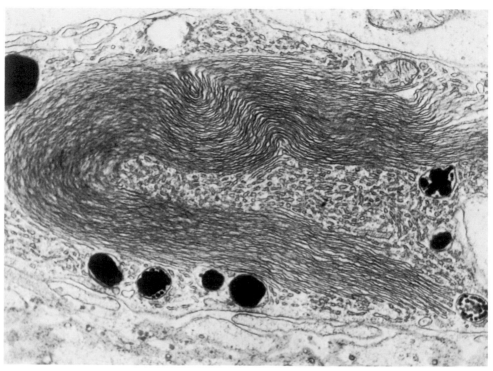

Fig. 39.17. Oval myelin-like structure formed from large focus of endoplasmic reticulum. ×27,200.

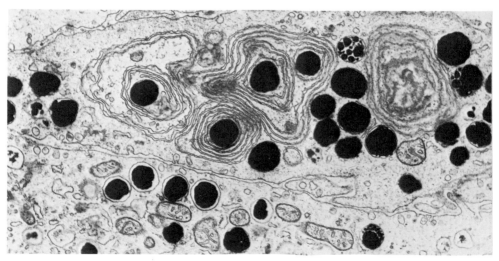

Fig. 39.18. Oval foci of endoplasmic reticulum surrounding pigment granules in a melanoma cell. ×17,000.

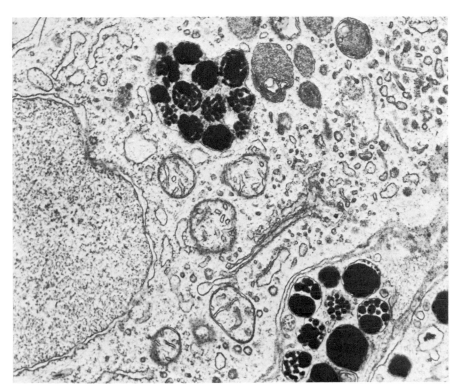

Fig. 39.19. Electron micrograph illustrating transitions in the formation of the large oval pigment granules by fusion of small electron-dense granules (lower right). A cell with organelles like those seen in the early melanoma cell contains dense bodies and a membrane-bound body containing pigment granules in various stages of development. It is felt that this is an early-to-intermediate melanoma cell exhibiting autophagocytosis with the formation of a compound melanosome. X24,000.

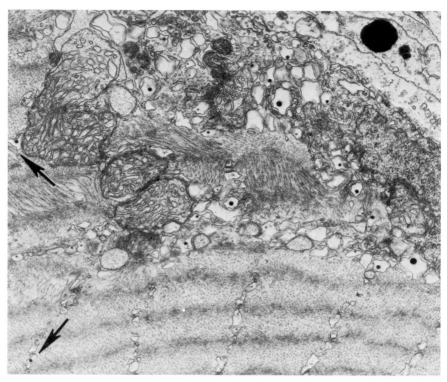

Fig. 39.20. Junction between the fish melanoma and muscle. The muscle is well preserved. Pinocyotic vesicles containing electron-dense material resembling that in the melanoma cell are noted in the extracellular space, and similar material is noted in the sarcoplasmic reticulum penetrating deep into the muscle (arrows). X17,300.

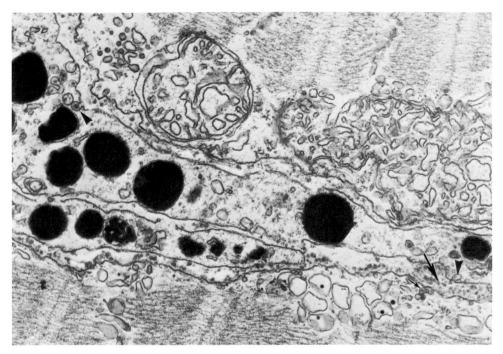

Fig. 39.21. Electron micrograph illustrating the apparent exocytosis of dense material from the melanoma cell (arrowhead), accumulating in the extracellular space (large arrow), and endocytosis into the sarcoplasmic reticulum of striated muscle (small arrow). ×24,700.

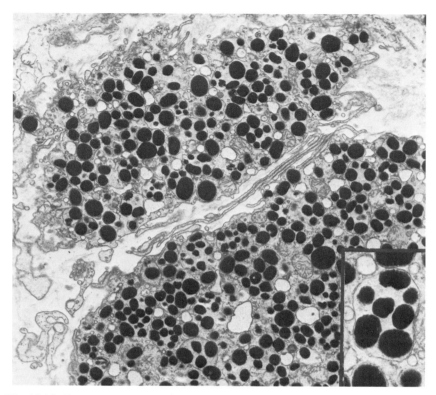

Fig. 39.22. Electron micrograph of a DMBA-induced hamster melanoma. The cells reveal prominent villous-like surface projections. The extracellular space is abundant. The unit membrane-delimited pigment granules contain many oval and elongated large electron-dense structures. X7,700.

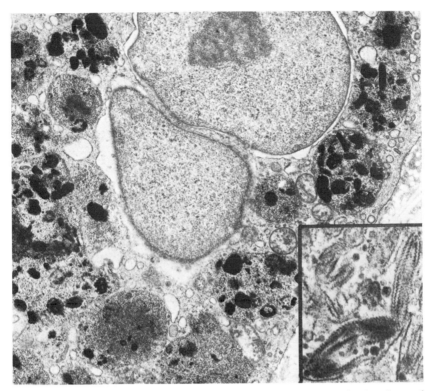

Fig. 39.23. Electron micrograph of a human melanoma cell, illustrating the abundance of compound melanosomes and the irregularity of the nucleus, suggesting the genesis of the frequent cytoplasmic invaginations. ×14,500.

Fig. 39.23, insert. Illustrates the fibrillar structure of the elongated granules before the deposition of pigment. ×44,000.

Discussion of Tumor Papers

R. Walker: I have a number of questions. First, with respect to the "kissing" carcinoma. It was said that the papillomas were not too much unlike the carcinomas in that characteristic, and there are certainly some papillomas, such as in the eels, in which there are opposing lesions on the mouth. You suggested that there had been viruses implicated in some of the lesions, in which case these papillomas could be caused by a transfer of virus. The question was whether in some of the "kissing" carcinomas there could be a transfer of cells rather than virus. There were also other pictures of various sorts of fish with lesions not on the same side but on opposite sides of the mouth. In lymphocystis we see that all the time. However, we know that lymphocystis is not a tumor. The question I am asking is, what must you have to make a "kissing" carcinoma? Must it be a carcinoma? Must it be without virus to make the definition legitimate? I am not sure that "kissing" carcinoma as such is such an important thing, but we really ask about the transfer mechanism. The much more general question is, what is the difference between metastasis and multiple tumor?

C. J. Dawe: We've been using that "kissing" term pretty loosely, and I don't know that there is an authoritative definition. I believe it is mostly a descriptive term meaning that a lesion, either a papilloma or a carcinoma, exists on both lips or both parts of the upper and lower jaw that correspond and make contact with each other. I don't think it was ever intended to mean that the disease was transmitted from one animal to another, either by biting or contact. I don't think there is much evidence that that happens with the papillomas of the bullhead, for example. Now, then the difference between metastasis and multiple tumors— I'm not sure what you are asking, Dr. Walker. Is it multicentric foci or is it transmission by virus?

R. Walker: Sometimes one doesn't know. You made a fairly clear statement with the lamprey. You said, here is the primary; and how do you know this if you have multiple tumors at the same time?

C. J. Dawe: It's a tough thing to decide, of course; we don't know always which is the primary tumor. In the case of the lamprey, just to take an example, the evidence was that in only one of the lesions did the neoplastic cells come up through the dermis, and form a fungating lesion that was ulcerating on the surface and was made up entirely of epithelial cells. Other cutaneous lesions were found below the dermis where they could have been multicentric, but the more logical way of explaining it would be that they traveled through the lymphatics. We see this in melanomas and many other tumors in man, and taking that together with the metastases we found in the branchial vessels and in the kidneys, I think that was the best way of putting it all together. It is true that we can't be 100 percent sure; we have no way of absolutely proving that, and we can only take the evidence as it stands and make it fit the facts as we see them. Do you have any other questions?

R. Walker: It's the same question all over again. Dr. Sonstegard showed pictures of a lot of small scale pockets and then something making a great big lesion which was deeper, as though it were the primary lesion. The question is how these multiple scale pocket tumors got their start.

C. J. Dawe: Was it not perhaps multicentric at the beginning, at least in multiple scale pockets? That's too fundamental a question to answer; if we could we would know so much more than anybody else that we really would be wasting our time here. I think you've put your finger on an extremely important phenomenon which has to do with the nature of neoplasms in animals in general. It hasn't really been brought to the fore and discussed as much as it should. When one is dealing with viral tumors, the proliferative process doesn't always have to be a cellular clone that is proliferating. There is another mechanism that can enter, a so-called recruitment mechanism, in which one cell carries virus and is transformed and can transmit virus to a neighboring cell, and it is transformed. This is recruitment, and this has been studied to some extent. Pontine was really the one who did the first work, with chickens, in which he showed that the Rous sarcomas which had been thought to have been transplanted through many years were really not transplanted at all but were re-recruitment tumors to males and showed that the sex chromatin changed according to the sex of the recipient after as little as six days, and yet the tumors were continuously growing. There was no period when it stopped growing and a new tumor was detected. It was as if it was a continuous growth of one cell line. Other people, such as Croft in England, have done some of this work with the T-6 chromosome and the mouse sarcoma viruses and the mouse leukemias, and have shown that some of the cells in these transplanted tumors are in fact ones that come from the host and have been recruited by the presence of virus. Nothing is known about that in any of the fish tumors that I know of.

M. M. Sigel: I believe that not only can you demonstrate multicentric tumors, but you can demonstrate different tumors arising at the same time in different kinds of cells. For cxample, without referring to specific references at the moment, I think there is at least one recent report of the co-existence of two myelo-mas in the same patient—different types of myelomas—suggesting two separate origins of neoplastic transformation. While I am up, may I ask a couple of questions? One to Dr. Sonstegard. Even though you didn't demonstrate any increase in immunoglobulin in your very exciting and new tumor, have you looked for heavy chains or light chains? Is it possible, as it occurs in some other mammalian higher vertebrate tumors, that you are getting incomplete molecules?

R. Sonstegard: On the basis of the electrophoretic studies, both these and by Dr. Jones, there is a very acute hypogammaglobulinemia and whether this, in fact, might be an explanation I wouldn't hazard a guess. It is hoped that, perhaps through protracted transmission and passage, we might come up with an individual fish, or perhaps a number of fish, that might give a clue on this. We might not have hit on the right individual animal to show the protein pattern that might be the real key to the characteristic syndrome of the disease.

Comment: You might also try placing your tumor in tissue culture to see if it does produce any immunoglobulins, that is, any immunoglobulin-like or heavy-chain-like protein.

R. Sonstegard: We have gone through the cell culture work, particularly looking for virus. I have attempted static suspension cultures of the neoplastic cells, and they don't, at least on the trials we have done so far, adapt too well to *in vitro* propagation, in that we lost these after about 20 days *in vitro*. I don't know if *in vitro* they might secrete, but this is something that is considered and is going to be tried. In regard to the cell culture studies I could say this: there is no evidence of any cytopathic type of effect or transformation that we have been able to demonstrate with infiltrates or with co-cultivation with the cell.

M. M. Sigel: Dr. Mulcahy's report causes two comments. She referred to the tumor as lymphoma, but then the cell is presumably a hematocytoblast and I am not very comfortable with the terminology of lymphoma, since there are really no lymphocytes or lymphoblast-like elements in the tumor. Wouldn't you be happier re-naming it?

Comment: Dr. Sigel, you know that with the pathologists' classifications of lymphoma, they call everything malignant lymphoma that comes from blood stem cells.

M. M. Sigel: We are entering a new era in fish pathology here, and we might as well start on the right foot. You illustrated your serum proteins which were apparently measured by means of acrylamide gel electrophoresis. This is fine, but since most of the fishes that we have studied contain macroglobulins as the major immunoglobulins, these proteins do not go into the gel, they stay at the very beginning, so what you are measuring is really not immunoglobulin; you are measuring other proteins. Perhaps you are missing an important one by using this method, and I would suggest using other procedures such as gel filtration or chromatography in DAE to illustrate the presence of immunoglobulins. I would like to say that even though Dr. Orr 20 years ago indicated the possible presence of

IgG in fish, this has not been confirmed; all the work done by Clem and myself and other investigators in recent years has agreed and shown that fish immuno-globulins are limited to IgM protein, with the exception, perhaps, of one fish. One fish does seem to have the precursor of IgG, but all the other studies so far are re-stricted to IgM, either 7S, 14S or 19S IgM.

C. J. Dawe: I would like to make a comment about multicentricity. There have been some very discriminating studies that I think are interesting. Linder and Gartler, Fialkow (*N. Engl. J. Med. 285:* 1198–1199, 1971), and others have done them on what appeared to be unicentric tumors, such as for example, leio-myomas of the uterus, neurofibromas, Burkitt lymphoma, and colon and cervical carcinoma. The studies were done on tumors from females known to be hetero-zygous on the X chromosome for glucose-6-phosphate dehydrogenase isozymes. In such persons there is mosaicism for two isozymes, one being repressed in some cells but not in the others. Tumors of single clone origin should therefore contain only one of the two possible isozyme types. Leiomyomas turned out to be single-clone tumors by this criterion, but individual neurofibromas associated with von Recklinghausen's disease were of multiclonal origin. Surprisingly, some tu-mors of viral origin that have been thought to be multicentric or polyclonal, be-cause many cells are generally thought to be transformed in a field, have actually turned out to be monoclonal. So some revolutionary ideas are turning up. I think the problem is more complicated than it might appear, because at the time a given tumor is tested it is pretty far advanced. It is possible that although the tumor may have been multiclonal at the beginning, a single clone was selected out and by the time the tumor was studied only a single clone persisted or predominated. So we don't know everything yet on this point. In fact, with murine myelomas, Michael Potter has shown that most late tumors are monoclonal, as indicated by their immunoglobulin-producing properties. But in the early phases some have been multiclonal, or mixed, so they probably can change as a result of selective processes. It is really difficult to see how we are going to obtain final answers to these questions.

W. E. Ribelin: I would like to ask two questions. The first to Dr. Budd. I was intrigued by the fact that in her survey of yellow perch she encountered al-most solely male perch. I think the fact that the testicular tumor was found only in males doesn't necessarily prove that it is sex-linked from a chromosomal viewpoint, since she was encountering only males. I wondered if there was some explanation as to why she got males, whether there could perhaps be a karyotypic effect of the tumor so that from a chromosomal point of view the population available for catching was predominantly male.

J. Budd: The population was not necessarily predominantly males. After the first year, when I found that these tumors occurred in males, the people who catch the fish for me like to eat yellow perch, and the yellow perch females are larger, so they took out the large ones, and I got the ones that were left.

W. E. Ribelin: The second question is to Dr. Sonstegard. I wondered if these histiocytic-type cells that are the primary cell in lymphoma in pike are present in normal pike scale pockets of fish that do not have tumors?

R. Sonstegard: No. The only time we see this type of cell is in the disease. I don't think I would call them a histiocyte, but perhaps we are dealing with a different terminology.

Question: Do you have any idea where the cell is coming from?

R. Sonstegard: I have just gone into a gross description of the progression of this disease. Now there is a very striking and marked seasonal and age distribution. This is very likely a contact-transplant transmission, but this is confounded by the fact that these cells in culture seem to grow amitotically, making karyotyping extremely difficult if not impossible. Mitotic cells are very, very rare, and there is no trouble doing a karyotype of the normal fish. I am saying this in view of a great number of unsuccessful attempts to demonstrate the evidence of virus, RNA, DNA, etc. These efforts have all been refractory. The evidence seems overwhelming that it is transplantation of neoplastic cells from one individual to another. This in itself has presented some real problems for confirmation.

C. J. Dawe: I would like to say that Dr. Sonstegard's slides showing the plasma cells in the blood didn't really do justice to the picture that you can see if you examine the smears yourself. A lot of the cells had visibly dilated cytoplasmic cysternae that were like those one sees in plasma cells that are loaded with protein. The amazing thing is that we can't explain where this protein, if it is being produced, is going, or if it is breaking down, or whether it may not be synthesized to the point where it is recognizable as immunoglobulin.

Contributors

Index

Contributors

LAURENCE M. ASHLEY, Western Fish Nutrition Laboratory, Bureau of Sport Fisheries and Wildlife, U.S. Department of the Interior, Cook, Washington 98605

R. A. BENDELE, JR., Department of Veterinary Pathology, Texas A & M University, College Station, Texas   77843

B. G. BLAYLOCK, Environmental Sciences Division, Oak Ridge National Laboratory, Oak Ridge, Tennessee   37830

JOAN BUDD, Department of Pathology, Ontario Veterinary College, University of Guelph, Guelph, Ontario, Canada

PHYLLIS H. CAHN, Graduate Department of Marine Science, Long Island University, P.O. Greenvale, Long Island, New York   11548

ROBERT H. CIULLO, Nasson College Springvale, Maine   04083

P. H. COHAN, Cooperative Science Education Center, Oak Ridge, Tennessee 37830

JOHN F. CONRAD, Oregon State Fish Commission, Clackamas, Oregon   97015

GLENNA J. CORLEY, Department of Pathology, College of Physicians and Surgeons, Columbia University, New York, New York   10032

G. E. COSGROVE, Biology Division, Oak Ridge National Laboratory, Oak Ridge, Tennessee   37830

JOHN A. COUCH, Gulf Breeze Laboratory, Environmental Protection Agency, Sabine Island, Gulf Breeze, Florida   32561

C. J. DAWE, National Cancer Institute, U.S. Department of Health, Education and Welfare, Bethesda, Maryland   20014

KAREN DAVEY DUKES, P.O. Box 9, Kemptville, Ontario, Canada

THOMAS W. DUKES, Veterinary Services Laboratory, Ministry of Agriculture and Food, Veterinary Services Branch, Kemptville, Ontario, Canada

LAFAYETTE L. ELLER, Fish-Pesticide Research Laboratory, Bureau of Sport Fisheries and Wildlife, U.S. Department of the Interior, Columbia, Missouri 65201

JOHN L. GAINES, JR., Department of Fisheries and Allied Aquacultures, Auburn University, Auburn, Alabama   36830

GEORGE R. GARDNER, National Marine Water Quality Laboratory, P.O. Box 277, West Kingston, Rhode Island   02892

J. E. HALVER, Western Fish Nutrition Laboratory, Bureau of Sport Fisheries and Wildlife, U.S. Department of the Interior, Cook, Washington   98605

J. C. HARSHBARGER, Registry of Tumors in Lower Animals, National Museum of Natural History, Smithsonian Institution, Washington, D.C.   20560

ROGER LEE HERMAN, Eastern Fish Disease Laboratory, Bureau of Sport Fisheries and Wildlife, U.S. Department of the Interior, Kearneysville, West Virginia   25430

JOHN G. HNATH, Hatchery Biology Service Center, Michigan Department of National Resources, Grayling, Michigan   49738

GLENN L. HOFFMAN, Fish Farming Experimental Station, Bureau of Sport Fisheries and Wildlife, U.S. Department of the Interior, Stuttgart, Arkansas 72160

RAYMOND T. JONES, Department of Pathology, University of Maryland School of Medicine, Baltimore, Maryland   21201

KLAUS D. KALLMAN, Osborne Laboratory of Marine Sciences, New York Zoological Society, New York, New York   11224

JOHN M. KING, Department of Veterinary Pathology, Cornell University, Ithaca, New York   14805

G. W. KLONTZ, Cooperative Fisheries Unit, College of Forestry, Wildlife, and Range Sciences, University of Idaho, Moscow, Idaho   83843

MARSHA L. LANDOLT, Department of Pathology, National Zoological Park, Washington, D.C.   20009

RICHARD T. LOVELL, Department of Fisheries and Allied Aquacultures, Auburn University, Auburn, Alabama   36830

EUGENE MARQUET, Department of Pathology and Max Wachstein Research Laboratory, Beth Israel Hospital, Passaic, New Jersey   07055

LIONEL E. MAWDESLEY-THOMAS, Huntingdon Research Centre, Huntingdon, England (*deceased September 1974*)

FRED P. MEYER, Fish Control Laboratory, Bureau of Sport Fisheries and Wildlife, U.S. Department of the Interior, La Crosse, Wisconsin 54601

GEORGE MIGAKI, Registry of Comparative Pathology, Armed Forces Institute of Pathology, Washington, D.C. 20305

MAIRE F. MULCAHY, Zoology Department, University College, Cork, Ireland

ROBERT G. PIPER, Fish Cultural Development Center, Bureau of Sport Fisheries and Wildlife, U.S. Department of the Interior, Bozeman, Montana 59715

JOHN A. PLUMB, Department of Fisheries and Allied Aquacultures, Auburn University, Auburn, Alabama 36830

H.-H. REICHENBACH-KLINKE, Zoologisch-Parasitologisches Institut der Universität München, Munich, Germany

WILLIAM E. RIBELIN, Department of Veterinary Science, University of Wisconsin, Madison, Wisconsin 53706

RONALD J. ROBERTS, Unit of Aquatic Biology, University of Stirling, Stirling FK9 4LA, Scotland

WILMER A. ROGERS, Department of Fisheries and Allied Aquacultures, Auburn University, Auburn, Alabama 36830

SOMPHONG SAHAPHONG, Department of Pathology, Faculty of Medicine, Ramethibodi Hospital Medical School, Bangkok-4 Thailand

THOMAS K. SAWYER, National Marine Fisheries Service, U.S. Department of Commerce, Oxford, Maryland 21654

J. D. SCHRODER, Department of Pathology, Ontario Veterinary College, University of Guelph, Guelph, Ontario, Canada

CHARLIE E. SMITH, Fish Cultural Development Center, Bureau of Sport Fisheries and Wildlife, U.S. Department of the Interior, Bozeman, Montana 59715

FREDERICK G. SMITH, Department of Anatomy and Radiology, College of Veterinary Medicine, University of Georgia, Athens, Georgia 30602

R. R. SMITH, Western Fish Nutrition Laboratory, Bureau of Sport Fisheries and Wildlife, U.S. Department of the Interior, Cook, Washington 98605

S. F. SNIESZKO, Eastern Fish Disease Laboratory, Bureau of Sport Fisheries and Wildlife, U.S. Department of the Interior, Kearneysville, West Virginia 25430

HAROLD J. SOBEL, Department of Pathology and Max Wachstein Research Laboratory, Beth Israel Hospital, Passaic, New Jersey 07055

RON SONSTEGARD, Department of Microbiology, University of Guelph, Guelph, Ontario, Canada

ROBERT C. SUMMERFELT, Cooperative Fishery Unit, Oklahoma State University, Stillwater, Oklahoma 74074

ROBERT TAFANELLI, Department of Biology, Tarleton State College, Stephenville, Texas 76401

BENJAMIN F. TRUMP, Department of Pathology, University of Maryland School of Medicine, Baltimore, Maryland 21201

G. U. ULRIKSON, Environmental Information Systems Office, Oak Ridge National Laboratory, Oak Ridge, Tennessee 37830

DAVID W. VALENTINE, Dames and Moore Company, 1100 Glendon Avenue, Los Angeles, California 90024

A. H. WALSH, Chas. Pfizer Company, Groton, Connecticut 06340

R. W. WISSLER, Department of Pathology, University of Chicago, Chicago, Illinois 60637

R. E. WOLKE, Marine Experiment Station and Department of Animal Pathology, University of Rhode Island, Kingston, Rhode Island 02881

WILLIAM T. YASUTAKE, Western Fish Disease Laboratory, Bureau of Sport Fisheries and Wildlife, U.S. Department of the Interior, Seattle, Washington 98115

Index

995

DESIGNED BY IRVING PERKINS
COMPOSED BY HORNE ASSOCIATES, INC., HANOVER, NEW HAMPSHIRE
MANUFACTURED BY NORTH CENTRAL PUBLISHING CO., ST. PAUL, MINNESOTA
TEXT IS SET IN PRESS ROMAN, DISPLAY LINES IN TRAJANUS AND TIMES ROMAN

Library of Congress Cataloging in Publication Data
Main entry under title:
The Pathology of fishes.
Includes bibliographies and index.
1. Fishes–Diseases and pests–Congresses.
I. Ribelin, William E., ed. II. Migaki, George, ed.
III. Registry of Comparative Pathology. IV. Universities
Associated for Research and Education in Pathology.
V. Wisconsin. University–Madison. Sea Grant Program.
SH171.P38   597'.02   73-15261
ISBN 0-299-06520-0